CW01023020

Constant Lambert
Beyond The Rio Grande

Constant Lambert
Beyond The Rio Grande

Stephen Lloyd

THE BOYDELL PRESS

First published 2014
The Boydell Press, Woodbridge

ISBN 978 1 84383 898 2

The Boydell Press is an imprint of Boydell & Brewer Ltd
PO Box 9, Woodbridge, Suffolk IP12 3DF, UK
and of Boydell & Brewer Inc.
668 Mount Hope Ave, Rochester, NY 14620-2731, USA
website: www.boydellandbrewer.com

A catalogue record for this book is available from the British Library

The publisher has no responsibility for the continued existence or accuracy
of URLs for external or third-party internet websites referred to in this book,
and does not guarantee that any content on such websites is,
or will remain, accurate or appropriate.

This publication is printed on acid-free paper

Designed and typeset in Hypatia Sans Pro and Warnock Pro
by David Roberts, Pershore, Worcestershire
Music origination by Jeanne Roberts

Contents

Illustrations & Music Examples

Frontispiece Constant Lambert, October 1937 (photo by Sasha/Hulton Archive/Getty Images)

A CONSTANT LAMBERT ICONOGRAPHY Appendix 11, pp. 537–42

MUSIC EXAMPLES

Elegiac Blues by Constant Lambert © Chester Music Ltd.

The Walk to the Paradise Garden by Frederick Delius © Copyright 1940 by Hawkes & Son (London) Ltd. Reproduced by Boosey & Hawkes Music Publishers Ltd.

Sonata for Pianoforte by Constant Lambert © Oxford University Press 1930. Extracts reproduced by permission. All rights reserved.

The Rio Grande music by Constant Lambert © Oxford University Press 1929. Music extracts reproduced by permission of Oxford University Press. All rights reserved.

Concerto for Solo Pianoforte and Nine Players by Constant Lambert © Oxford University Press 1933. Extracts reproduced by permission. All rights reserved.

Summer's Last Will and Testament' by Constant Lambert © Oxford University Press 1936. Extract reproduced by permission. All rights reserved.

'King Pest' from *Summer's Last Will and Testament* by Constant Lambert © Oxford University Press 1936. Extracts reproduced by permission. All rights reserved.

Extract from *Salomé* by Constant Lambert © Copyright by Peters Edition Limited, London. Reproduced by kind permission of Peters Edition Limited, London.

'Saraband' from *Summer's Last Will and Testament* by Constant Lambert © Oxford University Press 1936. Extract reproduced by permission. All rights reserved.

'Invocation to the Moon' from *Horoscope: A Ballet in One Act* by Constant Lambert © Oxford University Press 1938. Extract reproduced by permission. All rights reserved.

Dirge by Constant Lambert © Oxford University Press 1947. Extract reproduced by permission. All rights reserved.

Aubade héroïque by Constant Lambert © Oxford University Press 1944. Extract reproduced by permission. All rights reserved.

Extracts from *Tiresias* by Constant Lambert © Copyright by Peters Edition Limited, London. Reproduced by kind permission of Peters Edition Limited, London.

The author and publishers are grateful to all the institutions and individuals listed for permission to reproduce the materials in which they hold copyright. Every effort has been made to trace the copyright holders; apologies are offered for any omission, and the publishers will be pleased to add any necessary acknowledgement in subsequent editions.

Introduction & Acknowledgements

CONSTANT Lambert died on 21 August 1951, two days short of his 46th birthday. The following month Hubert Foss, until 1941 Head of the Music Department of Oxford University Press, having just written the first full-length study of Vaughan Williams,[1] sounded out his publisher, Harrap & Sons, about a book of tributes with which he was proposing to mark Vaughan Williams' 80th birthday the following year. At the same time, ever keen to promote his 'house composers', he mentioned another projected composer study:

> You may remember that there was a vague idea floating around that I ought to repair a serious omission in our musical literature by writing a book on Sir William Walton (no full-scale study exists).[2] Sir William demurred that it was too early – 'wait till fifty' was his plea. But he will be fifty next year, and the opera, *Troilus and Cressida*, on which he is working, will not be ready for production until a year from hence. No book could omit detailed consideration of this new major piece. Therefore concatenation of half-century and book may be ruled out.

But he went on to make a further suggestion:

> With Lambert the case is opposite. From every point of view, he is a subject for a biography. The quicker the job is tackled the better, and the readier vital information will be in coming forward (for memories are short). I do not exaggerate when I urge you to regard this brilliant young man's death as comparable historically in English music to the death of Purcell at the age of 36; so careless were Purcell's contemporaries that we have no exact record of his birth. Let us not err again.[3]

He put himself forward as Lambert's biographer as one who could write with personal knowledge of the 1920s – an essential ingredient, he argued, to a study of the man. He had also known Lambert personally as well as in a professional capacity.

Sadly, that year Foss suffered from very poor health and, although he was appointed editor of *The Musical Times* late in 1952, he never took up the post, dying from a stroke in May 1953. At the time he had other literary projects on the go. In 1952 he revised Philip Heseltine's book on Delius, and up to his death he was also working on a history of the London Symphony Orchestra, but got no further than the first two and a half chapters. Noël Goodwin completed the book which was published in 1954.

The book on Lambert had not even progressed that far, but Foss had already undertaken a fair amount of research, advertising in the press for information and contacting a number of Lambert's acquaintances. One person who had known him well, the novelist Anthony Powell, had offered any assistance he could give, and the composer Denis ApIvor had written a long account of their friendship. But very little by way of actual writing had been done by the time of Foss's death, so his widow Dora was left in a predicament as how to proceed with the book. The writer and music critic Edward Sackville-West was approached with a view to completing it, but he declined the task because, as he wrote to Dora, 'it is very difficult to write comprehensively

[1] Hubert Foss, *Ralph Vaughan Williams: A Study* (Edinburgh: Harrap, 1950).
[2] The first full study of Walton had to wait 14 years until Frank Howes, *The Music of William Walton* (London: Oxford University Press, 1965), appeared.
[3] Letter from Hubert Foss to J. H. H. Gaute, Harrap & Sons Ltd, 3 September 1951: Hubert Foss Archive.

about a contemporary without causing offence to living people. Also – this is the main reason why I feel obliged to refuse – in order to write well, or even adequately, at length on anything or anyone I have to feel a strong urge to do so; & this, in this particular instance, I must confess I do not feel.'[4]

Amy Lambert, Constant's mother, who had earlier given her support to Hubert Foss's book, writing that Constant's life 'could scarcely be in more discriminating hands', sympathised with Dora over the problem facing the would-be biographer: 'Contemporary interest carries with it contemporary difficulties & in reading recently John Buchan's *Life of Sir Walter Scott* I realized to the full the value of Time's perspective.'[5] In 1938 she had written a biography of her husband, the artist George Washington Lambert. It was published in Sydney, whither George had sailed from London in 1921, leaving behind his wife and two sons. It is a dry account, devoid of any real emotion, as curious for what it omits as for the manner in which certain facts are presented. It may have been intended as a mask for her true feelings; equally, much family detail may have been excluded out of respect for her sons who were then both reaching the peak of their careers. They were never to see their father again – Constant was 15 at the time of his departure – and while Amy went out to see him in 1926, she returned less than three years later on her own. He died in 1930. While her book tells us very little about Constant's childhood, it is at least the source for much information about his parents.[6]

Another to be considered for the planned book was Arthur Hutchings, Professor of Music at Durham University, who replied cautiously: 'I want to make it clear I was not one of Lambert's intimate circle, but that I was an admirer who enjoyed his conversation and company along with others on two or three occasions. ... You may easily find better help than mine.'[7] Nevertheless, he was given the documentation that Hubert Foss had accumulated to look through. In the meantime Dora had had a long chat with Amy Lambert about the writing of the biography, and she had also written to Angus Morrison, Constant's brother-in-law[8] and close friend from his Royal College of Music days, with whom she was anxious 'to discuss the distinctly involved situation which has arisen in consequence of Hubert's death'.[9]

But then, in November, Geoffrey Cumberlege of Oxford University Press, Lambert's publisher, threw a spanner in the works, writing to Dora:

> I have come to the conclusion that it is quite definitely not a book that we ought to do. For one thing the total output of music was small and if it is to be a Life then much of it will be sordid and of a kind that the scholar would not handle particularly effectively, while the journalist would tend to make it sensational.[10]

However, Anthony Powell thought otherwise, as he explained to Dora:

[4] Letter from Edward Sackville-West to Dora Foss, 7 July 1953: Hubert Foss Archive.

[5] Letter from Amy Lambert to Dora Foss, 9 September 1953: Hubert Foss Archive.

[6] Amy Lambert, *Thirty Years of an Artist's Life: The Career of G. W. Lambert, ARA* (Sydney: Society of Artists, 1938). 200 copies were printed but a large number were lost at sea *en route* to England during the war. Sparsely illustrated, in keeping with Amy's wishes before her death in 1963, it was reprinted in Sydney in 1977 for the Australian Artist Editions, with ten extra plates to illustrate George's work. The book, however, contains no family group pictures (see Appendix 11).

[7] Letter from Arthur Hutchings to Dora Foss, 28 October 1953: Hubert Foss Archive. Hutchings was to contribute an introduction to the 1966 Faber reprint of Constant Lambert's *Music Ho!*

[8] Stuart Angus Morrison (1902–89) studied at the Royal College of Music where he later taught from 1926 for 46 years. In 1926 Angus's sister Olga married Constant's brother Maurice.

[9] Letter from Dora Foss to Angus Morrison, 7 August 1953: RCM Library MSS 6961–6966.

[10] Letter from Geoffrey Cumberlege to Dora Foss, 25 November 1953: Hubert Foss Archive.

If Constant is a person who eventually will be written about a lot, it will be just as well to have some sort of a standard biography to which other writers can refer, even if they differ from it in their own opinions. If he turns out *not* to be a person the future is greatly interested in (personally I feel sure he will be, but one can never tell) it will not get easier to find someone to write the book, and it will not matter if it is not absolutely inspired in style.[11]

He advised Dora to get some agreement in writing from Lambert's two wives, his mother, his brother Maurice, and Hubert's literary executor before starting, and he offered to write a personal memoir. She lost no time in writing to Maurice to inform him that she was in discussion with a publisher about a book on Constant, possibly to be written by Hutchings 'on the lines visualised' by her husband and using the material he had collected. While she could not give an exact outline of the book, it would 'certainly emphasise the musical and intellectual aspects' of Lambert's life.[12]

With over two years having passed since Lambert's death and little progress made on the Foss book, matters became complicated when it became known that Angus Morrison was going to write the 'official' biography. Three days later Maurice Lambert tactfully replied to Dora:

As I see it, if two separate books are ultimately brought out, different in kind, but, one hopes, both excellent in quality, it would be all to the good: if they are very different in kind, as seems probable, there would be that much less danger of one adversely affecting the success of the other. We as a family are not likely to make any arrangements with Harrap's which would preclude us from providing you with material or information of which you, or an author working for you, might stand in need, assuming that you on your part would be prepared to act reciprocally regarding the availability of such material as you hold.[13]

Dora, still mourning her husband's death and naturally upset at the news of this rival book that Harrap had contracted, wrote to Morrison in January:

It has indeed come as a surprise to me to hear you are going to write Constant's biography for Harraps. The only information I have had was from your sister in December who said that no name had been mentioned as a possible writer. ... Please accept my good wishes to you in your task.

As to Hubert's material, this is the result of his work and personal contacts, and of the expenditure of his time, energy and money. It is, of course mine, and is needed for the book, based on his writings and research in which, as you know, I am interested.[14]

Regrettably, in the event neither book was completed. Foss had not left enough material for an outsider 'to put the book together' and Hutchings, who was already committed to finishing two books of his own, was relieved to learn that there was another projected biography. There were other problems. As Hutchings pointed out to Dora, 'the chief difficulty of the undertaking would be *not to cause offence*, and there is a great deal between the Lambert family's agreement "to a book on these lines" and their agreement to the publication of some of the material I was able to

[11] Letter from Anthony Powell to Dora Foss, 13 December 1953: Hubert Foss Archive.

[12] Draft of a letter from Dora Foss to Maurice Lambert, 20 December 1953: RCM Library MSS 6961–6966.

[13] Letter from Maurice Lambert to Dora Foss, 23 December 1953: Hubert Foss Archive.

[14] Draft of a letter from Dora Foss to Angus Morrison, January 1954: RCM Library MSS 6961–6966.

read even at a cursory scrutiny.'[15] It seems that biographical honesty and objectivity might be compromised. Morrison had probably discussed with the Lambert family how he intended to deal with the more sensitive aspects of Constant's life, sufficient for Kit Lambert, then at boarding school, to write: 'May I say how much I admired your level-headed yet sensitive treatment of the tragic theme of my father's ever increasing addiction to drink, ... and I thought that your attitude was both courageous and understanding.'[16]

Like Foss, Morrison went ahead and appealed in the press for personal reminiscences and had a good response from many who had known Lambert, both from his school days and later on in life. But as Marie Nielson, who had known Lambert professionally from the Vic-Wells days, commented to Morrison: 'It is a difficult task you have taken on. I imagine it will be easier to convey the brilliance than the sweetness that was & is Constant.'[17]

In April 1954 Dora, deeply disappointed when it seemed that her husband's intentions would not be realised, decided to hand over all the material to Morrison, except for some letters to Hubert that were more of a private nature. As an acquaintance commented, it was as if the Lambert family was terrified of anything coming out about Constant that they didn't want known and for that reason wanted to keep the writing of the biography in the family.

Morrison made a start on the book, dealing with the period during which he was closest to Lambert, the years that led to the composition of *The Rio Grande*. And then he seems to have gone no further. Although better equipped than most people to write about the music, when dealing with Lambert's life he may have been faced with the difficulty that Hutchings had predicted, of not causing offence either to the family or to persons still alive.

Nearly 20 years were to pass before the first book on Lambert appeared, in 1973, written by Richard Shead, who worked for the BBC Transcription Service and had heard Lambert conduct in the post-war years.[18] Angus Morrison made available his draft chapters and the material he had collected. Even more important, Shead was able to interview many people still living who had been close to Lambert and so he could present a fuller picture than might otherwise have been possible.[19] Yet even he encountered difficulties, the chief hurdle being unable to reveal the facts about Lambert's close relationship with Margot Fonteyn, who was then still alive and famously partnered with Rudolf Nureyev. All he did say was that Lambert 'had begun to fall in love with a dancer' with whom he had 'a deep and passionate affair'. He even found it necessary to omit sections from letters that mentioned other living people or, in a few cases, to replace their names by asterisks. Nevertheless, Shead's book still remains an excellent and sensitive study of Lambert, and an invaluable source for later writers.

Thirteen years later came the absorbing study by Andrew Motion of three generations of Lamberts in *The Lamberts: George, Constant and Kit*.[20] Besides interviewing the rather fewer people then alive who knew Constant well, Motion was

---

[15] Letter from Arthur Hutchings to Dora Foss, 5 January 1954: Hubert Foss Archive.

[16] Letter from Kit Lambert, Lancing College, to Angus Morrison, 22 January 1954: RCM Library MSS 6961–6966.

[17] Letter from Marie Nielson (MacDermott) to Angus Morrison, 19 February 1954: RCM Library MSS 6961–6966.

[18] Richard Shead, *Constant Lambert: His Life, His Music and His Friends* (London: Simon Publications, 1973).

[19] Both Amy and Maurice Lambert had died in 1964.

[20] London: Chatto & Windus, 1986.

able to draw upon Shead's book and present a much fuller account of his life, no longer having to shroud Fonteyn in anonymity as Shead did, now that she had retired and was living abroad with her husband.

M Y own interest in Constant Lambert was aroused by three performances: *Summer's Last Will and Testament* conducted by Sir Malcolm Sargent at the Royal Albert Hall in February 1965 (a work I had to wait seven years to hear again when Vernon Handley programmed it at Guildford in April 1972); *The Rio Grande* in August 1969 in a concert at Salzburg University given by young musicians attending a European summer school, with Maurice Miles conducting and a very young Simon Rattle the soloist; and in June 1977 at the Royal College of Music, *The Rio Grande* again, with which Angus Morrison celebrated his 75th birthday. With the composer known, if at all, to many people just by *The Rio Grande*, an extensive study of Lambert, examining all aspects of this remarkable man, seemed a natural progression after completing *William Walton: Muse of Fire* (Woodbridge: Boydell Press, 2001).

For this book I am deeply indebted to two people: Diana Sparkes, daughter of Hubert and Dora Foss, for making available to me the letters and documents in the Hubert Foss Archives, now in the British Library; and Elizabeth Panourgias, daughter of Angus Morrison, for allowing me to quote from all her father's material that was presented to the Royal College of Music Archives in 1990. I am also especially grateful to David Lloyd-Jones (who instigated this book) and Diana Sparkes for painstakingly reading every page and making many helpful suggestions as well as correcting numerous errors. Their help, encouragement and enthusiasm have been invaluable.

Many people have in different ways been extremely helpful in my research and I would like to thank the following: John Amis, Denis Aplvor, Felix Aprahamian, John Belcher, Stewart Craggs, Lewis Foreman, John France, James Gibson, Victor Gordon (son of Gavin Gordon), Kyla Greenbaum (sister of Hyam Greenbaum), Timothy Hands, Pauline Gray (daughter of Cecil Gray), Trevor Hoskins (for his research into Lambert's medical history), Nicola Humphries, my sister Jane Jones (in Australia), Leo Kersley (former Sadler's Wells dancer), Patricia Lambert (close friend of Isabel Rawsthorne), Alex Martin in Ohio (former Sadler's Wells dancer), Pamela May (former Sadler's Wells dancer and close friend of Margot Fonteyn), Edward Morgan, Helen Morgan (with regard to Thea Proctor), Norman Morrison, David Owen Norris, Kenneth Harvey Packer, Bruce Phillips, Arthur Ridgewell (for providing me with transfers of Lambert's commercial recordings), Anne Robinson (with regard to Penelope Spencer), Malcolm Riley, Malcolm Rudland, Barry Smith, Mrs Trundley (housekeeper for Patrick Hadley), Malcolm Walker (especially for discographical information) and Eric Wetherell.

I would like to thank many archivists and libraries who have patiently answered my enquiries and made material available to me: Richard Andrewes, Music Librarian, University of Cambridge; Dr Nicolas Bell, Curator of Music Manuscripts, British Library; John van Boolen, Barber Institute of Fine Arts, University of Birmingham; Jude Brimmer, Archivist, Britten-Pears Library; Alison Cable, East Kent Archives Centre; Julia Creed, Assistant Archivist, ROHCG; Sophie Currie, Oxford University Press; Diana Fasoli, Librarian, Buenos Aries; EMI Music Archive Trust, Hayes, Middlesex; Joanne Fitton, Archivist, RNCM, Manchester; Francesca Franchi, ROH Archivist; David Hannaford, Community Librarian, Margate; Dr Peter Horton, Reference Librarian, RCM; The Hyman Kreitman Research Centre, Tate Britain; Dr Paul Kuik, Nederlands Muziek Instituut; Peter Linnitt, BBC Music Library; Melanie Peart, Archivist, Rambert Dance Company; Dr Rupert Ridgewell, RCM; Eleanor Roberts, Hallé Development; Karen White, BBC Written Archives Centre, Caversham; and Simon Wright, Oxford University Press music department.

Extracts from Michael Ayrton's *Golden Sections* (Methuen & Co. Ltd.) are published with acknowledgement to the Ayrton estate; from Arthur Bliss's *As I Remember* (Faber & Faber) by kind permission of the Bliss Trust; from Harriet Cohen's *A Bundle of Time* (Faber & Faber) with acknowledgement to the estate of Harriet Cohen; from Tom Driberg's *The Best of Both Worlds* (Phoenix House Ltd) with acknowledgement to Messrs Bruce Hunter and John Rayner, Lord Bradwell's literary executors; from Andrew Motion's *The Lamberts* (Chatto & Windus) with acknowledgement to the author; from Anthony Powell's *Messengers of Day* and *Faces in my Times* by kind permission of David Higham Associates Ltd, and from Humphrey Searle's *Quadrille with a Raven* with acknowledgement to Fiona Searle. Extracts from Dame Ninette de Valois's *Come Dance with Me* and *Step by Step* are reproduced by kind permission of the Royal School of Ballet. Acknowledgements are also due for extracts from Mark Baring's *Por Lit'le Bleeder* (Graphic Type), Richard Buckle's *The Adventures of a Ballet Critic* (Cresset Press), Leslie Edwards' *In Good Company* (Dance Books), Nina Hamnett's *Is She a Lady?* (Allan Wingate), Elisabeth Lutyens' *A Goldfish Bowl* (Cassell & Co.), Anthony Phillips' *Sergey Prokofiev: Diaries, 1924–1933* (Faber & Faber), Peter Quennell's *The Marble Foot* (Curtis Brown), Richard Temple Savage's *A Voice from the Pit* (David & Charles), David Vaughan's *Frederick Ashton and his Ballets* (A. & C. Black) and Hugo Vickers' *Cecil Beaton: The Authorized Biography* (Weidenfeld & Nicolson). Thanks are also due to the Rawsthorne Trust and Friends of Alan Rawsthorne for permission to quote from their publication *The Creel*.

For permission to reproduce the following plates I am grateful to Getty Images (frontispiece, 8, 29, 37, 38), Victoria & Albert Museum, London (9, 25, 41), the Secretary to the Delegates of Oxford University Press (10), Elizabeth Panourgias (15), the Hubert Foss Archive (17), Pauline Gray (18), the National Portrait Gallery, London (20, 22), David Higham Associates Ltd (21), Tate Images (26), Julia Blake (28), Chetana Arya (36), ArenaPAL (39, 40), and Lola Marsden (43).

For permission to reproduce the following images in appendix 11, I am grateful to the Queensland Art Gallery, Brisbane (1), the Art Gallery of South Australia, Adelaide (2); the National Gallery of Australia, Canberra (3); the Kerry Stokes Collection, Perth (4), the Art Gallery of NSW, Sydney (6); the National Gallery of Victoria, Melbourne (8, plate 2), Christ's Hospital School, Horsham (10), Victor Gordon (11, 21, 23), Elizabeth Panourgias (12), the National Portrait Gallery (16, 19, 20), the Towner Art Gallery, Eastbourne (17), the Barber Institute of Fine Arts, University of Birmingham (18), the Victoria & Albert Museum (22), The Dancing Times (24), Charles Draught (25–7); the estate of Michael Ayrton (28–33), and John Minnion (34, 35).

Acknowledgement is also due to the collection of Sir Frederick Ashton (plate 7), Illustrated (plate 24), British Broadcasting Corporation (27), Baron (plates 31–3), Crown Copyright (plate 34), Ballet Today (plate 35), Penguin Music Magazine (plate 42) and Leicestershire County Council Artwork (app. 11 no. 13).

Finally, I am most grateful to the Vaughan Williams Trust and the John Ireland Trust for their generous financial support towards the publication of this book.

Stephen Lloyd
December 2013

Tributes from Lambert's Friends and Acquaintances

Denis Aplvor 'Lambert was the greatest, most lovable, and most entertaining personality of the musical world.'

Thomas Armstrong 'Those who remember Constant as a young man will remember that he was the most wonderful companion, a marvellous musician and a gay enchanting companion whose conversation was like a display of fireworks.'

Malcolm Arnold 'Had he lived into this time and he was given the opportunities, I think he had the makings of a great conductor.'

Frederick Ashton 'I remember that Maynard Keynes once said to me that [Constant Lambert] was potentially the most brilliant man he'd ever met. ... He was a tremendous influence on me musically and cultivated my musical tastes tremendously and I owe him a very big debt in that way.'

Michael Ayrton 'He simply had a human quality which made him enormously exciting company, on any subject, serious, absurd, grotesque, comic – simply to be in his company was a most extraordinary and stimulating experience and I've never known anyone else who could match it.'

Arthur Bliss 'Constant Lambert is almost kaleidoscopic in his talent. A sensitive composer, a brilliant pianist, an acid critic. And an accomplished conductor, his influence on English music is liberal and compelling.'

Kenneth Clark 'In the creation of what is now a world famous company, Ninette de Valois provided the drive and discipline, Constant Lambert the musicianship, Freddie Ashton the inventive genius. They were a perfect combination.'

Clement Crisp 'A musician of genius, a superlative conductor.'

Christian Darnton 'He will be remembered as a person, a fertilizing influence, of wide culture, with a flair for the bizarre in almost all spheres of living. ... His gifts as conversationalist, conductor, critic, writer, poet (tanto lascivo!), were, I think pretty equally divided. And what a richness!'

Margot Fonteyn 'That brilliant composer, conductor and champion of ballet in this country.'

Hubert Foss 'He was the idea of the artist incarnate, for while as a man and a musician he stood alone and unclassifiable, a single figure of genius, he embodied and expressed the ideas and thoughts of his time. ... He believed passionately in music and sought nothing but the best of its kind. Lambert had complete integrity.'

Cecil Gray 'A schizophrenic, Manichaean, ambivalent dichotomy, a Hegelian trinity of opposing subjects combined into a unity, at once a fin-de-siècle Frenchman and a bluff Englishman, a Baudelaire, a Fielding, an Erik Satie and a Henry Purcell, a Ronald Firbank and a Winston Churchill.'

Robert Helpmann 'I don't suppose anybody will ever really know how much he contributed to the success of the English Ballet as it stands today, not only being the most remarkable ballet conductor probably that there ever has been but in every way the way he contributed in every department of it, the décor, the musical taste, the standard of music, the playing of the orchestras.'

Robert Irving 'To his friends the recollection of him will always remain crystal-clear: of a great person, a man of very strong feelings and thoughts, an irrepressible wit, and a driving force whose influence on the British ballet was boundless and unique.'

Gordon Jacob 'He was the most brilliant musician I have known in my lifetime.'

Lydia Lopokova 'There's a genius there; it's rich and talented in spite of all that drink. I like it.'

Elisabeth Lutyens 'Amongst musicians Constant Lambert towered. ... The musical world shrank for me at his death. ... He was one of the most honest people, a person with the greatest integrity and the greatest generosity.'

Ralph Nicholson 'He was one of the most brilliant people I have known and one of the most splendid conductor-composers – a very good conductor.'

Harold Rutland 'The most stimulating conversationalist on music I've ever met.'

Edward Sackville-West 'He was among the most amusing people I have ever met and I often wake in the night and laugh over the joke postcards he used to send Gerald Berners.'

Osbert Sitwell 'When he was very young, even then it was impossible not to be astonished at his extraordinary knowledge of all that was going on in the arts in Europe. In this respect I do not think I ever met his equal.'

Ninette de Valois 'In Lambert lay our only hope of an English Diaghilev. ... Everyone loved him and respected him so enormously. He was quite unique. ... There were times when I used to say, "Please God, don't let anything happen to Constant." ... He was the greatest ballet conductor and adviser that this country has had.'

William Walton 'He was a fascinating companion, a wonderful talker and I learnt an enormous amount from him'

David Webster 'Constant Lambert was far more to Sadler's Wells Ballet than a Musical Director, or Adviser; he was a man of knowledge and taste in the visual and the literary, as well as in music, and we could gratefully look to Constant for advice in all kinds of problems of the ballet, sure that we would have a wise reply.'

Steuart Wilson 'You could not miss his vitality: it sparkled, it flowed like a torrent, it drenched like a fountain, it was real, and when it came it was spontaneous. He wrote criticism as he talked; ... when he thought a thing was good, no composer ever had a better champion.'

A Chronology

1905	23 Aug.	Born in Fulham
1909		The Lamberts move to 13 Margaretta Terrace, Chelsea
1910		Constant attends Mrs Spencer's school in Albert Bridge Road
1913		The Lamberts move to 25 Glebe Place, Chelsea
1914		Constant attends Manor House School, Clapham
1915	14 Sept.	Joins Christ's Hospital school, West Sussex
1916	29 July	Admitted to school's infirmary with what was later diagnosed as streptococcal septicaemia
	Sept.	Transferred to Royal Sea Bathing Hospital, Margate
1917	Apr.	Returns home from Margate
	Dec.	George Lambert leaves for Egypt and Palestine as Australian war artist
1918	Apr.	Constant returns to Christ's Hospital
	7 June	George Lambert home from abroad after contracting malaria
	Oct.	Constant's appendix removed at Middlesex Hospital
1919	Jan.	George Lambert leaves for Gallipoli
	Aug.	George Lambert returns home
1920	June	Constant's final operation, on tendons of right leg
1921	4 Feb.	George Lambert sails for Australia
1922	Aug.	Constant leaves Christ's Hospital
	Sept.	Enrols at the Royal College of Music
1923	May	Sees revue *Dover Street to Dixie* at London Pavilion
	28 June	*Green Fire* performed at RCM Patron's Fund Rehearsal
	8 Dec.	*Dance for Orchestra* performed at Pump Rooms, Bath
1924	6 Mar.	*The White Nightingale* and *Serenade* performed at RCM
1925	Mar.	In Spain with Walton and the Sitwells
	19 Mar.	Works by Lambert, Moeran and Hadley performed at RCM
	31 Mar.	Conducts Sibelius's Symphony No. 4 (slow movement) at RCM
	12/13 July	Timpanist in Strachey's *Son of Heaven* (music by Walton)
	14 July	Conducts his own suite from Glinka's *Ruslan and Ludmila*, inviting Diaghilev to attend
	Oct/Nov	Walton plays *Portsmouth Point* to Diaghilev at Savoy Hotel; Lambert, also present, plays his *Adam and Eve* which Diaghilev accepts
	Dec.	In Paris with Christopher Wood
1926	Jan.	With Wood in Paris and is painted by him
	Mar.	Leaves RCM; in Monte Carlo for *Romeo and Juliet* rehearsals.
	22 Apr.	Amy Lambert sails for Australia
	27 Apr.	Recites at second public performance of *Façade*, at New Chenil Galleries
	4 May	*Romeo and Juliet* premiere in Monte Carlo
	18 May	*Romeo and Juliet* performed in Paris – a political riot on the first night
	21 June	*Romeo and Juliet* performed in London
	29 June	Third public performance of *Façade*; Lambert sole reciter
	27 July	Maurice Lambert marries Olga Morrison; family home sold and Constant lives at 15 Cheyne Gardens, Chelsea
	3 Sept.	First broadcast, *The Wheel of Time*, with selection from *Façade*
	9 Sept.	*The Blackbirds*, with Florence Mills, opens at London Pavilion
	Oct.	First article, for *Apollo*
	27 Oct.	*Champêtre* conducted by Guy Warrack at the Aeolian Hall
	16 Nov.	*Divertimento* conducted by Anthony Bernard at Chelsea Music Club
	27 Nov.	Constant's article on Walton in *Boston Evening Transcript*

1927	14 May	Attends last night of *The Blackbirds*
	22 June	*Romeo and Juliet* in Diaghilev season at Princes Theatre, London
	Aug.	Moves to 189 High Holborn
	9 Sept.	*Pomona* first staged by the Company of the Colón Theatre, in Buenos Aires
	28 Nov.	Recites *Façade* at Arts Theatre Club, Great Newport Street, London
1928	27 Feb.	First performance of *The Rio Grande*, BBC broadcast
	17 Apr.	'I now have an accompanying job'
	10 July	Conducts *Leda and the Swan* (Gluck) at Apollo Theatre
	20 July	Article for *Radio Times*: 'The Future of Jazz'
	23 July	Second broadcast of *The Rio Grande* together with first performance of *Elegiac Blues*. Constant contributes article on jazz to *Life and Letters*
	14 Sept.	Recites *Façade* at the ISCM Festival in Siena
1929	16 Jan.	Article on William Boyce for first issue of *The Listener*
	16 Feb.	Amy Lambert sails home from Australia, arriving home on 24 April
	14 Mar.	Sees Anna May Wong in *The Circle of Chalk* at New Theatre
	Apr.	Moves to 42 Peel Street (mother's new house)
	29 Apr.	Recites *Façade* with Walton conducting at Salle Chopin, Paris
	14 June	First (broadcast) performance of Music for Orchestra conducted by Leslie Heward.
	12 July	First recording session of *Façade* for Decca (takes not used)
	22 July	Conducts *Music for Orchestra* at Covent Garden as a Ballets Russes 'Symphonic Interlude'
	13 Aug.	Second recording session of *Façade* (again takes not used)
	19 Aug.	Death of Diaghilev in Venice
	29 Aug.	Conducts first public concert performance of *Music for Orchestra* at Proms
	30 Oct.	*Seven Songs from the Chinese* at Gordon Bryan concert, Aeolian Hall.
	28 Nov.	Third *Façade* recording session (takes issued)
	12 Dec.	Conducts first concert performance of *The Rio Grande* at Manchester
	13 Dec.	*The Rio Grande* performed in London, Queen's Hall
1930	11 Jan.	Recording session of *The Rio Grande* for Columbia in Westminster Central Hall
	16 Feb.	Attends inaugural dinner for foundation of Camargo Society
	21 Mar.	Conducts and recites (*Façade*) at Contemporary Arts Festival in Bath
	12 Apr.	First article for *Nation and Athenæum*
	29 May	Constant's father dies in Australia
	15 June	Private performance of *The Rio Grande* at which Lambert plays percussion
	16 July	Lambert conducts the Frankfurt Symphony Orchestra
	21 Aug.	Suicide of Christopher Wood
	4 Sept.	Conducts *The Rio Grande* at the Proms
	19 Oct.	Conducts Camargo Society first programme (including *Pomona*) and appointed Camargo conductor
	17 Dec.	Suicide of Philip Heseltine (Peter Warlock)
1931	20 Jan.	First talk for the BBC
	3 May	Conducts first performance of Wilde's *Salomé* with incidental music by Lambert at Gate Theatre, London
	24 July	Conducts ballet matinée at ISCM Festival, Oxford
	27 July	Conducts *Music for Orchestra* at ISCM Festival in Queen's Hall
	5 Aug.	Marries Florence Chuter; they live at 15 Percy Street
	6 Nov.	Conducts Purcell's *Dido and Aeneas* at Sadler's Wells
	15 Nov.	First article for *Sunday Referee*
	29 Nov.	*A Day in a Southern Port* given by Camargo Society, Savoy Theatre
	18 Dec.	First performance (broadcast) of Concerto for Piano and Nine Players

1932	July	With Florence in Toulon
	Sept.	Conducts Vic-Wells in Copenhagen
	4&5 Dec.	Camargo Society performs *Adam and Eve*
1933	10 June	Conducts *Belshazzar's Feast* at ISCM Festival in Amsterdam
	29 June	Last presentation of Camargo Society
	June–July	Conducts for Edward James' Ballets of 1933
	Sept.	Appointed joint Professor of Conducting at RCM
	24 Nov.	Stands in for Schoenberg at BBC concert
	12 Dec.	First public performance of Concerto for Piano and Nine Players
1934		Moves to 4 Great James Street, Bloomsbury
		Awarded Collard Fellowship of the Musicians Company
	Apr.	*Music Ho!* published
	Aug.	In Toulon
	Sept.	In Venice for performance of Concerto for Piano and Nine Players
	Oct.	Margot Fonteyn joins Vic-Wells Company
1935	Jan.	Conducts in place of Beecham in Budapest
	15 Mar.	Conducts first performance of van Dieren's *Chinese Symphony*
	11 May	Son born, named Christopher – or Kit – after Christopher Wood
	Aug.	Conducts Vic-Wells Ballet Company's first provincial tour
1936		Moves to 10 Trevor Place, Knightsbridge
	29 Jan.	Conducts first performance of *Summer's Last Will and Testament*
	11 Feb.	Conducts first performance of ballet *Apparitions* (after Liszt)
	24 Apr.	Death of Bernard van Dieren
	Aug.	Conducts Vic-Wells' provincial tour of north of England and Scotland
	7 Oct.	Van Dieren memorial concert at Aeolian Hall
	8 Nov.	Takes part in Liszt concert at Oxford organized by Humphrey Searle
1937	4 Jan.	Conducts *Manon Lescaut* at Covent Garden (three performances)
	9 Apr.	Conducts van Dieren memorial concert at Broadcasting House, including second performance of the *Chinese Symphony*
	27 Apr.	Conducts first performance of Berners' ballet *A Wedding Bouquet*
	15 June	Conducts first performance of Bliss's ballet *Checkmate* in Paris
	Aug.	Alice von Hofmannsthal allows Lambert and Fonteyn the use of Hanover Lodge, Regent's Park. Constant and Florence are guests of the Hofmannstahls at Kammer Castle in Austria; break-up of their marriage
	Oct.	Music critic of short-lived magazine *Night and Day*
	9 Dec.	Operation on left ear
1938	27 Jan.	Conducts first performance of *Horoscope*
	16 Feb.	Treated in nursing home for bronchitis and pneumonia
	6 Mar.	Last article for *Sunday Referee*
	15 Mar.	Ill again with severe sinus infection and high temperature
	1 Apr.	Hyam Greenbaum conducts second performance of *Summer's Last Will and Testament*
	Summer	Short holiday in France with Cecil Gray
1939	5 Apr.	Conducts first performance of Britten's *Ballad of Heroes*
	27 Apr.	Conducts first performance of Berners' *Cupid and Psyche*
	May	Fonteyn meets Tito Arias at Cambridge
	3 May	Conducts *Turandot* at Covent Garden (two performances)
	July	Finishes teaching at RCM
	Sept.	Outbreak of war; tours with Sadler's Wells, accompanying on piano
1940	23 Jan.	*Dante Sonata* first staged
	May	Sadler's Wells' tour of Holland cut short by German advance

	21 June	Conducts National Gallery concert in a festival of English and French music
	Oct.	4-week ENSA tour
	24 Nov.	First performance of *Dirge for 'Cymbeline'* at Cambridge
1941		Still has use of Hanover Lodge
		On ENSA advisory council
	14 Jan.	Sadler's Wells opens at New Theatre
1942	12 Oct.	First performance (broadcast) of *Aubade héroïque*
	Nov.	On CEMA Music Panel
	6 Dec.	Conducts second UK performance of Britten's *Sinfonia da Requiem*
	Dec.	Moves back to Peel Street with his mother
1943	Apr.	Records music with LPO for documentary film *Battle for Music*
1944	Feb.	Moves into All Souls' Place with Michael Ayrton
	9 Mar.	Train journey to Hanley when he and Ayrton 'decorate' the compartment
	Nov.–Dec.	ENSA tour in Italy
1945		Florence remarries
	Jan.	ENSA tour in Belgium and France
	July–Sept.	Associate conductor of the Henry Wood Proms
	Oct.	Conducts in Poland
	Dec.	Conducts in Belgium
1946	20 Feb.	Gala reopening of Covent Garden with Tchaikovsky's *The Sleeping Beauty*
	July–Sept.	Assistant Conductor of the Henry Wood Proms
	29 Sept.	BBC Third Programme starts
	12 Dec.	Purcell's *The Fairy Queen* at Covent Garden
1947		Moves to 39 Thurloe Square
	Feb.	Holiday in Ischia. Conducts at Cannes Music Festival.
	29 May	Conducts *Turandot* at Covent Garden (8 performances)
	July	Resigns as music director of Sadler's Wells Ballet
	7 Oct.	Marries Isabel Delmer. Moves to Albany Street
1948	22 Jan.	Film *Anna Karenina* shown at Leicester Square Theatre, London
	28 June	Appointed joint artistic director of Sadler's Wells with de Valois and Ashton
	Sept.	Conducts Sadler's Wells Ballet in Paris
1949	24 Mar.	Return to Covent Garden greeted with ovation
	Apr.	Conducts at ISCM Festival in Sicily
	9 Oct.	Conducts Sadler's Wells Ballet's triumphant opening at Metropolitan Opera House, New York
1950	June	Holiday in France, composing *Tiresias*
1951	8 May	Conducts first concert of Purcell festival at Victoria & Albert Museum
	9 July	Conducts first performance of *Tiresias*
	15 July	Conducts *Summer's Last Will and Testament* for the last time
	15 Aug.	Last conducting engagement at the Proms
	21 Aug.	Dies of broncho-pneumonia and diabetes mellitus at the London Clinic
	25 Aug.	Burial service at St Bartholomew's the Great, Smithfield; interment of his ashes at Brompton Cemetery
	7 Sept.	Memorial concert at St Martin-in-the-Fields

1

A Meteor Fell …

TOWARDS the end of his comparatively short life, Constant Lambert was commissioned by the great film producer Sir Alexander Korda to provide a score for a new screen version of Tolstoy's classic, *Anna Karenina*. With its Russian setting, and with trains adding such an important and tragic element, Korda may not have realised how appropriate his choice of composer had been. Russian music had always been central to Lambert, and in his last years he had a favourite London pub with a garden where he would often sit and watch the trains pass by. When a year later he was invited by the Hallé Orchestra to conduct a series of concerts mainly of Russian music, he unusually took the opportunity to reveal something of his ancestry concerning Russia and trains. 'I have no Russian blood in my veins,' he wrote, 'nor have I ever visited the country. But it is perhaps not without significance that my father, the painter, was born in St Petersburg, both sides of his family being occupied either in engineering work on the Russian railways or in constructing the first locomotives made in the country itself.'[1]

Constant's grandfather, George Washington Lambert, born in Baltimore, had indeed been one of a group of American engineers involved in the construction of the first railways in Russia. It was there that he had met his second wife, Annie Matilda, his first having died. She was the only child of Thomas Firth, an English engineer whose family originally came from Yorkshire. Even at the time of their wedding (the bride being only 19[2] and the groom 35) George was experiencing warnings of heart trouble, and it was after the birth of three daughters that the seriousness of his condition caused Annie to travel with George to London to seek expert medical advice, leaving the children in the care of her step-daughter. As it turned out, she made a speedy return to Russia where her fourth child, a son, was born on 13 September 1873. George, who remained in London, died there on 25 July, aged only 40.

The baby was baptised George Washington Thomas in the British-American Congregational Church in St Petersburg. In 1875 George, grandparents, mother and sisters left Russia for Germany where Thomas Firth had been appointed Director of the Locomotive Works at Esslingen, in Würtemberg. There George enjoyed a pleasant upbringing in the local countryside of vineyards, fruit trees and woods, with his grandfather taking him for walks and instilling in him a love of nature. He was also taught to box. But before George was eight, with Thomas's retirement there was another family move, back to England, settling at Yeovil, in Somerset. There he found life less easy-going. He attended the local Kingston Grammar School as a day scholar and made good progress, but this went hand in hand with a certain conceit, for which he was admonished by his grandfather who made him clean the windows of his house. He found life at home unsatisfactory with its feminine domination and where it seemed his interests were secondary to those of his three sisters. (Constant's son Kit was also to suffer from the attention of female relatives who either dominated or spoilt him when left in their care following the break-up of his parents' marriage.) Their mother being a pianist, it was accepted that the girls should have music lessons, but George's

---

[1] Lambert, 'Myself and Russian Music', *Hallé Magazine*, 10 May 1948, p. 6.

[2] Amy Lambert, *Thirty Years of an Artist's Life*, p. 13. Annie's birthdate as given in the 'Family Tree' in Andrew Motion, *The Lamberts: George, Constant and Kit* (London: Chatto & Windus, 1986; paperback Hogarth Press, 1987), is clearly wrong, making her about nine at the time of marriage.

desire to learn the violin was not satisfied. However, his artistic talent first became apparent when he won a South Kensington drawing competition in the under-12 age group.

But this talent had little chance of blossoming as there was a further family upheaval in 1886. Thomas Firth's brother Robert had settled in Australia and his letters had convinced Thomas that it would be ideal for him in his retirement to settle there too. It was onboard ship that George executed his first watercolour sketch. 'From the time that I got this desire to do Art,' he recorded, 'I became a most objectionable kid in every way; moody, disobedient, dirty, noisy in flashes, a prig, a little beast, and it says much for the tolerance of both crew and passengers on board *The Bengal* that I was considered full of possibilities though difficult.'[3] Even at school he had earned himself the name 'Cocky Lambert'. On 20 January 1887 they reached Sydney.

To George, his early years in Australia seemed idyllic, roaming free on his granduncle's sheep station near Warren in New South Wales, with no desire for any further education. But when he was 14 it was felt that it was time he had a job, and so he was sent to Sydney where his mother and sisters were living. There he worked first as a clerk for a firm of textile merchants, and two years later as a clerk in the Shipping Master's Office. But the constraints of a city job and a crowded family house were not for him and he longed for the bush, returning to the sheep station in 1891. This time, however, life was harder than before because, with no money, he had to work as a hired-hand, dipping and shearing sheep, breaking in horses and doing any other job that was expected of him. Nevertheless, it was an environment that he enjoyed, with its open spaces and wild nature all around.

When he could he took up his sketch book, his subjects being mainly animals or men. He successfully submitted a few drawings to the *Sydney Bulletin*, a literary publication, which earned him some extra pocket money. He showed his sketches to a freelance artist who recommended that he studied with Julian Ashton, who was then recognised as the most important art teacher in Sydney. So, with a day job as a grocer's clerk, three times a week he attended evening classes on drawing and, on Saturday afternoons, painting classes. His first real success came in 1896 with a painting in oils, *A Bush Idyll*, depicting a young girl surrounded by goats in a country setting. He sent it to Sydney, somewhat doubtful whether it would be exhibited, and was delighted when the New South Wales Art Gallery bought it for £20. He also became a fairly regular contributor to the *Bulletin* which provided him with an income, and eventually he enrolled as a full-time student at the Sydney Art School under Ashton's direction. Then in 1899 his name became more widely known for the painting *Across the Black Soil Plains*, a study of a team of horses pulling a heavily laden wool wagon across the flat Australian terrain. It was bought by the same gallery for 100 guineas and additionally earned him the Wynne Prize.

For four years George shared a studio with fellow-artist Sydney Long, and when in 1898 Long left for another studio, George's mother moved in, bringing with her her piano and piano students: his grandfather had suggested that it was time that George supported his mother. George had a great mutual affection for her, just as Constant and his mother were to have, and he painted a striking portrait of her with which in 1900 he became the first person to win the New South Wales Society of Artists' travelling scholarship. But, despite his growing success as an illustrator and portrait painter, his income did not prove sufficient for him fully to care for his mother, and after a while she went back to live with her father.

Then one afternoon in 1898, a fellow Ashton student, Marian Absell, invited George

---

[3] Amy Lambert, *Thirty Years of an Artist's Life*, p. 15.

to tea. He had forgotten some equipment necessary for that evening's class and, as the Absells' home was nearer than his, Marian had offered him that item and had brought him home. There he met her sister, Amelia Beatrice, a talented young writer a year older than George, who had worked with her two sisters as photographic retouchers for a Sydney studio since arriving in Australia in the 1890s. George was immediately attracted to this stylish, dark-eyed young girl with jet-black hair. Amy, as she was known, had heard about this enthusiastic new student and she in her turn felt an exhilaration in the presence of this tall, fair-haired, blue-eyed and broad-shouldered, vital person. He was extremely swift in his movements, so swift in fact that a musician friend of Amy's called him a 'job-lot Apollo' and described a walk with him like 'being attached to a comet'. The fact that their families had been similarly uprooted from their home environment brought them together (the Absells having left London) and George and Amy soon became close friends. But even in those early days she sensed a remoteness about him, as if 'he was with us but not of us', she later wrote.

George and Amy, as illustrator and writer, both contributed to the monthly *Australian Magazine* that had been established as a rival to the *Sydney Bulletin* by a group of enthusiastic fellow Ashton students that included Thea Proctor, who occasionally modelled for George's illustrations,[4] and Sydney Long. First issued in March 1899, it embraced literature, music, drama and art, but it closed in September after six issues. However, on being awarded the travelling scholarship, with typical swiftness George told Amy, 'Well, I'm going to London and Paris – but not without you.' They were married on 4 September 1900 at St Thomas's Church in North Sydney, and two days later left Australia aboard the *SS Persic*, whose main cargo was a huge consignment of frozen meat for the soldiers fighting the Boer War in South Africa. They had good company on their journey when fellow artist Hugh Ramsay[5] boarded the liner at Melbourne, but it was to be a long and uncomfortable voyage. At Cape Town, because of the Boer War, their ship, like others, was 'commandeered to deport the undesirables from the colony, seditious Dutchmen, for the most part, with their wives and families'.[6] Then there were further delays, one being caused by the ship's water-condensers breaking down, another to take on board the crew of a boat whose cargo had burst into flames mid-ocean, and then an unscheduled call at Tenerife.

So they were much relieved when the boat docked in London on 11 November 1900. Ramsay had a brief trip to make to Scotland, the country of his birth, and George and Amy's plans were to go with him to Paris where he had been offered the share of a studio. Meanwhile, the Lamberts took a small furnished studio in the St Petersburg Mews, Bayswater, where George set to work, completing his first self-portrait, 'a frankly direct painting with a touch of youthful arrogance in the challenging eyes and dilated nostrils' as Amy described it. He illustrated two short stories for *Cassell's Magazine*, a popular monthly whose contributors at about that time included E. W. Hornung with his *Raffles* stories, and Rudyard Kipling, whose *Kim* was serialised throughout 1901. He also had a few commissions, for pencil portraits.

During their brief stay in London, Amy formed what was to be a valuable friendship,

---

[4] Alethea (Thea) Mary Proctor (1879–1966), printmaker, designer and painter, born in Armidale, New South Wales, to an English father and Australian mother who divorced in 1897. Although she was engaged for a while (until 1902) to the artist Sydney Long, she never married. She is especially known for her lithographs and woodcuts.

[5] Hugh Ramsay (1877–1906), Glasgow- born Australian artist whose family moved to Australia in 1878.

[6] Amy Lambert, *Thirty Years of an Artist's Life*, p. 27. Amy erroneously states that 'the Boer War was just over'. It did not end until 1902.

with Mrs Arthur Halford, one of whose daughters was married to Edmund Davis,[7] a prosperous Australian-born art collector and mining magnate who had made his money in South Africa and Northern Rhodesia. This friendship with the Halford family was, as Amy wrote, 'to prove on so many occasions a sure prop to our weakness, both spiritual and material'.[8]

As soon as Hugh Ramsay had returned from Scotland, on 3 February 1901 the three set off for Paris, leaving a London in mourning after the funeral of Queen Victoria the previous day. They found temporary accommodation at the Hôtel de Nice, Rue des Beaux-Arts, but soon George and Amy moved to a top-floor studio apartment with a moderate rent in the Latin quarter at 31 Boulevard Saint-Jacques. With Hugh close by at 51, they became part of a small but close-knit community of Australian artists studying in Paris. To keep fit, George practised boxing with his friends. It was probably in the first half of 1901 that he painted a group picture of five friends that included himself, Amy and Hugh Ramsay.

It was in Paris, on 25 June, that Amy gave birth to their first son, who was named Maurice Prosper Lambert. As their accommodation was not only too draughty for bringing up a baby but also infested with vermin, before long George found another studio in the Rue de la Tombe Issoire.

George and Hugh both enrolled at the Académie Colarossi, an establishment that had been set up as a rival to the more conservative École des Beaux-Arts. It was one of the cheapest of the Parisian academies, and although they found the atmosphere stimulating they were dissatisfied with the teaching and, in the summer of 1901, they progressed to the Atelier Délécluse, only to find the teaching there little better. The travelling scholarship provided George with £150 annually for three years, but one condition had been that he should produce a picture each year, and for his first he used his 'ready and willing model' for a Spanish-styled portrait of Amy which he called *La Guitariste* (1902). It is the warmest of his images of her, forward facing and half smiling as she sits clutching an upright guitar. The painting was exhibited in the Société National des Beaux-Arts before being sent to Sydney. It was to be the only painting he sent as part of his scholarship conditions during his two years in Paris. In that time he produced four other paintings that featured Amy: *Mother and Child* (1901, with the three-month-old Maurice) and *The French Landlady* (1901, also with Maurice), both influenced by Whistler whose work George had first come across at the home of Edmund Davis; *Déjeuner de la femme-de-menage* (1901–2, a pencil drawing with a rather anxious-looking Amy seated at a breakfast table full of plates, dishes and a wine bottle); and what Amy described as a portrait of poverty: a studio interior with her peeling potatoes and with baby Maurice eating a last biscuit. George painted at least two portraits of Ramsay who remained a good friend, writing to his brother in Australia:

> I stayed at home and worked and spent a quiet evening at Lambert's, nursing the baby. Maurice is growing like fun. ... Tell Auntie that Mrs Lambert is awfully good to me and darns my socks.[9]

Sadly, while in Paris, Ramsay contracted tuberculosis and was advised to return to Australia where he died four years later.

[7] Sir Edmund Gabriel Davis (1861–1939) was born in Melbourne and trained as an artist in Paris, but for health reasons went to Africa, where he embarked on a life of trading. Married in 1888, he and his wife became connoisseurs and patrons of the arts, and from 1918 lived at Chilham Castle, Kent.

[8] Amy Lambert, *Thirty Years of an Artist's Life*, p. 36.

[9] Letter from Hugh Ramsay in Paris to his brother Harry in Australia, 19 February 1902.

In addition to his scholarship money, George had been offered a weekly salary by the *Sydney Bulletin* for as long as he kept up a steady supply of illustrations for the material they sent him, so all the while he had the arduous task of fulfilling the weekly demands for illustrations for which he received £2 a week. But even with this additional income, with no buyers he found Paris too expensive, and in November 1902, short of money, the Lamberts had no option but to return to London where they felt their prospects would be sounder.

They had some unexpected luck when, at the suggestion of the Davises in London, the 'portrait of poverty' was bought for £10, and with that and what they could get from the sale of the contents of their Paris studio, they treated themselves to a brief holiday in a little fishing village near Boulogne.

Back in London, Edmund Davis offered them the temporary tenancy of an empty studio in a recently completed block of flats, Lansdowne House, in Lansdowne Road, Holland Park, and they managed to find two rooms in a house in Shepherd's Bush that was not too far from the studio. With his scholarship money slow in arriving, and George behind in supplying the second of the three required pictures, in Lansdowne House he produced *The Three Kimonos* (1905), with three friends as obliging sitters. So that Amy could help out in the studio, it became necessary to employ a part-time nursemaid who became involved in the last of the scholarship pictures, *Equestrian Portrait of a Boy* (1905), the boy being young Maurice astride a pony held by the new nursemaid who afterwards told Amy that 'it was not the posing that she objected to, but having to read *Brer Rabbit* aloud to Maurice and endure the corrections of his father'.[10]

The family were increasingly to be subjects in George's pictures. He illustrated books as well, including *Two Awheel and Some Others Afoot in Australia* (1903) by the historian Arthur (Wilberforce) Jose who, in November 1905, became his brother-in-law when he married Amy's other sister, Evelyn. Amy modelled for at least one of the illustrations in that book, and a group of father, mother and child with a landscape background, painted in Lansdowne House, became the first of a series of family paintings that brought George to the notice of the Royal Academy and they were exhibited annually at Burlington House.

However, his first canvas to be exhibited by the Royal Academy was completed in 1903: a portrait in oils of Thea Proctor, who had been a fellow-student at the Sydney School of Art. She arrived in London that summer, accompanied by her mother, and was to figure significantly in many of his paintings and in the Lamberts' lives. She had come to study at the St John's Wood School of Art in the hope of being accepted at the Royal Academy school. She already knew many of George's Australian friends in London and George even found time to give her some instruction. Amy somewhat ambiguously recorded that 'she was a daily visitor at both studio and home; at the former as student and model', implying that at their home she was something other than just a student and a model. She continued: 'The friendly interchange was of mutual benefit, as Lambert gained the services of an exceptionally graceful and artistic model, and Miss Proctor's drawings strengthened in line and directness of approach, and she rarely considered any design complete before it had been passed by Lambert.'[11] But their contact was clearly far more than one would normally expect between mere fellow artists or teacher and student. Six years younger than George, Thea had been born in Australia. Described by a friend as a 'breath-taking beauty', she was always well dressed with a keen fashion sense and, as painted by George, a tall and strikingly

[10] Amy Lambert, *Thirty Years of an Artist's Life*, p. 38.
[11] *Ibid.*, p. 40. Thea Proctor was by no means the only model that George used, although she can be seen in at least nine of his pictures until 1916.

elegant lady. The most surprising outcome of this friendship was her appearance in most of the Lambert 'family' portraits in which she often outshone Amy. But there seems to have been no bitterness as Amy hung George's portrait of Thea in her home, together with some of the family pictures in which Thea appeared.[12] That there were differences between the two is clear when, after Amy's death in 1963, Thea told a friend that Amy had no tolerance at all for a woman 'no matter how beautiful if she had no brains – whereas beauty meant so much to me I felt too much should not be expected, but that is an artist's point of view'.[13] However, Thea certainly did not lack intelligence, and her 1903 portrait, painted in a style similar to Gainsborough, wearing her own stylish summer outfit, remained for many years in the possession of the Lamberts until, in 1946, Amy gave it to the sitter.[14] With his flamboyance and boldness, George was beginning to create a stir in artistic circles and, according to Amy, a self-portrait he painted at this time caused much controversy when it was submitted to the International Society, the sculptor Francis Derwent Wood (whose portrait he painted in 1906) and another artist threatening to resign if it were rejected.

George became a member of the Chelsea Arts Club, 'a very necessary stimulus to a man whose early handicap had resulted in what might have been considered an inferiority complex,' Amy wrote with much candour, and when a permanent tenant was found for the loaned studio, he moved to Rossetti Studios in Chelsea where his best-known London work was to be done. Amy recalled how, after cleaning up the old studio, they had laughed at the number of spots of oil and paint that remained, ominously concluding, 'Somewhat ruefully we departed, feeling that we had bitten the hand that fed us. ... It is only after many years that I realise the hollowness of George's laughter'.[15] In 1904 Arthur Jose, then living in London, was appointed Sydney correspondent to *The Times*, and he offered them the remainder of the lease of a flat he occupied in Fulham, near Bishop's (now Fulham) Palace.

On the night of 23 August the following year, in St Clement's nursing home in Fulham Palace Road, their second son, Leonard Constant, was born. There was a thunderstorm that summer's evening and Amy wrote, as if reporting an omen, that a meteor fell the length of her window. The birth was registered at Lillie Road, Fulham. Constant was later to regard this with mock horror when he saw it on his Royal College of Music entry form – he would have much preferred Shoreditch (Amy's birth place) or even Pimlico!

Both boys were brought up in the atmosphere of the artist's studio. While Maurice was to be more influenced by his father, becoming a sculptor, Constant was closer to his mother and, although he was later to consider George's style dull and academic, he inherited a deep interest in the visual arts that never left him and was indeed to be of great value to him when working in ballet. When a visitor remarked to the three-year-old Constant, 'What thick hair you've got!' the child responded, 'That's because I've got a fertile brain.' Both his grandmothers had been musical, and at a very early age he seemed to have inherited a musical instinct. He would arrange his toys on the table in groups like an orchestra and conduct them with a hoop-stick. When, after a bout

---

[12] George did other portraits of Thea: in 1905 one in charcoal and *Study for Alethea* in oils, and in 1916 a striking *Portrait of a Lady*. In 1906 he did profile sketches in black chalk of both Thea and Amy both adopting a similar pose.

[13] Undated letter from Thea Proctor to Thea Bryant, *c.* 1966, quoted in Sarah Engledow, *The World of Thea Proctor* (Canberra: National Portrait Gallery of Australia, 2005), p. 27.

[14] Anne Gray, *George W. Lambert Retrospective* (Canberra: National Gallery of Australia, 2007). Thea was financially supported in old age by the sale of two Lambert pictures that Amy gave her as legacies (Engledow, *The World of Thea Proctor*, p. 27).

[15] Amy Lambert, *Thirty Years of an Artist's Life*, p. 39.

of whooping-cough, he was recuperating at Littlehampton, he was found at the end of a breakwater, alone, conducting the sea. Amy Lambert proudly told Mr Edwards, his housemaster at Christ's Hospital school, that even as a child he had had ambitions to become a conductor and that at the seaside he used to practise conducting the waves.

Constant was not a strong child and, with George quite often away from home on portrait commissions, Amy was grateful to have such a valuable friend in Mrs Halford, who had been widowed in 1903, and to whom she readily turned for help and advice. As she wrote, Mrs Halford 'had identified our interests with her own, treated our children as if they had been the grandchildren she had never known, advising and assisting in questions of health and education: indeed, I truly think that we owed the life of our younger son to the care she exercised during the first delicate year of his existence.'[16] She recommended that Maurice and Constant should have piano lessons when they were quite young and even helped by paying for them herself. They were taught by a fine pianist, Elsie Hall, an Australian who was a close friend of the family. As Angus Morrison has written of her:

> She always thought Maurice the more naturally musical of the two, and that had he wished, he could have become a professional pianist. Constant had tremendous facility and was a wonderful sight-reader but I don't think he had the patience to polish and perfect his performances as an instrumentalist has to do. He much preferred the excitement of conducting an orchestra – especially in the theatre or opera house, which he always maintained was his natural element.[17]

At seven Constant had a passion for Beethoven's sonatas, and at eight played Bach's Inventions by heart. Bach, Beethoven and Mozart were the only classical composers who inspired him in childhood.[18]

Even at an early age Constant was included in some of his father's pictures. The first of these was an elegantly dressed portrait group, called *The Mother* (1907), with Thea Proctor, looking every bit a member of the family, standing just behind Amy, their heads almost touching, with Maurice to the left gazing with a rather bored expression, and Constant standing in the foreground, his attention seemingly distracted by something on the floor.[19] Also that year, with the same four, was *The Holiday Group (The Bathers)*, Maurice walking naked with his clothes draped over one arm and Constant being carried by Amy. A family group the following year, without Thea, captures well the attention of all three subjects, with Maurice again mounted on a pony and Constant clutching a favourite toy as he is held by a rather voluptuous Amy baring her left shoulder. But the most striking of these 'family' pictures is *The Blue Hat* (1909) in which Thea, in a blue dress with a golden shawl, stands to the right with her back facing, looking across her left shoulder with an almost jealous expression to the family who are seated. Amy is wearing a golden dress and Constant, the centre of attention, is on her lap wearing a dark blue hat with a large feather. His golden locks are very visible. Maurice leans over Amy's right shoulder with a sullen expression. However much surprise there may be in seeing Thea in these pictures, she was considered family

---

[16] *Ibid.*, p. 67.

[17] Angus Morrison, 'The Family', in *Constant Lambert, 1905–1951: A Souvenir of the Exhibition at the South London Art Gallery*, ed. Kenneth Sharpe (London: London Borough of Southwark Council, 1976), pp. 26–7.

[18] Beryl de Zoete, 'The Younger English Composers: III, Constant Lambert', *The Monthly Musical Record*, vol. 59, issue no. 700 (1 April 1929), p. 97.

[19] *The Mother* (1907) was the subject of a ten-minute film produced by Film Australia in collaboration with the Queensland Art Gallery and the Queensland Film Corporation, 1980.

enough to be entrusted with the two boys when their parents were either out or away. She clearly regarded them with much affection, telling Amy that they 'had spoiled me for ordinary children'. She claimed with some pride to have been the first person to take Constant to a concert at the Albert Hall.[20]

Thea modelled for the *Study for Alethea* (1905, charcoal), *The Simpler Life (Study of Thea Proctor)* (1905, pencil) and for *Lotty and the Lady* (1906, oil, bought by the National Gallery of Victoria).[21] She is also seen in one of George's most daring pictures of the time, the allegorical and erotic *The Sonnet* (1907) that invariably caused some outcry whenever it was exhibited. Just as, after studying the paintings of Manet, *La Guitariste* had been a reworking of the latter's *Spanish Singer*, so *The Sonnet* was George's version of Manet's well-known *Le Déjeuner sur l'herbe*, with a fully dressed man (the artist Arthur Streeton) reading to a lady (Thea Proctor) who is facing forward, while seemingly oblivious to the couple, in between them, half-sitting in a thoughtful pose, lies a naked woman, possibly suggested by the words.[22] It was awarded a silver medal at the Exposicion Internacional de Arte in Barcelona in 1911. One painting that for some unknown reason caused greater controversy was a portrait of King Edward VII that had been commissioned by the Imperial Colonial Club. Amy only reveals that it 'got into difficulties for reasons best left in oblivion' and it was the only case of George taking 'legal steps to enforce his rights'. Although the picture was exhibited in Prince's Galleries, Piccadilly, it was never hung in the Imperial Club.

George's family group paintings attracted much attention when they were exhibited, even leading to a few commissions, and on the strength of one of them he and Amy enjoyed a short holiday in Belgium, leaving the children in the care of different friends. The warmest and most natural of these family paintings is *Mother and Sons* (1909). Amy, in a blue full-length dress, is sitting on a bed with Maurice[23] huddled on her back while Constant, naked and leaning backwards against her dress, looks upward affectionately into her eyes, one arm reaching around her neck. The last of these portraits is *Holiday in Essex* (1910) for which George received a prize of 1,600 francs from the Société Nationale des Beaux-Arts when he exhibited it in Paris in 1911. With a hint of Velasquez, it recalls a family holiday at Mersea Island, Essex, although it was executed in the studio, using a local milkman's pony that took some time to train to stand still.

In 1909 they moved to 13 Margaretta Terrace, a short walk off King's Road, Chelsea, where for about four years they looked after Amy's 11-year-old niece, Dulcie, after her parents had separated. She recalled 'little Constant, so pretty at four years old that he used to hide behind his curls with shyness when people took so much notice of him. ... [He] had long fair curls to his shoulders and wore smocks and little velvet pants.' She remembered there was much laughter in the house although George had 'terrible black moods of depression, and Amy, who would look after the boys in the evening, was often very tired.[24] From the age of five until eight Constant went to the nearby Albert Bridge School, many of whose pupils came from artistic families, such as the children of the

---

[20] Engledow, *The World of Thea Proctor*, p. 28.

[21] The housemaid Lotty was modelled by Lottie Stafford, a Cockney Chelsea washerwoman who was a popular model because of her naturalness.

[22] The nude was Kitty Powell, a regular model for George Lambert: Engledow, *The World of Thea Proctor*, p. 27.

[23] Apart from the family portraits, Maurice featured in several other pictures: in *The Shop* (1909, with George himself as the artist), *Seated Boy* (1912, in pencil), in *The Actress* (1913), *Boy with pipes* (1913, in imitation of George Frampton's sculpture of Peter Pan in Kensington Gardens), *Maurice Lambert* (1913) and *The Half-Back* (1920).

[24] Motion, *The Lamberts*, p. 52. (Page references are to the paperback edition.)

actors Sybil Thorndike and Lewis Casson. One pupil, Penelope Spencer, the daughter of the principal Edith Mary Spencer, became a good friend of Constant's, especially when in 1923 she was appointed ballet mistress at the Royal College of Music.[25]

George lived on his nerves, and the death of his mother, early in 1911, caused him much mental and emotional distress, especially because, for financial reasons, he had not been able to respond to a cable at Christmas summoning him to Australia. A portrait commission in Scotland which included a boating holiday in the Isle of Skye provided timely relief. 'I was rapidly approaching that state of health and nerves, in London, that spells disaster, at least mental disaster,' he wrote to Amy, who was staying with the boys at Mrs Halford's house at Cranleigh, in Surrey. He gave her detailed instructions for the tidying of his Chelsea studio in preparation for future work, but it is the absence of any expression of love or real affection in the conclusion to his letter that hints at the curious nature of their relationship and that remoteness which Amy had observed in the early days of their acquaintance: 'As to man's mortality, *il n'y a pas*, there are preferences, and the lady that a man prefers, nowadays, becomes his wife; and you are my pref.: I would sooner see you now than my washing.' This coolness was reciprocated when, after George's death in 1930, Amy came to write his biography. What emerged was a very dry account, devoid of any real emotion, as curious for what it omits as for the manner in which certain facts are presented.

To improve his income George began teaching at the London School of Art, and later at the Camberwell School of Art. Then in 1913 he gave up the tenancy of the Rossetti Studios and the family moved into 25 Glebe Place, Chelsea. A room on the first floor was cleared so that it could be used as a studio, and the house became the family home for the next 13 years. The following year, having just turned nine, Constant followed Maurice and progressed from Mrs Spencer's school to Manor House School in Clapham. He was only to remain there for one year. With the outbreak of war George's income was to decline and Constant was to move to another school where, towards the end of his first year, events were to leave their mark upon him and affect him for the rest of his life.

[25] Penelope Spencer (1901–93). Anne Robinson, 'The Influence of the Margaret Morris Movement on the career of Penelope Spencer', *Margaret Morris Movement Magazine*, no. 51 (Spring 2005), pp. 27–32.

2 1915–22
At Christ's Hospital

G EORGE Lambert was nearly 42 when war was declared; Constant was approaching nine. When it became clear that Australia was sending troops for the conflict, George reported to the Australian High Commission in London to be told that volunteers would only be accepted at recruiting offices in Australia. So, like many of his friends including Derwent Wood, he enlisted instead in the United Artists' Rifle Corps, a home defence unit specially created for those who found themselves in similar circumstances. In 1915 he became commander of 'A' Company and his skills at riding came to the fore, teaching men how to handle a horse.

At the time of the outbreak of war, the Lamberts were staying once again at Cranleigh in Surrey with their good friend Mrs Halford, whose house, as Amy described it, 'was transformed into a sewing party, servants and all. Great rolls of flannel were ordered, machines whirred, scissors flashed and needles flew. Even the children were set to rolling bandages or tearing up old linen into useful sizes.'[1] George's painting had not been bringing in substantial earnings; the war seemed likely to be a further drain on his income, and he was finding it difficult to maintain Maurice and Constant at Manor House School, even though he had been offered a reduction in fees. He had even painted a portrait of the headmaster which, as Amy delicately put it, was 'presented by the artist in recognition of much patience and forbearance with regard to school fees often in arrears per stress of circumstance, but always eventually defrayed.'[2] Matters were not helped by Maurice proving to be a very unwilling pupil. It is quite likely that Mrs Halford, who had already taken great interest in the welfare of the Lamberts, also suggested that Constant should move to the nearby Christ's Hospital school to ease George's financial burden.

Christ's Hospital, in Horsham, Sussex, sometimes referred to as the 'Bluecoat School' because of its distinctive uniform, was a charitable school that had been established by a royal charter in the City of London in 1552. Initially there were two sites, one for boys in Newgate Street, and a second for girls at Hertford that also included the boys' preparatory school. In 1902 the boys' preparatory and upper schools were moved to Horsham. The pupils' education was financed chiefly from investment endowments deriving from legacies and donations of property. Amidst the flurry of war preparation, Constant was taken to London to be interviewed as a possible pupil. George made good use of the contacts he had made with influential people in society. Speaking on Constant's behalf was the artist Walter J. James (1869–1932), later Lord Northbourne, a governor of Christ's Hospital, with whom George had become acquainted through the Chelsea Arts Club and whose portrait he had painted. Providing a reference was another artist, Philip Connard (1875–1958), whose wife had before the war presented elaborate pastoral plays that included both dancing and acting. There was an element of the actor in George, and in one of these plays, *The Awakening of Pan*, he had taken the part of Pan and, with a mask, skin-coloured tights, a goat-skin, pipes and a cluster of grapes, for 20 minutes 'stood immobile on his pedestal, and his sudden response to the embrace, and swift descent and capture and carrying off of Flora, left the audience breathless with surprise and admiration.'[3]

Constant's application for Christ's Hospital proved successful and he joined the

[1] Amy Lambert, *Thirty Years of an Artist's Life*, p. 68.

[2] *Ibid.*, p. 57

[3] *Ibid.*, p. 47

Preparatory School on 14 September 1915. He made an impressive start and by the end of his first school year he had scooped not only prizes for English, drawing and swimming but the prestigious all-round medal. But he was not to receive these awards at the summer prize-giving. The school's name was to take on an ironic ring: he had not quite completed the academic year when, on 29 July 1916, he was admitted to the school's infirmary with a rash and a temperature of 99°F. There were about 830 boys on the school roll and that term had seen 148 cases of rubella, 11 of scarlet fever – one resulting in a death, and 45 similar to Constant's that were diagnosed as 'fourth disease', also with a death.[4] There was good cause for concern. (Many years later, Constant, who always derived great pleasure from ambiguous sayings and comic combinations of words in headlines, received a copy of the Christ's Hospital magazine in which he saw a photograph of the churchyard with the curious caption: 'Boys who die during the term-time are usually buried in the churchyard.' According to Osbert Sitwell, he mused over the macabre import of that statement. How many boys died in an average term? What happened to the deceased who were not fortunate enough to be buried in the churchyard?)[5]

For four days his temperature remained steady so that Dr Gerald Friend, the school's medical officer, felt that there were would be no harm in asking his parents to take him home in a few days. But on 2 August his temperature rose to 103°F, causing Dr Friend to write to Constant's mother:

> I am afraid your boy will not be fit to come home on August 8th as I hoped. He has a rather severe form of the disease with a septic throat and nasal discharge. He is infectious and should not be visited if you have other children at home. But he is going on all right, and I do not think you need have any undue alarm about him. I will let you know again in a day or two how he is.[6]

He had in fact developed streptococcal septicaemia. The infection did not deter George from writing five days later:

> My wife & self propose visiting some friends at Cranleigh tomorrow who will motor us over to Christ's Hospital. We should like to either see the boy or hear the latest bulletin. Naturally we are very anxious but feel confident that everything possible is being done to restore him to health.

To Amy's great sorrow, Mrs Halford died suddenly during the first year of the war ('though we were glad to think that she was spared the knowledge of the suffering of a favoured child', she wrote),[7] and it was in the same house, inherited by her daughter

---

[4] After measles and scarlet fever, what was thought to be a second distinct form of rubella was classified as fourth disease.

[5] Osbert Sitwell, 'Portrait of a Very Young Man', in *Queen Mary and Others* (London: Michael Joseph, 1974), p. 80.

[6] For the correspondence between Dr Friend and the Lamberts, Christ's Hospital and other doctors concerned, and for much of the medical detail concerning Constant Lambert's treatment, I am indebted to Trevor Hoskins' article 'Constant Lambert: his illness at Christ's Hospital School and the role of Dr G. E. Friend', *Journal of Medical Biography*, vol. 11 (2003), pp. 14–20. Correspondence relating to Lambert's childhood illness, 1916–1924, chiefly between his parents and Dr G. E. Friend, the Medical Officer of Christ's Hospital, concerning Lambert's near-fatal attack of streptococcal septicaemia in 1916 and subsequent complications, together with a medical interrogatory signed by Lambert's mother and annotated by Friend, probably compiled in 1915, was presented by the governors of Christ's Hospital in 2006 through the offices of Dr T. W. Hoskins to the British Library: MS Mus. 1118, fols. 149–191.

[7] Amy Lambert, *Thirty Years of an Artist's Life*, p. 68.

and son-in-law, Edmund Davis, that George and Amy now stayed, only about ten miles from the school.

As Amy recorded: 'Once again it became our haven of refuge, being near the school where our child lay in the infirmary all through the long summer holidays. He heard the boys depart to their homes, he heard their return, without realising the lapse of time between. We had a car at our disposal by our kind friends and between our unsatisfactory visits to the school George put up some semblance of work.'[8] While staying at Cranleigh, George seized what opportunities there were to paint, producing an ingenious port-hole cottage interior, entitled *Convex Mirror*, that pictured the occupants, the artist and Amy as if seen reflected in a circular mirror. He also completed a portrait of the maid and two paintings of floral arrangements.

Constant's fever continued until Sunday 13 August when Dr Friend observed an abscess in the right ear and promptly called in a local surgeon from Horsham who straightway performed a partial mastoidectomy while Friend gave the anaesthetic. Matters became much more complicated when it was also found that Constant had septic arthritis in the left ankle and the right knee, and a week later Friend wrote to Rev Arthur William Upcott, the Headmaster, outlining his concerns:

> I am having a very anxious time with Lambert, Prep B. He developed an abscess in one ear last Sunday, and I had to get Jamison to operate on Sunday. This gave temporary improvement, but on Wednesday he developed symptoms of further trouble, and we had to operate again on a knee and an ankle joint which had become infected. The boy since then has held his own and there has been no further extension of the trouble, but of course he is very seriously ill, and at present it is impossible to tell what may happen. Should there be no extension of the poisoning through the blood, I think he has quite a good chance, but if further trouble shows itself the outlook will be a bad one, as he is very young and therefore has not any too much stamina. However at the moment things look fairly favourable.

It was an extremely anxious time, Amy writing:

> After the most serious of the many operations he underwent, we awaited in the school grounds the doctor's report of the result. 'Successful as far as we are able to carry it' was the best news they could give us. George threw his arms around me in an ecstasy of relief, thereby much shocking the doctor's maids, who, too, had shown some interest in the events of the morning.

With the worst over, George and Amy were able to return home. As a token of thanks George presented Friend with a painting of the doctor's house, which was near the infirmary, looking onto a small lake and trees, adding a few sheep, and a pencil sketch of Mrs Friend. He also obtained a job as part of the war effort. With so many young men going off to the war, while at Cranleigh he had made a small income from sketching miniature pencil portraits of soldiers in khaki. One of his subjects had been Henry, son of Sir Alfred Mond, the industrialist and politician who in 1928 became Lord Melchett. This fortuitous acquaintance led to an introduction to Sir Bamfylde Fuller, Director-General of Timber, and ultimately to the position for George as Divisional Works Officer in Wales for Home Timber Supplies. After some preliminary training near Tunbridge Wells, he was based at Bangor, although the districts under his control ranged as far as Aberystwyth and Haverfordwest, where he supervised the felling and sawing of trees for the production of trench supports and duck-boards on the Western Front. As a consequence he was often away from home, although he was

---

[8] *Ibid.*, p. 68.

joined by Amy during the school holidays. Constant, meanwhile, continued to receive daily care at Horsham, with no decline in his condition, but it seems that Edmund Davis had advised seeking a second opinion from Sir Alfred Fripp, the senior surgeon at Guy's Hospital. On 7 September Dr Friend wrote to Jamison to inform him of this step, adding that he had had to reinsert the tubes into the knee and the ankle to drain the fluids. The next day he wrote to George:

> Dr Jamison came out and saw your boy this morning and we have talked over his case at length. Our opinion is quite agreed, and amounts to this: the boy may now, bar accidents, be considered out of danger. He is making good progress, and considering how very ill he has been we are quite satisfied with his progress and condition – we think that the case will probably be a long one, and that it may be three or four months before he will have the use of his legs – also we cannot say what the ultimate condition of either knee or ankle will be, and we do not think anyone else could say either.
>
> In regard to treatment there is nothing to be done but continue as I am doing, the daily dressings and treatment, while ensuring that the drainage is sufficiently maintained, and it may prove necessary in the future to re-establish or provide new drainage, which might entail giving the boy Gas.
>
> We also think he would be better at Margate, and that he could be moved now by road so soon as arrangements can be made to place him where he can have the same amount of attention as he is receiving here, but we are sure he cannot do with less. In regard to your suggestion to call in another opinion, we neither of us think this necessary, but are quite willing to fall in with your wishes in the matter.

This letter clearly forestalled the need for any consultation with the Guy's Hospital surgeon, especially when George seemed so pleased with the treatment that Constant was receiving under Friend's supervision. He had written acknowledging 'the great kindness you and your charming wife extended to us so hospitably and sympathetically', adding that it 'enabled us to get through the days when the clouds looked pretty black'.

Friend continued to keep Jamison informed, writing to him on 10 September 1916:

> I got in a big pocket above the knee joint yesterday with a probe and got out about 2 oz of thick pus, and then managed to get a larger tube in quite easily, and it is now draining much more freely. I gave him 1/3 million autog vaccine on Friday with very little disturbance, so propose to give another on Tuesday. I think he is improving considerably otherwise.

At the end of the month Constant was moved to the Royal Sea Bathing Hospital in Margate, about 90 miles east of Horsham. This was a renowned publicly funded orthopaedic hospital, founded in 1791, that with its indoor salt-water baths had pioneered thalassotherapy as a treatment for tuberculosis and treated patients suffering from diseases of the hip, spine, bones and joints. At about the time of the move, Jamison wrote to Friend on 2 October, congratulating him on the fine progress that Constant had made under his care at Horsham: 'He has made a most remarkable recovery, & I have great hopes that his joints will regain almost all their proper function. Not a little of his recovery is due to the constant attention you gave him.' In November the School informed George that £40 had already been spent on Constant's operations and care.

The Royal Sea Bathing Hospital was an impressive classically designed building with 200 available beds, 116 of them being provided for children and about 50 for wounded soldiers. Most treatment was given charitably (patients had to be recommended by a governor of the charity) but fully paying patients and patients covered by insurance schemes were also accepted. The hospital looked on to the beach and, with a seaplane station close by at Westgate on Sea, there were some exciting sights in war time for the 11-year-old Constant, about which he wrote on 16 November 1916:

> Dear Dr Friend,
>
> I am ever so much better and my wounds are nearly healed up now. I can lift both legs at once without any support at all for a little while.
>
> A seaplane has just come down on the water and I am waiting for it to rise; I see lots down here as they have their base just round the corner of the cliff.
>
> I do not see many destroyers etc here as they are mostly up the other end of Margate.
>
> My mother and father came down to see me a little while ago and they may come down again at Christmas.
>
> We have just got a gramophone and it is playing now; we have got to raise eighteen bob for the records though.
>
> I have not seen many aeroplanes lately but on fine days I see lots.
>
> Waiting patiently for the day when I get up.
>
> Yours truly
>
> L. C. Lambert

With the hospital's emphasis on tuberculosis, there had initially been some confusion that may have caused the Lamberts to wonder whether Margate was the right place for Constant, as Friend reported to Jamison on 15 November:

> In a letter from Mrs Lambert to my wife, Mrs L said her husband has been down to Margate to see the boy & asked when he would be able to come home, the matron said probably not till after Xmas 'these tuberculous cases always take a long time'.
>
> The Lamberts are much worried about the 'Tuberculous' – also I am wondering if the Margate people know what they are talking about.
>
> Do you know the doctor men there, to find out what they are playing at?

Constant spent over six months at Margate and was eventually allowed home in April 1917. On 19 April George wrote to Dr Friend, on Chelsea Arts Club note-paper:

> I brought my youngster back last week. He is remarkably fit & fat & most cheerful; and it is very difficult to realize that he is the same poor little spark you laboured so skilfully to keep alive last summer. We have not yet called in a doctor for him. We are waiting for the statement from the Royal Sea Bathing [Hospital] which may be a guide as to future treatment. Anyway you can take it from me that there is no possibility of your taking him back this next term; but of course I will bring him along for examination if that is the regular thing to do.
>
> He gets round quite easily on crutches. On his right leg he wears a plaster splint, evidently to keep the knee straight. The left heel is still some distance from the ground but it is improving.
>
> I will write again as soon as we get a proper opinion.

He added a simple sketch of Constant's legs, showing the plaster splint and the left heel raised off the ground when he tried to stand. Once home, for much of the time Constant was confined to a bath chair in which he would be wheeled to the Chelsea Library where he could take out music scores to read – everything possible. While convalescing he even showed an interest in engineering and aeronautics, spurred on quite likely by the frequent sight of seaplanes at Margate, and with characteristic intensity he threw himself in studying engineering handbooks, fascinated by such structures as cranes, aircraft and skyscrapers.[9] Some of the time would also be spent by mother and son in their regular habit of reading together. The two were captured, sitting book-in-hand on a sofa, in a charming lithograph by Thea Proctor dating from 1915.[10] Angus Morrison, a close friend of the family, remembered Amy as 'a great and discriminating reader, with a phenomenally retentive memory for everything she had ever read and she passed on this quality to both her sons in full measure.'[11] Constant and Amy read French together, in particular Romain Rolland's *Jean-Christophe*, the ten-volume 1915 Nobel Prize-winning novel about a German composer that criticised the society of his time. Before long Amy did not need to translate as Constant had surpassed her.

Because of further complications Constant was not sufficiently mobile to return to school for some while. On 1 November Amy wrote to Dr Friend that, despite the regular syringing to the right ear that he had instructed, it was still discharging. An appointment was made with Harold Barwell, the ear, nose and throat surgeon at St George's Hospital, who carried out a revision of the mastoidectomy, about which he wrote to Dr Friend on 25 November:

> I re-opened Lambert's mastoid yesterday, and found several suppurating cells including some in the roof – an uncommon place. The ossicles were still there so I removed them.

Friend replied on 2 December:

> Many thanks for letting me know about Lambert. I am glad they decided to have it done, and the result shews I imagine that the operation was fully justified. I hope this will clear up the trouble and so allow him to return here by the summer. I am sorry I misled you about the ossicles. I certainly thought Jamison told me he had removed them.

One of Constant's most remarkable qualities was the way in which he overcame and even concealed his disabilities, in particular his partial deafness. His contemporary at Christ's Hospital, Michael Stewart (who became a prominent Labour politician, twice serving as Foreign Secretary, and ultimately created Baron Stewart of Fulham) remembered that 'his disabilities were exceptionally serious – one ear was a constant source of trouble to him and his feet were so injured that he could never put the whole of the foot to the ground and had to walk on his toes'.[12] The medical records seem to indicate that the hearing in his right ear was restored, and few of his friends and acquaintances in later life seemed to be aware of any deafness in that ear. Even his friend in his final years, Dr Denis ApIvor, composer and consultant anaesthetist, did not suspect any impaired hearing, while the artist Michael Ayrton, another close friend, later spoke of him as being only partially deaf in one ear. But when in 1937 Constant had to consult a Harley Street doctor because of severe pain in the other ear, it was, as that doctor wrote, 'vital to his career for me to cure the infection at once, as his right ear was completely deaf owing to the destruction of the drum some years

---

[9] De Zoete, 'The Younger English Composers', p. 97. Beryl de Zoete (1879–1962) was a dance critic and, like her life-long companion Arthur Waley, an Orientalist.

[10] Titled *Mother and Son* or *Portrait of Mrs G. W. Lambert and Constant Lambert*, it is Thea Proctor's earliest known lithographic work. It first appeared in the fifth number of *Art in Australia* (1918) and was exhibited in Melbourne in April 1919. See Plate 2.

[11] 'The Family', in *Constant Lambert, 1905–1951: A Souvenir of the Exhibition at the South London Art Gallery* (London: London Borough of Southwark Council, 1976), p. 26.

[12] Constant Lambert obituary in *The Blue*.

previous'.[13] When Osbert Sitwell first met Constant, aged about 17, he was immediately struck by the way his character established itself without difficulty or self-assertiveness. 'That which made this all the more remarkable,' he wrote, 'was that he suffered from partial deafness, which no doubt accounted for the eager look on his face, an expression which said clearly, "I don't want to miss anything", and for the manner in which his eyes followed the speaker.'[14] Partial deafness was unquestionably a serious handicap to his conducting, but it proved more difficult in conversation, especially in a crowded room with his conversationalists at close quarters, with some on his deaf side.

There still remains some mystery regarding his deafness. In his biography of the Sitwells, *Façades*, John Pearson tells how Iain Laing, later Foreign Editor of the *Sunday Times*, first saw Constant at one of Edith Sitwell's tea parties:

> His good looks alone would have marked him out, but what was equally unusual was that he did not react to anything that Edith said, nor for that matter did he speak a word until the time came when he bade her a brief good-bye.
> 'Who', I asked, 'is that extraordinarily beautiful youth?'
> 'Oh, didn't I introduce you?' said Miss Sitwell. 'His name is Constant Lambert – only eighteen years old but already a very gifted musician. Willie Walton thinks he has a brilliant future.'
> 'He's not very talkative, is he?'
> 'Well, no, it's sad,' replied Miss Sitwell gravely, 'but the poor boy's almost stone deaf ... Like Beethoven, you know.'

Laing did not see Constant again for several years until they were both regulars of the Fitzroy Tavern in Charlotte Street, London, and Constant was married.

> It was there one night that Lambert's first wife, Florence, said to me, 'Why do you shout at Connie so?'
> 'Well,' I replied, 'he's deaf, isn't he?'
> 'Deaf? He's no more deaf than you are, Iain.'[15]

As Michael Ayrton recalled, he was at least able to humour his condition. When he described himself as 'the only Francophile English composer-conductor born of an Australian painter from St Petersburg who could play God Save the King literally by ear, this was no idle boast, as he could demonstrate when weather conditions were favourable, by holding his nose and compressing his breath through a punctured right eardrum, to produce a recognizable if unfelicitous version of the National Anthem'.[16]

There were other disappointments for the 12-year-old Constant. His first Christmas at home in two years was not to be the happy family gathering he might have expected as his father had been appointed an official Australian war artist, first in Egypt and Palestine (and later in Turkey), where he was to make sketches of the operations of the Australian Imperial Forces.[17] The commission was initially for three months, but this

---

[13] Cyril Hereford, MD, FRCS Hon. RCM, in a letter to Hubert Foss, 27 January [1952]: Hubert Foss Archive.

[14] Sitwell, 'Portrait of a Very Young Man', pp. 77–8.

[15] John Pearson, *Façades: Edith, Osbert, and Sacheverell Sitwell* (London: Macmillan, 1978), p. 222.

[16] Michael Ayrton, 'Sketch for a Portrait', in *Golden Sections* (London: Methuen, 1957), p. 123.

[17] His first commission was for 'studies, sketches or drawings, which shall be not less than twenty-five in number, and which are to be and remain the sole property of the Commonwealth'. He was given £30 towards the cost of material and equipment. A second agreement called for 'a picture or composition of a battle-scene in which the AIF are represented, for the sum of £500, the subject to be decided by a committee appointed by the Commonwealth, to which the artist shall submit a sketch of the proposed picture for

was later extended. He was relieved to give up his chiefly office-based job in timber that had become a heavy administrative burden, and on a cold, damp Christmas morning, equipped with a Light Horseman's plumed hat, spurs, leggings and honorary commission as a Lieutenant, he left Waterloo Station for Southampton. After some delay, he was able to cross a heavily mined English Channel for Cherbourg. The sight of other officers' farewells at Southampton drove George to write in his diary with curious detachment: 'Why do they let their womenfolk see them off at the station! Say I, having got over my parting with my little lot two hours previously without unnecessary fuss.' After reaching Cairo he gave some thought to the family finances, instructing Amy how best to sell some of his paintings, including those done at Cranleigh, as much to settle his own debts as to help towards the family upkeep: 'Re pictures at the International, the prices could be, say, £150 for "The Convex Mirror", or £100 to Davis if he *really* wants it; the flower pieces £80 for the pair.[18] I owe Konody[19] some money; if you wrote him nicely he might help to bring about a sale, and I feel that the Chenil Gallery might sell some of my paintings and drawings and so get some money for their bill, also some for Chapman (frame-maker). If I make a success of this trip these damn creditors need not worry, and, anyway, they cannot attack you.'

From Cairo he went on to Palestine, from Jerusalem to Jericho, following the Australian army's advance against the Turks. His principal aim was to record the battlefields of Romani and Beersheba, two famous battles in the history of the Light Horse. This he did in March 1918, but when, on his return to Cairo, he learned that the battlefront was again active, he obtained approval to extend his duties by a visit to the Jordan Valley where he completed further sketches. He remained abroad for five months, longer than originally planned, returning on 7 June 1918. His stay might have been even longer as in May he was asked if he could remain a further six weeks in Palestine, but as well as suffering from the heat and the dust, he contracted malaria and had to be rushed to Cairo, and then home. He was to suffer from the after-effects of malaria for the rest of his life.

In April 1918, after an absence of five terms, Constant was considered well enough to return to school. But his medical problems were not over yet. On 1 May he went to London for a further consultation with Barwell who found there was still a small discharge from near the Eustachian tube, but he wrote that he expected it to dry up eventually, adding 'the hearing has improved'. The slight discharge continued but at the last meeting he had with Barwell in September 1918, the surgeon was still confident it would dry up.

Then one morning in October, Constant's dormitory companion woke early to hear him 'moaning, at times piteously crying out. This went on for quite an hour. No-one did anything. No boy would dare get out of bed before bell for dressing.' When eventually the morning bell rang, 'all got up but not Lambert. He was helpless and was rushed to hospital.'[20] He was taken first to the school's infirmary with symptoms of acute appendicitis which as quickly subsided, but Dr Friend felt in view of the severe infection he had had that he should not be left liable to a second attack. So he was admitted to the Middlesex Hospital, where his appendix was removed on 18 October. He made a sufficiently good recovery for Friend to declare him fit for physical training at the beginning of the January 1919 term.

Meanwhile, on top of the worries about Constant, having George home again

---

approval'. The subject eventually chosen was 'The Charge of the Australian Light Horse at Beersheba', commemorating the battle of 31 October 1917.

[18] *The Convex Mirror* was bought by Sir Edmund Davis and was hung in Chilham Castle.

[19] Paul George Konody (1872–1933), *The Observer* art critic and author.

[20] Letter from H. G. P. Davies to Hubert Foss, 25 January 1952: Foss Archive.

could not have been as easy a time as Amy might have wished because a number of factors plunged him into a mood of desperation. There was a conflict of interests as the Australian Imperial Forces had asked him to visit Palestine again, but the London authorities were suggesting that a large canvas depicting 'The Charge of the Australian Light Horse at Beersheba' should be tackled first. He was waiting to be informed of a military camp in England where he could work and where there would be available an Australian Light Horse and infantry dress and equipment that would feature in the painting. In the meantime he put off any private work, but after three months of hearing nothing he wrote with some understandable annoyance to his superiors: 'I have given to Australia the whole of my time and work, from December 25th up to about a month back, when I realised that I was being let down. That I am able to maintain myself and my family by private means is not in question, although some time must elapse before I can pick up what, for better name, I must call my clientèle.'

In December there came a request for him to go to Gallipoli and take some sketches of the battlegrounds and graves. He was to be accompanied by an officer who had taken part in the allied landings there. In his letter of acceptance he made several succinct demands: that the period of time for the journeys and his work should be a minimum of nine months but with the freedom for him to come home before that period was up if he saw fit; that his trip should include a return visit to Palestine; and a firm statement of what he expected as regards pay. He left at the end of January 1919, reaching Gallipoli by way of Lemnos on 16 February. 'I hope you and Maurice are managing all right and that there will be no difficulty about the separation allowance,' he wrote to Amy, adding, 'As usual, the voyaging has cost me dear.' George was a dutiful letter writer although, as reproduced by Amy in her biography of her husband, his letters and diary entries seem to contain very few references to the family. His own problems and feelings came first, and sometimes there is a hardness in passages where one might expect more devotion, as when he writes on 5 March: 'I am getting keen to reach Cairo and some news of you. This trip has indeed cut me off from you but I need not, I think, dwell on the fact that it would be good to have you alongside when I am working, even if I was snappy and even if you said the wrong thing about painting.' In April an attack of dysentery landed him for about six weeks in the 14th Australian General Hospital in Abbassia, on the outskirts of Cairo, from where he pronounced on Maurice's future. Constant's brother was considering entering the Royal Flying Corps but finally decided on 'some form of art'. Thinking of his own struggles and experiences, George gave Maurice no encouragement to follow a similar course but seemed instead more concerned in determining his own future. He had had thoughts of returning to Australia at the time of his mother's death in 1911 but could not then afford to make the journey. But Australia was now rarely absent from his thoughts.

> I don't want to express my thoughts too quickly on the subject. I am only just dragged back by medical skill and care, and possibly the news seems more of a blow at present than it really is. Further, I have had quite a stomachful of set-backs, beginning at the age of eleven or thereabouts, and I am determined to look a little after myself; try and find out if I have a self and what it really requires – if it really requires the grass-lands of Australia, the horses and other animals, I hope I shall realise it before I pass out.
>
> If the boy deliberately chooses Art as a career, it is not for me to stop him, even if it is possible, and by the same reason I don't see the call on me to assist him to go contrary to my advice. As an instructor – and I suppose I am one of

the best – I am perfectly willing to give him a short course of training, and there it ends, and he plunges or drifts. As long as he realises that it really is an abyss.[21]

In hospital George was forced to consider his own condition. He was now a weakened and worried man, troubled by his poor health, recurring bouts of malaria, and a weak heart. A few days later he added: 'It is up to Maurice to give me a still further improvement and easier mind. I am as much frightened of myself and the beastly family in me, the breed that goes stubborn and unforgiving, as I am of what *he* may do that is stupid.' Amy was fully aware of the hardships of an artist's life and understood George's concern for Maurice's future. As Thea Proctor wrote: 'I gave Maurice his first encouragement when both his parents were completely hostile about art as a profession for him – because they knew it was a hard life. He used to come to me for sympathy.'[22] Thea had returned to Sydney in 1912 to see her mother and grandmother and she was on her way back to England when war was declared. With George often away from home, her contact with the Lamberts was less frequent. Amy may have taken less kindly her supporting Maurice in his wishes, and his future was doubtless a topic of conversation when he sat for two lithographs, dating from about 1919, in which he was portrayed by Thea.[23]

Money at home was a constant worry, not just for the family's upkeep but to pay off George's artistic debts. The sale of the *Convex Mirror* helped to appease some creditors. By chance, while in Cairo, George saw a reproduction of the painting in a copy of the magazine *The Studio* and commented: 'I am glad the picture is sold and that Davis has it. There will be Chapmans' (framers) and Chenil (artist's materials), both firms to receive as much as possible; but leave enough for the momentary carry-on of your minute needs.' There was a softer tone in his letter of 4 June 1919 when he wrote: 'I am very sorry if my worrying about Maurice should have made you unhappy,' adding that he expected to be back home by the end of August. He included a letter to Maurice that went close to atoning for his earlier outburst:

> You must not be discouraged because I do not altogether swallow your choice of a profession. Seldom are father and son in agreement on this question; but acting on the memory of my own rather pathetic lack of sympathy and support from my own people, I do not wish to obstruct, but only to help. When I return we can go into the matter in a careful and friendly way, and find out if there is a way to help you, and a way to help your mother and myself to get some satisfaction in watching your progress.[24]

George had recovered sufficiently in June to leave the hospital and travel to Damascus, but he was soon exhausted again. On 18 July he hinted that his poor health might necessitate a brief rest on his way home, at either Marseille or Paris. 'But that doesn't concern you,' he continued bluntly. '... I must get away from London as soon as possible after I report to H.Q.,' and he went on to give Amy orders to go hunting for a suitable place where he could work on his larger canvases.

> Get sufficient money, even if a borrower you become, and, taking Maurice possibly, have a hunt around such places as Hounslow, Bushey and any other place that has paddocks and neglected, broken-down places that might be habitable and not too far from, or containing, a stable. ... Don't think that I

[21] Amy Lambert, *Thirty Years of an Artist's Life*, p. 122.

[22] Letter from Thea Proctor to Dulcie Stout, 15 September 1964, quoted in *Thea Proctor: The Prints* (Sydney: Resolution Press, 1980), p. 40.

[23] *Before Rehearsal* and *The Balcony*. Both are reproduced in *Thea Proctor: The Prints*, pp. 39, 41.

[24] Amy Lambert, *Thirty Years of an Artist's Life*, pp. 127–8.

want to take you away from your present drudgery and promote you to a more strenuous job of waiting hand and foot on an invalid. I want you about the place; I fear I shall want a lot of coddling.

At the same time, with equal bluntness, he made clear his long-term intentions: 'My castle in the air is to get through as much work as possible between August and March next, as I intend going to Australia about that time, either with or without the family – I hope with.' He ended with a rare personal greeting: 'My very best love to Constant'.[25]

In his next letter he spared Amy the task of studio hunting by suggesting that they took 'a roaming holiday' together in search for a suitable location. But on his return in August, after the intended rest, at Marseille, he was greeted with another commission, for a war memorial picture for the 14th King's Hussars officers' mess, which necessitated several visits to regiment's barracks near Salisbury Plain. The problem of finding a large enough studio for a short-term lease where he could complete his various commissions was solved by a spacious but gloomy property in Warwick Road, Kensington, and Maurice 'was pressed into service, and carried out many a job of squaring-up and transforming to larger canvases the sketches painted on the spot'. He, and a well-known Academy model, Luigi di Luca, had to pose for some of the pictures. But the lack of sunlight – and no horses available as models – made George look elsewhere, and that summer he accepted an offer from Algernon Talmage, RA,[26] to stay at his house at Bossiney, a small hamlet on the outskirts of Tintagel, in Cornwall.

Amy did not join him in Cornwall 'where truly Maurice would have been of more service, but our means did not warrant his travelling, especially as his father was expecting to be back in London very shortly', she has written, giving 'the health of our youngest son' a contributory reason for not having gone. But in September Constant was staying with the painter, illustrator and scene designer Charles Ricketts[27] at the Keep, Chilham Castle (between Ashford and Canterbury, in Kent). The castle had been bought in 1918 by Sir Edmund Davis who had amassed there a very considerable art collection about which he had sought Ricketts' advice, allowing him in return the tenure of the Keep with his life-long friend Charles Shannon. 'Young Lambert is here and lives at the Keep,' Ricketts wrote to a friend. 'He has grown and is very intelligent.'[28] It is likely that Constant spent several holidays at Chilham, an arrangement that would allow Amy to attend more readily to George's demands when he was home if, at the same time, making Constant's contact with his father even scarcer.

The stay in Cornwall did not provide George with the ideal solution. 'The place is perfect, but models unprocurable, so far, for either men or horses,' he wrote home. And to make matters worse the weather was 'damnable' with continual rain, turning his thoughts all the more to Australia. As Amy put it: 'His heart was largely with those new and old friends who had already returned to a country where he knew that sunlight, horses, and sympathetic assistance and whole-hearted appreciation awaited him. ... He could not face the continuance of such adverse conditions, and the drawing-on of winter, with the realisation that his health was not as good as before his experiences in the East.' So, quite likely without even discussing the matter with Amy, on 30 July 1920

[25] *Ibid.*, p. 130.

[26] Algernon Talmage (1871–1939), British impressionist painter.

[27] Charles de Sousy Ricketts (1866–1931), English artist, illustrator, author, printer and stage designer. He was a friend of Oscar Wilde, whose books he illustrated as well as being stage designer for the play *Salomé*, and a life-long friend of painter and lithographer Charles Shannon (1863–1937) whom he met at art school.

[28] Letter from Charles Ricketts to Mrs Muriel Lee Mathews, in *Self-Portrait, taken from the Letters and Journals of Charles Ricketts RA*, collected and compiled by T. Sturge Moore, edited by Cecil Lewis (London: Peter Davies, 1939), p. 320.

he put in an official request for a free passage 'to my country from which I have been so long exiled'. In feeble justification of his actions he wrote, 'The castle in the air is that things will go so well that you will either follow quickly or I shall come back quickly,' probably knowing that neither option would occur, and he returned to London to complete the commissions and free himself of any further restraints. On 4 February 1921, aged 47, he sailed for Australia aboard the *SS Mantua*, arriving at Sydney on 18 March. He was never to see his sons again.

In later years it was as if Constant wanted to forget the father he had too infrequently seen and really never known. The Australian writer and editor Jack Lindsay remembered his reaction when he called on him once and eagerly mentioned his father in conversation:

> 'Your father is the best realistic Australian artist,' I said, rather straining the term *realism* to be friendly, 'and mine is the most romantic.' I repeated the phrase a couple of times in the hopes of evoking some response, some admission of our both sharing an Australian element; but he kept on ignoring the remark. Neither he nor his sculptor brother, whose studio I visited, seemed to want to mention their father.[29]

T HE lack of a close father–son relationship was a Lambert family failing that Constant was to inherit, and the absence of a regular father presence and strong male guidance was to be an important factor in his adolescent years. At Christ's Hospital Dr Friend provided some of the missing paternal care. As one of Constant's contemporaries observed, '[Lambert] was a very close friend with his school doctor and spent a good deal of time at his home.' Friend clearly had great admiration for Constant, no doubt as much for the way he had faced an abnormal amount of suffering as for his strength of character. Thinking of the boy's future, it was only natural for Friend to want to save him from permanent disability in his left leg, and he appealed to the Treasurer of Christ's Hospital for financial assistance from the School for the necessary operation, writing in the summer of 1920:

> A boy named Lambert L. C. in 1916 got Osteomylitis after Fourth Disease. He had three operations done on him here by Dr Jamison and after nearly dying made a very good recovery. He subsequently had two more operations at home, one of which his parents paid for and the second was done free at Middlesex Hospital. Unfortunately the original disease has caused contraction on the tendons of one foot and the boy is lame in one leg. Dr Jamison saw the boy the other day and thinks the condition can be cured by an operation on the contracted tendons. He is willing to try and the parents are most anxious to have the chance given the boy. If his disability can be put right it will make the whole difference to his life and usefulness. The difficulty is the fee. The case is not one of urgency as regards life, but I think it is urgent as it will most probably convert a cripple into an able-bodied individual. The father is an artist and unable now to find the money. Dr Jamison is undoubtedly the right man to do the operation as he did the original one and knows the joint. And the matter is one that must be done by an expert to be successful. Dr Jamison has now left Horsham but is willing to come down and do the operation for £21, which is a very moderate fee in the circumstances. The operation ought to be done soon and is not in itself a big affair, provided it is properly done. I do not think it should be done locally, and strictly speaking it is not a matter that the School would do as a matter of course

---

[29] Jack Lindsay, *Fanfrolico and After* (London: Bodley Head, 1962), p. 94.

as it is not urgent in the sense of saving life. At the same time it will make the whole difference to the boy's future and the parents cannot afford the expense. The boy is a very promising pupil of the School and should ultimately do very well if he follows up his present promise. I am therefore asking you if under the special circumstances you will sanction the fee. There will be no extra charge as I shall be quite willing to give the anaesthetic and after treatment, and there will be no need for extra nurses for the case.

Fortunately, he received an immediate and sympathetic response from the Treasurer, who added:

I quite well remember the case in 1916, as it was a remarkable recovery after you had had so much anxiety about his operation & I think you told me the parents were very grateful to you for all the attention you gave to them.

The operation went ahead towards the end of June, with Amy writing to Friend at the beginning of the next school term: 'He is walking very well now, but the weak foot soon gets tired if he walks far or stands long.' Although Constant was to walk with a limp for the rest of his life, the success of the operation enabled him before long to go on more strenuous walks, as a friend at Christ's Hospital recalled:

I particularly remember one enjoyable outing I had with Lambert during the summer of 1922 on a whole holiday. We had intended to go for a walk in the immediate neighbourhood, but the surprise arrival of a 10/- note from my parents on the morning of the day enabled us to go farther afield. We went by train to Amberley, and having been already provided with sandwiches, we bought in the village two bottles of ginger beer and two cucumbers. After a swim in the Arun we laboriously climbed to the top of Amberley Mount where we sat and had our lunch, each devouring a whole cucumber. Surprisingly we were then able to walk to Arundel, where we had tea and another swim. Lambert was a keen swimmer.[30]

In later life Constant was to be a keen walker, if with a somewhat erratic gait.

Aₙ absence of five terms understandably made settling into life at Christ's Hospital very difficult for Constant, especially when he was not able to participate in most sports.[31] While he was not actively involved in cricket, he did occasionally score ('perhaps the most nauseating occupation designed to embitter an embryo artist')[32] though he enjoyed the schoolboy's pen-and-paper game known as dob-cricket. The two sports he did enjoy were swimming and, despite his weak ankle, boxing (one aspect in which he took after his father), at which he could be quite a fierce opponent. His housemaster, A. C. W. Edwards, remembered the effect all this had on Constant:

When I first made contact with Lambert, then about 13 years old, he had just recovered from a very serious illness, which inflicted upon him a lameness which

---

[30] Letter from R. Waller to Hubert Foss, 31 January 1952: Foss Archive.

[31] Lambert was probably delighted to be excused compulsory games. When much later discussing Honegger's *Pacific 231* and *Rugby*, he concluded: 'Sport is too old a friend to have much glamour and a composer who has been to an English public school is probably the last to be inspired by such a subject as "Rugby". I am glad, though, to hear of the English composer who is writing a lengthy and severe double-fugue for orchestra entitled "Compulsory Games"' ('Railway Music', *The Nation and Athanæum*, 16 August 1930). This could possibly refer to Edmund Rubbra's Triple Fugue, Op. 25, which was dedicated to Lambert.

[32] Lambert, 'Myself and Russian Music', p. 6.

lasted all his life and rendered him incapable of joining in the games of cricket & football with his fellows. It was this that set him apart – a little bitter tongued and affecting a cynical unboyish outlook – and forced him, in a sense, to prove that he was superior in other and more important fields. He was very grown-up in his language & ideas. He was a ready speaker with a remarkable quickness of repartee which he used to amuse, to amaze & often to hurt. ... He was a good English scholar whose essays were remarkable for freshness of expression and for daring of opinion.

He had his admirers and friends but I would not call him a popular boy. His lameness and his maturity of outlook were great handicaps to success in the philistine society of a public school.

He was, however, extremely fortunate to find at Christ's Hospital encouragement and opportunity to follow his bent. His main interest was music but debating & essay-writing interested him too.[33]

As another contemporary recalled,[34] one essay caused quite a stir.

The English master, Mr Goodwin, told the class to choose any person we liked to write an essay about and do it in Prep. We chose George V, Victoria, Wally Hammond [English cricketer] or Stanley Baldwin [who became Prime Minister in 1923] for we were boys. But Constant Lambert – nothing so mundane. To our wonderment he chose Trotsky! And such an essay. When I read it I was thunderstruck. It read like a book. It was easily the best essay and Mr Goodwin was so impressed he sent him to Mr Hamilton Fyfe, the Headmaster.[35]

Trotsky was then at the height of his powers and as an outsider Constant may well have felt some affinity, both by chance sharing Leon[ard] as a first name. A fellow-pupil saw Lambert very much as a cat who walked by himself:

He was quite the most out-of-the-ordinary person I have known, and by that I don't mean he was *extra*-ordinary. He was very aloof and appeared to take little interest in school activities or in individuals. He was just not in his element at a large public school and, as far as the boys were concerned, just did not bother to make himself naturally pleasant. He was not an easy boy to know. He was quite kindly in a limited sort of way. He certainly would never do a mean thing to anyone, but he just chose to live his own rarified life, and naturally had an air of detachment which made it difficult for the ordinary boy to have much to do with.[36]

Another pupil provided this most effective portrait:

I retain a vivid picture of his passing me in the lobby of Big School. We all keep these private picture galleries, I expect, in the attics of our minds; lumber, most of it. But this portrait has turned out to be a master. He had light proud eyes, clouded then with a trouble he was too haughty to share; a pale and handsome face; his hair grew off his forehead slightly wavy, and it gleamed and glinted as if in the sun, as the hair of young people often does. His lips, especially the

[33] Letter from A. C. W. Edwards to Angus Morrison, 16 April 1954: RCM Library MSS 6961–6966.

[34] Letter from H. G. P. Davies to Hubert Foss, 25 January 1952: RCM Library MSS 6961–6966.

[35] Rev. Arthur William Upcott was Headmaster at Christ's Hospital from 1902 until retiring in 1919. He was succeeded by Mr William Hamilton Fyfe (knighted 1942).

[36] Letter from Patrick Wood to A. C. W. Edwards, 30 December 1951: RCM Library MSS 6961–6966.

lower, were rather full, but set into supercilious curves which I knew were already habitual. He stalked past with a kind of stillness about him, as though he noticed none of his surroundings. ... He must have been about eighteen. I remember being somewhat awed by the beauty – no – by the power of his face; but attracted too, and friendly. He passed by.[37]

Michael Stewart, the future politician who was himself noted at Christ's Hospital for his intellect, remembered Constant's maturity of thought and interests:

At the age of sixteen, or even earlier, he had the mind and interests of a well-informed adult. ... In his company one was apt to be frequently and sharply reminded that outside school there was a real world, with manifold problems and interests, and that school life, however enjoyable, could not be more than a preparation for reality. This doesn't mean that he was a solemn person at all – he was an adult, but a gay, almost boisterous adult. ... My dearest memories of him belong to his last term, the summer term of 1922. I have a particularly vivid mental picture of a small group ... hurrying across Lamb A pitch to the Baths for 'early dip' with Lambert among us, reciting his own poems, or explaining the works of Ibsen or occasionally listening to what the rest of us had to say, but always a figure full of life and enjoyment.[38]

Being quick and incisive in speech and rather scornful of conventional thought made Constant a ready contributor to any debate. J. D. Jefferis, a member of his circle, remembered him as 'a fair speaker ... He argued for atheism, socialism, free-love and advanced views generally, but Shuffrey, who was some kind of distant cousin, used to say that he was simply repeating what his father said which used to enrage Lambert.'[39] He also shocked the Headmaster by declaring himself to be an agnostic. Another friend, R. Waller, experienced his readiness to engage in a discussion:

He always enjoyed an argument, and in any argument was always devastating.[40] He had an annoying habit of closing a discussion by saying 'I'm sorry, but it served you right – you asked for it.' – as if he had just dealt out some punishment. This mental superiority probably contributed to the fact that Lambert was not very popular at school – that and the fact that he appeared to be rather 'aloof'. However he took his share in the usual amount of ragging. He once put a quantity of breadcrumbs in a master's bed, and when the crime was traced to him, he was furious because the master refused to cane him 'on medical grounds'.[41]

As a member of Christ's Hospital Debating Society, two motions that he is on record as supporting were: 'In the opinion of this House the Officer Training Corps is deplorable' and 'This House approves of vivisection'. The latter occasion moved the reporter for the School's magazine, *The Outlook*, to remark: 'His taste exact for limitless fact amounts to a disease – and in this case comprised several diseases cured by vivisection – Statistics! Statistics! Statistics! He showed the number of experiments

---

[37] T. B. Radley, quoted in Shead, *Constant Lambert*, pp. 33–4.

[38] Quoted in *ibid.*, p. 34.

[39] Letter from J. D. Jefferis to A. C. W. Edwards, 11 December 1951: RCM Library MSS 6961–6966.

[40] Arthur Hutchings (1906–89), Professor of Music at Durham University, 1947–68, wrote to Angus Morrison of one encounter: 'I knew CL himself only from casual meetings, usually in pubs, at which I was the delighted victim of "My dear sir, you are talking b..." – which, I find, I usually was.' Letter, 27 April 1954, RCM Library.

[41] Letter from R. Waller to Hubert Foss, 31 January 1952: Foss Archive.

performed in one year, the usefulness of vivisection, attacked Rae, was answered, glared defiance and sat down'. The quest for precision in debate never left him. As Michael Ayrton wrote many years later:

> Constant, in particular, would, with a certain donnish pedantry, insist on minute accuracy in any descriptive statement. He liked facts to be exactly recorded, just as he would permit no licence in the proper construction either of musical or limerick form. ... 'Data, data, give me data!' was a quotation frequently upon his lips.[42]

Mr Edwards sometimes teased Constant about his intellectual superiority: 'I used to pull his leg when he entered my room by asking him to come down to my level for a minute or so and he would smile and reply. "I'll try, sir."'[43] Constant was a great admirer of G. K. Chesterton who was invited to address the Deputy Grecians Literary Society for which Constant was not eligible. Somehow he managed to get himself a special invitation and 'was simply unbearable for the next week'.

Constant's literary interests were extraordinarily mature. As Waller recalled: 'By the age of about fourteen Lambert was very familiar with all the works of Shaw, Chekhov, Ibsen, Dunsany,[44] on which he used to enthuse at length. We both went to the first performance of *Peer Gynt* at the Old Vic, with Russell Thorndike in the name part, during the holidays.'[45] Constant was particularly enthusiastic about the work of the Sitwells and he probably first read their poems in their annual anthology *Wheels*, six issues of which appeared between 1916 and 1921. He would save up his pocket money for weeks in order to buy remaindered copies. Waller was allowed to browse through an exercise book in which Constant wrote his own poems. Three poems and a short story were published in the July 1922 issue of *The Outlook*, a larger than normal representation that may have had something to do with the fact that not only was this Constant's last term but he was also chairman of the magazine's committee. Two of the poems in particular indicate Constant's versatility and range of tastes. 'Jazz Blues', which he instructed 'to be chanted with uniform rhythm', owes a heavy debt to Vachel Lindsay, most notably his poem 'The Congo',[46] but it shows Constant's early fascination for jazz rhythms and Negro and Dixie elements.

> *Jazz Blues*
>
> Cockatoos!
> Cockatoos!
> Swinging in chains from the painted roof
> Chatter and scream and flap their wings,
> Flinging their gaudy bodies in time
> To the ragtime tunes,
> The ragtime tunes,

---

[42] Ayrton, *Golden Sections*, pp. 123–4.

[43] Letter from A. C. W. Edwards to Hubert Foss, 28 December 1951: Foss Archive.

[44] Edward John Moreton Drax Plunkett Dunsany, 18th Baron (1878–1957), Irish poet, novelist and dramatist, his best-known plays being *The Glittering Gate* (1909), *The Gods of the Mountain* (1911), and *If* (1921).

[45] The first night of *Peer Gynt* was on 6 March 1922.

[46] Vachel Lindsay (1879–1931), an American pioneer of jazz poetry, was famous for the recitation of his own poems like *The Congo*, published in 1914, which begins: 'Fat black bucks in a wine-barrel room, / Barrel-house kings, with feet unstable, / Sagged and reeled and pounded on the table, / Pounded on the table, / Beat an empty barrel with the handle of a broom, / Hard as they were able, / Boom, boom, Boom, / With a silk umbrella and the handle of a broom, / Boomlay, boomlay, boomlay, Boom.' Even better known is his *The Daniel Jazz*.

Clots and blobs of
Syncopated melody
Shooting out in vermilion spirals,
Piccolo tunes, trombone glissandos,
Gurgling notes on the big bass clarinet,
Screaming, scraping, violins twanging,
'Coal-black mammy's down in Dixie' (nasally)
Oh! Oh!
Oh! Kentucky!
Swaying bodies, shuffling sideways,
Shimmying, twinkling, jazzing, stunting,
Parted lips and shining ear-rings,
Dancing to a band of
Fat buck niggers,
Playing on drums, trombones and saxophones,
Gongs and cymbals, bells and xylophones,
Thumping out in a clattering rhythm
Song-hits, dance-hits, tunes from Broadway,
Tunes for the shimmying couples dancing,
Dancing to the music of the ragtime tunes,
The ragtime tunes,
Clots and blobs of
Syncopated melody   (faster)
Syncopated melody
Syncopated melody
Syncopated melody
Oh! Oh!
Oh! Kentucky!

By contrast, 'Holy Moscow' suggests a familiarity with the Coronation Scene in Mussorgsky's *Boris Godunov*[47] or with *Khovanshchina*. (Elisabeth Lutyens' first encounter with Constant was to be only a year or two later, 'coming from the library at [the Royal] College [of Music] where he had been searching for the original – *not* the Rimsky-Korsakov – edition of *Boris Godunov*'.)[48]

Holy Moscow

Deeply-reverberating sounds
Green and black, come floating downwards
Swaying from side to side,
Pressing and jutting past each other,
Gong-like booming tones
Of ancient massive bells.
Crystalline metal jangles flutter by
Acute and piercing,
Spinning in shining vortices as if
The clustering golden domes which crown
The painted wooden church had tossed

---

[47] *Boris Godunov* was the first opera that Lambert heard: 'Myself and Russian Music', p. 6.

[48] Elisabeth Lutyens, *A Goldfish Bowl* (London: Cassell, 1972), p. 62. Elisabeth Lutyens (1906–83), a composer primarily of twelve-tone music, was daughter of the architect Sir Edwin Lutyens. Her second husband Edward Clark, whom she married in 1942, was a close acquaintance of Lambert's.

> Their heads together, pealing forth
> In joyous holy laughter.
> The music rings the sky, thrusting aside
> The canopied masses of white cloud,
> Flinging afar a happy paean, from the town
> Of painted wooden churches,
> Holy Moscow.

The published short story was somewhat in the manner of Conrad, with perhaps a hint of *The Heart of Darkness*. (According to Anthony Powell, Constant was an admirer of Conrad, especially *The Secret Agent*.)[49] It began:

> It was hot in the forest and the stout man, who had been tramping through it several hours by now, took out a large pocket handkerchief of gaudy design and mopped the sweat off his forehead.

and ended:

> An old charcoal burner who found him one morning a few days later was wont to say that the most horrible thing about the crumpled figure on the stone was the look of dull terror in the wide staring eyes.

But it was music that became the chief focus of Constant's activities. Even from an early age he had shown a musical interest. When, as a child, he was taken to the circus, he was laughed at for paying more attention to the brass band than to the horses.[50] Yet, as he explained in an interview,[51] he did not fully appreciate what music meant to him until his prolonged illness cut him off from the usual schoolboy pursuits. As he was later to realise, this illness affected the entire course of his life because, while he was indisposed, he had little else but music and books to occupy his attention. When the art teacher, H. A. Rigby, showed an interest in Constant's artistic talents and suggested his future might lie in that direction, there came a characteristic reply: 'Oh, no. There are too many artists in the family – my father, my brother and myself. I shall be a musician.' Because he could not take part in most games, he was given the run of the chapel organ and the school's many musical facilities. 'That was a critical opportunity for the development of his genius. He took full advantage of it,' the headmaster much later wrote in an obituary memoir.[52] N. R. Wilkinson, the Director of Music, taught him harmony and composition. The imprint he left on the mind of H. G. P. Davies, who played alongside Constant (on clarinet) in the School Band and the School Orchestra, was one of 'stern resolute purpose. He specialized increasingly in music from 15 years of age. Sitting next to me at every "Prep" he would be humming some notes – of a composition may be – while I, poor ordinary scholar – sought to do logarithms or learn irregular verbs.' Davies found him secretive. 'He had many letters. He never had a school pal as far as I recall. He was, however, separated and left to himself largely. Not unapproachable, polite if spoken to and I think always to the point.' Another put it sympathetically: 'I feel that under all was a spot of kindliness, and if he did not make many friends at school, it was as much our fault as his, in that we were not able to rise to his heights.' Waller claimed to be one of Constant's most intimate associates

[49] *To Keep the Ball Rolling: The Memoirs of Anthony Powell*, vol. 2: *Messengers of Day* (London: Heinemann, 1978), p. 113

[50] *Sunday Referee*, 9 January 1938.

[51] 'Constant Lambert', in Donald Brook, *Conductors' Gallery* (London: Rockliff, 1946), p. 85.

[52] Sir William Hamilton Fyfe, *The Times*, 24 August 1951.

at Christ's Hospital, being in the same school house, both studying music and having many other interests in common, and both leaving in 1922:

> We had many outings together and almost daily discussions (or I should say harangues). I was unique in being able to hear Lambert's earliest compositions, which he used to play to me on the grand piano in the Big School, I being the sole audience at the far end. I used to praise these efforts although in reality I did not like or understand them.
>
> I well remember Lambert returning from holidays after first being taken to the Diaghilev Ballet, and for weeks he could talk of nothing else. I got heartily tired of hearing the words 'Petrouchka', 'Rite of Spring', and 'Boutique Fantasque', all of which must have made a deep impression.
>
> He told me that his first musical compositions were criticized by the music master as 'not bad, but too Russian', and he decided not to submit them for criticism in future. It was about this time that the following conversation occurred while watching a cricket match:
>
> Housemaster (Teddy Edwards) – 'What are you thinking about, Lambert?'
>
> Me (interposing) – 'Russian Ballet I expect, as usual.'
>
> Lambert (sotto voce, his fury making it audible to all) – 'Shut up, you bloody little fool.'
>
> Lambert as a schoolboy was a brilliant pianist, but he always maintained that on leaving school he would give up playing and devote his time to composing. I enjoyed many hours listening to him playing at the music school. One of his favourites (and mine) was Mussorgsky's Prelude to Khovanshchina (Dawn over the River Moscow); others were Gopak by the same composer, and various excerpts from Don Giovanni and Pagliacci. I think he was fond of music in all its forms. Jazz: he enjoyed arranging contemporary hit tunes for performance at House concerts by a scratch band. Sullivan: he spent the whole of a Sunday afternoon playing through the score of the Gondoliers to the delight of a few of us enthusiasts. Classics: he once rated me soundly for speaking disparagingly of Bach.
>
> At his last school concert Lambert played Chopin's Polonaise in A flat (Op. 57 I think). He told me that this was the only decent thing that Chopin ever wrote, but he may not have meant this – he often made such remarks merely to be provocative. ...
>
> Finally I would say that I cannot over-rate Lambert's impact on me during school days, and his influence was immeasurable in helping me to form my taste and imparting some of the enthusiasm for music, literature and art.

The Russian Ballet, or Ballets Russes that had remained an artistic sensation in England since its first London season in 1911, was a frequent topic of Constant's conversation. As he remarked: 'I probably seemed to my school fellows something of a prig when I battened on reviews of the Russian Ballet while they were poring over the latest score from Lords or the Oval.'[53] Davies remembered how 'going back from London Bridge in the special train he talked continually of the shows he had seen.' In a broadcast talk on Chabrier that Constant gave in 1946, he spoke of hearing the composer's *Menuet pompeux* for the first time, adding that 'with luck I could just manage to get to the Diaghilev ballet on the first night and the last night – the rest of the season being spent, alas, at my school when instead of listening to Chabrier or watching the ballet I was made to spend my time scoring for cricket – a task which

---

[53] Lambert, 'Myself and Russian Music', p. 6.

I performed with considerable inaccuracy.'[54] It is possible that Constant was first taken to see the Ballets Russes by Thea Proctor. As early as 1911 she had painted a fan entitled 'Souvenir des Ballets Russes, Le Carnaval' and on her second and final return to Australia in 1921 she was quoted by the press as having found great inspiration in the Russian ballets. Her two lithographs of Maurice Lambert, dated about 1919, also include the ballerina Penelope Spencer who was to become a useful friend for Constant in the ballet world (her mother had run his first school in Albert Bridge Road). Angus Morrison suggested that Constant may have had his imagination fired by descriptions given to him by the stage-designer Charles Ricketts who was a passionate admirer of Diaghilev's work.[55] It was probably Ricketts to whom Constant was referring when he later wrote: 'I was fortunate enough to find myself in a country house where some enthusiast had bought the more outstanding works of the pre-war Diaghilev-Beecham repertoire. Here I was able to renew acquaintance with *Boris* and *Coq d'Or* while going through a host of works from *Prince Igor* to *Petrushka*. From then on Russian music became my special hobby.'[56] Ricketts maintained that even as a youth Constant's general artistic understanding was like that of an adult and his conversation superior to that of most of his own contemporaries, and it is probable that through him Constant heard a great deal about the Russian ballet before he ever saw a performance. Through his conversation and descriptions, Ricketts was the first really strong outside influence in Constant's life and one of the first to awaken his sense of the close connection and relationship between the different arts.

As he was on his own for so much of the time at school while others were involved in sports, Constant found the piano a great consolation and he even resolved to become a professional pianist. His first piano teacher at Christ's Hospital was Albert Bevan whose widow remembered that he 'adored Bach,[57] & his face would assume the expression of an angel when anything beautiful appealed to him. My husband often remarked what extraordinary insights & appreciation of music in all aspects Constant Lambert possessed.'[58] When Bevan left, he studied with Miss Ethel Wright with whom things did not start too promisingly:

> When he went to an audition with Miss Wright he played her a little piece by John Ireland, not with any intention of pleasing her for Miss Wright was certainly not pleased, and promptly told him to study quite the worst of the Chopin Nocturnes. When he protested it was cheap, he was asked who was he to judge, and told him that anyway it would do him all the good in the world.[59]

He studied with Ethel Wright for a few years and under her guidance in the spring of 1922 took the advanced grade of the Associated Board RCM and RAM, coming first in

[54] Lambert, 'Emmanuel Chabrier', BBC *Music Magazine*, 13 January 1946. Chabrier's *Menuet Pompeux* (orchestrated by Ravel) was played as a 'symphonic interlude' during the Alhambra Theatre season that lasted from 30 April until 30 July 1919.

[55] Angus Morrison, draft typescript forming part of his projected biography of Lambert, Royal College of Music Library, presented to the RCM by Morrison's daughter, Mrs Elizabeth Panourgias, 31 July 1990.

[56] Lambert, 'Myself and Russian Music', p. 6.

[57] Angus Morrison, in his obituary on Lambert, wrote: 'One day I happened to call upon him quite unexpectedly and found him reading through a volume of Bach's minor keyboard works with absolutely the same absorbed interest and concentration that he would have brought to a newly published work by Schönberg or Stravinsky.' *The RCM Magazine*, vol. 47 no. 8 (1951), p. 108.

[58] Letter from R. E. Bevan to Angus Morrison, 5 February 1954: RCM Library MSS 6961–6966.

[59] Letter from Patrick Wood to A. C. W. Edwards, 30 December 1951: RCM Library MSS 6961–6966.

all England with 147 marks out of 150 and winning the gold medal. 'I think he later tried for a composition scholarship but that must have been after he left Christ's Hospital; he did not get it, at any rate at his first trial. He wrote to me & blamed the examiners as being old fashioned! I believe one was Vaughan Williams but I am not sure!'[60]

At a school concert in March 1921 Constant played Chopin's Valse in A flat 'with his usual artistry, and showed the audience that we are the fortunate possessors of another pianist of distinction', reported the School's magazine, *The Blue*. A year later it was Liszt's *Waldesrauschen* [*Forest Murmurs*], in which he showed 'a nice touch, a good left hand and commendable restraint. His soft coda was excellent.' Davies recalled seeing him one Speech Day 'perched high up on the enormous organ loft with pipes up to the roof, playing without music a noisy though of course beautiful fugue or concerto or some such piece. This was in front of the Mayor and Sheriff of the City of London, not to mention all the visitors including Governors, the local squire and so on. We moved in awe of him after that.' On Speech Day in July 1922 Constant played Chopin's Polonaise in A flat to 'great applause which swelled to cheers when the Headmaster suggested that he should lay aside his diffidence and natural timidity and receive from the Lord Mayor the medal awarded him'. This was the Associated Board gold medal given for the highest marks in the highest grade examinations, a fact that received a mention in *The Times*. *The Blue* also recorded: 'He is at present, we understand, in the throes of orchestral composition.' When Constant was staying at Chilham Castle in 1919, Charles Ricketts had written: 'I am threatened with two compositions of his on the piano at the house when the house-party is away. He is less Stravinskyesque and seems genuinely interested in Weber and Liszt, the names least mentioned in recent years, both, I suppose, immense and forgotten influences on music. ... Judging from young Lambert, it would seem as if the young realized the need of movement and climax in music, the two things Debussy and his school tabooed.'[61]

Constant's introduction to contemporary music, in fact much of his musical education in general, was at the Henry Wood Promenade Concerts during the summer holidays. As he wrote much later:

> I have often wanted to describe myself as 'self-educated at the Proms'. We are so spoon-fed now by the gramophone and the wireless that we forget what the Proms meant in those days, particularly to someone like myself who was at school. Gramophone recording was bad and the catalogues scanty, wireless was in its infancy and had not set any musical standards, and the main symphony concerts took place in term-time. Had it not been for the Proms I would have been musically starved. I am sure that every musician of my generation will agree that he owes a greater debt to Sir Henry Wood than to any other individual.
>
> In my first Proms period I was still at school and could not, of course, afford to go to as many as I should have liked. The moment the precious programmes arrived I would feverishly count up my pocket money and then weigh the respective attractions of, say, 'Prince Igor Dances' and 'Night on the Bare Mountain'. In those days programmes were less segregated than they are now, otherwise I suppose I should have spent all my money on Russian nights. Fortunately the programmes were very mixed and as a result my education could not have been more liberal. Everything to me was a first performance, and hearing the moderns cheek by jowl with the classics it never struck me that

[60] Letter from Ethel Wright to Hubert Foss, 10 December 1951: Foss Archive.
[61] Ricketts, *Self-Portrait*, p. 320.

there was anything queer or difficult about them. I took to Bartók and Stravinsky as easily as I did to Mozart and Beethoven.[62]

After attending the Proms, Constant found Christ's Hospital's attitude to music old-fashioned. Nevertheless, as Patrick Wood commented, 'We learnt the rudiment of the Beethoven Symphonies, and many of the classical war-horses arranged for four hands, sitting side by side at various rather temperamental pianos. But he would always talk about and over-admire the modern works.'[63]

Even then Constant had ambitions to conduct, as one story recalls:

> The music master came as usual to the Big School on Friday evening for the choir practice. He was evidently much put out, nor could he keep the reason of his disquiet to himself. After reducing us to silence by rattling the keys he told us, in tones of irritation and shock, that Lambert had actually requested to conduct the school orchestra. The music master got what he needed: we laughed. A *boy* to conduct the orchestra, what a nerve; and I do not recollect that our laughter was sycophantic, as boys often are. We were in our fashion as shocked as the music master.[64]

Constant's musical abilities were much in demand for the more light-hearted school activities, such as playing the piano and providing the music and lyrics for concerts and shows. One number that stayed long in the memory of those involved was a syncopated 'Kipling Walk' written for an improvised jazz band consisting of combs with paper and other schoolboy instruments. Another, with the chorus 'We're four Bolsheviki from Russia the free, Iranavitch, Youranavitch, Popsky and me', satirised school life in comparison with Russia. He even belonged to a small group, that included the future Home Secretary, who found fun in writing songs about the schoolmasters, with Gilbertian words and tunes by Sullivan. A very detailed review he wrote for *The Outlook* in March 1922 of the School's production of *The Mikado* showed his enthusiasm for Gilbert and Sullivan, concluding: 'We can only hope that the rumours that we are to have no Gilbert and Sullivan next year are baseless as they are disturbing.'

As one friend remarked, he 'could mimic and burlesque a teacher's mannerisms and he was a great hand at the minor plots and conspiracies which engage so much time at boarding school.' While circumstances may not have contrived to make Constant a popular boy, he certainly made his mark and commanded respect, even admiration. He left Christ's Hospital on 3 August 1922.

[62] Lambert, 'My Promenading Life', *Radio Times*, 13 July 1945, p. 3.
[63] Letter from Patrick Wood to A. C. W. Edwards, 30 December 1951: RCM Library MSS 6961–6966.
[64] T. B. Radley, quoted in Shead, *Constant Lambert*, p. 34.

3 1922–6
The College 'Whizz-Kid'

CONSTANT entered the Royal College of Music on 18 September 1922.[1] His fellow students, soon to become firm friends, included the pianist Angus Morrison, the conductor Guy Warrack, a future Principal of the Royal Academy of Music Thomas Armstrong, and composers Gavin Gordon, Patrick Hadley and Gordon Jacob. Hadley later wrote: 'I knew [Constant] perhaps more intimately than most since the day he arrived (aged 17) at the RCM when we happened to share a lesson with old Ralph.'[2] The 49-year-old Vaughan Williams was their composition teacher, and many years later in a broadcast talk, Constant looked back on his first lesson:

> I well remember the trepidation with which I waited outside [Vaughan Williams'] door (oddly enough with Patrick Hadley) for my first lesson with him at the Royal College of Music. My admiration for him was as profound as my knowledge of my own technical shortcomings and I shall never forget the extraordinary kindliness with which he listened to the rag-bag of compositions I had produced at school. This was to begin a relationship between pupil and master which lasted for three years and was of the happiest. Vaughan Williams was above all a psychologist and realised that a strict and suddenly imposed course of theory would have been fatal to a student such as myself at that moment. Instead, he encouraged me to go on composing, at an alarming rate I admit.[3] For at one lesson, such was the time he devoted to detailed criticism, it was discovered that I was seven symphonic poems ahead of him. They were long ago pulped I need hardly say. The technical work was imposed later, of course, but the first few months were the most important to me and I can remember suddenly appreciating his kindly insight when he turned to me and said, 'I don't know if you are like what I was at your age. I thought then that my last work was the best piece of music ever written but that I should never write another. I was wrong both times.'
>
> Two things above all stand out in my memory of those weekly sessions in the somehow gloomy crypt assigned to him by the authorities, a crypt filled with the smoke of his perpetual pipe, and littered with the matchboxes he had stolen from his pupils. First, that he never encouraged his pupils to imitate his own style or mannerisms, and secondly that in the long run he had not only taught you but more important still had taught you to teach yourself.
>
> Being at that time a young student I was naturally attracted first of all by Vaughan Williams' early work. My introduction to his music was hearing his

---

[1] It is worth pointing out that Lambert did not enter the Royal College of Music with a composition scholarship, as stated by Richard Shead and Andrew Motion in their Lambert biographies. He did not gain a composition scholarship until 1924. Equally, he had not gone there on a piano scholarship, as later stated by Walton. Neither did he enter the College in the autumn of 1921 as Angus Morrison writes in his obituary of Lambert in the *RCM Magazine*.

[2] Letter from Patrick Hadley to Hubert Foss, 19 January 1952, in the collection of Foss's daughter, Mrs Diana Sparkes. Elsewhere he spoke of their friendship being 'as close as any I've had with my contemporaries': Eric Wetherell, *'Paddy': The Life and Music of Patrick Hadley* (London: Thames, 1997), p. 86.

[3] 'At the College he produced crude works at the rate of about ten a year', according to de Zoete, 'The Younger English Composers', p. 97.

lively but moving Overture 'The Wasps', a work which I subsequently arranged for piano duet when I was a pupil of his.[4]

According to Angus Morrison, Vaughan Williams said that the compositions Constant had first shown him, pieces that presumably he had written while still at Christ's Hospital, reflected 'the world of the Russian ballet',[5] and he spoke enthusiastically about his new pupil to the musicologist Edward Dent, shortly to become Professor of Music at Cambridge:

> It was Vaughan Williams who first discovered his marvellous musicianship. ... He called on me one day at Cambridge glowing with excitement to show me Constant's first attempt at a fugue, written without any previous knowledge of the rules. It was a most unorthodox fugue on a most unorthodox subject, but there could be no doubt that it was the product of an original and highly intelligent mind.[6]

Writing in 1951 to Hubert Foss, Vaughan Williams recalled that

> The first works he showed me were perfectly delightful tunes, songs, I think and pianoforte pieces very much in the folk song style. I wish they were extant still, but I expect he destroyed them as he soon became ashamed of them. ...
>
> Though he was so brilliant he was difficult to teach because he knew what he wanted and did not see the point of going through the ordinary mill, and I preached him a sermon once and told him that later on he would find the want of the 'stodge' which I was trying to make him do, and would then come back and ask me or someone else to teach him, which he countered with the invincible argument, 'Well, won't that be the time to do it?' I was non-plussed.[7]

Sir Thomas Armstrong, although seven years senior to Constant,[8] remembered with great affection their friendship and how they both became associated with Vaughan Williams:

> My friendship with Constant Lambert when he was a young man at the Royal College was a very great part of my life at that time. Those who remember Constant as a young man will remember that he was the most wonderful companion, a marvellous musician and a gay enchanting companion whose conversation was like a display of fireworks. I was associated with him a good deal because Vaughan Williams used to use us for trying out his new works and playing them on the piano.[9] All those who knew Lambert in those days will remember him as the most brilliant and wonderful creature.[10]

---

[4] 'Vaughan Williams as a teacher', Lambert's contribution to BBC *Music Magazine* edition on Vaughan Williams' 75th birthday, Home Service 12 October 1947: script in BBC Archives.

[5] Angus Morrison, draft typescript, RCM Library.

[6] Edward Dent (source not acknowledged), in Shead, *Constant Lambert*, p. 20.

[7] Letter from Ralph Vaughan Williams to Hubert Foss, 5 December 1951, in *Letters of Ralph Vaughan Williams, 1895–1958*, ed. Hugh Cobbe (Oxford: Oxford University Press, 2008), p. 491.

[8] Thomas Armstrong (1898–1994) had his Oxford studies interrupted by war service in France. After Oxford he joined the Royal College of Music in 1923, studying with Holst and Vaughan Williams.

[9] Possibly in connection with the arrangements for piano that Lambert made of Vaughan Williams' *Concerto Accademico* (Oxford University Press, 1927), *Fantasia on Sussex Folk Tunes* (not published) and *The Wasps*, for piano duet (Curwen, 1926).

[10] Sir Thomas Armstrong in *Desert Island Discs*, BBC Radio 4, 16/21 July 1989. At the age of 91, Sir Thomas chose *The Rio Grande* as one of his eight records.

While Armstrong became devoted to the music of Vaughan Williams, Constant was not to share his enthusiasm wholeheartedly, although he found much to admire in the *Pastoral Symphony*, which he referred to as 'one of the landmarks in modern English music',[11] and the Fourth Symphony, which at its first performance he hailed as 'a knock in the eye ..., all the old mannerisms have gone. The vigour, concision, and intellectual force of this symphony must have taken the composer's greatest admirers by surprise'.[12] In an article he wrote on contemporary English music for a 1929 Henry Wood Promenade Concert programme, he generously held up Vaughan Williams' compositions as 'undoubtedly the finest English works of their generation'.[13] He also considered *Flos Campi* 'one of the finest works written in any country since the War'.[14] But, like his fellow composer and close friend William Walton, he was not a follower of the folk-song school of English music. Walton, in one of his wittier moments, is reported as saying: 'There's no overwhelming reason why modern English music should chew a straw, wear a smock-frock, and travel by stage-coach. Folk tunes, like peas, bureaucrats, and Chinamen, are all the same.'[15] Constant held a similar view:

> The English folk song, except to a few crusted old farmhands in those rare districts which have escaped mechanization, is nothing more than a very pretty period piece with the same innocent charm as the paintings of George Morland.[16] ... Even in our day Elgar and Delius have, in their widely different ways, written music that is essentially English without having to dress it up in rustic clothes or adopt pseudo-archaic modes of speech.[17]

And there is, too, his much-quoted witticism that contains more than a grain of truth: 'To put it vulgarly, the whole trouble with a folk-song is that once you have played it through there is nothing much you can do except play it over again and play it rather louder,'[18] and he goes on to offer the delightful cartoon-like image of 'the hiker, noisily wading his way through the petrol pumps of Metroland, singing obsolete sea chanties with the aid of the Week-End Book, imbibing chemically flavoured synthetic beer.'[19] He is attributed with the following clerihew:

> The harmony of V.W.
> Is not of the kind to trouble you;
> Both yokels and driads
> Are represented by triads.

But Vaughan Williams was in no doubt of the importance of folk-song on British music when he fired this broadside:

---

[11] Lambert, *Music Ho! A Study of Music in Decline*, 2nd edn (London: Faber & Faber, 1937), p. 104.

[12] *Sunday Referee*, 14 April 1935.

[13] 'Contemporary English Music', Promenade Concert programme, 24 August 1929.

[14] *Sunday Referee*, 7 January 1934.

[15] Interview with Charles Stuart, *The Yorkshire Observer*, 21 December 1942, p. 2.

[16] George Morland (1763–1804) was a very successful painter of animals and rustic scenes. His profligate life-style put him in debt, and he frequently needed to flee from his creditors. He died from a brain fever.

[17] Lambert, *Music Ho!*, 2nd edn (1937), p. 120.

[18] Vaughan Williams quoted this in the programme note for the first performance of his Sixth Symphony (1948). Referring to 'an episodical tune' on the saxophone in the Scherzo that is 'repeated loud by the full orchestra', he commented: 'Constant Lambert tells us that the only thing to do with a folk tune is to play it soft and repeat it loud. This is not a folk tune but the same difficulty seems to crop up.'

[19] Lambert, *Music Ho!*, 2nd edn (1937), p. 114.

I know in my own mind that if it had not been for the folk-song movement of twenty-five years ago this young and vital school represented by such names as Walton, Bliss, Lambert, and Patrick Hadley would not have come into being. They may deny their birthright; but having once drunk deep of the living water no amount of Negroid or 'Baroque' purgatives will enable them to expel it from their system.[20]

Elgar, it seems, held a different view on folk-songs, once commenting that they 'are all very well for those who cannot invent their own tunes.'[21] Perhaps folk-song was one of the topics of the friendly disputes that Vaughan Williams and his pupil enjoyed, as mentioned by Hadley:

We used to get amusing accounts of [Constant's] differences of opinion with Vaughan Williams, always very good-natured – they never had a quarrel – but they were constantly arguing over maybe quite small points.[22]

As Vaughan Williams later wrote:

As he got to know more about French music [Lambert] got more and more away from the folk-song idiom. Indeed, at one of his early lessons he took me to task seriously for being influenced by folk song and told me I was all wrong. I took his rebuke quite meekly and kept my opinion to myself.

The first work which he showed me with the 'New look' was a very remarkable piece for clarinet solo without accompaniment. Again, I do not know what happened to that.[23]

In the same broadcast talk already mentioned Constant summed up his teacher warmly:

The late Charles Ricketts, the famous illustrator and scene designer, once said to me, 'The trouble about teachers is that they always teach what they were taught instead of teaching what they have learnt themselves'. He obviously could not have known Vaughan Williams. For the great quality of Vaughan Williams as teacher was the fact that he never taught in a doctrinaire manner. His teaching or, to put it more accurately, his tactful and kindly advice, was always based on his own hard and genuine practical experience.[24]

(It is probably worth pointing out here the origin of the description of Vaughan Williams's *Pastoral Symphony* as being like 'a cow looking over a gate' that has occasionally been attributed to Lambert. According to the poet Robert Nichols, it was the composer Philip Heseltine who commented after a performance of the work: 'A truly splendid work. You know I've only one thing to say about this composer's music: it is all just a little too much like a cow looking over a gate. None the less he is a very great composer and the more I hear the more I admire him.'[25] Elisabeth Lutyens went

[20] Ralph Vaughan Williams, 'The Evolution of the Folk-Song', in *National Music* (London: Oxford University Press, 1934); reprinted in *National Music and Other Essays* (London: Oxford Paperbacks, 1963), p. 47.

[21] In his tribute to Edward German, 16 February 1928. Brian Rees, *A Musical Peacemaker: The Life and Work of Sir Edward German* (Bourne End: Kensal Press, 1986), p. 219.

[22] *Constant Lambert Remembered (1905–1951)*, BBC Third Network, 25 June 1966.

[23] *Letters of Ralph Vaughan Williams*, ed. Cobbe, p. 491.

[24] Lambert, 'Vaughan Williams as a teacher', 12 October 1947.

[25] Cecil Gray, *Peter Warlock: A Memoir of Philip Heseltine* (London: Jonathan Cape, 1934), pp. 78–9. Robert Nichols was a friend of Heseltine when they were both studying at Oxford University.

further and dismissed English pastoral music as 'the cow-pat school' with its 'folky-wolky modal melodies on the cor anglais'.)[26]

Constant continued to study with Vaughan Williams until January 1925 when his professor of composition was Reginald Morris, Vaughan Williams' brother-in-law. 'R.O.', as he was known, was noted for his teaching of counterpoint. In 1922 he had a textbook published on the subject, *Contrapuntal Technique in the 16th Century*, and as Constant's style for a while became almost neo-classical – most noticeably in his first important ballet – so counterpoint became an important element in his writing. He stayed with Morris for the remainder of his College days.[27]

While composition was his first study, he continued with the piano for which his professor was Herbert Fryer, a one-time pupil of Busoni. Although five years Vaughan Williams' junior, Fryer's musical preferences were very conservative and hardly attuned to Constant's. According to Cyril Smith, one of his most distinguished pupils, Fryer 'hated any music which had been composed after 1910; the works of Walton, Stravinsky, and even Vaughan Williams were anathema to him. His enthusiasm was all for Chopin, Schumann and the impressionists ... and for the students he taught.'[28] This was probably one reason why Constant gave up the piano after four terms in order to concentrate on composition, but turning his attention also to conducting. However, there was no ill feeling, as Fryer recalled: 'My recollection is of his coming in his blue-coat & yellow stockings, aged about 16, I should imagine. One felt at once that he was extremely intelligent & musically gifted, but that his real interest was not in piano playing but in composition. ... The last time I saw CL was at Pagani's upstairs lunch-room where we had a meal together & I found him exceedingly pleasant & friendly.'[29]

It was during a lesson with Fryer that the pianist and critic Harold Rutland first met Constant:

> I went into Herbert Fryer's room one day to have a piano lesson, and there I found him showing a new pupil how to practise scales and arpeggios. The new pupil was Lambert, who was about seventeen at the time; he had just left school and was still wearing the uniform of Christ's Hospital, with its long blue coat and yellow stockings. We were introduced, and I was at once impressed by his handshake. The whole force of his personality seemed to be projected into it; it had an almost electrical effect.[30]

Constant also stood out because of his appearance – Hadley described him as

26 Notes for lecture 'Style and Integrity' in Elisabeth Lutyens' notebooks: Meirion and Susie Harries, *A Pilgrim Soul: The Life and Work of Elisabeth Lutyens* (London: Michael Joseph, 1989; paperback edn Faber & Faber, 1991), p. 52.

27 Shead, *Constant Lambert*, p. 37, states that Lambert studied with George Dyson, but the Royal College of Music records only show Vaughan Williams and R. O. Morris as his composition professors. If he did study with Dyson, it could only have been for a short while, perhaps during an absence of his official teacher and not long enough for the fact to be recorded.

28 Cyril Smith, *Duet for Three Hands* (London: Angus & Robertson, 1959), pp. 29–30. The pupils of Fryer (1877–1957) included Arthur Bliss, Kendall Taylor and Colin Horsley. A recital he gave of 'modern music' at the Aeolian Hall on 26 October 1921 consisted of some pieces of his own (including *Variations on a Theme by Purcell* and a *Prelude* to the tune of *The Vicar of Bray*), pieces by Balfour Gardiner and Sydney Rosenbloom, and Ravel's *Jeux d'eau* and Debussy's *La Cathédrale engloutie*.

29 Letter from Herbert Fryer to Angus Morrison, 14 June 1955: RCM Library MSS 6961–6966.

30 'Constant Lambert and a Story of Chelsea Reach: A Musical Diary by Harold Rutland in Reminiscent Mood', *Radio Times*, vol. 112, issue no. 1444 (13 July 1951), p. 9. Harold Rutland (1900–77), pianist, critic and composer, was on the BBC staff, 1940–56, and was Editor of *The Musical Times*, 1957–60.

'radiantly good-looking' – and what Rutland called his 'unusually incisive' manner of speaking, and he soon distinguished himself as 'a brilliant young musician'.[31] When he arrived at the Royal College he was already a very able pianist and an exceptionally good sight-reader, and, according to Michael Tippett who came a year after him, he 'was generally regarded as the whizz-kid'.[32]

Guy Warrack was one of Constant's circle of friends, soon to make a name for himself by presenting at the Chelsea Town Hall and the Aeolian Hall enterprising concerts that included early works by Lambert, Hadley and Walton.[33] He wrote of their friendship:

> Constant and I went to the RCM the same term & as students of composition & conducting we naturally saw a good deal of each other, especially as we both lived in Chelsea & often walked home together at the end of the day. Also we both went for a month to Germany together with Paddy Hadley & Michael Wilson one summer holiday.[34]

Another student who was to become a life-long friend was the pianist Angus Morrison.[35] Three years older than Constant, he began playing the piano at the age of four, and from nine studied under Harold Samuel. He won an open scholarship to the Royal College where his composition teachers were Thomas Dunhill and Vaughan Williams. In the term before Constant joined, he had been awarded the Dannreuther Prize for the best performance of a piano concerto (the Brahms D minor Concerto). Later, like Constant, he joined the teaching staff. As students they soon found that they shared a wide range of interests. After Constant's death, he wrote:

> All I can recollect now is the immense realisation I had that somebody very remarkable had come amongst us, and the ease and assurance with which he quickly took his place in my particular circle of friends. I think what drew us together so soon was the fact that both of us, over and above our main interest in music, were passionately interested in all the other arts. Perhaps it was just because we were less technically and professionally involved that we were even more ready to discuss and air our views about them than we were about music. Certainly in the first ten years of our friendship, many as were the hours spent together at concerts or in playing duets and two-piano arrangements of all the modern works we could get hold of, an even larger part of our time was spent in visiting exhibitions of painting, hunting out in obscure cinemas and theatres the first showings of the early German films such as *Dr Caligari*, *Warning Shadows*, *Waxworks*, etc and revivals of Chekhov, Strindberg and Ibsen, as well as in going to revues, musical comedies and music halls where his life-long interest in jazz and all forms of popular art and entertainment found continually renewed stimulation and enjoyment.[36]

[31] Harold Rutland, 'Recollections of Constant Lambert', 6pp typescript, 13 May 1952, Royal College of Music, in GB 1249 MSS 6961–6966.

[32] Michael Tippett, *Those Twentieth Century Blues: An Autobiography* (London: Hutchinson, 1991), p. 16.

[33] Guy Warrack (1900–86), Scottish conductor and composer, later associated with the BBC Scottish Orchestra and the Sadler's Wells Ballet. As he told the author, it was he who once commented: 'You should make a point of trying every experience once, except incest and folk-dancing', with which Lambert might well have concurred.

[34] Letter from Guy Warrack to Hubert Foss, 24 June 1952: Foss Archive.

[35] Angus Morrison (1902–89) made a brief appearance as a pianist in the 1940 film *Gaslight*.

[36] Morrison, 'Obituary: Constant Lambert August 21, 1951', pp. 107–8.

As Angus lived in Oakley Street, almost literally round the corner from the Lamberts, Constant would frequently drop in to play some improvements in the work on which he was then engaged. They also 'played duets by the hour, all the ballet scores: Debussy, Stravinsky, all music that was then modern.' As often as they could afford it they went to the gallery at Covent Garden, to 'a cheap high-brow cinema', to the theatre or a musical show.

In the summer months the Henry Wood Proms at Queen's Hall remained a strong attraction, although he became more selective in his attendance:

> At one time (like Sir Thomas à Malory) I always went to the gallery and thus had not savoured the full flavour of the Proms. This I did later as a student, when to go to anywhere but the actual promenade would have been out of the question. Those were my most pleasant days as a promenader. The audiences then were not so large and one could breathe and move comparatively freely. One could even make a rapid exit to avoid some work or artist one did not favour. Music by now being my daily life and not an occasional treat, I was already beginning to take it less earnestly. Instead of staying grimly on through the ballads in order to hear every note of the orchestra, I started the habit of coming for a particular work or works and concentrating on them alone. There was a friendly, informal atmosphere, and one was bound to run into a fellow student or an older composer, such as Peter Warlock, with whom one could stroll down Regent Street to discuss the whole thing over a drink.[37]

Yet, in spite of the many symphony concerts he attended, Constant's mind was always directed more to the theatre than to the concert hall. He had no desire to write symphonies; he was more interested in tone-poems based on a poetic idea. Walton remembered that 'around '23 to '26 he poured forth a steady stream of works such as the boxing ballet, piano concertos, symphonic poems, etc which unfortunately he later destroyed'.[38] Ballet fascinated him and was central to his musical thinking. It was then fashionable to construct ballets on the more classical plan of a series of separate, self-contained variations or episodes, using clearly defined musical or dance forms. Typical of these were the ballets by Poulenc, Milhaud and Auric[39] that appeared after the First War. According to Morrison, 'Constant had already written quite a number of these without having any very decided idea of what the ballet was to be about. Eventually I suggested a subject to him which seemed to fire his imagination, and soon after this the work was finished.'[40] The ballet, *Adam and Eve*, a *suite dansée* in three scenes with a scenario devised by Angus Morrison, was, in another guise, to bring Constant unexpected fame.

He had an invaluable friendship with Penelope Spencer, a prima ballerina at Covent Garden who, with Lady George Cholmondeley, was in charge of the ballet class at the College. In August 1922 she had choreographed and danced Stravinsky's *Pastorale* at the Glastonbury Festival. Constant hoped to interest her in his ballet scores. She remembered how

> he would bring me his compositions to see if I could dance to them. I had been

---

[37] Lambert, 'My Promenading Life'.

[38] William Walton, typescript, n.d. Fortunately, two of the works mentioned *have* survived: the boxing ballet (*Prize Fight*) and the early piano concerto (1924; reconstructed 1988).

[39] Poulenc's *Les Biches* (1923), Milhaud's *Le Bœuf sur le toit* (1919) and *Le Train bleu* (1924), and Auric's *Les Matelots* (1925) are examples.

[40] Morrison, 'Obituary: Constant Lambert August 21, 1951', p. 109. Elsewhere he said that 'between us – we were both fellow students then – [we] hit on the idea of a ballet based on Adam and Eve'.

taught to feel music 'flow through me', and I think Constant might possibly have been influenced by me … I was the only person he knew in the dancing world. He threw away masses and masses of work, and then would never allow me to talk about it. 'Oh that's no good, I've thrown it away,' he'd say.[41]

In an undated letter, almost certainly written just before joining the College, he informed her:

> Dear Penelope,
>   I have some compositions which I think might interest you. A Dance for orchestra which I wrote at school and a Spanish Rhapsody which I have just finished.
>   Could you hear them any time? I am going away for a week to Chilham but I hope to fix up something when I come back. I was sorry to miss your recital[42] but I saw several very good notices and heard good accounts from the family.
>   Yrs affectionately
>   Constant

Penelope choreographed and performed Constant's *Dance* in a recital she presented at the Pump Rooms in Bath in December 1923, making it his first work to receive a public performance.[43] In June the same year he wrote again:

> I wonder if you could come here some time and hear some stuff which might I think be suitable for you to dance to. I have got a Pastoral for flute, cla[rine]t, bassoon, horn, trumpet with accompaniment for strings and 3 percussion. The Pastoral is about 10 to 15 minutes long and is similar in form to the ballet though quite different in style. The Director is going to ask Anthony Bernard[44] if he could do it, so you may have a chance of hearing it on the orchestra. I have also two pieces for violin & piano one slow & soulful, the other very vigorous & quick & so on. I think they are both very suitable for dancing and if necessary they could be scored for a small orchestra (strings, piano, flute, clar[ine]ts, horns etc).
>   Will you have time to hear them fairly soon? If you are up at the College next Tuesday you could fix a time then.

Quite what the ballet is that he mentioned is not clear, but there is a note of pleasure in his postscript: 'Did I tell you I was having a work done at the next Patron's Fund Thursday 28th?'

The work in question was an orchestral piece that received its only performance on 28 June 1923 at the Royal College of Music at one of its Patron's Fund Rehearsals. Through the generosity of Sir Ernest Palmer, these were public rehearsals, usually three a term, lasting from 10 a.m. until just before noon after which the works were played straight through, often with the composer conducting. On this occasion Adrian

---

[41] Motion, *The Lamberts*, pp. 129–30.

[42] Aeolian Hall, 7 July 1922.

[43] 8 December 1923, The Pump Room Musicians, conductor Jan Hurst.

[44] Anthony Bernard (1891–1963) was one of a number of conductors who presented enterprising programmes, usually including new or unusual works. In 1921 he founded the London Chamber Orchestra with whom he gave concerts for the Chelsea Music Club and elsewhere. Lambert's two songs, sung by Phyllis James, were included on 1 December 1925 in a Contemporary Music Centre concert at the Court House, Marylebone, when Bernard conducted van Dieren's *Serenata*, Finzi's *Severn Rhapsody* and Hindemith's *Kleine Kammermusik*, and on 16 November 1926 for the Chelsea Music Club, when Bernard conducted the first performance of Lambert's *Divertimento*. A week later, at the American Women's Club, Mayfair, he gave the first performance of Warlock's *Capriol* Suite.

Boult conducted the Royal Albert Hall Orchestra in the first three works: a symphonic poem *Ireland* by Warwick Braithwaite, the last two movements of Lalo's *Symphonie espagnole* (with Leonard Hirsch as soloist) and Franck's Symphonic Variations (soloist Stephen Wearing), and the programme concluded with Constant's rhapsody *Green Fire*.

Green Fire was conducted by neither Boult nor its composer but a more senior student in Boult's conducting class, Gordon Jacob. Ten years older than Constant, he had done four or five years' war service before joining the College. 'But I got very friendly with Lambert,' he later recalled in an interview. 'I did a lot of work for him later, when he was conducting the ballet. He was the most brilliant musician I have known in my lifetime, I am bound to say. Extraordinary chap,'[45] adding on another occasion: 'His genius, charm of manner, ceaseless, but never boring talk and his extremely entertaining sense of humour did much to enliven the RCM.'[46] In a private memoir he summarised the young Lambert succinctly:

> C.L.'s approach to music was extremely serious and full of poetical imagination. But he kept a kind of defence-mechanism by which he never appeared superficially to be serious at all, though his writings showed an excellent judgement. … Those who only knew him in the later years could have no idea of what he was like in his youth and middle years – bright, scintillating, blessed with good looks and an engaging personality and extremely brilliant intellectually. Others knew more about his private life than I did … music mattered more to him than anything. … As far as I know he was a stranger to meanness, avarice, jealousy of others' success and his nature was generous and tolerant. Perhaps his most outstanding characteristic was the hiding of his feelings behind a mask of wit, paradox and humour.[47]

Although the score is no longer extant, *Green Fire* clearly made an impression. Its classification as a rhapsody would seem to align it with similarly titled works by Vaughan Williams and Delius, but its impact was very different from the pastoral effusions of those composers. Edmund Rubbra recalled 'the startling effect of his youthful *jeu d'esprit*' while Harold Rutland wrote that 'it was rumoured that Vaughan Williams had expressed himself as startled, and even bewildered, by Constant's trick of writing consecutive sevenths and ninths for trombones'. This may well have been the work that the critic Dyneley Hussey was thinking of when he wrote: 'I remember a performance of a piece by him at a College concert, which certainly displayed a determination to go his own way, if not to "cock a snook" at academic proprieties'.[48]

Although Constant was rarely wasteful of musical ideas, in the absence of the manuscript there is no evidence of him having revised *Green Fire* or reused its material elsewhere, as was often his habit. He was preoccupied with ballets and his earliest surviving attempt was *Prize Fight* (1923–4), a work closer in spirit to music hall (for which it was intended;[49] it was once listed 'for band') than the more outrageous products of Diaghilev's Ballets Russes than conventional ballet. Its subtitle, a 'satirical' or 'realistic' ballet in one act, and its flippant subject matter clearly betray the influence

[45] Gordon Jacob in interview with Lewis Foreman, July 1982, in 'Gordon Jacob in Interview', *British Music Society Journal*, vol. 7 (October 1985), p. 60.

[46] 'Personal View 5: Gordon Jacob', *RCM Magazine*, vol. 41 no. 3 (Christmas Term 1965), p. 72.

[47] 'Memoir by Dr Gordon Jacob, CBE', from a collection of essays, including selected articles by Lambert, intended for publication under the editorship of Mr J. Harvey Packer.

[48] Dyneley Hussey, 'Constant Lambert and the Ballet', *The Dancing Times*, no. 492 (October 1951), p. 9.

[49] Edwin Evans, 'Constant Lambert', *The Chesterian*, vol. 12, issue no. 95 (June 1951), p. 183.

of Erik Satie's 'ballet réaliste' *Parade*.[50] 'Ten minutes of sheer rowdiness,' he called it.[51] The action (with cue numbers) is as follows:

> The curtain goes up to show a boxing ring in a state of great confusion. The master of ceremonies (who is also the referee) tries to obtain silence [no. 3] and despite the interruptions of a noisy crowd eventually succeeds [6–7]. The two boxers, one black, the other a big American, are introduced to the audience [7] and the bell sounds for the first round [8]. In this round the black man gains precedence and the American is floored for a count of 9 but he is saved by the bell [13]. During the pause that follows, the seconds try to revive their exhausted champions with massage, cups of Bovril, magnums of champagne, etc while the referee has increasing difficulty in restraining the rowdy elements in the audience. At last the bell sounds [21] and the boxers proceed to fight with such extreme caution that not a blow is exchanged during the whole round. The disgusted audience start to whistle, boo, and throw things at the boxers. A lively group enters the ring and executes a bucolic dance [25]. The referee while trying to stop them [26] is violently attacked by the two boxers [29]; from his pocket he produces a large police rattle [30] and shakes it. As a result there is a charge of mounted police[52] [31] who also enter the ring, which unable to support so great a weight, suddenly collapses.

Constant played *Prize Fight* with Angus to Vaughan Williams at one of his composition lessons. Was it mere coincidence that his teacher had composed a ballad opera, *Hugh the Drover*, that centred on a boxing match and, although written before the war, had its first performances at the College in July 1924?[53] If *Hugh the Drover* uses both real and synthetic English folk-tunes, *Prize Fight* prominently quotes a variant of the American Civil War song 'When Johnny comes marching home', which is used in fugato style to accompany the two rounds of the fight, and may even have snatches of music hall tunes unfamiliar today. Other themes are labelled as representing the audience and the master of ceremonies. Constant completed *Prize Fight* in 1924 in two versions: a full score and a version for piano duet. On the reduced score of the first version he wrote and then crossed out: 'The Overture (not in this copy) is scored for the same orchestra but with 2 trumpets & no harmonium.' The Overture either has not survived or was re-used in another work. When three years later he made some small revisions and produced a new score, the synopsis and certain score directions were written in French, suggesting that he was hoping that it might be accepted by the Ballets Russes. But it was not performed in his life-time.[54] The final version calls for a small chamber orchestra including harmonium (or bass concertina) and an array of percussion with crécelle (rattle) and cloche (bell), to use some of the French terms favoured by Constant. As his close friend, the Scottish composer and critic Cecil Gray has written:

[50] The first English staging of *Parade* was given by Diaghilev on 14 November 1919 at the Empire Theatre. The young Walton saw that production.

[51] De Zoete, 'The Younger English Composers', p. 98.

[52] It is possible that the inclusion of mounted police came as a result of an incident at the first Cup Final held at the newly built Wembley Stadium in April 1923. The crowds had swollen to nearly twice the stadium's capacity by people climbing the boundary walls and spilling onto the pitch. Mounted police had to restore order.

[53] A ballet, *Le Boxing*, was presented by Ballet Rambert at the Mercury Theatre on 16 February 1931. With English and American champions and choreography by Susan Salaman, it used parts of Berners' *The Triumph of Neptune*.

[54] De Zoete ('The Younger English Composers', p. 98) states that the early version was given on the wireless, but no reference to this performance has been traced.

In his early years the French element was naturally in the ascendancy as the result of an adolescence passed in the atmosphere of the hectic, feverish, restless 'twenties, with the Russian Ballet of Diaghilev and the French school of composition as the preponderant influence.[55]

On 16 and 17 June 1924 Constant sat the final examinations for an open composition scholarship. It seems that it was almost a formality because, as Vaughan Williams later wrote, 'All who had to do with him realised at once his brilliant qualities and some of us insisted that he must be given a scholarship.'[56] His success was reported in the July issues of *The Musical Times* and Christ's Hospital's *The Outlook* and *The Blue*. Vaughan Williams told a delightful story of how, before being finally awarded the scholarship, Constant had to be medically examined and the doctor required a specimen. He duly brought one to the College but, finding no instructions as to where he was to leave it, carried it around with him all day in his music case.[57]

That June he completed another ballet that has survived, *Mr Bear Squash-You-All-Flat*. It lasts, like *Prize Fight*, for about 15 minutes and its seven characters are animals. The setting is a clearing in a wood with a large tree trunk. Mr Frog approaches the trunk, enquires whether anyone is living inside, and as nobody replies, hops in to make it his own. In turn Mr Mouse, Mr Hedgehog, Mr Duck, Mr Samson Cat and Mr Donkey enter, observe the trunk and are allowed in to share the home. Finally, a grizzly bear enters and on being told that the trunk is full up, calls out, 'I am Mr Bear Squash-You-All-Flat,' and sits on it, with obvious results. While Lambert called it 'a Ballet in One Act based on a Russian children's tale', he left no clue as to which tale he was using,[58] but he was almost certainly influenced by Stravinsky, especially *Renard* (1915) and *The Soldier's Tale* (1918), both of which derived from Alexander Afanasiev's collection of Russian folk tales. *Renard* was based on 'The tale about the Cock, the Fox, the Cat and the Ram' and although it was not given in England until July 1929, Constant would certainly have known about it. *The Soldier's Tale*, which was presented by Ernest Ansermet at a lecture-recital in the Wigmore Hall in August 1920, was among Stravinsky's earliest jazz-inspired pieces after he had been given some samples of ragtime music by Ansermet, on returning from an American tour in 1918. As Stravinsky himself acknowledged: 'My choice of instruments was influenced by a very important event in my life at that time, the discovery of American jazz,' adding that 'my knowledge of jazz was derived exclusively from copies of sheet music, and as I had never actually heard any of the music performed, I borrowed its rhythmic style not as played, but as written.'[59] Although Lambert had already developed an interest in jazz while at Christ's Hospital, for him it was a singularly important event – seeing the Negro revue *Dover Street to Dixie* in 1923 – that radically affected his compositional direction thereafter. If *Prize Fight* owes a debt to Satie, *Mr Bear Squash-You-All-Flat*

---

[55] Cecil Gray (1895–1951), *Musical Chairs, or Between Two Stools: An Autobiography* (London: Home & Van Thal, 1948; Hogarth Press, 1985), p. 291.

[56] Letter from Ralph Vaughan Williams to Hubert Foss, 5 December 1951, in *Letters of Ralph Vaughan Williams*, ed. Cobbe, p. 491.

[57] Letter from Ralph Vaughan Williams to Hubert Foss, 2 January 1952, *ibid.*, p. 494.

[58] The original Russian tale has not been identified, but in 1950 a children's story book *Mr Bear Squash-You-All-Flat* by Morrell Gipson and illustrated by 'Angela', was published by Wonder Books of New York. The author's inspiration had been a three or four-line entry in a classic Russian anthology. Gipson expanded the story, creating a bear that is mean but lovable and is taught an important lesson, so providing – unlike Lambert's version – a happy ending. This version was reprinted in 2000 by the Purple House Press of Cynthiana, Kentucky.

[59] Igor Stravinsky and Robert Craft, *Expositions and Developments* (London: Faber & Faber, 1962), pp. 91, 92.

has many touches of Stravinsky, particularly in the shape of the themes and their treatment. Ever present, too, is the influence of *Petrushka* that Sacheverell Sitwell considered to be in many ways the supreme Russian ballet, writing that 'no artist in any of the arts who saw it could have been unaffected by it'.[60] It left its mark on a number of composers at that time, including Arthur Bliss, William Walton and Gustav Holst, and Lambert was certainly not unaffected.

While neither *Prize Fight* nor *Mr Bear Squash-You-All-Flat* was to be performed in Lambert's lifetime, he did conduct a College performance of a similarly frivolous ballet written by his fellow student and another close friend, Gavin Gordon-Brown,[61] later to shorten his name to Gavin Gordon and become best known for his ballet *The Rake's Progress* that Constant premiered in May 1935. The frivolous work that provided Constant with his first experience of conducting ballet was *Les Noces imaginaires*, written specially for the newly formed Ballet Class, with golliwogs as the two principal characters and the others representing dolls. Constant conducted the first of four performances on 11 December 1924.[62] Gordon was multi-talented, sharing many of Constant's musical interests, particularly a fondness for Sousa marches. They were both delighted to discover that the 'March King' did not confine himself to a single art but wrote novels as well, notably *The Fifth String*, which Constant regarded as 'his *magnum opus* as a *romancier*', although he firmly stated that it was as a composer that Sousa would live.[63] It was in connection with Sousa that Gordon recalled one of those amusing 'happenings' that Lambert seemed able to conjure up:

> Constant was staying with me in my country cottage and although he liked high-brow music and so forth, he loved Sousa amongst other popular composers and we were playing duets, Sousa marches, and outside my window there was nothing but fields and we were blaring away at *Liberty Bell* or something or other when suddenly he stopped, and I turned round and said, 'What's the matter?' He was roaring with laughter, a really convulsed laughter, and he said, 'Look out of the window!' and there were about 200 cows who had come from all points of the compass and were all gawping at us.[64]

Besides being a composer, Gavin Gordon was a singer, taking many of the leading roles in the College productions (including John the Butcher in the first performance of Vaughan Williams' *Hugh The Drover*), a skilled caricaturist, an equally skilled writer of humorous poems such as clerihews, and an actor (but not to be confused with the American film star of the same name). Like Constant, his diversity of talents probably

---

[60] In his Prologue to *Gala Performance: A Record of The Sadler's Wells Ballet over Twenty-Five Years*, ed. Arnold Haskell, Mark Bonham Carter and Michael Wood (London: Collins, 1955), p. 15.

[61] Gavin Gordon-Brown (1901–70), RCM student, 1920–5. After the war he was a staff producer at Sadler's Wells.

[62] The other performances, all conducted by Lambert, were given on 24 February and 24 and 26 March 1925. The February performance was reviewed by *The Times*, its critic finding the music 'at once fanciful, piquant and danceable'. The new ballet class was under the direction of Lady George Cholmondeley and Penelope Spencer. The performances were prefaced by Guy Warrack conducting a ballet to Bax's *Mediterranean*, and followed by a scene from *Aida* conducted by H. Grunebaum who had recently joined the College staff. *Les Noces imaginaires* poked fun at Stravinsky's *Les Noces* (first performed in Paris in June 1923 by the Ballets Russes). When much later Stravinsky composed his *The Rake's Progress*, Gavin Gordon commented with much pleasure that he had got there first! In January 1928 the BBC invited Lambert to conduct *Les Noces imaginaires* at a 'try-over' rehearsal for new works.

[63] Lambert, 'Sousa, the Last of the Classicists', *Radio Times*, 8 July 1938, p. 12.

[64] *Constant Lambert Remembered*, BBC Third Network, 25 June 1966.

worked against his becoming outstanding in any single sphere. In later life he spoke about Constant in his College days:

> He was very shy; rather intense, and rather introvert, I suppose you would say; a little bit suspicious of people. Very quiet when he came into his lessons and went out when they had finished. He didn't really become the jolly hail-fellow-well-met until quite a lot later. It was perfectly obvious in his very early College days that he was a very brilliant person. He rebelled rather heartily against the general sort of trend very much based on I suppose the old Stanford sort of tradition still held of the German classics and which never meant anything to Constant and the kind of English folk song which he loathed and he sort of veered far more to the Russian-French school.[65]

Another sketch of Constant in his College days comes from Myfanwy Thomas, the youngest daughter of the poet Edward Thomas, who met him at a gathering of young people at a Chelsea dancing class:

> Once I went ... to a dance practice run by Jenny and Colin de la Mare and held in a Chelsea studio. ... The studio had a balcony overlooking the Thames. Harold and several friends from the Royal College of Music were already gathered round the pianist, whose name was Mark Anthony. Jenny de la Mare and her brother Colin were there, also Angus Morrison and Gavin Gordon-Brown, each later to make his name as pianist and composer of ballet music. Before long a young man asked me to dance. He had a slight limp, and looked like my idea of Pan, with fair loose curls from which budding horns might appear, and perhaps he limped because one elegant hoof had not quite changed back to a foot. I learned later that his name was Constant Lambert.[66]

In the Christmas term of 1923, Constant had joined the conducting class and on 1 April, under Boult's guidance – and still officially known as Leonard C. Lambert, he took the RCM Second Orchestra through the last movement of Borodin's Second Symphony. (The other student conductors that day were Patrick Hadley, Gideon Fagan, Doris Allen, Harold Davidson and Ivy Pugsley.) Harold Rutland felt that Lambert was 'completely at home on the conductor's rostrum where his force and vitality were an invaluable asset; he took to conducting as a duck to water; and his preferences for Russian, French and Spanish music soon declared themselves.[67] Even in the conducting class, his enthusiasms for which he was becoming known were evident. Gordon Jacob listed them as:

> Sousa's marches, jazz and blues, Liszt (especially late works which foreshadowed certain 20th century techniques of composition), Chabrier (very pronounced affection for his works), Sibelius of course, also Borodin (his two symphonies especially). He admired Elgar but was not in sympathy with the British folk music revival. He was keen on Purcell, Boyce, etc and his contrapuntal studies with R. O. Morris gave him a good grounding in live 16th century counterpoint.

[65] *Ibid.* Gavin Gordon sketched several caricatures of Lambert, as well as other composers including Walton, Vaughan Williams, Hadley, Ireland and Harty, and one delightful cartoon of Stravinsky tearing up a score with a gleeful Bliss on his knees picking up the scraps (reproduced in an issue of *The Sackbut*).

[66] Myfanwy Thomas, *One of These Fine Days: Memoirs* (Manchester: Carcanet New Press, 1982), pp. 157–8. Maurice Lambert made two sculptures *c.* 1928 of Myfanwy's older sister, Bronwen, who was a great friend.

[67] Rutland, 'Constant Lambert and a Story of Chelsea Reach', 13 July 1951, p. 9, and *Recollections of Constant Lambert*, 6pp typescript, 13 May 1952.

He was a very useful pianist and, I think, played the clarinet, too. I used to play piano duets with him, such as Chabrier, Les Six, *Rite of Spring*, etc.[68]

Walton summed up Lambert's taste in music as 'very unusual. He did not really like the classics, or indeed ever come to care for them, but preferred more the highways and byways of music; the Elizabethans, Purcell, Scarlatti, the Russian school – particularly Glinka and Mussorgsky – and amongst the French composers he had a particular predilection for Debussy and Erik Satie. He was one of the earliest Sibelius enthusiasts,'[69] and as Constant himself wrote: 'When two or three years ago someone said to me a trifle sneeringly, "I see you've joined the Sibelius cult," I replied with characteristic modesty, "I haven't joined it. I started it."'[70] Being such a close friend, however, Angus Morrison was in a position to make an important correction concerning the classics:

> Many people thought that his apparent neglect of the 'Great Composers' was wilful and due to some fundamental dislike or blind spot in his makeup, but that was far from the truth. He had the greatest affection and admiration for Handel, Haydn, Mozart, Beethoven (with certain reservations) and Schumann. *Carnaval* and *Kreisleriana* were two of his greatest favourites in all piano music.[71]

Two names notably absent from the list of his likes are Wagner and Brahms. With Wagner it was not a question of a strong dislike; rather that he preferred Liszt.[72] Brahms was another matter. With many British composers of the older generation having studied on the Continent in conservatoires like Leipzig, the Germanic influence at the Royal College was very strong and Brahms had been especially revered by the College's two figure-heads, Parry and Stanford. At the end of his life Sir Thomas Armstrong spoke of how he and other young British composers had to get Brahms 'out of our system'. Hubert Foss, in his *Music in My Time*, wrote of that composer as being 'a shadow over English music. He is recommended as a model to those whose natural mode of expression is the very antithesis of that of Brahms.'[73] Vaughan Williams remembered that Lambert 'hated Brahms and once told me that he longed to push as if by accident that plaster cast of Brahms which decorated one of the passages at the RCM and smash it for ever'.[74] He was never to conduct a Brahms symphony and indeed almost no work of his at all – the only exceptions possibly being the two

---

[68] 'Memoir' by Dr Gordon Jacob, CBE, written at the request of Mr K. Harvey Packer.

[69] William Walton, 'Constant Lambert (In Memoriam 21 August 1951)', in *Selections from the BBC Programme Music Magazine*, ed. Anna Instone and Julian Herbage (London: Rockliff, 1953), pp. 114–15; reprinted in Stephen Lloyd, *William Walton: Muse of Fire* (Woodbridge: Boydell Press, 2001), p. 273.

[70] Lambert, *Sunday Referee*, 5 December 1937. Walton claimed that 'it was he [Lambert] who introduced Cecil Gray at first to Sibelius'. But Gray gave a chapter to Sibelius in his *A Survey of Contemporary Music* (London: Oxford University Press, 1924), quoting the Fourth Symphony as 'one of the greatest things in modern music'. This may have spurred Lambert to conduct the slow movement at the Royal College the next year. Gray had possibly heard Sibelius conduct his Fourth and Fifth symphonies at Queen's Hall in February 1921, on his last visit to England.

[71] Obituary in *RCM Magazine*, p. 108.

[72] Ninette de Valois recalled 'a hilarious account of the acute discomfort that he had suffered when he found himself sitting through *The Ring* at Strasbourg': *Step by Step: The Formation of an Establishment* (London: W. H. Allen, 1977), p. 53.

[73] Hubert Foss, *Music in My Time* (London: Rich & Cowan, 1933), p. 75.

[74] Letter from Ralph Vaughan Williams to Hubert Foss, 5 December 1951, in *Letters of Ralph Vaughan Williams*, ed. Cobbe, p. 492.

piano concertos at the Royal College[75] when the choice of work would not have been necessarily his. When Toscanini came to London in 1937, Lambert wrote: 'When a man is the greatest living exponent of Italian music, why saddle us with the monumental mediocrity of the Brahms *Requiem* and *Tragic Overture?*'[76] His dislike of Brahms even caused a BBC producer to apologise in 1940: 'I am sorry to have harrowed your feelings by my Brahms suggestion.' Lambert used to say disparagingly that while many composers worked at the piano, Brahms worked at the double bass. He once told the pianist Frank Merrick that the only tune in all Brahms that he would like to have written himself was the F major tune in the intermediate section of the last movement of the second piano concerto. He could be equally scathing about German composers in general, writing in 1933:

> During the last century England became, musically speaking, a German colony, and although English composers have long ago declared a free state, English critics still maintain their old allegiance, and are to be found dotted about London like battered monuments of a past sovereignty. The tremendous force of the German nineteenth-century tradition has imposed the harmonic and melodic style of the German composers, not as one of many ways of writing music, but as the obviously correct way, the classic norm by which all other schools are judged, patronised, and condemned.[77]

For his conducting class on 15 July, this time with Geoffrey Toye in charge, the work was Borodin's First Symphony, of which he conducted only the last two movements (while quite probably much to his annoyance, Harold Davidson conducted the first two). His next conducting classes included Grieg's Symphonic Dance No. 4 (4 November, under Malcolm Sargent), Rossini's overture to *The Italian Girl in Algiers* (9 December, again under Sargent), Franck's Symphonic Variations (10 February 1925, with Josephine Dalmaine as soloist, repeating it at a Patron's Fund Rehearsal on 4 June), and the slow movement of Sibelius's then rarely played Symphony No. 4 (31 March, under Sargent). 'Ever since I first became acquainted with the score of Sibelius's Fourth Symphony,' he wrote seven years later, 'I have been convinced that the composer will ultimately prove to have been not only the greatest of his generation but one of the major figures in the entire history of music'.[78] On 16 June he was in charge of the slow movement of Mozart's Piano Concerto No. 23 in A. According to Angus Morrison, this movement became one of Constant's favourite pieces of music because of its Siciliana rhythm of which he was so fond and the almost Puccini-like melody with which the orchestra enters at the end of the long extended opening phrase for the solo piano.[79] In his remaining classes he conducted Handel's *Water Music* suite, Falla's *El amor brujo* ballet music, and Schumann's *Concertstück.*[80]

Sargent had initially joined the College staff as Boult's assistant with the conducting

[75] Brahms Piano Concerto No. 1, 12 June 1936 with Jean Morris, and Piano Concerto No. 2, 28 October 1938 with Maria Donska, in each case with the RCM First Orchestra.

[76] *Night and Day*, 25 November 1937, p. 243.

[77] *Sunday Referee*, 26 February 1933.

[78] *Sunday Referee*, 3 January 1932.

[79] 'I remember him saying he thought the slow movement of the A major one of the most beautiful single movements ever written'; Angus Morrison's memoir in the reissue of Lambert, *Music Ho!* (London: Hogarth Press, 1985), p. 16. Lambert also wrote of 'the Siciliana that forms the finale of [Mozart's] D minor quartet – a simple dance tune into which and its variations Mozart seems to have compressed the emotional experience of a lifetime': *Music Ho!*, 2nd edn (1937), p. 22.

[80] Respectively 27 October and 7 December 1925 (under Maurice Besley), and 16 February 1926 (under Sargent), The soloist in the Schumann was Millicent J. Silver, a RCM scholar.

class, but when in 1924 the latter became principal conductor of the City of Birmingham Orchestra, he took over so that Constant became mainly his student. Later he provided this short memoir:

> [Lambert] was a very charming person and as a member of my conducting class, I was happy to guide him in the right way, with regard to baton technique. He was a brilliant score reader and I well remember how easily and surprisingly he would play on the piano, the most complicated modern works. We had a system in which two students would undertake to play, for example, 'Petrouchka', or the 'Sacre du Printemps' – one taking over the wind parts on one piano, and the other the strings, on another piano, and then they would change places. He was exceptionally brilliant at this, and seemed to rejoice in the difficulties that such a job involves.
>
> With the stick, he was quick to learn anything that one had to teach him and he had a very definite idea always how everything should go. He was obviously more interested in modern music than in the classics and took a great joy and got rather excited in beating and understanding complicated rhythms.
>
> Of course, as a wit, he was exceptional and had a great flair for writing odd bits of nonsense poetry.[81]

With his strong leaning towards the Russian repertoire, for his conducting class on 14 July 1925 Lambert arranged a four-movement orchestral suite from Glinka's opera *Ruslan and Ludmila*. Leaving aside what he called 'the pleasing but quite uncharacteristic overture', the sections he chose were The Abduction of Ludmila, The Enchanted Palace, The Cortège and The Triumph of Ruslan. Always an avid reader, Constant had learned about the opera in Montagu-Nathan's monograph on the composer[82] and although he had not met the author he had written to tell him about the performance: 'Next Tuesday I am conducting at the RCM a suite which I have arranged from Ruslan and Ludmila. As it was your excellent little book which drew my attention to the opera, I should be very pleased if you could come. I have not had enough rehearsal time to ensure a really finished performance but I hope to give a good idea of the work. Included in the suite are the 5/4 chorus, the Persian chorus etc.' He gave fuller details the next year when writing to the conductor Edward Clark[83] in hope of another performance:

> The music, (which you probably know from the piano score) has never been heard in England and is, in my opinion astonishingly good. I have kept to Glinka as far as possible, the arrangement consisting merely of choosing & dovetailing the numbers, filling in the chorus parts & an occasional unavoidable touching up of the brass parts. The entire Suite (4 movements) lasts about 20 minutes, but a shorter, & possibly better, arrangement is to do the 3rd, 2nd, & 4th movements (about ¼ hr.) The score is for double wind (2nd flt. to picc. & 2nd oboe to C.I [*sic*]) 2 Trumpets, 4 Horns, 3 Trombones & gong ad lib.[84]

---

[81] Letter from Sir Malcolm Sargent to Angus Morrison, 8 June 1955: RCM Library MSS 6961–6966.

[82] M. Montagu-Nathan, *Glinka* (London: Constable, 1916). Montagu-Nathan was an expert on Russian music and had also written a study of Mussorgsky (London: Constable, 1916) and *An Introduction to Russian Music* (London: Palmer & Hayward, 1916) with which Constant was almost certainly familiar. Arnold Haskell described him as 'a man of exceptionally wide general culture'.

[83] Edward Clark (1888–1962), conductor and administrator. Born in Newcastle-upon-Tyne, he was the second husband of the composer Elisabeth Lutyens.

[84] Letter from Constant Lambert to Edward Clark, 5 October 1926: BL Add 52257, fols. 139–148b.

Edward Clark was an important figure, especially in the world of contemporary music. Having studied abroad with Arnold Schoenberg and the conductor Oskar Fried, he was acquainted with such composers as Busoni, Mahler, Webern, Stravinsky, Prokofiev and Bartók. During the war he had been interned in Germany with several thousand other civilians at Ruhleben Camp. In 1919 he was the first English conductor (with Adrian Boult) of the Ballets Russes in London and two years later he organised several ground-breaking concerts of contemporary music, also in London. In 1923 he was appointed conductor of the BBC's Newcastle station and much later he was to become music advisor for the BBC and, from 1945, president of the British section of the International Society for Contemporary Music.

Walton had generously provided Constant with an introduction to Clark at Newcastle where he had *Portsmouth Point* down for a broadcast. He had written: 'May I take the liberty of recommending to your attention the works of Constant Lambert, particularly a suite, which he has made from "Ruslan".'[85] Constant enclosed a letter of his own in which, as well as giving details of scoring, he informed Clark of a full set of parts at the Royal College. He ended with a bit of undisguised flattery: 'Excuse my hawking my wares like this but I thought you would be more interested in it than any other conductor in England.' Much to Constant's delight, Clark programmed the *Ruslan* Suite and he also proudly told Constant that in Newcastle he was about to give the first performance in England of Stravinsky's 'Tale of the Soldier', as he called it. Constant replied, asking if any programme notes were required for *Ruslan* and throwing in as an aside a suggestion: 'Do you know Glinka's *Valse Fantasie* by the way? I think it is charming but it is never done. The orchestra is quite small.' Then, ever a Francophile and a stickler for detail, he concluded almost as a corrective: 'I hope "L'Histoire d'un Soldat" went well.'[86]

Constant had also invited Serge Diaghilev[87] to his Royal College performance. Diaghilev regarded *Ruslan* as 'the Gospel of Russian music, forestalling Wagner and sometimes going even further than he did'[88] and Constant held Glinka in similarly high esteem: 'There is no Russian composition of importance – unless Scriabin's orchestral poems be considered important – that is not directly indebted to one or both of these operas [*A Life of the Tsar* or *Ruslan and Ludmila*]. ... Amongst nineteenth-century composers Glinka is second only to Liszt in historical importance. ... It would take a whole book to enumerate the technical devices – harmonic, orchestral and rhythmic – which, found for the first time in *Ruslan*, have altered the whole face of European music,' he later wrote in *Music Ho!*[89] This was not blind hero worship because he conceded one failing: 'Glinka changed and enriched every branch of music but one – construction – and this formal weakness is evidently part not only of Glinka's make-up but of the whole make-up of Russian music.' Just before Christmas Constant had the opportunity to conduct the last three movements of the Glinka suite again, this time with the London Symphony Orchestra at a Patron's Fund Concert presided over by Boult on 4 December 1925.

[85] Letter from William Walton to Edward Clark, 5 October 1926: BL Add 52257, fols. 139–148b.

[86] Letter from Constant Lambert to Edward Clark, 6 November 1926: BL Add 52257, fols. 139–148b.

[87] Both Angus Morrison and Walton have suggested that Lambert had an introduction to Diaghilev from the French illustrator Edmund Dulac, a friend of Charles Ricketts and the collector Sir Edmund Davis, and it may well have been that Lambert mentioned his acquaintance with Dulac when inviting Diaghilev to the Glinka performance. Lambert's letter of invitation is at the Lincoln Center, New York. See also chapter 5, n. 69.

[88] Richard Buckle, *Diaghilev* (London: Weidenfeld & Nicholson, 1979), p. 131.

[89] Lambert, *Music Ho!*, 2nd edn (1937), pp. 107, 108, 111.

Even before leaving Christ's Hospital Constant had formed one of his most important musical friendships – with William Walton. At the age of ten, Walton had won a scholarship to the Christ Church Cathedral School, Oxford, where for six years he was a chorister. Then, because he had shown considerable musical promise, through the Dean's intervention he joined Christ Church College as an undergraduate to continue his musical studies. It was there in 1919 that he was 'discovered' by the Sitwell trio, the self-appointed champions of all that was modern in art. Rather than see him go to the Royal College of Music, Osbert and Sacheverell Sitwell offered him a room in their London house[90] and the annual sum of £250 (to which a number of friends contributed). Three years older than Lambert, as a composer Walton was otherwise largely self-taught and no doubt sensed the difference between them, having forgone the thorough College musical education from which Constant was benefiting. He lacked too Constant's voracious mind and admired the way in which he was completely at ease when dealing with different art forms, not just music. He found him 'a fascinating companion, a wonderful talker, and I learnt an enormous amount from him. He led me into the many highways and byways of music, which I probably should not have explored much by myself, such as the Russian composers, and he was one of the first people to start the Sibelius craze.'[91] Later in life he spoke of him as 'one of my closest friends for nearly thirty years'[92] and of missing him more than anyone.[93] In the 1920s and 30s, when Walton and Lambert were seen as the rising young English composers, there was – on Walton's part at least – a degree of rivalry, even a little jealousy, between the two. When Constant's *The Rio Grande* (a setting for chorus, orchestra and solo piano of a poem by Sacheverell Sitwell) became popular, Osbert Sitwell wrote to one of Walton's patrons, the poet Siegfried Sassoon: 'Constant Lambert's success with his *Rio Grande* has, I am sorry to say, tinged a little their carefree friendship with a certain acerbity. In fact, I thought the other day that I distinctly heard him referred to as "that little beast".'[94] Nevertheless, he wrote warmly to his mother: 'The "Rio Grande" ... I see is having a huge & very well-deserved success, which makes me happy for Constant as he has not had much of a good life till now, & this ought to put him on his feet, both financially & otherwise.'[95] And before long Walton capped Constant's success with one of his own: *Belshazzar's Feast*, and it was through his single-mindedness that Walton ultimately was to emerge as the finer composer.

Constant came to know Walton through Osbert and Sacheverell Sitwell who lived in Carlyle Square, almost on the opposite side of King's Road from the Lamberts in Glebe Place. Walton recalled seeing him 'in the King's Road when he was still in Christ's Hospital as a boy, [with] this striking costume of the yellow stockings and this blue gown, and this extraordinary head that he had even in those young days. And

[90] First 5 Swan Walk, Chelsea and then 2 Carlyle Square, Chelsea, where Walton stayed with Osbert and Sacheverell Sitwell from 1919 until 1932.

[91] Walton's memoir of Lambert, sent to Hubert Foss, Hubert Foss Archives. In Duncan Hinnells, *An Extraordinary Performance: Hubert Foss, Music Publishing, and the Oxford University Press* (Oxford: Oxford University Press, 1998), p. 50.

[92] Walton, 'Constant Lambert (In Memoriam 21 August 1951)', p. 114.

[93] Angus Morrison, talk to the London University Music Diploma Society at the British Music Information Centre, London on 25 September 1987; text printed as 'Anyhow, about Walton and Lambert', *British Music*, vol. 15 (1993), pp. 16–32, at p. 22.

[94] Letter from Osbert Sitwell to Siegfried Sassoon, 17 January 1930, in Michael Kennedy, *Portrait of Walton* (Oxford: Clarendon Press, 1989), p. 55.

[95] 20 March 1930: *The Selected Letters of William Walton*, ed. Malcolm Hayes (London: Faber & Faber, 2002), p. 59.

then I got to know him, I think, through the Sitwells ...'[96] According to Osbert, 'it must have been in the winter of 1920 or 1921 ... that one day the front-door bell rang and I answered it. On the doorstep stood a pleasant-looking young, very young, man, who said, handing me an envelope, "I have a letter of introduction." I looked at him again, and noticed that he had a courageous look ... I said, "Come in, won't you?" And soon we were talking like old friends.'[97] Osbert was immediately struck by this 'prodigy of intelligence and learning, ... gifted with that particularly individual outlook and sense of humour which, surely were born in him and are impossible to acquire.'

The first product of Walton's Sitwellian patronage was *Façade*, a work of remarkable originality and maturity involving the recitation of poems by Edith Sitwell to a small instrumental ensemble. Edith described the poems as '*abstract* poems ... patterns in sound ... in many cases, virtuoso exercises in poetry (of an extreme difficulty) – in the same sense as certain studies of Liszt are studies in transcendental technique in music,'[98] a comparison that would have delighted Constant. *Façade* was originally intended merely as a piece of home entertainment in those days when society drawing rooms echoed with music-making. But Walton initially regarded it as a joke:

> They had great difficulty in persuading me to write the music[99] ... Osbert and Sachie were both very much excited and involved with it all once I had started, and they were the ones who were really keen on making me continue with the music. I remember thinking it was not a very good idea, but when I said so, they simply told me that they'd get Constant to do it if I wouldn't – and of course I couldn't possibly let that occur.[100]

It is unlikely that Constant (then only 16 and still at Christ's Hospital) attended the first private performance of *Façade* at 2 Carlyle Square on 24 January 1922, but he and Angus Morrison were both present the following year at the first public presentation at the Aeolian Hall on 12 June.[101] For those early performances Edith was the sole reciter,[102] and it may have been the strain on her that caused Constant to remark, 'Of course you made a great mistake. You ought to have had me reciting it.' And as Walton remembered: 'The next time we did [*Façade*], in 1925 or 6, *he* did it and of course it was a roaring success and he recited marvellously.'[103] First he shared the recitation, but

[96] *Constant Lambert Remembered*, BBC Third Network, 25 June 1966.

[97] Sitwell, 'Portrait of a Very Young Man', pp. 77–80.

[98] Decca sleeve note, LXT2977 and ECS560.

[99] *The Façade Affair*, BBC Radio 3, 12 June 1973: Sir William Walton, Angus Morrison, Peter Quennell and Ambrose Gauntlett talking with Bernard Keeffe. BBC Sound Archives MT41111, NSA M4959YBD1.

[100] Pearson, *Façades*, p. 180. However, Osbert states that Lambert was 17 at the time of their first meeting which – if true – would place it in 1922 or 1923, while Sacheverell's biographer, Sarah Bradford, in *Sacheverell Sitwell: Splendours and Miseries* (New York: Farrar, Straus, Giroux, 1993), p. 104, gives 'early in 1922'. Neither would allow credence to Walton's story of the brothers' threat to have Lambert set *Façade* if Walton refused.

[101] In 1927 Osbert Sitwell described this performance simply as 'not then a marked success, for it did not run smoothly enough', *All at Sea* (London: Duckworth, 1927), p. 32. At other times the Sitwells liked to mask *Façade*'s initial lack of success by describing the occasion as something of a riot that reviews clearly show it was not.

[102] In the early performances the reciter(s), instrumentalists and conductor were all concealed behind a painted curtain with a hole for the megaphone to be heard through. The original curtain, designed by Frank Dobson, was used for all performances until the Siena Festival in 1928 when the designer was Gino Severini. For the 1942 Aeolian Hall performance John Piper was the designer. Later performances dispensed with a curtain.

[103] BBC Sound Archives recording used in the documentary *An Extraordinary Relationship*, broadcast by BBC Radio 3 on 31 May 1990 and repeated on 29 August 1991. NSA B5928/07.

on the next occasion he took all of it upon himself, as became his habit whenever he performed the work. As a reciter of *Façade* Constant really came into his own. Walton, who admired his 'clear, rapid, incisive, tireless' voice with its 'extraordinary range of inflection', said that Constant 'always adored doing *Façade* and he maintained that he was by far the best interpreter – in which I agree with him. ... He would build in imitations of friends, common acquaintances and so on, and you never quite knew who he was going to be imitating ... though one remembers, in the last number ... he used this curious, rather sinister hissing voice that Professor Edward Dent, the Cambridge Professor of Music, used.'[104] Richard Shead has written that 'by the 1940s Lambert's interpretation and his voice had deepened, and he had also acquired the habit of introducing at what he conceived to be appropriate points imitations of such persons as Winston Churchill, John Ireland and the late Professor Dent – "moving in classical metres" in "When Sir Beelzebub" was recited in Lambert's "Dent" voice.'[105] As Constant himself wrote in 1928, 'The poems are recited, for the most part, "senza espressione", but with the utmost precision and variety of rhythm.'[106] For precision his interpretation, fortunately partly preserved on disc, has not been surpassed.

Constant cemented his friendship with the Sitwells by setting two of Sacheverell's poems, *The White Nightingale* and *Serenade*, that he would have come across in the annual anthology *Wheels*. They were first performed at an informal College concert on 6 March 1924 and repeated there on 2 April. Always avoiding the conventional, Constant scored these songs for soprano, flute and harp. The student performers were Bruce McLay (flute), Marjorie M. Buckle (harp), and Edna Kingdon (soprano) who remembered the first performance:

> Constant Lambert ... wrote a fearsome song – a setting for soprano, flute and harp of [Sacheverell] Sitwell's *The White Nightingale* – RVW gave us the unenviable task of singing this at a College Concert – I thought it was complete nonsense (youthful conceit) & it was very difficult – a lot of whole-tone scales, & no support at all from flute & harp. Later in my end of term report, Sir Hugh [Allen] scrawled – 'Had a tough nut to crack in the Lambert song'. Constant Lambert was in a frightful state of nerves – pacing up & down the corridors like a caged lion before the performance – the Sitwells were there, but I didn't see them.[107]

While at the College, he made several other Sitwell settings that have not survived: two poems by Edith Sitwell, *The King of China's Daughter* for voice and xylophone and *Serenade* for voice and glockenspiel, Osbert Sitwell's *Proud Fountains* for voice and orchestra and a symphonic poem based on the sequence of Osbert's poems *Argonaut and Juggernaut* first published in October 1919.[108] In 1925 he composed an overture for

---

Lambert's first recitation of part of *Façade* was on 27 April 1926.

[104] Motion, *The Lamberts*, pp. 147–8.

[105] Shead, *Constant Lambert*, p. 142.

[106] Lambert, 'Some Recent Works by William Walton', *The Dominant*, vol. 1 no. 4 (Feb. 1928), p. 18.

[107] Edna May Whitlock (née Kingdon) in conversation with Robert Gower, 10 November 1979, in Malcolm Riley, *Percy Whitlock: Organist and Composer* (London: Thames Publishing, 1998), pp. 28–9.

[108] De Zoete, 'The Younger English Composers', lists *The Queen of China's Daughter*, but no such poem by Edith seems to exist. She is probably referring to *The King of China's Daughter* that first appeared in *Wheels 1*, 1916, and then, in a revised form, in Edith's anthology *The Wooden Pegasus* published in June 1920. Osbert's *Proud Fountains* was probably *Fountains* from the anthology *Argonaut and Juggernaut*, although 'proud' is not a word that Osbert uses in that poem.

two pianos, at first untitled, which he dedicated to Gavin Gordon. He then used it as the finale of the ballet *Adam and Eve*, but in 1927 he extracted it as a short, bustling, contrapuntal orchestral overture in its own right, calling it *Bird-Actors* after a poem by Sacheverell.

Constant was soon accepted into the Sitwell circle and, by being seen to be joining in their antics, even taken as one. The young Cyril Connolly came across them at the Washington Irving Hotel in Granada at Easter 1925:

> They were really quite alarming – alarming rather than forbidding. All of them were wearing black capes and black Andalusian hats and looked magnificent. Dick Wyndham was with them and Constant Lambert and Willie Walton. I'd never met them before, but they *seemed* like Sitwells.[109]

He became a frequent guest at Renishaw Hall, the Sitwell family home in Derbyshire, usually in August. His first visit, according to Osbert, was in August 1925.[110] These visits were rarely without incident. Constant's encounter with the eccentric Sir George Sitwell on his first stay was one such instance. He had arrived late in the evening after Sir George had retired for the night. As this was his first experience of a large house-party (there were about 20 guests, including Walton and the author Peter Quennell) Constant was 'very alert and rather nervous. In consequence he was punctual to the minute in coming down to breakfast' the next morning. Finding the dining-room empty, he helped himself to eggs and bacon and was greatly surprised, on looking towards the garden, to see 'a dignified old gentleman, crawling on all fours, with a stick in his mouth'.[111] It was Sir George, apparently testing the soil for the new level of the lawn he was laying. (Lambert is famously said to have spread the malicious rumour that Walton, with his Sitwellian nose, was the illegitimate offspring of the union of Sir George Sitwell and Dame Ethel Smyth.) On another occasion Sir George was in the middle of a course of Nauheim carbonated baths to relieve his overstrained heart. Constant knew nothing of this and arriving for a few days' stay, 'very tired after conducting', he found to his delight a steaming bath that the nurse had prepared with salts and left to cool. Thinking that it was for him, he jumped in. As Osbert relates, Constant 'thoroughly enjoyed the bath, and stayed in a good while. But he developed a curious blue tinge in his complexion for all the remainder of the day, and for at least a week complained of singular palpitations and of a feeling of utter exhaustion'.[112] Sometimes the house would reverberate to the sound of his playing with Walton on two pianos. At other, quieter moments while at Renishaw he would turn to his own music. Part of a *Divertimento* that he wrote in 1926 was composed there.

While in Osbert's company, whether at Renishaw or Carlyle Square, there might have been some awkwardness with Constant having to run the gauntlet of Osbert's homosexual advances but fortunately, like Walton, he only once had to rebuff what he described as 'dormitory games – scuffling on the sofa'[113] for there to be no further

---

[109] Pearson, *Façades*, p. 189. Walton and the Sitwell brothers were touring Spain, visiting Cordoba, Cadiz, Seville and Granada where they were joined not only by Dick Wyndham and Constant Lambert but also by Edith, who was recovering from a recent operation for back trouble.

[110] Osbert Sitwell, *Laughter in the Next Room* (London: Macmillan, 1949; paperback edition, 1958), p. 248. Osbert again confuses the issue by stating that Constant was then 'only eighteen'.

[111] Sitwell, 'Portrait of a Very Young Man', p. 78.

[112] Sitwell, *Laughter in the Next Room*, pp. 259–60. This was, it seems, not the only time Sir George had his bath 'highjacked': Philip Ziegler ascribes a similar episode to Osbert's lover David Horner: *Osbert Sitwell* (London: Chatto & Windus, 1998), p. 171.

[113] Ziegler, *Osbert Sitwell*, p. 164, from an interview with Anthony Powell.

embarrassment. Walton similarly made it clear to Osbert that 'that sort of thing was not his cup of tea, and he had never asked again'.[114]

Lambert and Walton increasingly became regular companions, going to shows and various clubs and eating-places together. Walton valued Constant's 'companionship, his charm, his lively and amusing conversation, … his wit and the numerous other facets of this unique character'.[115] He went with the Sitwells to hear Constant's settings of Sacheverell's poems performed at the College and in turn Constant was probably present when Angus Morrison was pianist in the first performance of Walton's Toccata for Violin and Piano at Queen Square, Bloomsbury on 12 May 1925. When Walton wrote incidental music[116] for Lytton Strachey's play, *The Son of Heaven*, which was given two charity performances at the Scala Theatre, London on 12 and 13 July, Constant showed another of his talents, as timpanist in the theatre orchestra conducted by Walton. (In addition to the timpani, he once wrote of the bass drum being 'an instrument for which I have a natural talent'.)[117]

They studied each other's works in progress, and in November Lambert showed Walton his ballet *Adam and Eve* in which, according to Morrison, he had treated the biblical story 'rather frivolously', its scenario 'a very light-hearted affair … never very thoroughly worked out in detail or on paper.' The four characters were Adam, Eve, the Serpent and the Angel. Walton wrote excitedly to Sachie Sitwell about it, hoping that Diaghilev would accept it. He would be 'off his chump' if he didn't, he added. 'I think it's marvellous. In fact he [Lambert] is the genius amongst a lot of talent.'[118] This score was to be Constant's first stepping-stone to fame.

[114] Susana Walton, *William Walton: Behind the Façade* (Oxford: Oxford University Press, 1988), p. 51.

[115] Walton, 'Constant Lambert (In Memoriam 21 August 1951)', p. 117.

[116] In an article on Walton that Constant contributed to the *Boston Evening Transcript*, 27 November 1926, he wrote: 'So great, indeed, was [Walton's] obsession with ragtime that even when writing incidental music for Lytton Strachey's Chinese melodrama, *The Son of Heaven*, he was unable to prevent some unmistakable touches of Gershwin from entering the score!'

[117] Lambert, 'My Promenading Life', *Radio Times*, 13 July 1945, p. 3.

[118] Letter, 9 November 1925, in Bradford, *Splendours and Miseries*, p. 156.

4 1925–6
Diaghilev and Disagreement

L AMBERT and Walton shared an ambition not yet achieved by any British composer: to have a ballet accepted by Diaghilev. After the financial failure of *The Sleeping Princess* in 1921,[1] Diaghilev was looking to the wealthy press barons for support for his London seasons, something that he felt might be forthcoming if he were to choose an English subject with an English composer and an English painter. Through Eugene Goossens (who occasionally conducted for Diaghilev in London), Walton had met the Russian composer Vladimir Dukelsky, whose ballet *Zephyr and Flora* was being performed in November 1925 as part of the Ballets Russes' season at the Coliseum.[2] Knowing of Walton's hopes, Dukelsky arranged a meeting at the Savoy Hotel for him to play his overture *Portsmouth Point* to Diaghilev. (He had an ulterior motive in helping someone in the Sitwell circle: he was in love with the actress Frances Doble, soon to be Sachie's sister-in-law.) Walton wanted Lambert to come too, perhaps to provide some moral support. But, according to Richard Buckle, Diaghilev

> had taken a dislike to this young man who had begun haunting him, who had invited him to hear a performance of a suite from Glinka's *Ruslan* which he had arranged and conducted at the Royal College of Music, and who wore an orange shirt with a black tie. Dukelsky smuggled Lambert into the audition with Walton. The latter was no pianist and his rendering of *Portsmouth Point* left Diaghilev cold. Lambert then played [his *Adam and Eve*] and, being a better performer, gave a spirited rendering of what Dukelsky thought his 'mild' and 'skimpy' music. Dukelsky was surprised to see 'a beatific smile' on Diaghilev's face. 'Are you English?' he queried. 'Yes, I am. Why?' countered Lambert. 'That's most surprising. I don't like English music, yet I like your little ballet. I'm going to produce it, but not with that silly title.' He took a big red pencil, crossed out 'Adam and Eve' and wrote 'Romeo and Juliet' over it. Constant burst into uncontrollable tears.[3]

Later, in a humorous moment, Diaghilev told Tamara Karsavina, who danced Juliet, why he had changed the ballet's title. 'My dear Lambert,' he had exclaimed, 'how can you expect Madame Karsavina to appear as Eve? A married lady! But she won't hear of it!!'[4]

Walton put a different gloss on the audition, writing to Sachie that Diaghilev had praised *Portsmouth Point* as 'a most brilliant, fresh & exhilarating work', intimating that he might use his music for a ballet.[5] The work must have made some impression because it was chosen as one of the 'symphonic interludes'[6] played in June 1926 during

---

[1] *The Sleeping Princess* ran at the Alhambra Theatre from 2 November 1921 until falling audiences compelled Diaghilev to bring it to an end on 4 February 1922. The Ballets Russes did not return to London until November 1924.

[2] Vladimir Dukelsky (1903–69) is perhaps better known by the name Vernon Duke, under which he wrote musical comedies and songs like *April in Paris*.

[3] Buckle, *Diaghilev*, p. 460, from Vladimir Dukelsky, *Passport to Paris* (Boston: Little, Brown & Co., 1955), pp. 172–3.

[4] Tamara Karsavina (1885–1978), 'Serge Lifar and the Last Diaghilev Seasons', *The Dancing Times*, March 1967, p. 303.

[5] Letter, 26 November 1925, in Bradford, *Splendours and Miseries*, p. 156.

[6] Diaghilev had first introduced 'symphonic interludes' in 1919. These shorter pieces, played between ballets, considerably extended the range of music that he offered in any season, some works even receiving a first performance.

the intervals in the Ballets Russes summer season at His Majesty's Theatre (the work's first London performance, with Eugene Goossens conducting 'through the hum of conversation').

Writing many years later, Diaghilev's secretary Boris Kochno tells a slightly different story, suggesting that Diaghilev first approached Lambert for a ballet, rather than the other way round.

> When Diaghilev asked Lambert to compose a ballet score, he had no definite scenario to propose and suggested that he take his inspiration from some gouaches by an anonymous primitive artist, probably a nineteenth-century British seaman, which we had seen in Augustus John's studio. In November 1925, Lambert wrote to Diaghilev from London to say that John had agreed to design the ballet's mise-en-scène (for which he asked me to write a scenario) and would take these gouaches as a basis. The project did not materialise, however, and in 1926 I wrote a scenario for Lambert's ballet that was a choreographic version of *Romeo and Juliet.*[7]

While Walton was never to have a ballet commissioned by Diaghilev, Lambert's future now seemed assured. On 20 November he informed Diaghilev that Augustus John had agreed to do the designs for *Romeo and Juliet,*[8] but when the impresario visited John's studio he was not impressed by what he saw. After rejecting certain other English painters to whom he had been introduced by Sachie, he met the young Christopher Wood who was Constant's senior by four years.[9]

Christopher (or 'Kit' as he was often known) had one thing in common with Constant. It was while playing football at Marlborough College that he injured his leg. The wound developed into a case of septicaemia that was so serious that for nearly two years he was nursed at home by his mother. As with Constant, the illness prevented him from playing football and cricket again, and afterwards he too walked with a limp, often using a stick. While Christopher was convalescing, his father was absent for most of the time on war service, so that, again like Constant, a strong mother–son relationship developed with the result that Christopher became very mature for his age, with a clipped, fairly fast – almost nervous – manner of speech. He resumed his schooling in January 1918, and the following year he studied for a short time at the Liverpool University School of Architecture before moving to London. But it was Paris that opened the world to him. It was possibly through Augustus John that he was invited by the Jewish art collector Alphonse Kahn to stay in Paris where he established a lasting friendship with the Chilean diplomat Antonio de Gandarillas with whom he travelled widely in Europe, North Africa, Greece and Italy. Through these two influential people he became acquainted with George Auric, Jean Cocteau, Pablo Picasso and others artists who had connections with Diaghilev. Wood was talented but, unlike Constant, full of youthful arrogance, writing from Paris to his mother: 'You ask me what I am going to do: I have decided to try and be the greatest painter that has ever lived.' In April 1925 at Monte Carlo he became fascinated by the Ballet

---

[7] Boris Kochno, *Diaghilev and the Ballets Russes* (New York: Harper & Row, 1970), p. 236. The sections in *Romeo and Juliet* that Richard McGrady ('The Music of Constant Lambert', *Music & Letters*, July 1970, p. 243) cites as examples of 'Lambert's skill in creating effective mood music' more likely reflect Kochno's or Diaghilev's intuition in matching the music written for a different scenario to the Shakespeare plot.

[8] Buckle, *Diaghilev*, p. 466, from a letter, 20 November 1925, in the Bibliothèque Nationale, Opéra, Kochno collection.

[9] Christopher 'Kit' Wood (1901–30), bisexual artist whose paintings were chiefly landscapes, portraits and still life. He became an opium addict and was killed when he threw himself in front of a train on Salisbury station 'while of unsound mind'.

Russes ('The Russian Ballet is here also which is a great attraction and the most agreeable spectacle in the world. All the modern musicians are here too.'), and in May, while in Rome, he met Lord Berners who took him out in his car and they painted together.

Knowing of Diaghilev's interest in an English ballet, Wood hoped that with such influential friends and contacts a commission would come his way, making him the first Englishman to design for Diaghilev. He soon had two projects in hand, one probably of his own devising and the other for the Lambert score – if Diaghilev, as seemed likely, turned down Augustus John. On 16 December 1925 Kit wrote from Paris to his mother:

> I worked for three weeks day and night drawing out a very amusing English Ballet for a story arranged by Victor Spencer about English life, farm, race course, jockeys, gypsies, costermongers and so forth. It is a splendid thing and absolutely good to the end, but Diaghilev being a very complicated Russian has to be very carefully approached, as he refuses hundreds of ideas every day. The last day in London he came for lunch, and I showed him my paintings and drawings, and as I had to leave the next day the story and drawings of the ballet also which goes with the music of a boy called Lambert whose music he had already taken to go with a ballet by Augustus John.

According to Kit, John hesitated so much that he decided to have a go himself.

> I thought to myself 'There's no harm in trying, and I don't mind if he turns me down.' He seemed very impressed with my work, and said so, and later to Victor Spencer he said that he was prepared to do a ballet with the story and drawings by me, but he must think it over and it wouldn't be for some time. … If he wants it, he knows where to find me, so nothing will induce me to run after him.
>
> … Please say nothing about the Ballet to anybody, as I don't dare to myself. If I did so, it would ruin every chance I have with Diaghilev.[10]

The 'English Country Life' ballet, for which music by Berners was probably intended, never materialised, Kit writing home eight days later:

> I heard from Diaghilev that he liked my drawings the best of any he saw in England and thinks I have lots of talent, but won't accept the book of the ballet of Spencer. … Anyhow he made it quite clear that he thought I was the most interesting of all the young painters he had seen in England, and it is a very great deal to have his admiration and Tony and Jean Cocteau think that he will come back to me.

The precise nature of Lambert's relationship with Wood is unclear. Osbert Sitwell wrote that 'he was a great friend of the brilliant young English painter, Christopher Wood', and Anthony Powell, who became an intimate friend of Constant's and met Wood twice, went as far as writing that 'over and above his liking for Wood's designs, Lambert was a personal friend of Wood, for whom (in a quite unhomosexual manner) he had a certain hero-worship'.[11] But Wood's letters to his mother give no indication of any warmth on his part in their first meetings, in fact quite the opposite. Soon after Christmas Lambert stayed in Paris for several days in accommodation that Wood had found for him. On 29 December Kit wrote to his mother from Paris:

> Now I have young Lambert the little musician with whom I did the ballet, coming over to Paris and as he has never been here before and is too poor to

---

[10] Christopher Wood's letters are at the Hyman Kreitman Research Centre, Tate Britain, Millbank, London, with whose permission they are printed here.

[11] Powell, *Messengers of Day*, p. 58.

come otherwise I said he could live in the studio which ties me a good deal but I feel I am really doing someone a service by doing this so must put through with it for about 10 days. He rather bores me but I feel he may benefit so much from seeing this beautiful town and meeting some musicians cleverer than himself because I see that that is just what his musique lacks and find it a little too insular.

These letters give the impression of Wood being considerably inconvenienced by Lambert and wanting to separate him from his grander (and more senior) artistic friends, like Cocteau and Picasso, even if he might provide the way to Diaghilev and personal success. All the same, he made use of him while he was in Paris, taking the opportunity to paint some portraits, as he told his mother with a distinct tone of superiority – and even contempt – on 15 January 1926:

I have had this little musician staying. I took a cheap room in a hotel for him so as not to have the bother of him in the studio. He got dreadfully on my nerves and wanted to be with me all the time which I found very trying, and had to be very unselfish. He left yesterday.

I lunched with Diaghilev who is on his way to Monte Carlo. He was very nice and said he had liked my things very much, and thought I had a lot of talent. He says he hopes to do a ballet with me in the future …

I think in any case he is delaying this English Ballet for another year as he doesn't think Augustus John suitable. He wants me to be better known, and it is too great a risk for him for him if he did it now with Lambert who is lesser known than I am. So things couldn't be better in that direction, I think quite as good as could be expected.

I am working a good deal, I made my best portrait of Lambert while he was here, and a splendid drawing, so he served his purpose.[12] Besides, I feel it may have been a good turn to somebody by letting him be in Paris where I was able to introduce him to the best musicians here. I think he improved even during the short time he was here although he makes the great mistake of thinking he is a perfect little genius when he isn't really.

But having accepted Lambert's score for *Romeo and Juliet*, Diaghilev was for some time undecided as to whom he would choose for the designs, and on 2 February Wood wrote home:

Picasso is charming to me and said he couldn't understand why Diaghilev hadn't taken my ballet, that it couldn't have been done better or more beautiful. He loves it.

Constant meanwhile had returned to London, four days late for the start of the new College term. On 16 February he took up the baton at what was to be his last conducting class as a student, and then at the beginning of March, with a month of the term still remaining, he was summoned to Monte Carlo. On 3 March he wrote from 25 Glebe Place to Penelope Spencer:

I have just been wired for by Diaghilev to go to Monte Carlo immediately so I shall not be able to be present at your rehearsals.

Fortunately I have just finished the Berners, both score and parts. It was difficult to make it sound amusing with such a limited orchestra but I think it ought to come off alright. (I have put in an ad lib percussion part.)

If you are paying, the fee will be £4 but if you are going to dun the Lyric,

---

[12] Wood was also drawing Poulenc at this time, and that year he had already made a pencil sketch of Walton.

Hammersmith, I think I might well ask £5. I don't really think this is too much considering the extreme difficulty of the piece!

With best wishes for the success of the dance.

The ever-innovative Spencer was performing 'a startlingly original solo'[13] to Berners' *Funeral March for the Death of a Rich Aunt* at the Lyric Theatre, Hammersmith, as part of Nigel Playfair's *Riverside Nights* revue, written and arranged by A. P. Herbert and Playfair, with dances that she herself had arranged. As well as orchestrating for her the short and (despite its title) sprightly Berners piano piece, it is quite likely that Constant was her rehearsal accompanist, but he was now required to accompany Diaghilev's *corps de ballet* for the *Romeo and Juliet* rehearsals. His student days at the Royal College of Music were over.

Diaghilev had now conceived *Romeo and Juliet* as a ballet within a ballet. 'Since Shakespeare used no scenery, neither shall we,' he told Sergei Grigoriev, his manager,[14] an idea no doubt encouraged by his current shortage of money for new ballets. This was to cause the first crack in a relationship of conflicting temperaments. According to Buckle, when Diaghilev informed Lambert of his decision, there came a reply of youthful indignation: he might as well put sand on the stage in *Le Train bleu* because the scene was a beach.

The synopsis for the two tableaux, as outlined in the published piano score, is as follows, with the title of each section in brackets:

> 1. The action takes place in the classroom of a ballet. [I *Rondino*] Enter the premier danseur and the premiere danseuse, who, seeing that they are late, quickly change their clothes and get ready for the class. [II *Gavotte and Trio*: Women's Dance and III *Scherzetto*: Men's Dance] The professor teaches them a *pas de deux* [IV *Siciliana*], during which, forgetting their proper steps, they make no secret of their affection. [V *Sonatina*] The lovers are separated by their scandalised friends, who carry them off to the theatre where a rehearsal is due to start.
>
> 2. [Entr'acte] The stage is being prepared for a rehearsal of scenes from Romeo and Juliet.
>
>   a) [VI *Sinfonia*] The first meeting of Romeo and Juliet at the ball.
>   b) [VII *Alla Marcia*] The nurse and the servant.
>   c) [VIII *Toccata*] The duel between Romeo and Tybalt.
>   d) [IX *Musette*] The balcony scene.
>   e) [X *Burlesca*] Paris enters, accompanied by musicians, and searches for Juliet, his fiancée.
>   f) [XI *Adagietto*] The death of Juliet.
>
> [XII *Finale*] The curtain falls and the enthusiastic audience imitates and applauds the principal actors. The curtain rises, but Romeo and Juliet are not there to take their call. The spectators rush on to the stage and vainly search for the lovers, who elope by aeroplane.[15]

[13] Julie Kavanagh, *Secret Muses: The Life of Frederick Ashton* (London: Faber & Faber, 1996), p. 77. Spencer first danced the Berners piece at a RCM recital in 1924, and then in a matinée programme presented by the Cremorne Company (its only appearance) on 11 March 1926 at the Scala Theatre. On both occasions she probably had a piano accompaniment. She dressed as a male, with top hat, dressing gown and a grotesque mask, shedding crocodile tears at the aunt's demise. She later performed it in 1932 on BBC television.

[14] S. L. Grigoriev, *The Diaghilev Ballet, 1909–1929*, trans. and ed. Vera Bowen (London: Constable, 1953; Harmondsworth: Penguin Books, 1960), p. 221.

[15] *The Musical Times* review 1 June 1926 described the ending as 'a gay elopement, with a pantomime-charade of flight by motor-bicycle and aeroplane'.

Having the leading characters depart in leather coats and airmen's caps with goggles was certainly a novel touch; the flight by aeroplane was conveyed by having Romeo exit carrying Juliet poised horizontally over his shoulder.

The new scenario necessitated several changes and additions to the *Adam and Eve* score; among them, a short *Alla Marcia*, originally written for piano, was utilised for the nurse's scene. For these alterations Lambert had to travel to Monte Carlo. (The score is marked 'London 1925 – Monte Carlo 1926'.) At the same time Christopher Wood was in a quandary, still not knowing whether he was to be commissioned for the scenery. A further sequence of letters to his mother continues the sorry saga of his involvement, with a glimmer of hope that his *Romeo and Juliet* designs might be accepted:

March, n.d. [11 or 18], from Monte Carlo:

> It seems that there is once more a very good chance of my doing the Ballet, not mine, but another. If Derain refuses to do some scenes, which he probably will, there is a roundabout way I will possibly be asked to do it. All my friends like Cocteau and Auric have told Diaghilev that I am the only person and according to them it is practically settled, but here I am slaving away at these drawings which are extremely difficult as in this ballet all the scenes are set to represent the Rehearsal room of the Russian Ballet, which is a large empty room with white walls and behind the scenes of a theatre where there are nothing but ropes and bits of scenery to go on. So you can imagine that the subject is not very easy to make interesting.
>
> I don't care what it is as long as I do it simply for the advertisement it will bring, and I mean to have a small exhibition in London at the same moment as the ballet will be produced here. It is by no means decided yet and the exasperating thing is that after making the most awful fuss because I was going away, and also to show me what they wanted, and that I should go and make drawings at the rehearsals, etc now having done some work they don't seem to take any more interest in the thing or want to see what I have done – they are bound to do the ballet with someone, as Lambert is down here rehearsing it with the 'Corps de Ballet'. There is no other painter in England who understands the ballet as much as I do.
>
> I hope we shall leave for Paris on Monday with Diaghilev, and if he decides whilst in Paris for me to do the ballet I shall have to come back again which is a nuisance as I am tired of being here.[16]

24 March, from Paris:

> ... am lunching with Diaghilev tomorrow who is here three days arranging about his coming season. I hope I may hear something about the ballet. It is a long weary business waiting.

His surviving designs show a progression from a cluttered back-stage, with different-coloured flats, ropes, pieces of scenery and a costume basket, to a more geometric long rehearsal room, lined with chairs, merging to a point in the distance, with a balcony opening in the mid-distance on one side, and on the other side a representation of a rehearsal piano and an archway revealing – perhaps hoping to flatter the impresario – a seated Diaghilev surrounded by his entourage. Three days later it seemed that at last he had been successful:

---

[16] Letter from Christopher Wood, Monte Carlo to his mother, dated only 'Thursday', [11 or 18] March 1926.

27 March, from Paris:

> My long anxiety has come to an end today. Diaghilev asked me definitely to do the ballet after lunch just before he left for the train for Monte Carlo. He came with his manager and also his scene painter who is a Russian Prince and quite a nice fellow, who used to paint all the scenes before the war in Petrograd. They saw my designs which they discussed and asked me many questions, trying to change several things which I quite firmly refused, and which I think they appreciated as they saw that I understood and meant all that I had drawn. Apparently he'd more or less decided I should do it over a month ago. My work on the other ballet in London ['English Country Life'] which I cursed for a hopeless waste of time, proved just the contrary and it was on account of what I did then that they began to think of me. ... The whole of Paris is talking about it, and several people have told Tony [Gandarillas] even before he or I knew, that I was to do the ballet.

4 April, from Paris:

> I have heard nothing more about it since Diaghilev went back ... I am with Lambert to-day who is passing through Paris on his way back to London from Monte Carlo where he has been arranging the music. He will go down there again to conduct the final rehearsals.

But Wood's hopes were short lived. Whether Diaghilev took exception to his conceit or Kit's intolerance overreached itself, their working relationship soon broke down:

9 April, from Paris:

> I have so much work still to do tonight as Diaghilev is only here for two days, and I have many alterations to make. He is impossible to work for knowing nothing about painting, he wishes to poke his nose into everything, and makes the most ridiculous and useless changes. He has driven me so mad that I feel I would almost like to chuck the whole thing. I hate Russians almost as much as Americans. He will finish by ruining all my ideas and plans for the scenes, as it is there remains little of the originals which I planned to a great extent with Cocteau who has such wonderful ideas.

And five days later Wood's involvement was effectively over:

> To cut a long story short I began to think the whole affair scarcely worth while as he decided to have the curtain of my ballet painted by a young modern painter who had nothing to do with it, but who Diaghilev wished to employ to add another novelty to his season. To this I naturally made very strong protests and said in this case I would not do anything. He wanted to cut out a great deal of the technical part of my painting which if not there would have taken from the scenery the whole point of my painting and my character which after all makes it different from another. Had I simply got down to all these alterations it would have meant forsaking all my pride as an artist and made me look a very poor figure. Picasso and Cocteau who were even helping me get the ballet said under these conditions nothing would induce them to do it, and that if I had anything in me I would stick to my drawings or tell him to get someone else to do it. ... I have told Diaghilev that I had decided not to do it unless he gave me an absolutely free hand in the matter to do what I wished, which of course drove him mad, instead of being intelligent, and he said he would have no scenery at all. This is ridiculous, and the whole thing will collapse.

As Lydia Sokolova,[17] who played the Nurse, has written, Diaghilev always liked to feel that he was in touch with all that was new in music and painting, and he tried to bring something fresh and original to each season. In March while in Paris, he sent Serge Lifar, who was only a few months older than Lambert and was to take the Romeo lead, to view with Boris Kochno an exhibition in Montmartre of a group of surrealist painters that included Max Ernst and Jean Miró. In his memoirs Lifar wrote:

> We walked round in silence, and in silence looked at the pictures, of which we could make nothing. When he was seeing us off at the station: 'How did you like the surrealists?' asked Diaghilev.
>
> Kochno said something about 'all this nonsense not being worth the time spent on it.' Though inwardly entirely of the same opinion, I nevertheless, influenced by a sudden thought that perhaps there was something important underneath it all, which neither Kochno nor I was capable of seeing, more cautiously said: 'I didn't like Ernst and Miró, and I didn't understand surrealism at all, but you'd perhaps better go and see for yourself.'[18]

Diaghilev *did* go, and he was so interested in what he saw that, besides buying some pictures by the two artists (which he gave to Lifar),[19] he commissioned them for the *Romeo and Juliet* designs. Ernst painted two curtains representing Day and Night, while Miró was responsible for the front curtain and items that would suggest a ballet rehearsal room: a *barre*, two screens, and a pink dressing-gown hanging on a peg. According to Walton, Constant was 'disappointed and horrified' when Diaghilev chose the surrealists in favour of Wood.[20] But the question of who would provide the designs was not to be the only controversy surrounding *Romeo and Juliet*.

Rather than put the choreography in the hands of a new recruit, Georges Balanchivadze (to become better known as George Balanchine), Diaghilev entrusted it to the long-serving Bronislava Nijinska,[21] sister of the famous dancer Vaslav Nijinsky, who was on the point of leaving the company. Alicia Nikitina, a former ballet student at the Imperial Russian Ballet who had joined Diaghilev's company in 1923, was given the role of Juliet. In her autobiography she described the rehearsals:

> Back in Monte Carlo in spite of our tiredness we started at once rehearsing [the] new ballet. ... The whole troupe, including the soloists, took part in the general numbers. We had no time to waste as Nijinska was to leave us soon again for another assignment. Some of the scenes were really beautiful and full of invention. Lifar and I first entered the stage, dressed in ordinary street clothes. I had a suitcase in my hand. There was no décor. We were arriving for a rehearsal at a dancing school, running because we were late. The suitcase flew open, disclosing my pink tights and my dancing shoes which I had to pick up, Lifar helping me to do so. I remember that every time when I danced this ballet the audience believed this to be an accident. We then passed behind the

---

[17] Lydia Sokolova (1896–1974), born Hilda Munnings, was in 1913 the first English ballerina to join the Ballets Russes, staying with the company until it disbanded in 1929. She was the author of *Dancing for Diaghilev* (London: John Murray, 1960).

[18] Serge Lifar, *Serge Diaghilev: His Life, His Work, His Legend: An Intimate Biography*, (London: G. P. Putnam's Sons, 1940), p. 309.

[19] Earlier, Diaghilev had given similar gifts to Massine, including works by Matisse, Braque, Derain and some of the Italian futurists. Lifar was now in favour, writing: 'Thereafter, my own collection grew also with each first night and every holiday'. Lifar, *Serge Diaghilev*, p. 309.

[20] Walton, 'Constant Lambert (In Memoriam 21 August 1951)', p. 115.

[21] Bronislava Nijinska (1891–1972), dancer, choreographer and teacher. Born in Minsk, she joined the Ballets Russes in 1909 and died in the United States.

stage and I had just enough time to slip out of my dress. Then came the scene at the dancing school, followed by scenes in costume, the scene on the balcony, which provided great admiration both in the public and the press, the ball at the Capulets. The most successful was the death scene. The large bed was very stylised. Our acting was entirely directed by Nijinska whose way of presenting the scene was remarkable.[22]

Nikitina was also learning a principal role in *Les Biches* and she and Lifar often rehearsed at night, sometimes as late as 3 a.m., under Diaghilev's critical eye, 'almost to the point of fainting from fatigue.' Then, at the last moment, she was asked to hand over her leading part in *Romeo and Juliet* (as well as one that she had in *Les Sylphides*) to Tamara Karsavina whom Diaghilev had persuaded to return to the company for the Monte Carlo performances. When Nijinska heard of this she demanded that Lifar be given an examination before partnering the great Karsavina, who had been the leading ballerina of the Ballets Russes from its beginning in 1909 until 1922. Lifar was naturally indignant: 'When had a *premier danseur* ever had to pass an examination? What sort of conduct was this – treating him as someone quite unknown?'[23] Was it perhaps a test to see if the out-of-practice Karsavina would successfully partner the much younger Lifar? Nevertheless, Diaghilev managed to console Lifar, who passed the test with congratulations and embraces from all present, and the next day he began rehearsing. 'At the first performance I fell in love with my partner. Karsavina was very sweet to me and paid me plenty of compliments. During the first performance of *Roméo et Juliette* I danced with great fire. The success was considerable.' He received a bouquet from Diaghilev and some roses from Karsavina. After taking Tamara to supper he returned to his room to find that a jealous Diaghilev had thrown the flowers out of the window. 'I tied my sheets together and made a rope so that I could go and find my roses. I had hardly got one leg over the window-sill when my door opened violently. Diaghilev grabbed me by the hair and forced me back into the room. "I will not permit my theatre to be turned into a den of vice. I'll turn out these women who hang round the necks of my dancers …" Then there was a horrible row that kept the whole hotel awake for quite a considerable time.'[24]

Sergei Grigoriev had in recent years noticed a marked change in Diaghilev's behaviour, how he 'was inclined to be irritable and often lost his temper – a thing that never happened before.'[25] He was at this time having serious financial problems. Sir Oswald Stoll had financed the autumn 1921 London season, with his capital to be repaid by the box-office takings. But when the audiences failed to respond in numbers to the lavish full-length production of *The Sleeping Princess*, it was closed down and Stoll sequestered the scenery and costumes. It took some while before Diaghilev was able to settle matters with Stoll. Amongst other problems, there had been disagreements with Covent Garden, the management at Monte Carlo was restricting his presentations there, Léonide Massine[26] had left the company after a disagreement,

[22] *Nikitina by Herself*, trans. from the French by Baroness Budberg (London: Allan Wingate, 1959), pp. 57–8.

[23] Lifar, *Serge Diaghilev*, p. 52.

[24] Lifar, *Ma Vie: From Kiev to Kiev*, trans. James Holman Mason (London: Hutchinson 1970), p. 52, and Lifar, *Serge Diaghilev*, pp. 310–11. In spite of this, according to Lydia Lopokova, a few weeks later Lifar was confiding to her that 'he thought Karsavina in spite of her charm was really old', implying that she should have retired: *Lydia Lopokova*, ed. Milo Keynes (London: Weidenfeld & Nicolson, 1983), p. 27.

[25] Grigoriev, *The Diaghilev Ballet*, p. 167.

[26] Léonide Massine (1896–1979), choreographer and dancer, born Leonid Fyodorovich Myasin in Moscow. When Nijinsky left the Ballets Russes Massine replaced him in Diaghilev's favour.

and he had just lost Vera Nemtchinova, one of his leading classical ballerinas, to the theatrical producer C. B. Cochran[27] who occasionally used some of the leading dancers of the Ballets Russes in his revues. It was largely because of the loss of Nemtchinova that Diaghilev had persuaded Karsavina to return. The 1926 Monte Carlo season was certainly not without incident, especially when the ballet master, Nicolas Legat, also left after a row, and a Polish dancer tried to commit suicide for love of a pretty girl in the *corps de ballet.*

After the row with Lifar, calm was restored the next morning. But more was to come. Lydia Sokolova described one rehearsal that Constant attended:

> Constant Lambert was young, inexperienced, shy of the Russians and terrified of Diaghilev. ... One afternoon Constant had arrived to accompany a scene which Nijinska had arranged and which Diaghilev was coming to see at our two o'clock rehearsal. It was discovered that Thadeus Slavinsky [playing the Maestro], who opened the scene alone, was not present. After a few minutes of waiting the atmosphere grew very tense, and Diaghilev began walking about, banging his stick and haranguing Grigoriev. As Slavinsky made no secret of his private affairs some of us knew very well where he might be enjoying his afternoon siesta. At last Diaghilev turned on Grigoriev, who always got a red spot on his cheek when he was disturbed, and shouted, 'If you think you know where he is, go and fetch him!' Poor Grigoriev rushed away, and shortly afterwards Slavinsky appeared, making excuses. By this time Diaghilev was in such a state that he screamed abuse at Slavinsky. They nearly came to blows and some of the male dancers had to pull Slavinsky away. Florrie Grenfell, who was present to watch the rehearsal, told me that Diaghilev apologised to her afterwards for this degrading scene. Constant Lambert, seated at the piano, could not understand Russian and had never seen a Russian or a Pole in a rage before. I suppose his anxiety over the music, his animosity towards Diaghilev and his fear of the mad foreigners amongst whom he found himself, all came to a head: he went deathly pale and was about to faint. Noticing this, I grabbed a bottle of fizzy lemonade which I had brought to rehearsal, and poured it into his mouth as he was on the point of slipping from his chair. This brought him round.[28]

Lambert's near fainting was quite likely an early example of the undiagnosed medical condition that he was to suffer from, especially in later life: diabetes. The sugar content of the lemonade may well have aided his recovery.

More explosive still, and longer lasting, was the disagreement that Lambert had with Diaghilev. *Romeo and Juliet* was due to open at Monte Carlo on 4 May, but when Constant arrived two or three days in advance of the premiere, to his horror he found, as he wrote to his mother, that

> far from doing the ballet without a décor, Diaghilev had chosen two 10th-rate painters from an imbecile group called the 'surréalistes'. I cannot tell you how monstrous the décor is, both in itself and as an accompaniment to my music and the choreography of Nijinska. As you know, I am not academic in my point of view about painting but never in my life have I seen anything so imbecile.

[27] Sir Charles Blake Cochran (1872–1951), who liked to call himself a showman, occasionally incorporated a small-scale ballet in his revues with music by English composers, such as *The Rake* by Roger Quilter, *Lunar Park* by Lord Berners (1930) and *Follow the Sun* by William Walton. Lambert, however, was not commissioned for a score. Cochran was able to attract leading ballerinas as, according to Nikitina, Diaghilev's salaries were 'perhaps one-sixth' of those paid by Cochran.

[28] Sokolova, *Dancing for Diaghilev*, pp. 243–4.

Not only that, but Diaghilev has introduced disgraceful changes in the choreography, altering bits that Nijinska declared she would never be induced to change. For example, at the end of the 1st tableau, instead of the dance of 3 women which Nijinska designed, the lovers (who are supposed to be dragged apart) return and do a pas-de-deux, with all the rest staring at them. Can you imagine anything more stupid and vulgar? Of course I sent Nijinska a telegram immediately.[29]

The three dancers at the end of the first tableau were Felia Dubrovska, Alexandra Danilova and Tamara Gevergeva doing *fouettés*. According to Danilova, Diaghilev had cut this because its brilliance outshone the technical capabilities of Nikitina and Lifar.[30]
Lambert continued:

I was so upset by all this that I asked for and with great difficulty obtained an interview with Diaghilev. Instead of giving it to me alone he had Kochno and Grigoriev (the stage manager) with him. To frighten me, I suppose. He started off by saying that my letter to him was so rude that he didn't wish to speak to me, but as I was young he would pardon me. After a short pause in which I did not thank him I asked why he had rejected Kit Wood's décor. He became very angry and said, 'I forbid you to say a word about the décor.' I then tried to speak about the choreography but he said, 'I have known Madame Nijinska for 20 years and I forbid you to mention her name in my presence.' I naturally lost my temper and said I would withdraw the music entirely. I'm afraid it was rather a dreadful scene but then it is impossible to remain calm with a man like that.

The next morning I went to see a lawyer in Nice, who told me that unfortunately there was no way out of my contract. I went back to Monte-Carlo, quite calm by now, and went into the salle d'orchestre to listen to the only rehearsal for orchestra alone. To my surprise, they tried to stop me getting in, and when at last I 'effected an entry' I found all the orchestra waiting but no music put out. After about half an hour a sort of military funeral came in with the score and parts, and all during the rehearsal there were 2 concierges on each side of me to see I did not tear the work to pieces. After the rehearsal the parts were collected, carefully corded and sealed and taken up into a strong room! This ridiculous business has gone on ever since, and now Diaghilev has spread the report that I went quite insane at Monte-Carlo and had to be watched by 2 detectives! The orchestra were so annoyed by all this that they made a special point of cheering me at the dress rehearsal and at the 1st performance. It went down quite well at Monte-Carlo, but everyone I met thought that the décor spoiled everything, as indeed it does. It is not only a gross mistake artistically, but a most dreadful blunder from the business point of view, as it will be detested in England, particularly as every-one knows that Kit's scenery had been accepted.

Karsavina recorded her version of events:

---

[29] The present whereabouts of Lambert's letters to his mother, quoted extensively by Shead, *Constant Lambert*, pp. 56–7, 59, is not known, but Shead states that it was begun on 24 May while staying with friends at Giverny, between Paris and Rouen, and finished the following day at the Hôtel du Panthéon in Paris.

[30] In conversation with Richard Buckle, *Diaghilev*, p. 467. This may have also been a concession to Karsavina whom Nikitina described as coming to rehearsal with a rubber stocking to bandage her knee which was so sore that she could neither jump nor turn. 'She only performed a few steps and marked with hands the time of the *pirouettes*. All this was a terrible disappointment for me, who remembered her as such a great artist.' *Nikitina by Herself*, p. 64.

At the dress rehearsal, Diaghilev made a small cut in the score. The same afternoon, Constant Lambert came to see me. He was in a terrible state of agitation. Unless I could persuade Diaghilev to restore the cut, he said, he would at once remove the musicians' parts from their stands, and so prevent the performance. His motive was chivalrous: he deemed it an outrage to interfere with Nijinska's choreography. I could not have arbitrated as far as the music was concerned, but I felt that from the point of view of the staging, a cut might sometimes be doing a service to the choreographer. ... I could, however, prevent a scandal by giving an immediate warning to Diaghilev. As soon as Lambert was gone, I rang through to Diaghilev's room and in a matter of minutes he came (we stayed in the same hotel). At once he went to the theatre and gave orders to lock up the score. He told me afterwards that Lambert had to be kept back from fighting him.[31]

According to Kochno, Lambert pursued Diaghilev 'in the street and, when he was not received at the Hôtel de Paris, would wait for him at the entrance'.[32] Instead of accepting the fact that such last-minute changes were sometimes necessary and might even be an improvement, Lambert allowed his youthful impetuosity bordering on arrogance to get the better of him. In the absence of his revered Nijinska, he set himself up as her defender, permitting no deviation from her choreography.[33] But Kochno was not impressed by Nijinska's work. 'She took off from the premise that she was choreographing a dramatic work, and, by undertaking simply to substitute gesture for words she repeated for the greater part of the ballet the error she made with *Les Fâcheux* [Auric] and foundered in a conventional, realistic pantomime.' It was only saved, he added, by 'the magic of Karsavina's presence and the youthful, masculine charm of Lifar.'

There was to be still further disagreement, by which time communication between Lambert and Diaghilev had clearly broken down. He told his mother:

After the Monte-Carlo performance, Kochno came to see me and asked if I had any music for an entr'acte as they thought it would he more '*vivante*' if there was a passage of dancers from the class-room to the theatre. I was very annoyed at their trying to spoil Nijinska's work any more, so I said I would give him music[34] for an entr'acte but only on the understanding that not a note of it was to be danced. So they have now added a sort of comic march-past of the characters (without music) in very dubious taste and in a style which is the complete opposite of Nijinska's. It is really too sickening about the ballet – at one time it was going to be the best since *La Boutique Fantasque* or *Tricorne* but now it is just a dismal failure as far as I am concerned. What annoys me is for people to tell me that I am very lucky to have it done at all and shouldn't worry about anything else except the mere notes! When I get back to England I want it to be publicly known that I tried to withdraw the ballet on account of the décor and the changes in the choreography. I don't want people to think that I associate

[31] Karsavina, 'Serge Lifar and the Last Diaghilev Seasons', p. 303.

[32] Kochno, *Diaghilev and the Ballets Russes*, p. 236.

[33] Lambert singled out one section he admired as a highly successful example of choreographic counterpoint – 'the astonishing choreographic fugue which Nijinska arranged to a purely homophonic passage in the finale of *Romeo and Juliet*'; Lambert, 'Music and Action', in *Footnotes to the Ballet: A Book for Balletomanes*, ed. Caryl Brahms (London: Lovat Dickson, 1936), pp. 172–3.

[34] This was probably *Champêtre*, on the score of which he had written: 'On peut jouer ce morceau entre les deux tableaux du ballet "Romeo and Juliet".'

willingly with 10th-rate incompetent charlatans like Max Ernst and Joan Miró (the 'surréalistes').

The 'comic march-past' in between the tableaux, arranged in Nijinska's absence by Balanchine, was performed without music with the curtain lowered to within a few feet of the stage floor so that only the dancers' legs could be seen as they took up their position for the next episode.

A wounded Kit Wood took some solace from these disagreements surrounding the ballet, writing in early May from Paris to his mother, with a tone of superiority:

> I heard from Lambert this morning that the ballet is not a success at all. Everyone hated what they had arranged as scenery, trying in a foolish way to copy my ideas with no result. I am more than thankful to be well out of it. … Poor Lambert is broken-hearted about the ballet and tried to withdraw it and Laroy the great critic whom Diaghilev asked to come to Monte Carlo to write an article refused to go because I had not done the scenery. Diaghilev will find many people against him and that he has made a big mistake in interfering with my plans.

When *Romeo and Juliet* was premiered on 4 May 1926, as part of the company's short four-day run at the Théâtre de Monte Carlo, the dancers in the first tableau were Tamara Karsavina, Serge Lifar and Thadée Slavinsky (as the Maestro), and in the second tableau Karsavina (now as Juliet) and Lifar (Romeo), Lydia Sokolova (Nurse), Léon Woizikowsky (Pierre, servant to the Capulets), Slavinsky (the Maestro rehearsing as Tybalt) and Constantin Tcherkas (Paris). The corps de ballet in both tableaux consisted of 14 women (including newcomer 15-year-old Alicia Markova)[35] and 12 men. The curtains and stage pieces by Ernst and Miró were executed by Prince Alexander Schervashidze and the costumes by Georgette Vialet. The performance was under the baton of the theatre's resident conductor, Marc-César Scotto. *The Musical Times* thought it 'a matter of surprise' that Diaghilev had not commissioned an English score before, but 'now that he has turned our way, [he] has lighted upon an utterly unknown youth – and, be it added, a very clever one.' It considered the ballet itself 'a mere trifle, but a very spirited, agreeable and elegant trifle. … The fortunate youth,' the critic continued, 'has written a very pretty, engaging, piquant little score.' If the ballet's success was, in Lifar's words, 'considerable', the company were hardly prepared for the reception awaiting them at Paris.

And from Paris on 16 May, Kit Wood wrote to his mother: 'The Russian Ballet begins here on Tuesday, so I am curious to see what Romeo and Juliette [*sic*] will be like without my scenery. … Diaghilev is trying once more to be very pleasant to me and make up for his dishonest behaviour ….' He had asked Wood if he could print his portraits of Lambert and Auric in the programme and, pleased that at least some recognition would come his way, Wood agreed.[36]

For the opening of *Romeo and Juliet* two days later, the Théâtre Sarah-Bernhardt

---

[35] Alicia Markova (1910–2004), born Lilian Alicia Marks in London, joined the Ballets Russes in 1925. After Diaghilev's death she became principal ballerina of Marie Rambert's Ballet Club. She was later to form a notable dancing partnership with Anton Dolin.

[36] While the whole unhappy experience made Wood turn from the Continent to England for his home as an artist, this was not to be his last dealing with ballet. Towards the end of 1929 he designed the scenery for *Luna Park*, a ballet with music by Lord Berners that formed part of a Cochran revue which opened in Manchester in March the following year. 'Boris Kochno, Diaghilev's director, came to see my pictures and I was very happy about this after the unfortunate affair of 4 years ago,' he wrote. Five months after the revue reached London, Kit Wood took his own life by jumping in front of a train as it approached Salisbury Station.

was sold out. The police had warned Diaghilev that the surrealists and the communists were preparing a demonstration because Ernst and Miró had allied with this 'bourgeois capitalist', and Lifar advised the dancers what to do if any demonstrators rushed onto the stage. The programme opened with *Pulcinella* which passed without incident. Nikitina, restored to the role of Juliet, described what happened next:

> I was always very nervous on first nights, but on this particular one, because of the warning that such events might take place, my nervousness was at its peak. You will see that there was every reason for this. We had already danced one ballet and were to dance the new creation after the interval. [Roger] Désormière, who was conducting, struck the first bars and the curtain went up.
>
> I appeared on the stage, together with Lifar, and at once heard unusual sounds from the gallery of the Théâtre Sarah Bernhardt. The noise grew louder and louder and ended by completely drowning the music of the orchestra, which 'Deso' was still trying to conduct. I could see him gesticulating violently, but not a sound was able to reach us. It was impossible to dance. Désormière stopped his musicians and the curtain went down while in the auditorium the whistles of the demonstrators mingled with those of the police in an infernal din. The whole audience rose in protest. Through a hole in the curtain we saw the police invade the theatre, put an end to the rioting and expel the demonstrators. It lasted a quarter of an hour before order was re-established. Désormière struck again the first bars of *Romeo and Juliet*. But one can well imagine the state of my nerves, having to undergo twice the emotions of a first night! Luckily, after this appearance on the stage, the success was unprecedented. The next day the papers were full of eulogies and I had made a great personal success.[37]

Lifar noticed scuffling amongst the audience:

> From the gallery white leaflets, proclamations (a surrealist manifesto), began fluttering down till the house looked as though there had been a snowstorm. Meanwhile, in the auditorium, a pitched battle seemed to be raging. I saw one of Diaghilev's great friends, Iya, Lady Abdy (daughter of the dramatic artist and playwright and granddaughter of the painter Gué), slap a man's face, and at the same moment someone tore her dress. Then plain-clothes policemen began to appear from all sides, seized hold of the 'demonstrators', and removed them from the house ...
>
> All this had but one result, that Paris did nothing but talk of the new ballet, so that whenever it was given (May 20th and 27th) we played to crammed houses.[38]

Constant's own account is worth recording:

> As soon as the curtain went up about fifty men got up and blew on pea-whistles while others threw down thousands of leaflets from the roof. For three movements not a single note could be heard. It soon developed into a free fight, the most extraordinary scene you can imagine; eventually the police were called in and managed to throw most of the rioters out. Everybody yelled out 'Recommencez' so they started again but this time the leader of the surrealists jumped up and started a speech from one of the boxes, the only word I could hear was 'Merde' at the end. The performance didn't really quiet down until the second tableau. Naturally the ballet was cheered at the end, but that was chiefly reaction.

---

[37] *Nikitina by Herself*, pp. 64–5.
[38] Lifar, *Serge Diaghilev*, p. 313.

If the protest against the scenery had been because it was bad I should have heartily sympathised, but as the motive was purely a political one, I was furious, particularly as the protest being of an aural nature merely spoilt the music and left the scenery untouched. At the second performance everything went quite calmly, the orchestra (under Désormière) were much better than at Monte Carlo where Marc-Caesar Scotto who conducts like a porpoise in a rough sea didn't help matters much.[39]

Sergey Prokofiev, who was present, has also left a detailed account in his diaries of the uproar, going so far as to suggest that Diaghilev, seeking publicity, had engaged Ernst and Miró in anticipation of a demonstration. His report has an almost comic element in which he describes 'a large number of Englishmen present, magnificent gentlemen in full evening-dress complete with monocles' who, 'entirely ignorant of what the demonstration was actually about, jumped to the conclusion that it must be an anti-English protest against the staging of a ballet by an Englishman. ... From my balcony vantage-point I witnessed these superb tail-coated specimens deploying classic techniques of the noble art and landing fearsome blows on the unfortunate demonstrators. One of them, reeling from an uppercut to his cheekbone, cowered to the floor and buried his face in his hands while a lady in full *décolleté* pummelled him with her programme.'[40] When eventually the music was audible, Prokofiev was unimpressed, regarding it as 'rubbish, a feeble sort of sub-*Pulcinella*'.

Whatever the merits of the music, the scandal helped to bring about a capacity house on subsequent nights. News of the uproar circled the world. 'Free Fight in Theatre' ran the headlines in the New Zealand *Daily Times*, the Press Association release concluding that 'at the close Mr Lambert was called before the curtain and accorded vociferous applause'. Whatever the merit of the music, with a riot that rivalled that at the premiere of Stravinsky's *Le Sacre du printemps*, Lambert's *Romeo and Juliet* was assured a small place in ballet history. Even the *RCM Magazine* seemed less interested in congratulating one of its students on having a ballet score accepted by Diaghilev than reporting the scandal it had created. Without even mentioning the Monte Carlo premiere, it briefly touched on its London performance 'during the recent season of Russian Ballet' and then quoted in full a review of its Paris reception, 'Pandemonium in Theatre'.

The composer André Messager, known now for his operas and the ballet *Les Deux Pigeons*, put the spectacle aside and perceptively judged Lambert's music to be full of promise and displaying much dexterity in the handling of the orchestra, but ultimately lacking in individual character.[41] If the score lacks individuality, it has certain redeeming features. Its neo-classical style, in a somewhat similar vein to Stravinsky's ballet *Pulcinella* (based on music by Pergolesi) and with what Alan Frank called 'the clear lines of Scarlatti',[42] may not readily draw one's attention to any personal quality, pastiche rarely does; yet its harmonic piquancy, brilliant scoring and sheer energy bring it within the orbit of the contemporary French school of composers collectively known as Les Six. What may have attracted *Romeo and Juliet* (or *Adam and Eve* as it then was) to Diaghilev, desperate to present an English ballet, was not just its convenient

---

[39] Motion, *The Lamberts*, p. 151.

[40] *Sergey Prokofiev, Diaries, 1924–33*, trans. and annotated Anthony Phillips (London: Faber & Faber, 2012), pp. 312–14. Poulenc was also present.

[41] The review, in French, is quoted by Shead, *Constant Lambert*, p. 63.

[42] Alan Frank, 'The Music of Constant Lambert', *Disc*, vol. 5 no. 19 (1952), p. 104. Alan Frank worked for the music department of Oxford University Press from 1927 until 1975, being in charge for the last 25 years as successor to Hubert Foss.

division into short sections, making it the more easily adaptable, but quite likely its spirited rhythmic drive. All but four of the 13 movements are fast, and there is the frequent use of modish syncopation, in spite of what Lambert later called Diaghilev's 'almost pathological loathing' for American jazz which he avoided whenever possible. He 'only liked the fox-trots of Satie and Walton because they poked fun at it'.[43] He may even have felt, as one critic did on reviewing the published piano score of *Romeo and Juliet*, that 'the spirit of the early Italian *Commedia del'arte* presides over the whole piece'.[44] Others were less kind. *The Musical Times* (reviewing the piano arrangement) now found in it 'little but thinly-diluted Stravinsky'.[45] But at the time it mattered little to Constant that his first successful score embodied many of the qualities he was later to scorn, especially its affinity with Stravinsky and its determination to hang on to the shirt tails of Les Six.

Another of the Paris novelties was Auric's *Pastorale* on 29 May, and Constant joined the celebratory party that night. Lydia Lopokova[46] wrote at '2½ o'clock of night' to her future husband, the economist John Maynard Keynes: 'After the performance I drove with the composer Lambert to the party in honour of "Pastorale". Auric, Milhaud, Pruna, Picassos, Princesses and tytled [*sic*] Ladies were there.'[47] Lopokova was to know Lambert more closely when they were both involved in the Camargo Society, and she is reported as saying about him: 'There's a genius there: it's rich and talented in spite of all the drink. I like it.'

Diaghilev hoped that with 'an English ballet' now in his repertoire – and nothing for the stage could surely be more English than Shakespeare – with music by an English composer, he would be able to find a wealthy English businessman to underwrite his London season. He had his sights on Lord Rothermere, proprietor of the *Daily Mail*, who had a villa at Cap Martin on the French Riviera, and he had invited him to attend a rehearsal before the opening of the Monte Carlo season when Nikitina was still scheduled as Juliet. The company was told 'to rehearse urgently *Romeo and Juliet* to show it to an important person, an English millionaire'[48] whom Sokolova soon realised 'was prepared to take an interest in individual dancers as well as in the ballet.' The 58-year-old Lord Rothermere would lavish flowers and gifts on his favourite ballerinas, as Nikitina was to find out when, after the rehearsal, he asked to make her acquaintance. A close and lasting relationship developed. But it was Sokolova whom Diaghilev had used as 'bait'.

> Having noticed that Lord Rothermere liked me, [Diaghilev] sent for me and explained his plan. He had already approached Lord Rothermere about the backing, but nothing was settled, and he wanted me to clinch the deal for him at a supper party he was giving for the newspaper magnate and his principal dancers. ... Diaghilev seemed convinced that only I could persuade Lord Rothermere to give his word to back us and he said, 'You must realise that on your ability to get this support depends the whole future of the Russian Ballet.' The supper party took place at the Carlton Motel, Monte Carlo, and I was seated

[43] Lambert, *Sunday Referee*, 4 August 1935.
[44] *The Monthly Musical Record*, 1 December 1926, p. 363.
[45] *The Musical Times*, 1 October 1926, p. 909.
[46] Lydia Lopokova (1892–1981), born Lidia Vasilyevna Lopukhova in St Petersburg, studied under Fokine at the Imperial Ballet School. She joined the Ballets Russes at Paris in 1910 but left that same year for America. She rejoined Diaghilev's company in 1921, taking the roles of the Lilac Fairy and Princess Florine – and occasionally Aurora – in the ill-fated production of *The Sleeping Princess*. She married John Maynard Keynes (1883–1946) in August 1925.
[47] Keynes, *Lydia Lopokova*, pp. 26–7.
[48] *Nikitina by Herself*, pp. 60–1.

between Diaghilev and Lord Rothermere. At what he judged the right moment, the 'Old Man' whispered. 'Now you must go and dance with him.' I was very nervous and it was not until we had had two dances that I summoned the courage to approach the subject. Lord Rothermere did not make it easy for me. Eventually, after a little persuasion, he said, 'All right, I will do what you ask. But I want you to make it clear to Diaghilev that I am doing this for you personally.' I was dumbfounded.[49]

So keen was Diaghilev to retain the 'Englishness' of his presentation of *Romeo and Juliet* that he kept the English title from the outset, and when the score was to be published and Lambert wrote to Kochno asking permission to use his name as the author of the scenario, he 'refused, in agreement with Diaghilev, who at that point wanted to present his ballet as a work of young, exclusively English artists'.[50] The simple but effective cover design for the piano score was by Kit Wood, but this did not improve his relationship with Lambert. On 12 July he wrote from London to his mother: 'I am working very hard – have done the Drawing for Lambert's music cover, and am to be paid for it much to my surprise, not much it's true.' At the same time he had a commission from Lady Cunard to paint some drawing-room panels and he was on the point of going to see her. 'Just as I was leaving that wretched Lambert turned up and kept me which made me ten minutes late,' he wrote. He consequently missed his appointment. 'When I got there with the chauffeur who doesn't know London, Lady C was engaged, so I have not seen her since. ... Lambert always brings bad luck; he is an ass also.' Kit Wood had the distinction of being the only person who ever thought so.

The Ballets Russes 1926 London season opened at His Majesty's Theatre on 14 June with *Carnaval*, Stravinsky's *Les Noces* (for the first time in England) and *Les Matelots* (to music by Auric). A week later *Romeo and Juliet* was presented,[51] preceded by *Pulcinella* and followed by *The Three-Cornered Hat* (Falla). It received altogether nine performances, with Eugene Goossens conducting, and with Karsavina again in the role of Juliet, only to be replaced by Lydia Lopokova on two of the evenings. With the general strike and a consequent paper shortage, the Paris uproar had gone largely unreported in the English dailies, but Lambert had clearly made his disagreement with Diaghilev known to the Press. As the *Daily Telegraph* critic reported:

> As one listened to the young Englishman's music one felt that it bore but the remotest, if any, sort of relationship to the décor. Indeed, one would not be surprised to learn that to Mr Lambert the whole setting was antipathetic, that as a youngster he had done his bit, so to speak, in an operation over which he had no control. The flow of music, in general, seemed to have something to do with the choreography, but on the latter, it was all too obvious that certain 'stunts' had been grafted – such as the partially raised curtain revealing the feet of the players – that again had no connection with the musical ideas.[52]

But for many this seemed of lesser importance considering the quality of the performance. The review concluded: 'That a tragedy of William Shakespeare should be rendered into an inane farce matters to the audience not a straw. The technique of these "Russians" is so wonderful.' Another critic wrote: 'It pleased more than a little,

[49] Sokolova, *Dancing for Diaghilev*, p. 246.
[50] Kochno, *Diaghilev and the Ballets Russes*, p. 236.
[51] Boyd Neel, who saw it in London, said it was called 'A Rehearsal without Scenery in Two Parts', *My Orchestras and Other Adventures: The Memoirs of Boyd Neel* (Toronto: University of Toronto Press, 1985), p. 32.
[52] *Daily Telegraph*, 22 June 1926, p. 9.

though always in a mild way. ... It was graceful and witty, but there was not much in it – not enough to amuse one much after the first time of seeing. The music was attractive. It was light and vivacious in a modern way without having recourse to horse-play or the din of Dixieland.'[53] But *The Times* was dismissive:

> One wishes that Mr Lambert had seized the opportunity of writing music which could be called definitely English. He seems rather to have chosen to speak to us in French, and, like many foreigners, he speaks it even better than the Frenchman. At any rate, it contrasted very favourably with a tedious little piece by M. Auric, which was played as an entr'acte.

The audience, or the critic, at least found the interlude without music amusing; Karsavina, despite 'an obviously bandaged knee' after sustaining an injury, miraculously 'conveyed the impression that this *was* only a rehearsal and not the first night', but the review's conclusion echoed Constant's wishes:

> The decoration of the ballet had been entrusted to two Frenchmen of the latest 'advanced' school, which seems to be quite as silly as its predecessors. We wish that M. Diaghilev had seen fit to commission an English artist to provide the scenery for the first English ballet.[54]

The *Yorkshire Post* reported that because of his modesty Lambert was 'unable to obtain a seat for the first night of his own ballet' and that it was 'from "Standing Room Only" that he came after repeated calls for the composer to take his share of the applause'.[55] In doing so he 'blushed like a schoolboy'.[55]

Ninette de Valois,[56] with whom Lambert was to form one of the most important working partnerships in the history of English ballet, made an appearance during this London season. As she recalled:

> By chance rather than intent, I was in the cast, soon after the opening night of Lambert's *Romeo and Juliet* being thrust on as the nurse, as Sokolova was ill.[57] I appeared in the scene connected with the Monte Carlo dispute; consequently, it had no music, and had been choreographed by Balanchine – by Diaghilev's orders!

She had been on a short engagement with the Russian ballet and remembered the Paris affair as 'a theatrical *scandale* unequalled for noise'. She already knew Constant at that time and learned how, after his row with Diaghilev, he had threatened to 'take himself off, and with him his score'. He was 'left with us of course in a very bad mood – not quite as bad as Diaghilev's but a pretty bad mood. ... I felt sorry for him for he was frightfully young and full of courage and conviction.'[58] She touched on the humorous side of the row in her autobiography:

> Later he would tell, with delight, of his astonishment at the sight of his score,

[53] *The Monthly Musical Record*, 2 August 1926, p. 226.
[54] *The Times*, 22 June 1926, p. 14.
[55] *Yorkshire Post* and *Daily Express*, respectively, quoted in Shead, *Constant Lambert*, p. 61.
[56] Ninette de Valois (1898–2001), Irish dancer, teacher, choreographer and director of ballet, was born Edris Stannus in County Wicklow. She established the Vic-Wells Company, which became the Sadler's Wells Ballet Company and ultimately the Royal Ballet. She was created Dame in 1951, a Companion of Honour in 1982 and a member of the Order of Merit in 1992.
[57] Kathrine Sorley Walker, *Ninette de Valois: Idealist without Illusions* (London: Hamish Hamilton, 1987), p. 335, gives 10 June which is before the season started. It is more likely to have been 10 July.
[58] Ninette de Valois, in *Constant Lambert Remembered*, BBC Third Network, 25 June 1966.

heavily guarded by two of the casino gendarmes, in picturesque musical comedy uniforms, on its voyage from music library to rehearsal rooms! Diaghilev was the true autocratic Russian; he was not used to threats and displays of nonchalant independence: this fresh-complexioned young English man was treated with grave suspicion – he was either a revolutionary or else queer in the head. Again, Diaghilev could not, as a Russian, imagine the delight that the spectacle of this guard of honour gave Constant, making it impossible for him to carry out a threat that would spoil a good story.'[59]

Lord Rothermere also gave financial support to the company for its June 1927 London season, this time at the Princes Theatre where *Romeo and Juliet* was revived for five performances. Four were conducted by Eugene Goossens and the last one by Constant's former professor of conducting, Malcolm Sargent. That autumn the company toured Germany, giving seven further performances that became the cause for further disagreement, with Lambert suing Diaghilev for the non-payment of 1,050 francs.[60] As Walton said in a Lambert memorial broadcast: 'They did not speak for some years, but were eventually reconciled in what turned out to be Diaghilev's last season at Covent Garden, when he invited Constant to conduct his *Music for Orchestra* as an interlude during the season.'[61] On 22 July 1929, four days before Diaghilev, by then an ill man, gave his final London programme, Constant conducted the first public performance of this new work as an interlude between Auric's *Les Facheux* and *Le Sacre du printemps*. Less than a month later Diaghilev was dead.[62] Karsavina remembered how, after Diaghilev's memorial service, Lambert had gone up to her to say 'how deeply repentant he felt for his quarrel with Diaghilev; it gave him some measure of comfort to be reminded that no real harm had been done.' In a 1936 broadcast talk on 'Music and the Ballet' Lambert spoke of Diaghilev as 'the greatest producer of modern times', adding an interesting detail:

> I remember my surprise when he asked me to join him in reading at sight a difficult piano duet of Erik Satie, no easy task for a man who had not actually practised the piano for forty years, but a task which he accomplished with remarkable skill.

As for their differences, they were finally laid to rest:

> Some ten years ago I had the great honour of being asked to write a ballet for Serge Diaghilev and though from a purely musical point of view I did not always see eye to eye with him I have no hesitation in declaring myself a disciple of his as regards music for the ballet.[63]

---

[59] Ninette de Valois, *Come Dance with Me: A Memoir, 1898–1956* (London: Hamish Hamilton, 1957), pp. 116–17.

[60] Buckle, *Diaghilev*, pp. 518–19. A letter, dated 20 April 1928, from the Incorporated Society of Authors, Playwrights and Composers to Walter Nuvel, Diaghilev's administrator, is at the Lincoln Center.

[61] Walton, 'Constant Lambert (In Memoriam 21 August, 1951)', p. 116.

[62] Diaghilev died of diabetes, which was also to be the principal cause of Lambert's death.

[63] Lambert, 'The Vic-Wells Ballet', BBC Scottish Programme, 24 August 1936. The Satie duet could have been *Jack-in-the-Box* which was another novelty for Paris (3 July 1926).

5 1926–7
Early Ballets and Philip Heseltine

I N between his journeys to Paris and Monte Carlo in connection with the premiere of *Romeo and Juliet*, Constant became involved at short notice in the second public performance of *Façade*, described by the *Monthly Musical Record* critic as a 'Chelsea oddity'. This took place at the New Chenil Galleries in the King's Road on Monday 27 April 1926, at 8.45 p.m., with Walton once again conducting. *The Times* had announced the day before that the reciter would be 'Mr Neil Porter of the Old Vic Company', but although Porter was photographed, sengerphone in hand, outside the Chenil Galleries (possibly just before rehearsal) both with Edith and in a group with all three Sitwells and Walton, it seems that he was not the sole reciter.[1] Osbert wrote many years later that 'the words were chiefly spoken by that accomplished actor, Mr Neil Porter, my sister having decided only to recite a few of the slower poems',[2] but Constant informed his mother: '*Façade* was great fun just before I left [for Monte Carlo]. I ended up by doing about half the programme. The house was very crowded and most enthusiastic.'[3] The renumbering in Constant's hand of the surviving manuscripts of the poems for this performance would seem to confirm his participation. It is possible that in rehearsal Porter had found some of the poems difficult to recite in time with the instrumental ensemble (as did their author) and that Constant came to the rescue so that three reciters in fact took part. If this was so, it may well have strengthened the performance, making the poems which were not easily understood when declaimed through a sengerphone from behind a decorated cloth more audible to the audience. Alternatively, Osbert's memory was at fault and Porter withdrew. Whatever the circumstances, after the very mixed reception the work had received at its first public outing in June 1923 (though not the riot that the Sitwells would have everyone believe), this time it went down well with the very 'arty' audience. Arnold Bennett wrote in his diary: 'Crowds of people, snobs, high-brows, low-brows, critics and artists and decent folk. I enjoyed this show greatly. The verses are distinguished; the music (Walton) equally so.'[4] Another diarist, the photographer Cecil Beaton,[5] caught the atmosphere well:

> The Chenil Galleries were crowded with arty people and not a seat to be had in the place. There were masses of people standing and we had to stand. Everyone seemed very thrilled and expectant: the artiness of the place was terrific. Half the audience seemed nicely arty and the other half merely revoltingly arty. The poems started. They were recited through a megaphone put through a hole in a painted scene representing a face, and they were accompanied by modern music

---

[1] Both photographs appear in Elizabeth Salter, *Edith Sitwell* (London: Oresko Books, 1979), p. 55.

[2] Sitwell, *Laughter in the Next Room*, p. 200. Osbert began writing his sequence of five autobiographical volumes in 1941; *Laughter in the Next Room*, the fourth, was published in 1948.

[3] Letter from Constant Lambert to his mother, May 1926, in Shead, *Constant Lambert*, p. 48. No reviews identified the reciters.

[4] Quoted in Sitwell, *Laughter in the Next Room*, pp. 200–1.

[5] Cecil Beaton (1904–80), initially fashion and portrait photographer and later stage designer and diarist, worked for *Vogue* magazine and did his first stage designs for C. B. Cochran, including *Follow the Sun*. He is probably best known for his designs for the film (and stage version of) *My Fair Lady*.

by Walton. I rather liked the music. I rather liked the poems but I felt too restless to settle down properly to understand them. There were too many distractions – arty people moving about and arty people in the outer room talking too loud. I found the programme much too long and monotonous and didn't bother or couldn't concentrate to listen to the poems towards the end. The reception was extremely friendly and enthusiastic and the Sitwells were only too delighted to give repeated encores.[6]

With each successive performance *Façade* was progressively and often drastically revised, with certain numbers taken out, new ones inserted, and the order changed. For this presentation there were seven new numbers and, according to the 1951 published score, one of them, 'Four in the Morning', had been written 'in collaboration with C[onstant] L[ambert]' who is said to have been responsible for the first 11 bars. In fact, Lambert had adapted the lilting 12/8 opening of the Siciliana movement in his work of the moment, *Romeo and Juliet*.[7] It is difficult to be sure whether he had a hand in any other numbers, but one should certainly read bravado rather than truth in his sharp reply when the composer and conductor Erik Chisholm once asked him why Walton had suppressed so many of the original numbers in *Façade*: 'Because it was I and not Walton who wrote most of these.'[8]

At the next performance of *Façade* two months later, again at the New Chenil Galleries, Constant took on all the recitation himself. In their publicity the Sitwells announced the work as 'the success of the Sitwell Season' and advertised its presentation on 29 June as the 'positively final farewell performance before [a] Provincial Tour', even though no tour with *Façade* took place. Oddly enough, the announcements did not name the speaker. Had they done so, one wonders whether one distinguished figure in the audience, Serge Diaghilev, would have attended. Perhaps he had been urged to come by Walton, still hoping to be asked to compose a ballet, his hopes raised by the fact that *Portsmouth Point* had been performed as an entr'acte by the Ballets Russes at His Majesty's Theatre the previous evening. But Diaghilev was more likely to have been the guest of Sacheverell Sitwell with whom he was then working closely on the scenario for the only other English ballet to be accepted for the Ballets Russes, Lord Berners' *The Triumph of Neptune* that was premiered in December.[9] Diaghilev must have been surprised at the end of the performance when his *bête noire* emerged from behind the screen, especially when *Romeo and Juliet* was receiving its third London performance that very evening.

Façade brought Constant his first radio broadcast, for 2LO, on 3 September 1926 in a programme entitled *The Wheel of Time: A Fantasy in Three Parts*. Presented by Lancelot de G. Sieveking and J. H. Macdonell, the wordy billing for the programme explained: 'It has been designed to illustrate the idea that though time passes, today holds always an echo of yesterday and a note of tomorrow – these artists will illustrate

---

[6] Beaton's original diary entry, in Hugo Vickers, *Cecil Beaton: The Authorized Biography* (London: Weidenfeld & Nicolson, 1985), p. 70, which differs slightly from the published version in Cecil Beaton, *The Wandering Years: Diaries, 1922–1939* (London: Weidenfeld & Nicolson, 1961), pp. 89–90.

[7] I am indebted to David Lloyd-Jones for pointing out the similarity. The *Siciliana* movement is directed *quasi pizzicato*, while 'Four in the Morning' has *pizzicato* and is a tone higher.

[8] Erik Chisholm, 'William Walton and his Façade' (unpublished article).

[9] Walton was called in at the last moment to help out with some orchestrations. Stewart R. Craggs, in *William Walton: A Catalogue* (Oxford: Clarendon Press, 1990), p. 44, identifies seven numbers as being wholly or partly orchestrated by him. Bradford, *Splendours and Miseries*, p. 162, states that Lambert also helped with the score. Berners later rescored the whole ballet himself.

in their songs and recitations the difference between what was, what is and what will – or may – be.' Lambert described how 'the curiously quiet and refined vulgarity of jazz was strongly, though no doubt unconsciously, emphasised by an entertainment devised by the BBC, in which jazz songs of the present day were performed in the same programme as the Victorian songs popularised by Harold Scott and Elsa Lanchester,[10] and a selection from *Façade*.'[11] Lambert, Walton and the three Sitwells took part. Osbert, always one to seek an opportunity for publicity, had earlier created a rumpus in an interview by slighting stage actors so that those who had been booked for the programme withdrew and others had to be engaged.[12]

Whenever *Façade* was given, Constant was the obvious first choice as reciter, as he was on 28 November 1927, with Walton conducting, at the Arts Theatre Club in Great Newport Street in an evening's programme that also included the none-too-successful Sitwell play *First Class Passengers*, co-written by Osbert and Sachie, which had a short run of five nights.[13]

W ITH his mind very much on the premiere of *Romeo and Juliet*, Constant would have had little time to worry about family matters that were about to make big changes to his home life. In April 1926 his mother Amy, concerned about her husband George's health, decided to join him in Australia. Since his return to Sydney in March 1921, his health had steadily deteriorated. He had maintained an irregular correspondence with Amy, writing just before reaching Australia: 'I hope the boys are well and that Maurice is fast becoming a reliable sculptor, if not a worthy son, perhaps both.'[14] Constant was at that time still at Christ's Hospital with four terms remaining, while Maurice, with his mind now set on becoming an artist, had been studying drawing at the Chelsea Polytechnic. George's fellow artist Francis Derwent Wood, Professor of Sculpture at the South Kensington Royal College of Art, had offered to take Maurice on as a studio assistant.[15] 'I hope Maurice is becoming an able and efficient sculptor-assistant,' George wrote. 'I miss him quite a lot, both as a son and a useful possibility for the construction of the Palestine model, and also other things I have in mind', adding, as if for Amy's reassurance, 'I have only one old friend in the world – you.'[16] Later that year he informed her, with considerable frankness, that he remained celibate while in Australia, apart from occasional visits to prostitutes whom he regarded as 'hardfaced calculating' women who demanded 'large sums in advance'.[17] Meanwhile in his work, that had ranged from bush landscapes and portraiture to war

---

[10] Elsa Lanchester (1902–86), actress, married Charles Laughton in 1929. As a child she had studied dance in Paris under Isadora Duncan and in 1934 she appeared as a guest artist with the Vic-Wells Ballet. In 1931 the Laughtons let Lambert a flat off the Tottenham Court Road. Elsa played opposite her husband in the 1933 film *The Private Lives of Henry VIII* and starred in *The Bride of Frankenstein* (1935).

[11] Lambert, 'Jazz', *Life and Letters*, vol. 1 no. 2 (July 1928), p. 124.

[12] Osbert gave his own version of the whole affair at great length in 'A Few Days in an Author's Life', in *All at Sea*. For a less tedious account, see Pearson, *Façades*, pp. 208–9.

[13] Lambert and all three Sitwells performed *Façade* on Monday, Tuesday and Wednesday, 28, 29 & 30 November 1927: information kindly supplied by Stewart Craggs.

[14] Amy Lambert, *Thirty Years of an Artist's Life*, p. 139.

[15] Derwent Wood had urged George Lambert to allow his name to be put forward for membership of the Royal Academy, and he was elected an Associate in 1922.

[16] Amy Lambert, *Thirty Years of an Artist's Life*, p. 143.

[17] George Lambert to Amy Lambert, 10 November 1921, Lambert Family Papers, Mitchell Library, Sydney, quoted in Anne Gray, *George Lambert, 1873–1930: Art and Artifice* (Roseville East, NSW: Craftsman House, 1996), p. 117. This is a detail that Amy understandably omits when quoting from this letter in her biography of George.

studies, he had himself turned to sculpture, and in November 1921 he wrote to Amy: 'I am so glad that Maurice is getting on all right with Derwent Wood. I hope he finds time to do some modelling on his own. I don't know what your finances are. I have a horrid feeling that you are living on Maurice's wages and Constant's prospects of going bankrupt for millions like Beecham.'[18] He concluded by sending 'the most earnest good wishes to the boys from one who has left his stomach in Palestine and his heart at 25 Glebe Place, Chelsea'.[19]

By 1922 George's concern for his sons' future seemed to have evaporated, writing: 'I am delighted to get good reports of Maurice and Constant. Let 'em both do what they will, so [long] as they do it well. I feel that their desire to make a success of what they take up will help to keep them sober and wise.'[20] He maintained an interest in their progress: 'The last few days I have been practically paralysed by the thought of you and your welfare, and that of the boys. Result, stoppage of output, and therefore bad for you as well as myself. ... I think much of the work of the boys, but I feel that I have not bought the right to either advise or sympathise, still I have hopes. I really would be grateful if I could get copies of Constant's concert contributions, also photographs of Maurice's soldier.'[21] But relations soured when his suggestion that Maurice should go out to Australia as his father's assistant was not favourably received, and Maurice's announcement of his engagement to Olga, Angus Morrison's sister, brought a stern response: 'Marriage, for an artist, is recklessly stupid and unmoral. I cannot afford to think about it, for it means a loss of working power, and doctors, friends, and myself are helping me to overcome, not only the heart and stomach trouble – my little war souvenir – but the deadly aftermath, melancholia; but you will be pleased to learn that I am strong ...'[22]

Yet this was far from the truth. George had been suffering from exhaustion through overwork, with recurring attacks of malaria and heart strain, and this had resulted in spells in hospital. Amy's anxiety was aggravated by his increasingly sporadic letters home and, whether or not she was fully in the picture as regards his health, she decided to make the journey. With Constant having completed his Royal College studies and with a ballet accepted by Diaghilev, and with Maurice becoming established as a sculptor, she had fewer qualms about leaving them. In one of his last letters home George had made it clear that 'it was now time that the home should be broken up, since it had fulfilled its temporary purpose.' As she put it: 'I suddenly realised that this sale would help me to wind up our affairs in London and indulge my long-repressed desire to rejoin George in Sydney. ... The independence of our sons' actions, in shouldering the burden of their own decisions in matters directly concerning themselves, had unwittingly made for my freedom.'[23] So, on 22 April 1926, she boarded the P.&O. liner *Baradine* at Gravesend, determined to see Australia again after an absence of 25 years. Although she was to return to England three years later, at the time she may well have thought it was to be a permanent move.

---

[18] In the summer of 1920, following the death of his father and the collapse of the Beecham Estate, Sir Thomas Beecham was declared bankrupt and was out of music from 1920 until 1923. George was obviously alluding to Constant's intentions of joining the Royal College of Music and making music his career.

[19] [November 1921]. Amy Lambert, *Thirty Years of an Artist's Life*, p. 146.

[20] N.d., *ibid.*, p. 149.

[21] N.d., *ibid.*, p. 159. According to Amy Lambert, Maurice's soldier was a small memorial figure. It may have been in connection with the memorial Derwent Wood had been commissioned for Hyde Park and on which Maurice worked as an apprentice.

[22] N.d., *ibid.*, p. 166.

[23] *Ibid.*, p. 168.

En route she learnt by letter from Constant of his disagreement with Diaghilev and the problems with *Romeo and Juliet*, and soon after her arrival in Sydney she received a cable announcing Maurice's marriage. As she wrote later, George 'bowed to the inevitable, helped a little perhaps by my personal guarantee of the charm, health, common sense and general desirability of the new member of the family' and extended an olive-branch by asking to buy a specimen of Maurice's work. After seeing photographs of the two pieces offered, he chose the head of Walton which, on arrival, 'met with his qualified approval'.[24] To Constant, whose ballet had by now been staged in Monte Carlo, Paris and London, he wrote a typically dry letter that illustrates the distance between father and son:

> Dear Constant,
>
> You are now sworn to Music and all the history that the letters suggest to me. Quite a space. Mathematical construction is the human triumph. The space, the margin, the by-way for experiment. This is the great hope and goal today of the good student. But remember that it is better to bring your records back to humanity than to be killed by the adventure. I am honoured in being able to 'coff up' my fifty pounds. Your mother is well and I still work quite well.[25]

After their mother's departure, Constant and Maurice continued to live for a short while at 25 Glebe Place, but when on 27 July Maurice and Olga were married, the family house was sold and the couple moved to a large studio in Sussex Place that Maurice had taken a few months earlier. As brothers, it was their differences rather than any similarities that marked them out. Maurice, the quieter of the two, cultivated the air of a pipe-smoking man-in-the-street artist devoted to his work. While less at-ease than Constant in the circle of intellectuals – he would not seek out the company of the Sitwells and others of Constant's acquaintance – he was well educated in the arts and both read and wrote poetry. But, as he admitted in the early 1930s, 'I have up to date hated writing and writers, not because I'm a fool, but because I've had to in a kind of mental self-defence.'[26] Nevertheless, he gained a number of commissions from people with whom Constant was in contact.[27] Although he showed little of his father's flamboyance, he nevertheless inherited some of his traits. Often moody in appearance, he could be morose at times, and he and Constant had their arguments. He shared his father's interest in boxing, and enjoyed sailing too. His sculpture showed strong classical lines, while some of his most striking work, the bust of Edith Sitwell, for example, displayed modernistic tendencies. He and Constant went their separate ways, meeting infrequently probably on family occasions at their mother's instigation.

Constant went to live at 15 Cheyne Gardens, Chelsea, the home of Mrs Travers Smith. This was an arrangement that Amy had made before leaving, anxious that in spite of her absence Constant should not be deprived of the comforts and amenities of family life.

As an old friend of the Lamberts, Mrs Hester Travers Smith had taken an interest

---

[24] Amy Lambert, *Thirty Years of an Artist's Life*, p. 170.

[25] *Ibid.*, pp. 170–1.

[26] Undated letter to Adrian Stokes, Tate Archive, quoted in Vanessa Nicolson, *The Sculpture of Maurice Lambert* (Much Hadam: Henry Moore Foundation in association with Lund Humphries, 2002), p. 20.

[27] Besides his abstract sculptures, Maurice's subjects included a number of people connected with the arts, amongst them Angus Morrison (1924), Edith Sitwell (*c.* 1925), Jelly d'Aranyi (1925), Hermione Baddeley (1925), Sir Edmund Davis (1927), Peter Quennell (1927), Stephen Tennant (1928), Scott Goddard (1929), Adrian Stokes (*c.* 1935), J. B. Priestley (1949), Margot Fonteyn (three, *c.* 1956) and Sir Arthur Bliss (1954). The heads of his brother Constant and William Walton were completed in 1925.

in Maurice's and Constant's developing talents. She was also much involved in spiritualism and – as a medium – claimed not only to be in touch with the spirit of Oscar Wilde but to have transcribed an unknown full-length play by him by means of a planchette and Ouija board. This had much interested Constant, and while staying with Charles Ricketts at Chilham Castle in Kent, he had written to her:

> I have told Ricketts all about the Oscar Wilde affair. He is intensely interested.[28]
> He would like you, if you could to ask him
> (1) about the story of the Spanish crucifix – the sepulchre
> (2) about the play on the subject of Pharaoh[29]
> (3) why he altered the period of 'The Importance of Being Earnest'.
> He says that he would be very interesting on the subject of Beardsley, Flaubert, or his own (Ricketts') illustrations to the Sphinx.
>   I hope you had a good holiday. How are Dolly and Sparkshall?
>   When I come back I have a number of things, 4 songs, 2 foxtrots and a piece for piano duet to play you.[30]

He added a postscript: 'I believe Ricketts is the only man who knows about the 3 questions, so if you get a detailed answer, it would be pretty conclusive.' The reply, if there was any, has not been recorded.

Dabbling with the occult was for some a popular pastime, whether out of fun, serious intent or just curiosity. Fortunately, Constant did not, it seems, have much involvement with that infamous occultist Aleister Crowley,[31] who noted in his diary for 25 November 1937: 'Ran into Constant Lambert, with him talking till 12.30', only to follow it up on 11 February 1938: 'Thought I'd go to the Prada. There was Constant Lambert! I feigned not to notice him.' His entry two days later reads simply: 'Constant Lambert at Casa Prada.'[32] However, the novelist Anthony Powell has described one occasion in the early 1930s when he and Constant with his first wife took part in some 'spirit writing' with a planchette at the home of the economist and author Gerald Reitlinger. At first the session was unproductive and Constant, becoming bored, turned away to write some letters at a desk in the corner of the room.

> Suddenly planchette began to move, then to write. The 'influence', transcribed in a long sloping 18th century hand, announced itself as Mozart. Neither Reitlinger nor I being much up in musical matters, we asked Lambert to suggest an appropriate question for the great composer. 'Enquire who was his favourite mistress.'
>   We did so. Planchette wrote a reply. *La petite Carlotta.*
>   'When did this love affair take place?'

[28] Ricketts was a friend of Oscar Wilde and, like his friend Shannon, had been chosen by him to illustrate some of his books.

[29] *Pharaoh* was a play that Wilde contemplated while in prison but never committed to paper.

[30] Copy of the letter in the draft chapters by Angus Morrison at the RCM Library. Mrs Hester Travers Smith (1868–1949), also known by her maiden name Hester Dowden, claimed to have contacted Oscar Wilde via the Ouija board in June, July and December 1923 and January 1924, although the transcripts do not show that these questions were asked on any of those occasions. Her book, *Psychic Messages from Oscar Wilde* (London: T. Werner Laurie), was published in 1924. Oddly enough, when staying in Ireland in 1918, Philip Heseltine became acquainted with Hester Dowden and not only attended her seances with Ouija board but also composed some of his earliest songs in her Dublin home.

[31] Aleister Crowley (1875–1947), notorious occultist, author and practitioner of black magic.

[32] Casa Prada was a restaurant in the Euston Road, opposite Warren Street Station, much favoured by Elisabeth Lutyens and Edward Clark who, when working at the BBC, would entertain there foreign composers like Stravinsky, Bartók, Webern and Schoenberg.

'*A Napoli en 1789.*'[33]

Showing interest in this Mozartian manifestation, Constant stopped letter writing but did not take any active part. When he later looked up the details of Mozart's life he found that there was no substance at all in the 'spirit message'. For someone always concerned with factual accuracy his interest would have stopped there.

Living in another person's well-ordered home did require from Constant a certain discipline that had its rewards. As Harold Rutland much later recalled:

> Constant had an extraordinary facility with his pen. ... Thomas McGreevey [*sic*], the Irish poet, told me that he and Constant were staying at the house of Mrs Hester Dowden [Mrs Travers Smith] in Cheyne Gardens, Chelsea, and one Sunday afternoon Constant went up to his room, and in a couple of hours or so had written a first-rate article on music. 'I couldn't do it,' said McGreevey.[34]

But Constant soon realised that it did not allow him the freedom he wanted to compose, or to come and go as he pleased at any hour to see his friends, so instead he took two rooms at 59 Oakley Street, Chelsea, where he became an even closer neighbour to Angus Morrison, so close indeed that hardly a day went by without their meeting. Morrison felt that there was an element of 'the cat that walked by himself' in Constant's make-up, and that all along he had intended to live on his own but had decided to wait until his mother had left for Australia, and so avoid any protracted family discussion that might have given her extra worry at a sad time when they were giving up their home of many years. He would whenever possible avoid unpleasantness, especially in family and domestic matters, 'through the simple expedient of only announcing his actions when it was too late for outside influences to have any modifying effect on them'. Constant's departure from Cheyne Gardens had been hastened by an 'unfortunate encounter' one can only guess at, that took place on the stairs between Mrs Travers Smith's pet Pekinese and Walton, who was paying an unexpected visit.[35]

Living on his own in his new accommodation now gave Constant the independence he sought, especially to play the piano whenever and as loudly as he wanted, sufficient compensation for his not-so-comfortable surroundings and the lack of regular meals. Eating out and concert-going became regular patterns of his life-style. On the evening of Maurice's marriage [27 July 1926], he went with Angus Morrison and the critic Scott Goddard[36] to a 'supper party' at the Café de Paris in Coventry Street. Other regular eating haunts were Rules in Covent Garden, the Eiffel Tower in Percy Street, the Café Royal in Regent Street, and The Ivy in Covent Garden. The concerts he attended would naturally reflect his personal tastes, such as the one given by Beecham at Queen's Hall on 11 April 1927: Mozart, Symphony No. 34, Delius, *Sea Drift* and Berlioz, *Te Deum* – after which he had supper at the Café Royal with Angus, Goddard and Walton.

Angus remembered the frequency of their meetings:

> It was only natural we should continue to see a great deal of each other and for over a year, until he migrated to Bloomsbury in the autumn of 1927, hardly a day went by without a meeting of some sort. He had to pass my house every time

---

[33] Powell, *Messengers of Day*, pp. 176–7.

[34] Rutland, 'Recollections of Constant Lambert'.

[35] Angus Morrison's manuscript. He gave no explanation as to what exactly happened.

[36] Scott Goddard (1895–1965), for some time music critic of the *Daily News* and later of the *News Chronicle*, had been a student in Boult's conducting class at the Royal College of Music. He wrote to Hubert Foss in 1951 that 'Constant was quick-minded, assured, in every way brilliant; and I could not keep up with him.'

he went to and from the King's Road and would frequently drop in to play duets together and of course there was always endless talk about music and art in general, not to mention the more superficial pleasures of gossip and discussing one's friends. Constant was always a good talker and in those early years particularly brilliant, stimulating and responsive, and quite without the didactic element that began to creep into his views and judgment after writing *Music Ho!* We got to know a tremendous amount of orchestral music extremely unfamiliar to us both through that invaluable medium of musical education, the four-hand piano arrangement; and to a generation brought up passively to consider the long-playing record as the supreme and only means of acquiring musical literacy, the amount of skilled musicianship and pianistic dexterity required to read a complex modern orchestral work must indeed seem phenomenal.

Then, at the end of August 1927, Constant found new lodgings in Bloomsbury at 189 High Holborn, second floor rooms above a bookshop. The owner of the shop, who lived beneath him on the first floor, was Dorothy Varda, a tall, elegant, fair-haired young woman who had once been billed as 'The Beautiful Miranda' in C. B. Cochran's revues but had given up the stage for books. She had retained her surname after a brief, unsuccessful marriage to the Greek surrealist painter, Jean Varda, and her sharp and witty tongue prompted Constant to remark that she was the only woman he knew with a male sense of humour. During her occasional absences she relied on friends to stand in for her at the shop, a job that sometimes fell to Constant, who complained that he always struck a day when all the lunatics in London seemed to have been let out to buy books. He would, however, have enjoyed the story that went around about the stand-in who was asked by a customer if they had Shelley's *Prometheus Unbound*, to which came the hopeful reply: 'No, but I'm sure I've seen a bound copy on the shelves.' Dorothy Varda's evenings were often enlivened by friends calling in, usually resulting in trips to the Soho pubs and returning in the small hours, a homeless guest sometimes being discovered the next morning fast asleep among the book-shelves. It is hard to believe that Constant did not from time to time join that company as his life-style became increasingly Bohemian.

Above him, in slightly smaller rooms, was the author Peter Quennell, who earned Varda's disapproval by not joining in the pub crawls. He had these memories of Constant:

> He was a little younger than I was and I found him extremely good company. I can remember his room fairly distinctly: it was a small and rather bleak room with a somewhat grim-looking black upright piano at which he did a good deal of his work. There was a row of bottles of Chinese wine, earthenware bottles with large paper labels embellished with Chinese characters, and I soon discovered that these bottles of Chinese wine had a special significance for him. He was at the time very much in love with a beautiful Chinese film actress called Anna May Wong who had recently made her début in *The Thief of Bagdad* with Douglas Fairbanks. I don't think that at that time he'd ever met Miss Wong but she was his sort of Princesse Lointaine and in her honour he used to drink Chinese wine – which he also allowed me to drink. It was extremely nasty and I remember that the taste was rather like the taste of embalming fluid – not that I'd ever drunk embalming fluid but that is how I imagined it would taste. It had an unfortunate effect on Constant's metabolic system; in fact it made him

extremely constipated and nevertheless he went on drinking it in Miss Wong's honour.[37]

Neither his creative gifts nor his literary and critical intelligence were ever fully recognised; and, so long as I knew him, with his shapeless overcoat, his rough scarf and his heavy stick – he had a slightly lame leg – Constant remained a hard-working, hard-living and almost invariably hard-up Bohemian, whose powerful voice, whether he discussed the arts, sang a favourite folk-song or recited a ludicrous limerick, penetrated to the farthest recesses, and startled the drowsiest *habitués* of a London bar-parlour. He would have been perfectly at home in Paris during the Romantic 1930s.[38]

A strong literary friendship forged at about this time was with Anthony Powell, four months younger than Constant and best known today for his sequence of novels under the title *A Dance to the Music of Time* in which the character Hugh Moreland was in part modelled on Constant.[39] In a similar fashion to Constant who, unable to participate in games at Christ's Hospital, had used the time to widen his interest in the arts, so at Eton had Powell, not being a sporting person, found an escape in the 'Studio' where he learnt about modern art, attended lectures and took part in debates. He had also joined the select Eton Society of the Arts. After leaving Oxford in 1926 he had a basement flat in nearby Tavistock Square while serving a three-year apprenticeship with the publishing firm of Duckworth. It was soon after their first meeting in the autumn of 1927 – characteristically 'in a crowded pub' – that Powell suggested that Constant might contribute something of a musical nature to a series of essays by young writers that his publisher was contemplating.[40] Nothing came of the series, but a firm friendship was cemented, despite Powell inadvertently addressing his first letter to 'Constantine Lambert', believing the forename to be an abbreviation. From the start they got on well. Although, on his own admission, Powell lacked a musical sensibility, it was their shared interest in books and pictorial art that brought them together, even if their individual tastes sometimes differed. Both happened to be cat lovers, but it was Constant's unstuffy, unconventional attitudes that so appealed to Powell, especially when injected with a Rabelaisian wit.[41] He came, he later wrote, 'as a refreshing draught after Oxford self-consciousness about the arts.'[42] Powell was particularly struck by the ease with which Constant could expound freely upon the three arts without any of the snobbery or affectation he observed in many of his contemporaries. As Constant was a voracious reader, they were never short of topics for conversation, whether the familiar or the obscure, and it was through him that Powell first heard of the French novelist Claude Farrère and the city of Saigon that, according to Powell, had always

---

[37] Peter Quennell in *Constant Lambert Remembered*, BBC Third Network, 25 June 1966.

[38] Peter Quennell, *The Marble Foot: An Autobiography, 1915–1938* (London: Collins, 1976), p. 162.

[39] See Appendix 9.

[40] In the memoir he wrote for Richard Shead's biography of Lambert, Powell gave the date of their meeting as 'about the spring of 1928' but he corrected this in *Messengers of Day*, p. 55, adding that they met 'possibly in the company of [art critic Thomas] Earp, whom he always found sympathetic.'

[41] As Powell recalled in *Messengers of Day*, p. 59: 'Lambert loved discussing painters, Böcklin to Braque, Breughel to Brangwyn, especially enjoying to put forward subjects for Royal Academy pictures in the sententiously forcible manner of Brangwyn – once much imitated – of which two proposed canvases (titles in which perhaps Maurice Lambert too had a hand) were: *Blowing up the Rubber Woman*, and '*Hock or Claret, sir?': Annual Dinner of the Rectal Dining Society.*'

[42] *Ibid.*, p. 101.

been Constant's 'dream city' (probably because of Farrère's prize-winning novel *Les Civilisés* that was set in Saigon).[43]

The following June, to consecrate their friendship, and at the same time conveniently work off their various social obligations, they held a joint house-warming at Powell's flat that began as a cocktail party and went on until the early hours of the morning. Amongst Constant's guests were Frederick Ashton and William ('Billy') Chappell from the world of ballet. From then on they met quite frequently, in pubs, at parties, at eating places like Castano's Italian restaurant in Greek Street and the Eiffel Tower, or they would just go for walks. Powell found Constant to be a great walker despite his lameness, and he recalled one particular Sunday afternoon walk that they took together after first having tea in Constant's new rooms above the bookshop. Their first port of call was 'The Tiger' public house on Tower Hill. Then, after inspecting some buildings of architectural interest, they made their way to Wapping and Shadwell, and had dinner at a Chinese restaurant in Limehouse. They headed next for 'The Prospect of Whitby', taking in on their way several other riverside pubs, and well after midnight they crossed the Blackwall Tunnel to return home by the South Bank. Just after Rotherhithe, part of their remaining journey was considerably eased by the arrival of a tram. Back on their feet, they crossed the Thames to arrive home at about four in the morning. These long walks were not confined to London. One Christmas, they roamed the streets of Paris, stopping at a café that boasted a small orchestra with a list of pieces to be played on request. Constant took what Powell described as 'sadistic pleasure' in calling for the most difficult ones to be performed.[44]

It was through publishing that Powell first met Osbert Sitwell, and he and Constant were present at a Carlyle Square Sitwell dinner-party when the company also included William Walton, Harold Acton and Evelyn Waugh. While in later years their jobs were to prevent them from meeting as often as they would have liked, Constant remained one of Powell's closest friends, both gaining particular pleasure from the quirky literary exchanges in their occasional letters or postcards. Once or twice Constant would take Powell to visit another in his circle of friends, one who, for good and for bad, exerted the strongest influence on him: the composer Philip Heseltine, then living with his mistress in a very rundown area of Pimlico.[45] With his pointed beard and 'light-coloured eyes that were peculiarly compelling', he seemed to Powell to adopt a Mephistophelian appearance. 'His reputation,' he wrote in his memoirs, 'one not altogether undeserved, was that of *mauvais sujet*, but I always found him agreeable and highly entertaining; though never without a sense, as with many persons of at times malignant temper, that things might suddenly go badly wrong.'[46]

A T a Royal College of Music concert on 19 March 1925, Constant had given the first performance of his own Suite for Piano in Three Movements. Lasting about 12 minutes, this continuous suite is a remarkable work from someone not yet 20. A quiet opening on slowly rising fifths leads into softly repeated chords with a stretch of a ninth in each hand. This is followed by an eight-note sequence of falling and rising crotchets and dotted minims, repeated an octave higher and, with its lack of any clear

[43] *To Keep the Ball Rolling: The Memoirs of Anthony Powell*, vol. 4: *The Strangers All Are Gone* (London: Heinemann, 1982), pp. 131, 141. Claude Farrère was the pseudonym of Frédéric-Charles Bargone (1876–1957), a prolific author and French naval officer who wrote books in his spare time.

[44] *Ibid.*, p. 147.

[45] Philip Heseltine (1894–1930), composer, critic and author, was born in London's Savoy Hotel and composed under the pseudonym Peter Warlock.

[46] Powell, *The Strangers All Are Gone*, p. 147.

tonality, creating an aura of timelessness. Another important element is a contrapuntal sequence with a left-hand ostinato figure of five crotchets overlapping the bar and robbing this section of any feeling of definite time signature. After some treatment of these three ideas, the movement then plunges into a *prestissimo* passage, followed by a more meditative *andante*, a reprise of the *prestissimo* section and, after a fugal *presto*, the Suite finishes, as it began, quietly, with a repeat of the opening bars and the theme from the *andante* section. Much of the writing is in the upper register, and Mark Tanner, in his notes to his own recording of this work, makes the interesting suggestion that the work's opening fifths are a tongue-in-cheek reference to Liszt's *Mephisto Waltz*. The work, which reflects Constant's fascination with the Parisian world of ballet, and requires some degree of virtuosity in performance, was neither heard again nor generally known until, after his death, his widow donated the score, with others, to the BBC Library.

At the College concert, Constant was also the pianist in Patrick Hadley's *Ephemera*, a setting of W. B. Yeats for soprano, flute, oboe, string quartet and piano.[47] The programme also included a Theme and Variations for piano by E. J. Moeran, who in May and June that year arranged three chamber concerts at the Wigmore Hall, almost exclusively of English music.[48] Present at the last of these concerts was the soprano Dora Stevens, who remembered that 'Lambert, Heseltine and several other men sat in a row behind the one in which I was sitting. As they were both so striking in appearance, I own to having turned round on several occasions to look at them. … One time I was amazed to see a pipe being passed along from one to the other, each one having a puff or suck at it.'[49] This concert included a song-cycle by Hubert Foss, whom Dora was to marry in 1927.

Seven years older than Lambert and editor for the new music department of Oxford University Press, Foss had first met Constant in about 1923 or 1924 and became both his publisher and his friend, as he did for many of that generation of English composers: with his enquiring and perceptive mind, he proved to be for them an invaluable advocate.[50] He shared a number of musical interests with Constant – although jazz was a notable exception. He was then separated from his wife, Kate Carter Page. They had lived for a while in a small 18th-century cottage, formerly a bakery, that Foss had acquired in the Kent village of Eynsford in about 1921. Their home became the centre of many musical gatherings, with visits from two enigmatic composers, both of whom were to exert strong influences on Lambert: the Dutch-born Bernard van Dieren[51] who

---

[47] This was probably the only occasion when Lambert performed in public as solo pianist; for a while during the war he accompanied the ballet as part of a piano duo.

[48] Ernest John ('Jack') Moeran (1894–1950), composer and collector of folk-songs whose music belongs to the English pastoral tradition. The pianist on this occasion was Dorothy Aspinall. Moeran studied at the Royal College of Music but left in April 1921, a year before Lambert enrolled. His Wigmore Hall concerts included: 23 May: Debussy, String Quartet; Bax, Piano Quintet; Moeran, String Quartet; 7 June: R. O. Morris, Motet for String Quartet; van Dieren, 4th String Quartet; Warlock, *The Curlew*; Arthur Benjamin, Pastoral Fantasy for string quartet; 13 June: Moeran, Piano Trio; Hugo Anson, Two Poems for cello and piano; Hubert Foss, Song-cycle of 7 poems of Thomas Hardy; John Ireland, Piano Trio; Warlock, Sociable Songs.

[49] Hubert Foss Archives, British Library.

[50] Hubert J. Foss (1899–1953), composer, pianist, author, broadcaster and OUP Musical Editor 1923–41, was an important figure in the publication and performance of English music. He suggested the year of his meeting Lambert in a letter to J. H. H. Gaute of Harrap & Sons, 3 September 1951.

[51] In 1925 van Dieren composed a set of three studies for piano and dedicated them to Hubert Foss, who had just published some of his songs.

was living in England, and Philip Heseltine, who in January 1925 rented the cottage from Foss, sharing its tenancy with Moeran, and continuing the habit of week-end parties but on a more energetic scale. In Foss's words, 'bawdry, humour, and liquor were essential ingredients of life'.[52] 'The Warlock Gang', as he called them, from time to time included the conductors Hyam Greenbaum[53] and Leslie Heward, and the critic and composer Cecil Gray, who looked back on his days spent at Eynsford as among the happiest and most memorable of his life. Constant was an occasional visitor, even arriving in style one Sunday in Lord Berners' Rolls-Royce.[54] Berners became a good friend of Constant's. Composer, painter and writer, he too was well versed in the three arts. They shared a similar sense of humour and a similar dislike of pomposity. Like Heseltine, Berners was a skilled hand at humorous verse. Constant was to become closely associated with his orchestral music, conducting the premieres of three of his ballets, and he was to enjoy many a week-end at Faringdon House, Berners' home in Oxfordshire.

Another visitor to Eynsford was the Bohemian artist Nina Hamnett,[55] who stayed there for much of spring and early summer of 1927, and has left an account of one particularly high-spirited occasion in which Constant was involved. Heseltine had decided to disrupt an auction held in a neighbouring village by a rich, religious landlady whom he particularly disliked. The possessions of a poor girl who could not pay the rent were to be auctioned and Heseltine saw her eviction as an injustice that demanded a protest. He hired a large car and a chauffeur, and from a London theatrical shop bought masks, false noses and beards for his fellow conspirators whom he invited down for the week-end. For Constant he chose a nose attached to a small black beard that resembled a foreign conductor whom Heseltine disliked; for Nina he picked a white death mask, and for himself an enormous black hat – that was reputed at some time to have belonged to Augustus John – and a purple Moroccan robe. As a finishing touch he painted his nose bright red with lipstick. Even the chauffeur was provided with a false nose. The three of them, quite unrecognisable in their costumes, were driven to the pub where the auction was to take place, while Moeran, who had a car of his own, brought a girl-friend of Heseltine's, made up to look like a 12-year-old. The pranksters wisely took care not to drink too much because they learned that someone, sensing trouble, had already telegraphed the police at the nearest large town.

---

[52] Hubert Foss, 'Phases of the Moon: 1. The Warlock Gang', *London Symphony Observer*, November 1951, pp. 99–100. Foss himself had been offered an Elizabethan cottage some 5 miles south and took it.

[53] Hyam Greenbaum (1901–42), Brighton-born violinist, composer and conductor, affectionately known to his friends as 'Bumps' after a remark once made by a phrenologist about his cranium. A child prodigy, he played the Beethoven Violin Concerto at the age of seven and won an open scholarship to the Royal College of Music when only 11. He fought in the trenches by falsifying his age but was later discharged. He led the second violins in the Queen's Hall Orchestra until 1925, leaving to allow more time as second violin in the Brosa Quartet. He married Sidonie Goossens in 1924, their home at Wetherby Gardens, SW5 becoming a regular meeting place for musicians like Walton, Lambert, Rawsthorne, Hadley and Cecil Gray. The pianist Kyla Greenbaum, who in 1949 recorded *The Rio Grande* with Lambert conducting, was Hyam's sister.

[54] 6 March 1926. Fred Tomlinson, *A Peter Warlock Handbook*, 2 vols (London: Triad Press, 1974–7), vol. 1 p. 44.

[55] Born in Tenby, South Wales, Nina Hamnett (1890–1956) was a flamboyantly unconventional bisexual heavy-drinking artist who was equally at home in London and Paris. She frequented the Fitzroy Tavern, the Eiffel Tower and the Café Royal, and was known as the Queen of Bohemia.

As soon as the auctioneer started, Heseltine sprang forward in front of him and began to make a speech. We loudly applauded and each time the auctioneer protested, he was greeted by whistles and catcalls, several of the local inhabitants taking our part.[56]

Most of the auction lots were everyday things of little value and when Heseltine thought that their demonstration had gone far enough, he and his friends 'made a dash for the motorcars and drove away just as a detachment of mounted police were entering the village'.

Nina remembered another disruptive occasion when Constant was at Eynsford:

Constant Lambert, who came down often on Sundays, had found a Victoria duet called the 'Fairy Queen'. It contained runs up and down the piano and all kinds of curious trills and had the most ridiculous melody. Moeran and Lambert played together with very serious faces. They generally had an argument in the middle and one would push the other off the end of the piano stool. Next to our house was a chapel. It was surrounded by a small garden and on Sunday mornings we ran a rival show. When the service started, we began with several works by Max Reger, the noisy German composer, some of whose music sounds completely drunk. These were played on the pianola.[57] The 'Fairy Queen' was then played and we ended up by roaring sea songs, ending up with the unexpurgated version of 'Nautical William'.

The Sunday routine would consist of drinking in the garden of the Five Bells pub opposite their cottage while lunch was being cooked by Heseltine's faithful factotum, the Maori Hal Collins. Then they would take home for lunch a large jug of ale, and after the meal everyone would pile into Moeran's car for an exploration of the local pubs – with further drinking.

Walton was an occasional visitor. Osbert Sitwell observed that 'William entertained a high regard for [Heseltine] and greatly enjoyed his conversation, and, together with Constant, would go down to spend convivial evenings with him in Kent, where Heseltine was living; whence the two young composers would return very late, with footsteps faltering through the now uncertain immensity of night.'[58] Walton recalled one particular visit while Constant was still at the Royal College of Music:

There was one beautiful occasion when we started on a walk down the City one nice summer morning, stopped at every pub on the way and ended up at Eynsford with Philip Heseltine, that New Zealander [Hal Collins] and other people who were staying there. ... Next morning the police were more or less looking for us, so we disappeared. Constant had a lesson with VW that afternoon. He rang up to tell him that he couldn't come, during which time Philip extemporised very loudly in VW's best manner, or worst, as the case may be. He had something very odd to say about the telephone call the following lesson.[59]

---

[56] Nina Hamnett, *Is She a Lady? A Problem in Autobiography* (London: Allan Wingate, 1955), p. 32.

[57] The pianola (or player piano) played manufactured rolls of paper on which the music had been perforated. In his youth, Heseltine had become acquainted with many orchestral works by playing piano rolls.

[58] Sitwell, *Laughter in the Next Room*, p. 179.

[59] Typescript from Sir William Walton to Hubert Foss, n.d., Hubert Foss Archives. In Hinnells, *An Extraordinary Performance*, p. 50.

The critic Cyril Connolly recalled meeting Walton, Lambert and Heseltine one evening in Paris in the autumn of 1926 and together they 'all got very drunk'.[60] An excess of drinking was the undoing of a number who were drawn into the Heseltine circle, most prominently Moeran and Lambert. Walton wisely steered a clear course away from such influences: 'I knew [Heseltine] well enough to avoid his somewhat baleful influence. I couldn't keep up with his drinking luckily, whereas Moeran could, with, I feel, deleterious effects on him.'[61] And it was to Moeran in 1930 that Heseltine made this shrewd assessment of Walton and Lambert:

> Walton's work improves at every hearing. He is the best musician this country has produced for a long while. Lambert is perhaps more talented, but I do not feel that music is his ultimate mode of expression. His keen observation, sensibility, wit and critical intellect seem rather to point to literature as his medium, whereas Walton is specifically musical or nothing.[62]

During the seasons of Promenade Concerts at the Queen's Hall, a number of British composers invariably congregated in the interval in the bar behind the stalls, and Heseltine and Constant would often be found among them. While it would be unreasonable to suggest that without Heseltine Constant would not have developed a drinking problem, his close friendship with Philip ensured that he followed that downhill course. Other drinking friends like Patrick Hadley and Cecil Gray (whose own death was accelerated by excessive drinking) helped him on the way. But with Constant there was one important difference: in later life he suffered from undiagnosed diabetes, to the extent that his occasional faints and collapses would often be ascribed by onlookers to drink when in fact he had touched little or no alcohol for some while. Because of the many operations he had undergone in his youth, Constant avoided doctors whenever possible for the rest of his life, and so the diabetes went undetected.

Constant had the highest respect for Heseltine as a composer and recognised his brilliant mind, despite the mood swings and outrageous activities to which he was prone. After Philip's death he became one of his most devoted champions, in the concert hall, through broadcasts and in gramophone recordings. It was more than likely that Heseltine's scholarly researches into Elizabethan music encouraged Constant to follow in his footsteps with early composers like William Boyce and Thomas Roseingrave. They shared many interests, both musical and non-musical. Heseltine's enthusiasm for such composers as Bartók, Berlioz, Sibelius (whose Fourth Symphony had especially impressed him when he heard the composer conduct it in 1912), Delius and Liszt – according to Patrick Hadley, they played piano duet transcriptions of Liszt's symphonic poems[63] – drew them together, and both were devotees of van Dieren. Heseltine's skill in writing limericks (most of them unprintable)[64] almost certainly encouraged

---

[60] Pearson, *Façades*, pp. 211–12.

[61] Letter to Rhoderick McNeill, quoted in the latter's thesis, 'A Critical Study of the Life and Works of E. J. Moeran' (PhD diss., University of Melbourne, 1982).

[62] Letter from Heseltine to Moeran, 6 October 1930, in *The Collected Letters of Peter Warlock, vol. 4: 1922–1930*, ed. Barry Smith (Woodbridge: Boydell Press, 2005), p. 282.

[63] I. A. Copley, *The Music of Peter Warlock: A Critical Survey* (London: Denis Dobson, 1979), p. 241. In June 1925 Heseltine was planning a small book on Liszt, a technical study with analytical notes, but it never appeared.

[64] A collection of Warlock's 'limericks and other poems' was privately printed under the title *Cursory Rhymes* 'in the best interests of morality' by the Warlock Society in 2000 in a limited edition of 100 copies.

Constant to do likewise, and they both had a love of cats, which were very much in evidence at Eynsford.[65]

Like Heseltine, Constant had a taste for the grotesque, and the writer Jack Lindsay remembered being invited by him to see, with Nina Hamnett, one of the melodramas performed at Collins' Music Hall in Islington. After obligatory drinks at The Plough in Museum Street, they piled into taxis. Nina Hamnett continued the story:

> I heard that a season of melodramas was being held at Collins' Music Hall. Constant Lambert was most anxious to go, so a party of eight hired the two stage boxes, I think for 12s. 6d. each. It has a long bar at the back where you can both drink and watch the show. This is all right for music hall turns, but with the intimacy of melodrama one has, alas, to be near. The play was 'The Executioner's Daughter' and it was a masterpiece of horror. It was played by a stock company and the executioner's daughter was supposed to be sixteen and have a lame leg. She was in reality about 45. The villain was a splendid specimen. He had black, bushy eyebrows, fiery eyes and a large black moustache. He seemed to be fascinated by Constant Lambert and in the intervals of murdering people he would pop up his head into the box and glare into Constant's face. In the play nine people were bumped off and the General Post Office blown up. We were so enthralled that when we *did* meet in the bar for the interval, we rushed back to our boxes so as not to miss anything.[66]

Lindsay concluded:

> We had drunk copiously in the long bar during the intervals. After, we hurried to a nightclub and the party broke up. We went once again to Collins' with Constant, this time with a less noisy group, eating first at a Soho restaurant.[67]

When Lindsay called on Constant, it was usually in the company of Heseltine, and then it was poetry that they seemed to discuss rather than music. Jack Lindsay was present on 27 April 1926 with Nina Hamnett, Augustus John, Arnold Bennett and the young Cecil Beaton at the second public performance of *Façade* when Constant recited for the first time. Nina had further links with Constant; in her youth she had attended evening classes at the London School of Art where George Lambert was her favourite teacher.[68] After the war she had spent some time in Paris where she had become acquainted with Georges Auric (she knew all Les Six and had been to Satie's funeral), and Constant took her and Auric to visit Edmund Dulac in his studio.[69] She took the opportunity to draw Lambert, Poulenc and Auric (possibly when the latter two were in London for the English premieres of *Les Biches* and *Les Matelots*), and when she suddenly found herself short of money she offered the drawings to a friend for sale.

[65] Michael Ayrton once commented that Lambert only liked cats that didn't belong to anyone. Lambert proudly proclaimed to be president of the Kensington Kittens and Neuter Cats Club (*Who's Who in Music*, Shaw Publishing Co., 1949–50).

[66] Hamnett, *Is She a Lady?*, pp. 63–4.

[67] Lindsay, *Fanfrolico and After*, p. 94.

[68] 'George Lambert was the best professor I have ever had. He drew beautifully and took endless pains over anyone whom he thought had talent.' *Laughing Torso: Reminiscences of Nina Hamnett* (New York: Long & Smith, 1932), p. 21.

[69] Edmund Dulac (1882–1953), French artist – especially with watercolours – and illustrator of books. In a memorial broadcast talk on Lambert on 21 August 1951, Walton stated that Dulac brought Lambert to the notice of Diaghilev. But Dulac is not mentioned in either Lifar's or Buckle's biographies of Diaghilev, and there seems to be no further evidence to corroborate Walton's statement. See also chapter 3 n. 87.

AFTER leaving the Royal College of Music at the end of the Easter Term 1926, Constant had a productive period of composition. In August, while staying with the Sitwells in Derbyshire, he completed an orchestral seven-movement *Divertimento* that was soon to be reshaped into his next ballet, *Pomona*. In October he and Heseltine each orchestrated one of Delius's *Four Old English Lyrics*. In July the previous year Philip, with Moeran, had visited Delius at his home at Grez-sur-Loing in France. 'The poor old fellow is in a very bad state – completely blind and so paralysed that he cannot stand or walk even with assistance', he wrote.[70] Since his school days Heseltine had been a passionate devotee of Delius's, at a time when the older composer had not yet gained full recognition in England. Philip was two when his own father had died, and he increasingly turned to Delius for advice about his own future in music. He made piano transcriptions of many of Delius's works and wrote the first full-length study of the composer, which was published in 1923. Such an intense involvement inevitably brought a reaction, and his enthusiasm waned towards the end of his life. Constant's fondness for Delius's music was not quite as all-embracing as Philip's, but some of that enthusiasm must have rubbed off on him. Of the two Delius songs, Heseltine orchestrated 'So white, so soft, so sweet is she', while Constant took the setting of Thomas Nashe's 'Spring, the sweet Spring' that he was himself to set some years later in his largest work, *Summer's Last Will and Testament*. Songs were to form a very small part of his own œuvre; perhaps he felt himself too much in the shadow of Heseltine's extensive output in that genre, especially the latter's song-cycle *The Curlew* of which he was especially fond. After the Sitwell songs that he composed while at the Royal College, the only others he was to produce were the eight settings of Chinese poems by Li-Po that he dedicated to the Chinese actress Anna May Wong.

Constant's obsession for Anna May Wong[71] typified the kind of woman to whom he was most attracted, those who were somewhat oriental in appearance. This was to be true of both his wives, of the very young Margot Fonteyn with whom he was to have the longest lasting of his affairs, and the young Japanese (or Chinese) soprano he took on holiday to Ischia before his second marriage. There were also passing relationships with coloured women. As he was a keen film-goer, it is probable that his infatuation for the Chinese film star began after seeing her as the scantily dressed slave-girl in *The Thief of Bagdad*, made in 1924 and starring Douglas Fairbanks. A vogue for oriental mysteries helped elevate her to stardom, and she appeared in a number of silent films. In November 1928 Constant went with Angus Morrison to see her in *Show Life*. The following year she had a leading role in her first British silent film, *Piccadilly*, which was shown in London in February, and in March Constant went to the New Theatre to see her in the flesh, in *The Circle of Chalk*, a Chinese morality play, also starring Laurence Olivier, that capitalised on Miss Wong's cinematic fame. If critics found her dancing on stage entrancing, the same could not be said of her spoken voice (the cruel fate of many actors and actresses when they moved from silent films into the talkies).[72] According to Shead, Constant met his idol at the theatre 'but Miss Wong made it

---

[70] Letter from Philip Heseltine to Edward Clark, 26 July 1925, in Warlock, *Collected Letters*, vol. 4, p. 138.

[71] Anna May Wong (1907–1961) had appeared in a number of minor film roles before attracting attention as a slave girl in *The Thief of Bagdad* (1924). *Piccadilly* (1929) was her first British (silent) film. In 1932 she starred alongside Marlene Dietrich in Josef von Sternberg's *Shanghai Express*. Never married, she made few films after 1942.

[72] 'The voice was low, not unpleasing, but … possessed of only four usable tones, which she proceeded to exploit in every known musical variation. But oh! that Californian accent! As thick as the smog that now smothers their cities. Try as she might – and she did try – Anna May couldn't get rid of it.' Basil Dean, *Mind's Eye: An Autobiography, 1927–1972* (London: Hutchinson, 1973), p. 67. In *Cue for Music: An Autobiography* (London: Dennis Dobson, 1959),

painfully clear that enthusiasm, good looks and talent were not enough in an escort; money was necessary as well.'[73] Anthony Powell says that 'Constant did actually get as far as giving Anna May Wong dinner at the Savoy.'[74] Absorbed in all things Chinese, a month earlier on 26 September, he had gone with Angus to a cinema in Shaftesbury Avenue to see *Rose of Pu-Chul*, the first film with an all-Chinese cast and direction to be shown in England. The following evening they dined at a Chinese restaurant, and in July they had both been to Covent Garden to see *Turandot*. Constant went regularly with Angus to Chinese restaurants, and at home he drank quantities of Chinese wine in May Wong's honour (with unfortunate consequences). The musical culmination of this obsession was the dedication to her of his *Eight Poems of Li-Po*, and in February 1927 Heseltine wrote from Eynsford to his friend from Oxford days, the poet Robert Nichols:

> Do you by any chance know an address that would find one Anna May Wong, a Chinese actress who has worked with Fairbanks? A young composer who is staying with me at present – the only Englishman under 30 with any real ability for composition that I know – is so smitten with her beauty that he wants to write and ask if he may dedicate to her two books of songs which are settings of poems by Li-Po in the excellent translation of the Japanese Obata. The songs are really very charming.[75]

Originally composed for voice and piano, these Li-Po settings were not conceived as a cycle of eight songs. As soon as the first four were finished, in October 1926, Constant was anxiously trying to find a publisher. After at least one rejection, he was fortunate in having them accepted in 1927 by the music department of Oxford University Press, almost certainly through Hubert Foss. To these four by December 1926 he had added a further three which were published by J. & W. Chester in 1928. In October of the following year, after his rebuttal by Anna May Wong, he added an eighth, appropriately 'The Long-Departed Lover' (OUP 1930), scoring all except 'Lines Written in Autumn' for an ensemble of flute, oboe, clarinet, string quartet and double bass in time to conduct them himself at the end of the month in the Aeolian Hall, with soprano Odette de Foras, who had been a fellow student at the Royal College. ('Lines Written in Autumn' had to wait to be scored until 1947 when the whole sequence received its first performance in the Third Programme.)

Constant was not alone among composers in turning to Chinese poetry. Out of Heseltine's many songs only one, *Along the Stream* (1917), was a setting of a Chinese poem, also by Li-Po, in a translation by Lancelot Cranmer-Byng, but his melancholy 1924 Yeats cycle, *The Curlew*, scored for flute, cor anglais and string quartet, could not have been far from Constant's mind. Mahler had set four poems of Li-Po in *Das Lied von der Erde* (1908–9), a song-cycle of six Chinese poems, using free German translations by Hans Bethge, but it is unlikely that Constant knew this work at the time he was composing his own settings. First performed in England under Sir Henry Wood in January 1914, *Das Lied* was not heard again in this country until 1930. Yet when he did hear the work, in February 1936, conducted by Bruno Walter, he wrote that it had 'many unforgettable moments', picking out the second song, 'Solitude in Autumn',

---

Ernest Irving describes how he was asked to write the music for *The Circle of Chalk*. He also composed a Chinese song-cycle, *Love behind the Lattice*.

[73] Shead, *Constant Lambert*, pp. 70–1.

[74] Anthony Powell, 'Self-destruction the Lambert way' [a review of Motion, *The Lamberts*], *Daily Telegraph*, 25 April 1986, p. 14.

[75] Letter from Philip Heseltine (Eynsford, Kent) to Robert Nichols, 6 February 1927, in Warlock, *Collected Letters*, vol. 4, p. 169.

whose sentiments matched closely his own setting of 'Lines Written in Autumn', and commenting: 'A beautiful piece of writing but it is marred by a deliberate chinoiserie on the one hand, and an occasional lapse into conventional Teutonic sentiment on the other. The finale, for all its fine moments, suffers from a rather low theatrical parade of grief, like an actor manager moving the audience to tears while he counts the dead-heads in the stalls.'[76] He quite likely knew Stravinsky's *Three Japanese Lyrics*, scored for two flutes (one doubling piccolo), two clarinets (one doubling bass clarinet), string quartet, and piano. He was almost certainly acquainted with Bernard van Dieren's then unperformed *Chinese Symphony* (c. 1914),[77] a more or less continuous work with settings of eight poems, two of which were by Li-Po (including one that Mahler had used), and he would probably also have known Arthur Bliss's settings of Li-Po in *The Ballads of the Four Seasons*, for voice and piano (1923), and the song-cycle *The Women of Yueh* (1923–4), for flute, oboe, clarinet, bassoon, string quartet, double bass and percussion.[78] Constant followed Bliss in using the translations by Shigeyoshi Obata that had not long been published.[79] Yet his own settings were quite unlike any others. As Deryck Cooke has written, 'The subtle simplicity and exquisite fragility of [Li-Po's] brief poems … are beautifully reflected in Lambert's cool, fragrant, allusive settings. The music, like the verse, consists of strings of separate images loosely connected by feeling. As one can single out a phrase or a line of the poetry for special admiration, so can one isolate a single melodic twist or harmonic progression from the music for the same purpose.'[80] Almost every song is of less than two minutes' duration, and a line in the fifth song, 'Nothing remains but the moon above the river', may serve as a reminder that, like Giraud's Pierrot, Li-Po was moonstruck, believed to have drowned while attempting when drunk to kiss the moon's reflection in the Yellow River.

The Aeolian Hall concert that included the Li-Po settings was a show-case for new works by Lambert, Hadley and Walton, 'three young English composers who are fast establishing reputations for themselves,' announced Havergal Brian in *Musical Opinion*.[81] Besides the London premiere of Walton's Piano Quartet, also new was Constant's Piano Sonata, performed by Gordon Bryan who was promoting the concert.[82] Dedicated to Thomas Earp,[83] the art critic, heavy drinker and friend of Gray and Heseltine, and composed partly while on holiday in Toulon and partly in London, it was a work that almost denied the term 'sonata' and puzzled some listeners, embracing as it does idioms of jazz, ragtime and the blues. The *Monthly Music Record* critic found it 'hard, brilliant and clever', making 'heavy demands on the piano's percussive effects'.

---

[76] *Sunday Referee*, 9 February 1936, reviewing a BBC performance (in English) on 2 February conducted by Oscar Fried.

[77] Lambert conducted the first performance of van Dieren's *Chinese Symphony* on 15 March 1935.

[78] First performed in New York in November 1923 in both piano and instrumental versions, Bliss's *The Women of Yueh* was not heard in Britain in the latter version until recorded in June 1973 for a broadcast in April 1975. Rawsthorne, who became a close friend of Lambert's, also composed a Chinese song-cycle, to texts by the poetess Tzu-Yeh in translations by Arthur Waley, first performed in March 1929. Bliss also included a Li-Po verse in his choral symphony *Morning Heroes* of 1930.

[79] Shigeyoshi Obata, *The Works of Li Po, the Chinese Poet* (New York: Dutton & Co., 1922; London: Dent, 1923).

[80] Deryck Cooke, sleeve-note to Argo RG50.

[81] *Musical Opinion*, December 1929, p. 230.

[82] Gordon Bryan (originally Bryan-Smith, 1895–1957), composer and pianist, was born in London and studied with Oscar Beringer and, just before the First War, with Percy Grainger. His first London appearance was in 1919. He was later resident in Bournemouth where he was a frequent concerto soloist.

[83] Thomas Wade Earp (1895–1958).

A year later in the same paper, at the time of the Sonata's publication, Edmund Rubbra referred to 'its rhythmic monotony and its melodic paucity', hoping for a new work that would 'show forth a purely musical imagination over and above mere rhythmic and technical devices that titivate the ear but rarely enter the higher realms'.[84] Even Alan Frank, a friend of Lambert's and later head of the Oxford University Press music department, added in 1937 that 'a more justifiable criticism is that no single idea seems to last for more than a couple of bars. The resultant, and doubtless quite intentional, restlessness may end by becoming tiresome, as a perpetual stammer, though intelligent performance does much to dispel such an effect'.[85] The most sympathetic reviewer was Edwin Evans who wrote that 'to call it a "jazz" sonata as some have done is to exaggerate the significance of association' and looked instead at its ingenious structure.[86] Much later Richard McGrady, in *Music & Letters*, perceptively pointed out that in the first movement, 'whereas another composer might generate excitement and climax through the interaction of themes in their development, because of the nature of his material, this method is not available to Lambert' who turns instead to a cadenza for a central climax, a device he uses successfully in other piano works including *The Rio Grande*, not just simply for show but as a solution to a structural problem.[87] Nevertheless, the Sonata is a work that impresses by its almost restless energy and rhythmic drive, harmonic twists and chord clusters. A fast first movement is followed by a Nocturne with a bluesy *Lento e lugubre*, the dark mood occasionally being relieved by lighter, faster sections. The sombre mood persists in the opening to the third movement, also marked *lugubre*, that shares thematic material with the funereal passage in his later choral work *Summer's Last Will and Testament* to the words 'Farewell, earth's bliss'.

A MORE substantial work to emerge at this time was the ballet score *Pomona*, although it did not start as a ballet. In October 1926 Guy Warrack had included a short work of Constant's, *Champêtre*, in the first of three concerts he gave at the Aeolian Hall (with a first hearing of Walton's *Siesta* in his second concert). *Champêtre* had begun as one of two pastorals for piano composed earlier that year. Constant seems to have been dissatisfied with the second piece, *Paysage*, as he crossed through the manuscript, but he orchestrated *Champêtre* in London and Paris with the idea that it might serve as an entr'acte between the two tableaux in *Romeo and Juliet*. But when, as a result of his heated arguments with Diaghilev, a comic entr'acte without music was inserted instead, *Champêtre* became the promised 'new work' advertised for Warrack's concert on 16 October.[88] *The Monthly Musical Record* described it as 'a piquant little Anglo-French piece'[89] while the *Musical Times* critic merely reported that 'a little piece … by Mr Constant Lambert, a young hopeful of the Royal College of Music, said nothing much in a rather knowing and engaging way'. It eventually found its way into his next ballet.

[84] Edmund [Duncan-]Rubbra, 'Constant Lambert's Sonata', *The Monthly Musical Record*, December 1930, p. 35.

[85] Alan Frank, 'The Music of Constant Lambert', *The Musical Times*, vol. 78, issue no. 1137 (November 1937), p. 943. He went on to say that this criticism held also for the Concerto for Piano and Nine Players.

[86] Evans, 'Constant Lambert', p. 186.

[87] McGrady, 'The Music of Constant Lambert', *Music & Letters*, vol. 51 (1970), pp. 242–58.

[88] The concert also included an overture by Arne, Haydn's 'Le Matin' Symphony and Bliss's Rhapsody for soprano and tenor voices and small orchestra (soloists Odette de Foras and A. Winter).

[89] *The Monthly Musical Record*, 1 December 1926, p. 361.

In November the conductor Anthony Bernard put the seven-movement *Divertimento* into one of his Chelsea Music Club concerts. Constant, looking for publishers for his new works, was asking Heseltine's advice. As well as informing him of the forthcoming concert, he gave an amusing account of a visit he had made to the eccentric composer Kaikhosru Sorabji:

> Talking of comic composers I spent rather a ga-ga evening with Sorabji last night. He made one good remark which should appeal to Moeran. Pointing to a bar in one of his numerous concerti which seemed to be simultaneously in 1/1, 3/2, 7/4, 11/8, & 13½/16 rhythm I asked timidly 'What time is that bar in?' He said 'Oh that's in no particular time, it's just a swurge'!
>
> He has also written 64 variations & triple fugue on the theme 'Dies Irae' – the last 7 variations are labelled after the 7 deadly sins – he pointed out with undisguised glee the numerous trills in the Lechery section!
>
> Voigt,[90] I'm afraid, has returned Champêtre & the Chinese songs. What had I better do now? I had thought of trying Augeners for Champêtre & the Oxford Press for the songs. Will you do it or shall I? Anyhow write to me about it if you have time. Anthony Bernard is going to perform the Divertimento at the Chelsea Town Hall next Tuesday. It should be an auspicious occasion as the number of the date (16th) is the same as the number of movements (7) & of players (34)! I hope you will be able to come. Is he by any chance doing 'Capriol' at the same concert[?] I hope so.[91]

The *Divertimento* earned a favourable notice from the *Monthly Musical Record* critic who wrote: 'Mr Lambert's new Divertimento ... shows, as is natural in the work of a very young man, many fashionable influences, not omitting "The Six". But there is already skill in this pen, and there is plenty of time for a personality to develop. The "Pastorale" was agreeable hearing.'[92] Angus Morrison was convinced that Constant had the idea of a ballet in mind from the very beginning and had only given the collective title of *Divertimento* as a temporary measure, purely for the purpose of a concert performance, until he could find a suitable scenario. It was while staying at Mrs Travers Smith's that he met the Irish poet Thomas McGreevy who suggested the story of Pomona and Vertumnus. Converting the *Divertimento* into *Pomona* required little effort: he added 'Champêtre' as an Intrata, deleted the introductory five bars to the last movement, Marcia, stuck the two scores together and retitled the front cover.[93] As with *Romeo and Juliet*, it was a ballet for which the music had been written before the story attached to it had been planned. The classical tale of Pomona was slightly simplified for its eight individual movements:

> INTRATA (Andantino pastorale) – At the rise of the curtain, Pomona, goddess of fruits, and her nymphs are discovered in an orchard in a wood near Rome, the nymphs in little groups, Pomona apart.
>
> No. 1 CORANTE (Allegro deciso) – The sound of a hunting horn is heard. The god Vertumnus and his train of immortals, all wearing hunting attire, enter. Vertumnus makes attempts to gain favour with Pomona, but she repulses him

---

[90] Ernest R. Voigt, manager of Hawkes & Son, publishers.

[91] Letter from Lambert to Heseltine, 9 November 1926. Lambert may have met Sorabji through Sacheverell Sitwell who was a mutual friend. One of his earliest meetings was on 9 November 1925 when he, Sorabji and Heseltine were invited to tea with Walton and the Sitwell brothers.

[92] *The Monthly Musical Record*, 1 December 1926, p. 361.

[93] For this reason the presence of the autograph score of the *Divertimento* went undetected in the British Library until noticed by the present author.

and then, frightened by the bolder advances of Vertumnus and the immortals, she and her nymphs fly into the wood, Pomona with the eldest. Vertumnus watches her departure; then, disgusted with the failure of his disguise, expresses his chagrin in a dance. But it is with new decision that he leads his train away.

No. 2 PASTORALE (Andante tranquillo) – Pomona comes back timidly and expresses her sense of isolation in a dance. She goes.

No. 3 MENUETTO (Allegretto) – The nymphs re-enter timidly, but are disappointed to find the hunters gone and dance with melancholy. They are interrupted by the return of the immortals, who, having discarded their hunting attire, make a gentler entry this time. Pomona comes back quietly, and unnoticed, looks on while the immortals succeed little by little in gaining favour with the nymphs and leading them away one by one. At the end she is again alone.

No. 4 PASSACAGLIA (Serioso) – Vertumnus returns disguised as a lady of uncertain age. He endeavours to comfort Pomona. He succeeds, and casting off his disguise follows Pomona into the wood.

No. 5 RIGADOON (Vivace) – Divertissement danced by the nymphs and immortals.

No. 6 SICILIANA (Andantino dolce) – Vertumnus comes back to the orchard with Pomona. They dance a pas de deux expressive of their love for each other.

No. 7 MARCIA (Finale: Allegro, molto risoluto e pomposo) – Joyous return of nymphs and immortals. Nuptial dance. Procession. Solemn entry of Flamen Pomonalis, who gives the nuptial benediction and receives as a precious relic the woman's costume worn by Vertumnus. Curtain.

If the energy and bustle of *Romeo and Juliet* had partly masked its neo-classical anonymity, *Pomona* is altogether more personal, its beautiful opening suggesting a cool Arcadian pastoral scene, a mood echoed in the Siciliana, which was a favourite measure of Lambert's and Walton's.[94] The score alternates between movements of calm and vigour, and altogether has more unity and assurance than *Romeo and Juliet*. With a ground bass in the Passacaglia, the critic Eric Blom pointed out its classical design:

> *Pomona* falls into sections very much like Purcell's *Languished Lessons* or Bach's English Suites: a string of dances preceded by a prelude. The scheme is this: Intrata; No. 1 Corante; No. 2 Pastorale; No. 3 Minuetto; No. 4 Passacaglia; No. 5 Rigadoon; No. 6 Siciliana; No. 7 Marcia. All the numbered pieces, it will be noted, are dances, with the exception of Nos 2 & 7, and even they are bare movements of the kind the suite would admit in its more elastic examples, such as Bach's partitas.'[95]

Pomona pervades an aura of classic beauty that, by comparison, can make *Romeo and Juliet* seem slightly contrived.

When *Pomona* was revised by Sadler's Wells Ballet in September 1937, McGreevy was annoyed to see that his name had been omitted from the programme, and he pressed his claims of authorship to OUP, the publishers of the score. Lambert wrote to Hubert Foss:

---

[94] Angus Morrison wrote that Lambert 'always had a very special affection for [the Siciliana], and when I was asked to play pieces by Lambert and Walton at a musical party he made an exquisite little transcription of it for two hands as a companion piece to the Waltz from *Façade* arranged by Walton' (unpublished manuscript).

[95] Eric Blom, 'Constant Lambert as a Composer', *The Listener*, 12 September 1940, p. 393.

I was very amused to get the McGreevy letter. He seems to have wildly overestimated the part he played by the so-called 'author' in a ballet, particularly in the present instance.

'Pomona' is referred to as Lambert's 'Pomona' in exactly the same way as one speaks of Stravinsky's 'Petrouchka' or 'Sacre du Printemps' in spite of the fact that Benois in the first instance and Roerich in [the] second suggested many details in the scenario. It is one thing to write a libretto, another thing to suggest that a composer should write a ballet on an existing theme. Because Bakst suggested the theme of Daphnis and Chloe to Ravel does anyone seriously suggest that one should get in touch with Bakst's executor before staging a revival of the work?

In the present instance Mr McGreevy's part in the collaboration was even smaller than usual. He drew my attention to the old legend of Vertumnus and Pomona and suggested it might make a good ballet. I agreed but immediately suggested certain modifications in the story and adapted it to a previously existing orchestral suite which had already been performed. This side of the work was naturally carried out by myself for the simple reason that McGreevy is not a musician. McGreevy then suggested one or two small details (which incidentally have never been carried out by either of the choreographers) and wrote out a précis of the plot in English and French. That he, after spending an idle evening with Lemprière, should be given on the title page of Pomona the same acknowledgement as is due to Nijinska and myself is purely a matter of artistic politeness (a thing to which McGreevy coming from Dublin, is probably unused). 'Pomona' was performed first in Buenos Ayres, secondly in London. In each case McGreevy was employed in Paris which made it impossible to get his practical consultation even had he enjoyed the theatrical knowledge and experience which would have made this consultation necessary.

As regards the unsatisfactory 'elucidation' of certain points in his 'text' may I point out that the choreographer has the final say on what is theatrically and plastically effective. Nijinska introduced several modifications even at the first performance and Ashton has done no less than three versions of the choreography. (This of course is quite in order. Massine's version of the 'Sacre' was quite different from Nijinsky's and Roerich's name was not even mentioned.)

The modifications introduced by Ashton have naturally necessitated a slight alteration of McGreevy's text in the programme. This is no way due to any underestimation of McGreevy's gifts as a literary man, but one obviously can't describe in the programme things that don't happen on the stage.

That his name was omitted was purely an unfortunate oversight. It has already been apologised for and the mistake has been corrected.

If McGreevy has a financial claim to make I shall only be too pleased to consider it. But his artistic claims are both amateurish and untenable.[96]

The score bears a dedication 'To A.B.' Morrison, in the draft text of his proposed book on Lambert, wrote: 'I happen to know that these initials are those of a lady with whom he was very much in love at the time, but as he himself wished not to betray her identity more explicitly I can do no less than observe the same discretion.' Years later he must have revealed the name to Richard Shead who disclosed her to be Angela Baddeley.[97] She was the same age as Constant and, before becoming known

---

[96] Letter from Lambert to Foss, 31 October 1937. The credit in the published score (a piano duet arrangement by Lambert, OUP 1928) reads: 'Theme by Thomas McGreevy'.

[97] Angela Baddeley (1904–76) is probably best remembered for her portrayal of Mrs Bridges in the television period drama series *Upstairs, Downstairs*.

as an actress, had, with her sister Hermione, studied dancing at the Margaret Morris Club in Chelsea for which Constant was occasionally the accompanist. (The Club was often frequented by artists, and Maurice Lambert did a portrait in bronze of Hermione in about 1925, and two portraits of another dancer, Kathleen Dillon, whom Angus Morrison was to marry in 1931.)[98]

Like *Romeo and Juliet*, *Pomona* received its first performance abroad. Bronislava Nijinska, to whom Constant had been so devoted during the staging of *Romeo and Juliet* at Monte Carlo, was artistic director of the Colón Ballet at Buenos Aires. It may have been her sympathy for Constant after the treatment that he had received from Diaghilev that made her accept *Pomona*. However it came about, it was presented on 9 September 1927, with Aquiles Lieti conducting. The décor was by Rodolfo Franco and the leading roles of Vertumnus and Pomona were danced by Eugene Lapitsky and Leticia de la Vega. Altogether four performances were given. There had been hopes that *Pomona* would be included in Anton Dolin's season of ballet at the Théâtre des Champs-Elysées in Paris in March 1928.[99] An announcement to this effect was made, but in the event it was not given. Although it was to prove popular, *Pomona* was neither seen nor heard in England until a BBC broadcast in 1929 and a staging by the Camargo Society the following year with Dolin.

Writing in *Footnotes to The Ballet*, Basil Maine singled out *Pomona* as an example of a ballet being excellently served by its composer, noting how 'with an ingenious economy of means the music reflects the naïveté of the action' and commenting on the extreme clarity being achieved by the instrumentation and the skilful contrapuntal writing.[100] The score even won praise from Gerald Finzi when spending a weekend with Constant's former teacher R. O. Morris and his wife. 'Lambert's "Pomona" is a hundred-fold improvement on his "Romeo and Juliet",' he wrote to Howard Ferguson.[101]

However, the skilful contrapuntal writing and neo-classical lines of his ballet scores were to give way to another, very different style in his next work, one that was to prove his most famous, influenced by his love of jazz that had been stirred after seeing a particular London show.

---

[98] Kathleen Dillon, with whom the artist Edward Wadsworth had an affair in 1929, danced in the first English performance of Stravinsky's *Pastorale*, choreographed by Morris, at the Margaret Morris Club, London on 7 May 1917.

[99] Anton Dolin (1904–83), born Patrick Healey in Sussex, had a small part in Diaghilev's 1921 London production of *The Sleeping Princess*, and in 1923 joined the Ballets Russes in Monte Carlo, becoming for a while one of its leading male dancers. He later formed an important dance partnership with Alicia Markova.

[100] Basil Maine, 'The Score', in Brahms, *Footnotes to the Ballet*, p. 150.

[101] Letter from Finzi to Ferguson, in *Letters of Gerald Finzi and Howard Ferguson*, ed. Howard Ferguson and Michael Hurd (Woodbridge: Boydell & Brewer, 2005), pp. 44–5.

6

1927–30
The Rio Grande and Jazz

WHILE Walton, Morrison and Lambert were living so close together in Chelsea, they frequently enjoyed each other's company, with Constant quite likely providing light relief for William after the somewhat stifling atmosphere at nearby Carlyle Square with the Sitwells.[1] They would go to concerts and shows together, and one show in particular attracted their attention, one that for Constant, near the close of his first year at the Royal College of Music, was to affect his musical future.

At the end of May 1923 a Cochran revue called *Dover Street to Dixie* opened at the London Pavilion. It was a curious mixture of British entertainers and American Negro artists, kept in separate halves as if following Kipling's 'East is East' dictum. It ran for three months during the summer, creating little stir in the press. But for Constant it was the experience of a lifetime. Whether or not he attended the opening night, he certainly went the following week with Angus Morrison who retained clear memories of the show and the effect that it had on his companion. Of the first half he remembered only that 'the songs were dull, the sketches lacking in wit and point, and the artists second-rate'. But the second half more than made up for the inadequacies of the first, so much so that after seeing one performance many, like Constant and Angus, were so attracted to that part of the show that they would find out when the second half began and arrive just in time for it. As Morrison has described it:

> The scene was laid 'Way Down South' and the setting utterly simple and unpretentious. Some typical Dixie landscape I suppose, painted with the unobtrusive competence and complete lack of artistic self-consciousness of the professional music-hall scene designer. A view of hills and river in which (as I remember) the members of Will Vodery's [Plantation] orchestra were grouped at the back of the stage on an old river boat moored at the side of the bank – evoking the same atmosphere of the warm Southern States and 'Old Man River' that the Drury Lane musical comedy *Showboat* was to make so much more fashionable and popular a few years later.
>
> The arresting start of the whole performance was a sort of fanfare-like fantasia on the tune of 'Carry me back to old Virginia'. The Delius-like harmonies were made to sound even more lush and glowing by the clear, uninhibited playing of this magnificent Negro band in much the same way that 'The Last Rose of Summer' say, played on a cornet solo, can hit below the belt emotionally far more effectively than when heard under more musically respectable conditions. It was indeed the memory of the very opening flourish played by the superb first trumpeter, Johnny Dunn (described in the programme as 'the creator of Wa Wa') that remained with Constant all through his life ...[2]

The star of the show was the 27-year-old singer, Florence Mills. Born to ex-slave parents in the slums of Washington DC, she had risen to fame as the centre of an all-black show in the Plantation Restaurant on Broadway, and the British impresario C. B. Cochran brought her to London.[3] Morrison continued:

---

[1] Osbert and Sacheverell Sitwell. Edith lived apart at 22 Pembroke Mansions, Bayswater.

[2] Angus Morrison, draft manuscript, Royal College of Music library.

[3] The first all-Negro musical had been *In Dahomey*, with lyrics by Paul Dunbar and music by Will Marion Cook, a pupil of Dvořák. It came from Broadway to London and ran from mid-May through to Boxing Day 1903, returning in 1918.

The other strong impression made on [Lambert] by the performance, exciting an influence more general and all-embracing and with even deeper emotional repercussions – was the incomparable personality of Florence Mills herself. Personally I can never forget the particular quality of her charm and magnetism and always regard her as one of the most perfect artists in her own field that I have ever had the good fortune to hear and see ...

After the pungent, yet softly caressing quality of the coloured voices had plunged one straight into the right atmosphere, with an opening chorus of peculiarly haunting charms she made her first entrance, dressed (rather like a pantomime Dick Whittington) in conventional stage rags with a bundle on her shoulder, singing 'The Sleepy Hills of Tennessee'. Just another of the many songs on the theme of that longing to return to rustic simplicity so perennially popular in the world of light music – a song no better or worse than countless others of the same sort. ... Florence Mills brought tears to one's eyes purely by the quality of her voice and the sincerity of her acting.

The *Times* reviewer, finding the show 'a queer mixture of black and white and of East and West', did at least admit that the Dixie performers were 'easily the most entertaining and convincing part of the production'. Angus's diaries indicate that he and Constant went to see the show together on at least three occasions before it closed at the beginning of September, and Walton recalled 'going night after night with [Constant] to hear Florence Mills, that great coloured singer, and to hear Will Vodery's band'.[4]

On a number of occasions in his writings and broadcasts, Lambert referred to the show and how, 'after the rather hum-drum playing of the English orchestra in the first part it was an electrifying experience to hear Will Vodery's band play the Delius-like fanfare that preceded the second. It definitely opened up a whole new world of sound.'[5] That 'extremely beautiful prelude that, apart from its orchestration, might have been written by Delius' was to haunt him, and 'the change from the English theatre orchestra playing what was to all intents and purposes ragtime, to the negro jazz band was one of the most startling experiences of [his] life.'[6]

Morrison was in no doubt that this was a key experience for Constant, one that confirmed his life-long preoccupation with jazz and gave birth to ideas of blending many of its rhythmic inventions and subtleties into the texture of more serious music. Up till then no music had moved him quite so deeply and emotionally, and Morrison drew a parallel with Delius's experience of hearing Negroes singing on the plantations in Florida. From that moment jazz elements were to pervade most of Constant's scores, notably in works like *The Rio Grande*, *Elegiac Blues* and the Piano Sonata.

In September 1926 Florence Mills and the Plantation Orchestra returned to the London Pavilion with a new all-Negro show, *Blackbirds*,[7] but this time Angus was rather more restrained with his enthusiasm, later commenting:

[4] William Walton, *Constant Lambert: In Memoriam*, 7 October 1951, BBC Radio *Music Magazine* 1951. 'All of which,' Walton observed, 'left its mark when he came to write *The Rio Grande*, the Piano Sonata, the Concerto for piano and seven instruments [actually nine players] and the *Elegiac Blues* in memory of Florence Mills.'

[5] Lambert, *The New Statesman and Nation*, 27 February 1932, p. 274. In the same article Lambert was very critical of English jazz bands: 'If there is a band that actually supplies "swamp stuff" in this country then it is my hard lot never to have heard it, for to me the strains of the English jazz kings conjure up nothing more barbaric than a *thé dansant* at a seaside resort on a wet Sunday afternoon out of season.'

[6] Lambert, 'The Origins of Modern Dance Music', *The Listener*, 22 April 1936, pp. 792–3.

[7] Florence Mills never recorded for the gramophone, but on 12 January 1926, well in advance of the show's London opening, the Plantation Orchestra (actually the Pike Davies Orchestra

After the earlier show the later 'Blackbirds', with its greater sophistication and far more conscious sense of 'presentation' was in some ways a disappointment, and it was Florence Mills, alone of all the company, who still retained the essential simplicity and child-like quality that had made the whole Plantation performance so utterly endearing.

Nevertheless, the show took London by storm and he still went along with Constant on several occasions, especially towards the end of the show's eight-and-a-half month run, and they attended the last performance on 14 May 1927.[8] For his part Constant had lost nothing of this enthusiasm, writing:

> It is no exaggeration to say that if one wants a really perfect ensemble, whether in dancing, singing or orchestral playing, one should go to such an entertainment as *Blackbirds*, rather than to the Ballet, the Opera or the Queen's Hall.[9]

James Agate, in the *Sunday Times*, wrote of the show's star performer:

> Miss Florence Mills is a superb artist, whether she is imitating the epileptic frenzy of a witch-dance or indulging in her native melancholy. The notes she warbles are real wood notes, and you would say that her voice is untrained. This singer has taken her high C and come down again while more ponderous prima donnas are still debating the ascent ...[10]

But at the end of such a long run Mills was not just exhausted but ill. A tour of the provinces was cut short after her appearance at Liverpool when it became apparent that she needed serious medical attention. She had a rest in Germany but then flew back to America where she was admitted too late to hospital, dying there on 1 November. In her memory Constant was moved to write his *Elegiac Blues* in which he recalled the opening of the *Dover Street to Dixie* fanfare (Ex. 1)[11] that had so appealed to him when he first saw her on stage. Its rising flourish was so reminiscent of her that he used it to great effect throughout the piece (Ex. 2). Composed initially for the piano in the month of her death, he orchestrated it the following year.

Constant referred to the Fanfare as being Delius-like because rising triplets were a characteristic of that composer's style, found nowhere more effectively than in the popular *The Walk to the Paradise Garden* interlude from his opera *A Village Romeo and Juliet* (Ex. 3) where the bitter-sweet nature of the music depicts the doomed lovers enjoying their last moments of happiness. Rising triplets became a feature of much of Constant's music too, as, for example, in his Piano Sonata (Ex. 4).

---

named after its leader) cut four 78 sides of numbers from the *Blackbirds* revue (Columbia 4185 & 4238: *Silver Rose, Smiling Joe, Arabella's Wedding Day* and *For Baby and Me*). The band consisted of two trumpets (Pike Davies and Johnny Dunn), two violins, two clarinets doubling alto saxophone, tenor saxophone, trombone, bass brass, banjo, piano and drums.

[8] A fortnight later a pastiche revue, *White-Birds*, for which Bliss contributed *A Rout Trot* for piano, opened at His Majesty's Theatre. A 'short-lived ... theatrical disaster' (Anton Dolin, *Autobiography* (London: Oldbourne Book Co. 1960), p. 47) starring Maurice Chevalier, its best number involved the dancing of Anton Dolin and Ninette de Valois. It lasted two months.

[9] Lambert, 'Jazz', p. 127.

[10] James Agate, *Sunday Times*, 19 September 1926, reprinted in *Immoment Toys: A Survey of Light Entertainment on the London Stage, 1920–1943* (London: Jonathan Cape, 1945), p. 153.

[11] Reconstructed by Angus Morrison at the request of Christopher Palmer, *Delius: Portrait of a Cosmopolitan* (London: Duckworth, 1976), p. 35.

Ex. 1 *Dover Street to Dixie* Fanfare as reconstructed from memory by Angus Morrison

Ex. 2 Lambert, *Elegiac Blues*, bars 34–5

Ex. 3 Delius, *The Walk to the Paradise Garden*, fig. 11

Ex. 4 Lambert, Piano Sonata, opening

Another musician who went several times to see *Blackbirds* was 'Spike' Hughes,[12] son of the composer Herbert Hughes and a friend of Lambert and Walton. As an embryo jazz musician he was rather more fascinated by the pit orchestra, hearing for the first time 'Negro music played with all its characteristic colourfulness and vitality'.[13]

Constant was particularly annoyed at the general critical reaction. Referring to the Plantation Band in *Dover Street to Dixie*, he commented: 'Although they maintained an extraordinary high standard of musicianship throughout, it is hardly necessary to say that they were abused by the English press for their crudity and vulgarity.'[14] Jazz for most people at that time meant a new and exciting form of dance music, especially with the energetic dances styles that were sweeping across England after the gloom of the war. When in July 1919 a show opened in London with the title 'The Latest Craze', it was jazz dancing. The term jazz came to be used in a very broad sense but 'serious' musicians and critics generally viewed it with scorn and derision. In January 1919, at the London Coliseum, one critic was concerned at 'the effort of the orchestra to convert itself into a jazz band, one of those American peculiarities which threaten to make life a nightmare. The object of a jazz band, apparently, is to produce as much noise as possible; the method of doing so is immaterial.' When in April 1926 Paul Whiteman brought his band to London, the *Times* critic 'got rather weary after an hour of the queer noises produced, especially the muted brass and the trombone vibrato', and of

---

[12] Patrick 'Spike' Cairns Hughes (1908–87), jazz musician and music journalist. Studied composition with Egon Wellesz. Taught himself the double bass and formed his first jazz band in 1929. Much influenced by Duke Ellington.

[13] Spike Hughes, *Opening Bars: Beginning an Autobiography* (London: Pilot Press, 1946), p. 308.

[14] Lambert, *The New Statesman and Nation*, 27 February 1932, p. 274.

Gershwin's *Rhapsody in Blue*, one of the first attempts to amalgamate elements of jazz with symphonic music, that same critic wrote 'the composer does not know what to do with his themes'.[15]

Hamilton Harty, conductor of the Hallé Orchestra, was no more sympathetic towards jazz. Giving a presidential address to the Congress of the National Union of Organists' Association in Manchester on 31 August 1926, he told his audience that

> he had often listened to jazz with a sincere wish to find if it had any musical attraction whatever, but he had never found it to be anything but sensual, noisy and incredibly stupid. It possessed only two qualities that had anything to do with the art of music – rhythm and a certain cynical grotesqueness. The rhythm was generally far from subtle, and the grotesqueness was the result of treating instruments in a way that should result in three months' hard labour for the performers. The kindest thing to say about it was that it was just a noise for dancing, and the obligation that lay on musicians was to protest against such a travesty of music and find appropriate means of combating its vile influence.[16]

It is ironic, then, that Harty was soon to be largely responsible for the rise to fame of Constant's jazz-inspired *The Rio Grande*.

Walton and Lambert shared an early interest in jazz and dance music. In Walton's case this showed itself in the polka, waltz and other dance rhythms in *Façade*, and he once expressed a liking for such exponents of swing music and jazz as Duke Ellington, Spike Hughes and Benny Goodman,[17] while Constant was to have a strong admiration for Ellington, not just as a performer but as a composer. He came to know him personally, as Spike Hughes remembered:

> When the Duke first came here in 1933 I don't think that he [Ellington] and I and Constant ever went to bed at all. We used to go to little night clubs, real sort of night clubs in Soho with an iron door and a hole and southern fried pork chops, and we sat there always until dawn.[18]

(Ellington's *Rude Interlude* was apparently so named because of Constant's wife Florence's habit of calling his well-known number *Mood Indigo* as *Rude Indigo*.)[19] Both Lambert and Walton turned their hands to writing dance music, though without much success. Through Osbert Sitwell, Walton had met Richmond Temple, a director of the Savoy Hotel, who in turn introduced him to Debroy Somers who led the popular 11-piece dance band, the Savoy Orpheans, which started up in 1923,[20] Walton attempted some dance arrangements for Somers but, as he later admitted, he 'wasn't slick enough, somehow … to write those sort of tunes'. Constant had made similar attempts, much later confessing: 'At a time when I very foolishly imagined that I could write fox-trots, and even more foolishly imagined that I might be able to sell them, I played my latest

---

[15] *Rhapsody in Blue* was premiered in New York on 12 February 1924, and first heard in England on 15 June 1925 in a broadcast relayed from the Savoy Hotel with Debroy Somers conducting the Savoy Orpheans and the Savoy Havana Band, with Gershwin as soloist (*Radio Times*).

[16] *The Times*, 1 September 1926.

[17] Interview with Charles Stuart for *The Yorkshire Observer*, 21 December 1942, p. 2.

[18] *Constant Lambert Remembered*, BBC Third Network, 25 June 1966. Sidonie Goossens recalled Spike Hughes bringing Duke Ellington to the flat of her husband Hyam Greenbaum in July 1933.

[19] Derek Jewell, *Duke: A Portrait of Duke Ellington* (London: Hamish Hamilton, 1977), p. 50.

[20] The Savoy Orpheans consisted of piano, banjo, violin, soprano, alto and tenor saxophones, two trumpets, trombone, tuba and percussion. Somers left in 1926, and in 1928 Carroll Gibbons reformed the band as the Savoy Hotel Orpheans.

effort to a leader of a dance band. When I had finished he said with withering patronage, "I don't call that a 'number', I call that an 'etoode'."'[21]

But this did not stop them from attempting larger-scale works in jazz style. In 1926, in an article in the *Boston Evening Transcript*, Lambert revealed that 'for more than a year [Walton] did nothing but study jazz, writing and scoring foxtrots for the Savoy Orpheans Band and working at a monumentally planned concerto for two pianofortes, jazz band and orchestra. Although the concerto was finished and about to be performed, Walton suddenly abandoned the jazz style in a fit of disgust.'[22] This *Fantasia Concertante* was work in progress during 1923–5, before, it is worth pointing out, Gershwin's *Rhapsody in Blue* had been heard in England. Constant commented that 'those composers who have sought inspiration in jazz have not only made use of its exhilarating rhythmic qualities but have incorporated also the more obvious clichés', and in this work he accused Walton of being 'guilty of this himself'.[23] Walton wrote to his mother in May 1925: 'I have to see what can be done with my concerto with these Savoy people. Though I am afraid that there is only a remote chance of anything coming of it.'[24] And indeed it never materialised. The finest outcome of Walton's interest in jazz – with an equal debt to Stravinsky – was the breezy overture *Portsmouth Point* (1924–5) with its cross-rhythms and syncopation, in Constant's words 'the most violent syncopations of rhythm ... applied to his own melodic and harmonic basis' to steer clear 'of the monotonous four-square rhythm that is the depressing though essential feature of modern dance music'.

Walton's only surviving work for piano and orchestra was the result of another attempt, on 3 July 1927, to interest Diaghilev in a ballet score, a meeting confirmed by an entry in Angus Morrison's diary: 'Meeting with Diaghilev to play Willie's 3 movements on 2 pianos.' After a good lunch at Osbert's house, the company went over to Angus's house (where there were two pianos) and he and Walton played through a work written the previous autumn. Because of Constant's disagreement with Diaghilev it is quite likely that he was not present in case he spoiled Willie's chances, but, as Angus remembered, 'Diaghilev didn't bite ... He made some very charming remarks. I think he said, "You'll write better things later", ... [but] he was politeness and charm itself ..., thanking us for letting him come over to hear it. He was wonderfully courteous.'[25] However, by the new year Walton had transformed the score into his *Sinfonia Concertante* for piano and orchestra which received its first performance on 5 January 1928 in a Royal Philharmonic Society concert, with York Bowen the soloist and Ernest Ansermet conducting. Osbert's artistic friends supported the concert, with Stephen Tennant,[26] Cecil Beaton, Dick Wyndham and Rex Whistler[27] meeting at the Café Royal for a luncheon party before going on to Queen's Hall. Afterwards it was

[21] *Sunday Referee*, 3 July 1932. Philip Heseltine rewrote his piano send-up of César Franck's Symphony, *The Old Codger*, for Debroy Somers in November 1924, scoring it for piano, banjo, violin, soprano, alto and tenor saxophones, two trumpets, trombone and tuba: letter to Edward Clark, 8 November 1924, in Warlock, *Collected Letters*, vol. 4, p. 107.

[22] *Boston Evening Transcript*, 27 November 1926.

[23] Lambert, 'Some Recent Works by William Walton', p. 17. Curiously, a footnote in this same article states that the work was to be published by Oxford University Press.

[24] 4 May 1925: *Selected Letters of William Walton*, p. 35.

[25] Angus Morrison talk, in *British Music* 15 (1993), p. 27. His diary also records later that day: 'Dine with Hugh [Bradford] and Constant at the Ivy.'

[26] Stephen Tennant (1906–87), aristocratic member of the so-called 'Bright Young Things' and younger son of 1st Baron Glenconnor. Lover of Siegfried Sassoon and friend of William Walton, the Sitwells and others in their circle, Tennant led a generally decadent lifestyle.

[27] Rex Whistler (1905–44), painter, book illustrator, stage designer. Friend of the Sitwells, Cecil Beaton and Stephen Tennant, his work included designs for plays, revues, opera and ballet,

supper at the Savoy Grill and then on to the Chelsea Arts Ball. Angus and Constant chose instead to have supper at the long-established restaurant, Rules, in Covent Garden.

It is interesting to observe that at the same time that Walton was engaged on his scores involving piano and orchestra, Lambert was working on parallel pieces. While Walton was struggling with his large-scale *Fantasia Concertante*, Constant was completing a more modest 17-minute concerto for piano, two trumpets, timpani and strings, and while the ballet score intended for Diaghilev was being fashioned into the *Sinfonia Concertante*, Constant was composing what was to prove his most popular score, *The Rio Grande*, also a work for piano and orchestra – but with no woodwind. (A third concerted work for piano, with only nine players, was to follow in 1931.)

The earliest of Constant's three piano works, the Concerto of 1924, is a remarkably accomplished piece for someone only 18, and it remains a mystery why he never fully scored it and had it performed. Fortunately he left full details of its sparse instrumentation, but it wasn't heard until 1988 after the score had been realised by Edward Shipley and Giles Easterbrook. Whether or not, in having two trumpets, he was recalling Pike Davies and Johnny Dunn, the two trumpeters in the Plantation Orchestra for *The Blackbirds* show, there is nothing virtuosic or showy for that instrument in the Concerto, and it is unlikely that he was reworking the Overture that he had discarded from *Prize Fight* (which, unlike the remainder of that score, called for two trumpets) as the mood of the two works is very different. But, like *Prize Fight*, it is a work that could not have emerged without Constant's absorption of Stravinsky and the musical Parisian scene. Nevertheless it stands out as a personal score of much originality.

Cast in four continuous movements, its bold two-bar opening on timpani, *Allegro risoluto*, introduces a rhythm that is immediately taken up by the strings, leading soon to a short motif on violins that, like many Lambert ideas, is much repeated and varied, with the time signature altering from 3/4 to 4/4 and 5/4. An eerie rocking figure on the first violins leads eventually to the linked second movement, a whirlwind *Presto*, that is also heralded by two bars on timpani. The two trumpets, heard for the first time, pick up on repeated notes in thirds the rhythm of the timpani, and are followed by the piano with an important motif that dominates much of this movement. All then melts into a slow movement of great beauty and calm in which some earlier themes are recalled. Here the trumpets are at their most striking, as it were off-stage in Stravinskyian mood, the steady *piano* 3/4 tread of one against the 6/8 of the other. The last movement revisits the main themes, building to a *maestoso* statement and ending much as the work began, with the rhythm forcibly proclaimed on the same repeated note.

The solo piano, rather than take the lead as in a more conventional concerto, for much of the time weaves instead a decorative commentary throughout, and brilliant as the piano writing is in this work, it does not quite prepare one for the impact of *The Rio Grande*. In January 1929 Philip Heseltine wrote to his mentor Colin Taylor: 'The only other young Englishman under 25 is Constant Lambert – a more interesting composer and a much finer intelligence than Walton. He has written an admirable work *Rio Grande* (nothing to do with sea shantys!) for piano solo and orchestra (strings, brass and percussion only) with a mixed chorus; also an enchanting ballet-suite *Pomona* for small orchestra (OUP) ...'[28]

In contrast with Stravinsky's Concerto for Piano and Wind Instruments (1923–4) which has no strings (apart from double bass), *The Rio Grande* is scored for strings but

notably the ballet *The Rake's Progress* for Vic-Wells Ballet in 1935 and *The Wise Virgins* in 1940. He died in action while serving with the Welsh Guards.

[28] Philip Heseltine to Colin Taylor, 19 January 1929, in Warlock, *Collected Letters*, vol. 4, p. 217.

no woodwind, and with an impressive array of percussion.[29] Constant also broke away from the concerto mould by having a chorus, with a poem by Sacheverell Sitwell as its basis. It was to become the work by which he would be best known.

His initial choice of piano soloist came from an unexpected quarter. When *The Blackbirds* had completed its run at the London Pavilion, its place was taken by another Cochran revue, *One Dam Thing after Another*. One of its stars, alongside Jessie Matthews and Sonnie Hale, was the white American jazz pianist Edythe Baker who, according to the *Sunday Times* critic, 'contributed syncopated arabesques and fantasias, which showed that jazz only awaits its Chopin to become music.'[30] (Despite her great success, this turned out to be Edythe Baker's only professional engagement in England because she married a wealthy British banker and retired from the stage.)[31] Harold Rutland recalled how Constant

> came to see me one evening when I was living in Cheyne Walk, Chelsea, and brought the manuscript score of *The Rio Grande*, which he had just completed; so, as the River Thames flowed sedately by, I first heard those enlivening strains that celebrate the dancing in the city and the public squares 'as the great Rio Grande rolls down to the sea'. When he had played the work I asked him if he had anyone in mind as the soloist. To my surprise he mentioned Edyth[e] Baker, who was then delighting audiences (with her white piano) in a Cochran revue at the London Pavilion. ... Constant, I remember, left me that evening about 10 o'clock, saying that he was going on to a fancy-dress party at Augustus John's, and was thinking of dressing up as a sailor.[32]

According to Viva King (who, before the war, had an affair with the then-married Philip Heseltine) Constant was a regular visitor to John's home at Fryern Court, in Hampshire on the edge of the New Forest. She remembered him as being 'young, thin, and very good-looking and a non-stop talker; we got on extremely well together.'[33]

The Rio Grande was first heard in a BBC studio broadcast. Julian Herbage, one of the BBC programme planners, remembered first meeting Constant when he came to the Director of Music, Percy Pitt's office at Savoy Hill to play the work through.[34] It is quite likely that Edward Clark, by then also a programme planner for the BBC, was instrumental in having *The Rio Grande* accepted for broadcasting, but things at first did not run smoothly. On 9 January 1928, the BBC wrote to Lambert, informing him that the rehearsal of *The Rio Grande* had been arranged for Saturday 21 January

---

[29] See List of Compositions, Appendix 1. Beryl de Zoete, in her *Monthly Musical Record* article on Lambert written between the broadcasts and the first concert performance of *The Rio Grande*, besides mentioning 'eight brass instruments, five drum-players with about thirty drums', specifies nine strings, this presumably being the number suitable for broadcasting.

[30] *Sunday Times*, 29 May 1927, reprinted in Agate, *Immoment Toys*, p. 155. According to *The Times*, 21 May 1927: 'Miss Edythe Baker plays the piano, sings and dances cleverly and has distinct personality'.

[31] Fortunately, in the early 1920s in America, Edythe Baker cut a number of piano rolls for the Aeolian Company, and later in England she recorded a selection of her favourite numbers for the gramophone.

[32] Rutland, 'Constant Lambert and a Story of Chelsea Reach'.

[33] Viva King, *The Weeping and the Laughter* (London: Macdonald and Jane's, 1976), p. 159. Fryern Court was Augustus John's home from 1927. Viva King (née Booth), who was briefly engaged to Cecil Gray, described Heseltine as 'the only great passion' of her life (p. 95).

[34] Julian Herbage (originally Livingstone-Herbage, 1904–76) joined the BBC music staff in 1927 and was a programme planner until 1946, but he continued at the BBC for many years and is probably best remembered as co-editor with his wife Anna Instone (1912–78) of BBC's *Music Magazine*.

(4.30–5.30 p.m.) with the performance set for Monday. But the next day a BBC note bluntly announced: 'We very much regret to have to inform you that owing to a quite unforeseen but unavoidable programme change we will be unable to include your "Rio Grande" as we had hoped on January 23rd.' It was later announced that the performance was cancelled and the programme altered because of the 'imminent departure of Kathleen Long to America'. The alteration would seem to imply that Kathleen Long, who would have been known to Constant as she was on the staff of the Royal College of Music, was to have been the soloist in *The Rio Grande*. The premiere was rescheduled for over a month later, with Constant writing to Edward Clark:

> Is Feb. 27th official for the Rio Grande? I have received no notice. Would it be possible for me to be present at the last (or last two) <u>chorus</u> rehearsals. I think this is important & would save a great deal of time at the full rehearsal. I'm afraid I have let you in for a little extra expense as I find it is impossible to do with less than 5 percussion players (1 tympanist & 4 others). This looks a bit excessive but is, I think, necessary for this particular work. ... The parts could not be executed by 3 players without their leaping over each other's bodies like so many chamois & playing battledore & shuttlecock with gong & tambourine. I have been able to add a little more & the parts are now perfectly clear being divided as follows:

> 1st player: xylophone. Jeu de timbres. Δ (shared with 2nd)

> 2nd player: Δ. 1 Large Suspended Cymbal (Turkish crash). Castanets. Small Cow Bell (Mailloche, timp-sticks & large triangle beater or wooden hammer)

> 3rd player: 1 pair of Cymbals. Side Drum. Tambourine (shared with 4th player) optional Chinese tom-tom (wooden sticks & jazz brush)

> 4th player: Tambourine (shared with 3rd) Tenor Drum, Chinese Block, G.C. [Bass Drum] & Gong

> 5th player: 3 Timpani[35]

A week later Clark, concerned that the parts might not be ready, wrote to Constant: 'I fancy we arranged when we last met that you would write out all the wind and percussion parts necessary for the "Rio Grande" performance, and one copy each of the string parts, but that I would have the remainder of the last mentioned duplicated. ... Our librarian is beginning to get agitated.'[36] Eight days later Constant was enquiring about rehearsals: 'Can you let me know how much of this time I will have? A separate rehearsal of the cadenza (piano & percussion alone) would save a lot of time.'[37] In fact he was given a 'try-over rehearsal' six days before the broadcast, an hour's rehearsal with the chorus three days later, and a 90-minute rehearsal on the morning of the day itself.

The first performance of *The Rio Grande* took place on Monday 27 February 1928 in a late-evening 2LO broadcast from the BBC Savoy Hill studios. Constant conducted the Wireless Chorus and Orchestra in a 'Light Orchestral Concert' that also included works by Thomas, Verdi, Delibes, Rimsky-Korsakov and Johann Strauss. Angus Morrison, the work's dedicatee, was now the soloist, also playing *Three Spanish Dances* by Granados. Two days later Philip Heseltine wrote to his mother: 'I wonder if you

---

[35] Letter from Lambert to Clark, 31 January 1928: BBC Written Archives, Caversham.
[36] Letter from Clark to Lambert, 7 February 1928: BBC Written Archives, Caversham.
[37] Letter from Lambert to Clark, 15 February 1928: BBC Written Archives, Caversham.

heard Constant Lambert's "Rio Grande" on Monday last? He is the most interesting English composer under 30, and a great friend of mine.'[38]

Three days later Constant wrote to Kenneth Wright: 'Do I get paid anything for the Rio Grande and if so might I have it fairly soon as it would come in useful[?]' In his reply Wright outlined what then was the normal procedure as regards payment:

> I wish you had raised the question of fee before the show. In the ordinary way we do not pay composers for conducting their own work, particularly when as in your case we went to a certain amount of expense to have parts copied. On the other hand, if you had expressed desire that the point should be considered I would have had it put up, but they hate such applications being delayed until after the show is over. I would prefer therefore not to do so if you do not mind, but rather to make a case for a better fee than would have been approved for the repeat performance.[39]

Hoping to keep things sweet with the BBC, Constant had little option but to acquiesce, especially when he was hoping for the broadcast of another new work:

> As regards the fee I quite see your point of view. I had not expected anything for conducting. I only thought that works were automatically paid for according to length. Did Clark ever speak to you about my Symphonic Movement? I showed it to him about the same time as the Rio Grande – he seemed equally interested in it. The Oxford Press want to publish it but I naturally cannot let them do so until I am sure it comes off.[40]

Wright enlarged on the policy of payment ten days later:

> Works are paid for 'automatically' according to length in the case of those controlled by the P.R.S. with which we have a standing agreement arranged, it is true, on a rough basis of timing. On the other hand manuscript works of the nature of 'Rio Grande' are usually dealt with separately, as each arises. I suggest that the matter be dropped for the time being, and that when the next performance can be arranged we pay you a round figure of five guineas for the broadcasting right for the performance in question and for your conducting. The PRS rota is roughly 4/- per unit of three minutes.[41]

Constant's other new work, the *Symphonic Movement* – or *Music for Orchestra* as it was soon to be named – had been completed in 1927, and on 11 June of that year he had informed Kenneth Wright that the score was with the Oxford University Press. On 2 March 1928, four days after the first broadcast of *The Rio Grande*, the work was given a try-out at the BBC but, he was informed, 'circumstances made it impossible to have as large an orchestra as the score needs, particularly as regards strings'. He was anxious to have clear warnings of likely run-throughs as, he informed the BBC on 17 April, 'I now have an accompanying job and it is important for me to know when to get a substitute.' But nothing more happened until January 1929 when Wright, seeing that *Pomona* had been put down in a broadcast that Ernest Ansermet was to give in June of music by young British composers, thoughtfully suggested that, as *Pomona* was 'very light', the *Symphonic Movement* would make a better choice. But, to Constant's disappointment,

[38] Philip Heseltine to his mother, Edith Buckley Jones, 29 February 1928, from Eynsford, in Warlock, *Collected Letters*, vol. 4, p. 187.

[39] Letter from Wright to Lambert, 3 March 1928: BBC Written Archives, Caversham.

[40] Letter from Lambert to Wright, 5 March 1928; BBC Written Archives, Caversham.

[41] Letter from Wright to Lambert, 15 March 1928: BBC Written Archives, Caversham.

the programme went ahead as originally planned.[42] With uncharacteristic ingratitude he wrote to Edward Clark on 5 May:

> I am sorry that the B.B.C. do not consider my Symphonic Movement sufficiently interesting to perform. I was distinctly given to understand that Ansermet was to do this work in June & that I myself was to conduct 'Pomona' at some other concert. The Symphonic Movement was finished two years ago today and everyone who has studied the score has considered it my most important work. In spite of the many promises made by the B.B.C. it is still as far from performance as ever. I had always understood that it was to the B.B.C. that young English composers were to look for support & encouragement but the interest they have displayed has been of so tentative & grudging a nature that I am tempted to think that it is only abroad that the young English composer meets with any intelligent response to & enthusiasm for his work.

It was both unkind and unwise of him to have written so harshly to Clark in view of the support that he was giving to young British composers, especially Walton and Lambert. Clark was an extremely useful contact to have at the BBC. Later that year it was he who persuaded Hindemith to take up Walton's Viola Concerto for its first performance when Lionel Tertis had too hastily rejected it, and that same year it was to be Clark who approached Lambert and Walton for a work specifically designed for broadcasting.

As it turned out, Ansermet's broadcast received an encouraging notice from Ernest Newman who wrote: 'I know of no contemporary musical movement in any country that is better worth our sympathetic attention than that of the youngest British group. Two of these composers in particular, William Walton and Constant Lambert, seem to have the immediate future of our music on their shoulders.'[43] Edward Dent was equally encouraging in *Radio Times*:

> Wit and satire are qualities which foreign critics often name as peculiarly English. If their judgement is true, then the most English composer of today is Lord Berners; along with whom we may group William Walton and Constant Lambert. They have, like him, assimilated the techniques of Stravinsky and Casella; they are extremely clever and skilful, with all the modern determination to avoid pomposity or sentimentality. The general public, which adores sentimentality and is easily taken in by pomposity, has looked somewhat askance at these young composers, but they have gone their own way and have steadily developed their remarkable talents. It is time that the public took them seriously.[44]

In that same letter to Clark, Constant did at least thank him for putting him in touch with Ansermet who in January had included his transcription of William Boyce's Eighth Symphony in a 2LO broadcast. That same month he contributed an article on Boyce to the first issue of *The Listener*. Of the eight symphonies (published that year by OUP in his edited version) he wrote that 'they have all the vigour of Handel, but without his heaviness, all the lightness of Scarlatti, but with a greater force and emotional power. Among so great riches it is hard to choose, but perhaps the first and the last are the most entirely satisfying.' He was critical of the current performing

---

[42] The programme on 3 June 1929 consisted of Walton, *Sinfonia Concertante* (Hely-Hutchinson); Moeran, Second Rhapsody; Berkeley, Suite for Orchestra; Lambert, *Pomona*; Warlock, *Capriol* Suite and Hely-Hutchinson, *The Young Idea*.

[43] *Glasgow Herald*, 6 June 1929.

[44] 'Ask the Young! – Professor Dent on Our Young Composers', *Radio Times*, 31 May 1929, p. 452.

practices of such music: 'Many people approach eighteenth-century music with a curious preconceived notion of what the technical practices of the period were, and when faced with something which totally destroys this conception (which has its root, consciously or unconsciously, in nineteenth-century prejudices) they are forced to fall back on an elaborate theory of misprints.' (Much later Gerald Finzi wrote warmly of the edition: 'I think [OUP's] edition of the Boyce Symphonies, which Lambert edited, one of the most valuable contributions in the whole of their catalogue. Not all of them are, perhaps, first rate, but there can hardly be a string orchestra in England that does not make use of them and at least 4 of them are extremely good.')[45] Constant also touched on another 18th-century composer whose music he was to resurrect, Thomas Roseingrave, 'who managed to break more so-called rules of composition in four bars than anyone else, except perhaps Gesualdo, the Prince of Venosa'.

Constant did not have to wait much longer for his *Symphonic Interlude* to be performed as Leslie Heward included it in a 'Light Symphony Concert' on 2LO on 14 June 1929. Then, on 22 July under its new title *Music for Orchestra*, he conducted it himself as a Symphonic Interlude at Covent Garden in what was to be the last season of the Ballets Russes.[46] '[It is]', commented the *Observer* critic, 'a work more nearly mature than anything he has so far given us. The progress from the ballet *Romeo and Juliet* to this new work is altogether incommensurate with the lapse of the few years between. The two movements speak unhesitatingly. There is little evidence of ability only to express one side of a problem. Undoubtedly *Music for Orchestra* is the most interesting of the three orchestral works played as entr'actes this season.'[47] Not helped by its rather bland title, he himself described the work: 'It has no programme and consists of two interlinked movements: a slow introduction with two romantic themes, and a vigorous and more severe allegro in fugal style. At the end of the allegro the themes of both movements are combined in a broad climax for full orchestra.' He had presumably avoided the more apt title of 'Introduction and Allegro' to avoid confusion with the work of the similar name by Elgar. The published score contains much evidence of Lambert the Francophile with his use of a number of French terms and directions, such as *baguette d'éponge*, *baguette en bois*, *à la jante*, *se frottant* and *laissez vibrer*. Even the copy he gave to the work's dedicatee was partly inscribed in French: 'To Lord Berners from Constant Lambert Hommage affectueux, September 1930'. Although at the time he is said to have regarded it as his most important composition, and throughout his life he conducted it himself whenever the opportunity arose, it stands apart from his general output, like a contrapuntal exercise he had set himself as a challenge. Before it had been performed, Beryl de Zoete described it as 'an extremely intellectual, almost wintry work, remarkable for its bold architecture'.[48]

The work received rather more critical attention when Constant conducted its first concert performance on 29 August at a Queen's Hall Henry Wood Prom. 'Constant Lambert's *Music for Orchestra* stands a third hearing very well,' wrote the *Observer* critic. 'It is [a] really thoughtful, constructive work with exquisite moments in the orchestration. The three statements of fugal themes in the second part are the weakest

[45] Letter from Finzi to Cedric Thorpe Davie, 11 November 1946, in Stephen Banfield, *Gerald Finzi: An English Composer* (London: Faber & Faber, 1997; paperback edition, 1998), p. 406. On 22 February 1947 Finzi wrote to a friend: 'We do most of the Symphonies which Lambert edited', *ibid.*, p. 408, and with his Newbury String Players between 1940 and 1956 he gave nos. 1, 3, 4, 7 and 8.

[46] 29 June – 26 July 1929.

[47] *The Observer*, 28 July 1929. The other works were Rieti's *Noah's Ark* and Markevitch's Piano Concerto.

[48] De Zoete, 'Constant Lambert', p. 98.

part, or rather more weak.'[49] The Prom was largely of British music. Stanford, Delius and Holst were also represented, but Lambert and Heseltine conducted their own works. 'On the 29th I make my first and last appearance as a conductor, when "Capriol" will be given at the Prom,' Heseltine wrote to Colin Taylor. 'What a farce this silly "conducted by the composer" fetish is! One feels that one is merely stuck up at the desk to make the audience laugh, as though one were a dancing bear or something ...'[50] The occasion did almost turn into a farce as, according to Elizabeth Poston, Heseltine borrowed Lambert's trousers and John Ireland's tailcoat for the evening. 'Constant had got revoltingly fat, and safety-pinned up with reefs taken in, the lower half was all right. But John Ireland was rather a mingey little man and P couldn't move his arms. His conducting was a disaster, his chuckles audible to the players. The orchestra, going it alone, played like angels and the audience was not aware of anything unusual!'[51] But not Gerald Finzi, who was in the audience and wrote to Howard Ferguson: 'Lambert's work was a brilliant affair and "all London was there"; not, I think, a lasting work. Personally I liked the 2nd half with its lovely clashes better than the quiet and rather dull introduction. A good conductor, by the way. But the Warlock made a pitiful exhibition of himself. He was rather drunk and completely unable to give a beat of any sort. The baton just trembled and shook! I liked the work.'[52]

The *Daily Express* critic drew an interesting comparison between the two composer conductors:

> Mr Lambert, whose Music for Orchestra was scarcely recognisable as the piece performed a month or two ago at Covent Garden, so greatly improved was the playing of it,[53] formed an interesting contrast to Mr 'Warlock' both in appearance and manner. He is dark and sturdily built. He was a volcano of activity from the moment that he mounted the rostrum. His large head, which is usually inclined slightly to one side, jerked rapidly in every direction.[54] 'Peter Warlock' (whose real name is Philip Heseltine), on the other hand, is tall and fair, with a slight beard. He raised his hand in the air as though about to dive and brought it down energetically some three beats ahead of the orchestra.[55]

While Heseltine cut no figure as a conductor, it was a very different matter for the public and the critics with Constant. 'The audience ... were obviously impressed by the efficiency and assurance of this young man at the conductor's desk', noted the *Daily Telegraph. The Monthly Musical Record* concurred: [he] 'has indeed a clear beat for conducting.'[56] And the *Daily Mail* was equally impressed: 'Mr Lambert, who obviously has in him the makings of a conductor, gave us his new "Music for Orchestra" (Introduction and Fugal Allegro). Ever since Diaghileff produced this young man's ballet "Romeo and Juliet" three years ago he has been regarded as one of the

---

[49] *The Observer*, 1 September 1929.

[50] Letter from Heseltine to Taylor, 6 September 1929, in Barry Smith, *Peter Warlock: The Life of Philip Heseltine* (Oxford: Oxford University Press, 1994), p. 262.

[51] Letter from Elizabeth Poston to George Findlay, 8 December 1977, in *ibid.*, p. 263.

[52] Letter from Gerald Finzi to Howard Ferguson, September 1929, in *Letters of Gerald Finzi and Howard Ferguson*, p. 61. The work in question was *Music for Orchestra* and not *The Rio Grande* as the editors suggest.

[53] Shead, *Constant Lambert*, p. 80, suggests that *Music for Orchestra* had been inadequately rehearsed on that occasion because *Le Sacre du printemps* was in the ballet programme.

[54] The inclined head is an indication of Lambert's deafness in the right ear.

[55] *Daily Express* (Manchester Edition), 31 August 1929, quoted in *Peter Warlock: A Centenary Celebration*, ed. David Cox and John Bishop (London: Thames Publishing, 1994), pp. 236–7.

[56] *The Monthly Musical Record*, October 1929, p. 303.

hopes of British music.' The *Sunday Times* was of a similar opinion: 'In Mr Lambert and Mr Walton we have two British composers of the youngest generation who are proceeding with delightful certainty of aim and of touch towards a new goal. Will no concert society, by the way, give us this winter a performance of Mr Lambert's fine "Rio Grande"?'[57] Lambert was fast becoming a man of the moment.

C ONSTANT'S rather harsh words to Edward Clark about the BBC's patronage of British composers overlooked the fact that the Corporation had given a second performance of *The Rio Grande*, placing it in an unusual programme that could easily have been of Constant's devising. Kenneth Wright had not heard the work's first broadcast, but he wrote in a BBC memorandum that many of the BBC staff 'thought it came off very well and that it was a good novelty', suggesting another performance when Angus Morrison 'would also play a short Concertino by Mozart'. When *The Rio Grande* was given its second broadcast on 23 July 1928, it was in a late evening programme that could hardly have accommodated any Mozart. Entitled '*Blue on the Boulevard: A Study of Black and White*', it was described as 'a kind of miniature anthology showing "jazz" influences upon contemporary Western poets and musicians'. It was an enterprising mixture of jazz-inspired music and Negro poetry, with Satie's Fox-Trot from *Parade*, Milhaud's *Saudades*, Auric's *Adieu, New York*, a *Suite monégasque* by a friend of Constant's, Hugh Bradford,[58] and ending with *The Rio Grande*. Interspersed between the musical items were poems by Vachel Lindsay (*The Congo*), Carl Van Vechten, Countee Cullen and James Weldon-Johnson, and Louis Gruenberg's setting of Vachel Lindsay's *The Daniel Jazz* recited by Steuart Wilson with the Greenbaum String Quartet.[59] Constant conducted the whole programme that also included his *Elegiac Blues*. He also contributed an article to that week's issue of *Radio Times* (his first) on 'The Future of Jazz' in which he wrote:

> I see no reason why England should not eventually produce the most interesting examples of symphonic jazz. Sufficiently far removed from jazz to be able to view it with the necessary detachment, the English composer is yet sufficiently romantic to take the sentimentalities of jazz with more seriousness than does the Frenchman, and it is not to him the strange and alien product it is to the German. The English, too, possess a remarkably subtle sense of rhythm. ... Even Gershwin, who is a model of efficiency as far as ballroom jazz is concerned, showed a striking inability to cope with concerto-form in his rambling *Rhapsody in Blue*.[60]

The article acted like a red rag to arch-conservative Sir Henry Coward who replied emphatically with 'Jazz has no future!':

> For seventy years I have been acquainted with the salient features of the twangy strains and grotesque posturings of negro music and dancing. At that time

---

[57] *Sunday Times*, 1 September 1929.

[58] Hugh Bradford, five years older than Lambert, entered the Royal College of Music in 1917. Lambert may have met him through either Angus Morrison or Marie Rambert, for whose dancers all three accompanied, Bradford even composing some music for her. Lambert contributed an article on him to *The Monthly Musical Record*, 2 June 1930. Bradford later entered the church, becoming a vicar.

[59] Anthony Bernard had conducted *The Daniel Jazz* at a Chenil Galleries concert in 1926 with Steuart Wilson as reciter, together with works by Honegger, Vaughan Williams, Bloch, Berkeley and Warlock.

[60] *Radio Times*, 20 July 1928, pp. 95, 103. (Up to the war he generally received 8 guineas for a *Radio Times* article and 6 guineas for *The Listener*.) It seems he conducted *Rhapsody in Blue* once, with the LPO at Bristol in April 1943, with Sidney Harrison the soloist.

and for the next forty years it was considered derogatory to the white race to indulge in 'corked' (blacked) faces, and even when thus disguised there was only a limited amount of the crude 'plantation' business.[61]

Sir Henry Coward had made his views on jazz quite clear a year before when speaking at a luncheon of the Sheffield Rotary Club in September 1927. Jazz, he claimed, 'had led to a lowering of the prestige of the white races' and he went as far as calling for a ban 'to prevent further loss of prestige'. This had brought a letter to *The Times* from Carroll Gibbons, the new music director of the Savoy Orpheans, defending dance music – 'I refuse to call it jazz, which it is not' – for the pleasure it brought to so many people.[62] Sir Henry's latest outburst precipitated a correspondence in *Radio Times* that ran for several weeks, with at least one reader condemning Sir Henry's 'virulent onslaught upon jazz'. This was all sufficiently worrying for another dance band leader, Jack Payne, Director of BBC Dance Orchestra, fearful that his own style of music would be tarred with the same brush, to plead with readers of *Radio Times* in an article entitled 'A Fair Hearing for Syncopated Music'.[63]

In the same month as his *Radio Times* article, Constant wrote a much longer piece on jazz for the second issue of a new monthly publication, *Life and Letters*.[64] In it he shrugged off the widely held conception of jazz as being 'crude, barbaric and cacophonous', a fallacy, he suggested, that had arisen because of its origins in Negro folk music with the result that 'an essentially decadent and over-sophisticated art' was credited with 'the crude vigour and high spirits of its progenitors'. With what was to become a refreshing characteristic of his music journalism, he drew unexpected parallels between 'the inherent nostalgia and civilised melancholy of jazz music' and other types of popular music, such as Sousa marches and the sardanas of the Catalan composer Enric Morera. Jazz, he claimed, had lost its simple gaiety and sadness and had become 'a reflection of the nerves, sex-repressions, inferiority complexes, and general dreariness of the modern world. The nostalgia of the Negro who wants to go home has given place to the infinitely more weary nostalgia of the cosmopolitan Jew who has no home to go to.' Much of the general appeal of jazz, he argued, was in the association of its tunes with popular shows and revues that were fixed in people's minds 'by the attractions of one of the stars, or by the innocently promiscuous sex-appeal of the whole entertainment'. But for Lambert the appeal of jazz lay much deeper: in the technical side, in the virtuosity of both its performance and orchestration that he found 'little short of amazing', even if there was at times with the latter 'a tendency to over-emphasise the more grotesque timbres'. Jazz orchestration, he boldly claimed, provided 'the most intrinsically pleasing instrumental sound since the Haydn orchestra', and jazz piano playing marked 'the greatest advance in piano technique since Albeniz'. Turning to harmony he found 'a certain technical and spiritual similarity' between *The Sleepy Hills of Tennessee* (Florence Mills' hit song in *The Blackbirds*) and Delius's *On Hearing the First Cuckoo in Spring*. He suggested that *Hymns Ancient and Modern* were responsible for the 'richly sentimental harmony' shared by Negro spirituals and the music of Delius which was also imbued with nostalgia and the desire for escape, and that the best tunes of that great Victorian hymnist, the Reverend John Bacchus Dykes, 'must have possessed at the time they were written an extraordinary sensual

---

[61] *Radio Times*, 7 September 1928, pp. 415, 424. Sir Henry Coward (1849–1944) was widely known as a choral conductor in the Midlands and the north of England. He founded the Sheffield Musical Union in 1876.

[62] *The Times*, 26 September 1927.

[63] *Radio Times*, 14 September 1928, p. 470.

[64] *Life and Letters*, vol. 1 no. 2 (July 1928), ed. Desmond MacCarthy.

appeal'.[65] (It is interesting to note that eight years later Delius's amanuensis, Eric Fenby, was to comment that no essay on Delius would be complete without mention of Dykes.)[66]

Coming up to date with symphonic jazz, Lambert thought it unfortunate that those composers 'who have sought inspiration in jazz have not only made use of its exhilarating rhythmic qualities, but have incorporated also the more obvious harmonic clichés, the circumscribed form and the flat and uninspired melodic line that not even the utmost arabesque can save from deadness'. He quoted two notable exceptions: Stravinsky's *Les Noces*, and Walton's *Portsmouth Point* Overture for its 'interesting use of jazz rhythms adapted to a purely individual melodic and harmonic basis'. Other efforts had resulted 'in some such mélange as the *Rhapsody in Blue*, combining the more depressing mannerisms of jazz with all the formlessness of the nineteenth-century fantasia'. He found European efforts in jazz disappointing, with the French having 'too keen a sense of satire to approach it with sufficient seriousness' and the Germans approaching it 'with a kind of earnest depravity and sense of sin that is not without its humorous side'. He concluded:

> The failure of composers to produce jazz works of any importance or profundity is in reality due to the fact that jazz is itself an essentially decadent and derived art – at its best an ironic comment on Romanticism; at its worst a sentimental expression of a negative emotion – it is neither a vigorous nor an essentially new form of music, and any attempt to use it as a folk-tradition on which to form a style is about as intelligent as using plaster swags and ornamental ironwork for the foundation of a cathedral.

At the time that this article appeared, *The Rio Grande*, the most successful English example of symphonic jazz, was known to only a few through its two broadcasts. Constant's next moment of fame was to come with the work's first concert performance which most clearly signalled his arrival as a composer of importance.

A FEW weeks after the second broadcast of *The Rio Grande*, Constant was off to Italy for the first European performance of *Façade* as part of the International Society for Contemporary Music Festival in Siena in September 1928. The previous month he had joined the Sitwells at Renishaw in Derbyshire and now he was a guest at Sir George's castle of Montegufoni near Florence, some 40 miles' distance from Siena. The highlight of ten days of festivities that coincided with the ISCM festival was the Palio di Siena, a race between ten horses and their riders, preceded by a grand pageant, and all arranged in honour of the many visitors. Osbert recalled that 'just before the Palio was due to start, William and Constant, plainly after a very good luncheon, walked with dignity, though with a slight but telling lurch, across the Piazza del Campo, the centre of which had now been cleared for the imminent horse-race, and that their stately intrepidity won them a resounding cheer from the great crowds pressed but jostling behind the barriers.'[67] Probably more accurately, Spike Hughes wrote that 'feeling the heat, [they] had stopped off at a little wine shop we all knew where the wine was cheap

---

[65] According to Cecil Gray, Lambert's favourite hymn tune by Dykes was *Veni Cito* to the words 'O quickly come, dread Judge of all' by Lawrence Tuttiett. He wrote the following limerick: 'The Bishop of Central New Guinea / Never talked of Original Sin: he / Said, "Music's the art / To convert a man's heart"; / And he played J. B. Dykes on a "mini".'

[66] Eric Fenby, *Delius as I Knew Him* (London: Bell, 1936; Faber & Faber, 1981), p. 182.

[67] Osbert Sitwell, *Tales my Father Taught Me* (London: Hutchinson, 1962; Readers Union edition, 1963), p. 107. (Sitwell wrongly dates it as 1929.)

and strong, and had lost their way to their seats.'[68] The inexpensive wine was certainly an attraction, with Hubert Foss writing home to his wife Dora on 10 September: 'Yesterday evening … Lambert and Walton and I dined most pleasantly and cheaply (it's very cheap here – excellent wine at 1½d a glass!).'

Two performances of *Façade* were given on 14 September, with Walton conducting and Constant reciting Edith's poems through a megaphone from behind a painted drop curtain. There had been a mild panic beforehand as Walton had forgotten the address of the scene painter to whom he had entrusted the new curtain design to conceal the performers. Osbert's mother, Lady Ida, and Christabel Aberconway saved the day by tracking him down in the Florentine bar in which he had been commissioned for the task. Even then, Christabel had to convince an obstinate Sir George that it was possible for the rolled cloth to be carried in the car by laying it across the inside with one end projecting through a window.[69]

The work 'after some opposition (mostly Italian) met the success it deserves,' reviewed Hubert Foss in *The Musical Times*, the opposition coming from a section of the Italian audience who took offence to the treatment in the *Jodelling Song* of the well-known *Allegro vivace* tune from Rossini's *William Tell* Overture, although Spike Hughes who was present thought it was the irreverent parodying in the *Tarantella* of a national dance that caused shouts and calls, with hats and shoes being thrown at the stage. Despite the minor uproar, the *Popular Song* was twice repeated, and the 'shirt-sleeved conductor had to come from his back-stage hide-out and take a couple of calls'.[70] Other guests staying at Montegufoni for the festival included Arthur Waley, Stephen Tennant and Siegfried Sassoon, and when the rest of the house party had gone to bed, 'William and Constant would carouse with Henry Moat [Sir George's faithful butler].'[71]

W HILE Constant was enjoying himself on the Continent, his mother was still in Australia. Amy's reunion with her husband George was not to bring the pleasure she might have expected, if indeed she held any expectations. Firstly, after a 'long, tedious, noisy, crowded voyage' there was no George to greet her when she disembarked at Sydney on 16 June 1926. He was recovering at home from a fall that had injured his nose. One can only imagine her disappointment on receiving a rather cold letter from him in which he wrote: 'I cannot apologise for the situation that prohibits a holiday with you just now, for it is not of my making.' Amy used the accident as an excuse for 'his nervous condition' when, after a gap of five years, they eventually met. There is no mention in her biography of a warm meeting. 'But,' as she seemed to console herself, 'I had not come to make holiday, except in so far as was necessary for him, and there were plenty of odd jobs to occupy myself usefully both in and out of the studio.' There is little doubt that George put his work before family and even his marriage. A pencil sketch of his drawn the following year in George's Randwick studio in Sydney shows an unsmiling Amy, cup and saucer in hand, bringing tea for his two assistants. She has the appearance, as one Sydney reviewer commented, of a 'kindly matron'. What pleasures she had were taking trips by boat or tram to revisit various beauty spots around Sydney. Soon after her arrival she attended the opening of an exhibition of Thea Proctor's work

[68] Hughes, *Opening Bars*, p. 365.

[69] Christabel Aberconway, *A Wiser Women? A Book of Memories* (London: Hutchinson, 1966), pp. 90–2.

[70] Hughes, *Opening Bars*, p. 363. However, Hughes later wrote, in 'Nobody calls him Willie now' for *High Fidelity*, vol. 10 no. 9, (Sept. 1960), pp. 43–6, 116–17, that it was the *Tango-Pasodoble* that was 'cheered so wildly that the number had to be played three times'.

[71] Sitwell, 'Portrait of a very Young Man', p. 30.

and here again Amy may have had an uncomfortable reunion, knowing how much of a companion to George Thea had been – and still was, the two being occasionally associated in artistic ventures. For much of the time she stayed with her sister Marian, there being little in the way of comfortable accommodation in George's studio. It seems extraordinary that when George was busy with a large sculpture commission in Melbourne that Amy did not go with him, as his self-centred letters to her in April and June 1927 would suggest. He was in Melbourne again in September and it was only later that year, before he embarked on another commission, that she could write that George was 'determined to show me the Bush, which I had never seen and which meant so much to him. So we had five days' holiday ...' Once George was immersed in commissions, holidays were over. 'Those were busy but cheerful days in the studio, with all hands working with a will,' Amy recorded. 'It was my duty to cook and serve lunch for five men.'

After nearly three years Amy decided to return home. Disguising her obvious disappointment, she later gave her reasons for returning:

> Reports from home told of a successful exhibition of his son Maurice's sculpture at the Claridge Gallery,[72] and of much hopefulness and hard work. Our younger son was experiencing rather a stale and unprofitable period, after his earlier success with his ballet, and it is true that neither his parents was feeling particularly happy about either present circumstances or future prospects, and in view of the work which was rounding to completion in Australia, we came to the conclusion that it would be best for me to return to England next year, thus completing a three years' absence. I realised the necessity for providing some sort of pied-à-terre in London for George's obligatory return. He was himself anxious to sign his name at the Royal Academy, and renew contact with his fellow artists.

Whether or not George ever had any real intentions of returning to England as well, on 16 February 1929 Amy sailed from Sydney aboard the P.&O. liner *Barabool*. She was not to see him again. She took with her a typically formal message to the boys from their father:

> My message to the boys can, I think, be safely left to correspondence, though it would give me pleasure if you would convey personally my pride in their achievements to date, and my hope and trust for their correct and artistic development.[73]

England was having its coldest February for 40 years and Constant spent a week-end at Sacheverell Sitwell's home, Weston Hall in Northamptonshire, into which he and his wife Georgia had moved just over a year before. Amy arrived home from Australia on 24 April and moved into 42 Peel Street in Notting Hill, a small house between Campden Hill and Kensington Church Street. Constant was just able to greet her on her homecoming before dashing off to Paris to recite *Façade* with Edith six days later, Walton conducting, at the Salle Chopin in a concert promoted by the Pro Musica Society. With his mother home again, it was probably financial considerations and home comforts that made him move into Peel Street with her, and on hearing this George wrote to Amy on 10 June: 'Now that you are with him I shall be less worried.'

---

[72] In June 1927, the first of four important exhibitions of Maurice's work, the others being at Arthur Tooth in the summer of 1929, and two shows at Alex Reid & Lefevre in 1932 and 1934: Nicolson, *The Sculpture of Maurice Lambert*, p. 44.

[73] Letter from Maurice Lambert to his father, 28 June 1929, in Amy Lambert, *Thirty Years of an Artist's Life*, p. 180.

Near the end of the month Maurice, who now had a studio in Peel Street and kept his father informed of his own artistic progress, told him about a successful exhibition he had recently had, with excellent press reviews, adding rather morosely that his '[Mother']d like to see her family happy as anyone would. But I don't think she will, not in the accepted sense anyway. It's a word I don't know much about, nor does Constant. … In fact, I think we're both likely to get about as much as you've had, and I can't say fairer than that.'[74]

In July Constant had his first recording session for the gramophone. The new Decca Gramophone Company was recording part of *Façade* at the Chenil Galleries with Walton conducting and Edith sharing in the recitation, but the 'takes' were not good enough to be issued. A further session in August also failed to produce satisfactory 'takes', despite Walton writing, 'We made a new set of records, really good ones, last week, so things are getting a move on.'[75] It was from a third session in November that a two-record set comprising 11 of the poems was eventually issued. Constant wrote the accompanying notes.

In December Constant came into his own. The two broadcasts of *The Rio Grande* the previous year – both studio affairs and the work's only performances so far – would not have drawn a significantly large listening audience as in both instances the work had not been placed in an important concert. The BBC had decided against its inclusion in that year's Proms because of the cost of having a 40–50 strong chorus 'which would make it rather an expensive item'. Stanford Robinson had stated in a BBC memo back in April: 'If this is done at a Prom it must be in the same concert as the [Beethoven] Choral Symphony', adding that it was 'quite out of the question for the National Chorus to appear at two promenade concerts.' But the work had not escaped the notice of the *Sunday Times* critic who in September had thrown down the gauntlet: 'Will no concert society give us this winter a performance of Mr Lambert's fine "Rio Grande"?'[76]

It was Manchester, not London, that took up the challenge, and on 12 December 1929, in the (old) Free Trade Hall, Lambert conducted the first concert performance of *The Rio Grande* with the Hallé Orchestra,[77] the pianist being none other than the orchestra's principal conductor, Hamilton Harty who two years earlier had spoken publicly of his dislike of jazz. But that now seemed all forgotten. The work was an instant success. 'We take the risk of calling it a work of genius,' Neville Cardus wrote in the *Manchester Guardian*. 'Mr Lambert transfigures jazz into poetry; more wonderful still, he transfigures Mr Sitwell into poetry. … Beauty is the result. … Not a false touch is to be heard. Everything "comes off"; the score is perfectly poised,' and he described Harty's playing as 'delicious in its touch and masterful in its rhythmical control.'[78] *The Rio Grande* became a useful yardstick by which to judge other jazz-inspired works, and when Harty introduced the music of Ernst Krenek to Manchester the next season, Cardus wrote: 'He runs a poor second to Constant Lambert as an artist in idioms derived from jazz'.[79]

From Manchester the same players travelled to London to give a repeat performance

[74] Gray, *George Lambert*, p. 176.
[75] Letter from Walton to Christabel McLaren, 25 August 1929.
[76] *Sunday Times*, 1 September 1929.
[77] 'One of [Anthony] Burgess's lasting musical memories was attending the premiere of Constant Lambert's *Rio Grande* with his father in November [*sic*] 1929': Paul Phillips, 'The Music of Anthony Burgess', in *Anthony Burgess Newsletter*, no. 1.
[78] Quoted in Michael Kennedy, *The Hallé Tradition* (Manchester: Manchester University Press, 1960), p. 259.
[79] Krenek's *Potpourri*, 30 January 1931: Kennedy, *The Hallé Tradition*, p. 260.

the following day in Queen's Hall when not only the work itself but Lambert's conducting came in for praise.[80] 'Lambert is a first-rate conductor – in his own work and on this occasion at any rate,' reported the *Musical Opinion*.[81] 'Ease of style and knowledge of the orchestra were everywhere apparent.' The *Times* critic thought it 'the first completely successful example of a composer so absorbing the spirit, the rhythm and the instrumentation of jazz as to be able to use it naturally and in good faith to express ideas of his own which suit the medium.'[82] The *Musical Times* critic was equally enthusiastic, finding fault only with the chorus:

> Constant Lambert's *Rio Grande* was brilliantly successful, despite the inadequacy of the choral portion, sung by a small contingent of the Hallé chorus. Sir Hamilton Harty played dashingly in the exacting pianoforte part, and the composer conducted. This work should be heard again soon, and with a larger and better chorus. ... The work made a hit – perhaps the hit of the season – and provided one more proof that when it comes to the writing of really novel music, whether it be sublimated jazz (as in this case), 'juxtaposition of tonalities', or any other up-to-date development, we have a little group of young Englishmen who can play the Continentals at their own game and beat them all ends up.[83]

So successful was the work that Harty not only gave it again at Queen's Hall early in the new year but he also recorded it for Columbia the following day, 11 January, in the Central Hall, Westminster, with Lambert conducting on both occasions. The new recording was very soon broadcast, on 14 February.

In the words of *The Times*, the second London concert performance ended the programme 'with a final quarter of an hour of young exuberance'. That critic summed it up:

> The point of the work is not that it is very good or very new, perhaps it is neither, but that it is very natural. It is the work of a really young composer, one who has grown up among the present-day conditions of jazz and modern technique, takes what he wants from them, rejects the rest, and lets his imagination run free. The repetition after its first success was well justified.[84]

Such praise was not universal. On that occasion a different reviewer for *The Musical Times* took umbrage at the mere suggestion of any 'jazziness' about the work. 'The *Rio Grande*,' he claimed, 'owes next to nothing to jazz; its style, idiom, texture, and what-not are not founded on jazz; its rhythmic play is related to that of de Falla, Stravinsky, and other high-spirited Europeans, and not to that of jazz.' He did not ask himself whether those other composers had to any extent also been inspired by jazz, but summed up the work as 'a hotch-potch of good and bad, right and wrong, effective and ineffective, all thrown together in a riot of lively downrightness that makes it, quite comprehensibly, the hit of the season.'[85]

The jazz element quickly became a bone of contention. In his review Cardus had stated: 'It is all done by jazz; the work is a complete synthesis of jazz elements ... The

---

[80] The programme consisted of Wagner, *The Flying Dutchman* Overture; Beethoven, Violin Concerto (Jelly D'Aranyi); Lambert, *The Rio Grande* (with an extensive note with music examples by Hubert Foss); Berlioz, *Beatrice and Benedict* Overture, scenes from *Romeo and Juliet* and *Le Carnaval romain* Overture.

[81] *Musical Opinion*, January 1930, p. 321.

[82] *The Times*, 14 December 1929.

[83] 'G', *The Musical Times*, January 1930, p. 67.

[84] *The Times*, 11 January 1930.

[85] 'M', *The Musical Times*, 1 February 1930, p. 166.

jazz style is not once forgotten: we are conscious of it continuously, yet only as we are conscious of the presence of familiar idioms in a poem'. But *The British Musician and Musical News* critic differed.

> The truth is, not one third of *Rio Grande* derives from jazz. The last section is pure nocturnal loveliness, and hardly 'modern'. The cornet theme of the 'Comendador and Alguacil' passage is a jolly march. Certain choral passages are entirely English – as English as Prince Consort Road in 1900. The piano part is a delightful toccata of the neo-classical kind. The major portion of the work is actually Spanish. The piano solo that leads into the last section and establishes the tone there in considerable measure, is based on that loveliest of all Spanish (i.e. South American) rhythms, the tango, or habanera. The opening chords are in their rhythm exclusively Spanish; the music of no other race ever starts in just this way. And if the composer had left out his last two notes, the concluding cadence would have been the conventional Spanish. Jazz, glorified as perhaps never before, and rendered truly brilliant, invests *Rio Grande* with its animation; but among the elements of the work, it is at the most only first among equals.[86]

Today one would regard the work as 'jazzy' rather than a piece of jazz, but, as he was to do with the Concerto for Piano and Nine Players, Constant used many jazz 'effects', like syncopation, blue notes, trombone slides, glissandi on piano and xylophone, jazz-related instruments, and a piano style, all of which pointed to jazz derivations, and if there was any doubt about the connection, there was the instruction that 'the side-drum player should be provided with a wire-brush as used in Jazz Bands'.

When the records were released, the *Gramophone* reviewer was rather reserved, finding this 'very gay and amusing and thoroughly promising work which .... has had a great deal of deserved praise ... far too high-brow for the unadult sympathies of jazz-lovers (those, that is, who have little time for anything but dance music)', and he concluded that 'music such as this of Lambert's is very limited in scope'. Again, fault was found with the choir.[87]

For both the second London performance and the recording, the choir had not been the section of the Hallé chorus that had sung in December but the St Michael's Singers of Cornhill, London. Their conductor, Harold Darke, felt it necessary to defend his singers after they had 'received so many kicks from the press', including 'a nasty bruise' from the 'Gramophone Notes' section of *The Musical Times*:

> For some reasons unknown to me Sir Hamilton was unable to bring with him the contingent of the Hallé chorus ... The Oxford University Press, who were made responsible for supplying a choir, were thus in great difficulty, and after trying unsuccessfully several conductors, approached me as to whether I could help them in their dilemma. I immediately got in touch with my St Michael's Singers, and they very sportingly consented to take part. We had exactly one week in which to prepare the work. I was especially asked to supply thirty voices, and not the whole choir.[88]

The choir's contribution on record is in fact much better than the reviewers of the day would have one believe. In their Queen's Hall performance the St Michael's Singers may not have been able to disguise their difficulties in managing at such short notice so unfamiliar a choral idiom, with its jazz inflections and syncopated rhythms. (Only the following year the Leeds Festival Chorus faced similar difficulties when giving the

---

[86] *The British Musician and Musical News*, vol. 6 no. 3 [issue no. 50] (March 1930), pp. 59–60.

[87] *Gramophone*, March 1930, p. 453.

[88] *The Musical Times*, 1 April 1930, p. 351.

premiere of Walton's *Belshazzar's Feast*.) But on record these problems were largely overcome. The words may not be very clear and the big climaxes lack choral precision but the overall impact of the work is in no way lessened. As soloist, Harty brings a personal style of jazz pianism, in some respects rather more slurred than the brilliant staccato that soloists bring to the work today, and he was not beyond taking a few liberties, most noticeably the spread chord one bar before figure 13. This remained the only recording of *The Rio Grande* until Lambert rerecorded it 19 years later, with himself again as conductor.

Harty had done much to put *The Rio Grande* 'on the map' and when, in November 1934, he was awarded the Gold Medal of the Royal Philharmonic Society, Constant repaid his gratitude with some generous words of praise:

> It is impossible to think of anyone more deserving this great honour than Sir Hamilton Harty. Fame has come to him later than to some men, but his name stands all the more solidly because he has never sought the cheap and evanescent rewards of fashion. Unlike many famous conductors Sir Hamilton is a musician first and foremost. We never feel that he is using a piece of music as a vehicle for his own virtuosity; on the contrary, he draws attention not to himself but to the composer, and that surely is the highest degree of the conductor's art.[89]

As Angus Morrison remembered, the idea of setting Sacheverell Sitwell's poem *The Rio Grande*, which had first appeared in 1924 in the anthology 'The Thirteenth Caesar and other poems', had occupied Constant's thoughts for some while, and the rhythm of its arresting opening had been in his mind for two years before he actually wrote it down.[90] For him it was first and foremost an experiment which he felt he had successfully brought off even before it had gained a performance.

Sitwell's Rio Grande is not the familiar river that flows through the state of Colorado but instead one in Brazil that 'rolls down to the sea' and on whose banks 'they dance no sarabande … nor sing they forlorn madrigals' but instead join in festivities, with dancing and the playing of bands in the city squares. As Constant wrote in a programme note:

> The music of *Rio Grande* no more represents any actual scene or event than the atmospheric poem which inspired it. It is an imaginary picture that it conjures up, a picture of the gay life of a riverside town which may be in either South or North America, as the listener chooses to fancy. The poem is perhaps more definitely Spanish than the music which derives more from negro sources. The composer was very impressed by the coloured revues *Dover Street to Dixie* and *Blackbirds* that will always be remembered for the superbly moving singing of Florence Mills (to whose memory he has written an *Elegiac Blues*). The colour and rhythm of the singing was an absolute revelation of the possibilities of choral writing and thus *Rio Grande* is the first example of a serious and perfectly natural use of jazz technique in a choral work.

Alan Frank admirably summed up the work: 'With its combination of exhilarating rhythmic exuberance and lyrical warmth, *The Rio Grande* possesses both instant appeal and is intensely memorable.' And, in Edwin Evans' apt words, it is 'not only extraordinarily evocative, but it imbues the exotic scene it evokes with a strange poetical glamour. If it were French one would call it a blend of the nostalgia of Baudelaire with the festive glamour of Debussy's *Fêtes*.'[91]

---

[89] *Sunday Referee*, 25 November 1934. Nine days later Harty gave the first (incomplete) performance of Walton's first symphony.

[90] De Zoete, 'Constant Lambert', p. 98.

[91] Evans, 'Constant Lambert', p. 185.

Ex. 5 Lambert, *The Rio Grande*, chorus entry, fig. 1

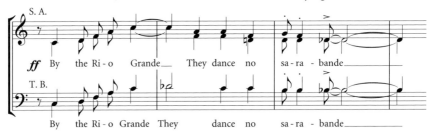

It is a work that never fails to make an effect, right from its lively opening of a repeated syncopated chord on pizzicato strings, followed by an excited flurry of piano and then orchestra in the build-up to the choirs *a cappella* entry (Ex. 5) on a rising figure similar (but without the triplet) to the Fanfare from *Dover Street to Dixie*.

An extensive cadenza, punctuated by a variety of percussion (four players), leads to a particularly haunting choral passage: 'The noisy streets are empty and hushed is the town', the rocking figure on the strings (hinted at earlier) with its chromatic harmonies being almost akin to a Negro spiritual. The work then builds to two choral climaxes which are followed by a second, shorter cadenza for solo piano. At the return of the gentle rocking figure, an alto soloist has a small but significant part backed by a humming semi-chorus, and the work comes to a quiet ending as the sounds of merry-making are lost in 'the soft Brazilian air', with the piano providing a brief, soft reminder of the choir's entry.[92]

Angus Morrison pointed out not only the curious geographical divergence between the poem and the music but also that the work betrays another love of Constant's, the music of Liszt, and in particular the *Faust* Symphony.

> A strange thing about *The Rio Grande* is that while the imagery of the poem is fundamentally South American, with its 'Comendador and Alguacil' and 'soft Brazilian air by those Southern winds wafted' the music is inspired largely by North American jazz and echoes from The Plantation. The music is, in fact, an extraordinary amalgam of many widely different elements, because there are also tango and samba rhythms as well as a phrase from Liszt's *Faust* Symphony which obsessed him at the time he was writing it. But somehow it works! ...
>
> Constant, from as long as I can remember, always had an immense admiration for this work [i.e. the *Faust* Symphony], although it is doubtful whether he could have possessed a full score during his student days as the work was then very infrequently played and Liszt orchestral [scores] were not always easy to come by. Nevertheless he knew the work well and became obsessed by these particular bars which he would play over and over again to himself and to his friends ... Obviously the passage must have been running in his head pretty continually while he was working at the Rio Grande because I can still remember him saying to me at a time when much of it was still very nebulous in his mind and only certain passages had emerged with sufficient finish and coherence to be played through on the piano that he wished he could use the Liszt passage as it was just the sound he wanted at a certain point in the work and he knew he wouldn't be able himself to think of anything different that was nearly so good or so 'right' in that particular context. At first ... he suffered scruples of conscience about taking something out of an already existing work and it was only after a struggle that he

---

[92] Alan Jenkins, in *The Twenties* (London: Heinemann, 1974), p. 146, suggests that 'at one point the chorus sings four complete bars from "I can't give you anything but love, baby".'

Ex. 6 Liszt, *A Faust Symphony*, slow movement, bar 188

Ex. 7 Lambert, *The Rio Grande*, fig. 6

succumbed to the temptation to incorporate the much-concealed passage into the body of his work.[93]

Morrison identified the passage in question (Ex. 6) as occurring at the 188th bar in the slow movement of *A Faust Symphony* (and again a few bars later). Its appearance in *The Rio Grande*, rhythmically altered so that it provides the choir with a lively syncopated accompaniment, is at the words 'By the river music, gurgling, thin' (Ex. 7), appearing again towards the end of the long piano cadenza (letter E), 'and, lastly, metamorphosed into a haunting Habanera, marked *Molto espressivo e rubato*' (figure 24).

Constant always hoped to have a Negro choir sing *The Rio Grande* and, unlike performances today, he did not want too much importance to be attached to the alto solo who is not listed in the score, which calls just for a mixed chorus. Morrison observed:

> I think Constant originally imagined the alto solo as suddenly emerging out of the choir, and that was how it was done in those first two studio performances. I don't believe he really wanted the majestic lady in a picture frock and white gloves who sits by the solo pianist throughout most of the work and only comes to life in the last two pages. It should be a wandering, disembodied voice, like somebody glimpsed in a crowd, and disappearing just as quickly.[94]

Constant may well have had in mind Delius's *Appalachia*, for which the score stipulates that the baritone soloist 'must be placed in the Chorus (not beside the conductor)'. For the first two concert performances, although not named on the programme, a contralto in the Hallé Chorus, Stephanie Baker, was the soloist. For Lambert's first recording of *The Rio Grande* the solo was, unusually, a male alto, Albert Whitehead,[95] who was also the soloist in a unique performance that took place on 15 June 1930 in Arthur Benjamin's[96] home at 66 Carlton Hill, London when Constant

[93] Angus Morrison, draft manuscript, Royal College of Music library.

[94] Angus Morrison, talk to the British Institute of Recorded Sound, 23 March 1970, published in *Recorded Sound*, nos. 70–1 (April–July 1978), p. 790.

[95] I am most grateful to Eleanor Roberts, of Hallé Development, for providing this information from the original vocal scores used. As the Hallé Chorus did not travel to London for the January 1930 performance, one assumes that Albert Whitehead, the soloist on the recording, replaced Stephanie Baker on that occasion.

[96] The Australian pianist and composer Arthur Benjamin (1893–1960) won a scholarship to the Royal College of Music in 1911. He saw war service, first with the Royal Fusiliers and then the Royal Flying Corps when he was shot down and taken prisoner at Ruhleben Camp near Berlin. After the war he went back to Australia but returned to England in February 1922 to become professor of piano at the RCM. As soloist he introduced a number of British piano concertos, including Lambert's Concerto for Piano and Nine Players in 1931.

alone took on all the percussion parts that normally require five players. As Dora Foss recorded in her memoirs:

> An exciting occasion I shall never forget was the party given by Arthur Benjamin at his home for the first chamber performance of Constant's 'Rio Grande'. The concert opened with Arthur Benjamin and Leslie Lasdun playing Arthur's 'Music for Dancing'. Then followed the Rio Grande. The music was arranged for two pianos (played by Julie Lasdun and Arthur Benjamin) and percussion, played by Constant, for alto solo, sung by Albert Whitehead, and a small group of six singers. Hubert conducted. The performance was exciting to a degree. Each and every performer gave of his or her best and I have never heard anything done with more urge and exuberance, and at the same time, with such beauty. Audience and musicians alike were carried away with enthusiasm, and to crown it all for me (and I laugh to think of it) after it was over, Hubert caught hold of me and danced me round the marquee in the garden. The only time I ever knew him to dance in or out of a ballroom.[97]

Walton, who was also present, got far more flustered having to turn over the pages for Constant.[98]

Much later this legendary feat resulted in the renowned percussionist James Blades being challenged to match it himself. So, after editing a part for single player, he performed it at an afternoon and evening performance at Dartington Hall. As he wrote in his autobiography:

> All went well as far as I was concerned, but at the afternoon performance certain members of the choir (and at least half the audience I was told) tended to watch my gymnastics rather than the conductor's beat, and so for the evening performance I played behind a large screen.[99]

In June, Harty played *The Rio Grande* yet again with the Hallé, at the Liverpool Promenade Concerts (his leader Alfred Barker taking over the conducting), and with the work proving a great success wherever it was given there was no question this time of it not being played at the 1930 Proms. It was featured in a 'British Composers' Night' on 4 September, Constant conducting, with Angus Morrison the piano soloist and Doris Owens the vocalist.[100] There was one caustic review, which came from *The Musical Times*:

> The Wireless Chorus put heart into its singing, but could not disguise the fact that this composer who sows wild oats in the pianoforte and paints the orchestra red has no idea how to make merry with a choir. He would learn a lot from Sir Hubert Parry, which is no doubt a dreadful accusation to bring against a young Georgian.[101]

[97] Another private performance of note was given 'At Home' at the RCM Union on 25 June 1931 with a small chorus, two pianos (Arthur Benjamin and Edwin Benbow) and three percussionists (Iris Lemare, Gordon Jacob and Guy Warrack). Whitehead once again was the alto soloist and Lambert conducted.

[98] Frank, 'The Music of Constant Lambert' (1952), p. 105.

[99] James Blades, *Drum Roll: A Professional Adventure from the Circus to the Concert Hall* (London: Faber & Faber, 1977), p. 202.

[100] The remainder of the programme was Berners' Fugue, Ethel Smyth's *Two Interlinked Melodies* and *Anacreontic Ode* (the composer conducting), Elgar's Cello Concerto (with Beatrice Harrison) and the *Enigma* Variations. Lambert had two rehearsals, one with piano and orchestra the day before, and a full rehearsal on the morning of the concert. Up to his death in 1951, *The Rio Grande* was performed 16 times at the Proms, with Lambert conducting on nine occasions. It received a further ten performances up to the 2005 season.

[101] *The Musical Times*, October 1930, p. 934.

The Rio Grande was the work that established Lambert as a composer, even if its popularity was to make the music public want more of the same at the expense of the remainder of his output. It soon become popular with choral societies and even met with success abroad. In January 1931 it was performed in New York by the Schola Cantorum under Hugh Ross with Colin McPhee at the piano, and the following April Serge Koussevtizky included it in the Boston Symphony Orchestra's 50th anniversary season, causing the critic of the *Boston Herald* to enthuse:

> Mr Lambert's *Rio Grande* is not only full of life that is contagious. ... Seldom in Symphony Hall has there been so instant, spontaneous, so prolonged, so tumultuous recognition of an unfamiliar composition signed with an unfamiliar name.

No one was more surprised by its success than Constant, who once told Alan Frank of OUP that because of its unorthodox scoring he had never expected it to have more than a handful of performances. It was, in fact, to achieve 200 performances in the ten years following its premiere.

W HILE 1930 proved in many ways to be a good year for Constant, it was not without its moments of sadness brought by three deaths. News of George Lambert's deteriorating health may have prompted Constant to write to his father, telling him about his new piano sonata, conducting *Music for Orchestra* at the Proms, and the Hallé performance of *The Rio Grande*. George in turn wrote to Amy: 'Everyone here of count congratulates me on Constant and his success, imagining, I suppose, that I have been a prime mover. If ever a youngster did it off his own bat, worse luck, he did.'

On 17 May George wrote ominously to Amy, 'My ticker is giving trouble ...' and 12 days later he died of heart failure. His death brought forward many tributes from people in the arts world, and his peers stressed his pre-eminence among Australian artists as the only one able to boast an international reputation. Amongst the mourners at his funeral service were his sisters and Thea Proctor. He was buried at South Head Cemetery, Vaucluse, Sydney.[102]

George had asked Amy to write his biography and this she undertook with a dry, detached, impersonal style that concentrated on his art, revealing very little of his home life and family relationships beyond what he had written himself in his occasional letters, or more precisely those parts that Amy chose to quote. Two hundred copies of the book were printed in Sydney in 1938 but a large number of these were lost when they were sent by sea to England during the Second World War. Before her death in 1963 Amy asked for the book to be reprinted and, with the addition of a few more plates, a thousand copies were printed in 1977 for the Australian Artist Editions.

The second death was of Kit Wood, who, on the afternoon of 21 August, 'while of unsound mind' had thrown himself in front of an incoming train at Salisbury Station. Although some people like Anthony Powell have commented that Constant thought highly of him, with even an element of hero-worship, there is little evidence to suggest that there was any real friendship.[103] Their personalities were too different and the two

---

[102] A headstone in Brompton Cemetery to the memory of George Lambert and to that of his father George Washington Lambert also marks the place where the ashes of Constant, Amy and their son Kit are buried.

[103] Lambert's admiration for certain people would often show itself in their being repeatedly mentioned in his articles and writings such as *Music Ho!* There is an isolated reference to 'Christopher Wood's early paintings' in his 1938 *Monthly Musical Record* article on Rawsthorne when comparing the sombre textures of artists of the 1930s with the bright tints of the 1920s.

seemed to have had little contact after Diaghilev dropped Kit's designs for *Romeo and Juliet*. Nevertheless, it has been suggested that when Constant's only son was born over four years later, he was named Christopher (or Kit) after the painter.

If Constant's reaction to Kit Wood's death was a muted one, later that year he was to be profoundly affected by the third death, also by suicide, of Philip Heseltine. In the meantime, he was becoming more and more involved in ballet, and while he was to emerge as one of its outstanding conductors, it was a world in which, sadly, he would find increasingly less time for composing.

T HE greater part of Lambert's life was devoted to ballet. Seeing Diaghilev's Ballets Russes in London while still a schoolboy had been the original inspiration. This led to him composing ballet music and to the great fortune of having one of his scores accepted by Diaghilev. But his wider involvement in the presentation of ballet began more humbly as a rehearsal accompanist for such ballet schools as Marie Rambert's,[1] nevertheless providing invaluable experience for someone who before long was to be involved in any production from its inception and planning, through its rehearsal stages as an accompanist, right up to its public performance as conductor. His earliest engagement as ballet conductor was on 10 July 1928 for part of an annual charity matinée in aid of the Sunshine Homes for Blind Babies at the Apollo Theatre, Shaftesbury Avenue, London. It was a ballet, *Leda* (later revised as *Leda and the Swan*), that Marie Rambert had devised for her dancers to the music of the 'Dance of the Blessed Spirits' from Gluck's opera *Orfeo ed Euridice*, and which she and her protégé, Frederick Ashton, had choreographed.[2] Leda was danced by Diana Gould (later Lady Menuhin), and the cast also included Harold Turner, Billy Chappell, Pearl Argyle, Andrée Howard and Ashton himself, all of whom were before long to work closely with Constant when the Vic-Wells Company was formed, the latter two chiefly as choreographers. Constant immediately became an admirer of Ashton's work and a friendship sprang up. '"Fred adored him", said Billy Chappell. "Constant was a very lovable man – so lively and funny and daft and wild." Right from the start of their association, Ashton was sufficiently impressed to allow Lambert to take his musical education in hand, steering him towards arcane enthusiasms, unjustly neglected composers, and contemporaries such as Peter Warlock, whose *Capriol* Suite was the score Lambert persuaded him would make a first-rate ballet'.[3] As Ashton himself recalled,

[Constant] was a tremendous influence on me musically and cultivated my musical tastes tremendously and I owe him a very big debt in that way. He would find exactly the right thing; if I said I would like to do a ballet to a certain piece of music he would reject it and say, 'You couldn't possibly use that!' [He was] absolutely unique – we've never had anyone like him, not only that but [someone] who fulfilled all the functions that he did: he was so extremely cultivated that

---

[1] Marie Rambert (1888–1982), one of the pioneers of British ballet, was born in Poland and briefly worked with Diaghilev. She emigrated to England in 1914, opening her own school at Bedford Gardens, London in 1920. In 1927 she moved to Ladbroke Road to what became known as the Mercury Theatre, and in 1930 created her Ballet Club to give performances to the public. Lambert's name was on the programme for the Apollo Theatre matinée in July 1928, and was almost certainly still the Ballet Club's pianist in 1931, but programmes did not generally list the pianist. (Information supplied by Melanie Peart, Archivist, Rambert Dance Company.) De Valois spoke of Lambert 'playing the piano at a dancing academy in Notting Hill for £2 a week and selling books in a friend's shop between those sessions': *Constant Lambert Remembered*, BBC Third Network, 25 June 1966.

[2] *Leda* had its first performance (with piano accompaniment) in June 1928 at a reception to celebrate the opening of Rambert's new premises in Ladbroke Road: Kavanagh, *Secret Muses*, p. 89).

[3] *Ibid.*, p. 110. *Capriol Suite* was first presented by Marie Rambert's pupils at a matinée performance at the Lyric Theatre, Hammersmith on 28 February 1930 to an accompaniment of two pianos. Ashton not only choreographed the ballet but performed in it.

when it came to scenarios or anything of that sort he could advise – he knew all about painting, about literature – he knew all about everything, really.[4]

It was while Constant was working as accompanist for Marie Rambert that a further important relationship came about, with someone who was to make her mark as another leading female figure in British ballet – Ninette de Valois. Marie Nielson, a member of the Rambert Ballet Club and a close friend of Constant's, wrote much later:

> I remember how Constant started with the [Vic-Wells] Ballet. Ninette [de Valois] wanted some music for a ballet orchestrated & as none of the conductors at the Vic could be bothered with ballet asked me if I thought that young man, Lambert, would do it. If so would I give her an introduction? I said that he was playing [the piano] for the Rambert ballet at Hammersmith that week & if we went to a performance we could go round in the interval. Both Constant & I were exceptionally shy in those days so muttering something I put her into his room & fled. She joined me a few minutes later looking rather worried & when I asked if Constant would do it said 'I don't know, a very vague young man. Says he is busy for ten days but will do it after that'. I said, 'He'll do it if he says he will.' At the end of the week she said, 'You see, nothing from that young man.' I pointed out that he had said ten days, & I thought she would hear from him then. 'Hm, I'll be very cross with you if I don't, I think I should have got someone more reliable.' Of course Constant did phone to make the appointment & after the interview Ninette was beaming – 'A most efficient young man – he's going to conduct for us too!' And that was the beginning & making of the Ballet ...[5]

This was a meeting that was both to provide a foundation for British ballet and to shape de Valois's and Lambert's futures. After dancing with Diaghilev's Ballets Russes for three years (as Nina Devalois), in 1926 Ninette de Valois opened her own school of ballet in London, known as The Academy of Choreographic Art. That same year she approached Lilian Baylis, Manager of the Old Vic Theatre that was then home to both Shakespearean productions and opera, with a proposal for a resident ballet company. Many operas contained ballet sequences and for these Baylis had depended on pupils from several dance schools and from a local church school. She recognised the need for a resident company and after visiting de Valois's school, an agreement was reached and Ninette became a staff member of the Vic-Wells Company, as it was to become, an organisation with which Lambert was soon to be closely associated for much of his life. At that time Baylis was tirelessly campaigning for the purchase of the once famous but dilapidated Sadler's Wells Theatre on the north side of the Thames in Rosebery Avenue, Islington. Her intention was to reconstruct its interior to provide another home for the Old Vic companies, the idea being for Shakespeare and opera to alternate a fortnight each between the two theatres. This was achieved by 1931, and the restored theatre opened on 6 January, appropriately to a performance of Shakespeare's *Twelfth Night* (with John Gielgud as Malvolio and Ralph Richardson as Toby Belch),

---

[4] *In Search of Constant Lambert*, BBC2, 26 July 1965.

[5] Letter from Marie Nielson to Angus Morrison, 19 February [1954]: RCM Archive. Marie Nielson (née Robertson; Nielson was her professional name) was a Scottish ballet dancer. In 1934 she married Cecil Gray, after he had been left by his first wife Tasha, a beautiful Russian woman who had once been married to Val Gielgud. As well as an illegitimate daughter, Perdita, from the poet Hilda Doolittle in 1919, Gray had a daughter Pauline (born 1929) from his first marriage and another, Fabia (born 1938), from his second marriage. Marie left Cecil in 1941 and later became Marie MacDermott.

followed a fortnight later by Bizet's *Carmen*, for which de Valois designed the ballet.[6]

The ballet score that de Valois had asked Lambert to orchestrate was *Les Petits Riens* and it was first presented at the Old Vic on 13 December 1928 as a curtain-raiser to the twice-weekly Christmas performances of Humperdinck's *Hansel and Gretel*, with Stanley Judson as Corydon and de Valois as Rosalind.[7] *Les Petits Riens* was Mozart's only full-length score for dance, and such was Constant's regard for that composer's music that this was to be the only occasion on which he agreed to its treatment for ballet. As Angus Morrison recalled, 'I remember Ninette de Valois telling me that throughout the many years Lambert was Musical Director of the Sadler's Wells, later the Royal Ballet, he was always adamant in refusing to allow anything by Mozart to be used for a ballet'.[8]

For the first months of the following year, with his mother still in Australia and *The Rio Grande* not yet the concert hall success it was to become, Constant earned his living piece-meal by writing the occasional article for music journals, and arranging or accompanying ballet. On 2 July he was at the piano when Penelope Spencer danced to his *Elegiac Blues* at the new Arts Theatre in Leicester Square.[9] That same month he was, as he wrote to Edward Clark, 'very busy over "Jew Süss" – I am arranging & conducting the music for the London run'.[10] *Jew Süss* was an historical novel by the German author Lion Feuchtwanger that Marie Rambert's husband, Ashley Dukes, had been commissioned to adapt for the stage. In the third scene, the guests at a great ball are entertained with a little opera and for this Rambert had devised *The Ballet of Mars and Venus*, choosing three sonatas by Dominico Scarlatti which she asked Constant to orchestrate and conduct and Ashton to choreograph. The play, a tragic-comedy with a cast that included Matheson Lang, Felix Aylmer and the 21-year-old Peggy Ashcroft, opened in Blackpool[11] on 29 July and, after a short tour of the north, went on to the Duke of York's Theatre, London on 19 September where it ran for six months before going on another provincial tour.[12]

As a curtain-raiser for the Old Vic's 1929 Christmas run of *Hansel and Gretel*, de Valois devised a new ballet, *Hommage aux belles Viennoises*, with waltzes and mazurkas by Schubert which she once again asked Constant to arrange and orchestrate.[13] Jobs

---

[6] During the opening ceremony at this 'spacious and beautiful' playhouse before the performance began, the audience was informed that Sadler's Wells still needed £21,000 and the Old Vic £7,000 to free them from debt (*The Times*, 7 January 1931).

[7] Charles Corri conducted *Hansel and Gretel* and probably the Mozart too. *Les Petits Riens* had already been used as a prelude to *Hansel and Gretel* by the British National Opera Company at Golders Green on 10 January 1927 with choreography by Penelope Spencer. The conductor was Aylmer Buest.

[8] Angus Morrison's memoir in *Music Ho!* (Hogarth Press, 1985), p. 16.

[9] *Elegiac Blues* was one of Penelope Spencer's most successful solo dances, and she frequently performed it, dedicating her part in 'Homage to the late Florence Mills'.

[10] Letter from Constant Lambert to Edward Clark, 26 August 1929.

[11] It is uncertain whether Lambert conducted at Blackpool or, indeed, that an orchestra was used in the pre-London run.

[12] Revised versions of *Mars and Venus* and *Leda* (as *Leda and the Swan*), together with the new *Capriol Suite* were among the five ballets at a matinée performed by Marie Rambert's Dancers on 25 February 1930 at the Lyric Theatre, Hammersmith as their first public production. The accompaniment was provided by a string quartet and Katherine Haworth and Norman Franklin on two pianos.

[13] The Vic-Wells files list a 'Divertissement: 1. *Etude* (Debussy); 2. *A Daughter of Eve* (Arensky), 3. *Hommage aux belles Viennoises* (Schubert)'. The conductor on this occasion may have been Vernon Corri, son of Charles Corri.

like these were probably more rewarding because of the contacts and the reputation they brought Constant rather than any financial gain, but in the coming year his contribution to ballet was to expand dramatically. In August 1929 the ballet world had been shaken by the death in Venice of Diaghilev. Ironically, the main cause of his death was also to be that of Lambert's – diabetes. Already overweight, Diaghilev was diagnosed too late in life as being diabetic at a time when insulin was only beginning to be widely available; in Lambert's case the diabetes went undiagnosed, with tragic results.[14]

If Lambert's albeit stormy relationship with Diaghilev had brought him fame as a composer of ballet, the latter's death indirectly helped pave the way for his career as a conductor – of ballet, and an outstanding one too. While Diaghilev was alive it was generally considered inconceivable that British ballet could offer serious competition, especially when most English dancers aspired to becoming members of his company, many of them changing their names to foreign-sounding ones. But with Diaghilev dying in poverty and the collapse of the Ballets Russes (with creditors claiming the company's properties), there was a need for something to fill the vacuum that could keep alive and feed the public's appetite for ballet and maintain the high standards that Diaghilev had set, as well as providing openings for English dancers. It was with these goals in mind that Philip Richardson, editor of *The Dancing Times*, the eminent ballet critic Arnold Haskell, and the music critic Edwin Evans proposed what became known as the Camargo Society, an organisation that depended on the financial contributions of its members. The founders held preliminary meetings on several Sundays to discuss the idea, inviting dancers, musicians and artists for their support.[15] These meetings were held over dinner, an inducement that clearly found favour with Lord Berners: 'I shall be delighted to put my name down as one of the supporters of the Camargo Society,' he wrote to Evans on 13 December, 'I enjoyed Sunday evening dinner so much.' Lambert was approached and replied three days later than Berners: 'I shall be delighted to do anything to help the society which naturally interests me very much. I am sorry not to have been at any of the meetings but as I now work at the theatre Sunday is my only free evening to see my friends & is usually booked up.'[16]

Once a sufficient number of supporters had been found, to mark the Society's foundation a dinner was held on Sunday 16 February 1930 at the Hotel Metropole, London. The impressive list of guests included most of the leading names in ballet and music, amongst them Tamara Karsavina, Lydia Lopokova (who after much persuasion joined the committee as choreographic adviser), George Balanchine, Boris Kochno, Ninette de Valois, Marie Rambert, Anton Dolin, John Maynard Keynes (husband to Lopokova), Mrs Henry McLaren (who became Lady Aberconway in 1934), Mr and Mrs Arnold Haskell, Gustav Holst and his daughter Imogen,[17] Mr and Mrs Arthur Bliss, Mr and Mrs Christian Darnton, and Dr and Mrs Malcolm Sargent. Among those who had promised their support were dancers Anna Ludmila, Phyllis Bedells, Tilly Losch,

---

[14] A Paris doctor informed Diaghilev in June 1929, two months before his death.

[15] Named, at the suggestion of Edwin Evans, after the celebrated French dancer Marie Anne de Camargo (1710–70) who made her début in 1727 and became a superstar in her day, known widely as 'La Camargo'.

[16] Correspondence to Edwin Evans concerning the Camargo Society 1930–33, British Library Add. 59814, fols. 1–38. *Jew Süss* was still running at the Duke of York theatre, Lambert conducting the short ballet. However, he would have had time off for the first two pubic performances of *The Rio Grande* that month, in Manchester and London.

[17] Gustav Holst had written on 23 December 1929: 'I am delighted with the scheme and am writing to give my cordial support. ... When the scheme develops and you need members, I think I know of a few recruits – my daughter Imogen for one.' Imogen Holst had been a student of Penelope Spencer's ballet class at the Royal College of Music.

Alicia Markova and Penelope Spencer; composers Herbert Howells, Arnold Bax, William Walton, Lennox Berkeley and Julius Harrison; and painters Augustus John, Rex Whistler, John Armstrong, Edward Wadsworth and Paul Nash. Chairman Mme Adeline Genée[18] proposed a silent tribute to the memory of Diaghilev and then Edwin Evans outlined the objects of the Society: it was not to take the place of Diaghilev; there was no suggestion of running a full season, but with a membership of 600–800 and using artists from the Vic-Wells Ballet and Marie Rambert's Ballet Club, it should be possible to hold productions four times a year in the West End on Sunday evenings and Monday afternoons before a subscription audience. It would produce ballet because ballet was a collaboration of the three arts: dancing, music and decorative design. The constitution did not allow the Society to make a profit for distribution to its subscribers; any money earned would be spent in furtherance of its objective. The watchword was economy, necessarily so as it turned out, because subscriptions barely covered production costs and there was a general financial crisis following the Wall Street crash. Lopokova's occasionally extravagant plans had to be reined in by her husband who, fortunately, was treasurer. In addition to the founders, the committee also included Marie Rambert, Ninette de Valois, Anton Dolin and Constant Lambert, with Montagu-Nathan as secretary. The Society's first production was set for October and Lambert's *Pomona* was among the ballets proposed.

M EANWHILE, Constant continued to be called upon to recite *Façade*. March 1930 saw the first gramophone release of 11 numbers that he and Edith had recorded the previous November in the Chenil Galleries. Walton had conducted, and he proudly wrote to Siegfried Sassoon, 'A de-luxe – signed by the author-&-composer edition of "Façade" is going to appear in the autumn, 300 copies at £3 3 0. Incidentally the records are out this month, & it is being "broadcast" to-morrow by Edith & Constant.'[19] This, the first complete broadcast of *Façade*, further revised and now with 18 songs divided into six groups, was given on 3 March at one of the BBC Concerts of Contemporary Music in Central Hall, Westminster. Writing beforehand from Amalfi, Walton had told Edward Clark, 'Each group should be announced by a separate voice and Constant will tell you anything you want to know about the conduct of the performance.'[20] In his own place as conductor Walton had recommended Leslie Heward, shortly to be appointed director of the City of Birmingham Orchestra in succession to Adrian Boult. The remainder of the programme included John Ireland accompanying nine of his songs, his Ballade played by Arthur Alexander, and a second broadcast of Constant's Piano Sonata, this time played by Angus Morrison. Fox Strangways, in *The Observer*, wrote of the Sonata: 'It has a fine first movement, which has lift and sometimes vision; after that it busies itself with this or that contrast, things of the moment, and the vision fades – as in life.'[21]

Later that same month Constant was both conducting and reciting at a

---

[18] Dame Adeline Genée (1878–1970), Danish-born ballet dancer, real name Anita Jensen, made her debut in Oslo and danced in the 1890s in Berlin and Munich before appearing regularly at the London Empire Theatre and from 1911 at the Coliseum and Alhambra. A charming, vivacious performer, her most famous role was as Swanilda in *Coppélia*.

[19] Letter from Walton to Sassoon, 2 March 1930, in Walton, *Selected Letters*, p. 57.

[20] Letter from Walton to Clark, 1 January 1930: Letters to Edward Clark, BL Add 52257, fols. 139–148b. The instrumentalists were Robert Murchie (flute), Frederick Thurston (clarinet), Walter Lear (saxophone), Ernest Hall (trumpet), Ambrose Gauntlett (cello) and Charles Bender (percussion).

[21] 9 March 1930.

Contemporary Arts Festival in Bath.[22] The opening programme included Hugh Bradford's Fugal March, a suite from *Pomona*, the *Elegiac Blues*, Walton's *Siesta* and Goossens' *Prelude to Philip II*, and *Façade* which was conducted by Edward Dunn. Montagu-Nathan, who first met Constant 'in the artists' room when he was trying to recover from his declamation of the *Façade* text',[23] reviewed the concert for *The Musical Times*:

> Later, having testified to his appreciation of a fellow-composer by conducting Hugh Bradford's very striking 'Fugal March' he abandoned the baton to the orchestra's permanent conductor, Mr Dunn, and proceeded to manifest his interest in a sister art by assuming the Sitwellian megaphone in a performance of *Façade*. ... Mr Lambert's declamation gave one the impression that only a consummate musician could have been capable of such a performance. One became aware that the poetry was being galvanised by an immensely strong sense of rhythm, without which Miss Sitwell's verse would be deprived of much of its point.[24]

At the end of April he took a short holiday in the south of France, staying first at Marseille from where he wrote to Anthony Powell:

> My dear Tony,
>   As I write I am surrounded by so many negros & dwarfs that I can hardly believe I am not in the heart of Old Bloomsbury. In fact the only real difference between Marseille night life & a Gt Ormond Street party is one of expense. One feels that at any moment the homely figure of Dick Wyndham may emerge from a bordel or that Wadsworth will be seen trying to retrieve his hat from some old hag or other. All the female whores look like Greta & all the male ones like Brian Howard.[25] There is an exact replica of Billy Chappell who dances a solo Charleston outside one of the homosexual bars – a cosy place whose principal attraction is a monkey that picks pockets & a boy with only one leg and one arm.
>   I expect you are now dressing for David Tennant's[26] Mozart-cum-bottle party. I meant to suggest that you should go as a character from the Magic Flute – there is a dragon in the 1st Act & 2 men in armour later on. 3 people between them could more or less finish off the Watteau atmosphere. I suppose Harry Walker will go as Leporello & Stephen [Tennant] as the Queen of the Night. You will excuse the shaky handwriting I'm sure – it's all I can do to hold a pen these days. My obsessions are becoming more pronounced I'm afraid but not quite so narrow. I feel rather like Walt Whitman – all races, all colours, all creeds, all sexes etc.
>   I find smoking Maryland has had an aggravating effect on my vomiting. Fortunately nobody minds a bit of retching here.
>   I leave for Toulon tomorrow where I may see Willie.[27]

---

[22] The Bath Festival lasted from 21 March until 5 April 1930.

[23] Letter to Foss, 20 March 1952.

[24] *The Musical Times*, May 1930, p. 457.

[25] Brian Howard, Eton and Oxford aesthete and a protégé of Edith Sitwell, on whom the character of Anthony Blanche in Evelyn Waugh's *Brideshead Revisited* is said to have been based.

[26] Hon. David Tennant (1902–68), elder brother of Stephen Tennant and first husband of Hermione Baddeley from 1928 until their divorce in 1936.

[27] Letter from Lambert to Powell, postmarked 1 May 1930, giving his address as 'Au rendezvous des Nauséabondes, Rue Crapoule, Vieux Port, Marseille'.

When the news of George Lambert's death near the end of May had reached home, Patrick Hadley was one of many to convey his sympathies to Amy. Constant, at the time engaged on a new work, his Concerto for Solo Piano and Nine Players (not to be completed for a year and a half), was quick to thank Paddy:

> Thank you very much indeed for your charming and generous letter in the Times.[28] It was very good of you. I rather liked the aesthetic fallacy in the first draft; it reminded me of my own articles. I must thank you too on behalf of my mother for your sympathetic letter. I'm afraid it has been rather a blow to her. She is a good deal better now but you naturally understand she isn't quite in the mood for letter writing. She was, I know, very pleased to hear from you.
>
> I do hope that you are composing a good deal. It would be the greatest pity if one of the few people in this country with any real genius for such an occupation should be prevented & hindered by routine work. My musical St Vitus dance gets worse & worse. My new concerto has now got out of 11/8 only to get into 13/8. However after this I am going to turn over a new leaf and in future my works will be noticeable for their morbid introspection, their extreme length, the paucity of notes to a bar and the remarkably deliberate tempi in which those few notes will be played.
>
> The Captain [Osbert Sitwell] told me a good story against myself which I feel you would be the first to appreciate. He played over one of my Façade records to his aunt who said when asked for an opinion 'Yes, my dear. I'm sure it's very pretty once you're used to it, but you know I've never cared for records in dialect'.
>
> Your idea about the Carlyle Square fagging suicide has kept us happy for some time .[29] (I was right, by the way about the cause of the Captain's bad temper. The Lewis book seems to have rattled him.[30] As I am one of the few people who have seen Lewis in the last year, I realise that everybody will think that I have supplied the more scandalous information. A grotesque theory as we never discuss personalities but sufficiently plausible to make my relations with half my friends fairly intolerable for a few months.) I never thanked you for the superb Bontoft item which is always with me.[31]

The following day was the occasion of the renowned first performance of a chamber version of *The Rio Grande*, at Arthur Benjamin's house when Constant took on all the percussion parts himself.

That summer he had an engagement abroad to conduct the Frankfurt Symphony Orchestra at a Festival of British Music. Part of one of the concerts, held on 16 July in the Rococo Theatre, Bad Homburg, was relayed at home by BBC London Regional: Boyce's Symphony No. 4, the *Idyll* from Bliss's *Serenade*,[32] and Bax's *Symphonic*

---

[28] This letter has not been traced. It is possible that Lambert received only a draft and the letter was never published.

[29] According to Susana Walton, *Behind the Façade*, p. 52, after reading a newspaper report of a boy committing suicide because of fagging at a public school, Lambert put the story about that Walton had committed suicide because of fagging at Carlyle Square. Osbert Sitwell would sometimes treat Walton rather like a fag, expecting him to run errands for him.

[30] Wyndham Lewis, *The Apes of God* (London: Arthur Press, 1930), which satirises the Sitwells, and in particular Osbert in the character of Lord Osmund.

[31] Letter to Patrick Hadley from Constant Lambert at 42 Peel Street, W8, 14 June (1930). The 'Bontoft item' may refer to a newspaper cutting of humorous interest, similar to the many that Lambert carried around with him to show friends.

[32] The *Idyll* is the purely orchestral movement from the *Serenade* for baritone and orchestra first performed on 18 March 1930 at a Courtauld-Sargent concert.

Variations in which the soloist was Harriet Cohen.[33] Constant was keen to include Walton's *Sinfonia Concertante* during 'English Music Week' and Walton wrote to Harriet: 'I hear from Constant that he hopes to play my *Sinfonia Concertante* with you, in the concert at Frankfurt in July.'[34] In her autobiography Harriet wrote: 'My rehearsals of the *Concertante* with Willie and Constant were often hilarious and brought joy to me during those sad, hard, though fundamentally satisfying months. Nothing could really extinguish the radiance of that roseate time; one was young and surrounded with love and work.'[35] It seems that during this rehearsal period Harriet even managed 'to dance a few times with … Willie and Constant'.

As the Festival grew closer she recalled that

> Constant now demanded many rehearsals for Bad Homburg; he had increased them to at least three a week, and interesting and happy times they were. Willie Walton often came along to hear how his *Concertante* was getting on. Tea-time was the hour of jokes and one occasion comes to mind when we talked of Elgar's 'descending sequences' and decided that he wrote out the initial phrase of one, high in the treble, and then went out for a walk leaving Lady Elgar to complete them right down to the last one in the bass. I remember looking at Walton very suspiciously and saying: 'You too, Willie, use a lot of sequences!' Constant broke in with: 'Perhaps he is the child of Sir Edward and Dame Ethel Smyth.'
>
> This light-heartedness continued for most of the time I was with Constant in Bad Homburg, although there were moments when his natural melancholy made itself felt. We often talked late into the night, principally about Debussy's later works. He considered Debussy the key figure of the century, the main influence of the period. Constant thought that in the *Nocturnes*, *La Mer* and *Images*, and perhaps notably in *Iberia* the most extended of the three, Debussy entered into a new emotional world. …
>
> The Mayors of Frankfort and Homburg gave us a banquet and, as I was exhausted and hot after my two concertos, I drank glass after glass of what seemed to be a lovely wine cup … I did not realise this was one of the finest and most potent of German wines and, of course, had not been diluted at all. Constant, knowing that I had not eaten all day, cast somewhat anxious glances at me during the dinner and when it had ended hurried over to me, as he saw I could hardly rise from the table on legs that suddenly dissolved. He gallantly put his arm round my shoulder and guided me away and back to the hotel; in fact, I remember nothing more until I awoke next morning … with my dress and shoes removed! Quickly recovered, I was joined by Constant for coffee on my balcony and we read the criticisms which were mostly kind, perhaps more to us than to the works.[36]

But her delight in his companionship was not shared by Constant, who wrote to Anthony Powell, first confiding in Powell the novelist his current reading matter:

> It's depressing how one works one's way through the modern English writers.

---

[33] Harriet Cohen (1895–1967) was chiefly associated with Arnold Bax with whom she had, from the age of 19, a long-lasting affair which waned, on Bax's part, later in his life. Many composers, including Lambert, dedicated works to her.

[34] Letter from William Walton to Harriet Cohen, Florence, n.d.: BL. Cohen was soon to visit America and Walton added: 'On Constant's suggestion I have cabled to Stokowski, though I only know him slightly.'

[35] Harriet Cohen, *A Bundle of Time: The Memoirs of Harriet Cohen* (London: Faber & Faber, 1969), p. 161.

[36] *Ibid.*, pp. 167–8.

After many years as a character from Firbank, the male Evelyn & Pierpoint I find myself imbedded in one of the more leaden passages in Eddie Sackville-West. The concert went quite well in spite of the fact that German players are actually far worse than English. The platform was draped with the flags of the British Mercantile Marine, most of them upside down. A week with Harriet Cohen is like being put next to one's bête-noire at school lunch – knowing you have to wait until the end of term. Shall recuperate in Paris, I need a little colour in my life.[37]

It was in Paris that Constant – in what he described as a moment of weakness – acquired from one of the bookstalls on the banks of the Seine a book of dubious character called *Slavey*, written by Gerald Reitlinger's brother under the pseudonym of Captain Teach. As Constant later recounted to Powell, he then ran into Lytton Strachey who was also on a visit to Paris.

Lambert, understandably, did not wish this recent acquisition to his library to fall under Strachey's satirical eye, and make a good story for spreading about Bloomsbury. Concealment was fairly easy in the street, where he tucked the book well under his arm. Strachey now complicated matters by inviting Lambert back to wherever he was staying in Paris. Even then *Slavey* might have been kept hidden without too much difficulty, had not something not at all bargained for by Lambert taken place; the making by Strachey of a determined physical pass. Nevertheless, all was well. Lambert managed to repulse Strachey – too concerned with his objective to think of other things – and escape without the detection of what appears to have been Captain Teach's sole publication under that pen-name.[38]

Constant was not usually to be found in Strachey's circles, and his biographer, Michael Holroyd, relates that on their next encounter Constant observed, 'Mr Strachey, do you realise it's five years since we met?' to receive the reply, 'Rather a nice interval, don't you think?'[39] Soon after his return home from the Continent, on 23 July Constant and Angus Morrison dined at the Carlton Grill with the French composer Reynaldo Hahn.[40]

That summer Constant and Ashton visited Lydia Lopokova at Tilton, the Keyneses' farmhouse under Firle Beacon on the South Downs, to discuss a masque of poetry, music and dancing that was to be presented at the Arts Theatre, London in December. Ashton remembered:

We arrived on the Friday, and Constant who loved his drink, found nothing but water. Then Saturday came and Maynard arrived, and with him was a full symphony of wonderful wines from Cambridge. He told us the pedigree of each, and the ensuing evening was one of great gaiety and laughter. On Sunday it was back to water. And Constant went off to the pub, which was a long way away, saying he must go for a walk.[41]

---

[37] Letter-card, postmarked 17.7.30, with views of Ritter's Park-Hotel, Bad Homburg. Powell has written: 'The "male Evelyn" refers to Evelyn Waugh, who was sometimes so called by his acquaintances to distinguish him from his first wife who was also called "Evelyn". "Pierpoint" is Wyndham Lewis, from a name for himself in one of his own books.' The British novelist Ronald Firbank (1886–1926) is probably best known for *Valmouth*.

[38] Powell, *Messengers of Day*, pp. 172–3.

[39] Michael Holroyd, *Lytton Strachey: A Biography* (Harmondworth: Penguin Books, 1971), p. 234.

[40] Reynaldo Hahn (1875–1947), composer, conductor and critic, born in Venezuela but became a naturalised French citizen. He was a life-long friend and for a while a lover of Marcel Proust.

[41] Ashton in Keynes, *Lydia Lopokova*, p. 120.

The *Masque* was to be directed by George Rylands and presented by Arnold Haskell, with choreography by Ashton and with Lambert the musical director. The cast consisted chiefly of Cambridge undergraduates, among them a young Michael Redgrave. The programme included two short ballets: *Follow your Saint: The Passionate Pavane* with music by Dowland transcribed by Warlock and arranged by Lambert for small orchestra, and the comical *The Tartans or Dances on a Scotch Theme* with music by Boyce also arranged by Lambert. The dancers were Lopokova, Ashton and Harold Turner. The spoken part of the programme consisted of excerpts from Shakespeare, from Milton's *Comus* and a masque on *Paradise Lost* to music by Purcell. Despite her distinct foreign accent, Lopokova was one of the speakers. Further planning meetings took place at Keynes's London house in Gordon Square where, after Lydia had raided Keynes's wine cellar, had Lambert and Ashton had their way, there would have been several frivolous additions to the programme, such as Lytton Strachey and Keynes sitting on armchairs by a fire, 'repeating the dialogue of Tilton on free trade, Lytton's voice gradually disappearing'.[42]

On 14 October 1930 a luncheon was held at the Waldorf Hotel to inaugurate the Camargo Society's first presentation five days later at the recently built Cambridge Theatre, London. Staunch vegetarian and teetotaller George Bernard Shaw disapproved of the gathering and wrote to Evans: 'The notion that a dinner can act as a send-off to a ballet season – unless they can make the Lord Mayor drunk enough to dance a hornpipe on the table among the walnut-shells – is beyond my patience.'[43]

Constant conducted the complete programme which consisted of an extract from *Robert the Devil* to music by Meyerbeer, a comedy number composed by Gavin Gordon and produced by Penelope Spencer entitled *A Toothsome Morsel (Scenes from a Dentist's Waiting-room)*,[44] Debussy's *Danse sacrée et danse profane* choreographed by Ninette de Valois, a Dance-Suite by Christian Darnton, Lambert's *Pomona* with Anton Dolin and Anna Ludmila, choreographed by Ashton, and, to conclude, de Valois and Dolin dancing a *pas de deux* to Glinka's *Variations and Coda*. Ashton had wanted to dance in *Pomona* but Lopokova, writing to her husband, was insistent that '*Pomona* should and must have Pat [Anton Dolin]'.[45] It was an immediate success, the *Dancing Times* critic rating it as 'a ballet worthy of the Diaghileff tradition'. Both the scenery and the costumes were designed by John Banting, instead of Augustus John who was busy with a commission elsewhere.[46] The setting, according to the *Dancing Times*, was one of 'fleecy clouds, shady trees, and amusing but anatomically impossible classic statues'. If the *Times* critic felt that the costumes 'deserved a better scene', Haskell later wrote that *Pomona* 'was of an extremely high standard, and in it Ashton showed his gift of being able to produce his dancers to full theatrical advantage.' Dolin's partner, Anna Ludmila, was a beautiful American blonde who 'translated sex-appeal into terms of ballet' and 'Ashton made full use of this and showed an adorable and very human little goddess who could move with immense charm and softness'.[47] In a similar fashion to Diaghilev's 'symphonic interludes', two orchestral items were inserted into the programme: Weber's Overture *Abu Hassan* and Hugh Bradford's *Fugal March*. At the conclusion of that first evening, Lopokova informed an enthusiastic audience that they

---

[42] Kavanagh, *Secret Muses*, p. 121.

[43] Arnold Haskell, *True Centre: An Interim Autobiography* (London: A. & C. Black, 1951), p. 100.

[44] First performed in 1927 at the Royal College of Music with Malcolm Sargent conducting.

[45] Lydia Lopokova to M. Keynes 25 May 1930, quoted in Kavanagh, *Secret Muses*, p. 118.

[46] John Banting also designed the cover designs for the piano duet score of *Pomona* (OUP, 1928) and the full and piano scores of *The Rio Grande* (OUP, 1930).

[47] Arnold Haskell, *Balletomania* (London: Gollancz 1934; revised edn Harmondsworth: Penguin Books, 1979), p. 173.

were witnessing the birth of British Ballet. 'We were able for half and hour to forget that Diaghilev was dead,' reported one critic. The whole programme was repeated the following afternoon.

On the success of the Society's first programme, Constant was officially appointed the Camargo conductor and, in Haskell's words, 'immediately established himself as the great musical leader of our ballet'. One day during the Camargo period, when Constant was being driven by Montagu-Nathan to a rehearsal, he mentioned that the Alhambra music hall had offered him its conductorship. He was quite hard up at the time but Montagu-Nathan had advised him 'to sit tight at his real job and await developments'. Financially the music hall would have been more advantageous for Constant. It was fortunate for British ballet that he followed Montagu-Nathan's advice.

A T this time Constant was involved in a prolonged discussion with the BBC about a new choral composition. In 1929 Edward Clark, in his capacity as a BBC programme planner, was keen on commissioning works specially suited for broadcasting, works that would take advantage of this relatively new medium. Nearly all the music written specially for the wireless had so far originated from Germany (with some on a much smaller scale from the Czechoslovakian broadcasting authorities) and Clark had been particularly impressed by some successful German scores, Kurt Weill and Paul Hindemith's collaboration, the 1929 radio cantata *Lindberg's Flight* among them, for the effective use it made of the spoken voice in contrast with the orchestra. He was looking to young British composers for new works on similar lines, written for a small choir, a soloist, and a small orchestra not exceeding 15, suitable for broadcasting with all its then inherent limitations. He had already sounded out Walton and Lambert, and on 21 August he reminded them both of his request, writing to Constant: 'With reference to the suggestion in discussion recently concerning the writing of special music for broadcasting I should be much obliged if you would let me know at the earliest possible moment the result of your cogitation.' Five days later he received a reply:

> I am afraid I haven't had much time for cogitating & am still very busy over 'Jew Süss' (I am arranging & conducting the music for the London run). I should certainly be pleased to write something particularly if I am allowed a free hand with effects & subject. Perhaps we might meet again to discuss this & I might show you my piano-sonata which I should like you to see. I am sorry I can't be more definite.

When on 12 January 1930 the whole question was discussed internally at the BBC, Clark was able to report that three composers had been approached and had informally agreed. Walton's subject was *Nebuchadnezzar, or the Writing on the Wall* (which became *Belshazzar's Feast*). Constant chose something typically outlandish, the story of Henri Christophe who, born a slave, became a mercenary and eventually King of Haiti, ultimately to take his own life. Constant was to make a text of his own from the recently published *Black Majesty (The Emperor of Haiti)* by John Vandercook.[48] The third composer was Victor Hely-Hutchinson[49] who was on the BBC staff. His work was to be *The Town*, to a text by Cecil Day Lewis. In an internal memo on 13 March, fees were set at 50 guineas each for Walton and Lambert and 20 guineas for

---

[48] John W. Vandercook, *Black Majesty: The Life of Christophe, King of Haiti* (New York: Harper & Brothers, 1928).

[49] The South African-born composer, pianist and administrator Victor Hely-Hutchinson (1901–47) joined the BBC in 1926 and was eventually to become its Director of Music from 1944 to 1947. Today he is probably best known for his *Carol Symphony*.

Hely-Hutchinson who, as a member of the Music Department, rather felt that he should receive no fee at all but hoped instead to be allowed time off to compose. Unfortunately, the whole matter quickly got out of hand when Walton let it be known to the Press that he had been definitely commissioned and furthermore was not satisfied with the fees proposed. Although the work was only half-finished, he was asking for £100. But the BBC were adamant about the £50 offered and suggested that he should write something else as his commissioned work. Walton, however, continued with *Belshazzar's Feast* which quickly outgrew the scale of the original commission. It was accepted for the 1931 Leeds Festival where it proved a resounding success.

The BBC now looked instead in Lambert's direction in the hope that he might fulfil the commission, and on 1 October 1930 Foss informed Richard Howgill that Lambert was 'very delighted and interested and would like to hear more'. Yet by 5 November, perhaps faced with the challenge of matching the success of *The Rio Grande*, he had changed his mind, with Foss writing to Howgill that 'after thinking it over at considerable length with great care, [Lambert] thinks there is very little chance of his being able to devote his attention to a choral work for some considerable time. In his present mood he finds that a choral work has little attraction for him'.

But Foss went on to mention that Constant was completing 'a new work of quite novel character, a Concerto for Piano & 8 instruments (flute, 3 clarinets, trumpet, trombone, cello & one perc. player) – planned originally to act as a prelude to William Walton's *Façade*' and wondered whether this might be suitable. In December a BBC memo from Adrian Boult stated that 'Constant Lambert spoke to us about his Piano Concerto, and is very anxious that should be his commissioned work.'[50] The BBC replied that they would prefer to keep to the original suggestion of a choral work, although by now they were in fact rather against the whole idea of the commission, and the scheme soon fizzled out. But the story of Henri Christophe was not to be forgotten; Lambert returned to it towards the end of his life as the subject of an orchestral tone-poem. Meanwhile, he completed his Piano Concerto, adding a double bass to the original listing. Walton wrote to Harriet Cohen on 26 November: 'Constant ... by the way, is continually asking after you – why from me I don't know. I think he's got it badly and is writing a Piano Concerto for you in 13/8 time.'[51] Whether or not there was any serious thought of dedicating the work to Harriet, a tragic event three weeks later was to decide the work's dedication.

On 27 November Constant had an engagement to conduct *The Rio Grande* at the Eastbourne Festival with Angus Morrison the soloist. In December Arnold Haskell's *Masque of Poetry and Music* ran for a week at the Arts Club Theatre, Constant conducting the two short ballets that included *The Passionate Pavane* with music by Dowland that Philip Heseltine had transcribed and Constant had arranged. On the morning following the last presentation of the *Masque*, Heseltine was found dead in his London flat under circumstances that suggested suicide by gassing. Constant was devastated. He was present three days later at the funeral at Godalming cemetery that was also attended by Bernard van Dieren, Anthony Bernard, Cecil Gray and Arthur Bliss. Then, as soon as he could, he escaped to Paris from where he wrote to Marie Nielson at Theatre Royal, Birmingham where she was performing:

---

[50] BBC memo, 10 December 1930, BBC Written Archives, Caversham.

[51] Letter from William Walton to Harriet Cohen, 26 November 1930: Harriet Cohen papers, BL Deposit 1999/10. This was the Concerto for Piano and Nine Players that made much use of irregular time signatures such as 7/4 and 11/8.

My dear Marie

I feel so guilty not having written before but just after I received your letter I had a great shock on hearing of the death of Peter Warlock who was one of my greatest friends. I was very upset and had to look after someone who was even more so [Cecil Gray] – the next few days were just a nightmare. I came to Paris on Sunday hoping to avoid the gloom of London. Not altogether successfully. Still I enjoy going for interminable walks in the more sinister and uncharted quarters of this town. I am sorry you are finding Birmingham so trying. I am glad you are not going to be away so long as you thought.

As for the Camargo – when I think of returning to it I am tempted to change my name and run away to sea.

I hope I shall see you when I come back.

Much love

Constant[52]

Heseltine's was one of two deaths to be commemorated in the Camargo Society's second production of ballets, with Constant conducting, at the Apollo Theatre, London on 25 January 1931, the whole programme being repeated the following afternoon. A ballet to the *Capriol* Suite was performed by Marie Rambert's dancers (who had included it in their three-week Christmas season of ballet), and to mark the recent death of the renowned Russian ballerina Anna Pavlova, Constant turned to the audience and announced that the orchestra would play *The Dying Swan* in her memory. The curtain rose to an empty stage with a single spotlight. The other ballet items were *Cephalus and Procris* to music by Grétry, a 'distressingly vapid' *Straussiana*, and Bliss's *Rout* (with a prologue spoken by Hedley Briggs) while, as an interlude, Madame Alice Cavoukdjian gave a display of solo dancing that, suggested *The Times* reviewer, showed greater rhythmic precision than anything else in the programme apart from

> Mr Constant Lambert's most excellent direction of the orchestra. He has the gift of imparting his own instinctive rhythm to his players, which is invaluable to anyone accompanying dancing. He also gave a piquant first performance of Gavin Gordon's amusing Polka from an orchestral Divertimento.

A month later, on 23 February, a Heseltine memorial concert was given at the Wigmore Hall (the latter part broadcast on the London Regional programme). Constant, who was involved in its planning, had written to Harriet Cohen: 'Like so many people I am still very depressed by Philip Heseltine's tragic death. I expect you may have heard from Arnold [Bax] that Gray and I are trying to arrange a memorial concert of his works.' After asking for her help with subscriptions, he added, 'We want to give a good and well rehearsed programme with small orchestra and singers.[53] I think it will not only be a personal tribute but will show to many people an unexpected variety and force in his music.'[54] Charles Kennedy Scott conducted the Oriana Singers, Arnold Bax at the piano accompanied some songs and Constant conducted a chamber

[52] Letter from Constant Lambert to Marie Nielson, 27 December 1930. From 1930 to 1932 she had minor roles with the Camargo Society and the Vic-Wells Company in such ballets as *Pomona* (1930), *Job* (one of the three daughters), *A Day in a Southern Port* (*The Rio Grande*), *Jew in the Bush*, *Narcissus and Echo*, *Rout*, *The Lord of Burleigh* and *The Origin of Design*.

[53] Among the many friends and admirers besides Lambert who gave financial support to the memorial concert were Arnold Bax, Anthony Bernard, Lord Berners, Adrian Boult, Harriet Cohen, Frederick Delius, Hyam Greenbaum, Cecil Gray, Patrick Hadley, Maynard Keynes, G. B. Shaw, Kaikhosru Sorabji and Ralph Vaughan Williams. For the full list, see Fred Tomlinson, *Warlock and van Dieren* (London: Thames Publishing, 1978), p. 37.

[54] Cohen, *A Bundle of Time*, p. 183.

orchestra in the *Serenade for Frederick Delius, An Old Song* and the *Capriol* Suite, and he was also in charge of *The Curlew*. With the concert behind him he found time to write to Marie Nielson:

> I am sorry to hear you have had the 'flu. I meant to write before but have been off my head with work for the Peter Warlock Concert – also a talk on the wireless (of all things). Are you up and about? Do let's fix up something next week. Perhaps you could ring me up as I have forgotten your number.[55]

The radio talk, on Debussy, was the first of many that he was to give over the years.[56] Broadcast on 20 February in the London Regional programme, it was the first of six half-hour programmes entitled 'New Friends in Music'. Others were given by Edwin Evans, Adrian Boult, Arthur Bliss, Percy Scholes and Victor Hely-Hutchinson.

In March, as a timely tribute, he recorded Warlock's *The Curlew* for the National Gramophone Society with the same artists as in the memorial concert: John Armstrong (tenor), Terence McDonagh (cor anglais), Robert Murchie (flute) and the International String Quartet. 'Its conductor was a brilliant young composer of salient promise and many gifts,' wrote Gordon Bottomley in *Gramophone*.[57] And with Heseltine very much in Constant's mind, the Piano Concerto, completed later that year, was dedicated to his memory.

The Camargo Society was now well established, and it gave its third presentation on Sunday 26 April at the Cambridge Theatre, again with Constant conducting. The programme, repeated the following afternoon, began with two short ballets arranged by Ashton: *Follow your Saint* (that had formed part of Haskell's *Masque* in December) and *Mars and Venus* (that had first appeared in 1929 in the play *Jew Süss* but now orchestrated for a 'full 18th-century orchestra'), Milhaud's *La Création du monde*, choreographed by de Valois,[58] a short *Valse-fantaisie* (Glinka) in which Ashton partnered Karsavina, and finally a new Ashton ballet, *Façade*, in which Lopokova, Markova and Ashton were among the performers. When Ashton had first shown an interest in the music of *Façade*, Constant prepared the ground by seeking the approval of Walton who was not initially drawn to ballet, and then introducing Ashton to Osbert Sitwell, Edith at first not wanting to be associated with the project.[59] Only when it had been successfully staged did she give it her seal of approval. Constant and Ashton probably discussed which numbers to choose, eventually adding two to the existing orchestral suite of five.[60] With a set designed by John Armstrong, this burlesque *divertissement* satirised various forms of dance. It had been intended for the Camargo's January programme but was not ready in time. When it was given in April it went down well with the audience and was quickly taken up by Marie Rambert for her

---

[55] Letter from Lambert (42 Peel Street) to Marie Nielson (1 Onslow Place, SW7), 25 February 1931.

[56] Lambert's radio talks are listed in Appendix 5.

[57] Gordon Bottomley, '"The Curlew" and Peter Warlock', *Gramophone*, December 1931, pp. 259–60.

[58] *La Création du monde* was commissioned as a ballet and premiered by the Ballet Suédois in 1923 at the Théâtre Champs-Elysées in Paris.

[59] The first ballet using the music of *Façade* (based on the First Suite for Orchestra) was given in September 1929 in Hagen to choreography by Günter Hess and conducted by Georg Lippert. Ashton's was the first English version and the one to stay in the repertoire.

[60] The *Façade* ballet, as presented by the Camargo Society, consisted of the following numbers: Scotch Rhapsody, Jodelling Song, Polka, Valse, Popular Song, Tango-Pasodoble, Finale – Tarantella Sevillana. The two items not in the *First Suite for Orchestra* were Scotch Rhapsody and Popular Song and the order was changed.

recently opened Ballet Club in Ladbroke Road. It was to find a permanent place in the Vic-Wells repertoire.

Nine days after the Camargo Society's third presentation came an even more significant occasion for Constant when he was invited to conduct the Vic-Wells Company's first complete evening of ballet, at the Old Vic. The whole venture was then considered something of a risk. The programme consisted of *Les Petits Riens* (Mozart), *Danse sacrée et danse profane* (Debussy), *Hommage aux belles Viennoises* (Schubert), *The Jackdaw and the Pigeons* (Hugh Bradford, with his Fugal March played as an overture), *Scène de ballet* from *Faust* (Gounod), *Suite of Dances* (Bach arranged by Goossens), *Spanish Dance* (Albeniz) and *The Faun* (Vaughan Williams).[61] Anton Dolin was the guest artist and, reported *The Times*, 'Mr Constant Lambert conducted the orchestra with his keen sense of the rhythm required by dance music.' In fact so successful was the occasion that it was repeated on 15 and 21 May at Sadler's Wells Theatre, with Constant conducting at a greatly reduced fee. On the third evening *Cephalus and Procris* (Grétry) was added to the programme with Lopokova appearing as a guest artist, generously donating her fees to a fund for repaying the theatre's building debts. While none of the ballets, all with choreography by de Valois, survived past the early days of the Vic-Wells, the public's response nevertheless emboldened Lilian Baylis to risk an evening of ballet once a fortnight for the coming season and engaged Constant as the Company's conductor and musical director.

While his future as a conductor of ballet was now on a firm foundation, Constant's next venture was on shakier ground. He had been asked to supply incidental music for Oscar Wilde's infamous play *Salomé* which was banned from the English stage both for reasons of immorality and because of its representation on the stage of biblical figures. When Beecham introduced the Strauss opera to London some absurd changes had to be made to comply with the Lord Chamberlain's demands. Private performances of the play or those given in 'clubs' were not subject to censorship and so *Salomé* could be presented at the Gate Theatre Studio on 27 May without interference. Produced by Peter Godfrey, the cast included Robert Speaight (Herod), Flora Robson (Herodias), John Clements, Norman Shelley and Esmond Knight. The leading role was taken by Margaret Rawlings and the climax of the play, her *Dance of the Seven Veils*, was arranged by de Valois who remembered Rawlings as 'an actress who could have been just as great a dancer. I know no actress with a greater sense of natural movement than hers.'[62] Constant's suitably sinister and lugubrious score, for clarinet, trumpet, cello and percussion, consisted of nine sections, the only extensive one being the *Dance of the Seven Veils*, its cumulative energy occupying nine pages of score. A nine-minute suite, skilfully arranged by Giles Easterbrook[63] and first performed in 1998, ends with a dramatic representation of the executioner's blow. As well as the opening trumpet call, several bars are recognisable as having been later reworked in Lambert's masterpiece, *Summer's Last Will and Testament*.

As Marie Nielson (who was one of Salomé's slaves in the production) remembered:

---

[61] This ballet should not be confused with an earlier one, also called *The Faun*, choreographed by de Valois at the Abbey Theatre, Dublin in 1928 to music by Harold White. The music was Vaughan Williams's *Charterhouse Suite* arranged for string orchestra.

[62] De Valois, *Come Dance with Me*, p. 98.

[63] 'As payment towards a large tax bill after Lambert's death, [the *Salomé*] music was confiscated by the Inland Revenue, who surprisingly did nothing with it. Eventually it fell in to the hands of Giles Easterbrook who … reconstructed the nine fragments (one with the percussion part missing) into a suite of three short movements, arranging the fragments into an order which matches the narrative of the play'. Claire Salmon, *BMS News, 81* March 1999 p. 284.

The Gate Theatre was so minute that the 'orchestra' sat on a shelf above the dressing-room. We had to get in early & shut the door so that a ladder could be propped up between stage & orchestra & Constant conducted perched on one of the rungs. A nerve-racking experience if one knew his habit of stepping backwards.[64]

The *Times* reviewer reserved his main criticisms for the text, suggesting that, writing the play in French, Wilde 'was so engrossed by the formal difficulties of his medium that he became a verbal decorator ... and when the play is dragged back from French into English the difficulties increase'. The music, which only played a small part in the production, received no comment at all, but the same reviewer wrote of Rawlings that she 'attained to a chill, feline evil very closely in the tradition of the Beardsley drawings' and that her dance 'is not a mere interlude, but greatly increases the dramatic tension'. The *Stage* critic thought that 'the dance was performed with grace, skill and as decorously as the circumstances allowed by the exiguously attired Miss Margaret Rawlings'. The play was followed by *Danses divertissements* performed by de Valois and Hedley Briggs.

Salomé ran for 32 performances, one of which was conducted by Spike Hughes who recalled in his autobiography:

I had spent some nights previously sitting in the wings while Constant conducted an orchestra consisting of a couple of wind instruments,[65] my West Indian friend Leslie playing the trumpet, and Bumps [Greenbaum], who sat surrounded by oriental drums, which he beat at unexpected moments with astonishing and typical virtuosity. During the run of the production the composer took a night off from his conducting and, believing that I knew the work by heart, I appointed myself to conduct in his place. Before the performance I drank nearly half a gallon of sherry at a conveniently situated wine-bar just opposite the stage door, and sat in the wings with my eyes shut, alternately humming long passages from Strauss' Salomé, and giving the orchestra what I pleased to consider a strong downbeat at the moments when they should perform the Lambert version. Needless to say, the entire incidental music was conducted by Bumps from behind his gongs and tom-toms. The orchestra, which played back stage, seemed to enjoy my performance, and bought me a lot of more sherry when the curtain came down.[66]

Fairly soon the censorship was relaxed and *Salomé* received its first public performance in England that same year, at the Savoy Theatre on 5 October. There were plans for the play to be staged at Cambridge with Constant's incidental music.[67] The composer Walter Leigh wrote to his mother in November 1931:

Trouble is now beginning about Salomé. I went up to London today to have lunch with Constant. ... His music for the Dance of the 7 Veils is quite effective but unnecessarily difficult, and necessitates getting players from London. This

---

[64] Letter from Marie Nielson (Marie MacDermott) to Angus Morrison, 19 February [1954].

[65] Alan Frank (1910–94), much later to become head of the music staff at Oxford University Press, played clarinet.

[66] Spike Hughes, *Second Movement: Continuing the Autobiography of Spike Hughes* (London: Museum Press, 1951), p. 136.

[67] According to Walker, *Ninette de Valois*, pp. 92–3, Terence Gray at the Cambridge Festival Theatre had tried to overcome the censorship and stage *Salomé*. He achieved a single private performance there in June 1929. 'De Valois was concerned only with the role of Salomé, taken by Vivienne Bennett. [Hedley] Briggs choreographed the rest of the movement.' The music (not Lambert's) is not identified.

the management again finds it can't face, so at present there is an impasse. Beatrice Lehmann has already learnt a dance (from Ninette) to the music, so that it more or less <u>has</u> to be done. I don't know what to do about it. I have to go to London again tomorrow. ... I have also to ... possibly write some substitute music for 'Salomé'. Life is a little difficult just now.[68]

Constant was now being given the occasional BBC studio broadcast and on 3 July for the London Regional he conducted a programme that included his own transcription of Boyce's Fourth Symphony, a Dowland Dance Suite arranged by Warlock and the latter's *An Old Song*, two pieces by Fauré, Mozart's A major Piano Concerto (with Angus Morrison) and Walton's *Façade* Suite. Two days later, at the Cambridge Theatre, he conducted the Camargo Society's fourth offering, beginning with *The Jackdaw and the Pigeons* (first performed two months earlier at the Vic-Wells' first evening of ballet) followed by *Pomona*, again with Dolin and Ludmila, preceded by the first performance of Constant's overture *The Bird-Actors*. But the undoubted success of the evening was Vaughan Williams' *Job*.

Had he seized the opportunity, Vaughan Williams – and not Lambert – would have been the first English composer to provide a ballet score for Diaghilev. In March 1913, in an interview for the *Daily Mail*, the Russian impresario spoke of his hopes 'on a future visit to produce an English ballet for which Dr Vaughan Williams is writing music; Mr Gordon Craig will be responsible for the scenery and staging.'[69] But at a Savoy luncheon the idea fell through. Vaughan Williams first objected to the story of Cupid and Psyche suggested by Craig (for which Nijinsky said he would dance both Cupid and Psyche) and then he rejected the proposal that he should write the music to which Craig would afterwards fit a story. He insisted, not unreasonably, on being given a scenario before writing the music.[70] And so the plan came to nothing.

Vaughan Williams' *Job* also nearly came to nothing. Geoffrey Keynes, younger brother of John Maynard Keynes, had written to Diaghilev on 27 June 1927, suggesting a ballet on the subject of Job, based on the engravings by William Blake.[71] Vaughan Williams would write the music while Gwen Raverat, Keynes' sister-in-law, would be responsible for the décor in the style of Blake.[72] Diaghilev, however, showed little interest, finding it too English and too old-fashioned, and Vaughan Williams was 'glad on the whole'. As he wrote to Gwen: 'Can you imagine Job sandwiched between *Les Biches* and *Cimarosiana* – and that dreadful pseudo-cultured audience saying to each other "My dear, have you seen God at the Russian Ballet?"'[73] Nevertheless, the first sketches for *Job* date from that year and he continued to work on them over the next three years. Not put out by Diaghilev's rejection, with the recent formation of the

---

[68] Walter Leigh (1905–1942), English composer, writing from the Festival Theatre, Cambridge to his mother, 17 November 1931. Leigh is probably best known for his operettas *The Pride of the Regiment* and *Jolly Roger*. Graduated at Christ's College, Cambridge in 1926, he studied composition with Hindemith in Berlin, 1927–9. He was killed in action in Libya.

[69] *Daily Mail*, 8 March 1913. See Buckle, *Diaghilev*, p. 245.

[70] Ursula Vaughan Williams, *RVW: A Biography of Ralph Vaughan Williams* (London: Oxford University Press, 1964), pp. 93–4.

[71] Sir Geoffrey Keynes (1887–1982) was a surgeon and a leading authority on the works of William Blake.

[72] Gwen Raverat's involvement went further. As Maynard Keynes explained in a letter to Edwin Evans, dated 13 February 1931 in which he promised £82 towards expenses: 'My sister-in-law, Mrs Raverat, who has made the design for the scenes, based upon Blake's engravings, is willing to do the necessary painting for the stage, provided that she can be given adequate assistance and facilities in a proper studio.'

[73] Michael Kennedy, *The Works of Ralph Vaughan Williams* (London: Oxford University Press, 1964), p. 202.

Camargo Society in mind Geoffrey Keynes invited Lilian Baylis and Ninette de Valois to look at a toy theatre that he and his sister-in-law had constructed with small cut-out figures of the *Job* characters and miniature backcloths based on Blake's drawings. They were won over.

Although *Job* was conceived for the stage, as its subtitle 'A Masque for Dancing' suggests, it was first heard in a concert performance at the Norwich Festival, the composer conducting, on 23 October 1930, under the title '*Job*, a pageant for dancing'. The critic Basil Maine later wrote that 'in spite of its coming at the end of a long morning programme, that concert performance was an intense experience'.[74] But the *Times* reviewer had reservations, writing that 'the new work suffered from being stage music without the stage ... A concert version of such a work can be little more satisfactory than is the orchestral accompaniment to a song-cycle without the singer. All that can be said is that the hearing of the music makes one want a realisation of the ballet worthy alike of Blake and of Vaughan Williams.'

Also attending that premiere was Gustav Holst, about whom Vaughan Williams was to write:

> I should like to place on record all that he did for me when I wrote *Job*. I should be alarmed to say how many 'Field Days' we spent over it. Then he came to all the orchestral rehearsals, including a special journey to Norwich, and finally, he insisted on the Camargo Society performing it. Thus I owe the life of *Job* to Holst ...[75]

After the first performance, when *Job* was being planned for the stage, Holst wrote to Edwin Evans:

> I have looked through the score of VW's *Job* and in my opinion it would have to be entirely re-scored for performance by a small orchestra. I have told him so, and at present I do not know whether he would cue in or follow my suggestion. He begs me to tell you that, if he is told in time, he would supply the fresh score if he thought it necessary, but he must be told as soon as possible if the work is wanted at all. He is only part owner as the inventor of the Ballet has to be consulted also. If the Camargo produced *Job*, VW would prefer them to do it in London first.[76]

Evans in turn wrote to Maynard Keynes:

> I should, of course, be very glad if the Camargo Society should find it practicable to perform it, either in connection with the Salzburg Festival or otherwise. Dr Vaughan Williams naturally has something to say about the music, and he has a complex about the word 'ballet' for which you would no doubt be willing to substitute 'masque'.[77]

Vaughan Williams in fact was insistent on using the word 'masque' and wrote to Evans:

> The only condition as far as I am concerned, and I am sure the mention of it is a mere formality – that I shall be allowed to veto anything in the production which in my mind does not agree with my music. ... One more stipulation – I

---

[74] Maine, 'The Score', pp. 150–1.

[75] Vaughan Williams, 'A Musical Autobiography (1950)', in *National Music and Other Essays* (1963), p. 194.

[76] Letter from Gustav Holst to Edwin Evans, 3 December 1930: BL Add. 59814, fols. 1–38.

[77] Letter from Edwin Evans to John Maynard Keynes, 16 December 1930: BL Add. 59814, fol. 1.

want the work called a '<u>Masque</u>' not a 'Ballet' which has acquired unfortunate connotations of late years, to me.[78]

As regards scaling down the score from symphony orchestra to pit orchestra proportions, he informed Evans:

> I think I had better get the 'boiling down' done & risk it – otherwise it might be too late – I think I shall ask Constant Lambert to do it if he is willing – he knows the conditions well – I will of course seek your confidence over all this.[79]

It says much for Vaughan Williams' confidence in Constant that he entrusted the task to him, who successfully pared down the score chiefly by eliminating the optional instruments and thinning out the brass. Edwin Evans, writing in *The Musical Times*, considered that 'Constant Lambert's arrangement for the smaller forces at his disposal was so skilfully done, that in proportion to the dimensions of the theatre it sounded exactly right, and was probably quite as effective as the larger orchestra in the larger building [Norwich Festival].'[80] Even Vaughan Williams commented that Constant had done the reduction 'wonderfully', getting over one particular difficulty 'when he added in a bass part for the harp, which was extremely effective'[81] while Constant himself modestly was to refer to it as 'a much-reduced orchestral arrangement which cannot be considered more than a postcard reproduction of the original'.[82]

In July 1930 Vaughan Williams had asked Vally Lasker, one of the staff of St Paul's Girls' School where Holst taught, to make a solo piano version of the score for the dancers to rehearse to, 'something simple and practical – I know it can't be all got in but something that will give the essentials. I can't spare the full score – but I think it wd. be all right to do it off the pfte duet copy.'[83] The work nevertheless presented considerable difficulties for the Camargo Society as it could only afford one theatre rehearsal with orchestra on the Friday preceding its two performances, especially when the lighting and the staging had to be sorted out at the same time. De Valois, who provided the choreography, remembered that they went through the ballet once with just enough rehearsal time left to do about a third of it again.[84] 'As far as I was concerned it did not matter which part we did repeat; it was all so bad and needed so much more work. Lambert, it appeared, was applying the same unhappy attitude to the score. We started again from the opening scene and got as far as we could before our time was up. I can remember clutching the rails of the orchestra pit; I did not dare to turn and face my fellow companions of the Camargo Society, for I was so deadly ashamed of the scene of chaos that I had just witnessed.'[85] Vaughan Williams recalled that the 'rehearsals were the only occasions on which I knew [Lambert] really worried and nervous. Rehearsal time was short, the orchestra was difficult, the clarinet said he

[78] Letter from Ralph Vaughan Williams to Edwin Evans, n.d. 'Sunday': BL Add. 59814, fols. 1–38.

[79] Letter from Ralph Vaughan Williams to Edwin Evans, n.d.: BL Add. 59814, fols. 1–38.

[80] *The Musical Times*, August 1931, p. 745.

[81] *Letters of Ralph Vaughan Williams*, ed. Cobbe, p. 491.

[82] *Sunday Referee*, 6 December 1931. Foss, *Ralph Vaughan Williams*, p. 184, erroneously refers to it being 'produced in full panoply, under Constant Lambert's stick, at the new Camargo Society'.

[83] 31 July 1930. Ursula Vaughan Williams, *RVW*, p. 184.

[84] This was not the first Vaughan Williams score that de Valois had used for a ballet. As a curtain raiser at the Old Vic on 9 May 1929 she had used the *Charterhouse Suite* for *The Picnic* (with different choreography also titled *The Faun*).

[85] De Valois, *Come Dance with Me*, p. 103.

could not, according to his trade union rules, double clarinet and saxophone & so on, but he triumphed over it all'.[86]

Holst's generosity fortunately saved the day. An onlooker at the rehearsal, he had been so distressed at the lack of rehearsal time for his fellow composer's work that – under stipulation of secrecy – he paid for an extra three hours' rehearsal on the Sunday morning.[87]

There was no doubting the highlight of the ballet. 'If one singles out for special praise the superb performance of Mr Anton Dolin as Satan, it is because his was the most spectacular and technically the most exacting part,' wrote *The Times* critic. 'He always assumed exactly the right postures, and his appearance with the clearly defined muscles was as close to the original as possible. The lighting contributed a great deal towards the effect ...'[88] Arnold Haskell concurred: 'There is one virtuoso role that stands apart from the pattern, dominates it, and makes the masque into a proper ballet – that of Satan. Dolin was Satan, superb in the powerful conception of a part, a Miltonic interpretation of the fallen angel.'[89] An important point made by ballet critic Cyril Beaumont is that '*Job* is not a choreographic version of the Biblical story, but of Blake's personal interpretation of it. Hence not only is the argument different, but the whole action is *symbolic*, not *material*.'[90] *Job* was to be the most important new ballet to transfer from the Camargo to the Vic-Wells repertoire.

Marie Nielson danced one of the three daughters of Job. When she went to America she was both amused and embarrassed one day to receive from Constant a highly coloured card of Blake's *Job* (with no envelope) on which he had written: 'As you can see Dolin has touched up his part considerably since you left!'

Later in July Constant was involved in the first festival in England of the International Society for Contemporary Music. Largely the brain-child of Edward Clark, the eight previous annual festivals had been held on the Continent and this one was divided between Oxford and London. In the opening concert, at Oxford on 21 July, Constant directed his *Music for Orchestra*, sharing the conducting of an eclectic programme with Gregor Fitelberg, Alfredo Casella and Hermann Scherchen in works by Roman Palester, Anton Webern, Virgilio Mortari, Vladimir Dukelsky and George Gershwin. On 24 July, at the New Theatre, Oxford, he conducted a matinée of ballet as part of the same festival. *Pomona* and *Job* were the British elements of the programme. Then three days later, Constant was at Queen's Hall, London for a repetition of the ISCM orchestral programme, with the BBC Symphony Orchestra and the same conductors, Constant's and the last two composers' works being the only ones to be broadcast. Aaron Copland, reviewing the concert for the American League of Composers Journal, *Modern Music*, wrote favourably about Constant's work:

> This work commanded particular attention as coming from a man of twenty-six, who, with William Walton, is generally looked upon as the 'white hope' of young British music. In spite of Lambert's youth, one can safely characterise him a born academician. ... It is good honest music built on clear-cut, honest themes that

---

[86] Letter from Ralph Vaughan Williams to Hubert Foss, 5 December 1951, in *Letters of Ralph Vaughan Williams*, ed. Cobbe, pp. 491–2.

[87] *Job* was chiefly financed by Geoffrey Keynes with the assistance of several friends, his brother John and Thomas Dunhill: Mary Clarke, *The Sadler's Wells Ballet: A History and an Appreciation* (London: A. & C. Black 1955, p. 71).

[88] *The Times*, 6 July 1931.

[89] Haskell, *Balletomania*, rev. edn, p. 171.

[90] Cyril W. Beaumont, *Sadler's Well Ballet: A Detailed Account of Works in the Permanent Repertory with Critical Notes* (London: Wyman & Sons, 1946), p. 102.

are interesting principally because of the way they avoid sounding like music by anyone else.'[91]

With Vaughan Williams the only other British composer to be featured in the two London ISCM orchestral concerts (with his *Benedicite*), the name of Lambert was becoming more widely known, not just in connection with ballet but with contemporary music as well.

On the evening of 4 August, Constant had another Regional broadcast, with the BBC Light Orchestra: ballet suites by Grétry, Hugh Bradford, and his own *Pomona* coupled with *The Bird-Actors* overture. Whether his mind was fully on the music is difficult to guess because the next morning was one of those momentous days in anyone's life – he was getting married.

---

[91] Reprinted in *Copland on Music* (London, 1961), p. 196, and quoted in McGrady, 'The Music of Constant Lambert', p. 244.

8 1931
Marriage and Journalism

ONE Sunday, while lunching with Anthony Powell, Constant casually commented: 'I have the most boring afternoon ahead of me you can imagine. I have to go and play the piano to a Russian female pianist who lives in St John's Wood. Can you think of anything one less wants to do on a Sunday afternoon?' But the outcome of his visit was far from boring. As Constant excitedly explained to Powell the next time they met: 'You never know what's going to happen in this life. You remember the dreary prospect ahead of me in St John's Wood? I arrived on the doorstep of the Russian's flat, and the door was opened by the most beautiful creature you ever saw in the world.'[1]

The person in question was a young girl little more than 14 or 15 years of age with striking oriental features.[2] Her name was Florence Chuter (or Kaye) and she was, according to one account, a model from Java.[3] Whatever her background and country of origin, she was certainly a young woman of great beauty. Walter Leigh later described her as Constant's 'exquisite Chinese wife – a rare jewel' and Lady Penelope Betjeman remembered her as his 'most attractive oriental wife'.[4] For a while Constant kept Flo (as she was familiarly called) a secret from his friends and acquaintances. The reason for this is clear – she was at least ten years younger than he was and under age. She was also intellectually very much his inferior but he set about educating her by suggesting books for her to read, talking about his own work, and discussing the pictures that he liked. Powell described how, soon after the marriage, Flo was 'reading only "good" books, seeing only "good" art, listening to only "good" music'.[5] When Constant eventually introduced this 'very young girl' to his friends, Driberg remembered that 'her frail, slightly fay and exotic looking beauty struck us all.'[6] Powell also recognised Flo's beauty and remembered how, whenever she felt untidy, she liked to gaze at a portrait in his house of a beauty known to his grandmother and 'make up her mind never again to fall short of it'.[7] Even Myfanwy Thomas had been struck by her beauty when they attended the same children's ballet school in Tottenham Court Road:

> One tiny elegant creature, her skin a warm olive colour, her glossy black hair knotted into a tight coronet above the almond-shaped eyes and high cheekbones, at once attracted my attention. … Tamara, as Madame called her, was often told to face the class and show us various steps and sequences. … I was sick with admiration and love for this child who moved so lightly and easily, performing the most impossible convolutions of her small, slender body with unsmiling and

---

[1] Powell, *Messengers of Day*, p. 122. The Russian musician was the pianist Elsa Karen who performed at the 1929 and 1930 Henry Wood Promenade Concerts (Honegger, Concertino and Liszt, Piano Concerto No. 2).

[2] Her marriage certificate of 15 August 1931 gives her age as 18, and her father, Frederick Chuter, as being deceased.

[3] Peter Wildeblood, Lambert obituary.

[4] In conversation with Peter Dickinson in his *Lord Berners: Composer, Writer, Painter* (Woodbridge: Boydell Press, 2008), p. 109.

[5] Powell, *Messengers of Day*, p. 176.

[6] In *Remembering Constant Lambert (1905–1951)*, BBC Radio 3 portrait of Lambert presented by Tom Driberg, 23 August 1975. BBC Sound Archives NP7054BL, National Sound Archives T8495/02.

[7] *To Keep the Ball Rolling: The Memoirs of Anthony Powell*, vol. 1: *Infants of the Spring* (London: Heinemann, 1976), p. 33. The picture was a reproduction of a portrait of Lady Cardigan, widow of the commander of the Light Brigade.

modest grace. ... There was great excitement the following week: Madame was rehearsing her girls for a matinée in a real theatre. Madame Tamara (as she was billed on the programme), dressed in a Turkish outfit, spangled trousers and long rainbow scarf, was to dance several solos. Then in a dazzling white tutu spattered with sparkling *diamenté* she did spectacular turns, her head twisting as though it were separate from her body.

Unfortunately for Myfanwy, her mother turned up for the dress rehearsal and took her home so she missed the performance.

But the dreams were mine and I thought often of the exquisite little Tamara, the octoroon, whose real name was Florence. When she grew up she became the wife of Constant Lambert the composer. He had been captivated by Anna May Wong, the film actress, and this elegant little creature closely resembled her.[8]

Constant and Flo even became gossip material, the *Evening News* social columnist reporting before their wedding:

I have often seen Mr Lambert and Miss Florence Chuter together and they are an arresting couple – he bare-headed, broad and almost burly, yet using a silver-mounted walking stick; she no taller than his shoulder, and *petite*. She usually wears a little knotted hat on the back of her head, and the hair is drawn back from an interesting brow mantling wide brown eyes. Twenty-five and eighteen they are: and Constant Lambert is likely to attain further distinction. ... Yesterday I found Mr Lambert deep in discussion on the ground floor while Miss Chuter was drinking iced coffee under the roof.[9]

Then one Sunday in 1931, probably after he had had quite a lot to drink at a celebration Anthony Powell was giving on the appearance of his first novel, *Afternoon Men*, he went down on one knee and proposed to her.[10] They were married at the Kensington Registry Office on 5 August. Powell was abroad in Toulon[11] at the time but April Gordon and Thomas Earp acted as witnesses. Gavin Gordon temporarily let the couple have the use of his home, Kenway Cottage in Kenway Road, near Earls Court, and much later Flo in an interview recalled both the proposal and the eventful day:

He actually got down on his knees and asked me to marry him. He had just had £50 worth of royalties which to him was an astronomical sum and so he thought, 'Right, this is marvellous. I can get married. £25 the wedding lounge, and £25 for the honeymoon.' But his mother didn't really like that. She said, 'No, you can't do this,' and she offered me a glass of milk and said, 'Constant is not the right sort of person to be married to.'

But it was quite incredible. He picked me up in a taxi, I was only sixteen [here she is almost in tears], and on the way to Chelsea [*sic*] Registry Office he said to me, 'My God! This is your wedding day. You haven't got any flowers. I must stop and get you some flowers.' And so he stopped at the florist and he bought me an enormous amount of carnations wrapped in paper, and he said to me, 'You know, this marriage is absolutely dead secret. Nobody is going to be there but Tommy

8 Thomas, *One of These Fine Days*, pp. 112–15. Myfanwy was born in 1910.
9 Quoted in Shead, *Constant Lambert*, p. 91.
10 Powell, *Messengers of Day*, p. 176.
11 Anthony Powell's first novel, *Afternoon Men*, had been partly written in Toulon. According to Powell, *Messengers of Day*, p. 156: 'Lambert had recommended the Hôtel du Port et des Négociants, where he had himself stayed several times, though we were never in Toulon together.'

Earp and Cecil Gray – those are our two witnesses – nobody will be there.' And so I arrived at the registry office clutching this terrible bouquet of carnations – it wasn't a bouquet, it was just wrapped in paper – I climbed out of the taxi and when I got out of the taxi there were eighteen press photographers and I was on the front of the *Evening Standard* that evening clutching my carnations wrapped in newspaper.

We go into the registry office and the registrar said to Constant, 'What profession? What does your father do?' and Constant's father happened to be a very famous painter and so Constant just said, 'Painter.' And so the registrar said, 'House painter?' and Constant said, 'Yes.' And then he said, 'Well, that is marvellous. May I be the first to congratulate you and call you Mrs Lambert? And that will be £2 19s 6d.' And Constant searched in his pocket and he couldn't find the money: it had all gone, he'd lost it on the way buying carnations.

Anyway, after the wedding we made a tour of London's police stations and nobody had found the wallet. We had already booked lunch at the Eiffel Tower which was in those days the very famous restaurant where Augustus John went and Stulik owned this place, and we thought, 'Right, we will go to Stulik's and we will get him absolutely so tight and then break the sad news to him that we couldn't pay the bill.' And this is what we did. And Stulik was so drunk it didn't matter.

And so we got on a train and we were going to France and we could only go to Toulon, we hadn't got enough money to go anywhere else. But when we came back Charles Laughton [and Elsa Lanchester] had lent us a flat in Percy Street which is off the Tottenham Court Road and it was above an Indian restaurant, and when we came back there was a man standing on the doorstep to offer Constant a job on the *Sunday Referee* to be the music critic. I think he was paid £7 a week.[12]

News about Florence quickly spread. As Dora Foss has written:

Avril Wood rang up and asked me to tea ... so I went up and had a very pleasant afternoon. I had a piece of Constant Lambert's wedding cake!! He'd sent a big piece to Sir Henry, complete with orange blossom and a silver shoe and a silver bell – and I got full particulars of Constant's romance. 'She' is a half Chinese-half Irish girl brought up in an East End Orphanage and was the little maid of Elsa Karen. Constant came to the flat to rehearse something with her, fell in love and has now married her.[13]

The offer of his own column in the *Sunday Referee* was a godsend for Constant who was invariably short of money and now had a wife to support. He had earlier taken tentative steps towards what was to become quite an extensive career in music journalism. Quite possibly taking a leaf out of Heseltine's book,[14] he had started with occasional articles, his first two being on a composer he much admired, Emmanuel Chabrier, writing for the monthly arts magazine *Apollo* in October 1926 and for the *British Musician* in July 1927. These articles may have been occasioned by Diaghilev's inclusion of five works by Chabrier as 'symphonic interludes' during his 1926 summer and winter London seasons. Right from the start Lambert displayed the style of not

---

[12] *Remembering Constant Lambert (1905–1951)*, BBC Radio 3, 23 August 1975.

[13] Letter from Dora Foss to Hubert Foss, 1931: Foss Archives. Avril was Sir Henry Wood's daughter.

[14] Heseltine was appointed music critic of the *Daily Mail* in February 1915, a position he only held for five months, but he contributed many journals and newspapers, and in 1920 founded the monthly journal *The Sackbut*.

just a well-seasoned writer but one with extraordinarily individual ideas and the means of expressing them. Here was someone with something fresh – and quite often controversial – to say, and not afraid of saying it. In the *British Musician* he suggested, with a typical Lambertian paradox, that the cause of Chabrier's lack of appreciation lay 'not in any obscurity or perversity of Chabrier's style and thought, but rather in the fact that his music is thoroughly pleasant to listen to and easy to grasp', and he ended with typical outspokenness by stating 'it is doubtful if [Chabrier's works] will be appreciated at their true worth in England until we have rid ourselves of the narrow and pompous outlook which still appears to form part of our musical heritage.'

In November 1926 he provided the first detailed assessment of Walton's output to appear anywhere, in a most unlikely quarter, the *Boston Evening Transcript*, a paper probably best known in England from the lines in T. S. Eliot's first published book of verse, *Prufrock and Other Observations*:

> The readers of the Boston Evening Transcript
> Sway in the wind like a field of ripe corn

Over a year later, in February 1928, he sang Walton's praises again, this time in the Oxford University Press's house journal, *Dominant*.[15] (In an article in a 1929 Promenade programme book, he defended Walton from accusations of flippancy and cynicism made by Dent.)[16] Before long he was offered a column in the *Nation and Athenæum* for which, from April 1930, he wrote monthly record reviews. These were remarkably catholic in their range, from the accepted classics to Sousa, Jimmy Dorsey, Duke Ellington and Cole Porter. When, in March 1931 the paper became *The New Statesman and Nation,* he continued with his 'Gramophone Notes' and the occasional book review until February 1935. For the *Nation and Athenæum* in December 1930 he had written a one-off film review, on René Clair's now classic *Sous les toits de Paris*.[17] A great lover of French cinema, indeed of almost all things French, he no doubt would have enjoyed becoming a regular film critic. The French language being no obstacle, he had even tried his luck with *Le Figaro*, writing in April 1929 under the pseudonym of C. Leonard, two reviews of a number of French films that were then showing in London. Reynaldo Hahn was music critic for *Le Figaro* and he may well have facilitated Constant's few film reviews for that paper.

But his most significant post was music critic for the *Sunday Referee*. From November 1931 until January 1938 he ran an extensive column, reviewing concerts and discussing topics of the moment or matters that he wanted to air. Here he was at his most opinionated, not afraid to ruffle a few feathers, resulting in a number of heated exchanges. But it all provided lively journalism. Other regular contributors to this paper included Aldous Huxley, Henry Williamson, Osbert Sitwell (and occasionally his sister Edith), Paul Dehn (its film critic), Humbert Wolfe (on books) and Barbara Cartland. Walton summed up Constant's journalism:

---

[15] Founded by Hubert Foss and edited by Edwin Evans, *The Dominant* was launched in November 1927 and at first was issued monthly, and then bi-monthly. It only lasted for two years. Lambert contributed one other article, on 'The Symphonies of Sibelius', for the May/June 1928 issue: Simon Wright, 'The Dominant: a Note on a Short-lived Periodical', *Brio*, vol. 41 no. 2 (Autumn–Winter 2004).

[16] Lambert, 'Contemporary English Music', Promenade Concert programme, 24 August 1929, p. 28.

[17] Lambert described René Clair as 'a man who seems miraculously to have absorbed the best features of other schools of production without losing his own individuality'. Lambert, *Music Ho!*, 2nd edn (1937), p. 183, suggests that 'films have the emotional impact for the twentieth century that operas had for the nineteenth', hailing René Clair as the successor of Offenbach.

Though he often found the work irksome, he managed to make his criticisms interesting, while preserving a just and unbiased, if provoking level. He was seldom unfair, and his championship of the music of Sibelius contributed to that great composer's reputation in England. He was unafraid to go against the fashions of the time, and he has since been often berated for his sometimes adverse criticism of the music of Stravinsky. But on the whole his opinions are still as valid now as at the time they were written.[18]

Gordon Jacob thought that 'his literary style was witty and always held the attention of the reader. He was never pompous and never perfunctory either in his writing or his conversation and he had a very clear, active and original mind'.[19]

His appointment to the *Sunday Referee* was heralded in that paper by an extraordinary introduction written by Cecil Gray (whom he had succeeded as music critic of *The Nation and Athenæum*), extraordinary both as a testimonial and for its length.[20] Lambert, he claimed, was the ideal critic of music, being 'that rarissima avis, the musician who is at the same time intelligent, for not only is he a composer and conductor of distinction but also a critic and writer of outstanding merit'. Gray's high regard for Lambert was more than reciprocated and Constant found in Cecil the ideal 'musical godfather'. He responded to him so readily because as a critic Gray held views that were for their time unorthodox and even controversial, championing composers that were not then widely accepted. His *Survey of Contemporary Music*, first published in October 1924, had chapters on, amongst others, Bartók,[21] Busoni, Delius, Sibelius and van Dieren, composers – especially the last two – that Constant was himself to champion, and he was undoubtedly influenced by many of Gray's views.

Gray had had an unhappy childhood, often bed-ridden as a result of various illnesses. He suffered three years of bullying at Haileybury School before being sent home in a very poor physical and mental state and with a diagnosed heart disease. Confined to bed, he spent the days reading and writing and, in a similar fashion to Constant, was largely self-educated in the areas that interested him. Realising that music was what mattered most to him, he moved to London during the First War and became acquainted with such artistic figures as Bernard van Dieren, Jacob Epstein, D. H. Lawrence and Philip Heseltine. Often testy and provocative, Cecil was to become one of Constant's closest friends, drinking companion and correspondent, and another composer friend, Denis ApIvor, has put on record that Cecil's second wife Marie 'spoke of Constant's almost child-like devotion to her and Cecil'.[22] In both *The Nation and Athenæum* and the *Sunday Referee* he would make warm, almost reverential references to Gray, and he would prove to be as opinionated as his predecessor.

He fully justified his appointment. As the tenor Sir Steuart Wilson, Head of Music at the BBC from 1948 until 1950, wrote in his obituary on Lambert:

[18] From a foreword written by Walton at the request of K. Harvey Packer to a collection of Lambert's essays that was never published.

[19] 'Memoir by Dr Gordon Jacob, CBE'.

[20] 'The Ideal Critic of Music – Mr Constant Lambert to write for the *Sunday Referee* – His Qualifications – by Cecil Gray', *Sunday Referee*, 8 November 1931. Cecil Gray (1895–1951), Scottish composer and critic, was the author of several books including *A Survey of Contemporary Music* (1926), two books on Sibelius (1931 and 1935), a biography of Philip Heseltine (1934), a play *Gilles de Rais* (1945) decorated by Michael Ayrton, and an autobiography, *Music Chairs* (1948).

[21] Cecil Gray and Philip Heseltine were among Bartók's most enthusiastic early supporters in Britain, both independently visiting him in Budapest in 1921.

[22] Denis ApIvor, 'Memories of "The Warlock Circle"', in *Peter Warlock: A Centenary Celebration*, ed. David Cox and John Bishop (London: Thames Publishing, 1994), p. 196.

You could not miss his vitality: it sparkled, it flowed like a torrent, it drenched like a fountain, it was real, and when it came it was spontaneous. He wrote criticism as he talked; only most of his talk could not be reproduced in print. It was pungent, his words were winged with good aim towards a known target which he was determined to hit – not by any means only to wound or destroy, for when he thought a thing was good, no composer ever had a better champion.[23]

Such was his distinction, or even notoriety as a critic that he earned a reference in Caryl Brahms and S. J. Simon's 1937 comedy crime novel, *A Bullet in the Ballet*, in which Detective Inspector Adam Quill muses that his chief

> ought to have been a ballet critic, for he had now reached the enviable position from which he had nothing to do but criticise the efforts of others. This duty he performed with the detachment of a Constant Lambert and the invective of a James Agate.[24]

Neither did Lambert the composer escape a mention in the same novel when an extravagant choreographer proposes a modernistic ballet for which 'all the best composers they all write the score. Stravinsky, Ravel, Prokofiev, Honegger, Poulenc and maybe Constant Lambert'.[25]

A FEW weeks after his marriage, with the couple settled in the Laughtons' flat at 15 Percy Street, Constant received a friendly letter from John Ireland:

> You wrote me some time since about the Camargo Society, but, much as I admire your work I really cannot afford these subscriptions in these hard times. I want to congratulate you on your marriage. I do not think I have ever met your wife, but I would be glad to do so some day, ere too long. Do come and dine with me here [Chelsea Arts Club] in the latter part of September. Your brother is a member here, altho' I haven't yet met him at the Club but he is very popular here, & you might like to see the pencil drawing of your father which is in our dining-room, it is a fine piece of work. Your name is often mentioned here, you might like to meet some of our members. I am very glad you had such a good show in the International Festival, the music was well worth the prominence given, tho' I could scarcely admit as much about the other British composer, who, however, may be an idol of yours, so I will say no more, except that Community Singing & shouting matches rather bore me.
>
> I have not seen friend Willie Walton for a long time; he is an elusive bloke. I saw his new choral work [*Belshazzar's Feast*] in sketch some time since, I think it ought to create a good impression. As you know I am a very great admirer of his work & I think it is rather a scandal that he did not appear in the International.
>
> Well, send me a p.c. when you are in town, & come along & dine – even if it bores you stiff, I think you will be doing us here a service.[26]

That year *The Rio Grande* was once again programmed for the Proms, as part of a 'British Composers' Night' on 10 September. Feeling that the choir at the previous year's performance had been too small, Constant had written suggesting that if six or eight sopranos were added it would make a 'vast difference'. (The ideal number he

---

[23] Sir Steuart Wilson, *Sunday Times* obituary on Lambert.

[24] Caryl Brahms and S. J. Simon, *A Bullet in the Ballet* (London: Michael Joseph, 1937; Harmondsworth: Penguin Books, 1942), p. 92.

[25] *Ibid.*, p. 90.

[26] Letter from John Ireland, Chelsea Arts Club, 143 Church Street, SW3, to Constant Lambert, 14 August 1931. It is not known whether Ireland's invitation was taken up.

had in mind was 40: 12 sopranos, 8 contraltos, 8 tenors, 12 basses.) Listening in to the Prom that night on the radio was a young Benjamin Britten who wrote in his diary: 'Lambert's *Rio Grande* very interesting, & beautiful'.[27]

Twelve days later the Vic-Wells Company opened its first season of 'periodical evenings of ballet organised by Miss Ninette de Valois' at the Old Vic, with Constant as its new musical director. The first London public staging of *Job* was on the bill, together with *Regatta* to a score by Gavin Gordon (Ashton's first ballet for the Vic-Wells Company), the Bach–Goossens Suite of Dances, *Scène de ballet* from Gounod's *Faust*, and *Hommage aux belles Viennoises*.[28] But the main attraction was undoubtedly Dolin and the programme was advertised as 'A Night of Ballet with Anton Dolin' who, after coming on as Satan in *Job*, took his curtain call dressed in evening trousers and patent leather shoes and went straight to the Hippodrome where he was appearing in the revue *Stand Up and Sing* with the popular entertainer Jack Buchanan. *Job* was conveniently placed early in the programme. It had two more performances in October.

As these Vic-Wells ballet evenings were at first only fortnightly, even with the occasional performance of one of his own works Constant's income was quite small. Journalism helped boost it a little but, with his marriage and the rent on the Percy Street flat lent by Charles Laughton and Elsa Lanchester, he occasionally turned to friends for a loan. Walton's patron, Christabel Aberconway (the 'Christabel' of his Viola Concerto) was one kind friend, and in October Constant wrote thanking her:

> My dear Christabel,
>
> I can't thank you too much for your cheque which arrived yesterday. I don't know what I should have done without you.
>
> Moving into a new flat with a premium and rent in advance etc has been rather a heavy expense and when I was faced with getting £50 in a couple of days I was really desperate. I just managed to scrape up £30 and your cheque has saved both of us. I felt very guilty about approaching you but felt at the same time that you were one of the few people I could rely on at such a time. Once all this business is over I shall be a little better off than usual and hope I shall be able to pay you back soon (if you don't mind being paid back by degrees).
>
> Have you seen Willie lately? Isn't it marvellous that he has had such notices for B's Feast? I'm afraid my only reply to it is a piano concerto of hideous gloom and necrophilistic atmosphere that is coming out in December.
>
> Hoping to see you again soon.[29]

Ten days earlier *Belshazzar's Feast* had had its triumphant first performance at Leeds. When, in December 1930, the question of an assistant conductor for the Leeds Festival had arisen (notably for the first performance of *Belshazzar's Feast*), Beecham had suggested that 'the most competent of the young men would be Constant Lambert'. The Leeds Committee ended up with two names: Lambert and Sargent.

---

[27] *Letters from a Life: The Selected Letters and Diaries of Benjamin Britten*, vol. 1: 1923–39, ed. Donald Mitchell and Philip Reed (London: Faber & Faber, 1991), p. 204. He also noted: 'Walton's wonderful Vla Concerto (beautifully played by Tertis) stood out as a work of genius.'

[28] Reviewing the first London concert performance of *Job* on 3 December 1931 in a Royal Philharmonic Society programme conducted by Basil Cameron, Lambert wrote that *Job* was 'the most important ballet I have seen outside the Diaghileff tradition' and, though impressive, the movements he typically found less interesting and the weakest were 'the "folk-song" Galliard and Altar dance': *Sunday Referee*, 6 December 1931. Because the Camargo Society was for a subscribing audience, the first staged performance of *Job* was not classified as a public one.

[29] Letter from Constant Lambert, 15 Percy Street, to Mrs Henry McLaren (Christabel Aberconway), 18 October 1931: BL Add 52556, fols. 121–23.

With his experience as a choral conductor, Sargent was chosen.[30] When *Belshazzar's Feast* received its first London performance in November, Constant hailed Walton's 'astonishing maturity' in his new *Sunday Referee* column, at the same time ticking off some commentators who, in their lavish praise for *Belshazzar's Feast*, had been 'blind to the genius' of his earlier works. He acutely noticed that, far from repeating himself, Walton was a composer who had 'chosen to concentrate one phase of experience in one particular work'. He tactfully reserved praise for Osbert Sitwell whose arrangement of the Biblical text showed 'a sense of musical form that is rare in a writer'.[31]

On 21 October *The Rio Grande* received another private performance, this time at the Park Lane home of Lady Louis Mountbatten. Anthony Bernard conducted the New English Choir and the London Chamber Orchestra, with Angus Morrison and Anne Wood the soloists. Coincidentally that same day the work received some unexpected praise when Elgar wrote to Constant: 'May I take this opportunity to say how much I have enjoyed your "Rio Grande" & how highly I think of it.' There were plans for Elgar's ballet *The Sanguine Fan* to be taken on tour in Canada by the choreographer Lady George Cholmondeley and, as her musical adviser, Constant was being consulted. Five days later he replied to Elgar:

> I have looked through your score again and have come to the conclusion that it is so carefully scored and cued that any touching up is quite unnecessary, unless of course one reduced it for a salon orchestra which would be undesirable. I have therefore told Lady George Cholmondeley that she may take it to Canada without a qualm, or at least with no more qualms than are caused by any provincial orchestra.
>
> Need I say how honoured I am by your opinion of 'Rio Grande'. I feel at times that it may almost come to be a millstone round my neck, as no one seems to want to hear my other pieces.[32]

Elgar's views were very soon to be echoed by Delius who wrote to Hamilton Harty several months later: 'I like Constant Lambert's "*Rio Grande*". I think he is the most gifted of the young lot. He has got something to say.'[33] If the work was in any way to become a millstone, much later Malcolm Arnold was in no doubt as to its achievements, commenting in an interview:

> I think that *The Rio Grande*, although it was a tremendous success, was really rather a tremendous and important mill-stone for any composer to have round their neck. I think that it did more in using jazz and popular elements of music in the most brilliant and simple way which is very much alive now because it is so much of its time and much more important than the sort of experiments that Gershwin was doing.[34]

On 5 November, possibly at Harriet Cohen's urging, Constant went to the Royal Philharmonic Society concert at Queen's Hall where John Barbirolli was conducting Bax's Second Symphony. If the concert had been programmed a week later he

[30] Richard Aldous, *Tunes of Glory: The Life of Malcolm Sargent* (London: Hutchinson, 2001), p. 48.

[31] *Sunday Referee*, 29 November 1931.

[32] Letter from Lambert (15 Percy Street) to Elgar, 26 October 1931, in *Edward Elgar: Letters of a Lifetime*, ed. Jerrold Northrop Moore (Oxford: Clarendon Press, 1990), p. 441.

[33] Letter from Delius to Harty, 26 February 1932, in Lionel Carley, *Delius: A Life in Letters*, vol. 2 (London: Scolar Press, 1988), p. 399. *The Rio Grande*, with Harty conducting, had been relayed by the BBC from Manchester the previous evening.

[34] *Constant Lambert Remembered*, BBC Third Network, 25 June 1966.

would quite likely have reviewed it in his first *Sunday Referee* column. However, he had reservations about the Bax symphonies or, more precisely, Bax as a symphonist. After a Proms performance of the Third Symphony the following year, he wrote that 'several hearings of this work have not lessened the charm of its many richly coloured and imaginative passages nor have they helped to elucidate its curious and rambling construction. Anybody who has heard the best of Bax's symphonic poems and chamber works must realise that he is amongst the most gifted and sensitive composers of our time ... [but] these gifts do not necessarily mean that he is a great symphonic writer. Unlike Sibelius, he has not found a formal expression to make his temperamental expression.'[35] When he heard Koussevitzky conduct the Second Symphony, he wrote that it 'contains the finest music in all Bax's symphonies, and up to the end of the second movement is without a dull patch. The finale disappointments us, not because it is any less good as music, but because it adds nothing to the emotional argument of the work'.[36] The Fifth he thought 'a dazzling work ... Taken as a whole the work is the best the composer has written since the grim and introspective second symphony. But one still doubts whether the form was the inevitable outcome of the material.'[37] And of the Sixth: 'I have always preferred his Symphonic Poems such as *The Garden of Fand* and *A Tale the Pine Trees Knew* to his symphonies, and his Sixth Symphony, pleasant though it was, has not changed my mind'.[38]

His first article for the *Sunday Referee*, on 15 November, opened with a strong defence of the BBC and its year-old Symphony Orchestra that had been under attack in some quarters for what, at a time of economic crisis, looked like lavish expense in having a larger than usual orchestra, for not employing more British musicians, and for its repertoire seeming to favour new European music. 'The BBC Orchestra is a fine example of the expenditure of public money in a constructive way that has increased our prestige abroad and created employment at home,' he argued. He did, however, weigh against programmes like all-British nights at the Proms: 'Vaughan Williams, the most English of our composers, has always, and rightly, expressed his detestation of a scheme by which British composers are segregated in a separate enclosure like the smaller mammals at the Zoo.' Criticism of the BBC's repertoire continued when that same month Schoenberg made a visit as the BBC were performing three of his works: *Verklärte Nacht*, *Variations for Orchestra*, and the *Five Orchestral Pieces* that had been famously booed when Sir Henry Wood introduced them at the Proms in 1912.[39] This found Constant in fine journalistic fettle, flying in the face of general public and critical opinion. 'We should be unusually grateful to the BBC for performing three of his most representative compositions in the course of one week', he wrote. 'The orchestra under Dr Adrian Boult played the extremely difficult score [*Five Orchestral Pieces*] remarkably well, though with a touch of the embarrassment and circumspection shown by a really polite Protestant who has found himself involved in a religious ceremony of some

---

[35] *Sunday Referee*, 21 August 1932.

[36] *Sunday Referee*, 21 May 1933.

[37] *Sunday Referee*, 21 January 1934. Courtauld-Sargent concert, 14 & 15 January 1934.

[38] *Sunday Referee*, 1 December 1935. First performance, conducted by Sir Hamilton Harty, Queen's Hall, 21 November 1935. Lambert had warmer praise when referring to the piano quintet as 'an unsatisfactory medium ... Of modern composers Arnold Bax seems to be the only one who has come near to solving the many problems it raises.' *The New Statesman and Nation*, 14 July 1934. By the time Bax's seventh and last symphony appeared in 1939, Lambert was no longer writing regularly for either the *Sunday Referee* or *The New Statesman*.

[39] *Verklärte Nacht* and *Variations for Orchestra* (first British performance) were broadcast from a studio on 13 November and the *Five Orchestral Pieces* from Queen's Hall on 18 November, Boult conducting all three works.

totally different creed.' He also seized the opportunity to lambast Stravinsky, whose Violin Concerto was performed in a Courtauld-Sargent concert the same week.

> Schönberg's revolution in musical technique has been far more sweeping and consistent than Stravinsky's, and to my mind this last week has once again proved him to be the more powerful and interesting personality. To find a parallel to his amazing technical virtuosity, his exasperated sensibility, and his strange, half-mathematical, half-sentimental outlook we have to turn to literature, where James Joyce provides an example of a remarkably similar mentality proceeding through much the same phases of thought and technique. ... To go from the Schönberg Variations to the Stravinsky Violin Concerto is an abrupt transition from a lecture on relativity to the 'twice two is five' of the village dunce. It is really hard to write of this work with patience. ... One sat down prepared for a piece of real hard listening, only to find that the work began with the naïvest of repetitive variations on a theme that might well have been drawn from the repertoire of Chico Marx.'[40]

Stravinsky was to bear the full brunt of his attack in his survey of music in the 1920s and 30s, *Music Ho!*, yet it was not a view idly reached. When in May 1928 the BBC were due to broadcast Stravinsky's *Oedipus Rex*, with the composer conducting, Constant had written to Kenneth Wright: 'I should be very obliged if you would arrange for me to listen in to "Oedipus" on Sunday afternoon.'[41] Such opinions added a considerable spice to his column and readers were quickly to learn what to expect.

The day after he attended the Royal Philharmonic Society concert came one of the rare occasions when Constant conducted opera. In fact it was his first opportunity. Opera at the Old Vic was normally entrusted to conductors like Charles Corri and Lawrance Collingwood, but Purcell's *Dido and Aeneas* was placed alongside two ballets: *Hommage aux belles Viennoises* and *Cephalus and Procris*, and Constant conducted the whole programme. The producer was Sydney Russell, and Joan Cross and Sumner Austin took the name parts. This was all repeated a week later with a matinée the following day. Then, in 1945 he recorded *Dido and Aeneas* for the British Council.[42]

The Camargo Society, now in its second year, presented its fifth programme of ballets at the Savoy Theatre on Sunday 29 November 1931, repeating it as usual the following afternoon. Constant was now on the executive committee, together with Lydia Lopokova, Edwin Evans, Marie Rambert, Ninette de Valois and treasurer John Maynard Keynes. Beecham conducted *A Woman's Privilege*, a ballet with music by Handel that he had arranged and orchestrated with the help of his assistant Henry Gibson, and Constant was in charge of the rest of the programme. This included two short ballets: *Fête polonaise* with Glinka's music arranged by Constant and with costumes by Edmund Dulac (six days earlier it had been added to the Vic-Wells repertoire), and a Chopin *Ballade* orchestrated by Bax; as an orchestral interlude there was a *Finnish Fantasy* by the Russian Alexander Dargomizhsky (whom Constant was to describe as 'Glinka's spiritual nephew').[43]

The other substantial ballet in the programme caused something of a stir. Under the

---

[40] *Sunday Referee*, 22 November 1931.

[41] 13 May 1928, 2LO, 4.50–5.50 p.m. Stravinsky *Oedipus Rex*, with the composer conducting the Wireless Chorus and Wireless Orchestra, with Walter Widdop, Astra Desmond, Harry Brindle, Frank Phillips, Hardy Williamson, Roy Henderson and Raymond Trafford (speaker).

[42] See Discography, Appendix 3. The first recording was made in 1936 for Decca, Clarence Raybould conducting.

[43] Lambert, *Music Ho!*, 2nd edn (1937), p. 107.

title of *A Day in a Southern Port*, it was none other than *The Rio Grande* brought to the stage and choreographed by Ashton, the principal dancers being Lydia Lopokova, Alicia Markova, Walter Gore and William Chappell. It was not the music that caused such a furore in the press but the subject matter. As Vaughan has written:

> The ballet's depiction of the seamy side of life in a tropical seaport was too strong for many people at that time. Instead of treating the subject frivolously, as in an 'exotic' revue number, Ashton attempted to create a genuinely *louche* and erotic atmosphere. It was not quite what people expected to see in a ballet, especially danced by classical ballerinas like Lopokova and Markova, supported by a corps de ballet of well-brought-up English girls, some of them hardly out of their teens. And Edward Burra's[44] décor and costumes were equally uncompromising: he was not given, in his paintings and drawings, to the sentimental portrayal of prostitutes.[45]

Cyril Beaumont was shocked by the women's costumes, with their 'skin-tight bodices, dresses about six inches long when seen from the front, bare thighs and stockinged legs'. Far removed from the Brazilian setting of Sacheverell Sitwell's verses, it was more likely inspired by a holiday that Ashton had taken that summer with William Chappell, Edward Burra and other friends in the sailors' port of Toulon. Burra in fact had based his backcloth on a fountain in one of the squares in Toulon. However, the 'undraped and over-developed ladies' on the back cloth, especially one naked lady who was sitting very inelegantly, pouring water over her head and down between her knees, proved too much for Lilian Baylis, who insisted that they be veiled by a stream of painted water.[46]

When the Society repeated the ballet six months later, the *Times* critic went so far as to say that Ashton had 'so completely misunderstood the character of Constant Lambert's music that it is astonishing that he, Mr Lambert, the composer, can bear to stand up in front of this crude travesty and conduct it'.[47] Yet Constant had had a hand in devising the scenario which reflected his own taste for exotic women. However, on the first night *The Times* had been less critical, with only one reservation: 'If we accept the new turn given to it, the ballet must be reckoned a success. Although the orchestra, with Mr Angus Morrison as pianist, played well under the composer's direction, the chorus was weak, thereby emphasising the departure from the original inspiration of the work.'[48] Lopokova had known and admired *The Rio Grande*, writing in February 1930 to her husband Maynard Keynes: 'I have bought [the records of] Rio Grande by Lambert, nobody else does. Even the salesman called it "complex music" but it is not, only influenced by moderns, Stravinsky, de Falla. ... It has real beauty in spite of influences and for a young man indeed a remarkable achievement.'[49]

On 4 December, a few days short of the anniversary of Heseltine's death, Constant was in the audience at the Wigmore Hall for a second memorial concert, this time consisting of his vocal and string transcriptions and his songs. Van Dieren's wife, Frida Kindler (a former pupil of Busoni) was among the performers. Reviewing it in the *Sunday Referee*, Constant commented on what he called a double melancholy: 'the

---

[44] Edward Burra (1905–76), British water-colourist who was chiefly drawn to low-life subjects such as night-clubs, bars and brothels. His earliest training had been at the Chelsea Polytechnic, and then the Royal College of Art.

[45] David Vaughan, *Frederick Ashton and his Ballets* (London: A. & C. Black, 1977), p. 67.

[46] William Chappell, *Fonteyn: Impressions of a Ballerina* (Spring Books, n.d.), p. 11.

[47] *The Times*, 14 June 1932.

[48] *The Times*, 30 November 1931.

[49] Quoted in Julie Kavanagh, *Secret Muses: The Life of Frederick Ashton* (London: Faber & Faber, 1996), p. 140.

loss of so rare and gifted an artist ... and that so fine a programme should meet with such poor response'.[50] Ten days later Anthony Bernard conducted *The Rio Grande* at Queen's Hall. The programme also included Lennox Berkeley's Symphony for Strings about which Constant wrote:

> Without wishing to be intolerably personal, I cannot help feeling that this lack of unity is due to an unsuitable milieu. The programme told us that Mr Berkeley has lived in Paris since 1926. When I think of the licensing laws of this country I cannot find it in me to urge anyone to come to England, but at the same time I should like to see a composer of Mr Berkeley's great sensibility surrounded by influences less sterile than those of Parisian musical thought.[51]

The following day the Camargo Society was involved in a charity event – Lady Wimborne's 'Midnight Ballet Party' – at the Carlton Theatre, Haymarket in aid of Queen Charlotte's Hospital. In addition to *Mars and Venus, Ballade, Capriol Suite* and *Façade* there were two new ballets: *The Lord of Burleigh*, with music by Mendelssohn arranged by Edwin Evans and orchestrated by Gordon Jacob, and *The Dancer's Reward* that utilised Constant's incidental music for *Salomé*[52] with choreography by William Chappell based on Beardsley's illustrations to Wilde's *Salomé*. The occasion also marked the opening of the Carlton cinema with a film by Ben Travers and, after the ballet, the guests danced on stage into the small hours. The musical socialite Lady Wimborne was soon to become the great love in Walton's life and the inspiration for the completion of his symphony.

Music for Orchestra was given a broadcast from Queen's Hall by the BBC Orchestra under Adrian Boult on 16 December, but of greater moment two days later was a BBC studio broadcast that Constant conducted of Contemporary Music that included Hadley's *Ephemera*, Bliss's *Rout* and three works of his own: a suite from *Romeo and Juliet*, seven of his Li-Po songs (sung by Odette de Foras), and the first performance of his Concerto for piano and small orchestra, or Concerto for Piano and Nine Players as it became known. Arthur Benjamin was the soloist.[53] Nine players should not be interpreted as nine instruments, as flute occasionally doubles with piccolo, the three clarinettists can vary from two in A and one in E flat to two in B flat and a bass clarinet; the single percussionist requires temple blocks, suspended cymbal, maracas, tom-tom, and both side and tenor drums, with wire brushes and wood and rubber-headed sticks; while trumpet, tenor trombone, cello and double-bass complete the roll-call.

Like the earlier (then unperformed) Concerto, this one does not fit into the conventional concerto mould and, with its unusual scoring, relates more closely to the world of jazz than any other substantial work of Lambert's, its mood suited more to that of a smoky jazz club than the concert hall. It has both a certainty of purpose and, at times, an almost improvisatory nature. Lambert had himself described it as being of 'of hideous gloom and necrophilistic atmosphere',[54] while Ayrton has said that the music was concerned, in part at least, with Constant's 'solitary prowling through

---

[50] *Sunday Referee*, 13 December 1931.

[51] *Sunday Referee*, 20 December 1931.

[52] Possibly *The Dance of the Seven Veils* alone. De Valois took the lead with Ursula Moreton and Marie Nielson.

[53] Benjamin was also the soloist in the first performances of Herbert Howells' First Piano Concerto (10 July 1914), Gordon Jacob's First Piano Concerto (30 May 1927) and his own Concertino for Piano (1 September 1928). He also premiered Bliss's four *Masks* for piano on 2 February 1926.

[54] In a letter to Christabel Aberconway, 18 October 1931.

the streets of Camden Town and Toulon'.[55] The dark mood that pervades much of the score can be related to the death of Heseltine to whose memory it was dedicated. Begun before his friend's suicide, there is no knowing how much of the concerto was written before the tragedy or indeed how much of it was reworked afterwards, but the mood of the last two movements suggests that they were written in 1931; certainly the second movement was completed in August 1931 while the whole work is dated as December 1931.

The piano dominates throughout. Opening with clarinet and double-bass oscillating rhythmically on two notes a semitone apart, the fast toccata-like first movement has an uneasy restless pulse, its time signature constantly alternating between 7/4, 11/8 and common time. (What Constant had referred to Patrick Hadley as his 'musical St Vitus dance' has been compared with the curious broken rhythm of his irregular manner of walking, in the way, according to Ayrton, that he was 'always stopping and lighting a cigarette, or turning away, or stopping to sing, or stopping to laugh, moving forward, or moving forward faster'.)[56] As usual with Lambert, the 'themes' are rhythmic rather than melodic, making themselves readily adaptable to repetition, inversion, combination or development, and four of these almost tumble over each other in the opening pages. A brilliant 68-bar cadenza for piano (which, as in *The Rio Grande*, comes unusually early) then leads into a much quieter, contemplative section marked '*andante espressivo* (almost twice as slow)' that builds steadily to a climax which, with maraca and cymbal with wire brush, dissolves in a cascade. The pace quickens in the brief coda, only to be brought to an abrupt ending in an unexpected key.

The second movement, Intermède, is a threnody in memory of Heseltine. If 'wa-wa' on muted trumpet and trombone, glissandi on trombone, various percussion effects, syncopation and piano riffs are some of the more familiar jazz borrowings in this movement, much less expected and not immediately detected is the almost improvisatory treatment – whether consciously or not – of motives from at least three of Heseltine's works. The movement opens like a hangover, with morning light filtering through the hazy atmosphere in the form of a slow blues melody, firstly with just a fragment on the cello and then in full on the trumpet (an intended suggestion, perhaps, of the Last Post), with the piano underlining the rhythm with *fortissimo* chords.[57] In the following section (in which the piano is silent), clarinets and cello in four-part harmony introduce a theme (Ex. 8) that hints at the cry on cor anglais in Warlock's *The Curlew* (Ex. 9), being the motive with which that work opens and with which the soloist later enters with the words 'O Curlew, cry no more in the air'. This theme is developed and, before long, flute enters, in counterpoint, with the blues melody. The piano then breaks in with a quicker pulse, *allegro scherzando*, in 11/8, soon to change to 5/8, 6/8, 5/4 and even 9/8 and 13/8, with a lively rhythmical idea first heard on flute and first clarinet becoming prominent. In a quieter moment, flute floats an expressive line over a syncopated *pianissimo* piano accompaniment (Ex. 10) similar to the rocking figure (Ex. 11) that accompanies part of Warlock's choral *Corpus Christi*. (While composition of the Concerto was in progress, both *The Curlew* and *Corpus Christi* were very much in Constant's mind: they both featured in the memorial concert that he organised and in part conducted in February 1931, and in March he was recording *The Curlew* for the gramophone.) Then the lively figure (Ex. 12) returns *fortissimo*, underlined by a trombone solo, with tom-tom, tenor drum, cello and bass setting a quick march

---

[55] According to Michael Ayrton, in *Constant Lambert Remembered*, BBC Third Network, 25 June 1955.

[56] *In Search of Constant Lambert*, BBC2, 26 July 1965.

[57] Rawsthorne seems almost to revisit the bleak opening to this movement at the beginning of the third movement of his Second Piano Concerto (1951).

Ex. 8 Lambert, Concerto for Piano and Nine Players, 'Intermède', fig. 23

Ex. 9 Warlock, *The Curlew*, opening

Ex. 10 Lambert, Concerto for Piano and Nine Players , 'Intermède', 1 bar after fig. 41

Ex. 11 Warlock, *Corpus Christi* , opening

Ex. 12 Lambert, Concerto for Piano and Nine Players, 'Intermède', fig. 45

Ex. 13 Lambert, Concerto for Piano and Nine Players, 'Intermède', fig. 53

Ex. 14 Warlock, *The Frostbound Wood*, bars 2–3

Ma - ry that was the Child's mo-ther, Met me in__ the frost-bound wood:

pulse. Before the movement fizzles out on pizzicato bass, the cello enters *piano* and *molto esspressivo* (Ex. 13) with a slow and rhythmically altered version of Ex. 12, that is recognisable as being almost identical to the opening line to one of Warlock's last songs, *The Frostbound Wood* (Ex. 14).

The sombre Finale, sapped of the energy so prominent in the first movement and marked (like parts of the Sonata) *lugubre*, opens with a short descending figure on the piano that dominates much of the movement. When heard in full on the piano it has been transformed into a slow plaintive rhythmic bluesy theme (very similar to that in the *Elegiac Blues* written in memory of Florence Mills) which proceeds with a funereal tread. In contrast, a slow and slightly sinister theme, first heard quietly on cello *marcato ma molto legato*, is taken up by trombone as this elegiac movement builds with intensity until finally dying away, unresolved, like mourners left speechless. The

Concerto was not the only work of Constant's to lie under the shadow of Heseltine's death: as will be seen, there are allusions to his funeral in the 'King Pest' movement of *Summer's Last Will and Testament*.

While it can now be seen as one of his finest works, the Concerto received a generally frosty reception. Perhaps the warmest review came from Ferruccio Bonavia in *The New York Times* who thought it only natural that Lambert, 'having been applauded for his use of jazz in [*The Rio Grande*] should try to repeat the experiment. The fault does not rest with Lambert, but with those who led him to believe that jazz rhythms could be used indefinitely without surfeiting the appetite.' Yet he felt that the Concerto held greater promise than *The Rio Grande*, for its orchestration and for 'the true dramatic instinct shown in the development of the movements', adding that 'the relation between the solo and orchestral instrument is always faultless – and this means much in an age when composers sometimes use orchestral instruments as if they hated them'.[58] Others, not unexpectedly, were less enthusiastic. *The Times* critic thought it 'not very satisfying music' with 'the actual writing for the piano not varied enough', and he drew comparisons with the previous work, the Sonata, suggesting that it suffered 'from the same short-windedness'. Lambert clearly rated both works highly, describing them characteristically to Foss as representing Cavalcanti[59] or the French films, while *The Rio Grande* was mere Hollywood.[60] Alan Frank dismissed them, suggesting 'that some deeply personal feeling underlying the Sonata and the Concerto makes them elusive and puzzling'.[61] Even Walton initially misjudged the Concerto, as he was much later to admit when asking Oxford University Press for a copy of the full score after hearing Richard Rodney Bennett's LP recording: 'It is a very remarkable piece – I fear I did not really appreciate it till now, nor I feel has anyone else except a few like R.R.B.'[62]

---

[58] Ferruccio Bonavia, *New York Times*, 17 January 1932.

[59] Alberto Cavalcanti (1897–1982), noted Brazilian film director who worked with the GPO Film Unit in the 1930s and in 1940 joined Ealing Studios. Walton and Berners provided scores for three of his films.

[60] Hubert Foss, *The Musical Times*, October 1951, p. 450.

[61] Alan Frank, *The Musical Times*, November 1937, p. 943.

[62] Letter to Christopher Morris at OUP from Sir William Walton, La Mortella, Ischia, 7 March 1978: OUP files.

9 1932–4
A Permanent Post

1932 began with healthy indications that Lambert was gaining wider recognition. These were conducting engagements with the Scottish Orchestra, in Edinburgh on 4 January and in Glasgow the following day. As was his habit when alone on tour, he snatched time to write to friends, and it was from the station hotel in the orchestra's home base of Glasgow that he wrote to Cecil Gray, congratulating him on his new book on Sibelius that he was reviewing for the *Sunday Referee*:

> I wanted to let you know how very much I enjoyed your brilliant book on Sibelius and at the same time apologize for the very inadequate review of it which will appear in tomorrow's Referee. It is a book which I would have liked to have digested and reviewed at my leisure but unfortunately the Referee found out where I had got to and sent the book on saying that the copy had to be in by Friday night. The book arrived at the end of a six hour rehearsal, I had to read it over dinner and review it that evening, so I feel sure you will excuse the patent inadequacy of the article. It was rather a slow starter and took about 8 brandies before it got into anything like top-gear.
>
> I am doing my best to cope with the Glasgow climate and architecture. Except that there is no running water this hotel is remarkably like a morgue. The pubs only seem to be open for about an hour on alternate days. The beer though is stronger and cheaper than in London. When I return we might perhaps celebrate the repeal of prohibition in Finland in a manner appropriate to the occasion.
>
> Please give my love to Tasha.[1]

In his review he agreed with Gray 'in considering Sibelius not only the greatest composer of today but the most inspiring to the younger generation of composers. ... I find it hard indeed to write of a book in which I am in such complete agreement. Ever since I first became acquainted with the score of Sibelius's Fourth Symphony I have been convinced that the composer will ultimately prove to have been not only the greatest of his generation but one of the major figures in the entire history of music'. This was a theme he was to expand in *Music Ho!* He also paid tribute to Sir Henry Wood for presenting the works of Sibelius 'at a time when few could be found to do so'. By a happy coincidence, in his own concerts with the Scottish Orchestra he was including the First Symphony.[2]

At the end of the month, at a Sadler's Wells matinée, Constant conducted the first performance of *Narcissus and Echo*, the first of four ballets by Bliss that he was to premiere throughout his career, although in this particular instance the music had not been specifically composed as a ballet but was an adaptation of Bliss's Rhapsody for two voices and small orchestra. Bliss's *Rout* was also given, another ballet treatment of an instrumental/orchestral score. (Although announced as a first performance, it was more likely its first London *public* performance.) The occasion was marked by the 'special appearance' of Alicia Markova who was making her début before a Sadler's Wells audience. Three already established ballets completed the programme.

Almost a month later, at the Savoy Theatre on 28 February, a Camargo Society

---

[1] Letter from Lambert, North British Station Hotel, Glasgow, to Cecil Gray, 2 January 1932. Tasha was Gray's first wife. The book Lambert was reviewing was *Sibelius* (OUP, 1931).

[2] These concerts also included works by Debussy, Glinka (his *Ruslan* Suite), Boyce, Gordon Jacob, Ian Whyte, Warlock's *Capriol* Suite, and his own *Music for Orchestra*.

matinée offered four ballets: *The Lord of Burleigh*, *La Création du monde*, *Valse-Fantaisie* (which 'Karsavina danced with incomparable grace') and *Façade*. By way of an entr'acte, Constant also conducted the *Variations on Cadet Rousselle*, the combined efforts of Arnold Bax, Frank Bridge, John Ireland and Eugene Goossens, who orchestrated the short work.

This was quickly followed by a Vic-Wells season, running from 4 to 23 March and consisting of 12 programmes from eight different ballets. The venue alternated between the Old Vic and Sadler's Wells, and opera was performed on the evenings when there was no ballet. The company was increased in number from 12 to 18, Markova and Dolin were the principals, and Constant's friend Marie Nielson was among the new recruits. The ballets new to the Vic-Wells were *Les Sylphides* (Chopin) and *Le Spectre de la rose* (Weber, danced by Dolin and de Valois), with premieres of *The Enchanted Grove* (using Ravel's *Le Tombeau de Couperin*), *Italian Suite* (Lalo) and *The Nursery Suite*, with Elgar attending the first of four performances on Saturday 19 March. He was delighted with the ballet, especially Dolin's performance as Georgie Porgie.[3] The Duchess of York, a dedicatee of the original suite, also graced the occasion. It was after the first performance of the *Nursery Suite* ballet that Constant had his only meeting with Elgar.

Constant continued to follow Diaghilev's habit of inserting 'symphonic interludes' between ballets; *The Bird-Actors* Overture was one such work that found its way into the programmes. The season opened and closed with *Job* which had five performances and on at least one evening drew a full house. The Company had made a promising start and Lilian Baylis was so impressed by Constant's achievements that she offered him a permanent job with the Vic-Wells Ballet for the coming season.

During the run Constant found time to give a talk to the Royal Musical Association on the 18th-century Anglo-Irish composer and organist Thomas Roseingrave.[4] He took up the theme more publicly in July and August by giving over the whole of his *Sunday Referee* column to an account of Roseingrave's life in three successive weeks, an extraordinary allowance of space to so unfamiliar – indeed, unknown – a composer whom Constant described as 'one of the most interesting and pathetic figures in English music'. (Typically, in the third article on Roseingrave he also managed to promote the music of van Dieren.) In March 1929 Diaghilev, contemplating an 18th-century ballet, had remembered Sacheverell Sitwell mentioning Roseingrave and had written to him, enquiring further about his music. To his dismay he learnt that the authority on this composer was Constant Lambert who only the previous year had sued him for the non-payment of royalties when *Romeo and Juliet* was staged in Germany. Sacheverell had replied:

> I received your letter this morning and have already written to Lambert. I think your composer was a certain Rosingrave or Roseingrave. He was Irish and a pupil of Domenico Scarlatti. Lambert has indeed copied some of his compositions, which are without exception in manuscript. I'm afraid that you'll find there is not enough music [for a ballet]. He wrote for the harpsichord and rather more for the organ, being organist at the church in Hanover Square in London. It is his extraordinary fugues – rather mad, as you say – that Lambert has copied.[5]

---

[3] According to Lambert, the ballet of *The Nursery Suite* was an adaptation which Elgar himself had suggested: *Sunday Referee*, 4 March 1934.

[4] Thomas Roseingrave (1688–1766). The text of Lambert's talk, given on 15 March 1932, was printed in the *Proceedings of the Royal Musical Association*, 58th Session (1931–2), pp. 67–83.

[5] Letter from Sacheverell Sitwell to Serge Diaghilev, 1 March 1929, quoted in Buckle, *Diaghilev*, pp. 518–19.

In response to Sacheverell's letter, Constant sent Diaghilev a postcard, in French, promising to send within a few days everything he had by Roseingrave. However, nothing came of Diaghilev's plans.

In June the Camargo Society took its boldest step and presented four weeks of ballet at the Savoy Theatre, with performances nightly from Monday to Saturday and one matinée each week. The changes were rung between 14 ballets.[6] Among the new ones was *The Origin of Design*, another Handel arrangement by Beecham who shared in the conducting on at least five occasions, not just with his own ballet score. Maynard Keynes wrote to Edwin Evans: 'Beecham wants to conduct on the first night, and Constant thinks that *Lac des cygnes* would be suitable for him.' *Job* opened the first programme (with Dolin 'as impressive as ever' as Satan), then Beecham took over, preceding a much abbreviated *Lac des cygnes* with, as an orchestral interlude, Boyce's Fifth Symphony (as resurrected by Constant). Finally, Constant offered as a breezy prelude the first performance of a 'simplified' version he had made of Walton's *Portsmouth Point* Overture[7] before Spike Hughes conducted his own new jazz ballet *High Yellow*.[8] This he had hastily assembled from gramophone recordings he had recently made, and nine jazz musicians joined eleven members of the London Symphony Orchestra.[9] The choreography was the joint efforts of Freddie Ashton and the black American dancer Buddy Bradley.[10] *High Yellow* received seven performances, *Job* ten and *The Rio Grande* a further four.

Another ballet new to the Camargo repertoire introduced one of Constant's favourite composers: Satie's *Mercure* that the Ballet Rambert had performed in June 1931 at the Lyric Theatre, Hammersmith, choreographed by Ashton. Constant later said in a Third Programme talk on Satie that he only saw *Mercure* twice but remembered it 'as being not only extremely funny but oddly beautiful. … I am the greatest admirer of Satie but even so at the first performance of *Mercure* I was quite unable to concentrate fully on the beauty of his music for the Graces bathing, owing to the fact that the Graces were represented by men from the corps-de-ballet with exaggerated bosoms of papier-mâché, appearing out of holes in a bright blue box representing the sea'. The

---

[6] Monday 6 June – Saturday 2 July 1932. The ballets included *Ballade*, *The Enchanted Grove*, *Façade*, *Fête polonaise*, *Giselle*, *High Yellow*, *Job*, *Le Lac des cygnes*, *The Lord of Burleigh*, *Mars and Venus*, *Mercure*, *The Origin of Design*, *Regatta* and *The Rio Grande*.

[7] Lambert rescored Walton's *Portsmouth Point* for a smaller orchestra, making it more accessible to orchestral societies not only by reducing the instrumentation to the minimum required but also by simplifying the work's rhythmic complexity with its tricky time-signatures by adapting frequent changes of 5/8 2/4 3/8 2/4 etc. to the more familiar 4/4 3/4 etc., with the cross-rhythms indicated by marks of phrasing and accentuation. Other 'interlude' music he conducted that season included his own *Romeo and Juliet* suite, Berners' *Luna Park* ballet music and *Three Lampoons* by Gavin Gordon. Special curtains by McKnight Kauffer, William Roberts and Walter Sickert were used as visual accompaniment to the musical interludes: Clarke, *The Sadler's Wells Ballet*, p. 59.

[8] Lambert had first suggested the title 'Coral Gables' and then 'Pink Palms' but it was Hyam Greenbaum who said: 'If this ballet's supposed to be a cross between black and white, why the hell don't you call the thing "High Yalla" and have done with it?' Hughes, *Second Movement*, p. 170.

[9] Recorded between 17 November 1931 and 1 April 1932, these have been reissued on CD: Largo 5129.

[10] Buddy Bradley (1908–72), presumably the 'well-known Negro-dance arranger' Lambert refers to in *Music Ho!*, 2nd edn (1937), p. 143, who was 'called in to produce a ballet for a highbrow company trained in the classical tradition. While all the Europeans flung aside their carefully won training to indulge in an orgy of pseudo-Charlestons the negro himself was moved to tears, not by his own work but by the classic elegance of *Lac des cygnes*.'

leading roles on this occasion were danced by Alicia Markova, Walter Gore and Pearl Argyle.

On the final evening Constant conducted *Mercure* and *Giselle* (in which Olga Spessiva was partnered by Dolin), and Beecham returned with the Boyce symphony and then took over *Façade* which had proved one of the Society's most successful productions. Constant conducted the seven other performances in the four-week series.

Eleven days after the final evening Constant gave a studio broadcast of 'music from the repertoire of the Camargo Ballet Company' with works by Walton (*Portsmouth Point* in Constant's rescoring), Mendelssohn (*The Lord of Burleigh*) and Glinka and the broadcast premieres of Satie's *Mercure*, Roseingrave's Overture in F (transposed and orchestrated by Constant) and Walter Leigh's *Interlude for Theatre Orchestra*.

Montagu-Nathan, the Camargo Society secretary, remembered that during this Savoy season 'the first Mrs Lambert used often to join me in the Secretary's Box. She possessed what appeared to be the smallest hands in London, but they were so powerful that between us we often succeeded in transforming a mere favourable reception into a veritable ovation.'[11] He also recalled a missed opportunity:

> In 1932, when we were about to embark on a month's season at the Savoy, I met Britten, then aged eighteen, at a small party. During conversation B divulged that he'd done a ballet. I suggested that as we were looking for novelties he'd better send me the score. It wasn't within my province to vet it, and so it was sent on to Evans, who should have gone through it and then got a second opinion from CL. I heard nothing further until after the season, when B asked me to let him have it back. Possibly, as B was then completely unknown, they never looked at the thing, but I've always since regretted that Camargo didn't collar the kudos of having produced BB for the first time ever![12]

Lennox Berkeley also approached Montagu-Nathan at this time, writing on 25 August 1932: 'I wonder if you could tell me whether there is any chance of the Camargo Society using the Ballet Music that I played to you and Constant Lambert some time ago, in the near future.' He had to wait six years before a ballet of his was staged.[13]

In July Constant snatched a holiday in the south of France with Flo, joined by Paddy Hadley. From Toulon he wrote to Anthony Powell:

> My dear Tony,
> I have just torn up a cheaply sensational letter I wrote you in which I said that there simply wasn't a single white settler in the whole town. Alas my pen was too optimistic.
> As I was sealing the envelope a grisly cortege headed by Baby Bera[14] and Boris Kochno passed along the quay. Still the hotel is amazingly free from pests and smells more of ozone than opium.
> Milhaud has just left Toulon for Aix, Reynaldo Hahn is at Cap Buon, Bera at

---

[11] Letter from Montagu-Nathan to Hubert Foss, 20 March 1952.

[12] *Ibid.* Montagu-Nathan related the story in an article in *Radio Times*, 31 July 1953, reprinted in Donald Mitchell, Philip Reed and Mervyn Cooke (eds.), *Letters from a Life: Selected Letters of Benjamin Britten*, vol. 3 (London: Faber & Faber, 2004), p. 70. The meeting actually took place on 15 November 1931 and the ballet was *Plymouth Town*.

[13] Lennox Berkeley's *The Judgement of Paris* was staged by the Sadler's Wells Company in 1938, choreographed by Ashton. This should not be confused with *Judgment of Paris*, with music by Kurt Weill and choreography by Antony Tudor, first performed at the Westminster Theatre, London, in 1938, a week after the Sadler's Wells ballet.

[14] Christian Bérard (1902–49), French artist and designer, lover of Boris Kochno.

les Sablettes, Cocteau at St Mandrian, Kochno's at Tamaris, the snail's on the thorn etc.

I can honestly claim to be the only English party-goer in the whole town, and can also congratulate myself in rather a Bellocian fashion on being the only intellectual here who is not a teetotal Jew. I feel some distinction should be awarded me. If not the Legion of Honour perhaps the 3rd Class Agricultural Palms.

The exchange is apt to sting one a bit as all prices seem to have gone up about 50% quite apart from only getting 88 or so to the pound.

Mechanical pianos seem to be on the wane but there are a thousand and one electric gramophones of unbelievable force. They are so loud that one just has to order drinks in dumb-show.[15] The only event of international interest has been a 'Grand Concours de Pyjamas'. The whole town is so quiet in fact that the whores just hang about in bunches in the street without even troubling to accost one. Wherever we go we have to take one of Patrick Hadley's wooden legs with us as he can't make up his mind which fits best.[16]

I expect I shall be home soon as money seems a bit short. Cedric Morris[17] disguised as a beggar has just passed playing the ukelele. Everyone here looks like Cedric Morris or D. H. Lawrence. It is most depressing.

I am getting nostalgic for the hectic life of old Bloomsbury (district of laughter, district of tears).

Yours truly,
Constant[18]

On 15 August he wrote to Marie Nielson, who had been dancing throughout June for the Camargo Society at the Savoy:

Thanks so much for the book and the letter. I had not read the Douglas[19] and enjoyed it immensely almost as much as South Wind. He is about the only writer I have patience with at the moment …

We should both love to come up for a day or two this month if it can managed without putting you to too much trouble. This weekend I am conducting what one paper describes as my 'renowned jazz-classic' but next week end we are free. Would that be alright for you?

Love
Constant

Three days short of his 27th birthday, he conducted that 'renowned jazz-classic' *The Rio Grande* at the Proms, where it was becoming a fairly regular item.

In September, at the instigation of Adeline Genée, a trip to Denmark for the Vic-Wells dancers was organised by the Association of Teachers of Operatic Dancing of Great Britain under the auspices of Anglo-Danish Society. Planned to coincide

---

[15] Lambert was to comment on 'the obsession with the wireless and the gramophone' and the effects of mechanical reproduction of music in 'The Appalling Popularity of Music' section of *Music Ho!*, 2nd edn (1937), pp. 163–8.

[16] As a result of an injury in France in the closing stages of the First War, Hadley had his right leg amputated below the knee, and in later years he would surprise people by removing his artificial leg which often gave him much pain.

[17] Probably Sir Cedric Lockwood Morris (1889–1982), Welsh artist and friend of Christopher Wood.

[18] Letter from Lambert (Grand Café de la Rade, Quai Cronstadt, Toulon) to Anthony Powell, 'le 26 Juillet 1932'.

[19] Norman Douglas (1868–1952), British writer best known for his novel *South Wind*.

with the British Trades and Arts Exhibition in Copenhagen, this was their first tour abroad. Constant was to share some of the conducting with Geoffrey Toye and they took with them a repertoire of eight ballets, including *Job*.[20] Dolin and Markova were the principal dancers and the company also included the 14-year-old Doris May, later better known as Pamela May. While Constant was abroad, Paddy Hadley took over his *Sunday Referee* column.

Just before leaving he wrote to Powell:

> Just a hurried note to let you know that I shall be in Copenhagen from the 14th to the end of the month. I suppose there is no chance of you coming that way is there?
>
> Letters may be addressed to me at 'the Kgl. Theater' Copenhagen and marked English Ballet in the corner. They are bound to be censored so don't send any photographs of some such everyday scene as 5 guards officers dressed as housemaids being flogged by 5 housemaids dressed as guards-officers.
>
> I have just received my sailing directions and they read very like the more depressing patches in Venusberg.[21] I go in a small boat which takes about 3 days and arrives in the small hours. The right Nordic note is struck, I think, by the sentence 'Captain Nellemose[22] – whom you will know by his scarred face – will meet you.'
>
> I shall have nothing to do there for about a week after my preliminary rehearsal so do write a card or fly over or something.[23]

Flo went to Denmark as well although, as Marie Nielson much later recalled, she was not readily accepted by everyone in the Company:

> In 1932 Genée & Geoffrey Toye with assistance of Danish & British Governments organised a series of gala performances at the Royal Opera House Copenhagen. Constant went a week before the Co to rehearse orchestra. The Co were, to say the least of it, 'snooty' about Florence & he asked me to stay with her in Percy St & bring her with me to Copenhagen. She was very charming & shy, & I remember read Conrad's 'Typhoon' on the crossing until we were both ill. Constant met us in the early morning at the station in very good spirits. I don't know whether Florence would still have the letters he wrote from Copenhagen to Percy St. So far as I remember he liked the orchestra but found Copenhagen 'clean & characterless' & not his cup of tea. After one of the performances a number of us were invited to the most fashionable night club – a very dignified place. Constant suddenly said 'I'd like to ask you to dance but I can't do these dances – I could if they played Sousa.' Without thinking I said – We'll ask them to, & the next minute he was threading his way across the ballroom to the band. The conductor recognising him beamed but his expression changed when he was asked if he knew Sousa & if so would he please play the Double Headed Eagle. However he did & we set off. The other dancers were completely bewildered but probably out of courtesy to the English one by one joined in sedately marching round while Constant charged down the ballroom doing a sharp turn at each

---

[20] The ballets were *Job*, *Les Sylphides*, *The Lord of Burleigh*, *La Création du monde*, *Regatta*, *Fête polonaise*, *Hommage aux belles Viennoises* and *Divertissement*.

[21] *Venusberg* was Powell's second novel, published in 1932 and set in 'a Baltic country'. It was dedicated to Constant and Florence Lambert.

[22] Captain M. W. Nellemose was the General Secretary of ICES, the International Council for the Exploration of the Sea established in Copenhagen.

[23] Letter from Lambert, 15 Percy Street, to Powell, 10 September 1932. At the time Powell was in Berlin.

corner & charged back again. He actually asked for & got an encore. We missed one of the official functions because he insisted that a Laurel & Hardy picture in the suburbs was not to be missed. ... Mention of Percy St reminds me that he used to spend an evening frequently at Wyndham Lewis'.[24]

For the King of Denmark's birthday the Vic-Wells Company shared a gala performance with Royal Danish Ballet. The police feared that there might be a socialist demonstration and Constant was informed that a police official would be sitting in the front of the stalls immediately behind him and if any trouble started he was to take instructions from the official.[25] Fortunately for him, with perhaps memories of *Romeo and Juliet* in Paris, nothing happened.

The trip to Denmark delayed the first night of the new Vic-Wells season which opened on 5 October with *The Nursery Suite*. The ballets introduced before the end of the year were *Douanes*, with music by Geoffrey Toye who conducted its first night, and *The Scorpions of Ysit*, an existing ballet for which Gavin Gordon had written a new score which Constant conducted.

Two days after the season's opening night Constant was among the expectant but not capacity audience in Queen's Hall for the first appearance of Beecham's London Philharmonic Orchestra. Beecham was a conductor for whom he usually had nothing but praise. But this time in the *Sunday Referee*, after saluting the 'electrifying performance of the *Carneval Romain*' and finding him 'equally brilliant in the *Brigg Fair* of Delius in which he secured exquisite gradations of tone from the strings, and in Strauss's *Heldenleben*, whose bombast he made, for the moment, seem significant', he continued in a less flattering manner:

> He also gave what is probably the worst performance of Mozart's Prague Symphony that has ever taken place in any covered building. The finale was without sparkle, the slow movement was invested with unimagined longueurs (each bloom was laboriously held up for inspection, but we were never allowed to look round the garden), the fiery introduction was made to sound like suave eighteenth century small talk, and as for the gear-change between the first and second subjects it would have made a French taxi-driver turn in his grave. Sir Thomas Beecham has in the past given us such inspired performances of Mozart that it would not be only insincere but definitely ungrateful to pretend that we do not recognise those rare moments when he definitely fails us.[26]

At the beginning of November, while Beecham was busy with his new orchestra, Constant conducted the first Sadler's Wells performance of the Handel–Beecham *Origin of Design*. That month he was asked to orchestrate a ballet sequence in

---

[24] Letter from Marie Nielson to Angus Morrison, 10 March 1954. In his autobiographical *Musical Chairs*, pp. 270–1, Cecil Gray recounts how a 'select audience' that included himself, Lambert and Thomas Earp would gather at Wyndham Lewis's rooms in Ossington Street, Notting Hill for evening discussions that would last until the early hours of the next morning. According to Powell, *Messengers of Day*, p. 150, Lewis's address was 'kept as a supposed secret from all but certain carefully selected associates, who themselves never knew when they might not fall out of favour. Lambert seems to have been one of the few from his age-group whom Lewis was from time to time prepared to meet. Although within reason an admirer of Lewis's work (the writing more than the pictures) Lambert always treated the relationship as rather a joke, often telling stories to illustrate Lewis's perpetual nervous tensions.' Lambert contributed 'An Objective Self Portrait' to a Wyndham Lewis double number of *Twentieth Century Verse*, November/December 1937. See Wyndham Lewis's drawing of Lambert (1932), Appendix 11, An Iconography.

[25] Clarke, *The Sadler's Wells Ballet*, p. 82.

[26] *Sunday Referee*, 9 October 1932.

a romantic comedy, *A Kiss in Spring*, that was to be given at the Alhambra Theatre. This was an adaptation by Julius Brammer and Alfred Grünwald of their operetta *Das Veilchen vom Montmartre* and the sequence in question was a pas de deux and variations in the third act that Ashton was choreographing.

In December the Camargo Society resumed its two-day programme of ballets, this time at the Adelphi Theatre. The new productions included *The Birthday of the Infanta* based on the Oscar Wilde story and with music by Elisabeth Lutyens who remembered in her autobiography:

> Then came a rather difficult lunch to be lived through with Lopokova still pressurising me and Constant Lambert, the musical director, who had to pass as well as conduct the score. I had only met Constant once before – beautiful and disdainful – coming from the library at College, where he had been searching for the original – *not* the Rimsky-Korsakov – edition of *Boris Godunov*. I disliked him as heartily at this lunch as I was beginning to dislike the once so adored Lopokova. He was extremely arrogant and patronising for someone only a year older than myself, proclaiming, didactically, that the only ballet requiring a chorus was the *Rio Grande*. ... First impressions can be misleading; Constant became one of the very best friends I ever had and the musical world shrank for me at his death.[27]

Her ballet was choreographed by Penelope Spencer and the costumes were designed by Rex Whistler. This was followed by the first performance of *Adam and Eve*, Constant's ballet that Diaghilev had taken and turned into *Romeo and Juliet*. This time it was choreographed by Antony Tudor with costumes and scenery by John Banting, and in this production the music was restored to its original form and sequence, with a few additions.[28] The bible story was given a burlesque twist and set in a futuristic Garden of Eden. As one reviewer wrote: 'Tudor approached the ballet lightly but not flippantly, using the flavour of the commedia dell'arte'. He was himself a great success as the Serpent, appearing as a masked Harlequin in black and white. Another reviewer recorded:

> The stars, Adam [Anton Dolin] and Eve [Prudence Hyman], looking like sun-bathers, are introduced to each other (Adam looks like a footballer and Eve like a soubrette) by the Fowls of the Air, with the approval of two Seraphim, there entered the Serpent (A. Tudor). When [Natasha] Grigorova was half way through her angel's duty of driving the erring pair from the garden, she relented. The serpent had another idea. He seized the avenging angel with her flaming sword and forced her to share a bite of the apple with him. All ended happily with a double marriage conducted by the Seraphim. Tudor's wry sense of humour and his 'jeu d'esprit' carry the story of its fruitful ending, as even the apple is given an effective part.[29]

Several critics pointed out the similarity between Dolin's Adam and his Job, both characters wearing a loin-cloth, the difference being a large fig-leaf. There were

[27] Lutyens, *A Goldfish Bowl*, p. 61.

[28] Antony Tudor (1908–1987), choreographer, teacher and dancer, born William John Cook, a member of Rambert's Ballet Club. He founded the London Ballet in 1938 and in 1939 was invited to New York where he became closely associated with the American Ballet Theatre and later the Metropolitan Opera Ballet School.

[29] *Christian Science Monitor*, 31 December 1932, quoted in Judith Chazin-Bennahum, *The Ballets of Antony Tudor: Studies in Psyche and Satire* (Oxford: Oxford University Press, 1994), p. 38.

mixed reviews. Arnold Haskell had reservations, finding Banting's décor 'infantile …
a crude imitation of Max Ernst at his worst'[30] while *The Times* thought it 'gay and
amusing, but ultimately the high spirits go one step too far'. It was not revived. The
whole programme, which began with *Les Sylphides* and also included the Dowland/
Warlock *The Passionate Pavane*, was conducted by Constant with the exception of a
short ballet *There is a Willow* to music by Frank Bridge who directed it himself.[31] An
'Overture' given as one of the interludes was described by *The Times* as 'a small suite
which [Lambert] had rescued from the forgotten English eighteenth-century composer,
Thomas Roseingrave'.

While *Adam and Eve* was to have only two performances, *Pomona* was to prove
more durable, and it received its first Vic-Wells production at Sadler's Wells on 17
January 1933, with Anton Dolin once again as Vertumnus but partnered this time
by Beatrice Appleyard (who had earlier been one of the nymphs). According to P. W.
Manchester,[32] it had been considerably altered since its presentation by the Camargo
Society but 'the Company as a whole were still not experienced enough to put over a
ballet which was of the smart-satirical type.'[33] The *Times* critic thought that Vanessa
Bell's costumes impeded the freedom of Pomona and her nymphs' dancing and also
felt that the slender character of the plot had not stimulated Ashton to 'any imaginative
feats of choreography'. Nevertheless, Constant later instanced Ashton's 'treatment of
a three-part fugato as a lyrical dance for a *solo* dancer' as a highly successful example
of choreographic counterpoint.[34] The Company's greatest success with this ballet was
to come later in revivals with Pearl Argyle and then Margot Fonteyn with whom she
alternated the lead role. But, as the ballet historian Mary Clarke observed, the inclusion
of *Pomona* in the repertoire undoubtedly attracted a smart and avant-garde audience
to the Wells whenever it was given.[35]

That season Dolin introduced his famous solo dance to Ravel's *Bolero* that had come
about with Constant's assistance. When Dolin had approached Lilian Baylis with the
idea of using *Bolero*, her reply had been, 'Never heard of it. Whose music is it, 'cos
I'll have to ask Constant Lambert, you know?' And when Dolin mentioned Ravel, he
was met with a similar response: 'Never heard of him. I'll telephone Constant and call
you back.' After a few minutes the telephone rang. 'Anton dear, Constant says it's a
wonderful idea. Marvellous music, so it doesn't matter what the dance is like 'cos he
says the music alone will fill the house.'[36]

The Company's next production, on 7 February, concerned a work close to
Constant's heart, Purcell's *The Faery Queene*, a project that he was only able to realise

---

[30] *The New English Weekly*, 15 December 1932.
[31] A young Benjamin Britten went with the Bridges to see his teacher's ballet and commented in
his diary: 'Pretty dismal show except for Wendy Toye's magnificent dance in F.B.'s "Willow".':
Letters from a Life: The Selected Letters and Diaries of Benjamin Britten, vol. 1, p. 293.
[32] P. W. Manchester, *Vic-Wells: A Ballet Progress* (London: Gollancz, 1942), pp. 15–16. Phyllis
Winifred ('Bill') Manchester (1907–98) was appointed dance critic of *Theatre World* in 1941
before becoming secretary to Marie Rambert (1944–6). In 1946 she started *Ballet Today*.
[33] The synopsis of *Pomona*, as given in Joseph Sandon, *Façade and Other Early Ballets by
Frederick Ashton* (London: A. & C. Black, 1954), omits the seventh section, *Marcia*. It is not
clear whether this was one of the changes made.
[34] Lambert, 'Music and Action', in *Footnotes to The Ballet: A Book for Balletomanes*, ed. Caryl
Brahms (London: Lovat Dickson, 1936), pp. 172–3. Another highly successful example he
cited (p. 173) was 'the astonishing choreographic fugue which Nijinska arranged to a purely
homophonic passage in the finale of *Romeo and Juliet*'.
[35] Clarke, *The Sadler's Wells Ballet*, p. 86. Seven performances were given in 1933, three in 1934,
six in 1937 and two in 1938.
[36] Dolin, *Autobiography*, pp. 57–8.

more substantially near the end of his life. For de Valois's *The Birthday of Oberon* he concentrated on the Masque of the Seasons in Act 4, inserting other music from elsewhere in the opera to make a satisfactory divertissement so that the Dance of the Seasons was preceded by an overture, a choral invocation, and five rural dances. The costumes and scenery were designed by John Armstrong, and 30 dancers and 40 singers were involved in this spectacular choral ballet that was well received by the press and a certain section of the audience but which did not stay long in the repertoire, having only six performances.

The Rio Grande was popular with provincial choral societies, and in March Constant conducted a performance in Leicester with Angus Morrison as soloist. He was also asked at short notice to deputise for Geoffrey Toye for the first of what were to have been Lydia Lopokova's three farewell performances (in the event two) as Swanilda in *Coppélia*.[37] Toye, declaring this to be his favourite ballet, had persuaded Constant to let him conduct, but a car accident then put him out of action. Not only was this the ballet's first production at the Wells (omitting the last act, as had become the general practice) but it was also the biggest production they had tackled so far. *The Times* reported that Constant 'secured an admirable performance from the orchestra'. In her curtain speech Lopokova indicated that her retirement might not be quite so definite as had been suggested and, with her husband Maynard Keynes, she continued to be very active in the promotion of ballet. Her social links with her friends in the ballet world remained as strong as ever and at the end of May, over Sunday lunch with Ninette, Constant and Flo, she was busy discussing Ashton's love life.[38] Lydia was known for her sense of humour and would sometimes shock and even outrage her friends by intentionally confusing words under the disguise of an imperfect grasp of English. At a dinner party Constant had told her about two rather curiously named Dutch liqueurs, Bols and Fockink. Later that evening she suddenly cried out, purposely mispronouncing the names, 'Have some more Bols! Have some more Fockink!' And when faced by a shocked silence she exclaimed with seeming innocence: 'Huh, and now you have done that to embarrass me.'[39]

Constant, now much preoccupied with the writing of *Music Ho!*, kept Marie Nielson, who was on a visit to America, up-to-date with news, writing in April:

> My dear Marie,
>   I am so sorry not to have written before but life has passed in a dreary whirl and I never seemed to have a moment. My beastly book which is now half done has kept me busy and the fact that Malcolm Sargent has had an operation and Uncle Geoffrey [Toye] has dislocated his arm has given me extra work to do.
>   Are you still functioning in Radio City and how is The Dance in America? When do you come back? Soon I hope.
>   The Camargo is at present following a policy of masterly inaction owing to the usual low funds. There is vague talk of a season after the opera but I very much doubt it.
>   Adam and Eve was quite mild fun, with some good choreography by Antony [Tudor] and some very post-war décor by Banting. I wrote some very devotional music for the angel and the music on the whole sounded better in its old form than in Romeo. Freddy redid Pomona for the Vic-Wells getting much more

---

[37] Lopokova danced Swanilda on 21 and 28 March but, because of an injured knee, she was replaced on 3 April by de Valois who was the leading peasant girl in the earlier performances. Later in the season de Valois fully took over the role of Swanilda.

[38] Kavanagh, *Secret Muses*, pp. 155–6.

[39] Keynes, *Lydia Lopokova*, p. 33.

shape and definition into the ensembles. Excellent décor by Vanessa Bell. Pat [Dolin] overacted disgracefully as the Widow Twankey and Stanley [Judson], who is coming on tremendously this season, was really much better in the part.

The best ballet this season has been 'The Birthday of Oberon' with Purcell music and a chorus of 40. Very good straight-forward choreography by Ninette (much better than 'Origin'). People objected to the chorus being in masks but, as I said, had they seen them without? It had excellent notices but wasn't a success after the first night.

The season rather fell off after that but was pulled together by Coppélia with Loppy (who was superb). Uncle Geoffrey was to have done it but ran into a car and only just escaped with his life so I had to do it at short notice.

The old Copenhagen gallop is to be revived for the last night after which I shall be out of a job unless I can get in with the Monte Carlo ballet which I hear is coming to the Coliseum in June.[40]

Stanley was excellent as the fool in Rimsky's Snow Maiden and Hedley [Briggs] was magnificent as the old man in Coppélia.

I am getting very bored with London and hope to get away when my book is finished and do some composing – I have about 40,000 more [words] to do though. How are you enjoying New York? Are you still at the same address? Are you drinking beer or gin? What is the feeling about the Scottsboro' trial (I have subscribed a wretched pound towards the defence so I expect I shall be stopped at Ellis Island if ever I go to New York).[41]

Do you go to Harlem? Is there anyone there better than Ellington? Have you met my New York bores Van Vechten and Max Ewing?[42] Answers please.

Love

Constant

PS The Concerto you asked about is just out. American agents Carl Fischer, 56 Cooper Square.

Florence sends her love.[43]

Among the *corps de ballet* in *Coppélia* was a newcomer, the Australian Robert Helpmann[44], who had come with a recommendation from Margaret Rawlings, by now well known as an actress, who had seen him dance while she was touring Australia. One morning at Sadler's Wells, de Valois noticed among the new arrivals this very pale

[40] The 'Copenhagen gallop' was a divertissement to music by Glinka that had been introduced during the visit to Denmark to involve the whole company.

[41] The Scottsboro' Trial was amongst the most infamous and most prejudiced trials in American legal history. In March 1931 two white girls alleged that they had been raped on a freight train by nine black youths. The defendants were hastily found guilty. Following an appeal and a stay of execution they were tried again in March 1933, once more with a guilty verdict. The case dragged on until 1937 when four of them were freed, the remaining five serving time in prison. It seems that for Lambert, with his fondness for Duke Ellington and Negro jazz musicians – and the recent staging of *High Yellow* – this highly emotive issue, which had much coverage in the English press, struck a sympathetic chord.

[42] Carl Van Vechten (1880–1964), American writer and photographer who, earlier in his career, was assistant music critic of the *New York Times*. He is remembered for his controversial novel on Harlem life, *Nigger Heaven*, published in 1926. He was Gertrude Stein's literary executor. Max Ewing (1919–79) also was an American photographer and writer.

[43] Letter from Lambert to Marie Nielson, 22 April 1933, from 15 Percy Street, W1. The Concerto he mentioned was his Concerto for Piano and Nine Players published by OUP in 1933.

[44] Sir Robert Murray Helpman(n) (1909–86). He later added the second 'n' to his family name. His first role was one of the seven sons in *Job*; by November he had advanced to Satan when Dolin was not available.

young man, wearing a huge camel-hair coat. 'I am struck by a resemblance in some strange way to Massine,' she recorded in her autobiography. 'Instinctively I know that this is Margaret Rawlings's Australian find. Everything about him proclaims the artist born. I get on the 'phone to Miss Baylis a little later and beg to be allowed to engage him at once.'[45]

Helpmann very quickly established himself as a key member of the Company, but in his eagerness from childhood to become a dancer he had evaded college and consequently now felt intellectually disadvantaged in the artistic company he was now keeping. Impressed by Constant's wide knowledge of the arts, he soon approached him as a possible mentor, an occasion he was not to forget:

> I went to him one day and said, 'I'm terribly sorry. I am completely uneducated. Will you help me?' And he laughed and just said, 'Oh no, I have a lot to do.' And then about a week later he said, 'Were you serious?' And I said that I was and he said, 'All right, I will. I will make you a list every month but you must do it, every thing that's in it, and then we'll discuss it.' And every month for about two years he prepared me a list of operas, paintings, museums, concerts, in fact I think everything I know now which isn't – I wasn't a very good pupil – but everything that I have done since I left the ballet Constant Lambert was completely responsible for. He actually educated me in every way in the theatre apart from the technique of dancing. I mean, you'd go to Constant and say, 'I want to do a new ballet, I'd like to do a romantic ballet,' and he'd come with seven or eight ideas, not one.[46]

While Helpmann's camp homosexuality put them poles apart temperamentally, they were to form an excellent working relationship, and some years after Constant's death, Helpmann spoke of his admiration for the man:

> I don't suppose anybody will ever really know how much he contributed to the success of the English Ballet as it stands today, not only being the most remarkable ballet conductor probably that there ever has been but ... the way he contributed in every department of it, the décor, the musical taste, the standard of music, the playing of the orchestra, he had a curious effect that – I never noticed it until he left and we had a second conductor – that when Constant played it sounded as though the orchestra had been doubled. It was quite remarkable. You never had to think 'Would Constant be with you?' He *was* with you. It was a curious relationship that he felt for dancing that I've never seen in another conductor, before or since. ... You were never bored with him for one second. You'd fight and argue, it wasn't easy at times, he would argue with you, quarrel. He was temperamental in the real sense of the word so much as the performance was the performance and everything had to centre on getting as near perfection as you possibly could, and he wouldn't tolerate any slacking, by the orchestra or the ballet. He would come round and criticise your performance just as much as the ballet master or mistress and he knew that he was always right, but he was not bad tempered. Never.[47]

He found Constant an inspiration. In a not dissimilar way to Diaghilev – but less extravagantly – Constant enriched his leading performers' appreciation of the arts. Ashton and Helpmann were not to be the only principal members of the Company for whom he acted as mentor.

---

[45] De Valois, *Come Dance with Me*, p. 108.
[46] Robert Helpmann talking in *In Search of Constant Lambert*, BBC2, 26 July 1965.
[47] *Constant Lambert Remembered*, BBC Third Network, 25 June 1966.

I N May, Constant stood in for his former teacher, Malcolm Sargent, at one of the Royal College of Music's Jubilee celebrations in the Parry Opera Theatre before the Prince of Wales.[48] It was essentially an evening of dance with 17 works, the majority of them having been composed by College ex-students or professors, among them Arthur Benjamin, Rutland Boughton, Hugh Bradford, Anthony Collins, Armstrong Gibbs, Gavin Gordon, Herbert Howells, Gordon Jacob, Malcolm Sargent and Guy Warrack. An exception was Lord Berners whose *Funeral March for a Rich Aunt*, orchestrated by Constant, was a party-piece of Penelope Spencer who not only choreographed all the dances but herself performed. Constant, whose *Elegiac Blues* was also included, conducted the whole programme. 'The dance in its various forms dominated an evening's diversion which everyone thoroughly enjoyed, from the Royal president to the most humble members of the staff,' wrote the *Daily Telegraph* critic. 'It was a light-hearted and thoroughly diverting evening.'[49] As if to recognise his growing stature among contemporary musicians, Constant's photographic portrait was taken by Bassano the day before the RCM celebrations.[50]

More prestigious was the invitation to conduct *Belshazzar's Feast* in the Amsterdam Concertgebouw as part of the ISCM Festival in June. 'It may be a rash choice, but I'm confident he will make a good job of it,' Walton, then busy with his first symphony, wrote to Edward Dent who had been President of the ISCM since its inception.[51] Under the circumstances Constant made an excellent job of it. The Rotterdam choir had been assembled at short notice and he 'had to conduct the choral rehearsals, for want of space, in the Post Office at Rotterdam, he one side of the counter and grills, and the choir the other'.[52] He called it 'a conductor's nightmare'.[53] The choir, who sang in English, 'could not conceal the fact that they had half-mastered the work. But Mr Roy Henderson was the singer, Mr Constant Lambert's knowledge of the score made up for all shortcomings, and the effect of the whole was electrical,' reported *The Times*.[54] Elsewhere in the Festival Constant conducted Erik Chisholm's *Dance Suite* with the composer at the piano but, according to *The Monthly Musical Record*, 'Walton's work had the one really great public success of the festival.'[55] Walton and Foss were both present, the latter writing to his wife, Dora:

> First of all Willie had a huge success last night. An ovation and half-a-dozen calls, and so did Constant. I don't think I've ever seen such a success at these Festivals. ... A very good performance considering all things. ... Constant did it with enormous drive and rather too fast if anything, but most thrillingly. The one trouble was lack of contrast in dynamics owing to lack of rehearsal.[56]

The day before the concert the three of them lunched together – 'Willie and Constant were most amusing', wrote Foss – before viewing the Van Gogh exhibition

---

[48] In April 1933 Malcolm Sargent underwent an operation for a tubercular abscess.

[49] *Daily Telegraph*, 11 May 1933.

[50] A popular society photography studio named after Alexander Bassano (1829–1913). Six Bassano studies of Lambert, dated 9 May 1933, are in the National Portrait Gallery, in addition to two of him with Florence Lambert and two of her alone, all taken the following day.

[51] 1 June 1933: Walton, *Selected Letters*, p. 99.

[52] Hubert Foss, Prom programme note, 13 September 1951.

[53] Letter from Hubert to Dora Foss, 10 June 1933: Hubert Foss Archives.

[54] Report from Amsterdam dated 11 June in *The Times* of 12 June 1933. The performance was on 10 June 1933.

[55] Henry Boys, *The Monthly Musical Record*, July–August 1933, p. 132.

[56] Letter from Hubert to Dora Foss, 11 June 1933: Hubert Foss Archives.

at the Rijksmuseum where there was also an exhibition of old instruments. Willie tried to match Constant's wit by behaving 'abominably – beating all the drums in ecstasy and turning a plaque of Richard Strauss to the wall!' Flo was with Constant for the Festival and the following day, after lunching with Foss, they were guests at a garden party given by a Dutch banker where they consumed much champagne cup.[57]

At the end of June the Camargo Society, in conjunction with the Vic-Wells Ballet, gave its final offering by staging two gala performances at Covent Garden for the delegates of the World Monetary and Economic Conference. The first evening was attended by the Queen and the Duke and Duchess of York; the second by the Prime Minister and members of the cabinet. Constant was to have shared the conducting with Beecham but Sir Thomas withdrew as he had engagements abroad, leaving *Le Lac des cygnes* and the two acts of *Coppélia* in Constant's capable hands.[58] It had become clear, with the rise of the Vic-Wells Company and Marie Rambert's Ballet Club, that the Camargo Society had largely fulfilled its aims and, at a time of economic depression, could no longer rely on the support of its subscribers and a small number of generous benefactors. Maynard Keynes' time was being increasingly taken up with economics and political matters, and so the Society was wound up.

T HAT same month Constant was excited by Duke Ellington's appearance at the London Palladium. This stirred him to a fulsome article in the *Sunday Referee*:

> That Duke Ellington's band is by far the best that has come to this country, few, I suppose, would deny. The ensemble of players is as remarkable as their individual virtuosity, and the most barbaric effects are executed with a surety and (curiously enough) restraint that every musician must admire, what ever his feelings about so-called 'hot-rhythm' music. The orchestration of nearly all the numbers show an intensely musical instinct, and after hearing what Ellington can do with fourteen players in pieces like 'Jive Stomp' and 'Mood Indigo', the average composer who splashes about with eighty players in the Respighi manner must feel a little chastened.'[59]

This resulted in a vigorous correspondence, with some of the paper's readers deriding jazz and Constant rising gallantly to the defence. His chief opposition came in the form of an 'Open Letter to Constant Lambert' from Roger Wimbush.[60] After expressing general praise for Lambert's 'virile criticism, and particularly for the stand you are putting up against the professional poseur' Wimbush continued:

> Your personal attitude towards jazz is somewhat disturbing. ... Surely, the sole interest in jazz lies in extemporisation and individual virtuosity. Stopping short at this I cannot see how jazz can be taken seriously as an influence on music. ... There can be little doubt that to Western minds jazz is definitely unhealthy. ... In genuine creative music ... jazz finds no place at all, simply because the latter is a Jew-ridden racket and the child of Mammon, whereas music is by nature a spiritual experience. ... It is essential to mention the lack of musicianship and fine feeling in jazz. ... Let Mr Armstrong tackle the trumpet part in the second Brandenburg before we start talking about artistry or even virtuosity.

[57] Letter from Hubert to Dora Foss, 12 June 1933: Hubert Foss Archives.

[58] 27 and 29 June 1933, with Lydia Lopokova returning to make her final appearance in *Coppélia*. Markova starred in *Lac des cygnes*.

[59] *Sunday Referee*, 25 June 1933.

[60] *Sunday Referee*, 9 July 1933. Roger Wimbush (1910–77) was probably best known as a regular contributor to *Gramophone* magazine.

The following week Constant faced his foes in an article he mockingly entitled 'Here we go round the Wimbush'. Dealing with one correspondent who had written that 'Ellington's music has neither movement, rhythm, nor form', he replied that 'it is a little difficult to know what to do. It is rather like discussing the finer gastronomic points with a man who prefers the cooking on English railways to that of "Les Trois Faisans" at Dijon.' Turning to Wimbush he first acknowledged that his letter had contained 'so many handsome bouquets that it may seem a little churlish to accept flowers and throw the maidenhair fern, the paper and the pins in the donor's face.' He continued: 'If Mr Wimbush had read my article on Ellington with eyes undimmed by honest Aryan tears he would have noticed that I was particularly careful to distinguish between "composed" jazz and jazz that consists of putting frills round the latest song hit.' And taking in turn the various points Wimbush had raised, he commented: 'To talk of Ellington and Armstrong as the same type of musician is like lumping together Ravel and Cortot. Ellington is a pianist, an arranger, and a composer. It is as a composer he interests me. ... If [Wimbush] feels so strongly about the Jewish influence on jazz, why is he not more pleased to find that its most distinguished exponent is coloured?' As for any lack of musicianship: 'I know of no English trumpeter who can hit bottom G without preparation and produce a round, firm tone, following it up a minute or two later with an F in alt that is clear and as unharsh as the same note played by the flute.' And he concluded: 'It is time people stopped speaking of jazz as if it was an unvaried stream of sound.'

In the vacuum created by the demise of Diaghilev's Ballets Russes, a number of ballet groups were to be seen in London that summer. Kurt Joos brought his company to the Savoy in June and the following month Colonel Vassily de Basil presented the first London season of the recently formed Ballets Russes de Monte Carlo at the Alhambra, with Léonide Massine as both choreographer and principal dancer.[61] Constant had hoped that he might be asked to conduct but that was a position given on tour to the Russian-born Efrem Kurtz. Instead, for a fortnight from the end of June at the Savoy, he shared with Maurice Abravanel the conducting of the recently formed London Philharmonic Orchestra for Georges Balanchine's company Les Ballets 1933. Their repertoire ranged from Kurt Weill's *Anna-Anna*[62] (with Lotte Lenya, Weill's wife), to Tchaikovsky's *Mozartiana, Errante* (mainly using Schubert's *Wanderer*), *Hymnes* (to a score by Igor Markevitch) and *Fastes* (a first performance in England with costume and décor by André Derain with music by Henri Sauguet).[63] Later, in October, Constant conducted the BBC Orchestra in a broadcast 'of music from the recent season ballet at the Savoy' that included *Mozartiana, Hymnes* and *Fastes*.

While *Anna-Anna* did not meet with much critical enthusiasm, Constant wrote

[61] Colonel Vassily de Basil's (Vassili Voskresensky) Ballets Russes de Monte Carlo (soon known simply as Ballets Russes and recalling memories of Diaghilev's company) was the most serious rival to the Vic-Wells Company in trying to establish a firm footing in English ballet. 'A magnificent company ... that would sweep into London like a forest fire' was how Fonteyn described them: Margot Fonteyn, *Autobiography* (London: W. H. Allen, 1975; Star Book paperback edition, 1976), p. 72. Later they had seasons at Covent Garden and the Theatre Royal, Drury Lane, when, in addition to their regular conductors Efrem Kurtz and Antal Dorati, Beecham had occasion to conduct them.

[62] *Anna-Anna* was an English version of the Weill-Brecht *Die sieben Todsünden der Kleinbürger* (*The Seven Deadly Sins of the Petits Bourgeois*) of which Maurice Abravanel had conducted the premiere with 'Les Ballets 1933' in Paris on 7 June 1933. Lotte Lenya, singing in German, was Anna I, while Tilly Losch was the dancing Anna II.

[63] Henri Sauguet (1901–89), described by Lambert as 'an insignificant but popular and typical Parisian composer': Lambert, 'Contemporary Music', in *Scrutinies: Critical Essays by Various Writers*, ed. Edgell Rickword, vol. 2 (London: Wishart & Co., 1931), p. 300.

most warmly about Weill in *Music Ho!*, describing him as 'undoubtedly the most successful and important of the Central European composers who have experimented with the jazz idiom' and 'almost the only composer who can evoke in music the odd, untidy, drably tragic background that is presented to us so forcibly by William Faulkner in *Sanctuary* and *Light in August*.' He held up *The Seven Deadly Sins* as the 'most important work in ballet form since *Les Noces* and *Parade*', and, while not claiming it to be 'a work of very great intrinsic or permanent value', he thought it had 'considerable strength in the way it manages to deal with a modern and emotional subject without chi-chi, false sentiment or mechanical romanticism'.[64]

Constant was unwell at the end of July – 'we wish him a speedy recovery' came the message from the *Sunday Referee*. To recuperate he and Flo went abroad in August, and by chance in Saragossa they ran into Anthony Powell on holiday with some friends, neither of them having known that the other was visiting Spain. 'We did no more than have a drink together, go our separate ways,' noted Powell.[65] On his return Constant informed his *Sunday Referee* readers:

> Having returned from Spain literally (yes, literally) only half an hour ago, I can hardly be expected to be au courant with the musical situation in London, such as it is, nor, I am afraid, can I embark on a vivid travel sketch of the type so much in vogue ("Through Andalusia with a Tuning-Fork") filled with purple patches about languorous tangos, care-free jotas, and what would you. To be quite frank I heard very little music in Spain, and such little as I did hear was strikingly lacking in either intrinsic or ethnological interest. As far as I could see the Spanish attitude towards music is a severely practical one. They realise that there is a place in life for music and they keep it there without allowing it to slop about the house ...[66]

In September Constant was appointed Professor of Conducting at the Royal College, a position he was to retain until the summer of 1939, and the following year he was awarded the Collard Fellowship with a three-year grant of £300 towards composition.[67] The additional income from this new post enabled Constant and Flo to move from the Percy Street flat lent to them by the Laughtons to accommodation of their own at 4 Great James Street, Bedford Row, on the fringe of Bloomsbury. That same month he conducted *Music for Orchestra* at the Proms with two rehearsals. Three weeks later the autumn season of ballet started, alternating between Sadler's Wells and Old Vic theatres with one programme each week, the other evenings being given to opera. *Pomona* remained in the repertoire, receiving altogether seven performances that year. The first night included *The Foolish Virgins*, choreographed by de Valois to music by Kurt Atterburg, and *Job* with Helpmann taking the role of Satan for the first time. Lambert, *The Times* reported, 'as usual, set a most admirable rhythm at exactly the right tempo'. Markova signed a contract with the Company for the whole season and Frederick Ashton became resident choreographer, giving him the security of a regular salary, something that he had not enjoyed before.

> One was always scrabbling around for what one could get, and I used to have to do things in revues, musical comedies, odd ballets and things which weren't very well paid, and all this was an extremely good discipline so that when you

[64] Lambert, *Music Ho!*, 2nd edn (1937), p. 160.
[65] Powell, *Messengers of Day*, p. 195.
[66] *Sunday Referee*, 20 August 1933.
[67] In his 1951 broadcast talk in memory of Lambert, Walton incorrectly refers to this as a Collett Scholarship.

came to use good dancers you were immensely appreciative of the luxury. I can remember the stimulation of working with Constant Lambert and with Sophie Fedorovitch and having the presence of de Valois there, and the whole thing was growing and what I used to find exciting was when Constant and I worked at a ballet from the beginning for he was a man of immense knowledge not only musically but in every other way and I think without him we would never have achieved what we did.[68]

At Sadler's Wells he, Lambert and de Valois were to form a triumvirate that was responsible for establishing British Ballet, and ultimately the Royal Ballet (an achievement towards which Helpmann also made a notable contribution). As Kenneth Clark has written:

> In the creation of what is now a world famous company Ninette de Valois provided the drive and discipline, Constant Lambert the musicianship, Freddie Ashton the inventive genius. They were a perfect combination, and received the benefice of a great star, Margot Fonteyn. All of them became our friends. We saw almost every one of Freddie Ashton's ballets, and watched the emergence of Margot with delight. In fact we made the mistake of asking her out to dinner when she was only sixteen, and was too embarrassed to speak. As she said when I reminded her of it 'I've made up for it since'.[69]

Fonteyn was soon to join the Company and become the most important person in Constant's life, yet, although their relationship was to span many years, it never fully blossomed. As Ashton later mused, 'I suppose I was [Constant's] closest friend – or at least his confidant. Every misery he went through I had to share. I saw him through it all with Margot.'[70] He saw the darker side of Constant's moods:

> He had great melancholy and great depressions, and oddly enough he used to cry quite a lot. Sometimes when things in his private life upset him I suppose I had his confidence more than anybody else over all that, and he was always coming to me in tears, or ringing up and saying I must see you at the most extraordinary hours. He was a very selfish man in that sense for he never thought whether it was convenient for me but he would come and then he would either burst into tears or go on at great length about his unhappinesses. But that was balanced again by this extraordinary liveliness and humour.[71]

Like Helpmann, Ashton admired Constant's ability as a conductor, especially the vitality he brought to a performance: 'The moment he went into the pit there was this very strong beat and strong rhythm – he would galvanize everybody into giving of their very best.' Later in his career, after Constant's death, Ashton felt keenly the lack of anyone of Constant's stature to advise him in musical and artistic matters.[72] De Valois was to recognise only too well the importance of Constant in the triumvirate:

> He really was the music foundation of the English Ballet. He was the one to put us on the right path in the very beginning, taste and style and approach, and our roots lie in the work that Constant Lambert did for us in the first twenty years of our life ...[73] He was terrifically rhythmical. Very strict. He disciplined

---

[68] *Royal Progress: The Vic-Wells Ballet*, BBC Radio 4 'Kaleidoscope', 4 April 1981.

[69] Kenneth Clark, *The Other Half: A Self Portrait* (London: John Murray, 1977), p. 46.

[70] Kavanagh, *Secret Muses*, p. 393.

[71] *In Search of Constant Lambert*, BBC2, 26 July 1965.

[72] Vaughan, *Frederick Ashton and his Ballets*, p. 274.

[73] *In Search of Constant Lambert*, BBC2, 26 July 1965.

the company very well, but again he had a very open mind, not only musically an open mind but an open mind to the sort of music he had to give to the dancer, and the dancer knew that in her own right she would always get as much assistance as possible. But if he considered anything was incorrect or unnecessary, musically he clamped down and there were no arguments whatsoever. But everyone loved him and respected him so enormously. He was quite unique.[74]

Elsewhere, she has left this delightful vignette of Constant:

the architect of English Ballet music and a figure prominent amid all our triumphs and disasters. The domestic picture conjured up by memory shows him in the ever shabby overcoat, complete with his stick, a score under his arm, a tattered newspaper peeping from his pocket, and the inevitable cigarette spraying his waistcoat with a cloud of fallen ash. Yet resolute and stalwart is the same figure on the rostrum, attired for many evenings of those early years in a morning coat that had once been the property of his father. I have seen him wield his baton on occasions both great and small, with an intensity that no circumstances diminished. He bestowed the same attack and energy on his piano playing during the early period of the war, resolute always that the best only should come forth from the orchestra pit. ... Loved by every orchestra player in London, he became a symbol of security when he entered the pit. As for the dancers, Constant in charge meant to them that all was well with the world; as director, I would sink back with a sigh of relief at the sight of the alert back and the raised arm – the signal for the onslaught of the surest of sure beats.[75]

As the critic Clement Crisp was to observe:

[Ninette de Valois] was blessed with Constant Lambert who was a vital figure. Lambert was, I think, a musician of genius; he was a superlative conductor, he was a very fine composer and he was also a man of very wide-ranging culture, and I do remember talking about Lambert to Dame Ninette and she said, 'You know, there were times when I used to think, "Please God, don't let anything happen to Constant."'[76]

While Constant's conducting career was now steadily progressing, his home life was far from steady. The next two or three years were to be increasingly unsettling ones for Constant and Flo. Whether for financial or other reasons they were to make further moves, first to 7 Mills Buildings, Park Row in Kensington where they stayed for most of 1935 and 1936, and then to 10 Trevor Place in Knightsbridge. Constant's Vic-Wells salary was only a modest one and, like all the Company salaries, dependant on the success of the ballets they presented. Now that he was married he became more reliant on his journalism and broadcasting to supplement his income. The intellectual gap between him and Flo was something that, despite initial efforts, could never be satisfactorily bridged, and the differences in their temperaments were becoming more marked. Marital disharmony was not helped either by his drinking, his habit of working late at night or his frequent absences from home through work, especially when the Company started to go on provincial tours, leaving Flo on her own for substantial periods. Quite simply, his self-centred life-style was not one that suited a married man, and the arrival

---

[74] *Constant Lambert Remembered*, BBC Third Network, 25 June 1966.

[75] De Valois, *Come Dance with Me*, p. 115.

[76] In *Call Me Madam*, TV documentary by Ross MacGibbon on Dame Ninette de Valois, BBC2, 30 July 1998.

of Margot Fonteyn was to shatter any possibility there may have been of holding the marriage together.

O N 21 October 1933 Constant was in charge of a Bax premiere at Queen's Hall: the small-scale *Saga Fragment* in which the piano soloist was Harriet Cohen who, obviously determined to be the star of the whole concert, also played concertos by Haydn and Bach as well as a continuo part that she contrived for Bach's Brandenburg Concerto in F, and Vaughan Williams' *Charterhouse* Suite.[77]

Near the end of the month the ballet *La Création du monde*, that had been presented both by the Camargo Society in 1931 and by the Vic-Wells Ballet on their visit to Denmark in 1932, was given at the Old Vic. Darius Milhaud's score was the result of hearing 'authentic' jazz in Harlem while on a trip to America. This African Negro view of the creation, choreographed by de Valois, in her words 'appealed to the minority and enraged the majority; Miss Baylis, I fear, heavily on the side of the majority'.[78] The *Times* critic, wrongly attributing the music to Auric, nevertheless found it 'the sort that Mr Constant Lambert well understands and can conduct with full effect'.[79] One of the earliest examples of 'symphonic jazz', it was a work that appealed to Constant, who rated it as 'a most remarkable example of the compromise possible between popular idiom and sophisticated construction'.[80] Then, at Sadler's Wells on 5 December, *Les Rendezvous*, Ashton's first ballet for de Valois, was premiered. Constant selected and arranged music from Auber's opera *L'Enfant prodigue*, and Billy Chappell designed the set and costumes. It was, as Clarke has described it, 'a piece of first-rate craftsmanship, beautifully constructed, concise, witty and admirably planned'[81] and as such has stayed in the repertoire.

In November Constant came to the BBC's rescue when Arnold Schoenberg had been programmed to conduct both *Pierrot lunaire* and his Suite Opus 29 for clarinets, strings and piano at the first of that season's Concerts of Contemporary Music. When in January 1931 his monodrama *Erwartung* was given by the BBC Orchestra under the composer's 'none-too-skilled direction', Constant had referred to him as 'one of the most important composers of our time'. He expounded an idea he was to elaborate on at length in *Music Ho!*:

> The remarkable thing about so much of Schönberg's music is that although it looks both scientific and discordant on paper, in performance it sounds purely impressionistic. The extreme elaboration of the orchestral texture tends to obscure the design, and the complete absence of any chord or progression related to common practice actually removes any feeling of excessive harshness. In spite of its apparent intellectuality, its appeal is primarily to our nerves. The purely physical effect is at times overwhelming; not through any excessive sonority but through the diabolical skill in the use of *outré* effects. Like *Pierrot Lunaire*, this work belongs spiritually not so much to our own times as to the 'nineties. It is the final and most elaborate presentation, in music, of the Edgar-Allan-Poe-cum-Aubrey-Beardsley spirit in art.[82]

---

[77] An arrangement for strings of Vaughan Williams' Suite of Six Short Pieces for Piano. Although the score includes a piano part, it is not meant to be played at a performance with orchestra.

[78] De Valois, *Come Dance with Me*, p. 119.

[79] *The Times*, 31 October 1933.

[80] Lambert, *Music Ho!*, 2nd edn (1937), p. 154.

[81] Clarke, *The Sadler's Wells Ballet*, p. 92.

[82] *The Musical Times*, 1 February 1931, p. 167.

Schoenberg returned in February 1933 and his *Variations* were heard again, 'under the somewhat nervous direction of the composer himself', and Constant devoted the whole of his *Sunday Referee* column to the work:

> When these *Variations* were first performed I drew a parallel between the various periods of development shown by Schönberg and Joyce.[83] They are both writers whose early work is feebly academic and sentimental, who have then revolutionised the technique of their arts, produced one outstanding masterpiece (*Ulysses* and *Pierrot Lunaire* respectively) and have finally become a prey to their own mannerisms, abandoning creative expression in favour of a dissection of technique.

He thought the Variations 'by far the most important work Schoenberg has written since the pre-war *Pierrot Lunaire*' and called for another performance soon: 'It is stupid to complain of modern works having no staying power if they are never asked to stay.'[84] By November, with the coming to power of the Nazi government, Schoenberg had been forced into exile and, deciding that America offered the best prospects for his future, had set sail in that direction, cancelling two concerts that Edward Clark had arranged for him to conduct for the BBC. A Queen's Hall programme was completely changed, but at two or three days' notice Constant was asked to step in and conduct *Pierrot lunaire*, with two sets of piano pieces by Schoenberg played by Eduard Steuermann now completing the programme. The reciter was Erika Wagner, and with string players from the Kolisch Quartet and wind players from the BBC Orchestra 'Mr Constant Lambert was able to secure a perfect performance,' reported *The Times*.[85]

On 12 December at the Grotrian Hall, Constant conducted the first public performance of his Concerto for Piano and Nine Players, with Arthur Benjamin again as soloist. Then, at Christmas, he indulged his habit of humorous literary and artistic exchanges by sending Anthony Powell a postcard of a Persian print entitled 'Alexander defeats Raja Fur of Kanauj' and inscribing on the reverse: 'An early ancestor of the Squire's leaving the hunting field to get a nice bit of firewood on the cheap. Best wishes from Constant and Florence for a nice psychic Xmas.' The Squire was the painter and writer Gerald Reitlinger, and the insertion of the word 'psychic' referred to the fact that Powell's flat in Tavistock Square was two doors away from the Institute of Psychical Research where he was sometimes asked in if they were short of people for a séance. In his memoirs Powell has made no mention of Constant accompanying him, but it is not beyond the bounds of possibility that he did so out of either curiosity or amusement.

---

[83] James Joyce (1882–1941), Irish writer and poet, best known for his experimental 'stream of consciousness' novel *Ulysses* (1921) which, because of censorship problems, was first published in Paris in 1922 in a limited edition. Imported copies were seized by the customs and the book did not appear in England until 1936. As Lambert wrote in *Music Ho!*, 2nd edn (1937), p. 13: 'Any printer can print *Ulysses* (if the law lets him), but not every orchestra can play *Erwartung*.' And continuing his comparison between Joyce and Schoenberg: 'Joyce's weakly sentimental *Chamber Music* and the dully realistic *Dubliners* are a parallel to the stodgy and academic imagination of *Verklarte Nacht*, and of Schoenberg's early work in general' (p. 207). Heseltine had greatly admired *Ulysses*, calling it 'a work of quite stupendous genius, a real masterpiece': 7 December 1922: Warlock, *Collected Letters*, vol. 4, p. 52.

[84] *Sunday Referee*, 12 February 1933.

[85] *The Times*, 25 November 1933. The concert, on Friday 24 November, was broadcast on the London Regional station 9.00–10.15 p.m. The piano pieces were Op. 9 and Op. 19.

10 1934
Let's to Billiards – *Music Ho!*

B Y December 1933 Constant had completed what he had described to Marie Nielson as his 'beastly book', which was published by Faber & Faber in April 1934 as *Music Ho!* Dedicated to his mother, it was subtitled 'A Study of Music in Decline', its title coming – with typical Lambertian tongue-in-cheek erudition – from a line in Shakespeare's *Antony and Cleopatra*, Act 2 scene 5:

> *All:* The music ho!
> [Enter Mardian the Eunuch]
> *Cleopatra:* Let it alone; let's to billiards.[1]

'The theme of this book,' he explained in the Preface, 'is modern music in relation to the other arts and in relation to the social and mechanical background of modern life. It is a study of movements rather than musicians and individual works are cited not so much on their own account as for being examples of a particular tendency.' And he ended with these words:

> The artist who is one of a group writes for that group alone, whereas the artist who expresses personal experience may in the end reach universal experience. He must not mind if for the moment he appears to be without an audience. He has no right to complain if Cleopatra prefers billiards. There is always the chance that she may become bored with billiards also, and when she returns to the musician, his song will be all the more moving for having been written to please not her but himself.

Unfortunately, the relevance of Cleopatra would have been lost on the readers of the 1948 Pelican edition because the opening quotation had been left out. It mattered little, too, that Shakespeare's reference to billiards was an anachronism: according to his *Who's Who* entry, billiards – or more precisely Russian billiards – was Constant's favourite pastime.

Having established himself as a music journalist of considerable flair, it was inevitable that he should exercise his pen in something wider than his weekly column in the *Sunday Referee*, for which he had been writing since November 1931, and his less frequent contributions to *The Nation and Athenæum* since April 1930. With his extensive knowledge of the arts, especially their more obscure corners, he was ideally equipped, and his book was keenly anticipated. As the critic Ralph Hill wrote:

> One feels that if he devoted himself entirely to criticism, there would possibly be no limitations to his achievements which are already considerable in quantity. His regular work as musical critic of the *Referee* has displayed an unusually active and original mind, a distinguished literary gift, and an exceptionally keen judgement. ...To my mind the finest short survey of contemporary music that has yet been written is that of his in *Scrutinies* which, for compression, comprehension, and sensitive discernment certainly stands unrivalled. He brings to his work a freshness of outlook that is the result of a wide sympathy with, and sensitive understanding of, the sister arts of painting, sculpture and literature. He is keenly appreciative of the relationship between, and significance

[1] Cleopatra asks her trusted servant and advisor, Charmian, to play but, having a sore arm, she suggests instead the eunuch Mardian. 'As well a woman with an eunuch play'd as with a woman,' Cleopatra replies, and then she changes her mind to fishing.

of, the various aesthetic movements in all the arts. It is therefore welcome news that he is at present engrossed in the writing of a book dealing with this subject as it affects modern music.[2]

Written with the minimum of technical language, without any music examples and without discussing in detail any individual work, *Music Ho!* was greeted with considerable acclaim. Edwin Evans, in *The Music Lover*, rated it as 'one of the most brilliant books written on modern music, in any country, and certainly the most brilliant in our language', while Richard Capell, in the *Daily Telegraph*, found it 'brilliant, and not merely brilliant, but also searching and knowledgeable to a rare degree'. M. D. Calvocoressi, who was challenged for making 'an interesting attempt to prove that the whole of *Boris* is based on the opening phrase', felt that, in seeing music against its social background, Lambert succeeded 'far better than any other writer on modern developments has done'.[3] The duo-pianist Joan Trimble recalled Herbert Howells giving her a copy of *Music Ho!*, telling her 'what a good book it was.'[4] And over 30 years later Arthur Hutchings could write: '*Music Ho!* still fascinates us, first because it is the artistic autobiography of an outstandingly sensitive young man, secondly because it is one of the best documentary revelations of a short but interesting era, thirdly because it is a projection (to borrow a geometrical term) rather than a prediction.'[5] Even today *Music Ho!* can entertain, inform, amuse, challenge and dazzle.

As more than one reviewer pointed out, the index to *Music Ho!* in itself made interesting reading, with *The Girl Friend* rubbing shoulders with *Die glückliche Hand*, and other striking juxtapositions such as *The Amazing Mandarin* and *Animal Crackers*, Al Capone and *Carmen*, T. S. Eliot and Duke Ellington, and van Dieren and Walt Disney. Few writers had previously brought literature and the visual arts so fully into the discussion of music (Cecil Gray being the other most notable example); fewer still had such an extensive range of interests. Many of the comparisons that Constant drew from the other arts would be lost on the average reader; Isaiah Berlin found his 'excessive love of a completely symmetrical parallelism' overdrawn.[6] Yet he was sufficiently up-to-date to comment on the rise of Hitler (in relation to the banning of the music of Alban Berg whom he rated highly), and sufficiently avant-garde to mention more than once Joyce's banned novel *Ulysses* and J. W. Dunne,[7] whose theories on time and dreams were then being much discussed amongst intellectuals.

Constant's underlying theme was that music in the 1920s and 30s was not just in decline but had lost direction. He began by declaring that

> to those who expect a sinister frisson from modern music, it is my melancholy duty to point out that all the bomb throwing and guillotining has already taken place. If by the word 'advanced' we mean art that departs as far as possible from the classical and conventional norm, then we must admit that pre-war music was considerably more advanced … than the music of our own days.

[2] Ralph Hill, 'Some Post-War Critics', *The Sackbut*, vol. 14 no. 5 (December 1933), pp. 122–6.

[3] *The Listener*, 2 May 1934.

[4] Christopher Palmer, *Herbert Howells: A Centenary Celebration* (London: Thames Publishing, 1992), p. 232.

[5] Arthur Hutchings' introduction to the third edition of Lambert, *Music Ho!* (London: Faber & Faber, 1966), p. 25.

[6] Isaiah Berlin, 'Music in Decline', *The Spectator*, 11 May 1934, p. 746.

[7] The Irish aeronautical engineer and author J. W. Dunne (1875–1949) became famous for his book *An Experiment with Time* (1927) in which recounted his own experiments with precognitive dreams.

This was quite likely a topic discussed by those in Constant's circle, as Hubert Foss had proposed much the same in his *Music in My Time*, published in October 1933:

> So many of the novelties of idiom are no more than foreshortened extensions of older practices, or recourse to practices of antiquity. They have grown, and not been grafted or remade, and that apostle of modernism, Mr Cecil Gray, can devote a whole essay to the proof that we are really not of our own age but an offshoot of the last century. If from that view one may differ, one cannot deny that there is nothing new under the sun.[8]

Cecil Gray had suggested in his *A Survey of Contemporary Music* (1924) that 'the music of the last twenty years or so, whether that of Debussy, Stravinsky, Schoenberg, or anyone else, despite all its appearance of novelty, is in reality only the last expression of expiring Romanticism'.[9] It was along these lines, according to Spike Hughes, that Constant had wanted 'to publish an album of Schoenberg waltzes, gavottes, and other essays in what the composer is pleased to call "dance forms", put them on the market with a pretty 1890 cover on them and then sit back and watch the fun.'[10] As a devoted Lisztian, Constant was keen to point out that, even in the harmonic revolution for which Debussy was supposed to be responsible, 'there are few actual harmonic combinations in Debussy that cannot be found in Liszt'. And he emphasised how old the 'new' was:

> The famous series of concerts given by Eugene Goossens in London in 1920 were historical in more ways than one. They apparently announced the dawn of a new era, but curiously enough their most potent arguments were drawn from the era which we all imagined to be closed.[11]

Constant regarded Debussy as a key figure, and while he found *Pelléas et Mélisande* 'one of his weakest and most mannered works' (Cecil Gray had excluded it from the composer's 'most significant works'), he rated most highly the orchestral *Images*, which he thought showed the composer's 'real strength as an artist'. It was impossible, he continued, not to draw the conclusion that the disruptive element in Debussy's impressionism provided the liberating force that led Stravinsky and Schoenberg to their own revolutionary style, and he identified Debussy's *Le Martyre de Saint Sébastian* ('the swan song of the 'nineties'), Stravinsky's *Le Rossignol* and Schoenberg's *Pierrot lunaire* as works that formed the culmination of – using a favourite word of his – 'the *neurasthenia* and preciosity of that impressionistic or disruptive period'.[12] There had been comparatively little critical examination of Debussy at that time, sufficient for

---

[8] Foss, *Music in My Time*, pp. 59–60.
[9] Gray, *A Survey of Contemporary Music*, pp. 255–6.
[10] Hughes, *Opening Bars*, p. 205.
[11] Lambert, *Music Ho!*, 2nd edn (1937), p. 13. Actually 1921, Eugene Goossens' first concert of 'contemporary music' at Queen's Hall on 7 June 1921, attended by Stravinsky, Diaghilev and Massine, included Berners' *Fantaisie Espagnole* (1919), Ireland's *The Forgotten Rite* (1913), Ravel's *La Valse* (1920) and the first concert performance in England of *Le Sacre du printemps* (1913). Four more concerts that followed towards the end of the year included Schoenberg's *Five Orchestral Pieces* (1909, revised 1922), Stravinsky's *Symphony for Wind Instruments* (1920) and a repeat of *Le Sacre*, Strauss's *Also sprach Zarathustra* (1896), Rimsky-Korsakov's *Antar* (1903), Malipiero's *Oriente immaginario* (1920) as well as many British works. Brahms's First Symphony was substituted for Stravinsky's *Song of the Nightingale* 'to bolster the sagging subscription list'.
[12] Lambert, *Music Ho!*, 2nd edn (1937), p. 36.

Edward Lockspeiser in his 1936 study of the composer[13] to cite Gray, Lambert and Foss as those who had attempted this 'difficult task'.

With his general antipathy to Stravinsky, Constant had little to say that was praiseworthy about his first two ballets: for him *The Firebird* was no more than 'a pleasant pantomime', and in *Petrushka* he found 'the composer playing – albeit with consummate brilliance – the role of effects man in music', although as a man of the theatre he did make the interesting comment that a concert performance of *Petrushka* was 'intolerable to those unacquainted with every detail of the stage action'. While he recognised such works as *Le Sacre du printemps*, *Pierrot lunaire* and Debussy's *Iberia* (from *Images*) as landmarks of the pre-war period, he felt that music in the 1920s had entered the age of pastiche. Stravinsky *le pasticheur* was the prime culprit, his first notable example being the ballet *Pulcinella* that Diaghilev introduced to Paris in 1920.[14] (Diaghilev himself was partly responsible for this trend towards pastiche, as he had unsuccessfully tried to interest Ravel in orchestrating first Scarlatti, and then Bach, for the ballet. Ultimately he presented Stravinsky with copies of Pergolesi's music and commissioned a ballet score from him.) If Foss saw Diaghilev as a 'mid-wife of contemporary art' for the way that he had fostered new music and radical art forms and combined them with exotic Russian dancing in ballet, Constant dubbed Diaghilev and Stravinsky 'time travellers', Stravinsky being 'by far the best person for Diaghileff to send time travelling in the eighteenth century because, both temperamentally and racially, he was out of touch with the whole period.'[15] He described this trend to pastiche:

> A great deal of pre-war music may have sounded, to use a dear phrase, 'like nothing on earth'. Most music of today sounds only too reminiscent of something that has previously been in existence. ... Today every composer's overcoat has its corresponding hook in the cloakroom of the past. Stravinsky's concertos (we have it on the composer's own authority) are 'like' Bach and Mozart; Sauguet's music is admired because 'c'est dans le vrai tradition de Gounod'; another composer's score is praised because in it 'se retrouvent les graces étincellantes de Scarlatti'. ... By 1913 music had already reached the absolute limit of complication allowed by the capacity of composers, players, listeners and instrument makers. With very few exceptions in detail – such as the piano writing of Sorabji, the polytonal choral writing of Milhaud[16] and the quarter-tone writing of Aloys Haba[17] – there is nothing in present-day music more complicated from any point of view than what we find in the music of twenty years ago.[18]

---

[13] Edward Lockspeiser, *Debussy* (London: J. M. Dent, 1936).

[14] The music, attributed to Pergolesi (1710–36), was reorchestrated by Stravinsky who later said: '*Pulcinella* was my discovery of the past, the epiphany through which the whole of my late work became possible. It was a backward look, of course – the first of many love affairs in that direction. ... I was therefore attacked for being a *pasticheur*.' Stravinsky and Craft, *Expositions and Developments*, p. 113.

[15] What Lambert, of course, chose to disregard was that, with *Romeo and Juliet* and especially *Pomona*, having sections imitative of 18th-century music and names of Elizabethan dance forms (and hautboy in the orchestra list), the epithet 'time traveller' could equally apply to him.

[16] Elsewhere in *Music Ho!* (2nd edn (1937), p. 140) Lambert wrote that 'Milhaud's earlier works, which jump sharply from the most academic euphony to the most startling cacophony, remind one of a host who having forgotten to put gin in the first round of cocktails puts methylated spirits in the second round to make up for it.'

[17] Alois Hába (1893–1973), Czech composer who studied in Prague, Vienna and Berlin.

[18] Lambert, *Music Ho!*, 2nd edn (1937), pp. 44, 45.

With a section in *Music Ho!* devoted to nationalism in music, and in particular Russian nationalists, a young Isaiah Berlin, writing in *The Spectator*, being Russian-born himself, understandably considered Russomania 'the most attractive form of musical extremism' and found that Constant betrayed all the symptoms:

> The greater part of the book consists of an onslaught upon the dominant schools; he is at his most violent and destructive when he attacks the group of Parisian *pasticheurs* gathered round the leading figure of Stravinsky; his tone grows almost personal, as of one who but lately was himself half a follower, but soon definitely revolted against the slick and lifeless formulae, the recipes for synthetic melody, which he found in place of any genuine will to create. He is perhaps particularly vehement because for him this represents a *corruptio optimi*, the betrayal of the nationalist movement in Russian music, which was begun by the genius of Glinka, and reached its apex in the great masterpieces of Mussorgsky and Borodin: it is quite plain that it is to the Russians that Mr Lambert has really lost his heart, far more than even to Debussy, whose crucial importance he fully recognises and on whom, indeed, he is very interesting; and this allegiance colours everything he writes.[19]

Constant's three years as a regular critic seem to have bred a certain impatience, if not an intolerance that showed in his writing, with the directions that contemporary music was taking, and he was running some risk in using his often abrasive journalistic style in a book that would have more permanence than a weekly paper. Fortunately, most reviewers realised that he was only being true to himself, although Rutland Boughton felt that in concentrating his adverse analysis upon what was bad in contemporary music, he conveyed a general feeling of music being, not so much in decline, as in 'excremental decay'.[20] Edwin Evans pointed out that Constant had 'set out with a bias': whereas most historians would approach the subject from the angle of German 19th-century music, Constant had taken the Russian nationalist school as a starting point. His main targets were Stravinsky and Hindemith. His patent dislike of the former might be seen as a rather hypocritical attitude for, as Isaiah Berlin indicated, Constant had himself undoubtedly been influenced by Stravinsky in his early works, with both *Romeo and Juliet* and *Pomona* having strong neo-classical lines; perhaps in attacking Stravinsky he was trying to disown any association.

Gray, who had no time for Stravinsky, had led the way in his *Survey of Contemporary Music* by describing him as 'simply an impersonal sum-total of pre-existing terms, a synthesis of all the separate and frequently conflicting tendencies which constitute that complex phenomenon we call the spirit of the age'. He discussed *Le Sacre du printemps* in terms of three interdependent elements – melody, harmony and rhythm – with colour as a possible fourth, and suggested that Stravinsky's 'obsession with rhythm ... has led, not only to the impoverishment of both harmony and melody, but to the loss of the very quality to which he sacrificed the other two – rhythmic vitality... Rhythm has here degenerated into metre.' Constant, following a similar thread, wrote that '[melody] is not only the most important element but an all-embracing one. Harmony without melody is only an aural tickling, and rhythm without melody is not even rhythm – it is only metre. ... A melody, though, is a complete work of art in itself and the unaccompanied Gregorian chants still remain among the most perfect and satisfying achievements in music'. He went on to suggest that 'Stravinsky's rhythm is not rhythm in the true sense of the term, but rather "metre" or

---

[19] Berlin, 'Music in Decline', pp. 745–6.
[20] Rutland Boughton, 'A Modernist Blows the Gaff', *New Britain*, 9 May 1934, p. 764.

"measure"',[21] and accused Stravinsky for 'his complete lack of any melodic faculty. ... We can recognise him immediately by his scoring, by his rhythm and by the setting he gives to his themes, but the themes themselves are either traditional or characterless.'[22]

The only work by Stravinsky for which he expressed any liking was *Les Noces*,[23] 'one of the masterpieces' of its period, he wrote in *Music Ho!*, 'and possibly the only really important work that Stravinsky has given us'.[24] Three years earlier, in an article on contemporary music that he had contributed to a collection called *Scrutinies*, he had set *Les Noces* apart from 'the elaborate series of pastiches with which [Stravinsky's] name is now chiefly associated', calling it his 'most valuable contribution to music and the one that shows most originality, ... his most moving composition' and the only one in which 'we find any real formal invention'.[25] But, he had continued, 'although *Les Noces* gave one the highest hopes, each succeeding work has only lowered them. Stravinsky has now become a sort of musical Dr Voronoff,[26] grafting the glands of various apes on to the withered body of his own inspiration. Occasionally he emulates Dr Moreau[27] ...',[28] analogies he wisely did not repeat in *Music Ho!* where he had this to say:

> Unlike Debussy, who was strong enough to conquer his early mannerisms and put his revolutionary technique to a flexibly expressive use, Stravinsky was caught in the mechanics of his technical mannerisms, and the deliberate exploitation of certain facets of musical thought for their own sake led him to a definite blind alley from which there was no escape except by a deliberate reaction. He is like a motorist who spends all his time with his head inside the bonnet. *Chi ha vissuto per amore, per amore si morì* ('Those who live for love are killed by love') sings the street musician in Puccini's *Il Tabarro* – and he might have added: 'Those who live for technique are killed by technique.'[29]

[21] Lambert, *Music Ho!*, 2nd edn (1937), pp. 68, 28. Cyril Beaumont, who attended the English premiere in 1913, described the music as 'formed of pure rhythm, a rhythm sometimes dull and monotonous, but sometimes attaining tremendous force, bludgeoning the audience', and added that 'not a few of the audience in the interval complained bitterly of splitting headaches': Cyril W. Beaumont, *The Diaghilev Ballet in London: A Personal Record* (London: Putnam, 1945), pp. 73, 75.

[22] *Ibid.*, pp. 67–8.

[23] *Les Noces* was first performed by the Ballets Russes in Paris in June 1923. The choreography was by Bronislava Nijinsky.

[24] Beaumont, *The Diaghilev Ballet in London*, p. 65.

[25] Lambert, 'Contemporary Music', pp. 296, 297. He was even later to admit that *Les Noces* was 'once one of my favourite pieces of music' (*The New Statesman and Nation*, 20 October 1934), a judgement possibly coloured by his devotion to Nijinska when he described the work as 'essentially two-dimensional ballet-music which requires the third dimension supplied by Nijinska's inspired choreography' (its first English presentation having been given by the Ballets Russes on 14 June 1926, a week before *Romeo and Juliet* had its English premiere). Oddly enough in *Music Ho!* he nevertheless commented on its 'monotonous peasant fragments' and that 'in the concert hall the ear soon wearies of a design on one plane only': 2nd edn (1937), pp. 68, 134.

[26] Serge Voronoff (1866–1951), Russian-born surgeon who gained notoriety in the 1920s for transplanting the glands of monkey testicles into elderly men to extend their lives and rejuvenate their sex drive. Although his theories were later ridiculed he has been recognised as a pioneer in organ transplant.

[27] The vivisectionist in H. G. Wells, *The Island of Doctor Moreau* (1896), who carried out his experiments on animals on a remote island.

[28] Lambert, 'Contemporary Music', p. 298.

[29] Lambert, *Music Ho!*, 2nd edn (1937), p. 67.

If his attacks on Stravinsky seem extreme, Constant was not alone among English critics as the composer's second wife, Vera, was to write much later: 'Ironically, the composer whom Ernest Newman, Constant Lambert, and others were belabouring was the only major foreign one ever to have become deeply attracted to English music', composers like Byrd, Bull, Gibbons and Purcell.[30]

However, by comparison, his vigorous debunking of Hindemith appears almost like a personal vendetta. In April 1929, six months before the German composer and viola player had stepped in for the premiere of Walton's concerto, Constant had written in an article in *The Listener* headed 'Doubts about the "Moderns"' that 'although [Hindemith] has a large and enthusiastic following in Germany, [he] has never impressed me as being a figure of real significance'.[31] The following year, in his article on contemporary music for *Scrutinies* in which he wrote that contemporary German composers suffered from uninspired facility and the tendency to overwrite, he added that 'Hindemith, the most typical and important German composer of today, is undoubtedly a man of immense talent and probably the most brilliant journalist in music that has been known. ... It is the absence of organic life and intrinsic form that we feel in Hindemith's by now almost weekly works.'[32] But the real attack began in February 1932 after the Courtauld-Sargent Concerts and the BBC had both presented a work of his.[33] Quoting Hindemith that a composer 'should never write unless he is acquainted with the demand for his work. The times of consistent composing for one's own satisfaction are probably gone for ever,' he mildly commented that 'it would be idle to inquire whether in refraining from writing for his own satisfaction Hindemith has necessarily incurred ours.'[34] He went on to deride what was termed as *Gebrauchsmusik* – 'bread-and-butter music, workaday, or utility music' as

> craft for craft's sake ... German Romantic music had come to resemble a stuffy drawing-room, over-decorated and encumbered with vast padded sofas and downy cushions. Hindemith and his followers have thrown open the double-windows, torn down the hangings, put sackcloth in the place of brocade, and replaced the upholstery with glass and aluminium. But there is still too much furniture about. German music has always suffered from a fatal facility and the new Gebrauchsmusik is no exception.

Just over a year later he condemned the oratorio *Das Unaufhörliche*:

> Hindemith's orchestral works may not be exactly inspired, but they are to be preferred to this oratorio for precisely the same reason that bad prose is to be preferred to bad poetry. ... His music is, indeed, an all too faithful interpretation

---

[30] Vera Stravinsky and Robert Craft, *Stravinsky in Pictures and Documents* (New York: Simon & Schuster, 1978), p. 160.

[31] Lambert's earliest acquaintance with the music of Hindemith was possibly at a Contemporary Music Centre concert in Marylebone on 1 December 1925 when Anthony Bernard conducted the *Kleine Kammermusik*. 'The intention is shallow and frivolous', reported *The Times* (3 December 1925). The concert also included works by van Dieren and Finzi and two songs by Lambert.

[32] Lambert, 'Contemporary Music', p. 304. He followed this up in *Music Ho!* by adding that 'his concertos, however varied in context, have the family resemblance of shape and texture that one edition of a newspaper bears to another and, as in journalism, Tuesday's edition irrevocably dates that of Monday' (p. 173).

[33] A Courtauld-Sargent concert on 9 February 1932 included the Concert Music for Piano, Brass and Harps, conducted by Otto Klemperer, while on 17 February 1932 with the BBC Orchestra Henry Wood conducted the Concert Music for Strings and Brass, op. 50.

[34] *Sunday Referee*, 21 February 1932. Quoted by Lambert from the composer's own note in the Courtauld-Sargent concert on 9 February 1932.

of the words, facile word-spinning is matched with facile counterpoint, and monotonous imagery is matched with monotonous melody.

He added:

> I must admit that by the end of the evening a more charitable explanation of the spiritual banality and musical nullity of this work presented itself to me. Perhaps, I thought, this is the supreme example of utility music and one written especially for England. Hindemith, having noticed the English liking for a highbrow atmosphere, combined with no intellectual effort, and realising their passion for (a) oratorio, (b) boredom, (c) choir-boys, (d) cheap philosophy, may have decided to write a work which would satisfy all these longings and yet not be too difficult or expensive to perform.[35]

This proved too much for Hindemith pupil Walter Leigh, who, on the day the review appeared, wrote to Constant (who only three weeks earlier had given him a very warm notice for his burlesque operetta *Jolly Roger*).[36] His letter has not survived but Constant straightway penned a lengthy reply:

> Dear Walter,
>
>   Your extremely interesting outburst has not only caused me to suspend operations on my book but actually to break one of the most cherished rules of my life viz: not to cover more than a sheet of foolscap unless substantially remunerated.
>
>   Your letter contains so many good points (together with a few red-herrings) that it would take several thousand words to deal with the various aesthetic problems raised. I hope indeed to deal with them fully in the book I am writing. Meanwhile I should like to answer some of your more sinister and far-reaching accusations.
>
>   To start with when I attack Hindemith I am not doing it from the point of view of obdurate tories like Newman or frank buffoons like P. P. I need hardly point out that I was one of the very few critics who wrote sympathetically about Schönberg's Variations for example and that I am the last person to lump 'Central European' music together as a thing to be either praised or blamed. I detest any sort of politico-artistic attitude towards music and feel that the critic who treats all new music as sympathetic and interesting because he wishes to be considered 'emancipated' does far more harm than the diehard who treats it all as so much or so many 'balls'.
>
>   It may be embarrassing to find oneself on the same side as the diehards but, if I may quote Jean Cocteau, 'One should not praise Wagner because Saint-Saens decries him'.
>
>   As a critic I should no doubt forget that I am a composer but as a composer I feel very strongly that the works of Hindemith and of the post-war Stravinsky are in their very different ways leading music 'up the garden' and that Hindemith

---

[35] *Sunday Referee*, 26 March 1933. Henry Wood conducted the first English performance of *Das Unaufhörliche* at Queen's Hall with the BBC Symphony Orchestra on 22 March 1933. After another performance on 7 May the following year with Boult conducting the BBC Symphony Orchestra, Lambert called the work 'the dullest oratorio since Parry's *Job*', *Sunday Referee*, 13 May 1934. By contrast, Hubert Foss, in his *Music in My Time* (1933), wrote more favourably about the work, saying that it marked 'a positive step' in Hindemith's development.

[36] 'Walter Leigh's Burlesque', *Sunday Referee*, 5 March 1933. 'In the theatre I know of no music that is more enjoyable both intrinsically and satirically than the music of "The Pride of the Regiment" and the recently produced "Jolly Roger". One has the rare and enjoyable sensation of both having one's cake and eating it.'

as the younger and more vital mind and as the more dextrous technician is the more nefarious influence of the two. Hindemith in writing so much 'occasional' music (a phrase which I think is better and fairer than 'gebrauchsmusik') is no doubt only reviving the traditions of the 18th century but is he not reviving one of the worst traditions of one of the least musical periods. A reference to the 18th century is to me no rap on the knuckles because I consider that the general level of music in that period was strikingly low and the general attitude towards music frankly deplorable. The music of the 18th century does not irritate us like the music of the 19th but isn't that because it is so often lacking in any content – a mere aural tickling like jazz? Half the people who go to hear 18th century music do so in the spirit of those who turn on dance music on the wireless. Admittedly much fine music in the 18th century was written to order but surely the reason why we find Mozart's later work so much finer than his earlier work is that he was writing more and more to please himself and less to please his audience or his patrons?[37] The Paris symphony was written to appeal to Paris but the Prague symphony was not as is generally believed written to please the people of Prague. It was written to please Mozart and as such it is no doubt from your point of view a piece of masturbation. But to extend your simile logically all music is masturbation and it is legitimate to consider masturbation in private, though blameworthy, a more dignified proceeding than masturbation to order in public.

You ask if I would write a concerto for Kreisler or a cantata for the BBC. The answer to the first is <u>no</u> because I dislike all fiddle concertos without exception[38] and God forbid I should add to their number. The answer to the second is yes because I happen to be writing a cantata[39] for my own pleasure and naturally hope to turn an honest penny with it. At the same time I feel that if I write to please myself and not to please Edward Clark for example it will be more likely to have a general and lasting appeal. A sculptor who designs a figure to please himself has more chance of creating a good (and therefore more truly speaking useful work of art) than the one who is commissioned to execute a portrait of Gladys Cooper or Lord Beaverbrook.

That The Lesson[40] is effective under certain specialized conditions is not in itself any praise of the work. The prose of James Douglas[41] undoubtedly has a great effect on the public it is designed for, but we don't take it seriously for that reason. If we are to adopt fitness for its purpose as the only standard then the articles of Dean Inge[42] assume a greater importance than the Work in Progress[43] of James Joyce.

I still feel that there is no such thing as musical furniture and that music is only 'useful' when it is aesthetically valuable. Hindemith's music strikes me as

---

[37] Here Lambert is touching on one of the main themes behind *Music Ho!*.

[38] Outside the Royal College of Music Lambert was true to his word and conducted few violin concertos: single performances of those by Giurne Creith (its premiere), Khachaturian, Mendelssohn, Dvořák, Barber, Vivaldi and Bartók No. 1. The Walton concerto was the only one he seems to have conducted more than once.

[39] *Summer's Last Will and Testament.*

[40] Hindemith's *Lehrstück*, which received its British premiere on 24 March 1933.

[41] Lambert was presumably referring to James Douglas (1867–1940), author, journalist and Editor of the *Sunday Express*.

[42] William Inge (1860–1954), Dean of St Paul's Cathedral. Nicknamed 'The Gloomy Dean', he was for 25 years a columnist for the *Evening Standard*.

[43] *Work in Progress* was the title given to James Joyce's *Finnegans Wake* when the first two parts were published in 1926 in serialised form. The novel was not completed and published until 1939.

being not so much an undecorated chair (which is to be preferred to a decorated one) but as an unpainted canvas or an armature to which the sculptor has not yet added clay.

His technical dexterity is enormous but I do not consider dexterity 'accomplishment'. Dyneley Hussey in the Week End Review this week says that Hindemith is a most powerful and accomplished composer and then goes on to say that he has no melodic appeal and that his fugues look well on paper but sound dull in performance. Such a view of 'accomplishment' is of course laughable. Any one can turn out counterpoint of a sort provided it doesn't have to be expressive. Similarly with music 'architecture' it only becomes a problem when you have to strike a balance between subjective emotion and objective form. For that reason I find the architecture of the Fantastic Symphony more interesting than that of The Art of Fugue – the shape of Sea Drift more interesting than that of The Perpetual.[44] There is no reason even to choose such contrasted works in period and technique. Surely Schönberg's Variations which have all Hindemith's technical and contrapuntal dexterity plus 'that something some others haven't got' and which were written to please himself, are a more valuable work than Hindemith's Philharmonic Variations[45] which seem to me merely slick 'occasional' music, fulfilling a certain but very limited purpose.

Nothing is so futile as musical criticism I quite realise. You look upon Hindemith as 'a sort of Palestrina' and so do I, but then I have always found Palestrina the most boring and least sympathetic of the great choral composers.

This letter then is far from being a 'gebrauchs-letter' (in fact I find that by adding up what I have lost by neglecting my book and what I get for a 1,000 words of nothing in particular from the Referee, this letter has cost me £10 and served no apparent purpose), at the same time I hope you will believe me when I say that when I attack Hindemith I am not so much showing mental laziness or English diehard-prejudice as defending one of the very few convictions I have left.

Yours ever,

Constant Lambert[46]

PS (Serial and cinema rights reserved).

Not put off by Leigh's letter – even possibly fired up by his own reply – Constant went into the attack again in his next *Sunday Referee* article entitled 'A Lesson to Us All', beginning: 'As a composer pure and simple, Hindemith is of little interest ...' This time it concerned the cantata *Lehrstück* (*The Lesson*), 'founded on a libretto whose pseudo-profundities are of a type which one hoped had found its last home in Hitler's speeches.'[47] (It is only fair to add that the text, by Berthold Brecht, had even been the subject of some controversy between author and composer, and after early performances in Germany the work was taken out of circulation for nearly thirty years.)[48]

His *Sunday Referee* and *New Statesman* articles provided useful recycling material for *Music Ho!* where, having dismissed Honegger's *Pacific 231* for its sentimentality

---

[44] Hindemith's oratorio *Das Unaufhörliche* (or 'The One Perpetual' in the translation by Mr and Mrs Cyril Scott of Gottfried Benn's text for the English premiere).

[45] *Philharmonic Concerto* (1932), variations for orchestra.

[46] Letter from Lambert (15 Percy Street, W1) to Walter Leigh, dated 'Monday' (27 March 1933).

[47] *Sunday Referee*, 2 April 1933. Adrian Boult conducted the work's first British performance at Broadcasting House on 24 March 1933.

[48] Geoffrey Skelton, *Paul Hindemith: The Man behind the Music* (London: Gollancz, 1977), p. 96.

in trying to 'capture the lyricism of an express train moving at top speed',[49] he continued:

> A far more disastrous example of mechanical romanticism is provided by the works of Hindemith. For whereas Honegger's works only affect the façade of the music as we know it, Hindemith's apply a pneumatic drill to its foundations, a pneumatic drill wielded by the most efficient and determined of mechanics.

'The supreme middle brow of our times' was how he summed up Hindemith. But he went a step too far when he added:

> Not only does Hindemith produce busy and colourless music without any distinguishing spiritual or national quality, but his followers and pupils, whether they write in Serbia or in Golders Green, produce precisely the same type of busy and colourless music. Their works differ as much from each other as a Cook's office in one town differs from a Cook's office in another.

It was an unkind swipe at Walter Leigh, who lived in Golders Green.[50] Hindemith was also a friend of Edward Clark and of Walton who was much later to repay his gratitude by dedicating his *Variations on a Theme by Hindemith* to the composer and his wife, and Constant was at risk of impairing several friendships. Yet what might appear today as rather savage attacks either did not seem so at the time or were regarded as acceptable. A decade earlier Cecil Gray, in his *Survey of Contemporary Music*, had written off contemporary German music as

> a wide ocean of notes in which no landmarks are audible. The only feature of interest, as in the fable, is the swollen and decomposed corpse of the Zauberlehrling [Sorcerer's Apprentice] himself, Richard Strauss. Otherwise nothing else shows above the surface; the most that can happen to us is to run aground on some nasty snag like Franz Schreker, some mud-shoal like Erich Korngold, or a sandbank like Paul Hindemith.[51]

Hubert Foss, in his *Music in My Time*, which preceded *Music Ho!* by six months, was more guarded in his appraisal of Hindemith whom he considered, for all his 'astonishing facility', to be 'at heart a light rather than a heavy thinker, occupied rather with problems of technique than the searchings of the soul. … Charm, consonance, and all the other ordinary parts of the musician's equipment are absent …'[52] But in summing up his review of *Music Ho!* Foss wrote: 'Few better expositions of Schönberg, Stravinsky, Debussy, Hindemith exist – I know of none that more clearly sum up jazz, the cinema, and our own funny ways of life as 'modern' people … It is especially an important document for all whose daily work in music has kept them aside from what has really been going on while they were not – could not be – looking.'[53]

With his rejection of Stravinsky and Hindemith in particular,[54] and Germanic music

---

[49] Lambert, *Music Ho!*, 2nd edn (1937), p. 170. Lambert had similarly discussed Honegger's *Pacific 231* in 'Railway Music', *The New Statesman and Athenæum*, 16 August 1930, pp. 620–1.

[50] David Drew, 'North Sea Crossings: Walter Leigh, Hindemith, and English Music', *Beiträge zur Musik des 20. Jahrhunderts*, ed. Susanne Schaal-Gotthardt, Luitgard Schader and Heinz-Jürgen Winkler, Frankfurter Studien 12 (Frankfurt am Main: Schott, 2009), pp. 127–54.

[51] Gray, *A Survey of Contemporary Music*, pp. 247–8.

[52] Foss, *Music in My Time*, p. 141.

[53] *The Musical Times*, June 1934 p. 515.

[54] Ironically, Lambert was to conduct the first English performance of Hindemith's *Symphonic Metamorphosis on Themes by Carl Maria von Weber* at a Henry Wood Prom on 3 September 1946. He also twice gave Hindemith's ballet overture *Cupid and Psyche* (Prom 3 August 1945 and a BBC 'Music of Our Time' concert 22 May 1946), while *Concert of Angels* (from *Mathis*

in general, one might have expected Constant to adopt a more sympathetic approach to English music which was itself going through a period of change. Elgar, Delius and Holst had less than six months to live, only the first three of Vaughan Williams' nine symphonies had been composed, and Walton, with the success of *Belshazzar's Feast* behind him, had yet to complete his shattering first symphony. Walton he classified as one of 'the most vital minds of the present generation',[55] but three years earlier in the *Sunday Referee*, touching the subject of nationalism in English music, he had cited dramatic intensity and formal coherence as

> the two qualities that most English composers are prepared to sacrifice or overlook in their obsession with an English mood. The complete gap in the English musical tradition and the absolute subjugation of English music to foreign influences not unnaturally produced a movement of rather exaggerated nationalism and a school of composers who seemed more intent on creating an English atmosphere than a solidly constructed piece of music. How well we know this typically English mood, the orchestration almost smelling of Harris tweed, the thematic landscape shrouded in mist, the brooding lyricism punctuated from time to time with a touch of that rugged heroism with which the Englishman plunges into a cold bath in January. The mood, I admit, is unsympathetic to me personally ... One feels that the composers are not constructing individual works but pouring out a synthetic 'mood paste' (to use an excellent phrase of Mr van Dieren's) into receptacles of different shapes and sizes.[56]

As he expanded in *Music Ho!*, it was particularly to the use of folk-song material that he objected, there being a sense of artificiality because 'folk songs in England are not a vigorous living tradition, as they were in Russia. ... The English folk song, except to a few crusted old farmhands in those rare districts which have escaped mechanization, is nothing more than a very pretty period piece with the same innocent charm as the paintings of George Morland'.[57]

Constant's real sympathies and enthusiasms become clear in the chapters on the Russian nationalists, Satie, films and jazz. Or as Isaiah Berlin put it, 'Rejecting the sincere and sterile, Mr Lambert receives with acclamation anything which seems to him to be eloquent and imaginative, from the hot jazz of Duke Ellington and the oddly moving underworld studies of Kurt Weill to the splendidly isolated figure of Sibelius.'[58] One of the most original chapters is that on Satie, whom he defends from a reputation as 'a farceur and an incompetent dilettante [which had] unfortunately outweighed his reputation as a composer'.[59] All his life Constant remained a keen and active supporter of the works of Satie. His section on films, however, is probably the most dated because at that time few 'serious' composers were writing for the cinema. Although Shostakovich had already produced his earliest film scores, Prokofiev and Walton were only about to embrace the medium and one of the most significant film scores of

---

der Maler) was in his Conductors' Class programme at the RCM on 10 December 1935, with Franz Reizenstein the student conductor.

[55] Lambert, *Music Ho!*, 2nd edn (1937), p. 232.

[56] *Sunday Referee*, 6 December 1931, reviewing Vaughan Williams' *Job*, in which he found 'the dramatic intensity and formal coherence ... all the more refreshing' for their presence.

[57] Lambert, *Music Ho!*, 2nd edn (1937), p. 120.

[58] Berlin, 'Music in Decline', p. 746.

[59] His chapter entitled 'Erik Satie and his Musique d'ameublement', translated into French, was included by Rollo Myers in his *Erik Satie: son temps et ses amis* (Paris: Richard–Masse, 1952) – not to be confused with Myers' *Erik Satie* in the 'Contemporary Composers' series, (London: Dennis Dobson, 1948).

the 1930s, Bliss's for the Korda–H. G. Wells epic *Things to Come*, was two years ahead. Yet who but Constant could have suggested that, with the cinema being the one art form that was in touch with the public, films had for 20th-century audiences the same emotional impact that operas had in the 19th century, and he nominated Pudovkin[60] and Eisenstein as the true successors of Mussorgsky, D. W. Griffiths of Puccini, Cecil B. de Mille of Meyerbeer, and René Clair of Offenbach? When he writes of the idea of a film as a musical entity vanishing with the first Al Jolson picture (the first of the 'talkies', made in 1927) he was referring to the old practice of having an orchestra accompany the silent screen, such as Edmund Meisel's score for Eisenstein's *Battleship Potemkin* which Constant thought a great improvement on the ordinary cinema music of the time if not 'quite a worthy counterpart of the film itself'.[61] He was alert to the surrealist potential of films, such as Walt Disney's *Silly Symphonies* cartoons and the Marx brothers films, a particular favourite of his, and he cited examples from Russian and American films in which sound was being imaginatively used as a counterpoint to the image on the screen. However, suggesting that post-war composers were 'cinema producers manqués' he could not refrain from adding: 'Instead of producing null and void concertos, Hindemith should be the camera man, Honegger should be in charge of the sound effects and Stravinsky, with his genius for pastiche, should be entrusted with the cutting.'

Turning to the racial origins of jazz and modern dance music, he delighted in pointing out to 'the crusty old colonels, the choleric judges and beer-sodden columnists … murmuring "swamp stuff", "jungle rhythms", "negro decadence"' that most modern jazz, far from being the province of the Negro, was in fact largely 'written and performed by cosmopolitan Jews' and that harmonically sophisticated European jazz was closer to a piece by Grieg than to native African music. He argued as before that the harmonic element in Afro-American music had derived from the religious music of the Anglo-Saxons, the hymns of John Bacchus Dykes and his followers with their 'juicy' harmony, all much enhanced by the religious nostalgia of the words of escaping to a better land. 'The nostalgia of the Negro who wants to go home,' he averred again, 'has given place to the infinitely more weary nostalgia of the cosmopolitan Jew who has no home to go to.'

> There is an obvious link between the exiled and persecuted Jews and the exiled and persecuted Negroes. … But although the Jews have stolen the negroes' thunder, although Al Jolson's nauseating blubber masquerades as savage lamenting, although Tin Pan Alley has become a commercialised Wailing Wall, the only jazz music of technical importance is that small section of it that is genuine Negroid.[62]

Commenting on the importance of the Jewish element in jazz, 'with over ninety per cent of jazz tunes being written by Jews', he remarked on the 'almost masochistic melancholy' of their 'curious sagging quality' being a product of the Jewish temperament. And it was his typical display of erudition in quoting at length in French

---

[60] Vsevolod Pudovkin (1893–1953), Russian film director whose techniques Lambert discusses with particular reference to his 1926 silent masterpiece, *The Mother*.

[61] Performed at the 1926 Berlin premiere of *Potemkin*. Because of the very late approval from the censorship board, Meisel had necessarily to repeat large sections of his score to complete it in time.

[62] Lambert, *Music Ho!*, 2nd edn (1937), pp. 142–9. Here Lambert was essentially repeating what he had written nearly six years ago in *Life and Letters*, vol. 1 no. 2 (July 1928), and was going to repeat in 'The Origins of Modern Dance Music', the first of two important illustrated talks on dance music (i.e. jazz) in April 1936. See Appendix 6.

from the Swiss poet Blaise Cendrars[63] that quite likely caused Gerald Finzi to write to Howard Ferguson: 'I thought of learning French in order to be able to read Constant Lambert's *Music Ho!*'[64]

But it was the artistry of Duke Ellington that he admired above all else, hailing him as the first jazz composer and the first Negro composer of distinction.

> I know of nothing in Ravel so dexterous in treatment as the varied solos in the middle of the ebullient *Hot and Bothered* and nothing in Stravinsky more dynamic than the final section. ... The exquisitely tired and four-in-the-morning *Mood Indigo* is an equally remarkable piece of writing of a lyrical and harmonic order.[65]

Ellington had prepared the way for 'those high-brow composers, whether American or European, who indulge in what is roughly known as "symphonic jazz".'

However controversial Constant is in much of *Music Ho!*, the one thing above all that he deplored, as Angus Morrison commented, was the widening gap between serious and popular music.[66] Nowhere else in *Music Ho!* does he write with greater sincerity than when he is describing what he referred to as 'the disappearing middlebrow', a statement probably even more true today with the average man-in-the-street ignorant of serious music:

> As far as we can concern any general social trend in the music of today it would appear that the middlebrow composer is disappearing. Music in this way is following much the same course as poetry. In the early nineteenth century one could be a great poet and yet a popular figure ... But now poetry of any merit has become the specialised enjoyment of the few and there is no great poet of our time who is genuinely in touch with the public as a whole. While the highbrow poet, through his no doubt sincere complexity, has lost all save a small section of the old middlebrow public, the lowbrow poet ... has, through his social and technical sophistication, gained the greater part of it. The middlebrow poet ... has been left stranded.
>
> The poetic atmosphere of our time may be likened to a severe winter that kills off all animals except those sufficiently sophisticated to live indoors and those sufficiently primitive to have tough hides. The sensitive nature-poet now presents the pathetic yet suitable spectacle of a frozen robin. Although middlebrow poetry drags on a kind of half-sentient existence, it is clear that poetry is now divided up between the unpopular and sophisticated highbrow. ... Anything between the two is a terrain vague – a deserted kitchen garden littered with rusty rakes and empty birdcages. Much the same process of splitting up is taking place in music.[67]

Broadcasting, a burgeoning business, was now taking an increasing share of the public's appreciation of music and he was alarmed at what he called 'the appalling popularity of music', with 'the loudspeaker ... little short of a public menace'. With only

[63] Blaise Cendrars, the nom-de-plume of the Swiss novelist and poet Frédéric Louis Sauser (1887–1961), who had written: 'Y a-t-il eu un peuple au monde plus profondément masochiste qu'Israël?'

[64] 30 April 1934: *Letters of Gerald Finzi and Howard Ferguson*, p. 93. Although Lambert's use of French in *Music Ho!* was by no means restricted to this instance (for example, a chapter heading is in French), this quotation was by far the most extensive.

[65] Lambert, *Music Ho!*, 2nd edn (1937), p. 151.

[66] 'Constant Lambert: A Memoir', an introduction to *Music Ho!* (Hogarth Press, 1985).

[67] Lambert, *Music Ho!*, 2nd edn (1937), p. 192.

a touch of exaggeration, he wrote of the average person's 'phenomenal indifference' to what he listened to:

> We board buses to the strains of Beethoven and drink our beer to the accompaniment of Bach. And yet we pride ourselves on the popular appreciation of these masters. … Now no one can avoid listening to music, whether in town or country, in a motor-car, train or restaurant, perched on a hilltop, or immersed in the river. It is even more trying for the musical than for the non-musical …[68]

The more people used the radio (or wireless as it was then called) 'the less they listen to it' (an observation perhaps more relevant today to television), and 'although excessive sonority has lost its thrill, we still demand it as an ever-increasing factor in our lives'. Constant summed up, somewhat crudely, the effect that the growth of broadcasting and gramophone records was having on concert-going:

> It is obvious that second-rate mechanical music is the most suitable fare for those to whom musical experience is no more than a mere aural tickling, just as the prostitute provides the most suitable outlet for those to whom sexual experience is no more than the periodic removal of a recurring itch. The loud speaker is the street walker of music.

He reserved the last section of his book for a suggested way out from the 'psychological cul-de-sac' in which he considered modern music to have found itself. Neo-classicism, he argued, was 'a bare framework, a stereotyped scaffolding designed to give to the inconsequent and devitalized ideas of the post-war composers a superficial air of logic and construction', while 'the feverish fashionable reactions of post-war Paris, the mathematical revolutionary formulas of post-war Vienna, indicate that the average post-war composer has either nothing to say or does not know how to say it'. The solution he offered to the 'symphonic problem' was the example of Sibelius – 'the most important symphonic writer since Beethoven'. After first bemoaning the popular success of such works as *Finlandia* and *Valse triste* (which he rated as 'excellent examples of their genre' unlike Gray who found such works banal) he turned to the Fourth Symphony as the 'least comprehended and most neglected of his works'.[69] He then briefly outlined Sibelius's complete symphonic canon and *Tapiola*, chiefly in terms of their formal structure, and ended with the belief that 'of all contemporary music that of Sibelius seems to point forward most surely to the future'.

At the time of Constant writing *Music Ho!*, the Sibelius 'boom' was only just underway. Although an eighth symphony was still expected, the composer's output had in fact ceased. The symphonies were beginning to appear on gramophone records, with Finnish government-sponsored issues of the first two in 1930, the remainder being spread across the six Sibelius Society volumes of 78s issued between 1932 and 1939.[70] Henry Wood, who had regularly championed the smaller popular works, had so far only programmed three of the symphonies at the Proms, and Beecham's advocacy, which was to reach its climax with a Sibelius Festival in London in 1938, had only just begun. One highlight was the visit to London in May and June 1934 of the Finnish National Orchestra under Georg Schneevoigt, performing five of the seven symphonies. Cecil Gray was prominent among the pro-Sibelius critics, devoting a chapter to him in his *A Survey of Contemporary Music* (1924) and first visiting the composer in 1929 prior to writing *Sibelius* (1931), to be followed by *Sibelius: The Symphonies* (1935). Another

---

[68] *Ibid.*, pp. 164, 166–7.

[69] Lambert's conducted the slow movement of Symphony No. 4 at the RCM on 31 March 1925.

[70] Lambert wrote the notes on *Oceanides* for vol. 4, Cecil Gray supplying the remainder for that issue.

influential voice was that of the senior critic Ernest Newman, with whom Constant was not afraid to cross swords regarding Sibelius. After praising a rare performance of the Sixth Symphony under Sargent, Constant defended both Sargent and Harty who had

> come in for some hard knocks (in connection with their recent performances of Sibelius) from Mr Ernest Newman, whose spiritual home has shifted suddenly and bewilderingly from Bayreuth to Helsingfors, and who, in addition to his many arduous duties, has now taken on the role of unofficial Finnish attaché to the arts. On some occasions, indeed, he has been 'plus royaliste que le roi', as when he rebuked Sir Hamilton Harty for introducing a thoroughly un-Finnish rubato at a point where Sibelius himself had indicated, I regret to say, this maudlin device.[71]

Music Ho! is not a book for prophesies, and Constant is no Cassandra, but his hope that Sibelius's example might be followed was not a vain one, as that influence can be detected in varying degrees in the symphonies of a number of non-Finnish composers, from William Walton, Arnold Bax and Ralph Vaughan Williams (each of whom dedicated his Fifth Symphony to Sibelius, in 1932 and 1943 respectively) to Malcolm Arnold, Granville Bantock, Arthur Butterworth, George Dyson, Patrick Hadley, Howard Hanson, Kenneth Leighton, Douglas Lilburn, E. J. Moeran, Edmund Rubbra (whose Second Symphony was hailed by one critic as Sibelius's Eighth), and contemporary figures like Peter Maxwell Davies and Per Nørgård. Even Michael Tippett acknowledged his influence. Whether, with or without this influence, modern music is in a healthier state than it was in 1934 is a debatable point.

Once it was published Constant declined requests to update *Music Ho!* in any way, wanting it remain simply a history of the 'troubled twenties'. In the preface to a second edition in 1936 he noted the passing of Berg with his 'elegiac violin concerto of astonishing mastery and haunting beauty', and when, in 1948, it was considered important enough by Penguin Books to reissue in the second batch of their new Pelicans, he acknowledged Britten and Rawsthorne as two of the most valuable figures of 'a vigorous young English school', but added that in the immediate post-war period many of the problems facing the contemporary composer remained, because of the difficulty there had been during the war in obtaining scores from abroad, with the result that the concert repertoire had become smaller and less enterprising.

O N 12 April 1934, the publication day of *Music Ho!*, Constant and Flo attended a Foyles Literary Luncheon at which he was expected to make a short speech. According to the *Daily Express* social columnist, he had never spoken in public before, and 'as zero hour approached, his nervousness became painfully infectious'. He fumbled with his cigarettes, he accidentally hit his neighbour on the shins with his stick, and his hands began to sweat. Nevertheless he 'spoke brilliantly'. Flo's table companion was a young boxer, Jack Doyle, who had a fondness for women and drink. It was possibly the latter that emboldened him to invite her to a party, adding: 'You're so like Katharine Hepburn!'[72] Another columnist credited Constant with the most amusing story of the luncheon: a fellow composer, on seeing on the cover of a book in a shop window the words 'English Comic Characters. J. B. Priestley' went inside and asked if they had 'Hugh Walpole' in the same series.

---

[71] *Sunday Referee*, 27 November 1932.
[72] *Daily Express*, 13 April 1934.

11 1934
Elgar and Delius; Enter Fonteyn

T HE new year, 1934, opened at the Old Vic with the Vic-Wells' first staging of *Giselle*, with Dolin, Markova, de Valois and Helpmann, and the *corps de ballet* filled out to 20 dancers. This ballet was not totally new to the Company because many of its dancers had taken part in it for the Camargo Society in June 1932. The evening began with *Pomona*, in which Helpmann now took Dolin's role. On the penultimate day of January *Casse-noisette*, soon to establish itself as a Christmas favourite, entered the Vic-Wells repertoire with only a few cuts. 'The orchestral performance under Mr Constant Lambert's direction was excellent,' wrote the *Times* critic. Elsa Lanchester (Mrs Charles Laughton) was cast in the Arabian Dance for the first few performances. Also on New Year's Day, the BBC mounted the first of six concerts of British Music to be given that month at Queen's Hall. This opening programme, conducted by Boult, placed *The Rio Grande* alongside Delius's *The Song of the High Hills*, the first performance of the Symphony in D by R. O. Morris (one of Constant's professors at the Royal College), and works by Elgar, Quilter, Scott and Mackenzie. 'Rio Grande reappeared with undiminished freshness and buoyancy,' commented Havergal Brian in *Musical Opinion*. But Constant was unhappy, not just with the company his work was sharing in the series of concerts but more specifically that British music should be treated as a special cause, and he aired his views in the *Sunday Referee*:

> A little ruthlessness on the part of the BBC would certainly have improved these programmes. The only thing that should be considered when building a programme is the actual value of the music itself. If a work is a bad one it should not be considered representative of British music merely because the composer has been writing long enough to know better. Unfortunately, the BBC have shown more consideration for the composer's feelings than for those of the audience. What I object to is the segregation of the British composer into a special compound, like the smaller animals at the zoo. Either we can produce good music in this country or we can't. If we can, then let it be played in company with the great masters.[1]

That month Wilhelm Furtwängler once again brought the Berlin Philharmonic Orchestra to London, but since Hitler's rise to power the previous year his position as chief conductor and his relationship with the Nazi party had become matters of considerable controversy. Prior to the visit, Sir Thomas Beecham as a professional colleague had written to *The Times* in his defence, stating that 'no changes have been made in [the orchestra's personnel] nor has any racial discrimination been permitted to prevail. Such prominent positions as the leader and two principal cellists, all of them Jews, retain their positions. The triumph of artistic impartiality over nationalistic dogma is due entirely to the sane judgement and personal influence of one man, Dr Furtwängler.' He concluded by asking that 'a more than usually warm welcome' be extended to the visitors.[2] But Constant was not prepared to be so trusting. On reviewing an earlier visit in February 1932, he had confined his comments largely to the quality of the orchestra's playing and Furtwängler's technique. This time, however, he was at his most outspoken. Carefully avoiding the word 'Jew', he began by challenging the cultural composition of the orchestra:

[1] *Sunday Referee*, 7 January 1934.
[2] *The Times*, 20 January 1934.

We are assured on every hand that the Berlin Philharmonic Orchestra has not suffered under the Nazi régime, and that Furtwängler, although semi-official head of Nazi music, has seen to it that the personnel has in no way been changed through Aryan prejudice. Yet, unless my usually retentive memory for grotesque surnames has failed me, it seemed to me that the list of players was not so colourful as it used to be.

After welcoming the fact that Simon Goldberg was still leader of the orchestra, he continued:

In connection with the retention of these players a number of questions arise, not all of them in the best of taste.

(a) Did Furtwängler keep these players on through racial broadmindedness; or, more simply, because he knew he could not replace them from a band of players more noted for solid musicianship than virtuosity?

(b) Was his action winked at by the higher authorities because they realised that the Berlin Philharmonic, as a touring orchestra, had its uses as a subtle if misleading form of propaganda?

(c) Has the same broadmindedness been shown in the case of orchestras permanently resident in Germany?

(d) Does the retention of one or two orchestral players console Germans for the fact that most German artists of international repute, and almost all German composers of merit, are either voluntary or (more often) involuntary refugees?

I am not implying any answer to these questions, I should quite simply like to know.[3]

He was able to report, however, that 'on Monday night there were none of the expected demonstrations, the hall had a fair sprinkling of palpable non-Aryans, and the reception was thoroughly friendly, if not wildly enthusiastic.'

T HE death of Elgar in February brought forth from Constant a *Radio Times* article and a brief report in the *Sunday Referee* in which he hailed him as 'the greatest English composer since the seventeenth century and one of the outstanding figures of his time' whose *Enigma* Variations 'showed that he was the technical equal of any of his foreign rivals, and that not even Strauss had a greater mastery of the orchestra.'[4] This was followed a week later by a longer one in which he described his only meeting with Elgar (after the first performance of the *Nursery Suite* ballet) when he had spoken of his early days and the music that had influenced him.

Curiously enough, he made no mention of the various symphonic and church composers he is held to resemble, and spoke only of Italian opera and how he used to long for the day when touring companies would come to the neighbourhood. Verdi was his favourite, apparently, but he spoke in the highest terms of Meyerbeer also. 'I was commissioned to write three operas by – (mentioning a famous Italian publisher), but I'm afraid it came to nothing. I don't know Italian well enough to set it satisfactorily, and who on earth wants to hear an opera in English?'[5]

[3] *Sunday Referee*, 28 January 1934.
[4] *Sunday Referee*, 25 February 1934.
[5] *Sunday Referee*, 4 March 1934.

Constant was to refer to Meyerbeer in a number of articles he wrote on Elgar, for example writing in *Radio Times* that 'Elgar's music has at times an almost Meyerbeer-like flamboyance'.[6] At a time when the composer's reputation had fallen into a decline, Constant was both selective and generally sympathetic in his appreciation. When in 1930 E. J. Dent had famously dismissed Elgar in an article on modern English music for a German publication, Constant had not added his name to the many who wrote to the press in his defence, even though Walton, Heseltine and Moeran were among the signatories. Perhaps he did not want to sour his relationship with Dent. However, in December 1932 at the time of Elgar's 75th birthday celebrations, he had contributed three articles in successive weeks to the *Sunday Referee* on the composer, in the first of which he qualified his stance. He began by expressing his displeasure of an article in the programme book for the first of the birthday concerts, written by Robert Lorenz, who saw Elgar merely in patriotic terms, conjuring up, as Constant mocked, 'a hearty picture of the composer as a fine old country gentleman huntin' and shootin' and fishin' and bettin' and occasionally doin' a spot of composin' (Devilish good fellow an' all that – never think to meet him in the golf club he was a composer at all ...).' He challenged Ernest Newman's suggestion that only those brought up in the English tradition could truly interpret Elgar's music, and then discussed the matter of nationalism and the English tradition in relation to Elgar, arguing that 'an unprejudiced Italian is interested in Elgar's music simply as music and it may be that he will find in it a lyricism, an emotionalism, a flamboyance even, that we have unconsciously blinded ourselves to, because they do not happen to fit into our preconceived idea of what English music should be'. He continued: 'That acute critic Professor E. J. Dent has noticed those "un-English" traits and duly registered his disapproval. I agree with his premises though not with his conclusion,' ending with a passing shot that the operatic or Italianate side to Elgar's music had been little observed.[7]

This thread he picked up in his second article, ingeniously taking the reader round the garden and invoking Sherlock Holmes (who 'would have made an ideal musical historian') before bringing the discussion back to Meyerbeer ('considered in this country as a kind of musical Moriarty'):

[Holmes's] lynx-like eye would not have overlooked a certain interview[8] published some months ago in which the highest praise of Meyerbeer was uttered by no less a person than Sir Edward Elgar. He might even have thought that if a composer of Sir Edward's genius can describe Meyerbeer's 'Struensee' Overture[9] as one of the finest overtures in the world, it is possible both that

[6] *Radio Times*, 9 March 1934. Unfortunately, with Meyerbeer's name split across two lines it appeared as 'Meyer-like'. Martin Cooper has written of Giacomo Meyerbeer (1791–1864) that 'no composer has achieved such universal fame in his lifetime and within a quarter of a century of his death, been so despised and then forgotten': *Fanfare for Ernest Newman*, ed. Herbert Van Thal (London: Arthur Barker, 1955), p. 38. Bernard van Dieren wrote a chapter in Meyerbeer's defence in *Down among the Dead Men, and Other Essays* (London: Oxford University Press, 1935). Lambert's fondness for Meyerbeer was to result in the ballet *Les Patineurs*, first performed in February 1937, for which he selected music from two of the composer's operas, *Le Prophète* and *L'Étoile du nord*.

[7] Lambert, 'On the Conductin' of Elgar's Celebration Concerts', *Sunday Referee*, 4 December 1932.

[8] 'Sir E. Elgar on the Music Crisis', *Daily Telegraph*, 5 November 1931, reprinted in *Edward Elgar: Letters of a Lifetime*, p. 442.

[9] Lambert conducted Meyerbeer's *Struensee* Overture himself in a BBC broadcast on 16 December 1935, and on several occasions he conducted the overture to the opera *L'Étoile du Nord*.

there is some truth in the remark, and that the composer himself has been slightly influenced by Meyerbeer.[10]

Perhaps, he concluded, some of the purpler passage in the symphonies could have derived from an operatic tradition.

On Elgar's death he returned to this theme, wondering whether, had he been born in another age or country, he would have been famous as a composer of operas. Although following Dent in finding a degree of theatricality in the oratorios[11] and symphonies, he thought Elgar's best music was in the *Enigma* Variations, the two concertos and *Falstaff*.[12] In *Music Ho!* (completed two months or so before Elgar's death) he had referred to him as 'the last serious composer to be in touch with the great public' and, while discussing the position of the composer in 'present-day England', he described Elgar as 'the first figure of importance since Boyce ... a composer in touch both with his audience and his period, expressing himself nationally in an international language.' He went on to suggest that it was 'more than probable that, but for the social and spiritual changes brought about by the war, Elgar would have been a more potent influence on English music than Vaughan Williams. ... In consequence much of Elgar's music, through no fault of its own, has for the present generation an almost intolerable air of smugness, self-assurance and autocratic benevolence' while 'owing to the late sprouting of nationalism in this country the inevitable post-war reaction to the spirit of Elgar took advantage of the world of escape provided by the folk-song revival'.[13] He doubted whether future critics would place his First Symphony alongside *Falstaff* and the *Enigma* Variations. Yet in 1946, not long after conducting that symphony, he gave a broadcast talk on Elgar in which he concentrated on that work, holding it up as the quintessence of his output. 'The second symphony,' he continued, 'is a fine and dignified work but to me less vital – except of course the third movement – the Rondo – which contains one of the most remarkable passages in modern music.' Harold Rutland wrote that 'Constant liked conducting Elgar No. 1',[14] in spite of what he once described as the 'frankly appalling melody that starts off the Symphony'.[15] A year later he wrote:

> I know there are many to whom this work is repellent in thought and colour, but even they must surely appreciate the absolute mastery of technique, the sureness of conception, and the way in which the themes instead of being repeated in a set mechanical frame are really given a new and more vital significance as the work proceeds.[16]

But it was *Falstaff* that Constant thought represented Elgar 'at his most English' and he could not understand why what was 'considered by most musicians to be Elgar's finest work, should not enjoy the same hold over the public as the symphonies'.[17] It

[10] Lambert, 'Meyerbeer and Elgar', *Sunday Referee*, 11 December 1932.

[11] In the *Sunday Referee* on 6 December 1936, Lambert wrote about *The Dream of Gerontius*: 'One of the patchiest of Elgar's works and does not live up to the consistent inspiration of its prelude. ... The Demons are Elgar's only complete failure on a large scale.'

[12] *Radio Times*, 9 March 1934.

[13] Lambert, *Music Ho!*, 2nd edn (1937), p. 199.

[14] Rutland, 'Recollections of Constant Lambert'. Lambert conducted Elgar's First Symphony in a BBC concert at People's Palace, London on 13 January 1946.

[15] Constant Lambert, gramophone review of Elgar's own recording of his First Symphony, *The New Statesman and Nation*, 25 April 1931.

[16] *Sunday Referee*, 17 April 1932, reviewing a performance with Wood conducting the BBC Symphony Orchestra.

[17] *Sunday Referee*, 10 September 1933, reviewing Prom performances of Elgar's *Falstaff* and Ireland's Piano Concerto, both works that 'are not only representative of each composer at

was while reviewing Elgar's own recordings that he made the interesting observation that 'only since Elgar's death have we realised how great his performances were'.[18] He regarded him as 'undoubtedly the finest interpreter of his works. ... He had an uncanny power of getting that extra ounce of tone from the players, and an Elgarian tutti under the composer's direction had a quite unforgettable sonority.'[19] He had even considered writing a book on Elgar, but in March 1934 in the Café Royal he met Hubert Foss who 'had a long talk with Constant and Florence (who was in black and powdered pearl colour).' Foss told his wife, Dora: '[Constant] doesn't think he is going to write a book on Elgar, so one day I may do so.'[20]

O N 21 April 1934, three days before the Vic-Wells' long London season ended, there was an occasion which, although not apparent at the time, was to be of great significance, not only in the life of the Company but in Constant's too. The afternoon programme of ballet opened with *Pomona*, continued with *Le Spectre de la rose* and ended with *Casse-noisette*. The stars of the programme were Markova, de Valois and Judson, but making her début in the last ballet as third snowflake was a very young Peggy Hookham, almost a month short of her 15th birthday.[21] As the Company consisted of only 36 dancers, students were brought in to swell its number for larger ballets and so, only a few days after her audition at the Wells, this young dancer found herself on stage, as she later recalled:

> Such an insignificant role as mine did not merit much rehearsal, so I was utterly confused by the time I got on stage. ... It was something of a nightmare until we reached near the end where we all knelt in a group waving our snowflake wands while paper snow rained about our heads. At this moment the opera chorus was singing, Tchaikovsky's inspired music had reached its most beguiling climax, the lights were dimmed to a soft blue and the curtains swung gently together, muffling the applause on the other side. I felt an incredible elation; this was theatre, this was the real thing. ... From this moment on there could be no turning back.[22]

Nor was there to be any turning back. Before long, under the name of Margot Fonteyn, she was to become not only the Vic-Wells' star ballerina but the central figure in Constant's life. He was then 28 and she was approximately the same age as Flo had been when Constant met her. He had a particular fondness for girls with an oriental appearance. As de Valois had observed on first seeing Margot: 'There is something about her ... she does not look English with those almond-shaped eyes. I inquired in a whisper about the little girl who looked Chinese. I asked where she came from and

his best, but can cheerfully take their stand beside Continental examples of the same genre. ... It is so rarely that I can enjoy the luxury of whole-heartedly praising two native works.' The author has not traced any instance of Lambert conducting Elgar's *Falstaff*.

[18] *Sunday Referee*, 14 November 1937.

[19] *The New Statesman and Nation*, 3 March 1934.

[20] Dora Foss's typescript, quoting from a letter from HJF to DMF, 1 March 1934. Foss was never to write a book on Elgar. One reason for Lambert declining to write a book on Elgar may well have been not wanting to endure again the pressures he had felt in completing *Music Ho!* alongside his ballet work.

[21] Margaret ('Peggy') Hookham, later (Dame) Margot Fonteyn, was born in Reigate, Surrey, on 18 May 1919 to an English father and an Irish mother with some Brazilian ancestry that may explain her exotic appearance. Nevertheless, while Peggy was between the ages of eight and 14 the Hookham family lived in Shanghai. She died of cancer in 1991.

[22] Fonteyn, *Autobiography*, pp. 47–8.

I was told Shanghai ... Chinese or not it was obvious that something wonderful and beautiful had come into our midst.'[23]

T HE death of Elgar was followed a little more than three months later by that of Delius whom Constant never met. He responded with an appreciation 'The Intimate Appeal of Delius' for *Radio Times*.

> It is true that most of Delius's works are settings of words, whether in theatrical or concert form, and that the best of his purely orchestral works are those built round some literary or pictorial idea, such as *Brigg Fair* or *In a Summer Garden*. In that sense he may not be a 'pure' musician. But when we examine the content of these works we see that no other medium could express it with such intensity. In that sense he is the most musical of all composers.[24]

When he went on to write that 'there is nothing in music more intensely evocative than the opening bars of *Brigg Fair*, as refreshing to the ear as an April morning to the nostrils, or that curiously moving passage for four horns which we hear in the distance when the curtain rises on the decaying Paradise Garden in *A Village Romeo and Juliet*', he was writing from experience because in the very week of penning these words he was rehearsing that opera for the three performances that Beecham was to give with student forces at the Royal College of Music.[25]

In November 1929, at the time of Beecham's Delius Festival in London, he had contributed an article on Delius to the arts magazine *Apollo* in which he summed up the festival as 'a great and fitting gesture to one of the foremost creative artists of our time', and in February 1935, for *The New Statesman*, he reviewed the first volume of Delius Society recordings, the main work being *Paris*,[26] which Constant had frequently conducted for the ballet *Nocturne*. 'The composer of *Paris*,' he boldly ventured, 'was potentially the greatest figure of his generation, showing a greater universality of outlook and a more flexible technique than the composer of the *Songs of Sunset*, for example.'[27] Constant would have been only too mindful of his great friend Philip Heseltine's championing of Delius. He would also have known how that enthusiasm had inevitably waned towards the end of Heseltine's life, but Constant's fondness for the music of Delius had none of the disciple's zeal that the young Philip had shown. In the *North Country Sketches* (which he heard in 1931), he curiously found much of the orchestral writing 'ungrateful' and the form 'scrappy and disorganised'[28] – with the exception of the 'exquisite' *Winter Landscape* (which he included, together with the *Fantastic Dance*, in a Conductors' Class programme at the Royal College in March 1935). 'The best Delius,' he argued, 'is to be found, not in his concertos and sonatas,

---

[23] De Valois, *Come Dance with Me*, p. 107.

[24] Lambert, 'The Intimate Appeal of Delius', *Radio Times*, 22 June 1934.

[25] Delius's *A Village Romeo and Juliet*, 27, 28 & 29 June 1934. The passage in question normally calls for six horns but the RCM Orchestra may have had only four for this occasion.

[26] In April 1934 Lambert cheekily rebuked Beecham for claiming that a performance he gave of Delius's *Paris* was 'by special request'. This, he wrote, 'can only have deceived the most trusting' as it was 'presumably a dress rehearsal for the recording' – which indeed took place the next day for the first of the Delius Society volumes.

[27] *The New Statesman and Nation*, 9 February 1935, p. 190.

[28] To be fair, this judgement may have had more to do with the performance, as Geoffrey Toye was replacing an indisposed Beecham at a London Symphony Orchestra concert on 9 November 1931. When reviewing the first volume of Delius Society recordings in 1935 he hoped that for the second volume 'the music throughout will be worthy of the extreme care [Beecham] has evidently expended' and suggested *Appalachia* and *North Country Sketches*', *The New Statesman and Nation*, 9 February 1935.

but in the exquisite series of works for chorus and orchestra (it would be a mistake to describe them merely as settings of poems); which includes *Sea Drift*, *Appalachia*,[29] *Songs of Sunset*, and *The Song of the High Hills*. It is in these that Delius finds his most intense emotional expression and, strangely enough, his most satisfactory expression. ... In spite of its almost unbearable melancholy and nostalgia, this mood cannot be described as pessimistic. There is a vein of sensuous beauty which runs through even the most tragic moments and saves them from bleakness or austerity.'[30] Reviewing Beecham's studio broadcast of *A Village Romeo and Juliet* two years earlier he had written: 'The whole opera seems to have been written with the same intensity of inspiration and as a piece of continuous lyricism it is without parallel in music.'[31]

Constant's fondness for Delius, or at least for certain works, provided the critic W. J. Turner[32] with an opportunity to retaliate after some strong digs Constant had made from time to time against him. In 1930, in a *Nation and Athenæum* article entitled 'The Writing in the Cheque-Book', Constant had weighed in on Ernest Newman's side when Turner was defending the programmes of the Courtauld-Sargent Concerts. There were three reasons for Constant's attack: the programmes showed a bias for what he termed 'the least inspired period of German music', too much prominence was being given to solo artists, and – nothing to do with the Concerts, but acting like a red rag to a bull – Turner had dared to state 'the age of jazz is dead'. The following year, in a book of essays[33] to which Constant contributed an article on 'Contemporary Music', he had rebuked Turner for holding up Rimsky-Korsakov as the most original composer he knew – 'a statement that would be unthinkable from anyone familiar with the score of *Ruslan and Ludmila* [Glinka]'. Now, after Constant had reviewed Beecham's rendering of Delius's *A Mass of Life* and the Royal Philharmonic Society's Delius Memorial Concert,[34] Turner wrote: 'This has proved a bit too much even for Mr Constant Lambert, who always tries hard to find as many good words to say about Delius as possible. I always read Mr Lambert with the interest due not only to his exceptionally able pen, but with the special interest that must be paid to a musician's criticism of music, but his tolerance with regard to Delius astonishes me.'[35]

Constant had probably best summed up his attitude to Delius in 1931 when reviewing a performance of *The Song of the High Hills*:

[29] Lambert used recordings of part of Delius's *Appalachia* and his opera *Koanga* in the first of his two 1936 BBC talks on jazz (or dance music) as 'the first important example of the negro influencing the white man, instead of the other way round'.

[30] Lambert, 'Delius and Sea-Drift', *Radio Times*, 27 January 1933.

[31] *Sunday Referee*, 22 May 1932.

[32] Walter James Redfern Turner (1884–1946), Australian poet, writer and critic, probably best known for his books on Beethoven (1927), Wagner (1933), Berlioz (1934) and Mozart (1938).

[33] *Scrutinies: Critical Essays by Various Writers*, ed. Edgell Rickword, vol. 2 (London: Wishart & Co., 1931).

[34] *A Mass of Life*, Queen's Hall, London 24 October 1934, reviewed *Sunday Referee*, 28 October; RPS Delius Memorial Concert, Queen's Hall 8 November 1934, reviewed 11 November.

[35] W. J. Turner, 'Delius and Sibelius', *The New Statesman and Nation*, 17 November 1934, p. 718. Lambert hit back a month later after Turner had written that Sibelius was like Grieg. 'As for Mr Turner's unwieldy and echolaliac syllogism: Wagner was a villain – Grieg was a minor composer – Delius derives from both – Sibelius derives from Grieg – people who like Delius like Sibelius, therefore, both Delius and Sibelius are villains and minor composers – it simply will not hold water at any point. There is more direct influence of Grieg to be discovered in the music of Erik Satie than in the music of Sibelius', *The New Statesman and Nation*, 15 December 1934, p. 914. Lambert's single reference to Turner in *Music Ho!* (2nd edn (1937), p. 215) was chiding him for 'actually describing *Tapiola* as "neo-Grieg"'.

To write of Delius's *The Song of the High Hills* is to realise the futility of musical criticism. It would be easy enough to analyse the weaker moments of this work, to question certain passages in the orchestration, or to doubt the 'purity' of the choral writing. It would be slightly more difficult, perhaps, to defend this work in the abstract, to answer those who maintain that it is not well made or logically constructed.

But how is one to convey one's feeling that the middle section of this work is not only the most inspired moment in Delius but one of the most moving passages in the whole of music? It is all very well to remind oneself of the one-sided nature of Delius's work, of his many deficiencies, but what do these matter when one is listening to works like *The Song of the High Hills* or *In a Summer Garden*?

Delius is the most aggravating composer for a critic to write about, for his work destroys all critical canons. I suppose there is no composer of modern times whose work is more inspired and no composer less able to disguise those moments when inspiration has failed him. We are hardly conscious of technique in his music, which seems a direct transcript of his emotional life and similarly closed to analysis. It is the intimately emotional quality of his music which makes it hard to explain his importance to anyone unsympathetically disposed towards the prevalent mood of his works.[36]

As he wrote in the same issue: 'I deliberately omitted to hear the Chausson Poème for Violin and Orchestra, as I wished to retain some slight powers of receptivity for the Delius.'

WHILE the 1934 spring season of ballet at the Sadler's Wells Theatre was replaced by opera and plays, Constant had some further involvement with Marie Rambert's Ballet Club. For their opening night on 15 May at the Mercury Theatre in Ladbroke Road, they presented *Bar aux Folies-Bergère*, choreographed by de Valois and based on the famous painting by Manet that had once been owned by Chabrier, whose music Constant arranged for the ballet. Alicia Markova, Pearl Argyle, Diana Gould and Ashton were the principal dancers. Almost a month later the Ballet Club presented *Mephisto Waltz*, Constant having suggested Liszt's *Mephisto Waltz* No. 1 to Ashton who remembered:

Constant felt that Liszt's music wasn't properly appreciated and started to speak out for it. He would talk about Liszt as one of the innovators of new music of that period and about the influence he had had on Wagner. People didn't agree with him, of course, but he had a very positive point of view.[37]

With choreography by Ashton and designs by Sophie Fedorovitch, and with Alicia Markova as Marguerite, Ashton as Mephisto, and Walter Gore as Faust, it was first presented on 13 June with Rica Offenhändem at the piano.

In August Constant and Flo took a holiday in Toulon during which Constant found time to review Cecil Gray's new book on Heseltine.[38] 'I can't tell you how much I am

---

[36] *Sunday Referee*, 13 December 1931. Lambert also wrote that 'it was once said of Delius that he divided English critics into two camps, those who did not know his works disputing the opinions of those who did': *Music Ho!*, 2nd edn (1937), p. 86.

[37] Kavanagh, *Secret Muses*, p. 174. A reviewer in *Gramophone* (August 1936, p. 12) of Roger Wimbush's book on Liszt wrote: 'There can be little doubt that the modern rediscovery of Liszt is largely due to the magnificent propaganda of Mr Lambert, and in a lesser degree to Mr Cecil Gray and the late Bernard van Dieren.'

[38] Gray, *Peter Warlock*, reviewed in *The New Statesman and Nation*, 10 November 1934, p. 672.

enjoying your book. I do think it is very well put together,' Flo wrote in a joint postcard. 'Toulon is so peaceful,' to which Constant added, 'Moi aussi. Writing more fully but in the meantime haven't you missed out *Lachrymae* in the list of transcriptions?'[39] He elaborated in his next letter:

> I want to say how much I have enjoyed your book on Philip. Enjoyed is perhaps hardly the word for it is both extremely moving and extremely depressing, but I do very much admire the way you have coped with what must have been a most trying problem, both objectively and subjectively. The book is bound to annoy the po-faced, who want to remember only the scholar-&-gentleman side; and the pub-spongers who want to remember only the supposed boon companion. But to any one who knew both sides it is magnificent and, I hope, will prove the same to the public who knew neither.[40]

He went on to make only two corrections – the first about *Capriol* being written first as a piano duet and then a string work – 'Of this I am certain as I arrived at Eynsford between the two' – and then he added, 'Also as the friend in question, I should like to point out that the motorbike which went in the saloon bar was not the high powered monster but the old 1-cylinder Ariel he bought for £10 when he was drunk. Otherwise I have no criticisms whatsoever.'[41]

According to the composer Denis Aplvor, the book was written during a turbulent moment in Gray's life:

> Part of the background to the completion of *Peter Warlock* is provided by some revealing letters to me from Cecil Gray's second wife, Marie Nielson, a charming Scottish dancer-friend of Constant, with whom Cecil suddenly fell in love that year, while working on the book. Believing himself rejected, he precipitately fled to South America on the *Almeida Star*, hinting darkly that he would throw himself and the book overboard. But Marie had relented[42] and he knew it, though he persisted with the trip. Carping critics of the memoir, for its 'bias' and 'incompleteness', can take time to conjecture that had the book sunk in the Atlantic, who else could have put Philip 'on the map' with the literary aplomb, humour, sympathy and personal knowledge, which has stood the test of time and bred several generations of enthusiasts for the work and the man?[43]

In the first week of September Constant and Flo moved on from Toulon to Venice where the Concerto for Piano and Nine Players was being performed in the Fenice Theatre as part of the Venice Biennale. The audience showed some hostility towards the work and an incensed Flo retaliated by making her own feelings clear. Reviewing the Festival in his *Sunday Referee* column, Constant wrote that 'what the Italians lack

---

[39] Postcard from Florence and Constant Lambert to Cecil Gray, postmark 28 August 1934. By *Lachrymae* Lambert is referring to Heseltine's transcriptions of John Dowland that Gray did not include in the List of Works.

[40] Letter to Gray from Lambert, Toulon, 1 September 1934.

[41] Gray had written (p. 279): 'The last of the series, I think, was an exceptionally powerful and wicked specimen at Eynsford on which, accompanied by a friend in a sidecar, he once spectacularly charged through the doors of the saloon bar of a public house, the throttle having refused to close and the brakes to act, appropriately enough just on opening time.'

[42] Marie Nielson married Cecil Gray in 1934. It was not a happy marriage: 'Arguments and rows were almost an everyday occurrence. Marie did not like her stepdaughter Pauline, and made this plain': Pauline Gray, *Cecil Gray*, p. 47. A daughter Fabia was born in 1938, but in 1941 Marie left Cecil, taking Fabia with her.

[43] Aplvor, 'Memories of "The Warlock Circle"', p. 189. This may explain Gray's own harsh views of women as expressed on page 233.

in organising ability they make up for generosity with their enthusiasm. In no other country, I like to think, would a composer be offered his first rehearsal at 12.30 on Saturday night after a long concert, and his second rehearsal at nine the next morning.' Despite the 'chaotic rehearsal arrangements' and the 'off-hand treatment of artists' he felt that 'the performance was as brilliant as it was sensitive'.[44] Arthur Benjamin was the soloist and the instrumentalists were from La Scala. One happy outcome of Constant's and Flo's stay in Venice was that their only child was conceived there.

They were back in London in time for Constant to conduct a Prom performance of *The Rio Grande* on 25 September, after which he, Flo, Gavin Gordon and Angus Morrison had supper together at the Café Royal. Then it was into rehearsals for the autumn ballet season which opened on 2 October with *Fête polonaise* and *Les Rendezvous*, both conducted by Constant, and in between *The Haunted Ballroom* (from which the Waltz became extremely popular), conducted by the score's composer, Geoffrey Toye. First presented in April, this time the part of Young Treginnis, which had been created by Freda Bamford, was taken by the Company's rising star, Miss Margot Fontes (as she was then known), for whom a *pas de deux* was added to *Les Rendezvous*.

The policy of the Old Vic and Sadler's Wells Theatres had been revised, partly because of the mechanical difficulties of transporting productions across London, but also because opera had proved more successful at Sadler's Wells and drama at the Old Vic, and that became the pattern for the future. For the new season at Rosebery Avenue, with opera predominant, ballet was limited to Tuesday evenings and every other Saturday matinée. It included an 'altogether beautiful performance' of *Job* of which 'the orchestra under Mr Constant Lambert gave a good, if not faultless, account of Vaughan Williams' score'[45] and, for a charity performance on 20 November in aid of the Queen Charlotte's Maternity Hospital, the first staging by an English company of the complete four-act version of *Le Lac des cygnes*. This was produced by Nicolai Sergeyev, who was able to bring to it his own experience of working in the old Imperial Theatre of St Petersburg, its 1895 revival there by Petipa and Ivanov being the model for productions by most later ballet companies.[46] Alicia Markova took the dual role of Odette-Odile.

The season's new work, on 9 October, was *The Jar*, with music by Alfredo Casella. If for the *Times* critic the music was 'of the kind called "modern"' it was second nature to Constant, who on 23 November conducted for the BBC a typically uncompromising programme of contemporary music that included works by de Root, Erik Chisholm, Igor Markevitch and Milhaud.[47] Just over three weeks earlier, amongst his students at the Second Orchestra and Conductors' Class had been John Cruft, conducting no doubt much to Constant's disapproval Brahms' *Academic Festival* Overture, Ralph Nicholson with Chabrier's *España* and Reginald Goodall the first movement of Beethoven's First Symphony. (Nicholson remembered Constant's pleasure in words and how on one occasion he asked his class for any amusing shop names they knew. He

[44] *Sunday Referee*, 23 September 1934.
[45] *The Times*, 7 November 1934.
[46] Nicolai Sergeyev (1876–1951) had been régisseur at the Imperial Theatre in St Petersburg from 1904 until 1917. He left Russia in 1918 and came to London to reconstruct *The Sleeping Princess* for Diaghilev's 1921 London production.
[47] De Root, *Five Studies* for piano and small orchestra; Erik Chisholm, Overture for chamber orchestra; Igor Markevitch, Partita for piano and small orchestra; and Milhaud, Suite *Maximilian* (first UK performance). Chisholm, 'William Walton and his Façade', wrote that 'Lambert conducted the first performances of a number of my own works in London and Amsterdam'.

was delighted when Nicholson came up with a shop in Dorking called Swaddling and Company that sold baby carriages.)[48]

On 1 December Anthony Powell was married to Lady Violet Pakenham at All Saints' Church, Ennismore Garden, London. Constant had a hand in the music for the wedding service which, as it turned out, he was not in a fit state to attend, as Powell recalled in his memoirs:

> There was no formal reception after the service, but a party had been given in the house the night before, which, beginning at 5.30 and extending to past 10 o'clock that night, had included every form of friend and relation. On the following morning Wyndham Lloyd, my best man (an old friend, reliable for such an occasion), arrived at Brunswick Square with half a bottle of champagne to ease the journey to the church. Constant Lambert had arranged the music (Handel's *Water Music*, and, he insisted, the *Lohengrin* Wedding March rather than Mendelssohn's), but he was himself too incapacitated by the party to attend the church.[49]

Before his wedding, during hours of insomnia from which he suffered at that time, Powell had been in the habit of writing verses of mock anti-Scottish satire in imitation of Burns's *Merry Muses of Caledonia*. 'They would be repeated,' he recalled, 'sometimes improved, at the Castano luncheon table; Lambert writing the section on Scotland's music.'[50] As a wedding gift a friend of Powell's, who had access to a printing press, arranged for a number of slim copies to be privately printed, bound in orange tartan boards, with the title *Caledonia: A Fragment*.[51] According to the introduction, these 154 lines, with their plea 'Against the Land of Porridge, Scones, and Slate, Let us rebuild THE WALL, before too late', were 'suggested by the sound of a Pibroch or Bag-Pipe played at an early hour in a London Square by an indigent Scotchman wearing the Plaid or National dress of that country'. It also acknowledges the contribution by an 'ingeniose graduate of the Royal College of Musick [Constant] for certain information herein contained and selected from the most approved and respectable musickal opinions of our time', and in some private copies Powell revealed Constant's authorship of 12 lines:

> In Musick's Realm this Race (the bitter fact is)
> Presume to *teach* an Art they cannot *practice*.
> Their *Rhapsodies* and *Rondos*, which abound,
> Pollute the Air with *Academick* sound;
> But better their morose, pedantic Strain
> Than those which to the sterner *North* pertain,
> Where ev'ry puling *Crofter's* lad of ten
> Aspires to be a BARTOK of the Glen.
> Belabour'd *Blackamoor* less harshly squeals
> Than *Highland Lasses*, dancing *Highland Reels*,
> And Ears go numb when *Scottish Neuropaths* play
> In Glasgow's Town the *Gaelick Snap* or *Strathspey*.

Always one to milk an idea – especially a humorous one – as much as possible,

---

[48] Ralph Nicholson speaking at a Delius Society meeting on 8 November 1994.
[49] *To Keep the Ball Rolling: The Memoirs of Anthony Powell*, vol. 3: *Faces in My Time* (London: Heinemann, 1980), pp. 17–18.
[50] Powell, *Messengers of Day*, p. 175.
[51] Eleven pages, with four pages of verse and one with an illustration by Edward Burra.

Constant later expanded his twelve lines into a grander onslaught against Scottish composers:

A few random lines on the subject of Scots composers

Near Regent's Park a stately building stands
The envy of the barren Pictish lands
To Saint Cecilia 'tis dedicate
And "R.A.M." the letters o'er its gate.
Here Caledonia's sons (the bitter fact is)
Presume to teach the art they cannot practise
Through graft attain the presidential chair
From whence they can pollute the vernal air.
The frail Cecilia sickens nigh to death
O'ercome by every presidential breath
(For Usquebaugh her errant sons pursues
And laughs as each successive dotard spews.)
Here tottered, tipsy e'er the day begun,
That Prince of bad composers H. MacCunn
Here sat in impotent and senile frenzy
That doddering old soaker A. Mackenzie
And here reclines, in ultimate blue ruin
That gruff and surly toper J. McEwen.
But better his morose pedantic strain
Than those which to the sterner North pertain
Where every slobbering crofter's lad of ten
Aspires to be the Bartok of the glen.
Bring wadding for my ears! Ah woe the night
When first I heard the works of Ian Whyte
Or saw a gang of Glasgow neuropaths play
Poor Erik Chisholm's version of a strathspay.

If Constant missed – by a glass or two – Powell's wedding ceremony, he was present two days later in Queen's Hall for the first (incomplete) performance of Walton's First Symphony of which he gave a very full review in the *Sunday Referee*, beginning with a characteristic literary analogy:

Following the example of Mr James Joyce, who wisely allows us to see from time to time fragments of his 'Work in Progress', Mr William Walton allowed us to hear three movements of his First Symphony at Monday's London Symphony Orchestra concert.[52]

'The course was justified by the result,' he continued, suggesting that the composer, unable to complete the last movement, was 'right in refusing to botch a potentially great work for the sake of a little extra réclame.' He excused the work's most apparent influence by saying that 'it is natural that any composer writing his first symphony should rely to some slight extent on his forerunners, and it is only to be expected that Sibelius, the greatest symphonic writer since Beethoven, should have some imprint on the present generation.' But, as he continued, 'although the first movement's epic quality recalls Sibelius in style, the construction which is what really gives this movement its great distinction is curiously individual.' He gave the opening movement

---

[52] *Sunday Referee*, 12 December 1934. It is interesting that Cecil Gray should also have referred to Joyce's *Work in Progress* in his book on Heseltine, pp. 276–7.

of Balakirev's Symphony as a precedent for the telescoping of the recapitulation and coda 'so that the last part of the movement moves forward in one great sweep ... but what Balakirev suggests Walton establishes.' He thought the scherzo and the slow movement pure Walton, and the latter 'one of the finest slow movements of our times'. Like everyone else he wondered how Walton would complete so impressive a symphony, and he concluded the review with a suggestion:

> It is to be hoped that the finale, without resorting to an academic device, will be more polyphonic in style than the rest, for if these three movements have a fault it is their great reliance on the sustained pedal in one form or another.

The following day *Coppélia* (in its two-act version) drew warm praise from the *Times* critic: 'The orchestra, under Mr Constant Lambert's direction, gave a thoroughly good performance of the music, in which the delicate ornamentation of the Variations in Act 1 were especially noteworthy.'

12 1935
Van Dieren and Walton

I N January 1935 Constant was called upon to stand in for an indisposed Beecham in Budapest. He conducted its Municipal Orchestra in an all-English programme that included works by Elgar, Delius and Vaughan Williams and one of his own, probably *Music for Orchestra*. 'All the posters announce my concert as an English "Hangoverszene". They've certainly come to the right conductor for it,' he scribbled on a postcard to the now-married Anthony Powell.[1] Back in England, on the 11 January he conducted *Music for Orchestra* at a Winter Prom, Henry Wood taking charge of the remainder of the programme.[2]

On 12 March the Wells programme included Milhaud's *La Création du monde* which, reported *The Times*, 'was well played under Mr Lambert's direction'. Three days later Constant shared with Leslie Woodgate the conducting of a concert at Broadcasting House in the BBC's Contemporary Music series.[3] Woodgate conducted the Wireless Chorus in three carols by Warlock and Two Motets for Double Chorus by Elizabeth Maconchy and then Constant conducted the first performance of van Dieren's *Chinese Symphony*. With hardly a year left to live, the composer was only just well enough to attend rehearsals, making the performance a great act of kindness in allowing him to hear his most substantial work before he died. As Lambert himself recalled, his illness did not prevent him from offering advice when needed:

> van Dieren was … quite obviously and distressingly ill, lying on a sofa in great pain with steam literally rising from him in a most alarming manner. The Chinese Symphony is a complex work and the orchestra were obviously baffled by its strange idiom. Eventually in the orchestral nocturne we came to a passage for violins where they were asked to use the bow in such an unusual fashion that completely nonplussed, they appealed to me.
>
> I, no violinist and equally nonplussed, appealed to the composer. In great pain and with an obvious effort he got up from the couch, went over to the orchestra, took the first violin's instrument from his hands and after executing the passage with complete ease, said very quietly, 'I think you'll find it quite simple if you hold the bow like that' and then returned to his couch. I need hardly mention with what confidence and respect he was treated by the orchestra from that moment on.
>
> At the end of the rehearsal one of the violins came to me and said, 'Was he

---

[1] Postcard from Lambert to Powell, undated, from The Royal Palace, Budapest. Powell later recorded: 'I remember Constant going to Hungary on this occasion and saying he could not make up his mind whether to wear his own clothes and go as a character out of one of my books, in a cloak and slouch hat as a character from William Le Queux, or in a "British Warm" as a character from Geoffrey Moss.' William Le Queux (1864–1927) was a writer of mystery and spy stories, while Geoffrey Moss was the *nom-de-plume* of the once popular author Major Geoffrey McNeill-Moss (1885–1954).

[2] Three Beethoven works, including the Choral Symphony, preceded *Music for Orchestra*, and Sullivan's *In Memoriam* followed it.

[3] BBC National Programme. BBC Concert of Contemporary Music – 6.10–11.15 p.m. Concert Hall, Broadcasting House. Margaret Godley, Betty Bannermann, Bradbridge White, Henry Cummings, Stanley Riley, Wireless Chorus, London Symphony Orchestra, conductors Leslie Woodgate and Constant Lambert. Cecil Gray contributed an article, 'A Chinese Symphony', to *Radio Times*, 8 March 1935.

by any chance a pupil of Ysaÿe, for I have never seen anyone since Ysaÿe hold the violin like that?'[4]

The full score of the *Chinese Symphony* had been written out by Philip Heseltine[5] who had also translated into English the Chinese poems that van Dieren had set to German translations by Hans Bethe.

Constant continued to hold his occasional conducting classes at the Royal College, his students at that time including Robert Irving, Franz Reizenstein, Lionel Salter, and Reginald Goodall, who in January 1936 conducted the first performance of Benjamin Britten's *Te Deum* at the Mercury Theatre. Constant was in the audience and reviewed the concert for the *Sunday Referee*. Under the banner of 'Young English Composer's New Triumph' he wrote that Britten

> displays that combination of a brilliant technique with ultimate greyness of effect that we have already come to expect from this young composer. Mr Britten is, I admit, rather a problem to me. One cannot but admire his extremely mature and economical method, yet the rather drab and penitential content of his music leaves me quite unmoved.[6]

In March 1935 the Camargo Society's ballet *A Day in a Southern Port* was added to the Vic-Wells repertoire under the music's original title, *The Rio Grande*. (On the demise of the Camargo Society all its ballets were bequeathed to the Vic-Wells Company.) Angus Morrison was again the solo pianist, Valetta Jacopi sang the alto solo, and the on-stage chorus was made up of members of the Vic-Wells Opera Company. The cast included Beatrice Appleyard, Walter Gore, William Chappell and a not quite 16-year-old Margot Fonteyn, taking over Markova's role as the Creole girl. It was a shrewd piece of casting on the part of de Valois, already seeing in the very young Fonteyn a successor to the Company's star who would be leaving in June.

The Rio Grande divided opinion and after ten performances that year it was not revived. Arnold Haskell thought it choreographically weak 'but theatrically admirable'[7] while P. W. Manchester declared it 'a detestable ballet' but nevertheless 'a good choice for Fonteyn's début'.[8] The action on stage was at odds with the poem being sung by the chorus, but this hardly worried Constant who was delighted with Ashton's interpretation as, in Haskell's words, an '*étude de mœurs* of the ladies of the court' which was well matched by Edward Burra's scenery and costumes. As Chappell recalled, 'Burra's fascinating act-drop, with its portside buildings whose windows were crowded with fabulous figures, always caused an astonished hush amongst the chattering audiences when the curtain rose.'

Fonteyn's mother, meanwhile, was 'faintly shocked at the completely transparent

---

[4] Lambert talking about van Dieren, BBC Third Programme, 5 December 1949.

[5] Fred Tomlinson, *Warlock and van Dieren* (London: Thames Publishing, 1978), p. 9, relates that a study of this score (in Heseltine's hand) has convinced him 'that BvD never scored the work himself and that PH wrote his score from the rough draft, no doubt with instructions and clarifications from BvD'.

[6] *Sunday Referee*, 2 February 1936. Just over two years earlier he had written: 'There are regrettably few young composers of any personality in England today, but in Miss Elizabeth Machonchy (sic) and Mr Benjamin Britten we have two whose future development should be of the greatest interest.' *Sunday Referee*, 12 November 1933.

[7] Haskell, *Balletomania*, rev. edn, p. 173. The ballet did not stay long in the repertoire, receiving only ten performances that year, the last on 9 December.

[8] Manchester, *Vic-Wells*, p. 24.

skirt of Margot's costume'[9] which no doubt contributed to the on-stage frisson between two of the principal dancers. As Fonteyn admitted in her autobiography, she had a crush on Chappell. 'Happily for me, the crush coincided with rehearsals of my first principal part, in … *Rio Grande*. Billy Chappell was a sailor and I the girl he picked up. Thus I was provided most opportunely with an excuse to regard him affectionately while acting my role.'[10] Chappell had similar feelings for Fonteyn. 'Made up the colour of a dark golden peach grown on some Southern shore, she glowed like a Mediterranean day and her wide radiant smile would have warmed a continent,' he wrote in his book on her, adding ruefully: 'When the little golden-skinned Fonteyn fell so gaily into my arms in *Rio Grande* she was too young to understand life's potentialities for happiness and despair …'[11]

But this was nothing compared with the relationship that was fast developing between the conductor (and composer) of the ballet score and the much younger dancer. After Constant's death, while Margot was alive it was a subject that was tactfully avoided. Richard Shead, Constant's first biographer, went no further than to say that he had 'begun to fall in love with a dancer'. Even after her death her friends closed ranks and said very little. Pamela May, one of Margot's closest friends, when asked about the affair, replied that anything that Margot had wanted to say on that matter she would have done so in her autobiography – where Lambert is only briefly mentioned six times.[12] As well as completely ignoring their affair, she does not even credit him with any of the ballets that he devised or for which he wrote the music. *The Rio Grande* is the only one of his scores that she mentions; there is no reference to *Horoscope* (which was dedicated to her) or to his last ballet, *Tiresias*, in which she had such an important role. His death is similarly passed by without a comment. It was only much later when a full-scale biography of Fonteyn and a television documentary[13] were being prepared that her friends were prepared to speak. Then it was also revealed that Constant had not been her first lover: she and Donald Hodson, ten years her senior and later to be the BBC's Controller of Overseas Services (for which Constant would record many programmes), had been, as his widow put it, 'bedfellows'.[14]

Yet Margot's silence is in part understandable. Her autobiography was published in 1975. In 1955, four year's after Constant's death, she married the Panamanian diplomat Roberto ('Tito') Arias.[15] Ten years later he was shot by a rival politician and remained a quadriplegic for the rest of his life. From then on Fonteyn devoted her life to caring for him in Panama, using her own earnings to pay the considerable expenses for his medical care and even extending her dancing career for that purpose. While before the marriage Arias could hardly have been unaware of Constant and Margot's affair, she

[9] Mrs Hookham, quoted in Meredith Daneman, *Margot Fonteyn* (New York: Viking, 2004), p. 78.

[10] Fonteyn, *Autobiography*, p. 55.

[11] Chappell, *Fonteyn*, pp. 12, 13.

[12] Pamela May in conversation with the author, 1 August 2003. References to Lambert in Fonteyn, *Autobiography* are confined to p. 60 ('[de Valois] had the brilliant advice of Constant Lambert as musical director'), p. 80 ('Constant Lambert was not a man to be ordered about by a handful of ballet dancers. He understood ballet as a genuine marriage between music and dance, with music the senior partner.'), and briefly on pp. 89, 91, 92, 93.

[13] Daneman, *Margot Fonteyn*, and Tony Palmer, *Margot* (2005), shown in two parts on ITV's South Bank Show on 17 & 24 August 2005. Lambert receives one brief mention in the filmed biography, *Margot Fonteyn*, produced and directed by Patricia Foy and narrated by Fonteyn, when she says, with a hint of awkwardness, 'then we had the really superb musical director, Constant Lambert.'

[14] Daneman, *Margot Fonteyn*, p. 104.

[15] Roberto ('Tito') Emilio Arias (1919–89), Panamanian ambassador. Fonteyn died in 1991.

suppressed any mention of it in her book, which was written while Arias was still alive. Even today the extent of the affair and the feelings of both parties are not entirely clear, but whatever the ups and downs of their relationship, Margot was to remain a central figure in Constant's life and he in hers.

M EANWHILE there were significant developments in Constant's married life. On 8 May he wrote to the composer Christian Darnton:[16]

> I must apologise for not having written before – I can only plead general distraction. As a matter of fact we would not have come as Florence, though well, is not going out at the moment and as I am forced to spend two or three evenings out myself I naturally stay in the rest of the time. It was very rude of me not to write, however.
>
> I am sorry that your harp concerto got such a poor show the other day. The performance was so obviously inadequate that it was difficult to form an idea of the work. I hope to hear it again in more favourable conditions.[17]

The performance in question was of Darnton's Concerto for Harp and Wind Instruments, given on 12 April in one of the BBC's Concerts of Contemporary Music, with Ansermet conducting. By all accounts it was a disastrous performance, Darnton himself calling it 'the worst performed programme in the annals of Broadcasting House ... never have I been so upset'.[18]

The reason for Constant having to stay at home became clear three days later, on 11 May, when Flo gave birth to their only child, a boy whom they named Christopher Sebastian; Christopher (or Kit) after the artist Christopher Wood who had died five years earlier in tragic circumstances, and Sebastian after J. S. Bach. (Ironically, Kit's death was to be equally tragic: remembered mostly for having been the manager of the pop group *The Who*, after a life of drinking and drugs, he died in April 1981 at an age almost identical to his father's – about a month short of his 46th birthday – of a cerebral haemorrhage after falling down the stairs in his mother's house.) Paddy Hadley wrote cheekily to Cecil Gray: 'I <u>didn't</u> know that Constant had become a father; of a son, or daughter, I wonder; and what colour? Species, Sex and Colour unknown so far perhaps.'[19] Eleven weeks on, Foss informed Dora: 'The C. Lambert baby is called Christopher Sebastian L. – both good names for their surname. He complains of it becoming vocal – well, <u>my</u> wee thing (Diana) sings 'Big bad wolf' very early in the morning and I love it!'[20] Walton was godfather to Kit, but as he wrote to Alan Frank in 1967: 'I've not seen him since I held him in my arms as his god-father & a fat lot of good I've been to him.'[21] Unfortunately, as if to repeat the experiences of his own upbringing, Constant was not to prove an attentive father. Whereas a child will bring joy to most families, for Constant, Kit's arrival was to cause disruption to his normal routine and ultimately be a factor in the failure of his marriage.

[16] Christian Darnton (1905–81) was born in Leeds and, after studying at Cambridge with Charles Wood and Cyril Rootham, entered the Royal College of Music in 1926. His left-wing – even Communist – sympathies caused him to be sidelined by the music authorities. Lambert favoured his opera *Fantasy Fair*, written for the 1951 Festival of Britain competition.

[17] Letter from Lambert, 7 Park Road, to Christian Darnton, 8 May 1935.

[18] Andrew Plant, 'Christian Darnton, 1905–1981: Discovering a Contemporary Legend' (1997), http://www.musicweb-international.com/darnton/darnton.htm.

[19] Letter from Patrick Hadley to Cecil Gray, 14 May 1935.

[20] Letter from Hubert to Dora Foss, 1 July. Their daughter, Diana, was born on 20 September 1933.

[21] Walton, *Selected Letters*, p. 379.

G AVIN Gordon's *The Rake's Progress* entered the Wells' repertoire on 20 May with Constant conducting.[22] It received seven performances in a fortnight of programmes that were billed as the 'Vic-Wells ballet with Markova', joined by Anton Dolin in the second week before moving to the Shaftesbury Theatre for a further week with four more performances. When *The Rake's Progress* was included in the opening night of the new season in September, *The Times* critic prophesied that it 'is going to prove one of the mainstays of the repertory, for it is a first-rate ballet, in which Gavin Gordon's music, Rex Whistler's stage translation of Hogarth's engravings, and Ninette de Valois's choreography achieve an instantaneous unity.' Constant, who was ever one to invest routine work with humour, added words to the big tune, heard on swannee whistles in the 'orgy' scene, that he and the cast cheerfully sang at rehearsal:

> O deary me,
> I do want to pee
> And I don't much care if the audience see;
> The pain's getting worse
> At the end of each verse
> ....[23]

When a recitation of *Façade* was imminent, he would almost involuntarily practise the words out loud if he happened to be conducting the *Façade* ballet.

On the day of Markova's last London appearance with Sadler's Wells, Constant found time to watch the annual Thames sailing barge races. Hubert Foss wrote to Dora: 'Well, C. Lambert and NJ [Norman Janes, the artist] turned up and got on well together. I was glad of Janes who broke the highbrow superiority of CL like a powerful breakwater ...'[24] The Company were then off for a week each in Blackpool and Bournemouth. From Blackpool Constant sent Powell a postcard with the following printed message, changing 'that' in the last line to 'what':

> Roses and a view of the front at Blackpool.
> Just arrived at Blackpool.
> A simple message here I send,
> A dainty picture too,
> To let you know just where I am
> And that I think of you.[25]

At Bournemouth he conducted the Municipal Orchestra nightly (with two matinées) in a programme that included *Job* with Maurice Brooke as Job, Dolin as Satan, and Margot Fonteyn among the Sons of the Morning, as well as dancing in *Lac des cygnes* and *Les Rendezvous*. As Leslie Edwards recalled, Ninette, Constant, Freddie and Bobby 'stayed at a rather posh hotel on the cliff-top; but in the socially-conscious thirties, even they were put in a wing of the hotel known as the "Pro's Annexe" and reserved for

---

[22] The ballet had been scheduled for April but this was postponed as de Valois had been taken ill in February and underwent an operation performed by Dr Geoffrey Keynes: Clarke, *The Sadler's Wells Ballet*, p. 102.

[23] Related to the author by former Sadler's Wells dancer Leo Kersley (1920–2012), 1 October 2005, who could not remember the last line.

[24] Letter from Hubert Foss to Dora Foss, 8 June 1935, in Dora Foss's typescript. Whether these were races or rehearsals is not clear as, according to *The Times*, the races took place on 25 June.

[25] Postcard from Lambert to Powell, postmarked 11 June 1935.

residents who were in the theatrical profession'. The others found accommodation in the town's many holiday boarding-houses.[26]

After taking a holiday in July, the Company went on its first provincial tour in August, taking them to Glasgow, Edinburgh, Manchester, Birmingham and Leeds, each for a week, and introducing *The Rake's Progress* to northern audiences. (At Leeds Markova and Dolin gave their last performances with the Company.) Powell received a typically Lambertian missive from Glasgow which had been stamped 'Telegrams "Attractive, Glasgow"', Constant having underlined the second word:

> Dear Tony,
>
> The enclosed snippets culled literally at random from the same copy of the same paper will give you some faint idea of the civilization by which I am surrounded. I hope you will share my ethnological interest in the influence of the Scottish climate on the Welsh temperament.[27]
>
> I can't thank you too much for recommending The Romantic Agony.[28] It is an ideal bed book combining pedantry and breeziness to a nicety. I can't decide which I prefer – that or Russia's Iron Age. I think in future I shall always travel with both.[29]

This was followed by another from Edinburgh:

> Dear Tony,
>
> Yesterday I started counting the cows in the pictures exhibited on the walls of this club. I had got up to 74 when my nerve gave way and I took to drink instead.
>
> The taps of the bathroom of my hotel are padlocked in case any one steals a bath on the sly.
>
> If ever you come here you should go to the Café Royal, a fish restaurant near Princes St. It contains a magnificent series of 1880 stained glass windows representing the sports. I am feeling too Strindbergian for words and am beginning to gibber in the streets.
>
> On two separate occasions drops of blood have appeared on my hand from no ascertainable provenance. Do you think I am going to get stigmata? I shouldn't be surprised.[30]

The provincial tours inevitably involved much tedious train travel. Leslie Edwards described a typical journey:

> Constant Lambert would be deep in his crossword puzzle and Miss de Valois making interesting observations on the passing scene, pointing out to Frederick Ashton, who was glumly slumped in a corner, missing his country house weekends, anyone she thought looked remotely Irish. Joy Newton would wind

[26] Leslie Edwards, with Graham Bowles, *In Good Company: Sixty Years with the Royal Ballet* (Binsted: Dance Books, 2003), p. 42.

[27] Anthony Powell had Welsh ancestry.

[28] *The Romantic Agony* by Mario Praz (1896–1982), first published in 1930 was a comprehensive survey of the erotic and morbid themes that characterised European authors of the late 18th and 19th centuries.

[29] Undated postcard from Lambert. Powell explained: 'The cuttings mostly represent various forms of journalistic facetiousness. The reference to the "Welsh temperament" is in connection with one of the cuttings about a man with a Welsh name who ran amok in a Glasgow Street with a sword.'

[30] Letter to Anthony Powell from Constant Lambert at the Scottish Art Club, 24 Rutland Square, Edinburgh, postmarked 15 August 1935.

up her portable gramophone in her compartment and she and her companions
would be deep into Delius.[31]

Accommodation on tour usually meant the traditional 'digs' – with landlady.
Edwards continued:

> It was not just the members of the *corps de ballet* who went into these digs, but
> also principals such as Ashton, Helpmann and Chappell and even Constant
> Lambert, until one day Chappell, with reference to his large and imposing figure,
> said to him, 'Constant, you're too big for digs', so Constant was banished to a
> hotel!

Constant had a National Programme broadcast scheduled for 20 September about
which he had written to Edward Clark:

> About the concert on the 20th I think on second thoughts I would like a soloist
> as I propose (unless the idea strikes you as too narcissistic) to give a programme
> of my own arrangements and would like to include my Handel Concerto.
> Although this is dedicated to dear little Hattie [Harriet Cohen] I certainly don't
> want her to establish a spiritual lien on it (as with the Bax and VW Concertos)
> and suggest Angus Morrison for the solo part (if he is prepared to do it).[32]

Asking for a fee of £20, in addition to the Handel he had suggested Boyce's
Symphony No. 6, Roseingrave's Overture in F minor, Hugh Bradford's Fugal Overture,
Walton's *Portsmouth Point* (in its reduced orchestration) and three movements of the
suite from Glinka's *Ruslan and Ludmila*, all works that he had either edited, arranged
or orchestrated. In the absence of Clark, abroad 'on urgent business', Kenneth Wright
replied that the BBC couldn't afford a soloist and suggested 'going back to Clark's
original suggestion and putting in a suite from *Romeo and Juliet*',[33] which is how the
broadcast went ahead.

A week after the broadcast, the autumn 1935 season opened at the Sadler's Wells
Theatre with two ballet programmes each week and an enlarged orchestra, so that
when on 15 October *Job* was staged, 'for the first time Mr Vaughan Williams' own
full score was used instead of Mr Lambert's clever reduction', reported *The Times*. So
skilful had his reduction of *Job* been that it seems at times some listeners were not
aware when the original score was being used, as he pointed out to *The Times* in 1946:

> Your critic in his notice of *Job* at Covent Garden gives the impression that my
> reduction of Vaughan Williams' score was in continuous use at Sadler's Wells
> and that ballet audiences are now hearing the original full orchestration for the
> first time. This is not the case. My reduction for an orchestra of fewer than 30
> players was a temporary expedient that proved useful to the Camargo Society
> (who gave the first performance) and later to the Vic-Wells ballet in its early days.
> The moment the Sadler's Wells orchestra became enlarged to symphonic stature
> my reduction was quite naturally dropped, having fulfilled its purpose. Ballet

---

[31] Edwards, *In Good Company*, p. 44.

[32] Letter from Lambert to Clark, 29 July 1935: BBC Written Archives. Harriet Cohen was very
possessive of works dedicated to her, especially when Bax, no doubt with some persuasion
on her part, gave her exclusive performance rights of his Symphonic Variations. Vaughan
Williams dedicated his Piano Concerto to Cohen, who had it to herself for a year, but who
was then much aggrieved when Vaughan Williams revised the solo part for two pianos, in
which version it was performed by Cyril Smith and Phyllis Sellick.

[33] Letter from Wright to Lambert, 7 August 1935: BBC Written Archives.

audiences were able to hear *Job* in its original full orchestration for at least six years before the war.[34]

A week earlier Ashton revived *Façade* for the Vic-Wells Company,[35] adding an extra number, 'Country Dance', and dancing the central character of the Dago himself. The same critic observed: 'One most commendable feature of the evening was the high standard of the orchestral playing – which is too often allowed to lapse into the second rate in the accompaniment of *ballets* – under Mr Constant Lambert's direction.' Fonteyn, who had been promoted to Markova's part in *Les Rendezvous* on the opening night, followed her in the 'Polka' in *Façade* and was now being noticed more and more by the critics: 'Miss Fonteyn moves gracefully and is already possessed of a high degree of technical accomplishment as well as of the personality to give character to her parts', the *Times* critic added in the same review.[36]

Constant was regarded, even by Walton, as something of an authority on *Façade*, and when a year later a second orchestral suite was being considered, his advice was naturally sought, with Hubert Foss writing:

> Dear Constant,
>   Willie and I were talking about Façade Second Suite today. I am keen to go on with it but I am not quite sure what numbers to publish in it. It appears that the only numbers that you use at Sadler's Wells which are not in the First Suite are Fanfare, which Willie does not want, I gather, to perpetuate, 'Scotch Rhapsody', a popular song [*sic*] and 'Country Dance'. Is that so? If so, I think we must find at least two other numbers to make a reasonable suite. So far Willie can only think of 'The Man from the Far Countree'. Let us meet and discuss this soon. I much want your advice.[37]

In October 1935 Constant was approached by the BBC to introduce a broadcast concert. He had already given one broadcast talk, in 1931 on Debussy, but the pressure of work (with a large choral score on the stocks) caused him to decline. 'I have never done an introductory talk to a concert,' he replied meekly, 'and I rather doubt if it is my forte. I shall be very busy arranging a new ballet in February and doubt if I could manage the concert you mention.'[38] Nevertheless he was persuaded to give an introductory talk in December to the BBC's series of winter promenade concerts, and occasional broadcast talks were soon to form an important part of his working schedule with a style very much of his own.[39]

In November he attended the first performance at Queen's Hall of Walton's completed symphony, now with a finale. In April he had reviewed the second

---

[34] Letter from Lambert (Midland Hotel, Manchester) to *The Times*, 22 May 1946, published in issue of 26 May.

[35] Ashton's version of *Façade* was first presented by the Camargo Society on 26 April 1931. It was then taken up in May that year by Marie Rambert for her Ballet Club, who also presented it early in 1935 in a season of ballet at the Duke of York Theatre.

[36] *The Times*, 9 October 1935.

[37] Letter from Foss to Lambert, 14 November 1936. The Second Orchestral Suite from *Façade*, published in 1938, consisted of 'Fanfare', 'Scotch Rhapsody', 'Country Dance', 'Noche Espagnôla (Long Steel Grass)', 'Popular Song' and 'Old Sir Faulk'. Lambert had scored the first three numbers and Popular Song, Walton the remaining two (*William Walton Edition*, vol. 8). He also made piano duet arrangements of both suites, published by OUP in respectively 1927 and 1939.

[38] Letter from Lambert to Barnes, 20 October 1935 (from 7 Mills Building, Park Road, SW1). The ballet in preparation was *Apparitions*.

[39] See Appendix 5.

performance of the symphony in its unfinished state at the Courtauld-Sargent concerts, reporting that

> The scherzo, which seemed at first hearing to be the least impressive movement, has been entirely rescored, and is now well able to stand by the others. In the first version Walton robbed the movement of its full effect by a rather finicking over-elaboration of scoring which has in the past detracted from other works of his. It is now immensely clarified, and scores its points directly, not by implication. The slow third movement (slightly but far less drastically rescored) still stands out as the finest of the three.[40]

After the unrelenting tension of the first three movements, Walton had written the opening two or three minutes and the coda of the finale and then come to a stop, uncertain how to continue. In July 1934 he had written to Dora Foss: 'In spite of my having progressed a little with this last movement, I feel at the end of my tether ... As a matter of fact I'm not at all sure that I shan't have to begin this movement all over again ...'[41] The solution apparently came from Constant who suggested a fugue. And when Walton claimed not to know how to write one (although he had already written *two* in the last movement of his first string quartet) Constant suggested that he consulted *Grove's Dictionary of Music and Musicians* where the article on Fugue was written by none other than Vaughan Williams, who had used one in his Fourth Symphony, first heard in April 1935 in between the two premieres of Walton's Symphony. Ironically, in 1932 Constant had touched on fugues in his *Sunday Referee* column:

> When it comes to music you can always knock [the Plain Man] on the head with a fugue. Actually, as Mr Gray has pointed out, there is nothing so easy to write as a fugue so long as you are not very particular as to the final quality of the music. Even a good fugue is on the whole a less remarkable exhibition of the musical faculty than a good operatic tune. In any case it must justify itself primarily as music, and the fact that when held up to a mirror it will combine with an augmented and inverted version of 'Rule Britannia' is neither here nor there.[42]

Constant had few reservations about the completed symphony, writing in the *Sunday Referee*:

> Let it be said at once that the finale is a rattling good piece of music. The two fugato sections show a few stains of midnight oil but the beginning is excellent and the coda has an irresistible drive. The last three minutes, indeed, are as good as anything Walton has written, which is saying much. It cannot be said, however, that the finale is quite up to the intellectual and emotional level of the first three movements. It would be unreasonable to expect a composer at the age of thirty-two to conquer a problem which neither Beethoven nor Sibelius resolved until late in life, and it is a remarkable tribute to the work that it should drag Beethoven and Sibelius into the argument at all. This, and Vaughan Williams' Fourth Symphony, are, to my mind, the two most important novelties of recent years, whether in this country or in Europe.'[43]

---

[40] *Sunday Referee*, 7 April 1935.
[41] 21 July 1934 at Weston: Dora Foss, 'Memoirs of Walton' (unpublished).
[42] *Sunday Referee*, 9 October 1932.
[43] *Sunday Referee*, 10 November 1935.

After the first performance Lady Wimborne gave a sumptuous buffet supper at Wimborne House (as she had after the first incomplete performance) and, with Walton having a whole page devoted to him in that day's *Evening Standard*, Florence was heard bemoaning the fact that Constant had no rich patroness to procure for him the attentions of the press.[44] When, a month later, the symphony was recorded for the gramophone, Constant noted that 'since its first performance the finale has been slightly touched up. A judicious cut of a few bars has been made, and the coda has been rescored so that the fugato subject stands out clearly as an accompaniment to the main tune.'[45] Much later Hubert Foss looked back on the recording sessions: 'My memory of the trials and tribulations of those grim hours is lightened by recalling the visits of distinguished guests who dropped in unheralded (especially for the last session) – Constant Lambert, Alan Rawsthorne, Spike Hughes and others ...'[46]

Despite his expressed aversion to Stravinsky, Constant conducted *Le Baiser de la fée*[47] which was given its first London performance at Sadler's Wells on 26 November, with Fonteyn creating her first leading role as the bride and Pearl Argyle as the fairy.[48] 'The music was excellently played under the direction of Mr Constant Lambert,' reported *The Times*; yet in *Music Ho!* he had regarded the score as an example of Stravinsky's neo-classical methods of fabrication here 'more openly avowed ... where a series of Tchaikovsky's lesser piano pieces are treated in the Procrustean manner once applied [in *Pulcinella*] to Pergolesi's innocent charm'. Nevertheless, he did admit that Stravinsky's 'brilliant sense of orchestral colour, which for some years he has rigorously suppressed, is here allowed full and charming play, and has much the piquant effect of Sickert's coloured transcriptions of Victorian engravings'.[49] Always one to bring forward works off the beaten track, Constant included Busoni's *Indian Fantasy* in a studio concert on 16 December with Eileen Joyce as soloist.[50]

At Christmas he sent Freddie Ashton a card entitled 'God of Love and Lover' with an illustration from *Le Roman de la rose*, a medieval allegory of love. The picture depicted Narcissus and Echo. Was Constant making some comment on the sexually ambivalent Ashton's current infatuation with a new male dancer in *Le Baiser de la fée*, Michael Somes? With the Company working literally in such close contact, it was inevitable that relationships, both heterosexual and homosexual, would easily form and just as easily fracture, often compounded by a degree of sexual jealousy. Ashton's card was signed 'With all good wishes for the New Year from Constant and Florence', but soon, however, there were to be serious ruptures in Constant's marriage.

---

[44] In fact it was Hubert Foss who, recognising the importance of the symphony, had seen to it that it was well covered in the press.

[45] *Sunday Referee*, 22 December 1935.

[46] Foss, *Gramophone*, February 1953, p. 228. The recording was made by Decca in a makeshift studio of the upper floor of a half-used warehouse near Cannon Street Station, London, on 9 and 10 December 1935 with Sir Hamilton Harty conducting the London Symphony Orchestra: Philip Stuart, *The London Philharmonic Discography* (London: Greenwood Press, 1997).

[47] First produced by Ida Rubinstein's company at the Paris Opéra on 27 November 1928, with choreography by Bronislava Nijinska and designs by Alexandre Benois.

[48] That year the Johannesburg-born Pearl Argyle (1910–47) took the role of Catherine Cabal in the Wells/Korda film *Things to Come* that was premiered in February 1936. Known for her beauty, she had earlier had a starring role in the 1934 film of *Chu Chin Chow* alongside Anna May Wong. In 1938 she married and moved to New York where she later died from a brain tumour.

[49] Lambert, *Music Ho!*, 2nd edn (1937), p. 74.

[50] Sir Henry Wood had included *The Indian Fantasy* in the Last Night of the Proms the previous year with the same soloist. Lambert's performance was the work's second broadcast.

13 1936
Pestilence and Apparitions

T HE large choral work with which Constant had been busy for many months was *Summer's Last Will and Testament*, and he conducted its first performance at Queen's Hall on 29 January 1936. The timing could not have been more unfortunate. The previous day had been one of national mourning, with the funeral of King George V at Windsor, and a work whose subject was the plague in 16th-century London could hardly have suited the mood of the hour. (When many years later Anthony Powell immortalised Constant as the composer Hugh Moreland in the *Dance to the Music of Time* sequence of novels, he placed the first performance of Moreland's symphony – something, of course, that Constant never wrote – at another time of national gloom, the abdication.) *Summer's Last Will and Testament* was suitably prefaced by Matthew Locke's *Music for the King's Cornets and Sackbuts* and it was followed by Mendelssohn's *Die erste Walpurgisnacht*, both conducted by Adrian Boult. Walton's patroness and lover Alice Wimborne threw a post-concert party (as she had after the first performances of his symphony in both its unfinished and finished states) and Hubert Foss provided Dora with a full account of the evening's events:

> Constant's concert was heavily papered but had a distinguished audience. I made friends again with [John] Ireland, and saw the world. I gather that white ties are taboo (your learned 'tabu' is only used by anthropologists!), but I knew no better, and was, thank God, covered by Lambert himself and Edward Marsh (CBE of Rupert Brooke fame). The performance was moderate, the work is much more difficult than CL thinks. C[harles] K[ennedy] S[cott][1] confirmed to me how hard it is for the choir, which he trained. CL had a job to pull it off and worked himself to death. I think it very good, but not a public hit, but vide The Times of today – a splash for us.
>
> The intellectual angle was so good – the classicised pictorialism (what a novelty of a cliché!) was beautifully done. Not liked by the wirelessites, according to my spies' accounts, but a good success in the hall. Not a popular work like Rio Grande or Belshazzar. We shall lose money. I cut the Mendelssohn, did my business jobs at the bar, and went to see Constant – rather tired and overwhelmed.
>
> The Wimborne party was only 30 or so – good food, mostly standing up but some sitting. Excellent champagne in floods, and whiskey if wanted. Alice, Lady W charming and enjoying the jokes of Willie and Constant. C not really fêted but quite caught up by sitting old ladies! It would have amused you. Paddy H[adley] especially nice to me about you. So kind and interesting at once. Bill Primrose came in full of beans and bursting with the [Walton] Viola Concerto which he is playing (eccentrically well) with Beecham on Feb. 27th (or so). Very brilliant. We sang the work together in forgotten corners, where Paddy and I had previously hymned in concert about Lord Wimborne (who is unwell).

> 'It is believed that God knew best
> When he created Ivor Guest.'[2]

[1] Charles Kennedy Scott (1876–1965), conductor of the Philharmonic Choir and the Oriana Madrigal Society.

[2] Ivor Churchill Guest, 1st Viscount Wimborne (1873–1939) was a MP from 1900 until 1910, when he became Baron Ashby St Ledgers. In 1914 he succeeded his father as Baron

Florence, in white brocade (rather the colour of old tennis shoes, unwashed) with a period turn-up colour, etc, accepted the bounty and attacked me – 'not a half-bad composer, I think, anyhow!' I duly agreed, if coldly.

Paddy and I got away at 12 or so, but I gather Willie and the rest drank on till 3 or more at WW's flat.[3]

Summer's Last Will and Testament, Constant's largest-scale work and in many ways his most impressive, was dedicated – whether out of appeasement or a sense of guilt – to Florence, who remembered that he worked at it right through the night when they lived at Percy Street.[4] Like most of his works that were written when his main preoccupations were conducting and arranging ballet – often on tour – it did not come easily, but this time composition was punctuated by interruptions of a different kind, those from baby Kit, who had been born eight months before the premiere.

In August 1932 Constant, often short of cash, thanked Paddy Hadley for helping him out and at the same time gave him an early account of the work's progress:

I hope that 'Elle s'apelle Youba' and 'Love for Sale'[5] [Cole Porter] arrived unscathed. They are difficult things to pack.

Please don't think I have forgotten the many and large sums I owe you. I would send you a cheque to-day were there the remotest chance of its being 'met' poor helpless thing. I feel most guilty about all this bilking and will really clear the whole thing up the moment I can.

At present I am wading my way through my choral work – a curiously English affair. I have done two movements – a dreary but quite pleasantly melancholy overture (late wet summer) and a choral movement (spring) of ghastly and Holst-like breeziness. To-day I have been trying to do a four-part motet vaguely based on Purcell[']s two in one canon Dance for the followers of night[6] but I find my technique is frankly not up to it.

The 1st two lines are champion – canons two-in-one, canons augmented, canons diminished, inverted, cancrisans, and arsyversy. Canons (in fact) to the right of them, canons (if I may use the phrase) to the left of 'em. But after that I can think of nothing but blocks of chords with a regrettable amount of doubled

Wimborne, and from 1915 until 1918 he served as Lord Lieutenant of Ireland. The family wealth came from steel works in South Wales. In 1902 he married Alice Grosvenor (1880–1948) who was extremely musical, and Wimborne House in London became home to many musical soirées. Later in their marriage they led independent lives, Alice preferring to associate with musicians and artists much younger than herself. She had an intense love affair with Walton (22 years her junior) who was devastated by her death from cancer.

[3] Letter from Hubert Foss to Dora Foss, 1 February 1936: typescript in Hubert Foss Archives.

[4] Letter from Mr K. Harvey Packer to David Lloyd-Jones, 14 February 1993.

[5] Rather daringly Lambert had recently reviewed this song for *The New Statesman and Nation*, 1 August 1931, writing that 'after the best of Ellington, the finest jazz record I have heard is *Love for Sale*, by Cole Porter, played by Waring's Pennsylvanians and sung by the Waring Sisters. This is melancholy, but not in the style of *Mood Indigo*. It has a rich nostalgia that expresses perfectly the curious mood evoked by certain towns, particularly ports like Marseille or Toulon. ... Unfortunately, this record is banned in this country because of the words which deal with the subject of prostitution. Prostitution is a theme that can be exploited with impunity in literature, the drama, and the plastic arts, but apparently cannot be used in connection with music. Not that prostitution is directly mentioned in *Love for Sale*, but its existence is, I regret to say, implied.'

[6] From the 'Masque of Night' in Purcell's *The Fairy Queen*. On 7 February 1933 the Vic-Wells Company performed *The Birthday of Oberon*, based on *The Fairy Queen* and choreographed by de Valois with the music selected by Constant Lambert (chiefly from the Masque of the Seasons but interpolating other music from the opera).

leading notes and outer parts moving from the minor ninth to the octave. It is all most disheartening. I think the plan of the work is good though – the words all taken from Nashe's 'Summer's Last Will & Testament'.

Seven sections falling into 3 groups.

A   I   Overture (pastorale and siciliana) orchestra

      II 'Fair summer droops' 4 part motet

B III 'Spring the sweet spring' the whole bloody shoot

    IV Scherzetto, mainly for orchestra with a silly little poem coming in from time to time on the chorus. A juicy bit of bouche fermée leading to –

C   V 'Autumn' Solo voice with chorus, a poem about London with references to the plague.

    VI Scherzo. 'King Pest' suggested by Poe's story of drunken sailors in the Great Plague. Orchestra only. A parody on the earlier movements.

   VII 'Adieu farewell Earth's bliss'. Winter. Unaccompanied chorus.

Composers, selections from whose works will be incorporated, include the following, Delius, Liszt, VW, Puccini, Fauré, Balfour Gardiner,[7] Purcell, Balakireff and Gesualdo.[8] The choice is not deliberate.[9]

That same day he wrote a very brief report to Marie Nielson: 'I am wading slowly and drearily through my choral work which is more like a wet English summer than you might think possible. I have done 2 movements but as there are going to be no less than 7 it doesn't get one very far.'[10]

He later made one or two changes to the initial plan. 'Autumn' alternated between female and male voices, and the soloist was reserved for the last section, with accompanied rather than unaccompanied chorus. If Constant was at all serious about including extracts from the works of other composers, he seems generally to have abandoned the idea, although one composer he did in part quote from is Delius, who died in June 1934. The bitter-sweet 'motto' theme representing summer (Ex. 15) with which the work opens and which recurs in various forms at key moments bears a strong resemblance to the opening figure in Delius's *In a Summer Garden* (Ex. 16), the same theme that Paddy Hadley was to quote some years later in *The Hills* at the words 'The hills bring back sweet memories'. *In a Summer Garden* was a work with which Constant was to have an unusual association. In a BBC broadcast in December 1937 he conducted the familiar revised version, but five years later on consecutive days he gave two broadcasts of the original version that had not been heard for nearly 30 years.[11]

[7] The composer and patron Henry Balfour Gardiner (1877–1950) was a friend of Hadley's whom he took to visit Delius at his home at Grez-sur-Loing in France. Lambert was never to meet Delius.

[8] Carlo Gesualdo (*c*. 1560–1613) was a composer in whom both Heseltine and Gray were interested and together they wrote a book, *Carlo Gesualdo: Prince of Verosa: Musician and Murderer* (London: Kegan Paul, 1926) which was largely expanded from articles that had appeared in *The Sackbut* and *The Chesterian*. In 1941 Gray unsuccessfully tried to interest Walton in an opera on the subject of Gesualdo.

[9] Letter from Constant Lambert to Patrick Hadley, 15 August [1932?] in the possession of Mrs Trundley, Hadley's house-keeper.

[10] Letter from Lambert (15 Percy Street, W1) to Marie Nielson, 15 August [1932].

[11] The score, which is in the BBC Music Library, is dated '23.5.42 London' and was copied by Henry Gibson from the original orchestral parts. The broadcasts, both in the Home Service with the BBC Symphony Orchestra, were on 12 December from Cambridge and 13 December from Bedford.

Ex. 15 Lambert, *Summer's Last Will and Testament*, opening

Ex. 16 Delius, *In a Summer Garden*, opening

Work on *Summer's Last Will and Testament* progressed slowly, and when in August 1935 Kenneth Wright at the BBC informed him of the date for its first performance, there was a slight sense of panic in Constant's reply:

> Your letter has only just reached me through devious ways hence the delay. January 29th gives me damned little time to get the work scored but I will manage it somehow. I have been held up by having to make another copy of the piano score but will make [a] start on the full score next week. The choir should be a large one at least 200. There is a baritone solo in the last movement for which Roy Henderson would be ideal. If you can't get him get an Empire singer of Roy Henderson type.[12]

The choir was the Philharmonic Choir, trained by Charles Kennedy Scott, and Roy Henderson was indeed the soloist. It is clear that Hyam Greenbaum played a significant part in getting the score ready in time as Alan Frank at OUP wrote to Constant in November: 'I have hesitated to write to Greenbaum about your chorus parts because I haven't quite known what to pay him? Would you advise?'[13] and Constant acknowledged his help as being rather more than just assisting with the chorus parts when he over-generously inscribed the vocal score he gave to 'Bumps': 'To Hyam Greenbaum (who as far as I remember wrote most of this work) from Constant Lambert'.[14] Spike Hughes was later to pay tribute to the help that Greenbaum gave to several composer friends including Lambert:

> When he died, one day after his 41st birthday, I realised what an enormous amount Bumps had meant in my life. There was scarcely a pub in London, a restaurant in Soho, an opera by Donizetti, a trick of orchestration that I had picked up which I had not originally discovered with Bumps. It was Bumps who first attracted me to the music of Sibelius. ... It was to Bumps that I instinctively turned for technical advice as William Walton and Constant Lambert and Alan Rawsthorne did. (A great deal of Willie Walton's [pre-war] film music was scored at great speed and with typical expertness by Bumps Greenbaum when the composer was pressed for time.)[15]

Greenbaum, knowing the work almost as well as its composer did, in fact took over the second performance of *Summer's Last Will and Testament* at short notice when Constant was too ill to conduct.

The work is subtitled both as 'The music by Constant Lambert for parts of Thomas Nashe's Masque' and 'A Masque for orchestra, chorus and baritone solo, to words

[12] Letter, n.d., replying to a letter of 7 August 1935.
[13] Letter from Alan Frank to Constant Lambert, 29 November 1935. OUP Archives.
[14] Score in the possession of Hyam's sister, Kyla Greenbaum.
[15] Hughes, *Opening Bars*, pp. 354–5.

taken from the Pleasant Comedy of that name written in 1593 by Thomas Nashe'. The play, probably written in the autumn of 1592 or 1593, is a pageant of linguistic virtuosity in which the transience of life is portrayed against a backdrop of the plague that heavily affected London in those years. Summer is personified as a dying man making his final testament in the presence of the other seasons as well as Harvest, Christmas and Bacchus. Even Vertumnus, the Roman god of the seasons (and a central figure in Lambert's *Pomona*), makes an appearance. The play's title is a pun on the name of King Henry VIII's court jester, Will Somers,[16] who assumes the role of Chorus, and the entertainment is interspersed with verses from which Lambert drew his text, including the two that are most frequently anthologised, 'Spring the sweet Spring' and 'Adieu, farewell Earth's bliss'. In choosing the former he was following Delius, Heseltine, van Dieren and Moeran, each of whom had set the poem either for solo voice or for unaccompanied chorus.[17] (Constant in all probability knew each of these versions, especially Delius's which he had orchestrated in 1926.)

One aspect of the play that would have particularly attracted Lambert was its Elizabethan setting, and he gave the seven movements of *Summer's Last Will and Testament* titles that belong essentially to Elizabethan music. His interest in early dance forms had been evident from the movement headings to his ballet scores *Adam and Eve* and *Romeo and Juliet*, written before he knew Heseltine, but the latter's scholarly researches into early music and the extensive transcriptions he had made, together with his settings of Elizabethan and Jacobean poets, much encouraged those in the 'Warlock' circle, such as Lambert and Moeran, to draw upon such a rich vein of music.

Another characteristic shared by Lambert, Heseltine and Moeran – and Walton too – was a fondness for the 6/8 rhythm, something that linked them with Delius. For Lambert and Walton this invariably took the form of the siciliana which Lambert had used in *Adam and Eve* (and *Romeo and Juliet*) – actually in 12/8 time – and then in *Pomona*, and which is also found in such Walton scores as *Siesta*, *The Quest* and the *Partita*. It is not surprising that the siciliana is very much in evidence in *Summer's Last Will and Testament*. (His fondness for the siciliana once almost won over his dislike for Brahms when reviewing a performance of the Brahms-Haydn Variations, 'a work,' he quickly added, 'whose texture sounds far better on two pianos than on the orchestra', in which he referred to the 'lovely Siciliana variation'.)[18]

Edmund Rubbra brought a composer's insight to this work in a programme note he wrote for a BBC performance in 1965:

> The Intrata (Pastorale and Siciliana) is an orchestral overture that brings forward various ideas that are used in later movements without, however, insisting upon them in any very developed form. The most developed idea is the triplet movement of the Siciliana, but towards the end the superimposition of the opening four-four idea brings a formal balance to the whole movement. The quiet ending, surprising yet beautifully logical in its use of a sort of distorted interrupted cadence in G major, has the practical advantage of giving the pitch for the unaccompanied choral opening of the second movement (Madrigal con ritornelli).
>
> This movement is a setting of words beginning 'Fair summer droops', the

---

[16] Sometimes spelt Summers. The pun is more pointed in the title used for its entry in the Stationers' Register (1600): 'A book called Summer's Last Will and Testament presented by Will Summers'.

[17] Settings for solo voice by Delius (1915), Heseltine (1922) and van Dieren (1926), and for unaccompanied chorus by Moeran (1929, in his *Songs of Springtime*) who in 1939 dedicated his choral *Phyllida and Corydon* to Lambert.

[18] Reviewing a performance by Mary and Geraldine Peppin, *Sunday Referee*, 29 May 1932.

latter word describing the shape of the imitative lines of the voices. Only a semi-chorus is used for the first four lines, and as the harmony and part-writing are fairly complex, pitch is helped by the orchestra joining in at the fourth bar. The last two lines of each verse are set as a choral refrain for full chorus. The nostalgic mood is forcefully interrupted by a *vivace* coda, based on ideas from the Siciliana, which goes straight into the third movement (Coranto), 'Spring, the sweet Spring'. Motives from the Introduction are again freely used and developed. The rhythmic vivacity is never-ceasing, and excitement is intensified by a combination of dual and triple rhythms, and textures diversified by legato choral writing against pungent orchestral dance-rhythms, e.g., the section beginning with divided sopranos, 'The fields breathe sweet'.

This leads without interruption into the fourth movement, Brawles *(allegro giocoso)*. Here the rhythmic interest is more characteristically Lambertian, being full of the restless and somewhat drunken syncopations that Walton developed in *Portsmouth Point*. Harmonically, too, it is an acute contrast, as shifting chromatic chords are largely rejected in favour of simple triads. The voices, used antiphonally, enter at the first Trio ('Trip and go'), but they are mainly additions to the continuously busy web of orchestral sound. Trio II begins in a steadier metre, and is a setting, for male voices, of 'Monsieur Mingo for quaffing doth surpass'. Its steadiness is, however, soon upset by the addition of contrary rhythms, and increases in complexity as it adds motive to motive. After the final 'Trip and go, heave and ho' the chorus is used instrumentally, and wordless vocal sound dominates the quiet ending.

Between this movement and 'King Pest' a quiet accompanied *Madrigal con ritornelli* intervenes, a setting of 'Autumn hath all the summer's fruitful treasure'. The menace of the succeeding movement *(vivace ma misterioso)* grows quietly out of the end of the Madrigal. It has cumulative force and excitement, again by reason of opposed rhythms and motives, and a tarantella-like drive and frenzy. This brilliant orchestral evocation is a wonderful foil for the final Saraband ('Adieu! Farewell Earth's bliss'), a movement of simple, poignant lyricism. The baritone solo is interspersed with choral commentaries that throw into relief the deep intensity of the soloist's phrases. Many recognizable motives are in this movement, not combined to create tension but transformed and shaped into the prevailing mood. It therefore has a fine sense of unity. The music ends pianissimo on a final A left high by a process of elimination, and thus turns full circle to the single note, A, with which the work begins.[19]

Constant was often drawn to darker subject matter, in this case understandable for someone whose childhood had been blighted by illness, near death and isolation, and for whom the plague would have had a sinister personal resonance. Reviewing a performance of *Summer's Last Will and Testament* for the *Sunday Times* in 1965, Felix Aprahamian saw the work in the wider context of Constant's life, commenting on its 'autobiographical overtones' and how 'Lambert was one of an ill-fated and tragically short-lived group of native composers.' Constant would have felt a more pleasurable affinity with another of the work's themes, that of drinking in the fourth movement to which he attached the title 'Brawles' after an old French dance – a variant of the term 'Bransles' used by Heseltine in his *Capriol* Suite, but here Constant may have delighted in its homophonic double meaning – just as two bars before figure 72 he

---

[19] Edmund Rubbra's programme note for a performance of *Summer's Last Will and Testament* given by Raimund Herincx, BBC Chorus and Choral Society and BBC Symphony Orchestra conducted by Sir Malcolm Sargent, Royal Albert Hall, 3 February 1965.

enjoyed directing the bass trombone to play *vibrato (quasi lampone)*, i.e. a raspberry. For 'Brawles' he combined two songs into one drunken revelry, 'Trip and Go' that in Nashe's play refers more soberly to Morris Dancers, and 'Monsieur Mingo in quaffing doth surpass' which praises Saint (Do)mingo, the patron saint of topers.

Constant came dangerously close to setting himself up as an authority on drinking when almost exactly a year later he reviewed the first London performance of Vaughan Williams' *Five Tudor Portraits*. Referring to drunken Alice in that work's opening movement, 'The Tunning of Elinor Rumming', he dared suggest that Vaughan Williams was the wrong person to catch the bawdiness of Tudor ale houses. 'Constant Lambert says: Tudor Teas are not the same as Tudor Pubs' ran the *Sunday Referee* headline. And he continued:

> I seem to have enjoyed this work rather less than most of my colleagues. … 'Exit the Folk-Song Society' must be the stage directions to any passage in this work. … Throughout the *Five Tudor Portraits* one feels the inevitable drawback of the time-lag that exists between poetry and its choral setting. As a result the work seems Tudor in the modernised or tea-house sense of the word. Vaughan Williams' temperament seems to me too elegiac, nostalgic, and individual to interpret the extrovert bawdy directness of that admirable poet Skelton. It is difficult to associate him with the English public-house, except in a remote Housmanish way.[20]

The emphasis on drinking in *Summer's Last Will and Testament* is made stronger by Lambert's interpolation of the purely orchestral movement, sub-titled *King Pest* after one of Edgar Allan Poe's more gruesome *Tales of Mystery and Imagination*. Set in London during the reign of King Edward III, the short story tells of two sailors who flee from an ale-house without paying and escape their pursuers by climbing the street barriers into a forbidden area of the city that has been affected by the plague. Having 'evidently reached the stronghold of the pestilence' they enter a 'tall and ghastly-looking building' and interrupt King Pest holding court in the house of an undertaker where he and his companions are drinking from skulls. For their intrusion the two sailors are sentenced to be drowned in ale but through sheer drunken bravado they manage to make their escape back to their ship. This brilliant orchestral tour-de-force is headed 'Rondo Burlesca'. Was Lambert reminded of the third movement, 'Rondo-Burleske', of Mahler's Ninth Symphony which he reviewed in February 1934 for the *Sunday Referee*, commenting that 'the two middle movements in particular reveal a mind of remarkable originality'?[21]

Alan Frank, in his programme note for the first performance of *Summer's Last Will and Testament*, disclosed that in 'Brawles' Lambert had used one theme that was not original but a fragment of a 16th-century Neapolitan tune. In *King Pest* he made rather more extensive use of traditional material. One of the main motifs is the Elizabethan drinking song known as *Watkins Ale* (Ex. 17) that Walton was to use so movingly in the 'Passacaglia: The Death of Falstaff' in his 1944 film score for *Henry V*. In *King Pest*

---

[20] *Sunday Referee*, 31 January 1937. The first performance of *Five Tudor Portraits* had been at the Norwich Triennial Festival on 25 September 1936. The first London performance was at Queen's Hall on 27 January 1937.

[21] In that review Lambert wrote: 'I must confess to having shared the usual English prejudice against Mahler, and having looked upon him as a symphonist manqué. But the Ninth Symphony, in spite of certain obvious weaknesses, is an astonishing piece of work. … Here is that rare thing, a modern work which is genuinely difficult to understand. The two middle movements in particular reveal a mind of remarkable originality': *Sunday Referee*, 11 February 1934.

Ex. 17 *Watkins Ale*

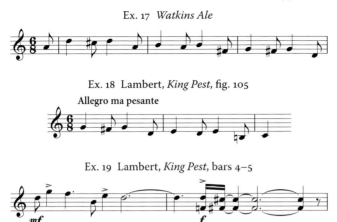

Ex. 18 Lambert, *King Pest*, fig. 105

Allegro ma pesante

Ex. 19 Lambert, *King Pest*, bars 4–5

Lambert treats this tune very freely, sometimes straightforwardly but at a faster tempo (Ex. 18) or elsewhere less recognisable in a much-altered fragmented form (Ex. 19).

But *King Pest* has more sinister allusions. In his biography of Heseltine, Cecil Gray wrote about one evening at Eynsford

> when Peter gave an impromptu performance of a little-known Sea Shanty in the collection of Sir Richard Terry, entitled *Walk him along, Johnny*, which he said he wished to be performed at his funeral [Ex. 20]. Caparisoned in his African witch-doctor's robe and a huge soft black hat, he intoned the choral lines in a hoarse whisper, hopping and capering grotesquely like a vulture, in a kind of *danse macabre*, imbuing the artless little ditty with a nameless sense of dread and horror, and seeming almost to gloat over the thought of his own imminent decease. On a certain dark and gloomy December day only a few years later, in the old cemetery at Godalming, I was to recall involuntarily this strange performance, and in my mind's eye seemed to see him leaping around his own coffin, croaking sardonically, 'Walk him along, Johnny, carry him along; carry him to the burying ground'.[22]

Ex. 20 *Walk him along, Johnny*

(Solo)   (Chorus)

Dan O' Con-nell died long a-go,   Walk him a-long, John-ny, car-ry him a-long;

Gray almost certainly discussed this incident with Constant who was also present at Heseltine's funeral and who would have read the above passage when he was composing *Summer's Last Will and Testament*.[23] On a copy that he gave to Tom Driberg[24] Constant marked several points in the score and against the following phrase (Ex. 21) wrote '"Walk him along to the burying ground" (Warlock's funeral)' and at one point (Ex. 22) 'Burying ground' (annotated thus on Driberg's score) becomes almost transformed as a chorale into the 'Dies Irae'. Beneath a jaunty 6/8 figure (Ex. 23) he had

---

[22] Gray, *Peter Warlock*, pp. 256–7.

[23] Lambert reviewed Cecil Gray's biography of Peter Warlock (Philip Heseltine) for *The New Statesman and Nation*, 10 November 1934.

[24] Inscribed 'To dear Tom (in recess as usual) with best wishes from Constant Lambert (House of Commons Jan. 15th '47)'.

Ex. 21 Lambert, *King Pest*, 2 bars before fig. 145

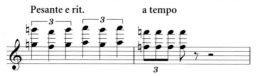

Ex. 22 Lambert, *King Pest*, 5 bars before fig. 103

Ex. 23 Lambert, *King Pest*, 6 bars after fig. 100

written the words of a late Victorian or early Edwardian music-hall song, 'As I was out walking beside the Royal Albert', that had suggested the passage to him.

There are also a few private jokes: in Driberg's score Constant had written 'parody of Ghiselle'[25] over the bass at fig. 98, 'Sir Arnold Bax'[26] at fig. 99, and an enigmatic 'W A' at fig. 113. His mind was clearly also full of literary allusions because, in addition to the title from Edgar Allan Poe, at the head of the movement he wrote 'James Joyce plus Hogarth' and against fig. 106 'Unfortunate traveller', a reference to Nashe's novel of the same name.

He also made use of self-quotation. In three places he quotes the prominent trumpet theme (Ex. 24) from his incidental music to *Salomé*, which in the third bar of *King Pest* becomes the figure shown in Ex. 25, perhaps drawing a grisly analogy between the head of John the Baptist and the drinking skulls which King Pest and his companions were brandishing. He quotes from *Salomé* again: the last 14 bars that lead directly into the Saraband are almost identical to letter E in the Dance (of the Seven Veils).[27] But what might seem to be the most prominent self-quotation is the opening to the last movement of his 1929 Piano Sonata (Ex. 26) which is almost identical to the principal theme of the Saraband (Ex. 27). Yet, as Alan Frank explained in his 1937 survey of Lambert's music, this was not a case of a quotation from an earlier work, because a rough and incomplete sketch for a setting of the Nashe poem already existed when the Sonata was being written and Lambert utilised it.[28]

As Hubert Foss informed his wife Dora, the first performance was well covered by the press who gave the new work a generally warm reception. William McNaught touched briefly on the difficulties it presented the choir, but after that one reservation he went on:

[25] The significance of the quotation is not clear. Giselle was a role that Alicia Markova included in her last season with the Sadler's Wells Ballet, her final performance being on 3 June 1935. It did not return to the repertoire until 19 January 1937 when Fonteyn took over Markova's role.

[26] This could have been a private retaliation against Bax, who at about this time had dedicated his tone-poem *Nympholept* to Constant, no doubt a hint at Constant's infatuation with the very young Margot Fonteyn.

[27] Lambert had also written 'Salomé' above figure 116 on Driberg's copy of the score.

[28] Frank, 'The Music of Constant Lambert' (1937).

Ex. 24 Lambert, *Salomé*, Prelude, opening

Ex. 25 Lambert, *King Pest*, bar 3

Ex. 26 Lambert, Piano Sonata, Finale, opening

Ex. 27 Lambert, *Saraband*, fig. 156

Mr Lambert's work can be praised without stint. It is music unclouded by any modern theory of procedure. All its various phases of action and expression are clear-spoken, intelligible, ardently worked out. When he is writing for the orchestra, that is to say in most of this work, Mr Lambert writes effects that come off, throws them out in rapid sequence – colour, rhythm, tune – and sees that his listeners enjoy themselves. And his chief aim is beauty.[29]

Beauty was the main feature commented on by the *Times* critic who thought the Introduction 'a very beautiful piece of orchestral writing' and concluded that 'beauty is not confined to the reflective opening; it strikes one in a number of expressive details and is the outstanding impression left by the finale'. Although in the *Morning Post* Francis Toye (brother of Geoffrey) thought the Introduction and the madrigals not altogether successful, regarding Brawles and 'the macabre scherzo' he commented that 'nothing could be more vivid, more entirely adequate to depict the various incidents of the scenes and emotions' and he considered the final number the best of all. 'Here the composer achieved a really remarkable procession of rhythm, emotional as well as physical, which made a most effective ending to the work.'

[29] *The Musical Times*, March 1936.

Richard Capell in the *Daily Mail* praised the score's ingeniousness and thought Lambert's 'repertory of devices' brilliant but wondered whether the restlessness of the style got in the way of its coherency. Edwin Evans, while recognising the work's brilliance with its skilfully contrived choral sections, was nonetheless baffled by its mood. 'What is one to make of a work which, beginning as a pastorale, greets the spring as "the year's pleasant king" then ends with Mr Roy Henderson singing of death's bitterness?' he asked.

The unkindest cut of all came, unexpectedly, from Spike Hughes who 'found it an unfriendly piece' and 'took a long time to assimilate the moods and get interested in what the composer was saying'. He did at least find some 'beautiful lyrical music' in the last movement and, like McNaught, suggested that the *rondo burlesca* might have a concert life as a separate work. Norman Peterkin of OUP was of a similar opinion, writing: 'After listening to the Rondo Burlesca it at once struck me that if we had separate full score and set of parts for this it could be done in orchestral concerts.'[30] Although Constant made it known that he did not wish *King Pest* to be let out on hire separately before further performances of the complete work had taken place, he was persuaded otherwise and *King Pest* was heard at that year's and the following year's Proms[31] before the whole work's second performance was given. *The Times* critic seemed to support Constant's doubts about detaching the movement when he described it as 'uncommonly clever but it does not stir the blood, at any rate when taken out of its context thus, any more than the nineteenth-century essay in diabolism which it somehow recalled'.[32]

Arthur Bliss, who was then on the BBC Music Advisory Committee, was impressed by the work and wrote: 'I have been studying Lambert's "Summer's Last Will & Testament" which has just been issued in piano score. I am convinced it is a work of rare and great beauty, and that we should take definite steps to arrange a second performance of it as soon as practical. ... I should like it put on the agenda for next mtg., so we can discuss the possibility of a special placing of it.'[33] Of the final chorus he wrote that 'with its superb ground bass [it] is not unworthy of Purcell.'[34] The next performance, which was also broadcast, did not take place until April 1938.[35]

Alan Frank was convinced that it was 'far and away' the finest work Lambert had yet produced, with its 'queer blend of grimly exuberant gaiety and utmost gloom', gathering 'impetus, emotionally, as it goes along'. He felt that *King Pest* suffered 'through being too tightly packed with thematic material and would be even more effective if thinned out and slightly shortened', although this is not the impression left by a good performance and certainly not a view shared by the present writer. Frank also found a very superficial resemblance to *L'Apprenti sorcier*, but he rated the work's final pages, with the chorus's recurring motive 'Lord have mercy upon us' interspersed

[30] Letter from Norman Peterkin to Constant Lambert, 4 February 1936: OUP files.

[31] 5 September 1936 and 19 August 1937, with Lambert conducting.

[32] *The Times*, 20 August 1937.

[33] Lewis Foreman, 'Arthur Bliss at the BBC', in *Arthur Bliss: Music and Literature*, ed. Stewart R. Craggs (Aldershot: Ashgate, 2002), p. 235.

[34] In 'Modern English Music', typescript of a lecture at Music Teachers National Association convention, Kansas City, Missouri, 27–30 December 1939, printed in *Bliss on Music: Selected writings of Arthur Bliss 1920–1975*, ed. Gregory Roscow (Oxford: Oxford University Press, 1991), p. 173.

[35] 1 April 1938, BBC National Programme, 9.40–10.35 p.m. BBC Chorus, BBC Orchestra (D), Roy Henderson, conducted by Hyam Greenbaum. (The introduction to *The Times* broadcasting listing on 1 April announced that Lambert was to conduct, but the detailed listing that followed below contradicted this by giving Greenbaum as the conductor.)

with the soloist's 'I am sick, I must die' to the distant tolling of the death-bell, as 'among the most moving things I know in contemporary music'.

Nowhere else in his output did Lambert maintain such an intensity of emotion achieved not just in the beauty of the melodic line but in the constantly shifting harmonies that alternate between moments of warm consonance and piercing dissonance. This deeply felt movement, in essence a threnody, forms a majestic climax to the whole work with a funeral cortège that slowly winds its way through the plague-infested streets of London (a coincidental point of contact with national events at the time of the premiere). The orchestral passage after figure 164 tellingly recalls the opening words of the first madrigal: 'Fair Summer droops, droop men and beasts therefore; So fair a Summer look for nevermore ...' The ending, with its reminiscence of the work's opening theme followed by the chord on the strings that gradually dissolves until only the high opening A is left hanging in the air, is a masterstroke. For its originality and mastery of effect *Summer's Last Will and Testament* has few parallels. Certainly there are a few similarities to be drawn with *Belshazzar's Feast* where jazz-like rhythms are employed, if to a different effect. Yet one could make a somewhat tenuous link with another original work that was to receive its first performance later that year, Benjamin Britten's *Our Hunting Fathers*. While in many respects these works are as different as their composers' personalities, one calling for a soprano solo while the other is essentially choral, they are both orchestral song-cycles, both end in funereal mood and both have a virtuosic *Totentanz* as a centrepiece. *Summer's Last Will and Testament* might even be seen as a forerunner to Britten's *Spring Symphony* (1946–9) which also incorporates a setting of Nashe's 'Spring, the sweet spring' and concludes in London, albeit in a happier May-time holiday mood.

T EN days before the death in January 1936 of King George V, Constant conducted the first night of a new version of the Handel–Beecham ballet *The Gods Go a'Begging*. Commissioned by Diaghilev and choreographed by Balanchine, it had been first given with Beecham conducting in July 1928. This new version, with choreography by de Valois, was to prove popular. The Royal death caused a brief suspension to the Sadler's Wells season and the postponement for three days of the first performance of Walton's *Siesta*, choreographed by Ashton as a *pas de deux*, in a programme that also included *Façade*, *Job* and *Les Sylphides*.[36] Walton conducted *Siesta* and, as an interlude, the ballet fragment from his film score *Escape Me Never*. But *Siesta* was not a great success and only had four performances. Following the transformation of *The Rio Grande* into a ballet, there had been some discussion in 1934 of giving Walton's *Belshazzar's Feast* similar treatment. Sponsorship was to have been provided by the Camargo Society that had been inactive since June 1933. When that idea fell through (probably because of the cost of the large choral forces that would be involved) Maynard Keynes and Montagu-Nathan, both officers of the Society, were keen on promoting a substantial new ballet and turned to Lambert for suggestions. After tossing around various possibilities using the music of Berlioz and Chabrier, he turned to another of his favourite composers and came up with an idea that he first tried out on Freddie Ashton, writing in July 1935:

> I was up in London last night and pursued you from theatre to theatre like a symbolist foot chasing a courtesan and equally in vain. My object was to bore you with my new idea for a ballet. I quite agree that we should have at least one new ballet that is not drawn from the repertoire of another company and I think that a Liszt ballet by you would be the ideal thing. My idea for it will sound

---

[36] 24 January 1936.

a little odd put down on paper – principally because I have conceived it more from the visual and aural point of view than from the literary point of view. I want as far as possible to use only unknown pieces mostly from the latest period though I may allow you Valse Oubliée and Consolation as a sop to your feelings.

The genre is 1830 romanticism of the fruitiest type plus a leavening of surrealism. Though not in detail entirely original (it derives slightly from Bien-Aimée, Errante[37] and Mephisto Waltz) I think the conception as a whole will come quite freshly to the audience.

It will be a longish affair[.] 3 big scenes with a prologue and epilogue. The prologue and epilogue a super-Gothic poet's study, the 3 scenes respectively a ballroom with a Polish accent, a snow clad plain and a brothel. I think it will suit very well the style you developed in Valentine's Eve[38] and Mephisto[39] (actually my two favourite ballets of yours).

For that reason I think Sophie [Fedorovitch] might be the best person for the décor if she can be juicy enough. The ball scene and brothel scene want to be as like Constantin Guys[40] as possible – the rest should be a little more fantastic.

The man's part will suit Bobby very well and the woman's part will be ideal for either Spessiva or Fonteyn (whom to my great surprise you don't seem to appreciate at her true level. Though obviously immature at the moment she is to my mind the only post-Diaghileff dancer, with of course the exception of Toumanova, to have that indefinable quality of poetry in her work.)

You may of course not like the idea at all. But if you do I hope we will be able to spend some time on it going through the piece again and again and really moulding the ballet into shape. All the Wells ballets suffer not only from being put on too quickly but from being too cut and dried. The best Diaghileff ballets were always the result of a long and close collaboration between the artists and boring though this may be I am sure it is necessary.

I am coming back to London on Thursday week for Les Cent Baisers[41] and will stay up for a few days. Then, probably back to the country for a week and of[f] to London again on the first.

I should like to go through the thing roughly with you some time before I go on tour.[42]

The two of them had for some time wanted to do a Liszt ballet and they had gone through all the music that they liked. But now that Constant had come up with a libretto (based on Berlioz's *Symphonie fantastique*) that interested Ashton, he wrote to Keynes: 'I have at last hit on a scheme which I really think is good … a mingling of romantic themes from Berlioz, Gautier, Villiers, etc,' stressing that it was 'ideally suited to Fred'.[43] He warned Keynes that the project was likely to be a costly one as

[37] *La Bien-Aimée* was a ballet created by Nijinska in 1928. *Errante* was presented by Les Ballets 1933 in Paris, with choreography by Balanchine and using Schubert's *Wanderer-Fantasie*, transcribed by Liszt and orchestrated by Charles Koechlin.

[38] Produced by Ballet Rambert on 4 February 1935 using Ravel's *Valses nobles et sentimentales*.

[39] *Mephisto Waltz*, a ballet by Ashton using Liszt's *Mephisto Waltz No. 1* (the second of *Two Episodes from Lenau's Faust*), first staged at the Mercury Theatre on 15 March 1933.

[40] French realist painter and illustrator, 1802–92.

[41] First performed at Covent Garden by De Basil's Ballets Russes, 18 July 1935, with music by Frederic d'Erlanger, choreographed by Nijinska and reviewed by Lambert in the *Sunday Referee* on 21 July 1935.

[42] Letter from Lambert at Woodgate Cottage, Beckley, Sussex, to Ashton, n.d.: ROHCG Archive.

[43] 16 September 1935: Vaughan, *Frederick Ashton and his Ballets*, p. 133.

all the music, selected from Liszt's late piano works, would have to be orchestrated. As Constant was completing *Summer's Last Will and Testament* he would not be able to take on the task himself and he suggested Gordon Jacob. 'I don't know how he can be offered less than £50,' he added, and as either of the two designers he suggested, Fedorovitch or Tchelitchev, would be expensive, he asked if Camargo funds could be made available for this new ballet.[44] When it emerged that the Society's constitution did not allow its funds to be used so freely, a committee meeting was held and it was agreed that an appeal should be sent out to members. As a cost-cutting move, Keynes rejected Constant's suggestions for the designer and instead in December 1935 commissioned the fashion photographer Cecil Beaton, informing him that not much money was available and that the sets would have to be very simple, not just to keep costs down but because of the limited storage space at the Wells' theatre. Beaton accepted for a fee of £50, and on 13 December he, Lambert, Ashton and de Valois met to discuss the ballet which by then had been given the title *Apparitions*. It says a great deal for the Vic-Wells team work and the devotion and enormous energy of its leading figures – de Valois, Ashton, Helpmann and Lambert – that the first performance took place less than nine weeks later. Such was Lambert's practicality that when writing out the piano scores he would write them in separate scenes so that if necessary different scenes could be rehearsed in different venues at the same time.

Just as the *Symphonie fantastique*, 'an episode in the life of an artist' with its theme of idealised love, had been inspired by Berlioz's infatuation for the actress Harriet Smithson, so might the libretto of *Apparitions* be seen to represent an episode in the life of Constant who at that time was falling in love with Margot. Yet, as Kavanagh has pointed out, the image of Michael Somes was not far from Ashton's thoughts as he worked on the choreography, so the ballet's theme had a personal resonance for him too.[45] In an interview in later years, he recounted the origins of *Apparitions* as he remembered them:

> I used to go to his house at two o'clock and we both had this great passion for Liszt who was very unfashionable at that time, and we used to play over and over things and in a sense that was *Apparitions* which was this marvellous arrangement he made of Liszt's music. Then when the opportunity came it was the first ballet I did when I joined Sadler's Wells Ballet. ... And when I was engaged I said, 'Well let's do our Liszt' and so we did it, and there were certain tunes that I liked very much which he put in for me. I said, 'I must have this one, I must have that one,' and he was at that time also a tremendous admirer of Berlioz and I'm not sure that he didn't identify himself a great deal with Berlioz because Berlioz was somebody for whom things were always going wrong. He would give a huge concert and the whole platform would collapse, and all this sort of side of him appealed tremendously to Constant and he took, which I thought was rather surprising at the time, he took the theme from the *Fantastic Symphony* and put it into the ballet which we did for *Apparitions*.[46]

The budgeting and the various expenses, over which Lilian Baylis kept a close watch, make interesting reading. As well as Beaton's fee, some of the scenery was painted at a professional studio at a cost of £53, while those for two other scenes were executed at the Old Vic for £43, four stronger lamps needed for the Cave Scene added £30, Gordon Jacob was paid £75, and Constant put in a meagre claim for £5 – 'I am not

---

[44] This correspondence, summarised in *ibid.*, pp. 133–5, is preserved in the library of the Royal Ballet School at White Lodge.

[45] Kavanagh, *Secret Muses*, pp. 189–90.

[46] *In Search of Constant Lambert*, BBC2, 26 July 1965.

asking anything for the scenario or the arrangement of the music – but for expenses of buying music, etc.'[47] Beaton asked for the principals' costumes to be made by Barbara Karinska who at that time was working on his designs for a short ballet with Walton music, *The First Shoot*, in a Cochran revue, *Follow the Sun*. In the end Karinska made all the dresses for the Ballroom Scene and, in view of the extra expense, Beaton generously returned his fee. Keynes suggested to Samuel Courtauld[48] that they each contribute £50 to which Courtauld agreed[49] (although, as the costs mounted, Keynes increased his own contribution to £75)[50] and the Camargo Society gave £250[51] to which Lord Rothermere added £100.

Ashton was also much involved in *Follow the Sun*, which opened in Manchester in December 1935.[52] As well as providing the choreography, he had to dance with the leading lady for two and a half weeks when the advertised star, filming in Hollywood, was delayed; when he eventually arrived, Ashton had to rehearse him. This added more pressure to the preparations and rehearsals of *Apparitions*. There were other interruptions. One cold wintry morning in February the Company travelled by bus to Cambridge where they gave a gala performance to mark the opening of the Arts Theatre, largely the result of the enterprise of Maynard Keynes and his wife Lydia Lopokova. Leslie Edwards has described how later that evening, after a meal in a nearby hall, they boarded the buses again,

> joined once more by Miss Baylis, Miss de Valois, Constant Lambert, Frederick Ashton, Margot Fonteyn and Robert Helpmann who had been dining as guests of Lydia Lopokova and Maynard Keynes in the newly opened restaurant in the theatre. We all made our frozen way back to London. It was the early hours by the time we reached town and our respective homes but nevertheless we had to be hard at it the next morning, rehearsing *Apparitions*.[53]

Fonteyn, who as Constant had suggested was cast opposite Helpmann as the woman representing idealised love, remembered how chaotic the final rehearsal had been, 'for the costumes were nowhere completed and everyone was very tense'. Afterwards, in a taxi on the way to the photographer's studio, Ashton had told her 'everything that was missing' from her interpretation and she promptly burst into tears. Even on the opening night while the first ballet (*Les Rendezvous*) was being danced, 'taxis were rushing up to the stage door with great clumps of ball dresses in the arms of frantic seamstresses. ... Some were still lacking bits of decoration, though there were plenty of loose pins.' Yet despite all the difficulties, *Apparitions* proved a great success. As Fonteyn put it, 'from the confusion emerged a ballet of intangible beauty, a melancholy, haunting, laudanum dream'.[54]

---

[47] Letter from Constant Lambert to Miss Harvey at the Old Vic, 5 February 1936. See Appendix 1 for the piano pieces by Liszt that Lambert chose for *Apparitions*.

[48] Letter from J. M. Keynes to Samuel Courtauld, 12 December 1935. Samuel Courtauld (1876–1947) was an art collector, best known for founding the Courtauld Institute for Art in London in 1932.

[49] Letter from Samuel Courtauld to J. M. Keynes, 18 December 1935.

[50] Letter from J. M. Keynes to Lilian Baylis, 19 February 1936.

[51] Letter from J. M. Keynes to Lilian Baylis, 10 January 1936. The Camargo Society's financial assistance was acknowledged in several of the reviews.

[52] *Follow the Sun* opened at the Manchester Opera House on 23 December 1935 and went on to the Adelphi in London on 4 February 1936.

[53] Edwards, *In Good Company*, p. 40. Edwards incorrectly dates it as 1935. The gala performance in question was on 3 February 1936 and consisted of *Les Rendezvous*, *The Rake's Progress* and *Façade*.

[54] Fonteyn, *Autobiography*, pp. 67–8.

Beaton had left for New York before the opening night on 11 February, but Constant gave him a full account of the triumphant outcome:

> Apparitions, you will be glad to hear, is the biggest success we have ever had at the Wells. The dress-rehearsal was too depressing. Half the costumes were unfinished, the atmosphere was dead, and one felt the awful weight of middle-brow opinion against the whole thing. But when we opened, there was a most marvellous atmosphere in the house, everyone was silent during the intervals, and the ballet went over as a whole with real dramatic suspense all the time.
>
> The curtains at the end were astonishing. I am sure you would have been delighted with how your work looked. Karinska, although dreadfully behindhand, did the costumes superbly (the only one that was no good was the one made at the Wells which Karinska re-made at the last moment). The Galop in the Ballroom Scene is the most exciting thing I have ever known and the Funeral Procession was equally good in its way.
>
> Without in any way altering your basic lighting we found it necessary to get a little more light on the dancers' faces in some of the scenes. I am sure you would have agreed. The only other changes we made were: Ballroom Scene – lights right up for Galop, down again for Pas de Deux. (Incidentally there are the most lovely shadow effects on the right wing in the scene.) Snow Scene – black masks for *all* the corps de ballet. Some people criticised these costumes but I thought them most successful. The sun effect we cut out entirely and we had a darker light for the funeral. Cavern Scene – no skirts for the women. They bunched up and looked too much like interfering with the lines of the choreography. One of the girls lost her skirt at rehearsal and the effect was so much better, we decided to remove them. I am sure you would have agreed. Incidentally, the scene was not the anticlimax I had feared; it came off splendidly. Freddie's choreography is the best that he had done – even better than 'Baiser' and quite different.
>
> By the way, I forgot to tell you how excellently it was danced. Helpmann was really excellent and sustained, and Fonteyn looked ravishing throughout. Freddie decided to cut the wreaths in the last scene and brought the corps de ballet on as a kind of tragic frieze in the purple frocks from Tableau 2 – Fonteyn, of course, in her own dress. We used your wreath on the funeral bier. I can't tell you how glad I am that after all the trials the ballet should have come out so well, and I am only sorry your weren't there to share in our success. It was a real collaboration and everyone agrees that it knocks spots off any ballet since 'Cotillon'.[55]

On his return from America, Beaton saw *Apparitions* several times and, besides being delighted with his own work, thought the music 'of an impossible romanticism and beauty'. Of Fonteyn's dancing he wrote: '[It] makes one weep a little for here is a combination of extreme youth, tenderness, elegance and virtuosity.[56] The *New Statesman* critic was of a similar opinion, writing: 'Miss Margot Fonteyn dances better every time we see her, and we now believe her to be more promising even than any of M. de Basil's chosen team.'

In taking the story behind Berlioz's *Symphonie fantastique* as a basis for *Apparitions*, Constant made several important changes. The protagonist, instead of being a composer, is a poet working on a sonnet entitled 'L'Amour suprème' when three figures in turn appear before him: a hussar, a monk, and a woman in a ball dress. She becomes

[55] Letter from Lambert to Cecil Beaton, in Cecil Beaton, *Ballet* (London: Wingate, 1951), pp. 58–60. *Cotillon* was a ballet choreographed in 1932 by Balanchine to a score by Chabrier for both Colonel de Basil and his own company, Les Ballets 1933.

[56] From Beaton's diary, May 1936, quoted in Vickers, *Cecil Beaton*, p. 188.

the symbol of the supreme love he is trying to enshrine in his poem, but once she has vanished, in despair he takes laudanum and falls into an uneasy sleep. The first tableau is a ball scene in which the poet finds that the hussar is a rival for his idealised woman. The vision fades and in the second tableau the poet find himself on a snowy plain. Bells announce a funeral procession led by the monk. Lying on the bier is the woman in the ball dress. The third tableau takes place in a cave where guests at the ball have become grotesque members of some unholy cult. The poet is drawn into an orgy until the woman appears, herself transformed into some hideous creature that now pursues him. He collapses in exhaustion. In the epilogue the poet realises that his dreams are but a reflection of his own tragic life and he kills himself. Gently and sorrowfully, the woman and her companions enter and bear him away.

It was, as Constant told Beaton, the biggest success at the Wells. The critics were almost unanimous in their high praise, with headlines that ranged from 'Sadler's Wells Triumph' to 'Brilliant New British Ballet'. They were united in their praise for Fonteyn and in regretting that she did not have a longer dancing part.

* * *

1936 was the 50th anniversary of Liszt's death and it was this anniversary that brought about the friendship between Constant and the composer Humphrey Searle,[57] in retrospect an unlikely alliance as Searle was to become an atonalist. As a member of the Oxford Musical Club he had sung in an early performance of *The Rio Grande* conducted by Trevor Harvey with Joseph Cooper[58] playing the solo piano part and with Robert Irving on percussion, but in his last year as an undergraduate at Oxford it was the music of Liszt that drew them together. Searle's interest had been stirred by the piano pieces *Années de pélerinage*, by Constant's Liszt-based ballet *Apparitions*, and by reading Sacheverell Sitwell's biography.[59] (Reviewing that book, Constant might unwittingly almost have been writing his own epitaph when he said of Liszt that his 'greatness lay in his variety of purpose, in the way he squandered his gifts, in the way he would drop his own work to put his burning enthusiasm to the service of others.')[60] To mark the anniversary Searle decided to organise a concert in Oxford consisting chiefly of piano solos and duets. But he also formed a small orchestra so that he could include the *Malediction* for piano and strings that had not yet received a performance in England. Not having met Lambert, he wrote asking if he would be willing to conduct, adding that he would not be able to offer any payment by way of expenses. Constant replied promptly with some helpful suggestions about the programme:

Dear Mr Searle,

Your Liszt concert sounds most interesting – and if you think your local strings can manage Malediction I should be pleased to conduct it (if free). As

---

[57] Humphrey Searle (1915–82), Oxford-born composer who studied at the RCM and, privately, with Anton Webern in Vienna. His compositions, that included five symphonies, employed a serial technique.

[58] Pianist and broadcaster Joseph Cooper (1912–2001) is widely remembered today as chairman of BBC2's *Face the Music* quiz in which, amongst other things, members of the panel had to guess the piece of music he played on his 'dummy keyboard'. The first Oxford performance of *The Rio Grande* was on 2 June 1932 with Frank Merrick as piano soloist.

[59] Sacheverell Sitwell, *Liszt* (London: Faber & Faber, 1934). As Sitwell later wrote, 'It was [Kaikhosru Sorabji's] knowledge and love for the music of Liszt that certainly prompted me, my musical ignorance notwithstanding, to attempt a life of that greatest of all virtuosi in the history of music'. Park Lane Group concert programme, 7 December 1976. Sitwell acknowledged Lambert's help in reading the manuscript and Lambert reviewed the book for the *News Statesman and Nation* on 12 May 1934.

[60] Lambert, 'The Great Virtuoso', *The New Statesman and Nation*, 12 May 1934, p. 718.

regards the piano pieces I don't know the 4th Mephisto nor the czardas. The Mephisto-Polka is a poor piece hardly worth doing. The 3rd Mephisto on the other hand is a masterpiece and though almost impossible for two hands makes a good duet. I should also include Nuages Gris and some of the short later pieces. You can find the best of the later Liszt in vols. 9 and 10 of the collected edition. As regards the Boccherini ballet I should like to see it but doubt if any ballet less than twenty-five minutes is a practical proposition at the Wells.[61]

A month later he wrote again with further practical advice:

About the Liszt programme. It is a mistake to begin with *Nuages Gris,* one of the most experimental and quietest of his pieces. If I were you I should start off with the *Weihnachtsbaum.* As regards this I imagine you are only doing a few of the best. Some of the Christmas ones are very bad and I suggest you confine yourself to *Polnisch, Hongroise, Abendglocken, Carillon* and *Jadis* Any more would be a mistake. I am interested to see about the recitation which I am told is remarkable.

I see you are doing the *Chromatic Galop* and the other one. In this case I suggest getting hold of the version for 2 pianos 8 hands which is a riot. The programme as a whole is most interesting and I very much hope to be able to help you. The only thing that would prevent me would be fuss concerning the new ballet [*Prometheus*] at Sadler's Wells which comes on the next Tuesday. So it would be as well to have someone to stand by in case. Gordon Jacob has my Liszt vols. still. Perhaps you could get in touch with him direct.[62]

They met several times before the concert and Searle took up all Constant's suggestions. Robert Irving (who had been in Constant's conductors' class at the Royal College and was much later to be his successor at the Royal Ballet) was the soloist in the *Malediction.*[63] A week before the concert Constant wrote again:

I am so glad to hear that Malediction is going alright. I have decided to spend Sunday night at Oxford so you can put it at the end of the programme. What time do you want me to rehearse? Is there a good train in the morning? (I'm afraid it is Sunday and my ABC is hopelessly out of date). Perhaps there's a good train on which I could get lunch. Cecil Gray is staying at the King's Arms and I shall probably go there. I hope you get the Elegy in time. Malediction I am going through with Irving on Wednesday. I should be most obliged if you could let me know exact time & place of rehearsal also suitable train etc.[64]

The concert, on 8 November at the Carfax Assembly Rooms, was a great success. The *Grand galop chromatique* (on one grand and one upright piano) was, as Constant had predicted, a riot and had to be repeated. Among the audience were many of Constant's friends and colleagues, including Lord Berners, Cecil Gray, Gavin Gordon, and Sacheverell and Georgia Sitwell who brought with them the great Liszt interpreter

---

[61] 7 September 1936, Park Row. The Boccherini work was a 'Ballet Espagnol' of which Searle brought back a photocopy from Germany where he was studying. As Lambert suggested, it proved to be too short for the Vic-Wells Company.

[62] 5 October 1936. Lambert would have lent his Liszt volumes, marked up so that Gordon Jacob could orchestrate the pieces he had selected for *Apparitions.*

[63] Irving was in Lambert's Conductors' Class from December 1934 until February 1936, and on 31 March 1936 he was the soloist in Walton's *Sinfonia Concertante* with Reginald Goodall conducting the Royal College of Music Second Orchestra. In the Oxford concert, as well as soloist in the *Malediction,* he played *La Lugubre Gondola* and *Csárdás macabre* (a first performance). Other pianists were Sydney Watson, John Gardner and Humphrey Searle.

[64] Letter from Constant Lambert, 7 Park Row, London, 1 November 1936: BL Add 71838.

Louis Kentner and his pianist wife Ilona Kabos. Only a month earlier Constant had hailed Kentner in his *Sunday Referee* column as 'among the first half-dozen masters of his instrument, while as an interpreter of Liszt he is second only to Petri',[65] and he and Flo entertained him to dinner. Kentner in turn regarded Constant as 'an inspiring conductor with whom it was a joy to play a concerto, versatile and tolerant, and, above all, a great craftsman'. He described him as 'a sort of Renaissance character, like Benvenuto Cellini, perhaps … who could talk with fascinating bravura on almost any subject'.[66] The following April Constant conducted him in the first of many concerts they were to share, on this occasion a BBC studio programme that included Liszt's *Totentanz* and the *Spanish Rhapsody* arranged by Busoni.[67]

Acknowledging the cheque and the notices that Searle sent him, Constant replied: 'I am so glad the concert went so well and that the notices were so good. Do let me know if you succeed in getting copies of the Elegy & the 4th Mephisto.'[68] They remained good friends, as Searle wrote in a memoir:

> After joining the BBC in 1938 I saw Constant regularly, sometimes in The George pub in Mortimer Street – a real *rendezvous des artistes* in those days – and usually on Saturdays at lunch in the now defunct Casa Prada in the Marylebone Road, where we often had long conversations; sometimes I accompanied him back to what he called his 'shooting-box', a small lodge belonging to a big house in Park Road. Here we often played piano duets, Satie, Chabrier and others, on his curious mini-piano. We saw each other less often during the war – he was mostly touring with the ballet playing the music on two pianos with Hilda Gaunt, while I was in the army; but he did conduct the first performance of my *Night Music* for the newly formed Committee for the Promotion of New Music (now the SPNM) in 1944.[69]

Casa Prada was also a favourite dining place of Edward Clark and Elisabeth Lutyens, who wrote in her memoirs. 'How well I remember many happy evenings there: Constant Lambert's latest clerihew, Parry Jones's stories …, Dallapiccola reciting Dante … and Edward's resounding laugh ringing out.'[70] It was a second home for many musicians.

I N March 1936, while the Vic-Wells London ballet season continued with two programmes a week and one every other Saturday (alternating with opera), Constant conducted the Liverpool Philharmonic Orchestra in *Music for Orchestra* and *Job*. Three days later with the BBC Orchestra he had a studio broadcast that began with

---

[65] *Sunday Referee*, 11 October 1936. The headline ran: 'A new – and great – pianist comes to England'. Egon Petri (1881–1962) was particularly known as an interpreter of the music of Busoni and Liszt. After hearing him play the Busoni Piano Concerto at a BBC concert in February 1934, Lambert wrote: 'Here was the most important concerto ever written played by a man who is head and shoulders above any other living pianist – Egon Petri.' On 1 December 1938 Lambert conducted Petri in Mozart's Piano Concerto No. 23 and Liszt's Piano Concerto No. 2 with the Hallé Orchestra in Manchester.

[66] Letter from Louis Kentner to Mr K. Harvey Packer, 2 August 1978.

[67] 28 April 1937, BBC National Programme. The concert included the British premiere of Roussel's *Petite suite*, Op. 39. Kentner was also to perform several works by Lambert, including his Concerto for Piano and Nine Players, the Piano Sonata and shorter piano pieces, and together they gave both Liszt Concertos and Rawsthorne's First Concerto.

[68] Postcard from Lambert to Searle, postmarked 16 November 1936: BL Add 71838.

[69] 'Constant Lambert by Humphrey Searle, CBE', typescript, sent to Mr K. Harvey Packer.

[70] Lutyens, *A Goldfish Bowl*, p. 84.

one of his favourite pieces of 'interlude' music, Grétry's Overture *L'Épreuve villageoise*, and two pieces from his *Ruslan* Suite.[71]

In April he gave his two broadcast talks on jazz to which a young Malcolm Arnold was a fascinated listener.[72] George Barnes of the BBC had reported internally that Lambert 'was very keen about the idea and was full of suggestions. ... He would give the talks in a light-hearted manner and yet his name would carry sufficient weight with those who connect "jazz" with frivolity and sex appeal.' Constant may not have realised that he was helping the BBC out of a spot. As Barnes continued: 'There is no doubt that two such talks by Lambert would help solve one of our problems, *viz* how to go on replying evasively to the suggestions put forward by rhythm clubs, swing music enthusiasts, Duke Ellington fans, etc.' Up to that time it had been the Corporation's policy to forbid such talks. The only concession to BBC taste was that in Constant's original titles, 'The Origins of Jazz' and 'Jazz today', the words 'Dance Music' were substituted for 'Jazz'.[73]

Other occasional BBC studio concerts included *Music for Orchestra* again in April (slipping in *Paysage*, a work by his friend Hugh Bradford), the first performance of Giurne Creith's Violin Concerto with Albert Sammons on 19 May (including Warlock's Serenade for Strings), and on 14 June the first English performance of Magnard's Third Symphony[74] in a programme that also included the Handel-Lambert Piano Concerto and Walton's *Sinfonia Concertante* with Angus Morrison as soloist. One Saturday mid-April he was in Brighton for matinée and evening performances of ballet, and for the first week of June the Vic-Wells Company made its usual visit to Cambridge.

Later that month he conducted the RCM First Orchestra in a performance of Vaughan Williams' *A London Symphony*,[75] a work to which from time to time its composer was making small cuts. When he conducted it at a mainly Vaughan Williams Prom on 27 September 1934, Lambert wrote: 'The *London Symphony* has been many times revised since its first performance and on Thursday night two further cuts were made, one at the end of the second movement, and one in the Epilogue. Though the passages cut were among the best in the symphony, intrinsically speaking I think the composer has been wise. The fine slow movement has no hint of a longueur and the Epilogue is more in proportion with the quick section of the finale.'[76] At the Royal College performance on 12 June 1936 two new cuts had been made, one in the slow movement and one in the Epilogue. In *Music Ho!* Lambert had hinted at a similarity between this work and Debussy's *La Mer*, writing: 'The direct, or indirect influence of Debussy is to be found in such outwardly differentiated works as the ballets of Stravinsky and the operas of Schönberg, the *London Symphony* of Vaughan Williams and the *Chinese Symphony* of van Dieren ...'[77] A startled Vaughan Williams famously wrote in his *Musical Autobiography*: 'I was quite unconscious that I had cribbed from

[71] 26 March 1936. Grétry; Haydn, Symphony No. 85, 'La Reine'; Grieg, Symphonic Dances Nos. 2 & 4; Glinka, March and Oriental Dance from *Ruslan and Ludmila*.

[72] See Appendix 6.

[73] David Papp, 'Save me from a week in Bootle, Bolton or Bacup', *BBC Music Magazine*, September 2001, p. 50.

[74] Albéric Magnard (1865–1914). Magnard composed four symphonies. He was killed resisting the German invasion of his home in 1914. Lambert wrote that 'almost alone among French composers [Magnard] thought naturally in symphonic terms': *Radio Times*, 7 April 1939.

[75] 12 June 1936. Boyce, Symphony No. 4; Mozart, Violin Concerto No. 4 (Ralph Nicholson); Brahms, Piano Concerto in D minor (Jean Morris); and Vaughan Williams, *A London Symphony*.

[76] *Sunday Referee*, 30 September 1934.

[77] Lambert, *Music Ho!*, 2nd edn (1937), p. 24.

La Mer in the introduction to my *London Symphony* until Constant Lambert horrified me by calling my attention to it.'[78]

Bernard van Dieren died in April. Constant, who had always held him in the highest regard, reacted typically in his *Sunday Referee* column:

> The musical world has suffered a greater loss than it probably realises through the death, at the age of 52, of Bernard van Dieren. Although his music will probably never be 'popular' in the ordinary sense of the word, there is no doubt that the circle which appreciates it has increased very largely during the last few years. Among the composers who have obviously been influenced by him in the past are Busoni and Peter Warlock, and it seems likely that he will be one of the greatest influences on the music of the future.
>
> He had the most amazingly versatile mind I have ever encountered, and would have easily taken his place among the great names of the Renaissance. His knowledge of every branch of art and literature was phenomenal. More unexpected was his wide knowledge of science and medicine – he once earned his living manufacturing surgical instruments.
>
> Even though hampered by long and appallingly painful series of illnesses he still found time to show his expertness at carpentry, photography, and revolver-practice. Yet he was far from being a dilettante. As a musician he was a complete professional. His complex scores were written out in copper-plate handwriting without any previous sketches or work at the piano nor did any detail have to be altered later. If any question arose as to the practicality of any passage, he would always show the player exactly how it could be done. Future generations will undoubtedly see in him one of the most remarkable figures of our times.[79]

He was echoing Gray who, 12 years earlier, had written: 'He is not only one of the few composers of the present day whose achievement is intrinsically of great value, but also one who is destined to exercise a profound influence in the future.'[80] For both of them it was to prove a false prophesy. Nevertheless, Constant's enthusiasm for van Dieren's music remained undaunted and he helped promote a commemorative concert at the Aeolian Hall on 7 October. He wrote to Christian Darnton about a week before the concert:

> As you may have heard a few friends of van Dieren's are giving a concert of his works next week (leaflet enclosed). The soloists of course are giving their services but the orchestra is proving rather an expense. It is hoped that beside clearing expenses we may have something over for Frida [his widow][81] who is very hard up. I realise of course that like most of Bernard's friends you are none too well off yourself. At the same time I thought that as a great admirer of Bernard's work you might care to join those who are backing the concert. Anything from £1 to £5 would I assure you be very gratefully received. I hate writing begging letters of this sort but I am sure you will understand.[82]

---

[78] Foss, *Ralph Vaughan Williams*, p. 32, and Vaughan Williams, *National Music and Other Essays* (1963), p. 118.

[79] *Sunday Referee*, 26 April 1936. The following day he attended van Dieren's cremation at Golders Green.

[80] Gray, *A Survey of Contemporary Music*, p. 222, in which Gray devoted a chapter to van Dieren.

[81] Frida van Dieren (née Kindler, 1879–1964), pianist and pupil of Busoni. They were married in 1910.

[82] Letter to Christian Darnton, 30 September 1936.

When Darnton gave his support, Constant, who was rarely well-off financially himself, replied: 'Many thanks for the cheque. As a recognised authority on overdrafts I fully appreciate the gesture.'[83] Constant shared the conducting with Hyam Greenbaum.[84] Denis ApIvor, who was to become a strong advocate of van Dieren's music, was at the concert and remembered Antonio Brosa's brilliant playing of the Sonata for Solo Violin, but for him 'even more memorable ... was the shining and translucent sounds extracted from the players of van Dieren's *Spenser Sonnet*, under the direction of Constant Lambert, an effect which, like Beecham's magic with Delius, appears not to have been equalled since.'[85]

Constant's championing of van Dieren continued the following April when he conducted the comedy overture *Anjou*[86] and only the second performance of the *Chinese Symphony* (of which he had given the first in March 1935) in another memorial concert, this time at Broadcasting House.[87] Towards the end of his life, on the Third Programme he directed the *Serenata* as well as the *Sonetto VII of Edmund Spenser's Amoretti* and also gave a broadcast talk as one who had been a personal friend of the composer.[88] He spoke first of the legend surrounding the man, as 'perhaps the most esoteric composer of our time' who, 'caring little for society, above all musical society, frequently confined to his house for long periods owing to the wretched state of his health ... was hardly ever seen in public'. He continued in true journalistic fashion:

> Some people even began to doubt his existence, imagining the propaganda for his music to be an elaborate hoax. I myself have heard Dr Vaughan Williams propound the theory, how seriously or not I cannot say, that van Dieren was the joint invention of his two great disciples, Peter Warlock and Cecil Gray, as a cloak for their more unconventional works.

He summed up van Dieren's elusive style as follows:

> Technically speaking his harmonic idiom may come as something of a surprise to those who first read of him as an incomprehensible 'modern'. It is true that in his early days before the 1914 war his harmonic style was as unconventional as that of Schönberg's but in the course of years it became gradually clarified

---

[83] Letter to Christian Darnton, 5 October 1936. He had added: 'I shall be delighted to do all I can to "write up" the chamber concerts which look most interesting. How is the Shadwick quartet turning out? Well I hope.'

[84] The artists involved were Megan Foster, Kathleen Long, Antonio Brosa, Parry Jones, the International String Quartet, a choir, and a chamber orchestra. The works performed were a Prelude and Coda for String Quartet with Villon's *Prayer to Our Lady*, *Sonnet VII of Edmund Spenser* (Parry Jones and 11 instruments), Serenade (Serenata) for Nine Instruments, Violin Sonata, Op. 5, some songs, and *Sketch* for piano in place of four Heine songs which were to have been sung by John Goss who was prevented by illness from taking part.

[85] ApIvor, 'Memories of "The Warlock Circle"', p. 191. In *Music Ho!* Lambert rated van Dieren's *Sonetto VII of Edmund Spenser's Amoretti* alongside Sibelius's Seventh Symphony and Berg's Lyric Suite as among three of the masterpieces of his time.

[86] Van Dieren's comedy overture *Anjou* had received a first broadcast on 29 November 1935 with Warwick Braithwaite conducting.

[87] 9 April 1937, National Programme 'Contemporary Music – 6', with Margaret Goodley, Betty Bannerman, Bradbridge White, Henry Cummings, Stanley Riley, BBC Chorus, BBC Orchestra 'D'. Cecil Gray wrote an article, 'Van Dieren: The Modern Leonardo', for *Radio Times*, 2 April 1937, p. 6.

[88] Third Programme, 5 December 1949. Cecil Gray intended to include the script of this talk in the book on van Dieren that he was contributing to, with others under the editorship of John Goss, until his own death in the same year as Lambert's. It was never published.

until in the end, as Warlock his great disciple pointed out to me, 'In van Dieren's music now you find no chord that by itself cannot be found in the works of a composer like Fauré, but the chords are approached in such a way as to give an impression of complete novelty.' Van Dieren had no desire to hit the listener below the belt. What he steadily aimed at and eventually achieved was neither a heady romanticism or a chilly neo-classicism, but a balance between polyphony, harmony and form which is truly classic.

But his admiration was not just for the music but for the man[89]:

> His generosity extended itself not only to his contemporaries but also to a younger generation. He would willingly sacrifice hours of his increasingly valuable time to give the benefit of his advice and experience to any young composer, singer or instrumentalist whom he considered worth the trouble, as I myself know with undying gratitude. At first our relations were rather formal and professional but later I became an intimate friend and one of the happy few who saw him at such intervals as his health would allow. ... Too many people in the room upset his nerves and he preferred to see his friends singly or at the most in pairs. That is why I was usually alone with him on those memorable afternoons I spent with him in his small music room in Maida Vale, sparsely furnished and decorated only by his own superb book bindings.

Frida van Dieren appreciated Constant's devotion, and when in 1951 Denis ApIvor took her to his funeral, 'she wept throughout'.[90] Soon after van Dieren's death, the violinist André Mangeot had written to the editor of *Gramophone*, suggesting that recordings of his works should be made as soon as possible by people who had worked with the composer when he was alive. 'Let us have all the possible orchestral works conducted by Constant Lambert and the piano variations played by Mrs van Dieren,' he pleaded, but to no avail.[91]

N EAR the beginning of August 1936 the Vic-Wells Company embarked on a provincial tour that took in Birmingham, Manchester, Nottingham, Edinburgh, Glasgow and Newcastle-upon-Tyne, spending a week in each town. Constant had a habit when on tour of sending friends picture postcards to which he would add a humorous inscription, so from Birmingham he sent to Anthony Powell's wife, Lady Violet Pakenham, a postcard of a tapestry 'Love and the Pilgrim' designed by Sir Edward Burne-Jones and woven by William Morris & Co, in which a cloaked pilgrim is being helped from a thicket of brambles by the winged figure of love. On the reverse Constant wrote: 'Lady Vi (r.) introducing Mr Powell, the well known Welsh novelist (l.) to the beauties of the Irish landscape.'

When they reached Edinburgh, Constant gave a talk for the BBC Scottish Region on 'Diaghilev, Tchaikovsky and the Ballet'. He began his broadcast by diplomatically hinting that the Scots had a keener appreciation of ballet than the English, adding a truism that holds even today that when ballet is discussed or reviewed, the conductor is the last person to be mentioned – if he is mentioned at all. This is something that he

---

[89] Arnold Bennett wrote, after meeting van Dieren on 3 January 1927: 'Looks frail and good-humoured and a bit sardonic. A marvellous brain. He indulged in an argumentative scrap with Bliss, who also is very intelligent, and beat him hollow. ... I liked van Dieren very much; or rather I admired him very much.' *The Journals of Arnold Bennett* (Harmondsworth: Penguin Books, 1954), p. 419.

[90] ApIvor, 'Memories of "The Warlock Circle"', p. 196.

[91] *Gramophone*, June 1936, p. 43.

clearly felt keenly himself, especially when he played such a strong part in shaping each ballet from conception to performance.[92]

> One of the pleasant features of coming to Scotland with the Vic-Wells Ballet and the Vic-Wells Orchestra is to know that the musical side of the ballet will be both appreciated and criticised at its true worth. Though London, with its enormous number and variety of concerts, may rightly be considered the musical centre not only of Britain, but Europe, there is no doubt that the further North you go the more musical appreciation you meet with generally speaking. This factor may not have worried the ballet conductor of a hundred years ago when music was little more than an amiable accompaniment to the dancing, praised if it helped a certain ballerina to display her particular branch of technical proficiency, and ignored if it did not. But it is a highly important factor to the ballet conductor of today when the music is, or should be, recognised as being an integral part of the art of the ballet, hardly less important than the choreography itself.

He had to leave the Company at Glasgow to conduct a studio broadcast in London on 1 September in which he gave the first broadcast performance of his edition of *The Power of Music*, then attributed to William Boyce but now ascribed to John Stanley. The programme also included Fauré's incidental music to *Shylock*, Dargomizhsky's Fantasia on Finnish Themes[93] and the complete ballet score for *Pomona*. Four days later he conducted *King Pest* at the Proms.

The provincial tour ended at Newcastle on 12 September, allowing only ten days before the opening of their autumn season in Rosebery Avenue. The first night found the Company in top form. 'The orchestra, directed by Mr Constant Lambert, played excellently so that it was possible to listen as well as to watch with pleasure,' reported *The Times*. The opening of the new season prevented Constant from conducting *The Rio Grande* at the Proms that same evening, Leslie Woodgate taking his place with Angus Morrison and Betty Bannerman the soloists.[94] Two new ballets were given this season. The first was *Prometheus*, on 13 October, with choreography by de Valois to Constant's arrangement of the Beethoven score. The costumes and scenery were designed by John Banting, who had been responsible for *Pomona*. But more significant was *Nocturne*, first given on 10 November at a gala premiere in aid of Queen Charlotte's Maternity Hospital, using Delius's evocative score *Paris* (subtitled 'The Song of a Great City'). In a programme note, Constant wrote:

> Delius's *Paris* is described by the composer as a Nachtstück or Nocturne. It is this aspect of the music rather than the purely local aspect, that has been stressed by the artists responsible for the present production. They have made no attempt at a realistic evocation of Paris itself. Instead, they have concentrated on a human drama to which the night life of a great city forms the background.

The ballet had arisen from an idea by Edward Sackville-West that Ashton developed in consultation with Lambert who at first had been opposed to the Delius score being

---

[92] A good example is M. H. Middleton's article on Lambert's 1946 presentation of *The Fairy Queen* at Covent Garden in 1946 and 1947, *Ballet Annual 2* (London: A. & C. Black, 1948), pp. 141–2. Despite the fact that he devised and conducted the whole production, Lambert receives no mention at all.

[93] Alexander Sergeyevich Dargomizhsky (1813–69) was a nationalist Russian composer who, as Lambert pointed out in *Music Ho!* (2nd edn (1937), p. 40), made rare use of the whole-tone scale in his opera *The Stone Guest*.

[94] On 20 April 1936, when the BBC Symphony Orchestra was on a European tour (planned by Edward Clark), Adrian Boult conducted *The Rio Grande* at the Salle Pleyel, Paris with Clifford Curzon.

used, as he felt that essentially symphonic music was not suited to balletic treatment.[95] He had made known his dislike of Massine's use of Brahms's Fourth Symphony for *Choreartium* and Tchaikovsky's Fifth for *Les Présages*. Notwithstanding his lack of sympathy for Brahms, he described the former ballet as 'a deplorable example of Massine's latest Roxy-cum-Delacroze manner', adding that 'in these two would-be symphonic works he has put back the whole art of ballet by many years'. In doing so he incurred Massine's wrath to such an extent that a battle of words between the two was waged in the *Sunday Referee* for several weeks.[96] One fault that could perhaps be fairly laid at Lambert's door was not knowing when to drop an argument. He was to raise the matter again two years later in an article he wrote for a book assembled by Caryl Brahms and called *Footnotes to The Ballet*. 'Is it less of an outrage,' he asks, 'when Massine represents the personal tragedy which lies behind the slow movement of Tchaikovsky No. 5 by a bogy-man with pantomime wings breaking in on a pair of lovers?'[97]

If he had been at least outwardly incensed by certain works being presented in ballet form, he relented in the case of *Paris*, partly because of his love of Delius's music but also because it appealed to the Francophile in him, especially when the backcloth offered a view that looked across the French capital. P. W. Manchester thought it 'one of the most wholly satisfying ballets arranged to existing music' and 'one of the very few ballets where ears and eyes are engaged in equal degrees' with costumes that were 'an inspiration'.[98] Set in Montmartre, the principal characters were a spectator, a young man, a rich girl and a poor flower girl – Ashton, Helpmann, June Brae and Margot Fonteyn (according to *The Times* 'admirably pathetic and looking like one of Manet's models'). Sophie Fedorovitch was responsible for the scenery and costumes, 'bringing to her work a certain mystical, evocative quality that no other designer ever quite matched,' recalled Fonteyn in her autobiography. It may have taken the orchestra a little time to settle into the Delius score, because the *Times* critic reported that on the first night 'the orchestral playing, under Mr Constant Lambert's direction, was less good than usual – the main theme was so inaccurately stated at its first appearance as to be hardly recognisable – but Delius's music is extraordinarily difficult to get at once precise and supple, and perhaps more rehearsal was needed than could be allowed.'[99] But Fonteyn had little difficulty getting into her new role, the third to be created for her.[100] '*Nocturne* was a glorious ballet for me,' she proclaimed in her autobiography. 'How completely I could lose myself in the heart of the poor Flower Seller, cast aside without thought by the Rich Young Man. I lived the story through anew at each performance.' As she herself recognised, *Apparitions* and *Nocturne* were 'the two ballets which put me on the crest of the wave'.[101]

(It was at a rehearsal of *Nocturne* on tour in Manchester just before the war that Constant showed, as always, that he was a man of the theatre. 'No, no, no!' he exclaimed to the Young Girl. 'If you put your hand there not a single member of the

---

[95] He elaborated on this theme in his article 'Music and Action'.

[96] The correspondence between Lambert and Massine ran in the 8 July, 29 July, 5 August and 12 August 1934 issues of the *Sunday Referee*.

[97] Lambert, 'Music and Action', p. 164.

[98] Manchester, *Vic-Wells*, p. 34.

[99] *The Times*, 11 November 1936. Eric Fenby, Delius's amanuensis, had warmer recollections of that premiere, writing: 'I recall the skilful doubling for reduced forces on that occasion, and how well the music was played in the pit': *Delius Society Journal*, April 1976, p. 22.

[100] The first had been the young bride in *Le Baiser de la fée* (26 November 1935) and the second the woman in the ball dress in *Apparitions* (10 March 1936).

[101] Fonteyn, *Autobiography*, pp. 70–1, 67.

stalls will be able to see your face. Push that hand into *my* face in the orchestra pit and then everyone will be able to see you.')

Just as Constant had been Helpmann's 'educator', so Fonteyn now turned to him in the hope of becoming less of the 'ignoramus' she found herself in the artistic company she was now placed. As Helpmann later acknowledged: 'Constant was one of the greatest influences on Fonteyn's life: he developed her tastes not only in painting but in literature, as he indeed did mine.' In her autobiography, as well as expunging any memories of her affair with Constant, when writing about her process of becoming better educated she did not name the one person who was largely responsible for bringing about this transformation:

> I began reading madly, and at random, all the classics I could lay hands on. Admirers were regarded first and foremost as a source of literary or musical information, to the point where I liked most the young man who could lend me the best books and records. Among other more suitable works he lent me James Joyce's *Ulysses*, which was at that time banned in Britain. De Valois boarded my bus one day as I was reading it on the way up Rosebery Avenue to Sadler's Wells. 'What's that, dear?' she asked, peering over at the book. She practically had a heart attack when she saw what it was. 'For God's sake, child, don't read that in public, you could be arrested!'[102]

Pamela May identified this educator: 'Ninette was hysterically funny about it. And a bit cross. "I'll bet it was Constant who gave it to you," she said. "If you must read it, take it home and read it there."'[103] May described Constant as Margot's guru, he feeding her with books and she keen to learn. The whole company were in awe of Constant's encyclopaedic knowledge of the arts. The ever tactful Leslie Edwards commented: 'He was a musical director such as one's rarely known. A great man. Terribly knowledgeable. And Margot was a very young girl. We all shared in his marvellous geniality. You could go to him and ask him questions about music. I remember him recommending books to read. I'm sure Margot's great love of reading stemmed from that time.'[104] Quite often during breaks in rehearsals she would be seen reading a work of literature that Constant had put on her list.

But beside guiding her artistic education, Constant was to have a profound influence on Fonteyn's development as a dancer, creating ballets with her in mind and suggesting roles for her to de Valois and Ashton. Although she was later to maintain a discreet silence about their close personal relationship – and indeed would hardly mention Constant's name at all – she clearly felt entirely safe when he was conducting (as did all the dancers), as she revealed in interview after his death in a rare breach of that silence:

> What I think he established so marvellously was that the music was the most important of the two between dancing and music, that we danced to the music and the conductor did not follow the dancers. He of course had the advantage; he had a marvellous sense of rhythm which is really essential to someone conducting for ballet. He knew how the music should go, he would be aware of what the dancers could do if they tried and he would know if he were really pushing us too far, and after that he was really – well – severe with us. One would definitely think twice about saying, 'Oh, could you take that piece a little slower?' – or a little quicker or something because you would be likely to get a

---

[102] *Ibid.*, p. 72.
[103] Daneman, *Margot Fonteyn*, p. 104.
[104] *Ibid.*, p. 103.

very sharp answer and be put very firmly in your place and told that was the way the music went and you danced it at that tempo and he certainly wasn't going to change the music to suit you and we were lucky we hadn't got Sir Thomas Beecham who would take it five times as fast as he did. ... But of course he could do it because he also did have this great sensitivity to the dance itself and if he saw someone getting into trouble with the music he always saved the situation and made it all right. He himself composed some of the ballets which were performed. That is a luxury that we have not had since. In fact as conductor-composer, the scores he composed were excellent for ballet and again that he understood so well the dramatic needs and the musical needs.[105]

Although Constant was to become an increasingly heavy drinker, it is said that he never drank before a performance in which Margot had a principal role.

The day after the premiere of *Nocturne*, the Vic-Wells Company ventured into a new medium. The BBC's first television programme from Alexandra Palace had gone out on 26 August 1936 and the official opening of a regular service took place on 2 November, alternating each week between the Baird and the Marconi-EMI systems. Nine days later the Vic-Wells Company made its first television appearance with Helpmann, Chappell and Somes among the dancers performing 25 minutes from *Job*.[106] This was done twice, at 3.35 and 9.35 p.m. Unfortunately, in those early days, only those living in the vicinity with a set would see these broadcasts, but the Company was to appear quite often. Hyam Greenbaum was appointed conductor of the Television Orchestra, and on most occasions he conducted and not Constant, who on this particular day had two engagements elsewhere, with the RCM Second Orchestra and Conductors' Class and an evening broadcast, both sharing Elgar's *Froissart* Overture and Sibelius's *King Christian II* Suite.

---

[105] Margot Fonteyn interviewed by Tom Driberg at the Royal Ballet School, Hammersmith for *In Remembering Constant Lambert (1905–1951)*, BBC Radio 3 portrait of Lambert presented by Driberg, 23 August 1975.

[106] Marie Rambert's was the first ballet company to appear on this regular service, on 5 November 1936.

14 1937–8
Checkmate and Horoscope

C ONSTANT'S first concert in 1937, on 2 January, was a broadcast to mark the centenary of one of his favourite composers, Balakirev.[1] Two days later came one of the highlights of his conducting career when for the first time he was invited by Sir Thomas Beecham to direct an opera at Covent Garden. The invitation inspired a short piece of verse:

> Though at last I've been honoured by Beecham
> I still may fall short of the prize
> Through war, epidemic, a fire in the theatre
> Riot or Royal Demise.[2]

It was in keeping with his musicianship that he was not in charge of a familiar score but of what was then a lesser known example of the Puccini canon, *Manon Lescaut*, that had not been heard there for ten years. The *Times* critic was complimentary:

> Last night's performance was competent rather than brilliant, and the chief credit for its good qualities must go to Mr Constant Lambert who was making his first appearance at Covent Garden. Mr Lambert kept the music always in motion and got the swing of Puccini's rhythms with their passionate onrush towards a held note. The climax of Act III was in particular splendidly done. If he was inclined at first to allow the orchestra to overwhelm the singers, that is only another way of saying that the voices were not always strong enough for the music.[3]

Francis Toye in the *Morning Post* was equally congratulatory: 'His interpretation had the great merit of bringing out all the life of the score. He played the music as if he loved (as I am sure he does) every bar of it; and that is the only way to do proper justice to Italian music in particular.' Even critic and recording manager Walter Legge noted that 'Lambert conducted with considerable skill and power.'[4] The soloists were Augusta Oltrabella, Pietro Menescaldi (both new to England), with Dennis Noble as Lescaut. There were only three performances and Angus Morrison was in the audience for the first night.[5] Constant was to conduct very little opera, the only other occasions being Purcell's *Dido and Aeneas* at the Old Vic in 1931 and, at Covent Garden, Puccini's *Turandot* in 1939 and 1947, and Purcell's *The Fairy Queen* in 1951.

On 14 January he was in charge of a typically unorthodox programme for the Royal Philharmonic Society at Queen's Hall that included Weber's *Ruler of the Spirits* Overture, two works for saxophone by Glazunov and Debussy, and, as a late anniversary gesture, *Two Faust Episodes* by Liszt. The *Times* critic, who disliked the saxophone as an instrument, which he thought sounded at its best 'like a badly-voiced

---

[1] 'A Centenary celebration under the direction of M. D. Calvocoressi', the fifth in a series of programmes on Balakirev: Overture on a Russian Theme; Incidental Music *King Lear*; Preludes to Acts 3 and 4, *A Song of Georgia* (Edward Reach, tenor); Symphonic Poem *En Bohème*.

[2] Shead, *Constant Lambert*, p. 115.

[3] *The Times*, 5 January 1937.

[4] Walter Legge, 'An Autobiography', p. 52, in Elizabeth Schwarzkopf, *On and Off the Record: A Memoir of Walter Legge* (London: Faber, 1982; paperback 1988).

[5] 4, 7 and 12 January 1937.

organ reed-stop on an uneven wind pressure', felt that the four composers were not shown at their best. But the Walton symphony, with which the concert ended, was a different matter. 'There were some rough details in the playing, but Mr Constant Lambert, who knows the work through and through, obtained an admirably vivid performance.' (Considering his standing as a conductor, it is perhaps surprising that he had to wait until January 1946 to be invited to conduct again for the Society.) While the programmes for Constant's concerts and broadcasts generally reflected his own preferences, occasionally a work with which one might not expect him to be in sympathy would be slipped in, such as Stanford's *Down among the Dean Men* that was included in a National Programme broadcast a fortnight later, with Maurice Cole as soloist.[6] He was more at home with the Walton symphony to which he returned for a Sunday broadcast with the BBC Orchestra at the end of February.[7]

Following her retirement as a dancer, Lydia Lopokova was pursuing a career as an actress and she planned to appear in Molière's *Le Misanthrope* as Célimène at the new Arts Theatre, Cambridge in February 1937. Because the play was quite short, her husband Maynard Keynes had invited Ashton to choreograph a ballet called *Harlequin in the Street* as a curtain-raiser. Rameau's *Fêtes d'Hebé* was suggested for the music, and Constant was asked to extract something suitable and arrange it for two harpsichords. But André Derain, who was to design the set and the costumes,[8] thought Rameau unsuitable and suggested Lully instead. Constant was not happy with the change and wrote to Keynes: 'Rameau has wit and humour and, above all, good dancing rhythm ... my impression is that Lully is inclined to sound a little "etiolated", as my dentist would say, whereas Rameau still retains his original savour.'[9] Eventually it seems that a compromise was reached with some pieces by Couperin arranged by Constant for two pianos. But the production was not a success at Cambridge, so when it transferred later that month to London further changes were made: the ballet was enlarged and the pianos replaced by an orchestra. Much later it was further expanded and *Harlequin in the Street* became a popular ballet in the Vic-Wells repertoire.

What was to become one of the Company's most successful ballets, *Les Patineurs*, had its first staging on 16 February. The idea had been Constant's after seeing an old programme advertising a ballet *Les Plaisirs de l'hiver; ou Les Patineurs* at Her Majesty's Theatre in 1849. (Always ready to find something humorous, Constant wrote on the programme 'With the maledictions of the "Old Master"' and underlined the name of Mr Sloman, who was responsible for the stage machinery for this production.)[10] He selected the music for this one-act ballet-divertissement from Meyerbeer's operas *Le Prophète* and *L'Étoile du nord*, and, as Leslie Edwards has written, from a dancer's point of view he had 'shaped it perfectly, as always, to suit each episode in the work, from the entrance of the skating couples to the exciting finale'.[11] It had originally been intended for de Valois to choreograph and after a matinée Constant was playing her the music in

[6] A recording of this performance exists in the National Sound Archive, T11657W2.

[7] 28 March 1937, also including Meyerbeer, Overture *Struensee*; Balakirev, *Russia*; and Delius, *Walk to the Paradise Garden*.

[8] According to Alexander Bland, *The Royal Ballet: The First Fifty Years* (New York: Doubleday & Co., 1981), p. 54, Dérain's 'memorable backdrops and costumes [were] fated to be discarded and painted over during the war'.

[9] Quoted in David Chadd and John Gage, *The Diaghilev Ballet in England*, programme book for an exhibition at the 45th Norfolk and Norwich Triennial Festival of Music and the Arts (Norwich: University of East Anglia, 1979), p. 61.

[10] Kavanagh, *Secret Muses*, p. 208

[11] Edwards, *In Good Company*, p. 53.

the conductor's room which was next to Ashton's dressing-room. When Ashton heard its well-pointed rhythms he instinctively felt that it was a ballet that suited him and, as it turned out, de Valois was at that time too busy with administrative matters, so she agreed to his taking it on. William Chappell designed the scenery and costumes. In May it was televised from Alexandra Palace with Hyam Greenbaum conducting the BBC Television Orchestra.[12]

In March Constant and Freddie Ashton were guests at Faringdon, the country house of Lord Berners, working with him on his new ballet, *A Wedding Bouquet*, a whimsical satire on the social conventions of marriage, for which he not only composed the music but also designed the sets. The idea had arisen over a lunch that Constant had with de Valois, Ashton and Berners. The story was based on a play by Gertrude Stein called *They Must. Be Wedded. To Their Wife*, and the libretto was the result of several enjoyable and luxurious weekends that Constant and Freddie spent at Faringdon. Berners had met Stein the previous summer, and while much of the score had been completed by the time of these meetings, it was 'brilliant and lovable Constant in charge of the music and the frenetic libretto', as Billy Chappell put it.[13] He was already familiar with Stein's work, writing prophetically in *Music Ho!* that 'writers like Gertrude Stein are aiming at rhythmic patterns and formal arrangements of sound that would have far more weight if expressed in musical form' and he quoted a typical Stein line from *Helen Furr and Georgine Skeene*: 'Everyday they were gay there, they were regularly gay there everyday'.[14]

Only a very small part of Stein's play was used, and the words, sung by a small chorus in period costume standing on the stage, form more of a witty commentary than a narrative link. Leslie Edwards found the rehearsals fascinating:

> They were attended in the final stages by Gertrude Stein and her friend Alice B. Toklas, who always followed three paces behind in a large, shady hat. Gertrude Stein, a very distinctive figure with her well-sculptured head topped with a grizzled Eton crop, seemed to favour wearing waistcoats, her thumbs firmly placed in the pockets. Lord Berners would sit at the piano with Constant Lambert while he hammered out a point or two of the score, and for me it was riveting to see this work in progress with such dynamic personalities. I admired the whole production, with members of the company dancing every role, whether large or small, to perfection.[15]

Fonteyn played Julia, the slightly demented guest who is seduced by the bridegroom (Helpmann), while de Valois was the maid Webster (her last role as a dancer). P. W. Manchester described how the scenario-cum-libretto was 'bellowed enthusiastically if at times incomprehensibly' by the chorus and that 'it was all terrific fun, in which audience and dancers joined'.[16] While *A Wedding Bouquet* did not have the immediate appeal of *Les Patineurs*, it was still a success. After the first performance on 27 April, conducted by Constant, there was a party at the Regent's Park home of Alice

---

[12] One of several ventures by the Vic-Wells Company into the television studios at this time was in March 1937 when the 'BBC made a film consisting of episodes from the final section of *Façade* for use as part of an exhibition film to be lent to television-set dealers': Clarke, *The Sadler's Wells Ballet*, pp. 125–6. It is not clear whether Lambert or, more likely, Greenbaum conducted.

[13] Haskell *et al.*, *Gala Performance*, p. 53.

[14] Lambert, *Music Ho!*, 2nd edn (1937), pp. 94, 66.

[15] Edwards, *In Good Company*, p. 54.

[16] Manchester, *Vic-Wells*, p. 36.

von Hofmannsthal,[17] with Gertrude Stein as a special guest. During the war, when it became difficult to muster a chorus, Constant had the idea of reciting the words himself. At least one critic had commented at the premiere that so few of the chorus lines were audible, so this new rendition clearly solved two problems. As David Vaughan has explained, Constant did it

> seated at a table to one side of the stage, sipping champagne and keeping an eye on the action. This was much more successful because the words, in his clear and caustic delivery, were finally audible; when the ballet was revived at Covent Garden after the war it was again possible to have the singing chorus, but soon afterwards the spoken narration was restored, from choice rather than necessity.[18]

Giselle and *A Wedding Bouquet* ended the season on 8 May, and for Coronation Week the Vic-Wells Company were off to Bournemouth for six days and then back at Rosebery Avenue. Constant conducted, although he had to miss one Bournemouth performance and the opening night of the new season because of studio broadcasts.[19] On such occasions either Joseph Chadwick, the leader, or John Fisher, viola, took over. Watching a Coronation firework display out at sea, Constant was heard to observe that 'the mass of stars falling from the rockets made the sky seem full of incandescent tresses of eighteenth-century wigs, their beauty being reflected in the sea'.[20]

After three evenings of ballet at Sadler's Wells, Constant enjoyed a relaxing Sunday at Cecil Beaton's Wiltshire home, Ashcombe, with Rex Whistler, Edith Olivier, Princess Marie of Luxembourg, Juliet Duff and David Herbert. 'Constant is *such* good company,' Edith recorded in her diary.[21] Five days later he conducted the Sadler's Wells Orchestra in a Nijinsky Gala Matinée at His Majesty's Theatre. Vaslav Nijinsky was in a Swiss nursing home, 'suffering from severe mental strain' as the press delicately reported it,[22] and the gala had been organised to raise money for his nursing expenses. With his friendship with Nijinska, Nijinsky's sister, Constant was only too willing to help arrange the gala. The Ballet Rambert, the Markova-Dolin Ballet (with Dolin but without Markova who was unable to appear because of a damaged foot) and the Sadler's Wells Ballet all performed, and there were solos from Lydia Sokolova and Serge Lifar. Tamara Karsavina, who had specially made the journey from Budapest, spoke a few words at the end of the afternoon's programme, and Fonteyn and Helpmann danced the *Pas de deux* from *Pomona* which the Company took with them in a new production to

[17] Born Ava Alice Muriel Astor in 1902, Alice was married four times, each ending in divorce: to Prince Oblensky in 1924, to Raimund von Hofmannsthal (the only son of Hugo von Hofmannsthal) in 1933, to Philip Harding in 1940, and to David Pleydell-Bouverie in 1946. She died in 1956.

[18] Vaughan, *Frederick Ashton and his Ballets*, pp. 152–3.

[19] 11 May 1937 National Programme: 'British Ballet Music' – *Pomona*, *The Rake's Progress*, *Façade*. (*Radio Times* credited the 'fine work' that Lambert was doing at Sadler's Wells.) 17 May 1937 Regional programme: Bizet, *L'Arlésienne* Suite No. 2; Busoni, *Indian Rhapsody* (Mark Hambourg); Lambert, *Music for Orchestra*.

[20] Edwards, *In Good Company*, p. 56.

[21] Entry for 23 May 1937. Penelope Middleboe, *Edith Olivier: From her Journals, 1924–48* (London: Weidenfeld & Nicolson, 1989), p. 193. Edith Maud Olivier (1872–1948), daughter of a Wiltshire rector, was a writer and diarist whose friends included many artistic and social figures, especially her protégé, the painter Rex Whistler.

[22] Nijinsky had had a nervous breakdown in 1919. He was diagnosed with schizophrenia and taken to Switzerland for treatment. He spent the rest of his life in hospitals and asylums, dying in London in April 1950.

Cambridge at the end of May.[23] There had been plans for Constant's *Romeo and Juliet* to be presented that same month by the Markova-Dolin Ballet, produced by Nijinska, but they came to nothing.[24]

The May visit to the Cambridge Arts Theatre was becoming an annual feature in the Company's calendar, and it was there that Margot first met her future husband, the Panamanian Tito Arias, who was a Cambridge undergraduate studying economics. It was a meeting that she romantically describes in her autobiography as being for her part one of love at first sight. Yet, as she wrote, 'it was obvious that his feelings were nothing like mine were for him', and after he had sailed home for his long vacation Margot began to wonder whether it had been mistaken love, and when she saw him again the following May at Cambridge her 'heart had hardened by a small but perceptible amount'. They briefly met twice in Paris later that year but, as she diplomatically put it, 'I had other companionable friends and admirers by now so I doubt whether anyone knew of my secret love for Tito.' Whatever the true depth of her feelings, 12 years were to pass before she heard from him again when she was on tour in America in 1950 – a single telephone call that was not followed as promised by another the next day. In fact they were not to meet for a further three years until September 1953 during the third American tour when a then married Arias presented himself during an interval in a performance of *The Sleeping Beauty*. The next morning, over a late breakfast, he suggested that they married. 'My wife will divorce me,' he added. Their wedding eventually took place in February 1955 at the Panamanian Consulate in Paris. Yet behind the glamour it was to be a sad relationship, with Arias increasingly relying on Margot's earnings, not only to support his extravagant life-style and his infidelities, but to finance his political intrigues that included his ill-fated coup against the Panamanian government of President Ernesto de la Guarda. When he died Margot was left effectively penniless. She herself died 15 months later.

If Arias's presence at Cambridge had sent Margot's 'world quivering', his entrance into her life was not to affect the affair she was having with Constant, and there were to be others before Arias claimed her. In the meantime the Company were off to Paris to take part in the Exposition Internationale des Arts et Techniques dans la Vie Moderne, to give the Paris Exhibition its full title. A new ballet with music by Bliss was in the programme.

'Dear Ninette,' Arthur Bliss had written towards the end of 1936, 'can you dine next Wednesday eight o'clock with Mr Ernst Makower [of the British Council] and myself at 75 Brook Street – to discuss a ballet for the forthcoming Paris exhibition? ... This is important and I hope you can manage it.'[25] This was the birth of *Checkmate* which was to be one of the most dramatic ballets in the Vic-Wells repertoire and the first of

[23] On 10 June 1937 in a short recital programme for BBC television that also featured Sidonie Goossens, Fonteyn danced a solo described in *Radio Times* as 'an extract from a new ballet by Constant Lambert, on which he is now working' and which was dedicated to the dancer: Vaughan, *Frederick Ashton and his Ballets*, p. 156. This may have been something from his forthcoming ballet *Horoscope* (which was dedicated to Fonteyn), or the 'Pastorale' from *Pomona*.

[24] In a letter to Miss Lynne, dated 14 April 1937, Hubert Foss confirmed the rights for the Markova-Dolin Ballet to produce Lambert's *Romeo and Juliet*, produced by Nijinska, for three performances during May and a further two performances each week for September to December 1937 at a London theatre. Two days later Foss was informed that 'owing to the shortage of time Nijinska has now decided she cannot do full justice to the production before the winter season' (letter heading of Vivian Van Damm Productions Ltd, of which Markova was a director): OUP files.

[25] Undated letter, Vic-Wells Archives.

the three ballet scores written by Bliss that Lambert was to premiere.[26] The Company had been invited to take part for one week in June in the 1937 Paris World Fair that ran from May to November, their appearance being followed by five nights of Bernard Shaw's *Candida*. When their participation was first mooted, Ninette de Valois wrote to Lilian Baylis: 'Ernst Makower tells me that he can arrange for the Vic-Wells Ballet to be presented by the British Council for 1 week in June next year. We would have to give 3 performances of all-English ballets and they want "The Rake" & Walton's "Façade" coupled with the 1st performance of a new ballet of Arthur Bliss.' When it was decided that they could take six ballets, Geoffrey Toye suggested *Façade, The Rake's Progress, Apparitions, Nocturne*, the new commission by Arthur Bliss, and his own *Les Douanes* that Ninette had not only choreographed but also taken the leading role. But the organising committee favoured Constant's *Pomona*, instancing de Valois's 'prejudice against dancing in *Douanes* in Paris',[27] something that she herself explained to Toye in January: 'Under the circumstances, with the number of excellent young dancers we have to show it is quite impossible that I as director should monopolise one entire ballet,' adding that '*Douanes* and *The Haunted Ballroom* meet with great success in their native theatre, but neither of them proved a success on our English tour.'[28] Lilian Baylis reasoned with Toye: 'At the moment Constant Lambert is very much before the musical world, and I do realise that the inclusion of *Pomona* should prove popular, especially as it can be adequately cast, which we do not feel that *Douanes* could be. Cambridge has specially asked for *Pomona*, so that it will entail additional rehearsals for Paris.'[29] Because *Les Patineurs* was a suitable ballet for showing off the whole Company, it was discussed as a possible alternative to *Pomona* and de Valois wrote: 'I might add that Constant Lambert has been most generous in ignoring his natural desire to figure as a composer during the season, and in pressing for the inclusion of *Les Patineurs* as being so good for the company as a whole.'[30] Lord Berners had even expressed a wish that *A Wedding Bouquet* might be included, but its need for a chorus in addition to the 30 members of the ballet (11 men and 19 women) ruled it out.

Eventually seven ballets were given at the Théâtre des Champs Elysées, opening on 15 June with *Les Patineurs*, the first performance of *Checkmate*,[31] and *Façade*, and followed later by *The Rake's Progress, Pomona, Apparitions* and *Nocturne*.[32] Constant, conducting the Lamoureux Orchestra, had asked for at least five three-hour rehearsals, as not only was the music unfamiliar to the orchestra but most of it was in manuscript, and he arrived in Paris a week before the first night, Flo staying at home with two-year-old Kit. It was arranged that the Company would stay at three hotels, with Constant, Margot and Ninette de Valois and three other females in one of them; Bobby Helpmann, Freddie Ashton, Billy Chappell, two other males and eight females in a second; and 12 other dancers in a third.

---

[26] The other two ballets were *Miracle in the Gorbals* (1944) and *Adam Zero* (1946). *Narcissus and Echo* (1932) was not originally written as a ballet.

[27] Letter from E. Makower to Miss Baylis, 8 January 1937.

[28] Letter from de Valois to Toye, 22 January 1937: Vic-Wells Archives.

[29] Letter from Baylis to Toye, 9 January 1937: Vic-Wells Archives. *Pomona* was presented at the Arts Theatre, Cambridge on 3 June 1937, with Fonteyn and Helpmann in the principal roles.

[30] 1 March 1937.

[31] Robert Helpmann was the Red King, June Brae the Black Queen, Frederick Ashton was Death, Harold Turner and William Chappell were Red Knights, Michael Somes was a Black Knight, and Margot Fonteyn led the Black Pawns.

[32] The programmes for the other evenings in June were 16th: *Pomona, Apparitions, Les Patineurs*. 17th: *Nocturne, Rake's Progress, Façade*. 18th: *Rake's Progress, Pomona, Nocturne*. 19th: *Apparitions, Pomona, Checkmate*. 20th: *Les Patineurs, Checkmate, Façade*.

Bliss had been under some pressure to complete *Checkmate* in time. On 30 April he wrote to the BBC: 'I am greatly pressed for time to finish my new Chess Ballet for Paris',[33] and the score was not completed until 31 May 1937. It may partly have been this pressure that made him expand 'The Building of the New World' section from his film music *Things to Come* into 'The Entry of the Red Castles'. On several levels *Checkmate* was a great success, the only general criticism being the length of some of the sections. (*The Times* critic instanced the final solo of the Black Queen.) The manuscript full score[34] has cuts written in Lambert's hand to six of the 12 sections, many of these probably made between the premiere and the first English performance. There was one problem in that some of the costumes, designed by the American artist Edward McKnight Kauffer (his only work for ballet), tended to be too bulky for dancing. Kauffer was more experienced in designing futuristic or cubist posters for such organisations as London Transport and various oil companies than in working for the stage.

Despite the pleasures of being in Paris, artistically the whole venture was a disappointment. Because of strikes by the French workmen, the specially constructed theatre for the visiting companies was not ready in time so they were rescheduled to the Théâtre des Champs-Elysées. Even then, as Bliss recalled, it was touch-and-go whether the opening night would proceed as planned:

> The almost inevitable last difficulties attending any new production were present in full force. There was considerable confusion in the front of the house over precedence, protocol, who should sit where, and whose bouquet should be largest, but it was nothing to the chaos behind the curtain, due to a sudden strike of scene shifters in the Parisian theatres. This is where the experience and panache of Bridges Adams, acting for the British Council, shone brightly. Ordering food and wine to be brought backstage, he addressed the scene shifters in fluent Stratford-atte-Bowe French, enlarging on the glories of the French dramatic tradition, and on this unique entente between them and a famous British Company. Mellowed by wine, and astonished at his oration, the scene shifters leapt to their feet, the stage was set just in time, and the curtain went punctually up on the first ballet of the evening, *Les Patineurs*, conducted by Constant Lambert.[35]

Attendances for the Vic-Wells ballets were disappointing because there had been little advance publicity, and while after the opening night the Company had a 'very plain' meal provided for them by the British Council, they were 'angry to read in Constant's *Times*, bought next day on the street corner, of the grand occasion at the British Embassy, brimming with exalted guests gathered to celebrate the first night of the Vic-Wells ballet' to which neither Ninette de Valois nor a single dancer had been invited.[36]

But as William Chappell recalled:

> The intoxication of the summer's day in Paris made everything else appear unimportant. In company with ... Ashton, Helpmann and Pamela May and a dear friend of all of ours, the elegant Alice Pleydell-Bouverie – then Alice von Hofmannsthal, a beautiful woman whose arched feet are more like a ballerina's

[33] BBC Written Archives, quoted in *Arthur Bliss: A Source Book*, ed. Stewart R. Craggs (Aldershot: Scolar Press, 1996), p. 231.

[34] *Checkmate*, manuscript full score, dated 31 May 1937: British Library, MS Egerton 3770.

[35] Arthur Bliss, *As I Remember* (London: Faber & Faber, 1970), pp. 114–15.

[36] Edwards, *In Good Company*, p. 59.

than any ballerina's – sometimes with Constant Lambert, we made our nightly rounds of the *boîtes*.[37]

Josephine Baker was to be seen at the Folies Bergère and Maurice Chevalier was performing at the Casino Theatre, but one particular night-club held a special attraction for Constant, as Arthur Bliss remembered:

> I spent a few days longer in Paris, often with Constant Lambert.[38] … He was very keen on spending one evening at a special Night Club in Montmartre – 'Brick Tops' I think it was called – where, he said, a wonderful coloured jazz group were playing. We toiled up thither, rather late, and I sat there with him for hours, listening to what was to me a most monotonous and depressive sound. As we came out into the street in the early morning a rickety fiacre was standing there, both horse and driver equally ancient. The driver was white-bearded and was holding a flute to his lips, on which he was blowing long sad notes. Before taking the cab Constant asked him why he was playing the flute at that hour. 'Pour la Mort' was the response. With a chill in our hearts we stole away. This was not the only macabre incident I have witnessed in Constant's company. He seemed to be a focal point for strange happenings, even to conjure them up. On this occasion I should not have been surprised to find, glancing back, the driver, horse and flute had all melted into the pale light of dawn.[39]

When he was back in England, in his weekly column in the *Sunday Referee* Constant conveyed to his readers the excitement he felt at coming across this jazz group. 'I make a find in a Night Club' his headlines declared with understandable eagerness when that group included Django Reinhardt, 'one of the most brilliant technicians on the guitar I have ever heard', and Stephane Grappelli, 'undoubtedly the most interesting figure in band music since Duke Ellington'.[40] When Lady Mendel gave a party at her house in Versailles in honour of the Vic-Wells Company's visit, Constant had sat 'entranced beside Stephane Grappelli and Django Reinhardt and the members of the Hot Club of France, who were playing during the party'.[41] A little while later, when Grappelli, Reinhardt and the Quintette du Hot Club de France were broadcast on the BBC, Constant recalled in *Radio Times* that moment of discovery:

> It was with a fairly jaded palette that, two years ago, I entered a small night club in Montmartre, not a district where one expects much in the way of jazz, anyway. But once inside I was delighted and surprised to hear a small band with an entirely new tone colour, and with a charming and original style of its own. Moreover, it was playing not an arrangement of a popular number, but a fascinating and exotic piece whose composer I was at a loss to place. They were the Quintette du Hot Club de France, and the composer was Django Reinhardt, the principal guitarist of the band. … Reinhardt is of French gypsy origin, does not read music, and is handicapped by having only two fingers on his left hand which function properly. Nevertheless he can do more with two fingers than

---

[37] Chappell, *Fonteyn*, p. 28.

[38] It was in Paris that Percy Grainger met Lambert and Bliss (who had first met Grainger in America a few years earlier): 'They were sitting at a pavement café sipping their coffee under the warm afternoon sun when Grainger chanced to walk past on his way to the Pyrenees.' John Bird, *Percy Grainger* (Oxford: Oxford University Press, 1999), p. 215.

[39] Bliss, *As I Remember*, p. 115.

[40] *Sunday Referee*, 1 August 1937. During Lambert's absence in France, Philip Page took over his column for two weeks in June, and also for two weeks in July.

[41] Chappell, *Fonteyn*, pp. 28–9.

most people with four and is the best jazz guitar player I know. He is partnered by Stephane Grappelly, a violinist who having started as a 'straight' player is now one of the most brilliant exponents of the jazz style.[42]

The very nature – and perhaps the appeal – of Constant's style of journalism was that he was often outspoken and even provocative. His criticism in June of Covent Garden's production of *Prince Igor*, under the heading of 'Opera at its worst',[43] resulted in the admission 'I am a Cad Critic: To judge by the somewhat dubious welcome I received at Covent Garden on Monday night, my recent remarks on the production of *Prince Igor* seem to have been taken none too kindly.'[44] But this did not stop him a week later from being highly critical of the opera he was attending that evening, Eugene Goossens' *Don Juan de Mañara*, and especially its librettist, Arnold Bennett:

> The utmost praise is due to the composer for so skilfully preserving the balance between stage and orchestra pit. There is only one thing wrong with this happy state of affairs. None of the words are worth listening to. Arnold Bennett was on the face of it the wrong calibre of writer to employ as a librettist. ... It is not until the third act that we get a tune we can get our teeth into, and it is typical of the whole opera that this tune should be played on the orchestra, because there are no suitable words to sing it to.[45]

His criticism was generally more negative than most critics, even to the point of occasionally being destructive, his particular *bêtes noires* being only too apparent and rather too frequently aired, sometimes to the point of tedium. But there was no question of him writing down to his readership, and when he despaired in *Music Ho!* of the 'disappearing middle brow', the decline of music criticism today in even the serious daily press, and the fact that no paper would carry a column like it of such erudition as his would seem to underline the point.

W HEN at the time of the Paris World Fair it was discovered that three great Russian ballerinas, Olga Preobrajenska, Lubov Egorova and Mathilde Kschessinska were resident in that city, Margot Fonteyn, Pamela May and June Brae went back to France during their long summer break to study with them. Meanwhile that summer Constant was invited by Ashton's great friend Alice von Hofmannsthal to stay at the Hofmannsthals' castle, Kammer, on the Attersee (famously painted by Gustav Klimt) about 30 miles from Salzburg. David Herbert and Cecil Beaton were among the other guests besides Ashton, and Florence was also invited – unwisely, as it turned out. This was a recipe for disaster because she had discovered that Alice had allowed Constant and Margot the use of her gate cottage at Hanover Lodge in Regents Park as their love nest. (Appropriately enough, Constant would often refer to it as 'Hangover' Lodge.) During her stay, Flo created some outrageous scenes, one of which centred on a missing earring. David Herbert was witness to the incident:

> Mrs Lambert admitted losing an opal earring. Alice – who was an eccentric character – became obsessed by the loss and spent a whole week looking for

---

[42] Lambert, 'Something New in Jazz', *Radio Times*, 17 March 1939, p. 15.

[43] *Sunday Referee*, 13 June 1937, reviewing the performance on 9 June 1937 of *Prince Igor* in a new arrangement of two acts with the tone poem *On the Steppes of Central Asia* as an epilogue, and the opera being sung in French. Eugene Goossens was the conductor. The production received generally poor reviews.

[44] *Sunday Referee*, 4 July 1937.

[45] *Sunday Referee*, 11 July 1937. *Don Juan de Mañara* was premiered on 24 June 1937, the composer conducting.

the missing jewel which Mrs Lambert said had dropped into the lake. Eventually Alice found it and handed it back to her. 'That opal had always brought me bad luck,' remarked Mrs Lambert. 'I didn't lose it, I threw it away.' And she tossed it back into the lake. I thought it cruel of her. Alice was more upset than ever.[46]

Florence had numerous rows with Constant, and her wedding ring soon followed the earring into the lake. Not wanting to tolerate any more of this behaviour, Alice's husband, Raimund von Hofmannsthal, bodily ejected Florence, depositing her and her luggage outside the front door. But Florence had the last say. As Cecil Beaton wrote in his diaries without naming names, 'The wife of a composer, upon being expelled from the castle, flounced out rudely exhibiting her behind'.[47]

After Florence's departure Constant settled down to work on his next ballet, *Horoscope*. His previous work, *Summer's Last Will and Testament*, had been dedicated to Flo, but this new ballet would be dedicated to Margot. Back in England, in August he escaped for a few days to Renishaw to enjoy the company of the Sitwells. Some days later he wrote to Ashton, principally to persuade him, after having had some tempting offers elsewhere, to stay at Sadler's Wells:

> I expect you have heard from Alice the gloomy story of my last few days. Florence discovering about Hangover – subsequent scenes – rapid departure – fall at the BBC – injured foot etc. I am too bored with my life even to describe it in short hand. Let's talk about yours for a change. It's now my turn to scold.
>
> I have been thinking a lot about your offers from de Basil and Massine and speaking quite objectively without any old school tie feeling, I think you would be a fool to take either. You must surely realise that they are only after you because you are in a stronger position than they. Think of the coming year. Massine will be taking all that time to form his company and de Basil will be in want of a really good choreographer. You on the other hand have your own theatre behind you with organisation and a growing reputation and if you produce two really striking ballets you will at the end of the year be in a far stronger position than either. Massine obviously only wants you to prevent de Basil from presenting a rival. You don't seriously imagine that you would get a 'fair deal' from him do you? Think what happened to Nijinska. Another thing to remember is *Massine has never yet succeeded on his own*. Mark my words. As you know I have an occasional gift of prophecy.
>
> Like most dancers he needs an artistic framework and that after all is what you get at the Wells in spite of its many deficiencies. I quite realise that the schoolroom atmosphere must irritate you even more than it does me but that is really only a minor point. You have much more there than de Basil could give you at the moment. At the same time I think it would be better to go to de Basil than to Massine. You would after all be their star choreographer and have a really big company even though they wouldn't as yet be familiar with your style. But don't go there and work with your left hand. That would be fatal.
>
> Don't do your equivalent of Cent Baisers.[48] Think how the people who know only that have underestimated Nijinska. People remember one failure or even one modified succès-d'estime far more than half-a-dozen successes. If I were you

---

[46] David Herbert, *Second Son: An Autobiography* (London: Peter Owen, 1972), pp. 68–9. Herbert would seem wrongly to imply that the year was 1935.

[47] Beaton, *The Wandering Years*, p. 287. Beaton would seem to imply that the year was 1935 but Vickers, *Cecil Beaton*, pp. 202, 604, dates the original diary as August 1937.

[48] The ballet *Les Cent Baisers*, with a score by Frederic d'Erlanger choreographed by Nijinska, was first performed at Covent Garden on 18 July 1935 by Colonel de Basil's company.

even if you want to go to de Basil eventually I should certainly stay at the Wells another year; after which your position will be ever stronger. After all even if you hate doing revues it is better to pot-boil with your left-hand than to do a second-rate ballet.

Excuse this long lecture but it comes from the heart. If it seems disconnected that is because two people are trying to describe the plot of the last Marx brothers film to me.

At the end of the week if I can hobble about enough, I hope to go down to Captain Berties where I shall be free from interruption and will be able to work at Horoscope which has naturally been at a standstill. I do hope it will turn out alright. I may not be back in London until the 18th. If you see Margot before I do, give her all my love and more, and try and persuade her I'm not such a beast as might appear.

I hope your life is proving pleasanter than mine. Give my love to Alice and Raimund.

Yours ever

Uncle Constant[49]

Fortunately for the Company, Constant's reasoning prevailed. Lawrance Collingwood stood in for him while he recovered from the fall.

That year Constant became associated with an adventurous but short-lived weekly magazine, *Night and Day*, that set itself up as an English equivalent to the *New Yorker*.[50] The first issue appeared in July 1937, but it was only to last six months, its demise being brought about by its literary editor and film critic, none other than Graham Greene, causing Twentieth Century Fox to bring a libel action against the magazine for his remarks about their young star, Shirley Temple. Among its more regular contributors were such literary figures as John Betjeman, Elizabeth Bowen, Alistair Cooke, Osbert Lancaster, Malcolm Muggeridge, Anthony Powell and Evelyn Waugh. In September Constant was announced as its music critic, but it wasn't until four issues later that his first article appeared, an amusing account of the phases he went through as a regular enthusiast of the Promenade Concerts, beginning as an enthusiastic schoolboy who endured 'a period of acute mental stress during which I would count up my money and weigh the respective merits of possible programmes', to the 'more genial phase as a concert-goer' taking his place in the promenade as a student and after, until now, as a critic, going 'in morose grandeur to the circle'. His only other piece, in which he gave vent to his dislike of Brahms and Sir Donald Tovey, was printed five weeks before the magazine folded.

In mid-August Constant conducted an all-Satie broadcast,[51] and he was back at Sadler's Wells on 28 September, fully recovered from his fall, for the first night of the season which included a revival of *Pomona*, using the original décor by John Banting. On the opening night Pearl Argyle was partnered by Robert Helpmann, while Fonteyn and Somes took the leading roles in two of the remaining six performances that year. 'This is an unpretentious little piece,' thought the *Times* critic, 'as modern in feeling

[49] Letter from Constant Lambert, c/o Mrs G. W, Lambert, 42 Peel Street, London W.8, to Frederick Ashton, Sunday [n.d. but between 7 and 27 September 1937]: original in ROHCG Archive. The identity of Captain Berties has not been ascertained.

[50] In 1985 Chatto & Windus published an anthology consisting of all 26 issues of *Night and Day* (without their covers) with an introduction by Christopher Hawtree and a preface by Graham Greene.

[51] 18 August 1937, National Programme: *Jack-in-the-Box* orchestrated by Milhaud, Suite *Relâche* (first British broadcast), *Trois valses du précieux dégoûte* orchestrated by Hyam Greenbaum, and Suite *Mercure*.

as Constant Lambert's music, and, because it does not aim too high, still deserves its place in the repertory of our young English ballet.'[52] Six days later Constant introduced Bliss's *Checkmate* to London audiences.[53] It was to be a long season, lasting until the following May, but ballet was still limited to two programmes in most weeks and his load was lightened by the appointment of Geoffrey Corbett, the Sadler's Wells chorus master, as assistant conductor. On 16 November Constant was involved with a charity matinée, held at the Savoy Theatre and arranged by Marie Rambert in aid of Child Psychology. The performers were members of the Vic-Wells and the Markova-Dolin companies and the ballets included *Le Foyer de danse*, a version of Berners' 'fantastic ballet' *Luna Park*. 'A large share of the credit for the success of the afternoon must be given to Mr Constant Lambert and the unnamed orchestra who played the various music with real liveliness,' wrote the *Times* critic.

Nine days later an era ended with the death from a heart attack of Lilian Baylis. It was announced that evening that performances of opera at Sadler's Wells and Shakespeare at the Old Vic would continue in accordance with her wishes, and the following evening in between the programme of ballet at Rosebery Avenue, Ninette de Valois delivered a spoken tribute.

With *Apparitions* now well established in the Vic-Wells repertoire, Constant included it as a ballet suite in a broadcast with the BBC Orchestra on 11 October, together with a rarer outing for Vaughan Williams' *Concerto accademico* with Henri Temianka as soloist, a score that he would have known well through the piano transcription he had made for its composer. Ever practical, he also added Dvořák's *Othello* Overture which he was to include in one of his Conductors' Class concerts next month.

In December severe pain in his left ear caused him to overcome his normal aversion to doctors and visit a specialist. As Cyril Hereford later recalled:

> In my official capacity as Hon. Laryngologist to the Royal Choral Society & the Royal College of Music, we often met & became great friends through our association with the musical world. … On Dec. 9th he came to see me and was greatly distressed. I told him it was vital to his career for me to cure the infection at once, as his right ear was completely deaf owing to the destruction of the drum some years previous. That very evening, however, he was due to conduct a concert at the Queen's Hall, so after treating his ear with soothing drops for the pain, I made him promise to come to me after the concert, which he did, about 11 p.m. and that night, under cocaine, I operated & punctured the drum & drew off all the infection, & I treated & watched it carefully for several days & much to his delight, & I may say mine also, the inflammation subsided & his hearing saved – I assure you if I had not done it that night his career would have been ruined.[54]

Meanwhile, another career was forging ahead. Under Constant's baton on 21 December, for the first time Fonteyn danced the dual role of Odette-Odile in a three-act *Lac des cygnes*, a date she proudly recorded in her autobiography. In the new year she was to have a triple association with the Company's next ballet, as inspiration, performer and dedicatee.

In January, among the ballets under discussion for future production were

[52] *The Times*, 29 September 1937.
[53] The first UK performance of *Checkmate* had been given while on tour at the Theatre Royal, Newcastle, on 2 September 1937.
[54] Letter from Cyril Hereford, MD, FRCS, Hon. RCM to Hubert Foss, 27 January [1952]: Hubert Foss Archive.

Prokofiev's *Sur le Borysthène* and Bartók's *The Miraculous Mandarin* and *The Wooden Prince*, though none was destined to enter the Company's immediate repertoire. The first new ballet that year was Constant's *Horoscope*, introduced at the Sadler's Wells Theatre on 27 January with designs by Sophie Fedorovitch and choreography by Ashton. P. W. Manchester wrote that 'it was created in the ideal manner of choreographer, composer and designer working together', resulting in 'an almost perfect unity'. She thought it Ashton's finest work so far.[55] That doyen of ballet, Arnold Haskell was of a similar opinion: 'Suddenly we were shown a work that represented a perfection of collaboration that we had not seen since Diaghilev. Lambert, Ashton and Sophie Fedorovitch worked as one. How well the music recalls to us the memory of Pamela May's shimmering moon and the lovers, Fonteyn and Somes, striving to overcome the writings in the sky.'[56] Margaret Dale remembered 'a general air of seriousness about the rehearsals as though everyone knew that they were engaged in the creation of a major work of greater depth than anything Ashton had hitherto attempted.'[57]

With a dedication 'To Margot Fonteyn' and a plot symbolic of the stress in their relationship brought about by outside forces, Constant's own programme note read as follows:

> When people are born they have the sun in one sign of the zodiac, the moon in another. This ballet takes for its theme a man who has the sun in Leo and the moon in Gemini, and a woman who also has the moon in Gemini but whose sun is in Virgo. The two opposed signs of Leo and Virgo, the one energetic and full-bodied, the other timid and sensitive, struggle to keep the man and woman apart. It is by their mutual sign, the Gemini, that they are brought together and by the moon that they are finally united.

Fonteyn danced the young woman. Helpmann had been given special leave to play Oberon at the Old Vic opposite Vivien Leigh's Titania in a Guthrie-Messel production of *A Midsummer Night's Dream*, so the young man making an impressive solo début was Michael Somes, now the centre of Ashton's sexual desires. Pamela May, then the object of Somes's desires, was the Moon.

While Constant held back from giving the two leads the star signs of the true protagonists (although Constant was born on 23 August at a point of transition from Leo to Virgo, Margot, born on 18 May, was a Taurus), the dedication of the score made his feelings only too clear. But fate was not to be kind to either the lovers or indeed the score. Constant and Margot were never to be fully united and *Horoscope*, sadly, was to receive only 29 performances before the costumes and set were lost in Holland when the Company were on tour in the early stages of the war. It is a great pity that this, one of the most beautiful of all British ballet scores, has not since been brought to the stage (although some of the original steps were used in later ballets). Nowhere else had Constant written with such passion and melodic, bittersweet charm, or with such brilliant orchestration. Fortunately, in January he selected five of the movements for an orchestral suite that was published that year and has since become his most popular work, alongside *The Rio Grande*.[58]

The ballet, in one act, is in nine sections. It begins with a quiet, evenly paced 'Palindromic Prelude' (*Molto sostenuto ma senza espressione*) that has a timeless, almost

[55] Manchester, *Vic-Wells*, p. 59.
[56] Arnold Haskell, 'A Short History of Ballet', in *The Decca Book of Ballet*, ed. David Drew, (London: Frederick Muller, 1958), p. 19.
[57] Vaughan, *Frederick Ashton and his Ballets*, p. 161.
[58] In his own recording of the Suite, Lambert cut the first nine bars of the 'Dance for the Followers of Leo'.

eerie quality. Lambert apparently told Humphrey Searle that this movement had been dictated to him by Bernard van Dieren after that composer's death in April 1936.[59] Next is a brilliant, energetic 'Dance for the Followers of Leo' (*Allegro energico*) with sharply accented almost trade-mark syncopated rhythms, followed by a more restrained 'Saraband for the Followers of Virgo' (*Andante espressivo*), reflecting *Pomona* in its cool classical lines, though not without moments of poignancy. The vigorous 'Variation for the Man' (*Allegro pesante*), the shortest movement lasting barely a minute (with a fanfare motto similar to the one he was later to use in his *Merchant Seamen* suite), contrasts with the wistful 'Variation for the Woman' (*Andante molto espressivo*) with its siciliana-like 6/8 middle section (*Allegretto piacevole*).[60] The 'Bacchanale for the Followers of Leo' (*Allegro barbaro*)[61] is another bold, energetic movement with strongly syncopated themes, followed by the graceful 'Valse for the Gemini' (*Allegretto*). The 'Pas de deux' (*Adagio amoroso*), that one commentator has described as 'a highly fragrant *billet-doux*',[62] rises to a passionate climax before the final section, 'Invocation to the Moon and Finale' (*Andante mysterioso*), with letter E of that section (Ex. 28) being appropriately marked *Amoroso*. At first *piano*, the *mf* eight bars later could equally be interpreted as MF. The ballet ends quietly, with a hint of the passions being ultimately unresolved rather than fulfilled, despite the leading characters being 'finally united'. Alan Frank has suggested the influence of Puccini on the score, and if so it was 'none the worse for that'.[63] It was given a tremendous reception on its first night, with Arnold Haskell writing: 'With *Horoscope* ballet, now truly indigenous in England, reaches a splendid maturity.'[64] The historian Mary Clarke rated it 'one of Ashton's loveliest ballets' and Lambert's score 'probably his finest for any ballet'.[65]

Constant continued to be in demand where contemporary music was concerned. In a broadcast on 24 January he gave the first performance of John Greenwood's[66] *Symphonic Movement*, and on 4 February, in the fifth of a series of BBC Concerts of Contemporary Music at Broadcasting House, he conducted Igor Markevitch's Suite *L'Envoi d'Icare*, Christian Darnton's *Swan Song* (with soprano May Blyth), the first British performance of Elizabeth Maconchy's Viola Concerto (with Bernard Shore) and the first UK performance of Vladimir Vogel's *Tripartita*.[67]

A Second Orchestra and Conductors' Class at the RCM on 8 February roamed

---

[59] In Humphrey Searle and Robert Layton, *Twentieth Century Composers*, vol. 3: *Britain, Scandinavia and the Netherlands* (New York: Holt, Rinehart & Winston, 1972), p. 52. According to Searle, 'Constant certainly believed in telepathic communication with other musicians (alive or dead) which indeed he often experienced.' The Palindrome bears an uncanny resemblance to the opening music (after the title sequence) to Bernard Herrmann's score for Alfred Hitchcock's 1960 film *Psycho*. Lambert's own initials LCL happen to be palindromic.

[60] *Piacevole* was a direction that Lambert quite likely borrowed from Elgar who had first used it in his Serenade for Strings, and much later for the slow movement of his String Quartet which Lambert reviewed for *The New Statesman and Nation*, 14 July 1934, quoting that direction. Lambert also used it in *Tiresias* for the female Tiresias's scenes.

[61] Simply *Allegro* in the piano score. There are a few minor differences between the full score and the piano reduction.

[62] Philip Lane, in his notes for the ASV recording of the complete *Horoscope*, CD DCA1168, 2004.

[63] Frank, 'The Music of Constant Lambert' (1952), p. 105.

[64] *Daily Telegraph*, 28 January 1938, quoted in Clarke, *The Sadler's Wells Ballet*, p. 137.

[65] Clarke, *The Sadler's Wells Ballet*, pp. 136–7.

[66] John Greenwood (1889–1975) studied at the RCM and is chiefly known for his many film scores.

[67] Vladimir Vogel (1896–1984), Russian composer.

Ex. 28 Lambert, 'Invocation to the Moon', from *Horoscope*, fig. E

through more familiar territory: Delibes' *Le Roi s'amuse*, Mozart's A major piano concerto, K488 (a favourite of his), and Sibelius's First Symphony; and similarly a London Regional broadcast five days later: Elgar Prelude to *The Kingdom*, Schubert–Liszt *Wanderer Fantasy* (with Kentner) and Balakirev's First Symphony. Then on 16 February he was taken ill again, seriously enough to send for Cyril Hereford, who found that he had bronchitis and pneumonia and put him at once in a London nursing home where he treated him for 12 days, visiting him daily. At Sadler's Wells Joseph Shadwick, the leader of the orchestra who always supported him most ably, conducted in his absence. At that time Constant was also due to give six weekly half-hour talks for the BBC on the instruments of the orchestra, but the first two were given instead by Scott Goddard. The day after the first broadcast Constant wrote from his nursing home to George Barnes of the BBC: 'I'm glad Scott's talk has gone off alright. Provided you don't mind a Tallulah Bankhead voice I am prepared to carry on from March 7th.'[68] For two weeks his familiar column in the *Sunday Referee* did not appear, and his next contribution, on 6 March, was to be his last for that paper. On 12 March he seemed well enough to stand in for Beecham (who had gone down with flu) at a London Philharmonic concert at The People's Palace, and then, as fate would have it, not fully recovered himself, three days later he went down again, this time with a severe sinus infection and a high temperature. Once more this caused Cyril Hereford considerable alarm as he was particularly anxious to protect the good ear. This time Constant was out of action for a much longer period, so that on 1 April Hyam Greenbaum took over the second performance of *Summer's Last Will and Testament*,[69] and six days later Shadwick was in charge of the new ballet at Sadler's Wells, *Le Roi nu*, to music by Jean Françaix. Fortunately in time, after careful treatment, all was cleared up, Hereford later commenting on

> how courageous [Lambert] was in overcoming the handicap of these serious infections, and loss of hearing in one ear, for I feel no one would have known he had such a handicap, he was such a brilliant musician. I admired him greatly & he always remained a most grateful & devoted friend.[70]

He was well enough in May to give a BBC broadcast that included his own *Music for Orchestra* and Ravel's jazz-influenced G major Piano Concerto, written only four years after *The Rio Grande*, of which he was later surprisingly critical, writing in *Radio Times*:

> It can't be said that Ravel's concerto is one of his major works. It is a tour-de-force of craftsmanship – a first-rate work of the second class. ... In comparison with the reflective movement, later Ravel at his best, the finale in toccata style

[68] Letter from Lambert to Barnes, 22 February 1938, from 23 Devonshire Street, W1.

[69] Roy Henderson, BBC Chorus, BBC Orchestra (Section D), broadcast on the BBC National service. According to a score in the BBC Music Library, the timing of Greenbaum's performance was 51' 45", compared with Lambert's 54' 40" (March 1944), 56' 35" (June 1947) and 55' 40" (July 1951).

[70] Letter from Cyril Hereford to Hubert Foss, 27 January [1952]: Hubert Foss Archive.

seems a little lacking in substance and though extremely effectively written hardly sustains the quality of the rest of the work.[71]

Five days later he and the Sadler's Wells Company came under the glare of the television cameras at Alexandra Palace for the first of two transmissions of *Checkmate* with Constant conducting.[72] Much innovative use was made of shadows, and June Brae, as the Black Queen, was allowed a wicked smile of secret satisfaction as she stabbed the Red Knight in the back.

In between the two TV presentations of *Checkmate*, a gala performance was held on 10 May in the presence of Queen Elizabeth in aid of both the Lilian Baylis Memorial Extension (following her death in November) and the Vic-Wells Ballet Fund. In addition to *Horoscope*, *Checkmate* and *Les Patineurs* there was the first performance of a ballet by Lennox Berkeley, *The Judgement of Paris* – 'very good' Benjamin Britten wrote in his diary. Afterwards 'with Freddy Ashton – the dancers – & C. Lambert' he went on to a party given by Alice von Hofmannsthal – 'very good too' he added.[73]

The London season which ended on 21 May (a little earlier than usual so that a start could be made on the much-needed extensions to the theatre) was immediately followed by a fortnight in Cambridge. Then, after a short holiday, it was off to Oxford and Bournemouth.

He revived his own suite from Glinka's *Ruslan and Ludmila* for a broadcast in July, and at the Proms on 8 August he introduced the concert suite from *Horoscope*. He included some Satie in a studio broadcast two days later, and that month he heard the Prom premiere of Britten's Piano Concerto, with the composer as soloist, which he reviewed for *The Listener*. Britten knew *The Rio Grande* when writing his concerto, and while influenced by Ravel, Prokofiev and even Liszt, he matched the pianism if not the jazz element of Constant's popular work. In his review, Constant praised Britten's playing and thought the concerto had 'one sterling merit – it is never boring.' But he voiced some disappointment: 'The first movement is admirable throughout and the second, a valse, is a fascinating psychological study. It is neither a "straight" valse nor a "cod" valse but hovers cynically and convincingly between the two. After the valse the composer seems to lose his grip on the work' which lacked 'a unifying conception of form and style' when compared with the *Frank Bridge Variations*.[74]

That summer Lambert and Gray enjoyed a short but relaxing holiday together in the Loire valley. On one particularly fine day, 'after an admirable lunch, embellished and fortified by many bottles of some of the noblest wines in the world', they visited

---

[71] *Radio Times*, 29 April 29 1938, p. 13, relating to the broadcast of 3 May in the National Programme.

[72] *Checkmate* was televised on 8 May 1938, 9.30–10.20 p.m., preceded at 9.20 p.m. by a ten-minute discussion about chess and the ballet between Arthur Bliss, Ninette de Valois and Edward McKnight Kauffer. A second, afternoon performance was given on 13 May. (*Times* review 16 May 1938, and Bruce Norman, *Here's Looking at You: The Story of British Television, 1908–1939* (London: BBC, 1984), p. 183.) Alexandra Palace Television Society document holdings include the acceptance of Lambert to conduct the orchestra. On four days in June the Company televised *Casse-noisette* Act 3, *The Gods Go a'Begging*, *Nocturne* and *Façade*, the last bringing forth the interesting observation from the *Times* critic: 'Televised ballet is not always the satisfying thing it ought to be … *Façade*, which is neat, crisp and witty in the theatre, came perilously near to being a music-hall turn on the screen: in fact the number *Popular Song* seemed to be the very thing it was taking off.' (13 June). For these ballets Hyam Greenbaum was probably the conductor.

[73] *Letters from a Life: The Selected Letters and Diaries of Benjamin Britten*, vol. 1, p. 565.

[74] *The Listener*, 25 August 1938, p. 412, reviewing the performance on 18 August 1938. In 1946 a revised version of the Concerto was given with a new third movement.

the 16th-century château of Azay-le-Rideau situated on an island in the River Indre. While Lambert 'indolently reclined on the green sward in the warm summer sunshine and indulged in a post-prandial siesta', Gray found a quiet spot known to him where he gained inspiration for one of the choruses for his opera *Women of Troy* that had eluded him.[75]

In the first week of October, Constant was a guest conductor at the Torquay Musical Festival, and while extensions to the Sadler's Wells Theatre were still in progress, the Company were performing for a week each in a variety of venues, from Manchester, Dublin and Cardiff to, nearer home, Streatham and Golders Green, before making a happy homecoming on 18 October with *Carnaval, The Rake's Progress* and *Horoscope*.[76] While 'Miss Margot Fonteyn as the young girl floated airily among the constellations … Mr Constant Lambert conducted and obtained a vivid performance of his own very attractive score,' reported *The Times*. On 10 November a revised and enlarged version of *Harlequin in the Street* was introduced. Constant had made a fresh selection of Couperin's music which Gordon Jacob orchestrated. 'It was,' reported *The Times*, 'very much Miss June Brae's evening' as, in addition to a leading role in *Harlequin*, she also appeared in *Nocturne* and *Checkmate*. 'The performance under Mr Lambert's direction was admirable.'[77] Five days later there was evidence of Fonteyn's growing stature as prima ballerina when she took on the double role of Odette-Odile in her first full-length four-act *Le Lac des cygnes*. *The Times* reported: 'Miss Margot Fonteyn has not yet acquired all the dramatic power nor developed the temperament to fulfil completely all the requirements of so exacting a part, but her dancing combines technical precision with a beautifully soft and fluent style, so that the heroine's part is adequately filled. … There were a few rough places in the playing, but the orchestra, under Mr Constant Lambert, contributed a good deal by its rhythmic verve to the dramatic success of the ballet.'[78]

Near the end of November Constant was the conductor of a children's charity matinée presented by the Ballet Joos at the Cambridge Theatre, in a mixed programme that included Berkeley's *The Judgement of Paris*. In between his ballet engagements he was fitting in the occasional recording session for Walter Legge, and now and again a broadcast. For the BBC on 27 November he paired Lizst's *Hungaria* with Falla's *Nights in the Gardens of Spain*, and in a short *Radio Times* article took the opportunity to defend Liszt who, he claimed, had 'become the butt of academic critics who ought to know better'. The Falla was a particular favourite of the soloist Harriet Cohen who wrote in her memoirs:

> No one conducted the *Nights in the Gardens of Spain* for me like Constant, not even the Spaniard Perez Casas. But where his art shone most as a conductor was in ballet, where he had an uncanny appreciation of the linked relationship of music and dance. As Sadler's Wells eventually took more and more of his time, I naturally saw less of him, especially as I was travelling so much, but our friendship remained taut and true to the end.[79]

---

[75] Gray, *Musical Chairs*, p. 317.

[76] Angus Morrison remembered Lambert once saying to him 'that he never liked the choreography of the finale of the ballet version of *Carnaval* because what happened on stage was merely a light-hearted romp; for him the music was tragic, expressing a profound and almost Elizabethan sense of doom and foreboding behind all human happiness' (Morrison's draft manuscript). See Appendix 13 for that season's programmes.

[77] *The Times*, 11 November 1938.

[78] *The Times*, 16 November 1938.

[79] Cohen, *A Bundle of Time*, pp. 138–9.

She recalled meeting Fonteyn for the first time, in the company of Constant and Willie Walton, at a Savoy Grill supper party hosted by Alice Wimborne, and she made this observation on Constant's attitude to the opposite sex:

> Constant was rather inclined to relegate women to the status of 'the Sex'. He admired, and indeed loved women, but rarely admitted them to a full male companionship. When, on one of our prowls pubwards after a concert, and certainly expecting a rebuff, I interrupted a monologue on 'the liberating influence of Debussy's impressionism' with: 'Don't you think the beginning of Stravinsky's *Rossignol* is awfully like the opening of Debussy's *Nuages*?', he looked at me with an awakened interest and agreed, I knew I was admitted to the Brotherhood.[80]

At about this time Constant wrote a short piano piece, *Elegy*, which he dedicated to Harriet. Lasting about five minutes, it was not published until 1940. Whether or nor its more serious mood was a reflection on the times, he inscribed the copy he gave to Lord Berners: 'To Gerald with apologies for this prophetic piece. With love from Constant.'

His Royal College First Orchestra concerts continued either to reflect his own tastes or include something unusual: on 28 October the programme ended with Balakirev's Symphony No. 1 while on 9 December Valerie Trimble, later to form a piano-duo with her sister Joan, was the soloist in Dohnanyi's *Konzertstück* for Cello and Orchestra. Then, in a BBC Christmas Eve broadcast, as if to thank Gordon Jacob for his Couperin orchestrations, he gave the first performance of his *Galop Joyeux* in a programme that also included pieces by Hérold, Delibes and Bizet.

By now Constant and Flo were living apart: he with Margot at 'Hangover' Lodge, she taking care of Kit at Trevor Place. Soon after their marriage, perhaps recognising the intellectual gap between herself and Constant and attempting to become more a part of his world, Flo became a pupil at Marie Rambert's school, as fellow student, Mark Baring,[81] who would sometimes join her for lunch at a nearby café, remembered:

> We had become friends. I think she pitied my poverty as life, I suspected, hadn't always been too easy for her either. ... However, she was now the bewitching Mrs Constant Lambert, photographed by *Vogue* and *Tatler*, and her portrait by Brockhurst hung at the Royal Academy.[82] She was on first name familiarity with the famous dancers, composers and artists of that time – and she was very beautiful. I loved her and basked happily in the reflected glory. We remained good friends until her untimely passing, although life battered us both about a bit in the interim.[83]

They briefly worked together in 1937 for a short TV ballet, *The Stained Glass Window*, choreographed by Sokolova, who was also one of the five dancers. Then, soon after Constant had moved out of Trevor Place, Flo asked Baring if he would like to stay with her for a while. He recalled spending several carefree months with her:

---

[80] *Ibid.*, p. 138. This was in fact a comparison that Lambert had already made in *Music Ho!*, 2nd edn (1937), p. 25.

[81] The actor and dancer Mark Baring joined the International Ballet Company in the 1940s and had an uncredited role in the 1948 film *The Red Shoes* as one of the *pas de quatre* in the 'Heart of Fire' ballet.

[82] Gerald Brockhurst (1890–1978), English portrait painter best known for his oils and small etched prints of beautiful, idealised women, many modelled by his first and second wives. The portrait of Florence Lambert has not been located.

[83] Mark Baring, *Por Lit'le Bleeder: An Autobiography* (Somerset: Graphic Type, 1998), p. 48.

Carefree because I didn't have to find the ten bob rent, but also carefree because life was never dull with La Lambert. But for poor, dear Flo this was a dismal time. She loved Constant dearly and was eternally raining curses on the head of the famous dancer who had blighted her marriage. Unhappy Flo, to shroud her misery, would go nearly every night to parties always looking a dream of enchantment, returning in the lean hours of the morning looking as awesome as a nightmare; in spite of a distinct alcoholic haze, she would always be up and ready for morning ballet class. Of course, we would be late for leaving and there was always a dash for the bus. One morning she managed to leap on before I could get on board. I was carrying her case of practice clothes at that time, which, in the rush, chose that moment to burst open! So there was I, left to gather up the bras, pants and tights that were scattered all along the Knightsbridge pavement. Much to the delight of the waving Flo and the amusement of the passing shoppers, I, red faced, mustered together Madame's unmentionables.[84]

While Flo was working, grandmother Amy and aunt Olga (who had no children of her own) would between them obligingly take care of Kit at Peel Street, which became his second home.[85] In 1939 he attended his first school, in Hampstead, and in November, in addition to her job as a model, Flo enrolled in the Vic-Wells School of Ballet.[86] Whether she seriously thought that this might bring about a reconciliation with Constant, or, more likely, out of jealousy hoped to make difficult any liaison between him and Fonteyn, by December she was listed as a member of the Company and her name appeared on a programme. It is possible that de Valois had her in the ballet to keep a check on Constant, and when they went on tour she found her a small part to justify her presence. One of the dancers recalled a vindictive streak in Flo and she only stayed with the ballet a short while.

Richard Shead has written that the marriage ended after Constant 'had provided grounds for divorce by spending a night in a hotel with a woman hired for the purpose (they played cards all night)'.[87] A petition for divorce was filed in the second year of the war and, despite their previous quarrels, a fairly amicable settlement was made.[88]

---

[84] Spring or summer 1938. *Ibid.*, p. 62.

[85] Maurice and Olga moved in late 1942 to Bosham, Sussex, where they stayed for the remainder of the war. After being discharged from the Parachute Regiment for health reasons, Maurice worked at a government department near Chichester building motor torpedo boats.

[86] The Vic-Wells Archives, Islington Museum, list her as having enrolled on 22 November 1939.

[87] Shead, *Constant Lambert*, pp. 116–17.

[88] Official records of their divorce have not survived.

15 1939–40
Double Bishops and Limericks

I T says much for Lambert's pre-war stature that he should even be considered as a possible successor to Hamilton Harty as principal conductor of the Hallé Orchestra. Harty had terminated his position in March 1933 and for the next six years, with no permanent appointment being made, a long list of guest conductors had filled the gap. On 26 November 1936 Lambert was on the rostrum at the Free Trade Hall, Manchester, with a programme of Borodin's Overture *Prince Igor*, Beethoven's Piano Concerto No. 4, Tchaikovsky's Overture *Romeo and Juliet* and Sibelius's Second Symphony. When two years later, on 1 December 1938, he returned with Elgar's Prelude to *The Kingdom*, Mozart's Piano Concerto No. 23 and Liszt's Piano Concerto No. 2 with Egon Petri as soloist, and Balakirev's Symphony No. 1 (with Bliss conducting a suite from *Checkmate*), Neville Cardus wrote in *The Manchester Guardian*: 'Mr Lambert controlled the orchestral part [Liszt] firmly and freely. ... Here is another conductor who would be a godsend to the Hallé Orchestra if he were put in charge'.[1] Even Philip Godlee, an influential member of the Hallé committee, wrote: 'If Monteux were at liberty he would fill the bill, but he is over 60. ... If Goossens were available we should be fortunate to get him. Lambert's claims should be seriously considered.'[2] Part of his appeal no doubt was his youth, but Malcolm Sargent and Basil Cameron were the favourites. Had Lambert broken his ties with the Vic-Wells Company and been appointed to the Hallé, the history of English ballet would have run a very different course. As it was, in April the position was offered to Sargent.

Constant continued to take the conductor's classes at the Royal College (among his pupils were Norman Del Mar,[3] George Malcolm and Bernard Stevens) and he was as busy as ever working for the BBC. In January 1939, as well as conducting two studio broadcasts,[4] he introduced a weekly half-hour radio programme of gramophone records of ballet music, a series that ran for six weeks.[5] Then in February the Vic-Wells Ballet made three visits to Alexandra Palace to televise once again a cut version of *Checkmate*. Conducting the augmented Television Orchestra, Constant upset the BBC authorities at rehearsal by having a bass trombonist replaced. The 40-minute

---

[1] Kennedy, *The Hallé Tradition*, p. 275.

[2] Memorandum, January 1939: *ibid.*, pp. 276–7.

[3] The RCM Conductors' Class programme on 30 May 1939 ended with Tchaikovsky's Fifth Symphony with four students each taking a movement, Norman Del Mar the last one. Much later in a radio talk, Del Mar recalled: 'I was desperately anxious to put in the cymbal crash which Mengelberg had introduced. [Lambert] wouldn't let me and I don't do it to this day': BBC Radio 3 *Third Ear*, 23 May 1991. In the same programme George Malcolm conducted John Ireland's *Legend* with Ruth Gipps the piano soloist.

[4] The broadcast on 2 January included the first performance of Lambert's arrangement of William Boyce's Overture *The Cambridge Ode*, together with Arthur Benjamin's *Romantic Fantasy* (Eda Kersey and Bernard Shore), Grieg's *Symphonic Dances* Nos. 2 and 4, and Elgar's Overture *Froissart*. The next broadcast, on 17 January, was the second of three performances Lambert was to give of Magnard's Third Symphony (also 14 June 1936 first English performance and 22 August 1940). Arthur Bliss wrote in *The Listener*: 'completely unknown to me, so that the performance had the excitement of a discovery. An austere and sternly self-critical personality stood revealed', 26 January 1939, p. 228, reprinted in *Bliss on Music: Selected Writings of Arthur Bliss, 1920–1975*, ed. Gregory Roscow (Oxford: Oxford University Press, 1991), pp. 165–6.

[5] See Appendix 5.

programme went out live the following evening, with an afternoon performance three days later.[6]

The poet W. B. Yeats died near the end of the month, and Arnold Bax (a poet himself) wrote to his brother Clifford: 'It seems almost unbelievable that Willie Yeats will never write another line of verse. As Constant Lambert said to me at lunch today, "He achieved a record in pleasing four generations of poetry lovers; even the most recent (Auden etc) reverenced him."'[7]

The first major event of the year was a Royal Gala charity performance at Sadler's Wells on 2 February, attended by Queen Mary and the Princesses Helena Victoria and Marie Louise (granddaughters of Queen Victoria). Constant conducted a complete *The Sleeping Princess*.[8] It was in effect an English premiere and the Vic-Wells' boldest enterprise. It had been a great ambition of de Valois's, not possible earlier because the Sadler's Wells theatre had simply not been large enough to accommodate such an undertaking but possible now because of the substantial addition that was named the Lilian Baylis Memorial.[9] Constant had worked with what was apparently the only copy of the full score in London, restoring cuts and eliminating alterations, such as those that Diaghilev had made for his ill-fated 1921 production in which two of the Company, de Valois and Ursula Moreton, had taken part, as well as Nicolai Sergeyev whom de Valois once again brought over from Paris as régisseur.[10] Not only had he been in the original St Petersburg production as a child but he had kept detailed records of the Maryinsky Theatre choreography that de Valois wanted to reproduce as faithfully as possible. She described him as a strange little man, completely devoid of any real stage sense and

> unmusical to a degree bordering on eccentricity; he always carried a blue pencil, and would carefully pencil out a bar of music, which, for some reason, wearied him. The offending bar would receive a long, strong blue cross through it. This would mean that I must 'phone Constant Lambert, who would come down in the lunch break and put the bars back. Sergeyev would return, and because, in his absence, I had extended some small choreographic movement to cover Mr Lambert's tracks, he would be unaware that the position was musically where it had been before the onslaught of the blue pencil! Crotchets would become quavers by the simple process of humming emphatically what he considered a reading of the piano score; this would lead to a show-down with Constant Lambert, and result in Sergeyev sadly murmuring, 'Mr Lambert ... he no good.'[11]

Margot Fonteyn excelled as Princess Aurora and, according to *The Times*, she was 'admirably partnered' by Robert Helpmann. Lambert's conducting was much praised.

---

[6] Rehearsal 18 February; with televised broadcasts 19 and 22 February 1939. Berners' *A Wedding Bouquet* was televised on 29 April.

[7] Foreman, *Bax*, p. 354.

[8] They followed Diaghilev in using this title rather than *The Sleeping Beauty*, which was too closely associated with Christmas pantomime versions of the traditional story.

[9] As a result of the completion fund, to which subscriptions were specifically asked as a tribute to Lilian Baylis, a new scene dock, a new wardrobe room, new sewing-rooms and rehearsal rooms for both the opera and ballet were added: Clarke, *The Sadler's Wells Ballet*, p. 136.

[10] The additions made by Diaghilev in 1921, mainly from *Casse-noisette*, were cut, and the restorations included Cinderella's dance to the series of fairy tales. 'It is almost a shock,' wrote *The Times* critic, 'to see the Farandole, for example, danced by the hunters and peasants, whom it suits much better than the nobles of the final scene, and to find that the music of the 'Three Ivans' is properly the climax of the grand *pas de deux*.'

[11] De Valois, *Come Dance with Me*, p. 112. Sergeyev insisted on having his own pianist at rehearsals.

Only the designs by Nadia Benois came in for criticism and here de Valois had gone against Constant's suggestion of using Edmund Dulac. The production was given 12 performances that season, and eight days after the Royal Gala Constant recorded a suite from the ballet for HMV in Kingsway Hall with the Sadler's Wells Orchestra. The first and third acts formed the framework of another gala performance (which was broadcast), this time at Covent Garden, on 22 March before the King and Queen and Queen Mary in honour of the visit of the President of the French Republic and Madame Lebrun. For this special evening the Royal Box was decorated to a design by Rex Whistler. Beecham opened and closed the musical proceedings with the National Anthem and *La Marseillaise*, and before the interval he conducted the London Philharmonic Orchestra in Debussy's *Iberia*. The ballet was conducted by Lambert and both he and de Valois were presented to the King and Queen.[12] Yet even de Valois admitted that they had not been entirely successful in trying quickly to adapt the production to Covent Garden's much larger stage.

Three days after the second gala Fonteyn, Helpmann and the Vic-Wells Company performed Act 1 before television cameras, with Lambert again conducting an augmented Television Orchestra. Four days later they were back at Alexandra Palace for Act 3. Live performances in hot cramped television studios brought their own difficulties, and it was during *The Sleeping Princess* that several dancers, after making a quick change, lost their way back to the studio so that Helpmann and Ursula Moreton had to dance the next scene on their own. As there were relatively few privately owned television sets at that time the viewing audience would have been a small one, but these occasions were at least financially rewarding for the Company which received £320 for two days' work. Such was the demand for televised ballet that in May they gave two further performances from Alexandra Palace of Act 3.

At Queen's Hall on 5 April Constant was in charge of the final event in a 'Festival of Music for the People'. Organised by Alan Bush, the Festival had opened with a pageant in the Royal Albert Hall and had also included a programme of folk music. For the closing concert Constant conducted the London Symphony Orchestra and a chorus made up of a dozen Co-Operative and Labour choirs in Beethoven's *Egmont* Overture, the slow movement and the choral finale of Bush's Piano Concerto[13] with the composer as soloist, John Ireland's *These Things Shall Be*[14] (in which 'Mr Lambert encouraged them to let their voices soar on its broad tunes'), and the first performance of Britten's *Ballad of Heroes*. Although the attendance was poor, the concert made some impression on the critics, especially the Britten work. Of its performance, Fox Strangways in *The Observer* commented that 'the inaccuracies could be forgiven because the work was published too late for serious study.'[15] In fact the full score had only been completed a week before the concert so it was a considerable achievement on Constant's part. It had been written 'to honour men of the British Battalion of the International Brigade who had fallen in Spain' and by a happy coincidence the Spanish Civil War had officially ended on 1 April. Constant was not a person who normally

[12] Peter Ustinov, son of Nadia Benois, related a humorous anecdote about this presentation in his televised one-man show, *An Audience with Peter Ustinov*, that has been released on video and DVD (Granada D23348).

[13] First performed on 4 March 1938 at a BBC Contemporary Music concert conducted by Boult with the composer as soloist.

[14] *These Things Shall Be* was orchestrated by Alan Bush (who had been a pupil of John Ireland's), the instrumentation being outlined by Ireland who dedicated the work to Bush.

[15] *The Observer*, 9 April 1939, quoted *Letters from a Life: Selected Letters and Diaries of Benjamin Britten* vol. 1, p. 613.

1 Constant: a pencil drawing by George Lambert, December 1913
2 Thea Proctor's portrait of mother and son, Amy and Constant, lithograph 1915

3, 4 *Romeo and Juliet*: rejected designs by Christopher Wood

6

Performers

Mr. CONSTANT LAMBERT

and

ORCHESTRA

Flute & Piccolo	R. MURCHIE
Clarinet & Bass Clarinet	PAUL DRAPER
Saxophone	A. COX
Trumpet	HERBERT BARR
Percussion	H. WESTON
Violoncello	WALTER BRITTON

Conductor : Mr. W. T. WALTON

The following selection of poems from Miss Sitwell's "Façade" are printed by courtesy of Messrs. Gerald Duckworth & Co., Ltd., and the Editor of "Vogue".

5 Serge Lifar and Alicia Nikitina in *Romeo and Juliet*, Paris, May 1926

6 The *Façade* programme for 29 June 1926, the New Chenil Galleries, Chelsea

7 *A Day in a Southern Port* (*The Rio Grande*) group: Lambert, Lydia Lopokova, Frederick Ashton, Edward Burra and Walter Gore (kneeling), 1931

8 Lambert and Fonteyn backstage before a performance of *Façade*, 1935

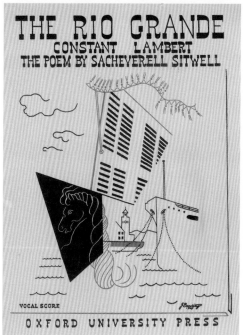

9 *The Rio Grande* dress rehearsal, Sadler's Wells, 1935. Centre group: William Chappell (Creole Boy), Fonteyn (Creole Girl), Beatrice Appleyard (Queen of the Port) and Walter Gore (Stevedore)

10 John Banting's cover design for the vocal score of *The Rio Grande* (Oxford University Press, 1930)

11 Florence Mills, star of *Dover Street to Dixie* and *Blackbirds*, to whose memory Lambert dedicated his *Elegiac Blues*

12 Anna May Wong, film star and dedicatee of Lambert's Li-Po settings

13 Florence Lambert, 1933

14 Margot Fontes, née Margaret (Peggy) Hookham, later to be better known as Margot Fonteyn, 1934

15 Angus Morrison

16 Christopher ('Kit') Wood, self-portrait, Paris 1927

17 Hubert Foss, publisher and friend to both Lambert and (*right*) Walton, 1932

18 Cecil Gray, at the Mill, Sussex *c.* 1943, with his future wife Margery
   Livingstone-Herbage

19 Lambert (*centre*) with Hal Collins, E. J. Moeran and Philip Heseltine in the garden of The Five Bells at Eynsford, 1928

20 Florence and Constant Lambert, May 1933

21 Lambert playfully posing as the jealous husband catching Anthony Powell with Florence Lambert

22 Lambert, 1933

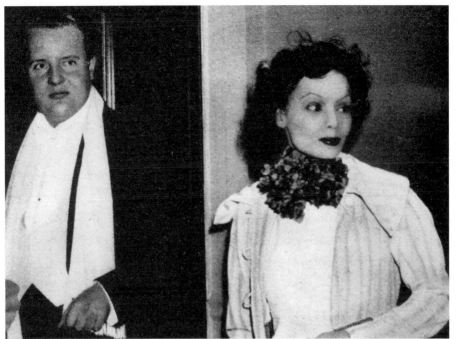

23 Constant and Florence Lambert arriving at Covent Garden for the first night of Weinberger's *Schwanda the Bagpiper*, 11 May 1934

24 Frederick Ashton, Lord Berners and Lambert at Berners' home, 1937

25 Robert Helpmann and Lambert planning a ballet

26 Jacob Epstein's *Isabel* in bronze

27 Lambert, Assistant Conductor, Henry Wood Proms 1946

28 Isabel Lambert, in later life (1967) when married to Alan Rawsthorne

29 Lambert working at the piano, July 1942

30 Lambert with Michael Ayrton, planning *The Fairy Queen*, 1946

31

32

33

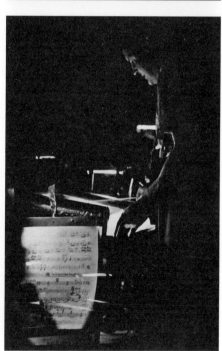

34

31–4 Studies of Lambert, typically with cigarette, at rehearsal and (*bottom right*) in performance at Covent Garden

35 Lambert, George Chaffee (dance teacher), Helen Dzhermolinska (editor of *Dance* magazine), Beryl Grey, Constantine (Hollywood photographer) and Mary Clarke at a party given on the occasion of Sadler's Wells' triumphant visit to New York, October 1949

36 Dame Ninette de Valois

37

38

37, 38 Lambert rehearsing the score of *Ballabile* in the crush bar at Covent Garden, May 1950.

39 The opening scene of *Tiresias*, with Michael Somes as young Tiresias and Margaret Dale as the Neophyte

40 Margot Fonteyn as the female Tiresias with John Field as her lover, *Tiresias*, scene 2

41 Isabel Lambert's costume designs for *Tiresias*

42 Lambert at the Zoo

43 Lambert with his pet cat, Captain Spalding, 1951

took any open political stance; he had more than likely become involved in the Festival through Edward Clark who assisted Alan Bush in its planning.

In the long seven-month season at Sadler's Wells that had lasted from 18 October 1938 until 18 May 1939, with two or three programmes a week, the most frequently performed ballets were *Harlequin in the Street, Checkmate, Les Patineurs, The Sleeping Princess, Horoscope, Les Sylphides* and *Lac des cygnes*.[16] A new ballet by Berners, *Cupid and Psyche*, premiered on 27 April, was not a success. As the Sadler's Wells historian Mary Clarke has written: 'The usual way of the Wells audience with an indifferent ballet was to cheer it loudly on the opening night and then gradually lose interest, but the gallery openly disapproved of *Cupid and Psyche* at its first performance, and booed it loudly.'[17] P. W. Manchester went as far as to write it off as a 'complete failure in which Ashton's invention seemed to have deserted him entirely.'[18] Over Easter Lambert and Ashton had discussed the new project with Berners at his home, Faringdon House in Berkshire, but Francis Rose, who designed the sets and the costumes, recalled that 'it was difficult for Gerald to conform to the hard work of the theatre, and as the ballet progressed, Constant Lambert, the great conductor, became more difficult.' Matters were made worse by Constant being ill a week before the premiere (with Boyd Neel replacing him for a BBC broadcast of works by Schubert, Haydn and Glinka). 'There were quarrels and at the end ... Lord Berners was nearly forced to conduct on the first night, but Constant Lambert regained health sufficiently to appear.' Things had hardly gone any better at rehearsals, with 'tights without slips, wings that fell off, wings that did not fit', and even at the dress rehearsal 'the costumes were only half there; in fact on the first night they arrived act by act.'[19] Berners had chosen a classical tale from Apuleius to which his satirical sense that had worked admirably in *A Wedding Bouquet* was not so well suited. Perhaps, too, frivolity was out of keeping with the darkening shadows of war, and there was a questionable lapse of taste in having Venus conceived as 'a vulgar little chit from the chorus of a non-stop revue' and Jupiter marching 'about the stage making Fascist salutes and hiccupping violently'.[20] As the *Times* critic observed, '[Berners] has not been able entirely to turn his back on the "amusing", and satire keeps breaking in until at the end the assembly of the classical gods degenerates into downright pantomime.' The ballet only survived four performances and Constant no doubt commiserated with Berners in June when he was once again staying at Faringdon.[21]

Constant's greatest personal success that year was conducting *Turandot* at Covent Garden in May, albeit only for two performances. He had first heard it together with Angus Morrison back in 1928[22] and it remained his favourite opera. The following year in an article on Puccini in the magazine *Milo* he had been prepared boldly to defy public opinion:

---

[16] Altogether the Company presented 66 programmes totalling 157 performances from a repertoire of 25 ballets. The ballets were generally staged on Tuesday and Thursday evenings, with a Saturday matinée. For the rest of the week, except Sunday and Monday, the theatre was given over to opera.

[17] Clarke, *The Sadler's Wells Ballet*, p. 144.

[18] Manchester, *Vic-Wells*, p. 43.

[19] Francis Rose, *Saying Life: The Memoirs of Sir Francis Rose* (London: Cassell, 1961).

[20] Manchester, *Vic-Wells*, p. 43.

[21] 27 April (premiere) and 2, 11 & 16 May. Lambert could not have conducted the third performance as he was conducting *Turandot* that evening at Covent Garden.

[22] At Covent Garden on 13 July 1928, conducted by Edoardo Fornarini. Afterwards Constant and Angus went on to Rules.

Puccini's music stands alone in modern times as being the only operatic music that is perfectly adapted to its medium. ... His best operas are equally satisfying both from the musical and dramatic point of view because almost alone amongst the composers of his time, he was able to express dramatic atmosphere in terms of melody. ... For too long Puccini has been contemptuously dismissed by the intellectual critics as a sentimental best-seller. That his works are occasionally vulgar may be true, but how much more refreshing is Puccini's full-blooded sentiment than the pretensions and pompous vulgarities of Strauss or the facetious and misguided vulgarities of the latest French school (which incidentally will probably have been superseded by the time this article appears). It is high time that Puccini was accorded the respect due to a remarkably original artist and a master of his craft.[23]

He approached *Turandot* with the same thoroughness and attention to detail as he had *The Sleeping Princess*, restoring some cuts that it had been the custom to make. As Spike Hughes observed: 'The cuts are inexplicable; they do not save more than a minute in time, all told, and are unjustifiable on artistic grounds.'[24] For Constant, to have his name listed alongside those of Beecham, Gui and Weingartner in Covent Garden's international season was evidence of his high standing as a conductor, and the *Times* review was one of commendation:

Mr Constant Lambert established himself at one stroke as a conductor who can handle opera as surely as he regularly manages the sister art of the theatre, the ballet. Singers, especially Italian singers, however, demand more tempo rubato than dancers, and Puccini with his trailing unison melodies is not the composer to cabin and confine them within the strict pulse of a metronome. Mr Lambert allowed them all the dramatic licence they needed without allowing the larger tension of the opera to slacken for a moment. Indeed, the way he built up the climax of the first act ... was contrived in successive waves of momentum and showed his right judgment of the nature and power of this particular opera.[25]

Eva Turner sang the title role for the only two scheduled performances.[26]

In April and May Sadler's Wells came under the wing of the London Music Festival, giving performances of *The Rake's Progress*, *Horoscope*, *Les Patineurs*, *A Wedding Bouquet*, *Checkmate*, *Façade*, *The Sleeping Princess* and *Job*, Constant conducting the last in an enterprising double-bill with Vaughan Williams' opera *Hugh the Drover* under Lawrance Collingwood. Five days later, on 18 May, the London ballet season ended with *The Sleeping Princess*. After a short break the Company went on tour, visiting first the Arts Theatre at Cambridge and then, for a week each, Oxford and Bournemouth, with Constant in between snatching a week-end at Faringdon House with Lord Berners.[27] In a memorial tribute he wrote of Berners' 'love of company when

[23] *Milo*, vol. 1 no. 3 (Christmas [December] 1929), pp. 9–11. See Appendix 4.
[24] Hughes, *Opening Bars*, p. 290n. Although Hughes does not make it clear whether he is referring to Lambert's 1939 or 1947 performances, it would be reasonable to suppose that he restored the cuts on both occasions.
[25] *The Times*, 4 May 1939.
[26] The two performances were given on 3 and 11 May 1939. The cast also included José Luccioni (Calaf), Mafalda Favero (Liu), Corrado Zambelli (Timur) and Octave Dua (Emperor).
[27] Lambert sent Anthony Powell a picture postcard, dated 12 June 1939, of Faringdon House with a meeting of the hounds, adding: 'I know that a broken collar-bone is the making of us. All at the same time I do wish I hadn't been bitten in the crutch by a fox.'

specially selected and nothing could have been gayer than his week-end parties where cuisine and conversation were on an equally high level'.[28]

In June Constant had a couple of studio concerts for the BBC[29] and a recording session for HMV. That same month *The Rio Grande* was down for performance at the Frankfurt Festival and Constant had been invited to conduct. He had conducted in Frankfurt in 1930 in a Festival of British Music, but this time because of the international situation he was against any involvement and in December had written from Hanover Lodge to Alan Frank of OUP:

> It has been suggested by a body called 'The Permanent Council for the International Co-Operation of Composers' that my 'Rio Grande' should be performed at a festival in Frankfurt next June. Personally speaking I have the very strongest objection to a note of mine being played in Germany under the present regime. I realise of course that I have no power of veto, that the work belongs legally to the OUP who may well feel that a composer's personal views should not stand in the way of a performance. I should like to know how Sir Humphrey Milford[30] and Hubert feel about it.

He added: 'I need hardly say that any money received from such a performance would immediately be sent to a refugee fund.' Frank wrote to the Frankfurt Festival organisers:

> I have been in touch with Constant Lambert and am sorry to inform you that he will under no circumstances conduct in Germany under the present political regime. He is anxious that even his work should not be performed, but this decision lies with us, as his publishers, and we do not consider it would be a good thing to withdraw it.[31]

So, despite Constant's concerns, the performance went ahead on 21 June 1939 but without his participation. One work that did not see performance as planned was the *Caprice péruvien*, a short orchestral piece that Constant had contrived using some of the interlude music in Berners' comic opera *Le Carrosse du Saint-Sacrement*.[32] It was to have been introduced at the Proms on 21 September, and in June Constant had sent a telegram to Julian Herbage, BBC programme planner: 'MUCH REGRET GRAMMATICAL HOWLER DUE LACK CLASSICAL EDUCATION STOP CAPRICE MASCULINE FOR PERUVIENNE READ PERUVIEN STOP WRITING STOP TELEPHONING LAMBERT.' But with the temporary suspension of the Proms at the outbreak of war on 3 September, that performance did not take place.

Other plans thrown to the winds by the outbreak of war concerned a production of *The Acharnians* of Aristophanes to be given by the Oxford University Dramatic Society in June 1940 with new incidental music. The producer, Robert Lewis, had first approached Vaughan Williams, who was unwilling to supersede his revered

---

[28] *The New Statesman and Athenæum*, 6 May 1930.

[29] The second broadcast, on 26 June, was titled 'Two hundred years ago: Music of 1739' and consisted of vocal, choral and orchestral works by Handel and Rameau.

[30] Sir Humphrey Milford was both the instigator and the head of the Music Department of Oxford University Press.

[31] Correspondence in the OUP files.

[32] Berners' only opera *Le Carrosse du Saint-Sacrement*, set in Peru with his own libretto based on the play by Prosper Mérimée, was first staged in Paris on 24 April 1924. The *Caprice péruvien* probably came about because there seemed little likelihood of the opera being staged again. It was completed on 12 July 1939. Lambert's copy of the vocal score, with his pencilled indications for the *Caprice*, is in the BBC Music Library.

teacher Parry's score[33], so he asked Lambert who had agreed, but the project was abandoned.[34]

On 7 July 1939 Constant took his last Conductors' Class of the term at the Royal College, Bernard Stevens being one of his students on that day. As it turned out, it concluded his teaching there, Gordon Jacob taking his place thereafter. In the remaining weeks of peace he had two more BBC studio broadcasts, including the first broadcast on 20 July of a Divertimento by Sándor Veress, a former pupil of Bartók and Kodály then on a study visit to London. At other times he did his bit in the civilian preparations against war by joining volunteers who were digging trenches for hastily constructed air-raid shelters in Regent's Park, a scene, Powell described, 'emblematic of the country's unpreparedness.'[35]

After a well-deserved holiday the Vic-Wells Company assembled in Manchester on 21 August for the start of a tour of northern England. 'Please excuse delay but Manchester always provokes extreme lethargy in me and I had to keep my mind off the crisis by playing Purcell all day,' Constant wrote to Herbert Murrill[36] at the BBC with whom he was hoping to arrange some Satie for a future broadcast: 'Having done Mercure & Relâche I would like to do Parade which has never yet been given here as a concert piece.[37] One could fit it in with something short, the Gymnopédies, Prélude de la Porte héroïque[38] (query scoring?) or that exquisite work La Belle Excentrique ... If this sounds too fantastic let me have alternative suggestions.' The Purcell he was playing may have been theatre music that he was selecting for a projected Ashton ballet on Pocahontas for which Rex Whistler was to design the décor, but this was abandoned when it became clear that future plans would have to be drastically curtailed because of war. (The next ballet for which he selected music by Purcell was to be *Comus*, in 1942.)

From Manchester the Company moved to Liverpool and on Saturday 2 September they concluded their week at the Royal Court Theatre with Constant conducting his last peace-time programme: *The Rake's Progress*, *Horoscope* and Act 3 of *The Sleeping Princess*. The next morning, amidst crowds of evacuees, they boarded a train to Leeds where on arrival they learned that war had been declared and that all theatres were to be closed by order of the Home Office. 'Fred Ashton was silent and gloomy,' Fonteyn wrote later. 'Constant Lambert, untypically, was at a loss for an amusingly highbrow comment to fit the occasion, and even Helpmann could think of no way to turn this situation into absurdity.'[39] Ashton, Helpmann and Billy Chappell, unsure of what to do, rang their good friend the writer and costume designer Doris Langley Moore who lived in Harrogate and they stayed with her for a few days until future plans were decided.

---

[33] *The Acharnians*, with incidental music by Parry, had been first staged by OUDS during the week of 18–24 February 1914. The conducting was shared between Hugh Allen and Adrian Boult, with Parry making only a brief conducting appearance on one of the days.

[34] Letter from Robert Lewis to Angus Morrison, 28 February 1954: RCM Archive.

[35] Powell, *Faces in My Time*, p. 87.

[36] Herbert Murrill joined the BBC staff in 1936, becoming Music Programmes Administrator 1942–6, Assistant Director (Head) of Music 1946–50, and eventually Head of Music 1950–2.

[37] On 18 August 1937 for the National Programme he conducted an all-Satie broadcast consisting of *Jack-in-the-Box* (orch. Milhaud), a suite from *Relâche* (first UK performance), *Trois valses du précieux degoûté* (orch. Greenbaum) and a suite from *Mercure*. Lambert had quite likely suggested *Mercure* when it was given on 22 June 1931 by the Marie Rambert Ballet at the Lyric Theatre, Hammersmith, with Ashton, Karsavina and Chappell.

[38] According to the catalogue, the copy in the British Library of Erik Satie's *Prélude de la porte héroïque du ciel*, orchestrated by Roland Manuel, has pencil annotations in the hand of Constant Lambert.

[39] Fonteyn, *Autobiography*, p. 89.

According to Helpmann's biographer, the three of them – and Constant – had had fun on an earlier occasion in going through Doris's collection of costumes and dressing up as suffragettes.[40] Doris herself remembered Constant's visits:

> He stayed at my house when playing in Bradford, Leeds (I think), and Harrogate where I lived. Later, for a time I saw a good deal of him in London. This was when the ballet was at the New Theatre and I was a frequent visitor. ... Constant's opinions always interested me greatly, and I appreciated immensely the fact that he would talk of music to me as if my being a music-lover was enough to entitle me to share in such conversation. ...
>
> ... At my house, he always played the pianola, which delighted me too, because it excited ill-concealed contempt in most of my friends, but Constant told me that his love of music had been very much stimulated in early days by a pianola.

With theatres closed, the Company had little option but to disband temporarily and return to London. The ban was lifted after a fortnight, only to be replaced by another restriction, that all performances across the country were to finish by 10 p.m., except in Central London where 6 p.m. was the closing time. (This ruling was abolished by December.)

In view of the prevailing circumstances the governors of Sadler's Wells felt that the best step would be to close down the ballet, but Kenneth Clark, William Walton and Ashton's close friend Alice von Hofmannsthal between them raised enough money to keep the ballet going and to fund a tour. So on 18 September, with Tyrone Guthrie's encouragement as Administrator of the Old Vic and Sadler's Wells, the Company reformed in Cardiff instead of London and then set off on an exhausting provincial tour, initially of uncertain length, that was to last until December, taking in Newcastle, Leicester, Leeds, Birmingham, Southsea, Brighton, Cambridge, Nottingham, Glasgow, Bradford and Hull, with a week's stay in each town. De Valois remained in London,[41] so the organisation of the tour fell largely on Ashton and Lambert whose artistic input was now to be greater than before. Irrespective of seniority, Constant and all the dancers were paid a flat rate of £5 a week, with the prospect of an increase if box-office takings were good.[42] In each town they gave six evening performances and three matinées with a repertoire that included *Les Sylphides*, *Harlequin in the Street*, *Checkmate*, *The Gods Go a'Begging*, *The Rake's Progress*, *Les Patineurs*, *Horoscope* and *Façade*. There was one big difference: instead of an orchestra, throughout the tour they were accompanied in the pit on two pianos by Constant Lambert and Hilda Gaunt, the Company's rehearsal pianist, Hilda taking the bass and Constant the treble.[43] Such was their workload that they necessarily also played for classes and rehearsals. As de Valois recalled:

> Our company had to work for nearly a year with two pianos. Constant Lambert became our first pianist, and forthwith his energy and musical integrity was

---

[40] Elizabeth Salter, *Helpman, The Authorised Biography* (Sydney: Angus & Robertson, 1978), p. 97.

[41] According to Kavanagh, *Secret Muses*, pp. 255–6, de Valois was helping out with her husband's medical practice, his partner having been conscripted. Neither de Valois herself nor her biographer, Kathrine Sorley Walker, mentions or explains her absence from this early war-time tour.

[42] Constant's salary for a week in each town was as follows: Cardiff £5, Newcastle £10 12 6, Leicester £22 10 0, Leeds £30, Birmingham £20, Southsea £20, Brighton £12 10 0, Cambridge £20, Nottingham £20, Glasgow £20, Bradford £20 and Hull £20. These totals presumably reflected the attendances in each town (Vic-Wells Archives).

[43] On a few occasions they used one piano and Lambert alone would accompany the Company.

transferred from the orchestral score to the pianoforte score. Hours were spent rehearsing and arranging with care, taste and forethought. No detail was too small, no problem too big to tackle in his approach to this change of medium; the standard of execution and arrangement had become of first importance to a mind that knew no 'second best'.[44] ... He was just as wrapped up in perfection – because he was a perfectionist, a great perfectionist – in performances with two pianos as he had been when he had an orchestra of his own, and a great sense of humour for the change in life and the roughness and the difficulties with our ENSA tours[45] and everything, and he was delighted when we arrived at one town to find a large poster saying 'At the piano Miss Constance Lambert'. He wanted to get hold of the poster and keep it.[46]

As Margaret Dale[47] remembered, there was no deprivation when performing to two pianos as

Hilda and Constant were playing all the things we used to hear on full orchestra. There was no difference as far as we were concerned because what matters most to dancers is tempo and rhythm, and Constant had rhythm. Constant understood what it was to dance even though he never danced himself. He had very clear ideas about choreography and dancing. He was a man of extraordinary energy. He was always con brio.[48]

Writing from Glasgow ('City of laughter, city of tears'), Constant provided Cecil Gray with a vivid account of the tour:

You have asked for autobiographical material. Very well you shall bloody well have it. Since Sept 17th I have been tickling the dominoes and/or punishing the keyboard for 8 hrs a day except Sundays when I have been making an exhilarating tour of industrial England the average train journey being 9 hrs. long (no restaurant car and an occasional 2 hr. wait out of hours at places like Doncaster & Trent.) The tour has consisted of the following towns <u>in this order</u>: Cardiff, Newcastle, Leicester, Leeds, Birmingham, Southsea, Brighton, Cambridge, Nottingham, Glasgow with a final <u>bonne bouche</u> of Bradford & Hull to look forward to. I spend my nights at the cheapest type of commercial hotel, the kind of place here they 'do you all in' (that I think is the phrase) for about 35/- a week. Perhaps it was the continuous and unrelieved Hades of my life which made me suggest to Fred a ballet on Liszt's 'Après une lecture de Dante'. Anyhow he has started and indeed almost finished it. It is very fine but involves my hammering the bloody thing out for 3 hrs. at a time on my rare free afternoons. (We rehearse every morning & do 3 matinées a week.) Tickling the dominoes involves being 90% on the wagon which is bad (a) for one's temper (b) for one's sex-mania.

You would enjoy Glasgow in November particularly in a black-out (which

---

[44] Ninette de Valois, 'Constant Lambert: An Appreciation of his Work', *The Dancing Times*, no. 492 (October 1951), pp. 7–8.

[45] ENSA, or Entertainments National Service Association, was an organisation set up in 1939 to provide entertainment for British munition workers and armed forces personnel both at home and abroad during World War II. Lambert was on the ENSA advisory council that also included Bax, Bantock, Hadley, Sargent, Walton and Wood: Wetherell, *'Paddy'*, pp. 50–1.

[46] Ninette de Valois, in *In Search of Constant Lambert*, BBC2, 26 July 1965.

[47] Margaret Dale (née Margaret Bolam) joined the Company in 1937.

[48] Margaret Dale talking at the Royal Opera House, Covent Garden in *Remembering Constant Lambert*, 14 March 2001. The occasion was recorded.

some might think a work of super-erogation). The fog swirls up the spiral stone staircases of the lodging houses at night and chokes one in the morning when in the empty theatre one sits practising Chopin with icy hands to the accompaniment of vacuum cleaners, one's classic beauty enhanced by the pot plants which stick into the back of one's neck.

I have retained my sanity by embarking on a series of limericks devoted to Bishops with double titles and have already done the Bishops of Glasgow & Galloway, Argyll & the Isles, Swansea & Brecon, Down & Connor, Kildare & Leighlin, Kimberly & Kuruman, Victoria & Hong-Kong, Kwangsi & Honan, Laburan & Sarawak and last but not least Ramnad & Madura. Can you suggest any more?

I return to London on December 11th and have a week out before starting rehearsals for a short season at the Wells (with orchestra thank God). Would there be any chance of coming down between the 12th & the 17th? It would be nice to make a contact with civilisation again. Apart from a couple of lunches with Walter Legge (I did some recording coming up from Brighton) and a pleasant glimpse or two of Paddy at Cambridge (he is now off the wagon and in champion form) I have been completely out of touch with my friends. Kit is apparently very well & happy. Flo in spite of a telegraphic barrage of the 'Foolish come Cambridge-writing' order insisted on coming up to Cambridge and creating one of her epic muddles. I didn't think the old girl was exactly at her best. Rumour has it that Bumps & Alan [Rawsthorne] sit drinking whiskey out of tin-helmets in the crypt of Bristol Cathedral. I see no reason to disbelieve this.[49]

Alan Rawsthorne and his wife Jessie Hinchliffe[50] were living in Bristol, whither the BBC Symphony Orchestra had been evacuated, Jessie being a violinist in the Orchestra. Alan was doing voluntary war work there and Constant had written a warm appreciation of him in *The Monthly Musical Record*, praising in particular his Theme and Variations for Two Violins and his Viola Sonata. (Of this work he once expressed astonishment that it contained so much double-stopping until he remembered that Rawsthorne had studied dentistry before turning to composition.) He admired Rawsthorne's 'sustained rhapsodical melodic invention' and the fact that his music was free from 'the traditional English influences: there is not a trace of folk-song in his work, still less of Anglo-Irish nostalgia or Chester-Belloc heartiness'.[51] He had possibly first become acquainted with Alan's music in February 1937 when a work of his was performed at a Wigmore Hall concert.[52] Before long they became close friends. They were both strong drinkers and lovers of cats – but these were not to be the only things that they were to share.

The double-bishop limericks, which eventually numbered about 50, were almost certainly influenced by Heseltine's equally bawdy and unprintable verses.[53] Constant cherished a collection of poems and quotations mainly relating to drinking that

[49] Letter from Lambert to Gray, 21 November 1939: RCM Archives. For the recording session, see Appendix 3.

[50] Alan Rawsthorne and Jessie Hinchliffe married in 1934, had an amicable separation in 1947, and were divorced in 1954. Alan married Isabel Lambert the following year.

[51] Lambert, 'The Younger English Composers: IV. Alan Rawsthorne', *The Monthly Musical Record*, September 1938, pp. 196–9.

[52] Gordon Green, 'The Friends of Alan Rawsthorne', *The Creel*, vol. 2 no. 1 (Spring 1992), pp. 127–8.

[53] Unprintable, that is, in those days. A comprehensive collection of Heseltine's verses, entitled *Cursory Rhymes: Limericks and Other Poems in the Best Interests of Morality*, edited by Brian Collins, was published by the Peter Warlock Society in 2000.

Heseltine had assembled under the appropriate pseudonym of Rab Noolas.[54] He himself had long enjoyed writing comic verse[55] and was quite likely encouraged too by Lord Berners' rather more refined efforts. He may also at that time been familiar with Norman Douglas's privately printed collection of limericks.[56] Two of Constant's, written on Casa Prada paper and thankfully preserved by Elisabeth Lutyens,[57] deserve further circulation:

> The first of two camp hippopotami
> To the second said, 'What are you? What am I?'
> Though our organs are massive
> As lovers we're passive.
> How can we resolve this dichotomy?

> Mr Westrup[58] tore *Lulu* to pieces,
> Declaring it atonal *faeces*.
> He said, 'I don't mind
> When the canon's behind,
> But I can't bear *per arsis et thesis!*'

Most of the double-bishop limericks, if less polished than Heseltine's, were unprintable in those far less liberal times and Constant circulated them amongst only his closest friends. They were the result of a chance visit to Newcastle in November by the *Daily Express* journalist Tom Driberg who was to become a good friend of Constant's.

Driberg,[59] who was only a few months older than Constant, was a journalist (he started the William Hickey column in the *Daily Express*) and a politician. Formerly a member of the Communist Party, he later joined Labour and became a member of parliament in 1942. Known amongst friends for his homosexual tendencies, he was educated at Lancing and gained an open scholarship to Christ Church, Oxford, where he formed a close (though chaste) friendship with W. H. Auden. He also knew the Sitwells on whose recommendation he was hired by the *Daily Express* as a reporter and he would attend Edith's poetry tea parties at her Bayswater home. In 1935, after a bizarre incident in which he shared his bed with two unemployed miners wanting accommodation for the night who later accused him of indecent assault, he narrowly escaped imprisonment, thanks to Lord Beaverbrook, who not only covered the cost of his defence but also used his powers to see that nothing got into the press. Driberg covered Spain for his paper during the civil war with fellow *Express* journalist Sefton Delmer.

[54] *Merry-Go-Down: A Gallery of Gorgeous Drunkards through the Ages: Collected for the Use, Interest, Illumination, and Delectation of Serious Topers* (London: Mandrake Press, 1929). Rab Noolas is, of course, 'saloon bar' in reverse.

[55] The 'blurb' for the Pelican edition of *Music Ho!* (1948) stated that 'his hobbies are few and mainly confined to playing Russian billiards and composing limericks'.

[56] Norman Douglas, *Some Limericks: Collected for the Use of Students, & Ensplendour'd with Introduction, Geographical Index, and with Notes Explanatory and Critical*. 1,000 numbered copies were privately printed in Germany, 1928 (reprinted Grove Press, 1967; Atlas Press 2009). Tom Driberg owned a copy that was annotated by Lambert.

[57] Harries, *A Pilgrim Soul*, pp. 81–2. The first was dedicated to 'Nobby Clarke [*sic*], August 2nd 1930'.

[58] Sir Jack Westrup (1904–75), music scholar, teacher, writer, critic and conductor.

[59] Tom Driberg was born on 22 May 1905 and died from a heart-attack in 1976. Amongst other writings *The Best of Both Worlds: A Personal Diary* was published in 1953 and his very frank autobiography, *Ruling Passions*, was published posthumously in 1977. In 1976 he became Lord Bradwell (or Baron Bradwell of Bradwell juxta Mare as he gazetted himself).

Driberg had known Constant before the war when they were both guests at 'wonderful week-ends at Tickerage with Dick Wyndham – week-ends compounded of long Sussex walks and crazy croquet, of magnums of château-bottled claret, of ninety-mile-an-hour drives to Lewes in Dick's Railton car, of all-night sessions of argument or Lexicon.'[60] These parties included such literary and journalistic figures as John Rayner, A. J. A. Symons, Peter Quennell and Cyril Connolly, who wrote that Constant's 'entries in Wyndham's visitors' book, accompanied by limericks and scraps of musical parody, run parallel to mine.'[61] As Driberg remembered:

> [Constant] came straight from the concert in his white tie and tail coat of a conductor looking very comical by the time he arrived and we sat there playing Lexicon, drinking certainly until dawn. ... He looked an extraordinary period figure like one of those great 19th century composers. It was very difficult to get him to go to bed because we used to play old gramophone records on an old portable gramophone. Two I remember in particular he used to like: one was 'The Big Noise from Winnetka'[62] which is indeed a marvellous record of its kind, and the other was a record by some big band – it may have been Paul Whiteman – of 'Love for Sale', and he used to go near the gramophone, because he was a bit deaf, and he used to lean over it, waiting intensely for the moment it started.[63]

Constant's second wife, Isabel, wrote in her unpublished memoirs:

> Tom Driberg and Constant both loved black American bands and singers of the great jazz era. Both frequented night clubs like the 'Nest'. Both liked the 'below the belt' hymn tunes such as those composed by J. D. Dykes. Both played word games with zest. When 'William Hickey' in the *Daily Express*, Tom Driberg would slip in news items about ballet or opera that Constant might tell him (in spite of the profound suspicion and dislike by Lord Beaverbrook of ballet or opera).[64]

Humphrey Searle also went with Constant to The Nest, in Kingly Street, off Regent Street, and remembered it as 'a simple, comparatively inexpensive club with Negro waitresses – who intrigued Constant who always fell for exotic-looking girls – and a small but superb Negro band which he liked as well. By about three in the morning the band had really reached its peak and the sound was terrifically exciting.' Performers like Fats Waller and the Mills Brothers would sometimes drop in after appearing at the Palladium and perform free of charge.[65]

Driberg was aware of Constant's late working hours:

> He seemed to withdraw into himself and it was difficult to coax him out because he was aware that he was late with some work that ought to have been delivered. He couldn't help sitting up late at night. In the inter-war period we used to go to cheap dives, sort of rather low night clubs around Carnaby Street and used to sit

[60] Tom Driberg, *The Best of Both Worlds: A Personal Diary* (London: Phoenix House, 1953), p. 70. Lexicon is a once-popular word-building card game.

[61] Cyril Connolly, 'March of Time', *Sunday Times*, 23 September 1973.

[62] Bob Crosby and his Orchestra, *The Big Noise from Winnetka* by Bob Haggart and Ray Bauduc (Decca F7005).

[63] *In Search of Constant Lambert*, BBC2, 26 July 1965.

[64] Isabel Rawsthorne's memoirs (unpublished), Hyman Kreitman Research Centre, Tate Britain. On a more personal level Lambert introduced Driberg to the songs of Peter Warlock.

[65] Humphry Searle, *Quadrille with a Raven: Memoirs* (www.musicweb-international.com/searle/titlepg.htm), chapter 6.

up until four or five. But of course like other artists he could work at any time of the day or night when he was forced to. ... Spike Hughes would sit up all night with him too, and some times Duke Ellington was with him.[66]

Another club they both frequented was the Shim-Sham Club, Driberg's favourite, in Frith Street, Soho. Most of its staff and customers were black and Constant struck up a close friendship with the club's cigarette girl, Laureen Sylvestre, whom he took to Toulon on at least one occasion. When Laureen gave birth to a daughter, Cleopatra, Tom and Constant both agreed to be godfathers. After Constant's death Laureen wrote:

> Mr Constant Lambert was a very dear and old friend of mine. ... He was also my little daughter's Godfather. It made me so happy when he wrote saying he would like to be her Godfather, for that was just what he would do, he was (as I suppose you know) always so kind, thoughtful and willing to do the things that he knew would bring happiness.

According to Driberg's biographer,[67] Tom always claimed that Constant was the girl's father. While Richard Shead allows space for a rumour that Constant had an illegitimate child with a black woman, Andrew Motion seems to dismiss the idea, there being 'no basis for this rumour'.

> Laureen, who lived in Conway Street, was an amusing, poorly educated woman, of much firmer principles that many of those with whom she surrounded herself. She refused to work at The Bag O'Nails night club, for instance, because the girls there were expected to sleep with customers as well as work as waitresses. ... As a godfather Constant fulfilled his duties conscientiously, regularly writing to Laureen, taking her out, and doing what he could for Cleo. (He tried to get her cast as the Indian Page in *The Fairy Queen* in 1951, but his efforts came to nothing.) Laureen, in return, could be relied on, he said, 'for information about night life', and for uncomplicated affection. When Constant died, Laureen wrote to Driberg: 'Oh, Tom, I feel so very unhappy ... Constant and I always had a joke about wearing a hat which I hate and I always said I hated to attend funerals because I would be compelled then to wear one. I feel so bewildered.'[68]

Constant and Driberg were in the habit of setting each other challenging limericks to complete and, as Driberg recalled, it was he who instigated the double-bishop limericks:

> Early in the war I unexpectedly had to spend a night in Newcastle. To my delight I found that the Ballet was performing there. It was impossible in those days to tour a whole orchestra: the accompaniment was provided by two pianos, played by Hilda Gaunt and Constant.
>
> I had just been visiting Glasgow, and had there noted, as something to tell Constant next time I saw him, that the title of the local Bishop – whose see is Glasgow and Galloway – was one that lent itself well to the limerick form. I decided to play a mild practical joke on Constant.
>
> Without letting him know I was in Newcastle I bought a seat in the front row of the stalls. I got to the theatre early, ascertained which piano Concert played, and unobtrusively leaned over the rail of the orchestra pit and placed on his music-stand a card on which I had written:

[66] *Constant Lambert Remembered*, BBC Third Network, 25 June 1966.

[67] Francis Wheen, *Tom Driberg: His Life and Indiscretions* (London: Chatto & Windus, 1990; reissued in association with Pan Books, 1992), p. 93.

[68] Motion, *The Lamberts*, p. 178.

> The Bishop of Glasgow and Galloway
> Preferred Artie Shaw to Cab Calloway …

It was perhaps unkind to risk 'putting him off' in this way, but the temptation was irresistible. It worked beautifully. Constant limped in, his head leonine and majestic as ever, his face stern. He made his stately bow to the audience. He sat down at the piano and put his stick on the floor. Then he glanced at the music before him. I saw his shoulders stiffen and his mouth twitch: he recognised my writing, looked around, and saw me. The audience could have noticed nothing, for this took only a moment and he began at once to play, and played superbly. By the first interval he had completed the last three lines of my limerick very creditably.[69]

The completed limerick (which betrays their shared loved of jazz) runs:

> The Bishop of Glasgow and Galloway
> Preferred Artie Shaw to Cab Calloway,
>   When it came to night life
>   He deserted his wife
> And tried it the blue, black and yaller way.

T HE recording work with Legge that Constant mentioned in his letter to Gray was of Liszt's *Hungarian Fantasia*, on 3 November at HMV's Abbey Road studios with Benno Moiseiwitsch and the London Philharmonic Orchestra, and by coincidence the music of Liszt was the basis of the new ballet, *Dante Sonata*, he was then working on. He gave a fuller account of its genesis in a radio talk in November 1948:

As we were touring the provinces for weeks on end, with a fairly established repertoire, all our spare time could be devoted to the endless discussion of new creations. In the case of *Dante Sonata*, the first of our war-time ballets and one whose symbolism is clearly inspired by the outbreak of war, Ashton suggested the theme of Dante's *Inferno*. I, after various ideas, settled on the Liszt piano piece which is used. The general layout, by which I mean not the dancing as such, but the association of various characters with various themes, and the general dramatic sequence was then established mutually by Ashton and myself. I played the piano at almost all the rehearsals while the choreography was being created, so that when it came finally to orchestrating the ballet, I had the whole stage picture in my mind. I am certain that, apart from whether people like *Dante Sonata* or not, it has a visual-cum-musical unity which could only have been achieved by this form of collaboration. The longer I work in ballet, and I have been doing it now for twenty-three years, the more convinced I am that ballets which endure are those in which no one collaborator can say, 'This is my ballet'. Nightly quarrels round the supper table are far more fruitful in the long run than polite letters from a distance.[70]

The piece he had chosen was the 15-minute *Fantasia quasi Sonata, après une lecture*

---

[69] Driberg, *The Best of Both Worlds*, pp. 71–2. Driberg also told the story in *Constant Lambert Remembered*, BBC Third Network, 25 June 1966. When a set of the Double Bishops limericks was auctioned at Christie's, Driberg bought them. See Appendix 12 for further examples. Ayrton, *Golden Sections*, p. 126, mentions 'the canto of ten stanzas known as *The Musical Peal of Ten Bells*' (a copy of which has not been found) that, with the Double Bishops verses, 'place Lambert among the great masters of the limerick form'.

[70] BBC broadcast 17 November 1948, with Lambert's contribution reprinted in *Dancing Times*, January 1949, under the title 'Music for Ballet'.

du Dante, from the *Deuxième Année* of Liszt's *Années de pèlerinage*. It was an apt choice to match Dante's *Inferno*, as Humphrey Searle was to suggest in his study of the music of Liszt (written in 1957 'In memory of Constant Lambert') when he wrote that 'though the title of the piece is actually taken from a poem by Victor Hugo, there is no doubt that in it Liszt expressed his own reactions to the "strange tongues, horrible cries, words of pain, tones of anger" which Dante describes in his Inferno.' Searle considered it 'not quite altogether satisfactory as a piano piece' but thought that the ballet brought out its qualities 'in a far clearer and more incisive manner'.[71]

As the tour continued, Constant kept Gray up-to-date with the itinerary, writing from the Royal Station Hotel in what he labelled 'the Biarritz of the North', Hull, and providing a travel commentary almost in a tongue-in-cheek imitation of one of his favourite guide books, Baedeker:

> Hull at first sight is not entirely unpleasant. One can at least breathe and there is an unexpected amount of tolerable 18th & early 19th [century] architecture in the streets. The theatre, a converted Assembly Rooms, is very pleasant outside & will I hope be equally nice within. It is a smallish repertory theatre run by the man who runs the Brighton theatre and should be a change from the monstrous pleasure domes and caves of ice[72] we usually play in. (Perhaps I am unduly elated merely because I am in a new town. When on tour one feels more than ever like Capt. Spalding[73] that one must be going.) Whether the intelligentsia of Hull will appreciate our faisandé fare remains to be seen. Anyhow anything must be better than my last fortnight. Glasgow as you know has never been my favourite town and there is less to be said for Bradford than might hastily be supposed.
>
> Your countrymen have an endearing habit of knocking out their pipes on the orchestra rail during the more intricate solo passages and while not denying for a moment the stirling work in the same field that has been put in by Hindus and Serbians I still maintain that nothing in the world can really touch the professional SCOTCH BORE. The architecture of Bradford has a Gothic exuberance, a Baroque extravagance, a Romantic frenzy which is striking even for an industrial town. The individual buildings hover, stylistically speaking, a little uneasily between Old Heidelberg and the Doges Palace at Venice but the tout ensemble is ravishing. But architecture apart the town & its inhabitants are a little damping and I'm not surprised that Delius was driven to nostalgia & negresses.
>
> I quite agree with you about the infernal beauty of the blackout and there I think I score over you for London is nothing to the Northern towns. The dock quarter of Liverpool with its dirty Doric buildings was quite seriously the most beautiful thing I have seen and Newcastle was nearly as good. Even the towns with bad architecture like Glasgow take on a certain nightmare quality (incidentally Scotch Masonic architecture needs a brochure to itself).
>
> I felt too tired to search for a commercial hovel on arriving here so am staying the night in temporary luxury before steeling myself for the worst. The continuous work plus the rehearsals of the Liszt is beginning to get me down. The new ballet is turning out splendidly but now Fred, after crucifying the whole company, is going to kill me off by bullying me into scoring the thing for piano & orchestra (a good idea incidentally). So I hope you have a refectory table and

---

[71] Humphrey Searle, *The Music of Liszt* (London: Williams & Norgate, 1954), p. 32.

[72] 'A sunny pleasure-dome with caves of ice!' from Samuel Taylor Coleridge's *Kubla Khan*.

[73] Captain Spalding was a character played by Groucho Marx in the film *Animal Crackers* (1930) and the name that Lambert was to give to one of his cats.

a lot of blotting paper at the Mill.[74] I return to London on Sunday and will in all probability get so monstrously blind that I shall be ill-equipped for the hazards of travel on Monday. So what about my coming down on Tuesday in time for lunch? Could you let me know a good train and send a card to the New Theatre Hull? I believe they have an air raid warning here every day so I shall have to spend a lot of the time playing the audience out. I propose buying a copy of that rightly renowned piece 'In the Shadows' by Herman Finck.[75]

In the early weeks of the war, while *Façade* had remained in the Company's repertoire since its introduction in 1935, Walton was keen on reviving the original version with reciter and in November sounded out Foss with an ingenious programme of his own devising. It consisted of what he referred to as a short curtain-raiser for *Façade* named *Canti carnascialeschi*, Constant's Chinese songs and piano concerto, and lastly *Façade*. He had some reservations, however, about Constant as reciter:

> Constant has I believe orchestrated his songs for the same combination as the Concerto & *Façade* [voice, flute, oboe, clarinet, string quartet, double bass], and the Canti Carnasc[h]ialeschi would be for the same, a few short pieces to act as a curtain-raiser so to speak. C would conduct his own pieces & I mine. About *Façade*, I'm afraid C's voice is not quite what it used to be & I doubt if it would stand the racket now, so if say, someone like Parry Jones was to sing the songs, he would in all probability be willing to do the reciting part in F. If guarantees were available we might arrange performances at the following universities, for that I think is where we should get most support.[76]

He suggested that such a scheme would have to wait until the summer to fit in before the black-out but, like many war-time plans, it never came about. Neither did Walton's curtain-raiser materialise, and it was not until May 1942 that the original *Façade* was revived.

Theatre life in London slowly began to pick up, especially once the early end of performances had been lifted, and the Vic-Wells Company felt justified in returning to its home venue and testing the water with a post-Christmas four week season with full orchestra again. Constant enjoyed a few days at Cecil Gray's windmill in Sussex, but he was preoccupied with the scoring of *Dante Sonata* as he explained to Gray in an (undated) letter of thanks:

> A thousand thanks for a very welcome oasis (using the word in all its senses, spiritual, temporal, and last but not least liquid). I was very sorry to leave on Sunday and found to my chagrin on returning that this wasn't really necessary. However, it landed me with a job for which I suppose I must be grateful. Beecham, after making a cheap success with Weinberger's never-sufficiently-to-be-derided Variations on Under the Fartarsing Chestnut Tree[77] has not unnaturally had qualms about recording it so I (as so often happens in my life) have been left to hold the baby. At first the music struck me as the kind of thing

[74] In 1938 Cecil Gray had bought a new home, The Old Mill, near Pulborough in Sussex.

[75] Letter undated [Sunday 3 December 1939]: RCM Archives. *In the Shadows* was probably the most popular piece by the theatre composer Herman Finck (1872–1939) and said to have been one of the last items played on board *The Titanic* before it sank.

[76] Letter from Walton to Hubert Foss, 7 November 1939, in Walton, *Selected Letters*, pp. 124–5. Walton suggested the universities of Oxford, Cambridge, Manchester, Liverpool, Birmingham, Cardiff, Bristol and London.

[77] Jaromir Weinberger's *Under the Spreading Chestnut Tree* which Lambert recorded in the Kingsway Hall, London on 21 December 1939: see Discography, Appendix 3.

that Geoffrey Toye might have written had he been born a Czech. I now think that this was a little hard on GT. Still, after all, £10 is £10 these days.

The only trouble is that it postpones my starting on the Liszt which is beginning to become a nightmare obsession with me. I suppose I shall just have to sit up all night, no new experience I grant you, but I have now reached the age when I quite frankly prefer drinking to scoring. However my tempo in both arts is as you know comparatively rapid so I suppose it will be alright in the end. It is difficult to work with everyone all round relaxing into a hideous Christmas spirit and the austere resolutions with which I returned to London have already met with a slight check owing to various encounters with among others Oliver [Messel][78] (outwardly cheerful but spiritually most gloomy) and the perennial Driftwood.

Constant's visit to the Grays' windmill could have been the occasion described by Marie:

That singular glow that went with (and I sometime thought – before) Constant. In the early days of the war we were sitting late one night in the Windmill talking with Walter Legge, who was our week-end guest. He suddenly asked if Constant was coming that week-end and we said no. Shortly after, the door handle banged and although I don't know how he got there at that time of night I wasn't surprised to hear Constant's voice. He had been to a wedding reception, then taken a negress[79] to a swimming bath and felt a proper conclusion would be to sleep in a windmill – so there he was. Could he have a toothbrush? His case contained a score he was working on and six ties. One never knew what kind of day the next one would be or what mood one would be in and it was necessary to have the appropriate tie.[80]

At Christmas he made his first entry in the visitors' book at Bradwell Lodge, a former rectory[81] that Tom Driberg had recently had renovated and moved into on a remote Essex peninsula at Bradwell-on-Sea (or Bradwell-juxta-Mare as it was also known and he liked to call it). There he frequently entertained his friends with good food and good wine and he took great pleasure in maintaining the house – at considerable expense. Constant was among the first party of house guests[82] and it might have been with some help from Driberg the epicurean that he made a contribution to a war-time publication, *A Kitchen goes to War: A ration-time cookery book with 150 recipes contributed by famous people*. Published the following year, its varied list of 'celebrities' of the day included Agatha Christie, Sir Kenneth Clark, Ernest Thesiger, Beverley Nichols, Beatrice Lillie, Isobel Baillie, Sir Malcolm Campbell, Cicely Courtneidge, John Gielgud,

[78] Oliver Messel (1904–78), English artist and stage designer.

[79] With a fondness for women of foreign appearance, he told Cecil Gray that he was haunted by Negroes and Negresses. Pauline Gray, *Cecil Gray: His Life and Notebooks* (London: Thames, 1989), p. 98.

[80] Letter from Marie Nielson to Angus Morrison, 19 February [1954].

[81] This house was the subject of a short film by Randon Film Productions Ltd in the Shell series *Discovering Britain with John Betjeman* screened by ITV on 4 November 1955. Betjeman was a friend of Driberg's from Oxford days.

[82] Driberg enjoyed inviting a mix of characters: the guests that Christmas were, besides Lambert, Tom's brother Jack, the writer Patrick Balfour (Lord Kinross) and Joan Rayner whose husband John was unable to come but sent the leather-bound visitors' book as a present. Constant was to have met him in 1944 when conducting in Italy but John was in hospital following a car accident. On another occasion at Bradwell Lodge the house party consisted of Constant, Isabel and Aneurin Bevan. Isabel remembered the guests at one time being entertained by Lena Horne singing.

Dr Marie Stopes and Margot Asquith. In print at least Constant was in notable company.

He was to spend several Christmases at Bradwell Lodge, but on this occasion he had to be back in Rosebery Avenue, Islington, on Boxing Day in time for the opening night with *Les Sylphides*, *Checkmate* and *Horoscope*. Four programmes of ballet were given each week, from Tuesday to Friday including a Thursday matinée, with opera on Thursday evenings and twice on Saturdays. The evening starting time was brought forward by two hours to 6.30 p.m. (although this was adjusted to 6.45 p.m. in the new year.)

Dante Sonata, with costumes and designs by Sophie Fedorovitch that were inspired by John Flaxman's illustrations for Dante's *Divina commedia*,[83] was first staged in the last week of the Christmas season, on 23 January 1940, and it created a sensation. That same day Constant sent the Grays a postcard suggesting that they came to London to see it: 'Despite dubiety growing artistic interest even best friends seriously suggest temporary suspension rural activities view viewing indubitably best ballet. Stop writing stop telephoning', adding the details of its only two other performances in what was the last week. 'Egocentric bugling apart what a shindy!' he concluded.

P. W. Manchester wrote of the first night of 'Ashton's great experiment in abstract ballet' that 'no-one who was there is ever likely to forget it'.[84] Cyril Beaumont considered it 'an impressive and moving composition', Ashton having devised 'a most effective panorama of writhing and contorted beings'.[85] These were two groups of spirits: in white the Children of Light, repentant sinners hoping for deliverance, and in black the Children of Darkness, 'with their snarling features, bared teeth and similar horrific attributes'[86]. With no resolution to the struggle between light and darkness and with striking crucifixion images (that were not to every critic's taste), it was easy to suppose that the ballet was intended as a comment on the present situation, but a note in the programme attempted to distance the creators from too literal a reading: 'The ballet is a freely symbolic interpretation of the moods and form of the music and, though it represents the warring attitudes of two different groups of equally tortured spirits, it tells no set story.'

With Fonteyn, Helpmann, Pamela May and June Brae in principal roles (dancing in bare feet), the three performances of *Dante Sonata* at least ensured that the season ended with better attendances. But the war was bringing other difficulties. The Company concluded their run with *The Sleeping Princess* and, as Clarke explained, 'already the Lord Mayor's Boy Players had been evacuated from London, so the pages had to be played by young girls from the ballet school. The flower waltz at the beginning of Act 1 was reduced from twelve couples to ten, and on one occasion Helpmann had to go on as the fourth prince in the Rose Adagio and then change himself into Prince Florimund. Bluebeard and Prince Hohlicke disappeared from the fairy-tale characters in the last act and Prince Hohlicke has never been restored.'[87] Losing dancers to the services was a serious worry, not just with the problem of replacing those that had been called-up but with the difficulty it posed of maintaining an equality of standard between the male and female dancers. Ashton, Lambert and de Valois had together approached the Secretary of State for Home Affairs, urging on him the damaging

---

[83] John Flaxman (1755–1826), illustrator, designer and sculptor, best known for his monument to Lord Nelson in St Paul's Cathedral.

[84] Manchester, *Vic-Wells*, p. 45.

[85] Ashton was to return to the music of Liszt in 1963 when he chose the Sonata in B minor for the ballet *Marguerite and Armand* he devised for Margot Fonteyn and Rudolf Nureyev.

[86] Beaumont, *The Sadler's Wells Ballet*, pp. 162–3.

[87] Clarke, *The Sadler's Wells Ballet*, p. 152.

consequences that conscription would have on English ballet still relatively in its infancy, only to be told that no exemption could be given.

At the end of January 1940 it was back to the provinces for another tour with two pianos, taking in Cambridge, Hull, Leeds, Liverpool, Leicester, Sheffield, Manchester, Brighton and Bristol. Constant had invited the pianist Harold Rutland to join him and Hilda Gaunt on this tour and to stand in for him when he had other engagements. Rutland remembered:

> I took over from him as pianist from time to time. Before doing so I not only had to learn the music, but watch the ballets carefully to find out what was happening on the stage. Many of the copies we played from, moreover, were so old and torn that it was a miracle that they held together. But Constant was marvellous, and equal to any emergency. I confess I had never thought of him as a pianist (he once told me that both he and Freyer [his piano teacher at the Royal College] had 'wept' during lessons because he was so bad, but that of course was a comic exaggeration); nevertheless he managed to get through the most complicated music with immense verve and aplomb. It is true that sometimes, through excitement, his fingers 'ran away with him' and he played too fast, making it difficult for the dancers. But that is also a fault of certain well-known pianists with far more experience. ...
>
> During this tour he and I shared a dressing-room, and we naturally saw a good deal of each other. What particularly used to astonish me was his physical endurance. In the intervals, after playing perhaps the formidable *Dante Sonata*, he would pace up and down the room, talking of musical matters. (Chabrier, I remember, was a favourite subject of conversation at that time.) Sometimes I urged him to sit down and take things easily; but he said he preferred to walk about. I couldn't help being struck by the contrast between his way of going on, and mine, when, at Leicester, I first played (with Hilda Gaunt) for the entire evening's programme. The attempt to make a not very good piano serve as a substitute for an orchestra, coupled with the inevitable nervous tension, proved so great a strain that in the interval between *Dante Sonata* and *Checkmate* I lay in the dressing-room, panting like a boxer between rounds.
>
> As we all know, there was a panache about Lambert. I remember a rehearsal at Hull (where I joined the Company), when he played the piano in the orchestra pit, and at the same time smoked a cigar. The ballet happened to be *Apparitions*, and when Robert Helpmann reproved him mockingly for his cigar, Constant at once retorted: 'Why not? It's a good Lisztian traditional.' He told me that one day, when he was leaving the stage door of the theatre, smoking a cigar, two small boys gazed at him with awe, and one said to the other: 'That's Mr Vic Wells'.[88]

At Hull, where at night the black-out was far worse than in London, the Company carried electric torches but Constant refused to do so. Stick in hand, he walked along the streets with his usual briskness, quite undeterred by the lack of light.

Taking *Dante Sonata* on tour incurred one problem, as Fonteyn recalled: 'It was created in the modern dance idiom in bare feet, and we were for ever coaxing splinters out of our bodies, since there was a lot of dragging each other across the stage and no-one ever thought to lay a covering over the ancient wooden floorboards of English provincial theatres.'[89]

At this time Constant wrote what has unfortunately become his most neglected work, the *Dirge*, a setting for tenor and baritone soloists, male chorus and strings of

[88] Rutland, 'Recollections of Constant Lambert'.
[89] Fonteyn, *Autobiography*, p. 96.

Ex. 29 Lambert, *Dirge from 'Cymbeline'*, opening

verses from Shakespeare's *Cymbeline*: 'Fear no more the heat o'the sun'. Rutland spoke of it as being written while on tour, with Constant 'searching for nearly a week at odd times for a suitable poem.' It is a simple but most effective setting, with a haunting, desolate beauty that is accentuated by the shifting chromatic harmonies (Ex. 29). Just as in *Summer's Last Will and Testament*, there are bitter-sweet Delian overtones, similar to E. J. Moeran's *Nocturne*, a work on a much larger scale[90] written in 1934 in memory of Delius. Both works open with a chromatic cadence, but in the *Dirge* the harmonies are at times more pungent, even discordant. Humphrey Searle thought it 'one of his most moving and beautiful works'[91] and the artist Michael Ayrton rated it a masterpiece and, after Constant's death, considered it 'a perfect epitaph'.[92] With a short duration of about seven minutes and its rather unconventional forces, it is not a work that fits easily into the average concert programme, and it is probably for that reason it has been overlooked. Hubert Foss considered it representative of the 'elegiac nostalgia that pervades the whole of Lambert's work' which at times has 'a poignancy that is almost unbearable', a quality he felt also present – 'less direct but no less poignant' – in the 'Intermède' in the Concerto for Piano and Nine Players, the *Nocturne* in the Piano Sonata, the *Elegiac Blues*, the *Aubade héroïque* and, clearest of all, in *Summer's Last Will and Testament*.[93] Such moments in his output contrast sharply with the more familiar passages of rhythmic vitality.

At Bristol on 30 March, within an hour or so of the last ballet of the tour finishing, Constant conducted the BBC Symphony Orchestra in the first of several war-time broadcasts he was to give there a short late-night programme of Meyerbeer, Fauré and Chabrier that was announced as 'good, popular music'. The orchestra had been evacuated from London to Bristol in November and Constant was initially on a BBC list of guest conductors who, it was suggested, might do one week in Bristol and one week alternatively in the Northern and Scottish regions.[94] But his ballet conducting did not always allow him sufficient flexibility and instead during the war years he was given the occasional studio concert in places like Bristol, Bedford or Cambridge.

At the beginning of April the Company were back in London for five weeks, opening – unusually on a Monday – with a complete *Swan Lake*. Fonteyn was very much the rising star, the *Times* critic observing that she had been 'steadily improving technically, dramatically, and in general command of the art. Her technical accomplishment had many moments of brilliance in the ballroom scene, the attractive softness of her dancing finds scope in the swans scene, and her dramatic grasp enables

---

[90] Moeran's *Nocturne* was written for solo baritone, chorus and orchestra.
[91] Searle and Layton, *Twentieth Century Composers*, vol. 3, p. 53.
[92] Ayrton, *Golden Sections*, p. 135.
[93] Hubert Foss, 'Constant Lambert', in *British Music of Our Time*, ed. A. L. Bacharach (Harmondsworth: Penguin Books, 1946), pp. 171–2.
[94] BBC memorandum, 12 October 1939. BBC Written Archives, Caversham.

her to sustain the whole ballet.' *Job* was revived for a single performance, 'excellently played by the orchestra under Constant Lambert' and with one critic left wondering whether 'the scene of Satan invading High Heaven and being cast down' had any 'special message for us'. There was a new production of *Coppélia*, enlarged to include the third act orchestrated by Gordon Jacob, while completely new was *The Wise Virgins* with music of Bach orchestrated by Walton.

Premiered on 24 April, the idea had arisen one evening near the end of January when the tour had begun at Cambridge[95] and Ashton and Lambert were staying with Boris Ord.[96] When the topic of conversation turned to Bach, Constant sat down at the piano and played the piece known popularly as *Sheep May Safely Graze* which impressed Ashton as something suitable for a ballet. As a way of countering the inevitable moments of boredom while on war-time tours, Ashton had announced his curious intention of reading the Holy Bible aloud every day from beginning to end. This may have given him the idea of using a biblical story for this new ballet and he chose the parable of the wise and foolish virgins. Constant meanwhile looked through Bach cantatas for seven other arias or chorales that could be adapted.

Things then developed quite swiftly. On 27 February Constant wrote to Hubert Foss: 'I am busy working out a religious ballet for Ashton based mainly on Bach choral preludes, vocal transcriptions etc. Alan Frank has been most helpful. ... I am hoping to get Willie to do the scoring. A good idea, don't you think?'

Walton enlisted Frank's help in obtaining copies of the music needed:

I've let myself in for scoring a Bach ballet for the 'Wells' so could you send me the following transcriptions. You don't happen to know where or from whom I could borrow a Bach Gesellschaft so I could look at the originals, as the transcriptions Constant showed me are rather obscure in places as to what the parts came from & go to.[97]

He added a list, and on 7 March Frank informed Foss:

I have now seen Walton who assures me that as far as the orchestration is concerned he will be working from the original and not from our transcriptions. I have therefore given him the copies he asked for in his letter, since the only use he will make of these is to refer to the number of bars which Lambert has specified are to be scored. I understand however that the ballet is also to be done on tour with two pianos, for which our published transcriptions will presumably be used.

Both Lambert and Walton, together with ten other English composers, had contributed a Bach transcription for solo piano to a collection published in 1932 as *A Bach Book for Harriet Cohen*. While Lambert's contribution was not used in *The Wise Virgins*, the chorale prelude that Walton had arranged, *Herzlich thut mich verlangen*, was included. The pressure was now on to have the orchestral version ready for the London premiere, with a two-piano version available when they went on tour, as Constant explained to Foss on 13 March:

The two piano version will not come into action until we go on tour again, which probably will not be for some months. In that version we will naturally be using

⁹⁵ The Sadler's Wells ballet were at Cambridge from Monday January 29 until Saturday 3 February 1940.

⁹⁶ Boris Ord (1897–1961), organist and choirmaster at King's College, Cambridge, 1927–57, and conductor of the Cambridge University Musical Society, 1938–54.

⁹⁷ Written from Alice Wimborne's country residence at Ashby St Ledgers, near Rugby. This sequence of correspondence is from the OUP Archives.

the OUP arrangements, as they stand. ... The three Rummel arrangements are, as you know, virtuoso arrangements for two hands, and rather heavy-handed at that. These I will re-arrange myself for two pianos after Willie has completed his score, but there seems no reason why Willie should not proceed with the orchestrations immediately, in fact he will have to if we are able to get the ballet ready in time.

At the beginning of March when the tour had reached Sheffield, Ashton, Helpmann and Lambert had conveniently stayed with the Sitwells at Renishaw. Edith wrote to her sister-in-law Georgia: 'Constant and Freddie and Bobbie have been here. It is so dreadful seeing all these poor young men on the brink of this ghastly catastrophe.' *The Wise Virgins*, which was no doubt discussed at Renishaw, was dedicated (by Ashton rather than by Walton)[98] to Edith.

With Ashton's choreography and with scenery and costumes by Rex Whistler, the ballet was first staged on Wednesday 24 April 1940 at the Sadler's Wells Theatre with Lambert conducting. 'It was *most* lovely', Edith told Ashton, 'and has a singular youthful innocence which is just like that of the Adorations of the Primitives. ... It moved me deeply. I am more proud than I can say that you should have dedicated it to me.'[99] Baroque in style, *The Wise Virgins* was in sharp contrast to *Dante Sonata*. Michael Somes and Margot Fonteyn were the bride and bridegroom, and while as a spectacle it was considered by some to be 'one of the most beautiful the Vic-Wells Ballet had ever presented',[100] it did not appeal so strongly to audiences and critics. *The Times* found it incongruous and lacking cohesion, and after the war it was dropped from the repertoire. Its main set proved too heavy to be transported from the Wells, one reason why this new ballet did not form part of the Vic-Wells' fateful visit to the Continent in May. After its opening night (which also included *Les Sylphides* and *Nocturne*) Constant spent a week-end at Driberg's,[101] returning to give two more performances of *The Wise Virgins* before the season ended on Friday 3 May.

[98] Walton had already dedicated his *Sinfonia Concertante* to the three Sitwells.
[99] Kavanagh, *Secret Muses*, p. 263.
[100] Vaughan, *Frederick Ashton and his Ballets*, p. 186.
[101] In his Visitor' Book Driberg noted, 'The Host defined goodness' to which Lambert added as a footnote 'as "socially useful single-mindedness".'

16 1940–3
Escape from Holland

I N May 1940 the Sadler's Wells Company (as they had now become known, dropping the 'Vic' tag so as to align them better with their home base at Sadler's Wells) had planned to go straight from London to Hull for a fortnight and then on to Swansea. But this was cancelled because the British Council and the Foreign Office decided to send them instead to Belgium and Holland as an exercise in cultural propaganda, despite the fact that an invasion of those countries was clearly imminent. This decision may have been hastened by the fact that a German ballet company had announced its intension of touring Holland in the second half of May.[1] This British gesture was considered important enough for the call-up of any male dancer to be waived for two months. As Bridges Adams of the British Council explained to Arthur Bliss (whose *Checkmate* was taken on the tour), the whole exercise came close to being a disaster:

> After many rebuffs, jibbing at further inertia, I persuaded a doubtful Lloyd[2] to let me send the Sadler's Wells Ballet to The Hague, Haarlem, Amsterdam, Brussels, and Antwerp. They got as far as Haarlem,[3] where they played to a rapturous and astonished house (it was in the danger zone) half an hour before the Germans marched in. They showed our flag and, much more important, the banner of all artists all over the word, to such effect that the Dutch cheered them to the roof when they had breath to spare from gasping at their pluck. I had based them, thank God, on The Hague throughout, with their own coach and scenery lorry. They got back, the drone of their own engine drowning all other sounds, to The Hague at about 3.0 a.m. and at 4 a.m. were awakened by the doings – they stood for an hour on the roof in their dressing gowns, watching dog fights and street battles, too excited to take care. Then a long journey under fire by night, a peaceful day in the deer park (this was full marks to the Legation) and at last an embarkation to the hold of a freighter where they lay on straw for 10 hours or so – no life belts, two life boats and 700 passengers – and so to Harwich and eventually Liverpool Street, where I met them at 2.30 a.m.
>
> The first to emerge was Constant Lambert, with an immense bandage round his head. 'My God,' I thought, 'they've been shot up.' 'You're hurt,' I said. 'Yes,' replied Lambert, 'cigarette ash in my eye!' The whole outfit, in fact, were unscathed. But I don't mean to go through it again. Seventy pretty legs, I kept thinking! I was on to the Legation eleven times, sometimes with strange noises sounding, but always the neutral world-weary diplomatic voice giving a shade more hope. Within an hour of the news I had a transport ready for them at Havre, but the road was bombed and they could not get there.
>
> The scenery and music are in a store at Haarlem. I am trying – what a hope! – to get it out.'[4]

The Company had set off cheerfully enough on Saturday 4 May, travelling by train to Harwich where they embarked for Rotterdam, not knowing what lay ahead, and when they arrived in Holland were 'laughing and sightseeing for all the world as

[1] Announced in *The Times*, 2 May 1940.
[2] Lord Lloyd of Dolobran, British Council chairman from 1937 to 1941.
[3] Adams' itinerary is not entirely accurate. They did not perform in Haarlem.
[4] Letter from Bridges Adams of the British Council to Arthur Bliss, 15 May 1940, in Bliss, *As I Remember*, pp. 128–9.

though nothing unusual was going on'.[5] Their first programme on the Monday at the Royal Theatre, The Hague, of *Checkmate*, *Les Patineurs*, *Dante Sonata* and *Façade*, was 'received with almost heartbreaking enthusiasm' with tulip petals raining down on the performers. *Dante Sonata* in particular proved a great success and the whole Company were entertained afterwards at the British Legation. The next day they were bussed to Hengelo which lay close to the German border. With barbed wire, concrete barricades and military activity everywhere the gravity of the situation became more apparent. As Fonteyn observed, 'Lambert tried to look cheerfully fatalistic, Ashton's hypersensitive imagination worked like an antenna to pick up new signs of the impending German invasion. Helpmann, the court jester, wrapped truth in humour in order to break the tension he perhaps felt more than anyone else.'[6] They reached Hengelo two hours before the performance was due to start. Constant had the difficulty of conducting a Dutch orchestra[7] unfamiliar with most of the repertoire, and one of the dancers, Annabel Farjeon, wrote in her journal[8] that in *Façade* 'violins raced to catch up, woodwind started and stopped in the middle of a phrase while some deep instrument boomed on steadily. … Finally to our horror Constant began to sing. Like many conductors his voice was not musical, hardly in tune.' Over 60 years later Pamela May remembered Constant's difficulties:

> He had terrible trouble conducting … they were a bit anti-English. You should have heard the noise they made of *Façade*; it wasn't music, it was noise. We were in hysterics, he was in hysterics trying to keep them and us together, without any sound that was familiar coming out of the orchestra. … So he had quite a battle.[9]

Nevertheless, they were given an enthusiastic reception at Hengelo by another packed audience, staying there for the night and moving the next morning to Eindhoven where they performed in the well-equipped theatre that was part of the large Philips factory. (As well as conductor, Constant may have been known to a few of the audience as a composer because *The Rio Grande* had been performed in Holland in February.) That night they returned to The Hague and on Thursday morning made an early start for Arnhem where they gave what was to be the last performance of their tour.[10] They left Arnhem at about 1 a.m., two hours ahead of the German invasion of that town, and reached The Hague at 3 a.m. The exhausted dancers had hardly been in bed an hour before they were roused by the sound of German aircraft flying overhead. Constant and Margot, in bed together, were rudely disturbed by one member of the Company, probably Helpmann who several days later related the whole frightening experience in a letter to his mother:

> I shall never forget the hell of Holland's invasion, which I saw at first hand. We finished our ballet season at Arnhem on the Thursday, and left that night for

---

[5] Fonteyn, *Autobiography*, p. 91. As well as in Fonteyn's autobiography, there are detailed first-hand accounts of the Holland tour in de Valois, *Come Dance with Me*, and Edwards, *In Good Company*. The experiences of one of the Company are recorded in Edith Olivier, *Night Thoughts of a Country Landlady* (London: Batsford, 1943), pp. 64–5.

[6] Fonteyn, *Autobiography*, p. 91.

[7] The orchestra was the 46-strong Haarlemsche Orkest-Vereeniging. The Dutch pianist Jan Odé was the soloist in *Dante Sonata*.

[8] Annabel Farjeon, *Dutch Journal*, quoted in Daneman, *Margot Fonteyn*, p. 147.

[9] Pamela May interviewed by the author, 1 August 2003.

[10] After the last ballet, *Façade*, bouquets were presented to de Valois and Fonteyn by an 11-year-old Audrey Ruston (Hepburn), a member of the ballet class at the Arnhem Conservatory of Music. Two more performances, planned for Haarlem and Amsterdam on 10 and 11 May, were cancelled.

The Hague. We say many troops moving past us, but as Holland had been on the alert for some time we merely thought it was manœuvres. Later we learnt we were only one hour before the Germans. We were lucky to get out alive, there were forty-nine of us in the troupe, so we split up into groups of seven, for convenience …

In the lounge of the hotel at The Hague we could hear distant gunfire. I called Constant Lambert who was in our group, and we went up on the roof. There, high above us in the dawn-reddening sky, there was a flight of planes, with white puffs of smoke bursting round them, then out of the east came the Dutch planes; while day slowly crept up the sky fighters, with machine guns blazing, whirled and swooped like some fantastic ballet …

Fascinated and stunned we stood watching; it seemed German planes would never stop coming. Some leaflets came falling down and Constant caught one; it was printed in Dutch, and called on the population to surrender. Then the German planes came thickly, and men tumbled from them, their parachutes billowing out behind them, floating gracefully down; this was a beautiful sight against the clear blue cloudless sky, it was hard to believe that this calm descent was the forerunner of destruction, terror and death.

Air-raid sirens were wailing, so we went down to the hotel lounge, people seemed too bewildered even to think of taking shelter, we hurried to have some food, and we went out to seek news. Nobody seemed to know anything, so we went to a café to drink coffee … Suddenly, in the middle of the conversation a bullet hit the pavement, and shot past Constant's eye, so we went back to the hotel and tried to sleep, without success.[11]

One gruesome sight seen from a window by two members was 'a dead German hanging from his parachute and careering with grim leaps and twists down an empty street in the light of early morning, like a marionette ballet dancer.'[12]

That morning, to the occasional background burst of gunfire, de Valois, Ashton and Lambert braved the walk to the British Embassy, where documents and files were hurriedly being burnt so they could not fall into enemy hands, to find how they might safely get back to England. De Valois boldly rejected any suggestion that the girls should return leaving the men behind. Back at their hotel they could only wait, and it was while they were sitting outside in the hotel's pavement café that they had the narrow escape when a stray bullet from a German plane passed between their heads and shattered the café window behind them. An Australian acquaintance of Helpmann's who was also outside that café described how 'while Constant, Bobby and I were talking a huge plate of glass window behind us was shot to pieces'.[13]

That night the Company slept wherever they could find room on the ground floor or on the stairs, and the next day everybody was confined to the hotel while overhead there was the steady roar of German aircraft on the way to their main target, Rotterdam. That Saturday afternoon they were instructed to make packs of food for themselves and to confine their essential belongings to one small suitcase: everything else would have to be left behind. (Out of kindness to a distraught Ashton, de Valois wore his expensive brand-new dinner jacket over her light summer coat and skirt.) Later they were transported on a nine-hour escape route that had many frightening moments, especially when, as Helpmann wrote: 'We had only got to the outskirts of the city when a plane swooped and machine-gunned our six lorries and the bus; the driver drove

---

[11] Mary Helpman, *The Helpman Family Story, 1796–1964* (Brisbane: Rigby, 1967), pp. 92–4.

[12] *Gramophone*, July 1940, p. 6.

[13] Billy McCann, writing to his father, quoted in Helpman, *The Helpman Family Story*, p. 94.

under some trees which hid us till the plane left.' They eventually arrived under cover of darkness at a large Dutch country house in the woods of Velsen. The building, which had been commandeered by the military, was, as Fonteyn recalled, so overcrowded with refugees that

> we went out to walk a little before trying to find a corner in which to lie down. The faintest grey light was breaking through the dense night sky. We were in a big garden. The chilly air was sweet and fresh, and trees took shape as the light grew. Slowly there came the miraculous unfolding of a picture so serene and exquisite, touched with morning dew and the promise of a fine warm day. It was like a Japanese landscape. A mist-laden lake, rushes, flowering shrubs, pathways and broad lawns came into view as the first vigilant birds alerted others to the hour of awakening. ... The day we spent in this blissfully rural paradise was disturbed by occasional bursts of gunfire .[14]

At about midnight the refugees were given orders to form into long lines with a hand on each other's shoulder and to file forward in the darkness as each group name was called out. The Sadler's Wells crocodile was led by a Dutch soldier through the woods to the waiting buses to take them to the port of Ymuiden. Even as they struggled up the gangway to board their ship they were fired at by machine-gun, fortunately without any casualties, and then they had the ordeal of an extremely uncomfortable 15-hour crossing by cattle boat to Harwich, arriving back in London very early on the Tuesday morning (the day on which Holland collapsed and Queen Wilhelmina and members of the Dutch government moved to England). Amazingly, everyone returned home unharmed, but the scenery, costumes, orchestral parts and scores of the six ballets they had toured with became the casualties of war as they had to be abandoned in the haste to escape. They were *Horoscope, Les Patineurs, Dante Sonata, Façade, The Rake's Progress* and *Checkmate*.[15]

There was one positive outcome from the drama of the tour.[16] Leslie Edwards suggested to Constant that he should write a piece of music to remind them of that blissful Sunday morning spent in the grounds of the Dutch chateau, and he responded with one of his most beautiful orchestral scores, *Aubade héroïque*. He later gave Edwards a copy of the score, inscribing it 'To Leslie Edwards, who suggested this piece.' The title echoes Debussy's *Berceuse héroïque* composed during the First World War and dedicated to the King of Belgium and his soldiers. It is quite likely that Constant used the work to fulfil a commission, as its first performance, on 12 October 1942, was in a broadcast celebrating Vaughan Williams' 70th birthday with works specially

---

[14] Fonteyn, *Autobiography*, p. 94.

[15] *The Times*, 5 June 1940, reported that they had also lost the costumes for *Les Sylphides*, although Clarke, *The Sadler's Wells Ballet*, p. 156, states that the Benois set 'had not been taken to Holland and was unharmed'. *Dante Sonata* was the first to be restaged, on 4 June 1940, with gramophone records as accompaniment; then *Façade* on 23 July 1940; *Les Patineurs* on 15 August 1940; *The Rake's Progress* on 27 October 1942; and *Checkmate* on 18 November 1947 (at Covent Garden, when the conductor was Hugo Rignold). *Horoscope* has never been restaged. According to Vaughan, *Frederick Ashton and his Ballets*, p. 136, a revival was discussed for the 25th anniversary performance of the Sadler's Wells Ballet in May 1956 but 'there proved to be too many gaps in peoples' memories' and the plan was dropped. After the war some of the scores were retrieved from Holland, having been kept safely by Baroness Ella van Heemstra, the mother of Audrey Hepburn who, brought up in Nazi-occupied Holland, later joined Marie Rambert's ballet school in London.

[16] The Dutch tour, and Lambert and Fonteyn's affair, became the subject of a BBC Radio 4 play, *An Unchoreographed World*, by Frances Byrnes, first broadcast on 22 May 2008. A Radio 4 feature on the tour, *Ballet behind the Borders*, was broadcast on 16 December 2002.

Ex. 30 Lambert, *Aubade héroïque*, letter D

written for the occasion, Clarence Raybould conducting the London Symphony Orchestra. The other contributors were Alan Bush, Patrick Hadley, Gordon Jacob, Elizabeth Maconchy, Robin Milford and Edmund Rubbra. Gerald Finzi attended the broadcast and wrote afterwards to Howard Ferguson: 'We went along to the Studio for the concert of tributes. I thought the results: Alan Bush, ghastly; Rubbra, like a bit of his 4th Symphony – I like it; Hadley, rather fussy and uninteresting; Constant Lambert, balls; Maconchy, not worth while but good fun.'[17] Whether or not Finzi's comments were coloured by the fact that he had not been invited to contribute, his scathing dismissal of the *Aubade* is certainly unfair. It was an appropriate birthday tribute as it is the closest that Constant came to the pastoral style of his former teacher.[18] It recalls most effectively and with great beauty the occasion that inspired it, that rare moment of peace suggested by solo flute *teneramente* and strings accompanied by a delicate harp ostinato (Ex. 30),[19] only to be interrupted by the ominous suggestions of distant war on muted trumpets.

Six days after his safe return home Constant gave a ten minute broadcast in the 'At Short Notice' slot that was reserved by the BBC 'for talks that cannot be announced in advance'. The daily papers listed it as 'Just Back from Holland by Constant Lambert' and he described how dangerous their escape had been:

> We had left Arnhem, a town on the border, just after midnight, only three hours before the Germans marched in. To hear that Holland had appealed to the Allies for help was at least a temporary relief, though we still didn't know what our chances were of getting out. Rotterdam, half in German hands, was being bombed and the way to the Hook of Holland was barred by parachutists. Eventually, after two days, we joined up with the refugees from Amsterdam, menaced all the time by the parachutists who were establishing themselves in the woods and were waiting to machine gun the cars. Every now and then as the firing broke out we would stop and duck down in the darkness. When we got to the port a great part of it was on fire and enemy planes were threatening us as we went on board. The Dutch guns and the British Navy got us safely out.[20]

In the BBC Written Archives at Caversham there is an annotated typescript headed 'At Short Notice' and clearly intended for that broadcast but differing substantially from

---

[17] *Letters of Gerald Finzi and Howard Ferguson*, p. 232.

[18] The work's dedication to Vaughan Williams was quite likely made at the suggestion of Oxford University Press, the two composers' publishers, as Shead quotes Lambert writing to Felix Aprahamian that the dedication was 'a fact which, to be quite frank, is relished by neither of us'. Shead, *Constant Lambert*, p. 128. The letter has not been located. Lambert conducted the first public performance at Oxford on 22 October 1942 and the first London performance at Golders Green on 21 February 1943.

[19] It may be purely coincidental that Stanford used an almost identical harp ostinato, with solo flute, in the third movement of his Symphony No. 4 of 1888.

[20] Extract from the BBC Sound Archives: BBC Home Service, 20 May 1940.

the extracts from the talk that exist in the BBC Sound Archives quoted above. The typescript is Lambert's most serious piece of journalism: it is less an account of how the ballet company escaped from a country under invasion than a chilling description – perhaps too chilling to broadcast – of how the German invasion was accomplished by 'parachutists disguised as Dutch and British officers; as clergymen, and peasants armed not only with machine guns, but with dummy soldiers which they leave on the ground in order to deceive people into thinking they are dead', how the enemy was assisted by Fifth Columnists, and how rumours circulated of prominent citizens being shot as spies. Its overall message was a clear warning: 'In this country we are apt to say, complacently, "Oh, that sort of thing can't happen here" ... We must not say "It can't happen here"; we must say, "It shall not happen here".' A more heroic – but still accurate – account was broadcast instead.

B EFORE the start in June of their six-week London season, the Sadler's Wells Company were sent on a short ENSA tour of the Aldershot district to entertain the troops. After their experiences in Holland they must have felt themselves almost fated when one of the military camps in which they were staying was the target of a night bombing raid, the bombs falling in the garden of the house where the dancers were billeted.[21] ENSA tours were sometimes sprung on them at short notice, much to Constant's irritation, as he told Gray:

> I was hoping to be able to come down to the Mill but have been landed with an ENSA tour (two pianos, with Nancy Evans attached to the company as light relief). We were to have started this Sunday but owing to the official inability to make our identity discs etc. in time the thing has been postponed for a week. I went this afternoon to get photographed and make out a few forms in quadruplicate and was ushered down to a cellar, a German aeroplane having been sighted off the Giant's Causeway. By the time they announced a "provisional release" it was too late to do anything so I have to go again tomorrow morning. There will (or so I am occasionally informed) always be an England.
>
> This tour obviously knocks our proposed collaboration on the head for the moment quite apart from the fact that my quill (always turgid) is now in a state of complete inanimation. I find it increasingly difficult to get the old brain to function at all – perhaps it will be better when I have some kind of fixed routine. The New Staggers & Naggers [*New Statesman and Nation*] has asked me to write for them again but in Christ's name what about?[22]

Constant spent the last weekend of May at Tom Driberg's,[23] ready to return to London for the reopening of Sadler's Wells on Tuesday 4 June. The financial losses incurred by the tour of Holland had raised doubts about the coming season. Tyrone Guthrie had sought compensation from the British Council who had, after all, instigated the tour, and de Valois and Lambert held long conferences discussing ways of securing an economic future. The first programme consisted of *Les Sylphides*, *The Wise Virgins* and *Dante Sonata*. Fortunately, Alexandre Benois's setting for *Les Sylphides* that the Company had bought in 1937 had not been taken on the tour and so

---

[21] De Valois, *Come Dance with Me*, p. 140.

[22] Letter from Lambert to Cecil Gray, n.d. [Thursday] from 'Hangover' Cottage. Once a regular contributor to the *New Statesman and Nation*, Lambert had last written for it in March 1937. Apart from an obituary on Lord Berners in 1950, he did not write again for that paper.

[23] A month later, after another week-end at Driberg's, Lambert wrote in the visitors' book: 'Oh! And Tom when you've finished getting the cheese from the post office you might decant the port!, a reference to an Italian servant at Bradwell Lodge whose name was also Tom.

remained unharmed, and although the autograph score and parts of *Dante Sonata* had been lost in Holland, by good fortune in March Constant had recorded the score for HMV with the Sadler's Wells Orchestra so, until he had time to reconstruct the score,[24] the Company performed to the gramophone records which, the *Times* critic reported, 'served their purpose reasonably well'. The set and costumes were fairly simple and so they were quickly renewed. The same critic reported that 'Mr Lambert takes *Les Sylphides* at a beautifully slow tempo which is somewhat trying on the *corps de ballet* though it puts no strain on the principals.'

Another loss in Holland was made good on 23 July with a redesigned *Façade*, with entirely new costumes and décor by John Armstrong and two more numbers added, 'Noche espagnola' (here called 'Nocturne péruvienne')[25] and 'Foxtrot' ('Old Sir Faulk').[26] Although some of the wit and subtlety of the ballet had given way to burlesque and even bawdiness (a full-bosomed lady painted on the back-cloth and underwear hanging on a washing-line), it was well received. 'Re-dressed and expanded, *Façade* is now one of the best things in the repertoire,' observed the *Dancing Times* critic.[27] Meanwhile de Valois had had in preparation a new ballet ironically called *The Prospect before Us* (with equal irony in its subtitle *Pity the Poor Dancers*) after a cartoon of the same title by Thomas Rowlandson (itself illustrating a ballet). Constant arranged music by William Boyce, from the trio sonatas and the eight symphonies that he had transcribed and edited for strings and optional woodwind (published by OUP in 1928).[28] With scenery and costumes by Roger Furse, it opened on 4 July and at the beginning of August for the gramophone Constant recorded a suite with the Sadler's Wells Orchestra. This period ballet, about two rival 18th-century London theatre managers competing to secure the best dancers and with both theatres going up in smoke, seemed to provide the necessary comic relief and proved a success, having more performances than any other ballet that season. Helpmann, who portrayed one of the managers, was at the same time appearing at the Ambassadors Theatre in the revue *Swinging the Gate*, dashing by taxi at the end of *The Prospect before Us* to go on stage in the last act of the revue to mimic either Margaret Rawlings or Margaret Rutherford. He kept up this double theatrical life for nearly six months.

What was at first to have been only a six-week season (of ballet and opera) eventually became 14 weeks, and when it ended on 6 September one enthusiast wrote to *The Times* that the opera and ballet companies had 'earned the gratitude of the Army, Navy and Air Force, and all war workers, who have come in great numbers to the performances. Sadler's Wells is indeed the home of our national opera and ballet, due to the foresight of that wonderful woman Lilian Baylis.'[29] Despite the mounting dangers of war, P. W. Manchester thought that 'those terrible nerve-wracking days of June and July saw some of the finest performances the Vic-Wells have ever given us'. In mid-August London had its first daylight air-raid warning and from time to time these were to punctuate performances, affecting audience numbers. Nevertheless the

---

[24] From memory, according to Morrison, 'Constant Lambert (1905–1951)', p. 790.

[25] According to Clarke, *The Sadler's Wells Ballet*, p. 158, Ashton's *Noche Espagnole* (originally *Long Steel Grass*) was 'a very wicked and very funny parody of Dolin's *Bolero*'.

[26] Ashton's 1931 *Façade* for the Camargo Society had seven numbers; 'Country Dance' was added in 1935.

[27] *Dancing Times*, September 1940.

[28] Antony Tudor had already used selections from William Boyce's symphonies arranged by Lambert (probably nos. 1 and 6), for his ballet *Paramour*, first performed on 20 February 1934 at the Town Hall, Oxford, for the Oxford University Dramatic Society's production of Marlowe's *Dr Faustus*.

[29] *The Times*, 12 September 1940.

Company continued, giving, during one 'alert' what Manchester considered 'the most superb *Giselle*' she ever saw.[30] For Constant and the dancers it had been a routine of three performances a week, at eight o'clock on Tuesdays and Thursdays and alternating between Friday evenings and Saturday matinées.[31] However, he voiced one concern in an article 'Ballet and Musical Interpretation' that he wrote for a book, *Ballet – To Poland*, published primarily to raise money for the Polish Relief Fund,[32] and this was picked up in the June issue of *Dancing Times*: that there were 'too few "experimental" works in "the present glorious revival of ballet" ... There is a danger,' he warned, 'that we may eventually finish up with a super body of executants living artistically speaking in the past.'

During that long London season Constant had several other engagements. At the National Gallery on Friday 21 June, he conducted the London Philharmonic Orchestra in one of ten concerts in a Festival of English and French Music. His programme as ever was a personal one, including works by Boyce, Purcell, Grétry, Satie and Chabrier, his own *Pomona* Suite and Moeran's *Lonely Waters*,[33] with Maggie Teyte singing songs by Berlioz and Duparc. Three days later he was in Bournemouth, conducting the recently formed Wessex Philharmonic, and on Thursday 8 August he shared with Walton and Sargent the conducting of a Queen's Hall concert in aid of the Red Cross and St John's Fund that was in part broadcast. Walton was in charge of a suite from *Façade*, but only the first two works in the programme formed the broadcast portion of the concert: Constant conducting a suite from *Horoscope* and Rachmaninov's Second Piano Concerto under Sargent. Even so, the 'Valse for the Gemini' was 'omitted because of lack of time', though it is not clear whether this was because of broadcasting considerations or so that Constant could be back at Sadler's Wells for the remainder of that evening's ballet of *Apparitions*, *Harlequin in the Street* and *The Prospect before Us*, three ballets for which he had chosen the music.

A fortnight later he had a broadcast from Bristol. It seems that Herbert Murrill who arranged the programmes was not aware of Constant's dislike of Brahms: 'I have chosen the Magnard Third Symphony,' he wrote in July, 'since it best suits our plans for the week, to have a French work in this period. I have put before it Grétry Overture *L'épreuve villageoise* with your favourite *Perpetuum Mobile* as an extra ... I am sorry to have harrowed your feelings by my Brahms suggestion'.[34] Constant flashed back a telegram: 'NATURALLY PLEASED CONDUCT MAGNARD 3 THOUGH PREFERRED BORODIN 1'. When Anthony Bernard conducted the BBC Orchestra in a broadcast of *Pomona* on 15 September, Eric Blom aptly commented in *The Listener*: '[Lambert] is not, as I have come to feel his contemporary William Walton is, an artist passionately absorbed in what he produces, absorbed, that is, to the exclusion of all regard for other people's music.'[35]

---

[30] Manchester, *Vic-Wells*, p. 49. The performance in question would have been on 27 August.

[31] 41 ballet programmes consisting of 92 performances drawn from 20 ballets. Opera was presented on other days, with Mondays reserved for rehearsals.

[32] As Harold Rutland wrote in 'Recollections of Constant Lambert': 'After one performance at Hull, I was having a drink with him, and he said that that night, before going to bed, he intended to write a two-thousand-word article on ballet music for a book to be published in aid of Polish forces. He had, as we all knew, an extraordinary facility with his pen.'

[33] Moeran's choral suite *Phyllida and Corydon* (1939) was dedicated to Constant Lambert.

[34] Letter from Herbert Murrill to Constant Lambert, 29 July 1940: BBC Written Archives, Caversham. The Magnard symphony seems to have been something of a speciality for Lambert. After giving the first English performance in June 1936, it was the only work in a broadcast on 17 January 1939. After the Bristol broadcast on 22 August 1940 his last performance of the work was on 30 December 1950.

[35] Blom, 'Constant Lambert as a Composer'.

On the last evening of the London summer season there was an air-raid alert between two scenes in *The Prospect before Us* (ironically just as the drop curtain depicting Rowlandson's 18th-century theatre in flames was being lowered), and the following evening the blitz on London began in earnest with severe and widespread damage. As the bombing intensified, the Sadler's Wells Theatre was commandeered as a rest centre for air-raid victims,[36] putting a question mark over the immediate future of the Company, as Constant, writing from his mother's address, informed Cecil Gray:

> My plans are uncertain – I was going to stay in Gloucestershire but on coming back to London from seeing Kit[37] I found that my hearty great sister-in-law, after barging about in gum-boots and a tin hat ever since the Czech crisis, has collapsed under the strain leaving my mother with no-one in the house hence the above address. God knows what is happening to the ballet. The theatre has been turned into a refuge for the homeless, but I suppose they may try & arrange some form of provincial tour. I hope so for financial reasons as I am now living on what for want of a better term is occasionally referred to as my capital. Should occasion permit perhaps I could pay a call at the mill.[38]

With the loss of their home theatre the Company had to make some radical changes and in October they went on a four-week ENSA tour. Fonteyn described how 'engagements at military camps were not always well received by soldiers who did not think that war meant having to watch fancy ballet dancing. They banged their seats loudly to express their disgust as they left the theatre during the quietest moments of *Les Sylphides*, which was normally first in the programme.'[39] Much of their comments could be clearly heard above the two-piano accompaniment. All this threw Constant into a mood of depression which he conveyed in a letter to Gray, carefully complying with security regulations by writing from 'the little town of N—':

> During the grimmer periods of my adult life it has always been my custom to console myself with the thought that anyway it isn't as bad as one's first term at a public school. But the other day I found myself quite seriously comparing the pros & cons of my life now & my life then. I don't wish to indulge in a wave of that self-pity which the austerer critics (yourself among them) so deplore in the works of Tchaikovsky but at the same time I feel that I am really beginning to experience altogether too many sides of this war.
>
> First of all the provinces in the black-out at a time when London was still gay & normal, then the bloody invasion of Holland, escaping from Hitler by a charabanc's length, then the blitzkrieg on London combined with total unemployment and finally the tedium of pseudo-military life. It needs the pen of a Verlaine to describe one's melancholy as one tramps through the mud & slush of Kitchener Road & Gant Lane on one's way to the Garrison Theatre there to hammer out Chopin on an out-of-tune upright with a squeaking pedal and a missing top octave. As well as being general manager of the company I have to accompany the singers and compère the whole show both of which I do with a

---

[36] While the stage, the stalls and the canteen were taken over for the care of air-raid victims, the two upstairs rehearsal rooms were still available for the opera and ballet companies when they moved to the New Theatre. From November 1940 the administration of both the Old Vic and Sadler's Wells companies was run from Burnley in Lancashire where the Victoria Theatre became their headquarters for two years.

[37] Kit's school had evacuated from Hampstead to Yarkhill, in Herefordshire: Motion, *The Lamberts*, p. 266.

[38] Letter, n.d. [Tuesday], from Lambert to Gray, headed 42 Peel Street.

[39] Fonteyn, *Autobiography*, p. 90.

sickening mixture of breeziness & diffidence. It would I feel afford you peculiar pleasure to watch the conductor of Pierrot Lunaire & The Chinese Symphony (not to mention your favourite Markevitch) bringing in the audience in the chorus of Land of Hope and Glory and 'Just a song at twilight'. The possibility that I may at some remote state inherit the Kingdom of Heaven is not, I find, sufficient consolation. Things cheered up a bit on Wednesday night when the officers threw a small party. They had I believe been told that the ballet hardly drank at all. Their beer bill the next day must have come as a salutary shock. (Incidentally among the palpable signs of the previous night's gaiety found outside the Garrison Theatre next morning was a set of false teeth.) I find myself now in Devizes which is one of those places like Wantage, Pitlochry, Avalon or Lyonesse that one associates with Literature rather than with life. It is not bad in a dull way and has a surprisingly high level of architecture. The tour takes us to Hereford where I shall be able to see Kit which will be pleasant. There is a chance I think that Nancy may be joining us there – she wasn't well enough to come out on the first week.

What happens after this month God knows. There is talk of a proper provincial tour with 2 pianos and a full repertoire which would at least bring in a little more than my present job which is barely paying expenses at that. And I need hardly say that I am completely in the cart financially. Excuse this long howl but life gets a little trying at times as you (with your critical flair) may have had occasion to observe. That staunch friend, the old Demon,[40] has to be pretty well cold shouldered these days for reasons both pianistic & financial. I find some consolation in Gorki's diary[41] which is now my favourite book. I expect you know it backwards.[42]

The early ENSA performances were an uneasy mixture of ballet and music hall, often with a comic or a popular singer in between each ballet which was danced to an upright piano. The audience reaction was mixed and it was felt that the performers were playing down to the troops. Once they had risked restricting themselves to ballet only, with an orchestra, scenery and costumes, the result was much more promising and the Company were sent to camps across the country.

In November they had a week each in Manchester and Stratford-upon-Avon. On 23 November Constant had two broadcasts on the same day at Bristol. The first, at 7.30 p.m., included works by Glinka, Saint-Saëns and Falla. The second, at 10 p.m., of 'favourite pieces from the repertoire of the BBC Orchestra' included items requested by Service listeners. Sousa and Suppé marches were favourites of Constant's, and as for Bizet's *L'Arlésienne* Suite, from Manchester he cabled agreement to Herbert Murrill: 'GIRLS FROM ARLES ALWAYS OKAY FOR ME.'

Now that the BBC Symphony Orchestra had evacuated to Bristol, Constant's great friend Hyam 'Bumps' Greenbaum and his wife Sidonie Goossens were sharing lodgings there with the Rawsthornes. On the night of the broadcast, Alan and Jessie were having a small gathering at their flat when the city experienced its heaviest air-raid. As one of those at the party remembered:

Constant Lambert looked out of the window … and said, 'Oh what pretty lights all around' … He didn't realise that they were flares any more than the rest of

---

[40] 'The Demon' was Lambert's name for alcohol.
[41] Maxim Gorki, *Fragments from My Diary: Autobiography* (Harmondsworth: Penguin Books, 1940), a selection from Gorki's journals first published in 1924 and translated into English in 1940 by his lifelong friend, Baroness Moura Budberg.
[42] 18 October 1940.

us did ... then a bit later he looked out again and said, 'Oh the roof's on fire' and Jessie's reaction ... was 'Never mind; have another drink', so we had another drink and so it went on. And then Constant looked up again and said, 'I'd better collect my scores' so he chased upstairs and brought down two suitcases with all his scores. A little bit later they decided they'd all better go off to the pub, because the building was clearly on fire and the fire brigade obviously wasn't coming because they had a thousand other fires to attend to ... so we all went to the pub.[43]

The pub was on the other side of the road and they stayed there all night, using its cellar for shelter. As Sidonie remembered, Constant did his share of fire-fighting, trying to stop the flames from reaching the cellar. He 'had found one of those little hoses that you use to wash glasses and was playing it against the wall of the furniture repository next door which was blazing away'.[44] When Alan, Jessie, Sidonie and Bumps emerged after the 'all-clear' they found their flat reduced to rubble, Alan's recently completed first violin concerto among the casualties.

In the week-end that Constant was in Bristol, his *Dirge from 'Cymbeline'* had its first performance at Caius College Cambridge in a reduced version with piano rather than string accompaniment. The male chorus was made up of College members and Patrick Hadley conducted an enterprising programme of British music that included, besides a piece of his own, choral works by Vaughan Williams and Moeran.

In December the Sadler's Wells Company were performing first in Newcastle and Blackpool and then, with little prospect of returning to London while the blitz was in progress and with no West Country theatre offering them a temporary home, they took up residence over Christmas at Dartington Hall in Devon. Most conveniently the estate had its own theatre and studios in which they could practise, and they put on six performances that delighted the public despite the 'bare economy of setting'. According to Joy Newton, the communal accommodation meant that 'everyone was in and out of each other's bed'.[45] One nightly ritual that involved Lambert, Ashton, Helpmann and Pamela May was a game of strip-poker.

When by the new year the bombing of London had become less regular, some semblance of normal life was attempted by keeping theatres going, and the Sadler's Wells Company took over the slightly smaller New Theatre[46] in St Martin's Lane for a five-week ballet season, to be followed by a season of opera. They opened on 14 January 1941 with *Les Sylphides*, *Façade* and *Dante Sonata*, giving seven programmes each week, from Monday to Friday at 2.30 p.m. and two performances on Saturday at 2 and 4 p.m. (a Thursday matinée was introduced in February). It was decided not to risk an orchestra (and not even to use gramophone records for *Dante Sonata*), so once again the dancers were accompanied by two pianists, usually Hilda Gaunt and Constant. 'Now that piano duettists are so good and theatre orchestras are often no better than they should be, this form of accompaniment to the ballet is very acceptable.

---

[43] Mollie Barger in interview with Tim Mottershead, in Mottershead, 'Alan Rawsthorne: the Fish with an Ear for Music: A Concise Biography', *The Creel*, no. 19 (Winter 2005/6), pp. 46–7.

[44] Carole Rosen, *The Goossens: A Musical Century* (London: Andre Deutsch, 1993), p. 193.

[45] Kavanagh, *Secret Muses*, p. 270.

[46] With the exception of one season at the Princes Theatre in 1944, the New Theatre (renamed the Albery Theatre in 1973) became their London home until July 1945. After the bombing in May 1941 of the Old Vic, it also became the temporary home of the Old Vic Company. See Appendix 13 for that season's programmes. Because of the theatre's smaller size, from September 1940 until May 1942 *The Wise Virgins* was performed without the Whistler set and danced instead in front of gauzes. As *The Times* critic reported, 'Whistler's setting loses something by being deprived of the original décor' (21 May 1941).

Even Walton's score lost little of its point by transference to the pianos,'[47] reported *The Times*. Angus Morrison stepped in occasionally,[48] as he did four days after the beginning of the run, playing with Hilda Gaunt when Constant had two broadcasts on the same day, an afternoon sequence for the Forces Programme and an evening broadcast conducting *The Triumph of Neptune* on the Home Service.[49] The busy schedule rang the changes between 15 ballets, the programmes being announced only a few days in advance, and Constant would have been delighted when one billboard read: '*The Wise Virgins* (subject to alteration)'. An inevitable result of the change of theatre and the short notice of programmes was that during the week they were often dancing to a half-empty house.

While at Dartington, Constant and Freddie Ashton had worked on a new ballet, *The Wanderer*, which was first staged at the New Theatre on 27 January 1941 with designs by Graham Sutherland. It was to be Ashton's last ballet before he was called to military service. He and Constant had discussed the project with Sutherland over lunch at Kenneth Clark's temporary home in Gloucestershire. The music was Schubert's *Wanderer Fantasy* played on two pianos by Hilda Gaunt and Constant but once the orchestra was reinstated Constant used Liszt's transcription for piano and orchestra. Julia Farren remembered how the quick-witted Constant solved a problem that Ashton was having with the last part of the ballet:

> It was early in the morning and Fred was having one of his sort of, 'Well, I don't know – you do something' days which he had occasionally. And suddenly Constant who had his umbrella and his overcoat and his cigarette permanently hanging out of his mouth, hung on to the piano and said, 'Play it, Hilda,' and so Hilda played it, and he said, 'Just listen. All you've got to do …' and with his poor foot [he stamped out the rhythm] and that started Fred off – and that was the final. He knew exactly how to get Fred moving.[50]

Although *The Wanderer* at first received mixed reviews, it grew in popularity and became the most performed ballet in that five-week run. To overcome any obscurity in the meaning of the ballet, Constant later added a more explicit programme note:

> The Wanderer in this ballet is not the physical traveller of the 19th century, but a mental and emotional traveller who belongs to all time. In the first movement we see him as a young man, turning his back on love and compassion, fascinated only by the glittering prizes of the external world. The second movement shows him in an internal world of doubts, despair, and distracting visions which clog his progress. The third movement shows him in the external world again, but this time he finds only disillusion in the prizes now within his grasp. In the fourth movement he summons up all the elements in his life, and conquers both the external and internal worlds by a supreme effort of the will.

Berners' *A Wedding Bouquet* was given two performances in February, to try out Constant's idea of dispensing with the chorus and having himself declaim the words. As *The Times* reported in May, 'As given now, the words supplied by Gertrude Stein are spoken, and very skilfully spoken, by Mr Constant Lambert, who places himself between the two pianists, whom he also directs, for the purpose. The first 10 minutes were exquisitely funny in their combinations of rhythmic music, rhythmic dance, and

---

[47] *The Times*, 15 January 1941.

[48] Later Geraldine Peppin and Marjorie Reed were occasionally supporting pianists.

[49] From the outbreak of war, all home broadcasting was either on the Home Service or the Forces Programme.

[50] *Remembering Constant Lambert*, Royal Opera House, Covent Garden, 14 March 2001.

rhythmic words. But brevity is not the soul of wit ... and it became laboured.' Constant enlivened things by adding extra humour, interpolating comments of his own, such as 'Webster! Your boots are squeaking!' directed at the Maid. Unlike Ashton, Gertrude Stein preferred this spoken version which received 22 performances in May and June.

In February Constant was present at Oxford where Walton was to receive an honorary doctorate, about which Berners wrote to Ashton: 'I hope Constant or Bobby told you about how we frightened Willie at Oxford where he came to be canonized or whatever it was. He has been getting above himself lately – owing, I presume, to adulation of ecstatic females.'[51] On 14 February Constant was in Bristol for a BBC 'lunch-hour' concert that included three movements from *Horoscope* and the Handel-Lambert Piano Concerto with Harriet Cohen as soloist. Near the end of the month he had a recording session in a bitterly cold Birmingham Town Hall that had suffered damage from recent air-raids. Such were the problems of war-time recording and Walter Legge is said to have used a hooter before each 'take' to scare away starlings, one take being spoiled by an air-raid siren going off on the Hall's roof.[52]

From March until May Constant was occupied with a provincial tour, visiting Harrogate, Bournemouth, Birmingham, Cardiff, Cheltenham, Bath, Exeter[53] and Cambridge, one week being for ENSA. The difficulties of train travel in war-time made these tours especially tiring but the natural resource of humour within the Company helped to lift people's spirits. Ninette thought that Constant, 'genial as a good-natured schoolboy ... was as much at home in a third-class railway carriage playing cards on the back of a music score (or on a crumpled *Times* drawn forth from the pocket of the ancient overcoat) with the humblest members of the Company, as in the presence of his particular cronies in the red plush of the old Café Royal. He detested humbug, and any form of false pride or intellectual snobbery.'[54] She recalled the 'agile monkey wit' of Helpmann the actor, and how

> we suffered gladly the invention of a rather grand touring *prima donna*, who had a landlady named Mrs Snodgrass (the latter was a true life name, an inspiration discovered on tour); these inventions enlivened many a train journey, for we would be given the highlights of a day in Mrs Snodgrass's select theatrical digs. There was also the terrible North Country mother 'spoilt by war' with her son Willie (obligingly played by Constant Lambert) who droned, groaned and grumbled her way across England on those slow wartime trains. These characters grew more and more alive in their solid topicality and we would await their further eccentricities with the greatest impatience.[55]

---

[51] Kavanagh, *Secret Muses*, pp. 280–1.

[52] Beresford King-Smith, *Crescendo! 75 Years of the City of Birmingham Symphony Orchestra* (London: Methuen, 1995), p. 71.

[53] While the Company were at Exeter, from Bristol on 30 April and 2 May 1941 Lambert gave two lunch-hour broadcasts (Berlioz, Balakirev and Elgar; Rossini, Liadov, Walton and Falla). The Walton was the *Sinfonia Concertante* with Angus Morrison. Other conductors in this regular series included Basil Cameron, Julius Harrison, Gideon Fagan, Adrian Boult, Herbert Menges, Warwick Braithwaite, Julian Clifford and William Walton. Also from Bristol, on 13 June he conducted a programme of Elgar, Delius, Ravel (Piano Concerto for the Left Hand with the one-armed pianist Douglas Fox) and Glazunov; and on 30 June an evening broadcast of Berlioz, Svendsen, Kodály and Smetana. From Evesham on 10–21 June he recorded a programme of Sadler's Wells ballets to be broadcast in the Latin-American Service.

[54] De Valois, *Come Dance with Me*, p. 113.

[55] Ibid., p. 109. It was Helpmann, not Lambert as suggested by Motion (*The Lamberts*, p. 222) who became the Company's entertainer.

Helpmann's 'mimicry of anyone and anything' often left Constant 'prostrate with merriment'. Both he and Ninette were jokers, sometimes at Helpmann's expense. Constant 'would spend hours with the Company, playing absurd games and listening to equally absurd stories'. But there were diversions of a more intellectual nature to while away the tedious train journeys. Rarely parted from his *Times* crossword (he was known to carry around several issues besides the one he was working on), Constant also enjoyed devising his own 'thematic' crosswords that would include the nicknames of members of the Company, the ballets they appeared in, and so on. Beryl Grey (née Groom), who first appeared with the Company in July 1941, even remembered being taught by Constant during war-time journeys how to read a score.

De Valois was only occasionally with the Company when on tour but one afternoon she arrived in Birmingham within hours of one of its biggest air-raids. The next morning she left early for the house allotted as their headquarters while they were performing at a nearby ENSA camp, only to find the area devastated by the night's raid. To her great relief they had been moved on the morning before the raid.[56]

They were back at the New Theatre on 19 May for another five weeks' stay, giving nine performances a week (every evening, except Sunday, at 7 p.m. and three matinées), this time with almost capacity attendances.[57] There was a change of programme every three days. De Valois's new two-act ballet treatment of Gluck's opera *Orpheus and Eurydice* was first given on 28 May, with Robert Helpmann and Pamela May taking the eponymous leads on stage with soloists Nancy Evans and Ceinwen Rowlands singing the arias in the pit beside Marjorie Reed and Constant, the two pianists. Having dancers mime actions sung by unseen singers proved an interesting if not an entirely successful experiment. The creation of this ballet became the subject of a BBC programme on 23 June in which, with a script partly written by Constant, he and Ninette, together with Helpmann, re-enacted the various stages of its growth, with Constant illustrating some of it on the piano.[58]

Many of the male members of the Company were now receiving their call-up papers and soon all the pre-war male soloists were lost to the services, except Helpmann who was exempt because of his Australian nationality.[59] On the last night of the five weeks' run, 21 June, Ashton had to go on as one of the Children of Light in the *Dante Sonata*, replacing a dancer who had left, and at the end of the evening de Valois informed the audience that several dancers, including Ashton, would be leaving.[60] In Ashton's absence Helpmann was appointed chief choreographer as well as being Fonteyn's dance partner. To fill the male gaps in the Company, boys as young as 16 were taken on, straight from the Ballet School and elsewhere, and they were able to stay for two years before their call-up came.

After another ENSA tour, they were back at the New Theatre for a further three weeks from 21 July able to announce 'The Full Orchestra under the direction of Constant Lambert'. This time three Saturday performances were given, at 2.00, 4.45 and 7.30 p.m. Near the end of the month Constant fitted in a recording session with the Hallé Orchestra in the Houldsworth Hall, Manchester. Afterwards they were on tour

---

[56] De Valois, *Come Dance with Me*, pp. 147–8.

[57] 135 performances drawn from 15 ballets, the most frequently performed being *A Wedding Bouquet* and *Les Sylphides*. See Appendix 13 for a list of that season's programmes.

[58] *Ballet First Night: The Reconstruction of the Production of a Ballet*, recorded 17 & 19 June, broadcast 23 June 1941, BBC Home Service. BBC Sound Archives; NSA ГL 3811–2.

[59] Constant's disabilities understandably ruled out military service; his brother Maurice served in the Royal Welsh Fusiliers during the war.

[60] Ashton was given leave to appear in the first fortnight of the July season, his last performance being on 2 August: Vaughan, *Frederick Ashton and his Ballets*, p. 195.

again for seven weeks: Liverpool (interrupted by a broadcast from Bedford), Burnley, Leeds, Harrogate and Manchester. As Arthur Bliss put it in an overseas broadcast:

> Constant Lambert has held the Vic-Wells Ballet together, touring all over the country giving performances to large audiences – two weeks in Manchester, two weeks in Liverpool, then back to London, then up to Glasgow and so forth. He tells me he knows more of England now than even J. B. Priestley. Finance does not run to an orchestra for the ballet, so you can imagine Lambert playing the piano nightly in the orchestral pit.[61]

From Burnley in Lancashire on 22 August Constant jokingly warned Cecil Gray by postcard, 'If I find you've bought all the Burmah cheroots in Harrogate it will be the end. My stocks are low and they are the only thing between me and the gas oven.' Postcards became a convenient way of keeping friends informed of his various movements, as with one sent to Gray from Harrogate on 3 September: 'Mr Constant Lambert is leaving Leeds (quite cheerfully) for Harrogate (the Royal Hall) where he will spend a few days with friends prior to departing for his shooting box at the Opera House Manchester where he will spend the last two weeks in September.'

The London autumn season opened at the New Theatre on 29 September with a complete four-act *Lac des cygnes* with Fonteyn and Helpmann. Then, after a four weeks' run,[62] they were off to Scotland and the north of England. When in Manchester Constant programmed Balakirev's *Russia* for a broadcast with the BBC Northern Orchestra, informing his programme arranger, 'Unlike most English conductors who are muscling in on the Anglo Soviet racket I am genuinely fond of Russian music and would like to include some in my programme.' Combining broadcasts with tours resulted in much travelling that was both difficult and tiring under war-time conditions, as, for example, taking a night train to London after the last ballet performance at Newcastle on Saturday 29 November, on to Bedford the next day for a rehearsal and late-night broadcast in the Corn Exchange (Berlioz's Overture *Benvenuto Cellini*, Balakirev's *Thamar* and Elgar's *Cockaigne*), and then back north to Sheffield in time for rehearsal for a week of ballet there starting the next day. Then, on 14 December, he introduced Manchester audiences to his suite from *Horoscope* in a Sunday Hallé concert that was otherwise conducted by Malcolm Sargent. Moments of escape were cherished, such as staying with Paddy Hadley and friends in Cambridge before Christmas, about which Bliss wrote to his wife Trudy:

> I had such a grand two days at Cambridge with Paddy Hadley; he put me up in Caius, while I conducted the Colour Symphony & Introduction and Allegro, with Walton taking the second half of the programme. You try & imagine Walton, Lambert, Alan Rawsthorne, Paddy & myself sitting in his room till the early hours, arguing and laughing and having a real grand set to – it did me good.[63]

For the five weeks' Christmas season at the New Theatre, beginning on Christmas Eve, the *Times* critic could report that 'the makeshift pianos are no more and Mr Constant Lambert has a capable orchestra at his disposal'. Four performances of *The Wanderer* were given with Angus Morrison the piano soloist. This season's new ballet, on 14 January 1942, Helpmann's first venture as choreographer, was *Comus*, based on the masque by Milton. Constant orchestrated various pieces that he selected

---

[61] Arthur Bliss, 'Music in Wartime', script for an untitled talk broadcast on BBC Overseas Service 3 October 1941; in *Bliss on Music*, pp. 176–80. The reference is to Priestley's *English Journey* (1934).

[62] Performances every day except Sunday and three matinées.

[63] Letter, 21 December 1941, in Bliss, *As I Remember*, p. 146.

from the operas and dramatic music of Purcell, and Oliver Messel designed the sets and costumes. Unusually the ballet included lines by Milton spoken by the character of Comus, which in this case was Helpmann himself. It was an immediate success, with 59 performances in London alone in the next six months. Cyril Beaumont commented that 'so adroitly has Lambert matched Purcell's music to the contrasting moods of the theme that it is difficult to believe that the music was not inspired by the actual situations presented,'[64] while *The Times* wrote that 'Constant Lambert's choice of music ... and his skill in orchestral adaptation makes this *Comus* a musical masterpiece'. In March, while the Company were in Manchester and Liverpool for three weeks, Constant recorded a ballet suite from *Comus* with the Hallé Orchestra.

In February the Company had made their customary visit to Cambridge. Constant's son Kit, now nearly seven, came over at the end of the week's stay and for much of the time was looked after by Fonteyn. Leo Kersley remembers being asked to take care of him while all the female dancers were on stage for *Les Sylphides* and how, afterwards, Kit went up to Fonteyn and gave her a tremendous hug, a show of love that was reciprocated.[65] It was as if Kit took the place of the child that Margot was never to have, and her maternal affection and care for him were to continue after Constant's death. She would visit Kit when he was at boarding school and take him out for the afternoon, and in the holidays too from time to time they would meet up. This only ended with her own marriage, when she tried to conceal any hint of her affair with Lambert. For Kit, Fonteyn's genuine warmth must have been a refreshing change from the uncertain attention he received when at home from school, at one time fitting into what Motion has described as 'the glamorous, flighty and peripatetic life of his mother' and his grandmother's 'severe, old-fashioned and strait-laced influence'.[66] After her short-lived life as a dancer with the Vic-Wells Company and with her career as a model waning, Flo had taken to buying, redecorating and selling flats to improve her income.

From Cambridge the Company went on to Oxford, Constant's week there being interrupted on 11 February by an afternoon broadcast 'from a concert hall in East Anglia' as *Radio Times* announced it, which was in fact back at the Arts Theatre, Cambridge. With the BBC Orchestra he gave a programme that included Britten's *Sinfonietta* (his Opus 1), his own Concerto for Piano and Nine Players, the first performance of Roberto Gerhard's ballet suite *Don Quixote*, and Milhaud's *La Création du monde*.[67] Then it was on to Bournemouth where at the Pavilion, after performances of *Les Patineurs*, *Horoscope* and *Checkmate*, Constant was approached at the stage door by a 14-year-old enthusiast asking him to autograph a copy of his Concerto for Piano and Nine Players. This he did, adding rather gruffly, 'I didn't think anyone even knew this existed any more.'[68] From Bournemouth he sent Cecil Gray a postcard on which he scribbled: 'I can't believe that Verlaine ever felt really at home here. Can you?' Then it was on to Manchester (where he fitted in the recording session with the Hallé Orchestra) and Liverpool, returning to the New Theatre for a three-week run that opened on 16 March with *The Sleeping Princess*.

On 27 March he travelled to the Bedford Corn Exchange for an afternoon broadcast of Dvořák's *Carnaval* Overture, Rimsky-Korsakov's *Fairy Tale* (*Skazka*), Op. 29, his

[64] Beaumont, *The Sadler's Wells Ballet*, p. 190.

[65] Leo Kersley in conversation with the author, 4 March 2008.

[66] Motion, *The Lamberts*, p. 264.

[67] Only the first two works were broadcast and Gerhard's *Don Quixote* received its first broadcast performance the next day under Raybould. Falla's Harpsichord Concerto had originally been planned but that was changed to the Lambert Concerto. Louis Kentner was the soloist.

[68] In a letter to the author from Dennis Andrews, 23 November 2003.

own *The Rio Grande* (with Margaret Good) and Falla's dances from *The Three-Cornered Hat*. 'It will be fun,' he had written to the programme supervisor, 'to follow up what is undoubtedly the worst scored work in 19th century music (viz Carnaval) with what is probably the best (to wit, Conte Féerie).'

Mid-April Constant stayed with Paddy Hadley before going on to Bedford to record a programme of English ballet music for the BBC Overseas Service (*Comus, The Prospect before Us, Checkmate, Pomona, Façade*) but first he met Angus Morrison at the Cambridge railway station where, in the refreshment room, he went through the piano part of *Dante Sonata* that Angus would be playing in the coming London season. Near the end of April the Sadler's Wells Ballet arrived at Bath just before an air-raid. Unable to find lodgings, Constant and several others decided to stay in the Theatre Royal for the night and within a few hours he was once again involved in fire-fighting, helping to save the famous theatre from being gutted. De Valois would have gone to Bath as well had she not been called to London on business, but hearing of the bombing and fearing the fate of the whole Company (80 strong with the orchestra), she travelled down by train the next day to find the city looking 'like a cracked bowl' but thankfully no-one hurt. The hotel she would have stayed in had taken a direct hit.[69] There were other problems. Next day they learned that the ballets were shut up in trucks on a siding at Bath station with two unexploded bombs close by. Fortunately there was no repetition of Holland and everything was eventually retrieved.

They were back at the New Theatre on 5 May, Helpmann's *Hamlet*[70] being the new production that was premiered a fortnight later with scenery and costumes by Leslie Hurry. The music was Tchaikovsky's fantasy-overture of the same name, a score that Constant was to record commercially with the Hallé Orchestra in October. As John Tooley remembered: 'At the New Theatre, with a tiny orchestra, [Lambert] would wring the last ounce out of his musicians as they played Tchaikovsky's *Hamlet* Overture. ... Few have equalled his conducting of Tchaikovsky.'[71]

The death on 13 May 1942 of 'Bumps' Greenbaum, aged only 41, came as a great shock to Constant and his circle of friends. In a long obituary Cecil Gray mourned the loss of one whom he called 'probably the most richly gifted interpretative artist, and certainly the best conductor of his generation in this country'. He wrote too of composers like Lambert, Walton and Rawsthorne frequently going to Greenbaum not only 'with their scores for advice on technical matters but also for constructive aesthetic criticism in the process of composition'.[72] Having first led the second violins in the Queen's Hall Orchestra, 'Bumps' had then joined the Brosa Quartet as second violin. His ambition had been to become a conductor but without any 'social influence or financial backing' it had not been easy, having to be satisfied with such jobs as musical director for C. B. Cochran's revues and recording manager for the Decca Record Company. His appointment as musical director for BBC Television had been abbreviated when the studios closed for the duration of war, and his last year was spent in charge of light variety for the BBC at Bangor, North Wales. His early death – the long-term result of alcoholism – might have served as a warning to Constant who was himself to die at a similar age and from similar causes. But it was a warning that went unheeded.

On 29 May Constant once again recited *Façade* at the Aeolian Hall, this time in

---

[69] De Valois, *Come Dance with Me*, pp 153–4.

[70] In 1944 Helpmann was also to take the 'straight' role of Hamlet in the play by Shakespeare.

[71] John Tooley, *In House: Covent Garden: 50 Years of Opera and Ballet* (London: Faber & Faber, 1999), p. 125.

[72] Cecil Gray, 'Hyam Greenbaum (1901–1942)', *The Music Review*, vol. 3 no.3 (August 1942), pp. 219–23.

a concert promoted by the music publishers Boosey & Hawkes. It was paired with Schoenberg's *Pierrot lunaire* conducted by Erwin Stein and with Hedli Anderson as the reciter. As Walton (who conducted *Façade*) remembered, for this performance, at Constant's suggestion, 'we decided as Schönberg had done three times seven poems in *Pierrot Lunaire* we should do a trick and have seven times three, a sort of typically Schönbergian inversion', and so the *Façade* poems were grouped accordingly. At the end Walton emerged from behind the screen in a pin-striped suit, while Lambert, in shirtsleeves, came out looking hot and flustered.[73] Benjamin Britten, who was in the audience, was not impressed by either work and wrote afterwards to Peter Pears, 'Friday's do … was pretty awful really. Horrible audience, snobby – and stupid. The pieces very faded & Constant Lambert completely inaudible.' According to one report[74] for some people 'the speech was unintelligible due to the inadequacy of the reproduction apparatus'. However, Richard Temple Savage, who was one of the instrumentalists, remembered that 'the verse was excellently spoken by Constant Lambert'[75] and the *Times* critic commented that *Façade* had 'a delightful silliness which pleased an audience that laughed frankly at 20-year-old jokes'. The whole programme was repeated a month later.

The ballet season at the New Theatre ended on 18 July and near the beginning of August there was a week of open-air performances in East London's Victoria Park, between Hackney and Bethnal Green, before touring Edinburgh and the north of England. When on tour and away from friends, Constant would as ever while away the tedious hours by sending humorous letters or postcards and he even turned his hand to verse. His current pre-occupation was completing the double-bishop limericks, and from Edinburgh on 11 August he informed Gray: 'Burmah situation is well in hand you will be glad (though envious) to hear. The Boys Blue Book of Bishops will be sent to you shortly.' From Newcastle 13 days later it was a simple greeting of 'Hoots Mon!', and two days on from Glasgow: 'I belong to Glesky, deir auld Glesky toon!' As the tour lengthened his mood became more impish and near the end of the month he selected a picture postcard of sheep against a mountain background to which he added the caption: 'A distinguished group of mourners at the funeral of the late Professor Tovey'.[76]

Lambert was rarely vindictive in either his private correspondence or his journalism but Sir Donald Tovey, who had died in Edinburgh in 1940, seems to have become a rare target of his rancour. In November 1937, reviewing the first performance of his Cello Concerto with Casals as soloist, he had written:

> I am told by those who had the moral physical and intellectual stamina to sit it out to the end that Professor Donald Tovey's Cello Concerto lasts for over an hour. This I cannot vouch for as, like several other musicians, I was compelled to leave at the end of the first movement, which seemed to last as long as my first term at school, but was probably a little shorter in fact. I therefore find myself in the melancholy position of not being able to delight my readers with an account of the work as a whole. All I can say is that the first movement is the most completely null and void piece of music I have ever heard at Queen's Hall. (And I have had some gruelling experiences in my day.)[77]

[73] Private information to the author from Robert Threlfall, 20 April 2003.

[74] The radio and television producer Dallas Bower, in a letter to Walton, 2 June 1942.

[75] Richard Temple Savage, *A Voice from the Pit: Reminiscences of an Orchestral Musician* (Newton Abbott: David & Charles, 1988), p. 98.

[76] Postcard 28 August 1942. Sir Donald Francis Tovey (1875–1940) had been professor of music at Edinburgh University and in that city he ran the Reid Orchestra concerts for which he wrote his well-known programme notes.

[77] *Sunday Referee*, 21 November 1937.

That same month, in the short-lived magazine *Night and Day*, he continued the attack:

> While in the mood to attack the BBC I should like to complain about the ever more frequent programme notes of Sir Donald Tovey which seem to me to perform no useful function. ... Professor Tovey would have been thoroughly at home in the theological circle of the middle ages when he could have argued about the number of angels who can dance on a pin-point to his heart's content. But I have yet to see that his laborious analyses show any appreciation of what goes on in a composer's mind. He seems to think that Beethoven was chiefly worried by trying to get back to the flattened super-tonic in time and he is quite capable of proving that Schubert's C major symphony is really not in C major at all but in B sharp or D double flat.[78]

In *Music Ho!* Constant had condemned 'the deplorable school of romantic analysts from Sir George Grove to Dr Hugo Leichtentritt' and when the fifth volume of Tovey's *Essays in Musical Analysis* was published in 1937, its author wrote to Foss:

> Constant Lambert, not content with being ill-tempered about my compositions (most critics are that) has flown out violently against my programme notes. All I wanted to complete their success was an honestly bad-tempered enemy, especially one who has some following. My next plan of campaign will be to produce some instrumental, not vocal, work of his next year and send him my perfectly polite notes on it. If he doesn't like them, he can write his own (for our programme). Could you produce me a list of his compositions?[79]

Other postcards from Edinburgh carried less venom. On one that had a picture of highland cattle Constant attached names: 'A Happy Snap at the Braemar Gathering (reading from left to right): – The Dinwiddie of Dinwiddie & children, The Hon. Mr. Norman McGlinkie, The Bishop of Galashiels (and friend)'. Touring from town to town, he often found himself staying, for convenience rather than by choice, at a railway hotel and this gave birth to a verse he sent from The Midland Hotel in Manchester to Anthony Powell, writing:

> My dear Tony
>
> It appears from your card that your Polish party is to last from Sept. 25th to 27th. It sounds rather like the one we gave in Tavistock Square and I am sorry not to be there – it should be warming up by now. But the above gloomy address tells its own tale. I feel exactly like a character in Priestley and am probably beginning to talk and walk like one.
>
> I whiled away a rainy Sunday afternoon here by composing the enclosed little ballad. Though not of a very high standard it has the following things to recommend it (a) it is factually true (b) it introduces <u>all</u> the L.M.S. hotels (c) it can be sung (with charming effect) to the tune of 'There are fairies at the bottom of my garden'.
>
> Give my love to Violet[;] also to little Flo if you see her.[80]

And he attached the following poem:

---

[78] *Night and Day*, 25 November 1937, p. 28

[79] Mary Grierson, *Donald Francis Tovey: A Biography Based on Letters* (London: Oxford University Press, 1952), pp. 314–15.

[80] Letter to Anthony Powell, 26 September 1942.

A BALLAD OF L.M.S. HOTELS

There are L.M.S. Hotels at Ayr & Dornoch,
There are L.M.S. Hotels at Leeds and Crewe;
  At Stratford-upon-Avon
  The salami's made of raven
And they charge you 10/6 for Irish Stew.
There's an L.M.S. Hotel at Kyle of Lochalsh
Where beds are cold & bathrooms far and few;
  At the hotel in Gleneagles
  They fricassée the beagles
And they charge you 10/6 for Irish Stew.
There's a squalid L.M.S. Hotel at Preston
(and the one at Stoke on Trent is pretty blue);
  At Derby or Turnberry
  One's not exactly merry
And they charge you 10/6 for Irish Stew.
At Holyhead & Liverpool & Euston
The halibut supreme is cooked in glue;
  At Edinburgh and "Glesgie"
  The supper's one kromeski
And they charge you 10/6 for Irish Stew.
At the one in Inverness the maids wear tartan
Which is rather hard on Sassenachs like you;
  At Dumfries and Strathpeffer
  They boil the aged heifer
And they charge you 10/6 for Irish Stew.
At Manchester & Morecombe, at Birmingham & Bradford
The food and drink would make an ostrich spew;
  But old Sir Arthur Towle[81]
  Has a gizzard like an owl
And he actually enjoys the Irish Stew.

Chorus: Aye Mon! and he actually enjoys the Irish Stew!

Most of Constant's BBC broadcasts now came from Bedford where, since July 1941, the BBC Symphony Orchestra had been relocated after the heavy bombing of Bristol. On 7 September 1942 he took a London train from Liverpool, where a fortnight of ballet had just begun at the Royal Court Theatre, and then on to Bedford for an evening broadcast the following day that included Alexander Dargomizhsky's *Kazatachok* and Borodin's Symphony No. 2. While such travel was unavoidable, he became increasingly frustrated with BBC bureaucracy that required him to write so many letters to different departments to make arrangements for a single broadcast. Eventually he challenged one BBC official:

I enclose my contracts for Nov 27th and Dec 12th & presume that the one for Dec 13th (only just confirmed) will arrive later.[82] As regards Dec 12th you will

---

[81] Arthur Towle was controller of the LMS Hotel Service from 1925 until 1944. Although he received a CBE he was not knighted.

[82] 27 November: BBC Home Service 1.15 p.m. Bedford. BBC Symphony Orchestra. Balakirev, *Overture on a Spanish March*; Lambert, *King Pest*; Ravel, Piano Concerto for the Left Hand (Douglas Fox). Chabrier, *España* and *Fête polonaise* played but not broadcast. 12 December: Home Service 2.30 p.m. Cambridge. BBC Symphony Orchestra. Berlioz, Overture *Benvenuto Cellini*; Liadov, *Kikimora*; Ibert, Concerto for Saxophone and Orchestra; Delius, *In a Summer*

note that the rehearsal times on the 10th have been altered thus involving me with a night in Bedford. Could you add this expense to my contract?

Incidentally in connection with these concerts I have been asked to write not only to (very naturally) Mr. Herbage but also to Mr. Tabb, Miss Duncan, Miss Wood, Miss Bennett & Mrs Waterman. I am as you know very busy & have no secretary.

Quite frankly is this expenditure of time, energy & notepaper really necessary? Wouldn't it be possible for me to write to one person in control who could pass the information on to the multifarious departments concerned?[83]

Fortunately, someone in the BBC hierarchy saw the sense in Constant's plea and the procedure was simplified.

The ballet moved on to Leeds for the second week of October but he was able to fit in recording sessions back in Manchester with the Hallé Orchestra to set down Tchaikovsky's *Hamlet* Overture and the Fourth Symphony, one of his most impressive recordings. He was happy to be back in London at the New Theatre for the start of the Christmas season that ran from 20 October until 19 December. *The Rake's Progress* was restored to the repertoire after the scenery and costumes had been lost in Holland. On 24 November he conducted the premiere of *The Birds*, Helpmann's first comic ballet, to music by Respighi, for which he had suggested Chinese décor from the designer Chiang Yee. Constant's *The Bird-Actors* was played as an overture and 'gave as much delight as anything that followed'.[84] For some time it had been apparent that Constant's work load was proving extremely arduous, and so in the first week of December, to relieve him of part of the burden, Julian Clifford[85] was appointed associate conductor, a position he held until the end of the following July.

At the end of that first week, on Sunday 6 December, Constant gave the second UK performance of Britten's *Sinfonia da Requiem*,[86] the composer having returned home from America in April. The orchestra was the London Philharmonic with whom Constant at that time had the occasional concert. The orchestra's bass clarinet, Richard Temple Savage, was critical of Constant's conducting, finding him

brilliant though he was, ... really at his best as a ballet conductor; to put it bluntly, he was incapable of following a singer or instrumentalist in a rubato. Jean Pougnet liked to play as encores little Kreisler 'lollipops' which I would orchestrate for him and we had to abandon one of these, *Schöne Rosmarin*, entirely because Lambert could not manage to follow Pougnet. He was particularly fond of light French music, reacted against the whole German tradition and thought a composer like Dvořák quite appalling. Nevertheless the Directors put him down to conduct Dvořak's cello concerto and between his

---

Garden (original version); Tchaikovsky, Symphony No. 4. 13 December: Home Service 2.30 p.m. Bedford. – same programme.

[83] Letter from Lambert (42 Peel Street) to Mr Wynn, 21 November 1942.

[84] Clarke, *The Sadler's Wells Ballet*, p. 176.

[85] Julian H. Clifford (1903–66), was the son of Julian Clifford (1877–1921), conductor of the Harrogate and Hastings Municipal Orchestras.

[86] The programme, at the Orpheum Theatre, Golders Green was Tchaikovsky, *Hamlet*; Beethoven, Piano Concerto No. 3 (soloist Solomon); Britten, *Sinfonia da Requiem*; Delius, *La Calinda* and *Irmelin* Prelude; and Copland, *El Salon Mexico*. The first UK performance of the *Sinfonia da Requiem* had been given on 22 July 1942 at a Henry Wood Prom in the Royal Albert Hall, with Basil Cameron conducting the same orchestra. The Orpheum was a venue much used by the London Philharmonic Orchestra during the war after the destruction, through bombing, of the Queen's Hall.

dislike of the music and his difficulty in accompanying the soloist we had all the ingredients for a disaster.[87]

However, it was with the London Philharmonic that he became involved in an unusual assignment. This was the film *Battle for Music*[88] that told the true story of the orchestra's war-time struggle for existence after becoming a self-governing body. It is an unusual film because instead of using professional actors throughout, most of the key figures were taken by members of the orchestra's committee who were themselves players.[89] This gives a rather wooden feel to much of the dialogue but at the same time, from an historical perspective, it adds much authenticity to what is after all a fascinating documentary. There are appearances by J. B. Priestley reading a 'musical manifesto' – in effect an appeal for public support[90] – and the impresario Jack Hylton,[91] and sequences with Malcolm Sargent, Adrian Boult and Warwick Braithwaite[92] conducting and with Eileen Joyce as soloist in the Grieg concerto. Constant's involvement is probably the only surviving film of him conducting. He is first seen coming on to take a bow, turning to the leader and commenting 'It's a good house' before conducting several intercut sections of Tchaikovsky's Overture *Romeo and Juliet* totalling just over five minutes on film. This sequence is particularly valuable because it gives a good view of Lambert's very clear conducting technique as well as showing him as looking particularly healthy, contradicting the suggestions made by some writers that he was at this time much overweight. Later he is seen accompanying Moiseiwitsch in substantial sections of Rachmaninov's Piano Concerto No. 2[93] with superimposed images of trains representing the orchestra on tour, together with the occasional glimpse of posters announcing concerts by the LPO and Lambert in places like Swansea, Bristol and Nottingham. As Thomas Russell, the orchestra's secretary and violist, wrote:

> The scenes in which a few of us from the Orchestra were starred were, of course, not acted in the ordinary sense of the word, but in spite of this they gave an impression of sincerity to which our naïve efforts added a truer quality. But the shape of the film was far from satisfactory. This was partly due to the delay in making the film, for during the long period spent over its preparation, the

[87] Savage, *A Voice from the Pit*, p. 95. Against this anecdote it should be said that in 1946 Lambert conducted an almost all-Dvořák Promenade concert that included the Violin Concerto; in June 1937 he had conducted the Dvořák Cello Concerto, and occasionally he conducted other shorter works of Dvořák, such as the overtures.

[88] The story of the making of the film was told in the chapter 'Making a Film' in Thomas Russell, *Philharmonic Parade* (London: Hutchinson, 1944), pp. 104–8; the film was also discussed in John Huntley, *British Film Music* (London: Skelton Robinson, 1947), pp. 124–8, although the sequence of events as described there are not quite as seen on film. Made at Elstree, the film lasts 75 minutes. The music was recorded 12–16 April 1943. The film was directed by Donald Taylor and the script written by St John L. Clowes.

[89] These included Thomas Russell (violist and the LPO's secretary), Frances Bradley (horn), Charles Gregory (horn), Francis Stead (trombone) and Maurice Ward (viola).

[90] 14 October 1941 at Cambridge at a LPO concert conducted by Boult (as in the film).

[91] In 1941 Jack Hylton gave the orchestra much support by promoting its tours and, by making available such venues as music halls (for which a special rostrum was built), brought the orchestra before a new audience.

[92] Warwick Braithwaite (1896–1971), born in New Zealand, was conductor of Sadler's Wells Opera, 1932–40, and Sadler's Wells Ballet, 1948–52.

[93] Totalling 7′21″, the sections of Rachmaninov's Second Piano Concerto seen are the first movement from the opening until 17 bars after figure 6, the slow movement from figure 27 leading into the first 20 bars of the last movement and then cutting to the soloist's *quasi glissando* entry into the last 46 bars.

story of the LPO had been changing and developing so that events recorded had lost or altered their significance. It was also due to the misplacing of the climax, which left the end of the film in the air.[94]

Made by Strand Films, it was released in February 1944.

T HE Sadler's Wells Company were in York over Christmas 1942 and from the Royal Station Hotel Constant wrote to the conductor Iris Lemare, a champion of Alan Rawsthorne's music:

> I have rather lost contact with people too, but owing to perpetual travelling Jessie [Hinchliffe, Rawsthorne's wife], who is in very good form I see whenever I am in Bedford. Alan who is now doing film work for the Army & is usually to be met in civilian clothes is his old self again.[95]

The first New Theatre season of 1943 was a three-week run starting on 25 January,[96] followed by two weeks in Bournemouth and a four week tour of Hanley, Coventry, Derby and Oxford. At the end of March it was back to the New Theatre for a further four weeks.[97] This was particularly notable for the temporary return of Frederick Ashton who had been given special six weeks' leave from the RAF to create a new ballet. There had been some disquiet about Helpmann's position within the Company, to the extent that Constant had threatened to resign unless Ashton was brought back to regain control. Kenneth Clark had even voiced his concern, writing: 'Helpmann is an admirable dancer, but he is a virtuoso, who does not command the confidence of the Company as a whole in the way that Ashton would do. If Constant Lambert leaves, I am afraid that Margot Fonteyn would leave also, and the whole Ballet would break up.'[98]

The new ballet that Ashton choreographed was *The Quest* with music by Walton, first staged on 6 April with Constant conducting. The idea had come to Ashton after seeing a particularly fine edition of Spenser's *Faerie Queene* one day while staying at the home of Doris Langley Moore. She offered to provide a scenario, and John Piper was chosen to design the scenery and the costumes. Walton dedicated the work to 'The Sadler's Wells Ballet Co and in particular to Ninette, Margot, Constant, Bobbie and Freddie' and two young dancers, Beryl Grey and Moira Shearer, were given their first important roles.

In the middle of the New Theatre run, Constant was involved in a Boosey & Hawkes chamber concert given at the Wigmore Hall on 11 June, the main item being the first performance of Elisabeth Lutyens' Chamber Concerto I,[99] and he took two days off in the final week to travel up to Manchester for further recording sessions with the Hallé Orchestra: Borodin's Second Symphony. Once their London season was over,

---

[94] Russell, *Philharmonic Decade*, p. 108.

[95] In 1931 Iris Lemare, a former student at the Royal College of Music, was co-founder with Anne Macnaghten and Elisabeth Lutyens of what became known as the Macnaghten-Lemare Concerts that championed young and relatively unknown British composers, among them Alan Rawsthorne who joined the Army in 1941 and was attached to the Education Corps.

[96] 56 performances of 13 ballets with 25 programmes spread over 19 days with two Sunday breaks. See Appendix 13 for a list of the programmes.

[97] See Appendix 13.

[98] Letter from Clark to unidentified source: Tate Gallery Archives, quoted in Kavanagh, *Secret Muses*, p. 288.

[99] Most works did not require a conductor; besides Bliss, Bax and Ravel, the programme included Warlock's *The Curlew*. The first two works only, Bax's *Nonet* and Bliss's *Rout*, were broadcast.

the Company were off again without a break for two weeks in Liverpool and one in Blackpool before another five back at the New Theatre.[100] For part of May Constant left the ballet in Julian Clifford's charge while he gave three concerts each in Norwich, Northampton and Newcastle with the London Philharmonic. Then from the New Theatre they went straight into another week at Hackney (Henry Wood conducted *The Rio Grande* at the Proms on the last evening of their week at the Open Air Theatre) before three weeks in Manchester[101] and two weeks in Newcastle. While in Manchester, Constant took the opportunity of visiting the zoo, as Gerald Iles, Superintendent of the Belle Vue Zoological Gardens, remembered:

I first met Constant Lambert in July 1943. Margot Fonteyn and Robert Helpmann had been to the Zoo to name two zebras but after Helpmann had seen a llama he insisted that he must name that animal, which bore such a striking resemblance to himself, rather than a zebra! Miss Fonteyn named the other zebra after herself and this animal is still with us. The following day Mr. Lambert 'phoned me from his hotel to say that the two ballet stars had told him that they had had a delightful day in the Zoo and that there was still a zebra spare without a name and he wondered, as he adored animals, whether he might come along to the Zoo and name the remaining animal. I was delighted with his suggestion and so it was arranged and we had two zebras named Margot and Constant and a llama 'Bobby'.

After this initial visit Mr. Lambert never failed to come to the Zoo as often as possible and as he was frequently in Manchester with either the Sadler's Wells Ballet or to conduct the Hallé Orchestra I saw quite a lot of him during the ensuing years.

His passion and love for animals was almost matched by his delight in riding on our amusement devices. One particularly devilish device we have here called 'The Octopus' captured his eye and he insisted on having a ride. I had previously sampled the machine and decided never to go on again but my duty as host compelled me to accompany Lambert on this occasion and the ride attendant gave us a particularly long session so that Lambert was soon calling for me to stop the thing as he was suffering from vertigo. I was pleased, however, that he was not very much upset by his experience for he conducted at the Ballet that night as well as ever.

Mr. Lambert was particularly interested in small animals and he was very much attached to a ring-tailed lemur called Lena which we had here at the time. I photographed him holding this animal and, on the same occasion, took one of him holding a python. This latter photograph is, I think, one of the nicest I have ever seen of him. ...

One other little story about Lambert which may be of interest – during one of his visits to the Zoo he saw our sea-lions go through one of their performances which concludes with a sea-lion playing 'God Save the King' on a 'Hornchestra', a specially made instrument consisting of trumpets which sea-lions can play by pushing the valves with their noses. Lambert was enchanted and promised to go straight back and write a special fanfare which the sea-lions could play at the forthcoming Circus. Unhappily he never lived to do this.[102]

After seven months' continuous work, even with an assistant conductor, Constant had good reason to write from the Midland Hotel in Manchester on 11 July, 'From the 8th to the 23rd I am having a much needed fortnight holiday. … I shall be staying in Norfolk with Patrick Hadley,' adding, 'Excuse these hasty notes but am very overworked as usual.' When Constant stayed with Paddy at Heacham they often enjoyed country walks together. He often took Margot with him, she providing the war-time luxury of pork pies that her mother made, and she would often cycle to the nearest beach for a swim. Sometimes there were other visitors, such as Maurice Bowra and his girl-friend, Sir Thomas Beecham's niece Audrey. When they were guests of Paddy's, Constant and Margot were discretely given adjacent bedrooms. At about this time Margot was using some form of contraception, this only becoming known when after one visit a packet was found beneath her bed by Paddy's housekeeper. But, whether through ineffectiveness or carelessness, this had not prevented her from becoming pregnant, it being generally accepted that in the late summer of 1943 she had an abortion.

Just before his Norfolk holiday, Constant had another concert with the LPO, in Bristol where on 4 August he introduced a suite from the music he had written for the film *Merchant Seamen* first shown in 1941. On 11 July from Manchester he had written to Felix Aprahamian, then acting as secretary for the LPO, putting in a plea for expenses:

> I enclose a receipt also my contract for the 4th [August]. Can you get these sent to the appropriate depts? As regards my contract can you get something added for my fare? Actually I am coming from Newcastle but if the firm doesn't feel up to coping with that then I shall be satisfied with a return from London to Bristol. I think this is only reasonable as with railway fares & hotel expenses to pay out of a reduced fee one is left with damned little & the whole affair combines the disadvantages of an arduous profession & an expensive hobby. The question of the right fee for Merchant Seamen I will raise, as you suggest, with Temple Savage.
>
> You will be glad to hear that I finished 'MS' yesterday. My aim has been not so much to arouse the neurasthenic susceptibilities of the audience as to blow the bastards out of their seats. I think I shall succeed. 4 movements are in the copyists hands and the 5th will be out this week. Cannot give you exact timing as 3 movements are in London but v. much doubt if it will go over the 15 minutes, may possibly be a fraction less but that doesn't matter.

He included full details of orchestration, jokingly adding to the percussion '(if it can be managed) 2 Kitchen Stoves – 1 large, 1 small'. The suite was first heard in London on 12 September in the Albert Hall, with Constant conducting, in an abbreviated three-movement form, as part of an elaborate ENSA pageant of music, verse and drama entitled 'Seascape' and devised by Basil Dean in aid of King George's Fund for Sailors. Two performances were given on the same day and Gracie Fields, Ralph Richardson and Edith Evans were among the big names appearing.

The film *Merchant Seamen* had begun, under the working title of *Able Seamen*, as a product of the enterprising and inventive GPO Film Unit, but when, after delays, it was

---

[102] Letter from Gerald T. Iles, Superintendent Belle Vue Zoological Gardens, to Angus Morrison, 5 February 1954. The two photographs mentioned, together with another of Lambert stroking a zebra, appeared in *Penguin Music Magazine II*, May 1947 between pp. 32 and 33. In a letter to his mother on 22 May 1948 Lambert mentions that he was hoping 'to write a piece for the sea-lions'.

completed in May 1941, it was released under the auspices of the Crown Film Unit.[103] Only 24 minutes long, it was a morale-boosting exercise showing, with a typical display of stoic humour, the work of the Merchant Navy in defending the Atlantic convoys from the ever-marauding U-boats. After a ship has been torpedoed, one of the youngest of the survivors makes up his mind that, when he has recovered from his injuries, he will go on a gunnery course and have his revenge on the enemy. After several months' training, he is back at sea, his ship guiding a convoy through a minefield in thick fog. The climax is the sinking of a U-boat. The film was more realistic than the Ealing Studios' 90-minute *Convoy*, first shown in July 1940 and dedicated to the Officers and Men of the Royal and Merchant Navies, the extra realism being added, in a similar fashion to *Battle for Music*, by the 'players' not being professional actors but serving British officers and Merchant Seamen, with the Narrator one of the crew represented. This clearly impressed the *Documentary News Letter* which considered that there had 'never been a documentary before quite so good in handling of people, whether actors or real men in the street.'[104] (Vaughan Williams was to make a similar contribution by writing the music for the 1942 Crown Film Unit documentary *Coastal Command* that also had serving officers and airmen instead of actors.) The soundtrack was recorded in the National Studios at Elstree[105] with Constant conducting the Sadler's Wells Orchestra, and the film was dedicated to The Orchestras of the Royal Marines. Music is used quite sparingly in the film. The Concert Suite consists of five movements (reduced if necessary to three) but not all the music that is heard in the film was used in the Suite and conversely not all the music in the Suite was used in the film. Reviewing a Prom performance of the Suite in the Lambert centenary, Andrew Clements wrote in *The Guardian*: 'Lambert … carried it off brilliantly. There are endless subtleties and imaginative touches in the orchestration of the *Merchant Seamen* concert suite that he later extracted from the film score.'[106]

The Company were back at the New Theatre from Thursday 26 August until Saturday 16 October 1943[107] with Alec Sherman[108] as the new assistant conductor. They opened, as was their custom, with *Les Sylphides* and Constant conducting, a shaky start, as *The Times* critic wrote that 'the only redeeming feature was Miss Fonteyn's exquisite dancing of her solos'. But although throughout the seven-week season Fonteyn's name appeared each day alongside that of Helpmann in the newspaper announcements, for ten days she was a noticeable absentee. 'On sick leave' was the official explanation[109] – but it is quite likely she was having an abortion. Yet she was back on 7 September for *Le Lac des cygnes* in which she danced the dual role of Odette/Odile, the first of the 14 performances in that run being given as a benefit for M. Sergueff, the ballet master responsible for this production to whom Helpmann paid tribute at the end of the evening.

[103] After the outbreak of war the Ministry of Information took over the GPO Film Unit which became the Crown Film Unit and the Colonial Film Unit.

[104] *Documentary News Letter* 2, May 1941, p. 88, quoted in Anthony Aldgate and Jeffrey Richards, *Britain Can Take It: The British Cinema in the Second World War* (Oxford: Blackwell, 1986), p. 247

[105] More precisely, the studios were situated at close-by Borehamwood, although they were usually referred to as being at Elstree.

[106] *The Guardian*, 11 August 2005.

[107] 66 programmes totalling 149 performances from 14 ballets, the most performed being *Lac des cygnes* and *Les Sylphides*, followed by *The Quest* and *Façade*. See Appendix 13.

[108] Alec Sherman (1907–2008) was for eight years violinist in the BBC Symphony Orchestra from its formation in 1930 until deciding to take up a career as a conductor. In 1941 he founded the 40-strong New London Orchestra.

[109] Clarke, *The Sadler's Wells Ballet*, p. 179.

Whether or not it was because of tension in the Company that may have arisen as a result of Fonteyn's absence, especially amongst those, like de Valois, who would have been in the know, the costumes became the catalyst for a major rift between Ninette and Constant. They were created by Leslie Hurry (who was also responsible for the scenery) and he came up with some splendid designs for the swans that varied in length and added a fine touch of grandeur at a gloomy time. However, on seeing them, de Valois, with a view only to their impracticality because of the war-time shortage of fabrics and the difficulties with clothes coupons, insisted that they all be the same length – the shortest. When Constant protested, she pointed to the pit, indicating that was as far as his job extended. From that day onwards he was no longer regarded as artistic director, making artistic decisions. He would only offer suggestions when asked.[110]

There were also attempts to bring an end to Constant's relationship with Margot. According to Meredith Daneman, Fonteyn's biographer, the chief plotter was the concerned mother, Mrs Hookham who, in league with Doris Langley Moore, under the pretext of having a film made about ballet, tried to interest Margot in the director, Charles Hassé. The idea, as Hassé recalled it, was that if Margot were to spend time with him 'it might break up the relationship with Constant'. In reality the scheme failed, developing instead more into a French farce. Perhaps they need not have bothered: in the ensuing months their relationship, more likely on Constant's part, was gradually to lose its intensity, though this was quite likely painful for Margot who attached greater sincerity to affairs of the heart, and would still have to maintain a daily working relationship with Constant on whom she was so dependant. It was a relationship that from the outset had seemed unlikely ever to end in marriage, with Constant already married and Margot not wanting anything that might hinder her career.

A T about this time Constant became acquainted with the painter and sculptor Michael Ayrton who became a close friend. They were even to share a house. Despite a difference in age of about 15 years (Ayrton being the younger)[111] they had much in common, not least their medical histories in which there are some remarkable parallels. When he was about 11 years old Ayrton suffered from a bout of osteomyelitis that started in the middle ear and then spread to the bone of his left leg, confining him to bed for a long period. According to Justine Hopkins, his biographer, 'he was referred to a specialist who infected him with scarlet fever to induce a cure. This failed; septicaemia developed, resulting in an abscess which had to be surgically opened, the upper end of the tibia being scraped and partially cut away. This left the boy with an ugly, depressed scar adhering to the bone beneath, and a slight but definite lameness. Although he returned to school in a fairly short time, he was forced initially to spend considerable periods in bed in the sanatorium'.[112] For a while, like Constant, he used a stick. Much later, after Constant's death, he was found to be suffering from an arthritic disorder known as ankylosing spondylitis and later still he was diagnosed as having diabetes. (His father had died in 1936 of cirrhosis of the liver and diabetes mellitus.) But Ayrton did not have to suffer, as Constant did, from an undetected condition, especially when they had something else in common: they were heavy drinkers. 'Matters are now in hand to put it right without taking me off the booze, thank God,' he wrote to a friend.[113]

---

[110] Leo Kersley in conversation with the author, 1 October 2005.
[111] Ayrton was born in London on 20 February 1921. He died in 1975.
[112] Justine Hopkins, *Michael Ayrton: A Biography* (London: Andre Deutsch, 1994), p. 18.
[113] Letter from Michael Ayrton to Charles Collingwood, 1 July 1973, quoted in *ibid.*, p. 387.

When only 14 Ayrton had seduced a French mistress in a haystack, putting into practice the facts of life that his father had told him, and he was consequently removed from school. He had a lonely and insecure adolescence but developed into a very precocious youth, able to talk eloquently at length on the arts – often outspokenly, and in the 1940s he became the youngest member of the BBC's 'Brains Trust'. He had quite likely been introduced to Constant by Cecil Gray[114] in the Café Royal and they instantly hit it off. They were kindred spirits, sharing many interests. Ayrton had a great passion for music, especially Berlioz,[115] a special love of France and a fondness for cats in common with so many of Constant's circle of friends (although, according to Ayrton, Constant only liked cats that didn't belong to anyone). He recognised Constant as 'a crack conductor who worked very hard at being one'. As drinkers they were to share that well-known watering hole, The George (also known affectionately as 'The Gluepot'), on the corner of Great Portland Street and Mortimer Street,[116] which, with its proximity to both Broadcasting House and, until it was destroyed in the war, Queen's Hall, was a favourite meeting place of writers, artists and musicians. Isabel Rawsthorne gave this account of The George and its habitués:

> *The George* which became the equivalent of the *Deux Magots* and the *Flore*, overcrowded, quite a struggle to the counter to get a drink, noisy, animated, in no way physically resembled the intellectual nests of Paris. Conveniently nearby was an Italian restaurant, Prada, where many Georgians took their lunch.
>
> Not far away was Fitzroy Street where Elisabeth Lutyens and Edward Clark lived. Both gregarious, their home always full of people and parties were frequent and immensely enjoyable. Edward, a slim elegant figure – he always wore a fresh flower in his button hole. Elisabeth, this aristocratic face, graceful slender hands, an appealing shrill aristocratic voice. They were both fond of Constant, were quick to defend him when he was attacked which was quite often. Elisabeth told me he made her feel shy but behind that ebullient non-stop talking screen she lived a retiring nervous existence.
>
> Many people went to The George to find jobs, as it was there were to be found BBC producers, people like R. D. Smith, Louis MacNeice, Lawrence Gilliam, those who made the Third Programme unique in European broadcasting. Also people from the film world. Elisabeth went there and did, in fact, get jobs this way. She was earning money for herself and Edward whose engagements for conducting were few so film jobs were particularly welcome. Alan Rawsthorne was also earning a living writing for films though he was in the 'feature' world and he went to The George more for conversation, though he did find a few writing for plays, for example for Louis MacNeice.[117]

As Ayrton has commented, just occasionally Constant composed in The George, sometimes for himself and sometimes in collaboration, as Rawsthorne remembered:

---

[114] Ayrton was to provide the decorations for an edition of Gray's play *Gilles de Rais* published in 1945 and it was possibly Gray's opera *The Temptation of St Anthony* that inspired Ayrton to take up the subject for his painting of 1942–3.

[115] Ayrton's passion for Berlioz developed, in his own words, into 'the project of a man singularly obsessed by a man singularly obsessed with that obsessed man'. He presented a programme on Berlioz for BBC2 in March 1969 (the centenary of Berlioz' death), gave an exhibition entitled *A Debt to Hector Berlioz* in November, and wrote *Berlioz, A Singular Obsession: A Personal Portrait of Hector Berlioz* (London: BBC Publications, 1969).

[116] The George was quite possibly disguised as the 'Mortimer' in the opening pages of Anthony Powell's *Casanova's Chinese Restaurant*, the pub in which Nicholas Jenkins (Powell) is said to have first met Hugh Moreland (Lambert). See Appendix 9.

[117] Isabel Rawsthorne, unpublished memoirs.

I think it was the first film for which I had to write any music. It was for the Post Office Film Unit ... so I walked into 'The Gluepot' I remember one day and said to Constant, 'You know, I'm rather perplexed because I have to write some music that sounds like a brown paper parcel (because the film was all about this) and he had a brown paper parcel and together we wrote a piece of music on the parcel. Unfortunately it had to go somewhere – so it was posted![118]

Elisabeth Lutyens, who once remarked that if a bomb had dropped on The George during the war it would have wiped out much of the musical profession, herself provided a vivid description of Constant there:

At lunch-time at The George one would see Constant, *The Times* under his arm, standing, one hand on the bar-rail, the other on his ivory-headed stick. Often he was obviously fighting out some mental Don Quixote battle with the philistines. With an expression of glowering concentration, his large, wide-spaced blue eyes focused on some imaginary enemy as he almost shook with righteous indignation. On those occasions I would take up my position at the further end of the bar, waiting until the inner argument ended – I hoped victoriously!

At other times, he would be shaking with inner laughter, to explode, when joined by friends, in lucid and uproarious descriptions of something ridiculous spotted in a newspaper, or his latest limerick or French poem. He was, in all, larger than life, and a life lived to the fullest and most all-embracing. Everything in his presence became more vital, more exciting and certainly more dramatic. The energy he expended on his mental fights, as the energy he put into his conducting, must have exhausted even his huge vitality.

As for his drinking, she added that his determination to walk upright with his permanent limp and the aid of a stick resulted in a somewhat rolling sailor-gait which was misinterpreted as intoxication.

All I can say is that in the twenty years or more that I knew Constant, I may have seen him tight, but never with his mind clouded or his wit blunted. Both Constant and Dylan [Thomas] – so very different from each other in every way – have suffered from over-emphasis in retrospect of stories of their drinking habit. ... Neither of them drank anything like the amount I have seen put back by some in homes and clubs, but both went without regular meals.[119]

Stick in hand, Constant had an almost Churchillian appearance and Lutyens remembered an occasion in the war when, being part of ENSA he came into The George wearing uniform, prompting his friends to greet him with 'Hello, Randolph' which annoyed him considerably.

According to Isabel, painters did not, as a rule, frequent The George so in this respect Ayrton was an exception. He found Constant

the most glamorous human being I've ever known (not in the Hollywood style) – it is something to do with heightening the pitch – he simply had a human quality which made him enormously exciting company, on any subject, serious, absurd, grotesque, comic – simply to be in his company was a most extraordinary and stimulating experience and I've never known anyone else who could match it.[120] ... I always felt he dominated *The George* when he came into it, whether

---

[118] *Constant Lambert Remembered*, BBC Third Network, 25 June 1966.
[119] Lutyens, *A Goldfish Bowl*, pp. 141–2.
[120] In an interview with John Amis, *Talking about Music*, recorded 18 September 1964.

he was talking or silent, and there were times when he was very silent. Even so I think his presence was felt by everyone in the place.[121]

Michael Ayrton soon became one of that close circle of friends with whom Constant kept up a cryptic correspondence when on tour, even confiding in him medical problems, as he did on 26 October from Edinburgh where the Sadler's Wells Company were performing for a fortnight directly after their London season: 'Remarkable and (even to me) unexpected attack on 1st night of Haydn ballet[122] following last week's attack after rehearsal of same. Any trouble your end?' These may have been early signs of undiagnosed diabetes from which Constant was increasingly to suffer. As Ayrton was to observe during the time they shared a house:

> After finishing the ballet at Sadler's Wells (without a drink – [he was] abstemious except for bottled cider) he often worked until 5 or 6 in the morning. He never drank in private. Promptly at 11.30 (opening time for the pubs in his area) he would be round at the pub; he would stand at the bar with eyes shut, trying to get used to the fact that another day had begun.[123]

Composition, it seemed, was done in the very early hours of the morning:

> He'd come home perhaps at about one o'clock in the morning and he would then sit down and play the larger arias of Puccini very loudly on the piano. It was fortunate he didn't live in a flat, really. And then he would stop, perhaps for an hour, and then he would play another piece of Puccini, perhaps from *The Girl of the Golden West*, and then it would stop again. And then I would go to sleep so I don't know what happened. But at the end of this the following morning there would be a couple of sheets of manuscript paper with something written on them which Constant would then hide so I gather that is how he composed.

Constant also suffered from insomnia, a condition on which the composer Denis ApIvor,[124] who at the time of their first meeting was studying medicine, was able to offer some advice. An admirer of Philip Heseltine and van Dieren (both of whom he never met), ApIvor followed in Walton's steps as a chorister at Christ's College, Oxford. It was after hearing *The Rio Grande* and being so affected by the work that he had wanted to meet Lambert and, if possible, to study with him. As he later recalled, 'In 1937 I begged Gray to introduce me to Constant Lambert and he arranged a dinner at the marvellous old Pagani's restaurant, behind Queen's Hall.'[125]

He had a vivid memory of their first meeting:

> As [Constant] came into the restaurant he indulged in a pantomime which was highly characteristic of him when he met one of his friends. Stopping at a distance he tapped his stick up and down with mock impatience while a large grin of pseudo-intolerance spread over his features as though to say, 'Well, damn it all, can't I come into this place without seeing Cecil sitting there like a gastronomical pontiff ready to stuff himself?'

[121] *Constant Lambert Remembered*, BBC Third Network, 25 June 1966.
[122] The ballet *Promenade* (with music by Haydn selected and arranged by Edwin Evans and orchestrated by Gordon Jacob) of which Lambert conducted the premiere – unusually outside London – at the King's Theatre, Edinburgh on 25 October 1943. The choreography was by de Valois.
[123] Michael Ayrton in *In Search of Constant Lambert*, BBC2, 26 July 1965.
[124] Denis ApIvor (1916–2004), a composer in his own right, in later life prepared performing editions of much of van Dieren's works, including the *Chinese Symphony*.
[125] Denis ApIvor, 'Composer's Anthology 7', *Recorded Sound*, nos. 66–7 (April–July 1977), p. 693.

On the way home [to Gray's home in Dorchester Gate] in the taxi, knowing that I was a medical student, he confided in me that he was suffering the tortures of insomnia and he made inquiry as to the merits of various sleeping potions. This was my first introduction to the battle which he must have waged all his life against an excessively nervous temperament and physical disabilities which would have daunted a lesser man. He told me too of the sufferings which he had endured as a child when he fell victim to what I believe was osteomyelitis of the bones of his leg. He had had to go through something like seven operations and his muscles were left permanently wasted. His leg pained him all his life and let him down sometimes, as on the occasion when, after conducting *The Curlew* at Maida Vale in the bitter winter of 1946–7, he came out of the 'Warrington' with Humphrey [Searle] and myself, and attempting to get into his car he fell prostrate in the snow.[126]

ApIvor saw two sharply contrasting sides to Constant' personality:

He was one of the most witty and gay and voluble people I have ever known and I do remember seeing him actually physically propelled by a joke which I had never seen anybody else in that way; that is to say he would come shall we say from the pub in Camden Town having savoured a joke, and you would see him on the way up to a pub in Regent's Park walking as it were sideways with his stick, truly bubbling and steaming like a sort of pot and at the same time sort of half speaking to himself and half laughing and going all the way up Park Way in this extraordinary state.

But there was another side to his personality like so many people of that sort of temperament – that at times he suffered from moods of the most intense depression and gloom.[127]

In a letter to Angus Morrison after Constant's death, ApIvor elaborated further on what he saw as his condition:

When one considers the matter dispassionately he was really ill equipped to have to contend with the appalling life of drudgery of the workaday ballet-conductor, and in that sense he was as much and more the victim of fate as any of us who have somehow to grub a living and find the time to compose. He was extraordinarily sensitive and nervous. If dipsomania is a psychoneurotic condition, a real illness as is believed in many quarters today, Constant was never fit to contend with life the way he had to. He used to say that he enjoyed drinking, and so to all appearances he did, – yet he always seemed to me of all people the one who really needed to drink to dull a sort of over awareness and over sensitivity. I am not a psychiatrist so I am on difficult ground here. He had fits of terrific depression and when not depressed his most frequent bane was 'boring' circumstances, or 'boring' people (an adjective you must yourself have heard him use many times). The volatile uproarious side of his character, of which I have never seen the like in any other human being, was probably at least fifty per cent of himself, but on the above analysis at least a part of it was due to the urgent necessity of avoiding the ever present abyss of ennui, leading to a vortex of depression. Towards the end of his life when he was conducting a concert of Contemporary Music at the BBC which included a work of mine I

---

[126] Letter (typed) from Denis ApIvor to Hubert Foss, 16 April [1952].
[127] *In Search of Constant Lambert*, BBC2, 26 July 1965.

went back before the show, and was appalled to find him in an absolute tremor of nervousness.[128]

ApIvor studied for six months with Patrick Hadley and then, at Gray's and Hadley's suggestion, went to Rawsthorne for two years until the outbreak of war. During that time he saw quite a lot of Constant:

Our steps frequently converged in the direction of Belsize Park where Alan Rawsthorne was living and where Constant himself stayed from time to time. Amusing incidents stick in my memory and could, I have no doubt, be added to by hundreds of people. I remember his gift of symphonic working up of a joke being well in evidence when, one bright summer night (my watch having stopped) I called round at the Rawsthorne's house and asked Constant to join me in a drink at the local some half hour after the last possible raucous shout of 'Time Please!' could have possibly rent the air. On another occasion I see him in my mind's eye giving a particularly unforgettable rendering of a song incorporating fantastic directions to the performer, by Percy Grainger, called I believe 'Mother of Mine'.[129]

During the war years ApIvor only met Constant once, 'at the house of Lord Berners in Wiltshire, where he and Margot Fonteyn were spending a short holiday',[130] but their friendship was resumed after the war. As well as being a composer and a doctor, ApIvor was also an expert on giving anaesthetics, and Constant delighted in telling friends that he knew a composer who put people to sleep during the day, unlike most composers who put them to sleep at night. ApIvor regarded Constant as 'probably the best conversationalist since Oscar Wilde'. When, after Constant's death (and through his recommendation) he was himself writing ballet scores, he came to appreciate the stress that Constant had been under:

It is a mystery to me that he ever got any composing done at all. The perpetual round of rehearsals and performances is enough in itself. But when one remembers that he was continually arranging and orchestrating music for them and putting on new works by other composers the strain must have been great.

N EAR the end of October 1943 Constant travelled from Edinburgh to Liverpool for a recording session with the Liverpool Philharmonic, and in November the Company had a week each in Glasgow, Leeds, Sheffield and Bristol. The first venue elicited a postcard greeting to Cecil Gray: 'Jist a braw Scots greeting frae the reeky lums o' Grey Glesgie', and to Ayrton: 'Extract from letter from my mother – "Kit has been indulging in black magic on Hallow E'en which he seems to have enjoyed." What a family.' Constant enjoyed receiving and sending newspaper cuttings that contained some amusing idiosyncrasy and, with reference to Ayrton's first stage work which had been designs for Gielgud's production of *Macbeth*[131] he wrote: 'I think you will agree with me that the witches scene in Macbeth is a pale piece of writing compared to the Fish Prices in the Glasgow Herald (ci-inclus). Please keep but do not destroy.'[132] The postcards he sent to Ayrton invariably contained some obscure artistic reference, such

---

[128] Letter (typed) from Denis ApIvor to Angus Morrison, 9 March 1954.
[129] The song *Dedication*, a setting by Percy Grainger of verses by Rudyard Kipling.
[130] ApIvor, 'Composer's Anthology', p. 693.
[131] *Macbeth* had opened in Manchester in January 1942, reaching London in July after a provincial tour. It used pre-recorded incidental music by Walton.
[132] Letter from Lambert to Michael Ayrton, from Central Hotel, Glasgow, 3 November 1943.

as one also from Glasgow: 'A good Scuola di Tadema I hope you agree. More [and worse] to follow,'[133] and from Leeds:

> This, I like to think, effectively disposes of our theory that the English landscape does not lend itself to plastic treatment. Do you know the work of F. H. Sikes? (You will soon). Thanks for pristine aeronauticalia. Yrs CL.[134]

When in Sheffield he was equally delighted to receive a cutting from Anthony Powell:

> Many thanks for the cutting by Judas Quennle [Peter Quennell]. What with Peter on the Cornhill,[135] Cyril [Connolly] on the Observer, Tom [Driberg] in Parliament and you in the War Office I feel like Verlaine in his declining years and have already embarked on personal reminiscences of Swinburne and Wilde. Do look me up at the theatre when we are back in London.[136]

From Leeds on 9 November he sent Cecil Gray a postcard with a photograph of deer on Exmoor to which he added: 'I thought an English note might be pleasantly struck for a change. Bien cordialement.' Then to Ayrton he dispatched a succession of cards, with some private joke about Cecil Gray:

> Hallowe'en C. Gray Esq (on Ilkla Moor baht aht [sic]) waiting for a rendezvous (manqué) with Miss Judy Cowell. [11 November]

> Unlike the rank imitations which you foist off on a credulous public this is a 'genuine' oil painting. (more and better Sikes and McIntyres to follow). Tartan crocodiles to you! [12 November]

> Hallowe'en C. Gray Esq disguises as a norn, waiting on Ilkla Moor baht aht for a rendezvous (manqué) with Mrs Maurice Ward. [13 November]

> 'Ill it is with my meal I fain must beg your bags to furnish me.' ('Gotterdammerung') [13 November]

And from Sheffield:

> The last of the McIntyres I'm afraid – no design at all in Sheffield not even good. Sorry about the vision of trellis work but it was not deliberate on my part. Next week Royal Hotel, Bristol. [16 November]

Illness struck the Company at the start of the new London season on Tuesday 30 November when they were without eight dancers and Constant.[137] Perhaps with good reason five days earlier he had written from Bristol to Ayrton: 'Perhaps it's just as well this tour is coming to an end. "Who's been at my Eno's?"' Such a large number of absentees obviously ruffled the Company as the *Dancing Times* critic commented on 'the worst piece of dancing the New Theatre has ever seen' with 'the general scramble for the exits after the big series of Sissones' and 'the poor ensemble in a most ragged performance of *Les Rendezvous*'. With Constant absent *A Wedding Bouquet* was replaced by *Façade* which the *Times* critic felt that 'excellent though it is, has become almost hackneyed'. Nevertheless Alec Sherman 'proved himself a capable deputy',

---

[133] Postcard from Lambert to Ayrton, from Glasgow, 5 November 1943.

[134] Postcard from Lambert to Ayrton, from Leeds, 9 November 1943. The mention of plastic refers to the manufacture of the postcard. Lambert sent a series of postcards with reproductions of paintings by such recondite artists as H. B. Wimbush, Sikes, McIntyre and Lasalle.

[135] *The Cornhill Magazine*, a literary journal of which Peter Quennell was at one time editor.

[136] Letter from Lambert to Anthony Powell, from Sheffield, 16 November 1943.

[137] See Appendix 13 for a list of that season's programmes.

and there was praise for one dancer in *The Rake's Progress*, Anne Lascelles, whose 'contribution as the dancer in the scene of the orgy requires commendation'.[138]

Anne Lascelles, whose real name was Sheila Fleming, was an attractive girl who had joined the Company in January 1942 and had not escaped Constant's attention. According to her friend, Celia Franca, 'She had a physique very much like Margot's … Constant had his eyes on her. She would be sitting on the stage as a fairy in the *Nutcracker*, and he would be conducting and looking at her the whole time. It was a little embarrassing but it was not a long-lived affair. Margot called me into her bedroom one day to speak about it – we were on tour somewhere and she would rest in the afternoons, so I went to her hotel. We chatted about it briefly – she was very cool and dignified.'[139]

Constant's absence was only a short one and *A Wedding Bouquet* was back in the repertoire on Friday 3 December. Nine days later he was conducting a 'Music of our Time' broadcast in the Home Service that consisted of Roussel's *Pour une fête de printemps* (Roussel's ballet *Le Festin de l'araignée* was soon to enter the Sadler's Wells repertoire), Walton's Viola Concerto with Frederick Riddle, and Kodály's *Dances of Galanta*, and just after Christmas he gave a talk on Puccini in the BBC Forces Programme.

---

[138] *The Times*, 1 December 1943.
[139] Daneman, *Margot Fonteyn*, p. 176.

17 1944–5
Small Fish and Large Cats

B Y 1944 Constant's relationship with Margot had entered a difficult stage, and he welcomed the male support that his new friendship with Ayrton brought him. At the same time Margot found a sympathetic ear in Michael's close friend Joan Walsh with whom he was living, Joan and Margot soon becoming, as Constant referred to them, 'the old girls'. He wrote to Michael from 42 Peel Street, his mother's house, where he was then living, commenting first, as was his habit, on something in a newspaper article that had amused him:

> What mouvementée lives lorry drivers seem to lead. On top of the man who stole (and in my opinion very reasonably) budgerigar seed in order to grow deadly nightshade, there is the lorry driver in to-night's Standard (actual cutting lost, alas,) who after being married for three weeks, got into his lorry and drove it at his wife. He was only given 4 months which must have been a disappointment. Did you notice, by the way, that the march in Barnby's 'Rebekah' is called 'The Brides March'? Not Bridal March or Wedding March as you might hastily be led to suppose. It shows more insight into 'feminine psychology' than I had previously credited the old boy with. I gather the old girls have got into a cabal (Kabal or gabal). Joan rang up Margot at tea-time. I gave intimations of FISH through the glass of the stage door and took down the conversation in shorthand on my shirt-cuff.
>
> In spite of all the turmoil and strife we hope to make that Feb. weekend if physically possible. It all depends, alas, on ENSA.
>
> If I don't see you before[,] we will meet at the Gluepot on Friday.
>
> Yours CL
>
> PS Many thanks for the drawing of Kit which we both much appreciate.
>
> PPS I never thought that I should fall in love with the daughter of an MP![1]

Two days later he had an afternoon broadcast from the Guildhall, Cambridge with the BBC Symphony Orchestra that included Rawsthorne's *Symphonic Studies*, first performed in 1939 at an ISCM concert in Warsaw.[2] Planning this concert back in November, he had written to Julian Herbage:

> I should like also to do something contemporary. The Rawsthorne Symphonic Studies I do not alas know, but have heard them very well spoken of. What do you feel about them? Also we might consider one of those Bax works we talked about ...[3]

Rawsthorne became affectionately known as 'Fish Face', and on a postcard he sent to Ayrton from Cambridge on 23 February he wrote: 'Have just found again that splendid *Country Life* article "Fish with an Ear for Music". Am showing it to a composer (who shall be nameless) stationed near here.' He also sketched a bat, adding:

---

[1] 13 January 1944. The MP's daughter, quite likely one of the dancers, has not been identified.

[2] In 1946, under the auspices of the British Council, Lambert made the first gramophone recordings of Rawsthorne's *Symphonic Variations* and the overture *Street Corner*.

[3] Letter 23 November 1943 from Lambert to Herbage: BBC Written Archives. The concert included no Bax but, in addition to the Rawsthorne, there was Rimsky-Korsakov, Overture *Ivan the Terrible* [*The Maid of Pskov*]; Haydn, Symphony No. 73; Delius, *Brigg Fair* and Borodin, Symphony No. 2.

'Can't remember the anatomy.' Constant's and Michael's drawing skills were soon to be put to the test.

The Sadler's Wells Company were in London at the New Theatre until 5 February, with a revival on 1 February of *Le Spectre de la rose* with Fonteyn and Alexis Rassine.[4] According to Clarke, the production had 'considerable help from Tamara Karsavina who created the ballet with Nijinsky for Diaghileff in 1911'.[5] Rex Whistler provided the décor and costumes but they were not to everyone's taste, especially the drop curtain with its nude male figure curled up asleep at the very heart of an enormous cabbage rose.[6] Constant chose Glinka's *Valse-Fantasie* as a prelude, quite likely prompted by the memory of Karsavina's Camargo Society performance of that work with Ashton in 1931.[7]

After London there were two ENSA weeks in garrison theatres in Eastbourne and Aldershot. For much of January Constant had been concentrating on the incidental music he was writing for *Hamlet* in which Helpmann, having taken the key role in the ballet of the same name, was now extending his career by acting the most famous of all stage roles.[8] On a piece of lavatory paper Constant expressed his disgust at what he was being paid: 'Offered £25. Asked for £100, with absolute minimum £75. Since offered £50 – still refusing. £75 – The sum refused me for the music of Hamlet. F*** their far from almighty souls.' He completed the fairly minimal score at the end of the month, and the play opened on 11 February at the New Theatre. Six days later at Bedford, for the BBC's 'Special Music Recording Service', he recorded his own *Merchant Seamen* Suite and Walter Leigh's overture *Agincourt*.

That month, finding that living with his mother restricted his freedom too much for his liking, he decided to move in with Michael Ayrton and Joan at 4 All Souls' Place, just off Great Portland Street and only a short walk from The George. He was to stay there for about three years. Touring took him first to Cambridge for a week and then to Derby, but in between, from London, he sent Michael a formal agreement that was laced with his own humorous touches:

> Formal agreement enclosed as requested. I also agree to the comparatively reasonable clauses in the codicil which, however, has certain lacunae you may have cause to regret when you are woken up by the sound of 'The Entry of the Gladiators' or 'Boy Scouts of Wisconsin, Forward Forever!' on the Marimbaphone (not to mention the dozen Singing Mice I purchased yesterday).[9]
>
> I am here (en route to Derby) to do a bit of eleventh-hour recording with the man Legge. My address next week will be the Midland Hotel, Derby, but the New Theatre is always a safe business address.
>
> Do get this week's 'Picture Post'. It has some photographs of that RCM rehearsal including 3 of VW which make Breughel look like Olive Snell[10] and one of myself, cutting my throat while conducting Humphrey Searle.

---

[4] Alexis Rassine joined the Company in March 1942.

[5] Clarke, *The Sadler's Wells Ballet*, p. 182.

[6] This was Rex Whistler's last work for the ballet. He was killed in action on 18 July 1944.

[7] Vaughan, *Frederick Ashton and his Ballets*, p. 58n.

[8] Robert Helpmann was also to have a career in films, amongst them Michael Powell's *One of our Aircraft is Missing* (1942), *The Red Shoes* (1948) and *The Tales of Hoffman* (1951), and Laurence Olivier's *Henry V* (1944), as well as *55 Days at Peking* (1963), *The Quiller Memorandum* (1966) and *Chitty Chitty Bang Bang* (1968).

[9] *The Entry of the Gladiators* is a march by the Czech composer Julius Fučík popularly associated with circuses, while *Wisconsin Forward Forever* is a march by John Philip Sousa.

[10] A portrait painter (late 19th – early 20th century).

I envy you your fires[11] – I am in an absolute fury at missing them. I was sorry to hear the RCM missed it but was consoled by the fact that all the windows have been blasted so that the professors have to teach in overcoats and catch influenza. The Fish with an Ear for Music gave me a slight jolt the other morning, first of all being introduced by one of the monoglot cretins at the University Arms as 'Mr Grossvoor' and then entering my bedroom in battle dress and a hangover carrying under his arm a framed Medici print which he presented to me with the conversational gambit 'Is this a Tintoretto?'

Without being a Borenius[12] I was able to assure him that it antedated Tintoretto by about 150 years being one of those typical Italian things with a parched landscape in the background, a rather ineffective miracle in the middle distance, the foreground occupied by a lot of pansies having a cocktail party, playing nap and getting off with the waiter etc. Apparently K. Clark or CEMA[13] or whoever is responsible send the paintings down with a list of the titles but fail to attach one to the other[,] so a good time is had by all with highbrow A[uxiliary]T[erritorial]S[ervice] labelling Reubens as Paul Nash and vice versa.

I am glad to hear that the costumes for Miss JC's Banquet[14] are finished – you must show them to me the next time we play Billiards Russe.[15] As regards the drop curtain I propose not shooting until I see the off-whites of their eyes. Please put your trust in a hardened old campaigner. The orchestration of the missing insects is being entrusted to Gordon Jacob who will do it well and carefully. I frankly can't manage it myself.

I am looking forward to a Roman Orgy at Etruria.

Constant concluded the letter with reference to Margot and Joan:

War on Two Fronts. This has now reached the stage of the second round of that famous welter-weight contest at Elsinore, viz. rapiers <u>and</u> daggers. To make things worse the two old girls in question are quite obviously going to GET TOGETHER with, I presume, pretty dire results for me. There are times when I seriously think of going back to my negress in the Fire Service.

Yours ever
Constant

PS The semi-bombed-out cloakroom at St Pancras has, pasted over it, the statement 'No one is more profoundly sad than he who laughs too much'. Without for one moment doubting the apothegm I can't really think the attendant has been burdened with undue hilarity on the part of his clients – he certainly wasn't this morning. CL[16]

The mention of *Picture Post* referred to an orchestral rehearsal sponsored by the

[11] London and parts of South-East England suffered several successive nights of being bombed by high explosives and incendiaries.

[12] Professor of History of Art at University College London.

[13] Council for the Encouragement of Music and the Arts, set up to provide war-time entertainment for the troops and civilians, often performed in military camps, and later to become the Arts Council.

[14] The ballet *Le Festin de l'araignée* (*The Spider's Banquet*) with music by Albert Roussel.

[15] Lambert cited Russian billiards as his favourite pastime in *Who's Who* and in the *Music Ho!* blurb which says that 'his hobbies are few and mainly confined to playing Russian billiards and composing limericks'.

[16] 27 February 1944. 'London (unexpectedly)'. The letter was signed with a drawing of a bat, labelled CL, and a cat, curling its tail around the letters MA, while gazing askance at a small singing mouse.

recently formed Committee for the Promotion of New Music at the Royal College of Music on 4 February.[17] Constant conducted the London Symphony Orchestra in the first performance of Humphrey Searle's *Night Music* and Norman Del Mar's Flute Concerto, while Francis Chagrin was in charge of his own piano concerto. A discussion of the works followed, and Vaughan Williams and Edwin Evans were among those present. As Searle observed, '[Lambert] didn't really like atonal or twelve-note music, with a few exceptions such as Schönberg's *Pierrot Lunaire*, Orchestral Variations and Berg's *Wozzeck*, but he was always prepared to give new music of all kinds sympathetic consideration.' Constant annoyed the College authorities by insisting on smoking throughout the rehearsals.

On Thursday 2 March, from Derby, he sent Ayrton a postcard: 'Will be up in London Wednesday. Travelling to Hanley on Thursday. We might go up with a bottle or two and blow raspberries at the O[ld] G[irl] [i.e. Margot] in Giselle. You can behave like Fortinbras and say "Bear up the bodies". There'll be plenty about.'[18]

On the Tuesday Constant had a late evening broadcast, introduced by Lydia Lopokova, in which he conducted the BBC Theatre Orchestra in music from the Sadler's Wells repertoire (*Horoscope*, *Les Patineurs*, *Harlequin in the Street* and *Apparitions*). Then two days later, as arranged, he travelled with Ayrton to Hanley where the Company were based that week. It was a journey never to be forgotten, thanks to the vivid account that Ayrton has left of the artistic challenge they set each other in extraordinary circumstances:

> At that time I was myself working on the designs for the ballet *Le Festin de l'araignée* for the company [with music by Albert Roussel], and had been asked, for reasons connected with the production, to travel up to discuss matters. Constant was going to rejoin the company as one of the two pianists who, during those bleak years, substituted for an orchestra. We decided to travel together and after a start which was delayed by Constant having inadvertently set alight to an armchair in his studio, and a late lunch at Pagani's Restaurant in Great Portland Street, we arrived at the railway terminus exactly one hour and twenty-two minutes before the train was due to leave. Constant insisted on being in time for trains. We seated ourselves in an empty carriage and became deeply involved in a discussion of the relative merits of cats and fish and their representation in Oriental art. To my surprise, Constant pleaded the cause of fish as ideal pictorial material, the reason, it became gradually apparent, being that he had spent many profitable hours while on tour with the ballet, in learning how to draw fish. Jealously, I proposed that my mastery of cat draughtsmanship was bound to exceed his amateur efforts even had he the advantage of that relatively easy vehicle for virtuosity, the stylised fish.
>
> As the train began to move, Constant produced paper and pencil and executed in outline a small but lively carp. Between us, alternating, we drew cats and fish for some time until the available paper was exhausted. The argument was not exhausted. As dusk fell, Constant inscribed in pencil above the carriage door a small goldfish seen head on. Gradually fish of many varieties and cats posed in numerous ways, came to decorate the available wall space. Night came on and we worked like the Cro-Magnon man in total darkness. Occasionally, by

---

[17] *Picture Post*, 26 February 1944, included an article by Martin Chisholm, 'A Chance for New Music to be Heard', pp. 14–16, with several photographs, including one of Lambert conducting the Searle work in short sleeves and, characteristically, with a cigarette in his mouth.

[18] 2 March 1944.

the light of matches, we inspected our work. Small cats appeared riding large fish. Small fish were revealed inside large cats. Fish bit cats. Cats sat on fish.

In due time, only the ceiling remained virgin and it was not without difficulty, for we were both heavily built, that we climbed each into a separate luggage rack to continue, like twin Michelangelos, to design upon the vault. At some time during this period of creative frenzy, the train drew up at a station, and an elderly lady entered our carriage. Seeing no seat occupied, she relaxed comfortably and took out her knitting. Poor lady, she had assumed that the carriage was empty. She was wrong. The luggage racks were filled with reclining draughtsmen, but it was not until Constant observed to me that the ceiling was becoming overcrowded that she became aware of this. She left hurriedly and one can only be thankful that the train was still standing in the station.[19]

Ayrton went on to relate one of those extraordinary happenings that Constant's close friends associated with him. He was back in time to accompany the ballet before they moved on to Bolton. But 'for some unexplained reason' he and Ayrton stayed on in The Potteries.

Constant and I began by being forbidden to play billiards in his hotel. The late morning was spent in a visit to the Great Tip, where a million broken cups and saucers make for rats a porcelain Chicago. Lunch must be passed over in silence. In later years the subject of Sunday lunch in Hanley was tacitly passed over by us both. But the grey and glacial public gardens of Stoke and the walk by the canal will always remain with me as one of the most macabre excursions ever shared by a painter and a musician. ... But we were only beginning our voyage *au bout de la nuit*. Only when towards evening we left the park and it occurred to us to seek the long-suffering friends who had given me hospitality did this macabre episode mount towards its climax.

Finding Ayrton's friends to be out, they were ushered by a maidservant into a darkening room. Lying on the piano were two scores: *Summer's Last Will and Testament* and Mussorgsky's *Sunless* song-cycle, and above the piano hung a large portrait of Christopher Wood.

The book which Constant was carrying at the time was the *Fêtes Galantes* of Paul Verlaine, and as he put it down it opened at the poem *Colloque Sentimental* which contains the unforgettable lines:

> Dans le vieux parc solitaire et glacé
> Deux spectres ont évoqué le passé.[20]

At the end of the month Constant conducted a broadcast of *Summer's Last Will and Testament* which was also recorded for the transcription services.[21] Hubert Foss introduced the work. Then on 5 April 1944, as a result of Constant's and William Walton's efforts of persuasion, the BBC gave a very rare broadcast from Bedford, with

---

[19] Ayrton, *Golden Sections*, pp. 128–9. Two broadcast accounts by Ayrton of this journey also exist: in *Constant Lambert Remembered*, presented by Ayrton, BBC Third Network, 25 June 1966, and *English Musical Eccentrics*, BBC Radio 3, 18 January 1976 (recorded November 1974), rebroadcast 17 November 1980.

[20] Ayrton, *Golden Sections*, p. 130.

[21] 29 March 1944, Home Service, 8 p.m. George Pizzey, BBC Chorus, BBC Symphony Orchestra. Ralph Hill wrote a brief article, 'Lambert's Masque', for *Radio Times*, 24 March 1944, p. 4. A copy of this recording has not been traced. According to a vocal score in the BBC Music Library, Lambert's timings for each movement were 1: 6′ 30″; 2: 6′ 10″; 3: 3′ 15″, 4: 8′ 25″, 5: 9′ 25″, 6: 9′ 25″; 7: 11′ 30″.

Constant conducting, of a work by Cecil Gray. It was part of his opera *The Women of Troy* that he had composed after completing his earlier music-drama *The Temptation of St Anthony* in 1937.[22] Joan Hammond, who sang in the broadcast, described Gray as 'a shy, sensitive man who shrank from asserting himself and his wishes' and remembered that 'the work, unfortunately, had to suffer large cuts as the time allotted for its performance proved to be too short. Daily one could see him shrinking further into himself as the premiere drew near and the opera was still running over time.'[23] In an effusive review of the broadcast, Sorabji claimed it to be 'without any doubt <u>the</u> outstanding work in operatic form produced in this country during the last forty or so years',[24] a view he repeated to Foss in 1951 after Gray's death.

In his autobiography, *Musical Chairs*, Gray described a French holiday he had taken in Touraine with Constant in the summer of 1938, and how, on a visit to Azay-le-Rideau, 'after an admirable lunch, embellished by many bottles of some of the noblest wines in the world' and with his companion stretched out on the grass in the grounds of the spectacular château, the scenery on that beautiful day had given him the inspiration for one of the choruses that had been eluding him in the opera.[25]

After spending March in Derby, Hanley and Bolton, the Company were back in London, at the Wimbledon Theatre, for part of April before going north again to Newcastle from where, on 3 May, Constant wrote to Ayrton:

> It is worth making the trek to Newcastle for various reasons (a) the dropcloth in the theatre which knocks the slats off Jean Lasalle and the boys (b) a show of John Martin which knocks the slats off Blake, Palmer and all <u>those</u> boys.[26] When you have finished hitting Joan on the head with a billiard cue because I'm too far away to reach, allow me to explain that I am referring <u>not</u> to bad copies of his less happy paintings made by inferior hacks but to the old sod's small original engravings the best of which are knock-outs. I have also got a theory about them which is going to knock the slats off K. Clark, Tancred Borenius and I need hardly say <u>the boys</u>.
>
> Also (c) an obscure bar, genuine barrel and sawdust genre, no girls admitted, where you can get jolly good sherry and superb Madeira in large tumblers for small sums: not to mention (d) a shop which sells Peacocks [a brand of cigarette] by the 100 at pre last budget prices.
>
> So life hasn't been too bad. You would have enjoyed hearing me (with a hangover and a debonair smile) compering Rake's Progress to the troops last

[22] In *Musical Chairs* (p. 313) Cecil Gray recalls an occasion when Leslie Heward and Constant Lambert played through *The Temptation of Saint Anthony* at the piano while Hyam Greenbaum followed with the full score. Hopkins, *Michael Ayrton*, p. 83, records another 'memorable evening' when Richard Gorer, Lambert and Ayrton rendered both *St Anthony* and *Women of Troy* 'to the best effect that a single piano and voices of assorted pitch and quality could contrive'.

[23] Joan Hammond, *A Voice, A Life* (London: Gollancz, 1970), p. 138. The performers were Noël Eadie, Joan Hammond, Gladys Ripley, Parry Jones, Stanley Riley, BBC Women's Chorus and the BBC Symphony Orchestra. The broadcast lasted one hour: the Prologue was condensed in the form of a narration and the first two scenes were omitted. In Pauline Gray, *Cecil Gray*, p. 86, there is a photograph of Constant Lambert, Cecil Gray, Arnold Bax and Parry Jones in Bedford for the broadcast.

[24] *The New English Weekly*, quoted in Pauline Gray, 'The Lesser Known Talents of Cecil Gray', *British Music Society Journal*, vol. 8 (1986), p. 4.

[25] Gray, *Musical Chairs*, pp. 316–17.

[26] John Martin (1789–1854), a popular Victorian artist whose bold canvases on biblical or heroic subjects were often on a large scale.

Sunday. I was cramped by having the Colonel's wife in the front row (Sorry that sentence didn't work out as intended).

Ninette is away examining so am keeping her letter till Monday. Re drop-cloth for Festin I will go and see Donald myself next week. It is much more likely to succeed than either writing to him or seeing Ninette.[27]

May was spent with more touring, first at Hammersmith and then Bournemouth, after which there was a dash to Bedford for a Sunday evening General Forces broadcast[28] before returning to the New Theatre at the end of the month for a long season that lasted until 5 August, with Alec Sherman still Constant's assistant conductor.[29] They opened with *Swan Lake*, with Beryl Grey establishing herself as 'prima ballerina in her own right' in place of Fonteyn, who had hurt her foot. 'Mr Constant Lambert, in charge of the orchestra, saw to it that the ear was satisfied,' was the verdict of *The Times*[30] which was also complimentary about *Le Festin de l'araignée* when it was first seen on 20 June with Constant conducting: 'Miss Andrée Howard's new ballet ... The union of the three arts of dance, design by Mr Michael Ayrton, and music is unusually complete ... Fascinating.' The ballet, lasting about half an hour, had been first staged in 1913 in Paris and it was characteristic of Constant's musical tastes that he should choose Roussel whom, in a radio talk in April 1946, he defended from being 'a minor follower of Debussy'. Taking the opening of *Le Festin de l'araignée* as an example, he went on:

> The sultry atmosphere of this Southern afternoon is as impressionistic as anything in Debussy, but the difference is that Roussel achieves his effect by his line more than his colour. For Roussel, like all typically French artists, was essentially a classicist. ... His music, though never 'juicy' enough perhaps to be popular with the man in the street, always has a firm lucidity that commands our admiration. He was a prose writer rather than a poet, but what a prose writer![31]

With the approach of the 50th anniversary of the Proms in 1944, a number of composers had been invited to write a work for the occasion, and a loosely titled 'symphonic poem' by Constant was advertised for Saturday 8 July. Henry Wood (whose last – brief – season of Proms it was to be; he died on 19 August) had asked him to conduct. He had promised to produce 'an overture of about the same length as [*Prince*] *Igor* or *Ivan the Terrible*, as I feel the English repertoire is very short of such pieces'.[32] For the subject of the piece he returned to the idea he had had when, together with Walton and Hely-Hutchinson, he was approached by the BBC in 1929 for a work especially suitable for broadcasting conditions as they then were. On 14 February Julian Herbage wrote to him:

> I have told Sir Henry that you will be writing a 15-minute Symphonic Poem on the subject of the Black Emperor – by the way, what was his name? Could you let me know how the work is progressing and by what date you think the score could be handed over to the copyists?

[27] From Royal Turk's Head Hotel, Newcastle upon Tyne.

[28] Leigh, *Agincourt*; Delibes, *La Source*, ballet suite no. 1; Delius, *Irmelin* Prelude and *La Calinda*; Dargomizhsky, *Kazachok*; and Auber, *Crown Diamonds* for which he was paid £27 15 1.

[29] 84 programmes, 207 performances, 18 ballets, the most frequent being *Les Patineurs* (21) and *Le Festin de l'araignée* and *Promenade* (19 each).

[30] *The Times*, 31 May 1944.

[31] Lambert, 'Albert Roussel', BBC *Music Magazine*, 7 April 1946.

[32] Arthur Jacobs, *Henry J. Wood, Maker of the Proms* (London: Methuen, 1994), p. 382.

While on tour with Sadler's Wells, he replied on 25 April from the Royal Turks Hotel, Newcastle-upon-Tyne:

> I am very worried about getting ready 'Henry Christophe' in time for July 8th. The trouble is that I intended to write a shortish overture – a sort of pièce d'occasion & I now find myself involved in a symphonic poem of quite formidable dimensions. Moreover it is complicated in style. Although superficially more like Horoscope or the Piano Concerto it is technically more like SLW&T, that is to say it is written in that musical prose style without formal patterns which take so much longer than musical poetic style, if you follow me.
>
> My pf. concerto took me 2 years & SLW 4 years[,] both written when I was far freer than I am now. These two heavy shows during my 'holiday' didn't help matters & no sooner have I got the Trojan girls [Cecil Gray's *Women of Troy*] out of my head than I find myself on tour with no proper place to work. I will certainly do my very best to get the thing finished in time. I have finished the introduction (about 5 mins.) & started the allegro & have innumerable small sketches but I have not got these really clarified yet. Even in normal times I should allow myself another 6 months or so on the sketches & 2 months on the score. I may get a sudden spurt which will enable me to finish it but you can see my reluctance to give final details or guarantee delivery. May I make the following suggestion – admittedly & reluctantly a compromise: that you put in the prospectus 'New Work' and <u>should</u> I fail to deliver the infernal <u>magnum opus</u> in time, that you substitute the full version of Merchant Seamen. This[,] it is true[,] has been performed outside London but it has never been broadcast & the full version would be entirely new to the London public (a truncated version was done at an ENSA pageant but the full version has only been recorded by the BBC for Latin America & still waits its 1st London performance). I only suggest this as a compromise & will continue of course my West Indian slavery ...
>
> '... To those who report I was a long time in finishing this tragedy, I confess, I do not write with a goose-quill winged with two feathers': – (no doubt you will be able to finish the quotation.) But I would rather be classed with Webster & Balakireff than with some I could mention. ... In the meantime wish me luck with my 20-minute development section![33]

The Times, announcing on 23 May the coming season of Promenade Concerts at the Royal Albert Hall, thought that 'a new work of unspecified nature by Constant Lambert will arouse interested curiosity'. But any curiosity that may have been aroused was not to be satisfied as *Henry Christophe* was never completed, and in the absence of a new work it was decided that, as he suggested, Constant would conduct the complete *Merchant Seamen* suite. However, the Proms had to face a far more serious problem: the menace of the V1 flying bombs, which put an end to that season from 30 June. In those days it was quite common for only part of the Prom concert to be relayed, and just those works that were to have been broadcast were played by the BBC Orchestra from its Bedford base, the *Merchant Seamen* suite not being among them.

Another work by Constant not to materialise was a small piece that had been requested by Felix Aprahamian, who wrote to Constant on 26 June: 'The French Committee of National Liberty have asked us to assist them by compiling an album of piano pieces by English composers as a Hommage à la France.' Constant replied on 8 July:

---

[33] In his address 'To the Reader' in *The White Devil* (1631; originally published in 1612), John Webster admitted that he had written the play slowly: 'I confesse I doe not write with a goose-quill, winged with two feathers'.

I shall be both delighted and honoured to write a piece for the 'Hommage à la France' album, this being arranged by the French Committee of National Liberation. I have not started on a piece yet but hope to do so next week. Perhaps you could let me know the final date for sending in the manuscript? As regards terms, etc., it will obviously be easier to discuss them with you personally.[34]

Ultimately the volume did not appear, as not all the composers who were approached, Constant among them, produced a piece. As late as October 1945, when he had other pressures of work, he was apologising:

I am sorry that I have led you up the garden about my piano piece, but it seems to be developing, alas, into a symphonic poem. As you know I have been very busy at the Proms, and am now engaged in a whirl of work for the British Council and ENSA. I would rather complete this piece to my own satisfaction than to turn out something hasty, and if by any possible means I can develop and polish the thing during the next week before I go abroad I will certainly do so and let you have it.[35]

Constant's 'whirl of work' was largely responsible for another failing – to attend the quarterly meetings of the Committee for the Encouragement of Music and the Arts. CEMA, formally appointed by the President of the Board of Education, had been established in December 1939 to help conserve Britain's cultural heritage. In 1942, under the chairmanship of John Maynard Keynes, it decided to set up two panels: one for Music and one for Art and Drama. In November certain musicians, including Arthur Bliss, Myra Hess, Thomas Wood and Constant Lambert, were sounded out as possible members of the music panel. In December the infuriated CEMA secretary, Mary Glasgow, wrote to Keynes: 'Has Constant Lambert ever answered properly? It is very rude of him not to, but I think the President might send him the formal invitation now and I will ask him to do so.'[36] However, ten days later R. A. Butler, President of the Board of Education, wrote to Constant: 'I want to say how glad I am to know that you are prepared to serve on the CEMA Music Panel. Your help as adviser will be considerable.'[37]

But Constant was not to be a regular attendant at these meetings, if he was present at any of them, and by August 1943 Keynes wrote: 'Yes, I think the time has come to drop Constant Lambert and Emlyn [Williams].'[38] Accordingly, on 1 September Butler wrote to Constant who replied seven days later with beguiling honesty:

I was not surprised to receive your letter & realise that all concerned must feel that I have let down my appointment to CEMA pretty badly. But, as you so kindly appreciate, the difficulties have been great and purely circumstantial.

Whenever a CEMA meeting has been called I have been either on tour or have had to conduct at the ballet owing to the lack of a deputy. Now, however, I hear that we are not going to do so much touring & I have got a good assistant conductor, Mr Alec Sherman, who has started very well & will, in a month or two's time, be able to take a lot of work off my shoulders. So I hope that I will then be able to give proper attention to my CEMA job.

---

[34] His letter was sent from 42 Peel Street.

[35] Letter from Lambert to Felix Aprahamian, 9 October 1945.

[36] 5 December 1942; Arts Council of Great Britain records, Victoria and Albert Museum Archives, EL 2/37.

[37] 15 December 1942; *ibid.*, EL 2/37.

[38] 11 August 1943; *ibid.*, EL 2/37. Emlyn Williams had served, if intermittently, on the Art and Drama Panel.

If I am not preventing anyone else being appointed to the panel I should be glad therefore if you could keep my name on <u>pro tem</u> as I look forward to being able to collaborate as I should.[39]

But this extension did nothing to improve Constant's record of attendance, and in February 1945 Butler was writing again, to say that he would have to be replaced by 'someone who will be able to take an active part in the affairs of the Panel'. Constant's reply was diplomacy itself:

Dear Mr Butler,

Please excuse my very late reply to your letter but my correspondence has been following me about all over Europe & now on my return I am in the throes of 'moving in'. As regards CEMA I entirely see your point & realise that I have done nothing to justify my position on the panel. I can assure you that at the beginning I fully intended to pull my weight, but as you know too well, as my work for the ballet I have had a lot of ENSA work involving perpetual travelling in the provinces & two long tours abroad. As a result it has been physically impossible for me to attend any of the meetings. It is clearly much better that my place should be taken by someone else. May I say how sorry I am that I have been of so little help to CEMA.[40]

During their 1944 summer season, from the end of June until the first week of August, the Sadler's Wells Company showed that they were not too easily put off by flying bombs. Their evening performances started at 6.45 p.m. but they were frequently interrupted by air-raid warnings. The dancers and audience displayed an admirable sangfroid during one performance of *The Gods Go a'Begging* when a V1 exploded a few hundred yards from the theatre and blew open the doors at the back of the Dress Circle. The dancers continued and the audience remained quietly in their seats.[41]

A three-week holiday was followed by three weeks at Manchester[42] and a week in Birmingham before returning to London, this time to the Princes Theatre in Shaftesbury Avenue.[43] The new ballet this season, premiered on 26 October, was *Miracle in the Gorbals* with music by Arthur Bliss, who had written in July: 'I have been asked to write a new ballet for Sadlers Wells, and have been given the subject Miracle in the Gorbals (the worst slum in Glasgow) ...'[44] By the first of August the score was about half-finished and Bliss sent 'a rather bare and crude scenario'. With designs by Edward Burra and scenario by Michael Benthall, a close friend of Robert Helpmann who provided the choreography, this was a stark uncompromising modern parable, or morality play, about a young girl who commits suicide by drowning and is brought back to life by a mysterious Christ-like figure who is himself ultimately done

---

[39] 8 September 1943; *ibid.*, EL 2/37.

[40] 4 All Souls' Place, 8 April 1945; *ibid.*, EL 2/3. At that time the Music Panel was drastically revised and among the large number who accepted a place were Ninette de Valois, Ferruccio Bonavia, Joan Cross, Herbert Howells, Michael Tippett, David Webster, Frank Howes, Benjamin Britten, Ernest Bullock, Victor Hely-Hutchinson and Percy Heming. Former members Myra Hess, Mary Ibberson and Reginald Jacques continued to serve.

[41] Clarke, *The Sadler's Wells Ballet*, p. 183.

[42] While in the Mersey region, on 30 August he recorded a General Forces Carnival Concert with the Liverpool Philharmonic Orchestra for broadcast on 24 September: Chabrier, Delius, Borodin, J. Strauss, Grainger and Dvořák.

[43] In 1963 the Princes Theatre was renamed the Shaftesbury Theatre.

[44] Letters from Bliss to William Bridges Adams, 20 July 1944, in Craggs, *Arthur Bliss: A Source Book*, p. 263.

to death by a gang of hooligans. Pauline Clayden played the suicide, Celia Franca the prostitute and Helpmann the stranger. Bliss provided another bold, dramatic score and he was delighted with the outcome, writing: 'The ballet has settled into a really great success. I went about the 5th performance to the back of the dress circle to watch, and the company has really got together, moving like a complex machine', although he did think 'the killing at the end is too long & brutal'.[45] *Miracle in the Gorbals* proved to be very popular among the dancers and received 20 performances before the end of the year.

There was a welcome return on 28 November when Frederick Ashton, on a week's leave from the RAF, resumed his original role as the Spectator in a revival of *Nocturne*, absent from the repertory for four years. Constant was not in the pit as he was conducting ENSA concerts in Italy.[46] As the *Times* reported, 'In the absence of Mr Constant Lambert ... the orchestra was in the charge of Mr Alec Sherman, who could not produce from an orchestra too small for Delius's score all its mystery, for which more strings would have been required, but he realized the shape of the work for the dancers. ... Miss Margot Fonteyn made the little flower girl movingly pathetic.'[47]

Constant flew to Italy, having had to wait three days at RAF Lyneham in Wiltshire for the air transport. His companion was the poet John Pudney[48] and the journey was not without incident. As Constant was leaving the plane at Naples, a sudden gust of wind caught most of the music he was carrying which ended up in the mud. Then the car driving him to Rome was involved in an accident from which he narrowly escaped injury. In his own inimitable style he provided his friends with a colourful account of the tour, writing to Ayrton:

> I had idly thought that a journey of some 100s of miles by 'plane would have transported me to a grove of oranges, lemons, buxom peasant girls and chianti rather in the style of the paintings near King or is it Duke St. Far from it. I am sitting in the freezing cold at an ebony wash-stand lit only by a dim ship's lantern, pestered by a charming but highly Baudelairian cat and surrounded by more books on Black Magic than I have ever seen before.
>
> My host, John Rayner is in hospital at the moment following a mild car accident between Naples and Rome. I myself am just recovered from a remarkable escape from death. (Details later: Miss JC would be a woolly English amateur here).
>
> The electric light (1 hr per day) has just been put on by the weeping Transylvanian maid so I hope my writing improves.
>
> Tomorrow I am going to see a surrealist red-head who it appears is a teetotal nymphomaniac surrounded by cats and engaged in doing drawings for private editions of the old Marquis de S. It all goes to show.
>
> Rome is even stranger than Wiltshire (where I spent 3 days waiting for a 'plane. Goodness me!)
>
> Had fun in Naples at the opera. Ever seen La Gioconda? It is full of property boats. Final par. in libretto goes 'As she falls to the ground the spy yells over

---

[45] Letter from Bliss to William Bridges Adams, 1 November 1944, in *ibid.*, p. 263. Benthall had been stationed near the Gorbals in the war.

[46] According to (Captain) Roger Wimbush (with whom before the war Lambert had an open dispute about jazz in the *Sunday Referee*), 'ENSA, who have done good work, but who lack imagination, made a fatal mistake in sponsoring Constant Lambert's Piano Concerto', *Gramophone*, October 1945, p. 11.

[47] *The Times*, 29 November 1944.

[48] John Pudney (1909–77), poet who wrote the poem 'Do not despair for Johnny-head-in-air' for the 1945 film *The Way to the Stars*.

her body, "Yesterday your mother offended me and I have drowned her!" but La Gioconda is already dead'.

Why is it that I can't lead a simple life?

Love to the old girl.

Yours truly, CL

P.S. Cassino[49] is remarkably like that painting you did of bad teeth inspired by Liszt's D[ance]. of D[eath].

From Naples on 5 December he wrote again to Ayrton:

You, dear Michael, are naturally conversant with 'Achilles in Scirro' by Pietro Metestano and Domenico Scarro which, as every schoolboy knows, opened the San Carlo on Nov 4th 1737. But did you know that it was 'a work subsequently hooted off the stages of almost every Opera House in Europe'? I like to think that the rare exceptions were due to <u>apathy</u> rather than admiration. Old Scarro seems to have had as much stamina as the brothers Ricci (or, for that matter, myself).

The Aquarium here is a dream, and contains a museum of skeleton catfish, cuttle-fish, octopods etc (looked after by a man like Spoletta) which knocks the slats of Ernst, Miro, Dali and the boys. The guide book (your Christmas present) is second only to Goya Popular Painter. In the section labelled 'Hermit Crabs' you get the following:- 'the anemone, too, gets her share, for she walks around on the agile legs of her friend; and this is not only an unexpected pleasure for a beast condemned to sit still throughout life – these promenades bring a more material gain'. ... The entire work is up to this standard.

If you see the man Gray, tell him I don't write because I don't wish to depress so typical a specimen of the 'diavolo incarnato' as himself. He will understand. The strains of the American national anthem are floating through the window as I write. Naples occasionally reminds one of a London Telephone box and for the same reason. Poltergeists temporarily under control but one should never boast too soon.

Love to the o[ld].g[irl].

CL

Three days later he had lunch with Evelyn Waugh[50] who was en route to Dubrovnik, Jugoslavia, as part of a British Military Mission, and he gave some concerts in Bari (at one of which the lights failed four times during the performance) from where he wrote to Gray:

Conducted last night in a charming opera house named after Piccinni[51] of all people. A good statue of him outside but not as funny as the statue of Mercadante in the other opera house. New Bari is like a Fascist edition of Bournemouth – Old Bari is fascinating. Having been both a Moorish & Norman colony the architects not un[n]aturally don't know whether they are coming or going & the results are a little surprising. Off tomorrow to Brindisi where I shall of course sing one. ('Le punch scintilla en reflets bleu' by Lecocq is my favourite). I believe there are good things to see on the way & I bullied them into letting me see Lecce the day afterwards.

---

[49] Site of the Battle of Monte Cassino, January–May 1944, in which the monastery overlooking the town was destroyed by American bombers.

[50] *The Diaries of Evelyn Waugh*, ed. Michael Davie (London: Weidenfeld & Nicolson, 1976; Phoenix paperback edition 1995), p. 596.

[51] Niccola Piccinni (1728–1800), Italian composer.

Do not imagine my life is a bed of roses – orchestra are rough – rehearsal conditions bad, travel gruelling – light heat & water hard to come by. However wine is cheap, good & plentiful & the old demon as you can imagine is frequently evoked in a moderately successful effort to palliate a series of frustrations & misadventures. BRANDED LIQUORS – STRONG DRINKS – NOBLEMAN ASSORTMENT as one of the wine shops here remarks.

Rome is by now quasi civilian & what with a few old 1920's friends a good time was had by all. Since Rome life has been less pleasant. But in spite of rain, cold, jeeps – Americans it is marvellous to be in stinking old Europe again & I wouldn't have missed it for worlds. Love to Marjorie & the usual wishes from your old fellow Diavolo Incarnato.

CL

For the censor's eyes he wrote on the envelope: 'Contains private affairs only.' On 10 December he wrote to Ayrton:

Sunny Italy to you! – the shindy made by the Adriatic plus complete lack of light, heat and water reminds one of a really ham version of Wuthering Heights by Cecil B. de Mille. Lights have just gone on hence late hour of script. Do you know this part of Italy? Superficially dull to begin with it ends up like a cross between the D[uchess]. of M[alfi]. and the more sinister parts of Wiltshire. Modern Bari is absolute hell – the old part is terrific. Every conceivable influence from Moorish to Norman with neither of them knowing whether they were coming or going. Tomorrow I go to Brindisi and hope to see some odd sights on the way. Particularly the Trulli or conical houses.

All the slang in the dialects here is derived from English or Celtic. The old slang, I mean, not the OKAYS with which you are greeted by the brats in the slums. All the players in this orchestra (and for that matter the instruments) remind one of early paintings by you, so I feel quite at home.

Statues here of Piccinni and Mercadente are knock-outs. 'YUGO-SLAVIAN WINE SHOP' 'Branded liqors [*sic*] – Strong Drinks – Nobleman Assortment' is an encouraging sign.

Do you know the Palermo guide 'Short history of the Catacombes'? The very curious sight HOW THEY DID THE MUMMIFICATION. (Tried to get a copy but have copied out best bits). Love to the old girl. Hope all goes well. Slightly harassed at the moment.[52]

The tour ended with concerts in Brindisi on 11 and 12 December, and then it was home. On Christmas Day he and the now nine-year-old Kit had tea with Angus Morrison.

At the end of January 1945 Constant found himself abroad again, this time taking the Sadler's Wells Ballet on a nine-week ENSA visit to the Belgium and France. This was their first trip abroad since their lucky escape from Holland in 1940. The Company, including staff and orchestra of 30, numbered over 80. Constant engaged a number of Belgian musicians to bring the orchestra up to sufficient strength. In addition to ballet in which Alec Sherman was assistant conductor, Constant conducted the Belgian National Orchestra with Arthur Grumiaux playing the Walton Violin Concerto, Walter Legge having secured the engagement of the Belgian violinist when his career was at a low ebb, giving him a copy of the score only three weeks before the performance.[53]

---

[52] 10 December 1944. Letter to Michael Ayrton from Bari, 3 a.m.

[53] The concert was arranged by the British Council in place of a suggested tour by the London Philharmonic Orchestra with Beecham, the Council feeling that Sir Thomas's 'irresponsible

The tour began with three weeks at the garrison variety theatre in Brussels, performing in front of many hundreds of service men and women, either on leave or stationed there. As Margot remembered, the Company were issued with 'straight khaki skirts, military jackets, sturdy overcoats, ghastly khaki stockings, flat-heeled shoes and a soft military cap.'[54] But the discomfort of the service uniform was nothing compared with the conditions in the only recently liberated cities.[55] *The Times* report gave some idea of what they had to put up with:

> For the first few days the company had some very dispiriting experiences. Their journey to Brussels was tediously delayed through gales in the Channel, and they arrived, behind scheduled time, having expected to come not to Brussels at all in the first place, but to Paris. They came at a time of intense cold and had to rehearse and later to dance in a theatre totally unheated (through lack of coal) where they and those who watched them shivered in sympathy; and with the thaw, a main water-pipe burst and flooded the auditorium for most of the day and made all the seats under the leaking balcony ceiling unusable for more than a week. Then, when coal arrived, and the central heating became effective, clouds of steam arose from the sodden carpets and seats. ... They had hoped to play a week at a forward centre in Holland [Eindhoven], but the idea had to be dropped because of the difficulties created by the size of the company and the volume of its impedimenta ...[56]

They were on the Continent in February and March, initially with two weeks in Brussels with a repertoire that consisted of *Les Sylphides*, *Carnaval*, *Les Patineurs*, *Promenade*, *The Rake's Progress*, *Hamlet*, *Miracle in the Gorbals*, *Nocturne*, *Façade*, *The Quest* and *Dante Sonata*. All programmes were sold out. As one young dancer much later described their final performance at the 1,600-capacity Théâtre Royale de la Monnaie:

> It was marvellous to see Constant Lambert – such an inspiring conductor – standing proudly on the podium. ... Constant was *simpatico* in the extreme. He was man who could talk about anything and we often used to sit at his feet and devour his knowledge of art, food, wine, history, women and, naturally, dancing. ... The performance was inspired for one and all.[57]

Such was their success that the British Council arranged a further week of performances in Paris before going on to Versailles, Ghent, Bruges and Ostend. The Council had hoped to follow the Continental tour directly with a 'goodwill mission' to South America, but that did not materialise, transport difficulties being given the reason at the time, so another season of ten weeks back at home at the New Theatre was scheduled instead.

Just before leaving for the ENSA tour, Constant had been invited to contribute an article on Alan Rawsthorne to *Tempo*, the new house magazine of the publishers Boosey & Hawkes. He replied that he would not be able to do so because of the two-month tour, but he added he would have liked to, not just because 'he happens to

---

utterances are more potentially dangerous than his musicianship can possibly outweigh': John Lucas, *Thomas Beecham: An Obsession with Music* (Woodbridge: Boydell Press, 2008), p. 312.

[54] Fonteyn, *Autobiography*, p. 104.

[55] A vivid account of the tour is given in de Valois, *Come Dance with Me*, pp. 157–63.

[56] *The Times*, 5 February 1945.

[57] Gillian Lynne, *A Dancer in Wartime* (London: Chatto & Windus, 2011; paperback Vintage, 2012) pp. 183–4. Gillian Lynne offers a fascinating insight into the life of dancers of the Sadler's Wells ballet during the war.

be one of my closest friends, but because I consider him to be the best young composer in England'. Curiously, besides just being close friends, their names were in time to be linked in an unexpected way. Isabel Delmer, a friend of Alan's, was soon to become the second Mrs Lambert and then, after Constant's death, the second Mrs Rawsthorne, a sequence of events that Constant would surely have found amusing. It was during the extended week in Paris that Constant and Isabel became closely acquainted.

18

1945–6
The Second Mrs Lambert

I N January 1940 the name of Isabel Delmer had made its first of many appearances in Tom Driberg's visitors' book. Sefton Delmer,[1] known to his friends as Tom was, like Driberg, a journalist on the staff of the *Daily Express*. He had been born in Berlin where his Tasmanian father was lecturer at the University. Educated at Oxford, Delmer was first a freelance reporter before being appointed head of the *Daily Express*'s Berlin bureau, gaining the distinction of being the first British journalist to interview Hitler. It was when he was in charge of the paper's Paris office that he met Isabel. She had been born in Hackney in 1912. Her father, Philip Llewelyn Nicholas, a master mariner of Welsh and Scottish descent, was more often than not abroad, usually in South America. But his homecomings were always great occasions, as he would bring back some exotic animal destined for a zoo. His wife would temporarily have to look after these creatures and in this way the young Isabel grew very fond of animals. When she was 12 her father's home port changed from London to Liverpool, so she was sent to school in Wallesey. In 1928 she enrolled at the Liverpool Art School where, as well as spending most of her time drawing from the nude, she gained valuable experience as a model. On her father's sudden death two years later, her mother and younger brother emigrated to Canada, but Isabel had meanwhile been accepted by the Royal Academy, so she moved to London. However, because of financial problems and her disappointment at the apparent lack of motivation among her fellow pupils, she soon left the Academy and sought work as a model. Jacob Epstein invited her to model for him at his studio at Hyde Park Gate, and in 1932 she went to live in the Epstein household as both a model and a studio assistant. Besides numerous drawings of her, Epstein made three portrait busts, one of which he considered to be among his finest works of art. At the age of 22 she had a son, Jackie, by him.[2]

Eventually, thanks to the proceeds of the sale in 1934 of her own drawings and watercolours, she was able to realise a long-held ambition to go to Paris. That same year, as Tom Delmer wrote in his autobiography:

> the latest passion of my imagination … was the bronze bust by Epstein of 'Isabel' – a long-necked girl with thick hair falling to her bare shoulders, a pouting almost Negroid mouth, high cheekbones, and those slanting Nefertiti eyes. They had always moved me, whether in life or in bronze, ever since I fell in love with a pair of them as an undergraduate at Oxford. When I had first seen them in the Tate Gallery my reactions were not at all that of a connoisseur of the Arts. It was that of a susceptible bachelor. 'You,' I said to the bust, 'are the girl I am going to marry – if ever I marry at all.'[3]

One day he saw her with friends at the Café du Dôme in Paris, introduced himself and they were married in 1936. He bought a new flat in the Rue de Castiglione, and Isabel had a studio in the courtyard.

Tom's job as foreign correspondent gave Isabel many opportunities for travel abroad. While they lived in Paris she continued her work as an artist and also returned

---

[1] Denis Sefton Delmer (1904–79).

[2] Jackie Epstein (1934–2009) became well known as a racing car driver and, for 15 years, general manager of Brands Hatch. Jacob Epstein created a bronze portrait of his son.

[3] Sefton Delmer, *Trail Sinister: An Autobiography*, vol. 1 (London: Secker & Warburg, 1961), p. 241.

to modelling. In 1936 a dealer suggested that her 'Eastern' looks might appeal to the French painter and illustrator André Derain, and in due course he made six portraits of her.[4] That same year she was also painted by Picasso, not a studio portrait but one done from memory. He would sit opposite her at a café they both frequented in the Boulevard Saint-Germain. 'One day after staring at me particularly hard he jumped up and said ... "Now I know how to do it." He then dashed back to his studio and started my portrait right away.' At the same time she was enjoying what was to become a life-long friendship with the Swiss sculptor and painter Alberto Giacometti who produced at least two portrait busts of her, a study of her in movement and some drawings.[5]

When Tom Delmer went to Spain to report on the Civil War, Isabel stayed in Paris until the German invasion of France when they both left for England. Tom was then put in charge of a Black Propaganda group based at Bletchley Park,[6] the work involving both radio broadcasts that purported to come from Germany and occupied countries, and also written propaganda for which Isabel designed the leaflets. It was in 1944 that signs of a break in their marriage came, when at about three o'clock one morning there appeared in their bedroom what Tom described as 'a blonde angel', a blue uniformed, breeched and high-booted dispatch rider with her corn-coloured curls peeping from under the crash helmet. As he wrote in his second volume of autobiography,

> All this soon became too much for Isabel. First she insisted on separate rooms so that she should not be awakened by my dawn visitor. Then she got herself a job as an artist designer for one of the department's productions in London. She went off to live there and only visited us ... at remote intervals. That was the beginning of the end of my first marriage.[7]

Towards the end of the war Isabel moved to London where she worked at Bush House[8] on a magazine *Il Mondo Liberto* designed for the Italian market. After the war, her marriage to Tom Delmer over, she returned to Paris where she worked on an English radio programme that was broadcast from France.

Isabel had already met Constant on two occasions. The first was before the war when she was an art student. 'I told him I thought I would be going to Paris fairly soon,' she wrote in her memoirs. 'He hoped that the ballet would go one day. When we said good-bye I had a curious feeling of seeing his face exceptionally clearly as though I were about to make a drawing.'

Their next meeting was just before returning to Paris after the war:

> One night before we started packing our bags John Rayner [a journalist friend] suggested we went to the ballet which was then performing at the New Theatre as the Sadler's Wells Ballet. Constant was conducting. John knew Constant. He had met him with Tom Driberg and he decided to leave a note and ask him for a drink the following day. I was in a state of great excitement when he arrived and knocked over my glass when pouring the drinks. This Constant noticed and remembered, interpreting it is as a good omen!

---

[4] André Derain (1880–1954), a friend of Henri Matisse and one of the leaders of the Fauvism movement, best known for his series of paintings of London.

[5] Alberto Giacometti (1901–66). Their correspondence is in the Tate Archive.

[6] War-time top-secret decryption establishment now famous for the breaking of German 'Enigma' codes.

[7] Sefton Delmer, *Black Boomerang: An Autobiography*, vol. 2 (London: Secker & Warburg, 1962).

[8] From 1940 the home of the BBC European Service department and, from 1958, of the BBC World Service.

Their friendship had little opportunity to develop until the end of February 1945 when Constant was with the ballet in Paris, a city that had been liberated only five months earlier. Isabel went to one performance[9] and afterwards

> Constant came with me to the City Hotel. He was enchanted with the place, especially the scaffolding which filled him with interesting and fanciful thoughts. In the café looking over the Seine it was clear that he was perfectly happy, his great love of France and most things French reduced him to a misty silence. Constant stayed on for a couple of days after the ballet had left. We met for dinner and spent whole nights walking about which can be so rewarding. Paris is even more beautiful at night than in the day. I took Constant to various all-night cafés that I knew. We went into The Halles[10] and along the [Boulevard de] Sébastopol.
>
> As Constant was lame and walked with a stick I was sometimes a little nervous on these night explorations in case he was jostled. He insisted on walking. It gave him the greatest pleasure, in fact two people could hardly be found to share such sweetness in walking about. I told him I was coming to England soon but the information did not seem to be of interest. I think he liked to think of me as living in Paris.

There occurred in Paris one incident which suggested that the Margot–Constant relationship had, superficially at least, finished. As Isabel described it:

> One evening without any warning Margot Fonteyn and Ninette de Valois arrived outside the café. There we both were, sipping what was probably a Pernod, when Margot turned towards Ninette smiling with glee, saying, 'Enfin il a trouvé son ambience!' They had brought with them Roland Petit who was astonished to find Constant frequenting such an unfashionable and broken down habitation as the City Hotel.

De Valois had introduced Margot to the 21-year-old choreographer and dancer Roland Petit with whom she was to have both an artistic and a personal relationship. 'I knew this girl from the pictures on the front of *Dancing Times* ... and I had already fallen in love with her, so it was a great emotion to meet her,' Petit recalled.[11] As for Isabel and Constant, with one living in Paris and the other in London, it was to be a little while yet before their friendship developed, but there had been a positive beginning.

Back from Belgium and France, on the day before the start of the new Sadler's Wells season, Constant recorded the first of five programmes of British Ballet Music for the BBC Transcription Service with the 'British Ballet Orchestra', the remaining programmes being recorded during May which, besides the ballet season, was a busy month.[12] Near the beginning and the end of the season there were BBC broadcasts;[13]

[9] Sadler's Wells performed in Paris from 21 February until 20 March 1945. In her memoirs Isabel mentions going to see *Job*, commenting that 'the Parisians did not like it'. Yet *Job* was not in the repertoire for that visit, but it was in 1948. It was possible that she was thinking of the later visit.

[10] Famous old covered central market of Paris, demolished in 1971.

[11] Quoted in Daneman, *Margot Fonteyn*, p. 185.

[12] 16 April 1945 *The Rake's Progress*, 1 May *Pomona*, 3 May *Miracle in the Gorbals*, 10 May *The Quest*, 18 May *Horoscope*. While this recording of *The Rake's Progress* has been issued on Dutton CDBP9761, none of the others seems to have survived.

[13] 5 May 1945 from Cambridge: Glinka, Overture *Ruslan and Ludmila*; Roussel, *Le Festin de l'araignée*; Liszt, Piano Concerto No. 2 (Kyla Greenbaum); Lambert, *Aubade héroïque*; and Sibelius, Symphony No. 1; 29 May: Borodin, Symphony No. 1 and finale from the composite opera *Mlada*, both with the BBC Symphony Orchestra.

on the 14th and 15th in Liverpool he had recording sessions for Sibelius' Second Symphony (that, sadly, was never issued), and on the 20th he gave an illustrated talk for BBC's *Music Magazine* on 'The Music of William Walton'.

The new season at the New Theatre, the first in peace-time, ran from 17 April until 23 June, with Geoffrey Corbett, who had been serving in the RNVR during the war, replacing Alec Sherman as assistant conductor. Constant was in command on the opening night and, as reported in *The Times*, 'obtained good performances, particularly of Gavin Gordon's music for *The Rake's Progress*, and of Tchaikovsky's *Hamlet* Overture'. The ten weeks at the New Theatre, with six nightly programmes and two matinées each week,[14] were followed by a week at the Finsbury Park open air theatre. Then, on 24 July, after an absence of five years, it was back to their old home, the Sadler's Wells Theatre in Rosebery Avenue, that had had a momentous reopening on 7 June with the premiere of Britten's *Peter Grimes*.

In the first week of July, before the start of the ballet season, Constant had had one of his most important recording sessions, sponsored by the British Council, that of Purcell's *Dido and Aeneas*: fourteen 78 rpm sides with an impressive line-up of soloists: Isobel Baillie, Joan Hammond, Joan Fullerton, Dennis Noble, Edith Coates, Edna Hobson, Gladys Ripley, Sylvia Patriss and Trefor Jones. Two days after the sessions were completed, he wrote to Margery Gray (formerly the first wife of Julian Livingstone-Herbage; she had married Cecil in 1944):[15]

> Thank you so much for sending the stamps, which Kit will adore, also for being so kind as to remember about Freda (patriotism is not enough) Cavell. I will get in touch with her the moment I am free. Have just spent an enjoyable but hard week recording the whole of 'Dido'. Otherwise I would have written before. I enjoyed my week at the mill enormously. It was most kind of you to put me up at such short notice & it made all the difference to my life. I am glad Fabia[16] is so well. I will try & arrange a family 'outing' when Kit comes back. Give the old epistomologist my love & tell him I have not forgotten about those cigars.[17]

In the spring of 1945 Flo married Peter Hole. As Constant's nickname for her had been 'mouse', the pairing of names caused him much amusement. More serious were thoughts for Kit's future education. Currently at Forres Preparatory School near Amersham, Buckinghamshire,[18] his name was put down for Lancing College in Sussex, which he entered in 1949, largely on the advice of Tom Driberg who was educated there himself. Constant wrote to his mother:

> As regards the conversation we had about Kit I realise that he is going through a difficult transitional period but refuse to believe that he is a neurotic or 'problem'

---

[14] 79 programmes, 20 ballets, 193 performances.

[15] Cecil and Margery lived together for a while until their respective divorces came through. Margery's was settled quite amicably, as Julian Herbage (as he became known) wrote to his former wife on 19 April 1944: 'Many congratulations! I hadn't heard of your marriage. It all sounds very good!' It was a happy marriage, although not all Cecil's friends liked her and she did not like all of them. She and Michael Ayrton had a long-running quarrel, which for a long time made it difficult for Cecil and Michael to meet. In 1947 Cecil and Margery went to live in Capri. Margery died the following year, after which Cecil's health quickly deteriorated and he drank heavily.

[16] Fabia, born 1938, was the daughter of Cecil Gray and Marie Nielson, who left him in 1941.

[17] Letter from Lambert to Margery Gray, 8 July 1945, from 4 All Souls' Place, W1.

[18] In the summer of 1945 Forres School moved back to its former location of Swanage, and in 1948, on Lambert's recommendation, Kit spent a year at Byron House, Cambridge, before entering Lancing College: Motion, *The Lamberts*, pp. 270–1.

child. On the contrary. And none of my intelligent and sympathetic friends would take up the idea.

I wish I could help him more and try all I can. But I think it would be *fatal* to take a sensitive child of his age and try and turn him into a crashing 'hearty'. God knows I don't want him to turn into a dreamy intellectual pansy nor do I want him sent to a crank school. I only want him to develop normally according to his own lights.

That is why I settled on a perfectly straightforward school like Lancing, which is almost humane. The only thing which *could* make Kit neurotic would be to shove him into some Kipling-like surrounding which would warp his life as it has done to so many of my friends.

As regards the Christmas holidays I think it is a good experiment. I only met Mr H[ole] for a few minutes but he seemed thoroughly nice though a little heavy-going.

As for Flo, no-one, least of all herself could turn her into the county figure she would like to be.

I think it might easily work out well particularly as there are other interests within close range.

At Kit's age there were only two things I really detested
  a) Children of my own age
  b) BOREDOM
Blame me not him if he takes after me.

While Kit's bringing up had largely been left to other hands than Constant's, Marie Nielson recalled a touching incident that illustrated, whatever his failings as a father, his feelings for his son:

I have a vivid memory of later years of going with him to a performance of 'Boris' at the Wells. (After he & Flo had separated.) I happened to look at him during the scene of Boris & his young son. The tears were streaming down his face. I always see it when I hear people say he hadn't much feeling for Kit, & wished then that something could have been done to preserve it for Kit to see when he got older. He used to take great care in choosing the books he took when he went to see Kit at school. I have never known an adult who could discuss the subtleties of Père Castor & Beatrice [*sic*] Potter as Constant could.[19]

There were now promising prospects for Constant's own career: on 13 April he had been invited, for a fee of £400, to become associate conductor of the 1945 Henry Wood Promenade Concerts which opened in July for the first time without their founder. He was given a share in ten programmes, with only one concert all to himself. Otherwise his co-conductors were Adrian Boult and Basil Cameron. But for someone invariably short of money the Prom season had one disappointing drawback: his part of the concert was not always broadcast, in which case he had to forego broadcasting fees. The works he was allocated very much reflected his own tastes: Liszt, Sibelius, Balakirev, Borodin, Chabrier, Ravel, etc.[20] That his favoured composers did not always match popular appeal is made clear by the *Times* review of his first Prom when he was in charge of the shorter second half of the programme: '[Mr Constant Lambert] secured lively playing from the orchestra in a work of his own [*Merchant Seamen* Suite] and in Liszt's *Les Préludes*. ... He is an advocate of Liszt and succeeded in imparting his convictions to the orchestra but hardly in convincing the sceptics. This was not

[19] Letter from Marie Nielson to Angus Morrison, 19 February [1954].
[20] See Appendix 8 for a complete list of the Promenade concerts that Lambert conducted.

for lack of eloquence, for many of us are born allergic to Liszt's particular brand of magniloquence.'[21] In an article for *Radio Times*, he looked ahead to what he termed his 'fourth period at the Proms' (having progressed from hard-up school-boy to a regular Promenader, then a critic and now a conductor):

> When I went to my first Prom as a child I had the ambition proper to my years. Even so I never envisaged myself as actually conducting any of them. So my first concert at the Proms this year will be another red-letter day in my life, except that on this occasion my excitement and pleasurable anticipation will be tempered by a certain amount of genuine fear. Fear, mainly, that I may not do justice to my favourite composers whose works, to my great good fortune, I have been entrusted with – a splendid selection ranging from Haydn, my favourite classic, through Borodin and the lesser-known Liszt, to Debussy, Sibelius and the concertos of my contemporaries Walton and Rawsthorne.[22]

At the conclusion of the Prom season Hely-Hutchinson, BBC's Director of Music, reported to the Controller of Programmes:

> Our own feeling is that Lambert's inclusion was abundantly justified, and that in a year or two, if we persevere with him (as I think we should), he will have won a permanent place in the series. He did make a positive contribution to the season, and materially confirmed his reputation in the musical world.[23]

Constant's elevation to associate conductor of the Proms brought warm appreciation from the soprano Sophie Wyss:[24]

> I wanted to talk with you at the 'Satie' concert but you had gone already when I had changed. I was wondering if you are not too busy, if you could arrange a few French folk-songs for me. I intended to give a recital of French folk-songs by British composers or perhaps contemporary composers later in the year. I have got some very good ones already arranged by VW, Gerhard, Britten, Seiber etc. If you feel like doing some, could we meet perhaps next week for lunch and we could talk about it. I am free all of the week from Tuesday the 7th of August.
>
> I was so delighted to see that you are conducting at the 'Proms'. For many years, I always thought you were the only man to do that job, once Henry Wood had gone. The others have not got enough personality.[25]

Constant was not able to respond to her request for a folk-song arrangement, but they remained good friends, with Sophie writing on 21 November: 'I am so glad to see that Edward Clark is conducting some concerts of contemporary music. The BBC has lost a lot in letting him go.'[26] Constant's Concerto for Piano and Nine Players was

[21] *The Times* review, 30 July 1945.
[22] Lambert, 'My Promenading Life'.
[23] David Cox, *The Henry Wood Proms* (London: BBC, 1980), p. 142.
[24] The Swiss soprano Sophie Wyss (1897–1983) tried to encourage many British composers to set French texts and arrange folk-songs for her, among them Berkeley, Racine Fricker, Gerhard, Maconchy, Rawsthorne and Seiber. She sang in the first performances of Britten's *Our Hunting Fathers* (1936) and *Les Illuminations* (1940) and Rawsthorne's *Three French Nursery Songs* (1938). Lambert engaged her for two Satie concerts and one Berners broadcast, all in the Third Programme.
[25] Letter to Constant Lambert from Sophie Wyss, 27 July 1945.
[26] In April 1936 the BBC Symphony Orchestra had its first Continental tour (Adrian Boult conducted *The Rio Grande* in the Salle Pleyel, Paris, with Clifford Curzon as soloist). The planning of the tour's programmes was largely the responsibility of Edward Clark, whose unorthodox methods did not meet with the BBC's approval, and he had resigned in March

given at Clark's second concert and he wrote to thank him: 'I am very grateful to you for all the help you gave me over that rarely played concerto of mine. Considering all the attendant difficulties I think the work went off extremely well and the concert as a whole was a most definite success.'[27]

Running simultaneously with the Proms was the eight-weeks' summer season of ballet with the Sadler's Wells Company now back in their own theatre in Rosebery Avenue. For this special opening night Constant asked to be released from his 'stand-by' commitment at the Proms to rehearse and conduct *Nocturne* at Sadler's Wells, as it 'had been unsatisfactorily done by other conductors in the past'. *Nocturne* was placed between *Promenade* and *Miracle in the Gorbals* which, reported *The Times*, 'were conducted by Mr John Fisher',[28] adding that 'Mr Constant Lambert … for this season has assumed the duties of musical director of the Company'.

Michael Ayrton and Joan were away while the Proms were in progress, leaving Constant more or less on his own in All Souls' Place. Michael was kept up-to-date with matters domestic by letter or postcard, often written late at night:

> Life at ASP is getting rather alarming. I have a saga which I will tell you later (rather like Casanova who as you well remember would refuse to tell of his escape from prison unless he knew that his listener had 3 clear hours in front of him).
>
> A sudden instinct made me go down to the kitchen about an hour ago. I found no less than <u>six</u> slugs on the wooden washboard of all places. Failing to find any Cerebos I managed to dissolve them in a rather slow and macabre manner with your Celery Salt. Disposing of the so-called bodies was a little unpleasant. We really must try the same effect on Miss Hawthorne.[29]

His health was now noticeably beginning to deteriorate, as Denis ApIvor observed: 'Constant was "for the high jump"' (as they say) in 1945–6 at the time he was living with Ayrton. I have never seen a man so ill, and at the same time so miserable.' Even Cecil Gray informed Ayrton:

> I have seen Constant several times lately. He still goes up and down in his usual disconcerting fashion. The last time I saw him – two days ago – he was in great form; the time before very much under the weather. But taking the situation by and large, I do not like the look of it all. His emotional instability is becoming 'chronic', as charwomen say. Of course we are all the same, but he takes it a stage further than the rest of us.[30]

Even Constant let slip, when writing to Ayrton in September, that in addition to a few domestic problems, things were not well with him:

> Excuse no letter beforehand but apart from professional fuss have been waylaid

before the tour started when the programmes were altered without him being consulted: Nicholas Kenyon, *The BBC Symphony Orchestra: The First Fifty Years, 1930–1980* (London: BBC, 1981), pp. 118–25.

[27] Letter from Lambert to Clark, 25 January 1946. Edward Clark gave a series of concerts of contemporary music on 14 December 1945 and 18 January and 15 February 1946 that included van Dieren, *Sonnet VII for Spenser's Amoretti*; Webern, *Five Movements* for string orchestra; Bartók, *Music for Strings, Percussion and Celesta*; Prokofiev, Overture for 17 Instruments; Lutyens, Bassoon Concerto; and Lambert, Concerto: Lutyens, *A Goldfish Bowl*, pp. 162–3.

[28] At the time John Fisher was leader of the Sadler's Wells Orchestra.

[29] Letter from Lambert to Ayrton, possibly 6 September 1945, headed 'Thursday (or rather Friday 2 a.m.)'.

[30] Letter from Cecil Gray to Michael Ayrton, 15 September 1945.

by the most formidable attack of the old complaint that I have ever known. Both physical and spiritual phenomena have reached a strange pitch. Please don't let Joan think that the house is going to rack and/or for that matter <u>ruin</u>. Mrs Smith (with whom I have attained <u>a modus vivendi</u>) – is keeping the place very clean and it is not her fault or mine that <u>all</u> the lights in the house have fused except the one distant exception by which I am writing. However I have been round to GTS and the whole thing will be put right before your return.

The slugs thank God have stopped. But otherwise life has required a strong effort of will to combat certain influences.

Oddly enough the last two 'Proms' have been an almost frightening success in spite of the fact that I was in a complete state of jitters. I look forward to settling down to a quiet life of composing with my 4th wife Cleopatra (a gay girl whom I met for the 1st time the other day).

Apart from the super-Strindberg quality of 4 ASP at the moment life has its consolations. Not having the time or energy of an 18th century novelist I can't tell you The Strange Story of Mr Ireland at the Albert Hall,[31] or The Abominable Episode of Mr Jay Pomeroy's Cocktail Party. Fortunately the irresistible jeer they have conjured up has helped me enormously. Must now stop and study Glière's 'Friendship of the Peoples'.[32]

Margot, alas, is in hospital having penicillin injections for her old trouble.[33]

Tiddlywinks[34] is having gastric catarrh like myself.

Give my love to Joan.

Yrs ever

CL

PS Margot's trouble isn't really bad. But she has to have injections every 3 hrs. so can't do it at home. She will be out in a couple of days I hope.

PPS No letters worth sending on. Only circulars (which as you know come under the same heading as musicians).[35]

One communication was prefaced with verse:

Good news from home, I read with tears
From friends I hadn't seen for years
(genuine ballad circa 1890)

Telephone (tenant's) was installed 3 p.m. by a sexagenarian midget (ex-French-Horn player in the Guards) who congratulated me on my playing of Prokofieff.[36] The extension is on its way. No lights yet. Only liver.[37]

Another letter followed the next day:

---

[31] This may refer to a performance of John Ireland's *Epic March* at the Proms on 8 September 1945.

[32] An overture, *Druzhba narodov*, by Reinhold Glière, written in 1941 to mark the fifth anniversary of the Soviet Constitution. It opened Lambert's Prom of Russian works on 13 September 1945.

[33] Exhaustion and a restricted diet had left Fonteyn quite ill for a while and an infection on her face was threatening to scar her for life. Fortunately, the penicillin treatment was successful. Fonteyn, *Autobiography*, p. 107.

[34] A cat.

[35] Letter from Lambert to Ayrton from 4 All Souls' Place, dated 'Monday night', possibly 10 September 1945.

[36] Prokofiev's Piano Concerto No. 3, with Kendall Taylor as soloist, was in Lambert's Russian Prom on 13 September 1945.

[37] Postcard from Lambert to Ayrton, 12 September 1945.

News slightly better. Lights (but not fires) restored by youthful Yidd from GTS accompanied by two telephone engineers and Slobodskaya[38] who did her exercises! (Vocal). It appears she was a genius for cooking but can only do it in the nude. Broke several neighbouring windows with 2 perf of Prok 3.

Yrs

Chico[39]

Six days later, with the Proms now behind him, there was a noticeable air of relief in his correspondence as he described to Ayrton the Last Night that he had shared with Boult and Cameron, his contribution – though not broadcast – being Dukas's *Sorcerer's Apprentice* and Rawsthorne's First Piano Concerto.

> I am not sending on any letters as I fear that they might cross with your return. They look pretty dull anyhow and seem to lack financial and/or sexual appeal. I gave your address to C. B. Rees whose Baroque-cum-Cymric charm grows from day to day.[40]
>
> The last night of the Proms was fantastic – rarely have the spectators been so dithyrambic. You have possibly read of the wild orgy in which 'the three conductors were pelted with flowers'. I have kept, as a souvenir, a large yellow chrysanthemum which caught Dame Adrian a neat whang on the nose. May I point out (in hasty parenthesis) that autumn treasures thrown by enthusiasts at short distance can be more painful than the casual observer might be led to suppose. My own theory is that the whole thing was led by a gang of highbrows who objected to our <u>tempi</u>. I beat a retreat before they got on to the earthenware.
>
> Old Fish-face had a good call after his concerto (which in my humble opinion knocks the slats off Darling Bengie,[41] Arseover Tippett and the Girls). It was very well played by Phyllis Sellick and I was delighted to see that it had a bad notice from W. Glock. I suppose that a good work by an old hetero, played by a woman, and conducted by his <u>bête noire</u> was too much for his so-called stomach.
>
> MEA CULPA, I broke (though very slightly) into your bottle of Ronsonol.[42] I think you will excuse me. I came back after the last night of the Proms <u>tout seul</u> and found I had damn all. Neurasthenia as usual had the better over my moral self. The <u>lacuna</u> will be restored ere you return. I have now got something of my own and in the immortal words of the late E. Lear

'He drinks a great deal of Marsala
  But never gets tipsy at all'.

NEWS FROM FAR AND NEAR

Philip Hendy[43] (!) is apparently going to be the successor to Sir K. Clark. How much is the job worth? It might solve the problem of what to do with my child.

---

[38] Oda Slobodskaya was singing Jaroslavna's aria from Borodin's *Prince Igor* at the Proms that evening.

[39] Postcard from Lambert to Michael Ayrton (c/o Mrs Jones, Dale School House, Dale (nr. Haverfordwest) Pembrokeshire, 13 September 1945.

[40] The journalist C. B. Rees contributed an affectionate portrait of Lambert in the second *Penguin Music Magazine*, 1947, reprinted as Appendix 10.

[41] Benjamin Britten.

[42] A brand of lighter fuel, but here referring to alcohol.

[43] Sir Philip Hendy (1900–80), art historian and Director of the National Gallery 1946–1967.

Your edition of the D of M[44] was reviewed in the Observer under the heading 'Black Magic'

The Emperor of Japan (bless his soul) is, we are told, renowned for his 'excursions into marine biology'.

Hoping this finds you as it leaves me viz. 47 sheets in the wind.

Yrs CL

PS Only the other day

> Mr Gray wrote a play
> The profits from which he pooled
> With Mr Ayrton Gould.

PPS Love to the OG and tell her not to worry. All is well on the upper floor.[45]

Although many of his friends in the ballet world were homosexual, Lambert had a particular dislike for Britten and Tippett, and the critic John Amis's last conversation with him

> was terminated by his discovery that I was a friend of the 'enemy'. We were talking à deux in The Gluepot, where he always stood on the same spot, and, after about half an hour, he happened to flick open an Everyman volume of Dostoevsky that I had laid on the counter. By mistake, instead of opening the book at the title-page, he arrived at the endpapers and saw the signature of the person I had borrowed it from – Michael Tippett. He rapped the book shut, finished his drink in one gulp and bustled out of the pub without ever uttering another word to me.[46]

C ONSTANT had only a week to recover from the exhaustion of the Proms (and the excitement of the Last Night) before giving the first London performance of Rawsthorne's Overture *Street Corner* (commissioned by ENSA) with the New London Orchestra in a Sunday concert at the Cambridge Theatre, together with Mozart's Symphony No. 38, Falla's *Nights in the Gardens of Spain* (with Harriet Cohen), his own *Aubade héroïque* and Sibelius's Symphony No. 2. 'His programme,' reported *The Times* the next day, 'showed much more adventure than is now usual at week-end concerts, but encountered the opposite difficulty of inadequate rehearsal. It is hard to believe that Mozart's *Prague* Symphony was not played at sight.'[47] Three days later, in a BBC Home Service evening broadcast, he once again conducted Arthur Grumiaux in the Walton Violin Concerto.[48]

After the Prom season, instead of joining the Sadler's Wells Company on their provincial tour, Constant recharged his batteries before another trip abroad, this time to Poland. It was one reason, in addition to his general disdain of folksong settings, why he felt unable to respond to Sophie Wyss's request, as he explained to her:

> Please excuse my rudeness in not having answered your letter before, but during the Promenade Season, which as you can well imagine was a rather anxious time

---

[44] John Webster's *The Duchess of Malfi*, an edition published by the Sylvan Press in 1945 with illustrations by Michael Ayrton.

[45] Letter from Lambert to Ayrton from '4 ASP ("Cheers and Tears" RF)', 19 September 1945.

[46] John Amis, *Amiscellany: My Life, My Music* (London: Faber & Faber, 1985; paperback, 1986), p. 75.

[47] *The Times*, 24 September 1945. Earlier that month Lambert conducted the first performance of *Street Corner* with the same orchestra at an ENSA concert in Leamington Spa.

[48] 26 September 1945. The broadcast also included Balakirev's *King Lear*, Haydn's Symphony No. 73 and Ravel's *La Valse*.

for me, I simply had to put all my correspondence on one side and concentrate on the scores. I would be very pleased indeed to make some arrangements for you later on when I am more free, but I am just about to go abroad for the British Council and do not expect to be back before Christmas.

May I say how much I enjoyed your singing of 'Socrate', a work which I have always admired and praised, but which I have never had the chance to actually hear.[49]

At Cracow on 22 October he conducted the Cracow Philharmonic in a concert of English music – Elgar, Purcell, Rawsthorne, Lambert and Walton. David Shillan, who organised the concert, described Constant's visit:

I had the job, as acting Cultural Attaché in Warsaw, where I was on an exploratory mission for the British Council, of putting on the first all-British concert in Poland; and we had Constant out to conduct it. It was at a difficult time in his life, and conditions out there were difficult and peculiar enough in themselves, so the whole experience was rather weird. It proved impossible, after some time of trying, to get the concert put on in Warsaw, so Constant and I were driven in an Embassy car (with a Sten gun ready in case of guerillas, etc) to Krakov, where we got an orchestra and a hall, and the thing was a success.

While in Warsaw we did odd bits of sight-seeing, and on a visit to a melancholy ruin of a palace with handsome ornamental waters, Constant wrote the enclosed poem and kindly inscribed it for me.

> *The Palace at Lazienki*[50]
>
> From the broken bridge
> The belvedere is sighted
> Pillars shattered and bored
> About to be dynamited
> The blown leaves blatant and yellow
> Are restrained by the pendant willow
> Pit props support the plaster
> Of ancient and baroque culture
> Yet who is now the master –
> The bleeding sheep or the vulture?
>
> > Constant Lambert
> > Warsaw, Oct 22nd 1945
> > For David Shillan for whom it was hastily improvised.[51]

Constant received much praise as a conductor of the highest rank, having prepared an extremely difficult programme in two short rehearsals. The Walton work was the First Symphony about which, according to Spike Hughes,

Willie himself announced that the main theme of the finale should be sung to the soldier's immortal words '–, and the same to you!' Once Willie had pointed out that the words fitted his music as well as they fitted 'Colonel Bogey' there was

[49] Letter from Lambert (4 All Souls' Place) to Sophie Wyss, 9 October 1945. He was to give the first performance in England of Satie's *Socrate* in a Third Programme broadcast on 17 June 1949 with Sophie Wysss and Megan Foster.

[50] This neo-classical Palace is situated on an island in a lake in Łazienki Park, a very beautiful part of Warsaw. In the war the Nazis wanted to blow up the Palace but because of the lack of time they only set fire to it.

[51] Letter from David Shillan to Hubert Foss, 4 February 1952.

no going back on it. Constant Lambert admits that whenever he conducts this movement he is compelled to sing the words to himself. When, in the autumn of 1945, Constant conducted the work in Cracow he found himself at last able to sing the words out loud. If the orchestra thought anything at all they probably imagined that the conductor was obviously moved to sing the words of an old English folk-song (which, indeed, he was); as it was, Constant's singing was broadcast the length and breadth of Poland and nobody was any the wiser.[52]

One outcome of his Polish trip was that the following year, on 22 May, he gave the first performance in England of a symphonic poem *Grünwald* by Jan Maklakiewicz, the score of which he had brought back from Poland.[53] Constant conducted the BBC Symphony Orchestra in one of the Home Service 'Music of Our Time' concerts, also including (surpisingly) Hindemith's ballet overture *Cupid and Psyche*, Khachaturian's Violin Concerto (with Max Rostal as soloist) and another Polish work, an overture by Antoni Szałowski.[54] 'As regards the proposed concert of Polish music, the BBC are, frankly, not being very helpful and in fact, are leaving me to cope with the whole thing,' Constant had confided to a colleague in January.[55]

Not long after his trip to Poland, there came an invitation on 14 November from much farther afield. The Managing Director of the Australian Consolidated Press, publishers of the *Sydney Daily Telegraph* and the *Sydney Sunday Telegraph*, invited Constant for a six- or seven-week stay from April to June the following year, conducting the newly formed Sydney Symphony Orchestra.[56] Although this offered him a new opportunity, he declined it because he was too busy. It would have taken him away at a time when there were about to be important developments with the Sadler's Wells Ballet Company.

He did not accompany them on their ten-week ENSA visit to Germany in November and December. Instead he had two BBC Home Service broadcasts, in one of which he conducted *Hail, Bright Cecilia* as part of the celebrations to mark the 250th anniversary of Purcell's death.[57]

In December he was approached by the *Daily Express* to judge scores for a 'Victory Music' prize.[58] He was also asked for an article on Edwin Evans who had died that year, and Francis Chagrin wrote to him, stressing the importance of his attending a concert for the Committee for the Promotion of New Music to assess the works that had been recommended for an international festival. But he declined all these requests because of another trip to the Continent, this time of just over a week's length, to Belgium that included a concert of mainly British music. And when on the day of his departure Rollo

---

[52] Hughes, *Opening Bars*, p. 319.

[53] Jan Maklakiewicz (1899–1954), Polish composer, teacher, critic and, from 1945–7, conductor of the Cracow Philharmonic.

[54] Antoni Szałowski (1907–73), Polish composer, was a pupil of Nadia Boulanger, the overture receiving high praise from Florent Schmitt when it was premiered in Paris on 15 October 1937. Lambert conducted this work again, on 30 July 1946 at the Proms.

[55] Letter from Lambert to David Cleghora Thomson, 3 January 1946.

[56] Established under the auspices of the Australian Broadcasting Commission, the Sydney Symphony Orchestra gave its first concert on 23 January 1946, and in November Eugene Goossens was appointed its first chief conductor.

[57] 22 November 1945, with soloists Margaret Field-Hyde, Alfred Deller, Charles Whitehead, René Soames, Stanley Pope, Stanley Riley and Eric Gritton. The other broadcast, two days later, consisted of Balakirev, Overture *King Lear*; Beethoven, Piano Concerto No. 3 (Noel Mewton-Wood); Debussy, *Printemps* and the Walton Symphony.

[58] Although Lambert's name was associated with the *Daily Express* prize, it is more likely that his fellow adjudicators Arthur Bliss and Malcolm Sargent did the actual judging. The first prize went to Bernard Stevens' *Symphony of Liberation*.

Myers of the British Council suggested that he might also like to conduct the Toulouse radio orchestra or even the Monte Carlo Orchestra, Constant replied: 'I frankly do not feel it worth while going all the way to Toulouse (whose only distinguished inhabitant, Mr Edmund Dulac told me in peace time was eight miles from anywhere). ... I would naturally like to go back to my old spiritual home Monte Carlo.' There was one matter, however, that he had to put right, writing to George Barnes of the BBC: 'Let me be the first person to hasten to point out that I am <u>not</u> living with Harriet Cohen! My present address is 4, All Souls' Place, W1 (Telephone Langham 2740), a precinct which I am occupying with the utmost and alas, regrettable celibacy.' He did agree, however, to a request from the Finnish Service of the BBC for his name to be added to the congratulatory messages that were being sent to Jean Sibelius on his 80th birthday.

At the beginning of January 1946 Constant found himself too busy even to contribute an article on 'Humour in Music' to an anthology entitled 'Music in Pictures', writing: 'I am already very much behind with various commitments, and can't possibly take on anything more.'[59] That month he had two recording sessions in London's Kingsway Hall with Walter Legge's recently formed Philharmonia Orchestra, and his second engagement for the Royal Philharmonic Society, conducting the London Symphony Orchestra in an afternoon programme that the *Times* critic recognised as 'reflecting the conductor's predilections' with works by Berlioz, Debussy, Liszt and Tchaikovsky, as well as his own *Aubade héroïque*.[60] To the older music he brought 'a fierce – one had almost written "ferocious" – intensity that drove it along with great effect, in spite of some evident shortcomings in the orchestral playing.'[61] Then in February he travelled north for five concerts with the Hallé Orchestra.[62]

But the most prestigious occasion was the reopening of the Royal Opera House, Covent Garden after the war under new management.[63] The Sadler's Wells Ballet were moving into a new and much larger home, and at the same time retaining their name.[64] As Alexander Bland put it in his history of the Royal Ballet, the company that the Covent Garden Trust acquired may have been 'war-weary but its assets were impressive. It consisted of an irreplaceable Director in Ninette de Valois, aided by a first-class choreographer, Frederick Ashton, and an inspired Music Director, Constant Lambert. The Company were led by two stars of growing magnitude, Margot Fonteyn and Robert Helpmann, and had a repertoire of sixty-seven ballets (of which sixteen were to be deemed suitable for Royal Opera House presentation).'[65] Their first challenge was to adapt to Covent Garden's larger stage. The ballet chosen for the grand opening on 20 February 1946 before the King and Queen, the Dowager Queen Mary and Princesses

---

[59] Letter to Sir George Franckenstein, 3 January 1946. Others approached for contributions were Sacheverell Sitwell, Julian Herbage, Alec Hyatt King, Desmond Shaw-Taylor and Edward Sackville-West.

[60] His first concert for the RPS had been on 14 January 1937.

[61] *The Times*, 21 January 1946, reviewing the concert of 19 January in the Royal Albert Hall.

[62] 12, 13, 15, 16 and 17 February in Manchester, Sheffield and Bradford. The main works were Vaughan Williams' Symphony No. 5 and Liszt's Piano Concerto No. 2 with Louis Kentner (three times each), and his own *Aubade Héroïque* and *Horoscope* Suite. He spoke to the Sheffield Philharmonic's Listening Club the evening before the Sheffield concert.

[63] During the war the Royal Opera House had been leased to Mecca Cafés which had run it as a dance hall.

[64] A second ballet company was formed at the Sadler's Wells Theatre, Rosebery Avenue. In 1956, by Royal Charter, the Sadler's Wells Company at Covent Garden became known as the Royal Ballet.

[65] Bland, *The Royal Ballet*, p. 83.

Elizabeth and Margaret was *The Sleeping Beauty*,[66] with designs by Oliver Messel. The *Times* critic wrote:

> Mr Constant Lambert obtained really disciplined playing of Tchaikovsky's enchanting score from an orchestra which Mr David Webster [Administrator] had somehow amassed for him. Mr Webster knows from his Liverpool experience how to raise orchestras, and he shares with Miss de Valois and the dancers whom she has trained the honours of last night's auspicious beginning of a new and difficult but very exciting adventure.[67]

On 18 March, Constant presented an evening of English ballet with *The Rake's Progress*, *Nocturne* and *Miracle in the Gorbals*. At about that time he was recording suites from two of these scores with the Covent Garden Orchestra, *The Rake's Progress* four days earlier and the Bliss on the morning of the all-English programme. Near the end of the month he was again in the recording studio, this time with the Philharmonia, for Rawsthorne's *Symphonic Studies* and *Street Corner* Overture and Bliss's march *The Phoenix (In Honour of France)*. Then in April he conducted two ballet premieres. The first new ballet to be presented at Covent Garden was *Adam Zero* with music by Bliss. This, the third (and last) of the Bliss ballet scores that Constant was to premiere, was dedicated to him and, as with *Miracle in the Gorbals*, the scenario was by Michael Benthall and the choreography by Helpmann.[68] Bliss himself described it as scenically the most ambitious of his three works:

> It was an allegory of the cycle of man's life: his birth, his passage through the spring, summer, autumn and winter of his existence, and his death. ... It was a splendid role for Helpmann, and might have had a long run if an early accident had not sent him from the cast. After a few performances there was a miscalculation, and he was sufficiently hurt to have to retire.[69]

Adam Zero was followed a fortnight later by *Symphonic Variations* which had been accompanied by a similar misfortune: the first performance had to be delayed because Michael Somes had torn a cartilage. With his general disapproval of using symphonic music for ballet Constant had had reservations about Ashton using César Franck's score for piano and orchestra (as he had been against Ashton using Debussy's *La Mer*).[70] After attending a performance of *Symphonic Variations*, Edward Dent wrote to Angus Morrison:

---

[66] As pointed out in Clarke, *The Sadler's Wells Ballet*, p. 202n, the title of the ballet was changed from *The Sleeping Princess* because it was a more exact rendering of the original fairy-tale name, *La Belle au bois dormant* and its Russian equivalent. *The Sleeping Beauty* ran until 18 March with Pamela May occasionally standing in for Fonteyn and Gordon Hamilton and David Paltenghi taking Helpmann's two parts of Carabosse and Prince Florimund.

[67] *The Times*, 21 February 1946. In fact Lambert had been much involved in auditioning the players.

[68] *Adam Zero*, premiered on 10 April 1946, was to be the last ballet that Helpmann choreographed until 1962 because, at the same time as continuing his dancing partnership with Fonteyn, he pursued his other desire to be an actor, performing regularly at the Old Vic and at Stratford-upon-Avon (frequently Shakespeare), often working in conjunction with his friend and director Michael Benthall. Helpmann was also to have a significant career in films.

[69] Bliss, *As I Remember*, p. 169. *Adam Zero* had 19 performances between 1946 and 1948, after which it was not revived. Elizabeth Salter, Helpmann's official biographer, does not mention a fall in *Adam Zero* but instead suggests that an earlier fall caused an abscess which 'drove him back to the clinic, where he was firmly immobilised for some months' (p. 130). June Brae was Helpmann's partner.

[70] Vaughan, *Frederick Ashton and his Ballets*, p. 206.

Constant is always right in these things. He is the best all-round musician we have in this country and it is a really great thing in our musical life that we have a man who is always unquestionably safe in scholarship, style, interpretation, sensitive understanding and complete professional accomplishment whatever he undertakes. I suppose most people would use that word 'safe' in a disparaging sense, but that is not at all what I mean – perhaps I should have said 'secure'.[71]

Nevertheless, *Symphonic Variations* was a great success and found a regular place in the repertoire. For the first two years Angus Morrison was the pianist, as he had been in March when *Dante Sonata* first came to the Covent Garden stage. In the spring Constant was doing more broadcasting, with talks on Roussel and Elgar, and a recording with the BBC Theatre Orchestra for the Corporation's Latin American service. In March Victor Hely-Hutchinson, BBC's Director of Music, had a meeting with Constant regarding the future of Covent Garden and afterwards informed R. J. F. Howgill, recently appointed Controller of Entertainment, that Constant 'was trying to make the Covent Garden orchestra into a thoroughly efficient and coherent entity, and with that in view he hoped to get them concert and recording work in due course apart from their work in the pit at Covent Garden.' Hely-Hutchinson added: 'It has since occurred to me that we might in due course find the orchestra useful for periodical studio bookings, if suitable terms can be arranged',[72] and on 8 May the Covent Garden Orchestra was booked by the 'Special Music Recording Service' at the BBC Maida Vale studios to record ten movements from *Adam Zero*.[73] With the same orchestra in June he recorded, this time for commercial release, suites from *Giselle* and *The Sleeping Beauty* and Bartók's *Two Portraits*. The first season of ballet finished on 29 June, and the following month Covent Garden played host to the International Society of Contemporary Music's 20th Festival. Although Constant did not conduct, he was a member of the jury[74] and it was doubtless on his recommendation that Alan Rawsthorne conducted his Fantasy Overture *Cortèges* in the second of the two orchestral concerts.[75]

When the Promenade Concerts came round again that month Constant was once

---

[71] Edward Dent, in Morrison, 'Constant Lambert: A Memoir', in *Music Ho!* (Hogarth Press, 1985), p. 19.

[72] Letter from Victor Hely-Hutchinson to R. J. F. Howgill, 10 March 1946, in Lewis Foreman, *From Parry to Britten: British Music in Letters, 1900–1945* (London: Batsford, 1987), pp. 269–71.

[73] This recording, made by the Special Music Recording Service (later the BBC Transcription Service), has been issued on CD APR5627 although it was not, as the accompanying notes state, of a world premiere broadcast – no such broadcast in this country has been traced. On the following day Lambert was due to record Delius's *Paris* (the music for the ballet *Nocturne*) and – if there was sufficient time – Rawsthorne's *Cortèges*. It is not known if either of these works was recorded as planned.

[74] The ISCM jury consisted of Samuel Dushkin (USA), Willem Pijper (Holland), Roland-Manuel (France), Gregor Fitelberg (Poland) and Constant Lambert (Great Britain). Lambert was also a member of the Committee (later Society) for the Promotion of New Music, and on 29 May 1946 recommended a quartet by 'an admirable, but little known, composer', George Linstead (1908–74).

[75] The conductors on 7 and 14 July were Boult, Fitelberg, Edward Clark (Lutyens, *Three Symphonic Preludes*), Bertus van Lier, Manuel Rosenthal and Alan Rawsthorne. *Cortèges* was first conducted by Basil Cameron at the Proms in July 1945. The composer Gerard Schurmann has written: 'I do remember Constant discussing the idea with Alan that he should write a kind of processional piece with balletic overtones, and it wouldn't surprise me if he had also suggested the French title': John McCabe, *Alan Rawsthorne: Portrait of a Composer* (Oxford: Oxford University Press, 1999), p. 98. *Cortèges* is dedicated to Lambert.

more engaged as assistant conductor, for a fee of £400. As David Cox wrote in his history of the Proms, there were 'objections by Cameron – not objections to Lambert personally, but disagreements with the Music Department about the need to have a post of associate conductor. Hely-Hutchinson wanted to establish the post on a secure basis, seeing the work of a younger conductor as being "the main plank at present in the forward-looking policy of the Proms", and continuing to recommend Lambert for the position.'[76] Boult had not been keen to carry on, but Hely-Hutchinson had persuaded him to continue for that year.

Constant's competence was not in question: Bernard Shore, for over ten years principal viola in the BBC Symphony Orchestra, later provided a player's assessment of Lambert and Bliss as conductors:

> Arthur Bliss and Constant Lambert share the honour of being the most efficient composer-conductors. Both are first-rate, with all the technique and experience necessary for the task their own music sets them. ... Constant Lambert is also completely master of his orchestra, he conducts other men's music as admirably as he does his own and possibly with more care. Less authoritative in manner than Bliss, he still has a strong grip and is extremely purposeful and definite about everything. He is not less clear and easy to follow than Bliss, but the two are dissimilar in method, Lambert being more imaginative in conception and less critical in execution. His ear is more than adequate and he always gets his way. A work of his composition receives no unduly favoured treatment at rehearsal, whatever its difficulty. His strong rhythmic sense and clear stick, together with his innate musicianship, makes him a refreshing personality to the orchestra.[77]

Constant shared the first night of the Proms with Boult and Cameron, conducting the last item, Borodin's *Polovstian Dances*.[78] This year he took part in 15 concerts, two of which he had sole charge.[79] The complete cycle of Sibelius symphonies was programmed, with Constant conducting numbers 1, 3, 4 and 6. His contribution also included a repeat performance of Szalowski's Overture, the first English performance of Hindemith's *Symphonic Metamorphosis on Themes by Carl Maria von Weber* (a curious fact for someone who had showed such an aversion to Hindemith in *Music Ho!*), the first performance of John Ireland's overture *Satyricon*,[80] and the Prom premiere of a suite from *Adam Zero*. The Bliss 'fairly galloped along under the sizzling baton of Constant Lambert,' remembered Alan Ridout, 'but it was the last piece, Howells' *Procession*, which crowned the evening and forever blessed the day for me'.[81] Nerves and drink got the better of Constant on at least one Prom occasion, according to Thomas Pitfield:

> I don't think it would be the first performance of Alan's First Piano Concerto, but I went to the Royal Albert Hall to hear it, played by Louis Kentner, with Alan's close friend, Constant Lambert conducting. It was in the second half, and I went round to the Green Room during the interval to wish them well, and could not

---

[76] Cox, *The Henry Wood Proms*, p. 143.

[77] Bernard Shore, *The Orchestra Speaks* (London: Longmans, 1948), pp. 143–4.

[78] 27 July 1946. He did not conduct Shostakovich's Symphony No. 9, as incorrectly listed in Alastair Mitchell and Alan Poulton, *A Chronicle of First Broadcast Performances of Musical Works in the United Kingdom, 1923–1996* (Aldershot: Ashgate, 2001); Basil Cameron was in charge of that UK premiere.

[79] See Appendix 8.

[80] Dedicated to Julian Herbage and Anna Instone, to whose BBC programme *Music Magazine* Constant was a frequent contributor.

[81] Alan Ridout, *A Composer's Life* (London: Thames, 1995), p. 41.

help noticing that both were rather the worse for strong liquor. I returned to my seat in the balcony above the pianist, in full view of operations, but it was obvious – in the Finale, I think, – that Lambert – brilliant musician that he was, had either lost his place in the score, or was temporarily incapable, and that the performance was rescued by Kentner's very fine communication with the orchestra.[82]

In between his Prom appearances, Constant was once again called to recite *Façade* at the Lyric Theatre, Hammersmith on 9 September, but this time in its original form from behind a painted curtain, using the design by John Piper that was first used in 1942. He was still, the *Times* reviewer seemed to suggest, the interpreter *par excellence* when he wrote: 'How much the ordinary reader never guesses of these "patterns in sound", these "virtuoso exercises in poetry (of an extreme difficulty)" is apparent only when they are delivered with Mr Constant Lambert's gusto and enjoyment and his widely varying pace and intonations. Behind the gaping satyr's mouth on Mr Piper's fantastic curtain ... Mr Lambert is a company of actors in himself, capable of making his part now incisively witty, now delightfully nonsensical, and now mysteriously pathetic.'[83]

---

[82] Thomas Pitfield, 'Some Recollections of Alan Rawsthorne', *The Creel*, vol. 1 no. 4 (Spring 1991), pp. 127–8. This was Lambert's second Prom performance of the concerto, on 14 August 1946. Announcements suggest that the piano concerto was actually in the first half of the programme.

[83] *The Times*, 10 September 1946. Other verses by Edith Sitwell, from *The Song of the Cold*, were spoken by Dorothy Green and the programme began with Poulenc's Sonata for Two Clarinets. A repeat performance was announced for 22 September.

19
1946–50
The Third Programme and *The Fairy Queen*

H ARDLY had the Prom season finished than one of the most important phases in Constant's last years began. On 29 September 1946 the BBC launched its cultural flagship, the Third Programme. Up until February 1950 Constant was to make a highly significant contribution, mainly in his own specialist areas of interest and largely at the invitation of Humphrey Searle who was one of the programme producers and a good friend. As well as conducting, Constant was occasionally narrator, he devised some programmes and contributed ideas to others, and gave talks. Considering how his friendship with Searle had started, it was only appropriate that his first offering for the Third Programme should be an all-Liszt concert. As Searle has explained:

> In the very first week of the Third Programme I put on a concert of rare orchestral works by Liszt, including the first English performance of 'Les Morts' which Liszt wrote in memory of his son Daniel, who was only twenty when he died; the song 'Die Vatergruft', the 2nd Mephisto Waltz and several other pieces. The conductor was Constant Lambert, and he was an able and willing collaborator in a number of programmes of unusual and exotic works over the next few years. ... Constant would conduct anything interesting, no matter in what style, though he was not keen on doing the standard Austro-German classics, and twelve-note music meant little to him, with a few exceptions such as Schönberg's 'Pierrot Lunaire', Orchestral Variations and Berg's 'Wozzeck', but he was always prepared to give new music of all kinds sympathetic consideration. He did once conduct a broadcast of the Bach–Webern Ricercare when one of Schönberg's pupils originally scheduled for the programme fell ill, and he told me afterwards how surprised he was when a score which looked so fragmentary on paper emerged so clearly in actual sound. We usually arranged these programmes over a drink in The George; it was no good writing him letters, and he was hopeless on the telephone, but once he was actually present he was full of ideas and most stimulating.[1]
>
> We often met in The George – he was staying with the painter and sculptor Michael Ayrton round the corner in All Souls' Place – and we usually arranged our programmes in the pub. ... I sometimes stayed in his flat – he had a curious spare bed which came down out of the wall – and when I went to bed he would usually start work at the piano upstairs, often playing from midnight 'till 4 a.m. He was a nocturnal man, and was never happy at morning rehearsals, but when he got to the evening performances he was brilliant. He could be an extraordinary conversationalist, but he never showed off for its own sake, and he would often relapse into silence. He was inclined to keep other people at arm's length until he got to know them well, but once he made friends he kept them. In spite of his brilliance he was sometimes melancholy, feeling perhaps that he had had to spend too much time on conducting and writing and not enough on composition. But his early death was a tragedy for us all.[2]

Constant was now very active in two spheres: broadcasting and ballet. Because of his many Prom appearances and his Third Programme engagements, Geoffrey Corbett had taken his place for the Sadler's Wells Company's autumn provincial tour and its

---

[1] Searle, *Quadrille with a Raven*, chapter 10.

[2] 'Constant Lambert by Humphrey Searle, CBE', typescript, sent to Mr K. Harvey Packer.

visit to Vienna. But on their return from abroad he opened the new Covent Garden season on 25 October with a revival of *Coppélia*. 'The actual dancing reached a high level under the inspiration of a fine orchestral performance conducted by Constant Lambert,' remarked *The Ballet Annual*,[3] and *The Times* critic was in agreement: 'The ballet has not had its music so well played for many years: Mr Lambert got precision and élan in the performance of Delibes' ingratiating score. This in turn enabled the Mazurka and the Czardas of the first act to be danced by the *corps de ballet* with greater verve and polish than formerly.'[4]

On 6 November, as part of an *Evening News* Festival of British Music at the Royal Albert Hall, Constant conducted *The Rio Grande* and Vaughan Williams his *A London Symphony*. Six days later he was in charge of the premiere of what was to be Berners' last ballet, *Les Sirènes*, to an idea by Frederick Ashton and with scenery and costumes by Cecil Beaton, who had worked on the designs at Faringdon while Berners composed at the piano in his drawing-room. It was not a success, 'sunk by the unnecessary lavishness of the venture' as Ashton's biographer put it[5] and perhaps by its over-cleverness with too many in-jokes. Even Beaton admitted that it was a flop, with much of the original idea having 'got lost'.[6] Leslie Edwards suggested that it might have been 'thought up too light-heartedly during a weekend country-house party'[7] and, after 19 performances, it was not revived. By comparison, the revival later that season on 6 February 1947 of *The Three-Cornered Hat*, with Constant conducting, was an undoubted success. Léonide Massine was the Miller (a role he had created back in 1919) with Fonteyn his wife. 'Lambert's superb sense of rhythm made him an ideal conductor for the de Falla music,' wrote the historian Mary Clarke.[8] *The Times* reported that 'the music was excellently played, except from some lack of synchronisation of the castanets, under Mr Constant Lambert's direction.'[9] One particular attraction was the use of Picasso's original décor.

Between these two productions came something much closer to his heart and the fulfilment of many years' ambition: the staging of Purcell's *The Fairy Queen*. It was a project that, as Constant himself said, had 'occupied my entire artistic life for well over six months. … It is because I have from my childhood been devoted both to the theatre and to the music of Purcell that I suggested to Covent Garden (and in particular because they were going through a transitional period from ballet to opera) that they should produce on a fully adequate scale Purcell's masterpiece.'[10] It was a task ideally suited to his talents, combining – in the tradition of the masque – drama, opera and ballet. With music by Purcell, *The Fairy Queen* was an adaptation of Shakespeare's *A Midsummer Night's Dream* (although significantly not titled as such). As Edward Dent wrote, '*The Fairy Queen* in its entirety might have taken well over four hours; it had to be

---

[3] *The Ballet Annual* (London: A. & C. Black, 1948), p. 7.

[4] *The Times*, 26 October 1946.

[5] Kavanagh, *Secret Muses*, p. 328.

[6] Beaton, *Ballet*, p. 67.

[7] Edwards, *In Good Company*, p. 110.

[8] Clarke, *The Sadler's Wells Ballet*, p. 216.

[9] *The Times*, 7 February 1947. Margot Fonteyn danced the miller's wife.

[10] Lambert, 'The Music of "The Fairy Queen"', in E. J. Dent *et al.*, *Purcell's The Fairy Queen as Presented by the Sadler's Wells Ballet and the Covent Garden Opera* (London: John Lehmann, 1948) pp. 25, 20. Lambert had previously worked on three theatrical productions involving the music of Purcell: *King Oberon's Birthday* (a choral ballet in 1933, founded mainly on the fourth act of *The Fairy Queen*), the ballet *Comus* (1942), and in 1931 he conducted *Dido and Aeneas*, something that he curiously omitted to mention in this article. For the Third Programme he was to continue his devotion to Purcell with many concerts of his music, including four performances of *Dido and Aeneas* and two performances each of *King Arthur*, *The Tempest* and *The Fairy Queen*: see Appendix 7.

reduced to little more than two. ... Constant Lambert courageously cut out practically the whole of the spoken play, leaving only a few curtailed scenes for the clowns, and a little dialogue between Oberon, Titania and Puck.'[11] Richard Temple Savage, Covent Garden's librarian, acquired a large stock of manuscript paper on which to prepare the score, but for him progress was slow: '(Lambert) did not bring me in much to work from and sometimes I even had to score passages myself from his verbal instructions. It also transpired later, when the bills began to come in, that he had farmed out a good deal of the work to others, in particular Professor Dent of Cambridge who scored several arias.'[12] Constant acknowledged Dent's help and expertise (as he did all the other contributors) in a book that commemorated the production, with numerous photographs and articles by Dent, Ayrton and Lambert himself.

The reason for some of the delay had not been the music, as Constant explained: 'I spent more time actually on the libretto than on the music, making no less than three versions before Malcolm Baker-Smith, the producer, collaborated with me on a fourth and final one.' He decided to ignore Theseus and the lovers and concentrate on the immortals and the clowns, reducing the original five acts to three. Constant always enjoyed close collaboration between those involved in a production. 'If *The Fairy Queen* proved a success I feel sure it was mainly due to the fact that the scene designer and myself, joined later by Malcolm Baker-Smith [co-producer with Ashton], and Frederick Ashton the choreographer, sat up night after night playing through the music and exchanging ideas until no one knew which idea was whose. ... By the time I had finally decided on the theatrical "lay-out" both my collaborators and, not unnaturally, myself felt slightly perturbed by the fact that not a note had been put on paper.'[13] One major problem was the placing of the chorus; he solved this by having them in boxes, two tiers high, on either side of the stage.

An even closer collaboration was possible with the designer, Michael Ayrton, while they were still sharing a house. After searching in vain for the designs used for the first production in 1692, Ayrton decided to base the scenery and costumes on the work of Inigo Jones. If, as he admitted, it was 'some departure from accuracy of the period', as Purcell and Jones could not possibly have collaborated, he felt it was nevertheless 'only fitting that the greatest English designer and composer, who complement each other so exactly in style, should ... collaborate in spirit'.[14] As his biographer relates, he also accompanied Constant on his various searches for the required music and for suitable copyists, this being often achieved 'by dint of scouring various hostelries (always a more profitable effort than ringing up music publishers)'. Notwithstanding the problems of the immediate post-war scarcity of certain materials, that Constant should mention 'the usual workaday reluctance to co-operate in a novel scheme' and that Ayrton in turn should refer to the designs being less ambitious at Covent Garden than the original stage directions required because of 'union restrictions on the activities of what men there were', suggests that both of them had to fight their corner.

Just before the opening night they were both involved in a fight of a very different and more serious nature. For some time Constant's health had been deteriorating and his drinking had become excessive. Back in June 1945 Ayrton had described him as 'spitting blood, and in every way worse'[15] and, with the help of the Sitwells, attempts

---

[11] Edward J. Dent, 'Preface', in Dent, *Purcell's The Fairy Queen*, p. 18. The spoken text that Lambert retained was as far as possible that by Shakespeare rather than by the anonymous adaptor.

[12] Savage, *A Voice from the Pit*, p. 113.

[13] Lambert, 'The Music of "The Fairy Queen"', pp. 22, 24.

[14] Michael Ayrton, 'The Design and Device', in Dent, *Purcell's The Fairy Queen*, p. 28

[15] Hopkins, *Michael Ayrton*, p. 98

were made to get Constant to see a Dr Child, an appointment, wrote Ayrton, that 'must be affected at the earliest opportunity. The middle of next week if possible. He can then be put out to grass for two full weeks. He *must be prevented* from working. Margot is frantic (and a party to our scheme)'.[16]

Denis ApIvor had been alarmed at the changes he had noticed in Constant. He remembered one particular evening in the pub when the seriousness of Constant's medical condition had become noticeable:

> One evening Constant came down to the RSBA [Royal Society of British Artists] Galleries to hear a new quartet of Elisabeth's and the Berg Lyric Suite. Afterwards we repaired to the little pub at the bottom of the Haymarket. At that time he had a particular 'thing' which he was exploiting (you remember it was the advertising matter of the Whitbread's brewery one week, and the translation of *Music Ho!* into Japanese, the next). This time it was Theme songs for important historical personages. He appeared to have got stuck with The Duke of Wellington. At this point my wife, whose mother was 'on the boards', and is well up in popular songs suggested 'Any old iron, any old iron, any any any old iron'. The incongruity of this struck Constant so forcibly that he began to laugh uncontrollably, then to cough: suddenly he swayed off his stool and fell with a crash like a smitten oak, prostrate on the floor. There was a moment of horrified silence, then everyone rushed to pick him up. I thought he had had a stroke. But as he was being helped up he suddenly recovered, shook away the supporting arms and was himself again. I made enquiries among the medical specialists and found that his attack was probably a 'laryngeal seizure' and indicative of a pretty grave state of health. ... That is the first time that it became evident to me that his health was deteriorating.[17]

David Webster, General Administrator of Covent Garden, not without reason, saw in this an approaching crisis and one that could damage the international reputation of the re-formed Covent Garden. So, to head off any possible incident, he approached the problem in the most unprofessional manner by appointing Karl Rankl, without any consultation, as conductor of *The Fairy Queen* in Constant's place.[18] The entire production team were appalled at such a step, not least Ayrton, who took it upon himself to rally support and organise a written declaration demanding that Constant be immediately reinstated with an apology, or else they would withdraw from the production.[19] Under the circumstances Webster had little choice but to retract, but the whole unpleasant matter must have shaken Constant considerably and laid the foundations for his eventual resignation.

Oberon was played by Helpmann (by now also established as an actor); his Titania was fellow Australian Margaret Rawlings who years back had recommended him to de Valois, and Bottom was Michael Hordern who remembered:

> It was a vast and complicated affair. ... We had a vast chorus of singers and dancers [who] performed all manner of bird ballets, night masques and seasonal frolics which altogether left the three of us (myself, Helpmann and Rawlings) as the primary speaking parts rather upstaged. I certainly felt much happier when

[16] Ayrton quoted in Daneman, *Margot Fonteyn*, p. 188.
[17] *In Search of Constant Lambert*, BBC2, 26 July 1965.
[18] Karl Rankl (1898–1968), Austrian-born conductor and composer, was appointed in June 1946 as the first music director of the new Covent Garden Opera Company. He left in 1951.
[19] Ayrton did not design for Covent Garden again.

I could hide behind my vast ass's head. ... Constant Lambert wrote me a little song, so there I was on the stage at Covent Garden, singing a solo:

> The Ousle cock so black of hue with orange tawny bill,
> The Throstle with his note so true, the wren with little quill ...

Constant Lambert kindly wrote at the bottom of the music, 'To be sung in any key'.[20]

The Fairy Queen proved to be a mixed success. There was general praise for Fonteyn and Somes as the Spirits of the Air, but *Ballet Today*, while giving credit to Constant's praiseworthy editing, felt that 'the main fault of the present adaptation is that it falls between stools'.[21] *The Spectator* damned it with faint praise, finding the spectacle 'delightful, though unevenly so' and the music 'which had been (inevitably) cut and adapted by Constant Lambert ... wholly suitable to the spectacle but no more than that'.[22] Mary Clarke later summed it up: 'The ballet audience was bored by the singing, the opera audience resented the dancers, and the Shakespeare enthusiasts who had been reared at the Old Vic were horrified by the whole proceeding.'[23] Constant, in the conclusion to his article on *The Fairy Queen*, took a side-swipe at the critics:

> The greatest and most intelligent tribute I received was not from any academic source but from my local greengrocer, Mr O'Leary of Great Titchfield Street, who said, 'What I liked about it was the balance of the thing. Not too much of anything. The right amount of singing, the right amount of speaking and the right amount of dancing.' What I have achieved was done for others.

Benjamin Britten had been invited by David Webster to be involved in *The Fairy Queen* but, as he wrote to his publisher, Ralph Hawkes: 'I have no faith in an organisation which has Lambert as assistant conductor, & on the committee behind it – Walton & Dent.'[24]

Herbert Fryer, Constant's piano teacher at the RCM, attended one performance and found it 'jolly good, surprisingly so as at the start [Lambert] was only just about able to climb into his seat & he didn't even make his bow! Sad – but the whole show was remarkably good, in spite of the inauspicious start & a terribly cold night. I was sorry for the dancers with, practically, nothing on!'[25] The production had a run of 25 performances, with Geoffrey Corbett designated 'second conductor'.[26]

On the last day of 1946, as well as conducting an evening performance of *The Fairy Queen*, Constant was to have taken a morning rehearsal of *King Pest* that was scheduled for the BBC Winter Proms just over a fortnight later. He did not turn up – the BBC records put his absence down to illness – and Boult had to find him alternative rehearsal time. His condition, which was now putting a strain on working relationships, could so easily have taken a fatal course but for a happy event the

[20] Michael Hordern, *A World Elsewhere* (London: Michael O'Mara Books, 1993), pp. 84–5.

[21] Alan Storey, '"The Fairy Queen" at Covent Garden', *Ballet Today*, January–February 1947, p. 14.

[22] Quoted in Hopkins, *Michael Ayrton*, p. 103.

[23] Clarke, *The Sadler's Wells Ballet*, p. 214.

[24] Letter from Benjamin Britten to Ralph Hawkes, 30 June 1946, quoted in Tooley, *In House*, p. 75. William Walton and Edward Dent were members of the Covent Garden Opera Trust.

[25] Letter from Herbert Fryer to Angus Morrison, 14 June 1955.

[26] 1946: December 12, 13, 14 (and matinée), 16, 17, 18, 23, 24, 27 (and matinée), 30, 31; 1947: January 1, 6, 7, 8, 15, 16, 17, 24, 25 (and matinée), 27 and 28. Corbett would at least have had to conduct on 25 January as Lambert had a Third Programme concert, relayed from People's Palace, in which he was conducting Liszt's *Dante* Symphony.

following year that – if not reversing the situation – at least delayed the inevitable: his second marriage.

J ANUARY 1947 began with *The Fairy Queen* on New Year's Day and 11 further performances that month, as well as two of *Les Sirènes*. From time to time he was plagued with irritating requests, such as providing the scripts for his many General Overseas Service broadcasts[27] or programme notes for an Albert Hall concert that Boult was giving that happened to include *Job*.[28] But it was the Third Programme that was now to make the heaviest demands on Constant's time: on successive evenings that month he conducted two live broadcasts of Purcell's *Dido and Aeneas* (edited by Dent and co-produced by Stanford Robinson and Lambert), with a recitation of *Façade* on the following evening; he was to conduct his Concerto for Piano and Nine Players with Kyla Greenbaum (sister to Hyam) as soloist and Leighton Lucas would conduct *Façade*. As programmes in those days generally went out live, Searle, the producer, asked Edith Sitwell to give a talk on the *Façade* poems in the interval 'while Constant took a short but necessary rest'. However, it seems that the short rest was not enough, as a displeased Walton later wrote to George Barnes: 'if, as I doubt, there should be another performance of the original "Façade" could it be either put on by itself & with no Concerto or speech beforehand? Either the Concerto or Façade, but not both, as C.L. was obviously exhausted by his exertions on the former, as to be at times almost incoherent. And he can do it so well especially if he has been on a diet of bread & water, at any rate on the latter if not the former.'[29] The whole programme was recorded and, whether or not to appease Walton, the two works were rebroadcast separately later in the year. When on 10 December 1948 Lambert recited *Façade* again, it was given on its own (again with Leighton Lucas conducting and a recorded repeat the following month). This may have encouraged Desmond Orland of the BBC to write to Walton on 25 July 1950 that the Third Programme was 'anxious to make a [final] authoritative recording[30] with Constant Lambert as speaker and yourself as conductor of *Façade*', adding a list of distinguished players. On 1 August Walton, then very involved with the composition of his opera *Troilus and Cressida*, replied: 'I should be delighted. … At the moment I'm preparing [*Façade*] for publication and as soon as a new set of parts is out we could begin to consider about dates. I'll let you know about this later on.' But it was not to be. Lambert died on 21 August 1951. When the score of *Façade* was eventually published, in the year of Lambert's death, it was fittingly dedicated to him.

In February, after the successful introduction of the Falla ballet *The Three-Cornered Hat* with Massine, followed by a Beethoven–Dvořák concert in the Royal Albert Hall, Constant had a short holiday on the island of Ischia (before Walton had settled there) where he joined up with Michael Ayrton and Joan. Then, taking a boat to nearby Capri, they all enjoyed a reunion with the author Norman Douglas and his new neighbour Cecil Gray who, with his wife Margery, had recently moved to that island, although, as Constant was to write, 'the boat journey from Ischia to Capri is of such rare occurrence and howling discomfort that only the strongest bonds of friendship … would induce anyone to set foot on the ship.' They had been regular friends in London during the war when Douglas had to leave his home in Capri. As he was short of money, Cecil, Constant and Michael had formed the Norman Douglas Dining Club to see to it that at least once a month their friend enjoyed a good meal with good drink and good

[27] The General Overseas Service became the World Service in 1964.

[28] 22 January 1947.

[29] 31 January 1947. BBC Written Archives.

[30] Sadly, neither of the two *Façade* performances with Lambert as reciter appears to have survived in the BBC Sound Archive.

company. As none of them was financially sound and Douglas's capacity for drink exceeded even that of his friends, funding the monthly meeting was not always easy.[31] Ayrton did not elaborate on what he mysteriously referred to on that short holiday as 'the Case of the Japanese Soprano which took place on the Island of Ischia in the Bay of Naples and in which the late Norman Douglas played a small but important role'.[32] But, as Isabel tells us, Constant had an oriental female companion on that holiday:

> Constant appeared in Paris accompanied by a young singer called Aki who I understood to be Japanese but later was told she was Chinese born in Hong Kong. She clearly saw herself as Madame Butterfly. They were on their way to holiday in Ischia. While the three of us were sitting in Les Deux Magots,[33] one of the young men selling horoscopes and prognostications of various kinds approached our table. Constant who was deeply superstitious asked for three. As the young man was placing them on the table he managed to switch the two destined for Aki and myself. The incident I heard later made an impression which he thought about afterwards.[34]

While on Ischia, Ayrton worked on several local scenes, three of which appeared as coloured prints in the November 1948 issue of *Lilliput*, a small-size monthly magazine of articles, pictures and stories to which for over a year Constant had been an occasional contributor, in this case by providing an article to accompany Ayrton's art work. This was to be the last of his five contributions to the magazine, as always broadening his piece by informing the reader that the cemetery at Casamicciola on the northern part of the island had inspired Böcklin's *The Isle of the Dead*, and adding not only that Ibsen had finished *Peer Gynt* on Ischia but that the island had inspired many details in Norman Douglas's well-known novel *South Wind*.[35] Another author with whom Constant was acquainted at about this time was Gerald Kersh, who gained some commercial success with his short stories, one of which, *Sad Road to the Sea*, he dedicated 'with affectionate regards' to Constant, giving him the autograph copy.[36]

The holiday abroad seemed to revive Constant's spirits, and Ayrton (who stayed on much longer in Italy) wrote afterwards to Gray: 'Constant is ... in wonderful form, he has given up smoking and drinks only Lacrimae Christi (non spirits). He is extremely well and coherent ... [and] if he can only remain in this happy state no one need worry.'[37] Constant conveniently combined his visit to Ischia with an engagement to conduct two concerts at the Cannes Music Festival.[38]

He had to be back in an unusually cold England in the first week of March as he was introducing and conducting a Warlock programme for the Third Programme in

[31] Hopkins, *Michael Ayrton*, p. 95.

[32] Ayrton, *Golden Sections*, p. 131.

[33] Les Deux Magots was one of the most fashionable cafés in Paris, patronised by Sartre and Hemingway, and situated next to its rival, the Café de Flore.

[34] Isabel Rawsthorne's unpublished memoirs.

[35] Lambert, '"The Face of Ischia": Three paintings by Michael Ayrton with a commentary by Constant Lambert', *Lilliput*, vol. 23 no.5 (November 1948), pp. 44–9.

[36] Gerald Kersh (1911–68). The story was published in *Argosy* (UK), December 1946, Heinemann 1947, and *The 8th Pan Book of Horror Stories*, ed. Herbert van Thal (Pan, 1967). The autograph, dated 29 January 1946, is in the RCM Archive.

[37] Letter from Gray to Ayrton, February 1947: Tate Gallery Archive, quoted in Hopkins, *Michael Ayrton*, pp. 128–9.

[38] 20 February: Purcell, Chaconne in G; Lambert, *Aubade héroïque*; Rawsthorne, Piano Concerto No. 1; Lambert, *Merchant Seamen* Suite; 23 February: Boyce, ed. Lambert, Symphony No. 1; Rawsthorne, Overture *Street Corner*; Walton, *Façade* Suite; Bliss, March *The Phoenix (In honour of France)*.

the BBC Maida Vale studios.[39] This was the occasion, remembered by ApIvor, when 'after conducting *The Curlew* at Maida Vale in the bitter winter of 1946–7, he came out of the "Warrington" with Humphrey and myself, and attempting to get into his car he fell prostrate in the snow.'[40] Later that month, in the Third Programme, he conducted the first full performance (with strings) of his *Dirge from 'Cymbeline'*, together with Elisabeth Lutyens' Bassoon Concerto,[41] and *Trois intermèdes* by Maurice Jaubert, a young French composer, known chiefly for his film music, who had been killed in action during the war. Reviewing the *Dirge*, W. R. Anderson wrote in *The Musical Times*:

> I am still unconvinced that the word-magic in Shakespeare wants, or can endure, other music than its own. Constant Lambert's setting is as good as one would expect, though this composer is not the readiest to find simplicity. I could not get the choir's harmony precisely: a frequent difficulty in radio choralism …[42]

At about this time Isabel decided to return to London, a decision in which Constant had played no small part. While she was in Paris he had been sending her postcards almost daily.

> Some were in the form of limericks, some like miniature crosswords, some were real quotations, some quotations from Beachcomber. Elisabeth Lutyens and Alan [Rawsthorne] observed this sport of cards going to France as they were written in the celebrated pub, The George, near Broadcasting House. Elisabeth told me afterwards that she said to Constant while listening to him talking to himself, 'I don't think Isabel will marry you because of some postcards – even yours!'
>
> One day I got a letter, a couple of lines in that inimitable handwriting at the top of a large page, asking me please to let him know the moment I arrived in London.
>
> We all met in The George, Elisabeth, Alan, Constant, Anna [Phillips] and myself. Alan I had met once for a moment after a concert of the ISCM where he had conducted a work of his own. I can remember thinking it had an effect of the sound being suspended and the instruments sounding individually with great clarity. I know that Constant had a great admiration for his music.[43]

Constant was almost certainly drawn to Isabel because of her 'Eastern' look that he found so attractive in women (accentuated by what her former husband Tom Delmer described as her 'Nefertiti eyes'). But they had certain things in common: they were both Francophiles, both had been through an unsatisfactory marriage, and while Constant had a deep knowledge of decorative art, Isabel also had an understanding of music, their artistic sensibilities thus enabling them to discuss matters of common interest at a similar intellectual level. Unfortunately, Isabel's ability to bring much-needed stability into Constant's life was limited because she too was a heavy drinker.

Not long after *The Three-Cornered Hat* had entered the Royal Opera House repertoire in February 1947, Fonteyn was absent for six weeks. It is not certain whether

---

[39] Full details of this broadcast are not available as, because of a paper shortage, *Radio Times* for 23 February – 8 March was not printed. *The Times* broadcasting listing merely gives 'Moeran and Warlock recital'.

[40] Letter (typed) from Denis ApIvor to Hubert Foss, 16 April [1952].

[41] Lambert was the dedicatee of Lutyens' *Three Improvisations for piano* (1948) for which he chose the titles: 'Adumbration', 'Obfuscation' and 'Peroration': Harries, *A Pilgrim Soul*, p. 282.

[42] W. R. Anderson, in 'Round About Radio', *The Musical Times*, May 1947, p. 164.

[43] Isabel Rawsthorne's unpublished memoirs.

this was because of illness or some physical disability, or indeed the emotional result of Constant's new liaison with Isabel. In Fonteyn's absence, Moira Shearer took the lead in the revival of *The Sleeping Beauty* on 27 March.[44] 'This is Tchaikovsky at his best and Mr Lambert plays it as though he recognises the fact,' commented the *Times* critic. On 10 April it was Beryl Grey's turn, *The Times* critic remarking: 'What care Mr Lambert bestows on the playing of Tchaikovsky's score! It is to be hoped that the dancers realise how great a part of their enchantments he creates for them.' The next day Fonteyn's return was announced, and three days later she was back, only to be off again in the middle of May, on her doctor's orders, for two months' rest. With the season ending in June, Roland Petit, with whom Margot had now formed a close relation ('We developed a deep but harmless crush on each other,' she wrote),[45] persuaded her to ask de Valois for leave of absence to study in Paris. This was granted and as Petit remembered:

> We were very young and we went together everywhere, doing the craziest things: we would take off our clothes and jump in [the Seine] and swim across and when we swam back our clothes were still on the bank.[46]

Her fling with Petit provided her with a much-needed emotional break, but she was back to rejoin the Company in August for a tour that took them to Poland.

I N the meantime, perhaps encouraged by Isabel to lead a more independent life instead of the rather Bohemian set-up in All-Souls' Place, Constant had moved to the smaller address of 39 Thurloe Square, South Kensington. But this led to little improvement, she describing his life style there as

> intolerably rigid – [his] pattern was one of hard work which was his nature, the dreary round of eating in familiar restaurants to sleep in a nasty little house in Thurloe Square. The only good thing to be said about this place was that it was near the Natural History Museum.

Unfortunately Constant, as usual in financial straits, now had to pay double rent until he had completed the terms of his tenancy with Michael and Joan. This was not the only problem. The new house was owned by Lilian Walker, a violinist, who had become widowed that year, and Constant was not the only lodger. Isabel continues:

> The house was occupied by a man called Otto who called himself Constant's agent. He proved to be an accomplished crook who cheated everyone he met … Otto managed to disappear before he was caught for fraud. We imagine he was swallowed by the Middle East.

Mrs Walker could fairly easily be persuaded by cunning lodgers to lower the rent. On one legendary occasion Otto made every effort to get her under the influence of alcohol, plying her with gin and orange in the hope that she would sign a deed, which he is alleged to have prepared in advance, which would have given both him and Constant

---

[44] Moira Shearer was soon to become famous for her starring role in the Powell and Pressburger film, *The Red Shoes*, released in 1948. In his autobiography, *A Life in Movies* (London: Heinemann, 1986), Michael Powell described the character in the film of Livy, the English conductor played by Esmond Knight, as 'a cross between Sir Thomas Beecham and Constant Lambert … with the polished rudeness of an upper-class Englishman and the keen perception of a perfectionist' (p. 644).

[45] Fonteyn, *Autobiography*, p. 114.

[46] Daneman, *Margot Fonteyn*, p. 200.

enhanced rights of rental and greatly lowered rates. As she would often later recount, to her great credit she resisted with vigour and clearheadedness.[47]

Constant gave his mother a fairly optimistic account of his move:

> Life is in a state of flux but definitely improving. Just moved into a new place which as yet is unfurnished but will eventually be much the best place I have found. Olga has the address.
>
> Sorry not to have called in before but only just back from France, plus two days in a gloomy hotel in Victoria, a performance of Boutique Fantasque tonight (without rehearsal) and a concert in Croydon tomorrow. 'Quelle Vie' as Berlioz once remarked.
>
> I am sending round an odd parcel consisting of lemons, sardines and some nougat (the latter for Kit). It will be brought you by my new factotum Mr Otto who is proving a great help.
>
> It is cold and the house is full of workmen. Why did I leave the South of France?[48]

On 29 May Constant conducted *Turandot* once again at Covent Garden, with Eva Turner and Walter Midgley in a new production that Richard Temple Savage rated as probably the most successful that year. *The Times* critic wrote that 'Mr Leslie Hurry's sets and costumes had the riot and fantastication of legend, of the orient, and of the perverted mind. Mr Constant Lambert read the score in the same light and drove the opera at a high and sustained pitch of intensity, which not only made it immediately effective, but called attention to the composer's fantasy and imagination at the end of his life. The audience, which was gripped from the start, applauded in no uncertain manner.'[49] Olivia Gollancz, who was playing horn in the orchestra, remembered Constant's conducting:

> The most vital memory I have of [Constant] was when ... he was conducting *Turandot* – Eva Turner and Walter Midgley were singing – it was a marvellous production, most exciting, and I found then that he really was one of the few conductors who could look at you and make you do what they wanted just by looking at you. He had the gift of putting across the way he wanted you to play without seemingly doing more than waving his arms up and down. He was a big, plump man; he wore always for rehearsal short sleeve shirts so you saw these rather large plump arms waving up and down and his absolutely seraphic face smiling away at the music and somehow or other you just had to give him what he wanted.[50]

On the other hand Richard Temple Savage, pre-war bass clarinettist in the London Philharmonic Orchestra and the Royal Opera House's orchestra's librarian, felt that Lambert 'primarily a ballet conductor ... always had difficulty in following singers'.[51] He remembered Walter Midgley asking him as librarian 'to mark various pauses he intended to make very clearly in the score so Lambert could not miss him'. 'Is he still having trouble following singers, then?' Temple Savage had inquired. 'Follow?' retorted

---

[47] Correspondence from Tim Hands of Portsmouth to the author, 13 February 2006.

[48] Letter from Lambert to his mother, undated and with no address.

[49] *The Times*, 30 May 1947.

[50] *Remembering Constant Lambert (1905–1951)*, BBC Radio 3, 23 August 1975. Olivia Gollancz also remembered quite the fastest Tchaikovsky Symphony No. 4 in her professional experience, with Lambert conducting the Hallé.

[51] Savage, *A Voice from the Pit*, p. 52.

Midgley. 'He couldn't follow an open bottle of Chanel down Piccadilly on a hot night!'[52] Constant, used to having his way in ballet, may have been less responsive to the demands and peculiarities of singers.

Malcolm Arnold thought that Constant was not able to express 'his enormous musicianship' because he didn't have the opportunities, although he 'had the makings of a great conductor'. Many of the concerts he conducted were on a single rehearsal, but Arnold did remember 'an afternoon concert in Cambridge with the LPO and he did Sibelius' First Symphony and all his inhibitions, everything broke down, and the place was set alight, audience and orchestra.'[53] Arnold had got to know Constant when playing for his conductor's class in the RCM second orchestra. 'I used to follow him after he had done the Second Orchestra to the *Queen's Elm* [South Kensington] where he took all his students and I used to play his [ballet] scores on the pub piano,' he recalled.[54] 'When I became a professional orchestral musician I would meet him for a drink in the Nag's Head in St. Martin's Lane. He was a lovely man, but strangely he was sometimes inhibited on the rostrum. When he gave himself a free rein he could do some really good performances.'[55]

Altogether there were eight performances of *Turandot* spread over a month,[56] in between which he had two important engagements for the Third Programme: a performance of *Summer's Last Will and Testament* on 7 June, and conducting *The Curlew* again four days later in the second of a series of Warlock programmes devised and introduced by Elizabeth Poston. Isabel remembered how Constant 'was busy most days and nights. He was pleased because he was always wanting to conduct opera.' She and Elisabeth Lutyens went to one performance and could not have helped matters when they 'behaved badly, stumbling into the wrong box and causing [a] disturbance'. Constant was known to stumble in and out of the pit, giving the impression of one who was incapable of self-control. The truth was rather different. However much he depended on drink, whether out of habit or to steady his nerves, once he was in front of the orchestra he was generally in control. Dame Eva Turner confirmed that he was always in command of a performance, even if he might be in a state of near collapse afterwards.[57]

Yet the *impression* that he gave – of one who was regularly drunk (irrespective of how much his then undiagnosed diabetes was contributing) – was what mattered as far as both the good name of the opera house and the confidence he could instil in the orchestra and performers were concerned, and there seems little doubt that the differences he had earlier had with David Webster during *The Fairy Queen* once again came to a head. Whether or not he was faced with an ultimatum and this was a means of saving face, on the day after his final performance of *Turandot* he resigned from the Sadler's Wells Ballet, a decision he confirmed in writing the next day:

> Dear David,
>
>   As I explained to you this afternoon, I have with the utmost regret decided to leave the Sadler's Wells Ballet Company with which, as you know, I have been associated intimately for the last 15 years and whom, if I may say so, I helped

[52] *Ibid.*, p. 117.

[53] Malcolm Arnold in *Constant Lambert Remembered*, BBC Third Network, 25 June 1966.

[54] Malcolm Arnold talking to Piers Burton-Page, BBC broadcast, 7 December 1993.

[55] Malcolm Arnold, 'My Early Life', *Music and Musicians*, October 1986, pp. 8–9.

[56] 29 May, 3 June, 5 June, 10 June, 13 June, 17 June, 28 June and 1 July 1947. When *Turandot* returned in November, it was conducted by Reginald Goodall.

[57] Shead, *Constant Lambert*, p. 147. Dame Eva Turner read a tribute to Lambert at St Paul's Church, Covent Garden, on 5 December 1981 in a service that launched a memorial appeal.

to carry through the very difficult war years at the expense of giving up my composing and conducting career. I feel now that the work is running on its own wheels and no longer needs the help of my experience. Among the many reasons which have induced me to take this decision have been the productions of 'The Fairy Queen' and Puccini's 'Turandot' in which, in sharp contradistinction to the balletic approach, I have received intimate collaboration and personal gratitude.

As I told you the other day I have taken on an important film which will involve my being free from the beginning of September to the end of November, so, apart from the preliminary work which I propose to start immediately after going abroad I will obviously be unable to give the hundred per cent support to the ballet which I have been able to give in the past. Since the situation has inevitably arisen I think it better that, howsoever regretfully, I should retire from my position as Musical Director and Conductor of the Sadler's Wells Ballet – though, as someone who has been connected with it intimately for so many years, I shall always be pleased to give them my musical advice.

I am very sorry to have made this heavy decision. Please convey my regrets to the Trustees who I am sure will appreciate the sincerity of my inevitable action.

With very best wishes for the future of the ballet,

Yours as ever,

Constant Lambert[58]

The reference to his two most recent productions leaves little doubt that the interference he had experienced from administrative quarters during the preparation of *The Fairy Queen* had not disappeared with *Turandot*. While his film commission for Alexander Korda's *Anna Karenina* was perhaps a convenient additional reason for resigning, Constant had very much understated the importance of his role in English ballet, something that Webster did not have the grace to correct in his less than effusive reply:

Dear Constant,

I read your letter to the Trustees at the last meeting and I know that Sir John Anderson is writing you officially as from the Trust.

I just want to add my own private word to the effect that the Sadler's Wells Ballet owes you an enormous amount of credit for the work they have done. Certainly no Ballet Company since Diaghileff has had such an outstanding list of musical works in their repertoire, and as far as English composers are concerned I am quite sure that never have they had such an innings with any other musical institution. It does you enormous credit.

I remember hearing you many times in the early part of the war thumping on those pianos and I cannot imagine any greater work and labour, nor can I think of anybody else in the country of your standing who would be willing to have given time to it.

I personally am extremely happy that it is likely you are going to do more composing and I am sure the whole musical world will be glad also.[59]

Webster showed particular insensitivity, not just in the inappropriate choice of the verb 'thumping', but in stating that Constant's resignation could engender in him extreme happiness, whether, as he stated, in the thought of him being able to devote more time to composition, or, as might be inferred, in the fact that no longer would he regularly

---

[58] Letter from Constant Lambert to David Webster, 2 July 1947.
[59] Letter from David Webster to Constant Lambert, 21 July 1947.

conduct at Covent Garden. Sir John Anderson, Chairman of the Covent Garden Trust, in his letter, did little more than echo Webster, if with more tact.

In its September issue, *The Musical Times* reported that 'a successor will not immediately be appointed and the conducting will be in the hands of Mr Geoffrey Corbett and Mr Hugo Rignold.' It was not until 1949 that his successor was appointed, it being Robert Irving, his former conducting student at the Royal College.

Leaving the Sadler's Wells Ballet was a devastating blow to Constant, terminating his career as the country's leading permanent conductor of ballet and considerably reducing his income. It was particularly poignant because only two weeks earlier he had been a guest speaker at a dinner at Claridge's given by the Dancing Profession in honour of Ninette de Valois. The other guest speakers were Kenneth Clark, Philip Richardson, Frederick Ashton, Robert Helpmann and David Webster. Constant's going was not to be marked by any such occasion.

Nor was this the only blow he was to receive that year. After two years as assistant (or associate) conductor of the Proms, he was dropped from the 1947 series. As Victor Hely-Hutchinson wrote:

> As to the identity of the Associate Conductor, I feel that in 1947 we should substitute Stanford Robinson for Lambert. I opposed this suggestion two years ago because Robinson was then specially associated with the Theatre Orchestra, but now that he is associated with the Symphony Orchestra, I think it would be unjustifiable not to allot this work to him. How much he would have to do would depend on the requirements of the individual conductors, and would probably vary with each of them. But the programmes could be built in such a way as to make it clear that he had a 'stake' in the Season as a whole. This recommendation does not imply a criticism of the work that Lambert has done in the last two years. His work on the whole has been very good, although he has not quite built himself up in the way that we hoped he would when he was originally appointed. In other words, I do not see Lambert developing into a Chief Conductor of the Proms one day ...[60]

In marked contrast to the two previous years he only made one Prom appearance that season, for a birthday performance of *The Rio Grande*, with soloists Gladys Ripley and Kyla Greenbaum; Adrian Boult and Stanford Robinson conducted the remainder of the concert. In September he consoled himself by visiting France to conduct at a music festival in Besançon, returning in time for a Third Programme 'Contemporary British Composers' broadcast on 2 October featuring himself and Tippett, in which Louis Kentner played piano transcriptions of the Siciliana from *Pomona* and two movements from *Horoscope*; Constant directed the first performance of the instrumental version of all *Eight Poems of Li-Po*, the manuscript of 'Lines Written in Autumn' (dated September) showing some signs of hurry. The soloist was Martin Boddey who knew Constant well and remembered his sense of humour and his delight in newspaper cuttings:

> One of the great things he used to like was the city editor's reports. Constant never really laughed – it was a little thing that went on in the back of the nose, and you'd know that he'd got something and he had to bring it to you and you would see 'Mr Rumbold on the spiral situation of rubber' and – this to him was desperately amusing – 'International rivets stand firm'.[61]

[60] Hely-Hutchinson to the Controller of Music BBC, in Cox, *The Henry Wood Proms*, p. 147.

[61] *In Search of Constant Lambert*, BBC2, 26 July 1965.

The one event of great moment that same month was his marriage to Isabel. On 11 October Ralph Hill wrote to Cecil and Margery Gray, now living in Capri:

> With regard to Constant, I have not yet run across him, but it was announced in the London press that he was engaged to be married to a Mrs. somebody or other (husband deceased, I believe!). According to unreliable testimony he now walks about with a wing collar, black tie, black vest and striped trousers, and drinks neat tonic water which is once again on the market!

According to Isabel, when Constant rang his mother to tell her whom he was to marry, he informed her: 'Anyway, she is not coloured, she is half Welsh, nor is she a ballerina.' They were married on 7 October in the Register Office, St Pancras Town Hall, and their witnesses were Elisabeth Lutyens and the artist Theyre Lee-Elliott. In her memoirs Isabel wrote that she could remember nothing of the day except going to her friend Anna Phillips' home for some drinks. Walton naughtily maintained that, with Constant full of drink, Alan Rawsthorne fulfilled the groom's duties on the wedding night. 'That night I slept in Thurloe Square,' was all that Isabel added.

After the wedding the first task was to search for a house in the Regents Park area that was in easy reach of Isabel's first floor studio let to her by Margaret Taylor, the wife of the historian A. J. P. Taylor.

> I knew this would appeal to Constant with Camden Town, with its mixed black and Irish population nearby. I discovered a house in Albany Street ideally situated between Camden Town and the Nash terraces. A Victorian house, floors were to let, with a small conservatory on the first floor. 197 became our house.[62] The ground floor was quite large. Upstairs there were 2 rooms, bedroom and a studio. The living room was large enough for 2 pianos. One was a small upright, a Kirkman, I believe Kirkman made harpsichords, this one sounded rather like a harpsichord, this no doubt was why Constant was so fond of it. The other was a baby grand, a most extraordinary instrument. It was of an elegant shape, the legs were slender, it made a sound like an unstrung harp. But it was great fun to have them both.
>
> In fact life now became great fun. Whenever I went out with Constant, it might be a small journey to the market, I always felt something extraordinary and exciting would happen. He carried about with him the aura of a conjuror. I was always conscious of being with a person of great physical beauty. His lameness possibly added to his distinction. It gave me great pleasure to watch him walking along Albany Street from the conservatory window. How revealing it is to see people from a distance. I still had my room at Margaret Taylor's house. He was to be seen in The George. Close by was a pub called The Edinburgh Castle with a small garden overlooking the railway. Constant was fond of this place because in his mind it had some connection with the music of Delius's *The Walk to the Paradise Garden*.[63] He alone among the other composers I had met had a great affection for Delius. Sometimes I would meet Constant at lunchtime. We would sit overlooking the trains.

The street they chose to live in was one of great character, with curious shops, and on

---

[62] On 30 October 1997 an English Heritage blue plaque was unveiled to Constant Lambert at 197 Albany Street, London NW1 by the Master of the Worshipful Company of Musicians, Antony Burnett, and Philip Jones CBE. The inscription reads: 'Constant Lambert 1905–1951 Composer lived here 1947–1951'.

[63] In Delius's opera *A Village Romeo and Juliet* 'The Paradise Garden' is a run-down inn with a wild garden frequented by vagabonds. It is here that the two lovers decide their own fate.

one side a large bomb site that became the subject of one of Isabel's paintings. But the move was not without expense, as Constant explained to Alan Frank when asking for the year's royalties in advance:

> The main reason is that we have had to move into a new place (with all the attendant expenses) while still paying for the old one. So you can see my difficulties. ... Excuse lop-sided writing but all the tables covered with pots of distemper, newspapers, or both.[64]

As a near neighbour, Denis ApIvor noticed the initial improvement that the marriage had on Constant:

> I don't think that one can overestimate the importance of his marriage to Isabel. His whole being seemed to change after that. They came to live in Albany Street a few hundred yards from where we lived and I inevitably saw a good deal of both of them. But physically things had gone too far. Do you think people realised what the strain of conducting and performing in public took out of his excessively nervous temperament?[65]

ApIvor, a frequent visitor to Albany Street, has described the 'gloomy front room, the chief decoration of [which] was strange faded newspaper clippings containing ridiculous jokes and cartoons which had amused [Constant]. Also scattered about the room were scraps of paper with cryptic messages to Isabel couched in terms of the profoundest obscurity.'[66] ApIvor was often a drinking companion:

> I visited nearly every pub within a wide radius of his Albany Street home with him. Occasionally he would make a tour starting in Albany Street, and working via the York and Albany and the Edinburgh Castle down Delancey Street to a pub the other side of the Camden High Road where there was usually a stall with shell-fish to which he was very partial. I used every now and again to come across him sitting alone in the Edinburgh Castle in their garden-like enclosure. One of the main reasons for his being there was that at the bottom of the said garden ran the main line expresses. Bad leg and all, he would suddenly spring up and go limping along to the edge to observe the spectacle of an interesting locomotive. This place also had a good expanse of sky looking west and he would observe the sunset on suitable evenings.

Isabel found the reaction of Constant's circle of friends to their marriage amusing:

> Lady Wimborne said, her eyes opening wide: 'Oh, you are so unlike all the others!'[67] Patrick Hadley invited us to dinner, and after a sidelong glance, he said to Constant, 'Where did you find her?' Lord Berners: 'Oh, such nice hand-made work' referring to an elegant black dress I had bought second-hand from a well-known shop in Paris.

But she was under no illusions as to the problems she had brought upon herself by marrying Constant:

> Constant thought that if he married me I would bring him back to life. His friends thought so too. He was a sad man and a sick man, and [a] lonely man. He had been a public figure since a young man, had acquaintances of all kinds, only

---

[64] Letter to Alan Frank, n.d., 39 Thurloe Square crossed out and 197 Albany St. written instead.
[65] Letter (typed) from Denis ApIvor to Hubert Foss, 16 April [1952]: Hubert Foss Archive.
[66] Letter (typed) from Denis ApIvor to Angus Morrison, 9 March 1954: RCM Archive.
[67] Alice Wimborne, Walton's companion, was soon to die, on 17 April 1948, from cancer of the bronchus.

four close friends. He was a loner. This was not apparent to most people. He hid behind a carapace of wit, sharp remarks and great vitality.

Constant used to go by himself on a pub crawl to somewhere where he was not known such as the Isle of the Dogs, which in those days was desolate and bombed, or Hackney, or elsewhere in the East End. He liked working class areas. He knew he was drinking too much and was prepared to try and drink less.

As a result of the move Anthony Powell now saw Constant more frequently, as he recorded in his memoirs:

> After their marriage Constant and Isabel Lambert took part of a house, 197 Albany Street, only a short way up the road from Chester Gate. I had come across Lambert only a few times during the war, but now began to see him again more regularly. By this period he was in rather a shaky condition. In general his drinking had not diminished, but he would have interludes when he hardly drank at all – that happened once when the Lamberts came to dinner, again when they themselves gave a party – but during such abstinences he would be in an odd state, sometimes silent, sometimes convulsed with laughter.
>
> Our chief exchanges, anyway most coherent ones, began to settle into a pattern of Lambert making long telephone calls to me relatively late at night. He would ring up between half-past eleven and midnight, discussing at great length things which had amused him during the day. This would happen especially on Sunday evenings, when Lambert liked to go through what had appeared on the book pages of the Sunday papers.[68]

It was in Albany Street that occurred one of those curious 'happenings' for which Lambert was renowned. As Ayrton remembered:

> Constant challenged those present to put on a show. Well, no-one could. 'Watch this!' he said. And round the corner of the turning out of Regent's Park came a compact group of Negroes of both sexes dressed from head to foot in tartan and all riding tricycles. 'The MacGregor tartan,' Constant said with great satisfaction.[69]

In November 1947, Hugo Rignold made his first conducting appearance with the Sadler's Wells Ballet, opening the season with *Giselle* and *Boutique fantasque* with Fonteyn. Ballets that Constant had premiered, *Checkmate* (its first staging since the Holland tour) and *Adam Zero*, followed soon after. But two weeks later, on 26 November, Constant was entrusted with the English premiere of Massine's ballet *Mam'zelle Angot* taken from Lecocq's operetta *La Fille de Mme Angot* with Fonteyn, Alexander Grant, Moira Shearer and Michael Somes. The décor was by Derain.

That month, in a Third Programme concert of Balakirev, Roussel and his own *Music for Orchestra*, he included Bax's *The Tale the Pine Trees Knew*. Constant had rather ambivalent views towards the music of Arnold Bax and rarely conducted any, but according to Harriet Cohen he particularly loved this work, probably because of its Sibelian sparseness.[70] After its first performance Bax had written to her that 'Constant was quite excited over it'[71] while, wearing his *Sunday Referee* hat, he had written that there were 'two very bad things about it: a) the whimsy title b) the unexpected loud

---

[68] Powell, *Faces in My Time*, pp. 221–2.

[69] *Constant Lambert Remembered*, BBC Third Network, 25 June 1966.

[70] Lewis Foreman, *Bax: A Composer and his Times*, 3rd edn (Woodbridge: Boydell Press, 2007), p. 409.

[71] *Ibid.*, p. 312

note with which it ends. Otherwise it is the best of the several new works by Bax we have heard this season.'[72]

Isabel and Constant's first Christmas together as a married couple was spent at Tom Driberg's, their host afterwards receiving the following letter, typically with an (unidentified) enclosure:

> My dear old torch-singing, strip-teasing, ex-stamp collecting, erstwhile Oxonian defender of our so-called (or should I say 'self-styled'?) liberties, I do so sincerely hope that you will find the enclosed brochure helpful.
>
> May I add (in hasty parenthesis) that the music (inspired equally by Adam & Addams) which I ever so turgidly penned at your cottage orné in that Ultima Thule of all rare artists Bradwell-juxta-Mare was of so macabre an order that even the ranks of Korda could scarce retain a tear.
>
> Toujours à vous
> CL [monogram][73]

The mention of Korda refers to the 'important' film score commission he had alluded to in his letter of resignation to David Webster and which Walton also mentioned just after Christmas when writing to Cecil Gray in Capri: 'Constant is as you may have heard, happily married & back composing if even only for the film "Anna Karenina". But he's altogether much better.'[74] He spent much of Christmas and Boxing Day in the octagon room at Bradwell Lodge working on the film music at a small old upright Bord piano that Driberg had resurrected from the old wing of his house.

Sadly, Alexander Korda's *Anna Karenina*, which had its London premiere on 22 January 1948, was to bring him little credit. The costumes were designed by Cecil Beaton and the principal characters were taken by Vivien Leigh, Kieron Moore and Ralph Richardson. The film might have had greater success had, as Korda had hoped, Laurence Olivier starred alongside Leigh, but Olivier was busy directing and taking the lead role in his own film of *Hamlet*. Moore proved to be a very weak Vronsky ('Mr Kieron Moore does not altogether succeed in making a full man out of Vronsky and Sir Ralph Richardson is allowed only to sketch in the outline of Karenin', wrote *The Times* critic), and the film suffered by comparison with the 1935 version in which Greta Garbo had starred with Fredric March. It had been a chance for Constant to prove his mettle against Walton, who had had great success with his score for Olivier's 1944 film of *Henry V*, soon to be followed by *Hamlet* for which he was also composing the music, and Constant had been eager to take on his first feature film score,[75] as Isabel remembered:

> Constant was extremely pleased and excited when he was offered the writing of a score for the film of *Anna Karenina*. ... He was longing to adventure into a new medium, felt he was destined to do this particular film as it was Russian. ... He immediately became fascinated by the studios and all the people who worked there. Like many people who work alone, he found it stimulating to be among

---

[72] *Sunday Referee*, 15 April 1934. After the score of *The Tale the Pine Trees Knew* was printed Bax altered the final chord to a *pianissimo*.

[73] Letter from Lambert to Driberg, 30 December 1947, with old notepaper headed 39 Thurloe Square, SW7.

[74] Letter from William Walton (at Ashby St Ledgers, Rugby) to Cecil Gray, 27 December 1947, in Walton, *Selected Letters*, p. 165.

[75] According to Francis Routh, this film was Humphrey Searle's introduction to the film industry because Lambert was unable to complete the score in time. Francis Routh, *Humphrey Searle*, http://www.musicweb-international.com/searle/routhhs.htm.

others, working on the same thing. The score was produced on time and pleased director Duvivier ... also apparently Vivien Leigh. I went to the studios with Kit Lambert to see the final showing in the studios. An interesting day.

The percussionist James Blades had memories of his involvement in the film score. Hubert Clifford, who was to conduct the sound track, had asked him to meet Constant and discuss the possibility of obtaining three bells that would match as near as possible the sound of those in St Ivan's Church in the Kremlin:

> Connie, a perfectionist, had carefully checked the pitch of these huge bells (the largest of which weighed nearly sixty tons) and had arranged a sequence in his score accordingly. Genuine church bells of the size of the Kremlin bells were out of the question, so Messrs. Boosey & Hawkes kindly experimented with bronze tubing, and tubular bells measuring up to fifteen feet in length proved satisfactory. They were suspended from a cross section in the roofing and a high platform erected to allow the percussionist to strike the tubes at the upper end. After the bell player nearly broke his neck in reaching the top of the platform, it was discovered that the bells sounded just the same when struck at the lower end.[76]

Probably the most sympathetic review came from Scott Goddard in *Penguin Music Magazine*:

> The one really considerable event in film music during January was Constant Lambert's score for *Anna Karenina*. Much had been expected of this, and with reason. The subject offered immense possibilities for the director of the film and so by implication for the composer of the music. The composer in question was known to be a musician of resource and great ability. There were those who for many years had regretted that so much of his time had been taken by executant's work instead of being given to the infinitely more exacting and rare work of creation. But now, we said, Lambert has left Covent Garden and our loss there will surely be our gain in other places, that is to say, in *Anna Karenina*.
>
> I went three times to this film within the space of a week. ... The first visit to *Anna Karenina* was nothing but acid disillusionment. But then, I had approached the film as an onlooker and not as a listener; the eye had usurped the rights of the ear. The second visit, when I forced myself to listen to the music, was more heartening, though I came away from that attempt hardly less clear in my mind as to the value of the music or rather its quality. ... It took a third visit to discover the real character and essential quality of Lambert's music. I don't think that the music will for long be remembered. The odds, the film odds, are too strong for it, seeing that in itself it is a subtle and delicate art. Seeing also that what surrounds it is so much less subtle or delicate and so much more instant in its appeal to the public, who will go to see Vivien Leigh and the astonishing performance of Sir Ralph Richardson.
>
> At that third hearing I began to try to face the problem of deciding what was and what was not Constant Lambert. Glinka, I said to myself during the scene in the ballroom, and was thankful to have this confirmed by one who knew (not Mr Tom Driberg, MP, who, I was relieved to find, had also discovered this fact for himself). But the absence of any music which one could, as it were, put one's finger on and say 'that is by Lambert' was intriguing and extraordinarily puzzling. He would be a foolhardy man who would vouch for having disentangled Glinka from Lambert, the quotations from the original text. In this film the two are

---

[76] Blades, *Drum Roll*, p. 202.

as close as some composers' English folk-music is close to their own type of utterance.

This is a bare score. The texture of the music is mainly transparent, a fact that will not surprise anyone who knows Lambert's work. ... And if I say that no one will remember this music, that is partly because no one in his senses will want to remember the film it so excellently and, alas! so adequately accompanies, and because it has either been given or has taken too little opportunity.[77]

If he was to make use of the music of any Russian composer, that he should choose Glinka comes as no surprise, and the extracts he selected came from the *Valse-fantaisie*, the overture to *Ruslan and Ludmila* and from *A Life for the Tsar*. He also used the prelude to Tchaikovsky's *Eugene Onegin*. As Richard Shead has pointed out, Constant used genuine Russian music for ball and theatre scenes; elsewhere it was his own original music. The score is effective enough for the purpose of film music to create moods, but it is hardly distinguished when separated from its visual counterpart. However, it took on a new lease of life when in 1975 the American conductor and composer Bernard Herrmann recorded a four-movement suite for a Decca LP of 'Great English Film Music'.[78] More recently, Philip Lane has arranged a more extensive suite of ten sections for a Chandos recording of film music by Lambert and Berners. With the sound of bells providing more than a hint of the opening of the Coronation Scene in Mussorgsky's *Boris Godunov*, the Overture (especially in Bernard Herrmann's recording of the Suite) also has the feel of a powerful locomotive pulling out of a station, with the cymbal clashes suggestive of great emissions of steam, appropriate for the important part that trains take in this tragic tale. Constant himself wrote that 'the St Petersburg–Moscow railway line is almost as important as the characters' and, remembering how his forebears had worked on the Russian railways, added: 'My feelings when writing the music for the railway sequences were naturally of a mingled mature. ... The only passage ...which I found actually galling was when the locomotive's wheels were slipping on the rails. A device to eliminate this unfortunate occurrence is still (or so I am informed) in use on the Trans-Siberian railway and is known as the "Lambert wet-sander".'[79]

After the release of *Anna Karenina*, Constant was relatively inactive in the first months of 1948, with only a handful of broadcasts. He and Isabel spent a few days at Driberg's at the end of March, but by contrast May was a very busy month indeed, beginning with BBC concerts on two consecutive days, and then, starting on the 7th, a tour of the north of England with the Hallé Orchestra, conducting nine concerts over 17 days with a mainly Russian repertoire.[80] He visited Wolverhampton, Sheffield, Morecambe, Preston, Middlesborough, Newcastle, Rochdale and Hanley, ending up at Manchester. Three days into the tour he wrote to his mother:

[77] Scott Goddard, 'Music of the Film' [*Anna Karenina*], *Penguin Music Magazine* no. 7 (1948), pp. 88–9.

[78] Writing in the *New York Herald Tribune*, December 1946, Herrmann grouped Lambert with Britten, Walton and Rawsthorne as those of the younger generation of English composers who were 'writing in a more universal modernism. Their music is eclectic, and brilliant, and stands exporting well.' On 15 March 1945, Herrmann wrote to Cecil Gray: 'My admiration grows for Lambert's *Summer's Last Will and Testament* the more I study it.'

[79] Lambert, 'Myself and Russian Music', p. 7.

[80] The repertoire for the tour with the Hallé Orchestra was Beethoven, Overture *Coriolan*; Borodin, *Polovstian Dances* (*Prince Igor*); Glinka, Overture *Ruslan and Ludmila*; Handel, Concerto Grosso; Prokofiev, *Peter and the Wolf* (speaker George Baker); Rimsky-Korsakov, *Dance of the Buffoons* and *Flight of the Bumble Bee*; Rimsky-Korsakov, *Scheherazade*; Shostakovich, Symphony No 9; Smetana, *Vltava* and Tchaikovsky, *Manfred* Symphony (first movement only).

My dear Mother,

So sorry not to have written before but this is my first free moment since I 'phoned you. The tour so far has been most successful and the general ambience far from unpleasant. The orchestra are not only first rate (particularly the strings) but an extremely pleasant crowd to be with. I stay in Manchester and go round with them by motor coach. Once out of Manchester it is lovely. Here to Sheffield over the moors and here to Morecambe through NW Lancashire are both very good trips, though Morecambe on a Sunday afternoon is not the ideal ambience for *Scheherazade*.

No concert to-day so went to the Art Gallery. Knock-out collection of Holman Hunts, and a very strange collection of medallion portraits in grisaille of poets by Blake. The portraits obviously copied from engravings, the fantastic decorations on each side obviously original. The gallery is more or less back to its old shape – Birds in Flight[81] is on view again but not too well placed. – Side view against a wall, most irritating, but what can you expect from a gallery that states on a painting of Derain's that he died in 1916. What will London think tomorrow? Dashed off an interim present to Kit (2 Puffin books – all I could get).

It's pleasant to be busy again. Will write later. Hope the rheumatism is much better.[82]

Even more pleasant had been the invitation to share with Ninette de Valois and Frederick Ashton the artistic direction of the Sadler's Wells Ballet Company, and while touring with the Hallé Orchestra he replied to David Webster:

Dear David,

You must think me very casual not having written before. But as you know I have been <u>literally</u> snowed under with scores & start working on my 3rd & most difficult programme tomorrow. ...

This cannot be a long business letter for obvious reasons. It is only to say that I shall be very pleased to accept the post you offer me at Covent Garden at the fee suggested (£500). ... I look forward very much to giving the ballet my utmost help.

My best wishes to Ninette & Fred.

This appointment took effect from 18 June and Constant confirmed the agreement in writing on 23 June. His services as stated were to involve 'general musical advice and supervision, the contacting of composers and publishers, examination of submitted scores, etc.' and 'as in the past close collaboration with Miss de Valois and Mr Frederick Ashton as regards general policy, choice of designers, etc.' Any appearances as guest conductor or the preparation of a score would be paid extra.

Things were at last beginning to look up and it was with some optimism that he was able to write of future plans to his mother who was assisting with his ever-present worry, finances.

My dear Mother,

So sorry not to have written before but this tour though extremely enjoyable and worthwhile in every way has been a little tiring and frequently after a long day's travelling and playing I have to sit up writing business letters including ones in French to Paris where I am conducting on June 3rd with an interesting

---

[81] *Birds in Flight* is a brass sculpture by Maurice Lambert first exhibited in February 1926 in London.

[82] Letter from Lambert to his mother, 10 May 1948, on Midland Hotel, Manchester notepaper.

modern English programme.[83] Writing the programme notes in French was difficult but Isabel has corrected the grammar and they have been sent off in time.

We go to Paris the day after my concert in London (Sunday week). It will be a great treat for both of us as we have had had no holiday since we married and hope to stay for a few days after my hectic rehearsing. I have my last and most important Hallé concert at the Opera House tomorrow.[84] I gather it is practically sold out which is not bad for Whit-week in Manchester when they close down on everything except religious processions. Have been asked to do several concerts here next season including a large scale choral, orchestral and brass band concert in the circus ring at Bellevue. Hope to write a piece for the sea-lions at the same time (I have now got the entrée to their training quarters).

The working days have been hard but interesting. Days off in Manchester have been very dull apart from the Zoo but I have managed to get through business letters and read some Shakespeares[85] which I knew only slightly or had forgotten. Troilus and Cressida is as marvellous as All's Well that Ends Well is boring. Now re-reading Measure for Measure.

Sent off a bird-book to Kit (serious illustrations and scientific notes) to atone for my rather perfunctory gesture.

Clifford (of London Films) wants to see me urgently re future prospects. So things seem to be looking up at last after a period which not unnaturally led to bitterness. Not that all is clear by any means but the combined invitations of the Hallé and the Orchestre Nationale have consoled me for neglect in my home town.

As regards finance (which I loathe discussing as you know) your suggested present will be more than welcome and I hope it won't embarrass you in any way. It was unfortunate that I should have to pay double rent at a time when jobs were fading away. But with your help I shall be able to start on clear ground once again and with my life settled we shall both be able to concentrate on our work without worry and interference. I can't tell you how grateful I am.

I hope Maurice appreciated my card. I would have got some others were it not for Whit-week closing.

I was very sorry to see about Dick Wyndham[86] and slightly irritated that all the papers referred to him as a reporter and never mentioned his painting which though not of great importance was very charming and highly competent. But after all even Andrew Marvell has a statue to him in which (I mean on which) he is described merely as M.P.

Must now brush up my Shostakovich and swallow what passes for food in this town. Will ring you when I get back.

With much love and many thanks.[87]

The hope of another film score commission led to nothing, but of greater immediacy was the London concert, on 30 May, the first of two at the Winter Garden Theatre,

---

[83] Boyce, Symphony No 1 (Vaughan Williams, *Tallis Fantasia* originally planned but replaced); Rawsthorne, *Symphonic Studies*; Walton, *Viola Concerto*; Lambert, *Music for Orchestra*.

[84] An all-Russian programme, including Shostakovich's Symphony No. 9.

[85] As Isabel Lambert wrote in her memoirs: '[Constant] never went on a journey without a pocket edition of one of Shakespeare's plays. He knew many of the poems by heart and would often recite them which was a great pleasure as he was a gifted reader with an eloquent delivery.'

[86] Richard Wyndham (1896–1948), artist.

[87] Letter from Lambert to his mother, 22 May 1948, from The Midland Hotel, Manchester.

Drury Lane with the London Symphony Orchestra. It consisted of Balakirev's *King Lear* Overture, Searle's *Night Music*, Liszt's *Malediction* (the work that had brought him and Searle together) with Kyla Greenbaum as soloist, the Suite from *Horoscope*, and Sibelius's Third Symphony. In the second concert, on 20 June, he shared an all-Liszt programme with Charles Brill: Constant conducted *Hamlet*, *Szardas Macabre* (orchestrated by Searle, a first performance); *Les Morts* with Valentine Dyall as the speaker (a first public performance in England)[88] and *Mephisto Waltz* No. 2. In the second half Brill conducted the *Faust* Symphony, no doubt much to Constant's annoyance as it was a work he himself had long wanted to conduct. (His opportunity was to come in the following year.) He later wrote a warm appraisal of Brill:

> Having known Mr Charles Brill for a number of years, mainly through his considerable reputation on the lighter side of music, I was very pleased to be asked to share with him a series of symphony concerts in London last year, in which the programmes showed great enterprise and in which he showed a complete grasp of the complex scores involved.

Such a recommendation was an act of kindness on Constant's part because, having, as a pacifist, deserted from the Royal Army Service Corps during the war, Brill had afterwards given himself up and served a spell in Dartmoor. These concerts, financed by a cousin of the designer Oliver Messel, were an attempt to rehabilitate him. Constant would have enjoyed the irony that the only choir available at the time for the choral finale in the *Faust* Symphony was the London Police Choir, especially when preliminary rehearsals had taken place in a police station.

When the Proms came round that year, Constant had only one engagement, to conduct his suite from *Horoscope*. As luck would have it, his part of the programme was not broadcast so he did not receive the additional broadcasting fee.[89] Four days short of his 43rd birthday *Rio Grande*, which had now become something of a favourite at the Proms, was also given, but conducted by Stanford Robinson. The birthday was passed instead at Tom Driberg's, Constant ruefully writing in the visitors' book:

> 'Tomorrow more's the pity, away we both must hie'[90] was written by (a) Keats (b) Gilbert (c) Skelton (d) Wilhelmina Stitch (e) T. S. Eliot? A composer's as old as he feels & this one feels a damn sight more than 43. CL [monogram]

In September Constant was in his element, back in Paris with Sadler's Wells for a fortnight at the Théâtre des Champs-Elysées, sharing the conducting with Warwick Braithwaite.[91] 'The music direction can be praised without reserve,' reported Ferdinand Reyna in *Ballet Today*. Isabel joined Constant and took the opportunity of introducing him to some of her French friends. She took him to visit Giacometti in his studio, and she later commented that he showed unusual reserve at the meeting, both men walking with sticks. But what amazed her was Constant's instant understanding of the artist's elongated sculptures: 'When we left he wrote down on a piece of paper his impression of what they were and the curious thing to me is that he understood the aim behind

---

[88] Lambert had given the first studio performance in England in his first concert for the Third Programme in October 1946.

[89] £13 2 6.

[90] From A. E. Housman's *Fancy's Knell*, set by Vaughan Williams in 1927 in the song-cycle *Along the Field*.

[91] The repertoire included *Miracle in the Gorbals*, a full length *Swan Lake*, *Les Sylphides*, *Dante Sonata*, *Symphonic Variations*, *Les Patineurs*, *Scènes de Ballet*, *The Rake's Progress*, *Checkmate* and *Job*. The Company were led by Fonteyn and Helpmann.

them, this question of space, and seeing things in distance; he just wrote it down in a sentence on a piece of paper.'

Constant then suggested that they visit Darius Milhaud whom he had known years before.

> He happened to be in Paris at that time and went up to see him in his flat in Montmartre and it was very moving because Milhaud was a fairly ill man and had been living in America for some time and when he saw Constant after all these years this was absolutely marvellous and they both enjoyed it like anything. Madame Milhaud grumbled at the lack of performances of her husband's music; otherwise it was a pleasant evening. We went to the Jeu de Paume where Constant felt like crying.[92] It was all over in about three days and we were home.[93]

Always keen to promote French music, only two months earlier Constant had written to Mrs Marie Riefenstahl, cousin of the composer Reynaldo Hahn (who, like Lambert, was often seen at the piano with a cigarette dangling from his mouth): 'I was a very great friend of Reynaldo Hahn's and when he died I suggested to the Third Programme a memorial concert of his works presented by myself. But they didn't seem sufficiently interested ...'[94]

The few days in Paris brought the couple together in their two common interests, art and things French. Isabel was particularly impressed by Constant's deep appreciation of art, and when back in London she took him to the Royal Academy for the first exhibition since before the war of the French impressionists, she noticed that he was moved to tears.

Constant did not go on with Sadler's Wells to Germany, but he was back on 25 November to open the London season with the premiere of *Don Juan*, an Ashton ballet with music by Richard Strauss and décor by Edward Burra. He approached the occasion with some trepidation, writing beforehand to his mother: 'Just off for the opening of the ballet at Covent Garden[,] a place where I feel still slightly ill at ease being received with the mingled welcome and suspicion that greets a cat that has been lost for a week.'[95] With a general air of concern at Constant's state, Markova, who danced three performances of *The Sleeping Beauty* that year, had been warned that he would not be his old self. But she found that she had no need to worry. 'I must say, in my performances he was just the same,' she recalled. 'I remember I had only two weeks to learn *Sleeping Beauty*, but I had such faith in him. ... He was a great musician; he was so reliable and yet it wasn't boring. It was always alive and fresh and yet I never had to worry about tempi.'[96] It was after mounting the podium for a performance of *The Sleeping Beauty* that he turned to Thomas Matthews, the leader of the orchestra, and said: 'When the pas de trois becomes the pas de six, I know that it's time for me to go home.'[97]

Nevertheless the opening night was marred by two happenings: one for which

---

[92] The Jeu de Paume was a French impressionist museum which the Nazis had used for storing their confiscated art. Hitler's henchmen kept photographic records of everything they stole, and the curator took the negatives home at night and copied them.

[93] From Isabel Rawsthorne's diaries and *In Search of Constant Lambert*, BBC2, 26 July 1965.

[94] Hahn died on 28 January 1947. Letter from Lambert at 197 Albany Street to Mrs Riefenstahl (formerly Marie Nordlinger), 13 July 1948. He did at least manage to have Hahn's *The Muses* included in the Third Programme on 7 July 1948.

[95] Letter from Lambert to his mother, 25 October 1948.

[96] Motion, *The Lamberts*, p. 244.

[97] Tooley, *In House*, p. 125. In *Step by Step*, p. 54, de Valois places this anecdote in New York after a performance of *Le Lac des cygnes*.

Warwick Braithwaite, who was in charge of the rest of the programme, was ticked off by a critic for not retrieving an error in *Les Patineurs* when one of the dancers led off her sequence of fouettés too soon; and the other, more serious, in *Don Juan* when Fonteyn strained a ligament, sufficient to put her out of action again for three months. In her autobiography she described her feelings at that time with unusual candour:

> The experience of being unable to dance and unable to find another direction in my life was a major personal crisis. It was turning point, in that I was forced to take stock of myself for the first time. I was twenty-nine years old ... emotionally my need to love far outweighed my need to be loved. The person whom I loved most and depended on most was Fred, but in the way of a friend, mentor and master, the man I could marry did not apparently exist, and without such a love I would descend into the abyss when my career ended.[98]

It was partly the success at Christmas of Ashton's new version of *Cinderella* (with music by Prokofiev), with the principal role alternating between Moira Shearer and Violetta Elvin, that fired Fonteyn's desire to return – which she did triumphantly on 25 March, with Braithwaite conducting.

Just before Christmas another side of Constant's musical tastes came to the fore when he conducted a 'Light Orchestral Concert' of Russian music in – rather unexpectedly – the Third Programme. In November, Compton Mackenzie, the novelist and co-founder of *Gramophone* magazine, had given a broadcast talk 'What is Light Music?', after which Beecham conducted a programme of light music. Perhaps in an attempt to relieve the station of its 'high-brow' tag, this was followed in the coming weeks by similar programmes, conducted in turn by Stanford Robinson, Josef Krips (with the Vienna Philharmonic Orchestra), Barbirolli and the Hallé, and Lambert in an all-Russian programme with the Philharmonia Orchestra. He was to be much associated with light music, as the following March he conducted the Philharmonia again in a Light Music Festival broadcast from the Kingsway Hall on the BBC's Light Programme. The other conductors in a week of programmes were Muir Mathieson, Sidney Torch, Michael Krein, Hugo Rignold and Stanford Robinson. Constant prefaced his concert with an article for *Radio Times* (and named, like Compton Mackenzie's talk, 'What is Light Music?') in which he wrote: 'During the war, when I did a number of concerts for ENSA, both for the Forces and for war-workers, it was my custom to play a Sousa march as an encore'[99] and he began his programme with Sousa's *Stars and Stripes Forever!*, including as well an overture by von Suppé (on whom he gave a radio talk in April) and his own *Elegiac Blues*. Then in January and February 1950 he was given a six-week series entitled 'Constant Lambert's Music at Eight' on Monday evenings in the BBC Light Programme. Lasting three-quarters of an hour, they were given with the Philharmonia Orchestra before an invited audience at the Kingsway Hall. As T. W. Chalmers, Controller of the Light Programme, had noted in a memo: 'Had lunch with Constant Lambert and discussed idea of a series of programmes of light music during the summer. Not British light music, Haydn Wood / Eric Coates stuff, but continental music that is often badly and inadequately played by orchestras that are far too small.' Sousa, Waldteufel, von Suppé, Chabrier, Delibes, Glinka, Rossini and Bizet were among the many composers represented.

Christmas 1948 was spent once again at Bradwell-juxta-Mare from where on Boxing Day Constant quite possibly listened in to his pre-recorded talk on 'Cats in Music' for the BBC *Music Magazine*. As Julian Herbage, the programme's co-presenter,

---

[98] Fonteyn, *Autobiography*, pp. 130–1.
[99] *Radio Times*, 25 March 1949.

remembered: 'Lambert was always dogged by technical failure whenever he broadcast. ... [He] contributed to *Music Magazine* splendid articles on such subjects as Sousa, Chabrier, Berners, Walton and Cats in Music. In recording the last he had to begin five or six times because of technical faults, and when at last he spoke, his voice quivered with suppressed anger.'[100]

In the new year, to his great delight he was asked back to conduct the Hallé Orchestra, beginning on 9 January with a large-scale choral concert in the King's Hall, Belle Vue, Manchester that included *Belshazzar's Feast* and *The Rio Grande*.[101] Four days later, in EMI's Abbey Road studios, he re-recorded *The Rio Grande* almost 19 years to the day after making the famous version with Hamilton Harty as pianist. This time the soloists were Gladys Ripley and Kyla Greenbaum, with the BBC Chorus and the Philharmonia Orchestra. He later told Kyla that he preferred her playing to Harty's – even though a prominent wrong note went uncorrected and was only digitally rectified many years later for one of its CD transfers. The following day he recorded movements from *Horoscope* and *Apparitions*. *Aubade héroïque* was also recorded at these sessions but, sadly, was not issued. Then in February he had five further dates with the Hallé, in Leeds, Harrogate and Sheffield.[102]

In March he was back at Covent Garden, conducting a revival of *Apparitions* with Helpmann and Fonteyn in their original roles, and with a new scenario by Cecil Beaton. The ballet had not yet been seen on the larger stage and such revivals were a test as to how these seasoned ballets would adapt. In this case the transition was very successful and Constant must have been warmed by the audience's response when he entered the pit. For Mary Clarke 'the abiding memory of that evening is of the great ovation which was accorded to him, quite spontaneously, by the audience. ... It was louder and longer than the applause which greeted the ballet itself when the curtain fell.'[103] As she had written in *Ballet Today*: 'The ovation that Lambert received when he conducted the first performances was an emphatic assertion by the audience (which is getting remarkably articulate these days) of how it had missed him, how it valued what he meant to Sadler's Wells and, perhaps, what it had thought of the orchestra during the rest of the spring season.'[104]

He continued to be heavily involved with the Third Programme, with a pre-recorded broadcast on New Year's Day of Handel's *Alexander's Feast* with the Philharmonia Orchestra, and later in January there followed two performances of John Dryden's *King Arthur* with music by Purcell that caused John Lowe of the BBC to write: 'I cannot hope to hear better conducting of Purcell than was done by Constant Lambert. The players provided by the New London Orchestra were not all of the first rank.' Also for the Third Programme, in March he conducted Handel's *Semele* (the performance was given a repeat broadcast a week later) and, showing his wide range of sympathies, a Vivaldi programme in April. He had also been asked to give Busoni's massive piano concerto with the young Noel Mewton-Wood as soloist,[105] but the proposed date clashed with

---

[100] Julian Herbage, '50 Years of Music Talks', BBC *Music Magazine*, 24 December 1972.

[101] Kyla Greenbaum and Marjorie Thomas were the soloists in *The Rio Grande*.

[102] The programmes included symphonies by Beethoven, Haydn, Sibelius and Tchaikovsky, piano concertos by Chopin, Grieg and Liszt, and smaller works by Balakirev, Berlioz, Bizet, Borodin, Debussy, Dukas, Glazunov, Grétry, Handel, Liadov and Rimsky-Korsakov, as well as his own *Aubade héroïque*. It is said that while conducting the latter work at Leeds, Lambert collapsed and the performance was not completed.

[103] Clarke, *The Sadler's Wells Ballet*, p. 234.

[104] Mary Clarke, *Ballet Today*, May–June 1949, pp. 5–6.

[105] Noel Mewton-Wood (1922–53), Australian pianist of considerable promise who took his own life. Beecham had conducted him in the Busoni concerto in the Third Progamme in January

his visit to Sicily in April where he was to conduct at the ISCM Festival. Humphrey Searle was involved in the Festival and wrote in his memoirs:

> The Palermo ISCM Festival took place in April 1949. The Italian Radio were providing the orchestra, and the preliminary rehearsals took place in Rome. Edward Clark and Elisabeth Lutyens went directly to Palermo, and my job was to supervise these rehearsals. This proved rather complicated, as no proper rehearsal schedule had been worked out, and all the conductors naturally wanted as much rehearsal time as possible. ...
>
> Constant Lambert arrived in Palermo to conduct the British works in the Festival. After a period of depression early in 1947, he had married Isabel Delmer whom he had known before the war, and he now seemed much happier. But he was not in a good state of health and it was as much as he could do to conduct the rehearsals and concerts.[106]

Isabel went with Constant, seizing the chance for them to travel through Italy on their way to Sicily. As she recalled:

> At that time Constant was already showing signs of illness so in that way it was a bit dodgy, but it was absolutely marvellous. We continued a whole week of just going to look at things we'd neither of us seen before, things like the Sistine Chapel and things like that, and then down to Sicily. There was a place called Aqua Santa which is outside Palermo and there we sat for a very long time just looking at the sea.'[107]

The second part of the Festival took place at Taormina where the guests were put in a luxury hotel with a spectacular view, with Mount Etna as a back-drop. However, the concert hall, which was in the hotel itself, was not very satisfactory. And there were other far from satisfactory features of the Festival, as Elisabeth Lutyens wrote:

> The programme here was described as a 'Concert for Small Orchestral Complexes and it is important to underline that it constitutes the first essay and the first step in the perspected direction without any pretence towards immediate efficacy'. The lack of 'pretence towards immediate efficacy' involved the absence of the harp (discovered, some two hours later, still at the station) and lack of any stands for the players. A prie-dieu was unearthed for Constant to conduct from and a 'Mickey Mouse' stand labelled 'Happy boys' for Max Rostal.[108] The rehearsal continued far into the night, just under our bedroom![109]

At the Festival Constant conducted works by Lennox Berkeley, Mátyás Seiber and Searle. One of the Palermo concerts was recorded by the BBC for a broadcast in July, with Constant conducting Searle's *Fuga giocoso* while other works were conducted by Carlo Maria Giulini and Roger Désormière (who in 1926 had conducted the Paris performances of Constant's *Romeo and Juliet*). As Isabel recorded in her

---

1948. Lambert had accompanied him in a broadcast on 24 November 1945 in Beethoven's Piano Concerto No. 3, the work with which he had made his London début in 1940. Lambert's Piano Sonata was in Mewton-Wood's repertoire.

[106] Searle, *Quadrille with a Raven*, chapter 11.

[107] Isabel Rawsthorne talking in *In Search of Constant Lambert*, BBC2, 26 July 1965.

[108] Max Rostal (1905–91), Austrian-born violinist who settled in England in 1934 and taught at the Guildhall School of Music from 1944 until 1958. Noted as an exponent of contemporary music.

[109] Lutyens, *A Goldfish Bowl*, p. 193.

memoirs, Constant's chance meeting with Désormière revealed some Covent Garden machinations of which he had been unaware:

> It was now over a year since David Webster, then General Administrator of the Opera House, had approached on behalf of the ballet the French conductor Roger Désormière if he would become the chief conductor for ballet. Désormière who knew Constant long ago in the Diaghilev days also knew of his reputation as conductor and musical director of the Royal Ballet and was astonished by this offer. We met Désormière who told Constant he had refused Sir David's offer as he was more interested in working with opera; nor did he want to come a lot to England. Later on he came to Covent Garden with a splendid performance of *Pelléas et Mélisande* with a French cast and a French designer. Constant was understandably disturbed by the encounter.

Constant stayed on in Sicily after the Festival to finish a commission for the British section of the ISCM, his *Trois pièces nègres sur les touches blanches* for piano duet. It received its first performance on 17 May in a Third Programme broadcast of contemporary music. Dedicated to Edward Clark, the work's performers were the sisters duo Mary and Geraldine Peppin. Written in the key of C to avoid any black notes, as the title suggests, the *Trois pièces* include a sprightly 'Aubade' (*vif et nerveux*), a more relaxed 'Siesta' (*calme*) and a lively, syncopated 'Nocturne' (*nonchalant, langoureux*) that puts one in mind of the popular *Jamaican Rumba* that Arthur Benjamin had written for another piano duo, Joan and Valerie Trimble. Constant had a special admiration for Geraldine Peppin, the wife of the English poet Randall Swingler,[110] she having occasionally played for the Sadler's Wells ballet while on tour without orchestra during the war; her sister, with Angus Morrison, had often accompanied for the Ballet Rambert. The broadcast also included the first performance of Searle's first large-scale serial composition, a setting for two speakers, male chorus and orchestra of an extensive narrative poem by Edith Sitwell, *Gold Coast Customs*, which he dedicated to Constant. As he himself wrote:

> I had asked Constant to conduct the work, but he preferred to share the speaking part with Edith. The performance took place before an invited audience in the Concert Hall of Broadcasting House; while in Palermo Constant had finished his *Trois Pièces Nègres sur les Touches Blanches* for the same concert. The pianists in both works were the Peppin twins, Geraldine and Mary, who had recently made their concert debut and were young and glamorous-looking. Constant and Edith sat at a table; Edith in a long gold cloak; Constant conducted Edith, and at times appeared to be conducting the conductor of the orchestra as well. The performance went very well and the audience seemed to be impressed; at any rate the BBC immediately arranged two further studio broadcasts of the work later in the year.[111]

Edith Sitwell gave an introductory talk. 'Did you ever see Constant do that "Gold-Coast Customs" thing of Humphrey's in which he had to shout, conduct, and keep an eye on Edith Sitwell for 35 minutes?' Denis ApIvor wrote to Hubert Foss. 'I was afraid seeing him after that he would collapse then and there.'[112] If Constant was exhausted

---

[110] Randall Swingler (1909–67) was a poet, an accomplished musician, and a member of the Communist Party. In the Second World War he saw active service in the Army in Italy, being awarded the Military Medal. He was a friend of Alan Rawsthorne, who was one of many composers to set his verses.

[111] Searle, *Quadrille with a Raven*, chapter 11.

[112] Letter (typed) from Denis ApIvor to Hubert Foss, 16 April [1952].

after the performance he was not the only one. 'Rehearsing with music is ghastly tiring and nerve-shattering,' wrote Edith,[113] and to John Lehmann she confessed: 'I was in such a state of exhaustion I had to take to my bed. *Gold Coast Customs* is *very* tiring. (In five days I had close on 10 hours of shouting above orchestra. Of course Constant did a lot of it, but there was a good deal of strain waiting for cues.)'[114] Constant's friendship with Edith had remained a warm one, and in later years he was on a few occasions amongst the artists and writers she invited to her Sesame Club meetings in Grosvenor Street, London.

Five days after the broadcast of *Gold Coast Customs*, Constant conducted a performance of Purcell's *Dido and Aeneas*, also for the Third Programme, in the Dent edition. The narration was written and spoken by Dennis Arundell, whose book on Purcell had appeared in 1927, and Constant was co-producer with Stanford Robinson. A live repeat performance was given two days later.

A Third Programme performance on 30 May of Satie's *Jack-in-the-Box* (in a concert that also included *The Rio Grande*) was the prelude to three programmes exclusively of Satie, devised by Constant, given over two weeks in June and including four first performances in England. The night before the first programme he gave a 20-minute talk in which he offered a serious defence of Satie, particularly his ballets. 'It was only at the end of his life he was acclaimed by his own countrymen, and then by only a few,' he began. 'I remember discussing this some years ago with his great follower Darius Milhaud who seemed both pleased and surprised to find a foreign composer who admired Satie as much as I did.' After these broadcasts he had a long restful weekend at Tom Driberg's, only to be back at the BBC at the end of the following week for a concert of Purcell and Rameau. Just over a month later, on successive days, he had two broadcasts with the BBC Symphony Orchestra, the first including what was then Lennox Berkeley's only symphony, and both concerts sharing Borodin's First Symphony.

C ONSTANT'S greatest joy at this time was being invited to accompany the Sadler's Wells Ballet on their first trip to America and Canada in October 1949. As Isabel wrote: 'It was essential that Constant should go with them. Fortunately his health had improved.' In preparation for this prestigious visit he conducted several times during the four-week Covent Garden autumn season which began on 1 August. Robert Irving, who was going to America as the second conductor, conducted the first three evenings with a programme that was all Lambert territory: *The Rake's Progress*, *Symphonic Variations* (with Angus Morrison as soloist), *Façade* (its first appearance at Covent Garden) and *The Miracle in the Gorbals*. *Cinderella* occupied the second half of the week. Constant took over for the whole of the next week with performances of *The Sleeping Beauty* with Moira Shearer and Ashton in which, the *Times* critic wrote, his 'experience gave fire and finish to the production as a whole.' He had lost nothing of his skill, the reviewer continuing: 'Mr Lambert's tempi, though occasionally too brisk for the dancers and sometimes, it is to be suspected, for the band itself, gave to Tchaikovsky's music the gloss and effervescence that it all too often lacks. ... Miss Margot Fonteyn ... was able to crown the evening with a grace and limpidity of line that need never falter for timing's sake. Mr Robert Helpmann, her ideal partner, and

[113] Victoria Glendinning, *Edith Sitwell: A Unicorn Among Lions* (London: Weidenfeld & Nicolson, 1981; paperback edition Phoenix 1993), p. 282.

[114] Letter from Edith Sitwell to John Lehmann, 19 December 1949 from Renishaw: in Edith Sitwell, *Selected Letters*, ed. John Lehmann and Derek Parker (London: Macmillan, 1970), p. 169.

Mr Lambert, her immaculate accompanist, were with her to the semiquaver.'[115] In the latter half of the following week he conducted *Swan Lake* (with Fonteyn and Somes), the same critic reporting that 'the honours of the evening are carried jointly by Miss Margot Fonteyn and Mr Constant Lambert [whose] presence, above all, assured a spirited and well-timed performance. His experience was as much a help to the dancers as it was a stimulus to the orchestra who responded with a dynamic and dashing execution of Tchaikovsky's splendid music.'[116]

P. W. Manchester, in *Ballet Today*, wrote that 'everyone greeted with joy the return of Constant Lambert, not only as conductor on certain nights, but as the narrator in *A Wedding Bouquet*,'[117] and she went on to describe his role:

> He now sits down stage left (audience right) at a table spread with a white cloth and decorated with a similar green creeper to that which adorns the tables for the wedding breakfast. There is a carafe of wine before him and he is reading his French newspaper having just concluded what we hope has been an extremely good dinner. He is then kind enough to explain the scene and story danced before us, and, as anticipated, makes plain many of the jokes obscured by the chorus singing. His return also brings back the 'clever saucer' explanation. To hear this, Helpmann leans with one hand on the table and listens with intense concentration. At first it seems beyond his comprehension, then understanding gleams across his face like a sunbeam and as he warmly shakes Lambert by the hand we realise that he has at last learnt something he has always wanted to know.[118]

That season Irving reintroduced the practice of playing an orchestral interlude between ballets, just as Constant had been in the habit of doing back in the Vic-Wells days, something that he had inherited from Diaghilev.

All seemed to augur well for the American tour. Near the beginning of September Constant conducted movements from *Horoscope* in a Home Service broadcast and in the last week of that month he gave another all-Satie programme for the Third. On 26 September he was a guest at Humphrey Searle's wedding at the Marylebone Registry Office, and three days later he went to the premiere of Bliss's opera *The Olympians*, also attended by Rawsthorne and Walton. Then on 3 October he flew to the United States.

The Company went in two aircraft, the women in one and the men (with the exception of Ninette to keep an eye on Constant) in another. The opening night six days later at New York's Metropolitan Opera House was to be followed by almost a month of performances there before moving on for short stays in Washington, Richmond, Philadelphia, Chicago and East Lansing (Michigan) – the longest being a

---

[115] *The Times*, Tuesday 9 August 1949.

[116] *The Times*, Friday 19 August 1949.

[117] According to the critic Felix Aprahamian, 'one of the "draws" for the ballet was lively speculation among the audience concerning the degree of Lambert's inebriation at any given performances': private conversation with Byron Adams, August 1992, in Byron Adams, 'High-Tea at Merlinford: Remembering Lord Berners', *Music & Letters*, vol. 91 (2010), p. 410.

[118] P. W. Manchester, *Ballet Today*, September–October 1949, p. 6. There were three performances, with Irving conducting, from 22–4 August 1949 with *Hamlet* and *Façade*. When *A Wedding Bouquet* was restored to the repertoire on 17 February 1949, Manchester had regretted 'that it was thought necessary to bring back the chorus which is largely unintelligible so that many of the jokes are completely lost' and she hoped too that 'second thoughts will restore Constant Lambert'.

week in Chicago – and then to Canada for a month.[119] On his third day in New York Constant gave his mother a brief account of his impressions of the city:

One's first two days in New York leave one with only two feelings:

(a) A maniacal and continuous desire for iced water

(b) An even more maniacal and continuous desire to be translated immediately to some odoriferous slum in the south of Europe.

Everybody is most kind and nice. But I could not (as yet) feel more a stranger. (Rends moi le Pausilippe et la mer d'Italie!) (Gerard de Nerval).[120] Perhaps I am still suffering from the overlong flight which I only overcame by doping myself with Dr Child's pills.

Had my first rehearsal today at the Metropolitan. Orchestra up to reasonable standard (about the equivalent to Covent Garden at its average) but most pleasant to deal with.

The town is extraordinarily beautiful by night, but during the day is rather drab. Not so modern or so chic as I had supposed. Rather suggesting a lot of buildings put up hastily for an International Exhibition and left there after the Exhibition had closed.

But as you know I am inclined to hasty prejudice.

More succinct details later.[121]

The opening night (brought forward by half an hour so the critics could attend the whole of *The Sleeping Beauty* and still meet their press deadlines for the morning papers) exceeded all expectations. For Fonteyn it was 'unimaginable success ... unlike anything we had experienced before'.[122] The critic Richard Buckle described it as one of the most exciting nights in theatrical history and 'a proud and glorious night for de Valois, for Lambert and for Fonteyn'.[123] A great outburst of applause greeted Constant when he took his place at the conductor's desk to open the proceedings with the two national anthems. The following day he informed his mother:

Opening night last night. Naturally great strain. First night nerves, no stage rehearsal, orchestra not too familiar with the music and a damp heat of over 80 degrees. But absolutely fantastic success from the start. Applause almost hysterical and a record number of curtains. To one's great relief and surprise New York has been knocked sideways by the ballet as a whole and quite rightly by Margot in particular.

Notices exceptionally good particularly for this town where critics are notoriously 'snooty'.

(a) Seen on the first night. Gent wearing leopard-skin dinner jacket with white bow tie. (Presumably <u>not</u> one of those Englishmen who always dress for dinner even in the jungle).

(b) The photograph of myself and cat in the programme bears the rather

[119] Their repertoire included *The Sleeping Beauty*, *The Rake's Progress*, *Symphonic Variations*, *Façade*, *Hamlet*, *Swan Lake*, *Miracle in the Gorbals*, *A Wedding Bouquet*, *Apparitions*, *Checkmate*, *Job* and *Cinderella*.

[120] Gérard de Nerval (1808–55), *nom-de-plume* of French poet, essayist amd translator Gérard Labrunie, whose translation of Goethe's *Faust* was used by Berlioz in his *La Damnation de Faust*.

[121] Letter headed 'Gladstone, 114–122 East 52nd Street New York 22' from Lambert to his mother, 6 October 1949.

[122] Fonteyn, *Autobiography*, p. 135.

[123] Richard Buckle, *The Adventures of a Ballet Critic* (London: Cresset Press, 1953), pp. 64–5.

ambiguous caption 'Constant Lambert, guest conductor, and one of the artistic directors'.

(c) 'Even before the performance began, there was the reassuring figure of Constant Lambert at the conductor's desk' (The New York Sun)

At what stage of the performance, may I ask, do American conductors deign to put in an appearance?

More news later.

Alexander Grant recalled the occasion, how 'Constant was in charge and he conducted in the most fantastic way which we all enjoyed, especially the Panorama. Every time he played the Panorama we all stood enthralled and on that very first visit in 1949 of the Company in New York, when he played the Panorama the audience went into thunderous applause.'[124]

Perhaps the finest praise came from the impresario Lincoln Kirstein who, with George Balanchine, had founded the New York City Ballet. He wrote to Richard Buckle:

> The hero of the occasion, according to Balanchine and myself, was Lambert; he had a fine band and the score never sounded so well; he is a genius for *tempi*; absolutely on the note in every variation; no boring bits; and he supports the dancers on the huge stage by giving them assurance from his authority. He whipped people up into applause, purely by sound; when nothing was really happening from a dancer he seduced everyone into somehow imagining that she was divine. Anyway, he got an ovation; many people knew what he had done.[125]

Eleven days later Kirstein still had nothing but praise:

> I loved Swan Lake; honest to God, I loved (almost) every moment of it. As far as performances went, it was superbly done. Marvellous music, exquisitely played by Lambert, a divine conductor, the greatest ballet man in the business. ... The ovation was COLOSSAL. It was deserved, every bit of it.[126]

Yet, despite the general acclaim of the critics, Constant's moods did not stay on a high. Only two days after the opening, in a letter to Isabel he revealed his true feelings of boredom and melancholy:

COLUMBUS DAY!!! [12 October]

Darling Isabel,

Autobiography Chaps III and IV (I don't think you've seen Chap II yet).

III Having spent 40 years before the mast I have no clear idea as to what it looks like, my behind having naturally been turned towards it. On the other hand I am an authority on the appearance of the bowsprit.

IV There are certain things in life such as birth, fornication, and death which have their ups and downs. The only thing in life which can maintain a continuous level is <u>cafard</u>. Talk about <u>cafard</u>! Fortunately I am getting gradually acclimatised and can even distinguish between one street and another (which is more than most Americans do). I live rather symbolically between two avenues (both of which I have explored) – Park Avenue, which tries to be like Gloucester Gate without succeeding and Lexington Avenue which is vaguely like Camden

---

[124] Alexander Grant talking at the Royal Opera House, Covent Garden in *Remembering Constant Lambert*, 14 March 2001. The occasion was recorded.

[125] Letter from Lincoln Kirstein to Richard Buckle, 10 October 1949, New York, in Buckle, *The Adventures of a Ballet Critic*, pp. 169, 57.

[126] *Ibid.*, p. 170.

Town High St and quite frankly lets the whole f***ing thing ride. I drink there rather gloomily after the show from time to time.

The only place in this curiously drab and <u>utterly dated</u> town (dated like an early UFA film or one of the more tedious works of Stravinsky) where I feel at home is the old Groucho Marx opera house, where fortunately I have to spend most of my time. ... Wildly comic supper given us by the Irish anti-British Mayor of NY in the garden of his super bungalow on East River. Telephone-pal Webster and Ralph Hawkes(!) literally crawling round me like lichen on an old church tower or slugs on a bunch of rhodedendrons.

... Tonight after two Sleeping Beautys I can relax a little as I am only doing the middle part of the show including Aubade Héroïque which they play v. well. In SB the Negro pages are done by actual Negro children who are solemn, wide-eyed and enchanting.

Social life obviously going to be intolerable. Everybody I have met during the last 24 hours took part in Romeo and Juliet 1926. The only tolerable conversationalists are the taxi drivers. ...

Gastronomic Notes

Food in general good and over copious but curiously tasteless and sweet. Much the best is the sea food which it is hard to spoil. They serve the blue-points with a tomato sauce to which has been added Lyles Golden Syrup in generous quantities but a really Churchillian scene will produce lemon and red pepper. Pompano, a flat fish like a small sole but with something of the texture of a tunny is well worth while. Deep sea scallops etc all excellent. Californian Burgundy disappointing. Chilian Riesling (no joking) excellent and is my staple beverage.

I am very lonely and miss you more than I can say. In spite of every conceivable pat on the back I could not feel more a stranger. Bobbie is at his worst and very sour at being overshadowed by Margot and myself. Margot in the beautiful but aloof world she had chosen. The only person of my own age and sex to whom I can talk is Pamela May with whom I have occasional coco-kolas.[127]

In her memoirs Isabel preserved a delightful anecdote of a lounging figure in a New York bar, on seeing Constant, shouting in a loud voice: 'Throw that man out. He looks like Oscar Wilde!' And keeping Constant as much as possible away from bars was the chief concern of the Company, so much so that Pamela May and June Brae took it upon themselves to look after him.

But their worst fears were realised when Constant blacked out during a performance of *Hamlet*. There are no clear accounts of what actually happened but, according to Daneman, he fell as he made his way into the orchestral pit and had to be helped to his feet. Thereafter his concentration and his beat wavered and the curtain was brought down. The next morning a number of the American musicians in the orchestra tried loyally to offer some excuse for the fall, one of them suggesting that it was the cable to the lights on his music stand that Constant had tripped over.[128] As Pamela May recalled: 'In New York, when he got so ill and collapsed, he came to us and said, "But I have not been drinking; I haven't had a drink all day." June Brae and I took him out and gave him dinner. He was terribly ill by then.'[129] There was no alternative: he had to return home and the American Robert Zeller took his place on the tour 'as guest

[127] As printed with Lambert's vagaries of spelling in Shead, *Constant Lambert*, pp. 158–9. The whereabouts of the original letter is not known. Shead added that it was 'unfortunately necessary to omit certain passages and names from this letter'.

[128] Daneman, *Margot Fonteyn*, pp. 249–50.

[129] In conversation with the author.

conductor'.[130] Isabel was at that time in France and Constant joined her there. 'The warrior appeared looking remarkably fresh,' she wrote in her memoirs. "He sat outside on the terrace, looked down the garden, gave a great sigh, and said, "You have no idea how wonderful it is to be back in France."' When the Company made a second visit to America the following year he did not go with them.

After his death, when it became generally known that he had been suffering from diabetes, friends would remember moments when – without their realising at the time – the symptoms had manifested themselves. As Driberg wrote: 'At once one recalled, almost with a sense of guilt, occasions when one had been faintly irritated by Constant's mannerisms in conversation – how he would suddenly become inattentive or quarrelsome, pass a hand over his forehead, squeeze his face up and shut his eyes, and not "come back" for some moments.'

A broadcast talk on Puccini he was going to give early in November was cancelled, but later that month he contributed to a BBC Music Magazine programme on that composer with Mosco Carner and Spike Hughes.[131] By December he was back in full swing in the Third Programme with two substantial programmes of Purcell's music (the last in a series of four arranged by Anthony Lewis), a talk on van Dieren[132] as an introduction to three programmes of the composer's songs and chamber music, and a second performance of Searle's *Gold Coast Customs* in which he once again shared the narration with Edith Sitwell. The broadcast was repeated three evenings later and a recording exists in the National Sound Archive. The two days before Christmas, another of Constant's life-long wishes came true: to conduct a performance of Liszt's *Faust* Symphony, thanks to Searle, who wrote in his memoirs:

> The BBC is normally helpful to members of its staff who have recently resigned by engaging them as outside producers, and early in 1950 I was asked by them to produce a comprehensive series of orchestral, choral and piano music by Liszt. I was thus able to fulfil Constant's long-cherished desire to conduct the Faust Symphony; he also conducted the rarely heard Funeral Ode, *La Notte*, and the first performance of the *Grand Solo de Concert* for piano and orchestra. This previously unknown version of the *Grosses Konzertsolo* for piano solo had turned up in MS at an auction at Sotheby's and I was asked to identify it. I obtained a photostat of the MS, which only contained the orchestral score, and was able to fill in the solo part from the solo piano version.

---

[130] *Ballet Today*, February 1950, p. 7. *A Wedding Bouquet* was subsequently dropped from the tour's repertoire. In a broadcast tribute to Berners, Lambert had said: 'I remember how pleased he was when I came back from America where I had been doing the voice part in *A Wedding Bouquet* and telling him that an orchestral player had said to me, "Who's this guy Berners? Is he really a lord or is it a name like Duke Ellington or Count Basie?"'

[131] BBC Home Service, 27 November 1949.

[132] Lambert's broadcast talk on van Dieren was to have been included in a collection of essays on the composer by Cecil Gray and others, edited by John Goss. Gray was working intermittently until his death on the van Dieren book which was never finished. On 7 October 1945 he wrote to the American composer and conductor Bernard Herrmann: 'My projected book on van Dieren has been held up indefinitely for several reasons, firstly the difficulty of getting in touch with certain sources of information which I require in Holland, and secondly the bottleneck which exists in this country at the present with everything concerning printing and publication.' Herrmann, who was interested in conducting works by both Gray and van Dieren, had written to Gray on 15 March: 'I have been conducting Bernard van Dieren's music quite steadily, and feel that one never reaches the end of the possibilities of his wonderful music. Do you know if the *Chinese Symphony* was ever published?'

The Symphony was a work of special significance to Constant as he had alluded to it in *The Rio Grande*.

To Searle's delight, one outcome of these programmes was the formation of a Liszt Society:

> A letter appeared in the *Radio Times* from Dr. Vernon Harrison suggesting the formation of a Liszt Society to publish, perform and, if possible, record his lesser known works. I seized on the idea and at once approached a number of people who were interested in or had worked actively for Liszt – Louis Kentner, the great Liszt pianist, Constant, of course, the Hon. Edward Sackville-West, who had written a radio play 'A Pipe for Fortune's Finger' about Liszt, Ralph Hill and Sacheverell Sitwell, both biographers of Liszt, and William Walton. Our President was Professor Edward Dent, the friend and biographer of Busoni and I was the Hon. Secretary.[133]

Christmas was spent at Driberg's, the routine on such occasions being that Constant, Isabel and Tom would first dine in London on Christmas Eve at the Casa Prada in Euston Road, and then drive on to Essex, taking in by a circuitous route midnight Mass at Thaxted, Driberg being Roman Catholic. The incumbent vicar, much to Tom's and no doubt Constant's delight, had inherited all the traits of his notorious socialist predecessor, the 'red' Conrad Noel.[134]

Before the end of the year Constant had two broadcast concerts, both including Haydn's 'London' symphony, Ravel's *La Valse* and Delius's *The Walk to the Paradise Garden* that he associated with *The Edinburgh Castle*. In January and February 1950 he was alternating between the Third and the Light programmes in his broadcasts, 'Constant Lambert's Music at Eight' being in their own way almost as prestigious as his programmes of *The Tempest* (with music by Purcell), Gluck and more Liszt. Probably the most demanding of them all was that of contemporary music in the concert hall of Broadcasting House on 21 February, with first performances of Aplvor's *The Hollow Men* (for baritone, chorus and orchestra) and Roberto Gerhard's Suite *Pandora*, and the first broadcast performance of Benjamin Frankel's song-cycle *The Aftermath*. As Aplvor later wrote:

> He was doing a whole concert of Contemporary Music at Broadcasting House including a fiendish work of Gerhard. Also Frankel, whose work he was conducting, was being beastly to him. He was in a terrible state of nerves shaking all over in the conductor's room. But he was alright afterwards and stayed here till 4 a.m. after the proceedings had been brought to an end by a four-handed performance of 'Gloire à Jupiter' (the one from Offenbach's *Orpheus*!) and bangings from the neighbours on the ceiling. I expect that you had noticed too Constant's partiality for finishing parties with piano duets; and I have memories of another remarkable performance, of a work of Liszt this time, given by Constant and Alan Rawsthorne in Lizzie Lutyens' top studio at Fitzroy St at about three in the morning.[135]

---

[133] Searle, *Quadrille with a Raven*, chapter 11. Searle wrote an article for *Radio Times*: 'Liszt, this many-sided Genius', 16 December 1949, p. 7.

[134] During the First World War, Conrad Noel (1896–1942) hung the flag of St George, the Sinn Fein tricolour and the Red Flag in Thaxted Church, and in 1921 he and his clergy, with the support of some of the congregation, backed the locked-out miners in their dispute over the reduction of wages, resulting in considerable local trouble. Noel had been a friend of Gustav Holst, who lived close by in Thaxted.

[135] Letter (typed) from Denis Aplvor to Hubert Foss, 16 April [1952]: Hubert Foss Archive.

ApIvor told Angus Morrison:

> [Constant] was apparently quite without unpleasant sentiments towards other composers. This also must have been almost unique. About 1950 he was gratuitously insulted by a composer called Frankel,[136] who tried to prevent his conducting a work of his, and stayed away from the performance, out of spite. This he never forgot, but such episodes were extremely rare, presumably because few composers would have wanted to treat him in that way.[137]

Regarding his setting of T. S. Eliot's *The Hollow Men*:

> Lambert had somewhat contentiously complained in his book that there was almost no settings of contemporary verse, and it was with a certain malign pleasure that I got him to conduct this work (the score of which he had seen some years earlier); I felt this was a suitable riposte for his habit of coming into the pub and announcing that 'April is the cruellest month ...'.[138]

On 9 March Constant was back at Covent Garden, sharing the conducting with Robert Irving at a 'Command Performance' given in honour of the French President. Irving conducted *Symphonic Variations* and the last act of *The Sleeping Beauty* while Constant directed *Façade* (with Ashton as the Dago in the Tango and Moira Shearer, just returned from her honeymoon) and, in between the first two ballets, his own *Aubade héroïque*, 'an allusive tribute to the political aspect of the occasion', commented *The Times*. Mid-April he spent a weekend at Driberg's, then in the first week of May he was conducting a Royal Opera House gala performance in aid of the Sadler's Wells Benevolent Fund. The evening included the premiere of *Ballabile*. The choreographer was Roland Petit with whom Constant had discussed the idea when they met in New York, the latter suggesting Chabrier whose music he had passionately espoused as far back as 1926 and 1927 in his earliest essays in journalism.[139] According to Shead, 'rehearsals were marred by a clash between Lambert and Petit in the presence of Lambert's son'[140] and things did not go too well in the actual performance, the *Times* critic remarking that it 'was like one of those awful dress rehearsals of which it is customary to say that "it is bound to be right on the night"', even adding that Chabrier's music 'might have been better played than it was'. Mary Clarke, in *Ballet Today*, clearly felt that it was Petit who was at fault, writing that 'one still gets the impression that M. Petit tosses off the choreography in hit-or-miss fashion after he has decided on the general stage spectacle ... [He] is obliged to carry the blame for the ballet's shortcomings simply because he has been so enormously fortunate in all his collaborators'.[141] One can only assume that any tension between the two had arisen from their respective interests in Fonteyn.

Everything went much better ten days later on 15 May when the Company gave a coming-of-age gala performance in the presence of Princess Margaret, the president

---

[136] The composer Benjamin Frankel (1906–73), son of Polish-Jewish parents, had earlier earned a living by playing jazz, and he may well not have forgiven Lambert for some comments he made in *Music Ho!* about the commercialising of jazz by Jews.

[137] Letter (typed) from Denis ApIvor to Angus Morrison, 9 March 1954: RCM Archive.

[138] ApIvor, 'Composer's Anthology', p. 694.

[139] Lambert, 'Chabrier', *Apollo*, October 1926, and 'A Plea for Chabrier', *The British Musician*, July 1927.

[140] Shead, *Constant Lambert*, p. 161.

[141] *Ballet Today*, July 1950, p. 5. The review included a photograph of Roland Petit, Constant Lambert and designer Antoni Clave taking a curtain call on the first night.

of the Sadler's Wells Foundation.[142] It was a nostalgic evening, with Fonteyn and Helpmann reprising their original roles in *The Haunted Ballroom*, de Valois (who had not danced since 1937) once again as Webster the parlour-maid in *A Wedding Bouquet* with Constant as speaker reciting from a table on the stage with real champagne, the orgy scene from *The Rake's Progress*, and *Façade*. Constant shared the conducting with Guy Warrack and Robert Irving.

There was an added poignancy to the evening as Lord Berners had died less than a month before at the age of 66. On 21 May, Constant presented a radio tribute, one of his finest broadcasts – and, as it turned out, the last subject on which he was to present a talk.[143] He probably understood Berners better than most people because they had much in common as regards their character and interests, their appreciation of art, their sensitivity and their humour, which Constant so much appreciated:

> I remember having gone down late for the weekend waking up on Sunday morning and being surprised at what at first sight seemed a flight of tropical birds, red, orange, bright blue and green. It turned out that Lord Berners had hit on the idea of dyeing his pigeons with gayer colours. The process which was done in the way you treat a drawing with fixative was entirely harmless and indeed seemed to please the birds considerably. But needless to say various female busybodies wrote to the local papers accusing him of cruelty to animals. Very typically he pointed out in reply that people who were hypersensitive about animals were notoriously callous about their fellow humans and accused the letter writers of the grossest brutality towards their nephews and nieces. Incidentally it may interest scientists and in particular the followers of Pavlov to know that after being dyed the pigeons no longer enjoyed the happy promiscuity for which their race is renowned but mated only with pigeons of the same colour. The fact that he dyed his pigeons in five different colours is possibly more remembered than the fact that he wrote amongst other things five important ballets. His eccentricity or to put it more accurately 'fantasy' was entirely spontaneous but at the same time it served as a guard against the outside world. Although the best of hosts, and nothing could have been gayer than his weekends when company, cuisine and conversation were all at an equally high level, he was at heart a rather shy and nervous man, given, like most famous wits, to bouts of melancholia, and quite wrongly distrustful of his own abilities. A typical example of his desire for solitude combined with his own individual humour was provided by his simple method of keeping a railway carriage to himself. Instead of employing the usual English tactics he would put on dark glasses and slyly beckon in the passers by. Those isolated figures who took the risk of entering the carriage became so perturbed by his habit of reading the newspaper upside down and taking his temperature every few minutes that they invariably changed carriages at the next station.[144]

With some feeling he added that 'in this country wit is always assumed to be a sign of superficiality and a suspicious nature. Versatility is even more suspect. "Jack of all trades and master of none" is the usual cry from the modern English critic.' Berners'

---

[142] On the day it was discovered that a mistake had been made and that it was only the Company's 20th birthday: Bland, *The Royal Ballet*, p. 100.

[143] Gerald Berners died on 19 April 1950 'of bad heart and blood pressure', according to Robert Heber Percy, his companion.

[144] 'Lord Berners: an appreciation by Constant Lambert', BBC *Music Magazine*, 21 May 1950, which was probably revised as 'Lord Berners (1883–1950): a tribute by Constant Lambert', BBC Third Programme, 16 February 1951, his last radio talk.

companion, Robert Heber-Percy, remembered when Berners was ill, 'driving Constant down, and we stopped at every pub for him to have a drink. We were meant to be at Faringdon by about eight, and got there at half-past ten. Gerald had gone to bed. ... He was happiest with Constant: he loved him. He was the greatest fun, terribly witty. Their sense of humour went very well together.'[145]

The talk on Berners was followed fairly soon by two important Third Programme broadcasts: on 28 May another performance of Handel's oratorio *Alexander's Feast* (which he had first given in January 1949), and six days later a fairly rare hearing of his *Summer's Last Will and Testament* with the Oxford Bach Choir.[146] A member of the choir had vivid memories of him on that occasion:

> I remember particularly the first time he came down for this – in the early summer of 1950. One was immediately struck by what a nervy and restless person he was – an impression which his rather harsh, jerky voice did nothing to mitigate. His face had somehow the fleshy pallor of ill-health, and I don't think it was merely the fact that we were singing about the plague that brought the word 'pock-marked' to my mind as a vague and no doubt ridiculous general impression – but singing those beautifully-set words 'I am sick, I must die' under Mr. Lambert seemed peculiarly impressive. He was always cheerful and unbelievably patient; but I had a strong impression of a man profoundly unwell in body, and, with that undeniable streak of genius running through him, strangely turbulent in mind and spirit. Much as one appreciated, respected and liked Constant Lambert from these encounters, one was left nevertheless with a feeling difficult to explain – that it must be an unhappy business for him to live perpetually with himself.[147]

The choir was prepared by its conductor, Constant's friend from RCM days, Thomas Armstrong, and he too remembered the occasion:

> He was then not well and I remember his conversations, a kind of frenzied gaiety, and I thought of the words of the music that he had composed for Thomas Nashe's poem written in the time of the pestilence. I remembered the words 'Come, come, the bells do cry, I am sick, I must die. Lord have mercy on us!' And I thought of his setting of these words and I had the awful feeling of a man really destroying himself, taking no care, making himself ill with overwork and worry. It's a memory I can't obliterate.[148]

---

[145] Robert Heber-Percy interviewed by Peter Dickinson, in Dickinson, *Lord Berners*, p. 79.

[146] The BBC recorded the performance and, as well as its live broadcast, played it in their Overseas Service on 3 January 1951. However, the recording does not seem to have survived.

[147] Letter dated 9 March 1952 from E. Joanna Cullen to Hubert Foss.

[148] Sir Thomas Armstrong speaking in *Desert Island Discs*, BBC Radio 4, 16 July 1989, rebroadcast 21 July 1989.

20 1950–1
Snakes and *Tiresias*

L ATER in June 1950 Constant took a much-needed holiday with Isabel in Valmandois, some 40 kilometres to the north of Paris. Here at last he was able to get away from all distractions and concentrate on the new ballet he had been commissioned by the Arts Council for the 1951 Festival of Britain. Its premiere was to be a Covent Garden Gala before royalty, and the subject was one that Constant had contemplated some 20 years earlier for the Camargo Society: the Greek myth of Tiresias. No-one could have predicted the uproar it was to produce, either for the damage it was to bring to the Company's reputation or the devastating effect it was to have on Constant himself at the very end of his life. Equally surprising is that no one seems to have questioned either the suitability of its subject for such an important occasion – including as it does copulating snakes, Tiresias changing into a woman and then back to a man, and the gods arguing as to whether the man or the woman derives the greater pleasure from the sexual act – or indeed whether this was something too difficult to be conveyed successfully in dance. (Michael Somes and Margot Fonteyn danced the principal roles.) An early draft of the synopsis that Constant prepared for Ashton was explicit enough (see Appendix 2). As Julie Kavanagh, Ashton's biographer, suggests, as an allegory of bisexuality it was a matter much closer to Ashton's heart than Lambert's, or was he acquiescing out of a sense of loyalty?

When it came to the Gala programme booklet, something much less explicit was clearly required. 'Enclosed is the *Tiresias* libretto,' wrote Constant. 'I have done my best to make the points of the story clear to the gallery while keeping it concealed from Royalty. A very difficult task I can assure you.'[1] And the following simplified version was printed:

Scene I In Crete. There lies the Scene.

Young girls in a gymnasium are attempting to somersault over the horns of a bull. The youthful Tiresias enters and displays his superior prowess. The young girls leave in mockery.

Tiresias executes a dance of athletic triumph. He is joined by his warrior friends who pay him homage. Their dance is interrupted by a young Neophyte who tells him that priestesses wish to give him a wand of honour. He accepts it with reluctance and is left alone.

Two snakes enter. Tiresias strikes the female snake with his wand and is transformed into a woman.

Scene II In the Mountains.

Tiresias, now a woman, is discovered alone. She is joined by a group of shepherds and shepherdesses but the shepherds do not appeal to her.

From behind a statue appears a stranger. They fall in love. The shepherds and shepherdesses celebrate the happiness of Tiresias and her lover. The Neophyte re-enters with the wand and the bacchanale is interrupted by the presence of two snakes. Tiresias strikes the male snake with her wand and is changed back to a man.

---

[1] Letter from Lambert to Michael Wood, Royal Opera House, 5 June 1951: ROH Archives.

Scene III A Palace.

Zeus, the God, and Hera, the Goddess are disputing the relative happiness of the two sexes, each maintaining that the other is the happier of the two. Tiresias is called upon for a decision. He states firmly that he preferred his life as a woman. Hera, furious at being contradicted, strikes Tiresias blind. Zeus as recompense gives Tiresias the gift of prophecy.

Interestingly enough, Cecil Gray had outlined the story of Tiresias in his autobiography *Musical Chairs*, completed in Capri in 1947 and published the following year. Discussing artists who practise two art forms, he wrote that 'while I am composing music I find it utterly impossible to write tolerably well, and *vice versa*; and every time I feel impelled to switch over from one to the other, I have to go to school again, as it were, and re-learn painfully the technique of whichever of the two crafts is involved, *ad initio* and *ab ovo* – and a very painful process it is, as I have said. One has to change one's aesthetic sex, like Tiresias of old', and he went on to relate the story.[2]

Tiresias had become a 'family' effort because Isabel was commissioned to create the designs, something that, according to her, had happened by chance when the painter and designer Leonor Fini[3] arrived in Paris just before the closing day of an exhibition of Isabel's work at the Hanover Galleries. As she explained in her memoirs:

Leonor Fini visited several art galleries while in London including the Hanover. Apparently she told Freddie Ashton that the only original works she had seen were mine. I learned about this much later. It was her remark that led directly to my being asked to design *Tiresias*. ... Sir David Webster told Constant that the ballet would like me to do the décor for his ballet. He insisted that it was not because I was his wife ... Constant was dead set on the story being set in Crete tho' strictly speaking it has nothing to do with Crete. It was for the purposes of décor. As soon as I started studying Crete I understood why Constant liked it so much. It was exotic – quite removed from the Central European, the Romano Germanic ideal. The style of beauty that really turned him off was the typical Nordic blonde. I think there must have connection with his lack of feeling for the classical Germanic music.

One of the striking features of Isabel's design was a large Minoan bull, and she visited the Ashmolean Museum in Oxford to see Sir Arthur Evans' Knossos collection and made a number of drawings and colour notes.

I was now working on quite large canvases, painting nudes, recollections of and extensions of my drawings made at Valmandois. Evening meals I would cook, lunch time we often went to Pagani's via The George. I would often return home through the zoo. [Isabel was a fellow of the Zoological Society.]

One evening Freddie Ashton came around for a necessary congratulation. For some reason we had on the table four candles alight. When Freddie saw these, he gasped: 'FOUR CANDLES' – there being, I learned, a great superstition in the theatre concerning candles bringing bad luck.

I cannot think that anyone designing anything had more pleasure designing than I creating *Tiresias*. As soon as I had paintings of the set and act drops which were in gouache I took them to Freddie. He seemed happy for me to continue. My intention was to bring into the theatre an atmosphere that was totally different from the familiar tutus and forest.

[2] Gray, *Musical Chairs*, p. 177.
[3] Leonor Fini (1907–96).

The costumes were not such a great problem for me, as most of them were in the Ashmolean, but [they] were for the wardrobe. The principle characters did require some inspiration. Margot's went through several trials and was finally arrived at in the last fitting and with Freddie's help.

Constant was kind enough not to tell me anything about working at Covent Garden. He let me find out for myself though he must have wanted to when I came home babbling especially as he was getting so pressed for time that he asked some friends to help out with copying …

According to Anya Linden, who was one of the Priestesses, 'We thought it was a tremendously exciting ballet. The stunning *pas de deux* which wasn't at all Fred's usual romantic style, the sexy snakes and the bare-bosomed designs by Constant's wild-looking wife … all seemed extraordinary to us.'[4] But Ashton apparently became so bored with the third scene, trying to translate the quarrel of the gods into dance form, that he handed the choreography over to Alfred Rodriguez (who played Zeus), saying, 'Just get on with it, but don't be too filthy.'[5] Alexander Bland thought 'the highly complicated story strained credibility to breaking point … and the hour-long entertainment had only a single *pas de deux* which was of interest.'[6]

While composing *Tiresias*, Constant had acquired a book on reptiles which he consulted for the mating habits of snakes. One day he went into The George and, finding Randall Swingler there, showed him the book. 'There ensued,' recalled ApIvor, 'a pantomime which was one of the funniest things I have ever seen in my life, in which both of them took part. The gist of this was the difference in the sexual behaviour of English and French snakes, and the views of the behaviour of the English held by the French, and the French by the English.' Swingler was the editor of a new monthly pocket-sized publication called *Circus* and Constant contributed a whimsical poem, *In Praise of Snakes*, to its first issue. Much to his annoyance, however, the line 'She hugs to her breast her withered dugs' was misprinted as 'She hogs to her breast her withered dogs' and to satisfy Constant's protestations a revised version of the poem was printed in the third issue.[7]

> *In Praise of Snakes*
>
> Praise be the asp
> Whose venomous grasp
> Refines to dust
> The gypsy's lust
> And willingly hugs
> Her dying dugs.
> Praise be the serpent who sloughs his skin
> And feels no more than the prick of a pin.
> Praised be the adder whose double tongue
> Gives innocent pleasure to old and young:
> The cobra, too, who bares his fang
> In self-defence, not that of the gang.
> And the all-embracing boa-constrictor
> Content to gorge without flaunting as victor.

[4] Kavanagh, *Secret Muses*, pp. 391–2.

[5] *Ibid.*, p. 391. In the manuscript, scene 3 (or Act 3 scene 1 in the revised score) is oddly titled with the gods' Roman equivalent, 'Juno and Jupiter'.

[6] Bland, *The Royal Ballet*, pp. 101, 104.

[7] The original is as remembered by Denis ApIvor. The revised version actually reads 'And willingly hugs / Her dying dugs': *Circus*, June 1950, p. 23.

> Reserve then our curses
> For kindly old nurses,
> Benevolent dons
> Devouring scones,
> The persons of wealth
> Concerned with their health,
> The cheery goodbye
> Of an old school tie,
> The pitying nod
> From those who like God.
> And the expert flaying knife
> Of the understanding wife.

The composition of *Tiresias* did not come easily, and even in Valmandois, as he explained to his mother, it took him a little time to settle to the task:

> Meant to write yesterday but got caught up by Tiresias. Am writing in a somewhat 'legarthic' [*sic*] mood after shelling the peas for tonight and after almost too good a Sunday lunch. We eat out on the terrasse and usually the meals though always good are simplicity itself but on Sundays we go slightly 'to town' and today we had smoked eels, jambonneau (delicious), new potatoes, peas from the garden, salad (garlic dressing), brie cherries and a bottle or two of a straightforward vin ordinaire.
>
> Work is going slowly but not too badly. I always find it difficult at first to write in a new situation and this extremely lush landscape with its incredible shindy of bird song is at first a little overwhelming. We have three rooms, a really large studio for Isabel, a spacious bedroom and a smaller room with a piano, presumably Pleyels experimental model, but just good enough to compose on. No modern conveniences, no h and c unusual offices in the garden. Life could not be more simple. Brood about work and/or take a walk in the morning. Lunch outside. Then tentative composing in the afternoon. Evening walk down to the village which is not beautiful but very human. The only bistro is filled with a series of characters (much hand shaking etc) for which any French film director would willingly sell his soul. Simple dinner and then non-professional music, ranging from Purcell to Chabrier. Isabel is working hard and has done some excellent drawings of Mary Rose Pelham. ...
>
> ... Tiresias is only just beginning to breed. Have sketched the prelude (which for final polishing I shall leave to the last), have finished the opening number (young girls in the nude somersaulting over bulls) and the last number in Scene 1 (Pas de deux for copulating snakes leading to Tiresias' first change of sex). Am pleased with the latter. Still 3 more numbers to do even to finish Scene 1!
>
> So much for egocentricity.
>
> I was very glad to have the letter from Kit who seems in good and improving form. I am very much on the side of his idea of a French holiday. Anyone vouched for by Dorothy Riddle would ipso facto be reliable. It is a good age to go abroad for the 1st time particularly if you are with people of your own age and living with a family in the country. I know that he longs to go to Paris with us but the idea is as you can see out of the question. Our whole ambience there is far too sophisticated and he wouldn't pick up a word of French from our high-speed highbrow friends.
>
> (Though I am still for being thrown head first into sophisticated society at the age of 20 as happened in my case).

I expect Dorothy Riddle will act as liaison officer but if there is anything I can do please let me know.

Flying to England on July 5th for a few days to conduct 'Semele' will ring you but doubt if rehearsals will allow time for a visit.

Isabel (trying to save a kitten's life with brandy) sends her love.[8]

Two more Third Programme performances of Handel's *Semele*[9] necessitated his return to London and brought an interruption to the 'holiday'. Although the broadcasts went well, as he informed his mother, they had been an annoying intrusion into any progress he had been making with *Tiresias*:

I have come to the conclusion that 14e Juillet is much more amusing in a small village than in Paris (where I spent it last year). It was great fun walking down to the village and joining in the local procession, small band of pompiers in front, children with Chinese lanterns etc. Then to the tiny square with a statue of Daumier[10] in it (he died here) where the fireworks were let off in somewhat haphazard but enthusiastic fashion by the local ironmonger (my namesake). Bal at the Mairie. 3 piece band. Accordion played by the tobacconist's daughter. Retraite des Pompiers. The combination of the 2 bands one inside, one out was indescribable.

Life here continues to be very simple. There are pleasant walks through the woods and more exhausting ones over the top of the hill to a completely pastoral plain high up, with no one in sight and with a superb panorama towards Paris.

Semele in London was a great success particularly the 2nd perf but five rehearsals and 2 shows in such a short time were not only exhausting but made a bad break with Tiresias.

The latter has reached rather a sticky point due not so much as to lack of ideas as to having <u>too</u> many fragmentary sketches. Will try and weed them out tomorrow. (Blast! On going upstairs to sharpen my pencil have just added another one!).

I hope you had a good time at Pulborough and that Connie was well. Any news of Kit and his holiday plans?

Returning on Aug 2nd after a couple of days in Paris.

He was absent from the Proms this year although he was represented by two works, the suite he had arranged from the ballet *Comus* (with music by Purcell) and the ever-popular *Rio Grande*, conducted respectively by Trevor Harvey and Stanford Robinson. On 17 August he directed a van Dieren and Warlock broadcast for the Third Programme that included van Dieren's *Serenata* for nine instruments and his *Sonetto VII of Edmund Spenser's Amoretti* for tenor and 11 instruments. He had two Kingsway Hall recording sessions with the Philharmonia in September that were to be his last (Waldteufel, Walton and Chabrier) and more Handel the following month for the Third programme – two performances of *L'Allegro ed Il Pensieroso*. In November for *The Times* he contributed a brief obituary on Ralph Hill: 'A first-rate editor, a man of eclectic tastes (who else could have been equally enthusiastic about Brahms and Liszt?), he was the ideal link between the professional world and "the man in the street",[11] and

---

[8] Letter from Lambert to his mother from Valmandois, Seine-et-Oise, dated only 'Sunday'.

[9] He conducted Handel's *Semele* with almost the same forces in 6 March 1949.

[10] Honoré Daumier (1808–79), French painter and political caricaturist.

[11] *The Times*, 1 November 1950. Ralph Hill was probably best known for his contributions to *Radio Times* and his editorship of the *Penguin Music Magazine* and Penguin books on *The Symphony* and *The Concerto*.

on 4 December, on hearing of Moeran's death, wrote to Alan Frank: 'I was sorry to read about dear old Raspberry'. Three days later he wrote to his mother:

I should have written before to thank you for your letter and for the most welcome cheque, but have been rounding an awkward corner in Tiresias.

I will look in at Barkers[12] the moment I can spare the time, meanwhile the old ENSA model (très chic, très snob, presque cad) is being put back on its penultimate legs by Mr Glicksman.

As regards Christmas I hope I have made it clear to all concerned that I am not playing at Christmas this year. We are going to shut ourselves in with a hare (as representing the best value for money these days).

I wish the ballet would move quicker but the subject is a complicated one. Haven't decided yet what disasters will overtake Tiresias as a woman. Most of my girl friends are abroad so am rather short of suggestions.

Hope the fish are ascending according to schedule. Love to Olga and Maurice.[13]

Three days before Christmas he recorded a programme to be broadcast in the Light Programme on Boxing Day, and then he was off to Driberg's for five days. His entry in the visitors' book was typically oblique: 'Quiz for later visitors. / "A smoky street, an open obelisk, an apple arbour, a prosperous port" / If you can't find the answer you jolly well ought!'[14] to which Isabel added: 'Memorable for food, wine, and the reopening of the dining and drawing rooms.' Just before the year was out he gave a Third Programme concert that included Bliss's *Adam Zero* ballet music and Magnard's Symphony No. 3, of which *Radio Times* reminded listeners that he had given the first performance in England back in June 1936.

Constant was one of five members on a selection panel for a new opera, commissioned by the Arts Council and to be staged in the Festival of Britain year.[15] Four operas emerged as contenders, although none of them was in fact to be produced during the Festival: Arthur Benjamin's *A Tale of Two Cities*, Alan Bush's *Wat Tyler*, Berthold Goldschmidt's *Beatrice Cenci* and Karl Rankl's *Deirdre of the Sorrows*. Constant had favoured Lennox Berkeley's *Nelson*, but another opera that was not seen by all the judges might well have been the subject of a court case had it not been for Constant's early death. This was Christian Darnton's *Fantasy Fair* that Constant was only to learn about after the results had been announced, when Darnton told him how sorry he was that his entry had not been accepted. As Darnton wrote later:

It was news to Constant that I had in fact sent in a work. A moment of natural embarrassment ensued; and then it came out that he, for one, had never seen my submission. Nor, as it later turned out, had 2 other of the judges. ... And so Constant made a big issue of this; and, as I say, behaved with that exemplary sense of honour and integrity on the matter of principle as such. He suffered in consequence considerable personal humiliations in public on this account; but remained to the end undeterred, his fine sense of equity and justice, artistic integrity and personal probity, flying mast-high ...

---

[12] A popular department store in Kensington High Street, London. It ceased trading in 1982.

[13] Letter from Lambert to his mother from 197 Albany Street, 7 December 1950.

[14] This was a reference to an old broadsheet advertisement for Windsor soap, with wood-cut pictorial letters for the word 'soap', that hung in the downstairs lavatory at Bradwell Lodge. Lambert's verse was an attempted solution to the meaning of the pictures on the broadsheet.

[15] The other members of the panel were Sir Steuart Wilson (chairman), Frederic Austin, Lawrance Collingwood and Edward Dent.

... His valiant partisanship on my behalf in attempting to expose a 'racket' in an adjudication in which he was concerned ... was unsuccessful; but events had gone so far that he was to have been my principal witness in a Court action which I was contemplating, but which, owing to his untimely death, had to be abandoned.[16]

While *Tiresias* continued to occupy most of Constant's time for the first part of 1951, he conducted two performances of *The Fairy Queen* for the Third Programme in February, and that month he gave again a broadcast tribute to Lord Berners by way of introduction to two memorial programmes of his works that Constant either arranged, introduced or conducted.[17] In March he was photographed at home for Festival of Britain programmes, the official caption of one portrait reading: 'Constant Lambert and Captain Spalding, his pet cat. Constant Lambert is at present working on the score of a new ballet which has been commissioned by the Arts Council in conjunction with the Festival of Britain.'[18]

On 8 May at the Victoria and Albert Museum, with the Covent Garden Chorus and the Philharmonia Orchestra, he conducted the first of eight Festival of Britain Purcell concerts arranged by Anthony Lewis. Then on 29 May at the recently opened Royal Festival Hall, with the Goldsmiths' Choral Union and the London Symphony Orchestra he gave what was to be his last public performance of *Summer's Last Will and Testament*.[19] *The Times* reported 'a tense performance ... and a rattling, vital performance of King Pest'. Ralph Nicholson, who sang in the choir, remembered that it was

> a very complicated work: it changes key and time almost every bar, and we were all horrified to see him shuffle on. ... We thought, 'How is he going to get through this complicated work?' Anyway, he shuffled on and was just able to step onto the small rostrum. And at that performance he never put a single beat in the wrong place. I don't know how he did it. He was practically sloshed yet he never made a single mistake.[20]

Such concerts as these only brought further interruptions to the composition of *Tiresias* and led ultimately to the great stress over its completion. As the time for its premiere grew nearer, one or two other concerts that he was scheduled to conduct were allocated to others. He was to have conducted his *Dirge* in a London Contemporary Music Centre concert broadcast in the Third Programme, but in the event the work was dropped. He did find time, however, to attend the first performance of Alan Rawsthorne's Second Piano Concerto in June at the Royal Festival Hall.[21] Dora Foss recalled seeing him there:

> We saw Constant twice in the last few weeks of his life – both fleeting meetings, the earlier, as we were leaving a party given to celebrate the first performance of Alan Rawsthorne's Second Piano Concerto, and then at the last performance he

[16] Letter from Christian Darnton to Hubert Foss, 8 January 1952: Hubert Foss Archive.

[17] See Appendix 7.

[18] 26 March. The photographer was Lola Walker (Lola Marsden) who also photographed Maurice Lambert on 12 April. Her three studies of Constant can be seen on the National Portrait Gallery website.

[19] A New Era concert. The first half, with Schubert's Overture *Rosamunde* and Bloch's *Shelomo*, was conducted by Richard Austin. George Pizzey was the baritone soloist.

[20] Ralph Nicholson speaking at a Delius Society meeting at the British Music Information Centre on 8 November 1994.

[21] 17 June 1951, Clifford Curzon, London Symphony Orchestra, Sir Malcolm Sargent.

conducted of the Rio Grande. We felt on both these occasions that his time was short. Nevertheless, his death came as a shock.[22]

At the end of June he attended what was for many people the most incredulous social event of the year: Tom Driberg's wedding, at the church of St Mary the Virgin, Pimlico. If the wedding announcement had surprised some of his friends, it shocked others, some of whom begged him to reconsider. His bride was a widow who had been a Labour activist. Driberg had insisted that the wedding service itself and the nuptial mass that followed should be as outrageously ornate as possible, and 400 guests were invited to the reception on the river terrace of the House of Commons. While the eclectic crocodile wound slowly towards the bride and groom, Constant was heard observing: 'All that's needed now is for the man to announce Burgess and Maclean!'[23] ApIvor recalled another instance of Constant humouring the occasion:

> It was at this time that one of his friends, noted for his homosexual propensities, got married. Constant took the very greatest interest in this episode. He was enormously impressed by the ritual of the high church ceremony which he declared to be choreographic in its complexity ... A few days after the marriage there was an accidental contiguity of news headlines in one of the papers ... 'MARRIED' and 'DUSTMEN THREATEN STRIKE' which I discovered for him. This he savoured like rare old wine as he had professed to observe that the bridegroom had a life-long partiality for dustmen.[24]

Nine days later, on 9 July, came the premiere of *Tiresias*, a production that was to prove, for different reasons, as controversial as *Romeo and Juliet* had 25 years earlier. *Tiresias* was one of three ballet commissions for the Festival of Britain, the other two being Arnell's *Harlequin in April* and Fricker's *Canterbury Prologue*. On its first night, a gala occasion in aid of the Sadler's Wells Ballet Benevolent Fund attended by the Queen and Princess Elizabeth, it was placed in between *Les Patineurs* (also choreographed by Ashton, conducted by Robert Irving) and *Ballet Imperial* (with music by Tchaikovsky, choreographed by Balanchine and conducted by John Hollingsworth). Gordon Watson was at the piano and Constant conducted.[25]

Completing the composition had caused him much trouble. It was seven or eight years since he had last produced a score of any substantial size (the *Aubade héroïque*) and he was under considerable pressure to prove himself since resigning as artistic director of the ballet.[26] According to Robert Irving, *Tiresias* had been planned 'as a satirical piece lasting about thirty minutes, but Lambert became so engrossed in the peculiarities of this legend, that the work which emerged ... was a brooding tragedy of some sixty-eight minutes. For some reason the timing of the earlier individual items

---

[22] Dora Foss typescript, Foss Archives.

[23] Driberg, *The Best of Both Worlds*, p. 57. Driberg had worked for MI5 during the war and in 1941 he was accused of being an informer by Anthony Blunt who himself was much later exposed as having been a Soviet spy. At the time of Driberg's wedding the news had only recently broken of the defection to Russia of the British diplomats Guy Burgess and Donald Maclean, two of the Cambridge Five spy ring (with Blunt). In 1956 Driberg, who had known Burgess casually, went to Moscow to interview him and that same year had published *Guy Burgess: A Portrait with Background* (London: Weidenfeld & Nicholson).

[24] Letter (typed) from Denis ApIvor to Hubert Foss, 16 April [1952]: Hubert Foss Archive.

[25] The dancers were Michael Somes and Margot Fonteyn (Tiresias), Margaret Dale (Neophyte), Pauline Clayden and Brian Shaw (Snakes), John Field (Lover), Alfred Rodrigues (Zeus) and Gerd Larsen (Hera).

[26] Not being either a concert or a stage work, his music for the film *Anna Karenina* falls into a separate category.

got out of hand, and from then on it became … a struggle to finish the work.'[27] To ApIvor his working methods seemed strange:

> Often he and Isabel would come out to the 'York and Albany' about seven, stay till getting near closing time, then go back and have food, and he would (one gathers) be intending to work after that. Whether he actually did I don't know.

Worst of all, he was very ill. How ill he had become was powerfully depicted in the pencil portraits Michael Ayrton sketched of him in those last years, and especially in the two canvases completed the year Constant died, the face bloated and one hand tightly clutching some crumpled paper close to his body.[28] In fact, as ApIvor recalled, 'he was so ill that the heavy work of the scoring … was beyond him, and a number of us helped him get it down on paper.'[29] Richard Temple Savage, the Royal Opera House librarian, anxiously awaited the orchestration so that he could prepare the orchestral parts.

> All he brought us was the first number on outsize manuscript paper that would not fit into any folder, the rest arrived in small sections which had been orchestrated by a number of his friends: Robert Irving, Denis ApIvor, Christian Darnton, Elisabeth Lutyens and Dr Gordon Jacob. Lambert had decided to use an orchestra without violins or violas, with a large wind section, cellos, basses, percussion and solo piano. As the first performance drew near I was away on tour and Tim Killar was copying day and night. At the final rehearsal Lambert decided that he needed a few more bars as an Interlude and this he dictated in the stalls to the hapless Tim who was obliged to lie on the floor as the only flat surface on which to write. He then copied the parts, passing them over to the players in the pit as he finished each one. … In the following years I took the opportunity of editing out some of the discrepancies in orchestration arising from its having been scored by a committee! I had to make a new full score anyway as every orchestrator seemed to have used a different size of paper and it was impossible to bind it all together in a presentable fashion.[30]

Yet despite the increasing pressures, ApIvor was in no doubt that writing *Tiresias* gave Constant 'tremendous happiness':

> He explored the humorous possibilities of the various situations in private, and recounted them to his friends. … He felt that he was going to épater les bourgeois sentiments of certain members of the ballet company and the public, which he certainly succeeded in doing; and also he took infinite delight in the domestic quarrel between Jupiter and Juno which he said reminded him of his first marriage.

For his part ApIvor regarded it as

> good fortune to work as other people did with him on *Tiresias* in helping him with the scoring, mechanical things – he gave full directions, and we just wrote it out for him. He knew what he wanted but his eyes were too bad at the end of his life, and I remember going to the dress rehearsal with him for *Tiresias* and standing on the stage before the curtain went up with all the scene shifters rushing about the place, … and he drew himself up to his full height – he had a

[27] Drew, *The Decca Book of Ballet*, pp. 185–6.
[28] See Iconography, Appendix 11.
[29] ApIvor, 'Composer's Anthology', p. 694
[30] Savage, *A Voice from the Pit*, p. 133.

habit of doing this, like a Roman emperor – and stamping his stick on the stage, he said, 'You know, when I get on the stage I feel like a tiger that's smelt blood.'[31]

Elisabeth Lutyens also made it clear those who assisted Constant were not involved in any composing or orchestrating:

> [Constant] had got behind with the scoring, and I and a few of his closest friends had come to the rescue as extra hands. We did *not* do any orchestration (as I read in some paper) for Constant either marked or gave specific instructions as to which instrument he wished for on which note. We merely were extra pens for his tired hands. I spent one whole day with him on this, and he talked with me, as never before, of his life and past, revealing new facts of his character.[32]

The much altered cut-and-paste manuscript score, in the Covent Garden archive, makes it clear which of Constant's friends were responsible for the scoring and the writing out of certain sections. As ApIvor observed, 'He was very careful in his directions and marked it all exactly as he wanted it.' Robert Irving, being close at hand at the Royal Opera House, made the major contribution, scoring 'Warrior's Dance', 'Cortège', 'Dance of the Priestesses', '1st entr'acte' and 'Bacchanale' (Act 2 scene 4). Christian Darnton undertook 'Snakes', Humphrey Searle 'Dance of the Shepherds and Shepherdesses' (Act 2 scene 2), Denis ApIvor 'Tiresias' Dance (woman)' (Act 2 scene 1) and 'Jupiter and Juno' (Act 3 scene 1), and Gordon Jacob 'Pas de deux' (Act 2 scene 3). The remainder Constant managed himself, with some assistance from Alan Rawsthorne[33] and Elisabeth Lutyens. Even Malcolm Arnold helped out:

> I did an intermezzo for him. It was easy because he had done all the ostinati and I just had to continue with the tune and transpose it. At the end I said, 'Constant, don't insult me by paying me for it. I'll buy you a whisky.' And he said, 'That's more like it!'

ApIvor remembered that Constant showed his gratitude for the help he had given by hiring a car to take him to the dress-rehearsal at the Royal Opera House.[34]

Lambert was paid £250 for *Tiresias*, 'not much for someone of his fame', considered ApIvor, who observed at close quarters that

> the effort of the work was too much for him in his state of health; he became very irritable at the end, and was drinking too much again. Still he was in great form, and the night before the first night I was with him and Alan Rawsthorne at his house until the small hours having a wonderful party, with Constant in uproarious mood. They left for Alan's place, ostensibly to write the interludes until dawn. In fact the interludes were written in the 'Nag' at lunch-time the next day.[35]

But to make matters worse, as Irving observed, on the first night Constant 'evidently found great difficulty in conducting the long and complicated score, and was far from maintaining the exactness of the tempo and rhythm which he himself intended.'[36]

---

[31] Denis ApIvor, in *In Search of Constant Lambert*, BBC2, 26 July 1965.

[32] Lutyens, *A Goldfish Bowl*, p. 202.

[33] In 1960 Rawsthorne composed *Improvisations on a Theme of Constant Lambert*, written for the Northern Sinfonia and premiered by them on 11 January 1961. The theme is the opening two bars of *Tiresias* (on trombones) and the work is dedicated to Isabel who was then Rawsthorne's wife.

[34] E-mail from Denis ApIvor to the author, 4 March 2003.

[35] Letter (typed) from Denis ApIvor to Angus Morrison: 9 March 1954.

[36] Drew, *The Decca Book of Ballet*, p. 186.

Tiresias received almost universally bad notices, although it was by no means comprehensively dismissed as history would have us believe. *The Dancing Times*, while admitting that the story was not an easy one, thought that the problems it raised had been 'brilliantly solved' and that it had 'a magnificent unity of style and purpose'. Lambert's music had given Ashton 'a wonderfully rhythmic and melodic base for his choreography' and he had 'excelled himself in the dances of Tiresias'. Although agreeing that it should be cut, the review ended by calling it 'wonderful theatre' that 'must be seen by all ballet-lovers'. Isabel's designs divided opinion, but there was special praise for Fonteyn, and for Pauline Clayden and Brian Shaw, the snakes. But, by contrast, in his diary Tom Driberg noted how violent some of the critics' reactions had been and catalogued their epithets: 'The *Express* headed its notice simply "Baffling, annoying, grim, savage." "Repulsive," yet merely "a frolic," said the *Herald*. There was also "sensational" (*Mirror*), "a work of the noblest stature … quite masterly … hieratic" (*Church Times*), and "a total loss" (*New Statesman*).'[37] The *Times* critic thought the ballet's weakness lay in its stylisation, with sets laid out in 'crude, harsh colours, steely blue and Indian red and glaring primrose yellow, so that they form no background, because moving or standing figures do not blend pleasurably into them' and Ashton's choreography 'so spare in invention as to border on dullness' (notwithstanding some 'moments of the real, thrilling Ashton'). The review concluded:

> Lambert's is true ballet music in that it supports and stimulates these moments and compels attention always. … He uses a large orchestra with chamber economy. … but even in the most vivid moments of music and choreography (which coincide since the collaborators are craftsmen) the ballet is not compensated for stretches of beautifully lit, grandiosely conceived, mediocrity.

Tiresias, like *Horoscope*, was an expression of love, if this time less overt, by its creator for one of its leading exponents, and it is significant that Margot's name (together with that of Michael Somes) appears in the first synopsis. As Julie Kavanagh has observed, the *pas de deux* was Constant's last love poem to her. Even some of the dancers sensed that there was 'still something lingering between Margot and Constant – we all felt it.'[38] Above all, there was his admiration for her art, a dancer now at the peak of her powers whom he had nurtured right from the very beginning, in a close working partnership of 17 years.

Some found much to admire. De Valois felt that *Tiresias* showed 'a powerful intellect at work that not even illness could overthrow',[39] Sophie Fedorovitch was insistent that it was a great ballet, and Lionel Bradley of Ballet Rambert thought it a masterpiece. But these were rare opinions. P. W. Manchester, editor of *Ballet Today*, was especially critical of its length:

> Unless Constant Lambert is prepared to be utterly ruthless and blue-pencil a full half-hour out of the present hour-long score of *Tiresias* I cannot see anything for the ballet but a speedy oblivion. The thirty minutes which would be left would give us a chance to appreciate the many individually fine moments of Ashton's choreography. As it stands at present, the ballet is like a hundred foot string of china beads amongst which some genuine pearls are almost lost to sight. In the first scene there is no need for the interminable dance of Tiresias after he has established his athletic supremacy with some excellent acrobatics (this could very well be extended and the dance cut altogether), the corps de

---

[37] In the 1970s, as 'Tiresias', Driberg compiled a scurrilous crossword for *Private Eye*.
[38] Kavanagh, *Secret Muses*, p. 391.
[39] De Valois, *Step by Step*, p. 118.

ballet play for time for minutes on end, while the waving back and forth of the wand of honour only induces hypnotic sleep in the audience. The second scene does not need so much attention, but could still be cut a little with advantage even though it would mean sacrificing a little of Fonteyn who is exquisite. The quarrel of Zeus and Hera and the manœuvrings of the corps de ballet in the last scene again threaten to go on forever, though since there is no dramatic tension in the story it is essential that Tiresias should appear as soon as possible and make the decision that strikes him blind. Somes had great dignity as the old, and subsequently blinded Tiresias and also started well with some hand springs and back somersaults, but became thoroughly bogged down in the well-nigh endless perambulatings round the stage necessitated by the music. I cannot imagine why Lambert ever thought that this Greek myth had any balletic possibilities, and one can only sympathise with Ashton at being given this story and an hour-long score with which to make his contribution to Ballet in Festival Year.[40]

Richard Johnson, in the *New Statesman and Nation*, found little to commend in either Ashton's, Constant's or Isabel's contribution. While at least finding Tiresias's dance of athletic triumph 'the most original and spirited part of the ballet', he concluded:

> It is a shame that Mr Ashton brings out none of the symbolism nor any of the overtones of this fascinating legend, for, unadorned, the story does not take happily to being a ballet. This is padded out with ritualistic passages of the utmost banality and dull dances for priestesses and warriors, athletes and shepherdesses that are sometimes folksy (there is a lot of business with staves) and too often merely gym. Perhaps the music that Constant Lambert has composed is to blame. His arid score with its faint flavour of Borodin's *Danses Polovtsiennes* is not worthy of a musician who, besides being our most distinguished ballet conductor, is an accomplished composer. Likewise, the décor. Isabel Lambert's drop curtain, ineptly and for no reason emblazoned with skeletons of reptiles and birds on squares, looks like nothing so much as a snakes and ladders board, while her garish sets in an entirely different style (a pastiche of ancient Middle-Eastern motifs) would do at a pinch for a provincial production of *Thaïs*. The costumes, a very long way after Minoan patterns, are not much better. Why does Covent Garden continue to employ artists with little idea, let alone experience, of the stage? With all respects for Messrs. Ashton and Lambert, I am afraid this ballet – the worst I have seen since the Swedish Ballet's *Medea* which it resembles – must be counted a total loss.[41]

After this review had appeared, Osbert Sitwell telephoned the critic Richard Buckle, asking his opinion of the ballet. When he replied that he had found it very dull, Osbert went on to say that, with Constant having telephoned him 'in a great state' about the *New Statesman* notice, he had let himself in to writing a letter in his defence. To this Buckle added that, as they were on opposite sides and he was reviewing the ballet for *The Observer*, Osbert would have to write an even stronger letter to that paper.

Osbert sprang vigorously to Constant's defence:

> Mr Richard Johnson's criticism of *Tiresias* calls for comment – or rather for flat contradiction which, in this case, is what it will obtain. In my opinion, and in that of other people qualified to judge, *Tiresias* is the most interesting and

[40] P. W. Manchester, 'Editorial Comment', *Ballet Today*, August 1931, p. 13.
[41] Richard Johnson, 'Tiresias', *The New Statesman and Nation*, 12 July 1951.

complete of modern ballets (and, by recent, I mean to indicate works of the last fifteen years). Its virtue is that it is continuously interesting throughout (though, as in the case of other works of art in their first stage, it may need light cutting). The whole ballet is superbly of one piece. Mr Lambert's music is always melodious, moving, suited to the theme, and its texture, as we should expect, is most agreeable. The choreography is unusually ingenious, full of surprises and delights and often beautiful, and the Cretan scenes and costumes of Isabel Lambert are particularly splendid, imaginative and fascinating.

Finally, to contradict Mr Richard Johnson once more, and where he most deserves it, may I express the hope that Covent Garden will now begin to employ such artists as Mrs Lambert – if there are others at work who have the same wealth of ideas, the same spontaneity and the same ability to express them, and that the Directors will decide to afford such designers an opportunity for experience?

But it was Buckle's review in *The Observer* that roused the most controversy. Some two years earlier Ashton had confided in him Constant's libretto for *Tiresias*. 'I said I thought he would be mad to do it: the story seemed utterly unsuited to ballet,' had been his reaction, and he later suggested that Ashton was probably too loyal to comment unfavourably. However, in his review Buckle attacked not just the ballet but the whole management of Sadler's Wells.

Blind Mice

Did you ever see such a thing in your life? Sadler's Wells has three artistic directors. See how they run. Ninette de Valois is too busy to supervise every detail of production; Frederic Ashton is too easily reconciled to compromise; Constant Lambert, one imagines, looks in occasionally with a musical suggestion. Lambert cannot take all the blame for the idiotic and boring Tiresias, which was given its first production on Monday, although the scenario and music were his, and the designs by his wife. Ashton must have undertaken the choreography of such a work with reluctance and out of duty to his colleague, but de Valois should have forbidden it. Experimental risks must be taken even with the taxpayer's money – and this ballet must have cost five thousand pounds – but certain enterprises are clearly doomed to failure from the start. Such was *Tiresias*.

What treatment other than a farcical one is suitable for this subject? ... There is no logic, no form, no dramatic conflict, no human interest, no possibility of characterisation, no truth and no beauty in this chronicle of nonsense.

The ballet lasts an hour. Its music is arid, and although it varies between the folksy and the syncopated, suggestive now of the Oriental Bazaar, now of Vaughan Williams in a religious mood, the main impression received is one of monotony. Isabel Lambert, whose speciality is to paint fish-bones, introduces these irrelevantly into her drop-curtain. Her sets are garish and monumental. Ashton's choreography, obliged to spin out long dances without dramatic relief, is the most uninspiring imaginable. The first scene, with soldiers rushing around, all out of time, clashing their shields, and with Somes hopping over their lances, seemed endless. Fonteyn was wasted on the scarf solo in Scene Two. Coming after the absurd wrangle of pedestalled deities, the blinding of Tiresias and his realistic tapping about the stage left us in puzzlement and disgust.[42]

---

[42] Richard Buckle, *The Observer*, 15 July 1951, reprinted in Buckle, *The Adventures of a Ballet Critic*, pp. 215–16.

Having seen the article and recognised the blind mice as Lambert, Ashton and herself, her comment some 25 years later was: 'When I am struck blind again may it be in such equally worthy company'.[43]

The following Friday *The Observer* and Buckle received letters from Constant's solicitor demanding an apology for a sentence in the article in which, it was alleged, the suggestion was made that Constant did not earn his salary as artistic director. Only four days later Harold Rutland encountered Constant in *The George* for what was to be their last meeting.

> I last saw him on 24th July 1951, less than a month before he died. I went to The George to have a drink with Daniel Jones, the Welsh composer, and there I saw Constant, wearing an open-necked shirt. A few weeks before, I had written a short article about him in the *Radio Times*, and I told him I hoped he had not minded what I said. His ballet *Tiresias* had been produced at Covent Garden shortly before, and he was evidently feeling a little bitter about some of the Press criticisms of it. 'Harold,' he said, 'I have so many libel actions on my hands at present, that I really can't add you to the list; otherwise I would.' Then in a more confidential tone, he added, 'Actually, it was very charming of you.' I then went off to talk to Daniel Jones, and when Constant left the pub, he called out to me, 'Good-bye, Harold: you wait for my "tu quoque".' I told him I would with the greatest of pleasure, but I shall have to wait a long time now.[44]

Buckle's article clearly called for some explanation and the following week he deflected his attack away from *Tiresias* and centred it on the running of the ballet.

> What is wrong with the artistic direction of Sadler's Wells? Is there any one person with the authority to say what shall be done and how it shall be done? Who failed to cut five minutes out of the middle act of *Cinderella*? Who allowed *Ballet Imperial* to be spoilt by an inadequate setting? Who thought *Don Quixote* would make a ballet? Who allows the conductors to play Tchaikovsky as if they were damming a stream of porridge? Who is content with Hurry's décor for *Swan Lake* and Chappell's for *Coppélia*? Who has spent tens of thousands of pounds and given us no successful new work, except Balanchine's with its feeble décor, in eighteen months? Who, possessing sole rights in the greatest ballerina in the Western world, gives her no role in which she can display her gifts to full advantage at the peak of her career?

A week later a third article followed, with Buckle now adopting the first person plural as if to suggest he was voicing a generally accepted viewpoint:

> Having diagnosed a deficiency of artistic direction in the Sadler's Wells Ballet we must propose some sort of remedy. No solution we suggest to the problem can be ideal: the ideal must be a benevolent despot with creative taste, like Diaghilev, and there is no evidence that such a one exists. Even if he did, one would hardly expect Dame Ninette de Valois, with Frederick Ashton and Constant Lambert, her artistic coadjutors, to appoint him over their heads – though he might conceivably be imposed on them by the Arts Council.

There were other factors to consider. In February 1951 the Company had returned from a second triumphant visit to America which, more ambitious than the first, had proved extremely tiring, and the strains of touring had resulted in two dancers having to return home early for medical treatment. Back in England there were a

---

[43] De Valois, *Step by Step*, p. 57.
[44] Rutland, 'Recollections of Constant Lambert'.

number of illnesses and, as David Vaughan has put it, 'there was a general feeling that the company had gone into a period of artistic decline, especially when the dancers returned exhausted by transcontinental touring. Creative juices seemed to be drying up, important roles were frequently undercast, performances in general were often lack-lustre.'[45] Ashton's staging of *Daphnis and Chloe* in April had not been a success and after the critical snipings at one Greek-based ballet, it was perhaps bold indeed to offer another. *Tiresias* had become an easy target for critics.

Yet Buckle's description of the music could hardly be farther from the truth. The splendid Hyperion CD, issued in 1999, has enabled listeners to rediscover the work and assess it for themselves without the paraphernalia of the staging and choreography. What emerges is one of Lambert's most fascinating scores in which he was exploring a new sound world, an extension, as it were, of the Concerto for Piano and Nine Players, with less emphasis on jazz rhythms but still with tremendous rhythmic drive and energy. With the absence of the upper strings there is none of the sweetness of *Horoscope*, and the audiences, accustomed to a lusher sound, may have found what Irving described as a 'harsh and somewhat "spiky" quality' uncomfortable, especially when having to endure it for over an hour. Searle thought that the 'acoustics of the orchestra pit at Covent Garden … failed to let it make its full effect.'[46] But under more ideal conditions, such as are possible with a recording, the scoring brings remarkable clarity, especially when Lambert generally contrasts the instrumental groups instead of using them en masse. Having no violins or violas brings a particularly clear focus on the woodwind and brass, while the piano has an unusually prominent role, used both for its percussive quality and as continuo. As in *The Rio Grande* and the Concerto, Lambert displays a flair for a wide array of percussion, and for all the hurry of its completion, it is a well-structured score.

It opens with an upward flourish on flutes and piano and (like Ravel's Piano Concerto in G) the crack of orchestral whips, followed by two important statements: one *fff* on trombones (Ex. 31) and the other, a fanfare-like figure on woodwind, repeated by horns (Ex. 32), that Constant had used in the last of his *Trois pièces nègres*. These two motifs, which in various forms represent the male Tiresias, are followed by quiet repetitions on brass of the first bar of Ex. 31 and a moment of pastoral calm (reminiscent of *Pomona*) in which solo oboe, *espressivo*, introduces a figure that is later to be associated with the female Tiresias. A bold inversion of those first four notes (or perhaps the four descending notes of the second bar, either way an important figure throughout the score) announces the appearance of young female athletes vaulting before a large Cretan bull. Other lithe, rhythmic ideas and repeated-note figures add to the energy and dynamism of this scene. A trumpet solo, *giocoso*, that for all its playfulness might have been lifted out of *Prize Fight*, heralds Tiresias's entry as he springs from behind the bull, with bold proclamations on brass and piano of his two motifs. He executes a dance (that was later much cut) which is followed by the Entry of the Warriors with their Sword Dance. The four-note descending figure, now prominent on the horns, is underlined on timpani and piano by sharply accented repeated-note rhythms. This figure is then eventually transformed into a plaintive cor anglais theme that marks the Entrance of the Young Virgin, who announces the Priestesses as they process in a stately triple-time Cortège. At the end of this scene, after a *maestoso* statement of the descending figure, the stage is cleared, leaving Tiresias alone with a wand that he has been given by a female neophyte. Flutter-tongued flutes then introduce the two copulating snakes represented by clarinets entwined in contrary motion – and

---

[45] Vaughan, *Frederick Ashton and his Ballets*, p. 252.
[46] Humphrey Searle, *Ballet Music: An Introduction* (London: Cassell, 1958), p. 153.

Ex. 31 Lambert, *Tiresias*, trombones, bars 2–4

Ex. 32 Lambert, *Tiresias*, horns, bars 12–14

Tiresias's anger is portrayed by tremolando brass, also in contrary motion, the crack of whips and staccato chords on piano and brass underlining each stroke of his stick. The first act ends with a bold statement of Ex. 32 as Tiresias is suddenly changed into a woman.

After the first interlude (whose bitonal rocking figure in contrary motion on the piano could easily have been the germ for Bernard Herrmann's title music for Hitchcock's 1958 film *Vertigo*), Act 2 opens with the female Tiresias's dance, a typical Lambertian siciliana movement, marked *piacevole*, in which the solo oboe brings back her theme. The Dance of the Shepherds and the Shepherdesses highlights the sexual ambiguity of the plot, with the gentle rocking figure on the woodwind contrasting with the bitonal and pentatonic interpolations of the piano. (Shead has pointed out that the bisexuality of the protagonist is also symbolised by the use throughout of the tritone.) After the female Tiresias is left alone, she is approached by a single male with whom she dances a passionate *pas de deux*. Here Constant makes uses of a beguiling, swaying theme borrowed from the 'Siesta' movement of *Trois pièces nègres* which has more than a hint of Falla's *El amor brujo*. Another stroke of the gong announces the Bacchanale, its sprightly opening theme being yet another borrowing from the *Trois pièces nègres*, this time its opening movement, 'Aubade'. At its climax, a restatement of Ex. 31 on horns is followed by the re-appearance of the snakes which the female Tiresias strikes as before, vanishes, and then returns – with heavily emphasised statements of Ex. 32 – as a man.

The shorter Act 3 opens with Zeus and Hera arguing as to who derives the greater pleasure from the sexual act. A snatch of the Dance of the Shepherds and the Shepherdesses is heard before Tiresias is summoned with Exx. 31 and 32 and a crash of the gong. Slowly he reappears, now an old man. As he ponders the question, there are brief reminiscence of the snakes, his solo dance, the female Tiresias's dance, and the beginning of the *pas de deux*. When he replies in favour of the female sex, he is struck with blindness by a furious Hera to emphatic exclamations of Ex. 32. Then a more forgiving Zeus offers him the gift of prophesy and, with the repeated descending figure on solo cello recalling the procession of Priestesses, the work dies away with final statements on cello of the two principal themes, soft chords on the piano supported by celesta, and the tapping of blind Tiresias's stick.

When writing her memoirs, Isabel could remember little of the first performance:

> As it was a command performance the audience was not a typical ballet audience. That they were surprised would be an understatement. I was told that the Duchess of Westminster left in the middle as she was shocked by the subject, namely a change of sex. In those days it was a taboo subject and above all for ballet tutus and sylphides. The following day we woke to criticisms that were violently abusive. ... After the dust had settled certain facts had to be accepted.

It was too [long]. The ballet would be greatly improved if ¼ hour had been taken out. This was the opinion of serious people including William Walton. The subject of the ballet was unsuitable for a command performance. My sets were either disliked, considered crude, clumsy, or much admired. The fact that I was immediately offered the opportunity to design another ballet 'Blood Wedding' and shortly an opera 'Elektra' proves this, I think.[47] When I appeared in the theatre the following day John Sullivan (lighting) found me drinking happily, he said, 'You seem to be taking all this very well.' I replied, 'If you are a painter, you have a rather distant view of criticism.'

C penned up in Margot's dressing room a piece of paper with the words 'famous flops – *Carmen, Swan Lake*'.

During the run of *Tiresias*, on Sunday 15 July Constant gave his last performance of *Summer's Last Will and Testament* in a Home Service broadcast, prefacing it with Borodin's Third Symphony.[48] He was worried that his mother might have been upset by the bad notices that had greeted *Tiresias*. She invited him and Isabel to lunch, but, as Isabel wrote in her memoirs, it wasn't the notices that upset her:

> Unfortunately partly out of nerves, and partly out of dislike of a change of scenery, Constant got drunk. She was much more troubled by the drink than the critics. I could see she was worried. I was also becoming worried. His conversation was wandering, his manner distant.
>
> After lunch brother Maurice and his wife arrived. They both disliked and disapproved of me. Maurice had seen my work and did not like it. Nor I his. ... Maurice had seen *Tiresias*, did not like it at all. As he never went to the ballet, or even to a concert, I suppose one can forgive his opinion.
>
> Constant had a respect for his brother's work; Maurice, I think, had not the faintest idea what his brother was about. Perhaps he was what people call tone-deaf. I was sorry for his mother. Constant was fond of her and in awe. The lunch was not a success.[49]

Eight performances of *Tiresias* were given at Covent Garden in July before it was taken to Liverpool, Leeds and the Edinburgh Festival.[50] It was seeing it at Edinburgh that left Dyneley Hussey 'amazed at the cold reception given to this remarkable

---

[47] *Blood Wedding*, with music by Denis ApIvor, was first staged at Sadler's Wells on 5 June 1953. Isabel Lambert also provided the designs for *Madame Chrysantheme*, with music by Alan Rawsthorne (by then her third husband), Covent Garden April 1955, and *Jabez and the Devils*, with music by Arnold Cooke, Covent Garden 1961. She was also considered for Walton's opera *Troilus and Cressida*, first produced at Covent Garden on 3 December 1954, Walton wrote to David Webster on 28 October 1953: 'I am glad you agree about Isabel Lambert. It struck me when I saw "Tiresias" that she would be excellent for T&C. So I hope negotiations are underway.' At the same time Walton wrote to Laurence Olivier (who was to be the producer): '[Isabel] Lambert is very good – her work very normal but with a good deal of distinction & personality. She did Constant's last ballet "Tiresias" & "Elektra" for Cov Gar. Both were excellent & it struck me when seeing them that she might be good for T&C. She is I'm told very practical & technically efficient. On the other [hand] she is a slightly awkward personality inclined to giggle for no particular reason, which is rather disconcerting I find.' Walton, *Selected Letters*, pp. 228, 230.

[48] 15 July 1951. Sunday Symphony Concert, BBC Home Service 6.15–7.45 p.m. George Pizzey (baritone), BBC Chorus, Philharmonia Orchestra. During the interval Alan Frank gave a talk on Lambert and *Summer's Last Will and Testament*. OUP had the *King Pest* movement privately recorded for sending to America in connection with a possible ballet based on Edgar Allan Poe.

[49] Isabel Rawsthorne, unpublished memoirs.

[50] 9–11 and 16–20 July 1951.

work by the majority of my colleagues who seem to be unable to see beyond its one or two obvious faults.'[51] One of these was clearly its length, and after the premiere Constant had been urged to shorten it, but he was not prepared to do so until it had been performed several times and had time to settle down. He was on the point of cutting it when he died and the task was done under Elisabeth Lutyens' direction. Hussey was also concerned with the subject matter. Although he considered Tiresias's metamorphosis suitable for balletic treatment, he thought the sexual discussion was not something that could be 'mimed with dignity' and wondered whether too much had been packed into three continuous scenes.

At the end of July, with the controversy over *Tiresias* still ringing in the press, Constant was back in the pit at Covent Garden for a fortnight's revival of *The Fairy Queen* with Saturday matinées.[52] On who observed him were both alarmed at his condition and amazed at his control. To the composer the penultimate day of this run he told David Webster that he had never been so happy,[53] but those Geoffrey Bush he 'looked like death as he hobbled into the orchestra pit on two sticks and his hand shook as he picked up the baton, but with the first notes of the overture he seemed to come to life again and to be in complete control of both music and the musicians.'[54] Sir Steuart Wilson watched from one of the stage boxes: 'In the reflected light from the orchestra desks I saw him in profile, bending over the score, waiting for the dialogue to end and his cue to come up. Intense concentration in that face, warm love for the music, complete certainty of control: the face of a scholar, a craftsman and a devotee.'[55] In his appreciation David Webster called Lambert 'the outstanding Purcell conductor of our time'.

His last two conducting engagements were for the Proms: the *Horoscope* Suite on Saturday 11 August (which was broadcast), and four days later he was in charge of the second half of the programme (which was not) – The Rio Grande, with Monica Sinclair and Kyla Greenbaum, and Ravel's *La Valse*. Joan Wilkinson, then a young violist in the BBC Symphony Orchestra, remembers how Constant lightened the atmosphere at rehearsal at Maida Vale by, instead of calling out straight cue letters, using phrases like 'L for leather' and 'O for the wings of a dove'. During a break in the rehearsal, much to the orchestra's amusement, he made great play of leaving his stick at the conductor's desk, walking slowly but steadily across to what was normally the announcer's table, pouring out a glass of water, and raising the glass to his head and drinking it slowly.[56] None there present realised, of course, that it was not so much the show of an alcoholic pretending to be 'on the wagon' but that of a diabetic quenching his thirst. Kyla Greenbaum remembered how, after that Proms performance, Constant 'staggered off', with some laughter from the orchestra.[57] Six days later he was dead.

Those close to him have left graphic accounts of those last days. Searle had been unable to attend the first night of *Tiresias* as a new work of his was being given at the Cheltenham Festival.[58] He recalled Constant's condition that year and on the last occasion he saw him:

[51] *The Dancing Times*, October 1951, p. 10.

[52] 31 July, 1–5 and 6–11 August 1951.

[53] David Webster, 'Constant Lambert: An Appreciation', *Opera*, vol. 2 no. 12 (November 1951), p. 656.

[54] Geoffrey Bush, 'Composer's Anthology 2', *Recorded Sound*, no. 40 (October 1970), pp. 692–3.

[55] Sir Steuart Wilson, *Sunday Times* obituary, 26 August 1951.

[56] In conversation with the author, 11 October 2003.

[57] Kyla Greenbaum in conversation with the author, 19 February 2003.

[58] Searle's *Poem for 22 Strings* was premiered at Cheltenham by the Boyd Neel Orchestra on 8 July 1951.

He was not well at the time, and kept having fainting fits for no apparent reason. On one occasion I was sitting with him in The George in the early evening when he had had little or nothing to drink. He suddenly felt unwell and I took him home by taxi. In August he came to a party in our studio after conducting a Prom; at the end of the party he suddenly passed out and had to be lifted into a car. We assumed that he must have been exhausted. The very next day he and Isabel, together with Lesley [Searle's wife] and I, had lunch with Edith Sitwell; he was in sparkling form, as if nothing had happened the night before. But a few days afterwards I received a late-night phone call from Denis ApIvor, who is a doctor as well as a composer, telling me that Constant had been taken to the London Clinic in a state of delirium. I telephoned his flat in the morning and was told that he had died in the night. This was a terrible shock; I could only walk aimlessly round the yard outside our house for the rest of the morning.[59]

ApIvor recalled:

In the week before he died he attended a round of parties and I was present at most of them. After conducting *Rio Grande* he went to the Searles. He was desperately ill that night, almost comatose, and should really (if one had known it) been taken to a nursing home and kept there for several weeks. But he recovered miraculously and I saw him at another party at Elisabeth Lutyens' where his son was present. He left precipitously in a temper, because that idiot Frank Dillon had insulted him or spilt beer on him.

Back home again the conversation turned on the subject which he not infrequently worked up to symphonic proportions, that of the preponderance of homosexuals at Covent Garden. He used to say that he only knew five normal men, as he also used to say that all his friends were Welshmen or Wykhemists. But all this was quite without malice either to Englishmen, queers, or old Etonians. He also on this last occasion asserted that he had himself been responsible for the rumour that the 'late Sir William' as he always called him since his knighthood, was a bastard son of Sir George Sitwell.[60]

… He suddenly rang up late on Saturday night and asked us to go over. He had at his house Andrée Howard who had been asking his advice about music for a new ballet which was to be on the lugubrious theme of witchcraft. My score *The Hollow Men* stood open on the piano and he had been playing some in an attempt to show Andrée what sort of grisly noises I could make. He was in very good form and bubbling with mirth. He insisted we should all go out for a drink before closing time. It was a hot night and a Saturday, and most of the pubs were crowded but we found one in Albany Street. It sticks in my mind that the women walked ahead coming back, and in the slow trek past that interminable expanse of empty wall to his house he spoke of *Pelléas et Mélisande* and particularly about Golaud. The theme was that he had always felt sorry for Golaud who was surely one of the most unfortunate characters in opera. This he worked up symphonically as only he could do until it became a joke of remarkable proportions.

Towards the end of the evening as it was getting pretty late and Isabel was tired we made moves to depart but Constant insisted on having some recordings of his of Waldteufel played (probably *Sur La Plage* and others). He sat there smiling away and conducting to himself. That was the last music he heard. Next morning I gather he didn't feel well and stayed in bed and in the early hours of

---

[59] Searle, *Quadrille with a Raven*, chapter 11.

[60] Letter (typed) from Denis ApIvor to Angus Morrison, 9 March 1954: RCM Archive.

Monday I was horrified to receive a distraught call from Isabel. We hurried over there to find him gravely ill. He was in a state of delirium tremens, seeing friends and terrible visions and threatening to jump out of the window. My wife did her best with him and she and Isabel held him in bed while I summoned his doctor. As I walked up and down the sitting room waiting for him to arrive I saw that *The Hollow Men* was still open on the piano where he had left it when he last sat down to play. His gramophone and records lay where he had left them. There were little notes on pieces of paper telling himself to do this and that, none of which he did I'm sure. He was looking forward to a tour in Edinburgh but never saw the mile of pubs, nor the French countryside which he promised himself after the Edinburgh Festival was over.

The ambulance came and took him away and I never saw him again. But the desolation which I feel when I think about all this in retrospect I was not so conscious of at the time. For some idiotic reason I expected he would be pulled out of it and get better. I must say that I have never missed anyone so much. There was no composer so close to one. I know the others well but I don't care for them as I did for him. In fact I sometimes wonder whether I care for them at all. But Constant was different. His admiration for van Dieren's work was just one of many points of contact. His sense of humour was certainly an all embracing quality and I believe in time a couple of hundred people used to save up their jokes for him knowing that he would savour them.[61]

He had intended going with the Company to the Edinburgh Festival but his doctor had advised against it. Nevertheless, to Isabel Constant appeared to be in a good state of mind in his last days.

He talked of writing an oratorio. … He chose to go out walking, always returned at the exact time arranged, but did not seem to remember where he had been. I believe this was genuine and not an act. Both Elisabeth and Alan[62] were aware of his change in behaviour. Elisabeth said, 'He is behaving exactly as he used to before you married him.'

We invited the lovely black Laureen and daughter Cleopatra to the ballet. Cleopatra must have been 7 or 8 years old, was a pupil at the Italia Conti School of dancing. We were in a box which was a good thing. When the curtain came down Constant suddenly collapsed onto the floor. Laureen took Cleopatra out and someone fetched brandy. After a few moments he recovered enough to be able to leave the theatre with help and we took [a] taxi home. I was now alarmed.

I was frightened of the barrier that closed separating one from the other. It was his loss of memory. He remembered nothing of his collapse and became angry when I told him of it.

I thought he would be angry when I told him he must see his doctor. No, not at all. He liked him as a person. The doctor knew it was no good to tell him to stop drinking altogether but did his best to frighten him into reducing his intake to a bottle of wine during the day. If he could work hard this would be the best help. Well, he had started working and for some time life became normal again, pleasant, amusing, busy. We made our journey on the 53 [bus] to Anna [Phillips] – spent some time strolling in the park down to Greenwich, that most beautiful place, that special shrine on the river. …

One evening we were invited to a party in a house the other side of Regent's Park. Kit was staying with us so the three of us went together. Kit had a good

---

[61] Letter (typed) from Denis ApIvor to Hubert Foss, 16 April [1952]: Hubert Foss Archive.

[62] Alan Rawsthorne was living for a while with Elisabeth Lutyens and Edward Clark.

effect on his father. They met regularly, always enjoyed themselves. They were alike in many ways, close as a family. The party was a merry one, Elisabeth and Constant were funny together. I managed to talk to Alan which I had not done for quite a long time, certainly not since the advent of *Tiresias*.

It was late when we got home. Kit was off early in the morning. I reminded Constant that Anna was expecting us for lunch. He said he did not feel like going, might come later.

I left him asleep, I thought, in bed and took a seat on the top deck of the 53. I enjoyed the journey – through south London, the Old Kent Road, up the long hill to the heath to Anna's lovely house in the Pentagon.

No sign of Constant and no telephone. So back home.

Opening the bedroom door I heard the most extraordinary noise. Constant was lying in bed with one arm stretched out in front of him, muttering in a voice unlike his own. Listening carefully I made out the words 'Don't let them take me away'. Then [']Look at the window[']. On the right hand side of the room was a glass door into the conservatory. It was at this that he was looking. I grabbed the telephone and was frantically grateful that Denis ApIvor who as well as being a composer was an anaesthetist, his wife a nurse. They lived very near, were round in a matter of minutes.

Denis telephoned Constant's doctor who again was around in minutes. It seemed to me that Constant was in hospital in an unbelievably short time. In occasions of shock it seems one's activities become automatic. I telephoned Elisabeth and Alan. They were both round in a few minutes. Now, a long way off, I wonder what would have happened if none of these people had been at home?

Through my sense of pain and disaster I kept thinking – but I have let them take him away! But then I remembered that before Denis and Irene arrived he had tried to get [out] of bed and move towards the window. I had no strength to stop such a strong man, especially one who was mad.

Alan [and] Elisabeth took me to the hospital[63] where we were told he was in bed, had been given sedatives and would sleep for some hours. We thought the best thing to do was to go and have something to eat and drink nearby. Elisabeth said she would [telephone] the few people who we thought ought to know. None of [us] had any sense of what was to happen.

We cannot have been out more than an hour or two before returning to Albany Street. The telephone rang, the hospital told me to come at once or it would be too late.

Arrived there, I was led to the room where Constant lay underneath a huge oxygen mask. He was still alive but it was obvious only just. He recognised me. In order to say something which sounded normal I asked who he would like to come and see him, Elisabeth, Alan? [']Yes. We have seen enough of you.['] The horror of these words did not really affect me until later. I was too shocked.

I was told that it is characteristic of this kind of delirium[,] leads the victim to turn against the closest to them. Had he not forgiven me for letting them take him away?

After this I remember nothing. All I know is that Alan and Elisabeth did everything, arranged everything. When Denis ApIvor was told what had happened he was astounded. He had talked to the doctor as a doctor and was assuming that once in hospital and under treatment there was no reason [why] Constant would not recover.

---

[63] The London Clinic, 20 Devonshire Place, London W1.

I know that Peter sent a telegram saying 'Come at once', that Pattie did come at once and faced a furious Maurice Lambert who understandably could not understand why he was not forewarned. Alan also faced the furious Maurice saying apparently, 'You don't like her, do you? Well I do.'

I must have told my mother. I always let her know if something critical was happening, and she and my brother were present at the funeral.

I can only just bring back into my memory the service at St. Bartholomew's – Alan was by my side as we followed the coffin. I remember seeing Ninette de Valois and Freddie Ashton and Randall Swingler in tears.[64]

After the funeral there was a cremation but I was told I need not go if I did not want to so I did not. After this my memory became a jumble of overlapping images.

Constant's death, on Tuesday 21 August, at such a relatively young age, stunned many people. As Elisabeth Lutyens was later to write so memorably: 'Amongst musicians Constant Lambert towered and the music world was duller with his dying. ... The musical world shrank for me at his death.' Even to some, like the critic Eric Blom who had not known him personally, he commanded respect as a true individual:

> And what a character he was. I hardly knew him beyond and nod and a beck, yet the impression remains indelibly of a unique person, a tragic mixture of aloofness and conviviality, stiffness and amicability, bohemianism and integrity, devastating wit and uncompromising seriousness. As a critic he was perhaps handicapped by his fine qualities as a conductor which could hardly fail to embarrass his judgement of other performers ...[65]

Geoffrey Bush, although he had never known him, heard on the radio the announcement of his death 'with a sense of personal shock' because 'he had contributed so much' to his musical life. Within a few hours there came to his head 'a theme for an elegiac blues in much the same mood as the one he had written for Florence Mills', and this eventually became the haunting slow movement of his first symphony.[66] Lambert had been his teenage musical hero.[67]

Among those who were deeply upset by his death were Malcolm Arnold, who years later confessed to having cried when he realised he would never see him again, and Paddy Hadley, whose friendship with Constant had been 'as close as any I've had with my contemporaries'.[68] He wrote to Angus Morrison, concerned about the financing of Kit's education. Walton had offered to be responsible for half of the school fees.[69] Cecil Gray, who had been heartbroken by the death of his wife Margery in 1948, became even more depressed after Constant's death and was himself to die in September. Robert Helpmann, sitting next to Nancy Mitford at a dinner part in December 1953, commented that he missed Constant more than anyone else in the world. Another, who was more inwardly moved by Constant's death, was Margot Fonteyn. The Company had only been at the Edinburgh Festival for a day or two when news of Constant's death broke. In *Tiresias*, Mary Clarke has recorded, she 'danced as one possessed. She

---

[64] According to Denis ApIvor, the only time he saw Rawsthorne in tears was on the day of Lambert's funeral.

[65] Eric Blom, *The Observer*, 2 September 1951.

[66] Bush, 'Composer's Anthology 2', p. 693. In the coda to the slow movement, Bush also alludes on the cellos to the choral entry in *The Rio Grande*.

[67] Sleeve note by Geoffrey Bush for Lyrita SRCS115 and SRCD252.

[68] Wetherell, '*Paddy*', p. 86.

[69] *Ibid.*, p. 89.

1950–1 • Snakes and *Tiresias* **411**

had a passionate intensity in this ballet which she had not equalled in any other role.'[70] Robert Irving, who conducted later performances, similarly observed that 'she seemed to bring a special intensity and pathos to this comparatively small role'.[71]

There were those who tried to see a direct link between Constant's death and the failure of *Tiresias*. Certainly ApIvor thought that 'the abuse which was hurled at *Tiresias* in the press affected him gravely.' But Osbert Sitwell, in the *New Statesman and Nation*, went further, writing that 'he would be alive today had it not been for the savage onslaughts of the critics … [who] jumped on him as if he were a criminal. And they felled him just at the moment when he was unwell and seriously overworked.' As a critic himself, Scott Goddard replied that Lambert 'was too big to be so grievously affected by what people said or wrote about his music' and suggested that Osbert had done him a disservice by asserting that 'he was killed by impolite criticism'. Edith, in the same paper, rose to the defence of her brother who had gone abroad: '[Constant Lambert] was *most* grievously affected, as I, with whom he lunched a few days before his death, know from his conversation,' concluding with a typical Sitwellian observation on manners: 'He did not mind adverse criticism. What he did mind was the extreme discourtesy with which it was worded.'[72] But, as the editor of *Ballet Today* tactfully put it: 'Sir Osbert, in understandable sympathy for an old friend, overstated his case', and Isabel firmly rejected any such suggestion:

> It was a disappointment but it had been greatly exaggerated. I mean, totally ridiculous things were said, you know, in the Press, by various individuals, I don't mean critics, but others. I mean the Sitwell family, for example, took it upon themselves to say this killed him which is an absolute utter lie – and you can record me saying that – and certainly he was disappointed. He least of all people who was so theatrically minded as a person. His life really was the theatre and he never had this ridiculous fashion pretending you don't mind criticism. This wasn't Constant's nature at all. He was the most honest man and said, 'We all want gorgeous praise all the time.' So he was disappointed, of course, but to say that it had anything to do with his death is totally and utterly and ridiculously wrong.[73]

Constant died intestate, leaving an estate valued at £2,514. The causes of death were recorded as broncho-pneumonia and diabetes mellitus. His funeral service was held on the morning of Saturday 25 August at the Anglican church of St Bartholomew the Great, Smithfield, followed by a private cremation. Walton had been asked to give the address but felt unable to do so and suggested Hubert Foss in his stead. As Dora wrote: 'I was not there myself, but several of those present told me how moving and inspired his words were. It was an ordeal indeed, and not only were his listeners touched, Hubert himself was almost overcome with emotion.' Denis ApIvor took Frida van Dieren who 'wept throughout'. His ashes were buried in Brompton Cemetery beneath a headstone that today records the deaths of George W. T. and George Washington Lambert, father and grandfather, of his mother, Amelia Beatrice, who ashes were buried alongside Constant's in 1963, and of Christopher Sebastian, who died in 1981.

If Constant had been able to conjure up strange events in his lifetime, according to Searle some curious phenomena occurred after his death. At the memorial service, which was held at the church of St Martin-in-the-Fields on 7 September, Louis Kentner was to have played the *Aubade héroïque* on the organ, an instrument that Lambert

---

[70] Clarke, p. 202n, p. 265.

[71] Drew, *Decca Book of Ballet*, p. 186.

[72] Edith Sitwell, *New Statesman and Nation*, 15 September 1951, p. 284.

[73] Isabel Lambert, in *In Search of Constant Lambert*, BBC2, 26 July 1965.

apparently loathed and, according to Helpmann, would get in a rage when he heard it being played. On this occasion, however, the instrument refused to emit a single note and so, instead, an out-of-tune piano had to be dragged out of the choir's practice room.[74] Needless to say, the organ performed normally afterwards. Helpmann was asked to read the lesson and, as he later commented, 'had the dreadful feeling that Constant was waiting just to trip me up as I went up the stairs to read'. Members of the Sadler's Wells Opera Company sang Bach's *Jesu, Joy of Man's Desiring* and the large congregation included many of the Sadler's Wells Company, including Dame Ninette de Valois, Margot Fonteyn and Frederick Ashton, as well as Sir William and Lady Walton, Edmund Dulac, and Anthony and Lady Violet Powell. In his last years his meetings with Anthony Powell had been less frequent but they had been in regular contact by telephone as Constant would ring up nearly every week for a chat.

Then, the following January, at a concert of the Society for Twentieth Century Music which included Constant's Li-Po poems in the chamber ensemble version and his piano concerto, a large black cat appeared on the platform and sat there throughout the performance. At the end of the concert it stalked off and was never seen again.

After the memorial service Isabel had a short holiday at Zenner in Cornwall where she was joined by Alan Rawsthorne. She went on to Paris, and then with Alan to Florence (her first visit) and Greece. They were married in 1955, she retaining her existing married name for professional purposes.

In October 1951 Walton gave a talk on Lambert in BBC's *Music Magazine* to which Constant himself had made many contributions,[75] and the following January two memorial programmes of his music were broadcast in the Third Programme, conducted respectively by Robert Irving and Norman Del Mar.

When the Covent Garden London season opened in September, three days before the memorial service, as a tribute to Constant a revised version of *Tiresias* was given on the opening night and the three successive evenings, with Margot still taking her leading role.[76] But when, in September 1953, Tito Arias came back into her life and saw the woman he planned to marry dressed revealingly in her Cretan-style bodice for *Tiresias*, he became so jealous that, as she told a friend, 'Tito has made such a carry-on, I just can't do it', and she relinquished the role to Violetta Elvin.[77] Even more tragic, if true, is the suggestion that, out of jealousy, Tito either burnt or made Fonteyn burn some unpublished manuscripts and letters that were in her possession at the time of her marriage.[78]

Tiresias was taken to America in 1955 where it found favour with at least one critic, who described it as 'rich, noble and underestimated ... as great a work as [Ashton] has ever accomplished'.[79] But it was afterwards dropped from the repertoire and largely forgotten until a BBC broadcast 40 years later and the commercial recording

[74] Both *The Times* and *The Dancing Times*, possibly copying what had been printed on the service sheet, reported that John Churchill played *Aubade héroïque* on the organ.

[75] Walton's talk was printed in *Selections from the BBC Programme Music Magazine*, ed. Instone and Herbage.

[76] *Tiresias* stayed in the repertoire for five years with a total of 34 London performances (12 in 1951, 10 in 1952; 7 in 1953; 3 in 1954, 2 in 1955). Somes danced in all but one of these performances, his understudy Alexander Grant appearing once; Fonteyn danced in 26 (1951–4), eventually relinquishing her role to Violetta Elvin. It was given in Paris in September 1954, during an exchange between the Théâtre Nationale de l'Opéra de Paris and the Royal Opera House, Covent Garden, and the following year in America.

[77] Kavanagh, *Secret Muses*, p. 391.

[78] Brian Masters, 'Margot Fonteyn', *Harpers & Queen*, April 1991, p. 169, and Daneman, *Margot Fonteyn*, p. 316.

[79] John Martin in *The New York Times*, quoted in Bland, *The Royal Ballet*, p. 111.

on compact disc in 1998.[80] Only then could it be readily assessed, emerging as a work with considerable strengths and, musically, far from the failure the critics had claimed it to be.

A s is often the case with composers, after his death Constant Lambert's reputation fell into a decline from which it has never really recovered. The diversity of his talents made it difficult for those commentators who engage in the popular pastime of pigeon-holing, to categorise him. Even in 1949 a critic in *Gramophone* could write:

> It is a truism, yet none the less regrettable, that Constant Lambert's gifts as a conductor, and his keen insight, brilliance and wit as a critic, have successfully distracted attention from his talents as a composer. Were he a foreign composer, we should be falling over our feet in efforts to perform his works: as it is, he is almost completely neglected in our concert halls and on our records. ... The incomprehensibility of our neglect becomes apparent when we hear [*Horoscope*]. The graceful *Saraband* contains the most soothing and heart-easing music, and the *Bacchanale* is full of Lambert's lively syncopated rhythms.[81]

From the melancholy of a simple work like *Elegiac Blues* to the searing climax of *Summer's Last Will and Testament*, from the lyrical beauty of *Horoscope*, the jazz rhythms of the mournful Concerto for Piano for Piano and Nine Players, the tender poignancy of the Li-Po settings, the pastoral calm of the war-time *Aubade héroïque*, the inventiveness of *Tiresias* (irrespective of its questionable libretto), to the sheer brilliance of *The Rio Grande*, his music deserves a regular place in concert planning. Yet even today his most substantial and arguably his finest work, *Summer's Last Will and Testament*, is seldom performed and the orchestral score remains unpublished. Unlike Walton, he did not develop a uniformly recognisable style as a composer. The continual and demanding hard work for the ballet and occasional bouts of melancholia may explain why his output, though consistently brilliant, is relatively small, while the instrumentation of many of his works does not make it easy for them to find a place in conventional programmes. In the almost half-century of seasons of the Henry Wood Promenade Concerts since his death until 2000 he received only 13 performances, nine of these being of *The Rio Grande*, and between 1965 and 1972 there were no Lambert performances at all at the Proms.[82] Neither was he well represented in the *Gramophone* catalogue: in the mid-1960s none of his works was available on record. Fine though his once popular choral work is, there are others beyond *The Rio Grande* that deserve to be known. Fortunately, almost all his significant works are now available on CD.[83]

Just as the public perception of Delius in his active years has been clouded – if not almost effaced – by the too familiar image of the blind and paralysed composer (the James Gunn portrait and Ken Russell's moving 1968 BBC film *Song of Summer*), so too does the mention of Lambert often conjure up a mental picture of him in his later years of heavy drinking – at the expense of any recognition of his earlier achievements.

---

[80] *Tiresias* received its first broadcast on 8 November 1995, with Barry Wordsworth conducting the BBC Concert Orchestra. It was recorded in April 1998 for Hyperion CDA67049, with David Lloyd-Jones conducting the English Northern Philharmonia.

[81] L[ionel].S[alter]., *Gramophone*, June 1949, p. 4. Sacheverell Sitwell similarly felt that 'so much work as conductor and musical adviser may have to some extent stultified [Lambert's] other talents': Haskell *et al.*, *Gala Performance*, p. 34.

[82] Between 2000 and 2011 six works by Lambert were given at the Proms, with only one performance of *The Rio Grande*.

[83] The one curious omission is the seldom-performed *Dirge (from 'Cymbeline')* that has never been recorded.

This was not helped in his centenary year when one writer, with an eye more to sensationalism than factual accuracy, irresponsibly reported that 'he collapsed in a gutter' before dying.[84]

In a radio talk on cats, Constant once commented that 'with one or two noteworthy exceptions I know of no composer or executant worth his salt who has not been devoted to the feline world'. The same might almost be said of composers of his generation and drink. Constant's tragedy was that his drinking problem was compounded by undetected diabetes. Even from his childhood he was dogged with misfortune. The operations that he underwent while a student at Christ's Hospital left their mark on him for life: deafness in the right ear and frequent pain in the right leg, with a permanent limp and the need to walk with a stick. While he claimed that the deafness affected his conversation more than his conducting – 'I can hear music easily; it is only so far as conversation is concerned that it affects me,' he is reported as saying[85] – as ApIvor observed, 'He had a wasted leg which let him down even when sober, and which caused him continued bouts of pain, I suppose throughout the whole of his life'. It was typical of Lambert that when the sensible recourse would have been to rest the leg as much as possible, in a pub for example, he was always seen standing at the bar. Drink for him became almost a necessity, to dull his pain and his nervousness – especially before conducting.

If drinking was one weakness, another concerned his close relationships, both as father and husband. Constant was not a family man, a failing that he inherited. His father's artistic manner and flamboyance could not have made easy any close father-son relationship, even if George Lambert had recognised its importance in a child's development. But then George had never known *his* father, and Constant was only 15 when George left permanently for Australia. Even when Constant was a child George was often away from home, and when only ten he was sent to boarding school. A warm family life was something he was not to experience. Both George's and Constant's devotion to their art was at the expense of their family – and ultimately their own health. It is hardly surprising that Kit endured a similar childhood that was regularly punctuated by the absence of his father. For him too boarding school was chosen, more as a convenience than an educational preference, and instead of having fond memories of a loving parent, he remembered Constant as being a rather formidable figure, and strongly eccentric:

> He'd quite often be seen walking round the streets where we lived in full evening dress at two o'clock in the afternoon before he went off to Covent Garden, yet somehow no-one seemed to be in the least surprised by this. ... He was completely occupied by his own thoughts and therefore not terribly aware of sometimes what was going on around him.[86]

As he told Angus Morrison, 'I only knew my father just well enough to realise what a great man he was.'[87] It was a great irony that Kit was to die at the same age as Constant, an end that in his case was hastened not by drink but by drugs.

Constant's life style and working routine were not conducive to married life, with the ballet frequently taking him away from home for long stretches, with his habit of

---

[84] Norman Lebrecht, *The Lebrecht Report*, 27 April 2005. Amongst other inaccuracies in the article, Lambert, an admirer of Elgar's *Falstaff*, is said to have 'ridiculed Elgarian romanticism' in *Music Ho!*

[85] *Evening Standard* obituary.

[86] *In Search of Constant Lambert*, BBC2, 26 July 1965. Kit's ultimately tragic life has been well told by Andrew Motion in *The Lamberts: George, Constant and Kit*.

[87] Letter to Angus Morrison, 22 January 1954.

working long into the night, and with his drinking. For all his appearance of a bon viveur and someone of a gregarious nature, Constant was in fact a very private person, even withdrawn and introverted. Those within his circle cherished his company and his humour, but despite his outward conviviality and bonhomie, he was, to quote Isabel again, 'a loner [who] hid behind a carapace of wit, sharp remarks and great vitality.' His affliction with streptococcal septicaemia, after his promising first successful year at Christ's Hospital, kept him away from school and his fellow students for five terms, and when on his return he was unable to participate in most sports, this and his level of intellect marked him out as a solitary figure, and close relationships were difficult. Throughout his life he seemed socially more at ease with people of a similar intellectual level and he had a small, select group of close friends, people like Cecil Gray, Michael Ayrton, Patrick Hadley, Alan Rawsthorne and Anthony Powell, whom he kept rather 'in compartments' according to their profession. They were, like himself and two friends of earlier years, Philip Heseltine and Bernard van Dieren, eloquent conversationalists. Frequent touring with the Vic-Wells/Sadler's Wells ballet company often made meetings with his friends difficult, yet even when stuck in some dull provincial town for a week of ballet, his humour never left him, showing itself in the postcards he sent them to combat his loneliness.

Humour was a powerful tool for Lambert the critic. It was almost certainly his frequent shortage of money that led him to diversify his talents and turn to journalism. A man of great sincerity, he despised pomposity and artifice, and he made no secret of what he disliked as far as music and the music profession were concerned. He was very much of his time, outwardly manifesting the flippancy of the 1920s but inwardly brooding over the troubled 1930s. With no published collection of his articles, his fame today as a critic rests on his one book, *Music Ho!* that has attained the status of a minor classic. Music criticism dates very quickly; it is for the moment, and even *Music Ho!* for all its brilliance does not give a full flavour of the wit and sometimes the acerbity of his weekly writing for papers like the *Sunday Referee* (to which he most regularly contributed and which in 1939 merged with the *Sunday Chronicle*) and *The New Statesman and Nation* (that from 1957 dropped the *Nation* suffix). He could at times seem unduly critical – even negative. But he meant what he wrote, and wrote what he felt, with the ability to hit his musical Aunt Sallies with a verbal dexterity that few of his contemporaries could match. He would sometimes overindulge his own particular preferences, but only because he felt they were worthy of attention and because nobody else was championing those causes. His criticism always had a purpose. Were he alive today, he would no doubt be horrified at the comparatively little space given to music criticism in the popular press, and just as he had prophesised the disappearance of the middle-brow composer, he would be horrified too at the disappearance of the middle-brow listener and the average man-in-the-street's seeming ignorance of serious music. Nearly 80 years since the writing of *Music Ho!* one prophesy is not far from the truth:

> Music written by composers whose individualism links them with the great composers of the past and whose work, being the result of a spiritual concentration, requires at least a modicum of this concentration from the listener, will become a specialised art like poetry, appreciated with the same intensity by an equally small public. Apart from this, music will be a definitely popular form of art, not revolving round the concert hall but adapting itself to wireless and the films. An easy-going, pleasant and exhilarating noise which will form a kind of *musique d'ameublement.*[88]

---

[88] Lambert, *Music Ho!* (Pelican Books, 1948), p. 199.

His friendship with Philip Heseltine was a turning point in Constant's life. While this was to have an adverse effect on his life-style, it nonetheless enriched his musical attitudes, deepening his appreciation of such composers as Liszt, Delius and van Dieren, and broadening his outlook by introducing him to composers of the Elizabethan period. The death of Heseltine affected him more deeply than anything else. Not for nothing did he once say to Frederick Ashton that he wanted to live like an Elizabethan and die young – which, alas, he did.

Lambert's posthumous reputation overlooks some aspects of his busy career for which he was known during his life-time: the unsurpassed reciter of *Façade*, a broadcaster, author, critic (although by the start of the Second World War he had ceased writing regular music criticism), teacher, conductor, recording artist, restorer of early music (even if by today's standards his work in that field might be regarded as more pioneering than scholarly), and jazz enthusiast. His radio talks were marked by a very individual delivery – the fairly rapid, slightly clipped speech with rolled 'r's that can be heard in the few broadcasts that remain in the BBC's sound archives, and with a clarity that distinguished his delivery of *Façade*. Although, sadly, no recording exists of his Third Programme broadcasts of *Façade*, one can have a fairly good idea of why he was so highly regarded, not least by Walton, from the extracts he recorded commercially in 1929.

His association with the Royal College of Music came to an end when he ceased teaching there at the outbreak of war, but in 1989 Mrs Camilla Hole (as Florence then called herself) endowed the College with a Constant and Kit Lambert Fund 'in memory of her husband Constant, a former Collard Fellow (1934–37) and liveryman, and son Kit'. Four studentships of £2,000 and two scholarships of £4,000 are awarded annually, together with one Fellowship worth £11,900. Amongst those in Constant's conducting class had been some familiar names like Reginald Goodall, Robert Irving, George Malcolm and Norman Del Mar, and two who were to be associated with Sadler's Wells Opera: James Robertson and Michael Mudie.

Too often overlooked is his legacy for the gramophone.[89] His efficiency in the recording studio resulted in 75 per cent of his issued record sides being first 'takes'. His recordings of many ballet scores, light pieces such as Waldteufel waltzes, more substantial works by Delius, Rawsthorne, Warlock, Borodin and Tchaikovsky, and his own music all deserve a wider circulation. As a conductor he probably spent more time in the radio studio than in the concert hall, for both home and overseas broadcasts. But his post-war appointment as assistant conductor at the Henry Wood Proms opened a new avenue for him and brought him a new audience. While he generally avoided the works of Germanic composers like Brahms, Schumann and Wagner, with the formation of the Third Programme he excelled in programmes that ranged from Purcell, Vivaldi and Handel to Liszt, Satie and van Dieren. From time to time his versatility resulted in him taking on certain modern works with which he was not in total sympathy or that others felt less inclined to tackle, and on one notable occasion he stepped in with a programme that Schoenberg was to have conducted. His sympathies were in many cases similar to those of Sir Thomas Beecham whom he greatly admired: Mozart, Delius, Sibelius, Berlioz, Liszt, Russian music and what could be described as light classical works. As Angus Morrison commented, a noticeable feature of Lambert's recordings is 'his wonderful sense of tempo. In slow music it is always flowing and alive, and in fast music clarity is never sacrificed to speed just for its own sake.'[90]

---

[89] See Appendix 3.
[90] Morrison, 'Constant Lambert (1905–1951)', p. 790.

But it was with ballet that he was, of course, most closely identified. While he is often mentioned as the first of only two English composers to have a ballet accepted by Diaghilev, it was not so much as a composer that he was fortunate in meeting the impresario. Although the ballet score that was accepted brought him some fame, it had already been composed with a different scenario in mind and it was just a case of Diaghilev shaping his ideas of *Romeo and Juliet* around the existing music, with little input from the composer – except disagreement. Had it not been for the riot on the night of its Paris presentation, it might have faded from the repertoire sooner than it did. What made Constant's collaboration with Diaghilev so invaluable was the insight that he gained into the creative process of ballet, how the Russian treated with equal importance the individual contributions of music, dance and design. This was to have the greatest influence on Constant and define his artistic future. In his youth he had witnessed the achievements of the Ballets Russes in their London seasons, but the insight he gained as a contributor gave him ideas of how a ballet company should function, ideas he was to carry through with the Camargo, Vic-Wells and Sadler's Wells companies. He was even to follow Diaghilev's practice of inserting fairly short pieces of music as interludes between ballets.

Apart from his compositions, Lambert's greatest achievement was unquestionably his work for the Vic-Wells/Sadler's Wells Ballet Company. From the early Camargo Society days, Constant learned the importance of seeing a ballet through from its beginning, of having regular discussions with, when possible, composer, choreographer and designer and ensuring a unity of those three arts. He guided the music from the start, often selecting the various pieces that would be used in a given ballet, even writing out the orchestral parts, and rehearsing with individual dancers so that when the orchestra was brought in he knew their personal strengths and requirements and would fashion the performance with this in mind. In this way the dancers knew they could totally rely on their conductor. He neither followed them, nor did they follow him; they worked together. Listening to the discussion between Lambert, de Valois and Helpmann in the admittedly scripted 1941 radio broadcast *Ballet Night*, it is clear how dominant a role Constant played in the Sadler's Wells planning. In a chapter in *Gala Performance: A Record of the Sadler's Wells Ballet over Twenty-Five Years*, Robert Irving, as a conductor of ballet, offered an astute assessment of his colleague:

> Apart from Lambert's expert musicianship, which contained that vital element of adventurousness and interest in 'lost' composers, he possessed that rare combination of creative force and a nimble and practical intelligence, which was ideal for the planning of a bold and varied musical policy. As a conductor, apart from his love of the ballet, he had that essential sense of movement, although he himself was physically handicapped by a severe illness as a child.
>
> This sense of movement was conveyed in his beat, which seemed to include within itself the inner components of the rhythm, while never losing sight of the dramatic significance of the music, as it affected the action of the ballet. Finally his warm humanity and burning enthusiasm were exactly the qualities required for working with a theatre orchestra, whose members are not constantly buoyed up by the public acclaim of the concert platform, and consequently need more encouragement to retain faith in their jobs. He was most ably supported by the violinist Joseph Shadwick.[91]

Constant was meticulous in all things, even to the layout of the orchestra in the pit, specifying the exact spacing between each player. Dame Ninette de Valois recognised

---

[91] Robert Irving, 'Music and the Ballet', in Haskell *et al.*, *Gala Performance*, p. 117.

as much as anyone what his contribution meant to the success of the ballet. In *Step by Step*, written in 1977, she outlined Constant's strengths:

> When new ballets had to be mounted, thick with wartime restrictions, Lambert was faced with many orchestral compromises, score reductions and difficult rehearsal schedules. Yet still came the demand for perfection, and the compromises were always handled skilfully. It was the echo of this frontal attack from the orchestra pit that became such a challenge on the stage. Somehow it compelled us to cope with the monthly sapping of our strength by the devastating military call-up. ...

> How am I to see him in retrospect as a friend, an adviser, and a man of intellect and personality in our midst? He was, as many a brilliant mind, distinctly volatile. At one moment you argued with an intellectual wayward 'bluecoat' boy; at another with an old head on young shoulders showing a depth of knowledge that left you blushing over your own shortcomings; another time he would be outrageous and not over-respectful of any elder or better, then you were confronted with an attack of acute conservatism, ridiculing his own avant-garde. ...

> Down through the years he wore his many-coloured coat, always hating any atmosphere of self-conscious intellectuality, and when such moments occurred this particular intellectual adopted a form of bucolic opposition. In spite of his fluctuating temperament, I maintain that Lambert's inborn common sense and knowledge of true values were always apparent.

> If temporarily irritated by the ballet classics, he would express his boredom with Tchaikovsky, and then go into the orchestra pit to conduct one of the composer's ballets as no one else has done since. When he had had too many drinks he was either exasperating, gloomy or very funny. ...

> He was observant, and possessed a shrewd judgement of his friends and acquaintances. I do not want the real Constant Lambert to get out of perspective. He had in him a strain of extraordinary logical reasoning powers, and if he had any interest or belief in the people that he was working with, they could only become even more aware of the great qualities that he was displaying. Thus for the years I watched a turbulent sea that had an undercurrent of a smooth waters, a gulf stream that could help balance the temperature with a sympathetic understanding of the rise and fall of thinking, planning and doing. ...

> Orchestral players adored him; his deft leadership and lack of pomposity went straight to the heart of even the most seasoned members of the orchestra. He was at his best when seated with us at the piano working out cuts, sequences, and the general development of a piano score that he was arranging. Long silences with a foot tapping, a hand conducting, a muffled hum through the cigarette with its endless fall of ash; there would be a sudden lean forward on to the score, and the appearance of several clear firm notation marks; once more the straightened position and the one-man band restarted.

> He had a carefully acquired knowledge of different types of dancers; an awareness, through his powers of observation, of weakness and strength in the all-over picture of technical prowess, and sympathetic understanding shown where licence could be permitted that was not to the detriment of the musical or choreographic flow. Yet he was a great disciplinarian, and generally insisted on discussing tempo with the choreographer concerned, or in the case of the classical revivals, with me. His word was law, and a law respected by all the artists. ... 'When Constant makes a tempo change it doesn't worry us, he always

makes you want to respond' ... in other words, he always knew when they could respond to his demands.

And she concluded:

> He was the greatest ballet conductor and adviser that this country has had, and the musical world has labelled him as such. Towards his end this was for him a very real frustration. I know through conversations with him how much he would have liked to have had far more musical interests outside ballet; he felt, and not without reason, that he was a victim of type casting. We, the ballet world, devoured him and drained him of everything that he had to give us from 1931 to within two years of his death. ...
>
> Even today ... there is no one to equal him in that all-round knowledge and intellectual understanding demanded of this eclectic side of the theatre world. He laid a foundation stone for us from which things could continue to spring, and here it can be seen in retrospect that he had all along shown second sight.[92]

Hubert Foss, who, had he lived longer, would have been his first biographer, knew Constant both in a professional capacity and as a friend, and he concluded his obituary with these words:

> The personality of Lambert was of such magnitude and vitality that this single pen would not attempt to express it. His humour, always bubbling up, had the rare quality of being informed by inside knowledge; always, he seemed to express life in a single joke. No man I have ever met had such singleness of purpose in art; he believed passionately in music and sought nothing but the best of its kind. Lambert had complete integrity. He could not tolerate self-seekers. He was a friend of all, a special friend of a wide circle of people who will never know his like. His cynical streak was a mere outcrop on a deep vein of love for art, life and people. Above all he was full-blooded, savoured life with the utmost relish, gorged on its beauties and good things. Save to add that Constant had genius, I will say no more.[93]

It was indeed a life which he fearlessly lived to the full because, as he wrote himself:[94]

> It's no good escaping your doom
> By taking a ticket to Spain;
> The bulging portmanteaux of gloom
> Will arrive by a later train.

---

[92] Ninette de Valois, *Step by Step*, pp. 52–6.
[93] Hubert Foss, *The Musical Times*, October 1951, p. 451.
[94] Sent to the author by Patricia Lambert (no relation), a close friend of Isabel Rawsthorne.

Appendix 1
The Compositions of Constant Lambert

* indicates a work that is no longer extant

* DANCE for orchestra
Composed: *c.* 1922 while at Christ's Hospital
First performance: 8 Dec. 1923, Pump Room, Bath, Pump Room Musicians, Jan Hurst, choreographed and danced by Penelope Spencer
Publication: Unpublished. Score probably lost.
Instrumentation: Not known
Note: 'I have some compositions which I think might interest you. A Dance for orchestra which I wrote at school and a Spanish Rhapsody which I have just finished.' (letter to Penelope Spencer, *c.* 1923).

* [Title not known] for solo clarinet
Composed: *c.* 1923
First performance: No performance known.
Publication: Unpublished. Score probably lost.
Note: A student work, the first one 'with the "New look"' that he showed his teacher Vaughan Williams who described it as 'a very remarkable piece' (*Letters of Ralph Vaughan Williams*, p. 491). Lambert played clarinet in the orchestra at Christ's Hospital.

* SPANISH RHAPSODY
Composed: *c.* 1923
First performance: No performance known.
Publication: Unpublished. Score probably lost.
Instrumentation: Not known
Note: See letter to Penelope Spencer under *Dance* above.

* GREEN FIRE Rhapsody for orchestra
Composed: 1923
First performance: 28 Jun 1923, Royal College of Music (RCM Patron's Fund Rehearsal), Royal Albert Hall Orchestra, Gordon Jacob. No further performances.
Publication: Unpublished. Score probably lost.
Instrumentation: Not known

* PASTORAL
Composed: 1923
First performance: No performance known.
Publication: Unpublished. Score probably lost.
Instrumentation: flute, clarinet, bassoon, horn, trumpet with accompaniment for strings and 3 percussion
Duration: '10 to 15 minutes' (letter to Penelope Spencer, June 1923)
Note: 'The Director [of the RCM] is going to ask Anthony Bernard if he could do it, so you may have a chance of hearing it on the orchestra.' (letter to Penelope Spencer, June 1923)

* TWO PIECES for violin and piano
Composed: 1923
First performance: No performance known.
Publication: Unpublished. Score probably lost.
Note: '... one slow & soulful, the other very vigorous & quick & so on. I think they are both very suitable for dancing and if necessary they could be scored for a small orchestra (Strings, piano, flutes, cla[rine]ts, horns, etc)' (letter to Penelope Spencer, June 1923)

TEMA for piano
   (*Tema* on title page; *Theme* at head of music)
Composed: n.d. (possibly a College exercise)
First performance: No performance known.
Publication: Unpublished. MS in BBC Library (BBC 9278). 2pp 73 bars written on 3 staves in
   pencil.
Duration: 1 minute
Note: The MS, with other scores, was presented by Lambert's widow to the BBC Library.

* TWO SONGS to poems by Edith Sitwell
   1. The King of China's Daughter (in *Wheels 1* (1916) and, revised, in *The Wooden Pegasus*
   (Blackwell, 1920); 2. Serenade (in *The Wooden Pegasus*)
Composed: Chelsea, *c.* 1923
First performance: No performance known.
Publication: Unpublished. MSS have not survived.
Instrumentation: 1. voice and xylophone; 2. voice and glockenspiel
Note: Listed in de Zoete, 'Constant Lambert'.

* PROUD FOUNTAINS Song to words by Osbert Sitwell
   'Fountains' (in *Wheels 2* (1917) and, with minor revisions, *Argonaut and Juggernaut* (1919))
Composed: Chelsea, *c.* 1923
First performance: No performance known.
Publication: Unpublished. MS has not survived.
Instrumentation: voice and orchestra
Note: Listed in de Zoete, 'Constant Lambert'.

* SYMPHONIC POEM based on Osbert Sitwell's Argonaut and Juggernaut
Composed: Chelsea, *c.* 1923
First performance: No performance known.
Publication: Unpublished. MS has not survived.
Instrumentation: orchestra (no further details known)
Note: Listed in de Zoete, 'Constant Lambert'.

TWO SONGS on poems by Sacheverell Sitwell
   1. The White Nightingale (as 'The Nightingale' in *Wheels 2* (1917) and as 'The Moon' in *The
   People's Palace* (Blackwell, 1918)); 2. *Serenade* (in *'Bird Actors'* in *Wheels 4* (1919) and *The
   Hundred and One Harlequins* (Grant Richards, 1922))
Composed: Chelsea, 1923
First performance: 6 Mar. 1924, Royal College of Music (repeated 2 Apr. 1924), Edna Kingdon
   (soprano), Bruce McLay (flute), Marjorie M. Buckle (harp); 8 Apr. 2001, Clore Studio, Royal
   Opera House, Covent Garden, Nicola Wydenbach and Holly Aisbitt (sopranos), Kate Kelly
   (flute), Serafina Steer (harp); 3 May 2005, Purcell Room, London, Sarah Leonard, Alwyn Duo
Publication: Maecenas Music MM0334. MSS in BBC Library (printed 'London Contemporary
   Music Centre').
Instrumentation: soprano, flute and harp
Duration: 3 minutes (1. 22 bars; 2. 37 bars)

PRIZE FIGHT Realistic Ballet in One Act
Composed: 1923–4; revised and rescored in 1927
First performance: first broadcast: 12 May 1969, BBC Midland Light Orchestra, Kenneth
   Montgomery; first staged performance: 15 May 1998, Christ's Hospital Theatre, Christ's
   Hospital Sinfonia, Peter Allwood; piano duet version 18 Nov. 2001, Linbury Theatre, Royal
   Opera House, Covent Garden, Waka Hasegawa and Joseph Tong
Publication: Full score on hire, Maecenas Music MM0333; piano duet (arr Lambert – no. 4 below),
   Maecenas Music MM0258.
MSS in BBC Library:
   1 'Satirical Ballet in One Act'. Piano duet. 25 Glebe Place (crossed out and 42 Peel Street
   added in pencil). Directions, in red, written in English.

2 'Realistic Ballet in One Act'. 1923–1924. Full score. Directions, in red, written in English. 1-page synopsis, typed in English.

3 'Ballet in One Act' 1924 (revised 1927). 'Partition d'orchestre.' 42 Peel Street. Directions, in red, written in French.

4 'Satirical Ballet in One Act'. 'Reduction pour pianoforte (4 mains)'. Directions, in red, written in French. 2-page synopsis, hand-written in French with cue numbers stuck inside cover. Also version in English.

Instrumentation: original version: piccolo, flute, oboe, 2 clarinets, bassoon, 2 horns, cornet, tenor trombone, harmonium, percussion (2 players), strings. 1927 version: piccolo, flute, oboe, 2 clarinets, bassoon, 2 horns, cornet, tenor trombone, percussion (2 players: xylophone, glockenspiel, tambour militaire, triangle, tambour de basque, piatti, GC, tam-tam, rattle (crécelle), cloche), harmonium (or bass concertina), and strings (6.6.4.4.2). *Baker's Biographical Dictionary of Musicians* (Schirmer, 1940), lists 'Prizefight, for band (1923)'.

Duration: 15 minutes

Note: On the first MS above is written and crossed out: 'The Overture (not in this copy) is scored for the same orchestra but with 2 trumpets & no harmonium.' The Overture has either not survived or was reused in another work. Beryl de Zoete, 'Constant Lambert', states that the early version was performed on the wireless but this performance has not been located. She also writes that it was rescored for Nijinska in America but never performed as a ballet. Both versions are scored for 6 woodwind, 4 brass, harmonium, percussion and strings, the later version requiring more extensive percussion.

MR. BEAR SQUASH-YOU-ALL-FLAT Ballet in One Act based on a Russian children's tale

Composed: 1923–4 (completed June 1924)

First performance: 22 Jun 1979, Manchester, students of the Royal Northern College of Music, Timothy Reynish; 23 Nov. 1997, Wigmore Hall (BBC broadcast 7 Dec. 1997), Eleanor Bron (narrator), Nash Ensemble, Martyn Brabbins; first staged performance: 15 May 1998, Christ's Hospital Theatre, Christ's Hospital Sinfonia, Peter Allwood; 8 Apr. 2001, Clore Studio, Royal Opera House, Covent Garden, Trinity College of Music Students, Lionel Friend

Publication: Maecenas Music MM0260. MS full score in BBC Library

Instrumentation: flute (doubling piccolo), clarinet, bassoon, trumpet, tenor trombone, percussion (2 players: xylophone, glockenspiel, side drum, tambourine, triangle, castanets, cymbals, bass drum, gong and rattle), piano

Duration: 15 minutes

CONCERTO for piano

Composed: 1924

First performance: orchestration by Shipley and Easterbrook: 2 Mar. 1988, St John's Smith Square, London, Jonathan Plowright, Redcliffe Chamber Orchestra, Christopher Adey; 29 Aug. 2001, Henry Wood Promenade Concert, Philip Fowke, Britten Sinfonia, Nicholas Cleobury

Publication: Original MS (two-piano score only), unpublished, in BBC Library. Realisation edited, arranged and orchestrated by Edward Shipley and Giles Easterbrook, facsimile, Maecenas Music MM0266MS.

Instrumentation: solo piano, 2 trum ets, timpani and strings (6.6.4.4.2)

Duration: 17 minutes

ALLA MARCIA for piano

Composed: n.d.

First performance: No performance known.

Publication: Unpublished. MS in BBC Library (BBC 9277). 3pp *Vif et net*.

Duration: 2 minutes

Note: Almost identical with *Alla Marcia* in piano score of *Romeo and Juliet* (Second Tableau) but written on 3 staves

OVERTURE for piano duet

Composed: 1925

Dedication: 'To G. M. Gordon Brown' (written in pencil)

First performance: No performance known.

Publication: Unpublished. MS in BBC Library (BBC 9619).

Duration: 4 minutes

Note: Orchestrated for use as the Finale of *Adam and Eve*; rescored in 1927 as *The Bird-Actors*

ADAM AND EVE Suite dansée

Scenario by Angus Morrison. Persons: Adam, Eve, The Serpent, The Angel

Scene I: Overture, Siciliana, Sonatina [details from faulty cover to Scene III]; Scene II: [score missing]; Scene III: Intermezzo Pastorale, Rondino, Passacaglia, Finale

As used by Antony Tudor for the Camargo Society: Scene I: Sinfonia, Siciliana, Sonatina, Intermezzo Pastorale; Scene II: Burlesca, Musette, Toccata, Intermezzo Pastorale; Scene III: Rondo, Sarabande, Finale

Composed: 1924–5, revised 1932

First performance: 4 Dec. 1932, Adelphi Theatre, Camargo Society, Constant Lambert, choreography by Antony Tudor, costumes and scenery by John Banting, 9 dancers including Anton Dolin (Adam and Serpent), Prudence Hyman (Eve) and Natasha Grigorova (Angel). ('Adam and Eve was quite mild fun. … I wrote some very devotional music for the angel and the music on the whole sounded better in its old form than in Romeo.' Letter to Marie Nielson, 22 Apr. 1933)

Publication: Unpublished in this form; partial MSS in BBC Library.

Note: Accepted by Diaghilev, becoming *Romeo and Juliet* (see below). Incomplete full score (Scene III one page of Intermezzo Pastorale and 3 pages of Passacaglia only) and four-hand piano score (Scene III Passacaglia starting at 6th bar and Finale only) in BBC Music Library (BBC 3795). Intermezzo Pastorale is the same as Adagietto in *Romeo and Juliet*; Passacaglia is no. 4 in *Divertimento* and *Pomona*; Finale is orchestrated version of Overture for piano duet (see above) later becoming *Bird-Actors* (see below).

ROMEO AND JULIET Ballet in two tableaux

'A rehearsal without scenery in two acts': Kochno, *Diaghilev and the Ballets Russes*, p. 234.

1st tableau: I Rondino; II Gavotte and Trio (Gavotte e Trio); III Scherzino (Scherzetto), IV Siciliana, V Sonatina

2nd tableau: Entr'acte, VI Sinfonia, VII Alla Marcia, VIII Toccata, IX Musette, X Burlesca, XI Adagietto, Xii Finale

Composed: MS full score dated 'Monte Carlo 1925–6'. Piano reduction dated 'London 1925 – Monte Carlo 1926'.

Dedication: 'à Madame Bronislava Nijinska'

First performance: 4 May 1926, Théâtre de Monte Carlo, Diaghilev Ballet, Marc-César Scotto; 18 May 1926, Théâtre Sarah-Bernhardt, Paris, Roger Désormière; 21 June 1926, His Majesty's Theatre, London, Eugene Goossens (also 23, 29, 30 Jun and 1, 9, 10, 17, 23 July)

Publication: OUP, 1926 (score and parts on hire); arr. solo piano by composer. Cover design by Christopher Wood. MS full score, in copyist's hand with annotations by Lambert, British Library (Music Loan 92.1.2).

Instrumentation: flute, piccolo, oboe, 2 clarinets, bassoon, 2 horns, 2 trumpets, tenor trombone, percussion (2 players: timpani, xylophone, glockenspiel, side-drum, tambourine, triangle, castanets, bass drum, cymbal), strings (8.6.4.4.2–4)

Duration: 30 minutes

Note: Based on *Adam and Eve* (see above) with omissions and additions; includes *Alla Marcia* (see above) directed 'menaciamente' in full score and 'mecanicamente' in two-piano version. Proposed performances of *Romeo and Juliet* in London in 1937 by the Markova-Dolin Ballet, produced by Nijinska, never materialized. Stewart R. Craggs, *William Walton: A Catalogue* (OUP, 1990), p. 42, suggests that Walton helped with some of the orchestration (probably more as a copyist than pure orchestrator). Excerpts from *Romeo and Juliet*, choreographed by Antony Tudor, were included in BBC television shows on 7 Jan. and 2 Feb. 1937.

THE BIRD-ACTORS Overture
Composed: 1925; reorchestrated 1927
First performance: 6 July 1931, Cambridge Theatre, London, Camargo Society, as an interlude
    preceding *Pomona*, conducted by the composer
Publication: Unpublished. Autograph full score and parts, British Library with 'Finale, *Adam and
    Eve*' partially erased (Music Loan 92.3).
Instrumentation: flute, piccolo, oboe, clarinet, bassoon, 2 horns, 2 trumpets, trombone,
    percussion (2 players), strings
Duration: 4 minutes
Note: Originally written as Overture for piano duet (see above); used as the Finale of *Adam and
    Eve*, but dropped when that work became *Romeo and Juliet* and rescored 1927 as *The Bird-
    Actors*. The title refers to a sequence of poems of that name by Sacheverell Sitwell, parts of
    which first appeared in *Wheels 4* (1919) and *Wheels 5* (1920) and then in *The Hundred and One
    Harlequins* (Grant Richards, 1922).

SUITE in three movements for piano
    1. Andante; 2. Prestissimo; 3. [Moderato], Presto
Composed: 1925
First performance: 19 Mar. 1925, Royal College of Music, by the composer; 22 Oct. 2005, Arts
    Centre, Pershore, Worcestershire, Mark Bebbington; first broadcast 17 Mar. 2006, BBC
    Radio 3 'In Tune', Mark Tanner
Publication: Maecenas Music MM0261; Edition Peters 71520. MS in BBC Library.
Duration: 12 minutes (although the printed score states only 8 minutes)

TWO PASTORALES for piano
    1. Champêtre; 2. Paysage
Composed: 1926
Publication: Unpublished. MSS in BBC Music Library.
Note: 'Champêtre' was orchestrated (see below). Second piece, 'Paysage', of 134 bars *Andante
    tranquillo*, completely crossed out.

CHAMPÊTRE pour petit orchestre
    'Idylle' crossed out on MS
Composed: London–Paris 1926
First performance: 27 Oct. 1926, Aeolian Hall, London, Guy Warrack
Publication: Unpublished in this form. Autograph full score and parts, British Library (Music
    Loan 92.8); MS (piano reduction) in BBC Library (P14462).
Instrumentation: 1 flute, 1 oboe, 2 clarinets, 1 bassoon, violins, violas, cellos, triangle
Duration: 4 minutes
Note: Written on title page and crossed out: 'On peut jouer ce morceau entre les deux tableaux
    du ballet "Romeo and Juliet"'. Reused as Intrata in *Pomona* (not in *Divertimento, pace* Motion,
    The Lamberts, p. 155).

DIVERTIMENTO FOR ORCHESTRA in seven movements
    I Corante; II Pastorale; III Menuetto; IV Passacaglia; V Rigadoon; VI Siciliana; VII Marcia
Composed: completed 1926, London and Renishaw, Derbyshire.
First performance: 16 Nov. 1926, Chelsea Music Club, Chelsea Town Hall, London Chamber
    Orchestra, Anthony Bernard (only known performance)
Publication: Unpublished. MS British Library (Music Loan 92.4, but catalogued as *Pomona*).
    Title page crossed through and 'Pomona. A Ballet in 1 Act' written in pencil, with *Intrata*
    movement stapled to title page, thus converting the score to *Pomona* with the first five bars of
    Marcia crossed out.
Duration: 17½ minutes
Note: Revised as *Pomona* (see below). The Passacaglia came from *Adam and Eve*.

POMONA An epicene ballet in one act (changed to 'a ballet in one act')
Intrata; I Corante; II Pastorale; III Menuetto; IV Passacaglia; V Rigadoon; VI Siciliana;
VII Marcia
Composed: MSS dated '1925–6, London, Paris and Renishaw' (BL Music Loan 92.4) and '1926–7'
(92.5); arr piano duet 'Chelsea and Renishaw 1926'.
Dedication: 'To AB' (Angela Baddeley)
First performance: 9 Sept. 1927, Company of the Estreno Teatro Colón, Buenos Aires, Aquiles
Lietti (Leticia de la Vega and Eugene Lapitsky, produced by Bronislava Nijinska, décor
by Rodolfo Franco) with further performances on 11 & 28 Sept. and 15 Nov.; first English
performance: 3 June 1929, BBC broadcast, BBC Symphony Orchestra, Ernest Ansermet; first
English staged performance: 19 Oct. 1930, first programme of Camargo Society, Cambridge
Theatre, London, Constant Lambert (with Anton Dolin and Anna Ludmila, choreography by
Ashton); 6 July 1931, Camargo Society, Constant Lambert (with Dolin and Ludmila), preceded
by *The Bird-Actors*; 17 Jan. 1933, Sadler's Wells (Beatrice Appleyard and Anton Dolin)
Publication: OUP, 1928; piano duet arranged by composer. Cover design by John Banting. MSS
British Library (Music Loans 92.4 and 92.5); orchestral parts (92.7).
Instrumentation: piccolo, flute, oboe, 2 clarinets, bassoon, 2 horns, 2 trumpets, tenor trombone, 3
timpani and triangle (1 player), strings (6.6.4.4.2)
Duration: 18½ minutes
Note: Adapted from *Divertimento* in seven movements (see above). Converted MS (BL Music
Loan 92.4) marked 'used by Vic-Wells Ballet'. The first movement of the ballet (Intrata)
is the piano Pastorale/orchestral Champêtre. The Siciliana also extracted as a solo piano
piece – 'made … partly at my request' (Angus Morrison) and published by OUP, 1930. First
performance probably at Cambridge by Harold Rutland, date unknown (Harold Rutland's
'Recollections of Constant Lambert'). Also privately recorded by the composer. *Pomona* was
announced for Dolin season at Théâtre des Champs-Elysées, Paris 31 Mar. 1928 but not given
(Vaughan, *Frederick Ashton and his Ballets*, p. 45).

EIGHT POEMS OF LI-PO
Li-Po translated by Shigeyoshi Obata
1. A Summer Day; 2. Nocturne; 3. With a Man of Leisure; 4. Lines Written in Autumn; 5. The
Ruin of the Ku-Su Palace; 6. The Intruder; 7. On the City Street; 8. The Long-Departed Lover
Composed: 1926–9. Nos. 1–4 October 1926; nos. 5–7 December 1926; no. 8 1929. 7 poems scored
14 Oct. 1929. No. 4 scored September 1947.
Dedication: 'To Anna May Wong'
First performance: instrumental version, seven poems only: 30 Oct. 1929, Aeolian Hall, London;
Odette de Foras (soprano) and ensemble, Constant Lambert; first broadcast performance:
(instrumental version, seven poems) 18 Dec. 1931, Odette de Foras, BBC Chamber Orchestra,
Constant Lambert; (eight poems) 2 Oct. 1947, Martin Boddey (tenor) and ensemble, Constant
Lambert, BBC Third Programme; 24 Aug. 1948, Victoria Sladen (soprano) and ensemble,
Constant Lambert, BBC Third Programme
Publication: Four songs with piano ('A Summer Day', 'Nocturne', 'With a Man of Leisure', 'Lines
Written in Autumn'), OUP, 1927; three songs with piano ('The Ruin of the Ku-Su Palace',
'The Intruder', 'On the City Street'), J. & W. Chester, 1928; one song with piano ('The Long-
Departed Lover'), OUP, 1930. The instrumental version available from Chester. MS No. 4
British Library (Music Loan 75.32)
Instrumentation: voice and piano; or voice and flute, oboe, clarinet, string quartet & double bass
Duration: 13 minutes

MUSIC FOR ORCHESTRA
Composed: 1927, London
Dedication: Lord Berners
First performance: 14 Jun 1929, Wireless Orchestra, Leslie Heward; as a Symphonic Interlude
during Diaghilev's Ballets Russes: 22 July 1929, Covent Garden, Constant Lambert; first
concert performance: 29 Aug. 1929, Queen's Hall, Henry Wood Proms, Constant Lambert
Publication: OUP, 1930. Autograph full score, British Library (Music Loan 92.9).

Instrumentation: 2 flutes, piccolo, 2 oboes, cor anglais, 3 clarinets, 2 bassoons, double bassoon, 4 horns, 3 trumpets, 3 trombones, tuba, timpani, percussion (3), strings
Duration: 12 minutes

ELEGIAC BLUES (In Memory of Florence Mills) for solo piano or orchestra
Composed: piano November 1927; orchestra 1928
First performance: 23 July 1928, Wireless Orchestra, Constant Lambert
Publication: (piano) J. & W. Chester 2164, 1928; in *The Joy of English Music for Piano* (London: Yorktown Music Press, 1996); in *A Century of Piano Music: 21 British Piano Works of the 20th Century*, ed. Richard Deering (Bosworth). Piano and orchestral MSS, British Library (Music Loan 75.31).
Instrumentation: solo piano; or 2 flutes, oboe, 2 clarinets, bassoon, 2 horns, 2 trumpets, trombone, percussion (1 player: side drum and tenor drum), strings
Duration: '3¾ mins.' in pencil on orchestral MS
Note: Selected for Associated Board of the Royal Schools of Music Grade 7: 2003–4

THE RIO GRANDE for chorus, alto solo, solo piano and orchestra
Text: 'The Rio Grande' by Sacheverell Sitwell, in *The Thirteenth Caesar and Other Poems* (London: Grant Richards, 1924).
Composed: 1927
Dedication: 'To Angus Morrison'
First performance: 27 Feb. 1928, BBC Savoy Hill, Angus Morrison (piano), and the Wireless Chorus and Orchestra, Constant Lambert; first concert performance: 12 Dec. 1929, Manchester, Sir Hamilton Harty (piano), Stephanie Baker (contralto), Hallé Chorus, Hallé Orchestra, Constant Lambert (repeated the following day in London at Queen's Hall); as ballet: (as *A Day in a Southern Port*) 29 Nov. 1931, Savoy Theatre, London, Camargo Society, Constant Lambert; (as *Rio Grande*) 26 Mar. 1935, Sadler's Wells Theatre, Vic-Wells Ballet, Vic-Wells Opera Chorus, Constant Lambert
Publication: OUP, December 1930. Full score, miniature score, vocal score and chorus edition. Cover design by John Banting. German text by Beryl de Zoete. A signed edition limited to 75 copies was also issued.
Instrumentation: solo piano, 2 trumpets, 2 cornets, 3 trombones, tuba, timpani and percussion (5 players), strings, alto solo, chorus. The percussion comprises bass drum; tenor drum; side drum (with wire brush); Chinese tom-tom; tam-tam; tambourine; castanets; triangle; cymbals; Turkish crash (1 large suspended cymbal); xylophone; jeu de timbres (keyed glockenspiel); small cow-bell (without clapper); Chinese block
Duration: 15 minutes
Note: The full score contains the following instructions:

> A large chorus is not necessary for this work and, indeed, if more than a hundred voices are used I recommend subdividing the choir into semi-chorus, medium chorus, and tutti, using the whole choir only for the more strenuous sections. The chorus is only a part of the work and no more important than, say, the piano part and it is essential that the singers should have absolute rhythmic precision as the least lagging behind will ruin the ensemble. The chorus should aim at a rather more theatrical and pungent style of singing than is usual with most choral societies.
>
> All instructions concerning the method of playing the percussion instruments should be meticulously followed and a separate rehearsal of the cadenza is recommended. There is a special arrangement of the percussion part (without tympani) for 3 players which may be used when absolutely necessary. When there are only 4 players this arrangement should be used with the addition of the tympani part. It is desirable, though, that the original 5 player version should be used.
>
> The cornet parts should not be played by trumpets. Fibre mutes in the brass instruments will be found to yield better results than brass mutes. CL

With a chorus of 50, the percussion was reduced to 3 players:
1st player: glockenspiel, xylophone, side drum (wooden sticks, soft sticks & jazz brush), tenor drum (or unsnared side drum), triangle and bell in C

2nd player: cymbals, bass drum, tambourine, castanets, gong

3rd player: 3 timpani

There is an alternative version for chorus, 2 pianos, timpani, and percussion players (3 or 5 players).

SONATA for pianoforte

I; II Nocturne; [III] Finale

Composed: 1928–9, Toulon–London

Dedication: 'To Thomas W. Earp'

First performance: 30 Oct. 1929, Aeolian Hall, London, Gordon Bryan

Publication: OUP, 1930.

Duration: 23 minutes

Note: The opening theme of the Finale came from an incomplete sketch for a setting of Nashe's poem 'Adieu, farewell earth's bliss' and was used again to the same words in *Summer's Last Will and Testament*.

CONCERTO for solo pianoforte and nine players

1. Overture; 2. Intermède; 3. Finale

Composed: 1930–1. Published score dated December 1931.

Dedication: 'To the memory of Philip Heseltine'

First performance: 18 Dec. 1931, BBC Studio broadcast, Arthur Benjamin (piano), ensemble, Constant Lambert; first public performance: 12 Dec. 1933, Grotrian Hall, London, Arthur Benjamin (piano), ensemble, Constant Lambert

Publication: OUP, 1933, full score and 2-piano score. 2-piano MS in BBC Music Library; end of second movement dated August 21 1931; first and third movements undated [42 Peel Street in pencil crossed out; 15 Percy Street added in blue]

Instrumentation: solo piano, flute (doubling piccolo), 3 clarinets (one doubling E flat, and one bass clarinet), trumpet, tenor trombone, percussion (2 miniature temple blocks, 4 ordinary temple blocks of increasing size, suspended cymbal, maraca (Cuban rattle), side drum, *tom-tom, tenor drum (wire brush, wood sticks, rubber-headed sticks)) cello, double bass. (*'The tom-tom should produce a note midway between the side drum and the tenor drum. A large unsnared side drum may be used instead.')

Duration: 25 minutes

Note: This work was originally planned as a prelude to Walton's *Façade* and on a very few occasions was performed as such.

SALOMÉ Incidental music to the play by Oscar Wilde

Nine sections, the most extensive being no. 7, 'Dance of the Seven Veils' (9 pages of score): I Prelude; II cue: The Princess rises; III cue: She is smiling like a little princess; IV cue: 'Ah!' (he kills himself); V cue: 'Salomé, thou art accursed!'; VI cue: 'He is too much afraid of the prophet'; VII cue: 'I am ready, Tetrarch' – The Dance; VIII cue: The executioner goes down into the sistern; IX cue: 'Kill that woman!'

Composed: completed 3 May 1931

First performance: 27 May 1931, Gate Theatre, London, Constant Lambert; 15 Dec. 1931 (32 performances); incidental music used for ballet *The Dancer's Reward* (midnight charity event), Carlton Theatre, Haymarket, Camargo Society, Constant Lambert; suite in 3 movements, arr. Easterbrook: 14 Nov. 1998, St Mary's Church, Putney, London, Fibonacci Sequence; suite presented as ballet *Gone Tomorrow* by Matthew Hawkins: 8 Apr. 2001, Clore Studio, Royal Opera House, Covent Garden, Trinity College of Music Students, Lionel Friend; as *Dance of the Seven Veils*: 15 May 1998, Christ's Hospital Theatre, Christ's Hospital Sinfonia, Peter Allwood

Publication: Unpublished. MS in BBC Library. Suite arr. Easterbrook, Maecenas Music 1998 MM0365, Peters Edition EP71518.

Instrumentation: clarinet, trumpet, cello and percussion: suspended cymbal, African tom-tom (low), Chinese tom-tom (high), rattle, Pan drums, Chinese tambourine (snake-skin head), sock cymbal, wire brush, felt-headed stick and rubber-headed stick

Duration: [Suite] 10 minutes

Note: 'As payment towards a large tax bill after Lambert's death, this music was confiscated by the Inland Revenue, who surprisingly did nothing with it. Eventually it fell in to the hands of Giles Easterbrook who … reconstructed the nine fragments (one with the percussion part missing) into a suite of three short movements, arranging the fragments into an order which matches the narrative of the play'. Claire Salmon, *BMS News* 81 (Mar. 1999), p. 284.

SUMMER'S LAST WILL AND TESTAMENT A Masque for chorus, baritone solo and orchestra, to words taken from the Pleasant Comedy of that name written in 1593 by Thomas Nashe

I Intrata (Pastorale and Siciliana); II Madrigal con Ritornelli ('Fair Summer droops'); III Coranto ('Spring, the sweet Spring'); IV Brawles ('Trip and Go'); V Madrigal con Ritornelli ('Autumn hath all the Summer's fruitful treasure'); VI Rondo Burlesca ('King Pest'); VII Saraband ('Adieu, Farewell Earth's Bliss!')

Composed: Summer 1932 – 27 Nov. 1935, London (concert ending for sixth movement dated 1936). MS British Library (Music Loan 92.11)

Dedication: 'to Florence' (Lambert)

First performance: 29 Jan. 1936, Queen's Hall, London, Roy Henderson (baritone), Philharmonic Choir, BBC Symphony Orchestra, Constant Lambert (broadcast)

Publication: OUP, 1937 (vocal score). MS and parts on hire. Limited edition two-piano score (150 copies), arranged by Archibald Jacob, with drawings by Michael Ayrton (OUP, 1946). Chorus edition (omitting I and VI).

Instrumentation: triple woodwind (including piccolo, cor anglais, bass clarinet, double bassoon), 4 horns, 3 trumpets, 2 cornets, 2 tenor and 1 bass trombones, tuba, timpani, percussion (3 players), 2 harps, strings

Duration: 52 minutes

Note: King Pest can be performed on its own with Lambert's 12-bar concert ending, starting at fig. 152 (3 flutes, 2 oboes, cor anglais, 2 clarinets, bass clarinet, contrabassoon, 4 horns, 3 trumpets, 2 cornets, 3 trombones, tuba, timpani, 3 percussion, strings).

HOROSCOPE Ballet in one act

1. Prelude (Palindrome); 2. Dance for the followers of Leo; 3. Saraband for the followers of Virgo; 4. Variation for the Young Man; 5. Variation for the Young Woman; 6. Bacchanale; 7. Valse for the Gemini; 8. Pas de Deux; 9. Invocation to the Moon and Finale

Composed: 1937, London and Austria

Dedication: 'To Margot Fonteyn'

First performance: 27 Jan. 1938, Sadler's Wells Theatre, London, Constant Lambert; first concert performance ('Four Dances'): 8 Aug. 1938, Henry Wood Proms, Constant Lambert.

Publication: Orchestral Suite (No. 1, Dance for the followers of Leo; No. 2, Saraband for the followers of Virgo; No. 3, Valse for the Gemini; No. 4, Bacchanale; No. 5, Invocation to the Moon and Finale): full score dated 'Jan 1938', OUP, 1939. Full ballet: piano arrangement by the composer: OUP, 1938. Autograph full score (lacking *Valse for the Gemini*), British Library (Music Loan 92.12). Autograph short score (with pencilled directions), ROHCG Archive.

Instrumentation: 3 flutes (doubling piccolo), 2 oboes (doubling cor anglais), 2 clarinets, 2 bassoons, 4 horns, 3 trumpets, 3 trombones, tuba, timpani, percussion (2 players: xylophone, glockenspiel, triangle, tambourine, castanets, jingles, Chinese block, maracas, side drum, bass drum, cymbals and gong), harp, strings. ('The entire parts can be executed by 2 players if the timpanist is willing to double xylophone, etc.')

Duration: 38 minutes (Suite 25 minutes)

Note: The orchestral parts and scenery for *Horoscope* were lost during Sadler's Wells' fateful tour of Holland in May 1940. It has never been staged again complete. 'Solo for the Moon' only danced by D. Vyvyan Lorrayne as a 'Tribute to Sir Frederick Ashton, Royal Opera House, 24 July 1970. Notes in the score: 'The composer recommends as a concert suite the following selection of movements. II [Dance for the followers of Leo], III [Saraband for the followers of Virgo], VII [Valse for the Gemini], VI [Bacchanale], IX [Invocation to the Moon and Finale].' (In his own recording of the Suite, Lambert cut the first nine bars of the *Dance for the Followers of Leo*.) 'The Horoscope chart reproduced on the cover [of both full score of the Suite and the piano arrangement of the full ballet] was specially drawn by Edmund Dulac'.

ELEGY **for piano**
Composed: 1938
Dedication: Harriet Cohen
First performance: earliest traced performance 22 May 1941, BBC Home Service, Harriet Cohen
Publication: OUP, 1940
Duration: 5 minutes

DIRGE **from Cymbeline**
Composed: 1940
Dedication: 'To Patrick Hadley'
First performance: with piano accompaniment: 24 Nov. 1940, Caius College, Cambridge, Walter Todd (baritone), Angus Morrison (piano), probably conducted by Patrick Hadley; first performance of full version: 23 Mar. 1947, BBC broadcast, with Martin Boddey (tenor), Hervey Alan (baritone), the BBC Men's Chorus and the Boyd Neel Orchestra, Constant Lambert
Publication: OUP, 1942. MS British Library (Music Loan 92.17)
Instrumentation: tenor and baritone soli, male chorus, strings
Duration: 7 minutes

MERCHANT SEAMEN **Film music**
I Fanfare; II Convoy in Fog; III Attack; IV Safe Convoy; V Finale: March 'Merchant Seamen' Crown Films production: director J. B. Holmes with assistant director Ralph Elton, photography by H. E. Fowle, editor Richard McNaughton. 24 minutes.
Composed: 1940; concert suite of five (or three) movements completed 9 July 1943
Dedication: The Orchestras of the Royal Marines
First shown: May 1941 (reviewed in *The Times* 30 May 1941)
First performance: full suite: 4 Aug. 1943, Colston Hall, Bristol, London Philharmonic Orchestra, Constant Lambert (an earlier performance, by the same forces, at the Theatre Royal, Norwich on 15 May 1943 has not been confirmed); shorter suite: 17 Sept. 1943, Royal Albert Hall ENSA 'Seascape' Pageant, Constant Lambert
Publication: (Full suite only): Boosey and Hawkes B&H8916, 1944. MS at Royal College of Music, 61pp.
Instrumentation: 2 flutes (2nd doubling piccolo) and piccolo, 2 oboes, cor anglais, 2 clarinets, bass clarinet, 2 bassoons, 4 horns, 3 trumpets, 3 trombones, tuba, timpani, percussion (2 or 3 players: cymbals, suspended cymbal, bass drum, side drum, triangle, jingles, gong, whip), xylophone, harp, piano, strings. The shorter suite omits flute (doubling piccolo), cor anglais, bass clarinet and xylophone.
Duration: Full suite 15 minutes; shorter suite 12½ minutes
Note: With a working title *Able Seamen* the film began with the GPO Film Unit but was released in 1941 as a Crown Film Unit production. It has been issued on video (VHS and PAL) and is available in both the *Fishermen at War* DVD and Imperial War Museum *Protect the Convoy* DVD. For the shorter suite Lambert reduced the last seven bars of the *Fanfare* from figure D to four bars, leading straight in *Safe Convoy*.

AUBADE HÉROÏQUE **for small orchestra**
Composed: 1942
Dedication: 'To Ralph Vaughan Williams on his seventieth birthday'
First performance: first studio performance: 12 Oct. 1942, BBC Studio, London Symphony Orchestra, Clarence Raybould; first public performance: 22 Oct. 1942, Oxford, London Philharmonic Orchestra, Constant Lambert; first London performance: 21 Feb. 1943, Golders Green, London, London Symphony Orchestra, Constant Lambert
Publication: OUP, 1944. Two autograph full scores (one incomplete and in poor condition) and parts, British Library (Music Loan 92.16).
Instrumentation: 2 flutes (2nd doubling piccolo), oboe, cor anglais, 2 clarinets, 2 bassoons, 2 horns, 2 trumpets, percussion (side drum, suspended cymbal), harp, strings
Duration: 7½ minutes. (Lambert informed Alan Frank of OUP, 8 Feb. 1947: 'The timing of the work varies slightly according to my mood but I would say that 7 minutes 30 seconds would be the safest bet.')

Note: 'This short piece was inspired by a daybreak during the invasion of Holland, the calm of the surrounding park contrasting with the distant mutterings of war.'

HAMLET Incidental music to the play by Shakespeare

Composed: completed 31 Jan. 1944

First performance: 11 Feb. 1944, New Theatre, London; 2 Fanfares, ed. and arr. Easterbrook: 3 May 2005, Purcell Room, London, trumpeters and drummer from RCM

Instrumentation: flute (doubling piccolo), 2 trumpets, percussion: side-drum (snared and unsnared with wood and timpani sticks), tabor & bell

Publication: Unpublished. MS in BBC Library.

Note: 30 short cues, together with Ophelia's songs ('He is dead and gone'; 'Valentine's Day', 'They bore him [barefaced on the bier]', 'And will he not come again?'), the Gravedigger's songs, and Hamlet's fragment (9 bars unaccompanied, 'Imperious Caesar' etc.). Robert Helpmann took the title role.

* HENRY CHRISTOPHE Symphonic Poem

Unfinished

Note: Commission for 1944 Proms. Letter from Lambert to Julian Herbage, 25 Apr. 1944: 'I will certainly do my very best to get the thing finished in time. I have finished the introduction (about 5 mins.) & started the allegro & have innumerable small sketches but I have not got these really clarified yet. Even in normal times I should allow myself another 6 months or so on the sketches & 2 months on the score.' Lambert referred to it as 'Black Slavery' after John W. Vandercook, *Black Majesty: The Life of Christophe King of Haiti* (New York: Harper & Brothers, 1928). It was a subject he had considered before. When in March 1930, together with Walton and Hely-Hutchinson, he was approached by the BBC for a work for broadcasting, he had suggested *Black Majesty (The Emperor of Haiti)* to a text of his own from the above book. By November 1930 he had lost interest in a choral work and offered instead his new Concerto for Piano and Eight [later changed to Nine] Players as a commissioned work, but the BBC wanted a choral work.

* ATROCITIES Film music

Note: Correspondence, 11 Dec. 1945, from Crown Film Unit to OUP about a film *Atrocities* using Lambert music A signed agreement, dated 1 March 1946, 'covering the use of the music composed by your good self for use in the above film'. This film has not been traced.

ANNA KARENINA Film music

43 music cues with the Ball Scene: la première polka, Glinka, orch. Lambert (approx. 47 secs)

Suite I (for Decca recording, arr Bernard Herrmann?) 11 mins: 1. Overture; 2. Forlane; 3. Love Scene; 4. Finale

Suite II (for Chandos recording, arr Philip Lane) 31 mins: 1. Main titles and opening scene; 2. Anna and Vronsky's first meeting; 3. Anna and Vronsky on the train; 4. Séance scene; 5. Anna and Vronsky discovered; 6. Anna's Garden; 7. Anna's illness; 8. Anna and Vronsky in Venice (Forlana); 9. Anna and Vronsky part acrimoniously; 10. Finale

Composed: 1947

Publication: Unpublished. Photocopies of MS in BBC Library with 128 pages of sketches.

First shown: Leicester Square Theatre, London, 22 Jan. 1948. Music recorded December 1947, London Film Symphony Orchestra, Dr Hubert Clifford

Publication: Unpublished. Photocopies of MS in BBC Library.

Duration: 11 minutes

Note: The film has been released on video and DVD.

TROIS PIÈCES NÈGRES POUR LES TOUCHES BLANCHES piano à 4 mains

I Aubade; II Siesta; III Nocturne

Composed: 1949, Camden Town–Palermo

Dedication: 'To Edward Clark'

First performance: 17 May 1949, Concert Hall, Broadcasting House, London (BBC/London Contemporary Music Centre Concert), Mary and Geraldine Peppin; as ballet *Three Words*

Unspoken by William Tuckett: 8 April 2001, Trinity College of Music Students, Lionel Friend, Clore Studio, Royal Opera House, Covent Garden
Publication: OUP, August 1950. Included in Aston, *Piano Duets: Twentieth Century British Composers.*
Duration: 8 minutes

TIRESIAS Ballet in three acts

Prelude; Scene 1; Scene 2, Tiresias' solo – Act 1 Entry of the Warriors – Sword Dance – Cortège – Snakes – Interlude – Act 2 Scene 1 – Scene 2, Dance of the Shepherds and Shepherdesses – Scene 3 Pas de deux – Scene 4 Baccahanale – Interlude – Act 3 Scene 1 Juno and Jupiter
Composed: 1950–1. On MS: July 1951 Seine-et-Oise and London (MSS, Royal Opera House, Covent Garden, Archives)
First performance: 9 July 1951, Royal Opera House, Covent Garden, Sadler's Wells Ballet, Covent Garden Orchestra and Gordon Watson (piano), Constant Lambert (sets and costumes by Isabel Lambert); first American performance: 16 Sept. 1955, Sadler's Wells Company (Royal Ballet), New York; first broadcast: (revised score) BBC Concert Orchestra, Barry Wordsworth, 8 Nov. 1995
Publication: FS (edited by John Abbott 1982–3) Maecenas Music MM0259 , Peters Edition EP71513.
MSS: (i) large FS in Lambert's hand, first in ink then pp. 8–32 in pencil: Prelude, pp. 1–10 and Scene 1, pp. 1–32, breaking off at 6 bars after M.
(ii) complete FS, 'July 1951 Seine et Oise & London', in ink and pencil with many cuts marked and written in various hands: Robert Irving: 'Warrior's Dance', 'Cortège', 'Dance of the Priestesses', '1st entr'acte', 'Bacchanale' (Act II scene 4); Christian Darnton: 'Snakes'; Humphrey Searle: 'Dance of the Shepherds and Shepherdesses' (Act II scene 2); Denis ApIvor: 'Tiresias' Dance (woman)' (Act II scene 1), 'Jupiter and Juno' (Act III scene 1); Gordon Jacob: 'Pas de deux' (Act II scene 3); The rest: Constant Lambert, Alan Rawsthorne, Elisabeth Lutyens (and Malcolm Arnold).
(iii) fair copy FS continuing from where (i) ended, written after Lambert's death and incorporating the cuts indicated in (ii).
Instrumentation: 3 flutes (all doubling piccolo), 3 oboes (3rd doubling cor anglais), 3 clarinets (3rd doubling E flat and bass clarinet), 3 bassoons (3rd doubling contrabassoon), 4 horns, 3 trumpets, 2 trombones, bass trombone, tuba, timpani, percussion (3 players: 2 whips, cymbals, glockenspiel, xylophone, side drum, tenor drum, bass drum, triangle, cow bell, gong, temple blocks, wood blocks, tambourine, castanets), piano, celesta, cellos, double basses
Duration: Original version 68 minutes; reduction reconstructed by John Abbott 54 minutes
Note: After the initial performances a number of cuts were made, totalling about 205 bars and bringing the playing time down to about 55 minutes. Lambert had started to make some cuts before his death and the task was completed by Elisabeth Lutyens. In 1982–3 John D. Abbott, a doctoral student at the University of Keele, took as his thesis project the editing of *Tiresias* and produced a piano reduction and then the full score which was used for the broadcast revival by the BBC in 1995 and was the basis for both the edition published by Maecenas and the Hyperion recording. Originally presented in three scenes, the published version of *Tiresias* is in three acts, with a prelude and two interludes. A 19-minute Suite for wind ensemble and piano, arranged by Timothy Reynish (Maecenas Music) has since been arranged of the following sections: 'Prelude and Dance of the Young Girls', 'Entrance of The Warriors and Sword Dance', 'Dance of the Shepherds and Shepherdesses', 'Bacchanale and Interlude' (no. 2) , Peters Edition EP71511.

* THE SLEEPING BEAUTY Film music
Unfinished
Note: 'When he collapsed on Sunday Mr Lambert was busy with the music he was composing for Robert Helpmann's new film based on the ballet "The Sleeping Beauty".' (Peter Wildeblood, in Lambert obituary)

⁂ Arrangements of Music by Other Composers

Auber, Les Rendezvous
ballet based on music from the opera *L'Enfant prodigue*
1. Entrance of Walkers Out; 2. Pas de six; 3. Variation; 4. Adagio of Lovers; 5. Pas de trios;
6. Variation; 7. Pas de six; 8. Exit of Walkers Out
First performance: 5 Dec. 1933, Sadler's Wells, Constant Lambert; first American performance:
7 Nov. 1951, Minneapolis, Sadler's Wells Company
Publication: Unpublished

Bach, Der Tag, der ist so freudenreich, вwv605 (chorale prelude O Hail This Brightest Day of Days)
arranged for piano
Dedication: 'Dedicated by the contributors to Harriet Cohen'
First performance: 17 Oct. 1932, Queen's Hall, Harriet Cohen (with the complete *Bach Book*)
Publication: In *A Bach Book for Harriet Cohen* (OUP, 1932); with arrangements by Bantock, Bax,
Ireland, Bliss, Berners, Bridge, Howells, Goossens, Vaughan Williams, Walton and Whittaker
(OUP, 2013)

Beethoven, Prometheus
from Beethoven's ballet score *The Creatures of Prometheus*
First performance: 13 Oct. 1936, Sadler's Wells, Constant Lambert
Publication: Unpublished
Note: The score was abbreviated and a new plot added with choreography by de Valois. 'In the
end the hero is shown in the unheroic aspect of a henpecked husband with a Potiphar's wife
joining in his discomfiture' (*The Times*, 14 Oct. 1936). Lambert wrote: 'The music [of the
original ballet] is of varying quality, containing a number of inferior dances cheek by jowl with
dances of real genius. The actual finale, for example, is a very poor affair indeed compared
with the march in Act II which is used as the finale in the present version. … It plays for
roughly forty-five minutes' (*Radio Times* 11 Dec. 1936).

* Berners, Funeral March for the Death of a Rich Aunt
orchestration of the third of *Trois petites marches funèbres for* piano (1916): 'Pour une tante à
heritage (For a wealthy aunt)'
Completed: March 1926
First performance: 10 April 1926, Lyric Theatre, Hammersmith, solo dancer Penelope Spencer;
10 May 1933, Royal College of Music, solo dancer Penelope Spencer, Constant Lambert.
According to Vaughan, *Frederick Ashton and his Ballets*, p. 10, Spencer first danced the
Berners *Funeral March* at the Scala Theatre, 11 Mar. 1926, in a matinée marking the first (and
only) performance of the Cremorne Company, but it is not clear whether the accompaniment
was provided by piano or orchestra. Lambert's letter to Spencer, 3 Mar. 1926, would seem to
suggest that the Hammersmith performance was the first of his orchestrated version.
Publication: Unpublished

Berners, Caprice péruvien for orchestra
based on the opera *Le Carrosse du Saint-Sacrement*
Completed: 12 July 1939. MS BL Music Loan 106.18: autograph score of the altered sections, with
instructions on where it links with Berners' score. Lambert's copy of the vocal score, with his
pencilled indications for the *Caprice*, is in the BBC Music Library.
First performance: earliest traced performance: 22 Oct. 1941, Oxford, London Philharmonic
Orchestra, Constant Lambert. (Prom performance planned for 21 Sept. 1939 did not take
place because of the cancellation of the Promenade Concerts due to the outbreak of war.)
Publication: J. & W. Chester

Boyce, Eight Symphonies
transcribed and edited for strings and optional woodwind
Publication: OUP, 1928. MS Symphony No. 8, transcribed and edited by Constant Lambert,
arranged for two pianos by Bernard Stevens, BL Add 69020, fols. 23–28

First traced performances in these editions:
Symphony No. 1 in B flat: 7 Jan. 1931, Bournemouth, Godfrey; 23 Feb. 1947, Cannes Festival,
    Lambert; 3 Jun 1948, Paris, Orchestre Nationale, Lambert
Symphony No. 4 in F minor: 16 July 1930, Bad Homburg, Frankfurt Symphony Orchestra,
    Lambert (relayed by BBC)
Symphony No. 5 in D: 27 Oct. 1928, BBC broadcast, London Chamber Orchestra, Anthony
    Bernard; 6 June 1932, Camargo Society, Savoy Theatre, London Symphony Orchestra,
    Beecham
Symphony No. 6 in F: 20 Sept. 1935, BBC Orchestra, Lambert
Symphony No. 7 in B flat: 29 Sept. 1942, Bedford, BBC Orchestra, Lambert
Symphony No. 8 in D minor: 18 Jan. 1929, BBCSO, Ernest Ansermet
Note: Selections from the Boyce Symphonies (probably nos. 1 and 6), as arranged by Lambert,
    were used in the ballet *Paramour* choreographed by Antony Tudor and first presented in the
    Town Hall Oxford on 20 Feb. 1934. Symphonies Nos. 1 and 6, arranged Lambert, were used in
    the television 'floor show' *Paleface* on 7 Jan. 1937, choreographed by Antony Tudor, also with
    music from Lambert's *Romeo and Juliet* (with Tudor and Maude Lloyd), Prokofiev's Third
    Piano Concerto and Boyce's Sonata No. 2. Hermione Baddeley was also one of the performers
    and Hyam Greenbaum conducted. *Paramour*, televised on 2 Feb. 1937, using the same music
    without the Prokofiev and also with chorography by Tudor, was a reworking of the ballet
    Paramour. It entered the Ballet Rambert repertoire on 22 April 1937.

Boyce, The Tartans or Dances on a Scotch Theme (ballet)
First performance: 10 Dec. 1930, Arts Theatre Club, London, in *A Masque of Poetry and Music*
    presented by Arnold Haskell, musical director Constant Lambert
Note: Music selected chiefly from the symphonies of Boyce

Boyce, Three Overtures transcribed and edited for strings and optional woodwind
The Power of Music [= John Stanley]; *The Cambridge Ode*; *Pan and Syrinx* [= John Stanley]
First performance: Concert Overture in 3 movements (*sic*): 5 Jan. 1932, Scottish Orchestra,
    Constant Lambert, Glasgow; *The Power of Music*: 1 Sept. 1936, BBC Orchestra, Constant
    Lambert; *The Cambridge Ode*: 2 Jan. 1939, BBC Orchestra, Constant Lambert
Publication: OUP (*The Power of Music* and *Pan and Syrinx* in 1937?)
Note: The MSS of *The Power of Music* and *Pan and Syrinx* have since been identified by Dr H. D.
    Johnstone as being in the hand of John Alcock and not William Boyce (see Ian Bartlett,
    'Lambert, Finzi and the Anatomy of the Boyce Revival', *The Musical Times*, Autumn 2003
    pp. 54–9).

Boyce, The Prospect before Us: ballet based on music by Boyce (the eight symphonies and trio sonatas)
First performance: 4 July 1940, Sadler's Wells, Constant Lambert; first American performance,
    3 Nov. 1951, Milwaukee, Sadler's Wells Company
Publication: Unpublished
Note: The music used is as follows: Scene 1: Symphony No. 2 mvts 1 & 2, Symphony No. 5 mvts 2
    & 3, Trio Sonata No. 3 mvts 3 & 4; Scene 2: Symphony No. 3 mvt 1; Scene 3: Symphony No. 3
    mvt 2, Symphony No. 5 complete; Scene 4: Symphony No. 7 opening *andante*, Symphony
    No. 1 complete; Scene 5: Overture to *The Cambridge Ode* opening *larghetto* only, Symphony
    No. 4 mvts 1 & 2; Scene 6: as Scene 2; Scene 7: Trio Sonata No. 1 mvt 3, Symphony No. 4 mvt 3,
    Symphony No. 7 mvt 3, Trio Sonata No. 2 mvt 2, Trio Sonata No. 3 mvt 4 (*Decca Book of
    Ballet*, p. 86). Suite recorded by Lambert, August 1940 (see Discography, Appendix 3).

Hugh Bradford, Fugal March (or 'Poet and Peasant') orchestrated by Lambert
First performance: 21 Mar. 1930, Bath, Constant Lambert
Publication: Unpublished. Autograph full score, British Library (Music Loan 92.15)

Chabrier, Bar aux Folies-Bergère
ballet based on *Dix pieces pittoresques*
First performance: 15 May 1934, Ballet Club, Mercury Theatre
Publication: Unpublished

Chabrier, Ballabile
ballet based on pieces by Chabrier, chosen by Lambert and orchestrated as follows: Lambert: *Valse romantique No. 1*; Mottl: *Sous bois* (*Dix pièces pittoresques*); Chabrier: *Bourrée fantasque*; Mottl: *Mélancolie* (*Dix pièces pittoresques*); Lambert: *Tourbillon* (*Dix pièces pittoresques*); Robert Irving: *Joyeuse Marche*, *España*
First performance: 5 May 1950, Royal Opera House, Constant Lambert
Publication: Unpublished in this arrangement

Chopin, Les Sylphides for piano, arranged and annotated by Lambert
1. Prelude (Overture), 2. Nocturne, 3. Valse, 4. Mazurka, 5. Mazurka, 6. Prelude, 7. Valse, 8. Valse (Finale)
Publication: J. & W. Chester

Couperin, Harlequin in the Street
ballet based on pieces by Couperin, chosen by Lambert and orchestrated by Gordon Jacob
First performance: 2 piano version: (as a prelude to *Le Misanthrope*) 8 Feb. 1937, Arts Theatre, Cambridge; enlarged and with orchestra: 23 Feb. 1937, Ambassadors' Theatre, London, Constant Lambert; further enlarged as separate ballet: 10 Nov. 1938, Sadler's Wells, Constant Lambert
Publication: Unpublished in this arrangement. Two-piano score, arranged Lambert, Royal Opera House Music Library.

Delius, Spring, the Sweet Spring orchestrated by Lambert
Completed: October 1926
Publication: Unpublished. MS Delius Trust
Note: The third of Delius's *Four Old English Lyrics* (*Four Elizabethan Songs*), 1915, with verses by Thomas Nashe that Lambert himself later set in *Summer's Last Will and Testament*. The orchestration agrees with the annotations on a MS fair copy by Philip Heseltine (Robert Threlfall, *Frederick Delius – A Supplementary Catalogue* (Delius Trust, 1986), p. 66).

Dowland, Follow your Saint: The Passionate Pavane transcribed by Warlock
from *Lacrymae, or Seven Teares figured in Seven Passionate Pavans, with divers other Pavans, Galliards, Almands* (1605) and arranged for small orchestra by Lambert
First performance: 10 Dec. 1930, Arts Theatre Club, in *A Masque of Poetry and Music* presented by Arnold Haskell, musical director Constant Lambert, choreography by Ashton

Glinka, Suite from Ruslan and Ludmila arranged by Lambert
1. The Abduction of Ludmila; 2. The Enchanted Palace; 3. Cortège; 4. Triumph of Ruslan
First performance: 14 July 1925, Royal College of Music, RCM Second Orchestra, Constant Lambert, Royal College of Music; repeat performance (mvts. 2, 3 & 4): 4 Dec. 1925, London Symphony Orchestra, Constant Lambert

Glinka, Fête polonaise
Polonaise and Mazurka
First performance: 23 Nov. 1931, Vic-Wells Ballet, Constant Lambert, Old Vic

Patrick Hadley, The Last Memory (Arthur Symons) 1929
Rhapsody for cello and orchestra with off-stage soprano, arranged by Lambert for cello, voice and piano. (See Wetherell, *'Paddy'*, p. 22.)
MS: Fitzwilliam Museum, Cambridge

Handel, Concerto in B flat for piano and small orchestra, arranged from 2nd and 6th Organ Concertos by Handel

First performance: 14 Jun 1936, Angus Morrison, BBC Orchestra, Lambert
Publication: OUP, 1934
Dedicated: 'To Harriet Cohen'
Note: Harriet Cohen, in *A Bundle of Time*, p. 228, wrote: 'Constant Lambert, taking the first movement from one of Handel's organ (or harpsichord) concertos and two shorter ones from another, had worked them into a single concerted work for me, with revised orchestration. I could have done without the "kaleidoscoping" but he had put such loving labour into it that I could not say anything and indeed, the little work was to become very useful in the second part of a programme where the first concerto was noticeably short.' Lambert wrote to Edward Clark on 29 July 1935 regarding a broadcast in September that ultimately did not include the Concerto: 'Although this is dedicated to dear little Hattie I certainly don't want her to establish a spiritual lien on it (as with the Bax and VW Concertos) and suggest Angus Morrison for the solo part (if he is prepared to do it).' Cohen's first performance of the work may have been at the Proms on 11 Aug. 1937.

Handel, Two movements from a sonata, arranged for small orchestra

First performance: first performance traced: 7 Feb. 1943, Piccadilly Theatre, London, New Symphony Orchestra

Kalman and Griffiths, The Ballet of Spring

a sequence in Act 3 of *Kiss in Spring*, a romantic comedy by Julius Brammer and Alfred Grünwald with music by Emmerich Kalman and Herbert Griffiths (an adaptation of Kalman's operetta *Das Veilchen vom Montmartre* premiered in Vienna in 1930); orchestration by Lambert of a *pas de deux* and variations only
First performance: 28 Nov. 1932, Alhambra Theatre
Publication: Unpublished
Note: Other orchestrations by Arthur Wood, Alfred Reynolds and Walford Hyden. Choreography by Frederick Ashton. Alicia Markova and Harold Turner were the principal dancers.

Liszt, Apparitions

ballet based on pieces by Liszt, chosen by Lambert, orchestrated by Gordon Jacob and choreographed by Frederick Ashton
1. *Consolation* No. 3 in D flat; 2. *Première valse oubliée*; 3. *Schlaflos*; 4. *Ungarisch* (*The Christmas Tree*); 5. *Polnisch* (*The Christmas Tree*); 6. *Jadis* (*The Christmas Tree*); 7. *Galop* in A minor; 8. *Elegy* No. 2; 9. *Evening Bells* (*The Christmas Tree*); 10. *Scherzoso* (*The Christmas Tree*); 11. *Carillon* (*The Christmas Tree*); 12. *Unstern*; 13. *Mephisto Waltz* No. 3; 14. *R[ichard] W[agner] – Venezia*
First performance: 11 Feb. 1936, Sadler's Wells Theatre, Vic-Wells Ballet, Constant Lambert; first American performance: 25 Oct. 1949, New York, Sadler's Wells Company
Publication: Unpublished in this arrangement. MS (two-piano score consisting of both printed and hand-written sections marked with cuts and links) ROHCG Archive.
Note: Ashton had previously used *Mephisto Waltz* No. 1 and *The Dance at the Inn* from *Lenau's Faust* in his ballet *Mephisto Waltz*, Mercury Theatre, 15 Jun 1934. Lambert recorded movements from *Apparitions*, January 1949 (see Discography, Appendix 3).

Liszt, Dante Sonata

ballet using an arrangement for piano and orchestra by Lambert of *D'après une lecture de Dante* for piano solo from Liszt's *Années de pèlerinage, deuxième année, Italie*.
First performance: 23 Jan. 1940, Sadler's Wells, Vic-Wells Ballet, Constant Lambert; first American performance, 23 Sept. 1950, New York, Sadler's Wells Company
Publication: Unpublished in this arrangement. MS FS ROHCG Archive
Note: The original score and parts were lost in Holland but Lambert reconstructed the score from memory and from the gramophone recording he had made in March 1940 (see Discography, Appendix 3).

Meyerbeer, Les Patineurs

ballet-divertissement in one act based on the music from the operas *L'Étoile du nord* and *Le Prophète* by Meyerbeer

1. Entries; 2. Pas seul; 3. Pas de deux; 4. Ensemble; 5. Pas de trios; 6. Duet; 7. Pas des patineurs; 8. Finale

First performance: 16 Feb. 1937, Sadler's Wells, Vic-Wells Ballet, Constant Lambert; first American performance, 2 Oct. 1946, New York, Ballet Theatre

Publication: (suite) Boosey & Hawkes

Note: The music Lambert selected was Waltz from Act 2, Prelude to Act 3 and Ismailov's aria 'Bel Cavalier' from *L'Étoile du nord* (1–3) and the ballet music and one aria from *Le Prophète* (4–8). Lambert recorded a suite from *Les Patineurs* in May 1939 (see Discography, Appendix 3).

Mozart, Les Petits Riens arranged and orchestrated by Lambert

First performance: 13 Dec. 1928, Old Vic, Vic-Wells Ballet

Publication: Unpublished

Note: Choreographed by Ninette de Valois as a curtain raiser to Humperdinck's *Hansel and Gretel.*

Purcell, The Birthday of Oberon

choral ballet based on Purcell's *The Fairy Queen*

First performance: 7 Feb. 1933, Sadler's Wells, Constant Lambert

Publication: Unpublished in this arrangement

Note: 'Lambert concentrated on the Masque of the Seasons (Act 4), interpolating other music from the opera, and making it into a comparatively self-sufficient divertissement.' [Clarke, 86–7]. 'The Dance of the Seasons [was] preceded by an overture, a choral invocation, and five rural dances.' (*The Times*, 8 Feb. 1933).

Purcell, Comus

ballet (18 numbers) based on music by Purcell from *The Indian Queen*, *The Fairy Queen*, The Masque in *Diocletian*, *The Tempest* (*The Enchanted Island*), *The Virtuous Wife*, *The Gordian Knot Unty'd*, *The Married Beau* (*The Curious Impertinent*)

First performance: 14 Jan. 1942, New Theatre, London, Vic-Wells, Constant Lambert

Publication: Suite (overture and 11 numbers): Boosey and Hawkes 8928

Note: Lambert recorded a suite from *Comus* in March 1942 (see Discography, Appendix 3).

Purcell, The Fairy Queen

edited by Lambert in association with Edward J. Dent

First performance: 12 Dec. 1946, Royal Opera House, Covent Garden, Constant Lambert

Instrumentation: 2 flutes (2nd doubling piccolo), 4 oboes (3rd and 4th doubling cor anglais), 2 bassoons, 4 trumpets, timpani, tabor, strings, harpsichord continuo

Publication: Unpublished in this arrangement

Note: *Purcell's 'The Fairy Queen' as presented by The Sadler's Wells Ballet and the Covent Garden Opera, a Photographic Record by Edward Mandinian with the Preface to the Original Text, a Preface by Prof. E. J. Dent and articles by Constant Lambert and Michael Ayrton* (London: John Lehmann, 1948), 96pp with 53 b&w plates.

Roseingrave, Overture in F

transposed and orchestrated by Lambert

First performance: studio broadcast: 13 July 1932, BBC Orchestra, Constant Lambert

Publication: Unpublished. Autograph full score, British Library (Music Loan 92.14)

Note: BL entry: THOMAS ROSEINGRAVE: selected pieces from the keyboard works of Thomas Roseingrave (*Eight Suits of Lessons*, 1729, and *Voluntarys and Fugues*, 1728), transcribed by Constant Lambert, with copies of some of the pieces in the hand of Millicent Silver; n.d. Both copies contain pencil annotations, mainly relating to registration. Lambert's manuscript was sent to M. Silver on 14 Mar. 1947 by Humphrey Searle for a broadcast on the BBC Third Programme on 13 April 1947. Apparently unpublished. Purchased from Mrs Sarah Johnson, daughter of Millicent Silver, 21 Jun 1988. Incorporated in 1989.

* Scarlatti, Mars and Venus
ballet arranged and orchestrated from the music of Domenico Scarlatti
First performance: *The Ballet of Mars and Venus* as an interlude during Ashley Dukes' *Jew
Süss*: 29 July 1929, Opera House, Blackpool; 19 Sept. 1929, Duke of York's Theatre, London;
revised as *Mars and Venus*: 25 Feb. 1930, Lyric Theatre, Hammersmith (with 2-piano and
string quartet accompaniment); (orchestrated for full 18th-century orchestra) 26 April 1931,
Camargo Society, Constant Lambert, Cambridge Theatre, London
Publication: Unpublished in this arrangement. Score probably lost.

Schubert, Hommage aux belles Viennoises
ballet arranged and orchestrated by Lambert from the piano music of Schubert
First performance: 19 Dec. 1929, Old Vic, Vic-Wells, Constant Lambert
Publication: OUP. Autograph full score, British Library (Music Loan 92.10).

Vaughan Williams, Fantasia on Sussex Folk Tunes for cello and orchestra
reduction for piano by Lambert
Publication: Unpublished. MS piano score, mostly in the hand of Constant Lambert, 1929, BL
57471, fols. 42–56.

Vaughan Williams, Job
reduced scoring; full score (in Lambert's hand) dated 1–18 Jun 1931, OUP
First performance: 5 July 1931, Cambridge Theatre, London, Camargo Society, Constant Lambert
Instrumentation: 2 flutes (2nd doubling piccolo), oboe, 2 clarinets, E flat saxophone (played by
2nd clarinet), 2 horns, 2 trumpets, trombone, timpani, percussion (3 players: cymbals, bass
drum, xylophone, glockenspiel, tam-tam) harp, strings. Lambert's version omits: bass flute,
2nd oboe (opt.), cor anglais, 3rd clarinet (opt.), bass clarinet (opt.), 2 bassoons, double bassoon
(opt.), 3rd & 4th horns, 3rd trumpet (opt.), 2nd & 3rd trombone, tuba, side drum, triangle, 2nd
harp (opt.), organ (opt.).
Publication: Unpublished

Vaughan Williams, The Wasps: Aristophanic suite
arranged for piano duet by Lambert, 1925.
Publication: Curwen, 1926. MS BL 63544 (presented by Mrs Ursula Vaughan Williams, 7 Mar.
1985)

Vaughan Williams, Concerto accademico
arranged for violin and piano
Publication: OUP, 1927

Walton, Façade Suite No. 1
arranged for piano duet
Publication: OUP, 1927
Note: In this version *Valse* wrongly bears a dedication 'To Mrs Beverley Baxter' that belongs to
Walton's arrangement for piano solo.

Walton, Façade Suite No. 2
arranged for piano duet
Publication. OUP, 1939
Note: As regards the orchestral suite (OUP, 1938), Lambert orchestrated 'Fanfare', 'Scotch
Rhapsody', 'Country Dance' and 'Popular Song', while Walton orchestrated 'Noche Espagnôle'
('Long Steel Grass') and 'Old Sir Faulk'.

Walton, Portsmouth Point
arranged for small orchestra
First performance: 6 Jun 1932, Savoy Theatre, Camargo Society, Constant Lambert
(6 performances in June and July 1932); 13 July 1932, BBC broadcast, BBC Orchestra, Constant
Lambert
Instrumentation: flute, piccolo, oboe, 2 clarinets, bassoon – 2 horns, 2 trumpets, trombone –
timpani, 1 or 2 percussion – strings

Publication: Unpublished. MS full score FRKF 588b, Frederick R. Koch collection, Beinecke Rare Book and Manuscript Library, Yale University. Score and parts on hire, OUP.

Walton, The Wise Virgins
arranged for piano duet for provincial tours
Publication: Unpublished
Note: As Lambert wrote to Foss on 13 Mar. 1940: 'The two piano version will not come into action until we go on tour again. … In that version we will naturally be using the OUP arrangements, as they stand. … The three Rummel arrangements are, as you know, virtuoso arrangements for two hands, and rather heavy-handed at that. These I will re-arrange myself for two pianos after Willie has completed his score.'

Warlock, Sleep
song (1922) with words by John Fletcher, arranged by Lambert for strings as *The Passionate Pavane*
First performance: 10 Dec. 1930, Arts Theatre Club, in ballet entitled *Follow your Saint: The Passionate Pavane*
Note: Recorded by Lambert with John Armstrong and International String Quartet, together with *The Curlew*, March 1931 (see Discography, Appendix 3).

Appendix 2
Synopsis of *Tiresias*

THIS synopsis was supplied by Lambert to Frederick Ashton and is as printed in Vaughan, *Frederick Ashton and his Ballets*, pp.421–3. The synopsis in the programme was considerably toned down for the Royal gala premiere.

Tiresias

Ballet in one act[1] and three scenes (after Lemprière)[2] by Constant Lambert

Scene I 'In Crete there lies the scene.'

An open air gymnasium in the outskirts of Knossos. Columns either side. Large Bull (flat) centre stage.

Dance I Young girls (nasty smelly little adolescents but don't tell this to the corps de ballet) are miming the old Cretan sport of vaulting in the nude over the horns of a bull. Fun, games and girlish laughter. At the climax of their hideous prank Tiresias enters in a carefree and slightly contemptuous manner. Executes a rather exhibitionist step. After which the little beasts run off half ashamed half mocking.

Dance II Tiresias slightly puzzled by his mingled reception pulls himself together and performs a dance of male triumph. (He is at this stage the typical athletic hearty of about 20.)

Dance III He is joined by a gang of other hearties who execute a 'danse guerrière' in his praise. Spears and double Minoan shields if possible. GLOIRE! The triumph of T's youth.

Dance IV Sudden change of key and lighting. A revolting young virgin (but revolting my dear!) enters and tells T that the priestesses are arriving. Solemn cortège of priestesses (this is a long number). In the middle the young virgin presents him with a wand of honour (sex symbols etc) which he accepts with slight apprehension. More GLOIRE. The captains and the queens depart. T (by now about 28) is left in a state of bewilderment.

Dance V Enter two snakes copulating. Tiresias for reasons known only to himself dashes at them in a puritanical fury and beats the female snake with his wand. Thunder and lightning! From behind the bull appears the figure of the female Tiresias wearing the mask of the young Tiresias. T is terrified. Margot takes off her mask and T disappears down trap. Black out.

Scene II (Pastoral Intermezzo)

Landscape with rocks and flowers. The Dove Goddess constructed by flat near the backcloth. Tiresias (by now an attractive girl of 30) discovered alone. Romantic solo. (Dance I.)

---

[1] When *Tiresias* was later revised, it was divided into three acts with linked scenes.

[2] John Lemprière (c. 1765–1824), author of the renowned encyclopaedia of mythology, *Bibliotheca Classica*.

<u>Dance II</u> Entrance of shepherds and shepherdesses. Ensemble. Solo for T in middle. Ineffectual passes by shepherds. Exit of shepherds and shepherdesses. Short solo for T.

<u>Dance III</u> From behind the Dove Goddess (sex symbol again) appears a luvlly man. Grand *pas de deux* starting off slowly but ending up in a state of erotic frenzy. Climax of T's sex life.

<u>Dance IV</u> T now a handsome woman of 40 invites her friends to a Bacchanale. 'A frenetic rumpus supervenes' (literal quotation from the Opera House, Palermo). Passes made all round but none to the hostess. At climax of orgy enter two gate crashers The SNAKES, and they're *at it again.* The disillusioned Tiresias seizes her wand and beats the male snake. The female Tiresias disappears as the elderly Tiresias appears as a man with a beard and breasts. (We must work out the technical details of this together.)

<u>Scene III</u>

An open courtyard in a Palace. Yellow backcloth. Two pedestals on which are placed Jupiter and Juno. Grouping of corps de ballet to be discussed later.

Argument between Jupiter and Juno on relative pleasure of being man or woman. Juno saying man and Jupiter saying woman. Tiresias is called in as only living authority. A man dances to his tune from Scene I. A girl dances to his tune from Scene II. T unhesitatingly says 'woman'!

Juno furious at losing her argument strikes him blind. (Thunder, lightning etc.) Jupiter as compensation gives him the gift of prophecy. Semi-religious finale. At the very end Michael and Margot enter in the same costumes as the snakes to form a triptych. END.

Appendix 3
A Constant Lambert Discography

1 Lambert's Commercial Recordings

Two books have been invaluable in the compilation of this discography: Philip Stuart, *The London Philharmonic Discography*, Discography no. 69 (London: Greenwood Press, 1997) and Alan Sanders, *Walter Legge: A Discography*, Discography no. 11 (London: Greenwood Press, 1984). (Feb. 2013. Dates in brackets refer to reviews in *Gramophone*.)

⁂ Session 1

Note: I am grateful to Alan Poulton, *The Recorded Works of William Walton: A Discography* (Kidderminster: Bravura, 1980), for the details of these *Façade* sessions.

12 July 1929 Chenil Galleries, London
Ensemble (six players), Edith Sitwell, Lambert*, William Walton

Walton, *Façade*

i Polka*; Fox-Trot*; Tango Pasodoble*	MA317 – IA – I – II – IIA	Unpub.
ii By the Lake; A Man from a far countree; Country Dance	MA318 – I – IA – IIA	Unpub
iii Valse*; Popular Song*	MA319 – I – IA – II – IIA	Unpub.

Fees: William Walton 10 guineas, Edith Sitwell 5 guineas, Constant Lambert 5 guineas, Ensemble 3 guineas each

'On the 12th I make gramophone records of "Façade" two-double-sided ones for the new "Decca" company. Unfortunately I get precious little for it. However it will be a good advertisement.' Letter from William Walton to Siegfried Sassoon, 3 July 1929: Walton, *Selected Letters*, p. 47.

⁂ Session 2

13 Aug. 1929 Chenil Galleries, London
Ensemble, Lambert*, William Walton

Walton, *Façade*

i Polka*; Fox-Trot*; Tango-Pasodoble*	MA317 – III – IV – V	Unpub.
ii Valse*; Popular Song*	MA319 – III – IV – V	Unpub.
iii By the Lake*	MA318 – III – IV – V	Unpub.
iv Black Mrs. Behemoth*; Jodelling Song*; Scotch Rhapsody*	MA392 – I – II – III – IV	Unpub.

Fees: William Walton 10 guineas, Constant Lambert 5 guineas, Ensemble 5 guineas each

'We made a new set of records, really good ones, last week, so things are getting a move on.' Letter from William Walton to Christabel McLaren, 25 Aug.

⁂ Session 3

28 Nov. 1929 Chenil Galleries, London
Ensemble, Edith Sitwell, Lambert*, William Walton

Walton, *Façade*

i Polka*; Fox-Trot*; Tango-Pasodoble*	MA317 – VI – VIIA – VIIIA	T124 (3/30)
ii Long Steel Grass; Man from a far countree; Tarantella*	MA723 – I – IIA	T125
iii Black Mrs. Behemoth; Jodelling Song; Scotch Rhapsody*	MA392 – VA – VIA – VIIA	T124
iv Valse*; Popular Song*	MA319 – VIA – VIIA – VII	T125

Fees: William Walton 10 guineas, Edith Sitwell 5 guineas, Constant Lambert 5 guineas, Ensemble 3 guineas each

78: Decca AK991–2; (US) Decca 25632–3 (accompanying notes written by Lambert)

441

EP: OUP110 (Walton 70th birthday de-luxe edition of *Façade* score, issued Mar. 1972 with original recording omitting *Valse*)

LP: Decca ECM834 (9/79); ECS560 (5/72); ECM834 (9/79)

CD: CDGSE78-50-65; Symposium 1203 (2/98); Living Era AJC8558; Dutton CDBP9761 (3/06)

'A de-luxe – signed by the author-&-composer edition of "Façade" is going to appear in the autumn 300 copies at £3 3 0. Incidentally the records are out this month, & it is being "broadcast" to-morrow by Edith & Constant [first complete broadcast, conducted by Leslie Heward].' Letter from Walton to Sassoon, 2 Mar. 1930: Walton: *Selected Letters*, p. 57.

Review, *Musical Times*, Mar. 1930, p. 232: 'I wish [the poems] hadn't been recited at all, for most of the words are inaudible, and the voices are generally so strident as to distract attention from the music. Occasionally the reciters have a hit with a kind of double-tongueing effect and some incisive rhythms, but the old problem of the combination of music and the speaking voice remains unsolved. Certainly the way out is not to monotone, as is done here almost throughout. The music is so engaging and piquant that it ought to be heard alone. Sitwellians, of course, will not agree; but as they are (I hope) in a small minority, they needn't be considered to the exclusion of normal beings. So please let us hear the music without the addition of vocal effects that suggest highly-cultured hawkers.'

Review, *Musical Opinion*, Mar. 1930, p. 517: 'The recording is excellent, and the rhythmic recitation by Edith Sitwell and Constant Lambert comes through well, although the words are not always distinct.'

℅ **Session 4**

11 Jan. 1930 Central Hall, Westminster. Producer: Joseph Batten

Albert W. Whitehead, St Michael's Singers, Hamilton Harty (pf), Hallé Orchestra

Lambert, *The Rio Grande*

i	WAX5330 – 1 – **2**	Columbia L2373 (3/30)
ii	WAX5331 – 1 – **2**	Columbia L2373
iii	WAX5332 – 1 – **2**	Columbia L2374
iv	WAX5333 – 1 – **2**	Columbia L2374

78: (US) C-68370/1D; set Col. X52; CM-230

LP: World Records SH227; EMI EH291343-1 (10/88)

Cassette: EMI EH291343-4 (10/88); BBC ZCR756 (9/90); Claremont 78-50-18

CD: BBC REH756 (9/90); Claremont 78-50-65; Symposium 1203 (2/98); Pristine PACO028 (+ download); Living Era AJC8558

Letter to Mr Brooke from Constant Lambert, 42 Peel Street, n.d. [Thursday]: 'This is to confirm your terms. 20 guineas for the session (1 to 5) and I agree not to conduct the Rio Grande for any other Gramophone Company. I think that the work should divide up very well into 4 parts. I hope it will be possible to get the piano–percussion cadenza on to a separate side which will mean that the drums can be grouped near the piano for that record thus getting a better ensemble than is possible in the concert room.'

℅ **Session 5**

24 Mar. 1931 Large Studio, Columbia, Petty France, London. National Gramophonic Society

John Armstrong (tenor), Terence McDonagh (cor anglais), Robert Murchie (fl), International String Quartet (André Mangeot, Walter Price, Eric Bray and John Shinebourne)

Warlock, *The Curlew*

i	AX6027 – 1	NGS 163 (12/31)
ii	AX6028 – 1	NGS 163
iii	AX6029 – 1	NGS 164
iv	AX6041 – 1 – **2**	NGS 164
v	AX6042 – 1 – **2**	NGS 165

Gordon Bottomley, '"The Curlew" and Peter Warlock', *Gramophone*, Dec. 1931, pp. 259–60

(6th side songs: *Sleep* and *Chop Cherry*, Armstrong & International String Quartet)

Cassette: ENS525 (*Peter Warlock: An Anthology of Recordings, 1931–1970*, compiled by John Bishop and made available exclusively to members of the Peter Warlock Society.)

CD: Pearl GEM0058, Symposium 1203 (2/98)

Download: Pristine NGS163-5

Lambert 'threw his whole being into its achievement, without pay'. Hubert Foss, *Gramophone*, Sept. 1951 p. 73. The same artists had performed *The Curlew*, under Lambert's direction, in the Heseltine memorial concert on 23 Feb. 1931, and also in a London Regional broadcast on 6 March.

⚅ Session 6

3 Apr. 1937 EMI Studio IA, Abbey Road, London. 10 a.m. Producer: Walter Legge
Constant Lambert String Orchestra (24 players: 8.6.4.4.2) £47.3.0

Warlock, *Capriol* Suite

i	2EA4721 – 1 – 2	HMV C2904 (5/37)
ii	2EA4722 – 1 – 2	HMV C2904

78: (US) Vic. 13497
CD: Pearl GEM0058; Divine Art DDH27811 (2 CDs)

Warlock, Serenade (To Frederick Delius on his 60th birthday)

i	2EA4723 – 1 – 2	HMV C2908 (6/37)
ii	2EA4724 – 1 – 2	HMV C2908

78: (US) Vic. 13554
CD: Divine Art DDH27811 (2 CDs)

⚅ Session 7

25 Oct. 1938 EMI Studio No. 1, Abbey Road. Producer: Walter Legge
London Philharmonic Orchestra
2 (+1).2.2.(CA).2 2.2. ten. tromb. sax. drum strings (12.10.8.6.6)

Delius, *On Hearing the First Cuckoo in Spring*

i	OEA6821 – 1 – 2	HMV B8819 (12/38)
ii	OEA6822 – 1 – 2	HMV B8819

78: (US) Vic. 4496
CD: Pearl GEM0058

Auber, Overture *Crown Diamonds*

i	2EA6824 – 1	unpub.

Session shared with Walton conducting *Siesta* (C3042) and *Façade* Suite 'Old Sir Faulk' and 'Noche espagnole' (unpublished)

⚅ Session 8

24 Nov. 1938 Kingsway Hall, London. 2.30 p.m. Producer: Walter Legge
London Philharmonic Orchestra
picc.1.2.2.2 4.2.2.1 3 perc. strings (12.10.8.6.6)
£80.5.0 + £10.10.0 conductor

Auber, Overture *The Bronze Horse*

i	2EA6946 – 1 – 2	HMV C3061 (3/39)
ii	2EA6947 – 1 – 2	HMV C3061

78: (US) Vic. 12511

Auber, Overture *Crown Diamonds*

i	2EA6948 – 1 – 2	HMV C3071 (3/39)
ii	2EA6949 – 1 – 2	HMV C3071

78: (US) Vic. 12806

[*Crown Diamonds*: 'The conductor has just the right poise and the piquant understanding of the style required.' *Gramophone*, Mar. 1939, p. 424.]

❧ Session 9

14 Dec. 1938 EMI Studio No. 1, Abbey Road. 2.30 p.m. Producer: Walter Legge
London Philharmonic Orchestra
2(picc.).2.2(CA).2 2.2. tenor trombone. sax. drums strings (12.10.8.6.6)
£81.1.3 orchestra + £10.10.0 conductor

Auber, Overture *Fra Diavolo*

i	2EA7192 – 1 – 2	HMV C3084 (4/39)
ii	2EA7193 – 1 – 2	HMV C3084

LP: (US) Past Masters 36 (11/81) ('The whole quality is of that agreeable crispness which Mr
Lambert, at his best, so surely draws.' *Gramophone*, Apr. 1939, p. 469.)

Delibes, *Le Roi l'a dit*

i	2EA7194 – 1 – 2	HMV C3080 (3/39)
ii	2EA7195 – 1 – 2	HMV C3080

78: (US) Vic. 12764

❧ Session 10

10 Feb. 1939 Kingsway Hall, London. 2.30–5.30 p.m. Producer: Walter Legge
Sadler's Wells Orchestra
3 fl. 2 ob. 2 clar. 2 bass. 4.2.3.1 2 pianos 1 harp strings (8.6.4.4.2)

Tchaikovsky, *The Sleeping Princess*

i	Introduction, Lilac Fairy	2EA7359 – 1 – 2	HMV C3081 (4/39)
ii	Six Fairies, Fairy Carabosse	2EA7360 – 1 – 2 trans – 4	HMV C3081
iii	Valse	2EA7361 – 1 – 2	HMV C3082
iv	Rose Adagio	2EA7362 – 1	HMV C3082
v	Puss in Boots, Diamond and Silver Fairies	2EA7363 – 1 – 2	HMV C3083
vi	Mazurka, Apotheosis	2EA7364 – 1 – 2	HMV C3083

Matrix 2EA7360 was transferred and issued as take 4 on C3081
78: auto C7525–7; (US) Vic. Set M673
LP: Victor Bluebird LBC1007
45: WBC1007
CD: [*Valse* only] Avid AMSC577; SOMMCD080 (12/08)

❧ Sessions 11 & 12

1 & 2 Mar. 1939 EMI Studio No. 1, Abbey Road. Producer: Walter Legge
London Philharmonic Orchestra

Tchaikovsky, Symphony No. 5

1 i	2EA7527 – 1 – 2	1.3.39	HMV C3088 (4/39; 8/40)
1 ii	2EA7528 – 1 – 2	1.3.39	HMV C3088
1 iii	2EA7529 – 1 – 2	1.3.39	HMV C3089
2 i	2EA7530 – 1 – 2	1/2.3.39	HMV C3089
2 ii	2EA7531 – 1 – 2	1/2.3.39	HMV C3090
2 iii	2EA7534 – 1 – 2	2.3.39	HMV C3090
2 iv; 3 i	2EA7535 – 1 – 2	2.3.39	HMV C3091
3 ii; 4 i	2EA7536 – 1 – 2	2.3.39	HMV C3091
4 ii	2EA7537 – 1 – 2	2.3.39	HMV C3092
4 iii	2EA7538 – 1 – 2	2.3.39	HMV C3092

78: auto C7528–32; HMV Album 327

n.b. Beecham was also to record this symphony with the same orchestra for Columbia on 18 Dec.
1939

Edward Greenfield, reviewing Igor Markevitch's recording of the symphony in *Gramophone*, Dec.
1966, wrote: 'I am afraid my memories of Constant Lambert's ancient 78 recording are rather dim,
but in principle his was exactly the same approach as Markevitch's. The point is that too often
we have swung from one extreme to the other: from the overemotional and sentimental reading

to the brittle, brilliant one. Markevitch, like Lambert, is a warm, affectionate Tchaikovskian, he encourages the sort of phrasing without which Tchaikovsky's melodies cannot really breathe, but like Lambert he will not abide sentimentality at any cost.'

※ Session 13

8 May 1939 Kingsway Hall. Producer: Walter Legge
Sadler's Wells Orchestra
2 fl. 2.2.2 4.4. 2 tenor trombones – bass trombone timp drums strings (8.6.4.4.2)

Meyerbeer–Lambert, *Les Patineurs* Suite: Entrée, Pas des Patineuses, Pas de deux, Pas de trois

i 2EA7739 – 1 – 2	HMV C3105 (7/39)	
ii 2EA7740 – 1 – 2	HMV C3105	

78: (US) Vic. 36238
45: 7P 102; 7PW 121
CD: Living Era AJC8558; SOMMCD080 (12/08)

Rossini, *William Tell* Ballet Music

i OEA7741 – 1	HMV B8900 (6/39)
ii OEA7742 – 1 – 2	HMV B8900
iii OEA7743 – 1 – 2	HMV B8901
iv OEA7744 – 1 – 2	HMV B8901

78: (US) Vic. 26743–4
CD: SOMMCD080 (12/08)

'Rossini's orchestral piquancies and gay rhythms lose none of their attraction under Lambert's experienced direction.' *Gramophone*, June 1939, p. 13.

※ Session 14

28 June 1939 Kingsway Hall. 10 a.m. Producer: Walter Legge
London Philharmonic Orchestra
picc.2.2.2 4.4.4. 2 ten. trombones bass trombone tuba triangle drums harp 2 perc strings (12.10.8.6.6)
£101.19.11 + £10.10.0 for conductor

Meyerbeer, Coronation March *Le Prophète*

2EA7924 – 1 – 2	HMV C3112 (9/39)

Chabrier, *Joyeuse marche*

2EA7925 – 1	HMV C3112

Offenbach, Overture *Orpheus in the Underworld*

i 2EA7926 – 1 – 2	HMV C3110 (8/39)
ii 2EA7927 – 1 – 2	HMV C3110

78: (US) Vic. 12604
LP: Camden CAL242 (11/55); CFL103 (9/55)

[Offenbach: 'One of the brightest of the series this conductor is making.' *Gramophone*, Aug. 1939, p. 103.]

※ Session 15

3 Nov. 1939 EMI Studio 1, Abbey Road.
Benno Moiseiwitsch, London Philharmonic Orchestra

Liszt, *Hungarian Fantasia*

i 2EA8139 – 1 – 2	HMV C3132	(1/40)
ii 2EA8140 – 1 – 2	HMV C3132	
iii 2EA8141 – 1 – 2	HMV C3133	
iv 2EA8142 – 1 – 2	HMV C3133	

78: (US) Vic. G19
Cassette: Koch 2 7035.4
CD: Koch 3 7035.2 (4/91); Naxos 8.110683 (9/02); Appian APR5529; Legacy 370352

iii 2EA8141 – 2	HMV C3113	Issued Jan 1950

⅜ Session 16

21 Dec. 1939 Kingsway Hall. 10 a.m. Producer: Walter Legge
Louis Kentner, London Philharmonic Orchestra
2.2.2.2 4.4.4 harp and timp 2 perc piano strings (12.10.8.6.4)
£123.2.6 (Kentner £5.5.0)

Weinberger, *Under the Spreading Chestnut Tree*

i Theme; Vars. 1, 2 & 3	2EA818 – 1 – 2	HMV c3148 (2/40)
ii Vars. 4 & 5	2EA8185 – 1 – 2	HMV c3148
iii Vars. 6 & 7	2EA8186 – 1 – 2	HMV c3149
iv Fugue	2EA8187 – 1 – 2	HMV c3149

78: (US) Vic. M654
CD: TIME MACHINE 0099; Dutton CDAX8005 (11/93)

Chabrier, *Le Roi malgré lui* – Danse slave

2EA8188 – 1 – 2   HMV c3218 (4/41)
(coupled with Tchaikovsky *Romeo and Juliet*)

78: auto C7550–2

⅜ Session 17

20 Mar. 1940 EMI Studio 1, Abbey Road. Producer: Walter Legge
Louis Kentner, Sadler's Wells Orchestra

Liszt, arr. Lambert, *Dante Sonata*

i CAX8760 – 1 – 2	Columbia DX967 (5/40)
ii CAX8761 – 1 – 2	Columbia DX967
iii CAX8762 – 1 – 2	Columbia DX968
iv CAX8763 – 1 – 2	Columbia DX968

CD: Pearl GEM 0069; Dutton CDBP9742; Naxos 8.111223

'The performance and recording are all that Columbia claims for them. Kentner has never done anything so absolutely first-rate in every way as this very vivid interpretation. ... Constant Lambert's extraordinary apt and picturesque orchestration might have been dictated to him by Liszt in a dream. It heightens and colours the dramatic and emotional elements of the music with sure instinct and often with superb effect.' A.R., *Gramophone*, May 1940, p. 419.

⅜ Session 18

1 Aug. 1940 EMI Studio 1, Abbey Road. Producer: Walter Legge
Sadler's Wells Orchestra

Boyce, arr. Lambert, *The Prospect before Us* Suite

i Rehearsal	2EA8717 – 1 – 2	HMV c3181 (10/40)
ii First scene; The Lawyers; The Urchins	2EA8718 – 1 – 2	HMV c3181
iii Ballet scene pt. 1	2EA8719 – 1 – 2	HMV c3182
iv Ballet scene pt. 2	2EA8720 – 1 – 2	HMV c3182
v Street scene	2EA8721 – 1 – 2	HMV c3183
vi Finale	2EA8722 – 1 – 2	HMV c3183

78: auto C7547–9; (US) Vic. M857; EB178–80
CD: TIME MACHINE 0099; SOMMCD080 (12/08)

⅜ Session 19

24 Feb. 1941 Town Hall, Birmingham. Producer: Walter Legge
City of Birmingham Orchestra

Tchaikovsky, *Romeo and Juliet* Overture

i 2ER449 – 1 – 2 – 3 – 4	HMV c3216 (4/41)
ii 2ER450 – 1 – 2 – 3	HMV c3216
iii 2ER501 – 1 – 2 – 3 – 4	HMV c3217 (matrix renumbered 2ER451)
iv 2ER502 – 1 – 2	HMV c3217 (matrix renumbered 2ER452)
v 2ER503 – 1 – 2	HMV c3218 (matrix renumbered 2ER453)

78: auto C7550–2
LP: Bluebird LBC1007
CD: CDLX7006 (1/94)

Walter Legge suppressed the name of the Birmingham Orchestra from appearing on the record labels. The *Gramophone* review, Apr. 1941, merely lists 'Symphony Orchestra'. One of the discs, however, states that it was 'Recorded in the Town Hall, Birmingham': Beresford King-Smith, *Crescendo! 75 years of the City of Birmingham Symphony Orchestra* (London: Methuen, 1995), p. 71.

※ Session 20

30 July 1941 Houldsworth Hall, Manchester. Producer: Walter Legge
Hallé Orchestra

Grieg, *Sigurd Jorsalfar* – Homage March

i CAX8901 – <u>1</u> – 2	Columbia DX1037 (11/41)	
ii CAX8902 – <u>1</u> – 2	Columbia DX1037	

Delius, *La Calinda*

i CAX8903 – <u>1</u> – 2	HMV C3273 (3/42)
	trans. to HMV series as 2EA9737 – <u>1</u>

45: 7P264 (11/60)
CD: Testament SBT1014 (5/93); Pearl GEM0058; Avid AMSC577; Danacord   DACOCD717

Delius, *Hassan* Intermezzo and Serenade

i CAX8904 – <u>1</u> – 2	HMV C3273 (3/42)
	trans. to HMV series as 2EA9736 – <u>1</u>

45: 7P264 (11/60)
CD: Testament SBT1014 (5/93); Pearl GEM0058

Schubert, *Overture in the Italian Style*

i CAX8905 – 1 – 2	unpublished

※ Session 21

6 Mar. 1942 Houldsworth Hall, Manchester. Producer: Walter Legge
Hallé Orchestra

Purcell–Lambert, *Comus* Ballet Suite

i The Attendant Spirit;	CAX9005 – <u>1</u> – 2	Columbia DX1076 (5/42)
The Rout and Comus		
ii The Lady and Comus;	CAX9006 – <u>1</u> – 2	Columbia DX1076
The Brothers		
iii Comus's Palace	CAX9007 – 1 – <u>2</u>	Columbia DX1077
iv The Brothers; Sabrina; Finale	CAX9008 – <u>1</u> – 2 – 3	Columbia DX1077

CD: Opera D'oro OPD-1220

※ Sessions 22 & 23

8 & 9 Oct. 1942 Houldsworth Hall, Manchester. Producer: Walter Legge
Hallé Orchestra

Tchaikovsky, Symphony No. 4

1 i	CAX9042 – 1 – <u>2</u> – 3 – 4	Columbia DX1096 (11/42)
1 ii	CAX9043 – 1 – 2 – <u>3</u> – 4	Columbia DX1096
1 iii	CAX9044 – <u>1</u> – 2	Columbia DX1097
1 iv	CAX9045 – <u>1</u> – 2	Columbia DX1097
2 i	CAX9046 – <u>1</u> – 2	Columbia DX1098
2 ii	CAX9047 – 1 – 2 – <u>3</u>	Columbia DX1098
3 i	CAX9048 – <u>1</u> – 2 – 3 – 4	Columbia DX1099
3 ii	CAX9049 – 1 – <u>2</u> – 3	Columbia DX1099
4 i	CAX9050 – 1 – <u>2</u>	Columbia DX1100
4 ii	CAX9051 – <u>1</u> – 2	Columbia DX1100

78: auto DX8185–9
CD: Dutton CDLX7006

⅋ **Session 23 [cont.]**

9 Oct. 1942 Houldsworth Hall, Manchester. Producer: Walter Legge
Hallé Orchestra

Tchaikovsky, *Hamlet* Overture

i	CAX9052 – <u>1</u> – 2	Columbia DX1101 (12/42)
ii	CAX9053 – <u>1</u> – 2	Columbia DX1101
iii	CAX9054 – <u>1</u> – 2	Columbia DX1102
iv	CAX9055 – <u>1</u> – 2	Columbia DX1102

78: Set X243
CD: Dutton CDLX7006

⅋ **Session 24**

22 Dec. 1942 Philharmonic Hall, Liverpool. Producer: Walter Legge
Liverpool Philharmonic Orchestra

Glazunov, *Stenka Razin* Op. 13

i	CAX9062 – 1 – 2 – 3 trans. – <u>4</u>	Columbia DX1107 (2/43)
ii	CAX9063 – 1 – <u>2</u> – 3	Columbia DX1107
iii	CAX9064 – <u>1</u>	Columbia DX1108
iv	CAX9065 – <u>1</u>	Columbia DX1108

CAX9062 transferred and issued as take 4 on DX1107

⅋ **Session 25 & 26**

23 & 24 June 1943 Houldsworth Hall, Manchester. Producer: Walter Legge
Hallé Orchestra

Borodin, Symphony No. 2

1 i	CAX9108 – <u>1</u> – 2 – 3	23.6.43	Columbia DX1125 (9/43)
1 ii	CAX9109 – <u>1</u> – 2	23.6.43	Columbia DX1125
2	CAX9110 – 1 – <u>2</u> – 3	23.6.43	Columbia DX1126
3 i	CAX9111 – 1 – <u>2</u>	24.6.43	Columbia DX1126
3 ii	CAX9112 – <u>1</u> – 2	24.6.43	Columbia DX1127
4 i	CAX9113 – <u>1</u> – 2	24.6.43	Columbia DX1127
4 ii	CAX9114 – <u>1</u> – 2	24.6.43	Columbia DX1128

(in 7 parts, coupled with Mozart Andantino, K251, conducted by Laurance Turner)
CD: Dutton CDAX8010 (2/95)

Also in 24 June session, Walton recorded his *Spitfire* Prelude and Fugue.

Letter from W. Legge to Mr Thomas, Record Sales, 10 Aug. 1943 (this correspondence is quoted with acknowledgement to the EMI Music Archive Trust, Hayes, Middlesex):

> As we agreed I have arranged with Lambert to record exclusively for us. He puts the screw on a bit for granting exclusivity for a year with options. So I have concluded with the following terms:
>> Period: I year with option for a second year
>> Minimum of 4 sessions per annum, the artist agreeing to conduct additional sessions above this number, on the same financial terms, if called upon by the Company to do so during the period of the contract.
>> Payment: 18 guineas per session
> May I have the contract please dated August 5th
> [Pencil note: Normal fee £10.10 per session]

Columbia contract signed by Lambert and Legge, dated 28 Aug. 1943: 'One year £18.18.0 per session. Duration of each recording session shall be approx. 3 hours.'

※ Session 27

29 Oct. 1943 Philharmonic Hall, Liverpool. Producer: Walter Legge
Joan Hammond, Liverpool Philharmonic Orchestra

Bizet, *Roma – Carnaval*

    i CAX9120 – 1 – <u>2</u>   Columbia DX1136 (12/43)
    ii CAX9121 – 1 – <u>2</u>   Columbia DX1136

['The orchestra plays much better here than in the other recordings this month ...; and Malcolm Sargent is just the man for this highly-coloured sort of music.' A[lec] R[obertson], *Gramophone*, Dec. 1943, p. 100.]

Rimsky-Korsakov, Overture *Ivan the Terrible*

    i CAX9127 – 1 – <u>2</u> – 3   Columbia DX1140 (1/44)
    ii CAX9128 – <u>1</u> – 2   Columbia DX1140

Tchaikovsky, *Eugene Onegin* – Tatiana's Letter Scene (sung in English)

    i CAX9129 – 1 – <u>2</u> – 3 – 4   Columbia DX1134 (12/43)
    ii CAX9130 – 1 – <u>2</u>   Columbia DX1134
    iii CAX9131 – 1 – <u>2</u> – 3 – 4 Columbia DX1135

CD: Testament SBT1013 (12/92)

1944

Letter 15 June 1944 from Columbia: contract extended for one year, from 5 Aug. 1944. Received, signed and dated by Lambert, 30 June 1944

Letter from Lambert to Columbia Graphophone Company, 30 June 1944:

> Referring to the agreement between us dated 28th August, 1943, as extended by letter dated 15th June, 1944, (hereinafter called 'the Principal Agreement') I hereby agree to the Principal Agreement being altered as follows:
>
> Clause 6
> The words 'a further successive period of one year' to be deleted from the clause and the words 'two further successive periods of one year each' to be substituted therefore.

※ Sessions 28 & 29

14 & 15 May 1945 Philharmonic Hall, Liverpool. Producer: Walter Legge
Liverpool Philharmonic Orchestra.

14 May 10.00 a.m.–12.30 p.m.; 2.00–5.00 p.m.

Sibelius, Symphony No. 2

1 i	CAX9290 – 1 – <u>2</u>	14.5.45	Columbia unpub. & destroyed 17.2.55
1 ii	CAX9291 – <u>1</u> – 2	14.5.45	do.
2 i	CAX9292 – <u>1</u> – 2 – 3	14.5.45	do.
2 ii	CAX9293 – <u>1</u> – 2 – 3	14.5.45	do.
2 iii	CAX9294 – <u>1</u> – 2	14.5.45	do.
3 i	CAX9295 – <u>1</u> – 2 – 3	14.5.45	do.
3 ii; 4 i	CAX9296 – <u>1</u> – 2	15.5.45	do.
4 ii	CAX9297 – 1 – <u>2</u>	15.5.45	do.
4 iii	CAX9298 – <u>1</u> – 2	15.5.45	do.

15 May 9.30 a.m.–1.00 p.m.

Lambert, *Horoscope*

Dance for the followers of Leo	CAX9299 – 1 – <u>2</u> – 3	Columbia DX1196 (7/45)
Valse for the Gemini	CAX9300 – 1 – <u>2</u>	Columbia DX1196
Invocation to the Moon	CAX9301 – 1 – <u>2</u>	Columbia DX1197
Finale	CAX9302 – <u>1</u> – 2	Columbia DX1197

LP/Cassette: [complete] EMI EH 291343-1; EMI EH291343-4 (10/88)
CD: EMI CDH763911-2 (9/92); Pearl GEM0069; Living Era AJC8558; B000CSTJZC

� Sessions 30, 31 & 32

4–6 July 1945 EMI Studio 1, Abbey Road. Producer: Walter Legge

Joan Hammond (Dido), Dennis Noble (Aeneas), Isobel Baillie (Belinda), Sylvia Patriss (Spirit), Edith Coates (Sorceress), Edna Hobson (1st Witch), Gladys Ripley (2nd Witch), Joan Fullerton (Woman), Trefor Jones (Sailor), Boris Ord (harpsichord) & Philharmonia String Orchestra

Purcell, *Dido and Aeneas* (British Council recording)

4 July EMI Studio 1

Pt. 1	10518 – 1 – 1a – 2 – 2A C3471 (12/45)	
Pt. 5	10522 – 1 – 1a – 2 – 2A – 3	C3473
Pt. 6	10523 – 1 – 1a – 2 – 2A – 3	C3473
Pt. 2	10519 – 1 – 1a – 2 – 2A – 3	C3471
Pt. 3	10520 – 1 – 1a – 2 – 2A – 3	C3472

5 July EMI Studio 1

Pt. 4	10521 – 1 – 1a – 2 – 3A C3472	
Pt. 9	10526 – 1 – 1a – 2 – 2A – 3	C3475
Pt. 10	10527 – 1 – 1a – 2 – 2A – 3	C3475
Pt. 13	10530 – 1 – 1a – 2 – 2A – 3	C3477
Pt. 12	10529 – 1 – 1a – 2 – 2A – 3	C3476
Pt. 8	10525 – 1 – 1a – 2 – 2A C3474	

6 July EMI Studio 1

Pt. 11	10528 – 1 – 1a – 2 – 2A – 3	C3476
Pt. 14	10531 – 1 – 1a – 2 – 2A C3477	
Pt. 7	10524 – 1 – 1a – 2 – 2A – 3	C3474

78: auto C7628–34

LP: [Side 5 only with Edith Coates] HLM7145

CD: Opera D'oro OPD1220

[The recording, which used E. J. Dent's edition, is complete, with additional repeats not marked in the vocal score, p. 75, of the *Vivace* and the *Allegro con spirito* sections. Alec Robertson concluded his review, *Gramophone*, Dec. 1945, p. 78: 'Thinking over the performance as a whole the orchestral playing, under Constant Lambert, stands in the first place. Here is a conductor who thoroughly understands his Purcell.']

Letter from Lambert to Margery Gray, 8 July 1945: 'Have just spent an enjoyable but hard week recording the whole of "Dido".'

Letter from Walter Legge to Lambert, 4 All Souls' Place, W1, 25 Sept. 1945:

As a mark of our appreciation of the work you have done for us [we] increase your session fee to twenty guineas' (with an exclusive contract the following October 1946–47 for 25 guineas). 'Repertoire to be
    Purcell Chaconne in G minor Gibbon Fantasia in F mi Grieg Elegiac Melodies Bartok Romanian Dances
    Scores of these will be sent to you this week.

� Session 33

12 Oct. 1945 EMI Studio 1, Abbey Road. 3.10–5.00 p.m. & 6.00–9.00 p.m. Producer: Walter Legge

Philharmonia String Orchestra

Purcell, arr. Whittaker, Chaconne in G minor

i	CAX9409 – 1 – 2	Columbia DX1230 (2/46)
ii	CAX9410 – 1 – 2	Columbia DX1230

Bartók, arr. Arthur Willner, *Roumanian Folk Dances*

i	CAX9411 – 1 – 2	Columbia DX1221 (12/45)
ii	CAX9412 – 1 – 2	Columbia DX1221

Grieg, *Two Elegiac Melodies* (1. 'Heart's Wounds'; 2. 'The Last Spring')
   i CAX9413 – <u>1</u> – 2   Columbia unpub.
   ii CAX9414 – <u>1</u> – 2   Columbia unpub.
Ole Bull–Svendsen, *Shepherd Girls' Sunday*
     CAX9415 – 1   Columbia unpub.

(Walton was also in the studio that day to record *Henry V* 'Death of Falstaff' and 'Touch her soft lips')

[Bartók: 'A record of excellent light charm.' *Gramophone*, Dec. 1945, p. 83.

Purcell: 'A record of uncommon style and vim, in which fine technique is to be deeply admired.' *Gramophone*, Feb. 1946, p. 105.]

Letter from Lambert to *New Statesman*, 3 Jan. 1946, on review of the Bartók Dances: 'If he had taken the trouble to borrow or buy the easily obtainable original he would have found that these dances have not been tampered with in any way by the arranger. They are a faithful transcription of the original piano pieces and the harmony has not been altered in any way what so ever.'

Letter 27 June 1945, extending contract for one year (from 5 Aug. 1945)

Letter from Walter Legge to Lambert at 4 All Souls' Place, w1, 3 Dec. 1945:

> Your formal contract is being prepared but as I promised you last night I am sending you this letter to confirm the agreement we reached on its details.
> 1. That during the remainder of your present contract which expires in August 1946 we will pay you for each recording session a fee of £21.
> 2. That you will record exclusively for this Company for a period of two years from August 1946 to August 1948
> 3. That during this period your fee per session will be 25 guineas.
> 4. That between now and August 1948 you will record for the Company the following of your own works:
>   a) one double-sided record of the Horoscope Suite
>   b) Merchant Seamen Suite, short version
>   c) Rio Grande
>   d) Aubade Héroïque
>   Let me also confirm that on January 25th 2 p.m. Kingsway Hall, you will record with the Philharmonia Orchestra 'On the Steppes of Central Asia', 'Jota Aragonese', and on the 30th January 1946 with the same orchestra 'Contes Féeriques'.
>   That I think is all for today. Have a good time in Belgium and let me know as soon as you are back.

Letter from Legge to Lambert, 15 Dec. 1945:

> to record in variant to your present contract or this new one 1 further double-sided record of:
>   Horoscope, Aubade Héroïque, Merchant Seamen Suite (short form) and to re-record Rio Grande
>   I look forward to this continuation of our happy association.

Exclusive contract from August 1946 to August 1948 – 25 guineas

⁂ Session 34

24 Jan. 1946 Kingsway Hall. 6.15–9.15 p.m. Producer: Walter Legge
Philharmonia Orchestra
2.2.1.(CA) 2 4.2.3.1 harp triangle 2 drums strings (10.8.6.6.4)

Borodin, *In the Steppes of Central Asia*

According to Searle, it was Lambert having once seen a score of this work with its title printed in three languages – *Im Mittelasien, Dans l'Asie Moyenne, In Average Asia* – that made him one winter call a snow and ice-bound part of London 'Average Asia' (Shead, *Constant Lambert*, p. 145).
   i CAX9443 – <u>1</u> – 2 – 3   Columbia DX1449 (1/48)
   ii CAX9444 – 1 – <u>2</u>   Columbia DX1449
78: (US) Col. 71956D

Glinka, *Jota Aragonese*

  CAX9445 – <u>1</u> – 2   Columbia unpub.

﷽ **Session 35**

30 Jan. 1946 Kingsway Hall. 2.00–5.00p.m. Producer: Walter Legge
Philharmonia Orchestra
2 + 1.2.2.2 (CA).2 4.2.3.1 triangle 3 drums 1 harp strings (10.8.6.6.4)

Rimsky-Korsakov *Fairy Tale [Skazka]*

  i CAX9448 – <u>1</u> – 2   Columbia DX1485 (6/48)
  ii CAX9449 – <u>1</u> – 2   Columbia DX1485
  iii CAX9450 – <u>1</u> – 2   Columbia DX1486
  iv CAX9451 – <u>1</u> – 2   Columbia DX1486

CD: Dutton BP9712

Dvořák, Overture *The Peasant a Rogue*

  i CAX9452 – 1 – 2   Columbia unpub.
  ii CAX9453 – 1 – 2   Columbia unpub.

Dvořák, *Scherzo capriccioso*

  i CAX9454 – 1   Columbia unpub.

﷽ **Session 36**

14 Mar. 1946 Kingsway Hall. Producer: David Bicknell
Royal Opera House Orchestra, Covent Garden
2 +1.2.2.2. 4.2.3.1 1 harp timp 2 drums strings (12.10.8.8.6)

Gordon, *The Rake's Progress*

  i Reception   CAX9469 – 1 – 2   Columbia DX1249 (6/46)
  ii Faithful Girl   CAX9470 – 1 – 2   Columbia DX1249
  iii Orgy Pt. 1   CAX9471 – 1 – 2   Columbia DX1250
  iv Orgy Pt. 2   CAX9472 – 1 – 2   Columbia DX1250

LP: (US) Col. ML4229; ML 2117 (10″)
CD: EMI CDH763911-2 (9/92); TIME MACHINE 0099

﷽ **Session 37**

18 Mar. 1946 EMI Studio 1, Abbey Road. Producer: David Bicknell
Royal Opera House, Covent Garden, Orchestra
2 +1.2.2.2. 4.2.3.1 1 harp timp 2 drums strings (12.10.8.8.6)

Bliss, *Miracle in the Gorbals*

  i The Street; The Girl Suicide   CAX9477 – <u>1</u> – 2   Columbia DX1260 (8/46)
  ii The Young Lovers; Discovery of the   CAX9478 – 1 – <u>2</u>   Columbia DX1260
    Suicide's Body
  iii Dance of Deliverance   CAX9479 – <u>1</u> – 2   Columbia DX1261
  iv Finale: Killing of the Stranger   CAX9480 – <u>1</u> – 2   Columbia DX1261

LP: (US) Col. ML2117 (10″)
CD: Dutton CDBP9761 (3/06)

﷽ **Sessions 38 & 39**

28 & 29 Mar. 1946 EMI Studio 1, Abbey Road Producer: Walter Legge
Philharmonia Orchestra

Rawsthorne, *Symphonic Studies* (recorded under the auspices of the British Council)

  i 2EA10942 – <u>1</u> – 2 – 3   28.3.46   HMV C3542 (1/47)
  ii 2EA10943 – <u>1</u> – 2 – 3   28.3.46   HMV C3542
  iii 2EA10944 – <u>1</u> – 2 – 3   28.3.46   HMV C3543
  iv 2EA10945 – <u>1</u> – 2   28.3.46   HMV C3543 [then Boult and BBCSO for
                     Vaughan Williams, *Job*]

v 2EA10953 – 1 – 2 – 3	29.3.46	HMV C3544
vi 2EA10954 – 1 – 2 – 3	29.3.46	HMV C3544

78: auto C7655–7
LP: HMV CLP1056 (12/55); MFP2069 (6/67)
CD: Pearl GEM0058

Rawsthorne, Overture *Street Corner* (recorded under the auspices of the British Council)

i 2EA10955 – 1 – 2 – 3	29.3.46	HMV C3502 (8/46)
ii 2EA10956 – 1 – 2 – 3	29.3.46	HMV C3502 [Pearl gives 10956 – 2]

Cassette: EMI EH291343-4 (10/88)
LP: EMI EH291343-1 (10/88)
CD: EMI CDH763911-2 (9/92); Pearl GEM0058

Bliss, March *The Phoenix (In Honour of France)* (recorded under the auspices of the British Council)

i 2EA10957 – 1 – 2 – 3	29.3.46	HMV C3518 (10/46)
ii 2EA10958 – 1 – 2	29.3.46	HMV C3518

Cassette: EMI EH291343-4 (10/88)
LP: EMI EH291343-1 (10/88)
CD: in EMI CZS569743-2 (4 CDs); in Dutton 2CDBP9818 (2 CDs)

∰ Session 40

6 Apr. 1946 EMI Studio 1, Abbey Road Producer: Walter Legge
Joan Hammond, Philharmonia Orchestra

Weber, *Der Freischütz* – Softly sighs

Part 1 2EA10970-1	HMV unpublished

A note on the recording sheet in Legge's handwriting reads: 'Lambert's inability to carry on through illness. James Whitehead happened to be in the building and Joan Hammond agreed to try to carry on with him.'

∰ Session 41

14 June 1946 Kingsway Hall. Producer: David Bicknell
Royal Opera House, Covent Garden, Orchestra
Zingra Bunbury (solo viola); Raymond Clark (solo cello)

Adam, *Giselle*

i Opening Scene: Giselle's Dance	CAX9555 – 1 – 2 – 3	Columbia DX1270 (9/46)
ii Mad Scene	CAX9556 – 1 – 2 – 3	Columbia DX1270
iii Pas de deux (Act 2)	CAX9557 – 1 – 2 – 3	Columbia DX1271
iv Closing Scene	CAX9558 – 1 – 2 – 3	Columbia DX1271

78: (US) Col. DX277
LP: Col. ML2117 (10″)

['A very favourable sample of bold, rich colouring in recording: I don't think anyone could ask for anything better.' *Gramophone*, Sept. 1946, p. 48.]

Letter from Legge to Copyright Department quoting an extract from a letter by Lambert:

With reference to Fraser's letter: the 'Giselle' ballet music arrangement is quite definitely mine and not Gordon Jacob's. Gordon Jacob was, of course, paid for his work on the score; even so, he deserves something for his share in the work.

This I am arranging with him personally and everything is, I need hardly add, on the most amicable basis. So you will instruct the Copyright Department to make the royalties payable to me direct and I will cope with the rest.

∰ Session 42

15 June 1946 Kingsway Hall. Producer: David Bicknell
Royal Opera House, Covent Garden, Orchestra; violin solo: Joseph Shadwick; cello solo: Raymond Clark

Tchaikovsky, *The Sleeping Princess Suite*

i	Panorama	CAX9524 – <u>1</u> – 2	Columbia DX1281 (11/46)
ii	Page's Dance; Aurora's solo (Act 1)	CAX9525 – <u>1</u> – 2	Columbia DX1281
iii	Vision Scene (Act 2)	CAX9526 – <u>1</u> – 2	Columbia DX1282
iv	Red Riding Hood; March (Act 3)	CAX9527 – 1 – <u>2</u>	Columbia DX1282

LP: (US) Col. ML4136

CD: [cello solo only] in CC1010 (2 CDs, The British Cello Phenomenon)

※ Session 43

22 June 1946 EMI Studio 1 Joseph Szigeti, Philharmonia Orchestra

Bartók, *Portrait*, Op. 5 No. 1

i	CAX9568 – <u>1</u> – 2 – 3	Columbia LX1531 (3/52)
ii	CAX9569 – 1 – <u>2</u> – 3	Columbia LX1531

LP: HMV HLM7016 (9/72); GR2254; (US) Col. ML2213; BWS715

CD: Naxos 8.110973; Pearl GEMO173

['Those of us who were friends of Constant Lambert could not have wished him to leave behind a finer legacy than this wonderful co-operation with Szigeti in a piece of music by a great contemporary composer that comes from, and goes to, the heart.' A.R., *Gramophone*, Mar. 1952, p.225.]

※ Session 44

24 Aug. 1946 EMI Studio 1, Abbey Road
Benno Moiseiwitsch, Philharmonia Orchestra

Delius, Piano Concerto

i	2EA11185 – 1 – <u>2</u> – 3	HMV C3533 (1/47)
ii	2EA11186 – 1 – <u>2</u> – 3	HMV C3533
iii	2EA11187 – 1 – <u>2</u> – 3	HMV C3534
iv	2EA11188 – <u>1</u> – 2 – 3	HMV C3534
v	2EA11189 – 1 – <u>2</u> – 3	HMV CS3535 (single side)

78: auto C7648–50

LP: World Records SH224 (8/75)

CD: Testament SBT1014 (5/93); Naxos 8.110689 (5/03)

Beecham attempted his first recording of this work, for EMI, on 3 Oct. 1945, but it was not issued.

※ Session 45

26 Aug. 1946 EMI Studio 1, Abbey Road
Joseph Szigeti, Philharmonia Orchestra

Berlioz, *Reverie and Caprice*

i	CAX9678 – 1 – <u>2</u>	Columbia LX946 (1/47)
ii	CAX9679 – <u>1</u> – 2	Columbia LX946

LP: HMV HQM1224 (8/70); GR2201; (US) Col. 72869D; BWS715

CD: LYS084

※ Session 46

7 Feb. 1947 Kingsway Hall. Producer: David Bicknell
Royal Opera House Orchestra, Covent Garden

Delibes, *Coppélia* Ballet Suite, Act 3 (orch. Jacob)

i	Marche de la cloche; La Prière	CAX9816 – <u>1</u>	Columbia DX1429 (12/47)
ii	Valse des heures; Danse villageoise	CAX9817 – <u>1</u>	Columbia DX1429
iii	Pas de deux; Les Fileuses	CAX9818 – <u>1</u>	Columbia DX1430
iv	Danse de fête; Galop final	CAX9819 – <u>1</u>	Columbia DX1430

LP: (US) Col. ML4145

Letter from Lambert to Alan Frank, 8 Mar. 1947: OUP files: 'I have heard no further news about the recording of the *Aubade* as Walter Legge seems to spend most of his time in Switzerland, for reasons best known to himself, but I have a definite promise on paper. The timing of the work varies slightly according to my mood but I would say that 7 minutes 30 seconds would be the safest bet.'

※ Session 47

25 Mar. 1947 EMI Studio 1, Abbey Road. Producer: David Bicknell
Royal Opera House Orchestra, Covent Garden
2.2.2.2 4.2.2 tenor tromb. 1 bass tromb.1 trgle. 1 drum strings (14.12.10.10.8)

Delibes, *Coppélia* Ballet Suite, Acts 1 & 2

i Prelude and Mazurka (Act 1)	CAX9855 – 1	Columbia DX1371 (6/47)
ii Swanhilda's Valse and Czardas (Act 1)	CAX9856 – 1	Columbia DX1371
iii Thème slave variée (Act 2)	CAX9857 – 1	Columbia DX1372
iv Valse de la poupée; Bolero; Gigue (Act 1)	CAX9858 – 1	Columbia DX1372

LP: (US) Col. ML4145

[2 Apr. 1947: Cheque for £26.5.0 for recording *Coppélia* on 25 Mar. with ROH Orch. CG]

1948

Lambert to Columbia Graphophone, 19 Jan. 1948:

> Dear Bicknell
>
> Thank you for your letter of December 10th. I am sorry for the delay in replying but I have been extremely busy on the music for the film "Anna Karénina".
>
> Your correspondent was right I am afraid. I can't imagine how the mistake occurred as we were both in contact over the correct labelling. Unfortunately I was not sent a complimentary copy or I could have detected the mistake at once.
>
> DX 1371 is labelled correctly
>
> DX 1372: for Act 1 read Act 2 and vice versa
>
> (Thème Slav Variée – Act 1
>
> Valse de la Poupée, Bolero, Gigue – Act 2)
>
> Act 3 is labelled correctly
>
> Could I in future be sent as usual a test – or complimentary copy of any record I make.

Inter-departmental memorandum from Legge to Miss Mathias, 26 Jan. 1948:

> There was attached to Constant Lambert's contract a letter in which we specifically agreed, with Mr Duncan's approval, to record his 'Rio Grande', 'Aubade Héroïque' and 'Merchant Seamen Suite', also I believe, the second 'Horoscope'. Can you find out, because he [Lambert] is reminding me of that stipulation and wants to know when we are recording the works.

Letter to Lambert, 28 Jan. 1948:

> Thank you very much for your letter of the 19th January giving us the correct label information for the 'Coppélia' Ballet records. We will see that the necessary alteration is made on the labels.
>
> We will also see that in future you receive a complimentary set of all the records you make with us.

Internal Memorandum to Mr B. Mitchell, 8 July 1948:

> Recording Commitments:
>
> In regard to conductors and orchestras, I think we should re-consider the value of the conductors that we have under contract and retain largely those that have international significance and who are primarily instrumental in selling orchestral records. I doubt whether we need Malko, Constant Lambert, George Weldon, Kubelick [*sic*], Sir Malcolm Sargent now that we have such conductors as Furtwängler, de Sabata, Karajan, not forgetting Sir Thomas Beecham. It might also be worth while considering whether we have any further need of the Liverpool Philharmonic Orchestra and the Halle Orchestra.

※ Session 48

13 Jan. 1949 EMI Studio 1, Abbey Road. 10.00a.m.–5.00 p.m. Producer: Walter Legge
Gladys Ripley (contralto), Kyla Greenbaum (pf), BBC Chorus, Philharmonia Orchestra

Lambert, *The Rio Grande*

i	CAX10427 – <u>1</u> – 2 – 3 – 4	Columbia DX1591 (9/49)
ii	CAX10428 – 1 – <u>2</u>	Columbia DX1591
iii	CAX10429 – <u>1</u> – 2	Columbia DX1592
iv	CAX10430 – 1 – <u>2</u>	Columbia DX1592

78: (US) set MX349
LP: Columbia 33SX1003 (3/53); HMV HQM1078 (6/67); Col. ML2145 (10")
CD: EMI CDH763911–2; Pearl GEM0069 (with wrong note corrected)

Lambert, *Aubade héroïque*

i	CAX10431 – 1	unpub.

※ Session 49

14 Jan. 1949 EMI Studio 1, Abbey Road 10.00a.m.–5.00 p.m. Producer: Walter Legge
Philharmonia Orchestra

Lambert, *Horoscope*

i	Bacchanale	CAX10432 – <u>1</u> – 2 – 3	Columbia DX1568 (6/49)
ii	Saraband for the followers of Virgo		
	i	CAX10433 – <u>1</u> – 2	Columbia DX1567
	ii	CAX10434 – <u>1</u> – 2	Columbia DX1567

LP: Columbia 33SX1003 (3/53); HMV HQM1078 (6/67); Col. ML2083 (10"); EMI EH291343-1
(10/88)
Cassette: EMI EH291343-4 (10/88)
CD: EMI CDH763911-2 (9/92); Pearl GEM0069; B000CSTJZC; Living Era AJC8558

['They are played most beautifully and sensitively by the Philharmonia Orchestra; the quality
of their performance is much superior to that of the Liverpool Phil., which recorded the other
movements. ... If there is a better recording than this, I have yet to hear of it.' L.S., *Gramophone*,
June 1949, p. 4.]

Liszt, arr. Lambert, orch. Jacob, *Apparitions*

i	Cave Scene i	CAX10435 – <u>1</u> – 2	Columbia DX1560 (4/49)
ii	Cave Scene ii	CAX10436 – <u>1</u> – 2	Columbia DX1560
iii	Galop	CAX10437 – <u>1</u> – 2	Columbia DX1568 (6/49)

LP: EMI EH291343-1 (10/88); Entre RL3056
Cassette: EMI EH291343-4 (10/88)
CD: EMI CDH763911-2 (9/92); Pearl GEM 0069; TIME MACHINE 0099; [*Galop* only] Living Era
AJC8558

['The performance is first-rate, and the recording ... – there is no other word for it – terrific.' L.S.,
Gramophone, Apr. 1949, p.175]

Memoir from BM to Walter Legge, 9 Apr. 1949: 'Rather than lose the services of Constant Lambert
I agree that you should increase your offer to a flat fee of 45 guineas per session.'

Draft Contract, 19 May 1949: '1 year. Minimum of 4 sessions per annum for either Columbia or
HMV £45 (in pencil – guineas: changed to £47.50 in full contract) Exclusively'

Agreement, 21 Sept. 1949: 'One year. 4 or more sessions £47.5.0 per session. Duration of each
recording session shall be approx. 3 hours.'

※ Session 50

22 Mar. 1950 Kingsway Hall
Philharmonia Orchestra

Waldteufel, *Les Patineurs* Waltz

i	CAX10760 – <u>1</u> – 2	Columbia DX1674 (9/50)
ii	CAX10761 – <u>1</u> – 2	Columbia DX1674

LP: Columbia 33S1006 (10", 10/53); Entre RL3054
45: SCD2097
CD: SOMMCD023 (5/02)

Waldteufel, *Estudiantina* Waltz
    i CAX10762 – <u>1</u>   Columbia DX1693 (12/50)
    ii CAX10763 – <u>1</u> – 2   Columbia DX1693
LP: Columbia 33S1006 (10", 10/53); Entre RL3054
45: SED5506; SEDQ113
CD: SOMMCD023 (5/02)

※ Session 51

24 Mar. 1950 Kingsway Hall Producer: Walter Legge
Philharmonia Orchestra

Suppé, *Pique Dame* Overture
    i CAX10775 – <u>1</u> – 2   Columbia DX1746 (5/51)
    ii CAX10776 -<u>1</u> – 2 – 3 Columbia DX1746
45: SED5506; SEDQ113
CD: SOMMCD023 (5/02)

Suppé, *Morning*, Overture *Noon and Night*
    i CAX10777 – <u>1</u> – 2   Columbia DX1665 (7/50)
    ii CAX10778 – <u>1</u> – 2   Columbia DX1665
LP: Entre RL3054
45: SED5504; SEDQ512
CD: SOMMCD023 (5/02)

Letter to Lambert, 13 July 1950: 'Referring to the agreement between us dated 21 September 1949, we wish the period of the agreement to be extended for a further period of one year from 20 September 1950 and on the same terms and conditions.'

Memoir from Walter Legge, 28 June 1950: 'Please prepare a contract for another year from the 20th September.'

※ Session 52

14 Sept. 1950 Kingsway Hall Producer: Walter Legge
Philharmonia Orchestra

Waldteufel, Waltz *Pomona*
    i CAX10895 – <u>1</u>   Columbia DX1713 (1/51)
    ii CAX10896 – <u>1</u>   Columbia DX1713
LP: Columbia 33S1006 (10", 10/53); Entre RL3054
CD: SOMMCD023 (5/02)

Waldteufel, Waltz *Sur la plage*
    i CAX10897 – <u>1</u> – 2   Columbia DX1755 (6/51)
    ii CAX10898 – <u>1</u>   Columbia DX1755
78: auto DX8374–6
LP: Columbia 33S1006 (10", 10/53)
45: SED5504; SEDQ512
CD: SOMMCD023 (5/02); TIME MACHINE 0099

※ Session 53

27 Sept. 1950 Kingsway Hall Producer: Walter Legge
Philharmonia Orchestra

Walton, *Façade* Suites 1 & 2
Fanfare, Polka, Swiss Jodelling Song	CAX10905 – <u>1</u> – 2	Columbia DX1734 (4/51)
Valse, Tango-Pasodoble	CAX10906 – <u>1</u> – 2	Columbia DX1734
Country Dance, Popular Song	CAX10907 – <u>1</u> – 2	Columbia DX1735
Scotch Rhapsody, Tarantella	CAX10908 – <u>1</u> – 2	Columbia DX1735

Noche espagnole; Old Sir Faulk   CAX10909 – <u>1</u> – 2   Columbia DX1736
78: auto DX8374–6
LP: Columbia 33SX1003 (3/53); ML4793
CD: SOMMCD023 (5/02)

Chabrier, orch. Lambert, *Ballabile (Pièces Posthumes)*
    CAX10910 – 1 – <u>2</u>   Columbia DX1736 (4/51)
78: auto DX8374–6
CD: EMI CDH763911-2 (9/92); SOMMCD023 (5/02); Living Era AJC8558
N.B.: Listed but not included in cassette EMI EH291343-4 (10/88)

✺ Index of works recorded by Lambert

Work	Session	Date
Adam, *Giselle*	[41]	June 1946
Auber, Overture *The Bronze Horse*	[8]	Nov. 1938
Auber, Overture *Crown Diamonds*	[7 & 8]	Oct. (unpub.) & Nov. 1938
Auber, Overture *Fra Diavolo*	[9]	Dec. 1938
Bartók, *Portrait*, Op. 5 No. 1	[43]	June 1946
Bartók, arr. Arthur Willner, *Roumanian Folk Dances*	[33]	Oct. 1945
Berlioz, *Reverie and Caprice*	[45]	Aug. 1946
Bizet, *Roma – Carnaval*	[27]	Oct. 1943
Bliss, *Adam Zero*	*	May 1946 [see Transcription recordings]
Bliss, *Miracle in the Gorbals*	[37]	Mar. 1946
Bliss, March *The Phoenix (In Honour of France)*	[39]	Mar. 1946
Borodin, *In the Steppes of Central Asia*	[34]	Jan. 1946
Borodin, Symphony No. 2	[25–6]	June 1943
Boyce, arr. Lambert, *The Prospect before Us*	[18]	Aug. 1940
Bull–Svendsen, *Shepherd Girls' Sunday*	[33]	Oct. 1945 (unpub.)
Chabrier, *Joyeuse marche*	[14]	June 1939
Chabrier, *Le Roi malgé lui – Danse slave*	[16]	Dec. 1939
Chabrier, orch. Lambert, *Ballabile (Pièces Posthumes)*	[53]	Sept. 1950
Delibes, *Coppélia* Ballet Suite, Acts 1 & 2	[47]	Mar. 1947
Delibes, *Le Roi l'a dit*	[9]	Dec. 1938
Delibes, orch. Jacob, *Coppélia* Ballet Suite, Act 3	[46]	Feb. 1947
Delius, *La Calinda*	[20]	July 1941
Delius, *Hassan* Intermezzo and Serenade	[20]	July 1941
Delius, *On Hearing the First Cuckoo in Spring*	[7]	Oct. 1938
Delius, Piano Concerto	[44]	Aug. 1946
Dvořák, Overture *The Peasant a Rogue*	[35]	Jan. 1946 (unpub.)
Dvořák, *Scherzo capriccioso*	[35]	Jan. 1946 (unpub.)
Glazunov, *Stenka Razin*, Op. 13	[24]	Dec. 1942
Glinka, *Jota Aragonese*	[34]	Jan. 1946 (unpub.)
Gordon, *The Rake's Progress*	[36]	Mar. 1946
	*	Apr. 1945 [see Transcription recordings]
Grieg, *Two Elegiac Melodies*	[33]	Oct. 1945 (unpub.)
Grieg, *Sigurd Jorsalfar* – Homage March	[20]	July 1941
Lambert, *Aubade héroïque*	[48]	Jan. 1949 (unpub.)
Lambert, *Horoscope* (4 mvts.)	[29]	May 1945
Lambert, *Horoscope* (2 mvts)	[49]	Jan. 1949
Lambert, *Merchant Seamen*	[video/DVD]	
Lambert, *Music for Orchestra*	*	2 July 1948 [see NSA recordings]

Lambert, *The Rio Grande*	[4]	Jan. 1930
Lambert, *The Rio Grande*	[48]	Jan. 1949
Liszt, *Hungarian Fantasia*	[15]	Nov. 1939
Liszt, arr. Lambert, *Dante Sonata*	[17]	Mar. 1940
Liszt, orch. Jacob, arr. Lambert, *Apparitions*	[49]	Jan. 1949
Meyerbeer, Coronation March *Le Prophète*	[14]	June 1939
Meyerbeer, arr. Lambert, *Les Patineurs*	[13]	May 1939
Offenbach, Overture *Orpheus in the Underworld*	[14]	June 1939
Purcell, *Dido and Aeneas*	[30–32]	July 1945
Purcell, arr. Lambert, *Comus* Ballet Suite	[21]	Mar. 1942
Purcell, arr. Whittaker, Chaconne in G minor	[33]	Oct. 1945
Rawsthorne, Overture *Street Corner*	[39]	Mar. 1946
Rawsthorne, *Symphonic Studies*	[38–39]	Mar. 1946
Rimsky-Korsakov, *Fairy Tale* [Skazka]	[35]	Jan. 1946
Rimsky-Korsakov, Overture *Ivan the Terrible*	[27]	Oct. 1943
Rossini, *William Tell* Ballet Music	[13]	May 1939
Schubert, *Overture in the Italian Style*	[20]	July 1941 (unpub.)
Sibelius, Symphony No. 2	[28–9]	May 1945 (unpub.)
Suppé, Overture *Morning, Noon and Night*	[51]	Mar. 1950
Suppé, Overture *Pique Dame*	[51]	Mar. 1950
Tchaikovsky, *Eugene Onegin* – Tatiana's Letter Scene	[27]	Oct. 1943
Tchaikovsky, Overture *Hamlet*	[23]	Oct. 1942
Tchaikovsky, Overture *Romeo and Juliet*	[19]	Feb. 1941
Tchaikovsky, *The Sleeping Princess* Suite	[10]	Feb. 1939
Tchaikovsky, *The Sleeping Princess* Suite	[42]	June 1946
Tchaikovsky, Symphony No. 4	[22–3]	Oct. 1942
Tchaikovsky, Symphony No. 5	[11–12]	Mar. 1939
Waldteufel, Waltz *Estudiantina*	[50]	Mar. 1950
Waldteufel, Waltz *Les Patineurs*	[50]	Mar. 1950
Waldteufel, Waltz *Pomona*	[52]	Sept. 1950
Waldteufel, Waltz *Sur la plage*	[52]	Sept. 1950
Walton, *Façade* [original version: as speaker]	[1–2 & 3]	July & Aug. (unpub.) & Nov. 1929
Walton, *Façade* Suites Nos. 1 & 2	[53]	Sept. 1950
Warlock, *Capriol* Suite	[6]	Apr. 1937
Warlock, *The Curlew*	[5]	Mar. 1931
Warlock, Serenade (To Delius on his 60th birthday)	[6]	Apr. 1937
Weber, *Der Freischütz* – Softly sighs	[40]	Apr. 1946 (unpub.)
Weinberger, *Under the Spreading Chestnut Tree*	[16]	Dec. 1939

2 Commercial Recordings of Lambert's Works

February 2013. **Bold type** denotes an issue on CD. The dates in parentheses refer to reviews in *Gramophone* (Aw denotes an Awards issue).

PRIZE FIGHT Realistic Ballet in One Act
BBC Concert Orchestra, Barry Wordsworth

	rec. 7.98	(2/00)	ASV **WHL2122**

English Northern Philharmonia, David Lloyd-Jones

	rec. 12.04	(Aw/05)	Hyperion **CDA67545**

– for two pianos
Mark Tanner and Allan Schiller   rec. 5.06   Priory **PRCD881**

MR BEAR SQUASH-YOU-ALL-FLAT
Nigel Hawthorne (narrator), Nash Ensemble, Lionel Friend

	rec. 5.94	(7/95)	Hyperion **CDA66754**
			CDH55397

PIANO CONCERTO (1924; ed. Easterbrook & Shipley)
David Owen Norris, BBC Concert Orchestra, Barry Wordsworth

	rec. 7.98	(2/00)	ASV **WHL2122**

Jonathan Plowright, English Northern Philharmonia, David Lloyd-Jones

	rec. 12.04	(Aw/05)	Hyperion **CDA67545**
			in **CDRSB505** (5 CDs)

OVERTURE FOR PIANO DUET
Peter Lawson and Alan MacLean   Albany **TROY142**

– orchestral version as THE BIRD-ACTORS
State Orchestra of Victoria, John Lanchbery

	rec. 2/6.99	(4/01)	**CHAN9865**

English Northern Philharmonia, David Lloyd-Jones

	rec. 12.04	(Aw/05)	Hyperion **CDA67545**

ROMEO AND JULIET Ballet in Two Tableaux
English Chamber Orchestra, Norman Del Mar

	rec. 7.77	(1/80)	Lyrita SRCS110
		(11/07)	Lyrita **SRCD215**

State Orchestra of Victoria, John Lanchbery

	rec. 2/6.99	(4/01)	**CHAN9865**

English Northern Philharmonia, David Lloyd-Jones

	rec. 12.04	(Aw/05)	Hyperion **CDA67545**

– Second Tableau
Royal Ballet Sinfonia, Barry Wordsworth   ASV **WHL2128**
                                                          in Resonance **CDRSB502** (5 CDs)
[Finale only]   in **RRCD641643** (3 CDs)

SUITE IN THREE MOVEMENTS
Mark Bebbington   rec. 8.05   (2/07)   **SOMM062**
Mark Tanner   rec. 5.06   Priory **PRCD881**

POMONA Ballet in One Act
English Chamber Orchestra, Norman Del Mar

	rec. 7.77	(1/80)	Lyrita SRCS110
		(11/07)	**SRCD215**

English Northern Philharmonia, David Lloyd-Jones

	rec. 4.98	(6/99)	Hyperion **CDA67049**

BBC Concert Orchestra, Barry Wordsworth

rec. 7.98	(2/00)	ASV **WHL2122**

State Orchestra of Victoria, John Lanchbery

rec. 2/6.99	(4/01)	**CHAN9865**

[See also *Siciliana* for piano solo: Lambert NSA recording]

EIGHT POEMS OF LI-PO

Alexander Young, Argo Chamber Ensemble, Charles Groves

(10/55)	Argo RG50
	Westminster XWN18254

Yvonne Kenny, Malcolm Martineau   rec. 5.92   Etcetera **KTC1140**
Philip Langridge, Nash Ensemble, Lionel Friend

rec. 5.94	(7/95)	Hyperion **CDA66754**
		CDH55397

MUSIC FOR ORCHESTRA

London Philharmonic Orchestra, Barry Wordsworth   (11/07)   Lyrita **SRCD215**
in **SRCD2338** (4 CDs)

[see also Lambert NSA recordings, Dutton **CDBP9761**]

ELEGIAC BLUES for solo piano

Richard Rodney Bennett

	(7/76)	Polydor 2383391
	(1/83)	HMV ESD7164;
		TC-ESD7164
	(5/06)	**586596-2**
		in **028989-2** (5 CDs)

Rhonda Gillespie   (2/75)   Argo ZRG786
Anthony Goldstone   (10/95)   **CHAN9382**
Mark Bebbington   rec. 8.05   (2/07)   **SOMM062**
[see also Lambert NSA recordings]

– for orchestra

BBC Concert Orchestra, Barry Wordsworth

rec. 1998	ASV **WHL2128**
	in Resonance **CDRSB502** (5 CDs)

English Northern Philharmonia, David Lloyd-Jones

rec. 12.04	(Aw/05)	Hyperion **CDA67545**

THE RIO GRANDE

Jean Temperley, Cristina Ortiz, London Madrigal Singers, London Symphony Orchestra, André
Previn

rec. 9.73	(5/74)	EMI ASD2990;
		TC-ASD2990
	(5/06)	**586596-2; 586595-2**

Sandra Browne, Peter Donohoe, BBC Singers, BBC Symphony Orchestra, James Loughran
p.p. Prom 15.9.79   BBC Classics **15656 9191-2**
Della Jones, Kathryn Stott, BBC Singers, BBC Concert Orchestra, Barry Wordsworth

rec. 6.91	(10/92)	Argo **436118-2**
	(1/03)	**473424-2**
		Ovation **4523242**

Sally Burgess, Jack Gibbons, Chorus of Opera North, English Northern Philharmonia, David
Lloyd-Jones

rec. 9.91	(6/92)	Hyperion **CDA66565**
		CDH55388

David Owen Norris, Kalamazoo Symphony Orchestra, Yoshimi Takeda

1996	Gilmore Festival Records

[see also Lambert sessions 4 & 47]

PIANO SONATA

Rhonda Gillespie		(2/75)	Argo ZRG 786
John McCabe			Continuum **CCD1040**
Ian Brown		(7/95)	Hyperion **CDA66754**
			CDH55397
Anthony Goldstone		(10/95)	**CHAN9382**
Benjamin Powell			**ENV038CD**
Mark Bebbington	rec. 8.05	(2/07)	**SOMM062**

CONCERTO FOR PIANO AND NINE PLAYERS

Menahem Pressler, ensemble, Theodore Bloomfield   MGM3081

Naxos **9.80286**

Gordon Watson, Argo Chamber Ensemble, Charles Groves

(10/55)   Argo **RG50**

Alessandro De Curtis, Harmonia Ensemble, Giuseppe Grazioli

rec. 1.89   Arts **47328-2**

Giulia **GS201009**

AS-5005

Richard Rodney Bennett, English Sinfonia, Neville Dilkes

	rec.12.75	(7/76)	Polydor 2383391
		(1/83)	HMV **ESD7164**;
			TC-ESD7164
		(5/06)	**586596-2**
			in **028989-2** (5 CDs)

Kathryn Stott, BBC Concert Orchestra, Barry Wordsworth

	rec. 6.91	(10/92)	Argo **436118-2**
		(1/03)	**473424-2**

Ian Brown, Nash Ensemble, Lionel Friend   rec. 5.94   (7/95)   Hyperion **CDA66754**

CDH55397

SALOMÉ Concert Suite

Nash Ensemble, David Lloyd-Jones   rec. 9.00   (9/01)   Hyperion **CDA67239**

SUMMER'S LAST WILL AND TESTAMENT

William Shimell, Chorus of Opera North, English Northern Philharmonia, David Lloyd-Jones

rec. 9.91   (6/92)   Hyperion **CDA66565**

CDH55388

– King Pest only

Royal Philharmonic Orchestra, Simon Joly (11/07)   Lyrita **SRCD215**

HOROSCOPE Ballet

– Complete Ballet (including Palindromic Prelude)

BBC Concert Orchestra, Barry Wordsworth

	rec. 6.91	(10/92)	Argo **436118-2**
		(1/03)	**473424-2**

BBC Concert Orchestra, Barry Wordsworth

rec. 3.03   (12/04)   ASV **CDDCA1168**

– Suite: Dance for the Followers of Leo; Valse for the Gemini; Invocation to the Moon and Finale; Saraband for the Followers of Virgo; Bacchanale

London Symphony Orchestra, Robert Irving

	rec. 2.53	(7/53)	Decca **LXT2791**
		(2/73)	**ECS657**

[*Valse for the Gemini* only] Royal Opera House Orchestra, Robert Irving

		(5/56)	HMV **CLP1070**
		(6/67)	**HQM1078**
		(6/73)	**SXLP30153**

	(6/81)	in ESDW713 (2 discs);	
		TC-ESDW713	
		in **9498192** (2 CDs)	
English Northern Philharmonia, David Lloyd-Jones			
rec. 6.90	(3/91)	Hyperion **CDA66436**;	
		KA66436	
		CDH55099	

[see also Lambert sessions 29 & 49]

ELEGY

Richard Rodney Bennett	(7/76)	Polydor 2383391
	(1/83)	HMV ESD7164;
		TC-ESD7164
	(5/06)	**586596-2**
		in **028989-2** (5 CDs)
Nicholas Unwin	(1/96)	Metier **MSVCD92009**
Anthony Goldstone	(10/95)	**CHAN9382**
Mark Bebbington rec. 8.05	(2/07)	**SOMM062**

MERCHANT SEAMEN Film Music

– Complete Film

Sadler's Wells Orchestra, Lambert   Video & DVD

– Suite

BBC Concert Orchestra, Barry Wordsworth

rec. 7.98	(2/00)	ASV **WHL2122**
BBC Concert Orchestra, Rumon Gamba rec. 9.07	(8/08)	**CHAN10459**

AUBADE HÉROÏQUE

English Northern Philharmonia, David Lloyd-Jones

rec. 9.91	(6/92)	Hyperion **CDA66565**
		CDH55388

ANNA KARENINA Film Music

– Complete film

London Film Symphony Orchestra, Hubert Clifford   S038132 (Video) & DVD

– Suite: Overture – Forlane – Love Scene – Finale

National Philharmonic Orchestra, Bernard Herrmann	(6/76)	Decca PFS4363;
		KPFC4363
		448 954-2
		ELQ4803787 (2 CDs)

– Suite arr. Philip Lane

BBC Concert Orchestra, Rumon Gamba rec. 9.07	(8/08)	**CHAN10459**

TROIS PIÈCES NÈGRES POUR LES TOUCHES BLANCHES

Peter Lawson and Christopher Scott	(4/82)	Auracle **AUC1001**
[*Nocturne* only] Isobel Beyer and Harvey Dagul	(9/87)	FMHD8046; FHMC843
		FHMD9673
Peter Lawson and Alan MacLean		Albany **TROY142**
David Nettle and Richard Markham		**303670017-2**
[*Siesta* only] David Nettle and Richard Markham		Netmark **NEMACD200**
John McCabe and Tamami Honma	(10/06)	Dutton **CDLX7167**
Priscilla Naish and Phil Cranmer		British Music Society
		BMS414 (cassette)

TIRESIAS Ballet
English Northern Philharmonia, David Lloyd-Jones

	rec. 4.98	(6/99)	Hyperion **CDA67049**

– Suite arr. Reynish
Depaul University Wind Ensemble, Donald Deroche

rec. 2.06–5.07		Albany **TROY1006**

※ Lambert as Arranger, etc. (selected listing)

Auber, *Les Rendezvous* – Ballet
English Chamber Orchestra, Richard Bonynge   in **4685782** (10 CDs)
[Allegro non troppo (No. 5) and Allegro (No. 6) only] Royal Opera House Orchestra, Covent
Garden, Robert Irving   (5/56)   HMV **CLP1070**
                                                                   HMV **ESDW713**
                                                                   (2 discs), TC-**ESDW713**

Bach, *Der Tag, der ist so Freudenreich*, BWV605 (Harriet Cohen Book)
Jonathan Plowright   Hyperion **CDA67767**
Antony Gray   ABC Classics **ABC4765171**

Berners, *Caprice péruvien*
RTE Sinfonietta, David Lloyd-Jones   rec. 1.95   (4/96)   Marco Polo **8.225155**
                                                     (4/01)   Marco Polo **8.223780**

Boyce, *The Prospect before Us* – Ballet
Royal Ballet Sinfonia, Barry Wordsworth   (1/02)   White Line **CDWLS255**
                                                               (2 CDs)

[see also Lambert session 18]
[Fugue in D major only] Royal Opera House Orchestra, Covent Garden, Robert Irving
                                                     (5/56)   HMV **CLP1070**
                                                     (6/81)   HMV **ESDW713**
                                                               (2 discs), TC-**ESDW713**

Couperin, *Harlequin in the Street* – Ballet
Royal Ballet Sinfonia, Barry Wordsworth   (7/04)   White Line **CDWLS273**
                                                               (2 CDs)

[Allegro only] Royal Opera Orchestra, Covent Garden, Robert Irving
                                                     (5/56)   HMV **CLP1070**
                                                     (2/59)   HMV **7EP7076**

Liszt, *Apparitions* – Ballet
Royal Ballet Sinfonia, Barry Wordsworth   (7/05)   Dutton **CDLX7149**
[Nos. 1 & 7 only] Royal Opera House Orchestra, Covent Garden, Robert Irving
                                                     (6/81)   HMV **ESDW713**
                                                               (2 discs), TC-**ESDW713**

[see also Lambert session 49]

Liszt, *Dante Sonata* – Ballet
Royal Ballet Sinfonia, Barry Wordsworth   (7/04)   White Line **CDWLS273**
                                                               (2 CDs)

[see also Lambert session 17]

Meyerbeer, *Les Patineurs* – Ballet
1. Entries, 2. Pas seul, 3. Pas de deux, 4. Ensemble, 5. Pas de trios, 6. Duet, 7. Pas des patineurs,
8. Finale
ROH Orchestra, John Hollingsworth   (11/50)   Columbia **DX8357-8**
London Symphony Orchestra, Robert Irving   (11/52)   Decca **LXT2746**
                                                               DLW5086
                                                               ACL62

Israel Philharmonic Orchestra, Jean Martinon	(12/58)	Decca SXL2021; LXT5456
	(5/66)	SDD139
		London STS15051
(1–5) Philharmonia, Charles Mackerras	(11/59)	Columbia SED5563,
		ESD7254
	(4/60)	SDD7115
	(2/82)	TC-ESD7115
National Philharmonic Orchestra, Richard Bonynge	(11/76)	Decca SXL6812;
		KSXC6812
	(1/90)	in **425468-2** (3 CDs)
		in **468578-2** (10 CDs)
Philadelphia Orchestra, Eugene Ormandy		Sony SBK46341
Cincinnati Pops Orchestra, Erich Kunzel		in Vox CDX5130
		(2 CDs)
Royal Ballet, Barry Wordsworth		Opus Arte OA1064D
		(DVD)
[see also Lambert session 13]		

Purcell, *Comus* – Ballet
[Overture and Minuet only] Royal Opera House Orchestra, Covent Garden, Robert Irving

	(5/56)	HMV CLP1070
	(6/81)	HMV ESDW713
		(2 discs), TC-ESDW713

Scarlatti, *Mars and Venus* – Ballet
Royal Ballet Sinfonia, Barry Wordsworth   (7/05)   Dutton CDLX7149

Vaughan Williams, Overture *The Wasps* transcribed for piano, four hands
Alan Rowlands and Adrian Sims   (12/10)   Albion ALBCD011

Walton, *Portsmouth Point* (reduced scoring)
London Philharmonic Orchestra, Jan Latham-Koenig   (1/94)   CHAN9148

Walton, *Façade* arr. for piano duet
David Nettle and Richard Markham   3036700172
[5 numbers only] David Nettle and Richard Markham   Netmark NEMACD200
Peter Lawson and Alan MacLean   Campion RRCD1353

3 Archive Recordings of Lambert Conducting

⁂ National Sound Archive (NSA) recordings and other off-air recordings

11 Nov. 1936 BBC National Programme
BBC Symphony Orchestra, Lambert

Elgar, Funeral March *Grania and Diarmid*
[NSA Leech Collection 375 T11556W4 1 disc, 2 sides, some 'wow']

Elgar, Overture *Froissart*
[NSA recording of first 2′ 25″, possibly from the same broadcast]

28 Jan. 1937 BBC National Programme

Stanford, *Down among the Dead Men* Maurice Cole, BBC Symphony Orchestra, Lambert
[NSA Leech Collection 424–5 T11657W2 2 discs, 4 sides, Incomplete with several breaks: 5′08″, 32″, 5′01″, 5′21″ & 3′43″ Good sound]

30 May 1937 BBC Regional and Scottish Programmes
Walton, *Crown Imperial* (fragment) BBC Symphony Orchestra, Lambert
[NSA Leech Collection 505 T11658R2 2′07″ Chiefly of the trio.]

n.d. 1937
Lambert (pf)
Lambert, *Elegiac Blues* [NSA M5017W C1]
Lambert, *Pomona: Siciliana* (arranged for piano) [NSA M5017R C1]
IBC Sound Recording Studios NSA NP10638W2

11 June 1943 Boosey & Hawkes Concert, Wigmore Hall
cond. Lambert [NSA recording]
Lutyens, Chamber Concerto I, for oboe, clarinet, bassoon, horn, trumpet, trombone, violin, viola and cello (first performance)

17 Feb. 1944 Bedford (Special Music Recording Service) 7.10 p.m.
BBC Symphony Orchestra
Lambert, Suite *Merchant Seamen*   [NSA 6821-2]
Walter Leigh, Overture *Agincourt*   [NSA 6823-4]

16 Apr. 1945
British Ballet Orchestra, Lambert
Gavin Gordon, *The Rake's Progress* Suite: The Reception; The Dancing Lesson, The Faithful Girl; The Orgy
From BBC Transcription discs 12PH 28861-9
Note: In 1945 Lambert recorded five programmes of British Ballet Music with the British Ballet Orchestra for the London (later BBC) Transcription Service. 16 Apr.: *The Rake's Progress*; 1 May: *Pomona*; 3 May: *Miracle in the Gorbals*; 10 May: *The Quest*; 18 May: *Horoscope*.
CD: Dutton CDBP9761 (3/06)

1 May 1945
British Ballet Orchestra, Lambert
Lambert, *Pomona*
(listed by Richard Shead as a BBC recording)

18 May 1945
British Ballet Orchestra, Lambert
Lambert, *Horoscope*

30037	1 Dance for the followers of Leo	4′21″
30037–8	2 Saraband for the followers of Virgo	5′29″
30040	3 Valse for the Gemini	4′07″
30041	4 Bacchanale	4′30″
30042	5 Invocation to the Moon and Finale	3′33″

(listed by Richard Shead as a BBC recording)

8 May 1946
'Special Music Recording Service' Studio C, Maida Vale 10.00 – 13.00
Royal Opera Covent Garden Orchestra, Lambert
Bliss, *Adam Zero*: Fanfare Overture, Dance of Spring, Love Dance, Bridal Ceremony, Dance of Summer, Approach of Autumn, Night Club Scene, Destruction of Adam's World, Dance of Death, Finale
CD: Appian APR 5627. This was not, as the accompanying notes state, a world premiere broadcast: no such broadcast in this country has been traced.

16 Jan. 1947 part of Winter Prom. RAH BBC Third Programme approx. 8.33 p.m.
BBC Symphony Orchestra, Lambert

Lambert, *King Pest*
(beginning of second half of concert, remainder conducted by Boult)

* A private recording of *King Pest*, possibly of this performance, was broadcast on 18 Oct. 1975 in a BBC Radio 3 feature, 'Man of Action: Michael Ayrton' (2.15–3.35 p.m.), introduced by Ayrton himself. When the programme was repeated, this recording was omitted. It is not known whether it still exists.

2 May 1948 BBC Home Service
BBC Symphony Orchestra, Lambert

Dukas, Symphony in G
[NSA Leech Collection. 2 sides only: CDR0006185; 1CDR0006465]

2 July 1948 [not broadcast]
Philharmonia Orchestra, Lambert (who introduces each work)

Rawsthorne, Overture *Cortèges*   [NSA B7085/02 9′21″]
(with copy donated by Mrs. Rawsthorne M4594R BD1)

Haydn, Symphony No. 101   [NSA B7085/03 23′38″]

Lambert, *Music for Orchestra*   [NSA B7085/04]

British Concert Hall – 23   [BBCX12385–12387]

CD: [Lambert only, with introduction] Dutton CDBP9761 (3/06)

9 Dec. 1949 BBC Third Programme
Edith Sitwell and Lambert, Mary and Geraldine Peppin (pf), Men's Chorus, Members of Philharmonia Orchestra, Leighton Lucas

Searle, *Gold Coast Customs*
[NSA recording: NP1541W 33′35″ with closing announcement; distorted at climaxes]

3 June 1950 BBC Third Programme 6.50–7.50 p.m.
George Pizzey, Oxford Bach Choir, BBC Symphony Orchestra, Lambert

Lambert, *Summer's Last Will and Testament*

OUP correspondence to Ann Arbor, 8.12.50: 'The BBC did take their own record of this performance under Lambert earlier this year, and they are playing it in their Overseas Service on January 3rd, 0300 hours GMT; among other countries, it will go to the US.' OUP files.

According to the OUP files, a BBC recording of 3 June 1950, LP 33 rpm 16″ disc was sent to Ann Arbor as a guide for a planned American performance and only to be used for rehearsals. It is not known whether this recording still exists.

21 Feb. 1950 BBC Third Programme
London Symphony Orchestra, Lambert

Gerhard, *Pandora* Suite   [NP155WBD1 24′20″ cut at end]

ApIvor, *The Hollow Men* Redvers Llewellyn, BBC Male Voice Chorus (first performance)
          [M5990W TR1]

※ Other recordings known to exist in private hands

BBC Orchestra, Lambert (n.d.)

Moskowski, *Boabdil*

4 Archive Recordings of Lambert's Works Conducted by Others

⅏ National Sound Archive (NSA) recordings and other off-air recordings

Mr Bear Squash-You-All-Flat
Eleanor Bron, Nash Ensemble, Martyn Brabbins
23 Nov. 1997. Wigmore Hall. BBC Radio 3 7 Dec. 1997. NSA H9508/1

Overture for piano duet
Alan MacLean and Peter Lawson
14 Nov. 1996. BBC Radio 3. NSA H8051/3

Pomona
BBC Concert Orchestra, Ashley Lawrence
n.d. (BBC Radio 3 13 Dec. 1988). NSA B3659/3
Northern Sinfonia, Odaline de la Martinez
n.d. (BBC Radio 3 25 Feb. 1990). NSA B5587/3

Music for Orchestra
BBC Scottish Symphony Orchestra, Norman Del Mar
n.d. (BBC Radio 3 1 Mar. 1982?). NSA NP5723BW
BBC Concert Orchestra, Barry Wordsworth
15 Oct. 1991. BBC Radio 3. NSA B8728/1
BBC Concert Orchestra, Barry Wordsworth
7 Feb. 1992. BBC Radio 3. NSA B9056/1

Elegiac Blues
Penelope Thwaites
n.d. NSA B5914/16
Anthony Goldstone
n.d. (Bristol 16 Nov. 1992, BBC Radio 3 22 Sept. 1998?). NSA H2078/12
BBC Concert Orchestra, Barry Wordsworth
n.d. (BBC Radio 3 24 Sept. 1998?). NSA ICD0179202

The Rio Grande
Bernadette Greevy, John Bingham, BBC Singers, BBC Symphony Orchestra, Norman Del Mar
15 Sept. 1973. Last Night of Henry Wood Proms. BBC Radio 3. NSA C1398/948
Shelley Alexander, Richard Chandler, New Zealand National Youth Choir and Youth Orchestra,
Doron Salomon
11 Aug. 1987. BBC broadcast of New Zealand Radio recording. NSA B2621/1
Christine Cairns, David Owen Norris, BBC Chorus and Symphony Orchestra, John Pritchard
22 Aug. 1987. Henry Wood Prom. BBC Radio 3. NSA B2666/2
Christine Cairns, Howard Shelley, BBC Singers, BBC Concert Orchestra, Barry Wordsworth
3 Aug. 1990. Henry Wood Prom. NSA ICD0047513
Kathryn Stott, BBC Symphony Chorus, BBC Singers, BBC Symphony Orchestra, Barry
Wordsworth
11 Sept. 1993. Henry Wood Prom. BBC2. NSA V2406/05
Paul Lewis, Karen Cargill, BBC Singers, BBC Symphony Chorus and Orchestra, Paul Daniel
10 Sept. 2005. Last Night of Henry Wood Proms. BBC Sound Archives LMCC651A

Piano Sonata
John Ogdon
BBC Radio 3 7 Apr. 1988. NSA B7971/04
John Clegg
n.d. NSA B2554/4

Concerto for Piano and Nine Players
Clifford Benson, Nash Ensemble, Elgar Howarth
10 Sept. 1975. Henry Wood Prom. BBC Radio 3 (rebroadcast 14 July 1995). NSA H7158/1

Summer's Last Will and Testament
Raimund Herincx, BBC Chorus & Choral Society, BBC Symphony Orchestra, Sir Malcolm Sargent
3 Feb. 1965. Royal Albert Hall. BBC Third Programme. NSA BD1
David Wilson-Johnson, Brighton Festival Chorus, BBC Concert Orchestra, Norman Del Mar
10 May 1986. Brighton Festival. BBC Radio 3. NSA C1398/1756 C7

Horoscope
(unspecified movements) BBC Concert Orchestra, Vilem Tausky
14 Mar. 1964. Tunbridge Wells. BBC Light Programme. NSA 1 CDR0011736
BBC Philharmonic, Nicholas Cleobury
(BBC Radio 3 22 Nov. 1988?) NSA B3565/02
[Palindrome only] BBC Concert Orchestra, Barry Wordsworth
30 Sept. 1992. BBC Radio 3. NSA H696/2
['Four Dances'] BBC Concert Orchestra, Barry Wordsworth
12 Aug. 1994. Henry Wood Proms. NSA H3676/1

Merchant Seamen – Film Music Suite
BBC Welsh Orchestra, Eric Wetherell
26 Apr. 1965. BBC broadcast. NSA M333R

Aubade héroïque
Academy of the BBC, Norman Del Mar
(n.d. BBC Radio 3 4 Nov. 1975?) NSA M7319BW

Trois pièces nègres
Richard Rodney Bennett and Malcolm Williamson
Cheltenham Festival. BBC recording
Priscilla Naish and Philip Cranmer
Guildhall School of Music. 15/16 Apr. 1992. NSA 1CA0006564

Tiresias
BBC Concert Orchestra, Barry Wordsworth
8 Nov. 1995. BBC Radio 3 (first broadcast). NSA H6053/2

Boyce, arr. Lambert, Overture The Power of Music
BBC Empire String Orchestra (with oboes), Hubert Clifford
recorded 19 Oct. 1944   NSA 8509–10 (BBC Transcription Discs)

Boyce, arr. Lambert, Symphony No. 4 in F
BBC Empire String Orchestra (with oboes), Hubert Clifford
recorded 19 Oct. 1944   NSA 8508–9 (BBC Transcription Discs)

Boyce, arr. Lambert, Symphony No. 8
BBC Empire String Orchestra (with oboes), Hubert Clifford
recorded 19 Oct. 1944   NSA 8511–13 (BBC Transcription Discs)

5 Other Recordings in Private Hands

Prize Fight
BBC Midland Light Orchestra, Kenneth Montgomery
12 May 1969. BBC Radio 3 (first broadcast)

Britten Sinfonia, Nicholas Cleobury
29 Aug. 2001. Henry Wood Prom. BBC Radio 3

Piano Concerto (1924)
Jonathan Plowright, Redcliffe Chamber Orchestra, Christopher Adey
2 Mar. 1988 (first performance). St John's Smith Square, London

Philip Fowke, Britten Sinfonia, Nicholas Cleobury
29 Aug. 2001 Henry Wood Prom. BBC Radio 3

David Owen Norris, BBC Concert Orchestra, Charles Hazlewood
24 Apr. 2004. BBC Radio 3 (analysis and performance)

Pomona
London Symphony Orchestra, Norman Del Mar
n.d.

BBC Symphony Orchestra, Elgar Howarth
27 June 1977. BBC Radio 3

Music for Orchestra
BBC Northern Symphony Orchestra, Maurice Handford
3 Oct. 1980. RNCM Manchester. BBC Radio 3 (rebroadcast 4 Oct. 1980)

BBC Northern Symphony Orchestra, Maurice Handford
19 Dec. 1980. BBC Radio 3

BBC Scottish Symphony Orchestra, Norman Del Mar
1 Mar. 1982. BBC Radio 3

Royal Philharmonic Orchestra, Norman Del Mar
10 June 1984. Royal Festival Hall. BBC Radio 3

BBC Concert Orchestra, Barry Wordsworth
15 Oct. 1991. BBC Radio 3 (rebroadcast 4 Oct. 1992)

The Rio Grande
(2 pianists), Harvard Glee Club, Radcliffe Choral Society, G. Wallace Woodworth
28 Feb. 1951

Helen Watts, Peter Katin, BBC Singers, BBC Concert Orchestra, Vilem Tausky
n.d. (introduced by Margot Fonteyn)

Elsa Kendal, Bernard Sumner, Hallé Choir, Hallé Orchestra, James Loughran
22 July 1975. Free Trade Hall, Manchester. BBC Radio 3

Sandra Browne, Peter Donohoe, BBC Singers, BBC Symphony Orchestra, Loughran
15 Sept. 1979. Henry Wood Prom. BBC Radio 3

Christine Cairns, David Owen Norris, BBC Symphony Chorus, BBC Concert Orchestra, Gareth Morrell
11 Dec. 1988. BBC Radio 3 (rebroadcast 12 Aug. 1991)

Jonathan Scott, Hallé Youth Choir, Hallé Orchestra, James Burton
30 Jan. 2008. Bridgewater Hall, Manchester. BBC Radio 3

Salomé – Suite
Psappha ensemble
2 Nov. 2000 Manchester. BBC Radio 3

Piano Sonata
Phillip Challis
21 Aug. 1972. BBC Radio 3

Julian Dawson-Lyell
31 Aug. 1982. BBC Radio 3

Summer's Last Will and Testament
Jeremy Huw Williams, City of Birmingham Symphony Chorus and Orchestra, Sakari Oramo
23 Sept. 1999. Symphony Hall, Birmingham. BBC Radio 3 5 Oct. 1999

Merchant Seamen – Film Music Suite
BBC Concert Orchestra, Carl Davis
28 Mar. 1995. BBC Radio 3

BBC Concert Orchestra, Barry Wordsworth
9 Aug. 2005. Henry Wood Prom. BBC Radio 3

Aubade héroïque
BBC Concert Orchestra, Barry Wordsworth
10 Sept. 1984. BBC Radio 3

BBC Concert Orchestra, Ashley Lawrence
8 Aug. 1984. BBC Radio 3

Ulster Orchestra, Colman Pearce
3 Mar. 1988. BBC Radio 3

Anna Karenina – Film Music Suite
BBC Concert Orchestra, John Wilson
14 July 2007. Henry Wood Prom. BBC Radio 3

6 Talks and Documentaries about Lambert

'**In Search of Constant Lambert**' TV documentary presented by Francis Coleman, with the recorded voices of Kit Lambert, Denis ApIvor, Isabel Rawsthorne, Michael Ayrton, Gavin Gordon, Angus Morrison, Bronislava Nijinska, William Walton, Duke Ellington, Ninette de Valois, William Chappell, Robert Helpmann, Frederick Ashton, Martin Boddey, Lesley Ayre, Alan Frank, Deryck Cooke, Julian Herbage, Randall Swingler, Tom Driberg, Malcolm Arnold, Elisabeth Lutyens, Peter Quennell and C. B. Rees. Directed by Barrie Gavin. Televised BBC2 26 July 1965 & 5 Sept. 1976. LMA7054S

'**Constant Lambert Remembered (1905–1951)**' Portrait of the composer presented by Michael Ayrton, with the recorded voices of Denis ApIvor, Malcolm Arnold, Frederick Ashton, Leslie Ayre, Deryck Cooke, William Chappell, Tom Driberg, Duke Ellington, Alan Frank, Gavin Gordon, Patrick Hadley, Robert Helpmann, Spike Hughes, Kit Lambert, Elisabeth Lutyens, Angus Morrison, Peter Quennell, Alan and Isabel Rawsthorne, Humphrey Searle, William Walton and Ninette de Valois. Produced by Maurice Brown. BBC Third Network 25 June 1966.

'**Remembering Constant Lambert (1905–1951)**' presented by Tom Driberg, with the recorded voices of Michael Ayrton, Isabel Rawsthorne, Margot Fonteyn, Anthony Powell, William Walton, Spike Hughes, Ninette de Valois and Malcolm Arnold. Produced by Derek Drescher. BBC broadcast 23 Aug. 1975. NSAT1024 T8495/02 TR1 C1

'**Four English Composers**' Alan Frank reminisces about his long association with Rawsthorne, Lambert, Vaughan Williams and Walton. In addition to music by Rawsthorne, Walton and Vaughan Williams, the programme also includes the finale of *Horoscope*, two movements from *Pomona* and two movements from Lambert's reduced scoring of Vaughan Williams' *Job* performed by the BBC Concert Orchestra conducted by Vilem Tausky. BBC Radio 3 broadcast (repeated 21 June 1973). NSA P1330BW

'**The Café Royal**' Michael Ayrton talking with Anthony Friese-Green about Cecil Gray, Constant Lambert, Philip Heseltine, Alan Rawsthorne and others who inhabited the Café Royal. Recorded Nov. 1974. Broadcast BBC Radio 3 18 Jan. 1976. NSA NP4421W

'**Remembering Constant Lambert**' Angus Morrison in interview with Michael Oliver. BBC Radio 3 Music Weekly 18 Sept. 1983. NSA NP7054BW

'**Lambert Ho!**' Lewis Foreman talking on Lambert, with the recorded voices of Michael Ayrton, Alan Rawsthorne, Malcolm Arnold, Alan Frank, William Walton, Robert Helpmann and Lambert himself. Promenade Concert interval talk, 12 Aug. 1994. NSA H3676/1

Appendix 4
Constant Lambert's Journalism

T HIS is a list of the principal articles located by the author that Constant Lambert contributed to a number of journals and papers, together with a short summary of their contents and some brief extracts. While this cannot claim to be a complete list, it gives some indication of the extraordinary range and depth of his journalism. His more substantial writings are included in the Bibliography. The journals and newspapers below are entered alphabetically.

※ Apollo
1926
  Oct. **'Chabrier'**

1929
  Nov., pp. 315–16 **'The Art of Frederick Delius'** (reprinted, without the final paragraph, in *A Delius Companion*, ed. Christopher Redwood (London: John Calder, 1976), pp. 75–7)

※ Boston Evening Transcript
1926
  27 Nov., section iv, p. 5 **'Fresh Hand; New Talent; Vital Touch – Brief Record of William Walton, Composer of 'Portsmouth Point' and a Score or Two Besides'** (reprinted in Stephen Lloyd, *William Walton: Muse of Fire* (Woodbridge: Boydell Press, 2001), pp. 267–70)

※ The British Musician
1927
  July, pp. 70–3 **'A Plea for Chabrier'**: 'For the real Chabrier one must go to the best passages in the operas and, above all, to the instrumental works, though it is doubtful if they will be appreciated at their true worth in England until we have rid ourselves of the narrow and pompous outlook which still appears to form part of our musical heritage.'

※ Circus
1950
  Apr. [vol. 1 no. 1] **'In Praise of Snakes'** [corrected version printed in issue 3 – see next item]
  June [vol. 1 no. 3] **'In Praise of Snakes'** [poem: 'This is the authentic version, gladly reprinted with our apologies to our author and readers, of the poem which appeared in the first number of Circus with two inexplicable nonsensical errors.']

※ Dancing Times
1949
  Jan. (pp. 192–3) **'Music for Ballet'**: transcript of Lambert's contribution to a BBC Third Programme broadcast on ballet in the 'Techniques' series consisting of a discussion between Arnold Haskell, Robert Helpmann and Michael Ayrton, with Michael Hordern as interlocutor, 17 Nov. 1948

※ Dominant
1928
  Feb. [vol. 1 no. 4], pp. 16–19 **'Some Recent Works by William Walton'**: 'He has already given proof of such vitality and fecundity of imagination that the musical world will look forward to his next important work; one can form but little idea of his future development save that of all modern composers he is the least likely to remain in a groove.'

1929

May–June [vol. 2 no. 3], pp. 14–17 '**The Symphonies of Sibelius**': 'He is one of the few great figures of our times, and even though his best work may not be widely known in his lifetime it is almost certain to have a profound influence on future generations.'

⁂ Le Figaro

1929

4 Apr., p. 3 **Films anglais** [writing as C. Leonard]: 'Bien qu'en Angleterre l'industrie de film est une activité sans exemple et qu'est disposé d'incomparables moyens techniques (on dit qu'il n'existe pas de studio mieux organisé que celui d'Elstree) on doit reconnaître à regret que le critique le plus patriote ne peut trouver grand'chose à louer dans les films auxmêmes.' *Piccadilly* (E. A. Dupont) 'Il est vrai que le roman d'Arnold Bennett n'avait aucune des qualities que conviennent au cinéma, mais la direction ne s'est pas distinguée et seul le jeu de Miss Anna May Wong, qui est une remarquable actrice, a donné un peu d'intérêt au film.' *Le Ring* (Hitchcock), *Le Métro* (Asquith), *Le Patrouille égaré* (Sommers)

5 Apr., p. 3 **Les Films français à Londres** [as C. Leonard]: *Thérèse Raquin* (after Zola; Eng.: 'Thou shalt not'); Cavalcanti's *Rien que les heures*, *En rade* and *La Petite Lilie*

⁂ Hallé: A Magazine for Music Lovers

1948

May [no. 10], pp. 6–7 '**Myself and Russian Music**': 'We are apt to be a puritan race particularly when it comes to music, and the fact that Russian music was first made sensationally popular by Diaghileff makes some people think that it is so much pseudo-oriental tinsel. They make, in my opinion, a profound mistake.'

⁂ Lilliput

1947

July [vol. 21 no. 1; issue no. 121], pp. 19–21 '**Baedeker et les Femmes**': 'No great artist … can work without a living muse, and I like to think that I have proved without question that what Frau von Wezensdonck was to Wagner, what George Sand was to Chopin, so was Mrs N. to Baedeker.'

Dec. [vol. 21 no. 6; issue no. 126], pp. 461–3 '**Have Auctioneers a Conscience?**' (reprinted in *The Bedside Lilliput*, ed. Richard Bennett (London: Hulton Press, 1950), pp. 283–6): 'I have just moved into an unfurnished flat on the fifth floor. Having spread my exiguous chattels round the place in such a manner as to give it (or so I vainly hoped) a "lived in" feeling I began to notice certain lacunae to say the least – … It was in this sombre mood, then, that I took the fatal plunge that has warped my life – and attended my first auction.'

1948

June [vol. 22 no. 6; issue no. 132], pp. 69–71 '**What, No Index?**': 'An index gains in humour in proportion to the seriousness of the book and for many years I thought that the best example of this incongruity was the index to Philip Heseltine's life of Delius, particularly as I knew the author so well.'

Oct. [vol. 23 no. 4; issue no. 136], pp. 97–9 '**All Alone on the Telephone**': 'At one period during the frivolous "twenties", I occasionally sought revenge by using the alphabet – deliberately designed by a symposium of fellow sufferers to fox the [telephone] operators as much as possible – beginning – "Aphorism, Beef or Mutton, See for yourself, etc." – of which my favourites were "Ell for leather" and "Oh for the wings of a dove".'

Nov. [vol. 23 no. 5; issue no. 137], pp. 44–9 '**The Face of Ischia: Three paintings by Michael Ayrton with a commentary by Constant Lambert**': 'Despite its attractions for the passing artist, this is no lotus land and that is why I feel that Michael Ayrton is so right, in his recent series of paintings, to have stressed the people of Ischia rather than their surroundings.'

⁂ The Listener

1929

16 Jan. [vol. 1 no. 1], p. 10 **'A Half-Forgotten Composer: William Boyce (1710–79)'** (Boyce arr. Lambert Symphony No. 8 conducted by Ansermet, broadcast on 18 Jan.): 'The Eight Symphonies, which are among the most delightful and original works of this period, have been strangely ignored. ... Many people approach eighteenth-century music with a curious preconceived notion of what the technical practices of the period were, and when faced with something which totally destroys this conception (which has its root, consciously or unconsciously, in nineteenth-century prejudices) they are forced to fall back on an elaborate theory of misprints.'

10 Apr. [vol. 1 no. 13], pp. 461–2 **'Doubts about the "Moderns"'**: after hearing the Chamber Music Concert on 3 Apr.: Martinů: 'unknown in England', Hindemith: 'although he has a large and enthusiastic following in Germany, has never impressed me as being a figure of real significance'; Stravinsky; Nabokoff

1936

22 Apr. [vol. 15 no. 380], pp. 792–3 **'The Origins of Modern Dance Music'** (talk broadcast on 15 Apr., reprinted in Appendix 6)

29 Apr. [vol.15 no. 381], pp. 844–5 **'Dance Music Today'** (talk broadcast on 24 Apr., reprinted in Appendix 6)

23 Sept. [vol. 16 no. 402], pp. 597–8 **'From Liszt to Honegger'**: the third of three articles forming a discussion of 'pure' music and programme music (previous articles by Ernest Newman, 9 Sept., and Donald Tovey, 16 Sept.)

1937

17 Feb. [vol. 17 no. 423], p. 335 **'Viola and Orchestra'** (broadcast of Walton's Viola Concerto and Berlioz' *Harold in Italy* on 24 Feb.): 'English audiences, when their tastes are not purely academic and stuffy, like romanticism to be morbid and passion to be torn to tatters. Perhaps it is the lack of this fine frenzy which accounts for the comparative unpopularity of "Harold" in this country.'

5 May [vol. 17 no. 434], p. 894 **'British Ballet Music'** (broadcast of *Pomona*, *Rake's Progress* and *Façade* conducted by Lambert on 11 May): 'It is always a surprise to me that Diaghilev did not commission a ballet from Walton.' [*Job*] 'Before the composer kills me for referring to it as ballet music, let me hasten to point out that it is no ordinary ballet and is actually described by the composer as A Masque for Dancing.'

1938

4 May [vol. 19 no. 486], p. 981 **'Strauss' Elektra'** (broadcast from Covent Garden on May 9): '*Elektra* is Wagnerian both in its consistency of mood and its pseudo-symphonic structure based on a number of leading motives. It is probably the last Wagnerian opera of any value, and though the material cannot compare with Wagner in musical quality, Strauss rivals his master in his treatment of it.'

4 Aug. [vol. 20 no. 499], p. 255 **'In Praise of Studio Programmes'**: 'It is only natural that the symphony concerts should be devoted to accepted masterpieces or to novelties by outstanding contemporaries, but between the two extremes lies a mass of music which, if not deserving a permanent place in the repertoire, is worth an occasional hearing. One cannot spend all one's time in the rarified atmosphere of the great masterpieces, and I'm always a little suspicious of the amateur who admires the mountain tops without having any knowledge of the pleasant countryside from which they came.'

11 Aug. [vol. 20 no. 500], p. 308 **'A French Week'** (several broadcasts of French music, including Leclair, Magnard 'the best of the later symphonists', Hahn and Dukas): 'I remember the contrasted sides of [Dukas'] music being aptly symbolized by his last appearance in London when, with the square-cut frock-coat and square-cut white beard, the very picture of a French President in some film by René Clair, he conducted with extreme rigidity the passionate strains of *La Péri*. ... It seems to me possible that when many more flashy reputations have faded, he may stand out as one of the most important figures of his generation not only in France but in Europe.'

18 Aug. [vol. 20 no. 501], p. 360 **'What is Wrong with English Composers?'**: 'When I am with foreign musicians I make a point of defending contemporary English music if only because their ignorance of it is usually abysmal. They may occasionally be right in their condemnations but, as Jean Cocteau has said, there are some people who make just criticism without having earned the right to make them ... My complaint about the average English composer is that he is content merely to evoke a mood – he does not necessarily go a stage further and crystallise it. And though he may give us precision of technique (which after all we have a right to expect from any professional) he rarely gives us precision of thought.' [Moeran's Symphony]: 'a man of undeniable talent who has a spontaneous lyrical gift that is all too rare in this generation. Moeran is never prolix in the academic sense, but he is inclined to be prolix in the imaginative sense. So many poetic ideas occur to him that he is apt to crowd them one upon another without allowing them space to develop naturally and logically. This is most noticeable in the first movement. The opening theme, though simple, is full of symphonic possibilities which are not allowed to come to full fruition. Like other English composers before him, Moeran seems to me to present in the first movement the variety of mood and colour which would be better separated into individual movements. When the first movement is full of rhapsodical "slow movement" material one does not want it to be followed by a full-length slow movement, even when this is as good as Moeran's slow movement undoubtedly is. Fortunately the last two movements redress the balance.'

25 Aug. [vol. 20 no. 502], p. 412 **'Britten's New Concerto'**: 'The concerto had one sterling merit – it is never boring – wit and invention are to be found in every movement, but to one listener at least it came as a slight disappointment after the same composer's brilliant variations for strings. ... I should not like it to be thought that what I have said is in any way a denigration of the undoubted effectiveness of Britten's [Piano] Concerto. Brilliantly written for both soloist and orchestra it is in every way a welcome addition to the very limited repertoire of modern English concertos. It is only because I feel that Britten has it in him to write a really great concerto that I take the trouble to criticise him from what may seem to others an over-exacting point of view.'

1940

18 Apr. [vol. 23 no. 588], p. 808 **'Liszt and his Songs'** (broadcast 21 Apr.): 'They are the songs of a great composer rather than the songs of a born song writer. That is to say, for all their fine qualities they rarely have the inevitability and concision that one associates with composers like Dowland, Wolf and Warlock who were song writers first and foremost.'

2 May [vol. 23 no. 590], p. 905 **'Tchaikovsky Today'** (centenary on 7 May): 'The first steps towards [his] rehabilitation came oddly enough from Diaghilev himself. Just as many Englishmen find Elgar, for all the German influences in his work, more truly English than the composers of the English folk-song school, so Diaghilev, a true Russian, in his heart of hearts, preferred Tchaikovsky to the nationalist composers. ... In my opinion Tchaikovsky has a gift for thinking naturally in musical terms which has been granted to few composers in the course of history.'

⁊⁊ MILO: Imperial League of Opera

1929

Christmas [vol. 1 no. 3 (Dec.)], pp. 9–11 **'Puccini: A Vindication'**: 'I once made a list of all the things that everyone lies about. Much of it is, alas, unprintable in this savagely Puritan age, but I remember that sandwiched between a reluctance to reveal the fact that one had not read *The Bridge of San Luis Ray* and that one couldn't compose away from the piano came the habit of disguising one's affection for the operas of Puccini. I have rarely met anyone who confessed to a whole-hearted admiration for Puccini, and yet, when I creep into a performance of *Tosca* or *Turandot* I find that the house is entirely filled with my acquaintances. If one has the bad taste to ask what they are doing here anyway, they either pretend to have mistaken the date or to have been reluctantly compelled to attend by rich and influential friends. ... Puccini's music stands alone in modern times as being the only operatic music that is perfectly adapted to its medium. ... His best operas are equally satisfying both from the musical and dramatic point of view because almost alone amongst the composers of his time, he was able to express dramatic atmosphere in terms of melody. ... Stravinsky is a case in point. His tunes by themselves have no individuality and little emotional power and he relies almost entirely on orchestral and rhythmic effect for any dramatic expression. As his dramatic works are chiefly in ballet form, this is not a serious drawback; but when we get a similar technical method applied to opera where lyrical expression is essential, the result is deplorable. Ravel's *L'heure espagnole* is, in this respect, one of the worst operas ever written. ... For too long Puccini has been contemptuously dismissed by the intellectual critics as a sentimental best-seller. That his works are occasionally vulgar may be true, but how much more refreshing is Puccini's full-blooded sentiment than the pretensions and pompous vulgarities of Strauss or the facetious and misguided vulgarities of the latest French school (which incidentally will probably have been superseded by the time this article appears). It is high time that Puccini was accorded the respect due to a remarkably original artist and a master of his craft.'

※ The Monthly Musical Record

1930
June, pp. 161–3 'The Young English Composers XIII – Hugh Bradford'

1938
Sept., pp. 196–9 'The Young English Composers IV – Alan Rawsthorne'

※ The Musical Times

1931
1 Feb., p. 167 '[**London Concerts**] **Schönberg's Erwartung**': BBC Symphony Orchestra, the composer: 'Even to those who are familiar with his style, Schönberg's work is extremely baffling on paper, and only actual performance can reveal the ingenuity and beauty of the music. Although I do not consider *Erwartung* as belonging to Schönberg's best period, there is no doubt that it is a tour de force without parallel.'

※ The Nation and Athenæum

1930
12 Apr. [vol. 47 no. 2], pp. 58, 60 **New Gramophone Records**: including Beethoven, Symphony No. 4 (Casals); Rimsky-Korsakov, *Scheherazade*; Chopin, Piano Concerto No. 2; Ellington ('after listening to this record [*Hot and Bothered*] it is quite impossible to tolerate the genteel and invertebrate performances which so often pass for jazz playing in this country')

31 May [vol. 47, no. 9], p. 298 **Recent Gramophone Records**: including Liszt, B minor Sonata (Cortot); Mozart; Beethoven; Tchaikovsky, Piano Concerto No. 1 (Solomon)

28 June [vol. 47, no. 13], p. 420 **June Gramophone Records**: including Mozart, 'Haffner' Symphony (Toscanini); Mozart; Brahms, Handel Variations (Moiseiwitsch)

9 Aug. [vol. 47, no. 19], pp. 598, 600 **Recent Gramophone Records** including Bach, '48' (Evlyn Howard-Jones); Schumann, *Carnaval* (Godowsky); Strauss, *Seven Veils* (Walter); Brahms, Symphony No. 3 (Stokowski); Auber (Godfrey)

16 Aug. [vol. 47, no. 20], pp. 620–1 **'Railway Music'**: Honegger, *Pacific 231* ('Honegger has, in fact, supplied us with a skilful series of onomatopæics [*sic*], and very little else') and *Rugby*: 'These two works ... suggest that the paraphernalia and external speed of modern life is beginning to become with him, as with so many contemporary artists, a dangerous obsession. It is interesting to read of the journalist who called on Honegger to discuss his latest oratorio and who was suddenly whisked into a sports-car and driven at breakneck speed through the suburbs of Paris while the composer dilated on stream-lining and super-charging.'
p. 628 **Recent HMV Records** including Sousa (Stokowski), Schumann, Wagner

20 Sept. [vol. 47, no 25], p. 772 **Recent Gramophone Records**: including Schumann, *Carnaval* (Landon Ronald); Bach; Ravel; Brahms; Auber (Godfrey)

27 Sept. [vol. 47, no. 26], p. 792 **'Prokofiev'**: Piano Concerto No. 3. 'Prokofiev is actually one of the few modern composers who primarily are melodists. That is to say, the thematic outline

is the main feature of the musical style and determines the harmonic, rhythmic and orchestral treatment.'

18 Oct. [vol. 48 no. 3], p. 104 **'Sibelius's Second Symphony'**

p. 116 **Recent Gramophone Records**: including Rossini, Tchaikovsky, Wagner, Liszt, Handel, Puccini, Jimmy Dorsey: 'shows extraordinary virtuosity on the saxophone and clarinet in a series of 10 in. records issued by Decca (accompanied by Spike Hughes and his orchestra).'

8 Nov. [vol. 48 no. 6], pp. 192–3 **'The Writing in the Cheque-Book'**: Courtauld-Sargent programmes and 'celebrity concerts'

29 Nov. [vol. 48 no. 9], pp. 302, 304 **Recent Gramophone Records**: including Mozart; Verdi, Requiem (Sabjano); Brahms; Elgar, Cello Concerto (Squire)

20 Dec. [vol. 48 no. 12], p. 406 **'Sous les Toits de Paris'** (René Clair, film review): 'In spite of the excellence of the acting and the photography, the real value of this film lies in the genius displayed by the director, Réné Clair, a man who seems miraculously to have absorbed the best features of other schools of production without losing his own individuality .'

1931

17 Jan. [vol. 48 no. 16], p. 520 **Recent Gramophone Records**: including Ravel, Falla, Wagner, Handel, Chopin

21 Feb. [vol. 48 no. 21], p. 676 **Recent Gramophone Records** including Schubert, 'Unfinished' Symphony; Beethoven, Symphony No. 1; Sibelius, Symphony No. 1; Albeniz, *Choo-choo* played by Frankie Trumbauer and his orchestra [one of the most original and modern jazz bands of the 1920s and early 1930s]: 'This is a more skilful and honest piece of work than *Pacific 231*'.

⁜ The New Statesman and Nation

1931

7 Mar. [vol. 1 no. 2], pp. 76, 78 **Gramophone Notes**: Liszt, Beethoven

28 Mar. [vol. 1 no. 5], pp. 194, 196 **Gramophone Notes**: Stravinsky, *Capriccio*; Franck, Ellington, *Mood Indigo* (Harlem Footwarmers): 'The harmony and orchestration are charmingly original. This record confirms my impression that Ellington is a quite outstanding popular composer.'

25 Apr. [vol. 1 no. 9], pp. 336, 338 **Gramophone Notes**: Stravinsky, *Rite of Spring*; Elgar, Symphony No. 1: 'frankly appalling melody that starts off the First Symphony'

30 May [vol. 1 no. 14], pp. 521–2 **Gramophone Notes**: Warlock; *Capriol* Suite (Anthony Bernard); Balakirev, *Islamay* (Goossens)

4 July [vol. 2 no. 19], pp. 24, 26 **Gramophone Notes**: Liadov, Sardana records

1 Aug. [vol. 2 no. 23], pp. 148, 150 **Gramophone Notes**: Ellington, *Creole Rhapsody*; Cole Porter, *Love for Sale* (Waring Sisters): 'It has a rich nostalgia that expresses perfectly the curious mood evoked by certain towns, particularly ports like Marseille or Toulon. … Unfortunately, this record is banned in this country because of the words which deal with the subject of prostitution. Prostitution is a theme that can be exploited with impunity in literature, the drama, and the plastic arts, but apparently cannot be used in connection with music.'

29 Aug. [vol. 2 no. 27], p. 260 **Gramophone Notes**: Debussy, and a plea for recordings of Warlock songs

3 Oct. [vol. 2 no. 32], pp. 414, 416 **Gramophone Notes**: Rachmaninov, Honegger

7 Nov. [vol. 2 no. 37], pp. 588, 590 **Gramophone Notes**: Russian music; Sibelius, *En Saga* and *Swan of Tuonela*; Delius, *Summer Night on the River* and *Walk to the Paradise Garden*. 'HMV have, with their Connoisseur catalogue & their October list, deluged the market (and the grateful but unfortunate reviewer) in a manner to which only our present Government lends a parallel.'

1932

2 Jan. [vol. 3 no. 45], p. 22 **Gramophone Notes**: Dvořák, 'New World' Symphony; Stravinsky, *Symphony of Psalms*: 'This work reeks of the self-consciously simple, fashionable religiosity first popularized by Jean Cocteau in the Home, Sweet Home straight talks with fishermen mood that preceded his flirtation with surrealism.'

30 Jan. [vol. 3 no. 49], pp. 126–8 **Gramophone Notes**: Russian composers

27 Feb. [vol. 3 no. 53], pp. 274, 276 **Gramophone Notes: English Jazz**. Ellington, 'Spike' Hughes: 'I am glad to see that H.M.V. have had the enterprise to add the name of Duke Ellington to their catalogue. ... Spike Hughes' band is one of the few English bands with a sense of jazz style and the sense to model itself on Harlem rather than Wimbledon. *A Harlem Symphony*, by Spike Hughes himself, disarms reminiscence hunting by being dedicated to Ellington. It is a pleasant essay rather in the style of Ellington's *Creole Rhapsody*, but it suffers from the two sides being insufficiently contrasted.'

26 Mar. [vol. 3 no. 57], pp. 399–400 **Gramophone Notes**: Debussy, *Rhapsodies*; Ellington

30 Apr. [vol. 3 no. 52], pp. 566, 568 **Gramophone Notes**: Brahms, Symphony No. 2; Mahler, *Kindertotenlieder*; Strauss, *Rosenkavalier* and *Salomé's Dance*: 'Those who find Richard Strauss's particular blend of abnormality repellent can always refresh themselves with the exquisite normality of Johann Strauss.'

4 June [vol. 3 no. 67], pp. 746, 748 **Gramophone Notes**: French music – Debussy and Berlioz

2 July [vol. 4 no. 71], pp. 22, 24 **Gramophone Notes**: Elgar, *Falstaff* and Programme Music: 'There is no term so ill-defined or so loosely applied as "Programme Music". It is made to cover a multitude of disparate works ranging from ballets that are little more than glorified noises off to symphonies that are classical in all but name; from pieces that cannot be followed without a plan of the battlefield, to others that would yield just as much pleasure if one were entirely ignorant of their literary associations.'

3 Sept. [vol. 4 no. 80], pp. 267–8 **Gramophone Notes: 'New French records'**: Milhaud

1 Oct. [vol. 4 no. 84], pp. 386, 388 **Gramophone Notes**: Berlioz, Beethoven, Bach: 'The Brandenburg String Concerto is so simple in construction and so tuneful that it can be easily memorized. It is thus a fit subject for the noiseless humming and ecstatic smiles of recognition of concert audiences. It seems a pity to take advantage of this. Why should an orchestra play Bach as if asking, "Do you remember this bit?" Of course I do, and I want to hear it played with care, not as if the orchestra were joyously running it over before beginning the real concert.'

29 Oct. [vol. 4 no. 88], pp. 526, 528 **Gramophone Notes**: Sibelius and Haydn Society volumes; Tchaikovsky, *Polish* and *Manfred* Symphonies; Prokofiev

26 Nov. [vol. 4 no. 92], pp. 670, 672 **Gramophone Notes**: Milhaud, *La Création du monde*; Beethoven

31 Dec. [vol. 4 no. 97], pp. 863–4 **Gramophone Notes**: 'Hot rhythm' music; Sibelius, Symphony No. 4 (Stokowski)

1933

4 Feb. [vol. 5 no. 102], pp. 140, 142 **Gramophone Notes**: Strauss, *Don Quixote*; Liszt

4 Mar. [vol. 5 no. 106], pp. 268, 270 **Gramophone Notes**: Stravinsky, *Soldier's Tale*; Verdi, *Otello*

18 Mar. [vol. 5 no. 108], pp. 336, 338 **Book review: 'The Joyce Book'**: 'The list of contents is undeniably impressive – less so the contents themselves. The only contribution that really stands out is the John drawing, an assured yet sensitive piece of virtuosity that puts to shame the drab mediocrity of most of the music.'

1 Apr. [vol. 5 no. 110], pp. 426, 428 **Gramophone Notes**: Prokofiev, *Love of Three Oranges*; Franck; Debussy; Ravel

6 May [vol. 5 no. 115], pp. 582, 584 **Gramophone Notes**: Donizetti, *Don Pasquale*; Mussorgsky, *Pictures at an Exhibition*: '... with two cycles of the *Ring* before us and with the Brahms

centenary around us on all sides, it is delicious to play truant for a day and put on Donizetti's *Don Pasquale.'*

10 June [vol. 5 no. 120], p. 772 **Gramophone Notes**: Ellington, Liszt, Poulenc: 'Composers like Ellington have set so high a standard in their particular genre that highbrow composers who attempt the same genre must needs go warily. ... The typically French *élan* of Poulenc's Caprice for pianoforte prevents too direct a comparison with the atavistic gaiety of the coloured composers, but there is no denying that this sort of thing falls a little flat after the more sharply defined and better constructed pieces of Ellington and Thomas ("Fats") Waller.'

28 Oct. [vol. 6 no. 140], pp. 528, 530 **Gramophone Notes**: Haydn Quartet Society 2nd album: 'supplied like the first with the most lucid of critical notes by Mr. Cecil Gray'; Sibelius Society (Kajanus): 'The introductory notes by Mr. Ernest Newman are, as might be expected, mainly about Wagner, but although one can hardly agree that Sibelius No. 7 is really Wagner No. 1, one can certainly agree with him when he says that this symphony is "one of the most difficult works in all music to analyse on paper".'; Kurt Weill, 2 Songs from *Mahagonny* 'sung by the incomparable Lottie Lenja – an antidote to Hitlerism'

2 Dec. [vol. 6 no. 145], pp. 712, 714 **Gramophone Notes**: Handel–Harty, Respighi, Bach

1934

20 Jan. [vol. 7 no. 152], pp. 96, 98 **Gramophone Notes**: Mendelssohn (Szigeti), Grieg (Backhaus), Elgar

3 Mar. [vol. 7 no. 158], pp. 320–1 **Gramophone Notes**: Elgar, Beethoven, 'Spike' Hughes

7 Apr. [vol. 7 no. 163], pp. 524, 526 **Gramophone Notes**: Mozart, Schubert, Stravinsky, Ellington, Maconchy, Elgar

5 May [vol. 7 no. 167], pp. 688, 670 **Gramophone Notes**: Weinberger, Polka and Fugue; Reginald Forsythe; Rimsky-Korsakov, *Antar*

12 May [vol. 7 no. 168], p. 718 **Book review: The Great Virtuoso – 'Liszt'** by Sacheverell Sitwell: 'It is indeed a curiously Lisztian work. Unequal and loosely built, if you will, but executed with a verve and a virtuosity that cannot be resisted. The ideal on the "vie trifurquée" of Liszt has yet to be written but, in the meanwhile, Mr Sitwell's biography is by far the best study we have of this strange, misunderstood figure who, by his brilliance, versatility and generosity, obscured his own greatness.'

16 June [vol. 7 no. 173], pp. 922, 924 **Gramophone Notes**: French music

14 July [vol. 8 no. 177], pp. 45–6 **Gramophone Notes**: Elgar, Piano Quintet; Fauré; Borodin. 'The piano quintet, from Schumann to Sorabji, has always been an unsatisfactory medium and of modern composers Arnold Bax seems to be the only one who has come near to solving the many problems it raises.'

20 Oct. [vol. 8 no. 191], pp. 560, 562 **Gramophone Notes**: Stravinsky, *Les Noces*; Shostakovich, *Age of Gold* dances; Mossolov: 'It is amusing to notice the way that Russians are beginning to look on machines as having exclusively Soviet virtues much as the English people always look on horses as having exclusively English virtues. Someone should tell Mossolov that his music would make just as good propaganda for Vickers-Armstrong as it does for Magnitogorsk.'

3 Nov. [vol. 8 no. 193], pp. 636, 638 **Gramophone Notes**: Bizet, *Fair Maid of Perth*; Mozart

10 Nov. [vol. 8 no. 194], p. 672 **'Warlock and Heseltine'**: review of Cecil Gray, *Peter Warlock: A Memoir of Philip Heseltine*: 'There was a sudden recrudescence before the end, however, notably in his setting of three poems by Bruce Blunt. I remember congratulating him on what seemed to me a complete recovery of his best form and his saying, "My dear sir, how ludicrous to think that after all these years one has merely got back to the same old thing – van Dieren and water." This description was, of course, absurdly denigrating, but at the same time one must admit that these songs, though beautiful, show little advance on the best of his earlier work. It was his feeling of moving in a circle, this sensation of spiritual staleness which was, I am convinced, the main factor in his suicide.'

15 Dec. [vol. 8 no. 199], pp. 914, 916 **Gramophone Notes**: Sibelius Society volume 3, Paganini

1935

12 Jan. [vol. 9 no. 203], pp. 46–7 **Book review: 'Heads I Win, Tails You Lose'** (Ernest Newman, *The Man Liszt*): 'Mr Newman's faults as a biographer we can forgive him, if only because they are so glaring. But it is less easy to forgive here his treatment of Liszt as a composer, the more as few of his readers (the book is clearly addressed to the non-technical public) will be in possession of sufficient knowledge to correct Mr Newman's biased statements.'

9 Feb. [vol. 9 no. 207], p. 190 **Gramophone Notes**: Delius Society volume 1 ('… the composer of *Paris* was potentially the greatest figure of his generation, showing a greater universality of outlook and a more flexible technique than the composer of the *Songs of Sunset*, for example'); Ravel, *Rapsodie espagnole*

1937

13 Mar. [vol. 13 no. 316], pp. 424, 426 **Book review: 'Swing that music' by Louis Armstrong**: 'So much nonsense has been written about "swing" in this country that it is a relief to get a few words straight from the horse's mouth (if Mr Armstrong will pardon this description of his genial features). … "Swing", in fact, is only a new fancy-name for a type of playing which has been familiar in England ever since the old "New-Rhythm Style" records came out on Parlophone. … We find the same principle at work in the variations of the Elizabethans and in the rubato ornaments of Chopin and Liszt. If we look at the two versions of Liszt's *Berceuse*, for example, we see that the 1862 version is a "swing" edition of the 1854 version.'

1950

6 May [vol. 39 no. 1000], p. 512 **Obituary: 'Gerald Berners'**: 'A good example of his desire for loneliness, combined with an extremely practical wit, was provided by his method of keeping a railway compartment to himself. Donning black spectacles he would, with a look of fiendish expectation, beckon in the passers by. Those isolated figures who took the risk became so perturbed by his habit of reading the paper upside down and taking his temperature every five minutes that they invariably got out at the next station.'

⚘ News Chronicle

1934

1 May **'Opera is still out of date'**: 'There was a time when a Royal Opera season was primarily an occasion for hearing new works …'

⚘ Night and Day

Reprinted in one volume, ed. Christopher Hawtree (London: Chatto & Windus, 1985)

1937

23 & 30 Sept. [vol. 1 nos. 13 & 14] [Lambert listed as music critic, but no contribution and no musical notes]

7 Oct. [vol. 1 no. 15] [announced as music critic but no Lambert contribution: 'Music Notes' by Patrick Ransome]

14 Oct. [vol. 1 no. 16] [Gramophone reviews by Jack Donaldson, on jazz]

21 Oct. [vol. 1 no. 17], pp. 35–6 [p. 188 in complete volume] **Music Notes by Constant Lambert**: *Positively the Last on the Promenades*. 'If it wasn't for the Proms, the music critic during the summer months would either have to give up his livelihood or review books on Wagner by Ernest Newman. A delicate choice. … I started my career in the balcony. In those days I was at school and, surprising though it may seem, quite genuinely fond of music. The moment the summer holidays began I dashed to the Queen's Hall to get a copy of the programmes. I was invariably told they would not be ready for another week. Somehow I never quite believed this and would usually make two or three further fruitless visits before the great day arrived. There then followed a period of acute mental stress during which I would count up my money and weigh the respective merits of possible programmes. … Russian music being my mania, I would spend harassed hours deciding whether I wanted to hear Rimsky's *Spanish Capriccio* more than Mussorgsky's *Night On the Bare Mountain*.

When the chosen day came I would arrive ridiculously early and stay to the bitter end. For the sake of the final orchestral item I even sat through the appalling ballads which still carried on at that period. ... Even when not accompanied by my family, I always went to the balcony. Why I can't think. ... My second and more genial phase as a concert-goer took place in the promenade when I was a student and after. Whether because the programmes were more varied and interesting or not I cannot say, but the Prom in those days was far less crowded and even lived up to its name. One could move about or even effect an exit during a boring work without being looked on as a howling cad. Those were the halcyon days of what is known as the 'bar-item'. One could go and listen to a little-known Haydn symphony or a new work by Bantock [misprint for Bartok?] or Milhaud and then during some weatherbeaten concerto played by an even more weatherbeaten virtuoso one would retreat to the bar which had then the atmosphere of a pleasantly informal club. I never quite rivalled the record of the late Peter Warlock who heard only ten minutes of Schubert's C Major Symphony (4 minutes of the first movement; 3 of the second, 2 of the third, and 1 of the fourth), but I certainly took my pleasures more lightly than the present generation. Now, in my third phase, I go in morose grandeur to the circle. ... It is melancholy to recall one's past enthusiasm. Now when the programmes arrive I open them more with apprehension than with any other feeling and wonder not how many I can afford to go to but how many I can afford to miss. For one thing I find it increasingly difficult to sit through a whole concert, partly because I concentrate more and partly because I concentrate less. During the few works I like, I concentrate to such an extent that I am mentally exhausted at the end. During that large majority of works I dislike, I find it almost impossible to concentrate at all.' [Lambert reworked this article as 'My Promenading Life' for *Radio Times*, 13 July 1945]

25 Nov. [vol. 1 no. 22], p. 28 [p. 243] **Music Notes by Constant Lambert**: *Toscanini and the BBC*: 'It is a pity when a genius like Toscanini comes here so rarely that his programmes should be so constricted. ... When a man is the greatest living exponent of Italian music why dabble us with the monumental mediocrity of the Brahms Requiem and Tragic Overture? It is true that Toscanini made these both sound better than one would have previously thought possible, but not even he could make the overture live up to its name or make the Requiem seem more than an impressive display of the trappings of woe, an undertaker's list expressed in terms of harmony. ... While in the mood to attack the BBC I should like to complain about the ever more frequent programme notes of Sir Donald Tovey which seem to me to perform no useful function. ... Professor Tovey would have been thoroughly at home in the theological circle of the middle ages when he could have argued about the number of angels who can dance on a pin-point to his heart's content. But I have yet to see that his laborious analyses show any appreciation of what goes on in a composer's mind. He seems to think that Beethoven was chiefly worried by trying to get back to the flattened super-tonic in time and he is quite capable of proving that Schubert's C major Symphony is really not in C major at all but in B sharp or D double flat. ...'; Nadia Boulanger concert including Fauré Requiem: 'one of the finest things in French music'

✼ Promenade Concert Programmes

1928
30 Aug. **'Modern French Music'**: 'Debussy, who towers above his contemporaries, and is by far the most important composer of the last fifty years, is sadly underestimated at the present day. ... Maurice Ravel is one of the most disappointing figures in modern music. Gifted with great sensitiveness and with undeniable technical mastery, he has yet failed to make any advance on his early work.'

1929
24 Aug. **'Contemporary English Music'**: Vaughan Williams' compositions 'are undoubtedly the finest English works of their generation'; Peter Warlock 'is something of a Jekyll and Hyde'.

※ Radio Times

1928

20 July [vol. 20 no. 251], pp. 95, 103 **'The Future of Jazz'** ('Blue on the Boulevard: A Study of Black and White', 2LO, 9.35–11.00 p.m. 23 July): 'By symphonic jazz I mean a serious musical work, not necessarily intended to be danced to, which draws its inspiration and technique from the dance music of today in much the same way that the composers of the eighteenth century (and earlier) used the dances of their time as a basis for their work.'

1929

29 Mar. [vol. 22 no. 287], pp. 759, 794 **'The Russian Ballet'** (Music for the Russian Ballet. Wireless Orchestra, Leslie Heward: Rossini-Respighi, Falla, Cimarosa, Rimsky-Korsakov, 2LO and 5XX, 9.35 p.m. 1 Apr.) 'Diaghilev, indefatigable in his search for new talent, has never been one to rely on the past, and with an uncanny perception he recognised in an early work of Stravinsky, then unknown, the latent genius which was to produce the series of ballets that include *Fire-Bird*, *Petrushka* and *Les Noces*. ... The two pitfalls for the artist are an academicism and a forced and eccentric modernity: the best Diaghilev ballets have always avoided both. ... I myself, far from being bored by the early ballets, consider *Thamar*, for instance, one of Diaghilev's finest creations.'

1931

4 Sept., p. 490 **'William Walton'** (British Composers at the Proms series): 'At an early age he went as a chorister to Christ Church, Oxford, where he created little short of sensation by his singing of the solo part in *The Woman of Samaria*. ... The [viola] concerto has a balance between intellect and emotion, a unity of thought and technique that are all too rare in contemporary music. He may be seen at the opening of a Picasso exhibition, but also at a cup-tie final; and although his batting may be as unorthodox in style as his piano-playing, it is no less far-reaching in its effect.'

1933

27 Jan., p. 188 **'Delius and "Sea-Drift"'**: 'All that one can do is to attempt some appreciation of that rare emotional quality, at one moment a reflection of the strange, inhuman beauty of elemental nature, the next moment a poignant expression of the transience of human emotion, which is the dominant characteristic of Delius's art. In spite of its almost unbearable melancholy and nostalgia, this mood cannot be described as pessimistic. There is a vein of sensuous beauty which runs through even the most tragic moments and saves them from bleakness or austerity.'

3 Feb., p. 38 **'At this week's Symphony Concert: a Constructive Anarchist'**: 'Schoenberg and Debussy are the two great revolutionists of modern music, and Debussy, underneath his disarmingly quiet manner, is actually the greater revolutionist of the two.'

1934

5 Jan., p. 9 **'What will be said of us in fifty years'** (British Music number, with contributions from Herman Klein, Percy Scholes, Clifford Bax and Dr Albert Einstein): 'If I live another fifty years I shall not be surprised to find that, for example, the exquisite Forlane of Ravel [from *Le Tombeau de Couperin*] has outlived the more grandiose symphonies of Sir Edward Elgar. The work of Elgar, and much of the work of Vaughan Williams and Bax is a statement in modern terms of the music which the English nineteenth century omitted to provide. ... English music is now returning to its classic state of unconscious nationalism modified by a certain enriching eclecticism. We are now free to choose without inhibition what we want from foreign tradition, and it is more unlikely that the English music of the future will be at all "folk-soggy".'

9 Mar., p. 709 **'Homage to Sir Edward Elgar'** (contributions from Herman Klein, Constant Lambert, Adrian Boult, Sir Richard Terry): 'It was one of Elgar's great qualities that he could write music indubitably English in feeling without adopting a rustic or archaic accent.'

22 June, p. 899 **'The Intimate Appeal of Delius: An appreciation by Constant Lambert'**: 'His music has been described, both in praise and blame, as a swan-song, and its dominant mood is certainly one of almost unbearable nostalgia. But it is not the facile disillusion of the nineties or the gather-ye-rosebuds moralising of the Elizabethans. There is no self-pity in Delius's music and no fear of death. He had a pagan acceptance of the world's beauty, and

the nostalgia of his music is like the curious melancholy that overcomes us when we look at a landscape the luxuriance of which is so great as to be almost oppressive.'

1936

7 Aug., p. 13 **'Some angles of the compleat Walton: Constant Lambert writes a lively literary overture to the Walton Prom to be broadcast on Tuesday'** (reprinted in Stephen Lloyd, *William Walton: Muse of Fire* (Woodbridge: Boydell Press, 2001), pp. 270–2)

11 Dec., p. 12 **'Prometheus Rebound'** – **Constant Lambert tells the story of Beethoven's ballet**

1937

8 Oct., p. 17 **'Checkmate'** (conducted by the composer, 15 Oct., BBCSO, National Programme): 'The Russian ballet had a strong prejudice against English musicians (understandable too, in view of the colourless and untheatrical nature of the average English composer …) The Red Knight left alone dances a joyous mazurka. In my opinion this solo and the later solo for the Black Queen (a tango) are the least successful numbers in the ballet. Short enough for the concert hall point of view, they are long and exacting from the purely physical point of view of the solo dancer. Their use of established dance rhythms seems at variance with the symphonic dance rhythms of the rest of the score.'

1938

29 Apr. [vol. 59 no. 761], p. 13 **'Ravel's Concerto'**: 'It can't be said that Ravel's [piano] concerto is one of his major works. It is a tour-de-force of craftsmanship – a first-rate work of the second class. … In comparison with the reflective movement, later Ravel at his best, the finale in toccata style seems a little lacking in substance and though extremely effectively written hardly sustains the quality of the rest of the work.'

13 May [vol. 59 no. 763], pp. 12–13 **'A Century of Music'** (on Gerald Abraham's *A Hundred Years of Music*): 'The only book I know which deals with the whole period from 1830 till today, both impartially and sympathetically. He can write with equal knowledge and enthusiasm on composers as different in style as Berlioz, Brahms, Wagner and Mussorgsky, and his final estimates seem to me remarkably sound and unbiased.'

20 May, pp. 12–13 **'Cathedral Hush'** (Toscanini conducts Verdi's *Requiem* and *Te Deum*): 'The most exciting performance I have heard of a Rossini overture was in a church in Siena. The audience was so excited that it broke into applause before the end.'

10 June, pp. 12–13 **'In Defence of Puccini'** (broadcast of *La Bohème*): 'I can remember the time when Puccini was looked on as the musical equivalent of the novels of Ethel M. Dell or the old Lyceum melodramas. Musical hostesses, always the lowest common denominator of the rag, tag and bobtail of the intellectual world, would throw up their hands in horror at the mention of his name.'

1 July, pp. 12–13 **'Master of English Song'** (recital of songs by Peter Warlock, with photo of Moeran, Hal Collins, Lambert and Heseltine at Eynsford): *The Curlew* 'the most poignant work in the whole of modern English music. … But he was, I know, acutely conscious of the fact that his creative gifts were waning, that he would never again be visited by the continuous flow of unalloyed inspiration that produced his earlier works. … He felt that as man and musician he had come full circle. And it was this haunting sense of spiritual weariness, far more than any set of circumstances, that drove him to his tragic end. … The key-note of his work is melancholy, and not the tragedy of the moment, but a curious timeless melancholy. … It is no exaggeration to say that his achievement entitles him to be classed with Dowland, Schubert, Mussorgsky and Debussy as one of the greatest song-writers that music has known.'

8 July, pp. 12–13 **'Sousa: The Last of the Classicists'** (broadcast of Sousa's Marches): 'Within his chosen medium what a master he was! Above all, in these days when popular music is formless in construction and neurasthenic in mood, how pleasant to turn to a composer who breathes such an air of gaiety, exuberance and self-confidence.'

26 Aug., pp. 16–17 **'Music of the Machine Age'** (Bliss's *Conquest of the Air* and Mossolov's *Factory* at the Proms): 'The trouble with music inspired by movement is that music by its very nature consists of movement. This makes it the most difficult medium of all in which to

describe external movement. For example, Debussy's piano piece *Mouvement* (inspired by machinery) is the most static piece and almost the worst piece he ever wrote.'

16 Sept., pp. 14–15 **'Enjoying Rachmaninoff'** (discussing first the Russian character and then his music): 'Technically speaking, it shows the utmost fluency and brilliance and his piano concertos in particular are a model to any contemporary composer in the contrast and balance of tone between soloist and orchestra. (I use the word brilliance advisedly, in spite of the general sombreness of Rachmaninoff's tone-colour, for his tone-colour is not only sombre but luminous – it never has the muddiness which comes from earnest incompetence.) But when one comes to look beneath this brilliance and elaboration of texture one finds a curious weakness and lack of drive in the main lines of the work. The melodies hover round two or three adjacent notes as though unwilling to leave a congenial atmosphere and the composer has to resort to mechanical means of an obvious kind in order to get things going. … His most impressive and typical passage is the finale of his choral work *The Bells* with its nostalgia for the silence of the grave.'

14 Oct., p. 14 **'Elgar at his most English'**: Falstaff – 'the most English of Elgar's works … it reminds me of the best paintings of Hogarth in which apparently incidental passages of illustration and caricature are essential parts of an unconventional but thoroughly ordered design.'

11 Nov., p. 15 **'Great Minor Art'** (Ravel Memorial Concert): 'with the exception of *Daphnis* his invention seems to exert itself within a deliberately restricted field. Together with Debussy's *Prélude à l'après-midi d'un faune*, [*Daphnis and Chloe*] is the greatest expression in modern times of the pagan ideal.'

18 Nov., pp. 24–5 **'Mendelssohn at his best'**: 'At a time when barbarians all over Europe are denouncing Jewish culture as something inimical and parasitic it is a good idea to recall those Jewish artists whose creative work has become identified with the land of their spiritual adoption. … As an orchestrator [Mendelssohn] was academic in the very best sense of the term. It is not for nothing that Sibelius, the greatest living orchestrator, holds up Mendelssohn as an example to his pupils.'

25 Nov., p. 13 **'Epic Music'** (Liszt's *Hungaria* conducted by Lambert on 27 Nov.): 'He had no use for formalism and that is why he is accused (and at times with justice) of being formless. But at his best he achieved that rare alchemy of inspiration and structure without which no music is truly great.'

2 Dec., pp. 14–15 **'Years of Pilgrimage'** (Liszt's *Années de Pèlerinage*): 'If, as an admirer of Liszt, I were to be asked which work of his I would choose to go down to posterity I would undoubtedly choose either the Faust Symphony or the Piano Sonata. … but if, as a lover of Liszt, I were asked which work out of his gargantuan output I could keep for myself I would undoubtedly choose the *Années de Pèlerinage*, for these piano pieces, less well known than his bravura works, give us the essential man.'

1939

3 Mar., pp. 12–13 **'Three Aspects of Nature'** (Debussy's three *Nocturnes*): 'The closing pages of *Nuages* and *Fêtes* are masterpieces of formal concision and it seems strange to think that they can ever have been looked upon as formless. But I suppose that in 1900 audiences were so deadened by listening to a school of symphonic writers who in Norman Douglas's words had "a passion for dissecting the obvious and squeezing the last drop out of a foregone conclusion" that they were unable to appreciate form unless it was knocked into their heads with a sledge-hammer.'

17 Mar., p. 15 **'Something New in Jazz'** (broadcast later in the week of the Quintette du Hot Club de France): 'Quite frankly I am a little tired a) of listening to jazz b) of writing about it. To start with, I have spent so much of my life doing both, and to go on with, I feel that jazz at the present is stagnating. … My complaint about present-day jazz is that we are always being presented with the same old tricks in a new guise, and that attention is concentrated on the performance, not on the music itself. I know of no interesting American composer who has come out since Ellington. This being so, you can imagine that it was with a fairly jaded palette that, two years ago, I entered a small night club in Montmartre, not a district where

one expects much in the way of jazz, anyway. But once inside I was delighted and surprised to hear a small band with an entirely new tone colour, and with a charming and original style of its own. Moreover, it was playing not an arrangement of a popular number, but a fascinating and exotic piece whose composer I was at a loss to place. They were the Quintette du Hot Club de France, and the composer was Django Reinhardt, the principal guitarist of the band. ... Reinhardt is of French gypsy origin, does not read music, and is handicapped by having only two fingers on his left hand which function properly. Nevertheless he can do more with two fingers than most people with four and is the best jazz guitar player I know, He is partnered by Stephane Grappelly, a violinist who having started as a 'straight' player is now one of the most brilliant exponents of the jazz style.'

7 Apr., pp. 12–13 **'The Symphony in Decline?' – Constant Lambert contends that the late nineteenth century was a bad period for the symphony** (broadcasts of symphonies by Franck, Rubinstein, Glazunov and Brahms): 'Symphonies written between Beethoven and Sibelius, whatever their incidental merits, almost invariably show a struggle between content and form which robs them of artistic completeness. Romantic material is forced into a chilly and archaic mould and the composers waver unhappily between story-telling and pattern-making.'

1944

11 Aug., p. 3 **'Tastes in Light Music'** (with contributions also from Bernard Buckham, Richard Addinsell, Edwin Evans and a 'Plain Mr Brown'): 'I would far rather give an unrehearsed performance of a Tchaikovsky symphony than one of a Waldteufel valse. A piece such as Chabrier's *Joyous March* demands even more preparation than one by Delius or Debussy. ... May I suggest that at next year's Proms, the second part be devoted entirely to a really adequate performance of the masterpieces of light music?'

1945

13 July, p. 3 **'My Promenading Life'** (a reworking of his article for *Night and Day*, 21 Oct. 1937)

1949

25 Mar., p. 2 **'What is Light Music?'**: 'During the war, when I did a number of concerts for ENSA, both for the Forces and for war-workers, it was my custom to play a Sousa march as an encore.'

✳ Sunday Referee

1931

8 Nov. [**'The Ideal Critic of Music – Mr Constant Lambert to write for the Sunday Referee – His Qualifications – by Cecil Gray**, with photo of Lambert']

15 Nov. **'Clear Politics Out Of Music – Panic Patriotism and its Repercussions'**: Music subsidy and the BBC; all-British nights at the Proms; Ballet Club

22 Nov. **'Music's Debt to the BBC – Schönberg, Joyce and Stravinsky – A Dramatic Contrast'**: Schoenberg's *Verklärte Nacht*, Variations for Orchestra and *Five Orchestral Pieces* all heard within the week: 'To find a parallel to [Schoenberg's] amazing technical virtuosity, his exasperated sensibility, and his strange, half-mathematical, half-sentimental outlook, we have to turn to literature where James Joyce provides an example of a remarkably similar mentality proceeding through much the same phases of thought and technique. ... The orchestra under Dr Adrian Boult played the extremely difficult score [*Five Orchestral Pieces*] remarkably well – though with a touch of the embarrassment and circumspection shown by a really polite Protestant who has found himself involved in a religious ceremony of some totally different creed.' Stravinsky's Violin Concerto: 'It is really hard to write of this work with patience. ... The *Symphony of Psalms* is a more pretentious but equally empty work.'

29 Nov. **'Belshazzar's Feast – William Walton's Astonishing Maturity'**: 'There is not a moment's hesitation or fumbling. The work "comes off" with a sureness and slickness that could do credit to a composer of forty-years' experience. ... But to me the finest feature of "*Belshazzar*" is not so much the brilliance of execution as the solidly-conceived and almost symphonic form in which the composer has cast a work that might easily have tended to

become a loosely-connected series of dramatic tableaux.' Bax, *Garden of Fand*: 'Both Bax's *Garden of Fand* and Sibelius's Fifth Symphony were given performances [LSO, Beecham] which down to every detail were so remarkable that one was left wondering with renewed amazement how it is that this strangely-moving early work of Bax has been allowed such a protracted rest, and that one of the few first-class symphonies of modern times is not yet in the regular repertoire.'

6 Dec. '**Vaughan-Williams's "Job" – A Symphony for Dancers – Tchaikovsky's War Horse**': *Job*, first London performance [RPS, Cameron]: 'the most successful theatrical work produced by a modern English composer ... a work of great power. Rachmaninov's Second Symphony: 'the long-winded and turgid emotionalism of this work must have left many with a disgust for any music written since Hucbald [*c.* 840–930].' *Northern Ballad*: 'typical Bax, but hardly Bax at his best.'

13 Dec. '**Composer who destroys all critical canons: Aggravating Delius – The Peter Warlock Memorial Concert – London Symphony Orchestra**': Delius's *Song of the High Hills*: 'the middle section of the work is not only the most inspired moment in Delius but one of the most moving passages in the whole of music. ... [Delius] is the most aggravating composer for a critic to write about for his work destroys all critical canons.' He compares the exoticism of Delius's *Appalachia* with the exoticism of Gauguin. 'It is quite possible that future generations examining the bare bones of Delius's music, without any realisation of its emotional life, will simply be unable to understand why we think of him as one of the greatest figures in all music.' Beecham: 'a fine performance of Elgar's First Symphony and a quite exceptionally good performance of Delius's *In a Summer Garden*. Unfortunately, between the two was sandwiched Strauss's empty and garrulous suite from *Le Bourgeois Gentilhomme*.'

20 Dec. '**Matters Musical: Vaughan-Williams's Mystical Songs – Parisian Musical Thoughts**': Berkeley, Symphony for Strings: 'a tantalising work'; Vaughan Williams's *Pastoral Symphony*: 'The first movement of the symphony ranks with the composer's very finest work – with the slow movement of the *London Symphony* and with all the opening of the last movement of the *Sea Symphony*, to take two examples.' With **Concert Notes** by Patrick Hadley that include a paragraph on four programmes that week that included works by Lambert.

27 Dec. ['Owing to a postal delay Constant Lambert's weekly notes had not arrived at the time of going to press.']

1932

3 Jan. '**Cecil Gray on Sibelius**': Gray, *Sibelius*: 'I find it hard indeed to write of a book in which I am in such complete agreement. Ever since I first became acquainted with the score of Sibelius's Fourth Symphony I have been convinced that the composer will ultimately prove to have been not only the greatest of his generation but one of the major figures in the entire history of music. ... [Gray's] unorthodox but brilliant essay on symphonic style in general is a remarkably profound and suggestive piece of writing.'

10 Jan. '**Music's Homage to Chaucer**': Dyson's *The Canterbury Pilgrims*: 'less satisfactory than the setting of Dunbar' [*In Honour of the City*]

17 Jan. '**Diversity of Programmes: Need for Enterprise**'

24 Jan. '**Music suffers a great loss**': Death of Mrs Samuel Courtauld

31 Jan. '**London Symphony Orchestra** – Great Performance at Queen's Hall – A New Pianist – Stravinsky': 'impossible not to be alarmed by the present [financial] condition of the LSO' and Beecham appeals to audience for support; Moeran, *Lonely Waters*: 'composer had made a mistake in introducing an actual singer at the end for the piece is essentially a reflection on something that has gone before.' Stravinsky, *Capriccio for Piano* and *Symphony of Psalms*: 'the performance only served to bring into greater prominence the laboriously short-winded nature of its construction ...'

7 Feb. '**The Berlin Philharmonic Orchestra' – Silly Snobbery – A Sense of Unity – The Poldowski** [memorial] **Concert**': 'To suggest, before the visiting orchestra has even given one concert, that to support it is merely snobbery is not only rude but silly. It really is time we

stopped making such tub-thumping fools of ourselves.' *A Night on the Bare Mountain*: 'The legend that Mussorgsky could not orchestrate is now completely shattered.'

14 Feb. **'Festival of French Music'**: 'One of the most moving things in the whole of Thursday's concert was a Conductus for Solo Voice by Perotin le Grand, the Maître de Chapelle at Notre Dame from 1180–1236.' **Mediaeval Masters – The "Rich Humanity" of the Earlier Composers**: 1st perf. of Bax's *Winter Legends* covered by Patrick Hadley

21 Feb. **'Craft for Craft's Sake' – Hindemith and his Works**: Hindemith's *Gebrauchsmusik*: 'it would be idle to inquire whether in refraining from writing for his own satisfaction Hindemith has necessarily incurred ours'; Harty's LSO concert with Sibelius Symphony No. 2: 'it really is astounding that this symphony should not have a permanent place in the repertoire'; Bax, *Picaresque Comedy Overture*: 'a dashing and brilliant work … in an unexpected but surprisingly successful vein'.

28 Feb. **'Ravel's New Concerto' – The Passing of a Great Trombonist** (Jesse Stamp): Ravel, with Marguerite Long and composer: 'like so much French music, the concerto is in painfully good taste throughout. On one occasion in his life Ravel forgot to be an apostle of French good taste and produced the rich and vigorous *Daphnis and Chloe*, undoubtedly his finest work. This pagan debauch, though, he has more than compensated for by a steady treatment of hock and soda water.' – Schubert Symphony No. 9 (BBC, Boult) – Goossens' Oboe Concerto: 'the material could definitely be made to yield more. There is some lovely writing in the slow section, but the work needs a real finale.'

6 Mar. **'Too Many Pianists'** and Harty/LSO Berlioz

13 Mar. **'Music and National Outlook'**: Verdi Requiem

20 Mar. **'Genius of Weingartner'**

27 Mar. Music Notes: **'Musical Vulgarity or Music-Hall Vulgarity – Lily Morris and Marinetti'**: 'Rachmaninoff's music strikes me as being vulgar because of his facile and deliberate emotionality, his continual wearing of a property heart on his sleeve'. 1st perf. of Delius's *Songs of Farewell*, with praise for Eric Fenby

3 Apr. Music Notes: **'New publications'** etc.; also Guy Warrack's Symphony at RCM

10 Apr. **'The performance of new works'**

17 Apr. **'Elgar and Prokofiev'**: 'I know there are many to whom this work [Elgar Symphony No. 1, BBC, Wood] is repellent in thought and colour, but even they must surely appreciate the absolute mastery of technique, the sureness of conception, and the way in which the themes instead of being repeated in a set mechanical frame are really given a new and more vital significance as the work proceeds.'

24 Apr. **'A period performance of Mozart'** (Bruno Walter) – **The Modern Pianissimo – Borovsky and Prokofiev**

1 May **'Delius and Berlioz – Mass of Life'**: 'Delius and Berlioz are the only two outstanding composers whose genius is almost hysterically acclaimed by half the intelligent musical world, while the other half refuses even to recognise it. … The work almost recalls certain books by D. H. Lawrence, when a somewhat tedious theorising about life interrupts the superbly written presentation of itself.'; Bliss's *Colour Symphony* reviewed

8 May **'A Poet on Mozart'**: Sacheverell Sitwell, *Mozart*

15 May **'"Tristan" at Covent Garden' – High-water Mark in Musical Achievement – Sir Thomas Beecham's Brilliance** (also BBC Contemporary Music, Henry Wood): Berg's *Wozzeck* Fragments: 'there is no composer in Europe more sure of himself or with greater technical ability'; Webern, Passacaglia; Krenek: 'his theme and thirteen variations … embraces every modern style from Elgar to Schönberg and falls between thirteen stools'

22 May **Matters Musical: 'Covent Garden Scenery and Criticism'**; also reviews Beecham's broadcast of Delius's *A Village Romeo and Juliet*: 'The whole opera seems to have been written with the same intensity of inspiration and as a piece of continuous lyricism it is without parallel in music.'

29 May '"Tannhauser" at Covent Garden' ('in many ways the least pleasing of Wagner's operas') – **Wagner's Programme Symphonies**: 'Nobody would be so foolish as to deny that Wagner was a magician; but it is open to question whether he was a white one or a black one.' Mary and Geraldine Peppin: 'the two-piano playing of these young sisters is most enjoyable'

5 June '**Extending the Concert Season**'

12 June '**The Royal Academy of Criticism**'

19 June '**Erik Satie – A misguided eccentric**'

26 June '**Erik Satie – Furniture Music and Music without Atmosphere**'

3 July '**Numbers and Etudes – What's wrong with Jazz?**: Duke Ellington 'is the one who stands out as a composer rather than an executant or arranger. He is, moreover, the only jazz composer … who has succeeded in striking a mean between a number and the étude.'

10 July [No entry]

17 July '**The Sibelius Concert**': Sibelius Society records

24 July '**Thomas Roseingrave: an Eighteenth Century Eccentric**'

31 July '**More Episodes in the Life of Thomas Roseingrave**'

7 Aug. '**Variety of Styles – Roseingrave's place in the English Tradition**': 'In the way that van Dieren's music may be said to lie between Delius and Schönberg in method, so Roseingrave's music lies between the Elizabethans and Scarlatti.'

14 Aug. **Matters Musical: 'These Dull Promenade Concerts' – A Stolid Set of Programmes – British Music at its Worst**: 'a lumbering and ill-chosen series of symphony concerts given nightly'. Bartók's Op. 4: 'given at a promenade concert about ten years ago. It is a splendid work, easy to grasp. … For some unaccountable reason it was shelved until the other day, when it was given at a studio concert of contemporary music. The work is fresh in the orchestra's mind, and could be put in the programmes with the minimum of trouble; but I need hardly say that Bartók, like so many modern composers of international importance, is not represented this year.'

21 Aug. '**A Musical Whipsnade' – British Night at the 'Proms' – Neglect of Novelties**: 'The first and best [course] is to scrap the British concerts entirely. The days are past when the English composer had to fight against racial prejudice, and it is false kindness to provide him with a nice railed-off enclosure of his own.'

28 Aug. '**Mozart without Preciosity – A Rarely Played Croation Symphony – Berners' Pastiche**'

4 Sept. '**Strauss's Waning Years**': *Intermezzo*

11 Sept. '**Three generations of English Music: German, Ireland and Walton**' (Sinfonia Concertante, Cohen/Wood): 'One looks forward with a certain amount of trepidation to the "heavy" works of a "light" composer. There is always the melancholy example of Chabrier, who wasted on his grand opera *Gwendoline* precious years that might have given us another *Roi malgré lui*. I am not setting up Sir Edward German as an English Chabrier, but I feel there is a spiritual likeness between his *Norwich* Symphony (played at Thursday's Prom) and Chabrier's grand opera. The best moments in *Gwendoline* are those when the composer forgets he is writing a grand opera and reverts to his characteristic manner, and the best moments in the *Norwich* Symphony are those in which Sir Edward forgets he is wearing an academic cloak and gives us such pure German as the delightful scherzo, for example.'

18 Sept. – 2 Oct. [Patrick Hadley took over while Lambert was conducting at the Anglo-Danish Exhibition at Copenhagen]

9 Oct. '**The Art and Craft of Fugue – New London Philharmonic**': Bach

16 Oct. '**Unexciting Novelties**': Martinů, Quartet for Strings

23 Oct. '**A Healthy Rivalry**': LPO and BBC

30 Oct. '**Sir Hamilton Harty, The Sibelius Symphony** [No. 2] **and Music Criticism**'

6 Nov. '**Walton's work as he intended it**': BBC's second performance of *Belshazzar's Feast*

13 Nov. '**French Composers and English Romanticism**'

20 Nov. **'Debussy and Stravinsky'**: 'The rapidity with which certain works have dated should prove to composers that works whose basis is intellectual rather than physical make up for their lack of immediate appeal by their greater staying power.'

27 Nov. **'Passports Please! – On the Interpretation of Sibelius'**

4 Dec. **'On the Conductin' of Elgar's Celebration Concerts'**: commenting on an article by Robert Lorenz who 'conjures up a hearty picture of the composer as a fat old country gentleman huntin' and shootin' and goin' and fishin' and bettin' and occasionally doin' a spot of composin'.'

11 Dec. **'Meyerbeer and Elgar'**

18 Dec. **'"The Kingdom" and Stainer – Genuine Gothic and Waterhouse'**

25 Dec. **'Sorabji and Pannain'**: on Sorabji's *Around Music* and Guido Pannain's *Modern Composers*

1933

1 Jan. **'Romanticism versus Form'**: 'There is a character in Peacock's *'Headlong Hall'* who, when told that the principle quality in a landscape garden was that of *surprise*, remarked, "And what happens when you go round the garden a second time?" (or words to that effect). His remark admirably sums up the difficulty of writing a romantic work in classical form.'

8 Jan. **'The Decay and Revival of the Symphony'**: Franck 'made such a mess of symphonic form'

15 Jan. **'English Landscape and Symphonies'**: Vaughan Williams' *A London Symphony*: 'There is little doubt that the sensuous melancholy and rich imagery of so much English poetry is best suited to a compact and lyrical form such as we find in the poems of Fletcher and in Peter Warlock's settings of them.'

22 Jan. **'Harold in Italy and Walton in Babylon'**: Courtauld-Sargent concert on 16 Jan., with Berlioz, Mozart and *Belshazzar's Feast*: 'In the *a cappella* passage they lost pitch with alarming rapidity.' Sargent, like Boult, 'makes a big hold up towards the end (figure 38) which is not marked in the piano score.'

29 Jan. **'Conductors and the Group-Mind'**: Ibert, *Escales*; Bliss, Two-Piano Concerto, with Victor Hely-Hutchinson and Ernest Lush soloists

5 Feb. **'The Modern Piano Concerto'**: Vaughan Williams, Piano Concerto (1st perf. 1 Feb. 1933); Poulenc, Concerto for 2 Pianos; Szymanowski

12 Feb. **'Schoenberg's Variations Again'**: conducted by the composer, 8 Feb. 1933: 'by far the most important work Schoenberg has written since the pre-war *Pierrot Lunaire*'

19 Feb. **'Hollywood and the Queen's Hall'**: a film 'short' of Walter conducting *Oberon* Overture; Berg, *Lyric Suite*: 'I am by no means a theoretical upholder of atonality, but a movement like this must surely convince the most academic critic.'

26 Feb. **'Beecham and Berlioz'**: *Symphonie fantastique*: 'one of the experiences that come very rarely'; Bax, *In the Faery Hills*: 'a subtle and finely wrought score'

5 Mar. **'Walter Leigh's Burlesque'**: 'I know of no music that is more enjoyable both intrinsically and satirically than the music of *The Pride of the Regiment* and the recently produced *Jolly Roger*. One has the rare and enjoyable sensation of both having one's cake and eating it.'

12 Mar. **'Contrasts of Two Centuries: Impure Music'**: Vittoria, Berg: 'If the rest of Wozzek [*sic*] comes off as well as these three fragments I cannot understand why we are denied a hearing of this opera in this country. ... I cannot understand anyone who has not been frightened off by Berg's reputation as a bogey-man failing to appreciate the direct expressiveness of these fragments.'

19 Mar. **'New Music at Wigmore Hall'**: Miaskovsky's and Prokofiev's Third Piano Sonatas

26 Mar. **'Gershwin and Hindemith on Foreign Ground'**: 'Gershwin's [second] rhapsody, just as it is going to develop into good jazz, slips back into Lisztian cliché as if the composer suddenly remembered he was supposed to be writing a serious work. ... Hindemith's orchestral works may not be exactly inspired, but they are to be preferred to this oratorio [*Das Unaufhörliche*] for precisely the same reason that bad prose is to be preferred to bad poetry.'

2 Apr. **'A Lesson to Us All'**: Hindemith, *Lehrstück*: 'As a composer pure and simple, Hindemith is of little interest.' '"The Lesson" – 'any part of the work may be omitted at will, pieces by other composers may be added if they conform to Hindemith's manner, and any instruments may be substituted for those in the full score. In other words, the music has no value as either form or colour.'

9 Apr. **'Late Debussy and Early Satie'**

16 Apr. **'Russian Opera at the "Wells"'**: 'The fact that I am occasionally associated with the Old Vic and Sadler's Wells Theatres in a non-critical capacity naturally prevents me from criticising the performance and production of Rimsky-Korsakov's *Snow Maiden* at Sadler's Wells on Wednesday. It would be carrying good taste to ludicrous lengths, however, were I to pass over this production, for it is not only the first excursion for the Vic-Wells company into Russian opera, but actually the first production in England of this particular work.'

23 Apr. **'A Forgotten Symphony'**: Borodin, Symphony No. 2

30 Apr. **'Berg's Chamber Concerto'**: 'the beauty of many of the passages, notably the opening of the slow movement, and the technical virtuosity of the work as a whole, convince me that the very considerable effort of concentrating for forty-five minutes on the alembicated texture of this concerto is in no way wasted, and that a second hearing should follow quickly.'

7 May **'At the Opera – A Leaden Rose'**: Strauss, *Der Rosenkavalier*

14 May **'Exotic Music – a New Isolde'**: Debussy's *Pagode* and Henny Trundt

21 May **'Koussevitzky, Sibelius and Bax'**: Bax's Symphony No. 2 'contains the finest music in all Bax's symphonies, and up to the end of the second movement is without a dull patch. The finale disappoints us, not because it is any less good as music, but because it adds nothing to the emotional argument of the work.'

28 May **'The Italian Opera Season'**

4 June **'Dramatic Music and Stage Music'**

11 June **'The Problem of Covent Garden'**: bad staging and lighting

18 June **'Musical Menshevism'**: ISCM Festival, with *Belshazzar's Feast* (which Lambert conducted)

25 June **'The Art of Duke Ellington'** (at the Palladium): 'That Duke Ellington's band is by far the best that has come to this country, few, I suppose, would deny. The ensemble of players is as remarkable as their individual virtuosity, and the most barbaric effects are executed with a surety and (curiously enough) restraint that every musician must admire, whatever his feelings about so-called 'hot-rhythm' music. ... The orchestration of nearly all the numbers show an intensely musical instinct, and after hearing what Ellington can do with fourteen players in pieces like *Jive Stomp* and *Mood Indigo*, the average composer who splashes about with eighty players in the Respighi manner must feel a little chastened.' [* This was followed on 2 July by an 'Open Letter to Constant Lambert' by Roger Wimbush (as well as two other anti-jazz letters). After expressing general praise for Lambert's 'virile criticism, and particularly for the stand you are putting up against the professional poseur' Wimbush continues: 'Your personal attitude towards jazz is somewhat disturbing. ... Surely, the sole interest in jazz lies in extemporisation and individual virtuosity. Stopping short at this I cannot see how jazz can be taken seriously as an influence on music. ... There can be little doubt that to Western minds jazz is definitely unhealthy. ... In genuine creative music ... jazz finds no place at all, simply because the latter is a Jew-ridden racket and the child of Mammon, whereas music is by nature a spiritual experience. ... Let Mr. Armstrong tackle the trumpet part in the second Brandenburg before we start talking about artistry or even virtuosity.']

2 July **'Taken from Life** (Part I)'. **The Art of Duke Ellington – An Open Letter to Constant Lambert** (Roger Wimbush)

9 July '**Here We Go Round the Wimbush**': a point-by-point reply: 'It is rather like discussing the finer gastronomic points with a man who prefers the cooking on English railways to that of "Les Trois Faisans" at Dijon. … Mr Wimbush's argument obscures the technical issue with vaguely defined sociological prejudices. … Ellington is a pianist, an arranger and a composer. It is as a composer he interests me.'

16 July '**Taken from Life** (Part II)': How far should the present day composer's work reflect 'his inward ideals' and 'the spirit of the age?'

23 July [sudden indisposition – 'we wish him a speedy recovery']

30 July '**Excelsior – Inspiration from the Contemporary Scene**': *Excelsior*, a ballet by Manzotti, with 'a happy snapshot' of Lambert at the recent Amsterdam International Festival of Contemporary Music

6 Aug. '**Critics of the Ballet**'

13 Aug. '**Lotte Lenya and Kurt Weill**': Lenya's recent appearance in England and issue of her records. 'What Nöel Coward has done for the debutante, what Cole Porter has done for the gigolo, Kurt Weill has done for the small racketeer, the poor white, the bum [in *Die Dreigroschenoper*].'

20 Aug. '**Decline of the Mechanical Piano**': 'The mechanical piano forms the ideal musique d'ameublement, and in certain instances is not only a solace to the ear but an ornament to the home. … The wireless provides precisely those two elements that are undesirable in café or bar music. The element of human personality and the element of monotony. Also, of course, the element of extreme unsuitability.'

27 Aug. '**Vaughan Williams, Liszt and Bartók**'

3 Sept. '**Egoism and the Symphony**': 'Berlioz was one of the world's finest egoists, and it is to this egoism as much as to any technical skill that we owe the formal unity of the Fantastic [Symphony].'

10 Sept. '"**Falstaff**" **and** "**Faust**"': 'I cannot understand why *Falstaff* which is considered by most musicians to be Elgar's finest work, should not enjoy the same hold over the public as the symphonies … the general level of thought strikes me as far more distinguished.' Ireland Piano Concerto: 'There are some concertos like hyenas, with tall shoulders dwindling down to a puny behind – others, like the diplodicus, whose head is a mere insignificant prelude to the more impressive hindquarters. The best concertos are like a lion – interest is centred in the head and shoulders, but the hind legs are sturdy and the tail is frisky. In this respect Ireland's concerto is leonine.'

17 Sept. '**Liszt Again**': *Hunnenschlacht*

24 Sept. '**Concerning Noise**'

1 Oct. '**Practical Surrealism**': Poulenc, Concerto for Two Pianos; The Marx brothers' films

8 Oct. '**Catalan Tunes and Song**': Gerhard, *Six Catalonian Folk-Songs*

15 Oct. '**London Symphony Orchestra**': Harty opens LSO season; Sibelius symphonies

22 Oct. '**The Pseudo-Classical Age**': Cyril Scott's *Disaster at Sea*: 'it would be easy enough to pillory this work did one not wish to forget about it immediately.'

29 Oct. '**Concerted Life**': piano concertos

5 Nov. '**Over-Production**': almost too much to hear; *Tapiola*: 'not only Beecham's finest performance of this work but probably the finest performance this work has ever had'

12 Nov. '**Bartók's Come-Back**': Piano Concerto No. 2; Maconchy, String Quartet

19 Nov. '**Miss Smithson and Lord Byron**', Berlioz, *Harold in Italy*; Tchaikovsky, *Manfred*

26 Nov. '**The Prodigal's Return**': Beecham and the BBC

3 Dec. '**Brer Bruckner**': '"Here I come a-bulging," remarked Brer Terrapin on a famous occasion, and I could not help being reminded of this the other night when Dr Adrian Boult gave us Bruckner's Ninth Symphony.'

10 Dec. '**Berlioz at his best**': *Hamlet* funeral march

17 Dec. '**Choral Colour**': Beethoven, Mass; Delius, *Songs of Sunset*; Sibelius, Symphony No. 3

24 Dec. **'Operatic Extracts'**: Dame Ethel Smyth, *Female Pipings in Eden*

31 Dec. **'A Reformed Rake'**: Honegger, *Les Cris du monde*

1934

7 Jan. **'A Seasonable Festival'**: BBC British Music concerts: *Flos Campi* 'in my opinion one of the finest works written in any country since the War'

14 Jan. **'"Smoke the Boots"!'**: welcomes Arthur Benjamin's Violin Concerto but finds Bridge's *Phantasm* 'most disappointing'; Elgar's First Symphony: 'While I can understand people disliking this symphony as a whole, I cannot understand anyone not recognising the sterling merit of the interlinked scherzo and slow movement which represents the very best of Elgar.'

21 Jan. **'Austerity and Luxuriance'**: Ireland, *Legend*; Hadley, *The Trees so High* – 'great sensibility and contains much fine music, and is at moments extremely moving. But I do not find that the emotional conception and the formal conception are quite in focus with each other' and Bax's Fifth Symphony – 'a dazzling work. ... Taken as a whole the work is the best the composer has written since the grim and introspective second symphony. But one still doubts whether the form was the inevitable outcome of the material.'

28 Jan. **'Near-Beethoven'**: Furtwängler and the Berlin Philharmonic Orchestra: Lambert challenges the composition of the orchestra under the Nazi régime: 'It is reassuring to see that Mr Simon Goldberg, that fine violinist, still holds his position as leader.'

4 Feb. **'A Poltergeist Concerto'**: Prokofiev, Fifth Piano Concerto: 'Prokofiev's redoubtable and individual pianistic technique has no human rival. It is as though Minnie Mouse were punishing the keyboard to the accompaniment of kitchen utensils.'

'Tragi-Comic Memories': reviews Lord Berners, *First Childhood*: 'This biting wit is the first impression one gets from the book. ... At a second reading, however, a different and more disturbing impression is made, and there slowly detaches itself from the comic background a rather tragic portrait of a sensitive child in the heartiest of huntin' circles.'

11 Feb. **'Subject to Alteration'**: on programme changes in general; on Mahler Symphony No. 9: 'I must confess to having shared the usual English prejudice against Mahler, and having looked upon him as a symphonist manqué. But the Ninth Symphony, in spite of certain obvious weaknesses, is an astonishing piece of work. ... Here is that rare thing, a modern work which is genuinely difficult to understand. The two middle movements in particular reveal a mind of remarkable originality.'

18 Feb. **'Diabolus in Musica'**: Vaughan Williams, *Job* (reprinted in Stephen Lloyd, 'Constant Lambert and RVW', *Journal of the RVW Society*, no. 34 (Oct. 2005), pp. 16–17)

25 Feb. **'The Passing of Elgar'**: 'the greatest English composer since the seventeenth century and one of the outstanding figures of his time'; Busoni, Piano Concerto

4 Mar. **'Elgar and the Theatre'**: It seems Lambert was taken to task by some readers for a short piece on Elgar. He wrote of his one meeting with Elgar after the ballet of *Nursery Suite* when Elgar spoke of his fondness for Verdi. 'He spoke only of Italian Opera and how he used to long for the day when the touring companies would come to his neighbourhood.'

11 Mar. **'Poderose "Consorts"'**: Locke

18 Mar. **'Wozzeck! At Last!'**: 'It is a grotesque comment on English musical life that Alban Berg's "Wozzeck", the finest opera of recent years, should have received its first English performance not on the stage at Covent Garden but in concert form at the Queen's Hall. ... While it is deplorable that the Holy Vehm who rule at Covent Garden show not the least interest in recent musical developments, it is consoling to think that the BBC has more intelligence, more enterprise, and more taste'. Referring to the section before the final scene – 'unsurpassed in contemporary music and places Berg in the highest rank. ... [He] treats atonalism as a means of expression, not as a theory.'

25 Mar. **'The Man in the Street'**: Ernest Newman's 'Plain Man' and Berg's *Wozzeck*

1 Apr. **'Some American Composers'**: Varèse, Thomson, Cowell

8 Apr. **'Composers and Publishers'**: also reviews Britten's *A Boy is Born*: 'A remarkable mature achievement for so young a composer. There are obvious weaknesses, of course; the tonal range is very narrow for so extended a work, one or two variations are too long, and much of the apparently contrapuntal writing is only thinly-disguised repetition of the same pentatonic chord. But the first effect is impressive and it is clear that the composer of the opening pages and the fifth variation has a future worth following.'

15 Apr. **'The Delius Society'**: urges readers to buy 78 recordings set(s); 1st perf. Bax, *The Tale the Pine Trees Knew*: 'has two very bad things about it: a) the whimsy title b) the unexpected loud note with which it ends. Otherwise it is the best of the several new works by Bax we have heard this season.'

22 Apr. **'Primitive Mussorgsky'**: *Boris Godunov*; picture of Walton but no article

29 Apr. **'Rachmaninoff Recollections'**: on a book of Rachmaninoff's reminiscences edited by Riesemann: Rachmaninoff 'the musician laureate to "Heartbreak House"'

6 May **'At Covent Garden'**: Beecham chastises the audience to stop talking during *Fidelio*

13 May **'Oh, Those Bells'**: London Musical Festival; Hindemith, *Das Unaufhörliche* ('the dullest oratorio since Parry's *Job*'); Scott's Festival Overture: 'It would be a matter of extreme psychological and scientific interest to hear the overtures that the judges considered less good. Mr Scott's lamp of inspiration can scarcely have flickered so feebly and dully.'

20 May **'Manners, Manners!'**: after Beecham reprimanded them the Covent Garden audience is too frightened 'to say boo to a goose'; Strauss's *Arabella* and Weinberger's *Schwanda the Bagpiper* (under Krauss). 'Is it not a sign of weakness in a light opera [*Arabella*] when one should have to listen to small details of workmanship to save one from boredom?'

27 May **'Rossini Revival'**: Francis Toye's book on Rossini

3 June **'Unusual Interpretations by Finnish Visits'**: Finnish National Orchestra and Sibelius

10 June **'Troubles and Trials of Italian Productions'**

17 June **'Secrets of Delius – Think of Keats and Shelley and Their Scented Poems'**: death of Delius; **Mephisto Waltz: A New Ballet**: at the Mercury Theatre

24 June **'The Ballets Russes'**: de Basil company not quite up to Diaghilev standards

1 July **' "The Village Romeo" – Dramatic value of Delius is now nearly established'**: Beecham's RCM performances

8 July **'Dancing Seconds – Innovation in the Russian Ballet is out of place'**: Dancing seconds: 'every detail of construction and figuration in the music is meekly followed by movements on the stage.' *Choreartium* based on Brahms's Symphony No. 4 – 'a deplorable example of Massine's latest Roxy-cum-Delacroze manner. … Massine, in spite of his extraordinary lapses, still remains the most technically efficient choreographer in Europe. But in these two would-be symphonic works [*Choreartium* and *Les Présages*] he has put back the whole art of ballet by many years. … Every note of Brahms's score is laboriously reflected on the stage. Yet the final result is less Brahmsian and less symphonic than can be imagined. Whatever else this grimly intellectual, intensely Nordic and introspective music suggests, it does not suggest monastery gardens, fête-galantes and precious Mediterranean athletics. However, it is above all things a symphony.' (Reprinted, with Massine's reply in the issue of 22 July and part of Lambert's reply the following week, in *Ballet Today*, Oct. 1951, pp. 5–7.)

15 July **'Railroad Ballet – Realism and Stylisation in "Union Pacific"'**: 'It is good easy-going "entertainment value" with one high spot in the shape of Massine's Chaplinesque dance as the postman. … However, M. Massine has only himself to blame for forcing us to judge his work by the very high standard set by his more important ballets. … It is evident that Massine had no very clear idea whether the ballet was going to be stylised or realistic, expressionist or safe "theatre" and probably decided that the present-day ballet audience doesn't care a hoot provided it is sufficiently amusing.'

22 July **'Mime and Ballet – Dolls that are human: humans that are dolls'**: *La Boutique Fantasque* (de Basil)

29 July **'Reply to Massine'**: 'There are only two things that can make an intelligent creative artist reply to a critic: a) a gross misstatement of facts; b) being flicked on the raw. I have, as far as I can tell, made no misstatement of facts. Mr Massine's letter [22 July, on the use of Delacroze methods in ballet], though illogical, is sufficiently important to demand an answer in full.'

5 Aug. [Letter from Massine: 'It is unfortunate that Mr Lambert does not restrict himself to criticising music. He is not sufficiently acquainted with choreography.']

5 Aug. **'Nought + Nought = Nought'**: de Basil ballet *Les Imaginaires*

12 Aug. **'Ballet – Farewell'**: 'I should have liked to have ended this series of articles on ballet in an atmosphere of moist eyes and handshakes, but ...' He gives 'Reply No. 2' to Massine's letter – 'so brilliant a piece of sidestepping I have not seen for many a day', and concluding: 'my readers will be relieved to hear that this is my last article on the subject.'

19 Aug. **'Composer and Fish'**: on critical labels attached to composers: 'A sculptor of my acquaintance who has made an exhaustive study of the behaviour of both fish and humans, has noticed that when humans go to watch fish in an aquarium the first thing they look as it not the fish but the label underneath.'

[no articles during his absence in Venice]

23 Sept. **'The Festival at Venice'**: 'What the Italians lack in organising ability they make up for generosity with their enthusiasm. In no other country, I like to think, would a composer be offered his first rehearsal at 12.30 on Saturday night after a long concert, and his second rehearsal at nine the next morning. ... Chaotic rehearsal arrangements, off-hand treatment of artists.'

30 Sept. **'Third Night at Venice Festival'**: Berg, *Der Wien*; Stravinsky, *Capriccio*; also covers the Proms: Bax, *The Tale the Pine Trees Knew* 'without offending chord'; 'The *London Symphony* [Vaughan Williams] has been many times revised since its first performance and on Thursday night two further cuts were made, one at the end of the second movement, and one in the Epilogue. Though the passages cut were among the best in the symphony, intrinsically speaking I think the composer has been wise. The fine slow movement has no hint of a longueur and the Epilogue is more in proportion with the quick section of the finale.'

7 Oct. **'Bartók's Work and the Public'**: Henry Wood conducting Suite Op. 3 (2nd movement in truncated form)

14 Oct. **'The Song of Joseph Marx'**

21 Oct. **'Handel and Arne'**

28 Oct. **'When Delius is not at his best'**: *A Mass of Life*: 'I doubt, if considered as a whole it is the equal of "*The* [sic] *Village Romeo and Juliet*". ... It still remains a great work.'; Elgar's Symphony No. 2

4 Nov. **'Some regrettable sounds'**: *Zarathustra* – 'thoroughly turgid' – and *Prometheus*; tells story, without mentioning names, about Balfour Gardiner and the Alps – see Stephen Lloyd, *H. Balfour Gardiner* (Cambridge University Press, 1984), p. 203

11 Nov. **'Delius and Caviar'**: RPS Delius concert, Beecham: 'I can remember few works which have moved me more than *Sea Drift* and *The Song of the High Hills* but I can also remember occasions when I have been given too much Delius, and Thursday night was one of them.'; Delius, *Paris*: 'I can honestly say that I have never heard a better performance of a modern composition.'

18 Nov. **'Vaughan Williams' New Suite'**: Suite for Viola and small orchestra

25 Nov. **'Out-of-date Programmes'**: Albert Coates gives Tchaikovsky Symphony No. 5 and Scriabin's *Prometheus* again; on Hamilton Harty receiving the Gold Medal of the Royal Philharmonic Society: 'It is impossible to think of anyone more deserving this great honour than Sir Hamilton Harty. Fame has come to him later than to some men, but his name stands all the more solidly because he has never sought the cheap and evanescent rewards of fashion. Unlike many famous conductors, Sir Hamilton is a musician first and foremost. We never feel that he is using a piece of music as a vehicle for his own virtuosity; on the contrary, he

draws attention not to himself but to the composer, and that surely is the highest degree of the conductor's art.'

2 Dec. **'Stravinsky and "Persephone"'**: 'so flaccid and invertebrate in the melodic invention of *Persephone* that the question of good or bad does not arise.'

9 Dec. **'Walton's First Symphony'**

16 Dec. **'A Fine Russian Opera'**: Tchaikovsky, *Eugene Onegin*

23 Dec. **'Is this Handel's best opera?'**: *Alcina*

30 Dec. **'The Democracy of Music'**: Purcell

1935

6 Jan. **'A Notable History of Music'**: Colles's *Oxford History of Music VII*: 'faced by Mussorgsky the author seems at a loss … [and] evades the problem by referring to Mussorgsky as little as possible'

13 Jan. **'Critic of Liszt's "Legends"'**: Newman, *The Man Liszt*: 'most of the time he is flogging a horse that has already been humanely dispatched by Mr Sacheverell Sitwell in his excellent study of the composer.'

20 Jan. [called to Budapest to replace Beecham]

27 Jan. **'Soviet Revolution – in Music Form'**: Borodin's Second Symphony, Albert Coates: 'the worst of many bad performances this symphony has suffered'; the opening 'instead of being hammered out at the proper speed was yawned over eight beats in the bar'; Shaporin's Symphony in C for chorus and orchestra: 'Mr Coates, the orchestra and chorus are to be congratulated on their clear-cut performance.'

3 Feb. **'London Symphony Success'**: Bach's *Art of Fugue* orch. Graeser; Sibelius, Symphony No. 4, LPO, Beecham: 'considerably quicker in many places than we are accustomed to but I am told on excellent authority that these tempi represent the composer's wishes'

10 Feb. **'Women Composers are so forceful'**: Macnaghten-Lemare Concert: 'Miss Elisabeth Lutyens, in her setting of Austin Dobson's very olde worde poem *The Dying of Tanneguy de Bois* is evidently determined that none of the Morris-wallpaper atmosphere of the words shall be reflected in the music, which is strained, angular and unconvincing.'

17 Feb. **'The Intelligent Concert-Goer'**

24 Feb. **'Hastings Festival Highlights'**: Queen's Hall Handel anniversary concert with Beecham replaced by Boult 'whose views on time do not seem to have been influenced by the theories of relativity'; tempi 'monotonously moderate'

3 Mar. **'The Art of Expert Conducting'**

10 Mar. **'BBC Orchestra at their best'**: Harty: Schumann, Sibelius and Berlioz

17 Mar. **'Are Music Hoaxes Worth While?'**: Wood/Klenovsky: 'not getting away with an imitation diamond – he was merely imitating paste, a sorry occupation'; Kreisler

24 Mar. **'Four Concerts of Real Merit'**: BBC, Boult, Malipiero and Berg: 'Once again Sir Landon Ronald has shown us that as a conductor of Elgar he was few rivals' (see also 24 Nov. 1935); Rachmaninov playing his Paganini Rhapsody: 'In musical content … it is even more empty and threadbare than the Fourth Concerto.'

31 Mar. **'First-Class Fare at Bournemouth'**: Boult conducts Vaughan Williams, Ireland, Holst and Schubert, Symphony No. 9

7 Apr. **'A Great Unfinished Symphony'**: two Courtauld-Sargent performances of Walton: 'There are some, I know, who think that the composer has piled Pelion on Ossa rather too soon in the first movement, but although I see that the movement risks anti-climax, I also think that it triumphantly avoids it. The scherzo, which seemed at first hearing to be the least impressive movement, has been entirely rescored, and is now well able to stand by the others. In the first version Walton robbed the movement of its full effect by a rather finicking over-elaboration of scoring which has in the past detracted from other works of his. It is now immensely clarified, and scores its points directly, not by implication. The slow third movement (slightly but far less drastically rescored) still stands out as the finest of the three. The performance by the

London Philharmonic Orchestra conducted by Malcolm Sargent, if a little less fiery than the first performance, was brilliantly clear and well-proportioned throughout.'

14 Apr. **'Surprises in a New Symphony'**: Vaughan Williams, Symphony No. 4: 'A knock in the eye ... all the old mannerisms have gone. The vigour, concision, and intellectual force of this symphony must have taken the composer's greatest admirers by surprise.'

21 Apr. **'Bach's "Passion" at Queen's Hall'**: 'Here we jib at playing Walton's *Belshazzar's Feast* in a cathedral but in Italy they play Rossini Overtures, and thoroughly enjoy them.'

28 Apr. **'Two New English Choral Works'**: Hadley's *La Belle Dame Sans Merci* and Moeran's *Nocturne*

5 May **'A Week of Opera'**: *La Cenerentola* and *Lohengrin*: the former 'has its moments of pomp and its flashes of "theatre" and at least is noisy enough to drown the dowagers and debutantes in the stalls'.

12 May **'Some Criticism of the Ring'**: 'In spite of the fact that the characters keep passing the plot on to each other in relay-race fashion, it is virtually impossible to understand it without previous study. ... The best of *Valkyrie* can be enjoyed in the concert hall without our having to suffer the monumental boredom of Act II (apart from the Prelude), and as for *Rheingold*, the less said the better.'

19 May **'Composers to be proud of'**: Tudor composers; *Italian Girl in Algiers*

26 May **'A Composer with no history'**: Sacheverell Sitwell, *A Background for Domenico Scarlatti*: 'He is also wrong when he describes Roseingrave as editing forty-two sonatas of Scarlatti, after the latter's death. The edition was published in London during the 1730s before Roseingrave went mad and at least twenty years before Scarlatti's death. It is a pity that this otherwise brilliant little book contains these blemishes.'

2 June **'A Bellini Revival is Due'**: centenary of his death

9 & 16 June [Cecil Gray replaces Lambert who is conducting the Vic-Wells Ballet]

23 June **'Critics who lose their heads over ballet'**: Adrian Stokes, *Russian Ballets*: Lambert quotes a sentence: '"In the orchestra a melody leaves on an errand, rising off the shimmer of strings and of plucked harps like a bird that flies from a lake with taut legs dripping." There are many comments I could make on this paragraph, but I will confine myself to the obvious and vulgar query, "How on earth does Mr Stokes imagine you play a harp if you don't pluck it? Does he think that you blow down it or hit it with a stick? Mr Stokes has evidently followed a number of ballets with rapt attention, and his book shows signs up to a point of the closest study. But a little common sense and a little less agonised sensitivity would have prevented him from harbouring a number of remarkable misconceptions, some of which I shall attempt to catalogue next week.'

30 June **'Lambert-Stokes Clash'**: 'Mr Constant Lambert's criticism last week of the book "Russian Ballets", by Adrian Stokes, has evoked a vigorous reply from the author, which, with Mr Lambert's further comment, is published below.'

7 July **'Opera and Ballet'**: criticises Massine's choreography of *Barabau*: 'but the story as a whole is not welded with other elements so as to produce a three-dimensional work of art'

14 July **'Artists can help the Ballet'**: Arnold Haskell: 'not a critic with whom I invariably find myself in agreement but I cannot help applauding a recent newspaper article of his which hits a number of nails on the head with great accuracy'

21 July **'Nijinska's Success in New Ballet'**: *Les Cent Baisers*. 'To my mind the most distinguished of modern choreographers. ... Construction, continuity, an impeccable taste and congruity of style are the fundamental qualities of her work. ... I may recall an occasion when she spent an entire rehearsal making the Diaghilev ballet walk round the stage to a march tune until she had got the precise type of walk she required.'

28 July **'New Ballet at Covent Garden'**: 'During the last few weeks a number of people have written to the *Sunday Referee* pointing out very kindly that I am past my prime and that I belong to the 1920s.'

4 Aug. **'The Truth about Diaghileff'**: Haskell, *'Diaghileff: His Artistic and Private* Life': 'Apart from the Introduction, "The Shade of Diaghileff" which is not very successful, and an

appendix of all the Diaghileff productions, which contains a number of slips, Mr Haskell's book is an admirably unbiased, soberly-written and well-documented account'; adding the corrective that 'Diaghileff had an almost pathological loathing for [American jazz], avoided it whenever possible, and only liked the fox-trots of Satie and Walton because they poked fun at it.'

11 Aug. −1 Sept. [Basil Maine took over. Lambert on holiday]

8 Sept. **'The Third Symphony of Saint-Saëns'**: 'the nadir of pretentiousness'

15 Sept. **'A Notable Liszt Concert'**: *Faust* Symphony Prom; Bliss conducts *Things to Come* Suite: 'here are all the old 1920 tricks brought out again, though admittedly in the most brilliant and dexterous fashion'

22 Sept. **'A Russian Concert'**: Prokofiev's Fifth Piano Concerto: 'he is obviously the biggest talent that has come out of Russia since *Petrushka*'

29 Sept. **'An Early Delius Opera'**: *Koanga* at Covent Garden: 'If there is one trait that links Delius with Conrad it is his treatment of nature as a background to human emotion.' (The whole article reprinted in *Delius Society Journal* no. 113 (Winter 1994), pp. 63–4; see Delius Society website)

6 Oct. **'"Boris" at Sadler's Wells'**

13 Oct. **'A Composer-Critic's View'**: van Dieren, *Down Among the Dead Men*: a 'remarkable essay on Meyerbeer'

20 Oct. **'Concerts of the Week'**

27 Oct. **'Opera without a dull bar'**: 'Puccini's *Il Tabarro* is a masterpiece' (at Sadler's Wells)

3 Nov. **'Highlights of Dukas's Best Work – A Philharmonic Triumph'**: *La Péri*

10 Nov. **'Walton's Symphony is Really Good Music'**: 'Let it be said at once that the finale is a rattling good piece of music. The two fugato sections show a few stains of midnight oil but the beginning is excellent and the coda has an irresistible drive. The last three minutes, indeed, are as good as anything Walton has written, which is saying much. It cannot be said, however, that the finale is quite up to the intellectual and emotional level of the first three movements. It would be unreasonable to expect a composer at the age of thirty-two to conquer a problem which neither Beethoven nor Sibelius resolved until late in life, and it is a remarkable tribute to the work that it should drag Beethoven and Sibelius into the argument at all. This, and Vaughan Williams' Fourth Symphony, are, to my mind, the two most important novelties of recent years, whether in this country or in Europe.'

17 Nov. **'Egon Petri: A Master Pianist'**

24 Nov. **'Britain's Music on Trial'**: visiting foreign music critics; 'in my opinion Sir Landon Ronald is unequalled as an interpreter of Elgar' (*Falstaff*; see also 24 Mar. 1935)

1 Dec. **'Bohemia brings her music to town'**: visit of the Prague Philharmonic Orchestra; 1st perf. of Bax, Symphony No. 6: 'I have always preferred his Symphonic Poems such as 'The Garden of Fand' and 'A [sic] Tale the Pine Trees Knew' to his symphonies, and his Sixth Symphony, pleasant though it was, has not changed my mind'; 1st perf. of Bliss, *Music for Strings*: '... an astonishingly efficient work, well planned and admirably conceived for its medium. In fact, there is nothing wrong about it except the music. ... Every note is in the right place but we are a little too conscious of the composer putting it there.'

8 Dec. **'Was Dvorak's Music Too High Hat?'**: Dvořák's Second (i.e. Seventh) Symphony

15 Dec. **'Magic of Purcell – England's Greatest Man of Music'**: Boult conducts *King Arthur*: 'I must confess that not until I actually heard this piece performed did I realise its astonishing romantic atmosphere – a kind of timeless, voluptuous melancholy that puts one in mind of a landscape by Richard Wilson or the finest passages in Tennyson.'

22 Dec. **'It brings this opera home'**: Decca recordings of *Dido and Aeneas* and Walton's Symphony recording: 'Since its first performance the finale has been slightly touched up A judicious cut of a few bars has been made, and the coda has been rescored so that the fugato subject stands out clearly as an accompaniment to the main tune.'

29 Dec. **'Hell-for-Leather Music'**: Markevitch's choral work *Paradise Lost*

1936

5 Jan. **'Pupil who beat his Teacher'**: death of Alban Berg: 'few composers, indeed, have produced anything more impressive than the closing scene [of *Wozzeck*]'

12 Jan. **'Liszt was as popular as Garbo'**

19 Jan. **'Music worth waiting for'**: English Music Society's records of Purcell

26 Jan. **'Britain's composers lack an Inspiration'**: Hindemith's *Trauermusik* written on the death of King George V: 'No [English] composer, ... without affectation or false pride, associates himself with the outward and visible life of the nation.'

2 Feb. **'Young English Composer's New Triumph'**: Britten's *Te Deum*: 'displays that combination of a brilliant technique with ultimate greyness of effect that we have already come to expect from this young composer. Mr Britten is, I admit, rather a problem to me. One cannot but admire his extremely mature and economical method, yet the rather drab and penitential content of his music leaves me quite unmoved.'

9 Feb. **'Jazz helps composer to write a classic'**: concert performance of Milhaud's *Christophe Colomb* postponed; Mahler's *Das Lied von der Erde*: '... has many unforgettable moments, notably the slow movement, "Solitude in Autumn". A beautiful piece of writing but it is marred by a deliberate chinoiserie on the one hand, and an occasional lapse into conventional Teutonic sentiment on the other. The finale, for all its fine moments, suffers from a rather low theatrical parade of grief, like an actor manager moving the audience to tears while he counts the dead-heads in the stalls.'

16 Feb. **'Two Revivals in Music'**: Stravinsky, *Oedipus Rex*; Debussy, *Images*

23 Feb. **'The kind of concert that empties halls'**: Albert Coates conducting Holler; Coates, *The Defence of Guinevere*; Tchaikovsky, Symphony No. 6

1 Mar. **'BBC making our Sundays Continental'**

8 Mar. **'Four Brass Bands played in this Symphony Concert'**: Harty conducts Berlioz' Requiem

15 Mar. **'Falstaff sings his way to fame'** (at Sadler's Wells)

22 Mar. **'Constant Lambert on Musical Jokes'**: *Wozzeck* and *Lady Macbeth of Mtensk* in concert rather than stage performances

29 Mar. **'Constant Lambert on Bartók's "Come-Back"'**: *Cantata Profana*: 'Critics and public cannot be expected to take in the complexities of a long work by, for instance, Schoenberg or van Dieren, at a first hearing. ... There seem hopes that Bartók may still fulfil the amazing promise of his early period. ... Before the War Bartók was to many people potentially the greatest composer in Europe. His early piano pieces, the first two string quartets and the opera *Bluebeard's Castle* are among the masterpieces of the twentieth century. But during and after the War his style underwent a strange process of desiccation, his melodic line became more and more cramped and he concentrated on purely percussive effect to an extent that became physically painful.'

5 Apr. **'Country that produces Composer-Pianists'**: Rachmaninov, Medtner, Prokofiev

12 Apr. **'A Composer in Blinkers'**: on Stravinsky's *Chronicle of My Life*: 'a sober book', an 'austere chronicle ... he makes the greatest mistake when he imagines that emotional content and logical architecture are necessarily antipathetic'

19 Apr. **'Constant Lambert on Romantic Music'**: continuing with Stravinsky

26 Apr. **'Constant Lambert says: The World has lost a great musician'** – death of Bernard van Dieren; Calvocoressi and Abraham's *Masters of Russian Music*: 'The musical world has suffered a greater loss than it probably realises through the death, at the age of 52, of Bernard van Dieren. ... Future generations will undoubtedly see in him one of the most remarkable figures of our times.'

3 May **'The Opera First Night'**

10 May **'Our Composers Can't Keep Pace with the Times'**: suggesting that the BBC, having done service to Berg, should similarly recognise van Dieren

17 May **'Constant Lambert: Wants to play an opera rôle – and why'**: Scarpia in *Tosca*

24 May **'Covent Garden's Best Singer This Season'**: Kirsten Flagstad

31 May **'Constant Lambert Prefers the Rockets to the Music'**: Charpentier's *Louise*

7 June **'The Sound of Things to Come'**: Cecil Gray, *Predicaments, or Music and the Future*

14 June **'They should sing French with an English accent!'**: *Les Contes d'Hoffmann*

21 June **'Why Ballet is Booming'**

28 June & 5 July [Philip Page: Lambert on holiday]

12 July **'A Composer who reformed Opera'**: Einstein's *Gluck*

17 July **'Stop all this ballet-hoo!'**: too many books on ballet

26 July **'So that's how ballet was born!'**: reviewing Prince Peter Lieven's *The Birth of Ballets-Russes*

2 Aug. **'Massine scores new triumph at Covent Garden'**: *Symphonie fantastique*

9 Aug. **'Ride wings of storm over the ballet'**: controversy over the symphonic ballet

16 Aug. **'Screen can provide new thrills in ballet'**: ballet in film

23 & 30 Aug. [Philip Page: Lambert on holiday]

6 Sept. **'Constant Lambert returns from holiday and says: Concertos should not be abolished'**

13 Sept. **'Lowbrow rules the BBC'**: in its programming

20 Sept. **'In defence of Tchaikovsky'**

27 Sept. **'Nobody Knows What Modern Music Is'**: Ireland, *London Overture*, 1st perf.

4 Oct. **'Man the Musicians Ignored'**: Balakireff

11 Oct. **'A new –and great – pianist comes to England'**: Louis Kentner: 'I have no hesitation in placing him among the first half-dozen masters of his instrument, while as an interpreter of Liszt he is second only to Petri.'

18 Oct. **'The Greatest Concert Season Ever Known'**: 'concert dates for the next few months would make the most hardened "concert-crawler" quail'

25 Oct. **'Vienna's Second Eleven Plays Well'**: Vienna Symphony Orchestra under Weingartner

1 Nov. **'Blind Spots That Hide Some Composers'**: Mahler, *Das Lied von der Erde* and Bruckner, Symphony No. 7

8 Nov. **Let's Have Some British Music!'**: 'I am not preaching a narrow chauvinism. Far from it, I only wish that England could return to the musical internationalism that reigned here ten years ago, for example.'

15 Nov. **'Strauss Writes Lifeless Music'**: *Ariadne in Naxos*

22 Nov. **'Cheap Tricks in New Opera Company's "Boris"'**: British Music Drama Opera Company

29 Nov. [Philip Page]

6 Dec. **'Gerontius – with no incense'**: BBC performance. 'One of the patchiest of Elgar's works and does not live up to the consistent inspiration of its prelude. ... The Demons are Elgar's only complete failure on a large scale.'

13 Dec. **'Alban Berg Writes His Own Elegy'**: performance of the Violin Concerto, Krasner and Wood: 'the most beautiful and significant piece of music written since the war'

20 Dec. **'English Music's Vice and Virtue – in three works'**: Vaughan Williams, *Flos Campi*; Bax, *Rogue's Comedy Overture*; Jacob, Violin Concerto

27 Dec. **'The Finest Modern Carol'**: Peter Warlock, *Bethlehem Down*

1937

3 Jan. **'Religion has inspired no great music'**, echoing Delius and commenting on Eric Fenby's 'interesting but priggish book' *Delius as I Knew Him*: 'Every admirer of Delius must feel nothing but admiration and gratitude for the self-sacrificing work that Mr Fenby did for Delius in his last years, taking down works by dictation in circumstances of the utmost difficulty. It is a pity, I feel, that in this book he did not confine himself to an account of this

work and an account of the gloomy household that surrounded it. Unfortunately he drags in a long and didactic section, pointing out what a much better composer Delius would have been had he been a true believer instead of a follower of Nietzsche. ... the best music of Delius and Elgar will live as long as anything produced in this generation, but it will not be because Elgar was a Catholic and Delius an atheist.' The article inadvertently referred to the *Moss of Life*!

10 Jan. **'The Real Plagiarists of Music'**: those who imitate a composer's style

17 & 24 Jan. [No entry]

31 Jan. **'Constant Lambert says: Tudor Teas are not the same as Tudor Pubs'**: Vaughan Williams, *Five Tudor Portraits*: 'I seem to have enjoyed this work rather less than most of my colleagues. ... "Exit the Folk-Song Society" must be the stage directions to any passage in this work. ... Throughout the *Five Tudor Portraits* one feels the inevitable drawback of the time-lag that exists between poetry and its choral setting. As a result the work seems Tudor in the modernised or tea-house sense of the word. Vaughan Williams' temperament seems to me too elegiac, nostalgic, and individual to interpret the extrovert bawdy directness of that admirable poet Skelton. It is difficult to associate him with the English public-house, except in a remote Housmanish way.'

7 Feb. **'Nordic Night at the Queen's Hall'**: Grieg, Delius and Sibelius; Beecham

14 Feb. **'Spirit of Beethoven'**: Beethoven, Mass; Rachmaninov, *The Bells*: 'orchestration magnificent and the choral writing splendid. Though not great music [it] makes most post-war choral works look pretty silly from the technical point of view' but no moments 'when we are really thrilled by the music *qua music* as apart from having our ears tickled by a master of the art.'

21 Feb. **'Radio beats concert stage'**: 'a good 50 per cent of the best music during the last 100 years is never heard at Queen's Hall simply because it doesn't fit into the traditional structure of a symphony concert'

28 Feb. **'First Time in England – and Last'**: Pfitzner's Piano Concerto, Beecham

7 Mar. [No entry]

14 Mar. **'Elgar Preferred Singers to Saints'**: *The Apostles*, 'least inspired of the larger works'

21 Mar. **'Why Busoni Can Never Be Popular'**: Boult's concert performance of Busoni's *Faust* at Queen's Hall

28 Mar. [No entry]

4 Apr. **'Flourish for Coronation'**: Beecham concert

11 Apr. **'Musicians Honour This Genius the Critics Scorn'**: van Dieren Memorial Concert: 'I am debarred from writing about the performances for the simple and excellent reason that I conducted it.'; tells how van Dieren had attended the first rehearsal for the 1st perf. of the *Chinese Symphony*

18 Apr. – 2 May [No entry]

9 May **'This Tenor Really Sings'**: Martinelli at Covent Garden

16 May **'Masterpieces They Left Out'**: too little Purcell in Coronation season

23 May **'Wagner's Ring Is Falling Off'**: empty seats for *Siegfried* at Covent Garden

30 May **'Perli, Queen of Opera'**: Lisa Perli [Dora Labbette] as Mélisande at Covent Garden

6 June **'Toscanini's Secret'**: on musical interpretation, including Beecham's Delius

13 June **'Opera at its worst'**

20 & 27 June [Philip Page replaces Lambert]

4 July **'I am a Cad Critic'**: 'To judge by the somewhat dubious welcome I received at Covent Garden on Monday night, my recent remarks on the production of *Prince Igor* seem to have been taken none too kindly.'

11 July **'You can hear every word'**: Goossens, *Don Juan de Mañara*: 'the utmost praise is due to the composer for so skilfully preserving the balance between stage and orchestra pit. There is only one thing wrong with this happy state of affairs. None of the words are worth listening to. Arnold Bennett was on the face of it the wrong calibre of writer to employ as a librettist. ...

It is not until the third act that we get a tune we can get our teeth into, and it is typical of the whole opera that this tune should be played on the orchestra, because there are no suitable words to sing it to.'

18 & 25 July [Philip Page]

1 Aug. **'I make a find in a Night Club'**: '… the excellent little band in Montmartre known as "Bricktop's" … [the leader] cannot actually read music [but] he is undoubtedly the most interesting figure in band music since Duke Ellington, and, like Ellington, he is not so much an arranger as composer.' Django Reinhardt: 'one of the most brilliant technicians on the guitar I have ever heard' playing with Grapelly [*sic*]

8 Aug. **'"Pub" Singers Could Teach High-Brows'**: amateur critics

15 Aug. **'Dictators are stupid about the Arts'**: André Gide, *Back from the USSR* and Kurt London, *The Seven Soviet Arts*

22 Aug. **'Banned Music'** (in Germany – with Hindemith 'sent to Coventry' – and Russia): 'I personally do not regard Shostakovich as an exceptionally good composer but he obviously has undoubted talent'

29 Aug. **'Left-Wings of Song'**: Rutland Boughton and Alan Bush: 'Neither of them, to be frank, is my favourite composer'; Boughton 'too saccharin' and Bush 'too ascetic to strike on my box'; Walton's Coronation March 'has not had words written to it, thank God, but it goes equally well to the phrase "My country, 'tis of thee" or "Hail to the I.L.P."'

5 Sept. **'In Praise of Prejudice'**: on William McNaught's *Modern Music and Musicians*

12 Sept. **'We Look, but Do Not See'**: on bad handwriting, etc.: 'I myself am infuriated when people address their envelopes to me as Constance Lambert or take my name over the telephone as Lambeth.'

19 Sept. **'Theatres Should Be Theatrical'**: good theatres: Leeds and Edinburgh

26 Sept. **'Strauss's Painful Music'**: *Wanderlust* and *Waltz* from *Intermezzo*

3 Oct. **'A High-Brow Dance Tickles Brain, But Not The Feet'**: Alan Bush's *Dance Overture*

10 Oct. **'Two New Names in Ballet'**: Karol Rathaus (composer) and Pierre Roy (painter) of de Basil's *Le Lion amoureux*

17 Oct. **'Tone With the Wind'** (Margaret Mitchell's *Gone with the Wind* was published in 1936, awarded the Pulitzer Prize in 1937, but not filmed until 1939): Prague Philharmonic Orchestra's tone 'so different from what we are accustomed in Western Europe'

24 Oct. **'Poker Ballet Won't Draw a Full House'**: Boult's *La Mer* 'the best I have heard so far'; Stravinsky's *Jeux de cartes*: 'It is impossible not to be intellectually entertained by the skill which has gone into Stravinsky's latest score. It is equally impossible to admit that it even comes into the same category as a work by a creative artist like Debussy or Berg.'

31 Oct. **'Beecham Worth a Guinea a Box'**: Rimsky-Korsakov, *Antar* Symphony; Tchaikovsky, *Romeo and Juliet* Overture

7 Nov. **'The Genius of Toscanini'**: Beethoven Symphonies 1 and 9: 'the best performance [of the first movement of the Ninth] ever given of the greatest symphonic movement ever written?'

14 Nov. **'Snub for Snobs'**: on Elgar's recordings, including *Falstaff*: 'only since Elgar's death have we realised how great his performances were'

21 Nov. **'Kitten on the Strings'**: 1st perf. of Tovey's Cello Concerto with Casals: 'I am told by those who had the moral physical and intellectual stamina to sit it out to the end that Professor Donald Tovey's Cello Concerto lasts for over an hour. This I cannot vouch for as, like several other musicans, I was compelled to leave at the end of the first movement, which seemed to last as long as my first term at school, but was probably a little shorter in fact. I therefore find myself in the melancholy position of not being able to delight my readers with an account of the work as a whole. All I can say is that the first movement is the most completely null and void piece of music I have ever heard at Queen's Hall. (And I have had some gruelling experiences in my day.)'

28 Nov. **'Britain is a German Colony'**: 'Most of the critics in England may be regarded as honorary German [in attitude]'; Monteux, 'one of the first half-dozen living conductors, has only appeared hear twice since the war'; Roger Désormière 'has never been given a single concert here'

5 Dec. **'The Music I Put on the Map'**: Beecham all-Sibelius concert: 'When two or three years ago someone said to me a trifle sneeringly, "I see you've joined the Sibelius cult," I replied with characteristic modesty, "I haven't joined it. I started it."

12 Dec. **'Brilliant, But Not Box-Office'**: Sargent concert of Haydn, 'Drum-Roll' Symphony; Dvořák, Violin Concerto; Bax, 5th Symphony

19 & 26 Dec. [No entry]

1938

2 Jan. **'Genius Looked Like Jockey'**: on the death of Ravel

9 Jan. **'Constant Lambert says that once the band was better than the circus, but now the circus BEATS THE BAND'**: 'When, as a child, I was taken to the circus, I remember I used to be laughed at for paying more attention to the brass band than to the horses.'

16 Jan. **'Great Britten'**: Britten's and Rawsthorne's Variations for Strings 'give one renewed faith in the younger generation of English composers'; Lambert was only able to hear the rehearsal for the first performance of Moeran's Symphony: 'the work as a whole is recognisably individual and recognisably English in style. It should have a great success.'

23 Jan. [No entry]

30 Jan. **'Song of an Eaglet'**: Prokofiev, Violin Concerto No. 2 and *Romeo and Juliet* Suite No. 2: 'someone said "He is not an eaglet who will become an eagle; he will always remain an eaglet"'

6 Feb. **'Old Colonel and Old Hat'**: Boult, replacing Harty in Elgar Symphony No. 2: 'never been heard to better advantage. He gave an interpretation that had both fire and continuity. … Those who look upon Elgar as the *brave bourgeois* of English music will eventually have to remodel their opinions.'

13 Feb. **'Three New Works'**: Bartók, Fifth String Quartet; Françaix, Piano Concerto; Stanley Bate, Concertino; Mahler, Symphony No. 8 ('bigger in quantity than in quality – the actual musical material … is often trivial and conventional, and not all the composer's consummate orchestral skills can disguise the fact.')

20 & 27 Feb. [No entry]

6 Mar. **'Malipiero Again'**: Boult conducts Malipiero's Symphony (No. 1)

Appendix 5
Constant Lambert's Talks for the BBC

T HE times given in some cases are the beginning and the ending of the programme (e.g. *Music Magazine*) and not necessarily of Lambert's contribution.

20 February 1931
'New Friends in Music – 1. Mr. Constant Lambert – Debussy': BBC London Regional 8.30–9.00 p.m. (The remaining talks, as announced in *The Times* on the day, were 2: Stravinsky by Edwin Evans, 27 February; 3: Vaughan Williams by Boult, 6 March; 4: *Morning Heroes* by Bliss, 13 March; 5: Bax by Percy Scholes, 20 March; 6: Holst by Hely-Hutchinson, 27 March) Script not found.

27 December 1935
Introductory talk to the Winter Proms: BBC National Programme after the 9 o'clock news. Script not found.

15 April 1936
'The Origins of Modern Dance Music' (first of two illustrated talks): National Programme 8.30–8.50 p.m. Script in BBC Archives. Printed in *The Listener*, 22 April 1936, pp. 792–3. Records used: *There are some things you never forget* (International Novelty Orchestra) and *Stack o'Lee Blues* (Warings Pennsylvanians). See Appendix 6.

24 April 1936
'Dance Music Today' (second of two illustrated talks): National Programme 9.05–9.25 p.m. Script in BBC Archives. Printed in *The Listener*, 29 April 1936, pp. 844–5. Records used: Duke Ellington *Mood Indigo* Parlophone R866 and *Hot and Bothered* R582 (Harlem Footwarmers = Duke Ellington Orchestra); *Donegal Cradle Song* (Spike Hughes and his Negro Orchestra) Decca F3717. See Appendix 6.

24 August 1936
'The Vic-Wells Ballet' ['Diaghilev, Tchaikovsky and the Ballet']: Scottish Programme 10.30–10.45 p.m. (on the occasion of the visit to Edinburgh of the Sadler's Wells Ballet). BBC Sound Archives, 12910, 3′15″ NSA NP9506/01; rebroadcast BBC Radio 3 on 9 March 1972 and 7 March 1994. CD: Dutton CDBP9761. Script in BBC Archives.

1938
'Music and the Ordinary Listener: The Instruments of the Orchestra': National Programme 6.30–7.00 p.m.

[21 February – 1 (on woodwind*) +

28 February – 2 (on woodwind*)] +

7 March – 3 (on brass) Script in BBC Archives.

14 March – [4, not numbered] (on strings) Script in BBC Archives.

21 March – 5 (on strings*) Script not found.

28 March [6, not numbered] (on percussion*) Script not found.

  * according to the introduction to the first programme (which suggested that the 14 March programme would be on brass)

  + Scott Goddard gave the first two talks as Lambert had to cancel because of bronchitis. Replying to Barnes' letter of February 22 CL wrote: 'Provided you don't mind a Tallulah Bankhead voice I am prepared to carry on from March 7th. As far as I remember this is on brass. Isn't it to be followed the next week by percussion, then strings? I think it will be better to take percussion before strings so as to stick to the usual order of the full score.'

9 January 1939
'Music and the Ballet – Tchaikovsky' (the first of six weekly programmes of gramophone records presented by Constant Lambert): National Programme 4.30–5.00 p.m. The scripts for the whole series do not seem to have survived.

16 January 1939
'Music and the Ballet – Ballet and the Masque' (the second of six weekly programmes of gramophone records presented by Constant Lambert): National Programme 4.30–5.00 p.m.

23 January 1939
'Music and the Ballet – Diaghilev: Pre-war' (the third of six weekly programmes of gramophone records presented by Constant Lambert): National Programme 4.30–5.00 p.m.

30 January 1939
'Music and the Ballet – Diaghilev: post-war' (the fourth of six weekly programmes of gramophone records presented by Constant Lambert): National Programme 4.30–5.00 p.m.

6 February 1939
'Music and the Ballet – Ballet in Opera' (the fifth of six weekly programmes of gramophone records presented by Constant Lambert): National Programme 4.30–5.00 p.m.

13 February 1939
'Music and the Ballet – Ballet Today' (the sixth of six weekly programmes of gramophone records presented by Constant Lambert): National Programme 4.30–5.00 p.m.

20 May 1940
'Escape from Holland' (not detailed in *Radio Times* but given in 'At Short Notice' series 'reserved for talks that cannot be announced in advance'): Home Service 7.05–7.15 p.m. BBC Sound Archives 14620. NSA NP9506/02. (Extract in *The BBC Scrapbook for 1940*, LP, Philips 6382 042.) Script in BBC Archives.

16 January 1941
'Constant Lambert and the Dante Sonata': for North American transmission. Script not found.

23 June 1941
'Ballet First Night': 'A reconstruction of the production of a ballet (in London in wartime) followed from its first conception, through the stages of discussion and rehearsal, ending with the opening bars of the overture. The material for the programme, which will include recordings of Constant Lambert, Ninette de Valois and Robert Helpmann taken in rehearsal, will be supplied by Constant Lambert, with the help of Ninette de Valois and the Sadler's Wells Ballet. Produced by Stephen Potter.' (The ballet was from Gluck's *Orfe ed Euridice*, with Lambert playing brief extracts at the piano.) Home Service 9.20–10.00 p.m. Recorded on 17 and 19 June. Leslie French and Lambert each contributed one-third of the script. BBC Sound Archives; NSA FE 3811–2. Script not found.

28 December 1943
'Puccini: Constant Lambert discusses, with gramophone records, some less familiar aspects of Puccini's music': Forces Programme 5.30–6.00 p.m. Script not found.

5 November 1944
'John Philip Sousa (born November 6 1854)': contribution to BBC *Music Magazine*, Home Service 11 a.m. (recorded London 3.15 p.m., 3 November); rebroadcast 9 March 1952 in *Music Magazine*, Home Service 11.30 a.m.–12.10 p.m. as 'Music Magazine remembers: John Philip Sousa, by the late Constant Lambert'. Script not found.

20 May 1945
'The Music of William Walton: an illustrated talk': contribution to BBC *Music Magazine*, Home Service 11.00–11.45 a.m. Script not found.

13 January 1946
'Emmanuel Chabrier (born January 18 1841)': contribution to BBC *Music Magazine*, Home Service 11.00–11.45 a.m. Recorded 8 January. Script not found.

7 April 1946
'Albert Roussel': contribution to BBC *Music Magazine*, Home Service 11.00–11.45 a.m. Script in BBC Archives.

2 June 1946
'Elgar's orchestral music': contribution to BBC *Music Magazine* edition on Elgar, Home Service 11.00–11.45 a.m. 10 guineas. Script in BBC Archives.

12 October 1947
'Vaughan Williams as a teacher': contribution to BBC *Music Magazine* edition on Vaughan Williams' 75th birthday, Home Service 7.15–7.45 p.m. Script in BBC Archives.

8 February 1948
'Two Operatic Manons'; contribution to BBC *Music Magazine*, Home Service 7.15–7.45 p.m. Script not found.

1948
Delius – possibly rehearsed/recorded 2 March and due to be broadcast on 17 March. Not located in *Radio Times*. 20 guineas. Script not found.

5 March 1948
'Musical Curiosities – 2: A programme of unusual music. Introduced by Constant Lambert, assisted by James W. Merrett and J. Edward Merrett (double basses), Ronald Smith and Lionel Salter (piano), and Frederick Stone (piano and harmonium)' (an occasional series, the first not located): BBC Third Programme 6.00–6.30 p.m. 10 guineas. Script not found.

18 April 1948
'Suppé (b. April 18 1819)': contribution to BBC *Music Magazine*, Home Service 7.00–7.45 p.m. Script not found.

7 July 1948
'Musical Curiosities – 4'. Assisted by Ronald Smith (pno.), Gwendolen Mason (harp), Isolde Alexis (mandoline), Frederick Stone (pno.) and BBC Women's Chorus. BBC Third Programme 6.20–6.50 p.m. (including *The Muses* by Hahn). Script not found.

17 November 1948
'Techniques: Ballet. Discussion by experts on various techniques whose fusion constitutes to techniques of ballet, with Arnold Haskell, Robert Helpmann, Michael Ayrton and Constant Lambert, with Michael Hordern as interlocuter.' Third Programme 10.00–11.00 p.m. repeated 18 November 7.15–8.15 p.m. and 12 January 1949 6.00–7.00 p.m. (Transcript of Lambert's contribution printed in *Dancing Times*, January 1949, pp. 192–3, as 'Music for Ballet'.)

16 December 1948
'Writers and Music No. 12: Music and the Nineties. An illustrated talk by Constant Lambert (BBC Recording)' (last talk in the series): BBC Third Programme 10.15–10.45 p.m. Recorded 14 December. 30 guineas. Script not found.

26 December 1948
'Cats and Music, recorded by Constant Lambert': contribution to BBC *Music Magazine*, Home Service 11.15–11.55 a.m. NSA recording BSA8123WR; B7085/1 6' 9"; rebroadcast 24 December 1972 and 3 August 1990. Printed in *Music Magazine: Selections from the BBC Programme*, chosen and edited by Anna Instone and Julian Herbage (London: Rockliff, 1953), pp. 53–7.

8 June 1949
'Erik Satie' (introductory talk to three programmes of his music): BBC Third Programme 10.35–10.55 p.m. (rehearsal 9.30 p.m.); producer, Alec Robertson. Script in BBC Archives.

27 November 1949
'Puccini (d. Nov. 29 1924): A commemoration for the 25th anniversary of his death, with contributions from Mosco Carner, Spike Hughes and Constant Lambert': contribution to BBC *Music Magazine*, Home Service broadcast 11.30 a.m.–12.10 p.m. (Rehearsal/recording 26 November instead of 8 November because of illness.) Script not found.

5 December 1949

'Bernard Van Dieren: Constant Lambert, who was a personal friend, sketches a portrait of the composer': BBC Third Programme 10.40–11.00 p.m. (rehearsal 9.40 p.m.); producer, Alec Robertson. Script in BBC Archives. Cecil Gray intended to include the script of this talk in the book on van Dieren that he was working on until his own death the same year as Lambert's. It was to be edited by John Goss.

21 May 1950

'Lord Berners: an appreciation by Constant Lambert': contribution to BBC *Music Magazine*, Home Service 11.30 a.m. – 12.10 p.m. Script not found.

16 February 1951

'Lord Berners (1883–1950): A tribute by Constant Lambert' as an introduction to two memorial programmes of his music: BBC Third Programme 6.35–7.15 p.m. Recorded 14 February 1951 and repeated 18 June 1956 in *Best of Yesterday* and 2 December 1972. BBC Sound Archives 18870–1. 13 mins. NSA recording NP9506/03. Script in BBC Archives.

Appendix 6
Constant Lambert's BBC Talks on Modern Dance Music (Jazz)

1 The Origins of Modern Dance Music

BBC National Programme, 15 April 1936
Printed in *The Listener*, 22 April 1936, pp. 792–3

Like most subjects about which people lose their tempers, jazz has never actually been defined. I shall certainly not attempt to define it here. I value my peace of mind too much, and I fear the avalanche of letters that would arrive from the innumerable Leagues, Societies and Clubs formed for the promotion of what is known as jazz, hot rhythm, or 'swing' music. It is odd that jazz, which is supposed to be a genial and popular form of art, should be taken with such immense seriousness, both by those who hate it, and those who admire it. On the one hand, we get angry old Colonels and pure-minded humourists talking about 'swamp stuff', 'Negro decadence', 'aping the manners of the jungle', and so forth. On the other hand we get the earnest jazz fans and Negro propagandists, who imagine that jazz is the most progressive music of our times, and who compare rival trombonists with all the solemnity of Wagnerians comparing rival Isoldes.

As usual, I find myself between two camps, two fires; not to mention two stools. To the angry old Colonel I should say that jazz, far from being 'swamp stuff', is not nearly barbaric enough for my taste. To the devotee of such music, I should say that jazz, far from being progressive, has not altered one bit for the last five years. But to both I should say, whatever jazz is – it is not African in any way. It is a product, not of the primitive jungle, but of the modern city.

I am not denying for one moment that the best jazz composers and players are Negroes, but they are sophisticated Americans, and not primitive Africans. If we look at African folk music we find that although it has an interesting melodic line and fascinating rhythmic sense, the tunes and rhythms have practically nothing in common with dance music as we know it. If they remind one of any European music, they remind one of Stravinsky's Russian peasant ballet, *Les Noces*, and, indeed, Paul Morand mentions in one of his books that African Negroes to whom he played them could make nothing of jazz records, and infinitely preferred listening to records of Russian folk songs. But more important than the question of tune or rhythm is the fact that nowhere in African folk music do we find any trace of harmony as we know it, and without its 'blue' harmony, modern jazz would not exist. That eminent Teutonic authority, Dr M. von Hornbostel, in the whole of his researches on African music, only found one example of harmony in the Western sense, and that was in a comic song about the local missionary, where the natives put in chords at the end to parody the lugubrious effect of his harmonium.

(Music example)[1]

Dr von Hornbostel has also stated that there is a distinct connection between African folk music and Indo-Chinese music, noticeably the music of the East Indies, which, as we know, has nothing in common with Western music, particularly Western dance music. The same conclusion has independently been arrived at by a less scientific

---

[1] The music examples have been omitted.

and more popular authority, Mr Paul Robeson. So I think that to some extent we can count Africa out when talking about jazz, but we cannot count the Negro out. The question is what exactly is it that the Negro has given to modern dance music.

Though the African slaves may have taken their folk music to the plantations, it is doubtful if in pure form it lasted any longer than their native language. What they certainly did take, however, was an astonishing musical instinct and aptitude for giving a peculiar individual twist to the European music they heard and tried to reproduce. In the case of Negroes who went to English and American possessions, they came into contact with the sentimental, not to say juicy, religious music of the Anglo-Saxons. The emotional impact of this richly harmonised music was, of course, enormously enhanced by the sentimental appeal of the words with their frequently expressed desire to escape from this vale of woe into a better land.

The Negro spiritual was the result of this impact, and for the first time we find Negroes singing spontaneously in Western harmony. But I think it is clear that these harmonic songs were completely acquired. If you go to the poor Negro dance halls in Paris, where the band consists of unsophisticated Negroes brought up in French Colonies, you will find that the band puts syncopations and rhythmic frills round the music in a most up-to-date fashion, but you will find that harmonically speaking, they get no further than the banal, threadbare harmonics of the music they have been brought up with – that is to say, French music-hall song.

Blue harmony, if I may be allowed the phrase, is the production of the English-speaking Negro, and, so far back as the nineteenth century, it was already beginning to influence highbrow music. I refer, of course, to the music of Delius, who spent much of his early life on a plantation in Florida where the Negroes used to come and sing to him in the evenings. He has recorded the vivid impression they made on him in two works, based on Negro subjects – *Appalachia*, variations on an old slave song, and *Koanga*, an opera whose hero and heroine are coloured. I should like to play one or two extracts from these works, because they are of great interest, and the first important example of the Negro influencing the white man, instead of the other way about.

The first is from *Koanga* – a wedding chorus sung by Negro slaves at the beginning of the second act –

(Music example)

I am not saying that this is an authentic record, but we know that Delius was trying to capture as far as possible the atmosphere of the Negro spiritual of his day. The influence of the hymn is obvious in the four-square construction, but we can see the Negro touch in the melancholy cadences and sensual harmonic elements which were later to crystallise into the blues.

The other example, rather more elaborate, is from the Finale of *Appalachia*, which deals with the tragedy of a Negro who has been transported to another plantation and has to leave his sweetheart.

(Music example)

The solo voice sings first, and is answered by the chorus. Here we get more of the syncopation, which, although unlike the rhythm of African folk music, is typical of the American Negro.

The rhythmic side of popular music, which most people would think of as the most important element in jazz, was, of course, being developed at the same time, but on the whole separately. Just as the Negro gave a melancholy and individual turn to the religious music of the nineteenth century, so he gave an equally individual but thoroughly cheerful tone to the old dances of the nineteenth century, such as the schottische. There is nothing melancholy or nostalgic about the cakewalk, with its clattering gaiety. *Rastus on Parade, Smokey Mokes*, and other tunes of the kind, which some of us can remember on old player piano rolls, are as resolutely cheerful as the marches of Sousa. Nevertheless, like the Negro spiritual, they represent one of the germs of modern jazz. In the course of time, the syncopations of the cakewalk became more exaggerated and stylised, and eventually produced what was known before the War as ragtime. *Alexander's Ragtime Band*, though not the best tune of its type, is possibly the best remembered, and we may take it as typical of its period. If we compare it with the old cakewalks written ten years before, we see a difference, but not in kind. But if we compare it with a post-war jazz tune, we find ourselves in another world altogether. Nobody would mistake *Alexander's Ragtime Band* for a work written by a highbrow composer of the day, any more than they would have mistaken Debussy's *Golliwogg's Cakewalk* for a popular dance tune. But when Florence Mills and the first Blackbirds Company came to the London Pavilion in 1923 or thereabouts, the band, Will Vodery's, played an extremely beautiful prelude that, apart from its orchestration, might have been written by Delius. The Negro revue only occupied the second half of the programme, and the change from the English theatre orchestra playing what was to all intents and purposes ragtime, to the Negro jazz band was one of the most startling experiences of my life.

To give an idea of how suddenly and dramatically modern jazz appeared on the scene, I am going to play a record of one of the first 'blues' tunes, *Stack o'Lee Blues*, played by Warings Pennsylvanians, always one of the best American bands. It is only fair to warn you in advance that it is an old pre-electric recording, and that it has had a rough life. I would like you to pay particular attention to the very original and charming passage at the end.

(Music example)

On the other side of the same record there is a tune called *There are some things you never forget*, played by the International Novelty Orchestra. I don't think we need play more than a few bars of the opening.

(Music example)

Now I expect you will agree with me that although the second tune I played is hardly any advance on the pre-war ragtime, the first tune, if it were only re-recorded and slightly touched up, would easily pass as one of this year's records. In fact, although produced in the same year, these tunes might have been separated by twenty years. *Stack o'Lee Blues* establishes a type of music which is with us still. *There are some things you never forget* represents a class of music that has already been forgotten.

You may ask what it is that distinguishes jazz from the earlier forms of dance music. The answer, I think, is this. The jazz composer has taken over the whole technical equipment of the contemporary highbrow composer and adapted it to a popular basis. Compared with all earlier forms of popular music, it is definitely self-conscious and sophisticated. The melancholy of the Negro spiritual, the syncopated rhythms of the cakewalk have played their part in its formation, but so, too, have the harmonics, rhythms and orchestral tricks of the most modern composers. Delius in the 'nineties imitated the simple Negro; the clever Negro has now taken to imitating Delius. For the first time in the history of music the gap between highbrow and lowbrow has disappeared. In the nineteenth century you could tell a waltz written by a highbrow composer like Chopin or Chabrier from the waltzes of the popular hack writers by the fact that it was obviously better and more sophisticated; but, today, the fox-trots and blues of the highbrow composer like Ravel can usually be distinguished by the fact that they are less good and less sophisticated than the genuine article turned out in Tin-Pan Alley.

But I see that I am already overstepping the subject of my first talk, which is the origins of Jazz only. I will try with Jazz as we know it today in my talk next week.

2. Dance Music Today

BBC National Programme, 24 April 1936
Reprinted in *The Listener*, 29 April 1936, pp. 844–5

In my first talk on the origins of Jazz I ended by saying that it was the most sophisticated form of popular music in the whole of history, the only lowbrow music which could tackle highbrow music on its own ground. Jazz, however, is not only sophisticated in technique, but sophisticated in emotion. If Duke Ellington had written one of his Blues, such as *Mood Indigo*, before the War he would have interested a few musical critics and a few followers of Debussy, but he certainly would not have been classed as a popular composer. It is only since the War that neurasthenia has had a popular appeal. Compared to the Edwardians we are a neurasthenic and repressed generation. This, after all, is hardly surprising. The surprising thing is that we seem to glory in it. When Noël Coward wrote *Twentieth Century Blues* he was, as usual, giving the public exactly what it wanted. Before the War people expected dance music to be definitely cheerful and exhilarating. The waltzes of Mr Archibald Joyce had a certain autumnal feeling it is true but, generally speaking, Edwardian dance music reflected the rather touching optimism of the period. In a vulgar way of course. The one-steps and two-steps of those days were the musical equivalents of *Comic Cuts*.[2] The Jazz tunes of today have a more intellectual appeal; their weary sophistication is very much that of the satirical post-war novelists, like Evelyn Waugh and Anthony Powell.

The extraordinary melancholy of the average Jazz tune may possibly be due to the fact that so great a proportion is written by Jews, a race whose natural melancholy always comes out particularly strongly in their music. Just as the Negro found it easy to express his exiled feelings by associating them with the melancholy formula of English hymns: 'There is a happy land, far, far away' and so forth, so the Jew has found it easy to express his exiled feelings by associating them with the equally alien formula of the Negro who wants to get back to his black-mammy – invariably situated in one of the remoter states.

But although the average Jazz tune is usually written by a polygot Jew, the best Jazz music is still written by the Negroes themselves, and the melancholy of their blues has a certain dignity and austerity which we don't find in the typical Tin Pan Alley song of the complaining type such as *Mean to Me*, or *Dancing with Tears in My Eyes*.

Of the Negro composers the most outstanding is undoubtedly Duke Ellington, and indeed he is one of the most interesting and charming composers of today, Jazz apart. I should like to play you a record of *Mood Indigo* – one of his earlier compositions, but still one of his best and most typical (*The Mooch* and *Rude Interlude* are other famous examples of his style); the harmony and orchestration of the opening and closing sections are most original and subtle – the solos in the middle section almost remind one of Debussy in the freedom of their arabesque. The piece as a whole is well formed, in fact it is a composition that any modern composer might be glad to have written.

(Music example)

In order not to give too gloomy a picture of modern Jazz, I should like to play another Ellington record illustrating his more vigorous and rhythmic style – *Hot and*

---

[2] A British comic book that lasted from 1890 until 1953.

Bothered. This is definitely a show-piece, designed to bring into prominence each individual member of the band in turn; much as Rimsky-Korsakov, in his *Spanish Capriccio*, brings into prominence each section of the Symphony Orchestra in turn. The end, in which the saxophones play the original tune in three-part harmony against an obstinate rhythm on the brass, is one of Ellington's best strokes; although sophisticated in actual technique, its mood has something of the simple gaiety of the pre-war dance tunes.

(Music example)

Hot and Bothered may at first hearing sound just one dam' thing after another; merely a string of pleasant but disconnected tunes. But actually, like so many Jazz pieces, it is written in a fairly strict, not to say old-fashioned, form; one much favoured by the Elizabethan composers – that is to say, variations over a ground. Both the variations and the ground are, of course, treated much more freely than they were in Elizabethan days, but the principle remains roughly the same: you establish your tune, with its accompanying harmonies, and then instead of repeating the tune you indulge in arabesques over the same harmonic scheme, the tune remaining as a sort of echo in the mind of the listener, but not actually in his ears. Anyone who has heard a modern version in the Harlem style of one of the old tunes like *Japanese Sandman* or *Limehouse Blues* will realise the kind of thing I mean. In lots of Jazz bands the individual player is more or less left to himself to improvise the right kind of arabesque on the spur of the moment, thus providing a link with oriental music where improvisation plays so great a part. At first you would think that this improvisation would give an effect of great freedom, but actually it ends by having rather a cramping effect: it stands to reason that two or three players can only improvise at the same time when they know exactly what basis they are working on, and when this basis is a fairly simple one. The first time I heard Louis Armstrong's records I was fascinated by the virtuosity of the frills he put round the tune; but after a few hearings I soon became bored by the monotony of the harmonic framework underneath.

I am speaking of course more from the listener's point of view than from the dancer's point of view. This, I think, is quite a legitimate attitude. Owing to the gramophone and wireless, Jazz is far more listened to as music pure and simple than any early dance music, and this is all to the good. It probably accounts for the very high level of technical sophistication which the best Jazz has reached: what will pass muster in a crowded night-club, with everybody dressed up to the nines – not to mention being one over the eight – will not necessarily sound so good when listened to dispassionately on the gramophone. Jazz has already split up into two main branches. First there are the songs in definite verse and chorus form, which appear first of all in Revues and are then subsequently arranged by each Dance Band as it pleases. Then secondly there are the pieces without words, specially composed for one particular band, intended to be listened to as music – free in form, but taking the one-sided or two-sided record as their formal framework. Ellington's *Creole Rhapsody*, the 10" version, is the best example I know of the second type: though it can be danced to, it is obviously better to listen to it.

Of the composers who have followed Ellington in treating the Jazz record as an art form (a horrid phrase, but unavoidable), the most interesting, in my mind, is Spike Hughes. Although greatly influenced by Ellington, he has a distinct style of his own, and though he is very much more up-to-date and American than his English rivals he is, curiously enough, the only Jazz composer to have introduced into Jazz a specifically English quality. To show you that Jazz need not necessarily recall a 'joint' in Harlem, or one of those peculiarly gloomy night-clubs we always see in English films, I should like to play you Spike Hughes's *Donegal Cradle Song*. This is an amusing example of New World and Old World influences blended together. It was written for and performed by a Negro band in America. Yet the opening phrase is so successful in its evocation of an Irish tune that it has actually been mistaken for a folk song by some people – much to the delight of the composer.

(Music example)

I think that if, after hearing that, you cast your mind back to *Alexander's Ragtime Band* you will agree with me that the progress made by modern dance music in only 25 years is one of the most remarkable things in musical history. The question is, will it take a similar advance in the next 25 years? Personally I think not, and for a number of reasons. It is a great mistake to imagine that musical progress in any sense goes on at a steady pace; as I remarked in my first talk, even high-brow Jazz has altered very little in the last five years. The sudden efflorescence of Jazz after the war was largely due to the low-brow composer's taking over the sophisticated technique of the high-brow composer. The harmonies of Debussy and Delius have now become a commonplace and form the stock-in-trade of the writer of Jazz: it might be thought that the same game of intellectual Pat-a-Cake would continue – the nineteenth-century Negro influencing Delius, Delius influencing the post-war Negro, the post-war Negro influencing the post-war European composer, like Darius Milhaud, and so on. But one must remember that the harmonies of Debussy and Delius, even when unfamiliar, always had a great element of purely sensuous appeal; they also lent themselves to a nostalgic and sentimental treatment. The same cannot be said of the highbrow composers of the succeeding generation. A foxtrot in the harmonic style of Bartók or Schönberg is, quite frankly, a ghastly thought.

It is possible, of course, that the next generation of modern composers will write music more acceptable to the unsophisticated ear and, in that case, I think the following will occur. The split between the two types of Jazz – Jazz to listen to and Jazz to dance to – will become more marked. Highbrow Jazz will continue to become more highbrow, by a process of cross-fertilisation with concert hall music, and may eventually produce something widely removed from our present-day foxtrot. But dance music pure and simple will probably remain much the same – at present the only rival to the ordinary Jazz band is the Rumba band, which, while it provides a pleasant change of colour, is not capable of such variety or development. The foxtrot in one form or another is probably in for as long an innings as the waltz which, after all, remained practically unchanged for a hundred years or so.

There is a limit to the complications of rhythm which the European man in the street can take in, and an even more marked limit to the complications of rhythm he can perform. Modern bands can play elaborate cross-rhythms, but the ballroom dancer still sticks to the steady 1–2–3–4 he was brought up on: even a professional tap-dancer would probably be flummoxed by the rhythms of modern ballet music, let alone the rhythms of an American ritual song. No, I do not think we shall see any startling change in our ballrooms. Even Mr H. G. Wells, that untiring prophet of change, has shown in his film, 'The Shape of Things to Come', that the shape of furniture to come will be very much the same. If, in the Wellsian future, people still sit about on triangular pieces of glass, like debutantes in a modernistic cocktail bar, I see no reason to suppose that the music they dance to will be very much different from what I have played you tonight.

Appendix 7
Constant Lambert's Third Programme Broadcasts

Humphrey Searle, one of the producers for the Third Programme, wrote in a memoir of Lambert:

> From 1946 onwards I saw a great deal of him. I had returned to the BBC, and was putting on programmes for the newly created Third Programme. Here anything went, and I asked Constant to conduct as many programmes as he had time for, mostly of exotic and unknown works. The programmes ranged from Purcell and Boyce via Glinka, Marschner and Balakirev to a number of modern works of all schools. Constant was not very interested in performing the standard classics – though he admired Haydn – and he boasted that he had never conducted a symphony of Brahms. He was always against anything or any character who seemed to him pretentious or boring, but he could be extremely kind to any genuine person who needed his help. We again often met in the George – he was staying with the painter and sculptor Michael Ayrton round the corner in All Souls' Place – and we usually arranged our programmes in the pub, as he was no good at telephoning or writing letters. I sometimes stayed in his flat – he had a curious spare bed which came down out of the wall – and when I went to bed he would usually start work at the piano upstairs, often playing from midnight 'till 4 a.m. He was a nocturnal man, and was never happy at morning rehearsals, but when he got to the evening performances he was brilliant.

Lambert was not personally involved in programmes marked ♩.

29 Sept. 1946 BBC Third programme begins

10 Oct. 1946 9.30–10.20; 10.40–11.20 p.m.
  'Music by Liszt'
  Valentine Dyall (orator), Henry Cummings, BBC Chorus, BBC Orchestra, cond. Lambert
    Two Episodes from Lenau's *Faust*: The Procession by Night; The Dance in the Village Hall –
      1st Mephisto Waltz
    Galop in A minor (orch. Jacob)
    Les Morts for orator, chorus and orchestra, 1st English performance
    Schubert–Liszt, *Cavalry March*
    Symphonic Poem *Hamlet*
    Es muss ein Wunderbares sein, song with orchestra
    Die Vätergruft, song with orchestra
    Hungarian Coronation March – Graduale for chorus and orchestra

17 Oct. 1946 7.40–8.30; 8.45–9.30 p.m.
  BBC Symphony Orchestra, cond. Lambert
    Balakirev, Overture *King Lear*
    Lambert, *Aubade héroïque*
    Sibelius, Symphony No. 6 (followed by interval)
    Rameau–Gevaert, Suite *Castor et Pollux*
    Chabrier, *Suite pastorale*

♩ 20 Nov. 1946 8.00–9.00 p.m.
  Emelie Hooke, Nikita Magaloff
    Lambert, *Seven Poems of Li-Po*
    Bliss, *The Women of Yueh*
    Prokofiev, Sonata No. 7
    Goossens, Five Songs
  Lambert and Prokofiev only rebroadcast on 16 January 1947

21 Nov. 1946 6.45–7.45; 8.00–8.45 p.m.
  'Romantic Composers'
  Guilhermina Suggia, Muriel Brunskill, BBC Symphony Orchestra, cond. Lambert
    Marschner, Overture *Hans Heiling*
    Tchaikovsky, *Variations on a Rococo Theme*
    Glinka, Incidental music to *Prince Kholmsky*
    Dargomizhsky, *Kazachok* (followed by interval)
    Berlioz, *Dance of the Slaves* (*The Trojans*)
    Berlioz, *La Captive* song with orchestra
    Liszt, Symphonic Poem *From the Cradle to the Grave*
    Liszt, *Mephisto Waltz* No. 2

4 Jan. 1947 8.00–9.00 p.m.
  Joan Cross, Isobel Baillie, Joan Fullerton, Phyllis Harrison, Gladwys Palmer, Dennis
  Noble, Trefor Jones; narrated by Dennis Arundell; spoken by Valentine Dyall; Boris Ord
  (harpsichord), BBC Theatre Chorus, Boyd Neel Orchestra, cond. Lambert
    Purcell, *Dido and Aeneas*, ed. E. J. Dent
  produced by Constant Lambert and Stanford Robinson
  'A Masterpiece in Miniature' by Dennis Arundell, *Radio Times* 27 Dec. 1946, p. 4

5 Jan. 1947 8.30–9.30 p.m.
  live repeat of Purcell, *Dido and Aeneas*

6 Jan. 1947 9.45–11.10 p.m.
  'Lambert and Walton'
  *Edward Walker (fl), Frank Hughes (E flat cl), *Bernard Walton (cl), *Wilfred Hambleton
    (bcl), *Walter Lear (a sax), *Harold Jackson (tpt), Stanley Brown (tbn), *James Blades (perc),
    Raymond Clark (vc), E. Chesterman (db), Kyla Greenbaum (pf) [players in *Façade*]
    Lambert: Concerto for Piano and Nine Players (Kyla Greenbaum)
    Edith Sitwell taking about *Façade* (approx. 10.15 p.m.)
    Walton, *Façade* (speaker Lambert, conductor Leighton Lucas)
  recording rebroadcast on 18 June

16 Jan. 1947 approx. 8.33 p.m. (from RAH)
  part of Winter Prom.
  BBC Symphony Orchestra
    Lambert, *King Pest* (cond. Lambert)
  beginning of 2nd half of concert; remainder conducted by Boult

❡ 16 Jan. 1947 11.30 p.m.
  Emelie Hooke, Nikita Magaloff
    Lambert, *Seven Poems of Li-Po*
    Prokofiev, Sonata No. 7
  recording of broadcast of 20 November 1946

25 Jan. 1947 7.30–8.15; 8.30–9.30 p.m. (from People's Palace)
  Marjorie Avis (sop), Kathleen Long (pf), BBC Symphony Orchestra, cond. Lambert
    Berlioz, Overture *Les Francs-Juges*
    Field, Piano Concerto No. 2 in A flat
    Liszt, *Symphony to Dante's Divina Commedia*

6 Mar. 1947 6.15–6.55 p.m.
  Warlock, *The Curlew*, introduced and conducted by Lambert
  Radio Times, 23 Feb – 8 Mar not printed due to paper shortage; in *Times* broadcasting listing
  given as 'Moeran and Warlock recital'

11 Mar. 1947 6.00–6.40 p.m.
  David Franklin (bass), BBC Symphony Orchestra, cond. Lambert
    Marschner, Incidental music to *The Goldsmith of Ulm*

23 Mar. 1947 10.05–11.00 p.m.
> Martin Boddey (tenor), Hervey Alan (bar), John Alexandra (bn), BBC Men's Chorus, Boyd
> Neel Orchestra, cond. Lambert
>> Purcell–Holst, *The Gordian Knot Untied* Suite No. 2
>> Lutyens, Concerto for bassoon and string orchestra
>> Lambert, *Dirge from 'Cymbeline'*, 1st performance full version
>> Maurice Jaubert, *Trois Intermèdes*

7 June 1947 7.30–8.30; 8.45–9.30 p.m.
> soloist not named, BBC Chorus, BBC Symphony Orchestra, cond. Lambert
>> Lambert. *Summer's Last Will and Testament*
> remainder of concert conducted by Boult

11 June 1947 10.05–10.50 p.m.
> one of a series of 5 programmes on Peter Warlock arranged and introduced by Elizabeth
> Poston
> Pierre Barnac (bar), Geoffrey Gilbert (fl), Leon Goossens (cor anglais), Aeolian String Quartet,
> cond. Lambert
>> Warlock, *Two Saudades* and *The Curlew*
> ❬ Prog. 1: 1 June 1947, 'The Root and the Flower' with soloists, Aeolian String Quartet, BBC
> Chorus, Welbeck Orchestra, cond. Maurice Miles
> ❬ Prog. 3: 17 June, 'Choral and Orchestral Works including Christmas Songs and Carols', cond.
> Anthony Bernard
> ❬ Prog. 4: 22 June, 'The Country Songs' with soloists and BBC Chorus, cond. Leslie Woodgate
> ❬ Prog. 5: 26 June, 'The Love Songs' with Heddle Nash

18 June 1947 7.45–8.35 p.m.
> repeat of broadcast of *Façade* from 6 January preceded by introductory talk by Edith Sitwell

13 Aug. 1947 7.45–8.40 p.m.
> 'Moeran and Lambert'
>> Moeran, Cello Sonata (Peers Coetmore and Frederick Jackson)
> repeat of broadcast on 5 June 1947
>> Lambert, Concerto for Piano and Nine Players
> repeat of broadcast on 6 January

2 Oct. 1947 6.30–7.30 p.m.
> 'Contemporary British Composers – Constant Lambert and Michael Tippett'
> Gareth Morris (fl), Natalie James (ob), Pauline Juler (cl), J. Edward Merrett (db), Zorian String
> Quartet, cond. Lambert
>> Tippett, String Quartet No. 2 (Zorian String Quartet)
>> Lambert, piano pieces (Louis Kentner): Siciliana (*Pomona*); *Elegy*; Saraband for the
>>   Followers of Virgo (*Horoscope*);
>> Lambert, *Eight Poems of Li-Po* for voice (Martin Boddey) and 8 instruments

14 Nov. 1947 9.30–10.25 p.m.
> Philharmonia Orchestra, cond. Lambert
>> Balakirev, Overture *King Lear*
>> Roussel, *Pour une fête de printemps*
>> Bax, *The Tale the Pine Trees Knew*
>> Lambert, *Music for Orchestra*

16 Feb. 1948
> 'Turning-Points in 20th Century Music – 5' (one of a series of programmes devised and
> introduced by Edward Clark)
> 7.15–8.05 p.m.
> Philharmonia Orchestra, cond. Lambert
>> Bartók, *Two Portraits* (soloist Leonard Hirsch)
>> Bartók, Second Suite Op. 4

❡ 8.25–9.35 p.m.

    Bartók, *Bluebeard's Castle* (Swiss Radio recording cond. Victor Reinshagen)

❡ Prog. 1: 19 January Schoenberg, String Quartet No. 1 (Philharmonic String Quartet)

❡ Prog. 2: 24 January Schoenberg, *Pelleas und Melisande* (BBC Symphony Orchestra, Scherchen)

❡ Prog. 3: 28 January Schoenberg, *Verklärte Nacht* and String Quartet No. 2 (Jacques String Quartet, Scherchen)

❡ Prog. 4: 9 February Bartók, piano pieces (Kyla Greenbaum)

5 Mar. 1948 6.00–6.30 p.m.

  'Musical Curiosities – 2' (one of a series devised by Searle with ideas from Lambert, Rawsthorne, Moeran and others)

  'A programme of unusual music. Introduced by Constant Lambert assisted by James W. Merrett and J. Edward Merrett (double bass), Ronald Smith and Lionel Salter (piano), and Frederick Stone (piano and harmonium).' Paid 10 guineas.

    Searle, *Quadrille with a Raven*

'The Third Programme was becoming somewhat solemn and esoteric – one Planner is reputed to have deleted Brahms' 4th Symphony from a proposed programme as being a "repertory work" – so I thought I might brighten it up by introducing some programmes of absurd or comic music. This led to a series called 'Musical Curiosities' which ran for several years. We had three main kinds of music; parodies or pastiches – like Fauré and Messager's Quadrilles on themes from Wagner's Ring or Chabrier's Quadrilles on themes from Tristran; works by people who were not normally thought of as composers, such as Jean-Jacques Rousseau, Samuel Butler and Nietzsche; and pieces which were so bad as to be funny, like [Sir Joseph] Barnby's Rebecca [Rebekah] or [George] Tolhurst's Ruth. I found some able collaborators in Constant Lambert and Alan Rawsthorne, who both came up with some brilliant suggestions, and also E. J. Moeran, who wrote an excellent script for one programme.'

1 May 1948 9.20–10.50 p.m.

  Trefor Anthony, BBC Symphony Orchestra, cond. Lambert

    Marschner, Overture *Hans Heiling*

    ❡ Bax, *The Bard of Dimbovitza*, 1st performance revised version Flora Nielsen – performance changed owing to indisposition of Flora Nielsen – Liszt substituted

    Liszt, Two Episodes from Lenau's *Faust*

    Weber, Wo berg' ich mich (from *Euryanthe*)

    Dukas, Symphony in G

7 July 1948 6.20–6.50 p.m.

  'Musical Curiosities – 4'

  assisted by Ronald Smith (pf), Gwendolen Mason (hp), Isolde Alexis (mandolin), Frederick Stone (pf), BBC Women's Chorus

    included Reynaldo Hahn, *The Muses*

  paid 15 guineas

❡ 24 Aug. 1948 6.00–7.00 p.m.

  'Chamber Concert'

  Victoria Sladen, Martin Boddey, Geoffrey Gilbert, Peter Newbury, Bernard Walton, Maria Korchinska, Jean Pougnet, Ernest Element, Frederick Riddle, William Pleeth, James W. Merrett

    Four pieces for flute, viola, cello and harp (Caldara, Rameau, Pergolesi, Vivaldi arr. Pilney)

    Hadley, *Ephemera*

    D'Indy, Suite for flute, viola, cello and harp

    Lambert, *Eight Poems of Li-Po*

7 Oct. 1948 8.10–8.50; 9.05–9.55 p.m.
    BBC Symphony Orchestra, cond. Lambert
        Marschner, Overture *The Goldsmith of Ulm*
        Barber, Violin Concerto (Frederick Grinke)
        Glazunov, Symphony No. 2

12 Oct. 1948 8.30–9.40 p.m.
    London Symphony Orchestra, cond. Lambert
        Rimsky-Korsakov, Overture *Ivan the Terrible*
        Berkeley, Piano Concerto (Colin Horseley)
        Sibelius, *Luonnotar* (Emelie Hooke)
        Sibelius, Symphony No. 6

❡ 30 Nov. 1948
    Compton Mackenzie 'What is Light Music?' – a talk, followed by a concert given by Royal
    Philharmonic Orchestra, cond. Beecham (Hérold, Saint-Saëns, Bizet, Fauré, Chabrier). This
    was an introduction to a series of light music programmes in the coming weeks, conducted
    by Stanford Robinson, Josef Krips and the Vienna Philharmonic Orchestra, Barbirolli and the
    Hallé, and Lambert.

10 Dec. 1948 6.20–7.05 p.m.
    Edward Walker, Bernard Walton, Wilfred Hambleton, Walter Lear, Harold Jackson, James
    Blades, Raymond Clark
        Walton, *Façade* (Lambert speaker; cond. Leighton Lucas)
    rebroadcast on 31 January 1949

16 Dec. 1948 10.15–10.45 p.m.
    'Writers and Music No. 12: Music and the Nineties. An illustrated talk by Constant Lambert
    (BBC Recording)' (final talk in the series, recorded on 14 December)

19 Dec. 1948 10.10–11.10 p.m.
    'Light Orchestral Concert No. 4'
    Philharmonia Orchestra, cond. Lambert
        Tchaikovsky, *Mazeppa – Gopak*
        Tchaikovsky, Symphony No. 3 – Alla tedesca
        Liadov, Eight Russian Folk Songs
        Glinka, *Valse-fantaisie*
        Rimsky-Korsakov, *Mlada: Cortège of the Nobles*
        Rimsky-Korsakov, *The Snow Maiden* Suite

23 Dec. 1948 8.30–9.25; 9.40–10.25 p.m.
    BBC Symphony Orchestra, cond. Lambert
        Berlioz, Overture *Les Francs-Juges*
        Bartók, Violin Concerto (Max Rostal)
        Balakirev, Symphony No. 1

1 Jan. 1949 8.15–9.20; 9.35–10.15 p.m.
    Margaret Ritchie, Joan Alexander, Richard Lewis, Trevor Jones, Owen Brannigan, Thurston
    Dart, George Thalben-Ball, BBC Chorus, Philharmonia Orchestra, cond. Lambert
        Handel, *Alexander's Feast*, ed. Basil Lam
    BBC Recording

12 Jan. 1949 6.00–6.50 p.m.
    'Techniques of the Ballet: A Discussion.' 'Discussion by experts on various techniques whose
    fusion constitutes to techniques of ballet, with Arnold Haskell, Frederick Ashton, Michael
    Ayrton and Constant Lambert, with Michael Hordern as interlocuter.'
    Transcript of Lambert's contribution printed as 'Music for Ballet' in *Dancing Times*, Jan. 1949,
    pp. 192–3

23 Jan. 1949 6.15–8.35 p.m. (with two 10-minute intervals)
   Boris Ord, BBC Chorus, Actors: Ralph Truman, John Chandos, Abraham Sofaer. Felix Felton,
   Geoffrey Wincott, Malcolm Graeme; singers: Margaret Field-Hyde, Ena Mitchell, Nancy
   Evans, John Kentish, Trevor Jones, Henry Cummings, Trefor Anthony, Norman Walker; New
   London Orchestra, cond. Lambert; producer Maurice Brown
      King Arthur or *The British Worthy* by John Dryden
      Music by Henry Purcell ed. Cyril Rootham and Dennis Arundell

25 Jan. 1949 8.50–11.10 p.m.
   live repeat of broadcast of 23 January
   In an internal BBC memo John Lowe wrote on 3 February 1949: 'I cannot hope to hear better
   conducting of Purcell than was done by Constant Lambert. The players provided by the New
   London Orchestra were not all of the first rank.'

31 Jan. 1949 10.50–11.30 p.m.
      Walton, *Façade*
   repeat of broadcast of 10 December 1948 with Lambert speaker and Leighton Lucas conductor

1 Feb. 1949 8.25–9.20 p.m.
   'Chamber Music'
   members of BBC Symphony Orchestra, cond. Lambert
      Guillaume de Machaut, *Double Hocquet*, arr. Malcolm Arnold
      Mozart, Divertimento No. 11 in D
      Stravinsky, *Octet for wind*

6 Mar. 1949 8.30–9.10; 9.25–10.05; 10.25–11.15 p.m.
   Margaret Ritchie, Audrey Strange, Catherine Lawson, Marjorie Thomas, Alfred Deller,
   Richard Lewis, George Armitage, Victor Harding, George James; continuo: Thornton
   Lofthouse and Raymond Clark; George Thalben-Ball, London Philharmonic Choir,
   Philharmonia Orchestra, cond. Lambert
      Handel, *Semele*

13 Mar. 1949 7.15–7.55; 8.15–9.00; 9.15–10.05 p.m.
   repeat of broadcast of 6 March

14 Apr. 1949 8.40–9.25 p.m.
   Vivaldi programme
   section of Philharmonia Orchestra, cond. Lambert
      Violin Concerto Op. 3 No. 9 (Campoli)
      Oboe Concerto in F (Terence MacDonagh)
      Concerto Grosso (1738)
   1st of 4 programmes – Trevor Harvey, 25 April; Boyd Neel, 11 May; Anthony Bernard, 27 May

17 May 1949 7.00–7.45; 8.05–8.50 p.m.
   'Contemporary Music' (London Contemporary Music Centre; before an invited audience in
   the Concert Hall, Broadcasting House)
   Mary and Geraldine Peppin (2 pf), BBC Chorus, section of Philharmonia Orchestra, cond.
   Leighton Lucas and Leslie Woodgate
      Stravinsky, Sonata for 2 pianos
      Wilfrid Mellers, 2 Motets (cond. Woodgate), 1st performance
      Lambert, *Trois pièces nègres pour les touches blanches*, 1st performance
   introductory talk by Edith Sitwell
      Searle, *Gold Coast Customs* (speakers Edith Sitwell and Constant Lambert; cond. L. Lucas)
         (dedicated to Lambert), 1st performance
   performed again 9 December; NSA recording NP1541W of that date

22 May 1949 9.35–10.40 p.m.
  (1st of 4 concerts arranged under the direction of Anthony Lewis)
  Joan Cross, Bettine Young, Esmie Smith, Elsie Boardman, Zilla Tregenna, Gladys Palmer, Joan
  Alexander, Trefor Jones, Dennis Dowling; continuo: Boris Ord and Raymond Clark; BBC
  Theatre Chorus, Philharmonia Orchestra, cond. Lambert; narration written and spoken by
  Dennis Arundell; produced by Constant Lambert and Stanford Robinson
      Purcell, *Dido and Aeneas*, ed. E. J. Dent
  Britten's realisation of *Dido and Aeneas* with the English Opera Group, Joan Cross and Peter
  Pears, was to be broadcast on 10 July 1951, conducted by Britten

24 June 1949 9.30–10.05 p.m.
  live repeat of *Dido and Aeneas*

30 May 1949 9.15–10.15 p.m.
  BBC Chorus, Philharmonia Orchestra, cond. Lambert
      Auber, Overture *Masaniello*
      Satie, *Jack in the Box*
      Ravel, *Pavane pour une infante défunte*
      Lambert, *The Rio Grande* (Kyla Greenbaum)
      Chabrier, Danse slave, Entr'acte, Barcarolle, Fête polonaise (from *Le Roi malgré lui*)

8 June 1949 10.35–10.55 p.m.
  broadcast of Lambert's talk on Erik Satie

❩ 9 June 1949 6.55–7.30 p.m.
  'Erik Satie' (1st of 3 concerts devised by Lambert, who did not participate)
  Robert Collet (pf); Mary and Geraldine Peppin (2 pf)
      Gymnopédie No. 1
      Sarabande No. 1
      Danse de travers; Air à fuir No. 2
      Trois valses
      Trois morceaux en forme de poire

14 June 1949 6.50–7.40 p.m.
  'Erik Satie' (2nd of 3 concerts)
  section of London Symphony Orchestra, cond. Lambert
      Prélude de la porte héroïque du ciel (orch. Roland-Manuel), 1st English performance
      Gnossienne No. 3 (orch. Poulenc)
      Je te veux (song)
      La Belle Excentrique, 1st English performance
      En habit de cheval, 1st English performance
      Les Aventures de Mercure
  '20 guineas incl. for devising programmes, provision of programme notes and presentation at
  the microphone'

17 June 1949 7.35–8.15 p.m.
  'Erik Satie' (3rd of 3 concerts)
  Megan Foster, Sophie Wyss, section of London Symphony Orchestra, cond. Lambert
      Socrate, 1st English performance

25 June 1949 9.10–10.25 p.m.
  'Purcell and Rameau' (2nd of 4 concerts arranged under the direction of Anthony Lewis)
  Ena Mitchell, Margaret Ritchie, Alfred Deller, William Herbert, Renê Soames, Gordon
  Clinton, Philip Hattey, Norman Walker; continuo: Boris Ord and Raymond Clark; BBC
  Chorus, Philharmonia Orchestra, con. Lambert
      Purcell, *The Yorkshire Feast Song*
      Rameau, Suite *Hippolyte et Aricie*
      Purcell, *The Masque in Dioclesian*

23 July 1949 8.10–9.05; 9.20–9.50 p.m.
 Orchestral concert recorded from ISCM Festival held at Palermo in April
  ◖ Marcel Mihelovici, Variations for strings and brass (cond. Robert Désormière)
  Searle, *Fuga giocoso* (cond. Lambert)
  ◖ Vladimir Vogel, Second Suite *Thyll Claes* (cond. Guilini)

29 July 1949 9.05–9.40; 10.00–11.00 p.m.
 BBC Symphony Orchestra, cond. Lambert
  Berkeley, Symphony (No. 1)
  D'Indy, Symphonic Variations *Istar*
  Borodin, Symphony No. 1

23 Sept. 1949 6.00–6.25; 6.45–7.25 p.m.
 'Erik Satie'
 Megan Foster, Sophie Wyss, London Symphony Orchestra, cond. Lambert
  Prélude de la porte héroïque du ciel (orch. Roland-Manuel)
  Gymnopédie No. 2 (orch. Debussy)
  Je te veux (song)
  La Belle Excentrique
  Socrate

4 Dec. 1949 6.00–6.25; 6.45–7.20 p.m.
 'Purcell' (3rd of 4 concerts arranged under the direction of Anthony Lewis)
 Margaret Field-Hyde, Ceinwen Rowlands, Marjorie Thomas, George Rizza, John Kentish,
 Henry Cummings, Owen Brannigan, Thurston Dart, Covent Garden Chorus, Boyd Neel
 Orchestra (leader Maurice Clare), cond. Lambert
  Welcome to all the pleasures (Ode to St Cecilia's Day 1683)
  Masque in Dioclesian

4 Dec. 1949 10.55 p.m.
  Walton, *Façade*
 repeat of broadcast of 10 December 1948

5 Dec. 1949 10.40–11.00 p.m.
 broadcast of Lambert's talk on van Dieren: 'Bernard van Dieren: Constant Lambert, who was
 a personal friend, sketches a portrait of the composer.'
  ◖ 6 Dec. Programme of van Dieren songs
  ◖ 9 Dec. Programme of van Dieren violin and piano music
  ◖ 15 Dec. Van Dieren, String Quartet No. 4

9 Dec. 1949 7.15–7.40; 8.00–8.45 p.m.
 'Contemporary Music'
 Edith Sitwell and Constant Lambert (speakers), Mary and Geraldine Peppin (2 pf), James
 Gibb (pf), BBC Men's Chorus, section of Philharmonia Orchestra, cond. Leighton Lucas
  ◖ Petrassi, *Song of the Dead*
 Introduction by Edith Sitwell
  Searle, *Gold Coast Customs*
 NSA recording: NP1541W 33′35″ with closing announcement; distorted at climaxes

12 Dec. 1949 9.00–9.25; 9.45–10.30 p.m.
 repeat of concert of 9 December

21 Dec. 1949 6.20–6.45; 7.05–8.00 p.m.
 'Purcell' (last of 4 concerts arranged under the direction of Anthony Lewis)
 Margaret Ritchie, Ceinwen Rowlands, Alfred Deller, George Rizza, John Kentish, George
 Pizzey, Owen Brannigan, Boris Ord, London Phiharmonic Choir, Boyd Neel Orchestra, cond.
 Lambert
  Purcell, *Ye Tuneful Muses*
  Purcell, *Masque in Dioclesian*

23 Dec. 1949 7.50–9.15 p.m.
  Trefor Jones, BBC Men's Chorus, BBC Symphony Orchestra, cond. Lambert
    Liszt, *A Faust Symphony*
    article by Searle: 'Liszt, this many-sided genius', *RadioTimes*, 16 Dec. 1949, p. 7

6 Jan. 1950 8.50–10.50 p.m.
  actors: Andrew Cruickshank, Cyril Cusack, Robert Harris, Dennis Arundell, J. Hubert Lelsie,
  Allan McClelland, Ivan Samson, Francis de Wolff, Norman Shelley, Ernest Jay, Maxine Audley,
  Cherry Cottrell, Marjorie Westbury, Bernard Miles, Vida Hope; singers: Margaret Field-Hyde,
  Margaret Ritchie, René Soames, William Parsons, Stanley Riley; continuo: Bernard Richards
  and John Wills; Covent Garden Chorus, Boyd Neel Orchestra, cond. Lambert; produced by
  Douglas Cleverdon
    The Tempest adapted from Shakespeare's comedy by William Davenant, John Dryden and
    Thomas Shadwell with music by Henry Purcell ed. Anthony Lewis

8 Jan. 1950 8.45–10.45 p.m.
  repeat performance of *The Tempest*

14 Jan. 1950 9.00–9.40; 9.55–10.45 p.m.
  Suzanne Danco, René Soames, Robert Irwin, Norman Platt, Covent Garden Chorus, New
  London Orchestra (leader Leonard Hirsch), cond. Lambert
    Gluck, *Alceste* Overture and Act 1
    Gluck, *Iphigénie en Tauride* Act 3

15 Jan. 1950 6.55–7.35; 7.55–8.30 p.m.
  repeat performance of 14 January

10 Feb. 1950 7.30–8.15; 8.35–9.15 p.m.
  'Liszt' (6th in a series devised by Humphrey Searle)
  Kyla Greenbaum, London Philharmonic Orchestra, cond. Lambert
    La Notte Funeral Ode, 1st English broadcast performance
    Grand Solo de Concert (with orchestra), 1st English broadcast performance
    Symphonic Poem *Héroïde funèbre*
    Totentanz
    Symphonic Poem *Hunnenschlacht*

21 Feb. 1950 7.45–8.20; 8.40–9.30 p.m.
  'Contemporary Music' (before an invited audience in the Concert Hall, Broadcasting House)
  Nancy Evans, George Chitty, Redvers Llewellyn, BBC Singers, BBC Men's Chorus, section of
  London Symphony Orchestra, cond. Lambert
    ¶ Copland, *In the Beginning* (cond. L. Woodgate)
    ApIvor, *The Hollow Men* (NSA recording M5990W), 1st performance
    Frankel, *The Aftermath*, 1st broadcast performance
    Gerhard, Suite *Pandora* (NSA recording NP1555W BD1; 24' 20" cut at end), 1st performance

28 May 1950 7.10–8.15; 8.35–9.55 p.m.
  Joan Alexander, Margaret Ritchie, Trefor Jones, Richard Lewis, Owen Brannigan, Carl and
  Marie Dolmetsch (recorders), continuo: Willem de Mont, Thurston Dart and George Thalban-
  Ball; Covent Garden Chorus, section of London Symphony Orchestra, cond. Lambert
    Handel, *Alexander Feast*, ed. Basil Lam

3 June 1950 6.50–7.50 p.m.
  George Pizzey, Oxford Bach Choir, BBC Symphony Orchestra, cond. Lambert
    Lambert, *Summer's Last Will and Testament*
    preceded by introductory talk by Alan Frank

8 July 1950 7.40–8.20; 8.35–9.20 p.m.
> Margaret Ritchie, Glenda Raymond, Catherine Lawson, Marjorie Thomas, Duncan Thomson, René Soames, George Armitage, Gordon Clinton; continuo: Thurston Dart and Raymond Clark; Geraint Jones (org), section of London Philharmonic Choir, Philharmonia Orchestra, cond. Lambert
>> Handel, *Semele*

9 July 1950 7.50–8.30; 8.50–9.35 p.m.
>> Handel, *Semele*
> 2nd of 2 performances before an invited audience

17 Aug. 1950 6.20–7.05 p.m.
> Edward Walker, George Walker, Roger Lloyd, Sidney Fell, Walter Lear, Ronald Waller, John Burden, George Eskdale, Philip Catalinet, David Martin, Neville Marriner, Max Gilbert, Eileen Grainger, Eugene Cruft, directed by Lambert
>> Van Dieren, *Serenata*, Op. 16, for nine instruments
>> Warlock, Seven songs
>> Van Dieren, *Sonetto VII of Edmund Spenser's Amoretti* for tenor and 11 instruments

1 Oct. 1950 8.40–9.35; 9.55–10.30 p.m.
> Margaret Field-Hyde, Margaret Ritchie, Betty Bannerman, William Herbert, William Parsons; continuo: Boris Ord and Geraint Jones; BBC Chorus, Philharmonia Orchestra, cond. Lambert
>> Handel, *L'Allegro ed Il Pensieroso*, ed. Norman Stone

2 Oct. 1950 7.35–8.30; 8.55–9.35 p.m.
> 2nd performance of programme of 1 October

30 Dec. 1950 8.45–9.20; 9.40–10.40 p.m. with interval
> 'Orchestral Concert'
> BBC Symphony Orchestra, cond. Lambert
>> Magnard, Symphony No. 3
>> Bliss, *Adam Zero*

5 Feb. 1951 8.30–9.45 p.m.
> 'Music from *The Fairy Queen* by Henry Purcell'
> adapted and arranged by Lambert
> Joan Alexander, Ena Mitchell, Nancy Evans, Janet Fraser, René Soames, Trevor Anthony, Boris Ord, BBC Chorus, Philharmonia Orchestra, cond. Lambert
> brief article by Harold Rutland in *Radio Times*, p. 11

9 Feb. 1951 7.00–8.15 p.m.
> repeat performance of *The Fairy Queen*

16 Feb. 1951 6.15–6.35 p.m. (recorded 14 February)
> 'Lord Berners (1883–1950)'
> A tribute by Constant Lambert
> NSA NP9506/03

16 Feb. 1951 6.35–7.15 p.m.
> 'Lord Berners (Memorial Programme)'
> Sophie Wyss, René Soames, Clifton Helliwell (pf), Angus Morrison, Joan and Valerie Trimble
>> *Trois petits marches funèbres*
>> *Trois chansons*
>> *Lullaby* (Dekker)
>> *Fragments psychologiques*
>> *The Lady Visitor in the Pauper Ward*
>> *The Rio Grande* (Berners)
>> *Theodore*
>> *Dialogue between Tom Filuter and his Man*
>> *Valses bourgeoises*
> programme arranged and introduced by Lambert

18 Feb. 1951 8.00–8.50 p.m.
  'Lord Berners'
  Royal Philharmonic Orchestra, cond. Lambert
      Caprice péruvien (arr. Lambert)
      Trois morceaux pour orchestre
      Suite: *The Triumph of Neptune*
      Fantaisie Espagnole

◀ 29 Jan. 1952 6.45–7.20; 7.40–8.35 p.m.
  'Constant Lambert Memorial Concert'
  London Philharmonic Orchestra, Robert Irving
      Pomona
      Music for Orchestra
      5 movements from *Horoscope*
      King Pest
  Arthur Jacobs, 'The Music of Constant Lambert', *Radio Times*, 25 Jan., p.13

◀ 30 Jan. 1952 10.05–11.00 p.m.
  'Constant Lambert Memorial Concert'
  Martin Boddey, Henry Cummings, Kyla Greenbaum; tenors and basses of the London
  Philharmonic Choir; London Symphony Orchestra Chamber Ensemble, Norman Del Mar
      Eight Poems of Li-Po
      Concerto for Piano and Nine Players
      Dirge from 'Cymbeline'

◀ 1 Feb. 1952 11.40 p.m.
  Gordon Watson
      Lambert, Piano Sonata
      repeat of broadcast of 26 May 1951

Appendix 8
Constant Lambert's Conducting Engagements at the Henry Wood Promenade Concerts

❧ **1929**

29 Aug. Queen's Hall
    Henry Wood Symphony Orchestra, Lambert
      Lambert, *Music for Orchestra*

❧ **1930**

4 Sept. Queen's Hall
    Angus Morrison, Doris Owens, BBC Singers, BBC Symphony Orchestra, Lambert
      Lambert, *The Rio Grande*

❧ **1931**

10 Sept. Queen's Hall
    Angus Morrison, Doris Owens, BBC Singers, BBC Symphony Orchestra, Lambert
      Lambert, *The Rio Grande*

❧ **1932**

20 Aug. Queen's Hall
    Angus Morrison, Doris Owens, BBC Singers, BBC Symphony Orchestra, Lambert
      Lambert, *The Rio Grande*

❧ **1933**

6 Sept. Queen's Hall
    BBC Symphony Orchestra, Lambert
      Lambert, *Music for Orchestra*

❧ **1934**

25 Sept. Queen's Hall
    Angus Morrison, Doris Owens, BBC Singers, BBC Symphony Orchestra, Lambert
      Lambert, *The Rio Grande*

❧ **1935**

11 Jan. Queen's Hall
    Winter Proms
    BBC Symphony Orchestra, Lambert
      Lambert, *Music for Orchestra*

18 Sept. Queen's Hall
    BBC Symphony Orchestra, Lambert
      Lambert, *Music for Orchestra*

❧ **1936**

5 Sept. Queen's Hall
    BBC Symphony Orchestra, Lambert
      Lambert, *King Pest*

❧ **1937**

19 Aug. Queen's Hall
    BBC Symphony Orchestra, Lambert
      Lambert, *King Pest*

⁂ 1938

8 Aug. Queen's Hall
　BBC Symphony Orchestra, Lambert
　　Lambert, *Horoscope* – Suite Premiere

20 Aug. Queen's Hall
　Angus Morrison, Astra Desmond, BBC Singers, BBC Symphony Orchestra, Lambert
　　Lambert, *The Rio Grande*

⁂ 1944

8 July Royal Albert Hall
　BBC Symphony Orchestra, Lambert
　　Lambert, Suite *Merchant Seamen*

⁂ 1945

　Appointed Assistant Conductor

28 July Royal Albert Hall
　London Symphony Orchestra (with Basil Cameron) – second half only, not broadcast
　　Lambert, Suite *Merchant Seamen* [instead of scheduled 'new work']
　　Liszt, *Les Préludes*

3 Aug. Royal Albert Hall
　London Symphony Orchestra (with Cameron) – second half, not broadcast
　　Hindemith, Overture *Cupid and Psyche*
　　Balakirev, *Tamara*

7 Aug. Royal Albert Hall
　Schubert-Liszt concert
　London Symphony Orchestra (with Adrian Boult) – broadcast
　　Schubert, Overture *Rosamunde*
　　Schubert–Liszt, *Wanderer-Fantasia* (Louis Kentner)
　　Liszt, *The Lorelei* (Oda Slobodskaya)
　　Liszt, Symphonic Poem *Hunnenschlacht*
　　[Boult–Schubert, Symphony No. 9]

9 Aug. Royal Albert Hall
　Wagner-Sibelius Concert
　London Symphony Orchestra (with Boult conducting Wagner) – not broadcast
　　Sibelius, *Night Ride and Sunrise*; *Luonnotar*; Symphony No. 3 (changed to *Night Ride and Sunrise*; Symphony No. 3; *Finlandia*, owing to the indisposition of Joan Hammand and then Eva Turner – slip in programme)
　[All Sibelius's symphonies were played in this season.]

21 Aug. Royal Albert Hall
　BBC Symphony Orchestra, all conducted by Lambert – only works marked * broadcast
　* Elgar, *Introduction and Allegro* [swapped by Lambert for *Cockaigne*]
　* Haydn, Recit. 'At once the earth opens her womb' and Aria 'Now heaven in fullest glory shone', from *The Creation* (Norman Walker)
　* Walton, *Sinfonia Concertante* (Phyllis Sellick) (changed from Walton Violin Concerto owing to indisposition of Arthur Grumiaux – slip in programme)
　　Sibelius, Symphony No. 5
　　Berlioz, *Royal Hunt and Storm*, from *The Trojans*
　　Debussy, *Iberia* (*Images*)

28 Aug. Royal Albert Hall
　BBC Symphony Orchestra (with Boult) – not broadcast
　　Lambert, *The Rio Grande* (Gladys Ripley, Kyla Greenbaum)
　　Kodály, *Dances from Galanta*

29 Aug. Royal Albert Hall
  BBC Symphony Orchestra (with Boult and Ian Whyte) – only works marked * broadcast
    Mozart, Symphony No. 32
    Haydn, Recit. 'At last the bounteous sun' and Aria 'With joy th'impatient husbandman',
      from *The Seasons* (George Pizzey)
  * Mozart, Piano Concerto No. 24 (Kathleen Long)
  * Haydn, Symphony No. 104

8 Sept. Royal Albert Hall
  BBC Symphony Orchestra (with Boult conducting Bax, Symphony No. 5) – not broadcast
    Borodin, Symphony No. 2
    Chabrier, *España*
    Ravel, *Pavane pour une infante défunte*
    Ravel, *Boléro*

13 Sept. Royal Albert Hall
  Russian Concert
  BBC Symphony Orchestra (with Boult) – only works marked * broadcast
    Glière, Overture *The Friendship of the Peoples*
  * Borodin, Jaroslavna's Aria 'A long time has passed', from *Prince Igor* (Oda Sloboskaya)
  * Prokofiev, Piano Concerto No. 3 (Kendall Taylor)
  * Tchaikovsky, *Romeo and Juliet*
    [Boult–Shostakovich, Symphony No. 5]

15 Sept. Royal Albert Hall
  Last Night of the Proms
  London Symphony Orchestra and BBC Symphony Orchestra (with Cameron and Boult) – not
  broadcast; Last Night broadcast only from approx. 8.00–9.00 p.m.
    Dukas, *Sorcerer's Apprentice*
    Rawsthorne, First Piano Concerto (Phyllis Sellick)

※ **1946**
  Engaged as Assistant Conductor £400

27 July Royal Albert Hall
  First Night of the Proms
  London Symphony Orchestra (with Cameron and Boult) – all broadcast
    Borodin, *Polovstian Dances* (last item)

30 July Royal Albert Hall
  London Symphony Orchestra (with Cameron conducting Sibelius) – not broadcast
    Walton, Viola Concerto (William Primrose)
    Szalowski, Overture

1 Aug. Royal Albert Hall
  Bach and Schubert programme
  London Symphony Orchestra (with Cameron) – not broadcast
    Schubert, Symphony No. 5 (last item)

8 Aug. Royal Albert Hall
  Haydn and Mendelssohn programme
  London Symphony Orchestra (with Cameron) – only works marked * broadcast
    Haydn, 'Representation of Chaos', from *The Creation*
  * Haydn, Symphony No. 73
  * Mendelssohn, Violin Concerto (Arthur Grumiaux)
    Mendelssohn, Symphony No. 4

10 Aug. Royal Albert Hall
  London Symphony Orchestra (with Boult) – not broadcast
    Walton, *Façade* Suite (Fanfare, Polka, Valse, Swiss Jodelling Song, Tango-Pasodoble, Scotch
      Rhapsody, Popular Song, Tarantella)
    Tchaikovsky, Overture *1812*

14 Aug. Royal Albert Hall
London Symphony Orchestra, all conducted by Lambert – only works
marked * broadcast
* Berlioz, Overture *Benvenuto Cellini*
* Verdi, Recit. and aria 'Arise! It was you who stained', from *A Masked Ball* (Dennis Noble)
    (replacing Verdi, Recit. and aria 'O tu Palermo', from *Sicilian Vespers* (Oscar Natzka))
* Rawsthorne, Piano Concerto (Louis Kentner)
* Sibelius, Symphony No. 1
    Schubert–Liszt, *Wanderer-Fantasia* for piano and orchestra (Louis Kentner)
    Ravel, *La Valse*

22 Aug. Royal Albert Hall
London Symphony Orchestra, all conducted by Lambert – only work
marked * broadcast
    Dvořák, Slavonic Dance, op. 72 no. 7 in C
    Dvořák, Violin Concerto (Ida Haendel)
* Dvořák, Symphony No. 4 (8) in G
    Franck, Symphonic Variations (Ivey Dickson)
    Sibelius, Symphony No. 3

29 Aug. Royal Albert Hall
BBC Symphony Orchestra (with Boult) – not broadcast
    Ireland, *Mai-Dun*
    Mussorgsky, *Song of the Flea* (Norman Allin)
    Kodály, *Dances of Galanta*

30 Aug. Royal Albert Hall
BBC Symphony Orchestra (with Boult) – not broadcast
    Sibelius, Symphony No. 4 (last item)

31 Aug. Royal Albert Hall
BBC Symphony Orchestra (with Boult) – not broadcast
    Bartók, *Portrait* No. 1 for Violin and Orchestra (Joseph Szigeti)
    Lambert, *The Rio Grande* (Gladys Ripley, Kyla Greenbaum)
    Chabrier, *Bourrée fantasque*
    Chabrier, *España*

3 Sept. Royal Albert Hall
BBC Symphony Orchestra (with Boult) – not broadcast
    Hindemith, *Symphonic Metamorphosis on Themes by Carl Maria von Weber* (first English
        performance)
    Weber, Overture *Ruler of the Spirits*

6 Sept. Royal Albert Hall
BBC Symphony Orchestra (with Boult conducting Vaughan Williams, Symphony No. 4) –
only works marked * broadcast
* Beethoven, Overture *Coriolan*
* Beethoven, Scena and Aria 'Vile devil!', from *Fidelio* (Edna Hobson)
* Beethoven, Symphony No. 2
    Beethoven, Piano Concerto No. 5 (Moiseiwitsch)

11 Sept. Royal Albert Hall
BBC Symphony Orchestra (with Cameron conducting Bax, Symphony No. 7) – second half
not broadcast
    Ireland, Overture *Satyricon* (first performance)
    Tchaikovsky, *Francesca da Rimini*

14 Sept. Royal Albert Hall
BBC Symphony Orchestra (with Boult) – not broadcast
    Prokofiev, *Peter and the Wolf* (George Baker)
    Walton, *Crown Imperial*

16 Sept. Royal Albert Hall
> BBC Symphony Orchestra (with Boult conducting Brahms) – not broadcast
>> Bliss Suite, *Adam Zero* (first concert performance)
>> Howells, *Procession*

19 Sept. Royal Albert Hall
> BBC Symphony Orchestra (with Boult conducting Wagner) – not broadcast
>> Sibelius, Symphony No. 6
>> Sibelius, *Lemminkäinen's Return*

21 Sept. Royal Albert Hall
> Last Night of the Proms
> London Symphony Orchestra and BBC Symphony Orchestra (with Boult and Cameron, conducting Sibelius, Symphony No. 7) – broadcast in Home Service
>> Walton, *Sinfonia Concertante* (Phyllis Sellick)
>> Milhaud, *Deux Marches: In memoriam; Gloria Victoribus* (first English performance)

※ 1947

16 Jan. Royal Albert Hall
> Winter Prom
> BBC Symphony Orchestra (with Boult) – beginning of second half broadcast in Third Programme
>> Lambert, *King Pest*

23 Aug. Royal Albert Hall
> Lambert Birthday Night
> BBC Symphony Orchestra (with Boult and Stanford Robinson) – broadcast in Light Programme
>> Lambert, *The Rio Grande* (Gladys Ripley, Kyla Greenbaum)

※ 1948

9 Aug. Royal Albert Hall
> BBC Symphony Orchestra (with Stanford Robinson)
>> Lambert, *Horoscope*

[19 Aug. Royal Albert Hall]
> [Stanford Robinson conducts *The Rio Grande* with Gladys Ripley and Eric Harrison]

※ 1949

[1 Aug. Royal Albert Hall]
> [Sargent conducts *The Rio Grande* with Nancy Evans and Eric Harrison – not broadcast]

※ 1950

[19 Aug. Royal Albert Hall]
> [Stanford Robinson conducts *The Rio Grande* (Eric Harrison, Gladys Ripley, BBC Opera Chorus)]

※ 1951

11 Aug. Royal Albert Hall
> London Symphony Orchestra (with Cameron) – broadcast in Light Programme
>> Lambert, *Horoscope* Suite

15 Aug. Royal Albert Hall
> BBC Symphony Orchestra (with John Hollingsworth) – Lambert conducts Part 2, not broadcast
>> Lambert, *The Rio Grande* (Monica Sinclair, Kyla Greenbaum) [15½' pencilled in programme]
>> Ravel, *La Valse* [12½' pencilled in programme]

Appendix 9
A Dance to the Music of Time: Anthony Powell, Hugh Moreland and Constant Lambert

T HE portrayal of British composers in fiction is rare. The few recognised cases include the character of Halliday in D. H. Lawrence's *Women in Love* and Coleman in Aldous Huxley's *Antic Hay*, both based on Philip Heseltine; and Francis Paltry in *Far from the Madding War* and Emmanuel Smith in *Count Omega*, both by Lord Berners, which are veiled references to William Walton. Berners represented himself as Lord FitzCricket in *Far from the Madding War* and as Miss Carfax in *The Girls of Radcliffe Hall*, while Lord Merlin, in Nancy Mitford's *The Pursuit of Love*, is also based on Berners. Cecil Gray was both Vane in Hilda Doolittle's semi-autobiographical novel *Bid me to Live* and, somewhat confusingly, 'Cyril Scott' in Lawrence's *Aaron's Rod*.[1] And to this brief list one can add James Farrar's short story *Episode in August* in which the wheelchair-bound grandfather is modelled on Delius.[2]

But none of these representations is as extensive as the character of Hugh Moreland, based on Constant Lambert, in Anthony Powell's *A Dance to the Music of Time*, the collective title for the sequence of 12 novels that follow the fortunes of a group of people over a period of 50 years, beginning just after the First World War. It is a work that, not surprisingly, has many autobiographical parallels for its author. The first novel, *A Question of Upbringing*, was published in 1951. Moreland is introduced in the fifth novel, *Casanova's Chinese Restaurant* (1960), and is present until his death at the end of the penultimate novel, *Temporary Kings* (1973).[3]

The beginning of *Casanova's Chinese Restaurant* is unusual because it breaks the narrative chronology of the previous novels. The fourth, *At Lady Molly's*, ends in 1934, but *Casanova's Chinese Restaurant* opens in post-war London with a description of a bombed-out public house, significantly 'The Mortimer' in which the narrator Nicholas Jenkins (Anthony Powell) had first met Hugh Moreland (Lambert) back in the late 1920s.[4] Over the rubble comes the voice of a woman singing, the same voice that Jenkins and Moreland heard years before, soon after their first meeting. (It is clear to the reader that Moreland is dead, music, we are told, being a 'natural accompaniment to Moreland's memory'.) A blonde woman on crutches[5] is singing a once-popular song from which Jenkins quotes the first two lines:

> Pale hands I loved beside the Shalimar,
> Where are you now? Who lies beneath your spell?

---

[1] Pauline Gray, *Cecil Gray*, pp. 18–19. Pauline Gray also suggests that Halliday in *Women in Love* may have been a caricature of her father.

[2] Christopher Palmer, *Spring Returning: A Selection from the Works of James Farrar* (London: Autolycus Press, 1986).

[3] Page references to *Casanova's Chinese Restaurant* are to the Penguin edition (1964), while those to *The Kindly Ones* and *Temporary Kings* are to the Fontana paperback editions (1977 and 1974 respectively).

[4] 'We first met, so far as I remember about the spring of the year 1928, in a crowded pub', Anthony Powell wrote in 'Constant Lambert: A Memoir', in Shead, *Constant Lambert*, p. 17. He corrected the date to autumn 1927 in his memoirs *Messengers of Day* (1978), p. 55.

[5] According to Powell, such a person frequented Gerrard Street in which Maxim's Chinese Restaurant, in part the model for Casanova's Chinese Restaurant, was to be found. The crippled woman's singing is also recalled in *The Kindly Ones* (p. 250).

These lines are from the *Kashmiri Song* (which Powell later refers to by name, p. 56), the third of a cycle of four *Indian Love Lyrics* composed in 1903 by Amy Woodford-Finden, the wife of an Indian Army brigadier. The second line could be seen as an allusion, not to Moreland, but to the person who inspired that character, Constant Lambert. '*Where are you now?*' the poet asks. Lambert had been dead nearly ten years when the novel appeared, a respectful distance, and he is now transformed into the character of Moreland. '*Who lies beneath your spell?*' Anthony Powell wrote of Lambert as being 'one of my greatest friends', and he dedicated his second novel, *Venusberg* (1932), to Constant and Florence Lambert. In the early years of their acquaintance they 'saw a great deal of each other', and if, later on, circumstances contrived to make their meetings less frequent than they would have wanted, during the last year or two of his life Lambert 'used to ring up most weeks and talk'.[6] One has only to look at Powell's four volumes of memoirs, *To Keep the Ball Rolling* – or even more significantly, his three volumes of *Journals* from 1982 to 1992 – to see the number of references to Lambert in each of these seven volumes; this can only speak of a person who made a strong impact on Powell. It would not be too fanciful to suggest that Powell came under the spell of Lambert's personality and intellect.

In these opening pages of *Casanova's Chinese Restaurant* Powell uses the singing as a clever device – appropriately a musical one – to bridge the decades and take the reader back to the late 1920s and the start of the friendship. In the subsequent pages, the fact that the relation between Time and Space was then a fashionable topic of discussion (*CCR*, p. 35) might allude to J. W. Dunne's 1927 book, *An Experiment with Time* (Lambert mentions Dunne in *Music Ho!*), while reference to the Delius Festival (pp. 26–7) firmly pins down the date to late 1929.

Hugh Moreland (usually just Moreland) is present throughout much of this novel, his being the first and the last name to be mentioned. The opening presents what later emerges as a small slip-up in chronology: with Moreland eventually dying in 1959 in the eleventh novel, it would be rather late for a bombsite still to exist in central London (although at the time of writing *Casanova's Chinese Restaurant*, Powell would quite likely not have known the span of life that he was going to allot to his character). The chronology is further confused when the reader is told of 'The Mortimer' being 'now rebuilt in a displeasingly fashionable style' (p. 15).

'The Mortimer' is quite possibly the renowned The George, a favourite watering hole of Lambert's, which stands on the corner of Mortimer Street and Great Portland Street. Although not actually bombed in the war[7] (unlike the closely adjacent Queen's Hall), one wonders if it had a mechanical piano that was 'the chief charm of the Mortimer for Moreland' (p. 15). The penny-slot mechanical piano, popular before the advent of the juke-box, was something Lambert had written about with enthusiasm in the *Sunday Referee*: 'There are few things in life so pleasant as sitting on the quay at Toulon, gazing out over the waters with a glass of wine beside one, and meditating to the strains of a mechanical piano.'[8]

The title of the novel, *Casanova's Chinese Restaurant*, and the fact that Moreland 'remained a hopeless addict of ... a "*princesse lointaine* complex"' (p. 14) reflect Lambert's Chinese phase, brought about by his infatuation with the film star Anna May Wong, when he was a frequent visitor to Chinese restaurants. The narrator Nicholas Jenkins is generally identified as being Anthony Powell himself who never denied that

---

[6] Letter from Anthony Powell to Hubert Foss, 1 December 1951: Hubert Foss Archive.

[7] Elisabeth Lutyens, *A Goldfish Bowl*, p. 140, remembered 'someone remarking that if a bomb dropped on The George a large proportion of the musical and literary world would be destroyed'.

[8] *Sunday Referee*, 20 August 1933.

the character of Moreland was, to some extent, based on Lambert. Even his wife, Lady Violet Powell, found *Casanova's Chinese Restaurant* 'an infinitely touching memorial to Constant Lambert' who had left 'an unfillable gap'.[9] Yet Powell was cautious in acknowledging too close a dependency:

> 'Moreland', friend of the Narrator (himself of equally mixed origins), is a musician, wit, sometimes exuberant, sometimes melancholy. Dark, rather than fair, he has the Bronzino-type features of Lambert's Bluecoat portrait by his father. There the resemblance to Lambert fades, invention, imagination, the creative instinct – whatever you like to call it – begins; ... the things that happen to 'Moreland' approximate to the things that happened to Lambert only so far as all composers' lives have something in common. ... In a thousand ways Lambert's career diverges utterly from that given to the character in the novel.[10]

Nevertheless, it is surprising how many points of contact there are between the two. Moreland is the same age as the narrator Nicholas Jenkins; Lambert and Powell were both born in 1905. He is introduced as a composer, conductor and pianist, all true of Lambert except that his main area of musical activity, ballet, is not alluded to. We are only told that the walls of his flat were 'hung with framed caricatures of dances [*sic*] in Diaghilev's early ballets. ... Pavlova, Karsavina, Fokine' (p. 12). In the next novel in the sequence, *The Kindly Ones*, we learn that Moreland is 'working on' a ballet (*TKO*, p. 96), this being in 1938, the year in which Lambert's ballet *Horoscope* was first performed. We are also told that he has written some film music (*CCR*, p. 14).

Moreland, like Lambert, was brought up in Fulham and, like Lambert, displayed 'juvenile brilliance – not an infant prodigy but showing alarming promise as a boy'. Both were 'destined to make a brilliant career in music' (p. 84) and both went to the Royal College of Music. Neither of them at any time was comfortably well off. Moreland shares Lambert's strong dislike for Brahms, advising one companion: 'I should certainly not go near the Albert Hall if I were you. ... It would be too great a risk. Someone might seize you and compel you to listen to Brahms', to which comes the rejoinder: 'Moreland, I wish to hear no more of your youthful prejudices – certainly no more of your sentiments regarding the orchestration of the Second Piano Concerto' (pp. 18–19). (In *Music Ho!* Lambert had disparaged 'the drab shades and muddy impasto' of Brahms' orchestration.) And in *The Soldier's Art* Moreland further damns Brahms by suggesting that a brothel would be a suitable place for playing his compositions – 'part of the Requiem perhaps'!'[11] Lambert's fondness for Sousa and his dislike of Hindemith are also touched on: '*Aut Sousa aut Nihil* has always been my motto in cases of that sort. Think if the man had played Hindemith. At least he wasn't a highbrow' (*CCR*, p. 152). One accidental bull's-eye was Moreland's liking of Chabrier – a detail that Powell said that he had attributed to Moreland without realizing it was true of Lambert. There are one or two references to Moreland being, like Lambert, a critic. In *Temporary Kings* he asks: 'Is "apodictic" the right word? I once used it with effect in an article attacking Honegger' (p. 275). Lambert did have occasion to write somewhat critically about Honegger, though not with the ferocity of his sustained attacks on Hindemith.[12]

Another close parallel is found with each composer's *magnum opus*. Moreland's symphony is greeted with a poor attendance because of the coincidence of the Abdication crisis (December 1936, *CCR*, p. 121). It is critically 'a success but not an

---

[9] Violet Powell, *The Departure Platform: An Autobiography* (London: Heinemann, 1998), p. 205.

[10] 'Constant Lambert: A Memoir' in Shead, *Constant Lambert*, pp. 19–20.

[11] Because of his family's poverty, the young Brahms is said to have played in brothels and music halls.

[12] Discussing Honegger's *Pacific 231*, *The Nation and Athenæum*, 16 August 1930, pp. 620–1.

overwhelming success'. In January 1936, the first performance of Lambert's largest work, *Summer's Last Will and Testament*, took place the day after the funeral of King George V, and at a time of national mourning its reception was understandably muted. Lambert was given a lavish party afterwards by Alice, Lady Wimborne, the *amour* and patron of fellow-composer William Walton. In *Casanova's Chinese Restaurant* Mrs Foxe fulfils a similar function for Moreland. It is interesting that Moreland should echo the theme in the last paragraph of *Music Ho!* ('[The composer] must not mind if for the moment he appears to be without an audience') when he asks: 'If action is to be one's aim, then is it action to write a symphony satisfactory to oneself, which no one else wants to perform?' (*TKO*, p. 79). The only other composition of Moreland's to be mentioned is a tone poem *Vieux Port*, significantly written in Marseille, a favourite resort of Lambert's (it could just have easily been Toulon), although we are also informed that he had written 'incidental music for a semi-private venture (a film version of *Lysistrata* made in France)', perhaps a parallel with Lambert's incidental music for the private staging of Oscar Wilde's *Salomé*.

Moreland has a number of Lambert's characteristics – 'a massive Beethoven-shaped head' (*CCR*, p. 21), the habit of persisting 'eternally with any subject that caught his fancy ...; a love of repetition sometimes fatiguing to friends' (p. 11), and being at times 'almost hysterical with laughter which he continually tried to repress by stuffing a handkerchief into his mouth' (p. 151). Just as typical is how Moreland and Jenkins, having 'not met for over a year', had been 'exchanging picture postcards ... (that) dealt usually with some esoteric matter that caught his attention – a peculiar bathing dress on the beach, peepshows on the pier, the performance of pierrots – rather than the material of daily life' (p. 89). Even more relevant, Moreland is blessed with Lambert's love of the visual arts: he 'liked painting and held stronger views about pictures than most musicians' (p. 29), while Jenkins, like Powell, did not have the interest in music that he had in writing and painting. Moreland has Lambert's devotion to music, as he explains: 'The arts derive entirely from taking decisions. ... Having taken the decision music requires, I want to be free of all others.' (*TKO*, p. 82)

Moreland, like Lambert, was 'subject to bouts of deep depression' (p. 116) and had 'to do a lot of hack work to keep alive' (p. 100). In *Books Do Furnish a Room* we learn that Moreland 'detested talking politics' (p. 31), and, like Lambert, he was a heavy drinker. When Jenkins says that Moreland lived 'with intensity' (*TKO*, p. 82), it might be Powell commenting on Lambert.

The two had some similarities in their dealings with women. 'Moreland could be secretive enough about his girls when he chose ...' (*CCR*, p. 152), just as Lambert was after first meeting the underage Florence, and as he had to be in the early stages of his relationship with Fonteyn. One is hardly surprised to learn that Moreland 'gravitated from one hopeless love affair to another, falling in love with women connected in one way or another with the theatre' (p. 14) and perhaps meriting the Casanova of the title. His stormy relationship with Matilda mirrors Constant's fractious marriage with Flo. But there is a reversal of roles in their married lives. With Matilda being an actress, for a while she is the one who is absent on tour, while Moreland is left alone in London. But when it is his turn to be travelling with work, with some displeasure she calls him 'Hugh the Drover', possibly an intentional reference to the opera of the same name by Lambert's teacher, Vaughan Williams. Matilda loses their only child (unlike Florence) and the break-up of their marriage disturbs Moreland so much that he might have 'given himself up increasingly to drink' had not an excess of war-time musical work 'kept him alive and busy'.

A friend – even an admirer – of Moreland's is the music critic Maclintick, who can be seen as a mixture of Philip Heseltine and Cecil Gray, an ironic dual personality, as Gray had attributed a similar duality to Heseltine/Warlock in his biography.[13] Maclintick, like Gray bespectacled and spirit-drinking (unlike the beer-swilling Heseltine), greatly values Moreland as a friend but suffers from melancholy and is disappointed with himself as a musician (*CCR*, p. 96). He is working on an 'unreadable book on musical theory' which he never finishes, tearing up the manuscript before turning on the gas and committing suicide. This greatly upsets Moreland, just as Lambert was devastated by Heseltine's very similar suicide. He is also quoted as saying: 'Maclintick doesn't like women, he likes tarts – indeed he once actually fell in love with a tart, who led him an awful dance' (*TK*, p. 260), which could be an allusion to Gray's unsuccessful marriage to the dancer Marie Nielson. Moreland later lives with Maclintick's wife, Audrey.

Moreland dies at the end of the penultimate novel, *Temporary Kings*, having made an appearance in almost all the intervening books. At a charity musical party, he has been conducting Mozart's *Die Entführung aus dem Serail* and advising on its production. (Elsewhere we learn of him having conducted *Pelléas et Mélisande* (*BDFR*, p. 29), not a work that Lambert rated very highly.) Audrey Maclintick warns that he should not be allowed another drink before the curtain goes up as it isn't good for him, and after the performance he has a blackout and a fall. When Jenkins sees him resting, he is surprised that he is drinking a glass of water, something that he had not seen him do before, apart from after a heavy evening the previous night. These are the only hints that Moreland, like Lambert, might be suffering from diabetes.

As Moreland is waiting to be driven home that evening, the topic of conversation turns to antique cars, and he quotes Omar Khayyam:

> For some we loved, the loveliest and the best
> That from His vintage rolling Time hath pressed,

But Powell does not complete the quatrain:

> Have drunk the Cup a round or two before,
> And one by one crept silently to rest.

Moreland's death comes a few months later, in hospital. Jenkins enjoys one last, typically literary, chat with Moreland, and, without giving any details, he merely states: 'That morning was the last time I saw Moreland.'

Powell is clearly not just bidding farewell to the character of Moreland but also to the spirit of Lambert. There is a telling sentence when Jenkins says: 'It was also the last time I had, with anyone, the sort of talk we used to have together', from which we may deduce that this was what Powell so valued in his friendship with Lambert, and what he had missed since his death in 1951. Just as Jenkins could have very few other acquaintances with whom he could discuss, for example, Stendhal as he did with Moreland (*TKO*, p. 80), so Powell mourned the loss of such intellectual exchanges and that 'unfillable gap' left by Lambert's death.

A Question of Upbringing, the first volume of *A Dance to the Music of Time*, appeared in July 1951. The question arises – at what point did Powell hit upon the idea of the character of Moreland? Michael Barber, in his excellent biography of Powell, quite reasonably suggests that Moreland was an afterthought. In keeping with the chronological sequence he should have been introduced in the second book, *A Buyer's Market* (published in 1952). In *Casanova's Chinese Restaurant* the narrative has advanced to about 1936, necessitating the flashback on the second page to Moreland's appearance. Having introduced him, there was quite likely an understandable reluctance to let him go, especially when Moreland is a character for whom Powell shows such sympathy. But to fashion him too closely on Lambert would have resulted

---

[13] Cecil Gray, *Peter Warlock: A Memoir of Philip Heseltine* (London: Jonathan Cape, 1934).

in too strong a character that would possibly have upset the balance of the novels. It may be for this reason that, generally speaking, Moreland seems to have inherited more of Lambert's weaknesses than his strengths. Powell was only too aware of the problem of trying to capture the brilliance of Lambert's conversation. 'If I have been skilful enough, lucky enough, to pass on an echo of Lambert's incomparable wit, then "Moreland" is like him,' he wrote in his *Memoir* for Shead's biography.

Why the name Moreland? Could it have any connection with that of the 18th-century London-born artist George Morland, whose paintings of 'innocent charm' Lambert mentions in *Music Ho!*? Despite his considerable success as a painter, Morland's profligate life-style and drunkenness often landed him in serious financial difficulty, a state that Lambert fortunately never found himself in despite his occasional shortage of money and the need to borrow from friends. The similarity of the names may be just a coincidence, or perhaps Powell had in mind the two men's dependence on drink.[14]

In the absence of any biography of Lambert at that time of writing *Casanova's Chinese Restaurant*, and in a literary parallel to Elgar's *Enigma* Variations with his 'friends pictured within', Powell was keeping alive Constant's spirit through the character of Hugh Moreland and paying tribute to a close friend.[15] Cyril Connolly has written that 'in Moreland is preserved not only Lambert's wit, but his warmth, humanity and love-life, his romantic interest in Chinese and coloured girls so typical of the fin de siècle'.[16] Lambert would surely have approved of the form of immortality that Powell had bequeathed him.

---

[14] Roger Quilter's light opera *Love at the Inn* was a romanticised version of part of George Morland's life. A reworking of his 1936 opera *Julia*, with lyrics by Rodney Bennett and based on the book by Jeffrey Lambourne, the first and last acts take place at the Blue Boar Inn.

[15] Richard Shead's biography of Lambert did not appear until 1973, the same year in which the penultimate novel, *Temporary Kings*, was published.

[16] Cyril Connolly, 'March of Time', *Sunday Times*, 23 September 1973.

Appendix 10
C. B. Rees on Constant Lambert

T HERE is a masculine strength about Constant Lambert. That is one of the first impressions he makes on you: broad shoulders and a fine torso, a large head and an expansive forehead, an alert face on which humour plays a number of good tunes, but on which, now and then, there settles a kind of stern gloom, not to be dispersed by any insensitive back-slapping. He is a too familiar figure in our musical life to need any 'biography' in these pages. You see him conducting ballet at Covent Garden, a studio concert at the People's Palace, Sibelius at the Proms, recording at Maida Vale, reciting the Sitwell poems in *Façade* at the Lyric, Hammersmith, playing billiards with a friend, lunching at Pagani's, discussing railways and railway engines in the 'local', laughing in the street over the latest quips in 'Beachcomber', arguing about pictures with Michael Ayrton, discussing the atom bomb with a couple of journalists, chewing the cud of a new score with Alan Rawsthorne, exchanging a funny story with an orchestral player ...

So he goes on. It has been said that he is not easy to get to know. May be. He is shy, anyway. He is a highly concentrated individual, lives a lot on his nerves, knows what it is to suffer the agonies that afflict the keyed-up artist before he 'walks the plank' up to the Albert Hall rostrum to meet the almost physical impact of a thousand faces flattening themselves against one's tensed awareness.

Conductor, composer (how one wishes the composer could organise forty-eight hours into the day), critic, talker, the friendliest of good companions. 'Constant' is a perpetual stimulus to those who delight in knowing him. You must be prepared, of course, to discover, in the middle of one of your sentences (and, frequently, one of his own) that he is – gone. He tilts his chin in the air, stares suddenly into the far distance, turns with ballet-like speed on his heel, and silently vanishes. I can't count the number of times when friends have come up to me and said, 'I thought you were talking to Constant.' 'Well,' I say, slightly baffled as by some conjuring trick, 'I was.'

He is a good listener – if you have anything to say. To the bores, an increasing affliction of our times, he presents an inflexible deafness and a cast-iron rigidity of inattention. It paralyses. They flee. So does he. His range of interests is extraordinarily wide, from Liszt to limericks, narrow-gauge obscure railway tracks to Italian opera, the latest theory about the subconscious to a roaringly comic sketch (of his own devising) for a new revue. There is something of Chestertonian gusto about him. No ivory towers, please. He loves life, and is one of the shrewdest appraisers I know of the human comedy – and tragedy. He gets through an enormous amount of work without ever seeming to. But when most people are asleep he is at his piano and his scores. A powerful constitution serves him well, and the vigour of his conducting both illustrates and reinforces the tireless vitality that is the first requisite of a conductor today. Yet there are people who talk as if navvying were the hardest work! And he enjoys a joke against himself, always an attractive characteristic in a world where morbid egotisms and too exposed nerves victimise and vitiate the artist. Some time ago my own carelessness (or a typographical mix-up, so I try to explain, at any rate) made me write of him in an American paper that 'Lambert produces the minimum of results with the maximum of effort.' When, rather nervously, I pointed this out to him, he hooted with glee – and spread the glad and twisted tidings all over the place. I like to think that, after that, our friendship was solidly cemented.

He is a young man, this greatly gifted person – only 41. And so we watch his career with keen expectancy, knowing, also, that whatever he does will be what he wants to do.

'Personality Corner', *The Penguin Music Magazine II* (1947), pp. 40–2.

The critic C. B. Rees, a regular in The George, was in the habit of wearing one of two black hats that Lambert called 'Rococo' and 'Baroque'. Having discerned that Rees was Welsh, Constant would come in on St David's Day with a large shopping bag out of which he would take a long leek. With a safety pin supplied by Isabel Lambert, he would pin the leek to the side of whichever hat Rees was wearing, insisting that he kept it on for as long as Constant was in The George that morning.

Appendix 11
A Constant Lambert Iconography

1 George W. Lambert
The Mother
[Maurice, Mrs Lambert, Constant and Miss Thea Proctor]
Oil on canvas 1907
Queensland Art Gallery, Brisbane

2 George W. Lambert
The Bathers
[*l. to r.:* Mrs Lambert, Constant, Miss Thea Proctor and Maurice]
Oil on canvas 1907
Art Gallery of South Australia, Adelaide

3 George W. Lambert
Portrait Group
[Maurice, Constant and Mrs Lambert]
Oil on canvas 1908
National Gallery of Australia, Canberra

4 George W. Lambert
The Blue Hat
[Maurice, Mrs Lambert, Constant and Miss Thea Proctor]
Oil on canvas 1909
Kerry Stokes Collection, Perth

5 George W. Lambert
Mother and Sons
[Maurice, Mrs Lambert and Constant]
Oil on canvas
1909
Private collection

6 George W. Lambert
Holiday in Essex
[Mrs Lambert, Constant and Maurice]
Oil on canvas 1910
Art Gallery of NSW, Sydney

7 George W. Lambert
Constant Lambert as a Young Boy
Pencil December 1913
Private collection

8 Thea Proctor
Mother and Son
[Mrs Lambert and Constant]
Lithograph 1915
National Gallery of Victoria

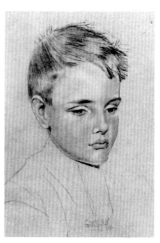

9 George W. Lambert
The Artist's son, Leonard Constant Lambert
Pencil 1916
Whereabouts unknown

10 George W. Lambert
Constant Lambert
Oil on canvas 1916
Christ's Hospital, Horsham

11 Gavin Gordon
[*Constant Lambert*]
Crayon n.d.
Victor Gordon

12 Maurice Lambert
Constant Lambert
Bronze 1925
Royal Opera House, London
bequeathed by Mrs Camilla Holt,
1989

13 Christopher Wood
The Composer
Oil on canvas 1925

14 Christopher Wood
Constant Lambert as a Young Man
Oil on canvas 1925
Leicestershire County Council Artworks

15 Christopher Wood
The Composer
Pencil January 1926

16 Christopher Wood
Portrait of Constant Lambert
Oil on canvas January 1926
National Portrait Gallery, London

17 Christopher Wood
The Composer
Oil on canvas 1927
Towner Art Gallery, Eastbourne

18 Edmond Kapp
Constant Lambert
Charcoal 1931
Barber Institute, University of Birmingham

19 (Percy) Wyndham Lewis
Constant Lambert
Pencil drawing & lithograph 1932
National Portrait Gallery, London

20 Oriel Ross
Constant Lambert
Pen and ink drawing 1930s
National Portrait Gallery, London

21 Gavin Gordon
[*Constant Lambert*]
Illustration *Radio Times*, July 1931

22 Guy Sheppard
Constant Lambert
Black and white painting 1938
V & A Museum, London

23 Gavin Gordon
[*Maynard Keynes, Ninette de Valois and Constant Lambert ?*]
Pencil drawing n.d.
Victor Gordon

24 Charles Reading
Constant Lambert
Illustration *The Dancing Times*, 1939

25 Kay Ambrose
Constant Lambert
Illustration *Balletomane's Sketch-Book*, 1941

26 Kay Ambrose
Constant Lambert
Illustration *Balletomane's Sketch-Book* 1941

27 Kay Ambrose
Constant Lambert
Illustration *Balletomane's Sketch-Book*, 1941

28 Michael Ayrton
Constant Lambert
Illustration *Radio Times*, 1945

29 Michael Ayrton
Studies for a Portrait of Constant Lambert
Pencil 1946

30 Michael Ayrton
Constant Lambert with a Cat
Pencil sketch for portrait 1948/9
Museum and Art Gallery, Salford

31 Michael Ayrton
Constant Lambert
Oil on canvas 1951
RCM, London

32 Michael Ayrton
Portrait of Constant Lambert
Oil on canvas 1951
Leicestershire Education
Authority collection

33 John Minnion
[Constant Lambert]
Pen and ink sketch for *The
Listener* 1983

Another family portrait by George W. Lambert, *The
Pond* (1908), oil on canvas, depicting mother and
two sons (Maurice and Constant), was unfortunately
found too late for inclusion in this appendix.

34 John Minnion
[Constant Lambert]
Pen and ink sketch in *Uneasy
Listening* 2003

Appendix 12
Lambert's Limericks and Other Verses

LIKE his close friend Philip Heseltine, Constant Lambert was a keen writer of limericks. During the war, encouraged by Tom Driberg, he embarked on a series of 'Double-Bishop Limericks', so called because they concerned bishops in the British Isles, the Dominions and the Tropics, most of whom had two or more dioceses. The collection was privately circulated under the alliterative title of 'The Boy[']s Blue Book of Bishops'; below is a selection of some of the more printable ones.

> The Bishop of Kimberley and Kuruman
> Had lusts that were strange and inhuman.
>   One night at Queen's Hall
>   He cried, 'Heaven may fall,
> But I simply *must* have Ernest Newman.'

> The Bishop (a frog) of Qu'Appelle
> Was renowned for his keen sense of smell.
>   When they bandaged his eyes
>   He sprung a surprise
> By telling Lord Keynes from Clive Bell.

> The Bishop of St Andrews, Dunkeld
> And Dunblane was once flogged till he yelled
>   By a Papist, whose grip
>   On a multi-thonged whip
> Was as firm as the tenets he held.

> The Bishop of Cork, Cloyne and Ross
> Was rarely, if ever, at loss
>   For a typical phrase
>   Explaining God's ways
> Such as calling Our Saviour 'The Boss'.

> The Bishop of Galway and Kilmacduagh
> Said, 'I'm not a fellow to rue a
>   Few nights on the tiles,
>   Though (because of my piles)
> Such pleasures get fewer and fewer.'

> The Bishop of Tuam, Killala
> And Achonry went to La Scala.
>   To the diva's surprise,
>   He nuzzled her thighs
> And murmured, 'Tonight's quite a gala.'

The Bishop of Newfoundland and Bermuda
Once painted himself in the nude – a
   Macabre little piece,
   Which reminded his niece
Of the morning he vainly pursued her.

The Bishop of Travancore and Cochin,
Having pushed back a barrel of scotch in
   The course of the day,
   Remarked, 'Let us pray
For the teetotal prigs who were watchin'.'

In addition to 'Jazz Blues' and 'Holy Moscow' (see chapter 2), the following poem, 'Dusk', was probably also written while Lambert was at Christ's Hospital. It shows the influence of Osbert Sitwell, bearing some similarity of mood to Sitwell's 'Rag-time', which appeared in *Wheels, Second Cycle*, December 1917 (reprinted in *Argonaut and Juggernaut* (London: Duckworth, 1919), p. 109), and to 'Metamorphosis', in *Wheels, Third Cycle*, January 1919 (*Argonaut and Juggernaut*, p. 79).

Dusk

A faery music floats upon the evening air
And ever changing chords of woodland harmony
Rise gently through the still translucent atmosphere.

Perfumes and sounds revolving in a misty haze
Caress with silken hands the far-off meadows dim
And trailing o'er the pools fall softly to the ground.

Steps in the village street break rudely on the ear
– Like hasty smudges on a rich bedizened book
The sound comes sharply through the softly stirring breeze.

Twilight enveloping all turns swiftly now to night
And swirling mists anoint the dark mysterious trees
Through which the wakeful owl cries out in hollow tone.

L. C. Lambert

Appendix 13
Vic-Wells / Sadler's Wells London Repertoire

T HESE samples of the Vic-Wells / Sadler's Wells ballet repertoire during the London seasons give some idea of the heavy work-load undertaken. The programmes are as advertised each day in *The Times*. They do not include the purely orchestral items that Constant Lambert often inserted between ballets. For the second and the third of these selected 'seasons', two pianos accompanied the dancers.

※ Season 1
At Sadler's Wells Theatre (30 weeks), alternating with Sadler's Wells Opera. Matinées at 2.30 p.m., evening performances at 8.30 p.m.

October 1938
Tues   18   *Carnaval, The Rake's Progress, Horoscope*
Thurs   20   *The Emperor's New Clothes, Les Sylphides, Checkmate*
Thurs   27   *Giselle, Les Patineurs*
Sat   29   matinée: *Les Rendezvous, Nocturne, Le Lac des cygnes 3*

November 1938
Tues   1   *Le Lac des cygnes 2, Nocturne, Checkmate*
Thurs   3   *A Wedding Bouquet, Apparitions, Les Patineurs*
Thurs   10   *Nocturne, Harlequin in the Street* (first performance), *Checkmate*
Sat   12   matinée: *Les Rendezvous, Horoscope, Harlequin in the Street*
Tues   15   *Le Lac des cygnes* (complete)
Thurs   17   *Harlequin in the Street, The Rake's Progress, Les Patineurs*
Thurs   24   *The Lord of Burleigh, Apparitions, Checkmate*
Sat   26   matinée: *Giselle, Façade*
Tues   29   *The Emperor's New Clothes, Horoscope, Casse-noisette 3*

December 1938
Thurs   1   *A Wedding Bouquet, Le Baiser de la fée, Nocturne*
Thurs   8   *Les Sylphides, The Judgement of Paris, Nocturne*
Sat   10   matinée: *Le Lac des cygnes* (complete)
Tues   13   *The Lord of Burleigh, Checkmate, Façade*
Thurs   15   *Casse-noisette* (complete), *Harlequin in the Street*
Thurs   22   *Les Sylphides, The Emperor's New Clothes, Le Baiser de la fée*
Mon   26   *Casse-noisette* (complete), *Les Patineurs*
Tues   27   *Les Rendezvous, Horoscope, Le Lac des cygnes 3*
Weds   28   *Façade* (preceding *Hansel and Gretel*)
Thurs   29   *Harlequin in the Street, Checkmate, Barabau*
Sat   31   matinée: *Façade* (preceding *Hansel and Gretel*)

January 1939
Tues   3   matinée: *Façade* (preceding *Hansel and Gretel*)
              evening: *The Rake's Progress, The Emperor's New Clothes, Le Baiser de la fée*
Thurs   5   *Carnaval, Horoscope, The Judgement of Paris, Façade*
Sat   7   matinée: *The Lord of Burleigh, Casse-noisette* (complete)
Tues   10   *Casse-noisette* (complete), *Horoscope*
Weds   11   matinée: *Façade* (preceding *Hansel and Gretel*)
Thurs   12   *Barabau, Les Sylphides, Checkmate*
Sat   14   matinée: *Façade* (preceding *Hansel and Gretel*)
Thurs   19   *Harlequin in the Street, Horoscope, Les Patineurs*
Sat   21   matinée: *Harlequin in the Street, Le Lac des cygnes 2, Checkmate*

Tues   24   *Le Lac des cygnes* (complete)
Thurs   26   *Casse-noisette* (complete), *Les Sylphides*

February 1939

Thurs   2   *The Sleeping Princess*
Sat   4   matinée: *Casse-noisette, Nocturne*
Mon   6   *The Sleeping Princess*
Tues   7   *Barabau, Apparitions, Les Patineurs*
Thurs   9   *The Sleeping Princess*
Thurs   16   *The Sleeping Princess*
Sat   18   matinée: *Harlequin in the Street, A Wedding Bouquet, Checkmate*
Tues   21   *The Sleeping Princess*
Thurs   23   *Les Sylphides, The Rake's Progress, Les Patineurs*

March 1939

Thurs   2   *Harlequin in the Street, Checkmate, The Judgement of Paris*
Sat   4   matinée: *The Sleeping Princess*
Tues   7   *Les Sylphides, Barabau, Horoscope*
Thurs   9   *The Emperor's New Clothes, Giselle*
Mon   13   *The Sleeping Princess*
Thurs   16   *Carnaval, Apparitions, Façade*
Sat   18   matinée: *Les Sylphides, The Gods Go a'Begging, Le Lac des cygnes* 3
Tues   21   *The Emperor's New Clothes, Checkmate, Harlequin in the Street*
Thurs   23   *The Gods Go a'Begging, The Rake's Progress, Les Patineurs*

April 1939

Sat   1   matinée: *The Sleeping Princess*
Mon   3   *The Sleeping Princess*
Tues   4   *Harlequin in the Street, The Haunted Ballroom, Les Patineurs*
Thurs   6   *The Sleeping Princess*
Thurs   13   *Carnaval, The Haunted Ballroom, A Wedding Bouquet*
Sat   15   matinée: *Le Lac des cygnes*
Tues   18   *The Gods Go a'Begging, Harlequin in the Street, Horoscope*
Thurs   20   matinée: *The Rake's Progress, Les Sylphides, Checkmate*
Thurs   27   matinée: *The Haunted Ballroom, Cupid and Psyche* (first performance), *Les Patineurs*
Sat   29   matinée: *The Rake's Progress, Horoscope, Les Patineurs*

May 1939

Tues   2   *Le Lac des cygnes 2, Cupid and Psyche, Horoscope*
Thurs   4   *A Wedding Bouquet, Checkmate, Façade*
Thurs   11   *Harlequin in the Street, Cupid and Psyche, Job*
Sat   13   matinée: *The Sleeping Princess*
            evening: *Job* (preceding *Hugh the Drover*)
Tues   16   *The Haunted Ballroom, Cupid and Psyche, Les Patineurs*
Thurs   18   *The Sleeping Princess*

※ Season 2

New Theatre (5 weeks) with two pianos, at 2.30 p.m.

January 1941

Tues   14   matinée: *Les Sylphides, Façade, Dante Sonata*
Weds   15   *Harlequin in the Street, The Wise Virgins, Façade*
Thurs   16   *Les Sylphides, The Prospect before Us, The Wise Virgins*
Fri   17   *Les Patineurs, The Prospect before Us, Les Sylphides*
Sat   18   2 p.m.: *Harlequin in the Street, Dante Sonata, Façade*
            4 p.m.: *Harlequin in the Street, Dante Sonata, Façade*
Mon   20   *The Gods Go a'Begging, The Sleeping Princess, The Prospect before Us*

Tues	21	*Le Lac des cygnes 2, The Wise Virgins, The Prospect before Us*
Weds	22	*Harlequin in the Street, The Sleeping Princess, Dante Sonata*
Thurs	23	*Les Sylphides, Dante Sonata, Façade*
Fri	24	*Harlequin in the Street, The Sleeping Princess, The Wise Virgins*
Sat	25	2 p.m.: *The Gods Go a'Begging, Le Lac des cygnes 2, Les Patineurs*
		4.15 p.m.: *The Gods Go a'Begging, Le Lac des cygnes 2, Les Patineurs*
Mon	27	*Harlequin in the Street, The Wanderer* (first performance), *Coppélia*
Tues	28	*The Gods Go a'Begging, The Wanderer, Façade*
Weds	29	*Les Sylphides, The Wanderer, The Gods Go a'Begging*
Thurs	30	*The Wise Virgins, The Prospect before Us, Les Rendezvous*
Fri	31	*Le Lac des cygnes, The Wanderer, Coppélia*

February 1941

Sat	1	2 p.m.: *Les Rendezvous, The Wanderer, Coppélia*
		4.15 p.m.: *Les Rendezvous, The Wanderer, Coppélia*
Mon	3	*Les Patineurs, Giselle 2, A Wedding Bouquet*
Tues	4	*Harlequin in the Street, The Prospect before Us, Dante Sonata*
Weds	5	*Le Lac des cygnes 2, A Wedding Bouquet, The Wise Virgins*
Thurs	6	2 p.m.: *The Gods Go a'Begging, Giselle 2, Dante Sonata*
		4.15 p.m.: *The Gods Go a'Begging, Giselle 2, Dante Sonata*
Fri	7	*The Wise Virgins, The Prospect before Us, The Wanderer*
Sat	8	2 p.m.: *Les Patineurs, The Wanderer, Façade*
		4.15 p.m.: *Les Patineurs, The Wanderer, Façade*
Mon	10	*Les Rendezvous, Le Lac des cygnes, The Wanderer*
Tues	11	*Harlequin in the Street, Le Lac des cygnes, Dante Sonata*
Weds	12	*The Gods Go a'Begging, The Wanderer, The Prospect before Us*
Thurs	13	2 p.m.: *Les Sylphides, The Wanderer, Les Patineurs*
		4.15 p.m.: *Les Sylphides, The Wanderer, Les Patineurs*
Fri	14	*Giselle 2, Façade, Dante Sonata*
Sat	15	2 p.m.: *Le Lac des cygnes 2, The Prospect before Us, The Wanderer*
		4.15 p.m.: *Le Lac des cygnes 2, The Prospect before Us, The Wanderer*

❦ Season 3

New Theatre (5 weeks) at 7 p.m. with two pianos

May 1941

Mon	19	*Fête polonaise, The Wise Virgins, A Wedding Bouquet*
Tues	20	*Fête polonaise, The Wise Virgins, A Wedding Bouquet*
Weds	21	matinée: *Fête polonaise, The Wise Virgins, A Wedding Bouquet*
		evening: *The Gods Go a'Begging, The Wanderer, Les Sylphides*
Thurs	22	matinée: *The Gods Go a'Begging, The Wanderer, Les Sylphides*
		evening: *The Gods Go a'Begging, The Wanderer, Les Sylphides*
Fri	23	*Le Lac des cygnes, The Prospect before Us, Dante Sonata*
Sat	24	matinée: *Le Lac des cygnes, The Prospect before Us, Dante Sonata*
		evening: *The Wise Virgins, The Wanderer, A Wedding Bouquet*
Mon	26	*Les Sylphides, The Prospect before Us, The Wanderer*
Tues	27	*Les Sylphides, The Prospect before Us, The Wanderer*
Weds	28	matinée: *Les Sylphides, The Prospect before Us, The Wanderer*
		evening: *Fête polonaise, Orpheus and Eurydice* (first performance), *A Wedding Bouquet*
Thurs	29	matinée: *Fête polonaise, Orpheus and Eurydice, A Wedding Bouquet*
		evening: *Fête polonaise, Orpheus and Eurydice, A Wedding Bouquet*
Fri	30	*The Gods Go a'Begging, Orpheus and Eurydice, Façade*
Sat	31	matinée: *Fête polonaise, Orpheus and Eurydice, A Wedding Bouquet*
		evening: *Le Lac des cygnes 2, Dante Sonata, Façade*

June 1941

Mon	2	matinée: *Harlequin in the Street, Les Sylphides, The Prospect before Us*
		evening: *Harlequin in the Street, Orpheus and Eurydice, Les Patineurs*
Tues	3	*Harlequin in the Street, Orpheus and Eurydice, Les Patineurs*
Weds	4	matinée: *Harlequin in the Street, Orpheus and Eurydice, Les Patineurs*
		evening: *The Wise Virgins, A Wedding Bouquet, Dante Sonata*
Thurs	5	matinée: *The Wise Virgins, A Wedding Bouquet, Dante Sonata*
		evening: *The Wise Virgins, A Wedding Bouquet, Dante Sonata*
Fri	6	*Fête polonaise, The Wanderer, Les Sylphides*
Sat	7	matinée: *Fête polonaise, The Wanderer, Les Sylphides*
		evening: *Harlequin in the Street, Orpheus and Eurydice, Façade*
Mon	9	*Le Lac des cygnes, Apparitions, Façade*
Tues	10	*The Wise Virgins, The Prospect before Us, Dante Sonata*
Weds	11	matinée: *The Gods Go a'Begging, Apparitions, Les Patineurs*
		evening: *Harlequin in the Street, The Wanderer, A Wedding Bouquet*
Thurs	12	matinée: *Les Sylphides, Orpheus and Eurydice, Façade*
		evening: *Les Sylphides, Orpheus and Eurydice, Façade*
Fri	13	*The Wise Virgins, Giselle 2, The Prospect before Us*
Sat	14	matinée: *The Gods Go a'Begging, Giselle, Les Patineurs*
		evening: *Les Sylphides, The Wanderer, A Wedding Bouquet*
Mon	16	*Les Sylphides, Harlequin in the Street, Apparitions*
Tues	17	*Les Sylphides, The Wise Virgins, Dante Sonata*
Weds	18	matinée: *The Gods Go a'Begging, Giselle, The Prospect before Us*
		evening: *Le Lac des cygnes, Orpheus and Eurydice, A Wedding Bouquet*
Thurs	19	matinée: *Harlequin in the Street, Apparitions, Façade*
		evening: *The Wise Virgins, The Wanderer, Les Patineurs*
Fri	20	*Harlequin in the Street, Orpheus and Eurydice, Façade*
Sat	21	matinée: *Le Lac des cygnes, The Wanderer, Apparitions*
		evening: *Les Sylphides, The Prospect before Us, Dante Sonata*

[The orchestra was used again from 21 July.]

⁊⁊ Season 4

New Theatre (3 weeks). Matinées at 2.30 p.m., evening performances at 6.45 p.m. Conductors: Constant Lambert and Julian Clifford

January 1943

Mon	25	*Coppélia*
Tues	26	*Comus, Les Sylphides, Hamlet*
Weds	27	matinée: *Coppélia*
		evening: *The Birds, The Rake's Progress, Façade*
Thurs	28	matinée: *Le Lac des cygnes*
		evening: *Le Lac des cygnes*
Fri	29	*The Birds, Comus, Dante Sonata*
Sat	30	matinée: *Les Rendezvous, Hamlet, Les Sylphides*
		evening: *Comus, Les Rendezvous, Dante Sonata*

February 1943

Mon	1	*Les Rendezvous, Apparitions, Façade*
Tues	2	*Coppélia*
Weds	3	matinée: *The Wise Virgins, Les Sylphides, Comus*
		evening: *Les Sylphides, The Wise Virgins, Hamlet*
Thurs	4	matinée: *The Birds, Giselle*
		evening: *Les Rendezvous, The Birds, The Rake's Progress*
Fri	5	*The Wise Virgins, Apparitions, Façade*
Mon	8	*The Birds, Giselle*
Tues	9	*The Wise Virgins, Apparitions, Façade*

Weds   10   matinée: *Le Lac des cygnes*
              evening: *Les Sylphides, Hamlet, Façade*
Thurs   11   matinée: *Coppélia*
              evening: *Le Lac des cygnes*
Fri   12   *The Rake's Progress, The Wise Virgins, Dante Sonata*
Sat   13   matinée: *The Birds, Comus, Les Rendezvous*
              evening: *Les Rendezvous, Giselle*

⁜ Season 5

New Theatre (4 weeks) at 6.45 p.m. Conductors: Constant Lambert and Julian Clifford

March 1943

Tues   30   *The Wise Virgins, Apparitions, Façade*
Weds   31   matinée: *The Wise Virgins, Hamlet, Casse-noisette*
              evening: *The Wise Virgins, Hamlet, Casse-noisette*

April 1943

Thurs   1   matinée: *Les Rendezvous, Apparitions, Casse-noisette*
              evening: *Les Rendezvous, Apparitions, Casse-noisette*
Fri   2   *Coppélia*
Sat   3   matinée: *Coppélia*
              Les Rendezvous, Hamlet, Façade
Mon   5   *Les Rendezvous, Hamlet, Façade*
Tues   6   *Les Sylphides, The Quest* (first performance), *Façade*
Weds   7   matinée: *Les Sylphides, The Quest, Façade*
              evening: *Les Sylphides, The Quest, Façade*
Thurs   8   matinée: *The Gods Go a'Begging, The Quest, Les Rendezvous*
              evening: *The Gods Go a'Begging, The Quest, Les Rendezvous*
Fri   9   *The Gods Go a'Begging, Giselle*
Sat   10   matinée: *The Gods Go a'Begging, The Quest, Casse-noisette*
              evening: *The Gods Go a'Begging, The Quest, Casse-noisette*
Mon   12   *Les Rendezvous, The Quest, Dante Sonata*
Tues   13   *Les Rendezvous, The Quest, Dante Sonata*
Weds   14   matinée: *Le Lac des cygnes*
              evening: *Le Lac des cygnes*
Thurs   15   matinée: *Les Sylphides, The Quest, Casse-noisette*
              evening: *Les Sylphides, The Quest, Casse-noisette*
Fri   16   *Comus, The Birds, The Rake's Progress*
Sat   17   matinée: *Les Rendezvous, Comus, Façade*
              evening: *Comus, The Birds, The Rake's Progress*
Mon   19   *The Birds, Giselle*
Tues   20   *Giselle*
Weds   21   matinée: *The Birds, Giselle*
              evening: *Le Lac des cygnes*
Thurs   22   matinée: *The Birds, The Quest, Dante Sonata*
              evening: *The Birds, The Quest, Dante Sonata*
Sat   24   matinée: *The Gods Go a'Begging, The Quest, Hamlet*
              evening: *The Gods Go a'Begging, The Quest, Hamlet*

⁜ Season 6

New Theatre (5 weeks) at 6.45 p.m. Conductors: Constant Lambert and Julian Clifford

May 1943

Tues   25   *The Birds, The Quest, Façade*
Weds   26   *The Birds, The Quest, Façade*

Thurs	27	matinée: *Le Lac des cygnes*
		evening: *Le Lac des cygnes*
Fri	28	*Les Sylphides, The Quest, Casse-noisette*
Sat	29	matinée: *Les Sylphides, Hamlet, Casse-noisette*
		evening: *Les Sylphides, Hamlet, Casse-noisette*
Mon	31	*Les Rendezvous, Hamlet, The Prospect before Us*

June 1943

Tues	1	*Les Rendezvous, Hamlet, The Prospect before Us*
Weds	2	matinée: *Coppélia*
		evening: *Coppélia*
Thurs	3	matinée: *The Gods Go a'Begging, The Quest, Façade*
		evening: *The Gods Go a'Begging, The Quest, Façade*
Fri	4	*The Birds, Giselle*
Sat	5	matinée: *The Birds, Dante Sonata, The Prospect before Us*
		evening: *The Birds, Dante Sonata, The Prospect before Us*
Mon	7	*The Wise Virgins, The Rake's Progress, Casse-noisette*
Tues	8	*The Wise Virgins, The Rake's Progress, Casse-noisette*
Weds	9	*Le Lac des cygnes*
Thurs	10	matinée: *The Wise Virgins, The Quest, Façade*
		evening: *The Wise Virgins, The Quest, Façade*
Fri	11	*The Wise Virgins, Dante Sonata, The Prospect before Us*
Sat	12	matinée: *Les Rendezvous, The Rake's Progress, Les Sylphides*
		evening: *Les Rendezvous, The Rake's Progress, Les Sylphides*
Mon	14	*The Gods Go a'Begging, Hamlet, A Wedding Bouquet*
Tues	15	*The Gods Go a'Begging, Hamlet, A Wedding Bouquet*
Weds	16	matinée: *Les Rendezvous, The Quest, Casse-noisette*
		evening: *Les Rendezvous, The Quest, Casse-noisette*
Thurs	17	matinée: *Coppélia*
		evening: *Coppélia*
Fri	18	*The Birds, The Rake's Progress, A Wedding Bouquet*
Sat	19	matinée: *The Birds, The Rake's Progress, A Wedding Bouquet*
		evening: *The Birds, Hamlet, A Wedding Bouquet*
Mon	21	*The Wise Virgins, Giselle*
Tues	22	*The Wise Virgins, The Quest, A Wedding Bouquet*
Weds	23	matinée: *Le Lac des cygnes*
		evening: *Le Lac des cygnes*
Thurs	24	matinée: *The Birds, The Quest, Façade*
		evening: *The Birds, The Quest, Façade*
Fri	25	*Les Sylphides, The Rake's Progress, A Wedding Bouquet*
Sat	26	matinée: *Les Sylphides, Hamlet, A Wedding Bouquet*
		evening: *Les Sylphides, Hamlet, A Wedding Bouquet*

※ Season 7

New Theatre (7 weeks). Conductors: Constant Lambert and Alec Sherman

August 1943

Thurs	26	*Les Sylphides, Hamlet, The Prospect before Us*
Fri	27	*Les Sylphides, Hamlet, The Prospect before Us*
Sat	28	matinée: *Comus, Les Sylphides, Hamlet*
		evening: *Comus, Les Sylphides, The Prospect before Us*
Mon	30	*Coppélia*
Tues	31	*Les Rendezvous, The Quest, Façade*

September 1943

Weds	1	matinée: *Les Rendezvous, Comus, Façade*
		evening: *Comus, Les Rendezvous, The Prospect before Us*
Thurs	2	matinée: *The Birds, The Quest, Façade*
		evening: *The Birds, The Quest, Hamlet*
Fri	3	*The Birds, The Quest, Façade*
Sat	4	matinée: *Coppélia*
		evening: *Coppélia*
Mon	6	*Les Rendezvous, Comus, Façade*
Tues	7	*Le Lac des cygnes*
Weds	8	matinée: *Le Lac des cygnes*
		evening: *Les Sylphides, A Wedding Bouquet, Dante Sonata*
Thurs	9	matinée: *Les Sylphides, A Wedding Bouquet, Comus*
		evening: *Comus, A Wedding Bouquet, Dante Sonata*
Fri	10	*Le Lac des cygnes*
Sat	11	matinée: *Le Lac des cygnes*
		evening: *Les Sylphides, A Wedding Bouquet, Dante Sonata*
Mon	13	*Le Lac des cygnes*
Tues	14	*Le Lac des cygnes*
Weds	15	matinée: *The Birds, The Quest, Façade*
		evening: *The Birds, The Quest, A Wedding Bouquet*
Thurs	16	matinée: *Le Lac des cygnes*
		evening: *Le Lac des cygnes*
Fri	17	*The Birds, Hamlet, The Prospect before Us*
Sat	18	matinée: *Les Sylphides, The Quest, A Wedding Bouquet*
		evening: *Les Sylphides, The Quest, Dante Sonata*
Mon	20	*Les Rendezvous, Giselle*
Tues	21	*Comus, Façade, The Rake's Progress*
Weds	22	matinée: *Le Lac des cygnes*
		evening: *Le Lac des cygnes*
Thurs	23	matinée: *Les Sylphides, Hamlet, Façade*
		evening: *Les Sylphides, The Rake's Progress, Façade*
Fri	24	*Comus, Giselle*
Sat	25	matinée: *Le Lac des cygnes*
		evening: *Le Lac des cygnes*
Mon	27	*Coppélia*
Tues	28	*Les Rendezvous, Hamlet, The Prospect before Us*
Weds	29	matinée: *Coppélia*
		evening: *Coppélia*
Thurs	30	matinée: *Le Lac des cygnes*
		evening: *Le Lac des cygnes*

October 1943

Fri	1	*Les Rendezvous, Hamlet, A Wedding Bouquet*
Sat	2	matinée: *The Birds, The Rake's Progress, Façade*
		evening: *The Birds, The Rake's Progress, Façade*
Mon	4	*Les Sylphides, The Quest, Dante Sonata*
Tues	5	*Les Sylphides, The Quest, Dante Sonata*
Weds	6	matinée: *Les Rendezvous, Giselle*
		evening: *Comus, Les Rendezvous, Dante Sonata*
Thurs	7	matinée: *Le Lac des cygnes*
		evening: *Le Lac des cygnes*
Fri	8	*Les Sylphides, Hamlet, The Prospect before Us*
Sat	9	matinée: *Les Sylphides, The Quest, Façade*
		evening: *Giselle, Façade*
Mon	11	*The Birds, The Rake's Progress, A Wedding Bouquet*

Tues   12   *The Birds, The Rake's Progress, A Wedding Bouquet*
Weds   13   matinée: *Coppélia*
             evening: *Coppélia*
Thurs   14   matinée: *Les Sylphides, The Quest, Hamlet*
             evening: *Les Sylphides, The Quest, Hamlet*
Fri   15   *Les Sylphides, The Quest, Dante Sonata*
Sat   16   matinée: *Le Lac des cygnes*
             evening: *Le Lac des cygnes*

⁂ Season 8
New Theatre (10 weeks). Conductors: Constant Lambert and Alec Sherman

November 1943
Tues   30   *Les Rendezvous, The Rake's Progress, Façade*

December 1943
Weds   1   matinée: *Coppélia*
             evening: *Coppélia*
Thurs   2   matinée: *Les Sylphides, The Quest, Les Rendezvous*
             evening: *Les Sylphides, The Quest, Façade*
Fri   3   *Les Rendezvous, The Rake's Progress, A Wedding Bouquet*
Sat   4   matinée: *Le Lac des cygnes*
             evening: *Le Lac des cygnes*
Mon   6   *The Wise Virgins, Giselle*
Tues   7   *The Wise Virgins, Promenade, Hamlet*
Weds   8   matinée: *Les Sylphides, Hamlet, Promenade*
             evening: *Les Sylphides, Hamlet, Promenade*
Thurs   9   matinée: *The Wise Virgins, Promenade, Façade*
             evening: *Promenade, The Rake's Progress, Façade*
Fri   10   *Le Lac des cygnes*
Sat   11   matinée: *Les Sylphides, The Quest, Promenade*
             evening: *Les Sylphides, The Quest, Promenade*
Mon   13   *The Wise Virgins, Promenade, Dante Sonata*
Tues   14   *Le Lac des cygnes*
Weds   15   matinée: *The Wise Virgins, Les Sylphides, Promenade*
             evening: *Promenade, Giselle*
Thurs   16   matinée: *The Wise Virgins, The Quest, Façade*
             evening: *The Wise Virgins, Promenade, Dante Sonata*
Fri   17   *Promenade, Hamlet, A Wedding Bouquet*
Sat   18   matinée: *Coppélia*
             evening: *A Wedding Bouquet, Promenade, Dante Sonata*
Tues   21   *Les Rendezvous, Giselle*
Weds   22   matinée: *Comus, Promenade, Job*
             evening: *Comus, Promenade, Job*
Thurs   23   matinée: *Les Rendezvous, Hamlet, Promenade*
             evening: *Les Rendezvous, Hamlet, Promenade*
Fri   24   *Les Sylphides, Promenade, Job*
Mon   27   *The Wise Virgins, Hamlet, The Prospect before Us*
Tues   28   *The Wise Virgins, Hamlet, The Prospect before Us*
Weds   29   matinée: *Le Lac des cygnes*
             evening: *Le Lac des cygnes*
Thurs   30   matinée: *Coppélia*
             evening: *Coppélia*
Fri   31   *Comus, Hamlet, Promenade*

January 1944

Sat   1   matinée: *Le Lac des cygnes*
            evening: *Le Lac des cygnes*
Mon   3   *Les Sylphides, Promenade, A Wedding Bouquet*
Tues   4   *Les Sylphides, Promenade, Job*
Weds   5   matinée: *Les Sylphides, Promenade, Façade*
            evening: *Promenade, The Quest, Dante Sonata*
Thurs   6   matinée: *Les Rendezvous, The Quest, Façade*
            evening: *Les Rendezvous, The Quest, Dante Sonata*
Fri   7   *Comus, Les Rendezvous, The Prospect before Us*
Sat   8   matinée: *Comus, Promenade, Job*
            evening: *Comus, Promenade, Job*
Mon   10   *Le Lac des cygnes*
Tues   11   *Le Lac des cygnes*
Weds   12   matinée: *Promenade, The Quest, Façade*
            evening: *Promenade, The Quest, Façade*
Thurs 13   matinée: *The Wise Virgins, Hamlet, Casse-noisette 3*
            evening: *The Wise Virgins, A Wedding Bouquet, Dante Sonata*
Fri   14   *Casse-noisette, Hamlet, Promenade*
Sat   15   matinée: *Coppélia*
            evening: *Coppélia*
Mon   17   *Casse-noisette, Façade, Job*
Tues   18   *Casse-noisette, Façade, Job*
Weds   19   matinée: *Les Rendezvous, The Quest, Casse-noisette 2*
            evening: *Les Rendezvous, The Quest, Casse-noisette 2*
Thurs 20   matinée: *Promenade, The Quest, Casse-noisette*
            evening: *Promenade, The Prospect before Us, Casse-noisette*
Fri   21   *Les Sylphides, The Prospect before Us, Promenade*
Sat   22   matinée: *Les Sylphides, A Wedding Bouquet, Job*
            evening: *Les Sylphides, A Wedding Bouquet, Job*
Mon   24   *Les Rendezvous, The Rake's Progress, Dante Sonata*
Tues   25   *Le Lac des cygnes*
Weds   26   matinée: *Coppélia*
            evening: *Coppélia*
Thurs 27   matinée: *Les Sylphides, The Quest, Promenade*
            evening: *Les Sylphides, The Quest, Promenade*
Fri   28   *Le Lac des cygnes*
Sat   29   matinée: *Casse-noisette, The Rake's Progress, Promenade*
            evening: *Casse-noisette, The Rake's Progress, Promenade*

February 1944

Tues   1   *Promenade, Casse-noisette, Dante Sonata*
Weds   2   *Promenade, Le Spectre de la rose, Le Lac des cygnes*
Thurs   3   matinée: *Les Sylphides, Le Spectre de la rose, Casse-noisette*
            evening: *Les Sylphides, Le Spectre de la rose, Job*
Fri   4   *Promenade, Le Spectre de la rose, Job*
Sat   5   matinée: *Promenade, Le Spectre de la rose, Job*
            evening: *Promenade, Le Spectre de la rose, Job*

Bibliography

Aberconway, Christabel, *A Wiser Women? A Book of Memories* (London: Hutchinson, 1966)

Acton, Harold, *Memoirs of an Aesthete* (London: Metheun, 1948)

Adams, Byron, 'High-Tea at Merlinford: Remembering Lord Berners', *Music & Letters*, vol. 91 (2010), pp. 406–11

Agate, James, *Immoment Toys: A Survey of Light Entertainment on the London Stage, 1920–1943* (London: Jonathan Cape, 1945)

Aldgate, Anthony, and Jeffrey Richards, *Britain Can Take It: The British Cinema in the Second World War* (Oxford: Blackwell, 1986)

Aldous, Richard, *Tunes of Glory: The Life of Malcolm Sargent* (London: Hutchinson, 2001)

Amis, John, *Amiscellany: My Life, My Music* (London: Faber & Faber, 1985; paperback, 1986)

—— *My Music in London, 1945–2000* (London: Amiscellany Books, 2006)

Amory, Mark, *Lord Berners: The Last Eccentric* (London: Chatto & Windus, 1998)

Anthony, Gordon, *The Vic-Wells Ballet: Camera Studies*, introduced by Ninette de Valois (London: Routledge, 1938) [first plate Constant Lambert]

ApIvor, Denis, 'A Personal Memoir of Constant Lambert', 8pp typescript [letter to Hubert Foss, 16 April 1952]

—— 'A Personal Memoir of Constant Lambert', 17pp typescript [letter to Angus Morrison, 9 March 1954]

—— 'Composer's Anthology 7', *Recorded Sound*, nos. 66–7 (April–July 1977), pp. 692–7 [transcription of 'Composer's Portrait', illustrated talk, BBC Music Programme, 19 April 1967]

—— 'Memories of "The Warlock Circle"', in *Peter Warlock: A Centenary Celebration*, ed. David Cox and John Bishop (London: Thames Publishing, 1994), pp. 187–96

Arnold, Malcolm, 'My Early Life', *Music and Musicians*, October 1986, pp. 8–9

Arundell, Dennis, *The Story of Sadler's Wells, 1683–1977* (London: Hamish Hamilton, 1965); extended second edition (Newton Abbott: David & Charles, 1978)

Ayrton, Michael, 'A Sketch for a Portrait of Constant Lambert', 11pp typescript [intended for publication in *The Book of the Year* (Dobson), and used with minor changes in *Ballet Annual*, no. 10 (1956); *Ballet Decade*, ed. Arnold Haskell (London: A. & C. Black, 1956); Ayrton, *Golden Sections* (London: Methuen, 1957), pp. 123–35]

Banfield, Stephen, *Gerald Finzi: An English Composer* (London: Faber & Faber, 1997; paperback, 1998)

Baring, Mark, *Por Lit'le Bleeder: An Autobiography* (Somerset: Graphic Type, 1998)

Baron [Stirling Henry Nahum], *Baron at the Ballet* [collection of photographs], introduction and commentary by Arnold L. Haskell, foreword by Sacheverell Sitwell (London: Collins, 1950)

Bartlett, Ian, 'Lambert, Finzi and the anatomy of the Boyce revival', *The Musical Times*, vol. 144, issue no. 1884 (Autumn 2003), pp. 54–9

Beaton, Cecil, *Ballet* (London: Wingate, 1951)

—— *The Wandering Years: Diaries, 1922–1939* (London: Weidenfeld & Nicolson, 1961)

—— *Self Portrait with Friends: The Selected Diaries*, ed. Richard Buckle (London: Pimlico, 1979)

Beaumont, Cyril W., *The Diaghilev Ballet in London: A Personal Record* (London: Putnam, 1940; first illustrated version, 1945)

—— *The Sadler's Wells Ballet: A Detailed Account of Works in the Permanent Repertory with Critical Notes* (London: C. W. Beaumont, 1946; revised and enlarged edition, 1947)

Bennett, Arnold, *The Journals of Arnold Bennett* (Harmondsworth: Penguin Books, 1954)

Berlin, Isaiah, 'Music in Decline', *The Spectator*, 11 May 1934, pp. 745–6

Bird, John, *Percy Grainger* (London: Paul Elek, 1976; London: Faber & Faber, 1982; Oxford: Oxford University Press, 1999)

Blades, James, *Drum Roll: A Professional Adventure from the Circus to the Concert Hall* (London: Faber & Faber, 1977)

Bland, Alexander, *The Royal Ballet: The First Fifty Years* (New York: Doubleday & Co., 1981)

Bliss, Arthur, *As I Remember* (London: Faber & Faber, 1970)

—— *Bliss on Music: Selected Writings of Arthur Bliss, 1920–1975*, ed. Gregory Roscow (Oxford: Oxford University Press, 1991)

Blom, Eric, 'Constant Lambert as a Composer', *The Listener*, 12 September 1940, p. 393

Boult, Adrian, *My Own Trumpet* (London: Hamish Hamilton, 1973)

Bradford, Sarah, *Sacheverell Sitwell: Splendours and Miseries* (New York: Farrar, Straus, Giroux, 1993)

Bradley, Lionel, *Sixteen Years of Ballet Rambert* (London: Hinrichsen Edition, 1946)

Britten, Benjamin, *Letters from a Life*: *The Selected Letters and Diaries of Benjamin Britten* (London: Faber & Faber), vol. 1: *1923–39*, ed. Donald Mitchell and Philip Reed (1991); vol. 3: *1946–51*, ed. Donald Mitchell, Philip Reed and Mervyn Cooke (2004)

Brook, Donald, *Conductors' Gallery* (London: Rockliff, 1946), pp. 85–7

Boughton, Rutland, 'A Modernist Blows the Gaff', *New Britain*, 9 May 1934

Buckle, Richard, *The Adventures of a Ballet Critic* (London: Cresset Press, 1953)

—— *Diaghilev* (London: Weidenfeld & Nicolson, 1979)

Bush, Geoffrey, 'Composer's Anthology 2', *Recorded Sound*, no. 40 (October 1970), pp. 688–94

Cannon-Brookes, Peter, *Michael Ayrton: An Illustrated Commentary* (Birmingham: Birmingham Museums and Art Gallery, 1978)

Chadd, David, and John Gage, '"A Native English Flower": The Camargo Society and the English Companies', in *The Diaghilev Ballet in England* (Norwich: University of East Anglia, 1979) [exhibition catalogue with separate addenda]

Chappell, William, *Fonteyn: Impressions of a Ballerina* (London: Rockliff, 1951)

Chazin-Bennahum, Judith, *The Ballets of Antony Tudor: Studies in Psyche and Satire* (Oxford: Oxford University Press, 1994)

Clark, Kenneth, *The Other Half: A Self Portrait* (London: John Murray, 1977)

Clarke, Mary, *The Sadler's Wells Ballet: A History and an Appreciation* (London: A. & C. Black, 1955)

Cochran, Charles B., *Cock-A-Doodle-Do* (London: Dent, 1941)

—— *Showman Looks On* (London: Dent, 1945)

Cohen, Harriet, *A Bundle of Time: The Memoirs of Harriet Cohen* (London: Faber & Faber, 1969)

Connolly, Cyril, 'March of Time', *Sunday Times*, 23 September 1973 [Connolly 'recalls an old antagonist with admiration']

Cooke, Deryck, 'Constant Lambert', liner notes for Argo RG50 LP (Lambert's Piano Concerto and *Eight Songs of Li-Po*), 1955

—— 'Another Look at *Music Ho!*', *The Listener*, 29 November 1962, pp. 910–11

Copley, Ian, *The Music of Peter Warlock: A Critical Survey* (London: Denis Dobson, 1979)

Coton, A. V., *A Prejudice for Ballet* (London: Methuen, 1938)

Cox, David, *The Henry Wood Proms* (London: BBC, 1980)

Craggs, Stewart R., *William Walton: A Catalogue* (Oxford: Clarendon Press, 1990) [superseding Craggs, *William Walton: A Thematic Catalogue* (Oxford: Oxford University Press, 1977)]

—— (ed.), *Arthur Bliss: A Source Book* (Aldershot: Scolar Press, 1996)

Crichton, Ronald, 'Lambert, (Leonard) Constant', in *The New Grove Dictionary of Music and Musicians*, ed. Stanley Sadie (Oxford: Oxford University Press, 1980), pp. 394–7

Daneman, Meredith, *Margot Fonteyn* (New York: Viking, 2004)

Dean, Basil, *Mind's Eye: An Autobiography, 1927–1972* (London: Hutchinson, 1973)

Delmer, Sefton, *Trail Sinister: An Autobiography*, vol. 1 (London: Secker & Warburg, 1961)

—— *Black Boomerang: An Autobiography*, vol. 2 (London: Secker & Warburg, 1962)

Delius, Frederick, Lionel Carley, *Delius: A Life in Letters*, vol. 2 (London: Scolar Press, 1988)

Demuth, Norman, *Musical Trends in the 20th Century* (London: Rockliff, 1952)

Dent, Edward, 'Constant Lambert: An Appreciation', in *Ballet, 1950–1952*, ed. Michael Wood, Covent Garden Books No. 6 (London: Royal Opera House, 1952), pp. 30–3

Dent, E. J., *et al.*, *Purcell's The Fairy Queen as presented by the Sadler's Wells Ballet and the Covent Garden Opera* (London: John Lehmann, 1948)

Dickinson, Peter, *Lord Berners: Composer, Writer, Painter* (Woodbridge: Boydell Press, 2008)

Dieren, Bernard van, *Down among the Dead Men, and Other Essays* (London: Oxford University Press, 1935)

Doctor, Jennifer, *The BBC and Ultra-Modern Music, 1922–1936* (Oxford: Oxford University Press, 1999)

Dolin, Anton, *Autobiography* (London: Oldbourne Book Co. 1960)

Doyle, Suzanne, 'Biography', and 'Isabel Rawsthorne: Paintings, Drawings and Designs', in *Isabel Rawsthorne, 1912–1992: Paintings, Drawings and Designs* (London: Harrogate Museum and Arts, 1997) [exhibition catalogue]

Drew, David, 'North Sea Crossings: Walter Leigh, Hindemith, and English Music', *Beiträge zur Musik des 20. Jahrhunderts*, ed. Susanne Schaal-Gotthardt, Luitgard Schader and Heinz-Jürgen Winkler, Frankfurter Studien 12 (Frankfurt am Main: Schott, 2009), pp. 127–54

——(ed.), *The Decca Book of Ballet* (London: Frederick Muller, 1958)

Driberg, Tom, *The Best of Both Worlds: A Personal Diary* (London: Phoenix House, 1953)

——*Ruling Passions* (London: Jonathan Cape, 1977)

Driver, Paul, '"Façade" Revisited', *Tempo*, new series 133/134 (September 1980), pp. 3–9

Dukelsky, Vladimir, *Passport to Paris* (Boston: Little, Brown & Co., 1955)

Easterbrook, Giles, liner notes for Hyperion CDA66754 (Concerto for Piano and Nine Players, etc.), 1995

——liner notes for ASV CD WHL2122 (*Prize Fight*, Piano Concerto, etc.), 1999

Edwards, Leslie, with Graham Bowles, *In Good Company: Sixty Years with the Royal Ballet* (Binsted: Dance Books, 2003)

Elgar, Edward, *Edward Elgar: Letters of a Lifetime*, ed. Jerrold Northrop Moore (Oxford: Clarendon Press, 1990)

Engledow, Sarah, *The World of Thea Proctor* (Canberra: National Portrait Gallery of Australia, 2005)

Evans, Edwin, 'Walton and Lambert', *Modern Music*, vol. 7 no. 2 (1930), pp. 26–31

——'Lambert's Autobiography, Chapter One' [review of *Music Ho!*], *The Music Lover*, 21 April 1934, p. 14

——'Constant Lambert' [obituary], *The Chesterian*, vol. 12, issue no. 95 (June 1951), pp. 181–7

Faulks, Sebastian, *The Fatal Englishman: Three Short Lives* (London: Hutchinson, 1996) [including Christopher Wood]

Fenby, Eric, *Delius as I Knew Him* (London: Bell, 1936; Faber & Faber, 1981)

Fifoot, Richard, *A Bibliography of Edith, Osbert and Sacheverell Sitwell*, 2nd revised edition (Hamden, CT: Archon Books, 1971)

Finzi, Gerald, and Howard Ferguson, *Letters of Gerald Finzi and Howard Ferguson*, ed. Howard Ferguson and Michael Hurd (Woodbridge: Boydell & Brewer, 2005)

Fonteyn, Margot, *Autobiography* (London: W. H. Allen, 1975; paperback Litton: Magna Print Books, 1976)

Foreman, Lewis, *From Parry to Britten: British Music in Letters, 1900–1945* (London: Batsford, 1987)

——liner notes for Hyperion CDA67049 (*Pomona, Tiresias*), 1999

——'Arthur Bliss at the BBC', in *Arthur Bliss: Music and Literature*, ed. Stewart R. Craggs (Aldershot: Ashgate, 2002), pp. 227–65

——*Bax: A Composer and His Times*, 3rd revised and expanded edition (Woodbridge: Boydell Press, 2007)

——liner notes for Lyrita SRCD215 (*Music for Orchestra, King Pest*), 2007

Foss, Hubert, *Music in My Time* (London: Rich & Cowan, 1933)

——'"Music Ho!" by Constant Lambert' [review], *The Musical Times*, vol. 75, issue no. 1096 (June 1934), pp. 514–15

——'Constant Lambert', in *British Music of Our Time*, ed. A. L. Bacharach (Harmondsworth: Penguin Books, 1946), pp. 168–74; new edition (1951), pp. 163–9

——'Constant Lambert', *Columbia Record Guide 9*, vol. 3 no. 10 (October 1947), pp. 9–11

——*Ralph Vaughan Williams: A Study* (Edinburgh: Harrap, 1950)

——'Constant Lambert' [obituary], *Gramophone*, September 1951, p. 73

——'Constant Lambert' [obituary], *The Musical Times*, vol. 92, issue no. 1304 (October 1951), pp. 449–51

——'*Horoscope*: A Study', *Hallé Magazine*, no. 41 (October 1951), pp. 18–20

—— 'Obituary of Cecil Gray (1895–1951)', *Music* (The Magazine of the London Musical Club), no. 3 (October 1951), pp. 4–5

—— 'Phases of the Moon: 1. The Warlock Gang', *London Symphony Observer*, November 1951, pp. 99–100

—— 'The Music of Constant Lambert', *The Listener*, 24 January 1952, p. 158

Frank, Alan, 'The Music of Constant Lambert', *The Musical Times*, vol. 78, issue no. 1137 (November 1937), pp. 941–5

—— 'Contemporary Portraits No. 5: Constant Lambert', *Music Teacher*, January 1951, pp. 19–20

—— 'The Music of Constant Lambert', *Disc*, vol. 5 no. 19 (1952), pp. 103–7

—— 'Constant Lambert', in *Modern British Composers* (London: Dobson, 1953), pp. 80–5

Gayford, Martin, 'More than a Face to Remember', *Daily Telegraph*, 25 July 1998 [on Isabel Lambert/Rawsthorne]

Geller, Eleanor, 'Constant Lambert and Ballet in Britain, 1923–1951' (Southampton University: unpublished BA dissertation, 2009)

Glendinning, Victoria, *Edith Sitwell: A Unicorn among Lions* (London: Weidenfeld & Nicolson, 1981; paperback Phoenix, 1993)

Goddard, Scott, 'Music of the Film' [*Anna Karenina*], *Penguin Music Magazine* no. 7 (1948), pp. 88–9

Goossens, Eugene, *Overture and Beginners: A Musical Autobiography* (London: Methuen, 1951)

Le Grand Baton, vol. 19 no. 3, issue no. 54 (September 1982) [Lambert special issue, including Kenneth DeKay, 'Constant Lambert: Genius and Tragedy'; Nathan E. Brown, 'Constant Lambert Discography'; 'Constant Lambert at the 1946 Proms' (Prospectus of Programmes)]

Gray, Anne, *George Lambert, 1873–1930: Art and Artifice* (Roseville East, NSW: Craftsman House, 1996)

—— *George W. Lambert Retrospective* (Canberra: National Gallery of Australia, 2007)

Gray, Cecil, 'The Music of Bernard Van Dieren', *The Sackbut*, vol. 2 no. 2 (July 1921), pp. 6–11

—— *A Survey of Contemporary Music* (Oxford: Oxford University Press, 1924)

—— 'A Young English Composer: Constant Lambert', *The Nation and Athenæum*, vol. 44 no. 5 (3 November 1928), pp. 174–5

—— *The History of Music* (New York: Kegan Paul, Trench, Trubner & Co., 1928)

—— *Peter Warlock: A Memoir of Philip Heseltine* (London: Jonathan Cape, 1934), 1938

—— 'A New Work by Constant Lambert', *The Listener*, 22 January 1936, pp. 187–8 [on *Summer's Last Will and Testament*]

—— 'Hyam Greenbaum (1901–1942)', *The Music Review*, vol. 3 no. 3 (August 1942), pp. 219–23

—— *Musical Chairs, or Between Two Stools: An Autobiography* (London: Home & Van Thal, 1948); reissued with an afterword by Pauline Gray (London: Hogarth Press, 1985)

Gray, Pauline, *Cecil Gray: His Life and Notebooks* (London: Thames, 1989)

—— 'The Lesser Known Talents of Cecil Gray', *British Music Society Journal*, vol. 8 (1986), pp. 1–9

Green, Gordon, 'The Friends of Alan Rawsthorne', *The Creel*, vol. 2 no. 1 (Spring 1992), pp. 127–8

Grierson, Mary, *Donald Francis Tovey: A Biography Based on Letters* (London: Oxford University Press, 1952)

Grigoriev, S. L., *The Diaghilev Ballet, 1909–1929*, ed. and trans. Vera Bowen (London: Constable, 1953; Harmondsworth: Penguin Books, 1960)

Hammond, Joan, *A Voice, A Life* (London: Gollancz, 1970)

Hamnett, Nina, *Laughing Torso: Reminiscences of Nina Hamnett* (New York: Long & Smith, 1932)

—— *Is She a Lady? A Problem in Autobiography* (London: Allan Wingate, 1955)

Harries, Meirion and Susie, *A Pilgrim Soul: The Life and Work of Elisabeth Lutyens* (London: Michael Joseph, 1989; paperback Faber & Faber, 1991)

Haskell, Arnold, *Balletomania* (London: Gollancz, 1934); revised edition (Harmondsworth: Penguin Books, 1979)

—— *True Centre: An Interim Autobiography* (London: A. & C. Black, 1951)

Haskell, Arnold, Mark Bonham Carter, and Michael Wood (eds.), *Gala Performance: A Record of The Sadler's Wells Ballet over Twenty-Five Years* (London: Collins, 1955)

Helpman, Mary, *The Helpman Family Story, 1796–1964* (Brisbane: Rigby, 1967)

Herbert, David, *Second Son: An Autobiography* (London: Peter Owen, 1972)

Heyes, David, 'Lambert and Rawsthorne', *British Music Society Newsletter*, no. 72 (December 1996), pp. 284–5; *The Creel* (Journal of the Rawsthorne Trust and Friends of Alan Rawsthorne), vol. 3 no. 4 (1997)

Hill, Ralph, 'Some Post-War Critics', *The Sackbut*, vol. 14 no. 5 (December 1933), pp. 122–6

Hinnells, Duncan, *An Extraordinary Performance: Hubert Foss, Music Publishing, and the Oxford University Press* (Oxford: Oxford University Press, 1998)

Holroyd, Michael, *Lytton Strachey: A Biography* (Harmondworth: Penguin Books, 1971)

Hopkins, Justine, *Michael Ayrton: A Biography* (London: Andre Deutsch, 1994)

Hordern, Michael, *A World Elsewhere* (London: Michael O'Mara Books, 1993)

Hoskins, Trevor, 'Constant Lambert: His Illness at Christ's Hospital School and the Role of Dr G. E. Friend', *Journal of Medical Biography*, vol. 11 (2003), pp. 14–20

Howes, Frank, *The English Musical Renaissance* (London: Secker & Warburg, 1966)

Hughes, Spike [= Patrick Cairns], *Opening Bars: Beginning an Autobiography* (London: Pilot Press, 1946)

—— *Second Movement: Continuing the Autobiography of Spike Hughes* (London: Museum Press, 1951)

Huntley, John, *British Film Music* (London: Skelton Robinson, 1947)

Hussey, Dyneley, 'Constant Lambert and the Ballet', *The Dancing Times*, no. 492 (October 1951), pp. 9–11

Hutchings, Arthur, 'Introduction', in Constant Lambert, *Music Ho!: A Study of Music in Decline*, reissued third edition (London: Faber & Faber, 1966), pp. 9–28

Inglesby, Richard, *Christopher Wood: An English Painter* (London: Allison & Busby, 1995)

Irving, Ernest, *Cue for Music: An Autobiography* (London: Dennis Dobson, 1959)

Jacob, Gordon, 'Personal View 5: Gordon Jacob', *RCM Magazine*, vol. 41 no. 3 (Christmas Term 1965), pp. 71–2

—— 'Gordon Jacob in Interview', *British Music Society Journal*, vol. 7 (October 1985), pp. 59–67

Jacobs, Arthur, 'The Music of Constant Lambert', *Radio Times*, 25 January 1952, p. 13

—— *Henry J. Wood, Maker of the Proms* (London: Methuen, 1994)

Jenkins, Alan, *The Twenties* (London: Heinemann, 1974)

Jewell, Derek, *Duke: A Portrait of Duke Ellington* (London: Hamish Hamilton, 1977)

Johnson, Richard, 'Tiresias', *The New Statesman and Nation*, 12 July 1951

Jones, Bryony, *The Music of Lord Berners (1883–1950): 'The Versatile Peer'* (Aldershot: Ashgate, 2003)

Jose, Arthur, *et al.*, *The Art of George W. Lambert, ARA* (Sydney: Art in Australia, 1924)

Karsavina, Tamara, 'Serge Lifar and the Last Diaghilev Seasons', *The Dancing Times*, vol. 57, issue no. 678 (March 1967), pp. 302–3, 314

Kavanagh, Julie, *Secret Muses: The Life of Frederick Ashton* (London: Faber & Faber, 1996)

Kennedy, Michael, *The Hallé Tradition: A Century of Music* (Manchester: Manchester University Press, 1960)

—— *The Works of Ralph Vaughan Williams* (London: Oxford University Press, 1964)

—— *Portrait of Walton* (Oxford: Clarendon Press, 1989)

Kenyon, Nicholas, *The BBC Symphony Orchestra: The First Fifty Years, 1930–1980* (London: BBC, 1981)

Keynes, Milo (ed.), *Lydia Lopokova* (London: Weidenfeld & Nicolson, 1983)

King, Viva, *The Weeping and the Laughter* (London: Macdonald and Jane's, 1976)

King-Smith, Beresford, *Crescendo! 75 Years of the City of Birmingham Symphony Orchestra* (London: Methuen, 1995)

Kochno, Boris, *Diaghilev and the Ballets Russes*, trans. Adrienne Foulke (New York: Harper & Row, 1970)

Kodicek, Ann (ed.), *Diaghilev: Creator of the Ballets Russes, Art, Music, Dance* (London: Barbican Art Gallery, 1996)

Lambert, Amy, *Thirty Years of an Artist's Life: The Career of G. W. Lambert, ARA, by his Wife* (Sydney: Society of Artists, 1938); reprinted (Sydney: Bloxham & Chambers, 1977)

Lambert, Constant, 'Jazz', *Life and Letters*, vol. 1 no. 2 (July 1928), pp. 124–31

—— 'Contemporary Music', in *Scrutinies: Critical Essays by Various Writers*, ed. Edgell Rickword, vol. 2 (London: Wishart & Co., 1931), pp. 290–314

—— 'Thomas Roseingrave (1688–1766)', *Proceedings of the Royal Musical Association*, 58th Session (1931–2), pp. 67–83 [text of a talk given by Constant Lambert, 15 March 1932]

—— *Music Ho! A Study of Music in Decline* (London: Faber & Faber, 1934; with new preface by Lambert, 1936; revised edition, 1937); third edition, with new preface by Lambert (London: Penguin, 1948); reissued with introduction by Arthur Hutchings (London: Faber & Faber, 1966; also October House: New York, 1966); reissued with introduction by Agnus Morrison (London: Hogarth Press, 1985) [The chapter on Satie was also reissued in French, in Rollo Myers, *Erik Satie: son temps et ses amis* (Paris: Richard – Masse, 1952)]

—— 'Foreword', in Kurt London, *Film Music: A Summary of the Characteristic Features of its History, Aesthetics, Technique; and Possible Developments*, trans. Eric S. Bensinger (Glasgow: Glasgow University Press, 1936), pp. 7–9

—— 'Music and Action', in *Footnotes to the Ballet: A Book for Balletomanes*, ed. Caryl Brahms (London: Lovat Dickson, 1936), pp. 161–74

—— 'The Oceanides Op. 73', analytic liner notes with music examples, *HMV Sibelius Society, Volume 4* (London: Gramophone Company, 1936), pp. 17–20

—— 'An Objective Self Portrait', *Twentieth Century Verse*, nos. 6–7, Wyndham Lewis double number (November–December 1937), 3pp.

—— 'Ballet and Musical Interpretation', in *Ballet To Poland, in Aid of the Polish Relief Fund*, ed. Arnold Haskell (London: A. & C. Black, 1940), pp. 39–43

—— contribution to *A Kitchen Goes to War: A Ration-Time Cookery Book with 150 Recipes Contributed by Famous People*, with contributions from Agatha Christie, Sir Kenneth Clark, Ernest Thesiger, Fougasse, Beverly Nichols, Beatrice Lillie, Isobel Baillie, Sir Malcolm Campbell, Cicely Courtneidge, John Gielgud, Dr Marie Stopes, Margot Countess of Oxford and Asquith, André L. Simon and Constant Lambert (London: John Miles, 1940)

—— 'Tchaikovsky and the Ballet', in Gordon Anthony, *The Sleeping Princess: Camera Studies* (London: George Routledge & Sons, 1940), pp. 15–26

—— 'The Music of "The Fairy Queen"', in E. J. Dent *et al.*, *Purcell's The Fairy Queen as presented by the Sadler's Wells Ballet and the Covent Garden Opera* (London: John Lehmann, 1948), pp. 19–27

—— 'Cats in Music', in *Selections from the BBC Programme Music Magazine*, ed. Anna Instone and Julian Herbage (London: Rockliff, 1953), pp. 53–7

[See also Appendix 4 for a comprehensive list of Lambert's writings for newspapers, journals, magazines, etc.]

Lane, Philip, 'The Film Music of Lambert and Berners', liner notes for Chandos CHAN10459 (Suites from *Merchant Seamen, Anna Karenina*, etc.), 2008

Legge, Walter, 'An Autobiography', in Elizabeth Schwarzkopf, *On and Off the Record: A Memoir of Walter Legge* (London: Faber, 1982; paperback 1988), p. 52

Leonard, Maurice, *Markova the Legend: The Authorised Biography* (London: Hodder & Stoughton, 1995; paperback 1996)

Lifar, Serge, *Serge Diaghilev: His Life, His Work, His Legend: An Intimate Biography* (London: G. P. Putnam's Sons, 1940)

—— *Ma Vie: From Kiev to Kiev*, trans. James Holman Mason (London: Hutchinson 1970)

Lindsay, Jack, *Fanfrolico and After* (London: Bodley Head, 1962)

Lloyd, Stephen, *William Walton: Muse of Fire* (Woodbridge: Boydell Press, 2001)

—— 'Constant Lambert and RVW', *Ralph Vaughan Williams Society Journal*, no. 34 (October 2005), pp. 12–18

—— 'The Constancy of Lambert and Some Lesser-Known Aspects of the Man', *British Music*, vol. 27 (2005), pp. 21–33

—— 'Rawsthorne and Lambert: Sharing a Centenary', *The Creel* (Journal of the Rawsthorne Trust and Friends of Alan Rawsthorne), vol. 5 no. 3, issue no. 19 (Winter 2005–6), pp. 15–18

Lockspeiser, Edward, *Debussy* (London: J. M. Dent, 1936)

Lucas, John, *Thomas Beecham: An Obsession with Music* (Woodbridge: Boydell Press, 2008)

Lutyens, Elisabeth, *A Goldfish Bowl* (London: Cassell, 1972)

Lynne, Gillian, *A Dancer in Wartime* (London: Chatto & Windus, 2011; paperback Vintage, 2012)

Maine, Basil, 'The Score', in *Footnotes to the Ballet: A Book for Balletomanes*, ed. Caryl Brahms (London: Lovat Dickson, 1936), pp. 129–60

—— 'Conversations: (iii) with Two English Critics' [Constant Lambert and Hubert Foss], in *Basil Maine on Music* (London: John Westhouse, 1945), pp. 123–6 [reprinted with minor changes from 'Das Unaufhörliche', *Musical Opinion* (June 1934), pp. 772–3]

Manchester, P[hyllis] W[inifred], *Vic-Wells: A Ballet Progress* (London: Gollancz, 1942)

Masters, Brian, 'Margot Fonteyn', *Harpers & Queen*, April 1991, pp. 164–71

McCabe, John, *Alan Rawsthorne: Portrait of a Composer* (Oxford: Oxford University Press, 1999)

McGrady, Richard, 'The Music of Constant Lambert', *Music & Letters*, vol. 51 (1970), pp. 242–58

McNeill, Rhoderick, 'A Critical Study of the Life and Works of E. J. Moeran' (PhD diss., University of Melbourne, 1982)

Middleboe, Penelope, *Edith Olivier: From her Journals, 1924–48* (London: Weidenfeld & Nicolson, 1989)

Middleton, M. H., 'The Fairy Queen', *Ballet Annual 2* (London: A. & C. Balck, 1948), pp. 141–2

Money, Keith, *Fonteyn: The Making of a Legend* (London: Collins, 1973)

Montagu-Nathan, M., 'The Empty Chair', *Music* (The Magazine of the London Musical Club), no. 3 (October 1951), pp. 4–5

Morrison, Angus, 'Obituary: Constant Lambert, August 21, 1951', *The RCM Magazine*, vol. 47 no. 3 (1951), pp. 107–10

—— 'The Family', in *Constant Lambert, 1905–1951: A Souvenir of the Exhibition at the South London Art Gallery*, ed. Kenneth Sharpe (London: London Borough of Southwark Council, 1976), pp. 25–7

—— 'Constant Lambert (1905–1951)', *Recorded Sound*, nos. 70–1 (April–July 1978), pp. 789–91 [based on an illustrated talk given on 23 March 1970]

—— 'Constant Lambert: A Memoir', introduction to Constant Lambert, *Music Ho! A Study of Music in Decline*, reissued third edition (London: Hogarth Press, 1985)

—— 'Anyhow, about Walton and Lambert', *British Music*, vol. 15 (1993), pp. 16–32 [transcript of a talk given at the British Music Information Centre, London, on 25 September 1987]

Motion, Andrew, *The Lamberts: George, Constant and Kit* (London: Chatto & Windus, 1986); reissued (London: Hogarth Press, 1987)

—— 'The Lovers of Constant Lambert', *The Observer*, 6 April 1986

—— 'Once More, with Feeling', *The Guardian*, 25 August 2001 [on Prom performances of Lambert]

Mottershead, Tim, 'Alan Rawsthorne: the Fish with an Ear for Music: A Concise Biography', *The Creel*, no. 19 (Winter 2005/6), pp. 46–7

Myers, Rollo, *Erik Satie: son temps et ses amis* (Paris: Richard–Masse, 1952) [includes translation of Lambert's chapter on Satie in *Music Ho!*]

Neel, Boyd, *My Orchestras and Other Adventures: The Memoirs of Boyd Neel* (Toronto: University of Toronto Press, 1985)

Newton, Eric, *Christopher Wood, 1901–1930* (London: Redfern Gallery, 1938)

Nicolson, Vanessa, *The Sculpture of Maurice Lambert*, with catalogue researched and compiled by Klio K. Panourgias (Much Hadam: Henry Moore Foundation in association with Lund Humphries, 2002)

Nikitina, Alice, *Nikitina by Herself*, trans. Baroness Budberg (London: Allan Wingate, 1959)

Norman, Bruce, *Here's Looking at You: The Story of British Television, 1908–1939* (London: BBC, 1984)

Olivier, Edith, *Night Thoughts of a Country Landlady* (London: Batsford, 1943)

Palmer, Christopher, 'Constant Lambert – a Postscript', *Music & Letters*, vol. 52 (1971), pp. 173–6

—— *Delius: Portrait of a Cosmopolitan* (London: Duckworth, 1976)

—— *Herbert Howells: A Centenary Celebration* (London: Thames Publishing, 1992)

—— liner notes for Hyperion CDA66565 (*The Rio Grande, Aubade héroïque, Summer's Last Will and Testament*), 1992

Papp, David, 'Save Me from a Week in Bootle, Bolton or Bacup', *BBC Music Magazine*, September 2001, pp. 49–51

Pearson, John, *Façades: Edith, Osbert, and Sacheverell Sitwell* (London: Macmillan, 1978)

Percival, John, 'The One and Only Constant', *The Independent*, 21 August 2001

Pitfield, Thomas, 'Some Recollections of Alan Rawsthorne', *The Creel*, vol. 1 no. 4 (Spring 1991)

Powell, Anthony, *Casanova's Chinese Restaurant* (London: Heinemann, 1960)

—— *The Kindly Ones* (London: Heinemann, 1962)

—— 'Constant Lambert: A Memoir by Anthony Powell', *The Times*, 30 December 1972, p. 9

—— 'Constant Lambert: A Memoir', in Richard Shead, *Constant Lambert* (London: Simon Publications, 1973)

—— *To Keep the Ball Rolling: The Memoirs of Anthony Powell*, 4 vols: *Infants of the Spring*; *Messengers of Day*; *Faces in My Time*; *The Strangers All Are Gone* (London: Heinemann, 1976–82); abridged, single-volume edition (Harmondsworth: Penguin Books, 1983)

—— 'Self-Destruction the Lambert Way', *The Daily Telegraph*, 25 April 1986, p. 14 [review of Andrew Motion, *The Lamberts: George, Constant and Kit*]

—— *Journals, 1982–1986 (*London: Heinemann, 1995)

—— *Journals, 1987–1989* (London: Heinemann, 1996)

—— *Journals, 1990–1992* (London: Heinemann, 1997)

Proctor, Thea, *The Prints*, introduced and catalogued by Roger Butler, with foreword and acknowledgements by Chris Deutscher and biography by Jan Minchin (Sydney: Resolution Press, 1980)

Prokofiev, Sergey, *Diaries, 1924–33*, trans. and annotated Anthony Phillips (London: Faber & Faber, 2012)

Quennell, Peter, *The Marble Foot: An Autobiography, 1915–1938* (London: Collins, 1976)

Rambert, Marie, *Quicksilver: An Autobiography* (London: Macmillan, 1972)

Rees, C. B., 'Personality Corner', *Penguin Music Magazine*, no. 2 (1947), pp. 39–45

Ricketts, Charles, *Self-Portrait, taken from the Letters and Journals of Charles Ricketts RA*, collected and compiled by T. Sturge Moore, edited by Cecil Lewis (London: Peter Davies, 1939)

Ridout, Alan, *A Composer's Life* (London: Thames, 1995)

Riley, Malcolm, *Percy Whitlock: Organist and Composer* (London: Thames Publishing, 1998)

Robinson, Anne, 'The Influence of the Margaret Morris Movement on the Career of Penelope Spencer', *Margaret Morris Movement Magazine*, no. 51 (Spring 2005), pp. 27–32

Rose, Francis, *Saying Life: The Memoirs of Sir Francis Rose* (London: Cassell, 1961)

Rosen, Carole, *The Goossens: A Musical Century* (London: Andre Deutsch, 1993)

Rubbra, Edmund [Duncan-], 'Constant Lambert's Sonata', *The Monthly Musical Record*, December 1930, p. 356

—— '*Summer's Last Will and Testament*', BBC Symphony Orchestra programme note, 3 February 1965

Russell, Thomas, *Philharmonic Decade* (London: Hutchinson, 1944)

Rutland, Harold, 'Constant Lambert and a Story of Chelsea Reach: A Musical Diary by Harold Rutland in Reminiscent Mood', *Radio Times*, vol. 112, issue no. 1444 (13 July 1951), p. 9

—— 'Recollections of Constant Lambert', 6pp typescript, 13 May 1952

Salter, Elizabeth, *Helpmann: The Authorized Biography* (Sydney: Angus & Robertson, 1978)

—— *Edith Sitwell* (London: Oresko Books, 1979)

Sanders, Alan, *Walter Legge: A Discography*, Westport Discographies no. 11 (London: Greenwood Press, 1984)

—— sleeve notes for SOMMCD 023 (Lambert's last recordings), 2001

Sandon, Joseph, *Façade and Other Early Ballets by Frederick Ashton* (London: A. & C. Black, 1954)

Savage, Richard Temple, *A Voice from the Pit: Reminiscences of an Orchestral Musician* (Newton Abbott: David & Charles, 1988)

Searle, Humphrey, *The Music of Liszt* (London: Williams & Norgate, 1954)

—— *Ballet Music: An Introduction* (London: Cassell, 1958)

—— 'Lambert, Constant' (1905–1951), in *The Oxford Dictionary of National Biography, 1951–1960 Supplement*, ed. E. T. Williams and H. M. Palmer (Oxford: Oxford University Press, 1971) pp. 602–4

—— *Quadrille with a Raven: Memoirs* (completed *c.* 1982), available online through www.musicweb-international.com/searle/titlepg.htm [accessed 13 August 2013]

Searle, Humphrey, and Robert Layton, *Twentieth Century Composers*, vol. 3: *Britain, Scandinavia and the Netherlands* (New York: Holt, Rinehart & Winston, 1972), pp. 49–55

Severn, Merlyn, *Sadler's Wells Ballet at Covent Garden: A Book of Photographs* (London: John Lane/Bodley Head, 1947) [includes photographs of *Sleeping Beauty*, *Miracle in the Gorbals*, *The Rake's Progress*, *Symphonic Variations* and *Adam Zero*]

Shead, Richard, *Constant Lambert: His Life, His Music and His Friends* (London: Simon Publications, 1973); reprinted with some additions but omitting Anthony Powell's memoir (London: Thames Publishing, 1986)

—— liner notes for Lyrita SRCD215 (*Romeo and Juliet*, *Pomona*), 1979

Shearer, Moira, 'Diaghilev', *Recorded Sound*, no. 78 (July 1980), pp. 5–21

Shore, Bernard, *The Orchestra Speaks* (London: Longmans, 1948)

Sitwell, Edith, *Selected Letters*, ed. John Lehmann and Derek Parker (London: Macmillan, 1970)

Sitwell, Osbert, *All at Sea* (London: Duckworth, 1927)

—— *Left Hand, Right Hand!: An Autobiography*, vol. 4: *Laughter in the Next Room* (London: Macmillan, 1949; paperback 1958)

—— 'Constant Lambert' [obituary tribute], *New Statesman and Nation* (August 1951)

—— *Tales my Father Taught Me* (London: Hutchinson, 1962; Readers Union edition, 1963)

—— 'Portrait of a Very Young Man', in Osbert Sitwell, *Queen Mary and Others* (London: Michael Joseph, 1974), pp. 77–80; reprinted in *Constant Lambert, 1905–1951: A Souvenir of the Exhibition at the South London Art Gallery*, ed. Kenneth Sharpe (London: London Borough of Southwark Council, 1976)

Sitwell, Sacheverell, *Liszt* (London: Faber & Faber, 1934)

Skelton, Geoffrey, *Paul Hindemith: The Man behind the Music* (London: Gollancz, 1977)

Smith, Barry, *Peter Warlock: The Life of Philip Heseltine* (Oxford: Oxford University Press, 1994)

—— 'Lambert, (Leonard) Constant', *Oxford Dictionary of National Biography* (Oxford: Oxford University Press, 2004), pp. 306–8

Smith, Carolyn J., *William Walton: A Bio-Bibliography* (London: Greenwood Press, 1988)

Smith, Cyril, *Duet for Three Hands* (London: Angus & Robertson, 1959)

Sokolova, Lydia, *Dancing for Diaghilev: The Memoirs of Lydia Sokolova*, ed. Richard Buckle (London: John Murray, 1960)

Storey, Alan, '"The Fairy Queen" at Covent Garden', *Ballet Today*, January–February 1947, p. 14

Stravinsky, Igor, and Robert Craft, *Expositions and Developments* (London: Faber & Faber, 1962)

Stravinsky, Vera, and Robert Craft, *Stravinsky in Pictures and Documents* (New York: Simon & Schuster, 1978)

Stuart, Philip, *The London Philharmonic Discography* (London: Greenwood Press, 1997)

Thomas, Myfanwy, *One of These Fine Days: Memoirs* (Manchester: Carcanet New Press, 1982)

Thomas, Roger, 'Constant Lambert: Passion and Pessimism', liner notes for *Constant Lambert: Conductor*, Pearl CD GEM0058 (1999)

—— 'Constant Lambert and the Joy of Perfection', liner notes for *Constant Lambert: Composer*, Pearl CD GEM0069 (2000)

Tippett, Michael, *Those Twentieth Century Blues: An Autobiography* (London: Hutchinson, 1991)

Tomlinson, Fred, *A Peter Warlock Handbook*, 2 vols (London: Triad Press, 1974–7)

—— *Warlock and van Dieren* (London: Thames Publishing, 1978)

Tooley, John, *In House: Covent Garden: 50 Years of Opera and Ballet* (London: Faber & Faber, 1999)

Valois, Ninette de, 'The Sadler's Wells Ballet in Holland', *The Dancing Times*, no. 357 (June 1940), p. 534

—— 'Constant Lambert: An Appreciation of his Work', *The Dancing Times*, no. 492 (October 1951), pp. 7–8

—— *Come Dance with Me: A Memoir, 1898–1956* (London: Hamish Hamilton, 1957)

—— *Step by Step: The Formation of an Establishment* (London: W. H. Allen, 1977)

Vandercook, John W., *Black Majesty: The Life of Christophe, King of Haiti* (New York: Harper & Brothers, 1928)

Vaughan, David, *Frederick Ashton and his Ballets* (London: A. & C. Black, 1977)

Vaughan Williams, Ralph, *National Music and Other Essays* (London: Oxford University Press, 1963)

—— *Letters of Ralph Vaughan Williams, 1895–1958*, ed. Hugh Cobbe (Oxford: Oxford University Press, 2008)

Vaughan Williams, Ursula, *RVW: A Biography of Ralph Vaughan Williams* (London: Oxford University Press, 1964)

Vickers, Hugo, *Cecil Beaton: The Authorized Biography* (London: Weidenfeld & Nicolson, 1985)

Walker, Kathrine Sorley, *Ninette de Valois: Idealiast without Illusions* (London: Hamish Hamilton, 1987)

Walton, Susana, *Behind the Façade* (Oxford: Oxford University Press, 1988)

Walton, William, 'Constant Lambert (In Memoriam, 21 August 1951)', in *Selections from the BBC Programme Music Magazine*, ed. Anna Instone and Julian Herbage (London: Rockliff, 1953), pp. 114–17; reprinted in Stephen Lloyd, *William Walton: Muse of Fire* (Woodbridge: Boydell Press, 2001), pp. 273–5

——*The Selected Letters of William Walton*, ed. Malcolm Hayes (London: Faber & Faber, 2002)

Warlock, Peter, *The Collected Letters of Peter Warlock*, vol. 4: *1922–1930*, ed. Barry Smith (Woodbridge: Boydell Press, 2005)

Waugh, Evelyn, *The Diaries of Evelyn Waugh*, ed. Michael Davie (London: Weidenfeld & Nicolson, 1976; Phoenix paperback 1995)

Webster, David, 'Constant Lambert: An Appreciation', *Opera*, vol. 2 no. 12 (November 1951), pp. 656, 664

Wetherell, Eric, *'Paddy': The Life and Music of Patrick Hadley* (London: Thames, 1997)

Wheen, Francis, *Tom Driberg: His Life and Indiscretions* (London: Chatto & Windus, 1990; reissued in association with Pan Books, 1992)

Wilson, Sir Steuart, 'Constant Lambert' [obituary], *Sunday Times*, 26 August 1951

Youens, F. G., 'An Appreciation of Constant Lambert', *Music Parade*, vol. 1 no. 11 (1948), pp. 5–6

Ziegler, Philip, *Osbert Sitwell* (London: Chatto & Windus, 1998)

Zoete, Beryl de, 'The Younger English Composers: III, Constant Lambert', *The Monthly Musical Record*, vol. 59, issue no. 700 (1 April 1929), pp. 97–9

Exhibition catalogues

Constant Lambert, 1905–1951: A Souvenir of the Exhibition at the South London Art Gallery (London: London Borough of Southwark Council, 1976) [includes Michael Ayrton, 'A Sketch for a Portrait of Constant Lambert' (from his *Golden Sections*); Angus Morrison, 'The Family'; Osbert Sitwell, 'Portrait of a Very Young Man' (from his *Queen Mary and Others*); and a 'Chronology of Family Background and Life']

Isabel Rawsthorne, 1912–1992: Paintings, Drawings and Designs (London: Harrogate Museum and Arts, 1997) [catalogue for exhibition at the Mercer Art Gallery, Harrogate and the October Gallery, London; includes foreword by Eduardo Paolozzi, introduction by Karen Southworth and biography and discussion of her work by Suzanne Doyle]

Maurice Lambert, 1901–1964 (London: Belgrave Gallery, 1988)

Index

References to illustrations appear in italics.